Total Language Accessibility

For over 150 years Oxford's hallmarks of integrity and authority have been adapted to meet the changing needs of dictionary users. Oxford–Hachette's range of French dictionaries are an integral part of this tradition and offer an unequalled range of carefully designed benefits to ensure maximum language accessibility.

Rapid Access Design

Oxford's new quick-access page designs and typography have been specially created to ensure exceptional clarity and accessibility. Paper and binding styles are carefully selected for their durability. Entries are written in clear, jargon-free language without confusing abbreviations.

Unrivalled practical help

Extended treatment of the core vocabulary offers the user step-by-step guidance on how to select, construct, and translate a given word correctly. Unrivalled practical grammatical help has been built into every dictionary within the range. Generous numbers of examples are carefully selected to illustrate the many different nuances of meaning and context. A clear, efficient system of translation signposting guides the user to the most appropriate translation.

Supplementary Information

All the dictionaries in the Oxford–Hachette range offer valuable additional help and information, which can include regular and irregular verbs tables, thematic vocabulary boxes, political and cultural information, guides to effective communication (how to write letters, CVs, book holidays, or take minutes), two colour texts, and pronunciation guidance.

Business, technical, and computing vocabulary

The editors of The Oxford–Hachette Language Programme have provided the widest and most accurate representation of the language of every notable specialist field. All translations were checked by a skilled team of specialist translators before being included.

The Oxford–Hachette Language Programme

The Oxford–Hachette Language Programme is the result of a unique partnership between two of the world's foremost reference publishers, and marks the start of a new age of bilingual dictionaries. The Programme has produced the only French dictionaries to be written using the evidence of scores of millions of words of English and French, drawn from every type of written and spoken language. Each dictionary provides a more accurate, up-to-date, and complete picture of real language than has ever been possible before.

The Bank of French

Capturing current French as it is truly used is the primary aim of The Bank of French, a unique 13 million word database of current French. The Bank shapes every dictionary entry and translation to meet the needs of today's users, highlighting important constructions, illustrating difficult meanings, and focusing attention on common usage.

The richest choice of words

Combining a comprehensive vocabulary with the full variety of idiomatic and colloquial French is a distinctive element of the Oxford-Hachette Language Programme. The Programme has captured standard, regional, and world French. In addition, variant pronunciations and the degree of formality for words, from formal right through to taboo, are signalled whenever necessary.

The library of French Literature

From Racine and Balzac to Gide and Camus, a library of the works of many of the greatest of France's playwrights, poets, and novelists has been included in the Bank of French, enabling the editors of the Programme to analyse and describe the vocabulary and usage of literary French – historical and contemporary – to assist readers and students of French literature.

The British National Corpus

Every English entry has been shaped by direct evidence from the British National Corpus, an unrivalled balanced collection of 100 million words of text representing every kind of writing and speech in English.

The Oxford Colour French Dictionary

Revised Edition

FRENCH–ENGLISH
ENGLISH–FRENCH

FRANÇAIS–ANGLAIS
ANGLAIS–FRANÇAIS

Michael Janes
Dora Carpenter
Edwin Carpenter

Word games prepared by Natalie Pomier

Oxford New York
OXFORD UNIVERSITY PRESS
1998

Oxford University Press, Great Clarendon Street, Oxford, OX2 6DP
Oxford New York
Athens Auckland Bangkok Bogota Bombay Buenos Aires
Calcutta Cape Town Dar es Salaam Delhi
Florence Hong Kong Istanbul Karachi
Kuala Lumpur Madras Madrid Melbourne
Mexico City Nairobi Paris Singapore
Taipei Tokyo Toronto Warsaw
and associated companies in
Berlin Ibadan

First published 1986 as The Oxford French dictionary
Second edition first published 1993
First issued as an Oxford University Press paperback 1989
Second edition first published 1994
Two-colour edition first published 1995
Revised edition published 1998

British Library Cataloguing in Publication Data
Data available

Library of Congress Cataloging in Publication Data
Data available

ISBN 0-19-8601913

10 9 8 7 6 5 4 3 2 1

Typeset by Pentacor PLC
Printed in Spain by
Mateu Cromo Artes Graficas S.A.
Madrid

Contents

Preface

The Oxford Colour French Dictionary is a dictionary designed for beginners of French. This revised edition includes word games specifically designed to build key skills in using your dictionary more effectively, and to improve knowledge of French vocabulary usage in a fun and entertaining way. You will find answers to all puzzles and games at the end of the section.

Acknowledgements

The Oxford Colour French Dictionary is based on the second edition of *The Oxford Paperback French Dictionary.* It remains largely the work of Michael Jane, the compiler of the first edition, but some entries have been substantially revised and we have been able to incorporate a large proportion of new material. We hope to have kept to the aim of the original: to provide users requiring a compact dictionary with the maximum amount of useful material.

Dora Latiri-Carpenter
Edwin Carpenter

Introduction

As an aid to easy reference all main headwords, compounds, and derivatives in this dictionary appear in blue. When you look up a word, you will find a pronunciation, a grammatical part of speech, and the translation. Sometimes more than one translation is given, and the material in brackets in *italics* is included to help you choose the right one. For example, under **cabin** you will see (*hut*) and (*in ship, aircraft*). When a word has more than one part of speech, this can affect the translation. For example **praise** is translated one way when it is a verb (*v.t.*) and another when it is a noun (*n.*).

A swung dash (~) represents the entry word, or the part of it that comes before a vertical bar (as in **libert|y**). You will see it in examples using the entry word and words based on it. For example, under **good** you will find **as ~ as** and **~ -looking**.

Translations are given in their basic form. You will find tables at the end showing verb forms. Irregular verbs are marked on the French to English side with †. This side also shows the plurals of nouns and the feminine forms of adjectives when they do not follow the normal rules.

Abbreviations • Abréviations

abbreviation	*abbr., abrév.*	abréviation
adjective(s)	*a. (adjs.)*	adjectif(s)
adverb(s)	*adv(s).*	adverbe(s)
American	*Amer.*	américain
anatomy	*anat.*	anatomie
approximately	*approx.*	approximativement
archaeology	*archaeol., archéol.*	archéologie
architecture	*archit.*	architecture
motoring	*auto.*	automobile
auxiliary	*aux.*	auxiliaire
aviation	*aviat.*	aviation
botany	*bot.*	botanique
computing	*comput.*	informatique
commerce	*comm.*	commerce
conjunction(s)	*conj(s).*	conjonction(s)
cookery	*culin.*	culinaire
electricity	*electr., électr.*	électricité
feminine	*f.*	féminin
familiar	*fam.*	familier
figurative	*fig.*	figuré
geography	*geog., géog.*	géographie
geology	*geol., géol.*	géologie
grammar	*gram.*	grammaire
humorous	*hum.*	humoristique
interjection(s)	*int(s).*	interjection(s)
invariable	*invar.*	invariable
legal, law	*jurid.*	juridique
language	*lang.*	langue
masculine	*m.*	masculin
medicine	*med., méd.*	médecine
military	*mil.*	militaire
music	*mus.*	musique
noun(s)	*n(s).*	nom(s)
nautical	*naut.*	nautique

oneself	*o.s.*	se, soi-même
proprietary term	*P.*	marque déposée
pejorative	*pej., péj.*	péjoratif
philosophy	*phil.*	philosophie
photography	*photo.*	photographie
plural	*pl.*	pluriel
politics	*pol.*	politique
possessive	*poss.*	possessif
past participle	*p.p.*	participe passé
prefix	*pref., préf.*	préfixe
preposition(s)	*prep(s)., prép(s).*	préposition(s)
present participle	*pres. p.*	participe présent
pronoun	*pron.*	pronom
relative pronoun	*pron. rel.*	pronom relatif
psychology	*psych.*	psychologie
past tense	*p.t.*	passé
something	*qch.*	quelque chose
someone	*qn.*	quelqu'un
railway	*rail.*	chemin de fer
religion	*relig.*	religion
relative pronoun	*rel. pron.*	pronom relatif
school, scholastic	*schol., scol.*	scolaire
singular	*sing.*	singulier
slang	*sl.*	argot
someone	*s.o.*	quelqu'un
something	*sth.*	quelque chose
technical	*techn.*	technique
television	*TV*	télévision
university	*univ.*	université
auxiliary verb	*v. aux.*	verb auxiliaire
intransitive verb	*v.i.*	verbe intransitif
pronominal verb	*v. pr.*	verbe pronominal
transitive verb	*v.t.*	verbe transitif

Pronunciation of French

Phonetic symbols

Vowels

i vie	ɑ bas	y vêtu	ɛ̃ matin
e pré	ɔ mort	ø peu	ɑ̃ sans
ɛ lait	o mot	œ peur	ɔ̃ bon
a plat	u genou	ə de	œ̃ lundi

Consonants and semi-consonants

p payer	f feu	m main	j yeux
b bon	v vous	n nous	w oui
t terre	s sale	l long	ɥ huile
d dans	z zéro	r rue	
k cou	ʃ chat	ɲ agneau	
g gant	ʒ je	ŋ camping	

Notes: ' before the pronunciation of a word beginning with *h* indicates no liaison or elision.

An asterisk immediately following an apostrophe in some words like **qu'*** shows that this form of the word is used before a vowel or mute 'h'.

Proprietary terms

This dictionary includes some words which have, or are asserted to have, proprietary status as trade marks or otherwise. Their inclusion does not imply that they have acquired for legal purposes a non-proprietary or general significance, nor any other judgement concerning their legal status. In cases where the editorial staff have some evidence that a word has proprietary status this is indicated in the entry for that word by the symbol P., but no judgement concerning the legal status of such words is made or implied thereby.

Français · Anglais
French · English

A

a /a/ *voir* avoir.

à /a/ *prép.* (*à + le = au, à + les = aux*) in, at; (*direction*) to; (*temps*) at; (*jusqu'à*) to, till; (*date*) on; (*époque*) in; (*moyen*) by, on; (*prix*) for; (*appartenance*) of; (*mesure*) by. **donner/***etc.* **à qn.,** give/*etc.* to s.o. **apprendre/***etc.* **à faire,** learn/*etc.* to do. **l'homme à la barbe,** the man with the beard. **à la radio,** on the radio. **c'est à moi**/*etc.*, it is mine/*etc.* **c'est à vous**/*etc.* **de,** it is up to you/ *etc.* to; (*en jouant*) it is your/*etc.* turn to. **à six km d'ici,** six km. away. **dix km à l'heure,** ten km. an *ou* per hour. **il a un crayon à la main,** he's got a pencil in his hand.

abaissement /abɛsmɑ̃/ *n.m.* (*baisse*) drop, fall.

abaisser /abese/ *v.t.* lower; (*levier*) pull *ou* push down; (*fig.*) humiliate. **s'~** *v. pr.* go down, drop; (*fig.*) humiliate o.s. **s'~ à,** stoop to.

abandon /abɑ̃dɔ̃/ *n.m.* abandonment; desertion; (*sport*) withdrawal; (*naturel*) abandon. **à l'~,** in a state of neglect. **~ner** /-ɔne/ *v.t.* abandon, desert; (*renoncer à*) give up, abandon; (*céder*) give (**à,** to). **s'~ner à,** give o.s. up to.

abasourdir /abazurdir/ *v.t.* stun.

abat-jour /abaʒur/ *n.m. invar.* lampshade.

abats /aba/ *n.m. pl.* offal.

abattement /abatmɑ̃/ *n.m.* dejection; (*faiblesse*) exhaustion; (*comm.*) allowance.

abattis /abati/ *n.m. pl.* giblets.

abattoir /abatwar/ *n.m.* slaughterhouse, abattoir.

abattre† /abatr/ *v.t.* knock down; (*arbre*) cut down; (*animal*) slaughter; (*avion*) shoot down; (*affaiblir*) weaken; (*démoraliser*) dishearten. **s'~** *v. pr.* come down, fall (down). **se laisser ~,** let things get one down.

abbaye /abei/ *n.f.* abbey.

abbé /abe/ *n.m.* priest; (*supérieur d'une abbaye*) abbot.

abcès /apsɛ/ *n.m.* abscess.

abdi|quer /abdike/ *v.t./i.* abdicate. **~cation** *n.f.* abdication.

abdom|en /abdɔmɛn/ *n.m.* abdomen. **~inal** (*m. pl.* **~inaux**) *a.* abdominal.

abeille /abɛj/ *n.f.* bee.

aberrant, ~e /abɛrɑ̃, -t/ *a.* absurd.

aberration /abɛrɑsjɔ̃/ *n.f.* aberration; (*idée*) absurd idea.

abêtir /abetir/ *v.t.* make stupid.

abhorrer /abɔre/ *v.t.* loathe, abhor.

abîme /abim/ *n.m.* abyss.

abîmer /abime/ *v.t.* damage, spoil. **s'~** *v. pr.* get damaged *ou* spoilt.

abject /abʒɛkt/ *a.* abject.

abjurer /abʒyre/ *v.t.* abjure.

ablation /ablɑsjɔ̃/ *n.f.* removal.

ablutions /ablysjɔ̃/ *n.f. pl.* ablutions.

aboiement /abwamɑ̃/ *n.m.* bark(ing). **~s,** barking.

abois (aux) /(oz)abwa/ *adv.* at bay.

abol|ir /abɔlir/ *v.t.* abolish. **~ition** *n.f.* abolition.

abominable /abɔminabl/ *a.* abominable.

abond|ant, ~ante /abɔ̃dɑ̃, -t/ *a.* abundant, plentiful. **~amment** *adv.* abundantly. **~ance** *n.f.* abundance; (*prospérité*) affluence.

abonder /abɔ̃de/ *v.i.* abound (**en,** in). **~ dans le sens de qn.,** completely agree with s.o.

abonn|er (s') /(s)abɔne/ *v. pr.* subscribe (**à,** to). **~é, ~ée** *n.m., f.* subscriber; season-ticket holder. **~ement** *n.m.* (*à un journal*) subscription; (*de bus, théâtre, etc.*) season-ticket.

abord /abɔr/ *n.m.* access. **~s,** surroundings. **d'~,** first.

abordable /abɔrdabl/ *a.* (*prix*) reasonable; (*personne*) approachable.

abordage /abɔrdaʒ/ *n.m.* (*accident: naut.*) collision. **prendre à l'~,** (*navire*) board, attack.

aborder /abɔrde/ *v.t.* approach; (*lieu*) reach; (*problème etc.*) tackle. ● *v.i.* reach land.
aborigène /abɔriʒɛn/ *n.m.* aborigine, aboriginal.
aboutir /abutir/ *v.i.* succeed, achieve a result. **~ à,** end (up) in, lead to. **n'~ à rien,** come to nothing.
aboutissement /abutismɑ̃/ *n.m.* outcome.
aboyer /abwaje/ *v.i.* bark.
abrasi|f, ~ve /abrazif, -v/ *a.* & *n.m.* abrasive.
abrégé /abreʒe/ *n.m.* summary.
abréger /abreʒe/ *v.t.* (*texte*) shorten, abridge; (*mot*) abbreviate, shorten; (*visite*) cut short.
abreuv|er /abrœve/ *v.t.* water; (*fig.*) overwhelm (**de,** with). **s'~er** *v. pr.* drink. **~oir** *n.m.* watering-place.
abréviation /abrevjɑsjɔ̃/ *n.f.* abbreviation.
abri /abri/ *n.m.* shelter. **à l'~,** under cover. **à l'~ de** sheltered from.
abricot /abriko/ *n.m.* apricot.
abriter /abrite/ *v.t.* shelter; (*recevoir*) house. **s'~** *v. pr.* (take) shelter.
abroger /abrɔʒe/ *v.t.* repeal.
abrupt /abrypt/ *a.* steep, sheer; (*fig.*) abrupt.
abruti, ~e /abryti/ *n.m., f.* (*fam.*) idiot.
abrutir /abrytir/ *v.t.* make *ou* drive stupid, dull the mind of.
absence /apsɑ̃s/ *n.f.* absence.
absent, ~e /apsɑ̃, -t/ *a.* absent, away; (*chose*) missing. ● *n.m., f.* absentee. **il est toujours ~,** he's still away. **d'un air ~,** absently. **~éisme** /-teism/ *n.m.* absenteeism. **~éiste** /-teist/ *n.m./f.* absentee.
absenter (s') /(s)apsɑ̃te/ *v. pr.* go *ou* be away; (*sortir*) go out, leave.
absolu /apsɔly/ *a.* absolute. **~ment** *adv.* absolutely.
absolution /apsɔlysjɔ̃/ *n.f.* absolution.
absor|ber /apsɔrbe/ *v.t.* absorb; (*temps etc.*) take up. **~bant, ~bante** *a.* (*travail etc.*) absorbing; (*matière*) absorbent. **~ption** *n.f.* absorption.
absoudre /apsudr/ *v.t.* absolve.
absten|ir (s') /(s)apstənir/ *v. pr.* abstain. **s'~ir de,** refrain from. **~tion** /-ɑ̃sjɔ̃/ *n.f.* abstention.
abstinence /apstinɑ̃s/ *n.f.* abstinence.
abstr|aire /apstrɛr/ *v.t.* abstract. **~action** *n.f.* abstraction. **faire ~action de,** disregard. **~ait, ~aite** *a.* & *n.m.* abstract.
absurd|e /apsyrd/ *a.* absurd. **~ité** *n.f.* absurdity.
abus /aby/ *n.m.* abuse, misuse; (*injustice*) abuse. **~ de confiance,** breach of trust. **~ sexuel,** sexual abuse.
abuser /abyze/ *v.t.* deceive. ● *v.i.* go too far. **s'~** *v. pr.* be mistaken. **~ de,** abuse, misuse; (*profiter de*) take advantage of; (*alcool etc.*) over-indulge in.
abusi|f, ~ve /abyzif, -v/ *a.* excessive; (*usage*) mistaken.
acabit /akabi/ *n.m.* **du même ~,** of that sort.
académicien, ~ne /akademisjɛ̃, -jɛn/ *n.m., f.* academician.
académ|ie /akademi/ *n.f.* academy; (*circonscription*) educational district. **A~ie,** Academy. **~ique** *a.* academic.
acajou /akaʒu/ *n.m.* mahogany.
acariâtre /akarjɑtr/ *a.* cantankerous.
accablement /akɑbləmɑ̃/ *n.m.* despondency.
accabl|er /akɑble/ *v.t.* overwhelm. **~er d'impôts,** burden with taxes. **~er d'injures,** heap insults upon. **~ant, ~ante** *a.* (*chaleur*) oppressive.
accalmie /akalmi/ *n.f.* lull.
accaparer /akapare/ *v.t.* monopolize; (*fig.*) take up all the time of.
accéder /aksede/ *v.i.* **~ à,** reach; (*pouvoir, requête, trône, etc.*) accede to.
accélér|er /akselere/ *v.i.* (*auto.*) accelerate. ● *v.t.*, **s'~er** *v. pr.* speed up. **~ateur** *n.m.* accelerator. **~ation** *n.f.* acceleration; speeding up.
accent /aksɑ̃/ *n.m.* accent; (*sur une syllabe*) stress, accent; (*ton*) tone. **mettre l'~ sur,** stress.
accent|uer /aksɑ̃tɥe/ *v.t.* (*lettre, syllabe*) accent; (*fig.*) emphasize, accentuate. **s'~uer** *v. pr.* become more pronounced, increase. **~uation** *n.f.* accentuation.
accept|er /aksɛpte/ *v.t.* accept. **~er de,** agree to. **~able** *a.* acceptable. **~ation** *n.f.* acceptance.
acception /aksɛpsjɔ̃/ *n.f.* meaning.
accès /aksɛ/ *n.m.* access; (*porte*) entrance; (*de fièvre*) attack; (*de colère*)

fit; (*de joie*) (out)burst. **les ~ de,** (*voies*) the approaches to. **facile d'~,** easy to get to.

accessible /aksesibl/ *a.* accessible; (*personne*) approachable.

accession /aksɛsjɔ̃/ *n.f.* **~ à,** accession to.

accessit /aksesit/ *n.m.* honourable mention.

accessoire /akseswar/ *a.* secondary. ● *n.m.* accessory; (*théâtre*) prop.

accident /aksidɑ̃/ *n.m.* accident. **~ de train/d'avion,** train/plane crash. **par ~,** by accident. **~é** /-te/ *a.* damaged *ou* hurt (in an accident); (*terrain*) uneven, hilly.

accidentel, ~le /aksidɑ̃tɛl/ *a.* accidental.

acclam|er /aklame/ *v.t.* cheer, acclaim. **~ations** *n.f. pl.* cheers.

acclimat|er /aklimate/ *v.t.*, **s'~er** *v. pr.* acclimatize; (*Amer.*) acclimate. **~ation** *n.f.* acclimatization; (*Amer.*) acclimation.

accolade /akɔlad/ *n.f.* embrace; (*signe*) brace, bracket.

accommodant, ~e /akɔmɔdɑ̃, -t/ *a.* accommodating.

accommodement /akɔmɔdmɑ̃/ *n.m.* compromise.

accommoder /akɔmɔde/ *v.t.* adapt (**à,** to); (*cuisiner*) prepare; (*assaisonner*) flavour. **s'~ de,** put up with.

accompagn|er /akɔ̃paɲe/ *v.t.* accompany. **s'~er de,** be accompanied by. **~ateur, ~atrice** *n.m., f.* (*mus.*) accompanist; (*guide*) guide. **~ement** *n.m.* (*mus.*) accompaniment.

accompli /akɔ̃pli/ *a.* accomplished.

accompl|ir /akɔ̃plir/ *v.t.* carry out, fulfil. **s'~ir** *v. pr.* be carried out, happen. **~issement** *n.m.* fulfilment.

accord /akɔr/ *n.m.* agreement; (*harmonie*) harmony; (*mus.*) chord. **être d'~,** agree (**pour,** to). **se mettre d'~,** come to an agreement, agree. **d'~!,** all right!, OK!

accordéon /akɔrdeɔ̃/ *n.m.* accordion.

accord|er /akɔrde/ *v.t.* grant; (*couleurs etc.*) match; (*mus.*) tune. **s'~er** *v. pr.* agree. **s'~er avec,** (*s'entendre avec*) get on with. **~eur** *n.m.* tuner.

accoster /akɔste/ *v.t.* accost; (*navire*) come alongside.

accotement /akɔtmɑ̃/ *n.m.* roadside, verge; (*Amer.*) shoulder.

accoter (s') /(s)akɔte/ *v. pr.* lean (**à,** against).

accouch|er /akuʃe/ *v.i.* give birth (**de,** to); (*être en travail*) be in labour. ● *v.t.* deliver. **~ement** *n.m.* childbirth; (*travail*) labour. **(médecin) ~eur** *n.m.* obstetrician. **~euse** *n.f.* midwife.

accoud|er (s') /(s)akude/ *v. pr.* lean (one's elbows) on. **~oir** *n.m.* armrest.

accoupl|er /akuple/ *v.t.* couple; (*faire copuler*) mate. **s'~er** *v. pr.* mate. **~ement** *n.m.* mating; coupling.

accourir /akurir/ *v.i.* run up.

accoutrement /akutrəmɑ̃/ *n.m.* (strange) garb.

accoutumance /akutymɑs/ *n.f.* habituation; (*méd.*) addiction.

accoutum|er /akutyme/ *v.t.* accustom. **s'~er** *v. pr.* get accustomed. **~é** *a.* customary.

accréditer /akredite/ *v.t.* give credence to; (*personne*) accredit.

accro /akro/ *n.m./f.* (*drogué*) addict; (*amateur*) fan.

accroc /akro/ *n.m.* tear, rip; (*fig.*) hitch.

accroch|er /akrɔʃe/ *v.t.* (*suspendre*) hang up; (*attacher*) hook, hitch; (*déchirer*) catch; (*heurter*) hit; (*attirer*) attract. **s'~er** *v. pr.* cling, hang on; (*se disputer*) clash. **~age** *n.m.* hanging; hooking; (*auto.*) collision; (*dispute*) clash; (*mil.*) encounter.

accroissement /akrwasmɑ̃/ *n.m.* increase (**de,** in).

accroître /akrwatr/ *v.t.*, **s'~** *v. pr.* increase.

accroup|ir (s') /(s)akrupir/ *v. pr.* squat. **~i** *a.* squatting.

accru /akry/ *a.* increased, greater.

accueil /akœj/ *n.m.* reception, welcome.

accueill|ir† /akœjir/ *v.t.* receive, welcome; (*aller chercher*) meet. **~ant, ~ante** *a.* friendly.

acculer /akyle/ *v.t.* corner. **~ à,** force *ou* drive into *ou* against *ou* close to.

accumul|er /akymyle/ *v.t.*, **s'~er** *v. pr.* accumulate, pile up. **~ateur** *n.m.* accumulator. **~ation** *n.f.* accumulation.

accus /aky/ *n.m. pl.* (*fam.*) battery.

accusation /akyzɑsjɔ̃/ *n.f.* accusation; (*jurid.*) charge. **l'~,** (*magistrat*) the prosecution.

accus|er /akyze/ *v.t.* accuse (**de,** of); (*blâmer*) blame (**de,** for); (*jurid.*) charge (**de,** with); (*fig.*) show, emphasize. **~er reception de,**

acknowledge receipt of. **~ateur, ~atrice** *a.* incriminating; *n.m., f.* accuser. **~é, ~ée** *a.* marked; *n.m., f.* accused.

acerbe /asɛrb/ *a.* bitter.

acéré /asere/ *a.* sharp.

achalandé /aʃalɑ̃de/ *a.* **bien ~,** well-stocked.

acharn|é /aʃarne/ *a.* relentless, ferocious. **~ement** *n.m.* relentlessness.

acharner (s') /(s)aʃarne/ *v. pr.* **s'~ sur,** set upon; (*poursuivre*) hound. **s'~ à faire,** keep on doing.

achat /aʃa/ *n.m.* purchase. **~s,** shopping. **faire l'~ de,** buy.

acheminer /aʃmine/ *v.t.* dispatch, convey. **s'~ vers,** head for.

achet|er /aʃte/ *v.t.* buy. **~er à,** buy from; (*pour*) buy for. **~eur, ~euse** *n.m., f.* buyer; (*client de magasin*) shopper.

achèvement /aʃɛvmɑ̃/ *n.m.* completion.

achever /aʃve/ *v.t.* finish (off). **s'~** *v. pr.* end.

acid|e /asid/ *a.* acid, sharp. ● *n.m.* acid. **~ité** *n.f.* acidity. **~ulé** *a.* slightly acid.

acier /asje/ *n.m.* steel. **aciérie** *n.f.* steelworks.

acné /akne/ *n.f.* acne.

acolyte /akɔlit/ *n.m.* (*péj.*) associate.

acompte /akɔ̃t/ *n.m.* deposit, part-payment.

à-côté /akote/ *n.m.* side-issue. **~s,** (*argent*) extras.

à-coup /aku/ *n.m.* jolt, jerk. **par ~s,** by fits and starts.

acoustique /akustik/ *n.f.* acoustics. ● *a.* acoustic.

acqu|érir† /akerir/ *v.t.* acquire, gain; (*biens*) purchase, acquire. **~éreur** *n.m.* purchaser. **~isition** *n.f.* acquisition; purchase.

acquiescer /akjese/ *v.i.* acquiesce, agree.

acquis, ~e /aki, -z/ *n.m.* experience. ● *a.* acquired; (*fait*) established; (*faveurs*) secured. **~ à,** (*projet*) in favour of.

acquit /aki/ *n.m.* receipt. **par ~ de conscience,** for peace of mind.

acquitt|er /akite/ *v.t.* acquit; (*dette*) settle. **s'~er de,** (*promesse, devoir*) carry out. **s'~er envers,** repay. **~ement** *n.m.* acquittal; settlement.

âcre /ɑkr/ *a.* acrid.

acrobate /akrɔbat/ *n.m./f.* acrobat.

acrobatie /akrɔbasi/ *n.f.* acrobatics. **~ aérienne,** aerobatics. **acrobatique** /-tik/ *a.* acrobatic.

acte /akt/ *n.m.* act, action, deed; (*théâtre*) act; (*de naissance, mariage*) certificate. **~s,** (*compte rendu*) proceedings. **prendre ~ de,** note.

acteur /aktœr/ *n.m.* actor.

acti|f, ~ve /aktif, -v/ *a.* active. ● *n.m.* (*comm.*) assets. **avoir à son ~f,** have to one's credit *ou* name. **~vement** *adv.* actively.

action /aksjɔ̃/ *n.f.* action; (*comm.*) share; (*jurid.*) action. **~naire** /-jɔnɛr/ *n.m./f.* shareholder.

actionner /aksjɔne/ *v.t.* work, activate.

activer /aktive/ *v.t.* speed up; (*feu*) boost. **s'~** *v. pr.* hurry, rush.

activiste /aktivist/ *n.m./f.* activist.

activité /aktivite/ *n.f.* activity. **en ~,** active.

actrice /aktris/ *n.f.* actress.

actualiser /aktɥalize/ *v.t.* update.

actualité /aktɥalite/ *n.f.* topicality. **l'~,** current events. **les ~s,** news. **d'~,** topical.

actuel, ~le /aktɥɛl/ *a.* present; (*d'actualité*) topical. **~lement** *adv.* at the present time.

acuité /akɥite/ *n.f.* acuteness.

acupunct|ure /akypɔ̃ktyr/ *n.f.* acupuncture. **~eur** *n.m.* acupuncturist.

adage /adaʒ/ *n.m.* adage.

adapt|er /adapte/ *v.t.* adapt; (*fixer*) fit. **s'~er** *v. pr.* adapt (o.s.); (*techn.*) fit, **~ateur, ~atrice** *n.m., f.* adapter; *n.m.* (*électr.*) adapter. **~ation** *n.f.* adaptation.

additif /aditif/ *n.m.* (*note*) rider; (*substance*) additive.

addition /adisjɔ̃/ *n.f.* addition; (*au café etc.*) bill; (*Amer.*) check. **~nel, ~nelle** /-jɔnɛl/ *a.* additional. **~ner** /-jɔne/ *v.t.* add; (*totaliser*) add (up).

adepte /adɛpt/ *n.m./f.* follower.

adéquat, ~e /adekwa, -t/ *a.* suitable.

adhérent, ~e /aderɑ̃, -t/ *n.m., f.* member.

adhé|rer /adere/ *v.i.* adhere, stick (**à,** to). **~rer à,** (*club etc.*) be a member of; (*s'inscrire à*) join. **~rence** *n.f.* adhesion. **~sif, ~sive** *a. & n.m.* adhesive. **~sion** *n.f.* membership; (*accord*) adherence.

adieu (*pl.* **~x**) /adjø/ *int. & n.m.* goodbye, farewell.

adipeu|x, ~se /adipø, -z/ *a.* fat; (*tissu*) fatty.
adjacent, ~e /adʒasɑ̃, -t/ *a.* adjacent.
adjectif /adʒɛktif/ *n.m.* adjective.
adjoindre /adʒwɛ̃dr/ *v.t.* add, attach; (*personne*) appoint. **s'~** *v. pr.* appoint.
adjoint, ~e /adʒwɛ̃, -t/ *n.m., f. & a.* assistant. **~ au maire,** deputy mayor.
adjudant /adʒydɑ̃/ *n.m.* warrant-officer.
adjuger /adʒyʒe/ *v.t.* award; (*aux enchères*) auction. **s'~** *v. pr.* take.
adjurer /adʒyre/ *v.t.* beseech.
admettre† /admɛtr/ *v.t.* let in, admit; (*tolérer*) allow; (*reconnaître*) admit; (*candidat*) pass.
administrati|f, ~ve /administratif, -v/ *a.* administrative.
administr|er /administre/ *v.t.* run, manage; (*justice, biens, antidote, etc.*) administer. **~ateur, ~atrice** *n.m., f.* administrator, director. **~ation** *n.f.* administration. **A~ation,** Civil Service.
admirable /admirabl/ *a.* admirable.
admirati|f, ~ve /admiratif, -v/ *a.* admiring.
admir|er /admire/ *v.t.* admire. **~ateur, ~atrice** *n.m., f.* admirer. **~ation** *n.f.* admiration.
admissible /admisibl/ *a.* admissible; (*candidat*) eligible.
admission /admisjɔ̃/ *n.f.* admission.
adolescen|t, ~te /adɔlesɑ̃, -t/ *n.m., f.* adolescent. **~ce** *n.f.* adolescence.
adonner (s') /(s)adɔne/ *v. pr.* **s'~ à,** devote o.s. to; (*vice*) take to.
adopt|er /adɔpte/ *v.t.* adopt. **~ion** /-psjɔ̃/ *n.f.* adoption.
adopti|f, ~ve /adɔptif, -v/ *a.* (*enfant*) adopted; (*parents*) adoptive.
adorable /adɔrabl/ *a.* delightful, adorable.
ador|er /adɔre/ *v.t.* adore; (*relig.*) worship, adore. **~ation** *n.f.* adoration; worship.
adosser /adɔse/ *v.t.* **s'~** *v. pr.* lean back (**à, contre,** against).
adouci|r /adusir/ *v.t.* soften; (*boisson*) sweeten; (*personne*) mellow; (*chagrin*) ease. **s'~r** *v. pr.* soften; mellow; ease; (*temps*) become milder. **~ssant** *n.m.* (fabric) softener.
adresse /adrɛs/ *n.f.* address; (*habileté*) skill.
adresser /adrese/ *v.t.* send; (*écrire l'adresse sur*) address; (*remarque etc.*) address. **~ la parole à,** speak to. **s'~ à,** address; (*aller voir*) go and ask *ou* see; (*bureau*) enquire at; (*viser, intéresser*) be directed at.
adroit, ~e /adrwa, -t/ *a.* skilful, clever. **~ement** /-tmɑ̃/ *adv.* skilfully, cleverly.
aduler /adyle/ *v.t.* adulate.
adulte /adylt/ *n.m./f.* adult. ● *a.* adult; (*plante, animal*) fully- grown.
adultère /adyltɛr/ *a.* adulterous. ● *n.m.* adultery.
advenir /advənir/ *v.i.* occur.
adverbe /advɛrb/ *n.m.* adverb.
adversaire /advɛrsɛr/ *n.m.* opponent, adversary.
adverse /advɛrs/ *a.* opposing.
adversité /advɛrsite/ *n.f.* adversity.
aérateur /aeratœr/ *n.m.* ventilator.
aér|er /aere/ *v.t.* air; (*texte*) lighten. **s'~er** *v. pr.* get some air. **~ation** *n.f.* ventilation. **~é** *a.* airy.
aérien, ~ne /aerjɛ̃, -jɛn/ *a.* air; (*photo*) aerial; (*câble*) overhead; (*fig.*) airy.
aérobic /aerɔbik/ *m.* aerobics.
aérodrome /aerɔdrom/ *n.m.* aerodrome.
aérodynamique /aerɔdinamik/ *a.* streamlined, aerodynamic.
aérogare /aerɔgar/ *n.f.* air terminal.
aéroglisseur /aerɔglisœr/ *n.m.* hovercraft.
aérogramme /aerɔgram/ *n.m.* air mail letter; (*Amer.*) aerogram.
aéronautique /aerɔnotik/ *a.* aeronautical. ● *n.f.* aeronautics.
aéronavale /aerɔnaval/ *n.f.* Fleet Air Arm; (*Amer.*) Naval Air Force.
aéroport /aerɔpɔr/ *n.m.* airport.
aéroporté /aerɔpɔrte/ *a.* airborne.
aérosol /aerɔsɔl/ *n.m.* aerosol.
aérospat|ial (*m. pl.* **~iaux**) /aerɔspasjal, -jo/ *a.* aerospace.
affable /afabl/ *a.* affable.
affaibl|ir /afeblir/ *v.t.,* **s'~ir** *v. pr.* weaken. **~issement** *n.m.* weakening.
affaire /afɛr/ *n.f.* matter, affair; (*histoire*) affair; (*transaction*) deal; (*occasion*) bargain; (*firme*) business; (*jurid.*) case. **~s,** affairs; (*comm.*) business; (*effets*) belongings. **avoir ~ à,** (have to) deal with. **c'est mon ~, ce sont mes ~s,** that is my business. **faire l'~,** do the job. **tirer**

qn. d'~, help s.o. out. **se tirer d'~,** manage.

affair|er (s') /(s)afere/ *v. pr.* bustle about. **~é** *a.* busy.

affaiss|er (s') /(s)afese/ *v. pr.* (*sol*) sink, subside; (*poutre*) sag; (*personne*) collapse. **~ement** /-ɛsmɑ̃/ *n.m.* subsidence.

affaler (s') /(s)afale/ *v. pr.* slump (down), collapse.

affam|er /afame/ *v.t.* starve. **~é** *a.* starving.

affect|é /afɛkte/ *a.* affected. **~ation**[1] *n.f.* affectation.

affect|er /afɛkte/ *v.t.* (*feindre, émouvoir*) affect; (*destiner*) assign; (*nommer*) appoint, post. **~ation**[2] *n.f.* assignment; appointment, posting.

affecti|f, ~ve /afɛktif, -v/ *a.* emotional.

affection /afɛksjɔ̃/ *n.f.* affection; (*maladie*) ailment. **~ner** /-jɔne/ *v.t.* be fond of.

affectueu|x, ~se /afɛktɥø, -z/ *a.* affectionate.

affermir /afɛrmir/ *v.t.* strengthen.

affiche /afiʃ/ *n.f.* (public) notice; (*publicité*) poster; (*théâtre*) bill.

affich|er /afiʃe/ *v.t.* (*annonce*) put up; (*événement*) announce; (*sentiment etc, comput.*) display. **~age** *n.m.* billposting; (*électronique*) display.

affilée (d') /(d)afile/ *adv.* in a row, at a stretch.

affiler /afile/ *v.t.* sharpen.

affil|ier (s') /(s)afilje/ *v. pr.* become affiliated. **~iation** *n.f.* affiliation.

affiner /afine/ *v.t.* refine.

affinité /afinite/ *n.f.* affinity.

affirmati|f, ~ve /afirmatif, -v/ *a.* affirmative. ● *n.f.* affirmative.

affirm|er /afirme/ *v.t.* assert. **~ation** *n.f.* assertion.

affleurer /aflœre/ *v.i.* appear on the surface.

affliction /afliksjɔ̃/ *n.f.* affliction.

afflig|er /afliʒe/ *v.t.* grieve. **~é** *a.* distressed. **~é de,** afflicted with.

affluence /aflyɑ̃s/ *n.f.* crowd(s).

affluent /aflyɑ̃/ *n.m.* tributary.

affluer /aflye/ *v.i.* flood in; (*sang*) rush.

afflux /afly/ *n.m.* influx, flood; (*du sang*) rush.

affol|er /afɔle/ *v.t.* throw into a panic. **s'~er** *v. pr.* panic. **~ant, ~ante** *a.* alarming. **~ement** *n.m.* panic.

affranch|ir /afrɑ̃ʃir/ *v.t.* stamp; (*à la machine*) frank; (*esclave*) emancipate; (*fig.*) free. **~issement** *n.m.* (*tarif*) postage.

affréter /afrete/ *v.t.* charter.

affreu|x, ~se /afrø, -z/ *a.* (*laid*) hideous; (*mauvais*) awful. **~sement** *adv.* awfully, hideously.

affriolant, ~e /afrijɔlɑ̃, -t/ *a.* enticing.

affront /afrɔ̃/ *n.m.* affront.

affront|er /afrɔ̃te/ *v.t.* confront. **s'~er** *v. pr.* confront each other. **~ement** *n.m.* confrontation.

affubler /afyble/ *v.t.* rig out (**de,** in).

affût /afy/ *n.m.* **à l'~,** on the watch (**de,** for).

affûter /afyte/ *v.t.* sharpen.

afin /afɛ̃/ *prép. & conj.* **~ de/que,** in order to/that.

africain, ~e /afrikɛ̃, -ɛn/ *a. & n.m., f.* African.

Afrique /afrik/ *n.f.* Africa. **~ du Sud,** South Africa.

agacer /agase/ *v.t.* irritate, annoy.

âge /ɑʒ/ *n.m.* age. **quel ~ avez-vous?,** how old are you? **~ adulte,** adulthood. **~ mûr,** middle age. **d'un certain ~,** past one's prime.

âgé /ɑʒe/ *a.* elderly. **~ de cinq ans/** *etc.*, five years/*etc.* old.

agence /aʒɑ̃s/ *n.f.* agency, bureau, office; (*succursale*) branch. **~ d'interim,** employment agency. **~ de voyages,** travel agency.

agenc|er /aʒɑ̃se/ *v.t.* organize, arrange. **~ement** *n.m.* organization.

agenda /aʒɛ̃da/ *n.m.* diary; (*Amer.*) datebook.

agenouiller (s') /(s)aʒnuje/ *v. pr.* kneel (down).

agent /aʒɑ̃/ *n.m.* agent; (*fonctionnaire*) official. **~ (de police),** policeman. **~ de change,** stockbroker.

agglomération /aglɔmerɑsjɔ̃/ *n.f.* built-up area, town.

aggloméré /aglɔmere/ *n.m.* (*bois*) chipboard.

agglomérer /aglɔmere/ *v.t.*, **s'~** *v. pr.* pile up.

agglutiner /aglytine/ *v.t.*, **s'~** *v. pr.* stick together.

aggraver /agrave/ *v.t.*, **s'~** *v. pr.* worsen.

agil|e /aʒil/ *a.* agile, nimble. **~ité** *n.f.* agility.

agir /aʒir/ *v.i.* act. **il s'agit de faire,** it is a matter of doing; (*il faut*) it is necessary to do. **dans ce livre il s'agit de,** this book is about. **dont il s'agit,** in question.

agissements /aʒismɑ̃/ *n.m. pl.* (*péj.*) dealings.

agité /aʒite/ *a.* restless, fidgety; (*troublé*) agitated; (*mer*) rough.

agit|er /aʒite/ *v.t.* (*bras etc.*) wave; (*liquide*) shake; (*troubler*) agitate; (*discuter*) debate. **s'~er** *v. pr.* bustle about; (*enfant*) fidget; (*foule, pensées*) stir. **~ateur, ~atrice** *n.m., f.* agitator. **~ation** *n.f.* bustle; (*trouble*) agitation.

agneau (*pl.* **~x**) /aɲo/ *n.m.* lamb.

agonie /agɔni/ *n.f.* death throes.

agoniser /agɔnize/ *v.i.* be dying.

agraf|e /agraf/ *n.f.* hook; (*pour papiers*) staple. **~er** *v.t.* hook (up); staple. **~euse** *n.f.* stapler.

agrand|ir /agrɑ̃dir/ *v.t.* enlarge. **s'~ir** *v. pr.* expand, grow. **~issement** *n.m.* extension; (*de photo*) enlargement.

agréable /agreabl/ *a.* pleasant. **~ment** /-əmɑ̃/ *adv.* pleasantly.

agré|er /agree/ *v.t.* accept. **~er à,** please. **~é** *a.* authorized.

agrég|ation /agregɑsjɔ̃/ *n.f.* agrégation (*highest examination for recruitment of teachers*). **~é, ~ée** /-ʒe/ *n.m., f.* agrégé (*teacher who has passed the agrégation*).

agrément /agremɑ̃/ *n.m.* charm; (*plaisir*) pleasure; (*accord*) assent.

agrémenter /agremɑ̃te/ *v.t.* embellish (**de,** with).

agrès /agrɛ/ *n.m. pl.* (gymnastics) apparatus.

agress|er /agrese/ *v.t.* attack. **~eur** /-ɛsœr/ *n.m.* attacker; (*mil.*) aggressor. **~ion** /-ɛsjɔ̃/ *n.f.* attack; (*mil.*) aggression.

agressi|f, ~ve /agresif, -v/ *a.* aggressive. **~vité** *n.f.* aggressiveness.

agricole /agrikɔl/ *a.* agricultural; (*ouvrier etc.*) farm.

agriculteur /agrikyltœr/ *n.m.* farmer.

agriculture /agrikyltyr/ *n.f.* agriculture, farming.

agripper /agripe/ *v.t.*, **s'~ à,** grab, clutch.

agroalimentaire /agrɔalimɑ̃tɛr/ *n.m.* food industry.

agrumes /agrym/ *n.m. pl.* citrus fruit(s).

aguerrir /agerir/ *v.t.* harden.

aguets (aux) /(oz)agɛ/ *adv.* on the look-out.

aguicher /agiʃe/ *v.t.* entice.

ah /ɑ/ *int.* ah, oh.

ahur|ir /ayrir/ *v.t.* dumbfound. **~issement** *n.m.* stupefaction.

ai /e/ *voir* **avoir.**

aide /ɛd/ *n.f.* help, assistance, aid. ● *n.m./f.* assistant. **à l'~ de,** with the help of. **~ familiale,** home help. **~-mémoire** *n.m. invar.* handbook of facts. **~ sociale,** social security; (*Amer.*) welfare. **~-soignant, ~-soignante** *n.m., f.* auxiliary nurse. **venir en ~ à,** help.

aider /ede/ *v.t./i.* help, assist. **~ à faire,** help to do. **s'~ de,** use.

aïe /aj/ *int.* ouch, ow.

aïeul, ~e /ajœl/ *n.m., f.* grandparent.

aïeux /ajø/ *n.m. pl.* forefathers.

aigle /ɛgl/ *n.m.* eagle.

aigr|e /ɛgr/ *a.* sour, sharp; (*fig.*) sharp. **~e-doux, ~e-douce** *a.* bitter-sweet. **~eur** *n.f.* sourness; (*fig.*) sharpness. **~eurs d'estomac,** heartburn.

aigrir /egrir/ *v.t.* embitter; (*caractère*) sour. **s'~** *v. pr.* turn sour; (*personne*) become embittered.

aigu, ~ë /egy/ *a.* acute; (*objet*) sharp; (*voix*) shrill. (*mus.*) **les ~s,** the high notes.

aiguillage /egɥijaʒ/ *n.m.* (*rail.*) points; (*rail., Amer.*) switches.

aiguille /egɥij/ *n.f.* needle; (*de montre*) hand; (*de balance*) pointer.

aiguill|er /egɥije/ *v.t.* shunt; (*fig.*) steer. **~eur** *n.m.* pointsman; (*Amer.*) switchman. **~eur du ciel,** air traffic controller.

aiguillon /egɥijɔ̃/ *n.m.* (*dard*) sting; (*fig.*) spur. **~ner** /-jɔne/ *v.t.* spur on.

aiguiser /eg(ɥ)ize/ *v.t.* sharpen; (*fig.*) stimulate.

ail (*pl.* **~s**) /aj/ *n.m.* garlic.

aile /ɛl/ *n.f.* wing.

ailé /ele/ *a.* winged.

aileron /ɛlrɔ̃/ *n.m.* (*de requin*) fin.

ailier /elje/ *n.m.* winger; (*Amer.*) end.

aille /aj/ *voir* aller[1].

ailleurs /ajœr/ *adv.* elsewhere. **d'~,** besides, moreover. **par ~,** moreover, furthermore. **partout ~,** everywhere else.

ailloli /ajɔli/ *n.m.* garlic mayonnais

aimable /ɛmabl/ *a.* kind. **~m** /-əmɑ̃/ *adv.* kindly.

aimant[1] /ɛmɑ̃/ *n.m.* magnet. **~er** /-te/ *v.t.* magnetize.

aimant[2], **~e** /ɛmɑ̃, -t/ *a.* loving.

aimer /eme/ *v.t.* like; (*d'amour*) love. **j'aimerais faire,** I'd like to do. **~ bien,** quite like. **~ mieux** *ou* **autant,** prefer.

aine /ɛn/ *n.f.* groin.

aîné, ~e /ene/ *a.* eldest; (*entre deux*) elder. ● *n.m., f.* eldest (child); elder (child). **~s** *n.m. pl.* elders. **il est mon ~,** he is older than me *ou* my senior.

ainsi /ɛ̃si/ *adv.* thus; (*donc*) so. **~ que,** as well as; (*comme*) as. **et ~ de suite,** and so on. **pour ~ dire,** so to speak, as it were.

air /ɛr/ *n.m.* air; (*mine*) look, air; (*mélodie*) tune. **~ conditionné,** air-conditioning. **avoir l'~ de,** look like. **avoir l'~ de faire,** appear to be doing. **en l'~,** (up) in the air; (*promesses etc.*) empty.

aire /ɛr/ *n.f.* area. **~ d'atterrissage,** landing-strip.

aisance /ɛzɑ̃s/ *n.f.* ease; (*richesse*) affluence.

aise /ɛz/ *n.f.* joy. ● *a.* **bien ~ de/que,** delighted about/that. **à l'~,** (*sur un siège*) comfortable; (*pas gêné*) at ease; (*fortuné*) comfortably off. **mal à l'~,** uncomfortable; ill at ease. **aimer ses ~s,** like one's comforts. **se mettre à l'~,** make o.s. comfortable.

aisé /eze/ *a.* easy; (*fortuné*) well-off. **~ment** *adv.* easily.

aisselle /ɛsɛl/ *n.f.* armpit.

ait /ɛ/ *voir* avoir.

ajonc /aʒɔ̃/ *n.m.* gorse.

ajourn|er /aʒurne/ *v.t.* postpone; (*assemblée*) adjourn. **~ement** *n.m.* postponement; adjournment.

ajout /aʒu/ *n.m.* addition.

ajouter /aʒute/ *v.t.* **s'~** *v. pr.* add (**à,** to). **~ foi à,** lend credence to.

ajust|er /aʒyste/ *v.t.* adjust; (*coup*) aim; (*cible*) aim at; (*adapter*) fit. **s'~er** *v. pr.* fit. **~age** *n.m.* fitting. **~é** *a.* close-fitting. **~ement** *n.m.* adjustment. **~eur** *n.m.* fitter.

alambic /alɑ̃bik/ *n.m.* still.

alanguir (s') /(s)alɑ̃gir/ *v. pr.* grow languid.

alarme /alarm/ *n.f.* alarm. **donner l'~,** sound the alarm.

alarmer /alarme/ *v.t.* alarm. **s'~** *v. pr.* become alarmed (**de,** at).

alarmiste /alarmist/ *a.* & *n.m.* alarmist.

albâtre /albɑtr/ *n.m.* alabaster.

albatros /albatros/ *n.m.* albatross.

album /albɔm/ *n.m.* album.

albumine /albymin/ *n.f.* albumin.

alcali /alkali/ *n.m.* alkali.

alcool /alkɔl/ *n.m.* alcohol; (*eau de vie*) brandy. **~ à brûler,** methylated spirit. **~ique** *a.* & *n.m./f.* alcoholic. **~isé** *a.* (*boisson*) alcoholic. **~isme** *n.m.* alcoholism.

alcootest /alkɔtɛst/ *n.m.* (P.) breath test; (*appareil*) breathalyser.

alcôve /alkov/ *n.f.* alcove.

aléa /alea/ *n.m.* hazard.

aléatoire /aleatwar/ *a.* uncertain; (*comput.*) random.

alentour /alɑ̃tur/ *adv.* around. **~s** *n.m. pl.* surroundings. **aux ~s de,** round about.

alerte /alɛrt/ *a.* agile. ● *n.f.* alert. **~ à la bombe,** bomb scare.

alerter /alɛrte/ *v.t.* alert.

algarade /algarad/ *n.f.* altercation.

alg|èbre /alʒɛbr/ *n.f.* algebra. **~ébrique** *a.* algebraic.

Alger /alʒe/ *n.m./f.* Algiers.

Algérie /alʒeri/ *n.f.* Algeria.

algérien, ~ne /alʒerjɛ̃, -jɛn/ *a.* & *n.m., f.* Algerian.

algue /alg/ *n.f.* seaweed. **les ~s,** (*bot.*) algae.

alias /aljɑs/ *adv.* alias.

alibi /alibi/ *n.m.* alibi.

aliéné, ~e /aljene/ *n.m., f.* insane person.

alién|er /aljene/ *v.t.* alienate; (*céder*) give up. **s'~er** *v. pr.* alienate. **~ation** *n.f.* alienation.

aligner /aliɲe/ *v.t.* (*objets*) line up, make lines of; (*chiffres*) string together. **~ sur,** bring into line with. **s'~** *v. pr.* line up. **s'~ sur,** align o.s. on. **alignement** /-əmɑ̃/ *n.m.* alignment.

aliment /alimɑ̃/ *n.m.* food. **~aire** /-tɛr/ *a.* food; (*fig.*) bread-and-butter.

aliment|er /alimɑ̃te/ *v.t.* feed; (*fournir*) supply; (*fig.*) sustain. **~ation** *n.f.* feeding; supply(ing); (*régime*) diet; (*aliments*) groceries.

alinéa /alinea/ *n.m.* paragraph.

aliter (s') /(s)alite/ *v. pr.* take to one's bed.

allaiter /alete/ *v.t.* feed. **~ au biberon,** bottle-feed. **~ au sein,** breast-feed; (*Amer.*) nurse.

allant /alɑ̃/ *n.m.* verve, drive.

allécher /aleʃe/ *v.t.* tempt.

allée /ale/ *n.f.* path, lane; (*menant à une maison*) drive(way). **~s et venues,** comings and goings.
allégation /alegɑsjɔ̃/ *n.f.* allegation.
allég|er /aleʒe/ *v.t.* make lighter; (*poids*) lighten; (*fig.*) alleviate. **~é** *a.* (*diététique*) light.
allègre /alɛgr/ *a.* gay; (*vif*) lively, jaunty.
allégresse /alegrɛs/ *n.f.* gaiety.
alléguer /alege/ *v.t.* put forward.
Allemagne /almaɲ/ *n.f.* Germany. **~ de l'Ouest,** West Germany.
allemand, ~e /almɑ̃, -d/ *a.* & *n.m., f.* German. ● *n.m.* (*lang.*) German.
aller†[1] /ale/ (*aux. être*) go. **s'en ~** *v. pr.* go away. **~ à,** (*convenir à*) suit; (*s'adapter à*) fit. **~ faire,** be going to do. **comment allez-vous?, (comment) ça va?,** how are you? **ça va!,** all right! **il va bien,** he is well. **il va mieux,** he's better. **allez-y!,** go on! **allez!,** come on! **allons-y!,** let's go!
aller[2] /ale/ *n.m.* outward journey; **~ (simple),** single (ticket); (*Amer.*) one-way (ticket). **~ (et) retour,** return journey; (*Amer.*) round trip; (*billet*) return (ticket); (*Amer.*) round trip (ticket).
allerg|ie /alɛrʒi/ *n.f.* allergy. **~ique** *a.* allergic.
alliage /aljaʒ/ *n.m.* alloy.
alliance /aljɑ̃s/ *n.f.* alliance; (*bague*) wedding ring; (*mariage*) marriage.
allié, ~e /alje/ *n.m., f.* ally; (*parent*) relative (by marriage).
allier /alje/ *v.t.* combine; (*pol.*) ally. **s'~** *v. pr.* combine; (*pol.*) become allied; (*famille*) become related (**à,** to).
alligator /aligatɔr/ *n.m.* alligator.
allô /alo/ *int.* hallo, hello.
allocation /alɔkɑsjɔ̃/ *n.f.* allowance. **~ (de) chômage,** unemployment benefit. **~s familiales,** family allowance.
allocution /alɔkysjɔ̃/ *n.f.* speech.
allongé /alɔ̃ʒe/ *a.* elongated.
allongement /alɔ̃ʒmɑ̃/ *n.m.* lengthening.
allonger /alɔ̃ʒe/ *v.t.* lengthen; (*bras, jambe*) stretch (out). **s'~** *v. pr.* get longer; (*s'étendre*) stretch (o.s.) out.
allouer /alwe/ *v.t.* allocate.
allum|er /alyme/ *v.t.* light; (*radio, lampe, etc.*) turn on; (*pièce*) switch the light(s) on in; (*fig.*) arouse. **s'~er** *v. pr.* (*lumière*) come on. **~age** *n.m.* lighting; (*auto.*) ignition. **~e-gaz** *n.m. invar.* gas lighter.
allumette /alymɛt/ *n.f.* match.
allure /alyr/ *n.f.* speed, pace; (*démarche*) walk; (*prestance*) bearing; (*air*) look. **à toute ~,** at full speed. **avoir de l'~,** have style.
allusion /alyzjɔ̃/ *n.f.* allusion (**à,** to); (*implicite*) hint (**à,** at). **faire ~ à,** allude to; hint at.
almanach /almana/ *n.m.* almanac.
aloi /alwa/ *n.m.* **de bon ~,** sterling; (*gaieté*) wholesome.
alors /alɔr/ *adv.* then. ● *conj.* so, then. **~ que,** when, while; (*tandis que*) whereas. **ça ~!,** well! **et ~?,** so what?
alouette /alwɛt/ *n.f.* lark.
alourdir /alurdir/ *v.t.* weigh down.
aloyau (*pl.* **~x**) /alwajo/ *n.m.* sirloin.
alpage /alpaʒ/ *n.m.* mountain pasture.
Alpes /alp/ *n.f. pl.* **les ~,** the Alps.
alpestre /alpɛstr/ *a.* alpine.
alphab|et /alfabɛ/ *n.m.* alphabet. **~étique** *a.* alphabetical.
alphabétiser /alfabetize/ *v.t.* teach to read and write.
alphanumérique /alfanymerik/ *a.* alphanumeric.
alpin, ~e /alpɛ̃, -in/ *a.* alpine.
alpinis|te /alpinist/ *n.m./f.* mountaineer. **~me** *n.m.* mountaineering.
altér|er /altere/ *v.t.* falsify; (*abîmer*) spoil; (*donner soif à*) make thirsty. **s'~er** *v. pr.* deteriorate. **~ation** *n.f.* deterioration.
alternati|f, ~ve /altɛrnatif, -v/ *a.* alternating. ● *n.f.* alternative. **~vement** *adv.* alternately.
altern|er /altɛrne/ *v.t./i.* alternate. **~ance** *n.f.* alternation. **en ~ance,** alternately. **~é** *a.* alternate.
Altesse /altɛs/ *n.f.* Highness.
alt|ier, ~ière /altje, -jɛr/ *a.* haughty.
altitude /altityd/ *n.f.* altitude, height.
alto /alto/ *n.m.* viola.
aluminium /alyminjɔm/ *n.m.* aluminium; (*Amer.*) aluminum.
alvéole /alveɔl/ *n.f.* (*de ruche*) cell.
amabilité /amabilite/ *n.f.* kindness.
amadouer /amadwe/ *v.t.* win over.
amaigr|ir /amegrir/ *v.t.* make thin(ner). **~issant, ~issante** *a.* (*régime*) slimming.
amalgam|e /amalgam/ *n.m.* combination. **~er** *v.t.* combine, amalgamate.

amande /amɑ̃d/ *n.f.* almond; (*d'un fruit à noyau*) kernel.

amant /amɑ̃/ *n.m.* lover.

amarr|e /amar/ *n.f.* (mooring) rope. **~es,** moorings. **~er** *v.t.* moor.

amas /amɑ/ *n.m.* heap, pile.

amasser /amɑse/ *v.t.* amass, gather; (*empiler*) pile up. **s'~** *v. pr.* pile up; (*gens*) gather.

amateur /amatœr/ *n.m.* amateur. **~ de,** lover of. **d'~,** amateur; (*péj.*) amateurish. **~isme** *n.m.* amateurism.

amazone (en) /(ɑ̃n)amazon/ *adv.* side-saddle.

Amazonie /amazɔni/ *n.f.* Amazonia.

ambages (sans) /(sɑ̃z)ɑ̃baʒ/ *adv.* in plain language.

ambassade /ɑ̃basad/ *n.f.* embassy.

ambassa|deur, ~drice /ɑ̃basadœr, -dris/ *n.m., f.* ambassador.

ambiance /ɑ̃bjɑ̃s/ *n.f.* atmosphere.

ambiant, ~e /ɑ̃bjɑ̃, -t/ *a.* surrounding.

ambigu, ~ë /ɑ̃bigy/ *a.* ambiguous. **~ïté** /-ɥite/ *n.f.* ambiguity.

ambitieu|x, ~se /ɑ̃bisjø, -z/ *a.* ambitious.

ambition /ɑ̃bisjɔ̃/ *n.f.* ambition. **~ner** /-jɔne/ *v.t.* have as one's ambition (**de,** to).

ambivalent, ~e /ɑ̃bivalɑ̃, -t/ *a.* ambivalent.

ambre /ɑ̃br/ *n.m.* amber.

ambulanc|e /ɑ̃bylɑ̃s/ *n.f.* ambulance. **~ier, ~ière** *n.m., f.* ambulance driver.

ambulant, ~e /ɑ̃bylɑ̃, -t/ *a.* itinerant.

âme /ɑm/ *n.f.* soul. **~ sœur,** soul mate.

amélior|er /ameljɔre/ *v.t.,* **s'~er** *v. pr.* improve. **~ation** *n.f.* improvement.

aménag|er /amenaʒe/ *v.t.* (*arranger*) fit out; (*transformer*) convert; (*installer*) fit up; (*territoire*) develop. **~ement** *n.m.* fitting out; conversion; fitting up; development; (*modification*) adjustment.

amende /amɑ̃d/ *n.f.* fine. **faire ~ honorable,** make an apology.

amend|er /amɑ̃de/ *v.t.* improve; (*jurid.*) amend. **s'~er** *v. pr.* mend one's ways. **~ement** *n.m.* (*de texte*) amendment.

amener /amne/ *v.t.* bring; (*causer*) bring about. **~ qn. à faire,** cause sb. to do. **s'~** *v. pr.* (*fam.*) come along.

amenuiser (s') /(s)amənɥize/ *v. pr.* dwindle.

amer, amère /amɛr/ *a.* bitter.

américain, ~e /amerikɛ̃, -ɛn/ *a.* & *n.m., f.* American.

Amérique /amerik/ *n.f.* America. **~ centrale/latine,** Central/ Latin America. **~ du Nord/Sud,** North/ South America.

amertume /amɛrtym/ *n.f.* bitterness.

ameublement /amœbləmɑ̃/ *n.m.* furniture.

ameuter /amøte/ *v.t.* draw a crowd of; (*fig.*) stir up.

ami, ~e /ami/ *n.m., f.* friend; (*de la nature, des livres, etc.*) lover. ● *a.* friendly.

amiable /amjabl/ *a.* amicable. **à l'~** *adv.* amicably; *a.* amicable.

amiante /amjɑ̃t/ *n.m.* asbestos.

amic|al (*m. pl.* **~aux**) /amikal, -o/ *a.* friendly. **~alement** *adv.* in a friendly manner.

amicale /amikal/ *n.f.* association.

amidon /amidɔ̃/ *n.m.* starch. **~ner** /-ɔne/ *v.t.* starch.

amincir /amɛ̃sir/ *v.t.* make thinner. **s'~** *v. pr.* get thinner.

amir|al (*pl.* **~aux**) /amiral, -o/ *n.m.* admiral.

amitié /amitje/ *n.f.* friendship. **~s,** kind regards. **prendre en ~,** take a liking to.

ammoniac /amɔnjak/ *n.m.* (*gaz*) ammonia.

ammoniaque /amɔnjak/ *n.f.* (*eau*) ammonia.

amnésie /amnezi/ *n.f.* amnesia.

amnistie /amnisti/ *n.f.* amnesty.

amniocentèse /amniɔsɛ̃tɛz/ *n.f.* amniocentesis.

amocher /amɔʃe/ *v.t.* (*fam.*) mess up.

amoindrir /amwɛ̃drir/ *v.t.* diminish.

amollir /amɔlir/ *v.t.* soften.

amonceler /amɔ̃sle/ *v.t.,* **s'~** *v.pr.* pile up.

amont (en) /(ɑ̃n)amɔ̃/ *adv.* upstream.

amorc|e /amɔrs/ *n.f.* bait; (*début*) start; (*explosif*) fuse, cap; (*de pistolet d'enfant*) cap. **~er** *v.t.* start; (*hameçon*) bait; (*pompe*) prime.

amorphe /amɔrf/ *a.* (*mou*) listless.

amortir /amɔrtir/ *v.t.* (*choc*) cushion; (*bruit*) deaden; (*dette*) pay off; (*objet acheté*) make pay for itself.

amortisseur /amɔrtisœr/ *n.m.* shock absorber.

amour /amur/ *n.m.* love. **pour l'~de,** for the sake of. **~-propre** *n.m.* self-respect.
amouracher (s') /(s)amuraʃe/ *v. pr.* become infatuated (**de,** with).
amoureu|x, ~se /amurø, -z/ *a.* (*ardent*) amorous; (*vie*) love. ● *n.m., f.* lover. **~x de qn.,** in love with s.o.
amovible /amɔvibl/ *a.* removable.
ampère /ɑ̃pɛr/ *n.m.* amp(ere).
amphibie /ɑ̃fibi/ *a.* amphibious.
amphithéâtre /ɑ̃fiteɑtr/ *n.m.* amphitheatre; (*d'université*) lecture hall.
ample /ɑ̃pl/ *a.* ample; (*mouvement*) broad. **~ment** /-əmɑ̃/ *adv.* amply.
ampleur /ɑ̃plœr/ *n.f.* extent, size; (*de vêtement*) fullness.
ampli /ɑ̃pli/ *n.m.* amplifier.
amplif|ier /ɑ̃plifje/ *v.t.* amplify; (*fig.*) expand, develop. **s'~ier** *v.pr.* expand, develop. **~icateur** *n.m.* amplifier.
ampoule /ɑ̃pul/ *n.f.* (*électrique*) bulb; (*sur la peau*) blister; (*de médicament*) phial.
ampoulé /ɑ̃pule/ *a.* turgid.
amput|er /ɑ̃pyte/ *v.t.* amputate; (*fig.*) reduce. **~ation** *n.f.* amputation; (*fig.*) reduction.
amuse-gueule /amyzgœl/ *n.m. invar.* appetizer.
amus|er /amyze/ *v.t.* amuse; (*détourner l'attention de*) distract. **s'~er** *v. pr.* enjoy o.s.; (*jouer*) play. **~ant, ~ante** *a.* (*blague*) funny; (*soirée*) enjoyable, entertaining. **~ement** *n.m.* amusement; (*passe-temps*) diversion. **~eur** *n.m.* (*péj.*) entertainer.
amygdale /amidal/ *n.f.* tonsil.
an /ɑ̃/ *n.m.* year. **avoir dix/***etc.* **ans,** be ten/*etc.* years old.
anachronisme /anakrɔnism/ *n.m.* anachronism.
analgésique /analʒezik/ *a.* & *n.m.* analgesic.
analog|ie /analɔʒi/ *n.f.* analogy. **~ique** *a.* analogical, (*comput.*) analogue.
analogue /analɔg/ *a.* similar.
analphabète /analfabɛt/ *a.* & *n.m./f.* illiterate.
analy|se /analiz/ *n.f.* analysis; (*de sang*) test. **~ser** *v.t.* analyse. **~ste** *n.m./f.* analyst. **~tique** *a.* analytical.
ananas /anana(s)/ *n.m.* pineapple.
anarch|ie /anarʃi/ *n.f.* anarchy. **~ique** *a.* anarchic. **~iste** *n.m./f.* anarchist.
anatom|ie /anatɔmi/ *n.f.* anatomy. **~ique** *a.* anatomical.
ancestr|al (*m. pl.* **~aux**) /ɑ̃sɛstral, -o/ *a.* ancestral.
ancêtre /ɑ̃sɛtr/ *n.m.* ancestor.
anche /ɑ̃ʃ/ *n.f.* (*mus.*) reed.
anchois /ɑ̃ʃwa/ *n.m.* anchovy.
ancien, ~ne /ɑ̃sjɛ̃, -jɛn/ *a.* old; (*de jadis*) ancient; (*meuble*) antique; (*précédent*) former, ex-, old; (*dans une fonction*) senior. ● *n.m., f.* senior; (*par l'âge*) elder. **~ combattant,** ex-serviceman. **~nement** /-jɛnmɑ̃/ *adv.* formerly. **~neté** /-jɛnte/ *n.f.* age; seniority.
ancr|e /ɑ̃kr/ *n.f.* anchor. **jeter/lever l'~e,** cast/weigh anchor. **~er** *v.t.* anchor; (*fig.*) fix. **s'~er** *v.pr.* anchor.
andouille /ɑ̃duj/ *n.f.* sausage filled with chitterlings; (*idiot: fam.*) nitwit.
âne /ɑn/ *n.m.* donkey, ass; (*imbécile*) ass.
anéantir /aneɑ̃tir/ *v.t.* destroy; (*exterminer*) annihilate; (*accabler*) overwhelm.
anecdot|e /anɛkdɔt/ *n.f.* anecdote. **~ique** *a.* anecdotal.
aném|ie /anemi/ *n.f.* anaemia. **~ié, ~ique** *adjs.* anaemic.
ânerie /ɑnri/ *n.f.* stupidity; (*parole*) stupid remark.
ânesse /ɑnɛs/ *n.f.* she-ass.
anesthés|ie /anɛstezi/ *n.f.* (*opération*) anaesthetic. **~ique** *a.* & *n.m.* (*substance*) anaesthetic.
ang|e /ɑ̃ʒ/ *n.m.* angel. **aux ~es,** in seventh heaven. **~élique** *a.* angelic.
angélus /ɑ̃ʒelys/ *n.m.* angelus.
angine /ɑ̃ʒin/ *n.f.* throat infection.
anglais, ~e /ɑ̃glɛ, -z/ *a.* English. ● *n.m., f.* Englishman, Englishwoman. ● *n.m.* (*lang.*) English.
angle /ɑ̃gl/ *n.m.* angle; (*coin*) corner.
Angleterre /ɑ̃glətɛr/ *n.f.* England.
anglicisme /ɑ̃glisism/ *n.m.* anglicism.
angliciste /ɑ̃glisist/ *n.m./f.* English specialist.
anglo- /ɑ̃glɔ/ *préf.* Anglo-.
anglophone /ɑ̃glɔfɔn/ *a.* English-speaking. ● *n.m./f.* English speaker.
anglo-saxon, ~ne /ɑ̃glɔsaksɔ̃, -ɔn/ *a.* & *n.m., f.* Anglo- Saxon.

angoiss|e /ɑ̃gwas/ *n.f.* anxiety. **~ant, ~ante** *a.* harrowing. **~é** *a.* anxious. **~er** *v.t.* make anxious.
anguille /ɑ̃gij/ *n.f.* eel.
anguleux, ~se /ɑ̃gylø, -z/ *a.* (*traits*) angular.
anicroche /anikrɔʃ/ *n.f.* snag.
anim|al (*pl.* **~aux**) /animal, -o/ *n.m.* animal. ● *a.* (*m. pl.* **~aux**) animal.
anima|teur, ~trice /animatœr, -tris/ *n.m., f.* organizer, leader; (*TV*) host, hostess.
anim|é /anime/ *a.* lively; (*affairé*) busy, (*être*) animate. **~ation** *n.f.* liveliness; (*affairement*) activity; (*cinéma*) animation.
animer /anime/ *v.t.* liven up; (*mener*) lead; (*mouvoir, pousser*) drive; (*encourager*) spur on. **s'~** *v. pr.* liven up.
animosité /animozite/ *n.f.* animosity.
anis /anis/ *n.m.* (*parfum, boisson*) aniseed.
ankylos|er (s') /(s)ɑ̃kiloze/ *v. pr.* go stiff. **~é** *a.* stiff.
anneau (*pl.* **~x**) /ano/ *n.m.* ring; (*de chaîne*) link.
année /ane/ *n.f.* year.
annexe /anɛks/ *a.* attached; (*question*) related. (*bâtiment*) adjoining. ● *n.f.* annexe; (*Amer.*) annex.
annex|er /anɛkse/ *v.t.* annex; (*document*) attach. **~ion** *n.f.* annexation.
annihiler /aniile/ *v.t.* annihilate.
anniversaire /anivɛrsɛr/ *n.m.* birthday; (*d'un événement*) anniversary. ● *a.* anniversary.
annonc|e /anɔ̃s/ *n.f.* announcement; (*publicitaire*) advertisement; (*indice*) sign. **~er** *v.t.* announce; (*dénoter*) indicate. **s'~er bien/mal,** look good/bad. **~eur** *n.m.* advertiser; (*speaker*) announcer.
Annonciation /anɔ̃sjɑsjɔ̃/ *n.f.* **l'~,** the Annunciation.
annuaire /anɥɛr/ *n.m.* year-book. **~ (téléphonique),** (telephone) directory.
annuel, ~le /anɥɛl/ *a.* annual, yearly. **~lement** *adv.* annually, yearly.
annuité /anɥite/ *n.f.* annual payment.
annulaire /anylɛr/ *n.m.* ringfinger.
annul|er /anyle/ *v.t.* cancel; (*contrat*) nullify; (*jugement*) quash. **s'~er** *v. pr.* cancel each other out. **~ation** *n.f.* cancellation.
anodin, ~e /anɔdɛ̃, -in/ *a.* insignificant; (*blessure*) harmless.
anomalie /anɔmali/ *n.f.* anomaly.
ânonner /ɑnɔne/ *v.t./i.* mumble, drone.
anonymat /anɔnima/ *n.m.* anonymity.
anonyme /anɔnim/ *a.* anonymous.
anorak /anɔrak/ *n.m.* anorak.
anorexie /anɔrɛksi/ *n.f.* anorexia.
anorm|al (*m. pl.* **~aux**) /anɔrmal, -o/ *a.* abnormal.
anse /ɑ̃s/ *n.f.* handle; (*baie*) cove.
antagonis|me /ɑ̃tagɔnism/ *n.m.* antagonism. **~te** *n.m./f.* antagonist; *a.* antagonistic.
antan (d') /(d)ɑ̃tɑ̃/ *a.* of long ago.
antarctique /ɑ̃tarktik/ *a.* & *n.m.* Antarctic.
antenne /ɑ̃tɛn/ *n.f.* aerial; (*Amer.*) antenna; (*d'insecte*) antenna; (*succursale*) agency; (*mil.*) outpost; (*auto., méd.*) emergency unit. **à l'~,** on the air. **sur l'~ de,** on the wavelength of.
antérieur /ɑ̃terjœr/ *a.* previous, earlier; (*placé devant*) front. **~ à,** prior to. **~ement** *adv.* earlier. **~ement à,** prior to. **antériorité** /-jɔrite/ *n.f.* precedence.
anthologie /ɑ̃tɔlɔʒi/ *n.f.* anthology.
anthropolo|gie /ɑ̃trɔpɔlɔʒi/ *n.f.* anthropology. **~gue** *n.m./f.* anthropologist.
anthropophage /ɑ̃trɔpɔfaʒ/ *a.* cannibalistic. ● *n.m./f.* cannibal.
anti- /ɑ̃ti/ *préf.* anti-.
antiadhési|f, ~ve /ɑ̃tiadezif, -v/ *a.* non-stick.
antiaérien, ~ne /ɑ̃tiaerjɛ̃, -jɛn/ *a.* anti-aircraft. **abri ~,** air-raid shelter.
antiatomique /ɑ̃tiatɔmik/ *a.* **abri ~,** fall-out shelter.
antibiotique /ɑ̃tibjɔtik/ *n.m.* antibiotic.
anticancéreu|x, ~se /ɑ̃tikɑ̃serø, -z/ *a.* (anti-)cancer.
antichambre /ɑ̃tiʃɑ̃br/ *n.f.* waiting-room, antechamber.
anticipation /ɑ̃tisipɑsjɔ̃/ *n.f.* **d'~,** (*livre, film*) science fiction. **par ~,** in advance.
anticipé /ɑ̃tisipe/ *a.* early.
anticiper /ɑ̃tisipe/ *v.t./i.* **~ (sur),** anticipate.
anticonceptionnel, ~le /ɑ̃tikɔ̃sɛpsjɔnɛl/ *a.* contraceptive.
anticorps /ɑ̃tikɔr/ *n.m.* antibody.

anticyclone /ɑ̃tisiklon/ *n.m.* anticyclone.
antidater /ɑ̃tidate/ *v.t.* backdate, antedate.
antidote /ɑ̃tidɔt/ *n.m.* antidote.
antigel /ɑ̃tiʒɛl/ *n.m.* antifreeze.
antihistaminique /ɑ̃tiistaminik/ *a.* & *n.m.* antihistamine.
antillais, ~e /ɑ̃tijɛ, -z/ *a.* & *n.m., f.* West Indian.
Antilles /ɑ̃tij/ *n.f. pl.* **les ~,** the West Indies.
antilope /ɑ̃tilɔp/ *n.f.* antelope.
antimite /ɑ̃timit/ *n.m.* moth repellent.
antipath|ie /ɑ̃tipati/ *n.f.* antipathy. **~ique** *a.* unpleasant.
antipodes /ɑ̃tipɔd/ *n.m. pl.* antipodes. **aux ~ de,** (*fig.*) poles apart from.
antiquaire /ɑ̃tikɛr/ *n.m./f.* antique dealer.
antiqu|e /ɑ̃tik/ *a.* ancient. **~ité** *n.f.* antiquity; (*objet*) antique.
antirouille /ɑ̃tiruj/ *a.* & *n.m.* rustproofing.
antisémit|e /ɑ̃tisemit/ *a.* anti-Semitic. **~isme** *n.m.* anti- Semitism.
antiseptique /ɑ̃tisɛptik/ *a.* & *n.m.* antiseptic.
antithèse /ɑ̃titɛz/ *n.f.* antithesis.
antivol /ɑ̃tivɔl/ *n.m.* anti-theft lock *ou* device.
antre /ɑ̃tr/ *n.m.* den.
anus /anys/ *n.m.* anus.
anxiété /ɑ̃ksjete/ *n.f.* anxiety.
anxieu|x, ~se /ɑ̃ksjø, -z/ *a.* anxious. ● *n.m., f.* worrier.
août /u(t)/ *n.m.* August.
apais|er /apeze/ *v.t.* calm down, (*douleur, colère*) soothe (*faim*) appease. **s'~er** *v. pr.* (*tempête*) die down. **~ement** *n.m.* appeasement; soothing. **~ements** *n.m. pl.* reassurances.
apanage /apanaʒ/ *n.m.* **l'~ de,** the privilege of.
aparté /aparte/ *n.m.* private exchange; (*théâtre*) aside. **en ~,** in private.
apath|ie /apati/ *n.f.* apathy. **~ique** *a.* apathetic.
apatride /apatrid/ *n.m./f.* stateless person.
apercevoir† /apɛrsəvwar/ *v.t.* see. **s'~ de,** notice. **s'~ que,** notice *ou* realize that.
aperçu /apɛrsy/ *n.m.* general view *ou* idea; (*intuition*) insight.
apéritif /aperitif/ *n.m.* aperitif.
à-peu-près /apøprɛ/ *n.m. invar.* approximation.
apeuré /apœre/ *a.* scared.
aphone /afɔn/ *a.* voiceless.
aphte /aft/ *n.m.* mouth ulcer.
apit|oyer /apitwaje/ *v.t.* move (to pity). **s'~oyer sur,** feel pity for. **~oiement** *n.m.* pity.
aplanir /aplanir/ *v.t.* level; (*fig.*) smooth out.
aplatir /aplatir/ *v.t.* flatten (out). **s'~** *v. pr.* (*s'allonger*) lie flat; (*s'humilier*) grovel; (*tomber: fam.*) fall flat on one's face.
aplomb /aplɔ̃/ *n.m.* balance; (*fig.*) self-possession. **d'~,** (*en équilibre*) steady, balanced.
apogée /apɔʒe/ *n.m.* peak.
apologie /apɔlɔʒi/ *n.f.* vindication.
a posteriori /apɔsterjɔri/ *adv.* after the event.
apostolique /apɔstɔlik/ *a.* apostolic.
apostroph|e /apɔstrɔf/ *n.f.* apostrophe; (*appel*) sharp address. **~er** *v.t.* address sharply.
apothéose /apɔteoz/ *n.f.* final triumph.
apôtre /apotr/ *n.m.* apostle.
apparaître† /aparɛtr/ *v.i.* appear. **il apparaît que,** it appears that.
apparat /apara/ *n.m.* pomp. **d'~,** ceremonial.
appareil /aparɛj/ *n.m.* apparatus; (*électrique*) appliance; (*anat.*) system; (*téléphonique*) phone; (*dentaire*) brace; (*auditif*) hearing-aid; (*avion*) plane; (*culin.*) mixture. **l'~ du parti,** the party machinery **c'est Gabriel à l'~,** it's Gabriel on the phone. **~(-photo),** camera. **~ électroménager,** household electrical appliance.
appareiller[1] /apareje/ *v.i.* (*navire*) cast off, put to sea.
appareiller[2] /apareje/ *v.t.* (*assortir*) match.
apparemment /aparamɑ̃/ *adv.* apparently.
apparence /aparɑ̃s/ *n.f.* appearance. **en ~,** outwardly; (*apparemment*) apparently.
apparent, ~e /aparɑ̃, -t/ *a.* apparent; (*visible*) conspicuous.
apparenté /aparɑ̃te/ *a.* related; (*semblable*) similar.
appariteur /aparitœr/ *n.m.* (*univ.*) attendant, porter.

apparition /aparisjɔ̃/ *n.f.* appearance; (*spectre*) apparition.

appartement /apartəmɑ̃/ *n.m.* flat; (*Amer.*) apartment.

appartenance /apartənɑ̃s/ *n.f.* membership (**à,** of), belonging (**à,** to).

appartenir† /apartənir/ *v.i.* belong (**à,** to) **il lui/vous/***etc.* **appartient de,** it is up to him/you/*etc.* to.

appât /apɑ/ *n.m.* bait; (*fig.*) lure. **~er** /-te/ *v.t.* lure.

appauvrir /apovrir/ *v.t.* impoverish. **s'~** *v. pr.* grow impoverished.

appel /apɛl/ *n.m.* call; (*jurid.*) appeal; (*mil.*) call-up. **faire ~,** appeal. **faire ~ à,** (*recourir à*) call on; (*invoquer*) appeal to; (*évoquer*) call up; (*exiger*) call for. **faire l'~,** (*scol.*) call the register; (*mil.*) take a roll-call. **~ d'offres,** (*comm.*) invitation to tender. **faire un ~ de phares,** flash one's headlights.

appelé /aple/ *n.m.* conscript.

appel|er /aple/ *v.t.* call; (*nécessiter*) call for. **s'~er** *v. pr.* be called. **~é à,** (*désigné à*) marked out for. **en ~er à,** appeal to. **il s'appelle,** his name is. **~lation** /apelɑsjɔ̃/ *n.f.* designation.

appendic|e /apɛ̃dis/ *n.m.* appendix. **~ite** *n.f.* appendicitis.

appentis /apɑ̃ti/ *n.m.* lean-to.

appesantir /apəzɑ̃tir/ *v.t.* weigh down. **s'~** *v. pr.* grow heavier. **s'~ sur,** dwell upon.

appétissant, ~e /apetisɑ̃, -t/ *a.* appetizing.

appétit /apeti/ *n.m.* appetite.

applaud|ir /aplodir/ *v.t./i.* applaud. **~ir à,** applaud. **~issements** *n.m. pl.* applause.

applique /aplik/ *n.f.* wall lamp.

appliqué /aplike/ *a.* painstaking.

appliquer /aplike/ *v.t.* apply; (*loi*) enforce. **s'~** *v. pr.* apply o.s. (**à,** to). **s'~ à,** (*concerner*) apply to. **applicable** /-abl/ *a.* applicable. **application** /-ɑsjɔ̃/ *n.f.* application.

appoint /apwɛ̃/ *n.m.* contribution. **d'~,** extra. **faire l'~,** give the correct money.

appointements /apwɛ̃tmɑ̃/ *n.m. pl.* salary.

apport /apɔr/ *n.m.* contribution.

apporter /apɔrte/ *v.t.* bring.

apposer /apoze/ *v.t.* affix.

appréciable /apresjabl/ *a.* appreciable.

appréc|ier /apresje/ *v.t.* appreciate; (*évaluer*) appraise. **~iation** *n.f.* appreciation; appraisal.

appréhen|der /apreɑ̃de/ *v.t.* dread, fear; (*arrêter*) apprehend. **~sion** *n.f.* apprehension.

apprendre† /aprɑ̃dr/ *v.t./i.* learn; (*être informé de*) hear of. **~ qch. à qn.,** teach s.o. sth.; (*informer*) tell s.o. sth. **~ à faire,** learn to do. **~ à qn. à faire,** teach s.o. to do. **~ que,** learn that; (*être informé*) hear that.

apprenti, ~e /aprɑ̃ti/ *n.m., f.* apprentice.

apprentissage /aprɑ̃tisaʒ/ *n.m.* apprenticeship; (*d'un sujet*) learning.

apprêté /aprete/ *a.* affected.

apprêter /aprete/ *v.t.,* **s'~** *v. pr.* prepare.

apprivoiser /aprivwaze/ *v.t.* tame.

approba|teur, ~trice /aprɔbatœr, -tris/ *a.* approving.

approbation /aprɔbɑsjɔ̃/ *n.f.* approval.

approchant, ~e /aprɔʃɑ̃, -t/ *a.* close, similar.

approche /aprɔʃ/ *n.f.* approach.

approché /aprɔʃe/ *a.* approximate.

approcher /aprɔʃe/ *v.t.* (*objet*) move near(er) (**de,** to); (*personne*) approach. ● *v.i.* **~ (de),** approach. **s'~ de,** approach, move near(er) to.

approfond|ir /aprɔfɔ̃dir/ *v.t.* deepen; (*fig.*) go into thoroughly. **~i** *a.* thorough.

approprié /aprɔprije/ *a.* appropriate.

approprier (s') /(s)aprɔprije/ *v. pr.* appropriate.

approuver /apruve/ *v.t.* approve; (*trouver louable*) approve of; (*soutenir*) agree with.

approvisionn|er /aprɔvizjɔne/ *v.t.* supply. **s'~er** *v. pr.* stock up. **~ement** *n.m.* supply.

approximati|f, ~ve /aprɔksimatif, -v/ *a.* approximate. **~vement** *adv.* approximately.

approximation /aprɔksimɑsjɔ̃/ *n.f.* approximation.

appui /apɥi/ *n.m.* support; (*de fenêtre*) sill; (*pour objet*) rest. **à l'~ de,** in support of. **prendre ~,** support o.s. on.

appuie-tête /apɥitɛt/ *n.m.* headrest.

appuyer /apɥije/ *v.t.* lean, rest; (*presser*) press; (*soutenir*) support, back. ● *v.i.* **~ sur,** press (on); (*fig.*) stress. **s'~ sur,** lean on; (*compter sur*) rely on.

âpre /ɑpr/ *a.* harsh, bitter. **~ au gain,** grasping.

après /aprɛ/ *prép.* after; (*au-delà de*) beyond. ● *adv.* after(wards); (*plus tard*) later. **~ avoir fait,** after doing. **~ qu'il est parti,** after he left. **~ coup,** after the event. **~ tout,** after all. **d'~,** (*selon*) according to. **~-demain** *adv.* the day after tomorrow. **~-guerre** *n.m.* postwar period. **~-midi** *n.m./f. invar.* afternoon. **~-rasage** *n.m.* aftershave. **~-ski** *n.m.* moonboot. **~-vente** *a.* after-sales.

a priori /aprijɔri/ *adv.* in principle, without going into the matter. ● *n.m.* preconception.

à-propos /aprɔpo/ *n.m.* timeliness; (*fig.*) presence of mind.

apte /apt/ *a.* capable (**à,** of).

aptitude /aptityd/ *n.f.* aptitude, ability.

aquarelle /akwarɛl/ *n.f.* water-colour, aquarelle.

aquarium /akwarjɔm/ *n.m.* aquarium.

aquatique /akwatik/ *a.* aquatic.

aqueduc /akdyk/ *n.m.* aqueduct.

arabe /arab/ *a.* Arab; (*lang.*) Arabic; (*désert*) Arabian. ● *n.m./f.* Arab. ● *n.m.* (*lang.*) Arabic.

Arabie /arabi/ *n.f.* **~ Séoudite,** Saudi Arabia.

arable /arabl/ *a.* arable.

arachide /araʃid/ *n.f.* peanut.

araignée /areɲe/ *n.f.* spider.

arbitraire /arbitrɛr/ *a.* arbitrary.

arbitr|e /arbitr/ *n.m.* referee; (*cricket, tennis*) umpire; (*maître*) arbiter; (*jurid.*) arbitrator. **~age** *n.m.* arbitration; (*sport*) refereeing. **~er** *v.t.* (*match*) referee; (*jurid.*) arbitrate.

arborer /arbɔre/ *v.t.* display; (*vêtement*) sport.

arbre /arbr/ *n.m.* tree; (*techn.*) shaft.

arbrisseau (*pl.* **~x**) /arbriso/ *n.m.* shrub.

arbuste /arbyst/ *n.m.* bush.

arc /ark/ *n.m.* (*arme*) bow; (*voûte*) arch. **~ de cercle,** arc of a circle.

arcade /arkad/ *n.f.* arch. **~s,** arcade, arches.

arc-boutant (*pl.* **arcs-boutants**) /arkbutɑ̃/ *n.m.* flying buttress.

arc-bouter (s') /(s)arkbute/ *v. pr.* lean (for support), brace o.s.

arceau (*pl.* **~x**) /arso/ *n.m.* hoop; (*de voûte*) arch.

arc-en-ciel (*pl.* **arcs-en-ciel**) /arkɑ̃sjɛl/ *n.m.* rainbow.

archaïque /arkaik/ *a.* archaic.

arche /arʃ/ *n.f.* arch. **~ de Noé,** Noah's ark.

archéolo|gie /arkeɔlɔʒi/ *n.f.* archaeology. **~gique** *a.* archaeological. **~gue** *n.m./f.* archaeologist.

archer /arʃe/ *n.m.* archer.

archet /arʃɛ/ *n.m.* (*mus.*) bow.

archétype /arketip/ *n.m.* archetype.

archevêque /arʃəvɛk/ *n.m.* archbishop.

archi- /arʃi/ *préf.* (*fam.*) tremendously.

archipel /arʃipɛl/ *n.m.* archipelago.

architecte /arʃitɛkt/ *n.m.* architect.

architecture /arʃitɛktyr/ *n.f.* architecture.

archiv|es /arʃiv/ *n.f. pl.* archives. **~iste** *n.m./f.* archivist.

arctique /arktik/ *a.* & *n.m.* Arctic.

ardemment /ardamɑ̃/ *adv.* ardently.

ard|ent, ~ente /ardɑ̃, -t/ *a.* burning; (*passionné*) ardent; (*foi*) fervent. **~eur** *n.f.* ardour; (*chaleur*) heat.

ardoise /ardwaz/ *n.f.* slate.

ardu /ardy/ *a.* arduous.

are /ar/ *n.m.* are (= *100 square metres*).

arène /arɛn/ *n.f.* arena. **~(s),** (*pour courses de taureaux*) bullring.

arête /arɛt/ *n.f.* (*de poisson*) bone; (*bord*) ridge.

argent /arʒɑ̃/ *n.m.* money; (*métal*) silver. **~ comptant,** cash. **prendre pour ~ comptant,** take at face value. **~ de poche,** pocket money.

argenté /arʒɑ̃te/ *a.* silver(y); (*métal*) (silver-)plated.

argenterie /arʒɑ̃tri/ *n.f.* silverware.

argentin, ~e /arʒɑ̃tɛ̃, -in/ *a.* & *n.m., f.* Argentinian, Argentine.

Argentine /arʒɑ̃tin/ *n.f.* Argentina.

argil|e /arʒil/ *n.f.* clay. **~eux, ~euse** *a.* clayey.

argot /argo/ *n.m.* slang. **~ique** /-ɔtik/ *a.* (*terme*) slang; (*style*) slangy.

arguer /argɥe/ *v.i.* **~ de,** put forward as a reason.

argument /argymɑ̃/ *n.m.* argument. **~er** /-te/ *v.i.* argue.

aride /arid/ *a.* arid, barren.

aristocrate /aristɔkrat/ *n.m./f.* aristocrat.

aristocrat|ie /aristɔkrasi/ *n.f.* aristocracy. **~ique** /-atik/ *a.* aristocratic.

arithmétique /aritmetik/ *n.f.* arithmetic. ● *a.* arithmetical.

armateur /armatœr/ *n.m.* ship-owner.

armature /armatyr/ *n.f.* framework; (*de tente*) frame.

arme /arm/ *n.f.* arm, weapon. **~s,** (*blason*) arms. **~ à feu,** firearm.

armée /arme/ *n.f.* army. **~ de l'air,** Air Force. **~ de terre,** Army.

armement /arməmɑ̃/ *n.m.* arms.

armer /arme/ *v.t.* arm; (*fusil*) cock; (*navire*) equip; (*renforcer*) reinforce; (*photo.*) wind on. **~ de,** (*garnir de*) fit with. **s'~ de,** arm o.s. with.

armistice /armistis/ *n.m.* armistice.

armoire /armwar/ *n.f.* cupboard; (*penderie*) wardrobe; (*Amer.*) closet.

armoiries /armwari/ *n.f. pl.* (coat of) arms.

armure /armyr/ *n.f.* armour.

arnaque /arnak/ *n.f.* (*fam.*) swindling. **c'est de l'~,** it's a swindle *ou* con (*fam.*). **~r** *v.t.* swindle, con (*fam.*).

arnica /arnika/ *n.f.* (*méd.*) arnica.

aromate /arɔmat/ *n.m.* herb, spice.

aromatique /arɔmatik/ *a.* aromatic.

aromatisé /arɔmatize/ *a.* flavoured.

arôme /arom/ *n.m.* aroma.

arpent|er /arpɑ̃te/ *v.t.* pace up and down; (*terrain*) survey. **~eur** *n.m.* surveyor.

arqué /arke/ *a.* arched; (*jambes*) bandy.

arraché (à l') /(al)araʃe/ *adv.* with a struggle, after a hard struggle.

arrache-pied (d') /(d)araʃpje/ *adv.* relentlessly.

arrach|er /araʃe/ *v.t.* pull out *ou* off; (*plante*) pull *ou* dig up; (*cheveux, page*) tear *ou* pull out; (*par une explosion*) blow off. **~er à,** (*enlever à*) snatch from; (*fig.*) force *ou* wrest from. **s'~er qch.,** fight over sth. **~age** /-aʒ/ *n.m.* pulling *ou* digging up.

arraisonner /arɛzɔne/ *v.t.* inspect.

arrangeant, ~e /arɑ̃ʒɑ̃, -t/ *a.* obliging.

arrangement /arɑ̃ʒmɑ̃/ *n.m.* arrangement.

arranger /arɑ̃ʒe/ *v.t.* arrange, fix up; (*réparer*) put right; (*régler*) sort out; (*convenir à*) suit. **s'~** *v. pr.* (*se mettre d'accord*) come to an arrangement; (*se débrouiller*) manage (**pour,** to).

arrestation /arɛstɑsjɔ̃/ *n.f.* arrest.

arrêt /arɛ/ *n.m.* stopping (**de,** of); (*lieu*) stop; (*pause*) pause; (*jurid.*) decree. **~s,** (*mil.*) arrest. **à l'~,** stationary. **faire un ~,** (make a) stop. **sans ~,** without stopping. **~ maladie,** sick leave. **~ de travail,** (*grève*) stoppage; (*méd.*) sick leave. **rester** *ou* **tomber en ~,** stop short.

arrêté /arete/ *n.m.* order.

arrêter /arete/ *v.t./i.* stop; (*date, regard*) fix; (*appareil*) turn off; (*appréhender*) arrest. **s'~** *v. pr.* stop. **(s')~ de faire,** stop doing.

arrhes /ar/ *n.f. pl.* deposit.

arrière /arjɛr/ *n.m.* back, rear; (*football*) back. ● *a. invar.* back, rear. **à l'~,** in *ou* at the back. **en ~,** behind; (*marcher*) backwards. **en ~ de,** behind. **~-boutique** *n.f.* back room (of the shop). **~-garde** *n.f.* rearguard. **~-goût** *n.m.* after-taste. **~-grand-mère** *n.f.* great-grandmother. **~-grand-père** (*pl.* **~-grands-pères**) *n.m.* great-grandfather. **~-pays** *n.m.* backcountry. **~-pensée** *n.f.* ulterior motive. **~-plan** *n.m.* background.

arriéré /arjere/ *a.* backward. ● *n.m.* arrears.

arrimer /arime/ *v.t.* rope down; (*cargaison*) stow.

arrivage /arivaʒ/ *n.m.* consignment.

arrivant, ~e /arivɑ̃, -t/ *n.m., f.* new arrival.

arrivée /arive/ *n.f.* arrival; (*sport*) finish.

arriver /arive/ *v.i.* (*aux. être*) arrive, come; (*réussir*) succeed; (*se produire*) happen. **~ à,** (*atteindre*) reach. **~ à faire,** manage to do. **en ~ à faire,** get to the stage of doing. **il arrive que,** it happens that. **il lui arrive de faire,** he (sometimes) does.

arriviste /arivist/ *n.m./f.* self-seeker.

arrogan|t, ~te /arɔgɑ̃, -t/ *a.* arrogant. **~ce** *n.f.* arrogance.

arroger (s') /(s)arɔʒe/ *v. pr.* assume (without justification).

arrondir /arɔ̃dir/ *v.t.* (make) round; (*somme*) round off. **s'~** *v. pr.* become round(ed).

arrondissement /arɔ̃dismɑ̃/ *n.m.* district.

arros|er /aroze/ *v.t.* water; (*repas*) wash down; (*rôti*) baste; (*victoire*) celebrate with a drink. **~age** *n.m.* watering. **~oir** *n.m.* watering-can.

arsen|al (*pl.* **~aux**) /arsənal, -o/ *n.m.* arsenal; (*naut.*) dockyard.
arsenic /arsənik/ *n.m.* arsenic.
art /ar/ *n.m.* art. **~s et métiers,** arts and crafts. **~s ménagers,** domestic science.
artère /artɛr/ *n.f.* artery. **(grande) ~,** main road.
artériel, ~le /arterjɛl/ *a.* arterial.
arthrite /artrit/ *n.f.* arthritis.
arthrose /artroz/ *n.f.* osteoarthritis.
artichaut /artiʃo/ *n.m.* artichoke.
article /artikl/ *n.m.* article; (*comm.*) item, article. **à l'~ de la mort,** at death's door. **~ de fond,** feature (article). **~s d'ameublement,** furnishings. **~s de voyage,** travel requisites *ou* goods.
articul|er /artikyle/ *v.t.*, **s'~er** *v. pr.* articulate. **~ation** *n.f.* articulation; (*anat.*) joint.
artifice /artifis/ *n.m.* contrivance.
artificiel, ~le /artifisjɛl/ *a.* artificial. **~lement** *adv.* artificially.
artill|erie /artijri/ *n.f.* artillery. **~eur** *n.m.* gunner.
artisan /artizɑ̃/ *n.m.* artisan, craftsman. **l'~ de,** (*fig.*) the architect of. **~al** (*m. pl.* **~aux**) /-anal, -o/ *a.* of *ou* by craftsmen, craft; (*amateur*) home-made. **~at** /-ana/ *n.m.* craft; (*classe*) artisans.
artist|e /artist/ *n.m./f.* artist. **~ique** *a.* artistic.
as[1] /a/ *voir* avoir.
as[2] /ɑs/ *n.m.* ace.
ascendant[1], **~e** /asɑ̃dɑ̃, -t/ *a.* ascending, upward.
ascendant[2] /asɑ̃dɑ̃/ *n.m.* influence. **~s,** ancestors.
ascenseur /asɑ̃sœr/ *n.m.* lift; (*Amer.*) elevator.
ascension /asɑ̃sjɔ̃/ *n.f.* ascent. **l' A~,** Ascension.
ascète /asɛt/ *n.m./f.* ascetic.
ascétique /asetik/ *a.* ascetic.
aseptique /asɛptik/ *a.* aseptic.
aseptis|er /asɛptize/ *v.t.* disinfect; (*stériliser*) sterilize. **~é** (*péj.*) sanitized.
asiatique /azjatik/ *a.* & *n.m./f.*, **Asiate** /azjat/ *n.m./f.* Asian.
Asie /azi/ *n.f.* Asia.
asile /azil/ *n.m.* refuge; (*pol.*) asylum; (*pour malades, vieillards*) home.
aspect /aspɛ/ *n.m.* appearance; (*fig.*) aspect. **à l'~ de,** at the sight of.
asperge /aspɛrʒ/ *n.f.* asparagus.
asper|ger /aspɛrʒe/ *v.t.* spray. **~sion** *n.f.* spray(ing).
aspérité /asperite/ *n.f.* bump, rough edge.
asphalt|e /asfalt/ *n.m.* asphalt. **~er** *v.t.* asphalt.
asphyxie /asfiksi/ *n.f.* suffocation.
asphyxier /asfiksje/ *v.t.*, **s'~** *v. pr.* suffocate, asphyxiate; (*fig.*) stifle.
aspic /aspik/ *n.m.* (*serpent*) asp.
aspirateur /aspiratœr/ *n.m.* vacuum cleaner.
aspir|er /aspire/ *v.t.* inhale; (*liquide*) suck up. ● *v.i.* **~er à,** aspire to. **~ation** *n.f.* inhaling; suction; (*ambition*) aspiration.
aspirine /aspirin/ *n.f.* aspirin.
assagir /asaʒir/ *v.t.*, **s'~** *v. pr.* sober down.
assaill|ir /asajir/ *v.t.* assail. **~ant** *n.m.* assailant.
assainir /asenir/ *v.t.* clean up.
assaisonn|er /asɛzɔne/ *v.t.* season. **~ement** *n.m.* seasoning.
assassin /asasɛ̃/ *n.m.* murderer; (*pol.*) assassin.
assassin|er /asasine/ *v.t.* murder; (*pol.*) assassinate. **~at** *n.m.* murder; (*pol.*) assassination.
assaut /aso/ *n.m.* assault, onslaught. **donner l'~ à, prendre d'~,** storm.
assécher /aseʃe/ *v.t.* drain.
assemblée /asɑ̃ble/ *n.f.* meeting; (*gens réunis*) gathering; (*pol.*) assembly.
assembl|er /asɑ̃ble/ *v.t.* assemble, put together; (*réunir*) gather. **s'~er** *v. pr.* gather, assemble. **~age** *n.m.* assembly; (*combinaison*) collection; (*techn.*) joint. **~eur** *n.m.* (*comput.*) assembler.
assener /asene/ *v.t.* (*coup*) deal.
assentiment /asɑ̃timɑ̃/ *n.m.* assent.
asseoir† /aswar/ *v.t.* sit (down), seat; (*affermir*) establish; (*baser*) base. **s'~** *v. pr.* sit (down).
assermenté /asɛrmɑ̃te/ *a.* sworn.
assertion /asɛrsjɔ̃/ *n.f.* assertion.
asservir /asɛrvir/ *v.t.* enslave.
assez /ase/ *adv.* enough; (*plutôt*) quite, fairly. **~ grand/rapide** *etc.*, big/fast/*etc.* enough (**pour,** to). **~ de,** enough. **j'en ai ~ (de),** I've had enough (of).
assid|u /asidy/ *a.* (*zèle*) assiduous; (*régulier*) regular. **~u auprès de,** attentive to. **~uité** /-ɥite/ *n.f.* assiduousness; regularity. **~ûment** *adv.* assiduously.

assiéger /asjeʒe/ *v.t.* besiege.

assiette /asjɛt/ *n.f.* plate; (*équilibre*) seat. **~ anglaise,** assorted cold meats. **~ creuse/plate,** soup-/dinner-plate. **ne pas être dans son ~,** feel out of sorts.

assiettée /asjete/ *n.f.* plateful.

assigner /asiɲe/ *v.t.* assign; (*limite*) fix.

assimil|er /asimile/ *v.t.*, **s'~er** *v. pr.* assimilate. **~er à,** liken to; (*classer*) class as. **~ation** *n.f.* assimilation; likening; classification.

assis, ~e /asi, -z/ *voir* asseoir. ● *a.* sitting (down), seated.

assise /asiz/ *n.f.* (*base*) foundation. **~s,** (*tribunal*) assizes; (*congrès*) conference, congress.

assistance /asistɑ̃s/ *n.f.* audience; (*aide*) assistance. **l'A~ (publique),** government child care service.

assistant, ~e /asistɑ̃, -t/ *n.m., f.* assistant; (*univ.*) assistant lecturer. **~s,** (*spectateurs*) members of the audience. **~ social, ~e sociale,** social worker.

assist|er /asiste/ *v.t.* assist. ● *v.i.* **~er à,** attend, be (present) at; (*scène*) witness. **~é par ordinateur,** computer-assisted.

association /asɔsjɑsjɔ̃/ *n.f.* association.

associé, ~e /asɔsje/ *n.m., f.* partner, associate. ● *a.* associate.

associer /asɔsje/ *v.t.* associate; (*mêler*) combine (**à,** with). **~ qn. à,** (*projet*) involve s.o. in; (*bénéfices*) give s.o. a share of. **s'~** *v. pr.* (*sociétés, personnes*) become associated, join forces (**à,** with); (*s'harmoniser*) combine (**à,** with). **s'~ à,** (*joie de qn.*) share in; (*opinion de qn.*) share; (*projet*) take part in.

assoiffé /aswafe/ *a.* thirsty.

assombrir /asɔ̃brir/ *v.t.* darken; (*fig.*) make gloomy. **s'~** *v. pr.* darken; become gloomy.

assommer /asɔme/ *v.t.* knock out; (*tuer*) kill; (*animal*) stun; (*fig.*) overwhelm; (*ennuyer: fam.*) bore.

Assomption /asɔ̃psjɔ̃/ *n.f.* Assumption.

assorti /asɔrti/ *a.* matching; (*objets variés*) assorted.

assort|ir /asɔrtir/ *v.t.* match (**à,** with, to). **~ir de,** accompany with. **s'~ir (à),** match. **~iment** *n.m.* assortment.

assoup|ir (s') /(s)asupir/ *v. pr.* doze off; (*s'apaiser*) subside. **~i** *a.* dozing.

assouplir /asuplir/ *v.t.* make supple; (*fig.*) make flexible.

assourdir /asurdir/ *v.t.* (*personne*) deafen; (*bruit*) deaden.

assouvir /asuvir/ *v.t.* satisfy.

assujettir /asyʒetir/ *v.t.* subject, subdue. **~ à,** subject to.

assumer /asyme/ *v.t.* assume.

assurance /asyrɑ̃s/ *n.f.* (self-) assurance; (*garantie*) assurance; (*contrat*) insurance. **~-maladie** *n.f.* health insurance. **~s sociales,** National Insurance. **~-vie** *n.f.* life assurance *ou* insurance.

assuré, ~e /asyre/ *a.* certain, assured; (*sûr de soi*) (self-)confident, assured. ● *n.m., f.* insured. **~ment** *adv.* certainly.

assurer /asyre/ *v.t.* ensure; (*fournir*) provide; (*exécuter*) carry out; (*comm.*) insure; (*stabiliser*) steady; (*frontières*) make secure. **~ à qn. que,** assure s.o. that. **~ qn. de,** assure s.o. of. **~ la gestion de,** manage. **s'~ de/que,** make sure of/ that. **s'~ qch.,** (*se procurer*) secure *ou* ensure sth. **assureur** /-œr/ *n.m.* insurer.

astérisque /asterisk/ *n.m.* asterisk.

asthm|e /asm/ *n.m.* asthma. **~atique** *a. & n.m./f.* asthmatic.

asticot /astiko/ *n.m.* maggot.

astiquer /astike/ *v.t.* polish.

astre /astr/ *n.m.* star.

astreignant, ~e /astrɛɲɑ̃, -t/ *a.* exacting.

astreindre /astrɛ̃dr/ *v.t.* **~ qn. à qch.,** force sth. on s.o. **~ à faire,** force to do.

astringent, ~e /astrɛ̃ʒɑ̃, -t/ *a.* astringent.

astrolo|gie /astrɔlɔʒi/ *n.f.* astrology. **~gue** *n.m./f.* astrologer.

astronaute /astrɔnot/ *n.m./f.* astronaut.

astronom|ie /astrɔnɔmi/ *n.f.* astronomy. **~e** *n.m./f.* astronomer. **~ique** *a.* astronomical.

astuce /astys/ *n.f.* smartness; (*truc*) trick; (*plaisanterie*) wisecrack.

astucieu|x, ~se /astysjø, -z/ *a.* smart, clever.

atelier /atəlje/ *n.m.* workshop; (*de peintre*) studio.

athé|e /ate/ *n.m./f.* atheist. ● *a.* atheistic. **~isme** *n.m.* atheism .

athl|ète /atlɛt/ *n.m./f.* athlete. **~étique** *a.* athletic. **~étisme** *n.m.* athletics.

atlantique /atlɑ̃tik/ *a.* Atlantic. ● *n.m.* **A~,** Atlantic (Ocean).

atlas /atlɑs/ *n.m.* atlas.

atmosph|ère /atmɔsfɛr/ *n.f.* atmosphere. **~érique** *a.* atmospheric.

atome /atom/ *n.m.* atom.

atomique /atɔmik/ *a.* atomic.

atomiseur /atɔmizœr/ *n.m.* spray.

atout /atu/ *n.m.* trump (card); (*avantage*) great asset.

âtre /ɑtr/ *n.m.* hearth.

atroc|e /atrɔs/ *a.* atrocious. **~ité** *n.f.* atrocity.

atroph|ie /atrɔfi/ *n.f.* atrophy. **~ié** *a.* atrophied.

attabler (s') /(s)atable/ *v. pr.* sit down at table.

attachant, ~e /ataʃɑ̃, -t/ *a.* likeable.

attache /ataʃ/ *n.f.* (*agrafe*) fastener; (*lien*) tie.

attach|é /ataʃe/ *a.* **être ~é à,** (*aimer*) be attached to. ● *n.m., f.* (*pol.*) attaché. **~é-case** *n.m.* attaché case. **~ement** *n.m.* attachment.

attacher /ataʃe/ *v.t.* tie (up); (*ceinture, robe, etc.*) fasten; (*étiquette*) attach. **~ à,** (*attribuer à*) attach to. ● *v.i.* (*culin.*) stick. **s'~ à,** (*se lier à*) become attached to; (*se consacrer à*) apply o.s. to.

attaque /atak/ *n.f.* attack. **~ (cérébrale),** stroke. **il va en faire une ~,** he'll have a fit. **~ à main armée,** armed attack.

attaqu|er /atake/ *v.t./i.,* **s'~er à,** attack; (*problème, sujet*) tackle. **~ant, ~ante** *n.m., f.* attacker; (*football*) striker; (*football, Amer.*) forward.

attardé /atarde/ *a.* backward; (*idées*) outdated; (*en retard*) late.

attarder (s') /(s)atarde/ *v. pr.* linger.

atteindre† /atɛ̃dr/ *v.t.* reach; (*blesser*) hit; (*affecter*) affect.

atteint, ~e /atɛ̃, -t/ *a.* **~ de,** suffering from.

atteinte /atɛ̃t/ *n.f.* attack (**à,** on). **porter ~ à,** make an attack on.

attel|er /atle/ *v.t.* (*cheval*) harness; (*remorque*) couple. **s'~er à,** get down to. **~age** *n.m.* harnessing; coupling; (*bêtes*) team.

attelle /atɛl/ *n.f.* splint.

attenant, ~e /atnɑ̃, -t/ *a.* **~ (à),** adjoining.

attendant (en) /(ɑ̃n)atɑ̃dɑ̃/ *adv.* meanwhile.

attendre /atɑ̃dr/ *v.t.* wait for; (*bébé*) expect; (*être le sort de*) await; (*escompter*) expect. ● *v.i.* wait. **~ que qn. fasse,** wait for s.o. to do. **s'~ à,** expect.

attendr|ir /atɑ̃drir/ *v.t.* move (to pity). **s'~ir** *v. pr.* be moved to pity. **~issant, ~issante** *a.* moving.

attendu /atɑ̃dy/ *a.* (*escompté*) expected; (*espéré*) long-awaited. **~ que,** considering that.

attentat /atɑ̃ta/ *n.m.* murder attempt. **~ (à la bombe),** (bomb) attack.

attente /atɑ̃t/ *n.f.* wait(ing); (*espoir*) expectation.

attenter /atɑ̃te/ *v.i.* **~ à,** make an attempt on; (*fig.*) violate.

attenti|f, ~ve /atɑ̃tif, -v/ *a.* attentive; (*scrupuleux*) careful. **~f à,** mindful of; (*soucieux*) careful of. **~vement** *adv.* attentively.

attention /atɑ̃sjɔ̃/ *n.f.* attention; (*soin*) care. **~ (à)!,** watch out (for)! **faire ~ à,** (*professeur*) pay attention to; (*marche*) mind. **faire ~ à faire,** be careful to do. **~né** /-jɔne/ *a.* considerate.

attentisme /atɑ̃tism/ *n.m.* wait-and-see policy.

atténuer /atenɥe/ *v.t.* (*violence*) tone down; (*douleur*) ease; (*faute*) mitigate. **s'~** *v. pr.* subside.

atterrer /atere/ *v.t.* dismay.

atterr|ir /aterir/ *v.i.* land. **~issage** *n.m.* landing.

attestation /atɛstɑsjɔ̃/ *n.f.* certificate.

attester /atɛste/ *v.t.* testify to. **~ que,** testify that.

attifé /atife/ *a.* (*fam.*) dressed up.

attirail /atiraj/ *n.m.* (*fam.*) gear.

attirance /atirɑ̃s/ *n.f.* attraction.

attirant, ~e /atirɑ̃, -t/ *a.* attractive.

attirer /atire/ *v.t.* draw, attract; (*causer*) bring. **s'~** *v. pr.* bring upon o.s.; (*amis*) win.

attiser /atize/ *v.t.* (*feu*) poke; (*sentiment*) stir up.

attitré /atitre/ *a.* accredited; (*habituel*) usual.

attitude /atityd/ *n.f.* attitude; (*maintien*) bearing.

attraction /atraksjɔ̃/ *n.f.* attraction.

attrait /atrɛ/ *n.m.* attraction.

attrape-nigaud /atrapnigo/ *n.m.* (*fam.*) con.

attraper /atrape/ *v.t.* catch; (*habitude, style*) pick up; (*duper*) take in; (*gronder: fam.*) tell off.
attrayant, ~e /atrɛjɑ̃, -t/ *a.* attractive.
attrib|uer /atribɥe/ *v.t.* award; (*donner*) assign; (*imputer*) attribute. **s'~uer** *v. pr.* claim. **~ution** *n.f.* awarding; assignment. **~utions** *n.f. pl.* attributions.
attrister /atriste/ *v.t.* sadden.
attroup|er (s') /(s)atrupe/ *v. pr.* gather. **~ement** *n.m.* crowd.
au /o/ *voir* à.
aubaine /obɛn/ *n.f.* (stroke of) good fortune.
aube /ob/ *n.f.* dawn, daybreak.
aubépine /obepin/ *n.f.* hawthorn.
auberg|e /obɛrʒ/ *n.f.* inn. **~e de jeunesse,** youth hostel. **~iste** *n.m./f.* innkeeper.
aubergine /obɛrʒin/ *n.f.* aubergine; (*Amer.*) egg-plant.
aucun, ~e /okœ̃, okyn/ *a.* no, not any; (*positif*) any. ● *pron.* none, not any; (*positif*) any. **~ des deux,** neither of the two. **d'~s,** some. **~ement** /okynmɑ̃/ *adv.* not at all.
audace /odas/ *n.f.* daring; (*impudence*) audacity.
audacieu|x, ~se /odasjø, -z/ *a.* daring.
au-delà /odla/ *adv.*, **~ de** *prép.* beyond.
au-dessous /odsu/ *adv.*, **~ de** *prép.* below; (*couvert par*) under.
au-dessus /odsy/ *adv.*, **~ de** *prép.* above.
au-devant (de) /odvɑ̃(də)/ *prép.* **aller ~ de qn.,** go to meet s.o.
audience /odjɑ̃s/ *n.f.* audience; (*d'un tribunal*) hearing; (*intérêt*) attention.
Audimat /odimat/ *n.m.* (P.) **l'~,** the TV ratings.
audiotypiste /odjɔtipist/ *n.m./f.* audio typist.
audio-visuel, ~le /odjɔvizɥɛl/ *a.* audio-visual.
audi|teur, ~trice /oditœr, -tris/ *n.m., f.* listener.
audition /odisjɔ̃/ *n.f.* hearing; (*théâtre, mus.*) audition. **~ner** /-jɔne/ *v.t./i.* audition.
auditoire /oditwar/ *n.m.* audience.
auditorium /oditɔrjɔm/ *n.m.* (*mus., radio*) recording studio.
auge /oʒ/ *n.f.* trough.
augment|er /ogmɑ̃te/ *v.t./i.* increase; (*employé*) increase the pay of. **~ation** *n.f.* increase. **~ation (de salaire),** (pay) rise; (*Amer.*) raise.
augure /ogyr/ *n.m.* (*devin*) oracle. **être de bon/mauvais ~,** be a good/bad sign.
auguste /ogyst/ *a.* august.
aujourd'hui /oʒurdɥi/ *adv.* today.
aumône /omon/ *n.f.* alms.
aumônier /omonje/ *n.m.* chaplain.
auparavant /oparavɑ̃/ *adv.* before (-hand).
auprès (de) /oprɛ(də)/ *prép.* by, next to; (*comparé à*) compared with; (*s'adressant à*) to.
auquel, ~le /okɛl/ *voir* lequel.
aura, aurait /ora, orɛ/ *voir* avoir.
auréole /oreɔl/ *n.f.* halo.
auriculaire /orikylɛr/ *n.m.* little finger.
aurore /orɔr/ *n.f.* dawn.
ausculter /ɔskylte/ *v.t.* examine with a stethoscope.
auspices /ospis/ *n.m. pl.* auspices.
aussi /osi/ *adv.* too, also; (*comparaison*) as; (*tellement*) so. ● *conj.* (*donc*) therefore. **~ bien que,** as well as.
aussitôt /osito/ *adv.* immediately. **~ que,** as soon as. **~ arrivé/levé/*etc.*,** as soon as one has arrived/got up/*etc.*
aust|ère /ostɛr/ *a.* austere. **~érité** *n.f.* austerity.
austral (*m. pl.* **~s**) /ostral/ *a.* southern.
Australie /ɔstrali/ *n.f.* Australia.
australien, ~ne /ostraljɛ̃, -jɛn/ *a.* & *n.m., f.* Australian.
autant /otɑ̃/ *adv.* (*travailler, manger, etc.*) as much (**que,** as). **~ (de),** (*quantité*) as much (**que,** as); (*nombre*) as many (**que,** as); (*tant*) so much; so many. **~ faire,** one had better do. **d'~ plus que,** all the more since. **en faire ~,** do the same. **pour ~,** for all that.
autel /otɛl/ *n.m.* altar.
auteur /otœr/ *n.m.* author. **l'~ du crime,** the person who committed the crime.
authentifier /otɑ̃tifje/ *v.t.* authenticate.
authenti|que /otɑ̃tik/ *a.* authentic. **~cité** *n.f.* authenticity.
auto /oto/ *n.f.* car. **~s tamponneuses,** dodgems, bumper cars.
auto- /oto/ *préf.* self-, auto-.

autobiographie /otɔbjɔgrafi/ *n.f.* autobiography.

autobus /otɔbys/ *n.m.* bus.

autocar /otɔkar/ *n.m.* coach.

autochtone /otɔktɔn/ *n.m./f.* native.

autocollant, ~e /otɔkɔlɑ̃, -t/ *a.* self-adhesive. ● *n.m.* sticker.

autocratique /otɔkratik/ *a.* autocratic.

autocuiseur /otɔkɥizœr/ *n.* pressure cooker.

autodéfense /otɔdefɑ̃s/ *n.f.* self-defence.

autodidacte /otɔdidakt/ *a. & n.m./f.* self-taught (person).

auto-école /otɔekɔl/ *n.f.* driving school.

autographe /otɔgraf/ *n.m.* autograph.

automate /otɔmat/ *n.m.* automaton, robot.

automatique /otɔmatik/ *a.* automatic. **~ment** *adv.* automatically.

automat|iser /otɔmatize/ *v.t.* automate. **~ion** /-mɑsjɔ̃/ *n.f.* **~isation** *n.f.* automation.

automne /otɔn/ *n.m.* autumn; (*Amer.*) fall.

automobil|e /otɔmɔbil/ *a.* motor, car. ● *n.f.* (motor) car. **l'~e,** (*sport*) motoring. **~iste** *n.m./f.* motorist.

autonom|e /otɔnɔm/ *a.* autonomous. **~ie** *n.f.* autonomy.

autopsie /otɔpsi/ *n.f.* post-mortem, autopsy.

autoradio /otɔradjo/ *n.m.* car radio.

autorail /otɔrɑj/ *n.m.* railcar.

autorisation /otɔrizɑsjɔ̃/ *n.f.* permission, authorization; (*permis*) permit.

autoris|er /otɔrize/ *v.t.* authorize, permit; (*rendre possible*) allow (of). **~é** *a.* (*opinions*) authoritative.

autoritaire /otɔritɛr/ *a.* authoritarian.

autorité /otɔrite/ *n.f.* authority. **faire ~,** be authoritative.

autoroute /otɔrut/ *n.f.* motorway; (*Amer.*) highway.

auto-stop /otɔstɔp/ *n.m.* hitch-hiking. **faire de l'~,** hitch-hike. **prendre en ~,** give a lift to. **~peur, ~peuse** *n.m., f.* hitch-hiker.

autour /otur/ *adv.,* **~ de** *prép.* around. **tout ~,** all around.

autre /otr/ *a.* other. **un ~ jour**/*etc.*, another day/*etc.* ● *pron.* **un ~, une ~,** another (one). **l'~,** the other (one). **les ~s,** the others; (*autrui*) others. **d'~s,** (some) others. **l'un l'~,** each other. **l'un et l'~,** both of them. **~ chose/part,** sth./somewhere else. **qn./rien d'~,** s.o./nothing else. **quoi d'~?,** what else? **d'~ part,** on the other hand. **vous ~s Anglais,** you English. **d'un jour**/*etc.* **à l'~,** (*bientôt*) any day/*etc.* now. **entre ~s,** among other things.

autrefois /otrəfwa/ *adv.* in the past.

autrement /otrəmɑ̃/ *adv.* differently; (*sinon*) otherwise; (*plus*) far more. **~ dit,** in other words.

Autriche /otriʃ/ *n.f.* Austria.

autrichien, ~ne /otriʃjɛ̃, -jɛn/ *a. & n.m., f.* Austrian.

autruche /otryʃ/ *n.f.* ostrich.

autrui /otrɥi/ *pron.* others.

auvent /ovɑ̃/ *n.m.* canopy.

aux /o/ *voir* à.

auxiliaire /oksiljɛr/ *a.* auxiliary. ● *n.m./f.* (*assistant*) auxiliary. ● *n.m.* (*gram.*) auxiliary.

auxquel|s, ~les /okɛl/ *voir* lequel.

aval (en) /(ɑ̃n)aval/ *adv.* downstream.

avalanche /avalɑ̃ʃ/ *n.f.* avalanche.

avaler /avale/ *v.t.* swallow.

avance /avɑ̃s/ *n.f.* advance; (*sur un concurrent*) lead. **~ (de fonds),** advance. **à l'~, d'~,** in advance. **en ~,** early; (*montre*) fast. **en ~ (sur),** (*menant*) ahead (of).

avancement /avɑ̃smɑ̃/ *n.m.* promotion.

avanc|er /avɑ̃se/ *v.i.* move forward, advance; (*travail*) make progress; (*montre*) be fast; (*faire saillie*) jut out. ● *v.t.* (*argent*) advance; (*montre*) put forward. **s'~er** *v. pr.* move forward, advance; (*se hasarder*) commit o.s. **~é, ~ée** *a.* advanced; *n.f.* projection.

avanie /avani/ *n.f.* affront.

avant /avɑ̃/ *prép & adv.* before. ● *a. invar.* front. ● *n.m.* front; (*football*) forward. **~ de faire,** before doing. **~ qu'il (ne) fasse,** before he does. **en ~,** (*mouvement*) forward. **en ~ (de),** (*position, temps*) in front (of). **~ peu,** before long. **~ tout,** above all. **bien ~ dans,** very deep(ly) *ou* far into. **~-bras** *n.m. invar.* forearm. **~-centre** *n.m.* centre-forward. **~-coureur** *a. invar.* precursory, foreshadowing. **~-dernier, ~-dernière** *a. & n.m., f.* last but one. **~-garde** *n.f.* (*mil.*) vanguard; (*fig.*)

avant-garde. **~-goût** *n.m.* foretaste. **~-guerre** *n.m.* pre-war period. **~-hier** /-tjɛr/ *adv.* the day before yesterday. **~-poste** *n.m.* outpost. **~-première** *n.f.* preview. **~-propos** *n.m.* foreword. **~-veille** *n.f.* two days before.

avantag|e /avɑ̃taʒ/ *n.m.* advantage; (*comm.*) benefit. **~er** *v.t.* favour; (*embellir*) show off to advantage.

avantageu|x, ~se /avɑ̃taʒø, -z/ *a.* attractive.

avar|e /avar/ *a.* miserly. ● *n.m./f.* miser. **~e de,** sparing of. **~ice** *n.f.* avarice.

avarié /avarje/ *a.* (*aliment*) spoiled.

avaries /avari/ *n.f. pl.* damage.

avatar /avatar/ *n.m.* (*fam.*) misfortune.

avec /avɛk/ *prép.* with; (*envers*) towards. ● *adv.* (*fam.*) with it *ou* them.

avenant, ~e /avnɑ̃, -t/ *a.* pleasing.

avenant (à l') /(al)avnɑ̃/ *adv.* in a similar style.

avènement /avɛnmɑ̃/ *n.m.* advent; (*d'un roi*) accession.

avenir /avnir/ *n.m.* future. **à l'~,** in future. **d'~,** with (future) prospects.

aventur|e /avɑ̃tyr/ *n.f.* adventure; (*sentimentale*) affair. **~eux, ~euse** *a.* adventurous; (*hasardeux*) risky. **~ier, ~ière** *n.m., f.* adventurer.

aventurer (s') /(s)avɑ̃tyre/ *v. pr.* venture.

avenue /avny/ *n.f.* avenue.

avérer (s') /(s)avere/ *v. pr.* prove (to be).

averse /avɛrs/ *n.f.* shower.

aversion /avɛrsjɔ̃/ *n.f.* aversion.

avert|ir /avɛrtir/ *v.t.* inform; (*mettre en garde, menacer*) warn. **~i** *a.* informed. **~issement** *n.m.* warning.

avertisseur /avɛrtisœr/ *n.m.* (*auto.*) horn. **~ d'incendie,** fire-alarm.

aveu (*pl.* **~x**) /avø/ *n.m.* confession. **de l'~ de,** by the admission of.

aveugl|e /avœgl/ *a.* blind. ● *n.m./f.* blind man, blind woman. **~ement** *n.m.* blindness. **~ément** *adv.* blindly. **~er** *v.t.* blind.

aveuglette (à l') /(al)avœglɛt/ *adv.* (*à tâtons*) blindly.

avia|teur, ~trice /avjatœr, -tris/ *n.m., f.* aviator.

aviation /avjɑsjɔ̃/ *n.f.* flying; (*industrie*) aviation; (*mil.*) air force. **d'~,** air.

avid|e /avid/ *a.* greedy (**de,** for); (*anxieux*) eager (**de,** for). **~e de faire,** eager to do. **~ité** *n.f.* greed; eagerness.

avilir /avilir/ *v.t.* degrade.

avion /avjɔ̃/ *n.m.* plane, aeroplane, aircraft; (*Amer.*) airplane. **~ à réaction,** jet.

aviron /avirɔ̃/ *n.m.* oar. **l'~,** (*sport*) rowing.

avis /avi/ *n.m.* opinion; (*renseignement*) notification; (*comm.*) advice. **à mon ~,** in my opinion. **changer d'~,** change one's mind. **être d'~ que,** be of the opinion that.

avisé /avize/ *a.* sensible. **bien/mal ~ de,** well-/ill-advised to.

aviser /avize/ *v.t.* notice; (*informer*) advise. ● *v.i.* decide what to do (**à,** about). **s'~ de,** suddenly realize. **s'~ de faire,** take it into one's head to do.

aviver /avive/ *v.t.* revive.

avocat[1]**, ~e** /avɔka, -t/ *n.m., f.* barrister; (*Amer.*) attorney; (*fig.*) advocate. **~ de la défense,** counsel for the defence.

avocat[2] /avɔka/ *n.m.* (*fruit*) avocado (pear).

avoine /avwan/ *n.f.* oats.

avoir† /avwar/ *v. aux.* have. ● *v.t.* have; (*obtenir*) get; (*duper: fam.*) take in. ● *n.m.* assets. **je n'ai pas de café,** I haven't (got) any coffee; (*Amer.*) I don't have any coffee. **est-ce que tu as du café?,** have you (got) any coffee?; (*Amer.*) do you have any coffee? **~ à faire,** have to do. **tu n'as qu'à l'appeler,** all you have to do is call her. **~ chaud/faim/***etc.*, be hot/hungry/*etc.* **~ dix/***etc.* **ans,** be ten/*etc.* years old. **~ lieu,** take place. **~ lieu de,** have good reason to. **en ~ contre qn.,** have a grudge against s.o. **en ~ assez,** have had enough. **en ~ pour une minute/***etc.*, be busy for a minute/*etc.* **il en a pour cent francs,** it will cost him one hundred francs. **qu'est-ce que vous avez?,** what is the matter with you? **on m'a eu!,** I've been had.

avoisin|er /avwazine/ *v.t.* border on. **~ant, ~ante** *a.* neighbouring.

avort|er /avɔrte/ *v.i.* (*projet etc.*) miscarry. **(se faire) ~er,** have an abortion. **~é** *a.* abortive. **~ement** *n.m.* (*méd.*) abortion.

avou|er /avwe/ *v.t.* confess (to). ● *v.i.* confess. **~é** *a.* avowed; *n.m.* solicitor; (*Amer.*) attorney.
avril /avril/ *n.m.* April.
axe /aks/ *n.m.* axis; (*essieu*) axle; (*d'une politique*) main line(s), basis. **~ (routier),** main road.
axer /akse/ *v.t.* centre.
axiome /aksjom/ *n.m.* axiom.
ayant /ɛjɑ̃/ *voir* avoir.
azimuts /azimyt/ *n.m. pl.* **dans tous les ~,** (*fam.*) all over the place.
azote /azɔt/ *n.m.* nitrogen.
azur /azyr/ *n.m.* sky-blue.

B

ba-ba /beaba/ *n.m.* **le ~ (de),** the basics (of).
baba /baba/ *n.m.* **~ (au rhum),** rum baba. **en rester ~,** (*fam.*) be flabbergasted.
babil /babi(l)/ *n.m.* babble. **~ler** /-ije/ *v.i.* babble.
babines /babin/ *n.f. pl.* **se lécher les ~,** lick one's chops.
babiole /babjɔl/ *n.f.* knick-knack.
bâbord /bɑbɔr/ *n.m.* port (side).
babouin /babwɛ̃/ *n.m.* baboon.
baby-foot /babifut/ *n.m. invar.* table football.
baby-sitt|er /bebisitœr/ *n.m./f.* babysitter. **~ing** *n.m.* **faire du ~ing,** babysit.
bac[1] /bak/ *n.m.* = **baccalauréat.**
bac[2] /bak/ *n.m.* (*bateau*) ferry; (*récipient*) tub; (*plus petit*) tray.
baccalauréat /bakalɔrea/ *n.m.* school leaving certificate.
bâch|e /bɑʃ/ *n.f.* tarpaulin. **~er** *v.t.* cover (with a tarpaulin).
bachel|ier, ~ière /baʃəlje, -jɛr/ *n.m., f.* holder of the *baccalauréat.*
bachot /baʃo/ *n.m.* (*fam.*) = **baccalauréat. ~er** /-ɔte/ *v.i.* cram (for an exam).
bâcler /bɑkle/ *v.t.* botch (up).
bactérie /bakteri/ *n.f.* bacterium.
badaud, ~e /bado, -d/ *n.m., f.* (*péj.*) onlooker.
badigeon /badiʒɔ̃/ *n.m.* whitewash. **~ner** /-ɔne/ *v.t.* whitewash; (*barbouiller*) daub.
badin, ~e /badɛ̃, -in/ *a.* lighthearted.
badiner /badine/ *v.i.* joke (**sur, avec,** about).
badminton /badmintɔn/ *n.m.* badminton.
baffe /baf/ *n.f.* (*fam.*) slap.
baffle /bafl/ *n.m.* speaker.
bafouer /bafwe/ *v.t.* scoff at.
bafouiller /bafuje/ *v.t./i.* stammer.
bâfrer /bɑfre/ *v.i.* (*fam.*) gobble. **se ~** *v.pr.* stuff o.s.
bagage /bagaʒ/ *n.m.* bag; (*fig.*) (store of) knowledge. **~s,** luggage, baggage. **~s à main,** hand luggage.
bagarr|e /bagar/ *n.f.* fight. **~er** *v.i.*, **se ~er** *v. pr.* fight.
bagatelle /bagatɛl/ *n.f.* trifle; (*somme*) trifling amount.
bagnard /baɲar/ *n.m.* convict.
bagnole /baɲɔl/ *n.f.* (*fam.*) car.
bagou(t) /bagu/ *n.m.* **avoir du ~,** have the gift of the gab.
bagu|e /bag/ *n.f.* (*anneau*) ring. **~er** *v.t.* ring.
baguette /bagɛt/ *n.f.* stick; (*de chef d'orchestre*) baton; (*chinoise*) chopstick; (*magique*) wand; (*pain*) stick of bread. **~ de tambour,** drumstick.
baie /bɛ/ *n.f.* (*géog.*) bay; (*fruit*) berry. **~ (vitrée),** picture window.
baign|er /beɲe/ *v.t.* bathe; (*enfant*) bath. ● *v.i.* **~er dans,** soak in; (*être enveloppé dans*) be steeped in. **se ~er** *v. pr.* go swimming (*ou*) bathing. **~é de,** bathed in; (*sang*) soaked in. **~ade** /bɛɲad/ *n.f.* bathing, swimming. **~eur, ~euse** /bɛɲœr, -øz/ *n.m., f.* bather.
baignoire /bɛɲwar/ *n.f.* bath(-tub).
bail (*pl.* **baux** /baj, bo/ *n.m.* lease.
bâill|er /bɑje/ *v.i.* yawn; (*être ouvert*) gape. **~ement** *n.m.* yawn.
bailleur /bajœr/ *n.m.* **~ de fonds,** (*comm.*) backer.
bâillon /bɑjɔ̃/ *n.m.* gag. **~ner** /bɑjɔne/ *v.t.* gag.
bain /bɛ̃/ *n.m.* bath; (*de mer*) bathe. **~(s) de soleil,** sunbathing. **~-marie** (*pl.* **~s-marie**) *n.m.* double boiler. **~ de bouche,** mouthwash. **mettre qn. dans le ~,** (*compromettre*) drop s.o. in it; (*au courant*) put s.o. in the picture. **se remettre dans le ~,** get back into the swim of things. **prendre un ~ de foule,** mingle with the crowd.
baiser /beze/ *n.m.* kiss. ● *v.t.* (*main*) kiss; (*fam.*) screw.
baisse /bɛs/ *n.f.* fall, drop. **en ~,** falling.

baisser /bese/ *v.t.* lower; (*radio, lampe, etc.*) turn down. ● *v.i.* go down, fall; (*santé, forces*) fail. **se ~** *v. pr.* bend down.
bajoues /baʒu/ *n.f. pl.* chops.
bakchich /bakʃiʃ/ *n.m.* (*fam.*) bribe.
bal (*pl.* **~s**) /bal/ *n.m.* dance; (*habillé*) ball; (*lieu*) dance-hall. **~ costumé,** fancy-dress ball.
balad|e /balad/ *n.f.* stroll; (*en auto*) drive. **~er** *v.t.* take for a stroll. **se ~er** *v. pr.* (go for a) stroll; (*excursionner*) wander around. **se ~er (en auto),** go for a drive.
baladeur /baladœr/ *n.m.* personal stereo.
balafr|e /balafr/ *n.f.* gash; (*cicatrice*) scar. **~er** *v.t.* gash.
balai /balɛ/ *n.m.* broom. **~-brosse** *n.m.* garden broom.
balance /balɑ̃s/ *n.f.* scales. **la B~,** Libra.
balancer /balɑ̃se/ *v.t.* swing; (*doucement*) sway; (*lancer: fam.*) chuck; (*se débarrasser de: fam.*) chuck out. ● *v.i.*, **se ~** *v. pr.* swing; sway. **se ~ de,** (*fam.*) not care about.
balancier /balɑ̃sje/ *n.m.* (*d'horloge*) pendulum; (*d'équilibriste*) pole.
balançoire /balɑ̃swar/ *n.f.* swing; (*bascule*) see-saw.
balay|er /baleje/ *v.t.* sweep (up); (*chasser*) sweep away; (*se débarrasser de*) sweep aside. **~age** *n.m.* sweeping; (*cheveux*) highlights. **~eur, ~euse** *n.m., f.* road sweeper.
balbut|ier /balbysje/ *v.t./i.* stammer. **~iement** *n.m.* stammering.
balcon /balkɔ̃/ *n.m.* balcony; (*théâtre*) dress circle.
baleine /balɛn/ *n.f.* whale.
balis|e /baliz/ *n.f.* beacon; (*bouée*) buoy; (*auto.*) (road) sign. **~er** *v.t.* mark out (with beacons); (*route*) signpost.
balistique /balistik/ *a.* ballistic.
balivernes /balivɛrn/ *n.f. pl.* balderdash.
ballade /balad/ *n.f.* ballad.
ballant, ~e /balɑ̃, -t/ *a.* dangling.
ballast /balast/ *n.m.* ballast.
balle /bal/ *n.f.* (*projectile*) bullet; (*sport*) ball; (*paquet*) bale.
ballerine /balrin/ *n.f.* ballerina.
ballet /balɛ/ *n.m.* ballet.
ballon /balɔ̃/ *n.m.* balloon; (*sport*) ball. **~ de football,** football.
ballonné /balɔne/ *a.* bloated.
ballot /balo/ *n.m.* bundle; (*nigaud: fam.*) idiot.
ballottage /balɔtaʒ/ *n.m.* second ballot (*due to indecisive result*).
ballotter /balɔte/ *v.t./i.* shake about, toss.
balnéaire /balneɛr/ *a.* seaside.
balourd, ~e /balur, -d/ *n.m., f.* oaf. ● *a.* oafish.
balustrade /balystrad/ *n.f.* railing(s).
bambin /bɑ̃bɛ̃/ *n.m.* tot.
bambou /bɑ̃bu/ *n.m.* bamboo.
ban /bɑ̃/ *n.m.* round of applause. **~s,** (*de mariage*) banns. **mettre au ~ de,** cast out from. **publier les ~s,** have the banns called.
banal (*m. pl.* **~s**) /banal/ *a.* commonplace, banal. **~ité** *n.f.* banality.
banane /banan/ *n.f.* banana.
banc /bɑ̃/ *n.m.* bench; (*de poissons*) shoal. **~ des accusés,** dock. **~ d'essai,** test bed; (*fig.*) testing-ground.
bancaire /bɑ̃kɛr/ *a.* banking; (*chèque*) bank.
bancal (*m. pl.* **~s**) /bɑ̃kal/ *a.* wobbly; (*raisonnement*) shaky.
bandage /bɑ̃daʒ/ *n.m.* bandage. **~ herniaire,** truss.
bande[1] /bɑ̃d/ *n.f.* (*de papier etc.*) strip; (*rayure*) stripe; (*de film*) reel; (*radio*) band; (*pansement*) bandage. **~ (magnétique),** tape. **~ dessinée,** comic strip. **~ sonore,** sound-track. **par la ~,** indirectly.
bande[2] /bɑ̃d/ *n.f.* (*groupe*) bunch, band, gang.
bandeau (*pl.* **~x**) /bɑ̃do/ *n.m.* headband; (*sur les yeux*) blindfold.
bander /bɑ̃de/ *v.t.* bandage; (*arc*) bend; (*muscle*) tense. **~ les yeux à,** blindfold.
banderole /bɑ̃drɔl/ *n.f.* banner.
bandit /bɑ̃di/ *n.m.* bandit. **~isme** /-tism/ *n.m.* crime.
bandoulière (en) /(ɑ̃)bɑ̃duljɛr/ *adv.* across one's shoulder.
banjo /bɑ̃(d)ʒo/ *n.m.* banjo.
banlieu|e /bɑ̃ljø/ *n.f.* suburbs. **de ~e,** suburban. **~sard, ~sarde** /-zar, -zard/ *n.m., f.* (suburban) commuter.
bannière /banjɛr/ *n.f.* banner.
bannir /banir/ *v.t.* banish.
banque /bɑ̃k/ *n.f.* bank; (*activité*) banking. **~ d'affaires,** merchant bank.
banqueroute /bɑ̃krut/ *n.f.* (fraudulent) bankruptcy.

banquet /bɑ̃kɛ/ *n.m.* dinner; (*fastueux*) banquet.
banquette /bɑ̃kɛt/ *n.f.* seat.
banquier /bɑ̃kje/ *n.m.* banker.
bapt|ême /batɛm/ *n.m.* baptism; christening. **~iser** *v.t.* baptize, christen; (*appeler*) christen.
baquet /bakɛ/ *n.m.* tub.
bar /bar/ *n.m.* (*lieu*) bar.
baragouin /baragwɛ̃/ *n.m.* gibberish, gabble. **~er** /-wine/ *v.t./i.* gabble; (*langue*) speak a few words of.
baraque /barak/ *n.f.* hut, shed; (*boutique*) stall; (*maison: fam.*) house. **~ments** *n.m. pl.* huts.
baratin /baratɛ̃/ *n.m.* (*fam.*) sweet *ou* smooth talk. **~er** /-ine/ *v.t.* (*fam.*) chat up; (*Amer.*) sweet-talk.
barbar|e /barbar/ *a.* barbaric. ● *n.m./f.* barbarian. **~ie** *n.f.* (*cruauté*) barbarity.
barbe /barb/ *n.f.* beard. **~ à papa,** candy-floss; (*Amer.*) cotton candy. **la ~!,** (*fam.*) blast (it)! **quelle ~!,** (*fam.*) what a bore!
barbecue /barbəkju/ *n.m.* barbecue.
barbelé /barbəle/ *a.* **fil ~,** barbed wire.
barber /barbe/ *v.t.* (*fam.*) bore.
barbiche /barbiʃ/ *n.f.* goatee.
barbiturique /barbityrik/ *n.m.* barbiturate.
barboter¹ /barbɔte/ *v.i.* paddle, splash.
barboter² /barbɔte/ *v.t.* (*voler: fam.*) pinch.
barbouill|er /barbuje/ *v.t.* (*peindre*) daub; (*souiller*) smear; (*griffonner*) scribble. **avoir l'estomac ~é** ou **se sentir ~é** feel liverish.
barbu /barby/ *a.* bearded.
barda /barda/ *n.m.* (*fam.*) gear.
barder /barde/ *v.i.* **ça va ~,** (*fam.*) sparks will fly.
barème /barɛm/ *n.m.* list, table; (*échelle*) scale.
baril /baril/ *n.m.* barrel; (*de poudre*) keg.
bariolé /barjɔle/ *a.* motley.
barman /barman/ *n.m.* barman; (*Amer.*) bartender.
baromètre /barɔmɛtr/ *n.m.* barometer.
baron, ~ne /barɔ̃, -ɔn/ *n.m., f.* baron, baroness.
baroque /barɔk/ *a.* (*fig.*) weird; (*archit., art*) baroque.
baroud /barud/ *n.m.* **~ d'honneur,** gallant last fight.
barque /bark/ *n.f.* (small) boat.
barrage /baraʒ/ *n.m.* dam; (*sur route*) road-block.
barre /bar/ *n.f.* bar; (*trait*) line, stroke; (*naut.*) helm.
barreau (*pl.* **~x**) /baro/ *n.m.* bar; (*d'échelle*) rung. **le ~,** (*jurid.*) the bar.
barrer /bare/ *v.t.* block; (*porte*) bar; (*rayer*) cross out; (*naut.*) steer. **se ~** *v. pr.* (*fam.*) hop it.
barrette /barɛt/ *n.f.* (hair-)slide.
barricad|e /barikad/ *n.f.* barricade. **~er** *v.t.* barricade. **se ~er** *v. pr.* barricade o.s.
barrière /barjɛr/ *n.f.* (*porte*) gate; (*clôture*) fence; (*obstacle*) barrier.
barrique /barik/ *n.f.* barrel.
baryton /baritɔ̃/ *n.m.* baritone.
bas, basse /bɑ, bɑs/ *a.* low; (*action*) base. ● *n.m.* bottom; (*chaussette*) stocking. ● *n.f.* (*mus.*) bass. ● *adv.* low. **à ~,** down with. **au ~ mot,** at the lowest estimate. **en ~,** down below; (*dans une maison*) downstairs. **en ~ âge,** young. **en ~ de,** at the bottom of. **plus ~,** further *ou* lower down. **~-côté** *n.m.* (*de route*) verge; (*Amer.*) shoulder. **~ de casse** *n.m. invar.* lower case. **~ de laine,** nest-egg. **~-fonds** *n.m. pl.* (*eau*) shallows; (*fig.*) dregs. **~ morceaux,** (*viande*) cheap cuts. **~-relief** *n.m.* low relief. **~-ventre** *n.m.* lower abdomen. **mettre ~,** give birth (to).
basané /bazane/ *a.* tanned.
bascule /baskyl/ *n.f.* (*balance*) scales. **cheval/fauteuil à ~,** rocking-horse/-chair.
basculer /baskyle/ *v.t./i.* topple over; (*benne*) tip up.
base /bɑz/ *n.f.* base; (*fondement*) basis; (*pol.*) rank and file. **de ~,** basic.
baser /bɑze/ *v.t.* base. **se ~ sur,** base o.s. on.
basilic /bazilik/ *n.m.* basil.
basilique /bazilik/ *n.f.* basilica.
basket(-ball) /baskɛt(bol)/ *n.m.* basketball.
basque /bask/ *a. & n.m./f.* Basque.
basse /bɑs/ *voir* bas.
basse-cour (*pl.* **basses-cours**) /bɑskur/ *n.f.* farmyard.
bassement /bɑsmɑ̃/ *adv.* basely.
bassesse /bɑsɛs/ *n.f.* baseness; (*action*) base act.

bassin /basɛ̃/ *n.m.* bowl; (*pièce d'eau*) pond; (*rade*) dock; (*géog.*) basin; (*anat.*) pelvis. **~ houiller,** coalfield.

basson /bɑsɔ̃/ *n.m.* bassoon.

bastion /bastjɔ̃/ *n.m.* bastion.

bat /ba/ *voir* battre.

bât /bɑ/ *n.m.* **là où le ~ blesse,** where the shoe pinches.

bataill|e /batɑj/ *n.f.* battle; (*fig.*) fight. **~er** *v.i.* fight.

bataillon /batajɔ̃/ *n.m.* battalion.

bâtard, ~e /bɑtar, -d/ *n.m., f.* bastard. ● *a.* (*solution*) hybrid.

bateau (*pl.* **~x**) /bato/ *n.m.* boat. **~-mouche** (*pl.* **~x-mouches**) *n.m.* sightseeing boat.

bâti /bɑti/ *a.* **bien ~,** well-built.

batifoler /batifɔle/ *v.i.* fool about.

bâtiment /bɑtimɑ̃/ *n.m.* building; (*navire*) vessel; (*industrie*) building trade.

bâtir /bɑtir/ *v.t.* build; (*coudre*) baste.

bâtisse /bɑtis/ *n.f.* (*péj.*) building.

bâton /bɑtɔ̃/ *n.m.* stick. **à ~s rompus,** jumping from subject to subject. **~ de rouge,** lipstick.

battage /bataʒ/ *n.m.* (*publicité: fam.*) (hard) plugging.

battant /batɑ̃/ *n.m.* (*vantail*) flap. **porte à deux ~s,** double door.

battement /batmɑ̃/ *n.m.* (*de cœur*) beat(ing); (*temps*) interval.

batterie /batri/ *n.f.* (*mil., électr.*) battery; (*mus.*) drums. **~ de cuisine,** pots and pans.

batteur /batœr/ *n.m.* (*mus.*) drummer; (*culin.*) whisk.

battre† /batr/ *v.t./i.* beat; (*blé*) thresh; (*cartes*) shuffle; (*parcourir*) scour; (*faire du bruit*) bang. **se ~** *v. pr.* fight. **~ des ailes,** flap its wings. **~ des mains,** clap. **~ en retraite,** beat a retreat. **~ la semelle,** stamp one's feet. **~ pavillon britannique/***etc.*, fly the British/*etc.* flag. **~ son plein,** be in full swing.

battue /baty/ *n.f.* (*chasse*) beat; (*de police*) search.

baume /bom/ *n.m.* balm.

bavard, ~e /bavar, -d/ *a.* talkative. ● *n.m., f.* chatterbox.

bavard|er /bavarde/ *v.i.* chat; (*jacasser*) chatter, gossip. **~age** *n.m.* chatter, gossip.

bav|e /bav/ *n.f.* dribble, slobber; (*de limace*) slime. **~er** *v.i.* dribble, slobber. **~eux, ~euse** *a.* dribbling; (*omelette*) runny.

bav|ette /bavɛt/ *n.f.*, **~oir** *n.m.* bib. **tailler une ~ette,** (*fam.*) have a chat.

bavure /bavyr/ *n.f.* smudge; (*erreur*) mistake. **~ policière,** (*fam.*)police cock-up. **sans ~,** flawless(ly).

bazar /bazar/ *n.m.* bazaar; (*objets: fam.*) clutter.

bazarder /bazarde/ *v.t.* (*vendre: fam.*) get rid of, flog.

BCBG *abrév.* (*bon chic bon genre*) posh.

BD *abrév.* (*bande dessinée*) comic strip.

béant, ~e /beɑ̃, -t/ *a.* gaping.

béat, ~e /bea, -t/ *a.* (*hum.*) blissful; (*péj.*) smug. **~itude** /-tityd/ *n.f.* (*hum.*) bliss.

beau *ou* **bel*, belle** (*m. pl.* **~x**) /bo, bɛl/ *a.* fine, beautiful; (*femme*) beautiful; (*homme*) handsome; (*grand*) big. ● *n.f.* beauty; (*sport*) deciding game. **au ~ milieu,** right in the middle. **bel et bien,** well and truly. **de plus belle,** more than ever. **faire le ~,** sit up and beg. **on a ~ essayer/insister/***etc.*, however much one tries/insists/*etc.*, it is no use trying/insisting/*etc.* **~x-arts** *n.m. pl.* fine arts. **~-fils** (*pl.* **~x-fils**) *n.m.* son-in-law; (*remariage*) stepson. **~-frère** (*pl.* **~x-frères**) *n.m.* brother-in-law. **~père** (*pl.* **~x-pères**) *n.m.* father-in-law; stepfather. **~x-parents** *n.m. pl.* parents-in-law.

beaucoup /boku/ *adv.* a lot, very much. ● *pron.* many (people). **~ de,** (*nombre*) many; (*quantité*) a lot of. **pas ~ (de),** not many; (*quantité*) not much. **~ plus/***etc.*, much more/*etc.* **~ trop,** much too much. **de ~,** by far.

beauté /bote/ *n.f.* beauty. **en ~,** magnificently. **tu es en ~,** you are looking good.

bébé /bebe/ *n.m.* baby. **~-éprouvette,** test-tube baby.

bec /bɛk/ *n.m.* beak; (*de plume*) nib; (*de bouilloire*) spout; (*de casserole*) lip; (*bouche: fam.*) mouth. **~-de-cane** (*pl.* **~s-de-cane**) door-handle. **~ de gaz,** gas lamp (*in street*).

bécane /bekan/ *n.f.* (*fam.*) bike.

bécasse /bekas/ *n.f.* woodcock.

bêche /bɛʃ/ *n.f.* spade.

bêcher /beʃe/ *v.t.* dig.

bécoter /bekɔte/ *v.t.*, **se ~** *v. pr.* (*fam.*) kiss.

becquée /beke/ *n.f.* **donner la ~ à,** (*oiseau*) feed; (*fig.*) spoonfeed.
bedaine /bədɛn/ *n.f.* paunch.
bedeau (*pl.* **~x**) /bədo/ *n.m.* beadle.
bedonnant, ~e /bədɔnɑ̃, -t/ *a.* paunchy.
beffroi /befrwa/ *n.m.* belfry.
bégayer /begeje/ *v.t./i.* stammer.
bègue /bɛg/ *n.m./f.* stammerer. **être ~,** stammer.
bégueule /begœl/ *a.* prudish.
béguin /begɛ̃/ *n.m.* **avoir le ~ pour,** (*fam.*) have a crush on.
beige /bɛʒ/ *a.* & *n.m.* beige.
beignet /bɛɲɛ/ *n.m.* fritter.
bel /bɛl/ *voir* beau.
bêler /bele/ *v.i.* bleat.
belette /bəlɛt/ *n.f.* weasel.
belge /bɛlʒ/ *a.* & *n.m./f.* Belgian.
Belgique /bɛlʒik/ *n.f.* Belgium.
bélier /belje/ *n.m.* ram. **le B~,** Aries.
belle /bɛl/ *voir* beau.
belle|-fille (*pl.* **~s-filles**) /bɛlfij/ *n.f.* daughter-in-law; (*remariage*) stepdaughter. **~-mère** (*pl.* **~s-mères**) *n.f.* mother-in-law; stepmother. **~-sœur** (*pl.* **~-sœurs**) *n.f.* sister-in-law.
belligérant, ~e /beliʒerɑ̃, -t/ *a.* & *n.m.* belligerent.
belliqueu|x, ~se /belikø, -z/ *a.* warlike.
belote /bəlɔt/ *n.f.* belote (*card game*).
belvédère /bɛlvedɛr/ *n.m.* (*lieu*) viewing spot, viewpoint.
bémol /bemɔl/ *n.m.* (*mus.*) flat.
bénédiction /benediksjɔ̃/ *n.f.* blessing.
bénéfice /benefis/ *n.m.* (*gain*) profit; (*avantage*) benefit.
bénéficiaire /benefisjɛr/ *n.m./f.* beneficiary.
bénéficier /benefisje/ *v.i.* **~ de,** benefit from; (*jouir de*) enjoy, have.
bénéfique /benefik/ *a.* beneficial.
Bénélux /benelyks/ *n.m.* Benelux.
benêt /bənɛ/ *n.m.* simpleton.
bénévole /benevɔl/ *a.* voluntary.
bén|in, ~igne /benɛ̃, -iɲ/ *a.* mild, slight; (*tumeur*) benign.
bén|ir /benir/ *v.t.* bless. **~it, ~ite** *a.* (*eau*) holy; (*pain*) consecrated.
bénitier /benitje/ *n.m.* stoup.
benjamin, ~e /bɛ̃ʒamɛ̃, -in/ *n.m., f.* youngest child.
benne /bɛn/ *n.f.* (*de grue*) scoop; (*amovible*) skip. **~ (basculante),** dump truck.
benzine /bɛ̃zin/ *n.f.* benzine.
béotien, ~ne /beɔsjɛ̃, -jɛn/ *n.m., f.* philistine.
béquille /bekij/ *n.f.* crutch; (*de moto*) stand.
bercail /bɛrkaj/ *n.m.* fold.
berceau (*pl.* **~x**) /bɛrso/ *n.m.* cradle.
bercer /bɛrse/ *v.t.* (*balancer*) rock; (*apaiser*) lull; (*leurrer*) delude.
berceuse /bɛrsøz/ *n.f.* lullaby.
béret /berɛ/ *n.m.* beret.
berge /bɛrʒ/ *n.f.* (*bord*) bank.
berg|er, ~ère /bɛrʒe, -ɛr/ *n.m., f.* shepherd, shepherdess. **~erie** *n.f.* sheep-fold.
berlingot /bɛrlɛ̃go/ *n.m.* boiled sweet; (*emballage*) carton.
berne (en) /(ɑ̃)bɛrn/ *adv.* at half-mast.
berner /bɛrne/ *v.t.* hoodwink.
besogne /bəzɔɲ/ *n.f.* task, job, chore.
besoin /bəzwɛ̃/ *n.m.* need. **avoir ~ de,** need. **au ~,** if need be.
best|ial (*m. pl.* **~iaux**) /bɛstjal, -jo/ *a.* bestial.
bestiaux /bɛstjo/ *n.m. pl.* livestock.
bestiole /bɛstjɔl/ *n.f.* creepy-crawly.
bétail /betaj/ *n.m.* farm animals.
bête[1] /bɛt/ *n.f.* animal. **~ noire,** pet hate, pet peeve. **~ sauvage,** wild beast. **chercher la petite ~,** be overfussy.
bête[2] /bɛt/ *a.* stupid. **~ment** *adv.* stupidly.
bêtise /betiz/ *n.f.* stupidity; (*action*) stupid thing.
béton /betɔ̃/ *n.m.* concrete. **~ armé,** reinforced concrete. **~nière** /-ɔnjɛr/ *n.f.* cement-mixer, concrete-mixer.
betterave /bɛtrav/ *n.f.* beetroot. **~ sucrière,** sugar-beet.
beugler /bøgle/ *v.i.* bellow, low; (*radio*) blare.
beur /bœr/ *n.m./f.* & *a.* (*fam.*) young French North African.
beurr|e /bœr/ *n.m.* butter. **~er** *v.t.* butter. **~ier** *n.m.* butter-dish. **~é,** *a.* buttered; (*fam.*) drunk.
bévue /bevy/ *n.f.* blunder.
biais /bjɛ/ *n.m.* (*fig.*) expedient; (*côté*) angle. **de ~, en ~,** at an angle. **de ~,** (*fig.*) indirectly.
biaiser /bjeze/ *v.i.* hedge.
bibelot /biblo/ *n.m.* curio.
biberon /bibrɔ̃/ *n.m.* (feeding-) bottle. **nourrir au ~,** bottle-feed.
bible /bibl/ *n.f.* bible. **la B~,** the Bible.
bibliographie /biblijɔgrafi/ *n.f.* bibliography.

bibliophile /biblijɔfil/ *n.m./f.* book-lover.

biblioth|èque /biblijɔtɛk/ *n.f.* library; (*meuble*) bookcase; **~écaire** *n.m./f.* librarian.

biblique /biblik/ *a.* biblical.

bic /bik/ *n.m.* (P.) biro (P.).

bicarbonate /bikarbɔnat/ *n.m.* **~ (de soude),** bicarbonate (of soda).

biceps /bisɛps/ *n.m.* biceps.

biche /biʃ/ *n.f.* doe.

bichonner /biʃɔne/ *v.t.* doll up.

bicoque /bikɔk/ *n.f.* shack.

bicyclette /bisiklɛt/ *n.f.* bicycle.

bide /bid/ *n.m.* (*ventre: fam.*) belly; (*théâtre: fam.*) flop.

bidet /bidɛ/ *n.m.* bidet.

bidon /bidɔ̃/ *n.m.* can. ● *a. invar.* (*fam.*) phoney. **c'est pas du ~,** (*fam.*) it's the truth, it's for real.

bidonville /bidɔ̃vil/ *n.f.* shanty town.

bidule /bidyl/ *n.m.* (*fam.*) thing.

bielle /bjɛl/ *n.f.* connecting rod.

bien /bjɛ̃/ *adv.* well; (*très*) quite, very. ● *n.m.* good; (*patrimoine*) possession. ● *a. invar.* good; (*passable*) all right; (*en forme*) well; (*à l'aise*) comfortable; (*beau*) attractive; (*respectable*) nice, respectable. ● *conj.* **~ que,** (al)though. **~ que ce soit/que ça ait,** although it is/it has. **~ du,** (*quantité*) a lot of, much. **~ des,** (*nombre*) many. **il l'a ~ fait,** (*intensif*) he did do it. **ce n'est pas ~ de,** it is not right to. **~ sûr,** of course. **~s de consommation,** consumer goods. **~-aimé, ~aimée** *a.* & *n.m., f.* beloved. **~-être** *n.m.* well-being. **~-fondé** *n.m.* soundness. **~-pensant, ~-pensante** *a.* & *n.m., f.* (*péj.*) right-thinking.

bienfaisan|t, -te /bjɛ̃fəzɑ̃, -t/ *a.* beneficial. **~ce** *n.f.* charity. **fête de ~ce,** fête.

bienfait /bjɛ̃fɛ/ *n.m.* (kind) favour; (*avantage*) benefit.

bienfai|teur, ~trice /bjɛ̃fɛtœr, -tris/ *n.m., f.* benefactor.

bienheureu|x, ~se /bjɛ̃nœrø, -z/ *a.* happy, blessed.

bienséan|t, ~te /bjɛ̃seɑ̃, -t/ *a.* proper. **~ce** *n.f.* propriety.

bientôt /bjɛ̃to/ *adv.* soon. **à ~,** see you soon.

bienveillan|t, ~te /bjɛ̃vɛjɑ̃, -t/ *a.* kind(ly). **~ce** *n.f.* kind(li)ness.

bienvenu, ~e /bjɛ̃vny/ *a.* welcome. ● *n.f.* welcome. ● *n.m., f.* **être le ~, être la ~e,** be welcome. **souhaiter la ~e à,** welcome.

bière /bjɛr/ *n.f.* beer; (*cercueil*) coffin. **~ blonde,** lager. **~ brune,** stout, brown ale. **~ pression,** draught beer.

biffer /bife/ *v.t.* cross out.

bifteck /biftɛk/ *n.m.* steak.

bifur|quer /bifyrke/ *v.i.* branch off, fork. **~cation** *n.f.* fork, junction.

bigam|e /bigam/ *a.* bigamous. ● *n.m./f.* bigamist. **~ie** *n.f.* bigamy.

bigarré /bigare/ *a.* motley.

big-bang /bigbɑ̃g/ *n.m.* big bang.

bigot, ~e /bigo, -ɔt/ *n.m., f.* religious fanatic. ● *a.* over-pious.

bigoudi /bigudi/ *n.m.* curler.

bijou (*pl.* **~x**) /biʒu/ *n.m.* jewel. **~terie** *n.f.* (*boutique*) jeweller's shop; (*comm.*) jewellery. **~tier, ~tière** *n.m., f.* jeweller.

bikini /bikini/ *n.m.* bikini.

bilan /bilɑ̃/ *n.m.* outcome; (*d'une catastrophe*) (casualty) toll; (*comm.*) balance sheet. **faire le ~ de,** assess. **~ de santé,** check-up.

bile /bil/ *n.f.* bile. **se faire de la ~,** (*fam.*) worry.

bilieu|x, ~se /biljø, -z/ *a.* bilious; (*fig.*) irascible.

bilingue /bilɛ̃g/ *a.* bilingual.

billard /bijar/ *n.m.* billiards; (*table*) billiard-table.

bille /bij/ *n.f.* (*d'enfant*) marble; (*de billard*) billiard-ball.

billet /bijɛ/ *n.m.* ticket; (*lettre*) note; (*article*) column. **~ (de banque),** (bank)note. **~ d'aller et retour,** return ticket; (*Amer.*) round trip ticket. **~ de faveur,** complimentary ticket. **~ aller simple,** single ticket; (*Amer.*) one way ticket.

billetterie /bijɛtri/ *n.f.* cash dispenser.

billion /biljɔ̃/ *n.m.* billion (= 10^{12}); (*Amer.*) trillion.

billot /bijo/ *n.m.* block.

bimensuel, ~le /bimɑ̃sɥɛl/ *a.* fortnightly, bimonthly.

bin|er /bine/ *v.t.* hoe. **~ette** *n.f.* hoe; (*fam.*) face.

biochimie /bjɔʃimi/ *n.f.* biochemistry.

biodégradable /bjɔdegradabl/ *a.* biodegradable.

biograph|ie /bjɔgrafi/ *n.f.* biography. **~e** *n.m./f.* biographer.

biolog|ie /bjɔlɔʒi/ *n.f.* biology. **~ique** *a.* biological. **~iste** *n.m./f.* biologist.

bipède /bipɛd/ *n.m.* biped.
bis[1], **bise** /bi, biz/ *a.* greyish brown.
bis[2] /bis/ *a.invar.* (*numéro*) A, a. ● *n.m.* & *int.* encore.
bisbille (en) /(ɑ̃)bisbij/ *adv.* (*fam.*) at loggerheads (**avec**, with).
biscornu /biskɔrny/ *a.* crooked; (*bizarre*) weird.
biscotte /biskɔt/ *n.f.* rusk.
biscuit /biskɥi/ *n.m.* (*salé*) biscuit; (*Amer.*) cracker; (*sucré*) biscuit; (*Amer.*) cookie. **~ de Savoie,** sponge-cake.
bise[1] /biz/ *n.f.* (*fam.*) kiss.
bise[2] /biz/ *n.f.* (*vent*) north wind.
bison /bizɔ̃/ *n.m.* (American) buffalo, bison.
bisou /bizu/ *n.m.* (*fam.*) kiss.
bisser /bise/ *v.t.* encore.
bistouri /bisturi/ *n.m.* lancet.
bistre /bistr/ *a.* & *n.m.* dark brown.
bistro(t) /bistro/ *n.m.* café, bar.
bit /bit/ *n.m.* (*comput.*) bit.
bitume /bitym/ *n.m.* asphalt.
bizarre /bizar/ *a.* odd, peculiar. **~ment** *adv.* oddly. **~rie** *n.f.* peculiarity.
blafard, ~e /blafar, -d/ *a.* pale.
blagu|e /blag/ *n.f.* joke. **~e à tabac,** tobacco-pouch. **~er** *v.i.* joke; *v.t.* tease. **~eur, ~euse** *n.m., f.* joker; *a.* jokey.
blaireau (*pl.* **~x**) /blɛro/ *n.m.* shaving-brush; (*animal*) badger.
blâm|e /blɑm/ *n.m.* rebuke, blame. **~able** *a.* blameworthy. **~er** *v.t.* rebuke, blame.
blanc, blanche /blɑ̃, blɑ̃ʃ/ *a.* white; (*papier, page*) blank. ● *n.m.* white; (*espace*) blank. ● *n.m., f.* white man, white woman. ● *n.f.* (*mus.*) minim. **~ (de poulet),** breast, white meat (of the chicken). **le ~,** (*linge*) whites. **laisser en ~,** leave blank.
blancheur /blɑ̃ʃœr/ *n.f.* whiteness.
blanch|ir /blɑ̃ʃir/ *v.t.* whiten; (*linge*) launder; (*personne: fig.*) clear; (*culin.*) blanch. **~ir (à la chaux),** whitewash. ● *v.i.* turn white. **~issage** *n.m.* laundering. **~isserie** *n.f.* laundry. **~isseur, ~isseuse** *n.m., f.* laundryman, laundress.
blasé /blɑze/ *a.* blasé.
blason /blazɔ̃/ *n.m.* coat of arms.
blasph|ème /blasfɛm/ *n.m.* blasphemy. **~ématoire** *a.* blasphemous. **~émer** *v.t./i.* blaspheme.
blatte /blat/ *n.f.* cockroach.
blazer /blɛzœr/ *n.m.* blazer.
blé /ble/ *n.m.* wheat.
bled /blɛd/ *n.m.* (*fam.*) dump, hole.
blême /blɛm/ *a.* (sickly) pale.
bless|er /blese/ *v.t.* injure, hurt; (*par balle*) wound; (*offenser*) hurt, wound. **se ~er** *v. pr.* injure *ou* hurt o.s. **~ant, ~ante** /blɛsɑ̃, -t/ *a.* hurtful. **~é, ~ée** *n.m., f.* casualty, injured person.
blessure /blesyr/ *n.f.* wound.
blet, ~te /blɛ, blɛt/ *a.* over-ripe.
bleu /blø/ *a.* blue; (*culin.*) very rare. **~ marine,** navy blue. ● *n.m.* blue; (*contusion*) bruise. **~(s),** (*vêtement*) overalls. **~ir** *v.t./i.* turn blue.
bleuet /bløɛ/ *n.m.* cornflower.
bleuté /bløte/ *a.* slightly blue.
blind|er /blɛ̃de/ *v.t.* armour (-plate); (*fig.*) harden. **~é** *a.* armoured; (*fig.*) immune (**contre**, to); *n.m.* armoured car, tank.
blizzard /blizar/ *n.m.* blizzard.
bloc /blɔk/ *n.m.* block; (*de papier*) pad; (*système*) unit; (*pol.*) bloc. **à ~,** hard, tight. **en ~,** all together. **~-notes** (*pl.* **~s-notes**) *n.m.* note-pad.
blocage /blɔkaʒ/ *n.m.* (*des prix*) freeze, freezing; (*des roues*) locking; (*psych.*) block.
blocus /blɔkys/ *n.m.* blockade.
blond, ~e /blɔ̃, -d/ *a.* fair, blond. ● *n.m., f.* fair-haired *ou* blond man *ou* woman. **~eur** /-dœr/ *n.f.* fairness.
bloquer /blɔke/ *v.t.* block; (*porte, machine*) jam; (*freins*) slam on; (*roues*) lock; (*prix, crédits*) freeze; (*grouper*) put together. **se ~** *v. pr.* jam; (*roues*) lock.
blottir (se) /(sə)blɔtir/ *v. pr.* snuggle, huddle.
blouse /bluz/ *n.f.* smock.
blouson /bluzɔ̃/ *n.m.* lumber-jacket; (*Amer.*) windbreaker.
blue-jean /bludʒin/ *n.m.* jeans.
bluff /blœf/ *n.m.* bluff. **~er** *v.t./i.* bluff.
blush /blœʃ/ *n.m.* blusher.
boa /bɔa/ *n.m.* boa.
bobard /bɔbar/ *n.m.* (*fam.*) fib.
bobine /bɔbin/ *n.f.* reel; (*sur machine*) spool; (*électr.*) coil.
bobo /bobo/ *n.m.* (*fam.*) sore, cut. **avoir ~,** have a pain.
bocage /bɔkaʒ/ *n.m.* grove.
boc|al (*pl.* **~aux**) /bɔkal, -o/ *n.m.* jar.
bock /bɔk/ *n.m.* beer glass; (*contenu*) glass of beer.
body /bodi/ *n.m.* leotard.

bœuf (*pl.* **~s**) /bœf, bø/ *n.m.* ox; (*viande*) beef. **~s,** oxen.
bogue /bɔg/ *n.m.* (*comput.*) bug.
bohème /bɔɛm/ *a.* & *n.m./f.* unconventional.
boire† /bwar/ *v.t./i.* drink; (*absorber*) soak up. **~ un coup,** have a drink.
bois [1] /bwa/ *voir* boire.
bois [2] /bwa/ *n.m.* (*matériau, forêt*) wood. **de ~, en ~,** wooden.
boisé /bwaze/ *a.* wooded.
bois|er /bwaze/ *v.t.* (*chambre*) panel. **~eries** *n.f. pl.* panelling.
boisson /bwasɔ̃/ *n.f.* drink.
boit /bwa/ *voir* boire.
boîte /bwat/ *n.f.* box; (*de conserves*) tin, can; (*firme*: *fam.*) firm. **~ à gants,** glove compartment. **~ aux lettres,** letter-box. **~ de nuit,** night-club. **~ postale,** post-office box. **~ de vitesses,** gear box.
boiter /bwate/ *v.i.* limp; (*meuble*) wobble.
boiteu|x, ~se /bwatø, -z/ *a.* lame; (*meuble*) wobbly; (*raisonnement*) shaky.
boîtier /bwatje/ *n.m.* case.
bol /bɔl/ *n.m.* bowl. **un ~ d'air,** a breath of fresh air. **avoir du ~,** (*fam.*) be lucky.
bolide /bɔlid/ *n.m.* racing car.
Bolivie /bɔlivi/ *n.f.* Bolivia.
bolivien, ~ne /bɔlivjɛ̃, -jɛn/ *a.* & *n.m., f.* Bolivian.
bombance /bɔ̃bɑ̃s/ *n.f.* **faire ~,** (*fam.*) revel.
bombard|er /bɔ̃barde/ *v.t.* bomb; (*par obus*) shell; (*nommer*: *fam.*) appoint unexpectedly (as). **~er qn. de,** (*fig.*) bombard s.o. with. **~ement** *n.m.* bombing; shelling. **~ier** *n.m.* (*aviat.*) bomber.
bombe /bɔ̃b/ *n.f.* bomb; (*atomiseur*) spray, aerosol.
bombé /bɔ̃be/ *a.* rounded; (*route*) cambered.
bomber /bɔ̃be/ *v.t.* **~ la poitrine,** throw out one's chest.
bon, bonne /bɔ̃, bɔn/ *a.* good; (*qui convient*) right; (*prudent*) wise. **~ à/pour,** (*approprié*) fit to/for. **tenir ~,** stand firm. ● *n.m.* (*billet*) voucher, coupon; (*comm.*) bond. **du ~,** some good. **pour de ~,** for good. **à quoi ~?,** what's the good *ou* point? **bonne année,** happy New Year. **~ anniversaire,** happy birthday. **~ appétit/voyage,** enjoy your meal/trip. **bonne chance/nuit,** good luck/night. **bonne femme,** (*péj.*) woman. **bonne-maman** (*pl.* **bonnes-mamans**) *n.f.* (*fam.*) granny. **~-papa** (*pl.* **~s-papas**) *n.m.* (*fam.*) grand-dad. **~ sens,** common sense. **~ vivant,** bon viveur. **de bonne heure,** early.
bonbon /bɔ̃bɔ̃/ *n.m.* sweet; (*Amer.*) candy. **~nière** /-ɔnjɛr/ *n.f.* sweet box; (*Amer.*) candy box.
bonbonne /bɔ̃bɔn/ *n.f.* demijohn; (*de gaz*) canister.
bond /bɔ̃/ *n.m.* leap. **faire un ~,** leap in the air; (*de surprise*) jump.
bonde /bɔ̃d/ *n.f.* plug; (*trou*) plughole.
bondé /bɔ̃de/ *a.* packed.
bondir /bɔ̃dir/ *v.i.* leap; (*de surprise*) jump.
bonheur /bɔnœr/ *n.m.* happiness; (*chance*) (good) luck. **au petit ~,** haphazardly. **par ~,** luckily.
bonhomme [1] (*pl.* **bonshommes**) /bɔnɔm, bɔ̃zɔm/ *n.m.* fellow. **~ de neige,** snowman.
bonhom|me [2] /bɔnɔm/ *a. invar.* good-hearted. **~ie** *n.f.* good-heartedness.
bonifier (se) /(sə)bɔnifje/ *v. pr.* improve.
boniment /bɔnimɑ̃/ *n.m.* smooth talk.
bonjour /bɔ̃ʒur/ *n.m.* & *int.* hallo, hello, good morning *ou* afternoon.
bon marché /bɔ̃marʃe/ *a. invar.* cheap. ● *adv.* cheap(ly).
bonne [1] /bɔn/ *a.f. voir* bon.
bonne [2] /bɔn/ *n.f.* (*domestique*) maid. **~ d'enfants,** nanny.
bonnement /bɔnmɑ̃/ *adv.* **tout ~,** quite simply.
bonnet /bɔnɛ/ *n.m.* hat; (*de soutien-gorge*) cup. **~ de bain,** swimming cap.
bonneterie /bɔnɛtri/ *n.f.* hosiery.
bonsoir /bɔ̃swar/ *n.m.* & *int.* good evening; (*en se couchant*) good night.
bonté /bɔ̃te/ *n.f.* kindness.
bonus /bɔnys/ *n.m.* (*auto.*) no claims bonus.
boom /bum/ *n.m.* (*comm.*) boom.
boots /buts/ *n.m. pl.* ankle boots.
bord /bɔr/ *n.m.* edge; (*rive*) bank. **à ~ (de),** on board. **au ~ de la mer,** at the seaside. **au ~ des larmes,** on the verge of tears. **~ de la route,** roadside. **~ du trottoir,** kerb; (*Amer.*) curb.

bordeaux /bɔrdo/ *n.m. invar.* Bordeaux (wine), claret. ● *a. invar.* maroon.
bordée /bɔrde/ *n.f.* **~ d'injures,** torrent of abuse.
bordel /bɔrdɛl/ *n.m.* brothel; (*désordre*: *fam.*) shambles.
border /bɔrde/ *v.t.* line, border; (*tissu*) edge; (*personne, lit*) tuck in.
bordereau (*pl.* **~x**) /bɔrdəro/ *n.m.* (*liste*) note, slip; (*facture*) invoice.
bordure /bɔrdyr/ *n.f.* border. **en ~ de,** on the edge of.
borgne /bɔrɲ/ *a.* one-eyed; (*fig.*) shady.
borne /bɔrn/ *n.f.* boundary marker. **~ (kilométrique),** (*approx.*) milestone. **~s,** limits.
borné /bɔrne/ *a.* narrow; (*personne*) narrow-minded.
borner /bɔrne/ *v.t.* confine. **se ~** *v. pr.* confine o.s. **(à,** to).
bosquet /bɔskɛ/ *n.m.* grove.
bosse /bɔs/ *n.f.* bump; (*de chameau*) hump. **avoir la ~ de,** (*fam.*) have a gift for. **avoir roulé sa ~,** have been around.
bosseler /bɔsle/ *v.t.* emboss; (*endommager*) dent.
bosser /bɔse/ *v.i.* (*fam.*) work (hard). ● *v.t.* (*fam.*) work (hard) at.
bossu, ~e /bɔsy/ *n.m., f.* hunchback.
botani|que /bɔtanik/ *n.f.* botany. ● *a.* botanical. **~ste** *n.m./f.* botanist.
bott|e /bɔt/ *n.f.* boot; (*de fleurs, légumes*) bunch; (*de paille*) bundle, bale. **~s de caoutchouc,** wellingtons. **~ier** *n.m.* boot-maker.
botter /bɔte/ *v.t.* (*fam.*) **ça me botte,** I like the idea.
Bottin /bɔtɛ̃/ *n.m.* (P.) phone book.
bouc /buk/ *n.m.* (billy-)goat; (*barbe*) goatee. **~ émissaire,** scapegoat.
boucan /bukɑ̃/ *n.m.* (*fam.*) din.
bouche /buʃ/ *n.f.* mouth. **~ bée,** open-mouthed. **~ d'égout,** manhole. **~ d'incendie,** (fire) hydrant. **~ de métro,** entrance to the underground *ou* subway (*Amer.*). **~-à-bouche** *n.m.* mouth-to-mouth resuscitation.
bouché /buʃe/ *a.* **c'est ~,** (*profession, avenir*) it's a dead end.
bouchée /buʃe/ *n.f.* mouthful.
boucher[1] /buʃe/ *v.t.* block; (*bouteille*) cork. **se ~** *v. pr.* get blocked. **se ~ le nez,** hold one's nose.
bouch|er[2]**, ~ère** /buʃe, -ɛr/ *n.m., f.* butcher. **~erie** *n.f.* butcher's (shop); (*carnage*) butchery.
bouche-trou /buʃtru/ *n.m.* stopgap.
bouchon /buʃɔ̃/ *n.m.* stopper; (*en liège*) cork; (*de bidon, tube*) cap; (*de pêcheur*) float; (*de circulation*: *fig.*) hold-up.
boucle /bukl/ *n.f.* (*de ceinture*) buckle; (*forme*) loop; (*de cheveux*) curl. **~ d'oreille,** ear-ring.
boucl|er /bukle/ *v.t.* fasten; (*terminer*) finish off; (*enfermer*: *fam.*) shut up; (*encercler*) seal off; (*budget*) balance. ● *v.i.* curl. **~é** *a.* (*cheveux*) curly.
bouclier /buklije/ *n.m.* shield.
bouddhiste /budist/ *a. & n.m./f.* Buddhist.
boud|er /bude/ *v.i.* sulk. ● *v.t.* steer clear of. **~erie** *n.f.* sulkiness. **~eur, ~euse** *a. & n.m., f.* sulky (person).
boudin /budɛ̃/ *n.m.* black pudding.
boudoir /budwar/ *n.m.* boudoir.
boue /bu/ *n.f.* mud.
bouée /bwe/ *n.f.* buoy. **~ de sauvetage,** lifebuoy.
boueu|x, ~se /bwø, -z/ *a.* muddy. ● *n.m.* dustman; (*Amer.*) garbage collector.
bouff|e /buf/ *n.f.* (*fam.*) food, grub. **~er** *v.t./i.* (*fam.*) eat; (*bâfrer*) gobble.
bouffée /bufe/ *n.f.* puff, whiff; (*méd.*) flush; (*d'orgueil*) fit.
bouf† /bufi/ *a.* bloated.
bouffon, ~ne /bufɔ̃, -ɔn/ *a.* farcical. ● *n.m.* buffoon.
bouge /buʒ/ *n.m.* hovel; (*bar*) dive.
bougeoir /buʒwar/ *n.m.* candlestick.
bougeotte /buʒɔt/ *n.f.* **la ~,** (*fam.*) the fidgets.
bouger /buʒe/ *v.t./i.* move; (*agir*) stir. **se ~** *v. pr.* (*fam.*) move.
bougie /buʒi/ *n.f.* candle; (*auto.*) spark(ing)-plug.
bougon, ~ne /bugɔ̃, -ɔn/ *a.* grumpy. **~ner** /-ɔne/ *v.i.* grumble.
bouillabaisse /bujabɛs/ *n.f.* bouillabaisse.
bouillie /buji/ *n.f.* porridge; (*pour bébé*) baby food; (*péj.*) mush. **en ~,** crushed, mushy.
bouill|ir† /bujir/ *v.i.* boil. ● *v.t.* **(faire) ~ir,** boil. **~ant, ~ante** *a.* boiling; (*très chaud*) boiling hot.
bouilloire /bujwar/ *n.f.* kettle.

bouillon /bujɔ̃/ *n.m.* (*aliment*) stock. **~ cube,** stock cube. **~ner** /-jɔne/ *v.i.* bubble.
bouillote /bujɔt/ *n.f.* hot-water bottle.
boulang|er, ~ère /bulɑ̃ʒe, -ɛr/ *n.m., f.* baker. **~erie** *n.f.* bakery. **~erie-pâtisserie** *n.f.* baker's and confectioner's shop.
boule /bul/ *n.f.* ball; (*de machine à écrire*) golf ball. **~s,** (*jeu*) bowls. **jouer aux ~s,** play bowls. **une ~ dans la gorge,** lump in one's throat. **~ de neige,** snowball. **faire ~ de neige,** snowball.
bouleau (*pl.* **~x**) /bulo/ *n.m.* (silver) birch.
bouledogue /buldɔg/ *n.m.* bulldog.
boulet /bulɛ/ *n.m.* (*de canon*) cannon-ball; (*de forçat*: *fig.*) ball and chain.
boulette /bulɛt/ *n.f.* (*de papier*) pellet; (*aliment*) meat ball.
boulevard /bulvar/ *n.m.* boulevard.
bouleversl|er /bulvɛrse/ *v.t.* turn upside down; (*pays, plans*) disrupt; (*émouvoir*) distress, upset. **~ant, ante** *a.* deeply moving. **~ement** *n.m.* upheaval.
boulier /bulje/ *n.m.* abacus.
boulimie /bulimi/ *n.f.* compulsive eating; (*méd.*) bulimia.
boulon /bulɔ̃/ *n.m.* bolt.
boulot[1] /bulo/ *n.m.* (*travail*: *fam.*) work.
boulot[2], **~te** /bulo, -ɔt/ *a.* (*rond*: *fam.*) dumpy.
boum /bum/ *n.m.* & *int.* bang. ● *n.f.* (*réunion*: *fam.*) party.
bouquet /bukɛ/ *n.m.* (*de fleurs*) bunch, bouquet; (*d'arbres*) clump. **c'est le ~!,** (*fam.*) that's the last straw!
bouquin /bukɛ̃/ *n.m.* (*fam.*) book. **~er** /-ine/ *v.t./i.* (*fam.*) read. **~iste** /-inist/ *n.m./f.* second-hand bookseller.
bourbeu|x, ~se /burbø, -z/ *a.* muddy.
bourbier /burbje/ *n.m.* mire.
bourde /burd/ *n.f.* blunder.
bourdon /burdɔ̃/ *n.m.* bumble-bee.
bourdonn|er /burdɔne/ *v.i.* buzz. **~ement** *n.m.* buzzing.
bourg /bur/ *n.m.* (market) town.
bourgade /burgad/ *n.f.* village.
bourgeois, ~e /burʒwa, -z/ *a.* & *n.m., f.* middle-class (person); (*péj.*) bourgeois. **~ie** /-zi/ *n.f.* middle class(es).
bourgeon /burʒɔ̃/ *n.m.* bud. **~ner** /-ɔne/ *v.i.* bud.
bourgogne /burgɔɲ/ *n.m.* burgundy. ● *n.f.* **la B~,** Burgundy.
bourlinguer /burlɛ̃ge/ *v.i.* (*fam.*) travel about.
bourrade /burad/ *n.f.* prod.
bourrage /buraʒ/ *n.m.* **~ de crâne,** brainwashing.
bourrasque /burask/ *n.f.* squall.
bourrati|f, ~ve /buratif, -v/ *a.* filling, stodgy.
bourreau (*pl.* **~x**) /buro/ *n.m.* executioner. **~ de travail,** workaholic.
bourrelet /burlɛ/ *n.m.* weather-strip, draught excluder; (*de chair*) roll of fat.
bourrer /bure/ *v.t.* cram (**de,** with); (*pipe*) fill. **~ de,** (*nourriture*) stuff with. **~ de coups,** thrash. **~ le crâne à qn.,** fill s.o.'s head with nonsense.
bourrique /burik/ *n.f.* ass.
bourru /bury/ *a.* surly.
bours|e /burs/ *n.f.* purse; (*subvention*) grant. **la B~e,** the Stock Exchange. **~ier, ~ière** *a.* Stock Exchange; *n.m., f.* holder of a grant.
boursoufler /bursufle/ *v.t.*, **se ~** *v. pr.* puff up, swell.
bouscul|er /buskyle/ *v.t.* (*pousser*) jostle; (*presser*) rush; (*renverser*) knock over. **~ade** *n.f.* rush; (*cohue*) crush.
bouse /buz/ *n.f.* (cow) dung.
bousiller /buzije/ *v.t.* (*fam.*) mess up.
boussole /busɔl/ *n.f.* compass.
bout /bu/ *n.m.* end; (*de langue, bâton*) tip; (*morceau*) bit. **à ~,** exhausted. **à ~ de souffle,** out of breath. **à ~ portant,** point-blank. **au ~ de,** (*après*) after. **~ filtre,** filter-tip. **venir à ~ de,** (*finir*) manage to finish.
boutade /butad/ *n.f.* jest; (*caprice*) whim.
boute-en-train /butɑ̃trɛ̃/ *n.m. invar.* joker, live wire.
bouteille /butɛj/ *n.f.* bottle.
boutique /butik/ *n.f.* shop; (*de mode*) boutique.
bouton /butɔ̃/ *n.m.* button; (*pustule*) pimple; (*pousse*) bud; (*de porte, radio, etc.*) knob. **~ de manchette,** cuff-link. **~-d'or** *n.m.* (*pl.* **~s-d'or**) buttercup. **~ner** /-ɔne/ *v.t.* button

(up). **~nière** /-ɔnjɛr/ *n.f.* buttonhole. **~-pression** (*pl.* **~s-pression**) *n.m.* press-stud; (*Amer.*) snap.

boutonneu|x, ~se /butɔnø, -z/ *a.* pimply.

bouture /butyr/ *n.f.* (*plante*) cutting.

bovin, ~e /bɔvɛ̃, -in/ *a.* bovine. **~s** *n.m. pl.* cattle.

bowling /boliŋ/ *n.m.* bowling; (*salle*) bowling-alley.

box (*pl.* ~ *ou* **boxes**) /bɔks/ *n.m.* lock-up garage; (*de dortoir*) cubicle; (*d'écurie*) (loose) box; (*jurid.*) dock.

box|e /bɔks/ *n.f.* boxing **~er** *v.t./i.* box. **~eur** *n.m.* boxer.

boyau (*pl.* **~x**) /bwajo/ *n.m.* gut; (*corde*) catgut; (*galerie*) gallery; (*de bicyclette*) tyre; (*Amer.*) tire.

boycott|er /bɔjkɔte/ *v.t.* boycott. **~age** *n.m.* boycott.

BP *abrév.* (*boîte postale*) PO Box.

bracelet /braslɛ/ *n.m.* bracelet; (*de montre*) strap.

braconn|er /brakɔne/ *v.i.* poach. **~ier** *n.m.* poacher.

brad|er /brade/ *v.t.* sell off. **~erie** *n.f.* open-air sale.

braguette /bragɛt/ *n.f.* fly.

braille /braj/ *n.m.* & *a.* Braille.

brailler /brɑje/ *v.t./i.* bawl.

braire /brɛr/ *v.i.* bray.

braise /brɛz/ *n.f.* embers.

braiser /breze/ *v.t.* braise.

brancard /brɑ̃kar/ *n.m.* stretcher; (*bras*) shaft. **~ier** /-dje/ *n.m.* stretcher-bearer.

branch|e /brɑ̃ʃ/ *n.f.* branch. **~ages** *n.m. pl.* (cut) branches.

branché /brɑ̃ʃe/ *a.* (*fam.*) trendy.

branch|er /brɑ̃ʃe/ *v.t.* connect; (*électr.*) plug in. **~ement** *n.m.* connection.

branchies /brɑ̃ʃi/ *n.f. pl.* gills.

brandir /brɑ̃dir/ *v.t.* brandish.

branle /brɑ̃l/ *n.m.* **mettre en ~,** set in motion. **se mettre en ~,** get started. **~-bas (de combat)** *n.m. invar.* bustle.

branler /brɑ̃le/ *v.i.* be shaky. ● *v.t.* shake.

braquer /brake/ *v.t.* aim; (*regard*) fix; (*roue*) turn; (*banque*: *fam.*) hold up. **~ qn. contre,** turn s.o. against. ● *v.i.* (*auto.*) turn (the wheel). ● *v. pr.* **se ~,** dig one's heels in.

bras /bra/ *n.m.* arm. ● *n.m. pl.* (*fig.*) labour, hands. **à ~-le-corps** *adv.* round the waist. **~ dessus bras dessous,** arm in arm. **~ droit,** (*fig.*) right-hand man. **en ~ de chemise,** in one's shirtsleeves.

brasier /brɑzje/ *n.m.* blaze.

brassard /brasar/ *n.m.* arm-band.

brasse /bras/ *n.f.* (breast-)stroke; (*mesure*) fathom.

brassée /brase/ *n.f.* armful.

brass|er /brase/ *v.t.* mix; (*bière*) brew; (*affaires*) handle a lot of. **~age** *n.m.* mixing; brewing. **~erie** *n.f.* brewery; (*café*) brasserie. **~eur** *n.m.* brewer. **~eur d'affaires,** big businessman.

brassière /brasjɛr/ *n.f.* (baby's) vest.

bravache /bravaʃ/ *n.m.* braggart.

bravade /bravad/ *n.f.* **par ~,** out of bravado.

brave /brav/ *a.* brave; (*bon*) good. **~ment** *adv.* bravely.

braver /brave/ *v.t.* defy.

bravo /bravo/ *int.* bravo. ● *n.m.* cheer.

bravoure /bravur/ *n.f.* bravery.

break /brɛk/ *n.m.* estate car; (*Amer.*) station-wagon.

brebis /brəbi/ *n.f.* ewe. **~ galeuse,** black sheep.

brèche /brɛʃ/ *n.f.* gap, breach. **être sur la ~,** be on the go.

bredouille /brəduj/ *a.* empty-handed.

bredouiller /brəduje/ *v.t./i.* mumble.

bref, brève /brɛf, -v/ *a.* short, brief. ● *adv.* in short. **en ~,** in short.

Brésil /brezil/ *n.m.* Brazil.

brésilien, ~ne /breziljɛ̃, -jɛn/ *a.* & *n.m., f.* Brazilian.

Bretagne /brətaɲ/ *n.f.* Brittany.

bretelle /brətɛl/ *n.f.* (shoulder-)strap; (*d'autoroute*) access road. **~s,** (*pour pantalon*) braces; (*Amer.*) suspenders.

breton, ~ne /brətɔ̃, -ɔn/ *a.* & *n.m., f.* Breton.

breuvage /brœvaʒ/ *n.m.* beverage.

brève /brɛv/ *voir* bref.

brevet /brəvɛ/ *n.m.* diploma. **~ (d'invention),** patent.

brevet|er /brəvte/ *v.t.* patent. **~é** *a.* patented.

bribes /brib/ *n.f. pl.* scraps.

bric-à-brac /brikabrak/ *n.m. invar.* bric-à-brac.

bricole /brikɔl/ *n.f.* trifle.

bricol|er /brikɔle/ *v.i.* do odd (do-it-yourself) jobs. ● *v.t.* fix (up). **~age** *n.m.* do-it-yourself (jobs). **~eur, ~euse** *n.m., f.* handyman, handy woman.

brid|e /brid/ *n.f.* bridle. **tenir en ~e,** keep in check. **~er** *v.t.* (*cheval*) bridle; (*fig.*) keep in check, bridle; (*culin.*) truss.

bridé /bride/ *a.* **yeux ~s,** slit eyes.

bridge /bridʒ/ *n.m.* (*cartes*) bridge.

briève|ment /brijɛvmɑ̃/ *adv.* briefly. **~té** *n.f.* brevity.

brigad|e /brigad/ *n.f.* (*de police*) squad; (*mil.*) brigade; (*fig.*) team. **~ier** *n.m.* (*de police*) sergeant.

brigand /brigɑ̃/ *n.m.* robber. **~age** /-daʒ/ *n.m.* robbery.

briguer /brige/ *v.t.* seek (after).

brill|ant, ~ante /brijɑ̃, -t/ *a.* (*couleur*) bright; (*luisant*) shiny; (*remarquable*) brilliant. ● *n.m.* (*éclat*) shine; (*diamant*) diamond. **~amment** *adv.* brilliantly.

briller /brije/ *v.i.* shine.

brim|er /brime/ *v.t.* bully, harass. **se sentir brimé,** feel put down. **~ade** *n.f.* vexation.

brin /brɛ̃/ *n.m.* (*de corde*) strand; (*de muguet*) sprig. **~ d'herbe,** blade of grass. **un ~ de,** a bit of.

brindille /brɛ̃dij/ *n.f.* twig.

bringuebaler /brɛ̃gbale/ *v.i.* (*fam.*) wobble about.

brio /brijo/ *n.m.* brilliance. **avec ~,** brilliantly.

brioche /brijɔʃ/ *n.f.* brioche (*small round sweet cake*); (*ventre*: *fam.*) paunch.

brique /brik/ *n.f.* brick.

briquer /brike/ *v.t.* polish.

briquet /brikɛ/ *n.m.* (cigarette-) lighter.

brisant /brizɑ̃/ *n.m.* reef.

brise /briz/ *n.f.* breeze.

bris|er /brize/ *v.t.* break. **se ~er** *v. pr.* break. **~e-lames** *n.m. invar.* breakwater. **~eur de grève** *n.m.* strikebreaker.

britannique /britanik/ *a.* British. ● *n.m./f.* Briton. **les B~s,** the British.

broc /bro/ *n.m.* pitcher.

brocant|e /brɔkɑ̃t/ *n.f.* second-hand goods. **~eur, ~euse** *n.m., f.* second-hand goods dealer.

broche /brɔʃ/ *n.f.* brooch; (*culin.*) spit. **à la ~,** spit-roasted.

broché /brɔʃe/ *a.* paperback(ed).

brochet /brɔʃɛ/ *n.m.* (*poisson*) pike.

brochette /brɔʃɛt/ *n.f.* skewer.

brochure /brɔʃyr/ *n.f.* brochure, booklet.

brod|er /brɔde/ *v.t.* embroider. ● *v.i.* (*fig.*) embroider the truth. **~erie** *n.f.* embroidery.

broncher /brɔ̃ʃe/ *v.i.* **sans ~,** without turning a hair.

bronch|es /brɔ̃ʃ/ *n.f. pl.* bronchial tubes. **~ite** *n.f.* bronchitis.

bronze /brɔ̃z/ *n.m.* bronze.

bronz|er /brɔ̃ze/ *v.i.*, **se ~er** *v. pr.* get a (sun-)tan. **~age** *n.m.* (sun-)tan. **~é** *a.* (sun-)tanned.

brosse /brɔs/ *n.f.* brush. **~ à dents,** toothbrush. **~ à habits,** clothes-brush. **en ~,** (*coiffure*) in a crew cut.

brosser /brɔse/ *v.t.* brush; (*fig.*) paint. **se ~ les dents/les cheveux,** brush one's teeth/hair.

brouette /bruɛt/ *n.f.* wheelbarrow.

brouhaha /bruaa/ *n.m.* hubbub.

brouillard /brujar/ *n.m.* fog.

brouille /bruj/ *n.f.* quarrel.

brouill|er /bruje/ *v.t.* mix up; (*vue*) blur; (*œufs*) scramble; (*radio*) jam; (*amis*) set at odds. **se ~er** *v. pr.* become confused; (*ciel*) cloud over; (*amis*) fall out. **~on**[1], **~onne** *a.* untidy.

brouillon[2] /brujɔ̃/ *n.m.* (rough) draft.

broussailles /brusɑj/ *n.f. pl.* undergrowth.

brousse /brus/ *n.f.* **la ~,** the bush.

brouter /brute/ *v.t./i.* graze.

broutille /brutij/ *n.f.* trifle.

broyer /brwaje/ *v.t.* crush; (*moudre*) grind.

bru /bry/ *n.f.* daughter-in-law.

bruin|e /brɥin/ *n.f.* drizzle. **~er** *v.i.* drizzle.

bruire /brɥir/ *v.i.* rustle.

bruissement /brɥismɑ̃/ *n.m.* rustling.

bruit /brɥi/ *n.m.* noise; (*fig.*) rumour.

bruitage /brɥitaʒ/ *n.m.* sound effects.

brûlant, ~e /brylɑ̃, -t/ *a.* burning (hot); (*sujet*) red-hot; (*ardent*) fiery.

brûlé /bryle/ *a.* (*démasqué*: *fam.*) blown. ● *n.m.* burning. **ça sent le ~,** I can smell sth. burning.

brûle-pourpoint (à) /(a)brylpurpwɛ̃/ *adv.* point-blank.

brûl|er /bryle/ *v.t./i.* burn; (*essence*) use (up); (*signal*) go through *ou* past (without stopping); (*dévorer*: *fig.*) consume. **se ~er** *v. pr.* burn o.s. **~eur** *n.m.* burner.

brûlure /brylyr/ *n.f.* burn. **~s d'estomac,** heartburn.

brum|e /brym/ *n.f.* mist. **~eux, ~euse** *a.* misty; (*idées*) hazy.
brun, ~e /brœ̃, bryn/ *a.* brown, dark. ● *n.m.* brown. ● *n.m., f.* dark-haired person. **~ir** /brynir/ *v.i.* turn brown; (*se bronzer*) get a tan.
brunch /brœnʃ/ *n.m.* brunch.
brushing /brœʃiŋ/ *n.m.* blow-dry.
brusque /brysk/ *a.* (*soudain*) sudden, abrupt; (*rude*) abrupt. **~ment** /-əmɑ̃/ *adv.* suddenly, abruptly.
brusquer /bryske/ *v.t.* rush.
brut /bryt/ *a.* (*diamant*) rough; (*soie*) raw; (*pétrole*) crude; (*comm.*) gross.
brut|al (*m. pl.* **~aux**) /brytal, -o/ *a.* brutal. **~aliser** *v.t.* treat roughly *ou* violently, manhandle. **~alité** *n.f.* brutality.
brute /bryt/ *n.f.* brute.
Bruxelles /brysɛl/ *n.m./f.* Brussels.
bruy|ant, ~ante /brɥijɑ̃, -t/ *a.* noisy. **~amment** *adv.* noisily.
bruyère /bryjɛr/ *n.f.* heather.
bu /by/ *voir* boire.
bûche /byʃ/ *n.f.* log. **~ de Noël,** Christmas log. **(se) ramasser une ~,** (*fam.*) come a cropper.
bûcher [1] /byʃe/ *n.m.* (*supplice*) stake.
bûch|er [2] /byʃe/ *v.t./i.* (*fam.*) slog away (at). **~eur, ~euse** *n.m., f.* (*fam.*) slogger.
bûcheron /byʃrɔ̃/ *n.m.* woodcutter.
budg|et /bydʒɛ/ *n.m.* budget. **~étaire** *a.* budgetary.
buée /bɥe/ *n.f.* mist, condensation.
buffet /byfɛ/ *n.m.* sideboard; (*réception, restaurant*) buffet.
buffle /byfl/ *n.m.* buffalo.
buis /bɥi/ *n.m.* (*arbre, bois*) box.
buisson /bɥisɔ̃/ *n.m.* bush.
buissonnière /bɥisɔnjɛr/ *a.f.* **faire l'école ~,** play truant.
bulbe /bylb/ *n.m.* bulb.
bulgare /bylgar/ *a.* & *n.m./f.* Bulgarian.
Bulgarie /bylgari/ *n.f.* Bulgaria.
bulldozer /byldozɛr/ *n.m.* bulldozer.
bulle /byl/ *n.f.* bubble.
bulletin /byltɛ̃/ *n.m.* bulletin, report; (*scol.*) report; (*billet*) ticket. **~ d'information,** news bulletin. **~ météorologique,** weather report. **~ (de vote),** ballot-paper. **~ de salaire,** pay-slip. **~-réponse** *n.m.* (*pl.* **~s-réponses**) reply slip.
buraliste /byralist/ *n.m./f.* tobacconist; (*à la poste*) clerk.
bureau (*pl.* **~x**) /byro/ *n.m.* office; (*meuble*) desk; (*comité*) board. **~ de location,** booking-office; (*théâtre*) box-office. **~ de poste,** post office. **~ de tabac,** tobacconist's (shop). **~ de vote,** polling station.
bureaucrate /byrokrat/ *n.m./f.* bureaucrat.
bureaucrat|ie /byrokrasi/ *n.f.* bureaucracy. **~ique** /-tik/ *a.* bureaucratic.
bureautique /byrotik/ *n.f.* office automation.
burette /byrɛt/ *n.f.* (*de graissage*) oilcan.
burin /byrɛ̃/ *n.m.* (cold) chisel.
burlesque /byrlɛsk/ *a.* ludicrous; (*théâtre*) burlesque.
bus /bys/ *n.m.* bus.
busqué /byske/ *a.* hooked.
buste /byst/ *n.m.* bust.
but /by(t)/ *n.m.* target; (*dessein*) aim, goal; (*football*) goal. **avoir pour ~ de,** aim to. **de ~ en blanc,** point-blank. **dans le ~ de,** with the intention of.
butane /bytan/ *n.m.* butane, Calor gas (P.).
buté /byte/ *a.* obstinate.
buter /byte/ *v.i.* **~ contre,** knock against; (*problème*) come up against. ● *v.t.* antagonize. **se ~** *v. pr.* (*s'entêter*) become obstinate.
buteur /bytœr/ *n.m.* striker.
butin /bytɛ̃/ *n.m.* booty, loot.
butiner /bytine/ *v.i.* gather nectar.
butoir /bytwar/ *n.m.* **~ (de porte),** doorstop.
butor /bytɔr/ *n.m.* (*péj.*) lout.
butte /byt/ *n.f.* mound. **en ~ à,** exposed to.
buvard /byvar/ *n.m.* blotting-paper.
buvette /byvɛt/ *n.f.* (refreshment) bar.
buveu|r, ~se /byvœr, -øz/ *n.m., f.* drinker.

C

c' /s/ *voir* ce[1].
ça /sa/ *pron.* it, that; (*pour désigner*) that; (*plus près*) this. **ça va?,** (*fam.*) how's it going? **ça va!,** (*fam.*) all right! **où ça?,** (*fam.*) where? **quand ça?,** (*fam.*) when? **c'est ça,** that's right.

çà /sa/ *adv.* **çà et là,** here and there.

caban|e /kaban/ *n.f.* hut; (*à outils*) shed. **~on** *n.m.* hut; (*en Provence*) cottage.

cabaret /kabarɛ/ *n.m.* night-club.

cabas /kabɑ/ *n.m.* shopping bag.

cabillaud /kabijo/ *n.m.* cod.

cabine /kabin/ *n.f.* (*à la piscine*) cubicle; (*à la plage*) (beach) hut; (*de bateau*) cabin; (*de pilotage*) cockpit; (*de camion*) cab; (*d'ascenseur*) cage. **~ (téléphonique),** phone-booth, phone-box.

cabinet /kabinɛ/ *n.m.* (*de médecin*) surgery; (*Amer.*) office; (*d'avocat*) office; (*clientèle*) practice; (*pol.*) Cabinet; (*pièce*) room. **~s,** (*toilettes*) toilet. **~ de toilette,** bathroom.

câble /kɑbl/ *n.m.* cable; (*corde*) rope.

câbler /kɑble/ *v.t.* cable.

cabosser /kabɔse/ *v.t.* dent.

cabot|age /kabɔtaʒ/ *n.m.* coastal navigation. **~eur** *n.m.* coaster.

cabotin, ~e /kabɔtɛ̃, -in/ *n.m., f.* (*théâtre*) ham; (*fig.*) play-actor. **~age** /-inaʒ/ *n.m.* ham acting; (*fig.*) play-acting.

cabrer /kabre/ *v.t.*, **se ~** *v. pr.* (*cheval*) rear up. **se ~ contre,** rebel against.

cabri /kabri/ *n.m.* kid.

cabriole /kabrijɔl/ *n.f.* (*culbute*) somersault. **faire des ~s,** caper about.

cacahuète /kakaɥɛt/ *n.f.* peanut.

cacao /kakao/ *n.m.* cocoa.

cachalot /kaʃalo/ *n.m.* sperm whale.

cache /kaʃ/ *n.m.* mask; (*photo.*) lens cover.

cachemire /kaʃmir/ *n.m.* cashmere.

cach|er /kaʃe/ *v.t.* hide, conceal (**à,** from). **se ~er** *v. pr.* hide; (*se trouver caché*) be hidden. **~e-cache** *n.m. invar.* hide-and-seek. **~e-nez** *n.m. invar.* scarf. **~e-pot** *n.m.* cache-pot.

cachet /kaʃɛ/ *n.m.* seal; (*de la poste*) postmark; (*comprime*) tablet; (*d'artiste*) fee; (*fig.*) style.

cacheter /kaʃte/ *v.t.* seal.

cachette /kaʃɛt/ *n.f.* hiding-place. **en ~,** in secret.

cachot /kaʃo/ *n.m.* dungeon.

cachott|eries /kaʃɔtri/ *n.f. pl.* secrecy. **faire des ~eries,** be secretive. **~ier, ~ière** *a.* secretive.

acophonie /kakɔphɔni/ *n.f.* cacoph-ny.

us /kaktys/ *n.m.* cactus.

cadavérique /kadɑverik/ *a.* (*teint*) deathly pale.

cadavre /kadɑvr/ *n.m.* corpse.

caddie /kadi/ *n.m.* trolley.

cadeau (*pl.* **~x**) /kado/ *n.m.* present, gift. **faire un ~ à qn.,** give s.o. a present.

cadenas /kadnɑ/ *n.m.* padlock. **~ser** /-ase/ *v.t.* padlock.

cadenc|e /kadɑ̃s/ *n.f.* rhythm, cadence; (*de travail*) rate. **en ~e,** in time. **~é** *a.* rhythmic(al).

cadet, ~te /kadɛ, -t/ *a.* youngest; (*entre deux*) younger. ● *n.m., f.* youngest (child); younger (child).

cadran /kadrɑ̃/ *n.m.* dial. **~ solaire,** sundial.

cadre /kɑdr/ *n.m.* frame; (*milieu*) surroundings; (*limites*) scope; (*contexte*) framework. ● *n.m./f.* (*personne*: *comm.*) executive. **les ~s,** (*comm.*) the managerial staff.

cadrer /kɑdre/ *v.i.* **~ avec,** tally with. ● *v.t.* (*photo*) centre.

cadu|c, ~que /kadyk/ *a.* obsolete.

cafard /kafar/ *n.m.* (*insecte*) cockroach. **avoir le ~,** (*fam.*) be feeling low. **~er** /-de/ *v.i.* (*fam.*) tell tales.

caf|é /kafe/ *n.m.* coffee; (*bar*) café. **~é au lait,** white coffee. **~etière** *n.f.* coffee-pot.

caféine /kafein/ *n.f.* caffeine.

cafouiller /kafuje/ *v.i.* (*fam.*) bumble, flounder.

cage /kaʒ/ *n.f.* cage; (*d'escalier*) well; (*d'ascenseur*) shaft.

cageot /kaʒo/ *n.m.* crate.

cagibi /kaʒibi/ *n.m.* storage room.

cagneu|x, ~se /kaɲø, -z/ *a.* knock-kneed.

cagnotte /kaɲɔt/ *n.f.* kitty.

cagoule /kagul/ *n.f.* hood.

cahier /kaje/ *n.m.* notebook; (*scol.*) exercise-book.

cahin-caha /kaɛ̃kaa/ *adv.* **aller ~,** (*fam.*) jog along.

cahot /kao/ *n.m.* bump, jolt. **~er** /kaɔte/ *v.t./i.* bump, jolt. **~eux, ~euse** /kaɔtø, -z/ *a.* bumpy.

caïd /kaid/ *n.m.* (*fam.*) big shot.

caille /kɑj/ *n.f.* quail.

cailler /kɑje/ *v.t./i.*, **se ~** *v. pr.* (*sang*) clot; (*lait*) curdle.

caillot /kajo/ *n.m.* (blood) clot.

caillou (*pl.* **~x**) /kaju/ *n.m.* stone; (*galet*) pebble. **~teux, ~teuse** *a.* stony. **~tis** *n.m.* gravel.

caisse /kɛs/ *n.f.* crate, case; (*tiroir, machine*) till; (*guichet*) pay-desk; (*bureau*) office; (*mus.*) drum. **~ enregistreuse,** cash register. **~ d'épargne,** savings bank. **~ de retraite,** pension fund.

caiss|ier, ~ière /kesje, -jɛr/ *n.m., f.* cashier.

cajol|er /kaʒɔle/ *v.t.* coax. **~eries** *n.f. pl.* coaxing.

cake /kɛk/ *n.m.* fruit-cake.

calamité /kalamite/ *n.f.* calamity.

calandre /kalɑ̃dr/ *n.f.* radiator grill.

calanque /kalɑ̃k/ *n.f.* creek.

calcaire /kalkɛr/ *a.* (*sol*) chalky; (*eau*) hard.

calciné /kalsine/ *a.* charred.

calcium /kalsjɔm/ *n.m.* calcium.

calcul /kalkyl/ *n.m.* calculation; (*scol.*) arithmetic; (*différentiel*) calculus. **~ biliaire,** gallstone.

calcul|er /kalkyle/ *v.t.* calculate. **~ateur** *n.m.* (*ordinateur*) computer, calculator. **~atrice** *n.f.* (*ordinateur*) calculator. **~ette** *n.f.* (pocket) calculator.

cale /kal/ *n.f.* wedge; (*de navire*) hold. **~ sèche,** dry dock.

calé /kale/ *a.* (*fam.*) clever.

caleçon /kalsɔ̃/ *n.m.* underpants; (*de femme*) leggings. **~ de bain,** (bathing) trunks.

calembour /kalɑ̃bur/ *n.m.* pun.

calendrier /kalɑ̃drije/ *n.m.* calendar; (*fig.*) timetable.

calepin /kalpɛ̃/ *n.m.* notebook.

caler /kale/ *v.t.* wedge; (*moteur*) stall. ● *v.i.* stall.

calfeutrer /kalføtre/ *v.t.* stop up the cracks of.

calibr|e /kalibr/ *n.m.* calibre; (*d'un œuf, fruit*) grade. **~er** *v.t.* grade.

calice /kalis/ *n.m.* (*relig.*) chalice; (*bot.*) calyx.

califourchon (à) /(a)kalifurʃɔ̃/ *adv.* astride. ● *prép.* **à ~ sur,** astride.

câlin, ~e /kɑlɛ̃, -in/ *a.* endearing, cuddly. **~er** /-ine/ *v.t.* cuddle.

calmant /kalmɑ̃/ *n.m.* sedative.

calm|e /kalm/ *a.* calm ● *n.m.* calm(ness). **du ~e!,** calm down! **~er** *v.t.*, **se ~er** *v. pr.* (*personne*) calm (down); (*diminuer*) ease.

calomn|ie /kalɔmni/ *n.f.* slander; (*écrite*) libel. **~ier** *v.t.* slander; libel. **~ieux, ~ieuse** *a.* slanderous; libellous.

calorie /kalɔri/ *n.f.* calorie.

calorifuge /kalɔrifyʒ/ *a.* (heat-) insulating. ● *n.m.* lagging.

calot /kalo/ *n.m.* (*mil.*) forage-cap.

calotte /kalɔt/ *n.f.* (*relig.*) skullcap; (*tape*: *fam.*) slap.

calqu|e /kalk/ *n.m.* tracing; (*fig.*) exact copy. **~er** *v.t.* trace; (*fig.*) copy. **~er sur,** model on.

calvaire /kalvɛr/ *n.m.* (*croix*) calvary; (*fig.*) suffering.

calvitie /kalvisi/ *n.f.* baldness.

camarade /kamarad/ *n.m./f.* friend; (*pol.*) comrade. **~ de jeu,** playmate. **~rie** *n.f.* good companionship.

cambiste /kɑ̃bist/ *n.m./f.* foreign exchange dealer.

cambouis /kɑ̃bwi/ *n.m.* (engine) oil.

cambrer /kɑ̃bre/ *v.t.* arch. **se ~** *v. pr.* arch one's back.

cambriol|er /kɑ̃brijɔle/ *v.t.* burgle. **~age** *n.m.* burglary. **~eur, ~euse** *n.m., f.* burglar.

cambrure /kɑ̃bryr/ *n.f.* curve.

came /kam/ *n.f.* **arbe à ~s,** camshaft.

camée /kame/ *n.m.* cameo.

camelot /kamlo/ *n.m.* street vendor.

camelote /kamlɔt/ *n.f.* junk.

camembert /kamɑ̃bɛr/ *n.m.* Camembert (cheese).

caméra /kamera/ *n.f.* (*cinéma, télévision*) camera.

caméra|man (*pl.* **~men**) /kameraman, -mɛn/ *n.m.* cameraman.

camion /kamjɔ̃/ *n.m.* lorry, truck. **~-citerne** *n.m.* tanker. **~nage** /-jɔnaʒ/ *n.m.* haulage. **~nette** /-jɔnɛt/ *n.f.* van. **~neur** /-jɔnœr/ *n.m.* lorry *ou* truck driver; (*entrepreneur*) haulage contractor.

camisole /kamizɔl/ *n.f.* **~ (de force),** strait-jacket.

camoufl|er /kamufle/ *v.t.* camouflage. **~age** *n.m.* camouflage.

camp /kɑ̃/ *n.m.* camp; (*sport*) side.

campagn|e /kɑ̃paɲ/ *n.f.* country (side); (*mil., pol.*) campaign. **~ard, ~arde** *a.* country; *n.m., f.* countryman, countrywoman.

campanile /kɑ̃panil/ *n.m.* belltower.

camp|er /kɑ̃pe/ *v.i.* camp. ● *v.t.* plant boldly; (*esquisser*) sketch. **se ~er** *v. pr.* plant o.s. **~ement** *n.m.* encampment. **~eur, ~euse** *n.m., f.* camper.

camphre /kɑ̃fr/ *n.m.* camphor.

camping /kɑ̃piŋ/ *n.m.* camping. **faire du ~,** go camping. **~-car** *n.m.* camper-van; (*Amer.*) motorhome.

~-gaz *n.m. invar.* (P.) camping-gaz. **(terrain de) ~,** campsite.
campus /kɑ̃pys/ *n.m.* campus.
Canada /kanada/ *n.m.* Canada.
canadien, ~ne /kanadjɛ̃, -jɛn/ *a.* & *n.m., f.* Canadian. ● *n.f.* fur-lined jacket.
canaille /kanɑj/ *n.f.* rogue.
can|al (*pl.* **~aux**) /kanal, -o/ *n.m.* (*artificiel*) canal; (*bras de mer*) channel; (*techn., TV*) channel. **par le ~al de,** through.
canalisation /kanalizɑsjɔ̃/ *n.f.* (*tuyaux*) main(s).
canaliser /kanalize/ *v.t.* (*eau*) canalize; (*fig.*) channel.
canapé /kanape/ *n.m.* sofa.
canard /kanar/ *n.m.* duck; (*journal: fam.*) rag.
canari /kanari/ *n.m.* canary.
cancans /kɑ̃kɑ̃/ *n.m. pl.* malicious gossip.
canc|er /kɑ̃sɛr/ *n.m.* cancer. **le C~er,** Cancer. **~éreux, ~éreuse** *a.* cancerous. **~érigène** *a.* carcinogenic.
cancre /kɑ̃kr/ *n.m.* dunce.
cancrelat /kɑ̃krəla/ *n.m.* cockroach.
candélabre /kɑ̃delabr/ *n.m.* candelabrum.
candeur /kɑ̃dœr/ *n.f.* naïvety.
candidat, ~e /kɑ̃dida, -t/ *n.m., f.* candidate; (*à un poste*) applicant, candidate (**à,** for). **~ure** /-tyr/ *n.f.* application; (*pol.*) candidacy. **poser sa ~ure pour,** apply for.
candide /kɑ̃did/ *a.* naïve.
cane /kan/ *n.f.* (female) duck. **~ton** *n.m.* duckling.
canette /kanɛt/ *n.f.* (*de bière*) bottle.
canevas /kanva/ *n.m.* canvas; (*plan*) framework, outline.
caniche /kaniʃ/ *n.m.* poodle.
canicule /kanikyl/ *n.f.* hot summer days.
canif /kanif/ *n.m.* penknife.
canin, ~e /kanɛ̃, -in/ *a.* canine. ● *n.f.* canine (tooth).
caniveau (*pl.* **~x**) /kanivo/ *n.m.* gutter.
cannabis /kanabis/ *n.m.* cannabis.
canne /kan/ *n.f.* (walking-)stick. **~ à pêche,** fishing-rod. **~ à sucre,** sugar-cane.
cannelle /kanɛl/ *n.f.* cinnamon.
cannibale /kanibal/ *a.* & *n.m./f.* cannibal.
canoë /kanɔe/ *n.m.* canoe; (*sport*) canoeing.
canon /kanɔ̃/ *n.m.* (big) gun; (*d'une arme*) barrel; (*principe, règle*) canon. **~nade** /-ɔnad/ *n.f.* gunfire. **~nier** /-ɔnje/ *n.m.* gunner.
canot /kano/ *n.m.* boat. **~ de sauvetage,** lifeboat. **~ pneumatique,** rubber dinghy.
canot|er /kanɔte/ *v.i.* boat. **~age** *n.m.* boating. **~ier** *n.m.* boater.
cantate /kɑ̃tat/ *n.f.* cantata.
cantatrice /kɑ̃tatris/ *n.f.* opera singer.
cantine /kɑ̃tin/ *n.f.* canteen.
cantique /kɑ̃tik/ *n.m.* hymn.
canton /kɑ̃tɔ̃/ *n.m.* (*en France*) district; (*en Suisse*) canton.
cantonade (à la) /(ala)kɑ̃tɔnad/ *adv.* for all to hear.
cantonner /kɑ̃tɔne/ *v.t.* (*mil.*) billet. **se ~ dans,** confine o.s. to.
cantonnier /kɑ̃tɔnje/ *n.m.* roadman, road mender.
canular /kanylar/ *n.m.* hoax.
caoutchou|c /kautʃu/ *n.m.* rubber; (*élastique*) rubber band. **~c mousse,** foam rubber. **~té** *a.* rubberized. **~teux, ~teuse** *a.* rubbery.
cap /kap/ *n.m.* cape, headland; (*direction*) course. **doubler** *ou* **franchir le ~ de,** go beyond (the point of). **mettre le ~ sur,** steer a course for.
capable /kapabl/ *a.* able, capable. **~ de qch.,** capable of sth. **~ de faire,** able to do, capable of doing.
capacité /kapasite/ *n.f.* ability; (*contenance*) capacity.
cape /kap/ *n.f.* cape. **rire sous ~,** laugh up one's sleeve.
capillaire /kapilɛr/ *a.* (*lotion, soins*) hair. **(vaisseau) ~,** capillary.
capilotade (en) /(ɑ̃)kapilɔtad/ *adv.* (*fam.*) reduced to a pulp.
capitaine /kapitɛn/ *n.m.* captain.
capit|al, ~ale (*m. pl.* **~aux**) /kapital, -o/ *a.* major, fundamental; (*peine, lettre*) capital. ● *n.m.* (*pl.* **~aux**) (*comm.*) capital; (*fig.*) stock. **~aux,** (*comm.*) capital. ● *n.f.* (*ville, lettre*) capital.
capitalis|te /kapitalist/ *a.* & *n.m./f.* capitalist. **~me** *n.m.* capitalism.
capiteu|x, ~se /kapitø, -z/ *a.* heady.
capitonné /kapitɔne/ *a.* padded.
capitul|er /kapityle/ *v.i.* capitulate. **~ation** *n.f.* capitulation.
capor|al (*pl.* **~aux**) /kapɔral, -o/ *n.m.* corporal.

capot /kapo/ *n.m.* (*auto.*) bonnet; (*auto., Amer.*) hood.
capote /kapɔt/ *n.f.* (*auto.*) hood; (*auto., Amer.*) (convertible) top; (*fam.*) condom.
capoter /kapɔte/ *v.i.* overturn.
câpre /kɑpr/ *n.f.* (*culin.*) caper.
capric|e /kapris/ *n.m.* whim, caprice. **~ieux, ~ieuse** *a.* capricious; (*appareil*) temperamental.
Capricorne /kaprikɔrn/ *n.m.* **le ~,** Capricorn.
capsule /kapsyl/ *n.f.* capsule; (*de bouteille*) cap.
capter /kapte/ *v.t.* (*eau*) tap; (*émission*) pick up; (*fig.*) win, capture.
capti|f, ~ve /kaptif, -v/ *a.* & *n.m., f.* captive.
captiver /kaptive/ *v.t.* captivate.
captivité /kaptivite/ *n.f.* captivity.
captur|e /kaptyr/ *n.f.* capture. **~er** *v.t.* capture.
capuch|e /kapyʃ/ *n.f.* hood. **~on** *n.m.* hood; (*de stylo*) cap.
caquet /kakɛ/ *n.m.* **rabattre le ~ à qn.,** take s.o. down a peg or two.
caquet|er /kakte/ *v.i.* cackle. **~age** *n.m.* cackle.
car[1] /kar/ *conj.* because, for.
car[2] /kar/ *n.m.* coach; (*Amer.*) bus.
carabine /karabin/ *n.f.* rifle.
caracoler /karakɔle/ *v.i.* prance.
caract|ère /karaktɛr/ *n.m.* (*nature, lettre*) character. **~ères d'imprimerie,** block letters. **~ériel, ~érielle** *a.* character; *n.m., f.* disturbed child.
caractérisé /karakterize/ *a.* well-defined.
caractériser /karakterize/ *v.t.* characterize. **se ~ par,** be characterized by.
caractéristique /karakteristik/ *a.* & *n.f.* characteristic.
carafe /karaf/ *n.f.* carafe; (*pour le vin*) decanter.
caraïbe /karaib/ *a.* Caribbean. **les C~s,** the Caribbean.
carambol|er (se) /(sə)karɑ̃bɔle/ *v. pr.* (*voitures*) smash into each other. **~age** *n.m.* multiple smash-up.
caramel /karamɛl/ *n.m.* caramel. **~iser** *v.t./i.* caramelize.
carapace /karapas/ *n.f.* shell.
carat /kara/ *n.m.* carat.
caravane /karavan/ *n.f.* (*auto.*) caravan; (*auto., Amer.*) trailer; (*convoi*) caravan.
carbone /karbɔn/ *n.m.* carbon; (*double*) carbon (copy). **(papier) ~,** carbon (paper).
carboniser /karbɔnize/ *v.t.* burn (to ashes).
carburant /karbyrɑ̃/ *n.m.* (motor) fuel.
carburateur /karbyratœr/ *n.m.* carburettor; (*Amer.*) carburetor.
carcan /karkɑ̃/ *n.m.* (*contrainte*) yoke.
carcasse /karkas/ *n.f.* carcass; (*d'immeuble, de voiture*) frame.
cardiaque /kardjak/ *a.* heart. • *n.m./f.* heart patient.
cardigan /kardigɑ̃/ *n.m.* cardigan.
cardin|al (*m. pl.* **~aux**) /kardinal, -o/ *a.* cardinal. • *n.m.* (*pl.* **~aux**) cardinal.
Carême /karɛm/ *n.m.* Lent.
carence /karɑ̃s/ *n.f.* inadequacy; (*manque*) deficiency.
caressant, ~e /karɛsɑ̃, -t/ *a.* endearing.
caress|e /karɛs/ *n.f.* caress. **~er** /-ese/ *v.t.* caress, stroke; (*espoir*) cherish.
cargaison /kargɛzɔ̃/ *n.f.* cargo.
cargo /kargo/ *n.m.* cargo boat.
caricatur|e /karikatyr/ *n.f.* caricature. **~al** (*m. pl.* **~aux**) *a.* caricature-like.
car|ie /kari/ *n.f.* cavity. **la ~ie (dentaire),** tooth decay. **~ié** *a.* (*dent*) decayed.
carillon /karijɔ̃/ *n.m.* chimes; (*horloge*) chiming clock. **~ner** /-jɔne/ *v.i.* chime, peal.
caritati|f, ~ve /karitatif, -v/ *a.* **association ~ve,** charity.
carlingue /karlɛ̃g/ *n.f.* (*d'avion*) cabin.
carnage /karnaʒ/ *n.m.* carnage.
carnass|ier, ~ière /karnasje, -jɛr/ *a.* flesh-eating.
carnaval (*pl.* **~s**) /karnaval/ *n.m.* carnival.
carnet /karnɛ/ *n.m.* notebook; (*de tickets etc.*) book. **~ de chèques,** cheque-book. **~ de notes,** school report.
carotte /karɔt/ *n.f.* carrot.
carotter /karɔte/ *v.t.* (*argot*) swindle. **~ qch. à qn.,** (*argot*) wangle sth. from s.o.
carpe /karp/ *n.f.* carp.
carpette /karpɛt/ *n.f.* rug.

carré /kare/ *a.* (*forme, mesure*) square; (*fig.*) straightforward. ● *n.m.* square; (*de terrain*) patch.

carreau (*pl.* **~x**) /karo/ *n.m.* (window) pane; (*par terre, au mur*) tile; (*dessin*) check; (*cartes*) diamonds. **à ~x,** check(ed).

carrefour /karfur/ *n.m.* crossroads.

carrel|er /karle/ *v.t.* tile. **~age** *n.m.* tiling; (*sol*) tiles.

carrelet /karlɛ/ *n.m.* (*poisson*) plaice.

carrément /karemɑ̃/ *adv.* straight; (*dire*) straight out.

carrer (se) /(sə)kare/ *v. pr.* settle firmly (**dans,** in).

carrière /karjɛr/ *n.f.* career; (*terrain*) quarry.

carrossable /karɔsabl/ *a.* suitable for vehicles.

carrosse /karɔs/ *n.m.* (horse-drawn) coach.

carross|erie /karɔsri/ *n.f.* (*auto.*) body(work). **~ier** *n.m.* (*auto.*) body-builder.

carrure /karyr/ *n.f.* build; (*fig.*) calibre.

cartable /kartabl/ *n.m.* satchel.

carte /kart/ *n.f.* card; (*géog.*) map; (*naut.*) chart; (*au restaurant*) menu. **~s,** (*jeu*) cards. **à la ~,** (*manger*) à la carte. **~ blanche,** a free hand. **~ de crédit,** credit card. **~ des vins,** wine list. **~ de visite,** (business) card. **~ grise,** (car) registration card. **~ postale,** postcard.

cartel /kartɛl/ *n.m.* cartel.

cartilage /kartilaʒ/ *n.m.* cartilage.

carton /kartɔ̃/ *n.m.* cardboard; (*boîte*) (cardboard) box. **~ à dessin,** portfolio. **faire un ~,** (*fam.*) take a pot-shot. **~nage** /-ɔnaʒ/ *n.m.* cardboard packing. **~-pâte** *n.m.* pasteboard. **en ~-pâte**, cardboard.

cartonné /kartɔne/ *a.* (*livre*) hardback.

cartouch|e /kartuʃ/ *n.f.* cartridge; (*de cigarettes*) carton. **~ière** *n.f.* cartridge-belt.

cas /kɑ/ *n.m.* case. **au ~ où,** in case. **~ urgent,** emergency. **en aucun ~,** on no account. **en ~ de,** in the event of, in case of. **en tout ~,** in any case. **faire ~ de,** set great store by. **~ de conscience** matter of conscience.

casan|ier, ~ière /kazanje, -jɛr/ *a.* home-loving.

casaque /kazak/ *n.f.* (*de jockey*) shirt.

ascade /kaskad/ *n.f.* waterfall; (*fig.*) ate.

cascad|eur, ~euse /kaskadœr, -øz/ *n.m., f.* stuntman, stuntgirl.

case /kɑz/ *n.f.* hut; (*compartiment*) pigeon-hole; (*sur papier*) square.

caser /kaze/ *v.t.* (*mettre*) put; (*loger*) put up; (*dans un travail*) find a job for; (*marier*: *péj.*) marry off.

caserne /kazɛrn/ *n.f.* barracks.

cash /kaʃ/ *adv.* **payer ~,** pay (in) cash.

casier /kɑzje/ *n.m.* pigeon-hole, compartment; (*meuble*) cabinet; (*à bouteilles*) rack. **~ judiciaire,** criminal record.

casino /kazino/ *n.m.* casino.

casqu|e /kask/ *n.m.* helmet; (*chez le coiffeur*) (hair-)drier. **~e (à écouteurs),** headphones. **~é** *a.* wearing a helmet.

casquette /kaskɛt/ *n.f.* cap.

cassant, ~e /kɑsɑ̃, -t/ *a.* brittle; (*brusque*) curt.

cassation /kasasjɔ̃/ *n.f.* **cour de ~,** appeal court.

casse /kɑs/ *n.f.* (*objets*) breakages. **mettre à la ~,** scrap.

cass|er /kɑse/ *v.t./i.* break; (*annuler*) annul. **se ~er** *v. pr.* break. **~er la tête à,** (*fam.*) give a headache to. **~e-cou** *n.m. invar.* daredevil. **~e-croûte** *n.m. invar.* snack. **~e-noisettes** *ou* **~e-noix** *n.m. invar.* nutcrackers. **~e-pieds** *n.m./f. invar.* (*fam.*) pain (in the neck). **~e-tête** *n.m. invar.* (*problème*) headache; (*jeu*) brain teaser.

casserole /kasrɔl/ *n.f.* saucepan.

cassette /kasɛt/ *n.f.* casket; (*de magnétophone*) cassette; (*de video*) video tape.

cassis[1] /kasis(s)/ *n.m.* black currant.

cassis[2] /kasi(s)/ *n.m.* (*auto.*) dip.

cassoulet /kasulɛ/ *n.m.* stew (of beans and meat).

cassure /kɑsyr/ *n.f.* break.

caste /kast/ *n.f.* caste.

castor /kastɔr/ *n.m.* beaver.

castr|er /kastre/ *v.t.* castrate. **~ation** *n.f.* castration.

cataclysme /kataklism/ *n.m.* cataclysm.

catalogu|e /katalɔg/ *n.m.* catalogue. **~er** *v.t.* catalogue; (*personne*: *péj.*) label.

catalyseur /katalizœr/ *n.m.* catalyst.

cataphote /katafɔt/ *n.m.* reflector.

cataplasme /kataplasm/ *n.m.* poultice.

catapult|e /katapylt/ *n.f.* catapult. **~er** *v.t.* catapult.
cataracte /katarakt/ *n.f.* cataract.
catastroph|e /katastrɔf/ *n.f.* disaster, catastrophe. **~ique** *a.* catastrophic.
catch /katʃ/ *n.m.* (all-in) wrestling. **~eur, ~euse** *n.m., f.* (all-in) wrestler.
catéchisme /kateʃism/ *n.m.* catechism.
catégorie /kategɔri/ *n.f.* category.
catégorique /kategɔrik/ *a.* categorical.
cathédrale /katedral/ *n.f.* cathedral.
catholi|que /katɔlik/ *a.* Catholic. **~cisme** *n.m.* Catholicism. **pas très ~que,** a bit fishy.
catimini (en) /(ɑ̃)katimini/ *adv.* on the sly.
cauchemar /kɔʃmar/ *n.m.* nightmare.
cause /koz/ *n.f.* cause; (*jurid.*) case. **à ~ de,** because of. **en ~,** (*en jeu, concerné*) involved. **pour ~ de,** on account of.
caus|er /koze/ *v.t.* cause. ● *v.i.* chat. **~erie** *n.f.* talk. **~ette** *n.f.* **faire la ~ette,** have a chat.
caustique /kostik/ *a.* caustic.
caution /kosjɔ̃/ *n.f.* surety; (*jurid.*) bail; (*appui*) backing; (*garantie*) deposit. **sous ~,** on bail.
cautionn|er /kosjɔne/ *v.t.* guarantee; (*soutenir*) back.
cavalcade /kavalkad/ *n.f.* (*fam.*) stampede, rush.
cavalerie /kavalri/ *n.f.* (*mil.*) cavalry; (*au cirque*) horses.
caval|ier, ~ière /kavalje, -jɛr/ *a.* offhand. ● *n.m., f.* rider; (*pour danser*) partner. ● *n.m.* (*échecs*) knight.
cave[1] /kav/ *n.f.* cellar.
cave[2] /kav/ *a.* sunken.
caveau (*pl.* **~x**) /kavo/ *n.m.* vault.
caverne /kavɛrn/ *n.f.* cave.
caviar /kavjar/ *n.m.* caviare.
cavité /kavite/ *n.f.* cavity.
CD (*abrév.*) (*compact disc*) CD.
ce[1], **c'*** /sə, s/ *pron.* it, that. **c'est,** it *ou* that is. **ce sont,** they are. **c'est moi,** it's me. **c'est un chanteur/une chanteuse/***etc.*, he/she is a singer/*etc.* **ce qui, ce que,** what. **ce que c'est bon/***etc.***!,** how good/*etc.* it is! **tout ce qui, tout ce que,** everything that.
ce[2] *ou* **cet*, cette** (*pl.* **ces**) /sə, sɛt, se/ *a.* that; (*proximité*) this. **ces,** those; (*proximité*) these.
CE *abrév.* (Communauté européenne) EC.
ceci /səsi/ *pron.* this.
cécité /sesite/ *n.f.* blindness.
céder /sede/ *v.t.* give up. ● *v.i.* (*se rompre*) give way; (*se soumettre*) give in.
cédille /sedij/ *n.f.* cedilla.
cèdre /sɛdr/ *n.m.* cedar.
CEE *abrév.* (*Communauté économique européenne*) EEC.
ceinture /sɛ̃tyr/ *n.f.* belt; (*taille*) waist; (*de bus, métro*) circle (line). **~ de sauvetage,** lifebelt. **~ de sécurité,** seat-belt.
ceinturer /sɛ̃tyre/ *v.t.* seize round the waist; (*entourer*) surround.
cela /səla/ *pron.* it, that; (*pour désigner*) that. **~ va de soi,** it is obvious.
célèbre /selɛbr/ *a.* famous.
célébr|er /selebre/ *v.t.* celebrate. **~ation** *n.f.* celebration (**de,** of).
célébrité /selebrite/ *n.f.* fame; (*personne*) celebrity.
céleri /sɛlri/ *n.m.* (*en branches*) celery. **~(-rave),** celeriac.
céleste /selɛst/ *a.* celestial.
célibat /seliba/ *n.m.* celibacy.
célibataire /selibatɛr/ *a.* unmarried. ● *n.m.* bachelor. ● *n.f.* unmarried woman.
celle, celles /sɛl/ *voir* celui.
cellier /selje/ *n.m.* store-room (*for wine*).
cellophane /selɔfan/ *n.f.* (P.) Cellophane (P.).
cellul|e /selyl/ *n.f.* cell. **~aire** *a.* cell. **fourgon** *ou* **voiture ~aire,** prison van.
celui, celle (*pl.* **ceux, celles**) /səlɥi, sɛl, sø/ *pron.* the one. **~ de mon ami,** my friend's. **~-ci,** this (one). **~-là,** that (one). **ceux-ci,** these (ones). **ceux-là,** those (ones).
cendr|e /sɑ̃dr/ *n.f.* ash. **~é** *a.* (*couleur*) ashen. **blond ~é,** ash blond.
cendrier /sɑ̃drije/ *n.m.* ashtray.
censé /sɑ̃se/ *a.* **être ~ faire,** be supposed to do.
censeur /sɑ̃sœr/ *n.m.* censor; (*scol.*) assistant headmaster.
censur|e /sɑ̃syr/ *n.f.* censorship. **~er** *v.t.* censor; (*critiquer*) censure.
cent (*pl.* **~s**) /sɑ̃/ (*generally* /sɑ̃t/ *pl.* /sɑ̃z/ *before vowel*) *a.* & *n.m.* (a) hundred. **~ un** /sɑ̃œ̃/ a hundred and one.

centaine /sɑ̃tɛn/ *n.f.* hundred. **une ~ (de),** (about) a hundred.
centenaire /sɑ̃tnɛr/ *n.m.* (*anniversaire*) centenary.
centième /sɑ̃tjɛm/ *a. & n.m./f.* hundredth.
centigrade /sɑ̃tigrad/ *a.* centigrade.
centilitre /sɑ̃tilitr/ *n.m.* centilitre.
centime /sɑ̃tim/ *n.m.* centime.
centimètre /sɑ̃timɛtr/ *n.m.* centimetre; (*ruban*) tape-measure.
centr|al, ~ale (*m. pl.* **~aux**) /sɑ̃tral, -o/ *a.* central. ● *n.m.* (*pl.* **~aux**). **~al (téléphonique),** (telephone) exchange. ● *n.f.* power-station. **~aliser** *v.t.* centralize.
centr|e /sɑ̃tr/ *n.m.* centre. **~e-ville** *n.m.* town centre. **~er** *v.t.* centre.
centuple /sɑ̃typl/ *n.m.* **le ~ (de),** a hundredfold. **au ~,** a hundredfold.
cep /sɛp/ *n.m.* vine stock.
cépage /sepaʒ/ *n.m.* (variety of) vine.
cèpe /sɛp/ *n.m.* (edible) boletus.
cependant /səpɑ̃dɑ̃/ *adv.* however.
céramique /seramik/ *n.f.* ceramic; (*art*) ceramics.
cerceau (*pl.* **~x**) /sɛrso/ *n.m.* hoop.
cercle /sɛrkl/ *n.m.* circle; (*cerceau*) hoop. **~ vicieux,** vicious circle.
cercueil /sɛrkœj/ *n.m.* coffin.
céréale /sereal/ *n.f.* cereal.
cérébr|al (*m. pl.* **~aux**) /serebral, -o/ *a.* cerebral.
cérémonial (*pl.* **~s**) /seremɔnjal/ *n.m.* ceremonial.
cérémon|ie /seremɔni/ *n.f.* ceremony. **~ie(s),** (*façons*) fuss. **~ieux, ~ieuse** *a.* ceremonious.
cerf /sɛr/ *n.m.* stag.
cerfeuil /sɛrfœj/ *n.m.* chervil.
cerf-volant (*pl.* **cerfs-volants**) /sɛrvɔlɑ̃/ *n.m.* kite.
ceris|e /sriz/ *n.f.* cherry. **~ier** *n.m.* cherry tree.
cerne /sɛrn/ *n.m.* ring.
cern|er /sɛrne/ *v.t.* surround; (*question*) define. **les yeux ~és,** with rings under one's eyes.
certain, ~e /sɛrtɛ̃, -ɛn/ *a.* certain; (*sûr*) certain, sure (**de,** of; **que,** that). ● *pron.* **~s,** certain people. **d'un ~ âge,** past one's prime. **un ~ temps,** some time.
certainement /sɛrtɛnmɑ̃/ *adv.* certainly.
certes /sɛrt/ *adv.* indeed.
certificat /sɛrtifika/ *n.m.* certificate.
certif|ier /sɛrtifje/ *v.t.* certify. **~ier qch. à qn.,** assure s.o. of sth. **~ié** *a.* (*professeur*) qualified.
certitude /sɛrtityd/ *n.f.* certainty.
cerveau (*pl.* **~x**) /sɛrvo/ *n.m.* brain.
cervelas /sɛrvəla/ *n.m.* saveloy.
cervelle /sɛrvɛl/ *n.f.* (*anat.*) brain; (*culin.*) brains.
ces /se/ *voir* ce².
césarienne /sezarjɛn/ *n.f.* Caesarean (section).
cessation /sɛsɑsjɔ̃/ *n.f.* suspension.
cesse /sɛs/ *n.f.* **n'avoir de ~ que,** have no rest until. **sans ~,** incessantly.
cesser /sese/ *v.t./i.* stop. **~ de faire,** stop doing.
cessez-le-feu /seselfø/ *n.m. invar.* cease-fire.
cession /sɛsjɔ̃/ *n.f.* transfer.
c'est-à-dire /setadir/ *conj.* that is (to say).
cet, cette /sɛt/ *voir* ce².
ceux /sø/ *voir* celui.
chacal (*pl.* **~s**) /ʃakal/ *n.m.* jackal.
chacun, ~e /ʃakœ̃, -yn/ *pron.* each (one), every one; (*tout le monde*) everyone.
chagrin /ʃagrɛ̃/ *n.m.* sorrow. **avoir du ~,** be distressed. **~er** /-ine/ *v.t.* distress.
chahut /ʃay/ *n.m.* row, din. **~er** /-te/ *v.i.* make a row; *v.t.* be rowdy with. **~eur, ~euse** /- tœr, -tøz/ *n.m., f.* rowdy.
chaîn|e /ʃɛn/ *n.f.* chain; (*de télévision*) channel. **~e de montagnes,** mountain range. **~e de montage/fabrication,** assembly/production line. **~e hi-fi,** hi-fi system. **en ~e,** (*accidents*) multiple. **~ette** *n.f.* (small) chain. **~on** *n.m.* link.
chair /ʃɛr/ *n.f.* flesh. **bien en ~,** plump. **en ~ et en os,** in the flesh. **~ à saucisses,** sausage meat. **la ~ de poule,** goose-flesh. ● *a. invar.* **(couleur) ~,** flesh-coloured.
chaire /ʃɛr/ *n.f.* (*d'église*) pulpit; (*univ.*) chair.
chaise /ʃɛz/ *n.f.* chair. **~ longue,** deck-chair.
chaland /ʃalɑ̃/ *n.m.* barge.
châle /ʃɑl/ *n.m.* shawl.
chalet /ʃalɛ/ *n.m.* chalet.
chaleur /ʃalœr/ *n.f.* heat; (*moins intense*) warmth; (*d'un accueil, d'une couleur*) warmth. **~eux, ~euse** *a.* warm.
challenge /ʃalɑ̃ʒ/ *n.m.* contest.

chaloupe /ʃalup/ *n.f.* launch, boat.
chalumeau (*pl.* **~x**) /ʃalymo/ *n.m.* blowlamp; (*Amer.*) blowtorch.
chalut /ʃaly/ *n.m.* trawl-net **~ier** /-tje/ *n.m.* trawler.
chamailler (se) /(sə)ʃamɑje/ *v. pr.* squabble.
chambarder /ʃɑ̃barde/ *v.t.* (*fam.*) turn upside down.
chambre /ʃɑ̃br/ *n.f.* (bed)room; (*pol.*, *jurid.*) chamber. **faire ~ à part,** sleep in different rooms. **~ à air,** inner tube. **~ d'amis,** spare *ou* guest room. **~ à coucher,** bedroom. **~ à un lit/deux lits,** single/double room. **~ forte,** strong-room.
chambrer /ʃɑ̃bre/ *v.t.* (*vin*) bring to room temperature.
chameau (*pl.* **~x**) /ʃamo/ *n.m.* camel.
chamois /ʃamwa/ *n.m.* chamois. **peau de ~,** chamois leather.
champ /ʃɑ̃/ *n.m.* field. **~ de bataille,** battlefield. **~ de courses,** racecourse.
champagne /ʃɑ̃paɲ/ *n.m.* champagne.
champêtre /ʃɑ̃pɛtr/ *a.* rural.
champignon /ʃɑ̃piɲɔ̃/ *n.m.* mushroom; (*moisissure*) fungus. **~ de Paris,** button mushroom.
champion, ~ne /ʃɑ̃pjɔ̃, -jɔn/ *n.m., f.* champion. **~nat** /-jɔna/ *n.m.* championship.
chance /ʃɑ̃s/ *n.f.* (good) luck; (*possibilité*) chance. **avoir de la ~,** be lucky. **quelle ~!,** what luck!
chanceler /ʃɑ̃sle/ *v.i.* stagger; (*fig.*) falter.
chancelier /ʃɑ̃səlje/ *n.m.* chancellor.
chanceu|x, ~se /ʃɑ̃sø, -z/ *a.* lucky.
chancre /ʃɑ̃kr/ *n.m.* canker.
chandail /ʃɑ̃daj/ *n.m.* sweater.
chandelier /ʃɑ̃dəlje/ *n.m.* candlestick.
chandelle /ʃɑ̃dɛl/ *n.f.* candle. **dîner aux ~s,** candlelight dinner.
change /ʃɑ̃ʒ/ *n.m.* (foreign) exchange.
changeant, ~e /ʃɑ̃ʒɑ̃, -t/ *a.* changeable.
changement /ʃɑ̃ʒmɑ̃/ *n.m.* change. **~ de vitesses** (*dispositif*) gears.
changer /ʃɑ̃ʒe/ *v.t./i.* change. **se ~** *v. pr.* change (one's clothes). **~ de nom/voiture,** change one's name/car. **~ de place/train,** change places/trains. **~ de direction,** change direction. **~ d'avis** *ou* **d'idée,** change one's mind. **~ de vitesses,** change gear.
changeur /ʃɑ̃ʒœr/ *n.m.* **~ automatique,** (money) change machine.
chanoine /ʃanwan/ *n.m.* canon.
chanson /ʃɑ̃sɔ̃/ *n.f.* song.
chant /ʃɑ̃/ *n.m.* singing; (*chanson*) song; (*religieux*) hymn.
chantage /ʃɑ̃taʒ/ *n.m.* blackmail. **~ psychologique,** emotional blackmail.
chant|er /ʃɑ̃te/ *v.t./i.* sing. **si cela vous ~e,** (*fam.*) if you feel like it. **faire ~,** (*délit*) blackmail. **~eur, ~euse** *n.m., f.* singer.
chantier /ʃɑ̃tje/ *n.m.* building site. **~ naval,** shipyard. **mettre en ~,** get under way, start.
chantonner /ʃɑ̃tɔne/ *v.t./i.* hum.
chanvre /ʃɑ̃vr/ *n.m.* hemp.
chao|s /kao/ *n.m.* chaos. **~tique** /kaɔtik/ *a.* chaotic.
chaparder /ʃaparde/ *v.t.* (*fam.*) filch.
chapeau (*pl.* **~x**) /ʃapo/ *n.m.* hat. **~!,** well done!
chapelet /ʃaplɛ/ *n.m.* rosary; (*fig.*) string.
chapelle /ʃapɛl/ *n.f.* chapel. **~ ardente,** chapel of rest.
chapelure /ʃaplyr/ *n.f.* breadcrumbs.
chaperon /ʃaprɔ̃/ *n.m.* chaperon. **~ner** /-ɔne/ *v.t.* chaperon.
chapiteau (*pl.* **~x**) /ʃapito/ *n.m.* (*de cirque*) big top; (*de colonne*) capital.
chapitre /ʃapitr/ *n.m.* chapter; (*fig.*) subject.
chapitrer /ʃapitre/ *v.t.* reprimand.
chaque /ʃak/ *a.* every, each.
char /ʃar/ *n.m.* (*mil.*) tank; (*de carnaval*) float; (*charrette*) cart; (*dans l'antiquité*) chariot.
charabia /ʃarabja/ *n.m.* (*fam.*) gibberish.
charade /ʃarad/ *n.f.* riddle.
charbon /ʃarbɔ̃/ *n.m.* coal. **~ de bois,** charcoal. **~nages** /-ɔnaʒ/ *n.m. pl.* coal-mines.
charcut|erie /ʃarkytri/ *n.f.* pork-butcher's shop; (*aliments*) (cooked) pork meats. **~ier, ~ière** *n.m., f.* pork-butcher.
chardon /ʃardɔ̃/ *n.m.* thistle.
charge /ʃarʒ/ *n.f.* load, burden; (*mil.*, *électr.*, *jurid.*) charge; (*mission*) responsibility. **~s,** expenses; (*de locataire*) service charges. **être à la ~ de,** be the responsibility of. **~s sociales,** social security contributions. **prendre en ~,** take

charge of; (*transporter*) give a ride to.

chargé /ʃarʒe/ *a.* (*journée*) busy; (*langue*) coated. ● *n.m., f.* **~ de mission.** head of mission. **~ d'affaires,** chargé d'affaires, **~ de cours,** lecturer.

charger /ʃarʒe/ *v.t.* load; (*attaquer*) charge; (*batterie*) charge. ● *v.i.* (*attaquer*) charge. **se ~ de,** take charge *ou* care of. **~ qn. de,** weigh. s.o. down with; (*tâche*) entrust s.o. with. **~ qn. de faire,** instruct s.o. to do. **chargement** /-əmɑ̃/ *n.m.* loading; (*objets*) load.

chariot /ʃarjo/ *n.m.* (*à roulettes*) trolley; (*charrette*) cart.

charitable /ʃaritabl/ *a.* charitable.

charité /ʃarite/ *n.f.* charity. **faire la ~,** give to charity. **faire la ~ à,** give to.

charlatan /ʃarlatɑ̃/ *n.m.* charlatan.

charmant, ~e /ʃarmɑ̃, -t/ *a.* charming.

charm|e /ʃarm/ *n.m.* charm. **~er** *v.t.* charm. **~eur, ~euse** *n.m., f.* charmer.

charnel, ~le /ʃarnɛl/ *a.* carnal.

charnier /ʃarnje/ *n.m.* mass grave.

charnière /ʃarnjɛr/ *n.f.* hinge. **à la ~ de,** at the meeting point between.

charnu /ʃarny/ *a.* fleshy.

charpent|e /ʃarpɑ̃t/ *n.f.* framework; (*carrure*) build. **~é** *a.* built.

charpentier /ʃarpɑ̃tje/ *n.m.* carpenter.

charpie (en) /(ɑ̃)ʃarpi/ *adv.* in(to) shreds.

charretier /ʃartje/ *n.m.* carter.

charrette /ʃarɛt/ *n.f.* cart.

charrier /ʃarje/ *v.t.* carry.

charrue /ʃary/ *n.f.* plough.

charte /ʃart/ *n.f.* charter.

charter /ʃartɛr/ *n.m.* charter flight.

chasse /ʃas/ *n.f.* hunting; (*au fusil*) shooting; (*poursuite*) chase; (*recherche*) hunt. **~ (d'eau),** (toilet) flush. **~ sous-marine,** underwater fishing.

châsse /ʃɑs/ *n.f.* shrine, reliquary.

chass|er /ʃase/ *v.t./i.* hunt; (*faire partir*) chase away; (*odeur, employé*) get rid of. **~e-neige** *n.m. invar.* snow-plough. **~eur, ~euse** *n.m., f.* hunter; *n.m.* page-boy; (*avion*) fighter.

[cha]ssis /ʃasi/ *n.m.* frame; (*auto.*) [cha]ssis.

chaste /ʃast/ *a.* chaste. **~té** /-əte/ *n.f.* chastity.

chat, ~te /ʃa, ʃat/ *n.m., f.* cat.

châtaigne /ʃɑtɛɲ/ *n.f.* chestnut.

châtaignier /ʃɑtɛɲe/ *n.m.* chestnut tree.

châtain /ʃɑtɛ̃/ *a. invar.* chestnut (brown).

château (*pl.* **~x**) /ʃɑto/ *n.m.* castle; (*manoir*) manor. **~ d'eau,** water-tower. **~ fort,** fortified castle.

châtelain, ~e /ʃatlɛ̃, -ɛn/ *n.m., f.* lord of the manor, lady of the manor.

châtier /ʃɑtje/ *v.t.* chastise; (*style*) refine.

châtiment /ʃɑtimɑ̃/ *n.m.* punishment.

chaton /ʃatɔ̃/ *n.m.* (*chat*) kitten.

chatouill|er /ʃatuje/ *v.t.* tickle. **~ement** *n.m.* tickling.

chatouilleu|x, ~se /ʃatujø, -z/ *a.* ticklish; (*susceptible*) touchy.

chatoyer /ʃatwaje/ *v.i.* glitter.

châtrer /ʃɑtre/ *v.t.* castrate.

chatte /ʃat/ *voir* chat.

chaud, ~e /ʃo, ʃod/ *a.* warm; (*brûlant*) hot; (*vif: fig.*) warm. ● *n.m.* heat. **au ~,** in the warm(th). **avoir ~,** be warm; be hot. **il fait ~,** it is warm; it is hot. **pour te tenir ~,** to keep you warm. **~ement** /-dmɑ̃/ *adv.* warmly; (*disputé*) hotly.

chaudière /ʃodjɛr/ *n.f.* boiler.

chaudron /ʃodrɔ̃/ *n.m.* cauldron.

chauffage /ʃofaʒ/ *n.m.* heating. **~ central,** central heating.

chauffard /ʃofar/ *n.m.* (*péj.*) reckless driver.

chauff|er /ʃofe/ *v.t./i.* heat (up). **se ~er** *v. pr.* warm o.s. (up). **~e-eau** *n.m. invar.* water-heater.

chauffeur /ʃofœr/ *n.m.* driver; (*aux gages de qn.*) chauffeur.

chaum|e /ʃom/ *n.m.* (*de toit*) thatch.

chaussée /ʃose/ *n.f.* road(way).

chauss|er /ʃose/ *v.t.* (*chaussures*) put on; (*enfant*) put shoes on (to). **se ~er** *v. pr.* put one's shoes on. **~er bien,** (*aller*) fit well. **~er du 35/***etc.*, take a size 35/*etc.* shoe. **~e-pied** *n.m.* shoehorn. **~eur** *n.m.* shoemaker.

chaussette /ʃosɛt/ *n.f.* sock.

chausson /ʃosɔ̃/ *n.m.* slipper; (*de bébé*) bootee. **~ (aux pommes),** (apple) turnover.

chaussure /ʃosyr/ *n.f.* shoe. **~s de ski,** ski boots. **~s de marche,** hiking boots.

chauve /ʃov/ *a.* bald.

chauve-souris (*pl.* **chauves-souris**) /ʃovsuri/ *n.f.* bat.

chauvin, ~e /ʃovɛ̃, -in/ *a.* chauvinistic. ● *n.m., f.* chauvinist. **~isme** /-inism/ *n.m.* chauvinism.

chaux /ʃo/ *n.f.* lime.

chavirer /ʃavire/ *v.t./i.* (*bateau*) capsize.

chef /ʃɛf/ *n.m.* leader, head; (*culin.*) chef; (*de tribu*) chief. **~ d'accusation,** (*jurid.*) charge. **~ d'équipe,** foreman; (*sport*) captain. **~ d'État,** head of State. **~ de famille,** head of the family. **~ de file,** (*pol.*) leader. **~ de gare,** station-master. **~ d'orchestre,** conductor. **~ de service,** department head. **~-lieu** (*pl.* **~s-lieux**) *n.m.* county town.

chef-d'œuvre (*pl.* **chefs-d'œuvre**) /ʃɛdœvr/ *n.m.* masterpiece.

cheik /ʃɛk/ *n.m.* sheikh.

chemin /ʃmɛ̃/ *n.m.* path, road; (*direction, trajet*) way. **beaucoup de ~ à faire,** a long way to go. **~ de fer,** railway. **en** *ou* **par ~ de fer,** by rail. **~ de halage,** towpath. **~ vicinal,** by-road. **se mettre en ~,** start out.

cheminée /ʃmine/ *n.f.* chimney; (*intérieure*) fireplace; (*encadrement*) mantelpiece; (*de bateau*) funnel.

chemin|er /ʃmine/ *v.i.* plod; (*fig.*) progress. **~ement** *n.m.* progress.

cheminot /ʃmino/ *n.m.* railwayman; (*Amer.*) railroad man.

chemis|e /ʃmiz/ *n.f.* shirt; (*dossier*) folder; (*de livre*) jacket. **~e de nuit,** night-dress. **~ette** *n.f.* short-sleeved shirt.

chemisier /ʃmizje/ *n.m.* blouse.

chen|al (*pl.* **~aux**) /ʃənal, -o/ *n.m.* channel.

chêne /ʃɛn/ *n.m.* oak.

chenil /ʃni(l)/ *n.m.* kennels.

chenille /ʃnij/ *n.f.* caterpillar.

chenillette /ʃnijɛt/ *n.f.* tracked vehicle.

cheptel /ʃɛptɛl/ *n.m.* livestock.

chèque /ʃɛk/ *n.m.* cheque. **~ de voyage,** traveller's cheque.

chéquier /ʃekje/ *n.m.* cheque-book.

cher, chère /ʃɛr/ *a.* (*coûteux*) dear, expensive; (*aimé*) dear. ● *adv.* (*coûter, payer*) a lot (of money). ● *n.m., f.* **mon ~, ma chère,** my dear.

chercher /ʃɛrʃe/ *v.t.* look for; (*aide, paix, gloire*) seek. **aller ~,** go and get *ou* fetch, go for. **~ à faire,** attempt to do. **~ la petite bête,** be finicky.

chercheu|r, ~se /ʃɛrʃœr, -øz/ *n.m., f.* research worker.

chèrement /ʃɛrmɑ̃/ *adv.* dearly.

chéri, ~e /ʃeri/ *a.* beloved. ● *n.m., f.* darling.

chérir /ʃerir/ *v.t.* cherish.

cherté /ʃɛrte/ *n.f.* high cost.

chéti|f, ~ve /ʃetif, -v/ *a.* puny.

chev|al (*pl.* **~aux**) /ʃval, -o/ *n.m.* horse. **~al (vapeur),** horsepower. **à ~al,** on horseback. **à ~al sur,** straddling. **faire du ~al,** ride (a horse). **~al-d'arçons** *n.m. invar.* (*gymnastique*) horse.

chevaleresque /ʃvalrɛsk/ *a.* chivalrous.

chevalerie /ʃvalri/ *n.f.* chivalry.

chevalet /ʃvalɛ/ *n.m.* easel.

chevalier /ʃvalje/ *n.m.* knight.

chevalière /ʃvaljɛr/ *n.f.* signet ring.

chevalin, ~e /ʃvalɛ̃, -in/ *a.* (*boucherie*) horse; (*espèce*) equine.

chevauchée /ʃvoʃe/ *n.f.* (horse) ride.

chevaucher /ʃvoʃe/ *v.t.* straddle. ● *v.i.,* **se ~** *v. pr.* overlap.

chevelu /ʃəvly/ *a.* hairy.

chevelure /ʃəvlyr/ *n.f.* hair.

chevet /ʃvɛ/ *n.m.* **au ~ de,** at the bedside of.

cheveu (*pl.* **~x**) /ʃvø/ *n.m.* (*poil*) hair. **~x,** (*chevelure*) hair. **avoir les ~x longs,** have long hair.

cheville /ʃvij/ *n.f.* ankle; (*fiche*) peg, pin; (*pour mur*) (wall) plug.

chèvre /ʃɛvr/ *n.f.* goat.

chevreau (*pl.* **~x**) /ʃəvro/ *n.m.* kid.

chevreuil /ʃəvrœj/ *n.m.* roe(-deer); (*culin.*) venison.

chevron /ʃəvrɔ̃/ *n.m.* (*poutre*) rafter. **à ~s,** herring-bone.

chevronné /ʃəvrɔne/ *a.* experienced, seasoned.

chevrotant, ~e /ʃəvrɔtɑ̃, -t/ *a.* quavering.

chewing-gum /ʃwiŋgɔm/ *n.m.* chewing-gum.

chez /ʃe/ *prép.* at *ou* to the house of; (*parmi*) among; (*dans le caractère ou l'œuvre de*) in. **~ le boucher**/*etc.*, at the butcher's/ *etc.* **~ soi,** at home; (*avec direction*) home. **~-soi** *n.m. invar.* home.

chic /ʃik/ *a. invar.* smart; (*gentil*) kind. **sois ~,** do me a favour. ● *n.m.* style. **avoir le ~ pour,** have the knack of. **~ (alors)!,** great!

chicane /ʃikan/ *n.f.* zigzag. **chercher ~ à qn,** needle s.o.

chiche /ʃiʃ/ *a.* mean (**de,** with). **~ (que je le fais)!,** (*fam.*) I bet you I will, can, *etc.*

chichis /ʃiʃi/ *n.m. pl.* (*fam.*) fuss.

chicorée /ʃikɔre/ *n.f.* (*frisée*) endive; (*à café*) chicory.

chien, ~ne /ʃjɛ̃, ʃjɛn/ *n.m.* dog. ● *n.f.* dog, bitch. **~ de garde,** watch-dog. **~-loup** *n.m.* (*pl.* **~s-loups**) wolfhound.

chiffon /ʃifɔ̃/ *n.m.* rag.

chiffonner /ʃifɔne/ *v.t.* crumple; (*préoccuper: fam.*) bother.

chiffonnier /ʃifɔnje/ *n.m.* rag-and-bone man.

chiffre /ʃifr/ *n.m.* figure; (*code*) code. **~s arabes/romains,** Arabic/roman numerals. **~ d'affaires,** turnover.

chiffrer /ʃifre/ *v.t.* set a figure to, assess; (*texte*) encode. **se ~ à,** amount to.

chignon /ʃiɲɔ̃/ *n.m.* bun, chignon.

Chili /ʃili/ *n.m.* Chile.

chilien, ~ne /ʃiljɛ̃, -jɛn/ *a.* & *n.m., f.* Chilean.

chim|ère /ʃimɛr/ *n.f.* fantasy. **~érique** *a.* fanciful.

chim|ie /ʃimi/ *n.f.* chemistry. **~ique** *a.* chemical. **~iste** *n.m./f.* chemist.

chimpanzé /ʃɛ̃pɑ̃ze/ *n.m.* chimpanzee.

Chine /ʃin/ *n.f.* China.

chinois, ~e /ʃinwa, -z/ *a.* & *n.m., f.* Chinese. ● *n.m.* (*lang.*) Chinese.

chiot /ʃjo/ *n.m.* pup(py).

chiper /ʃipe/ *v.t.* (*fam.*) swipe.

chipoter /ʃipɔte/ *v.i.* (*manger*) nibble; (*discuter*) quibble.

chips /ʃips/ *n.m. pl.* crisps; (*Amer.*) chips.

chiquenaude /ʃiknod/ *n.f.* flick.

chiromanc|ie /kirɔmɑ̃si/ *n.f.* palmistry. **~ien, ~ienne** *n.m., f.* palmist.

chirurgic|al (*m. pl.* **~aux**) /ʃiryrʒikal, -o/ *a.* surgical.

chirurg|ie /ʃiryrʒi/ *n.f.* surgery. **~ie esthétique,** plastic surgery. **~ien** *n.m.* surgeon.

chlore /klɔr/ *n.m.* chlorine.

choc /ʃɔk/ *n.m.* (*heurt*) impact, shock; (*émotion*) shock; (*collision*) crash; (*affrontement*) clash; (*méd.*) shock.

colat /ʃɔkɔla/ *n.m.* chocolate; (*à ...e*) drinking chocolate. **~ au lait,** milk chocolate. **~ chaud,** hot chocolate.

chœur /kœr/ *n.m.* (*antique*) chorus; (*chanteurs, nef*) choir. **en ~,** in chorus.

chois|ir /ʃwazir/ *v.t.* choose, select. **~i** *a.* carefully chosen; (*passage*) selected.

choix /ʃwa/ *n.m.* choice, selection. **au ~,** according to preference. **de ~,** choice. **de premier ~,** top quality.

choléra /kɔlera/ *n.m.* cholera.

chômage /ʃomaʒ/ *n.m.* unemployment. **en ~,** unemployed. **mettre en ~ technique,** lay off.

chôm|er /ʃome/ *v.i.* be unemployed; (*usine*) lie idle. **~eur, ~euse** *n.m., f.* unemployed person. **les ~eurs,** the unemployed.

chope /ʃɔp/ *n.f.* tankard.

choper /ʃɔpe/ *v.t.* (*fam.*) catch.

choquer /ʃɔke/ *v.t.* shock; (*commotionner*) shake.

choral, ~e (*m. pl.* **~s**) /kɔral/ *a.* choral. ● *n.f.* choir, choral society.

chorégraph|ie /kɔregrafi/ *n.f.* choreography. **~e** *n.m./f.* choreographer.

choriste /kɔrist/ *n.m./f.* (*à l'église*) chorister; (*opéra, etc.*) member of the chorus *ou* choir.

chose /ʃoz/ *n.f.* thing. **(très) peu de ~,** nothing much.

chou (*pl.* **~x**) /ʃu/ *n.m.* cabbage. **~ (à la crème),** cream puff. **~x de Bruxelles,** Brussels sprouts. **mon petit ~,** (*fam.*) my little dear.

choucas /ʃuka/ *n.m.* jackdaw.

chouchou, ~te /ʃuʃu, -t/ *n.m., f.* pet, darling. **le ~ du prof.,** the teacher's pet.

choucroute /ʃukrut/ *n.f.* sauerkraut.

chouette[1] /ʃwɛt/ *n.f.* owl.

chouette[2] /ʃwɛt/ *a.* (*fam.*) super.

chou-fleur (*pl.* **choux-fleurs**) /ʃuflœr/ *n.m.* cauliflower.

choyer /ʃwaje/ *v.t.* pamper.

chrétien, ~ne /kretjɛ̃, -jɛn/ *a.* & *n.m., f.* Christian.

Christ /krist/ *n.m.* **le ~,** Christ.

christianisme /kristjanism/ *n.m.* Christianity.

chrom|e /krom/ *n.m.* chromium, chrome. **~é** *a.* chromium-plated.

chromosome /krɔmozom/ *n.m.* chromosome.

chroniqu|e /krɔnik/ *a.* chronic. ● *n.f.* (*rubrique*) column; (*nouvelles*) news; (*annales*) chronicle.

~eur *n.m.* columnist; (*historien*) chronicler.
chronolog|ie /krɔnɔlɔʒi/ *n.f.* chronology. **~ique** *a.* chronological.
chronom|ètre /krɔnɔmɛtr/ *n.m.* stop-watch. **~étrer** *v.t.* time.
chrysanthème /krizɑ̃tɛm/ *n.m.* chrysanthemum.
chuchot|er /ʃyʃɔte/ *v.t./i.* whisper. **~ement** *n.m.* whisper(ing).
chuinter /ʃɥɛ̃te/ *v.i.* hiss.
chut /ʃyt/ *int.* shush.
chute /ʃyt/ *n.f.* fall; (*déchet*) scrap. **~ (d'eau),** waterfall. **~ du jour,** nightfall. **~ de pluie,** rainfall. **la ~ des cheveux,** hair loss.
chuter /ʃyte/ *v.i.* fall.
Chypre /ʃipr/ *n.f.* Cyprus.
-ci /si/ *adv.* (*après un nom précédé de ce, cette, etc.*) **cet homme-ci,** this man. **ces maisons-ci,** these houses.
ci- /si/ *adv.* here. **ci-après,** hereafter. **ci-contre,** opposite. **ci-dessous,** below. **ci-dessus,** above. **ci-gît,** here lies. **ci-inclus, ci-incluse, ci-joint, ci-jointe,** enclosed.
cible /sibl/ *n.f.* target.
ciboul|e /sibul/ *n.f.,* **~ette** *n.f.* chive(s).
cicatrice /sikatris/ *n.f.* scar.
cicatriser /sikatrize/ *v.t.,* **se ~** *v. pr.* heal (up).
cidre /sidr/ *n.m.* cider.
ciel (*pl* **cieux, ciels**) /sjɛl, sjø/ *n.m.* sky; (*relig.*) heaven. **cieux,** (*relig.*) heaven.
cierge /sjɛrʒ/ *n.m.* candle.
cigale /sigal/ *n.f.* cicada.
cigare /sigar/ *n.m.* cigar.
cigarette /sigarɛt/ *n.f.* cigarette.
cigogne /sigɔɲ/ *n.f.* stork.
cil /sil/ *n.m.* (eye)lash.
ciller /sije/ *v.i.* blink.
cime /sim/ *n.f.* peak, tip.
ciment /simɑ̃/ *n.m.* cement. **~er** /-te/ *v.t.* cement.
cimetière /simtjɛr/ *n.m.* cemetery. **~ de voitures,** breaker's yard.
cinéaste /sineast/ *n.m./f.* film-maker.
ciné-club /sineklœb/ *n.m.* film society.
cinéma /sinema/ *n.m.* cinema. **~tographique** *a.* cinema.
cinémathèque /sinematɛk/ *n.f.* film library; (*salle*) film theatre.
cinéphile /sinefil/ *n.m./f.* film lover.
cinétique /sinetik/ *a.* kinetic.
cinglant, ~e /sɛ̃glɑ̃, -t/ *a.* biting.
cinglé /sɛ̃gle/ *a.* (*fam.*) crazy.
cingler /sɛ̃gle/ *v.t.* lash.
cinq /sɛ̃k/ *a. & n.m.* five. **~ième** *a. & n.m./f.* fifth.
cinquantaine /sɛ̃kɑ̃tɛn/ *n.f.* **une ~ (de),** about fifty.
cinquant|e /sɛ̃kɑ̃t/ *a. & n.m.* fifty. **~ième** *a. & n.m./f.* fiftieth.
cintre /sɛ̃tr/ *n.m.* coat-hanger; (*archit.*) curve.
cintré /sɛ̃tre/ *a.* (*chemise*) fitted.
cirage /siraʒ/ *n.m.* (wax) polish.
circoncision /sirkɔ̃sizjɔ̃/ *n.f.* circumcision.
circonférence /sirkɔ̃ferɑ̃s/ *n.f.* circumference.
circonflexe /sirkɔ̃flɛks/ *a.* circumflex.
circonscription /sirkɔ̃skripsjɔ̃/ *n.f.* district. **~ (électorale),** constituency.
circonscrire /sirkɔ̃skrir/ *v.t.* confine; (*sujet*) define.
circonspect /sirkɔ̃spɛkt/ *a.* circumspect.
circonstance /sirkɔ̃stɑ̃s/ *n.f.* circumstance; (*occasion*) occasion. **~s atténuantes,** mitigating circumstances.
circonstancié /sirkɔ̃stɑ̃sje/ *a.* detailed.
circonvenir /sirkɔ̃vnir/ *v.t.* circumvent.
circuit /sirkɥi/ *n.m.* circuit; (*trajet*) tour, trip.
circulaire /sirkylɛr/ *a. & n.f.* circular.
circul|er /sirkyle/ *v.i.* circulate; (*train, automobile, etc.*) travel; (*piéton*) walk. **faire ~er,** (*badauds*) move on. **~ation** *n.f.* circulation; (*de véhicules*) traffic.
cire /sir/ *n.f.* wax.
ciré /sire/ *n.m.* oilskin; waterproof.
cir|er /sire/ *v.t.* polish, wax. **~euse** *n.f.* (*appareil*) floor-polisher.
cirque /sirk/ *n.m.* circus; (*arène*) amphitheatre; (*désordre: fig.*) chaos.
cirrhose /siroz/ *n.f.* cirrhosis.
cisaille(s) /sizɑj/ *n.f.* (*pl.*) shears.
ciseau (*pl.* **~x**) /sizo/ *n.m.* chisel. **~x,** scissors.
ciseler /sizle/ *v.t.* chisel.
citadelle /sitadɛl/ *n.f.* citadel.
citadin, ~e /sitadɛ̃, -in/ *n.m., f.* city dweller. ● *a.* city.
cité /site/ *n.f.* city. **~ ouvrière,** (workers') housing estate. **~ universitaire,** (university) halls of residence. **~-dortoir** *n.f.* (*pl.* **~s-dortoirs**) dormitory town.

cit|er /site/ *v.t.* quote, cite; (*jurid.*) summon. **~ation** *n.f.* quotation; (*jurid.*) summons.
citerne /sitɛrn/ *n.f.* tank.
cithare /sitar/ *n.f.* zither.
citoyen, ~ne /sitwajɛ̃, -jɛn/ *n.m., f.* citizen. **~neté** /-jɛnte/ *n.f.* citizenship.
citron /sitrɔ̃/ *n.m.* lemon. **~ vert,** lime. **~nade** /-ɔnad/ *n.f.* lemon squash *ou* drink, (still) lemonade.
citrouille /sitruj/ *n.f.* pumpkin.
civet /sivɛ/ *n.m.* stew. **~ de lièvre/lapin,** jugged hare/rabbit.
civette /sivɛt/ *n.f.* (*culin.*) chive(s).
civière /sivjɛr/ *n.f.* stretcher.
civil /sivil/ *a.* civil; (*non militaire*) civilian; (*poli*) civil. ● *n.m.* civilian. **dans le ~,** in civilian life. **en ~,** in plain clothes.
civilisation /sivilizɑsjɔ̃/ *n.f.* civilization.
civiliser /sivilize/ *v.t.* civilize. **se ~** *v. pr.* become civilized.
civi|que /sivik/ *a.* civic. **~sme** *n.m.* civic sense.
clair /klɛr/ *a.* clear; (*éclairé*) light, bright; (*couleur*) light; (*liquide*) thin. ● *adv.* clearly. ● *n.m.* **~ de lune,** moonlight. **le plus ~ de,** most of. **~ement** *adv.* clearly.
claire-voie (à) /(a)klɛrvwa/ *adv.* with slits to let the light through.
clairière /klɛrjɛr/ *n.f.* clearing.
clairon /klɛrɔ̃/ *n.m.* bugle. **~ner** /-ɔne/ *v.t.* trumpet (forth).
clairsemé /klɛrsəme/ *a.* sparse.
clairvoyant, ~e /klɛrvwajɑ̃, -t/ *a.* clear-sighted.
clamer /klame/ *v.t.* utter aloud.
clameur /klamœr/ *n.f.* clamour.
clan /klɑ̃/ *n.m.* clan.
clandestin, ~e /klɑ̃dɛstɛ̃, -in/ *a.* secret; (*journal*) underground. **passager ~,** stowaway.
clapet /klapɛ/ *n.m.* valve.
clapier /klapje/ *n.m.* (rabbit) hutch.
clapot|er /klapɔte/ *v.i.* lap. **~is** *n.m.* lapping.
claquage /klakaʒ/ *n.m.* strained muscle.
claque /klak/ *n.f.* slap. **en avoir sa ~ (de),** (*fam.*) be fed up (with).
claqu|er /klake/ *v.i.* bang; (*porte*) slam, bang; (*fouet*) snap, crack; (*se casser*: *fam.*) conk out; (*mourir*: *fam.*) snuff it. ● *v.t.* (*porte*) slam, bang; (*dépenser*: *fam.*) blow; (*fatiguer*: *fam.*) tire out. **~er des doigts,** snap one's fingers. **~er des mains,** clap one's hands. **il claque des dents,** his teeth are chattering. **~ement** *n.m.* bang(ing); slam(ming); snap(ping).
claquettes /klakɛt/ *n.f. pl.* tap-dancing.
clarifier /klarifje/ *v.t.* clarify.
clarinette /klarinɛt/ *n.f.* clarinet.
clarté /klarte/ *n.f.* light, brightness; (*netteté*) clarity.
classe /klɑs/ *n.f.* class; (*salle*: *scol.*) class(-room). **aller en ~,** go to school. **~ ouvrière/moyenne,** working/middle class. **faire la ~,** teach.
class|er /klɑse/ *v.t.* classify; (*par mérite*) grade; (*papiers*) file; (*affaire*) close. **se ~er premier/dernier,** come first/last. **~ement** *n.m.* classification; grading; filing; (*rang*) place, grade; (*de coureur*) placing.
classeur /klɑsœr/ *n.m.* filing cabinet; (*chemise*) file.
classif|ier /klasifje/ *v.t.* classify. **~ication** *n.f.* classification.
classique /klasik/ *a.* classical; (*de qualité*) classic(al); (*habituel*) classic. ● *n.m.* classic; (*auteur*) classical author.
clause /kloz/ *n.f.* clause.
claustration /klostrɑsjɔ̃/ *n.f.* confinement.
claustrophobie /klostrɔfɔbi/ *n.f.* claustrophobia.
clavecin /klavsɛ̃/ *n.m.* harpsichord.
clavicule /klavikyl/ *n.f.* collar-bone.
clavier /klavje/ *n.m.* keyboard.
claviste /klavist/ *n.m./f.* keyboarder.
clé, clef /kle/ *n.f.* key; (*outil*) spanner; (*mus.*) clef. ● *a. invar.* key. **~ anglaise,** (monkey-)wrench. **~ de contact,** ignition key. **~ de voûte,** keystone. **prix ~s en main,** (*voiture*) on-the-road price.
clémen|t, ~te /klemɑ̃, -t/ *a.* (*doux*) mild; (*indulgent*) lenient. **~ce** *n.f.* mildness; leniency.
clémentine /klemɑ̃tin/ *n.f.* clementine.
clerc /klɛr/ *n.m.* (*de notaire etc.*) clerk; (*relig.*) cleric.
clergé /klɛrʒe/ *n.m.* clergy.
cléric|al (*m. pl.* **~aux**) /klerikal, -o/ *a.* clerical.
cliché /kliʃe/ *n.m.* cliché; (*photo.*) negative.
client, ~e/klijɑ̃, -t/ *n.m., f.* customer; (*d'un avocat*) client; (*d'un*

médecin) patient; (*d'hôtel*) guest. **~èle** /-tɛl/ *n.f.* customers, clientele; (*d'un avocat*) clientele, clients, practice; (*d'un médecin*) practice, patients; (*soutien*) custom.

cligner /kliɲe/ *v.i.* **~ des yeux,** blink. **~ de l'œil,** wink.

clignot|er /kliɲɔte/ *v.i.* blink; (*lumière*) flicker; (*comme signal*) flash. **~ant** *n.m.* (*auto.*) indicator; (*auto., Amer.*) directional signal.

climat /klima/ *n.m.* climate. **~ique** /-tik/ *a.* climatic.

climatis|ation /klimatizɑsjɔ̃/ *n.f.* air-conditioning. **~é** *a.* air-conditioned.

clin d'œil /klɛ̃dœj/ *n.m.* wink. **en un ~,** in a flash.

clinique /klinik/ *a.* clinical. ● *n.f.* (private) clinic.

clinquant, ~e /klɛ̃kɑ̃, -t/ *a.* showy.

clip /klip/ *n.m.* video.

clique /klik/ *n.f.* clique; (*mus., mil.*) band.

cliquet|er /klikte/ *v.i.* clink. **~is** *n.m.* clink(ing).

clitoris /klitɔris/ *n.m.* clitoris.

clivage /klivaʒ/ *n.m.* cleavage.

clochard, ~e /klɔʃar, -d/ *n.m., f.* tramp.

cloch|e[1] /klɔʃ/ *n.f.* bell. **~ à fromage,** cheese-cover. **~ette** *n.f.* bell.

cloche[2] /klɔʃ/ *n.f.* (*fam.*) idiot.

cloche-pied (à) /(a)klɔʃpje/ *adv.* hopping on one foot.

clocher[1] /klɔʃe/ *n.m.* bell-tower; (*pointu*) steeple. **de ~,** parochial.

clocher[2] /klɔʃe/ *v.i.* (*fam.*) be wrong.

cloison /klwazɔ̃/ *n.f.* partition; (*fig.*) barrier. **~ner** /-ɔne/ *v.t.* partition; (*personne*) cut off.

cloître /klwatr/ *n.m.* cloister.

cloîtrer (se) /(sə)klwatre/ *v. pr.* shut o.s. away.

clopin-clopant /klɔpɛ̃klɔpɑ̃/ *adv.* hobbling.

cloque /klɔk/ *n.f.* blister.

clore /klɔr/ *v.t.* close.

clos, ~e /klo, -z/ *a.* closed.

clôtur|e /klotyr/ *n.f.* fence; (*fermeture*) closure. **~er** *v.t.* enclose; (*festival, séance, etc.*) close.

clou /klu/ *n.m.* nail; (*furoncle*) boil; (*de spectacle*) star attraction. **~ de girofle,** clove. **les ~s,** (*passage*) zebra *ou* pedestrian crossing. **~er** *v.t.* nail down; (*fig.*) pin down. **être ~é au lit,** be confined to one's bed. **~er le bec à qn.,** shut s.o. up.

clouté /klute/ *a.* studded.

clown /klun/ *n.m.* clown.

club /klœb/ *n.m.* club.

coaguler /kɔagyle/ *v.t./i.*, **se ~** *v. pr.* coagulate.

coaliser (se) /(sə)kɔalize/ *v. pr.* join forces.

coalition /kɔalisjɔ̃/ *n.f.* coalition.

coasser /kɔase/ *v.i.* croak.

cobaye /kɔbaj/ *n.m.* guinea-pig.

coca /kɔka/ *n.m.* (P.) Coke.

cocagne /kɔkaɲ/ *n.f.* **pays de ~,** land of plenty.

cocaïne /kɔkain/ *n.f.* cocaine.

cocarde /kɔkard/ *n.f.* rosette.

cocard|ier, ~ière /kɔkardje, -jɛr/ *a.* chauvinistic.

cocasse /kɔkas/ *a.* comical.

coccinelle /kɔksinɛl/ *n.f.* ladybird; (*Amer.*) ladybug; (*voiture*) beetle.

cocher[1] /kɔʃe/ *v.t.* tick (off), check.

cocher[2] /kɔʃe/ *n.m.* coachman.

cochon, ~ne /kɔʃɔ̃, -ɔn/ *n.m.* pig. ● *n.m., f.* (*personne: fam.*) pig. ● *a.* (*fam.*) filthy. **~nerie** /-ɔnri/ *n.f.* (*saleté: fam.*) filth; (*marchandise: fam.*) rubbish.

cocktail /kɔktɛl/ *n.m.* cocktail; (*réunion*) cocktail party.

cocon /kɔkɔ̃/ *n.m.* cocoon.

cocorico /kɔkɔriko/ *n.m.* cock-a-doodle-doo.

cocotier /kɔkɔtje/ *n.m.* coconut palm.

cocotte /kɔkɔt/ *n.f.* (*marmite*) casserole. **~ minute,** (P.) pressure-cooker. **ma ~,** (*fam.*) my sweet, my dear.

cocu /kɔky/ *n.m.* (*fam.*) cuckold.

code /kɔd/ *n.m.* code. **~s, phares ~,** dipped headlights. **~ de la route,** Highway Code. **se mettre en ~,** dip one's headlights.

coder /kɔde/ *v.t.* code.

codifier /kɔdifje/ *v.t.* codify.

coéquip|ier, ~ière /kɔekipje, -jɛr/ *n.m., f.* team-mate.

cœur /kœr/ *n.m.* heart; (*cartes*) hearts. **~ d'artichaut,** artichoke heart. **~ de palmier,** heart of palm. **à ~ ouvert,** (*opération*) open-heart; (*parler*) freely. **avoir bon ~,** be kind-hearted. **de bon ~,** with a good heart. **par ~,** by heart. **avoir mal au ~,** feel sick. **je veux en avoir le ~ net,** I want to be clear in my own mind (about it).

coexist|er /kɔɛgziste/ *v.i.* coexist. **~ence** *n.f.* coexistence.

coffre /kɔfr/ *n.m.* chest; (*pour argent*) safe; (*auto.*) boot; (*auto., Amer.*) trunk. **~-fort** (*pl.* **~s-forts**) *n.m.* safe.
coffrer /kɔfre/ *v.t.* (*fam.*) lock up.
coffret /kɔfrɛ/ *n.m.* casket, box.
cognac /kɔɲak/ *n.m.* cognac.
cogner /kɔɲe/ *v.t./i.* knock. **se ~** *v. pr.* knock o.s.
cohabit|er /kɔabite/ *v.i.* live together. **~ation** *n.f.* living together.
cohérent, ~e /kɔerɑ̃, -t/ *a.* coherent.
cohésion /kɔezjɔ̃/ *n.f.* cohesion.
cohorte /kɔɔrt/ *n.f.* troop.
cohue /kɔy/ *n.f.* crowd.
coi, coite /kwa, -t/ *a.* silent.
coiffe /kwaf/ *n.f.* head-dress.
coiff|er /kwafe/ *v.t.* do the hair of; (*chapeau*) put on; (*surmonter*) cap. **~er qn. d'un chapeau,** put a hat on s.o. **se ~er** *v. pr.* do one's hair. **~é de,** wearing. **bien/mal ~é,** with tidy/untidy hair. **~eur, ~euse** *n.m., f.* hairdresser; *n.f.* dressing-table.
coiffure /kwafyr/ *n.f.* hairstyle; (*chapeau*) hat; (*métier*) hairdressing.
coin /kwɛ̃/ *n.m.* corner; (*endroit*) spot; (*cale*) wedge; (*pour graver*) die. **au ~ du feu,** by the fireside. **dans le ~,** locally. **du ~,** local. **le boulanger du ~,** the local baker.
coincer /kwɛ̃se/ *v.t.* jam; (*caler*) wedge; (*attraper*: *fam.*) catch. **se ~** *v. pr.* get jammed.
coïncid|er /kɔɛ̃side/ *v.i.* coincide. **~ence** *n.f.* coincidence.
coing /kwɛ̃/ *n.m.* quince.
coït /kɔit/ *n.m.* intercourse.
coite /kwat/ *voir* coi.
coke /kɔk/ *n.m.* coke.
col /kɔl/ *n.m.* collar; (*de bouteille*) neck; (*de montagne*) pass. **~ roulé,** polo-neck; (*Amer.*) turtle-neck. **~ de l'utérus,** cervix.
coléoptère /kɔleɔptɛr/ *n.m.* beetle.
colère /kɔlɛr/ *n.f.* anger; (*accès*) fit of anger. **en ~,** angry. **se mettre en ~,** lose one's temper.
colér|eux, ~euse /kɔlerø, -z/, **~ique** *adjs.* quick-tempered.
colibri /kɔlibri/ *n.m.* humming-bird.
colifichet /kɔlifiʃɛ/ *n.m.* trinket.
colimaçon (en) /(ɑ̃)kɔlimasɔ̃/ *adv.* spiral.
colin /kɔlɛ̃/ *n.m.* (*poisson*) hake.
colin-maillard /kɔlɛ̃majar/ *n.m.* **jouer à ~,** play blind man's buff.
colique /kɔlik/ *n.f.* diarrhoea; (*méd.*) colic.
colis /kɔli/ *n.m.* parcel.
collabor|er /kɔlabɔre/ *v.i.* collaborate (**à,** on). **~er à,** (*journal*) contribute to. **~ateur, ~atrice** *n.m., f.* collaborator; contributor. **~ation** *n.f.* collaboration (**à,** on); contribution (**à,** to).
collant, ~e /kɔlɑ̃, -t/ *a.* skin-tight; (*poisseux*) sticky. ● *n.m.* (*bas*) tights; (*de danseur*) leotard.
collation /kɔlɑsjɔ̃/ *n.f.* light meal.
colle /kɔl/ *n.f.* glue; (*en pâte*) paste; (*problème*: *fam.*) poser; (*scol., argot*) detention.
collect|e /kɔlɛkt/ *n.f.* collection. **~er** *v.t.* collect.
collecteur /kɔlɛktœr/ *n.m.* (*égout*) main sewer.
collecti|f, ~ve /kɔlɛktif, -v/ *a.* collective; (*billet, voyage*) group. **~vement** *adv.* collectively.
collection /kɔlɛksjɔ̃/ *n.f.* collection.
collectionn|er /kɔlɛksjɔne/ *v.t.* collect. **~eur, ~euse** *n.m., f.* collector.
collectivité /kɔlɛktivite/ *n.f.* community.
coll|ège /kɔlɛʒ/ *n.m.* (secondary) school; (*assemblée*) college. **~égien, ~égienne** *n.m., f.* schoolboy, schoolgirl.
collègue /kɔlɛg/ *n.m./f.* colleague.
coll|er /kɔle/ *v.t.* stick; (*avec colle liquide*) glue; (*affiche*) stick up; (*mettre*: *fam.*) stick; (*scol., argot*) keep in; (*par une question*: *fam.*) stump. ● *v.i.* stick (**à,** to); (*être collant*) be sticky. **~er à,** (*convenir à*) fit, correspond to. **être ~é à,** (*examen*: *fam.*) fail.
collet /kɔlɛ/ *n.m.* (*piège*) snare. **~ monté,** prim and proper. **prendre qn. au ~,** collar s.o.
collier /kɔlje/ *n.m.* necklace; (*de chien*) collar.
colline /kɔlin/ *n.f.* hill.
collision /kɔlizjɔ̃/ *n.f.* (*choc*) collision; (*lutte*) clash. **entrer en ~ (avec),** collide (with).
colloque /kɔlɔk/ *n.m.* symposium.
collyre /kɔlir/ *n.m.* eye drops.
colmater /kɔlmate/ *v.t.* seal; (*trou*) fill in.
colombe /kɔlɔ̃b/ *n.f.* dove.
Colombie /kɔlɔ̃bi/ *n.f.* Colombia.
colon /kɔlɔ̃/ *n.m.* settler.
colonel /kɔlɔnɛl/ *n.m.* colonel.

colon|ial, ~iale (*m. pl.* **~iaux**) /kɔlɔnjal, -jo/ *a. & n.m., f.* colonial.
colonie /kɔlɔni/ *n.f.* colony. **~ de vacances,** children's holiday camp.
coloniser /kɔlɔnize/ *v.t.* colonize.
colonne /kɔlɔn/ *n.f.* column. **~ vertébrale,** spine. **en ~ par deux,** in double file.
color|er /kɔlɔre/ *v.t.* colour; (*bois*) stain. **~ant** *n.m.* colouring. **~ation** *n.f.* (*couleur*) colour(ing).
colorier /kɔlɔrje/ *v.t.* colour (in).
coloris /kɔlɔri/ *n.m.* colour.
coloss|al (*m. pl.* **~aux**) /kɔlɔsal, -o/ *a.* colossal.
colosse /kɔlɔs/ *n.m.* giant.
colport|er /kɔlpɔrte/ *v.t.* hawk. **~eur, ~euse** *n.m., f.* hawker.
colza /kɔlza/ *n.m.* rape(-seed).
coma /kɔma/ *n.m.* coma. **dans le ~,** in a coma.
combat /kɔ̃ba/ *n.m.* fight; (*sport*) match. **~s,** fighting.
combati|f, ~ve /kɔ̃batif, -v/ *a.* eager to fight; (*esprit*) fighting.
combatt|re† /kɔ̃batr/ *v.t./i.* fight. **~ant, ~ante** *n.m., f.* fighter; (*mil.*) combatant.
combien /kɔ̃bjɛ̃/ *adv.* **~ (de),** (*quantité*) how much; (*nombre*) how many; (*temps*) how long. **~ il a changé!,** (*comme*) how he has changed! **~y a-t-il d'ici à ...?,** how far is it to ...?
combinaison /kɔ̃binɛzɔ̃/ *n.f.* combination; (*manigance*) scheme; (*de femme*) slip; (*bleu de travail*) boiler suit; (*Amer.*) overalls; (*de plongée*) wetsuit. **~ d'aviateur,** flying-suit.
combine /kɔ̃bin/ *n.f.* trick; (*fraude*) fiddle.
combiné /kɔ̃bine/ *n.m.* (*de téléphone*) receiver.
combiner /kɔ̃bine/ *v.t.* (*réunir*) combine; (*calculer*) devise.
comble[1] /kɔ̃bl/ *a.* packed.
comble[2] /kɔ̃bl/ *n.m.* height. **~s,** (*mansarde*) attic, loft. **c'est le ~!,** that's the (absolute) limit!
combler /kɔ̃ble/ *v.t.* fill; (*perte, déficit*) make good; (*désir*) fulfil; (*personne*) gratify. **~ qn. de cadeaux/** *etc.*, lavish gifts/*etc.* on s.o.
combustible /kɔ̃bystibl/ *n.m.* fuel.
combustion /kɔ̃bystjɔ̃/ *n.f.* combustion.
comédie /kɔmedi/ *n.f.* comedy. **~ musicale,** musical. **jouer la ~,** put on an act.
comédien, ~ne /kɔmedjɛ̃, -jɛn/ *n.m., f.* actor, actress.
comestible /kɔmɛstibl/ *a.* edible. **~s** *n.m. pl.* foodstuffs.
comète /kɔmɛt/ *n.f.* comet.
comique /kɔmik/ *a.* comical; (*genre*) comic. ● *n.m.* (*acteur*) comic; (*comédie*) comedy; (*côté drôle*) comical aspect.
comité /kɔmite/ *n.m.* committee.
commandant /kɔmɑ̃dɑ̃/ *n.m.* commander; (*armée de terre*) major. **~ (de bord),** captain. **~ en chef,** Commander-in-Chief.
commande /kɔmɑ̃d/ *n.f.* (*comm.*) order. **~s,** (*d'avion etc.*) controls.
command|er /kɔmɑ̃de/ *v.t.* command; (*acheter*) order. ● *v.i.* be in command. **~er à,** (*maîtriser*) control. **~er à qn. de,** command s.o. to. **~ement** *n.m.* command; (*relig.*) commandment.
commando /kɔmɑ̃do/ *n.m.* commando.
comme /kɔm/ *conj.* as. ● *prép.* like. ● *adv.* (*exclamation*) how. **~ ci comme ça,** so-so. **~ d'habitude, ~ à l'ordinaire,** as usual. **~ il faut,** proper(ly). **~ pour faire,** as if to do. **~ quoi,** to the effect that. **qu'avez-vous ~ amis**/*etc.*?, what have you in the way of friends/*etc.*? **~ c'est bon!,** it's so good! **~ il est mignon!** isn't he sweet!
commémor|er /kɔmemɔre/ *v.t.* commemorate. **~ation** *n.f.* commemoration.
commenc|er /kɔmɑ̃se/ *v.t.* begin, start. **~er à faire,** begin *ou* start to do. **~ement** *n.m.* beginning, start.
comment /kɔmɑ̃/ *adv.* how. **~?,** (*répétition*) pardon?; (*surprise*) what? **~ est-il?,** what is he like? **le ~ et le pourquoi,** the whys and wherefores.
commentaire /kɔmɑ̃tɛr/ *n.m.* comment; (*d'un texte*) commentary.
comment|er /kɔmɑ̃te/ *v.t.* comment on. **~ateur, ~atrice** *n.m., f.* commentator.
commérages /kɔmeraʒ/ *n.m. pl.* gossip.
commerçant, ~e /kɔmɛrsɑ̃, -t/ *a.* (*rue*) shopping; (*personne*) business-minded. ● *n.m., f.* shopkeeper.
commerce /kɔmɛrs/ *n.m.* trade, commerce; (*magasin*) business. **faire du ~,** trade.

commerc|ial (*m. pl.* **~iaux**) /kɔmɛrsjal, -jo/ *a.* commercial. **~ialiser** *v.t.* market. **~ialisable** *a.* marketable.

commère /kɔmɛr/ *n.f.* gossip.

commettre /kɔmɛtr/ *v.t.* commit.

commis /kɔmi/ *n.m.* (*de magasin*) assistant; (*de bureau*) clerk.

commissaire /kɔmisɛr/ *n.m.* (*sport*) steward. **~ (de police),** (police) superintendent. **~-priseur** (*pl.* **~s-priseurs**) *n.m.* auctioneer.

commissariat /kɔmisarja/ *n.m.* **~ (de police),** police station.

commission /kɔmisjɔ̃/ *n.f.* commission; (*course*) errand; (*message*) message. **~s,** shopping. **~naire** /-jɔnɛr/ *n.m.* errand-boy.

commod|e /kɔmɔd/ *a.* handy; (*facile*) easy. **pas ~e,** (*personne*) a difficult customer. ● *n.f.* chest (of drawers). **~ité** *n.f.* convenience.

commotion /kɔmosjɔ̃/ *n.f.* **~ (cérébrale),** concussion. **~né** /-jɔne/ *a.* shaken.

commuer /kɔmɥe/ *v.t.* commute.

commun, ~e /kɔmœ̃, -yn/ *a.* common; (*effort, action*) joint; (*frais, pièce*) shared. ● *n.f.* (*circonscription*) commune. **~s** *n.m. pl.* outhouses, outbuildings. **avoir** *ou* **mettre en ~,** share. **le ~ des mortels,** ordinary mortals. **~al** (*m. pl.* **~aux**) /-ynal, -o/ *a.* of the commune, local. **~ément** /-ynemɑ̃/ *adv.* commonly.

communauté /kɔmynote/ *n.f.* community. **~ des biens** (*entre époux*) shared estate.

commune /kɔmyn/ *voir* commun.

communiant, ~e /kɔmynjɑ̃, -t/ *n.m., f.* (*relig.*) communicant.

communicati|f, ~ve /kɔmynikatif, -v/ *a.* communicative.

communication /kɔmynikɑsjɔ̃/ *n.f.* communication; (*téléphonique*) call. **~ interurbaine,** long-distance call.

commun|ier /kɔmynje/ *v.i.* (*relig.*) receive communion; (*fig.*) commune. **~ion** *n.f.* communion.

communiqué /kɔmynike/ *n.m.* communiqué.

communiquer /kɔmynike/ *v.t.* pass on, communicate; (*mouvement*) impart. ● *v.i.* communicate. **se ~ à,** spread to.

communis|te /kɔmynist/ *a. & n.m./f.* communist. **~me** *n.m.* communism.

commutateur /kɔmytatœr/ *n.m.* (*électr.*) switch.

compact /kɔ̃pakt/ *a.* dense; (*voiture*) compact.

compact disc /kɔ̃paktdisk/ *n.m.* (P.) compact disc.

compagne /kɔ̃paɲ/ *n.f.* companion.

compagnie /kɔ̃paɲi/ *n.f.* company. **tenir ~ à,** keep company.

compagnon /kɔ̃paɲɔ̃/ *n.m.* companion; (*ouvrier*) workman. **~ de jeu,** playmate.

comparaître /kɔ̃parɛtr/ *v.i.* (*jurid.*) appear (**devant,** before).

compar|er /kɔ̃pare/ *v.t.* compare. **~er qch./qn. à** *ou* **et** compare sth./s.o. with *ou* and; **se ~er** *v. pr.* be compared. **~able** *a.* comparable. **~aison** *n.f.* comparison; (*littéraire*) simile. **~atif, ~ative** *a.* & *n.m.* comparative. **~é** *a.* comparative.

comparse /kɔ̃pars/ *n.m./f.* (*péj.*) stooge.

compartiment /kɔ̃partimɑ̃/ *n.m.* compartment. **~er** /-te/ *v.t.* divide up.

comparution /kɔ̃parysjɔ̃/ *n.f.* (*jurid.*) appearance.

compas /kɔ̃pa/ *n.m.* (pair of) compasses; (*boussole*) compass.

compassé /kɔ̃pɑse/ *a.* stilted.

compassion /kɔ̃pɑsjɔ̃/ *n.f.* compassion.

compatible /kɔ̃patibl/ *a.* compatible.

compatir /kɔ̃patir/ *v.i.* sympathize. **~ à,** share in.

compatriote /kɔ̃patrijɔt/ *n.m./f.* compatriot.

compens|er /kɔ̃pɑ̃se/ *v.t.* compensate for, make up for. **~ation** *n.f.* compensation.

compère /kɔ̃pɛr/ *n.m.* accomplice.

compéten|t, ~te /kɔpetɑ̃, -t/ *a.* competent. **~ce** *n.f.* competence.

compétiti|f, ~ve /kɔ̃petitif, -v/ *a.* competitive.

compétition /kɔ̃petisjɔ̃/ *n.f.* competition; (*sportive*) event. **de ~,** competitive.

complainte /kɔ̃plɛ̃t/ *n.f.* lament.

complaire (se) /(sə)kɔ̃plɛr/ *v. pr.* **se ~ dans,** delight in.

complaisan|t, ~te /kɔ̃plɛzɑ̃, -t/ *a.* kind; (*indulgent*) indulgent. **~ce** *n.f.* kindness; indulgence.

complément /kɔ̃plemɑ̃/ *n.m.* complement; (*reste*) rest. **~ (d'objet),** (*gram.*) object. **~ d'information,** further information. **~aire** /-tɛr/ *a.*

complementary; (*renseignements*) supplementary.

compl|et[1], **~ète** /kɔ̃plɛ, -t/ *a.* complete; (*train, hôtel, etc.*) full. **~ètement** *adv.* completely.

complet[2] /kɔ̃plɛ/ *n.m.* suit.

compléter /kɔ̃plete/ *v.t.* complete; (*agrémenter*) complement. **se ~** *v. pr.* complement each other.

complex|e[1] /kɔ̃plɛks/ *a.* complex. **~ité** *n.f.* complexity.

complex|e[2] /kɔ̃plɛks/ *n.m.* (*sentiment, bâtiments*) complex. **~é** *a.* hung up.

complication /kɔ̃plikɑsjɔ̃/ *n.f.* complication; (*complexité*) complexity.

complic|e /kɔ̃plis/ *n.m.* accomplice. **~ité** *n.f.* complicity.

compliment /kɔ̃plimɑ̃/ *n.m.* compliment. **~s,** (*félicitations*) congratulations. **~er** /-te/ *v.t.* compliment.

compliqu|er /kɔ̃plike/ *v.t.* complicate. **se ~er** *v. pr.* become complicated. **~é** *a.* complicated.

complot /kɔ̃plo/ *n.m.* plot. **~er** /-ɔte/ *v.t./i.* plot.

comporter[1] /kɔ̃pɔrte/ *v.t.* contain; (*impliquer*) involve.

comport|er[2] (se) /(sə)kɔ̃pɔrte/ *v. pr.* behave; (*joueur*) perform. **~ement** *n.m.* behaviour; (*de joueur*) performance.

composé /kɔ̃poze/ *a.* compound; (*guindé*) affected. ● *n.m.* compound.

compos|er /kɔ̃poze/ *v.t.* make up, compose; (*chanson, visage*) compose; (*numéro*) dial. ● *v.i.* (*scol.*) take an exam; (*transiger*) compromise. **se ~er de,** be made up *ou* composed of. **~ant** *n.m.*, **~ante** *n.f.* component.

composi|teur, ~trice /kɔ̃pozitœr, -tris/ *n.m., f.* (*mus.*) composer.

composition /kɔ̃pozisjɔ̃/ *n.f.* composition; (*examen*) test, exam.

composter /kɔ̃pɔste/ *v.t.* (*billet*) punch.

compot|e /kɔ̃pɔt/ *n.f.* stewed fruit. **~e de pommes,** stewed apples. **~ier** *n.m.* fruit dish.

compréhensible /kɔ̃preɑ̃sibl/ *a.* understandable.

compréhensi|f, ~ve /kɔ̃preɑ̃sif, -v/ *a.* understanding.

compréhension /kɔ̃preɑ̃sjɔ̃/ *n.f.* understanding, comprehension.

comprendre† /kɔ̃prɑ̃dr/ *v.t.* understand; (*comporter*) comprise. **ça se comprend,** that is understandable.

compresse /kɔ̃prɛs/ *n.f.* compress.

compression /kɔ̃prɛsjɔ̃/ *n.f.* (*physique*) compression, (*réduction*) reduction. **~ de personnel,** staff cuts.

comprimé /kɔ̃prime/ *n.m.* tablet.

comprimer /kɔ̃prime/ *v.t.* compress; (*réduire*) reduce.

compris, ~e /kɔ̃pri, -z/ *a.* included; (*d'accord*) agreed. **~ entre,** (contained) between. **service (non) ~,** service (not) included, (not) including service. **tout ~,** (all) inclusive **y ~,** including.

compromettre /kɔ̃prɔmɛtr/ *v.t.* compromise.

compromis /kɔ̃prɔmi/ *n.m.* compromise.

comptab|le /kɔ̃tabl/ *a.* accounting. ● *n.m.* accountant. **~ilité** *n.f.* accountancy; (*comptes*) accounts; (*service*) accounts department.

comptant /kɔ̃tɑ̃/ *adv.* (*payer*) (in) cash; (*acheter*) for cash.

compte /kɔ̃t/ *n.m.* count; (*facture, à la banque, comptabilité*) account; (*nombre exact*) right number. **demander/rendre des ~s,** ask for/ give an explanation. **à bon ~,** cheaply. **s'en tirer à bon ~,** get off lightly. **à son ~,** (*travailler*) for o.s., on one's own. **faire le ~ de,** count. **pour le ~ de,** on behalf of. **sur le ~ de,** about. **~ à rebours,** countdown. **~-gouttes** *n.m. invar.* (*méd.*) dropper. **au ~-gouttes,** (*fig.*) in dribs and drabs. **~ rendu,** report; (*de film, livre*) review. **~-tours** *n.m. invar.* rev counter.

compter /kɔ̃te/ *v.t.* count; (*prévoir*) reckon; (*facturer*) charge for; (*avoir*) have; (*classer*) consider. ● *v.i.* (*calculer, importer*) count. **~ avec,** reckon with. **~ faire,** expect to do. **~ parmi,** (*figurer*) be considered among. **~ sur,** rely on.

compteur /kɔ̃tœr/ *n.m.* meter. **~ de vitesse,** speedometer.

comptine /kɔ̃tin/ *n.f.* nursery rhyme.

comptoir /kɔ̃twar/ *n.m.* counter; (*de café*) bar.

compulser /kɔ̃pylse/ *v.t.* examine.

comt|e, ~esse /kɔ̃t, -ɛs/ *n.m., f.* count, countess.

comté /kɔ̃te/ *n.m.* county.

con, conne /kɔ̃, kɔn/ *a.* (*argot*) bloody foolish. ● *n.m., f.* (*argot*) bloody fool.

concave /kɔ̃kav/ *a.* concave.

concéder /kɔ̃sede/ *v.t.* grant, concede.

concentr|er /kɔ̃sɑ̃tre/ *v.t.*, **se ~er** *v. pr.* concentrate. **~ation** *n.f.* concentration. **~é** *a.* concentrated; (*lait*) condensed; (*personne*) absorbed; *n.m.* concentrate.

concept /kɔ̃sɛpt/ *n.m.* concept.

conception /kɔ̃sɛpsjɔ̃/ *n.f.* conception.

concerner /kɔ̃sɛrne/ *v.t.* concern. **en ce qui me concerne,** as far as I am concerned.

concert /kɔ̃sɛr/ *n.m.* concert. **de ~,** in unison.

concert|er /kɔ̃sɛrte/ *v.t.* organize, prepare. **se ~er** *v. pr.* confer. **~é** *a.* (*plan etc.*) concerted.

concerto /kɔ̃sɛrto/ *n.m.* concerto.

concession /kɔ̃sesjɔ̃/ *n.f.* concession; (*terrain*) plot.

concessionnaire /kɔ̃sesjɔnɛr/ *n.m./f.* (authorized) dealer.

concevoir† /kɔ̃svwar/ *v.t.* (*imaginer, engendrer*) conceive; (*comprendre*) understand.

concierge /kɔ̃sjɛrʒ/ *n.m./f.* caretaker.

concile /kɔ̃sil/ *n.m.* council.

concil|ier /kɔ̃silje/ *v.t.* reconcile. **se ~ier** *v. pr.* (*s'attirer*) win (over). **~iation** *n.f.* conciliation.

concis, ~e /kɔ̃si, -z/ *a.* concise. **~ion** /-zjɔ̃/ *n.f.* concision.

concitoyen, ~ne /kɔ̃sitwajɛ̃, -jɛn/ *n.m., f.* fellow citizen.

concl|ure† /kɔ̃klyr/ *v.t./i.* conclude. **~ure à,** conclude in favour of. **~uant, ~uante** *a.* conclusive. **~usion** *n.f.* conclusion.

concocter /kɔ̃kɔkte/ *v.t.* (*fam.*) cook up.

concombre /kɔ̃kɔ̃br/ *n.m.* cucumber.

concorde /kɔ̃kɔrd/ *n.f.* concord.

concord|er /kɔ̃kɔrde/ *v.i.* agree. **~ance** *n.f.* agreement; (*analogie*) similarity. **~ant, ~ante** *a.* in agreement.

concourir /kɔ̃kurir/ *v.i.* compete. **~ à,** contribute towards.

concours /kɔ̃kur/ *n.m.* competition; (*examen*) competitive examination; (*aide*) aid; (*de circonstances*) combination.

concr|et, ~ète /kɔ̃krɛ, -t/ *a.* concrete. **~ètement** *adv.* in concrete terms.

concrétiser /kɔ̃kretize/ *v.t.* give concrete form to. **se ~** *v. pr.* materialize.

conçu /kɔ̃sy/ *a.* **bien/mal ~,** (*appartement etc.*) well/badly planned.

concubinage /kɔ̃kybinaʒ/ *n.m.* cohabitation.

concurrenc|e /kɔ̃kyrɑ̃s/ *n.f.* competition. **faire ~e à,** compete with. **jusqu'à ~e de,** up to. **~er** *v.t.* compete with.

concurrent, ~e /kɔ̃kyrɑ̃, -t/ *n.m., f.* competitor; (*scol.*) candidate. ● *a.* competing.

condamn|er /kɔ̃dɑne/ *v.t.* (*censurer, obliger*) condemn; (*jurid.*) sentence; (*porte*) block up. **~ation** *n.f.* condemnation; (*peine*) sentence. **~é** *a.* (*fichu*) without hope, doomed.

condens|er /kɔ̃dɑ̃se/ *v.t.*, **se ~er** *v. pr.* condense. **~ation** *n.f.* condensation.

condescendre /kɔ̃desɑ̃dr/ *v.i.* condescend (**à,** to).

condiment /kɔ̃dimɑ̃/ *n.m.* condiment.

condisciple /kɔ̃disipl/ *n.m.* classmate, schoolfellow.

condition /kɔ̃disjɔ̃/ *n.f.* condition. **~s,** (*prix*) terms. **à ~ de** *ou* **que,** provided (that). **sans ~,** unconditional(ly). **sous ~,** conditionally. **~nel, ~nelle** /-jɔnɛl/ *a.* conditional. **~nel** *n.m.* conditional (tense).

conditionnement /kɔ̃disjɔnmɑ̃/ *n.m.* conditioning; (*emballage*) packaging.

conditionner /kɔ̃disjɔne/ *v.t.* condition; (*emballer*) package.

condoléances /kɔ̃dɔleɑ̃s/ *n.f. pl.* condolences.

conduc|teur, ~trice /kɔ̃dyktœr, -tris/ *n.m., f.* driver.

conduire† /kɔ̃dɥir/ *v.t.* lead; (*auto.*) drive; (*affaire*) conduct. ● *v.i.* drive. **se ~** *v. pr.* behave. **~ à,** (*accompagner à*) take to.

conduit /kɔ̃dɥi/ *n.m.* (*anat.*) duct.

conduite /kɔ̃dɥit/ *n.f.* conduct; (*auto.*) driving; (*tuyau*) main. **~ à droite,** (*place*) right-hand drive.

cône /kon/ *n.m.* cone.

confection /kɔ̃fɛksjɔ̃/ *n.f.* making. **de ~,** ready-made. **la ~,** the clothing industry. **~ner** /-jɔne/ *v.t.* make.

confédération /kɔ̃federɑsjɔ̃/ *n.f.* confederation.

conférenc|e /kɔ̃ferɑ̃s/ *n.f.* conference; (*exposé*) lecture. **~e au sommet,** summit conference. **~ier, ~ière** *n.m., f.* lecturer.

conférer /kɔ̃fere/ *v.t.* give; (*décerner*) confer.

confess|er /kɔ̃fese/ *v.t.*, **se ~er** *v. pr.* confess. **~eur** *n.m.* confessor. **~ion** *n.f.* confession; (*religion*) denomination. **~ionnal** (*pl.* **~ionnaux**) *n.m.* confessional. **~ionnel, ~ionnelle** *a.* denominational.

confettis /kɔ̃feti/ *n.m. pl.* confetti.

confiance /kɔ̃fjɑ̃s/ *n.f.* trust. **avoir ~ en,** trust.

confiant, ~e /kɔ̃fjɑ̃, -t/ *a.* (*assuré*) confident; (*sans défiance*) trusting. **~ en** *ou* **dans,** confident in.

confiden|t, ~te /kɔ̃fidɑ̃, -t/ *n.m., f.* confidant, confidante. **~ce** *n.f.* confidence.

confidentiel, ~le /kɔ̃fidɑ̃sjɛl/ *a.* confidential.

confier /kɔ̃fje/ *v.t.* **~ à qn.,** entrust s.o. with; (*secret*) confide to s.o. **se ~ à,** confide in.

configuration /kɔ̃figyrɑsjɔ̃/ *n.f.* configuration.

confiner /kɔ̃fine/ *v.t.* confine. ● *v.i.* **~ à,** border on. **se ~** *v. pr.* confine o.s. (**à, dans,** to).

confins /kɔ̃fɛ̃/ *n.m. pl.* confines.

confirm|er /kɔ̃firme/ *v.t.* confirm. **~ation** *n.f.* confirmation.

confis|erie /kɔ̃fizri/ *n.f.* sweet shop. **~eries,** confectionery. **~eur, ~euse** *n.m., f.* confectioner.

confis|quer /kɔ̃fiske/ *v.t.* confiscate. **~cation** *n.f.* confiscation.

confit, ~e /kɔ̃fi, -t/ *a.* (*culin.*) candied. **fruits ~s,** crystallized fruits. ● *n.m.* **~ d'oie,** goose liver conserve.

confiture /kɔ̃fityr/ *n.f.* jam.

conflit /kɔ̃fli/ *n.m.* conflict.

confondre /kɔ̃fɔ̃dr/ *v.t.* confuse, mix up; (*consterner, étonner*) confound. **se ~** *v. pr.* merge. **se ~ en excuses,** apologize profusely.

confondu /kɔ̃fɔ̃dy/ *a.* (*déconcerté*) overwhelmed, confounded.

conforme /kɔ̃fɔrm/ *a.* **~ à,** in accordance with.

conformément /kɔ̃fɔrmemɑ̃/ *adv.* **~ à,** in accordance with.

conform|er /kɔ̃fɔrme/ *v.t.* adapt. **se ~er à,** conform to. **~ité** *n.f.* conformity.

conformis|te /kɔ̃fɔrmist/ *a.* & *n.m./f.* conformist. **~me** *n.m.* conformism.

confort /kɔ̃fɔr/ *n.m.* comfort. **tout ~,** with all mod cons. **~able** /-tabl/ *a.* comfortable.

confrère /kɔ̃frɛr/ *n.m.* colleague.

confrérie /kɔ̃freri/ *n.f.* brotherhood.

confront|er /kɔ̃frɔ̃te/ *v.t.* confront; (*textes*) compare. **se ~er à** *v. pr.* confront. **~ation** *n.f.* confrontation.

confus, ~e /kɔ̃fy, -z/ *a.* confused; (*gêné*) embarrassed.

confusion /kɔ̃fyzjɔ/ *n.f.* confusion; (*gêné*) embarrassment.

congé /kɔ̃ʒe/ *n.m.* holiday; (*arrêt momentané*) time off; (*mil.*) leave; (*avis de départ*) notice. **~ de maladie,** sick-leave. **~ de maternité,** maternity leave. **jour de ~,** day off. **prendre ~ de,** take one's leave of.

congédier /kɔ̃ʒedje/ *v.t.* dismiss.

cong|eler /kɔ̃ʒle/ *v.t.* freeze. **les ~elés,** frozen food. **~élateur** *n.m.* freezer.

congénère /kɔ̃ʒenɛr/ *n.m./f.* fellow creature.

congénit|al (*m. pl.* **~aux**) /kɔ̃ʒenital, -o/ *a.* congenital.

congère /kɔ̃ʒɛr/ *n.f.* snow-drift.

congestion /kɔ̃ʒɛstjɔ̃/ *n.f.* congestion. **~ cérébrale,** stroke, cerebral haemorrhage. **~ner** /-jɔne/ *v.t.* congest; (*visage*) flush.

congrégation /kɔ̃gregɑsjɔ̃/ *n.f.* congregation.

congrès /kɔ̃grɛ/ *n.m.* congress.

conifère /kɔnifɛr/ *n.m.* conifer.

conique /kɔnik/ *a.* conic(al).

conjectur|e /kɔ̃ʒɛktyr/ *n.f.* conjecture. **~er** *v.t./i.* conjecture.

conjoint, ~e[1] /kɔ̃ʒwɛ̃, -t/ *n.m., f.* spouse.

conjoint, ~e[2] /kɔ̃ʒwɛ̃, -t/ *a.* joint. **~ement** /-tmɑ̃/ *adv.* jointly.

conjonction /kɔ̃ʒɔ̃ksjɔ̃/ *n.f.* conjunction.

conjonctivite /kɔ̃ʒɔ̃ktivit/ *n.f.* conjunctivitis.

conjoncture /kɔ̃ʒɔ̃ktyr/ *n.f.* circumstances; (*économique*) economic climate.

conjugaison /kɔ̃ʒygɛzɔ̃/ *n.f.* conjugation.

conjug|al (*m. pl.* **~aux**) /kɔ̃ʒygal, -o/ *a.* conjugal.

conjuguer /kɔ̃ʒyge/ *v.t.* (*gram.*) conjugate; (*efforts*) combine. **se ~** *v. pr.* (*gram.*) be conjugated.

conjur|er /kɔ̃ʒyre/ *v.t.* (*éviter*) avert; (*implorer*) entreat. **~ation** *n.f.* conspiracy. **~é, ~ée** *n.m., f.* conspirator.

connaissance /kɔnɛsɑ̃s/ *n.f.* knowledge; (*personne*) acquaintance. **~s,** (*science*) knowledge. **faire la ~ de,** meet; (*personne connue*) get to know. **perdre ~,** lose consciousness. **sans ~,** unconscious.

connaisseur /kɔnɛsœr/ *n.m.* connoisseur.

connaître† /kɔnɛtr/ *v.t.* know; (*avoir*) have. **se ~** *v. pr.* (*se rencontrer*) meet. **faire ~,** make known. **s'y ~ à** *ou* **en,** know (all) about.

conne|cter /kɔnɛkte/ *v.t.* connect. **~xion** *n.f.* connection.

connerie /kɔnri/ *n.f.* (*argot*) (*remarque*) rubbish. **faire une ~,** do sth. stupid. **dire une ~,** talk rubbish. **quelle ~!,** how stupid!

connivence /kɔnivɑ̃s/ *n.f.* connivance.

connotation /kɔnɔtɑsjɔ̃/ *n.f.* connotation.

connu /kɔny/ *a.* well-known.

conquér|ir /kɔ̃kerir/ *v.t.* conquer. **~ant, ~ante** *n.m., f.* conqueror.

conquête /kɔ̃kɛt/ *n.f.* conquest.

consacrer /kɔ̃sakre/ *v.t.* devote; (*relig.*) consecrate; (*sanctionner*) establish. **se ~** *v. pr.* devote o.s. (**à,** to).

consciemment /kɔ̃sjamɑ̃/ *adv.* consciously.

conscience /kɔ̃sjɑ̃s/ *n.f.* conscience; (*perception*) consciousness. **avoir/prendre ~ de,** be/become aware of. **perdre ~,** lose consciousness. **avoir bonne/mauvaise ~,** have a clear/guilty conscience.

consciencieu|x, ~se /kɔ̃sjɑ̃sjø, -z/ *a.* conscientious.

conscient, ~e /kɔ̃sjɑ̃, -t/ *a.* conscious. **~ de,** aware *ou* conscious of.

conscrit /kɔ̃skri/ *n.m.* conscript.

consécration /kɔ̃sekrɑsjɔ̃/ *n.f.* consecration.

consécuti|f, ~ve /kɔ̃sekytif, -v/ *a.* consecutive. **~f à,** following upon. **~vement** *adv.* consecutively.

conseil /kɔ̃sɛj/ *n.m.* (piece of) advice; (*assemblée*) council, committee; (*séance*) meeting; (*personne*) consultant. **~ d'administration,** board of directors. **~ des ministres,** Cabinet. **~ municipal,** town council.

conseiller[1] /kɔ̃seje/ *v.t.* advise. **~ à qn. de,** advise s.o. to. **~ qch. à qn.,** recommend sth. to s.o.

conseill|er[2]**, ~ère** /kɔ̃seje, -ɛjɛr/ *n.m., f.* adviser, counsellor. **~er municipal,** town councillor.

consent|ir /kɔ̃sɑ̃tir/ *v.i.* agree (**à,** to). ● *v.t.* grant. **~ement** *n.m.* consent.

conséquence /kɔ̃sekɑ̃s/ *n.f.* consequence. **en ~,** consequently; (*comme il convient*) accordingly.

conséquent, ~e /kɔ̃sekɑ̃, -t/ *a.* logical; (*important: fam.*) sizeable. **par ~,** consequently.

conserva|teur, ~trice kɔ̃sɛrvatœr, -tris/ *a.* conservative. ● *n.m., f.* (*pol.*) conservative. ● *n.m.* (*de musée*) curator. **~tisme** *n.m.* conservatism.

conservatoire /kɔ̃sɛrvatwar/ *n.m.* academy.

conserve /kɔ̃sɛrv/ *n.f.* tinned *ou* canned food. **en ~,** tinned, canned.

conserv|er /kɔ̃sɛrve/ *v.t.* keep; (*en bon état*) preserve; (*culin.*) preserve. **se ~er** *v. pr.* (*culin.*) keep. **~ation** *n.f.* preservation.

considérable /kɔ̃siderabl/ *a.* considerable.

considération /kɔ̃siderɑsjɔ̃/ *n.f.* consideration; (*respect*) regard. **prendre en ~,** take into consideration.

considérer /kɔ̃sidere/ *v.t.* consider; (*respecter*) esteem. **~ comme,** consider to be.

consigne /kɔ̃siɲ/ *n.f.* (*de gare*) left luggage (office); (*Amer.*) (baggage) checkroom; (*scol.*) detention; (*somme*) deposit; (*ordres*) orders. **~ automatique,** (left-luggage) lockers; (*Amer.*) (baggage) lockers.

consigner /kɔ̃siɲe/ *v.t.* (*comm.*) charge a deposit on; (*écrire*) record; (*élève*) keep in; (*soldat*) confine.

consistan|t, ~te /kɔ̃sistɑ̃, -t/ *a.* solid; (*épais*) thick. **~ce** *n.f.* consistency; (*fig.*) solidity.

consister /kɔ̃siste/ *v.i.* **~ en/dans,** consist of/in. **~ à faire,** consist in doing.

consœur /kɔ̃sœr/ *n.f.* colleague; fellow member.

consol|er /kɔ̃sɔle/ *v.t.* console. **se ~er** *v. pr.* be consoled (**de,** for). **~ation** *n.f.* consolation.

consolider /kɔ̃sɔlide/ *v.t.* strengthen; (*fig.*) consolidate.

consomma|teur, ~trice /kɔ̃sɔmatœr, -tris/ *n.m., f.* (*comm.*) consumer; (*dans un café*) customer.

consommé[1] /kɔ̃sɔme/ *a.* consummate.

consommé[2] /kɔ̃sɔme/ *n.m.* (*bouillon*) consommé.

consomm|er /kɔ̃sɔme/ *v.t.* consume; (*user*) use, consume; (*mariage*) consummate. ● *v.i.* drink. **~ation** *n.f.* consumption; consummation; (*boisson*) drink. **de ~ation,** (*comm.*) consumer.

consonne /kɔ̃sɔn/ *n.f.* consonant.

consortium /kɔ̃sɔrsjɔm/ *n.m.* consortium.

conspir|er /kɔ̃spire/ *v.i.* conspire. **~ateur, ~atrice** *n.m., f.* conspirator. **~ation** *n.f.* conspiracy.

conspuer /kɔ̃spɥe/ *v.t.* boo.

const|ant, ~ante /kɔ̃stɑ̃, -t/ *a.* constant. ● *n.f.* constant. **~amment** /-amɑ̃/ *adv.* constantly. **~ance** *n.f.* constancy.

constat /kɔ̃sta/ *n.m.* (official) report.

constat|er /kɔ̃state/ *v.t.* note; (*certifier*) certify. **~ation** *n.f.* observation, statement of fact.

constellation /kɔ̃stelɑsjɔ̃/ *n.f.* constellation.

constellé /kɔ̃stele/ *a.* **~ de,** studded with.

constern|er /kɔ̃stɛrne/ *v.t.* dismay. **~ation** *n.f.* dismay.

constip|é /kɔ̃stipe/ *a.* constipated; (*fig.*) stilted. **~ation** *n.f.* constipation.

constitu|er /kɔ̃stitɥe/ *v.t.* make up, constitute; (*organiser*) form; (*être*) constitute. **se ~er prisonnier,** give o.s. up. **~é de,** made up of.

constituti|f, ~ve /kɔ̃stitytif, -v/ *a.* constituent.

constitution /kɔ̃stitysjɔ̃/ *n.f.* formation; (*d'une équipe*) composition; (*pol., méd.*) constitution. **~nel, ~nelle** /-jɔnɛl/ *a.* constitutional.

constructeur /kɔ̃stryktœr/ *n.m.* manufacturer.

constructi|f, ~ve /kɔ̃stryktif, -v/ *a.* constructive.

constr|uire† /kɔ̃strɥir/ *v.t.* build; (*système, phrase, etc.*) construct. **~uction** *n.f.* building; (*structure*) construction.

consul /kɔ̃syl/ *n.m.* consul. **~aire** *a.* consular. **~at** *n.m.* consulate.

consult|er /kɔ̃sylte/ *v.t.* consult. ● *v.i.* (*médecin*) hold surgery; (*Amer.*) hold office hours. **se ~er** *v. pr.* confer. **~ation** *n.f.* consultation; (*réception: méd.*) surgery; (*Amer.*) office.

consumer /kɔ̃syme/ *v.t.* consume. **se ~** *v. pr.* be consumed.

contact /kɔ̃takt/ *n.m.* contact; (*toucher*) touch. **au ~ de,** on contact with; (*personne*) by contact with, by seeing. **mettre/couper le ~,** (*auto.*) switch on/off the ignition. **prendre ~ avec,** get in touch with. **~er** *v.t.* contact.

contag|ieux, ~ieuse /kɔ̃taʒjø, -z/ *a.* contagious. **~ion** *n.f.* contagion.

container /kɔ̃tɛnɛr/ *n.m.* container.

contamin|er /kɔ̃tamine/ *v.t.* contaminate. **~ation** *n.f.* contamination.

conte /kɔ̃t/ *n.m.* tale. **~ de fées,** fairy tale.

contempl|er /kɔ̃tɑ̃ple/ *v.t.* contemplate. **~ation** *n.f.* contemplation.

contemporain, ~e /kɔ̃tɑ̃pɔrɛ̃, -ɛn/ *a. & n.m., f.* contemporary.

contenance /kɔ̃tnɑ̃s/ *n.f.* (*contenu*) capacity; (*allure*) bearing; (*sang-froid*) composure.

conteneur /kɔ̃tnœr/ *n.m.* container.

contenir† /kɔ̃tnir/ *v.t.* contain; (*avoir une capacité de*) hold. **se ~** *v. pr.* contain o.s.

content, ~e /kɔ̃tɑ̃, -t/ *a.* pleased (**de,** with). **~ de faire,** pleased to do.

content|er /kɔ̃tɑ̃te/ *v.t.* satisfy. **se ~er de,** content o.s. with. **~ement** *n.m.* contentment.

contentieux /kɔ̃tɑ̃sjø/ *n.m.* matters in dispute; (*service*) legal department.

contenu /kɔ̃tny/ *n.m.* (*de contenant*) contents; (*de texte*) content.

conter /kɔ̃te/ *v.t.* tell, relate.

contestataire /kɔ̃tɛstatɛr/ *n.m./f.* protester.

conteste (sans) /(sɑ̃)kɔ̃tɛst/ *adv.* indisputably.

contest|er /kɔ̃tɛste/ *v.t.* dispute; (*s'opposer*) protest against. ● *v.i.* protest. **~able** *a.* debatable. **~ation** *n.f.* dispute; (*opposition*) protest.

conteu|r, ~se /kɔ̃tœr, -øz/ *n.m., f.* story-teller.

contexte /kɔ̃tɛkst/ *n.m.* context.

contigu, ~ë /kɔ̃tigy/ *a.* adjacent (**à,** to).

continent /kɔ̃tinɑ̃/ *n.m.* continent. **~al** (*m. pl.* **~aux**) /-tal, -to/ *a.* continental.

contingences /kɔ̃tɛ̃ʒɑ̃s/ *n.f. pl.* contingencies.

contingent /kɔ̃tɛ̃ʒɑ̃/ *n.m.* (*mil.*) contingent; (*comm.*) quota.

continu /kɔ̃tiny/ *a.* continuous.

continuel, ~le /kɔ̃tinɥɛl/ *a.* continual. **~lement** *adv.* continually.

contin|uer /kɔ̃tinɥe/ *v.t.* continue. • *v.i.* continue, go on. **~uer à** *ou* **de faire,** carry on *ou* go on *ou* continue doing. **~uation** *n.f.* continuation.

continuité /kɔ̃tinɥite/ *n.f.* continuity.

contorsion /kɔ̃tɔrsjɔ̃/ *n.f.* contortion. **se ~ner** *v. pr.* wriggle.

contour /kɔ̃tur/ *n.m.* outline, contour. **~s,** (*d'une route etc.*) twists and turns, bends.

contourner /kɔ̃turne/ *v.t.* go round; (*difficulté*) get round.

contracepti|f, ~ve /kɔ̃trasɛptif, -v/ *a. & n.m.* contraceptive.

contraception /kɔ̃trasɛpsjɔ̃/ *n.f.* contraception.

contract|er /kɔ̃trakte/ *v.t.* (*maladie, dette*) contract; (*muscle*) tense, contract; (*assurance*) take out. **se ~er** *v. pr.* contract. **~é** *a.* tense. **~ion** /-ksjɔ̃/ *n.f.* contraction.

contractuel, ~le /kɔ̃traktɥɛl/ *n.m., f.* (*agent*) traffic warden.

contradiction /kɔ̃tradiksjɔ̃/ *n.f.* contradiction.

contradictoire /kɔ̃tradiktwar/ *a.* contradictory; (*débat*) open.

contraignant, ~e /kɔ̃trɛɲɑ̃, -t/ *a.* restricting.

contraindre† /kɔ̃trɛ̃dr/ *v.t.* compel.

contraint, ~e /kɔ̃trɛ̃, -t/ *a.* constrained. • *n.f.* constraint.

contraire /kɔ̃trɛr/ *a. & n.m.* opposite. **~ à,** contrary to. **au ~,** on the contrary. **~ment** *adv.* **~ment à,** contrary to.

contralto /kɔ̃tralto/ *n.m.* contralto.

contrar|ier /kɔ̃trarje/ *v.t.* annoy; (*action*) frustrate. **~iété** *n.f.* annoyance.

contrast|e /kɔ̃trast/ *n.m.* contrast. **~er** *v.i.* contrast.

contrat /kɔ̃tra/ *n.m.* contract.

contravention /kɔ̃travɑ̃sjɔ̃/ *n.f.* (parking-)ticket. **en ~,** in contravention (**à,** of).

contre /kɔ̃tr(ə)/ *prép.* against; (*en échange de*) for. **par ~,** on the other hand. **tout ~,** close by. **~-attaque** *n.f.*, **~-attaquer** *v.t.* counter-attack. **~-balancer** *v.t.* counterbalance. **~-courant** *n.m.* **aller à ~-courant de,** swim against the current of. **~indiqué** *a.* (*méd.*) contra-indicated; (*déconseillé*) not recommended. **à ~-jour** *adv.* against the (sun)light. **~-offensive** *n.f.* counter-offensive. **prendre le ~-pied,** do the opposite; (*opinion*) take the opposite view. **à ~-pied** *adv.* (*sport*) on the wrong foot. **~plaqué** *n.m.* plywood. **~-révolution** *n.f.* counter-revolution. **~-torpilleur** *n.m.* destroyer.

contreband|e /kɔ̃trəbɑ̃d/ *n.f.* contraband. **faire la ~e de, passer en ~e,** smuggle. **~ier** *n.m.* smuggler.

contrebas (en) /(ɑ̃)kɔ̃trəbɑ/ *adv. & prép.* **en ~ (de),** below.

contrebasse /kɔ̃trəbɑs/ *n.f.* double-bass.

contrecarrer /kɔ̃trəkare/ *v.t.* thwart.

contrecœur (à) /(a)kɔ̃trəkœr/ *adv.* reluctantly.

contrecoup /kɔ̃trəku/ *n.m.* consequence.

contredire† /kɔ̃trədir/ *v.t.* contradict. **se ~** *v. pr.* contradict o.s.

contrée /kɔ̃tre/ *n.f.* region, land.

contrefaçon /kɔ̃trəfasɔ̃/ *n.f.* (*objet imité, action*) forgery.

contrefaire /kɔ̃trəfɛr/ *v.t.* (*falsifier*) forge; (*parodier*) mimic; (*déguiser*) disguise.

contrefait, ~e /kɔ̃trəfɛ, -t/ *a.* deformed.

contreforts /kɔ̃trəfɔr/ *n.m. pl.* foothills.

contremaître /kɔ̃trəmɛtr/ *n.m.* foreman.

contrepartie /kɔ̃trəparti/ *n.f.* compensation. **en ~,** in exchange, in return.

contrepoids /kɔ̃trəpwa/ *n.m.* counterbalance.

contrer /kɔ̃tre/ *v.t.* counter.

contresens /kɔ̃trəsɑ̃s/ *n.m.* misinterpretation; (*absurdité*) nonsense. **à ~,** the wrong way.

contresigner /kɔ̃trəsiɲe/ *v.t.* countersign.

contretemps /kɔ̃trətɑ̃/ *n.m.* hitch. **à ~,** at the wrong time.
contrevenir /kɔ̃trəvnir/ *v.i.* **~ à,** contravene.
contribuable /kɔ̃tribɥabl/ *n.m./f.* taxpayer.
contribuer /kɔ̃tribɥe/ *v.t.* contribute (**à,** to, towards).
contribution /kɔ̃tribysjɔ̃/ *n.f.* contribution. **~s,** (*impôts*) taxes; (*administration*) tax office.
contrit, ~e /kɔ̃tri, -t/ *a.* contrite.
contrôl|e /kɔ̃trol/ *n.m.* check; (*des prix, d'un véhicule*) control; (*poinçon*) hallmark; (*scol.*) test. **~e continu,** continuous assessment. **~e de soi-même,** self-control. **~e des changes,** exchange control. **~e des naissances** birth-control. **~er** *v.t.* check; (*surveiller, maîtriser*) control. **se ~er** *v. pr.* control o.s.
contrôleu|r, ~se /kɔ̃trolœr, -øz/ *n.m., f.* (bus) conductor *ou* conductress; (*de train*) (ticket) inspector.
contrordre /kɔ̃trɔrdr/ *n.m.* change of orders.
controvers|e /kɔ̃trɔvɛrs/ *n.f.* controversy. **~é** *a.* controversial.
contumace (par) /(par)kɔ̃tymas/ *adv.* in one's absence.
contusion /kɔ̃tyzjɔ̃/ *n.f.* bruise. **~né** /-jɔne/ *a.* bruised.
convaincre† /kɔ̃vɛ̃kr/ *v.t.* convince. **~ qn. de faire,** persuade s.o. to do.
convalescen|t, ~te /kɔ̃valesɑ̃, -t/ *a. & n.m., f.* convalescent. **~ce** *n.f.* convalescence. **être en ~ce,** convalesce.
convenable /kɔ̃vnabl/ *a.* (*correct*) decent, proper; (*approprié*) suitable.
convenance /kɔ̃vnɑ̃s/ *n.f.* **à sa ~,** to one's satisfaction. **les ~s,** the proprieties.
convenir† /kɔ̃vnir/ *v.i.* be suitable. **~ à** suit. **~ de/que,** (*avouer*) admit (to)/that. **~ de qch.,** (*s'accorder sur*) agree on sth. **~ de faire,** agree to do. **il convient de,** it is advisable to; (*selon les bienséances*) it would be right to.
convention /kɔ̃vɑ̃sjɔ̃/ *n.f.* convention. **~s,** (*convenances*) convention. **de ~,** conventional. **~ collective,** industrial agreement. **~né** *a.* (*prix*) official; (*médecin*) health service (*not private*). **~nel, ~nelle** /-jɔnɛl/ *a.* conventional.
convenu /kɔ̃vny/ *a.* agreed.
converger /kɔ̃vɛrʒe/ *v.i.* converge.
convers|er /kɔ̃vɛrse/ *v.i.* converse. **~ation** *n.f.* conversation.
conver|tir /kɔ̃vɛrtir/ *v.t.* convert (**à,** to; **en,** into). **se ~tir** *v. pr.* be converted, convert. **~sion** *n.f.* conversion. **~tible** *a.* convertible.
convexe /kɔ̃vɛks/ *a.* convex.
conviction /kɔ̃viksjɔ̃/ *n.f.* conviction.
convier /kɔ̃vje/ *v.t.* invite.
convive /kɔ̃viv/ *n.m./f.* guest.
conviv|ial (*m. pl.* **~iaux**) /kɔ̃vivjal, -jo/ *a.* convivial; (*comput.*) user-friendly.
convocation /kɔ̃vɔkɑsjɔ̃/ *n.f.* summons to attend; (*d'une assemblée*) convening; (*document*) notification to attend.
convoi /kɔ̃vwa/ *n.m.* convoy; (*train*) train. **~ (funèbre),** funeral procession.
convoit|er /kɔ̃vwate/ *v.t.* desire, covet, envy. **~ise** *n.f.* desire, envy.
convoquer /kɔ̃vɔke/ *v.t.* (*assemblée*) convene; (*personne*) summon.
convoy|er /kɔ̃vwaje/ *v.t.* escort. **~eur** *n.m.* escort ship. **~eur de fonds,** security guard.
convulsion /kɔ̃vylsjɔ̃/ *n.f.* convulsion.
cool /kul/ *a. invar.* cool, laidback.
coopérati|f, ~ve /kɔɔperatif, -v/ *a.* co-operative. ● *n.f.* co-operative (society).
coopér|er /kɔɔpere/ *v.i.* co-operate (**à,** in). **~ation** *n.f.* co-operation. **la C~ation,** civilian national service.
coopter /kɔɔpte/ *v.t.* co-opt.
coordination /kɔɔrdinɑsjɔ̃/ *n.f.* co-ordination.
coordonn|er /kɔɔrdɔne/ *v.t.* co-ordinate. **~ées** *n.f. pl.* co-ordinates; (*adresse*: *fam.*) particulars.
copain /kɔpɛ̃/ *n.m.* (*fam.*) pal; (*petit ami*) boyfriend.
copeau (*pl.* **~x**) /kɔpo/ *n.m.* (*lamelle de bois*) shaving.
cop|ie /kɔpi/ *n.f.* copy; (*scol.*) paper. **~ier** *v.t./i.* copy. **~ier sur,** (*scol.*) copy *ou* crib from.
copieu|x, ~se /kɔpjø, -z/ *a.* copious.
copine /kɔpin/ *n.f.* (*fam.*) pal; (*petite amie*) girlfriend.
copiste /kɔpist/ *n.m./f.* copyist.
coproduction /kɔprɔdyksjɔ̃/ *n.f.* co-production.
copropriété /kɔprɔprijete/ *n.f.* co-ownership.
copulation /kɔpylɑsjɔ̃/ *n.f.* copulation.

coq /kɔk/ *n.m.* cock. **~-à-l'âne** *n.m. invar.* abrupt change of subject.

coque /kɔk/ *n.f.* shell; (*de bateau*) hull.

coquelicot /kɔkliko/ *n.m.* poppy.

coqueluche /kɔklyʃ/ *n.f.* whooping cough.

coquet, ~te /kɔkɛ, -t/ *a.* flirtatious; (*élégant*) pretty; (*somme: fam.*) tidy. **~terie** /-tri/ *n.f.* flirtatiousness.

coquetier /kɔktje/ *n.m.* egg-cup.

coquillage /kɔkijaʒ/ *n.m.* shellfish; (*coquille*) shell.

coquille /kɔkij/ *n.f.* shell; (*faute*) misprint. **~ Saint-Jacques,** scallop.

coquin, ~e /kɔkɛ̃, -in/ *a.* naughty. ● *n.m., f.* rascal.

cor /kɔr/ *n.m.* (*mus.*) horn; (*au pied*) corn.

cor|ail (*pl.* **~aux**) /kɔraj, -o/ *n.m.* coral.

Coran /kɔrɑ̃/ *n.m.* Koran.

corbeau (*pl.* **~x**) /kɔrbo/ *n.m.* (*oiseau*) crow.

corbeille /kɔrbɛj/ *n.f.* basket. **~ à papier,** waste-paper basket.

corbillard /kɔrbijar/ *n.m.* hearse.

cordage /kɔrdaʒ/ *n.m.* rope. **~s,** (*naut.*) rigging.

corde /kɔrd/ *n.f.* rope; (*d'arc, de violon, etc.*) string. **~ à linge,** washing line. **~ à sauter,** skipping-rope. **~ raide,** tightrope. **~s vocales,** vocal cords.

cordée /kɔrde/ *n.f.* roped party.

cord|ial (*m. pl.* **~iaux**) /kɔrdjal, -jo/ *a.* warm, cordial. **~ialité** *n.f.* warmth.

cordon /kɔrdɔ̃/ *n.m.* string, cord. **~-bleu** (*pl.* **~s-bleus**) *n.m.* first-rate cook. **~ de police,** police cordon.

cordonnier /kɔrdɔnje/ *n.m.* shoe mender.

Corée /kɔre/ *n.f.* Korea.

coreligionnaire /kɔrəliʒjɔnɛr/ *n.m./f.* person of the same religion.

coriace /kɔrjas/ *a.* (*aliment*) tough. ● *a. & n.m.* tenacious and tough (person).

corne /kɔrn/ *n.f.* horn.

cornée /kɔrne/ *n.f.* cornea.

corneille /kɔrnɛj/ *n.f.* crow.

cornemuse /kɔrnəmyz/ *n.f.* bagpipes.

corner[1] /kɔrne/ *v.t.* (*page*) make dog-eared. ● *v.i.* (*auto.*) hoot; (*auto., Amer.*) honk.

corner[2] /kɔrnɛr/ *n.m.* (*football*) corner.

cornet /kɔrnɛ/ *n.m.* (paper) cone; (*crème glacée*) cornet, cone.

corniaud /kɔrnjo/ *n.m.* (*fam.*) nitwit.

corniche /kɔrniʃ/ *n.f.* cornice; (*route*) cliff road.

cornichon /kɔrniʃɔ̃/ *n.m.* gherkin.

corollaire /kɔrɔlɛr/ *n.m.* corollary.

corporation /kɔrpɔrɑsjɔ̃/ *n.f.* professional body.

corporel, ~le /kɔrpɔrɛl/ *a.* bodily; (*châtiment*) corporal.

corps /kɔr/ *n.m.* body; (*mil., pol.*) corps. **~ à corps,** hand to hand. **~ électoral,** electorate. **~ enseignant,** teaching profession. **faire ~ avec,** form part of.

corpulen|t, ~te /kɔrpylɑ̃, -t/ *a.* stout. **~ce** *n.f.* stoutness.

correct /kɔrɛkt/ *a.* proper, correct; (*exact*) correct; (*tenue*) decent. **~ement** *adv.* properly; correctly; decently.

correc|teur, ~trice /kɔrɛktœr, -tris/ *n.m., f.* (*d'épreuves*) proof-reader; (*scol.*) examiner. **~teur d'orthographe,** spelling checker.

correction /kɔrɛksjɔ̃/ *n.f.* correction; (*punition*) beating.

corrélation /kɔrelɑsjɔ̃/ *n.f.* correlation.

correspondan|t, ~te /kɔrɛspɔ̃dɑ̃, -t/ *a.* corresponding. ● *n.m., f.* correspondent; (*au téléphone*) caller. **~ce** *n.f.* correspondence; (*de train, d'autobus*) connection. **vente par ~ce,** mail order.

correspondre /kɔrɛspɔ̃dr/ *v.i.* (*s'accorder, écrire*) correspond; (*chambres*) communicate.

corrida /kɔrida/ *n.f.* bullfight.

corridor /kɔridɔr/ *n.m.* corridor.

corrig|er /kɔriʒe/ *v.t.* correct; (*devoir*) mark, correct; (*punir*) beat; (*guérir*) cure. **se ~er de,** cure o.s. of. **~é** *n.m.* (*scol.*) correct version, model answer.

corroborer /kɔrɔbɔre/ *v.t.* corroborate.

corro|der /kɔrɔde/ *v.t.* corrode. **~sion** /-ozjɔ̃/ *n.f.* corrosion.

corromp|re† /kɔrɔ̃pr/ *v.t.* corrupt; (*soudoyer*) bribe. **~u** *a.* corrupt.

corrosi|f, ~ve /kɔrozif, -v/ *a.* corrosive.

corruption /kɔrypsjɔ̃/ *n.f.* corruption.

corsage /kɔrsaʒ/ *n.m.* bodice; (*chemisier*) blouse.

corsaire /kɔrsɛr/ *n.m.* pirate.

Corse /kɔrs/ *n.f.* Corsica.

corse /kɔrs/ *a.* & *n.m./f.* Corsican.

corsé /kɔrse/ *a.* (*vin*) full-bodied; (*scabreux*) spicy.

corset /kɔrsɛ/ *n.m.* corset.

cortège /kɔrtɛʒ/ *n.m.* procession.

cortisone /kɔrtizɔn/ *n.f.* cortisone.

corvée /kɔrve/ *n.f.* chore.

cosaque /kɔzak/ *n.m.* Cossack.

cosmétique /kɔsmetik/ *n.m.* cosmetic.

cosmique /kɔsmik/ *a.* cosmic.

cosmonaute /kɔsmɔnot/ *n.m./f.* cosmonaut.

cosmopolite /kɔsmɔpɔlit/ *a.* cosmopolitan.

cosmos /kɔsmos/ *n.m.* (*espace*) (outer) space; (*univers*) cosmos.

cosse /kɔs/ *n.f.* (*de pois*) pod.

cossu /kɔsy/ *a.* (*gens*) well-to-do; (*demeure*) opulent.

costaud, ~e /kɔsto, -d/ *a.* (*fam.*) strong. ● *n.m.* (*fam.*) strong man.

costum|e /kɔstym/ *n.m.* suit; (*théâtre*) costume. **~é** *a.* dressed up.

cote /kɔt/ *n.f.* (classification) mark; (*en Bourse*) quotation; (*de cheval*) odds (**de**, on); (*de candidat, acteur*) rating. **~ d'alerte,** danger level.

côte /kot/ *n.f.* (*littoral*) coast; (*pente*) hill; (*anat.*) rib; (*de porc*) chop. **~ à côte,** side by side. **la C~ d'Azur,** the (French) Riviera.

côté /kote/ *n.m.* side; (*direction*) way. **à ~,** nearby; (*voisin*) nextdoor. **à ~ de,** next to; (*comparé à*) compared to; (*cible*) wide of. **aux ~s de,** by the side of. **de ~,** aside; (*regarder*) sideways. **mettre de ~,** put aside. **de ce ~,** this way. **de chaque ~,** on each side. **de tous les ~s,** on every side; (*partout*) everywhere. **du ~ de,** towards; (*proximité*) near; (*provenance*) from.

coteau (*pl.* **~x**) /kɔto/ *n.m.* hill.

côtelette /kotlɛt/ *n.f.* chop.

coter /kɔte/ *v.t.* (*comm.*) quote; (*apprécier, noter*) rate.

coterie /kɔtri/ *n.f.* clique.

côt|ier, ~ière /kotje, -jɛr/ *a.* coastal.

cotis|er /kɔtize/ *v.i.* pay one's contributions (**à**, to); (*à un club*) pay one's subscription. **se ~er** *v. pr.* club together. **~ation** *n.f.* contribution(s); subscription.

coton /kɔtɔ̃/ *n.m.* cotton. **~ hydrophile,** cotton wool.

côtoyer /kotwaje/ *v.t.* skirt, run along; (*fréquenter*) rub shoulders with; (*fig.*) verge on.

cotte /kɔt/ *n.f.* (*d'ouvrier*) overalls.

cou /ku/ *n.m.* neck.

couchage /kuʃaʒ/ *n.m.* sleeping arrangements.

couchant /kuʃɑ̃/ *n.m.* sunset.

couche /kuʃ/ *n.f.* layer; (*de peinture*) coat; (*de bébé*) nappy. **~s,** (*méd.*) childbirth. **~s sociales,** social strata.

coucher /kuʃe/ *n.m.* **~ (du soleil),** sunset. ● *v.t.* put to bed; (*loger*) put up; (*étendre*) lay down. **~ (par écrit),** set down. ● *v.i.* sleep. **se ~** *v. pr.* go to bed; (*s'étendre*) lie down; (*soleil*) set. **couché** *a.* in bed; (*étendu*) lying down.

couchette /kuʃɛt/ *n.f.* (*rail.*) couchette; (*naut.*) bunk.

coucou /kuku/ *n.m.* cuckoo.

coude /kud/ *n.m.* elbow; (*de rivière etc.*) bend. **~ à coude,** side by side.

cou-de-pied (*pl.* **cous-de-pied**) /kudpje/ *n.m.* instep.

coudoyer /kudwaje/ *v.t.* rub shoulders with.

coudre† /kudr/ *v.t./i.* sew.

couenne /kwan/ *n.f.* (*de porc*) rind.

couette /kwɛt/ *n.f.* duvet, continental quilt.

couffin /kufɛ̃/ *n.m.* Moses basket.

couiner /kwine/ *v.i.* squeak.

coulant, ~e /kulɑ̃, -t/ *a.* (*indulgent*) easy-going; (*fromage*) runny.

coulée /kule/ *n.f.* **~ de lave,** lava flow.

couler[1] /kule/ *v.i.* flow, run; (*fromage, nez*) run; (*fuir*) leak. ● *v.t.* (*sculpture, métal*) cast; (*vie*) pass, lead. **se ~** *v. pr.* (*se glisser*) slip.

couler[2] /kule/ *v.t./i.* (*bateau*) sink.

couleur /kulœr/ *n.f.* colour; (*peinture*) paint; (*cartes*) suit. **~s,** (*teint*) colour. **de ~,** (*homme, femme*) coloured. **en ~s,** (*télévision, film*) colour.

couleuvre /kulœvr/ *n.f.* (grass *ou* smooth) snake.

coulis /kuli/ *n.m.* (*culin.*) coulis.

couliss|e /kulis/ *n.f.* (*de tiroir etc.*) runner. **~es,** (*théâtre*) wings. **à ~e,** (*porte, fenêtre*) sliding. **~er** *v.i.* slide.

couloir /kulwar/ *n.m.* corridor; (*de bus*) gangway; (*sport*) lane.

coup /ku/ *n.m.* blow; (*choc*) knock; (*sport*) stroke; (*de crayon, chance, cloche*) stroke; (*de fusil, pistolet*) shot; (*fois*) time; (*aux échecs*) move. **à ~ sûr,** definitely. **après ~,** after the event. **boire un ~,** have a drink. **~ de chiffon,** wipe (with a rag). **~ de coude,** nudge. **~ de couteau,** stab. **~ d'envoi,** kick-off. **~ d'état** (*pol.*) coup. **~ de feu,** shot. **~ de fil,** phone call. **~ de filet,** haul. **~ de frein,** sudden braking. **~ de grâce,** coup de grâce. **~ de main,** helping hand. **avoir le ~ de main,** have the knack. **~ d'œil,** glance. **~ de pied,** kick. **~ de poing,** punch. **~ de sang,** (*méd.*) stroke. **~ de soleil,** sunburn. **~ de sonnette,** ring (on a bell). **~ de téléphone,** (tele)phone call. **~ de tête,** wild impulse. **~ de théâtre,** dramatic event. **~ de tonnerre,** thunderclap. **~ de vent,** gust of wind. **~ franc,** free kick. **~ sur coup,** in rapid succession. **d'un seul ~,** in one go. **du premier ~,** first go. **sale ~,** dirty trick. **sous le ~ de,** under the influence of. **sur le ~,** immediately. **tenir le coup,** take it.

coupable /kupabl/ *a.* guilty. ● *n.m./f.* culprit.

coupe[1] /kup/ *n.f.* cup; (*de champagne*) goblet; (*à fruits*) dish.

coupe[2] /kup/ *n.f.* (*de vêtement etc.*) cut; (*dessin*) section. **~ de cheveux,** haircut.

coupé /kupe/ *n.m.* (*voiture*) coupé.

coup|er /kupe/ *v.t./i.* cut; (*arbre*) cut down; (*arrêter*) cut off; (*voyage*) break; (*appétit*) take away; (*vin*) water down. **~er par,** take a short cut via. **se ~er** *v. pr.* cut o.s.; (*routes*) intersect. **~er la parole à,** cut short. **~e-papier** *n.m. invar.* paper-knife.

couperosé /kuproze/ *a.* blotchy.

couple /kupl/ *n.m.* couple.

coupler /kuple/ *v.t.* couple.

couplet /kuplɛ/ *n.m.* verse.

coupole /kupɔl/ *n.f.* dome.

coupon /kupɔ̃/ *n.m.* (*étoffe*) remnant; (*billet, titre*) coupon.

coupure /kupyr/ *n.f.* cut; (*billet de banque*) note; (*de presse*) cutting. **~ (de courant),** power cut.

cour /kur/ *n.f.* (court)yard; (*de roi*) court; (*tribunal*) court. **~ (de récréation),** playground. **~ martiale,** court martial. **faire la ~ à,** court.

courag|e /kuraʒ/ *n.m.* courage. **~eux, ~euse** *a.* courageous.

couramment /kuramɑ̃/ *adv.* frequently; (*parler*) fluently.

courant[1]**, ~e** /kurɑ̃, -t/ *a.* standard, ordinary; (*en cours*) current.

courant[2] /kurɑ̃/ *n.m.* current; (*de mode, d'idées*) trend. **~ d'air,** draught. **dans le ~ de,** in the course of. **être/mettre au ~ de,** know/tell about; (*à jour*) be/bring up to date on.

courbatur|e /kurbatyr/ *n.f.* ache. **~é** *a.* aching.

courbe /kurb/ *n.f.* curve. ● *a.* curved.

courber /kurbe/ *v.t./i.,* **se ~** *v. pr.* bend.

coureu|r, ~se /kurœr, -øz/ *n.m., f.* (*sport*) runner. **~r automobile,** racing driver. ● *n.m.* womanizer.

courge /kurʒ/ *n.f.* marrow; (*Amer.*) squash.

courgette /kurʒɛt/ *n.f.* courgette; (*Amer.*) zucchini.

courir† /kurir/ *v.i.* run; (*se hâter*) rush; (*nouvelles etc.*) go round. ● *v.t.* (*risque*) run; (*danger*) face; (*épreuve sportive*) run *ou* compete in; (*fréquenter*) do the rounds of; (*filles*) chase.

couronne /kurɔn/ *n.f.* crown; (*de fleurs*) wreath.

couronn|er /kurɔne/ *v.t.* crown. **~ement** *n.m.* coronation, crowning; (*fig.*) crowning achievement.

courrier /kurje/ *n.m.* post, mail; (*à écrire*) letters; (*de journal*) column.

courroie /kurwa/ *n.f.* strap; (*techn.*) belt.

courroux /kuru/ *n.m.* wrath.

cours /kur/ *n.m.* (*leçon*) class; (*série de leçons*) course; (*prix*) price; (*cote*) rate; (*déroulement, d'une rivière*) course; (*allée*) avenue. **au ~ de,** in the course of. **avoir ~,** (*monnaie*) be legal tender; (*fig.*) be current; (*scol.*) have a lesson. **~ d'eau,** river, stream. **~ du soir,** evening class. **~ magistral,** (*univ.*) lecture. **en ~,** current; (*travail*) in progress. **en ~ de route,** on the way.

course /kurs/ *n.f.* run(ning); (*épreuve de vitesse*) race; (*entre rivaux: fig.*) race; (*de projectile*) flight; (*voyage*) journey; (*commission*) errand. **~s,**

(*achats*) shopping; (*de chevaux*) races.
coursier, ~ère /kursje, -jɛr/ *n.m., f.* messenger.
court[1]**, ~e** /kur, -t/ *a.* short. ● *adv.* short. **à ~ de,** short of. **pris de ~,** caught unawares. **~-circuit** (*pl.* **~s-circuits**) *n.m.* short circuit.
court[2] /kur/ *n.m.* **~ (de tennis),** (tennis) court.
courtier, ~ière /kurtje, -jɛr/ *n.m., f.* broker.
courtisan /kurtizɑ̃/ *n.m.* courtier.
courtisane /kurtizan/ *n.f.* courtesan.
courtiser /kurtize/ *v.t.* court.
courtois, ~e /kurtwa, -z/ *a.* courteous. **~ie** /-zi/ *n.f.* courtesy.
couscous /kuskus/ *n.m.* couscous.
cousin, ~e /kuzɛ̃, -in/ *n.m., f.* cousin. **~ germain,** first cousin.
coussin /kusɛ̃/ *n.m.* cushion.
coût /ku/ *n.m.* cost.
couteau (*pl.* **~x**) /kuto/ *n.m.* knife. **~ à cran d'arrêt,** flick-knife.
coutellerie /kutɛlri/ *n.f.* (*magasin*) cutlery shop.
coûter /kute/ *v.t./i.* cost. **~e que coûte,** at all costs. **au prix ~ant,** at cost (price). **~eux, ~euse** *a.* costly.
coutume /kutym/ *n.f.* custom. **~ier, ~ière** *a.* customary.
couture /kutyr/ *n.f.* sewing; (*métier*) dressmaking; (*points*) seam. **~ier** *n.m.* fashion designer. **~ière** *n.f.* dressmaker.
couvée /kuve/ *n.f.* brood.
couvent /kuvɑ̃/ *n.m.* convent; (*de moines*) monastery.
couver /kuve/ *v.t.* (*œufs*) hatch; (*personne*) pamper; (*maladie*) be coming down with, be sickening for. ● *v.i.* (*feu*) smoulder; (*mal*) be brewing.
couvercle /kuvɛrkl/ *n.m.* (*de marmite, boîte*) lid; (*d'objet allongé*) top.
couvert[1]**, ~e** /kuvɛr, -t/ *a.* covered (**de,** with); (*habillé*) covered up; (*ciel*) overcast. ● *n.m.* (*abri*) cover. **à ~,** (*mil.*) under cover. **à ~ de,** (*fig.*) safe from.
couvert[2] /kuvɛr/ *n.m.* (*à table*) place-setting; (*prix*) cover charge. **~s,** (*couteaux etc.*) cutlery. **mettre le ~,** lay the table.
couverture /kuvɛrtyr/ *n.f.* cover; (*de lit*) blanket; (*toit*) roofing. **~ chauffante,** electric blanket.
couveuse /kuvøz/ *n.f.* **~ (artificielle),** incubator.
couvreur /kuvrœr/ *n.m.* roofer.
couvrir† /kuvrir/ *v.t.* cover. **se ~ir** *v. pr.* (*s'habiller*) cover up; (*se coiffer*) put one's hat on; (*ciel*) become overcast. **~e-chef** *n.m.* hat. **~e-feu** (*pl.* **~e-feux**) *n.m.* curfew. **~e-lit** *n.m.* bedspread.
cow-boy /kobɔj/ *n.m.* cowboy.
crabe /krab/ *n.m.* crab.
crachat /kraʃa/ *n.m.* spit(tle).
cracher /kraʃe/ *v.i.* spit; (*radio*) crackle. ● *v.t.* spit (out).
crachin /kraʃɛ̃/ *n.m.* drizzle.
crack /krak/ *n.m.* (*fam.*) wizard, ace, prodigy.
craie /krɛ/ *n.f.* chalk.
craindre† /krɛ̃dr/ *v.t.* be afraid of, fear; (*être sensible à*) be easily damaged by.
crainte /krɛ̃t/ *n.f.* fear. **de ~ de/que,** for fear of/that.
craintif, ~ve /krɛ̃tif, -v/ *a.* timid.
cramoisi /kramwazi/ *a.* crimson.
crampe /krɑ̃p/ *n.f.* cramp.
crampon /krɑ̃pɔ̃/ *n.m.* (*de chaussure*) stud.
cramponner (se) /(sə)krɑ̃pɔne/ *v. pr.* **se ~ à,** cling to.
cran /krɑ̃/ *n.m.* (*entaille*) notch; (*trou*) hole; (*courage: fam.*) pluck.
crâne /krɑn/ *n.m.* skull.
crâner /krɑne/ *v.i.* (*fam.*) swank.
crapaud /krapo/ *n.m.* toad.
crapule /krapyl/ *n.f.* villain. **~eux, ~euse** *a.* sordid, foul.
craquer /krake/ *v.i.* crack, snap; (*plancher*) creak; (*couture*) split; (*fig.*) break down; (*céder*) give in. ● *v.t.* **~er une allumette,** strike a match. **~ement** *n.m.* crack(ing), snap(ping); creak(ing); striking.
crasse /kras/ *n.f.* grime. **~eux, ~euse** *a.* grimy.
cratère /kratɛr/ *n.m.* crater.
cravache /kravaʃ/ *n.f.* horsewhip.
cravate /kravat/ *n.f.* tie.
crawl /krol/ *n.m.* (*nage*) crawl.
crayeux, ~se /krɛjø, -z/ *a.* chalky.
crayon /krɛjɔ̃/ *n.m.* pencil. **~ (de couleur),** crayon. **~ à bille,** ball-point pen. **~ optique,** light pen.
créancier, ~ière /kreɑ̃sje, -jɛr/ *n.m., f.* creditor.
créateur, ~trice /kreatœr, -tris/ *a.* creative. ● *n.m., f.* creator.
création /kreɑsjɔ̃/ *n.f.* creation; (*comm.*) product.
créature /kreatyr/ *n.f.* creature.

crèche /krɛʃ/ *n.f.* day nursery; (*relig.*) crib.
crédibilité /kredibilite/ *n.f.* credibility.
crédit /kredi/ *n.m.* credit; (*banque*) bank. **~s,** funds. **à ~,** on credit. **faire ~,** give credit (à, to). **~er** /-te/ *v.t.* credit. **~eur, ~euse** /-tœr, -tøz/ *a.* in credit.
credo /kredo/ *n.m.* creed.
crédule /kredyl/ *a.* credulous.
créer /kree/ *v.t.* create.
crémation /kremɑsjɔ̃/ *n.f.* cremation.
crème /krɛm/ *n.f.* cream; (*dessert*) cream dessert. ● *a. invar.* cream. ● *n.m.* **(café) ~,** white coffee. **~ anglaise,** fresh custard. **~ à raser,** shaving-cream.
crémeu|x, ~se /kremø, -z/ *a.* creamy.
crém|ier, ~ière /kremje, -jɛr/ *n.m., f.* dairyman, dairywoman. **~erie** /krɛmri/ *n.f.* dairy.
créneau (*pl.* **~x**) /kreno/ *n.m.* (*trou, moment*) slot; (*dans le marché*) gap; **faire un ~,** park between two cars.
créole /kreɔl/ *n.m./f.* Creole.
crêpe[1] /krɛp/ *n.f.* (*galette*) pancake. **~rie** *n.f.* pancake shop.
crêpe[2] /krɛp/ *n.m.* (*tissu*) crêpe; (*matière*) crêpe (rubber).
crépit|er /krepite/ *v.i.* crackle. **~ement** *n.m.* crackling.
crépu /krepy/ *a.* frizzy.
crépuscule /krepyskyl/ *n.m.* twilight, dusk.
crescendo /kreʃɛndo/ *adv. & n.m. invar.* crescendo.
cresson /kresɔ̃/ *n.m.* (water)cress.
crête /krɛt/ *n.f.* crest; (*de coq*) comb.
crétin, ~e /kretɛ̃, -in/ *n.m., f.* cretin.
creuser /krøzɛ/ *v.t.* dig; (*évider*) hollow out; (*fig.*) go deeply into. **se ~ (la cervelle),** (*fam.*) rack one's brains.
creuset /krøzɛ/ *n.m.* (*lieu*) melting-pot.
creu|x, ~se /krø, -z/ *a.* hollow; (*heures*) off-peak. ● *n.m.* hollow; (*de l'estomac*) pit.
crevaison /krəvɛzɔ̃/ *n.f.* puncture.
crevasse /krəvas/ *n.f.* crack; (*de glacier*) crevasse; (*de la peau*) chap.
crevé /krəve/ *a.* (*fam.*) worn out.
crève-cœur /krɛvkœr/ *n.m. invar.* heart-break.
crever /krəve/ *v.t./i.* burst; (*pneu*) puncture burst; (*exténuer: fam.*) exhaust; (*mourir: fam.*) die; (*œil*) put out.
crevette /krəvɛt/ *n.f.* **~ (grise),** shrimp. **~ (rose),** prawn.
cri /kri/ *n.m.* cry; (*de douleur*) scream, cry.
criant, ~e /krijɑ̃, -t/ *a.* glaring.
criard, ~e /krijar, -d/ *a.* (*couleur*) garish; (*voix*) bawling.
crible /kribl/ *n.m.* sieve, riddle.
criblé /krible/ *a.* **~ de,** riddled with.
cric /krik/ *n.m.* (*auto.*) jack.
crier /krije/ *v.i.* (*fort*) shout, cry (out); (*de douleur*) scream; (*grincer*) creak. ● *v.t.* (*ordre*) shout (out).
crim|e /krim/ *n.m.* crime; (*meurtre*) murder. **~inalité** *n.f.* crime. **~inel, ~inelle** *a.* criminal; *n.m., f.* criminal; (*assassin*) murderer.
crin /krɛ̃/ *n.m.* horsehair.
crinière /krinjɛr/ *n.f.* mane.
crique /krik/ *n.f.* creek.
criquet /krikɛ/ *n.m.* locust.
crise /kriz/ *n.f.* crisis; (*méd.*) attack; (*de colère*) fit. **~ cardiaque,** heart attack. **~ de foie,** bilious attack.
crisp|er /krispe/ *v.t.,* **se ~er** *v. pr.* tense; (*poings*) clench. **~ation** *n.f.* tenseness; (*spasme*) twitch. **~é** *a.* tense.
crisser /krise/ *v.i.* crunch; (*pneu*) screech.
crist|al (*pl.* **~aux**) /kristal, -o/ *n.m.* crystal.
cristallin, ~e /kristalɛ̃, -in/ *a.* (*limpide*) crystal-clear.
cristalliser /kristalize/ *v.t./i.,* **se ~** *v. pr.* crystallize.
critère /kritɛr/ *n.m.* criterion.
critique /kritik/ *a.* critical. ● *n.f.* criticism; (*article*) review. ● *n.m.* critic. **la ~,** (*personnes*) the critics.
critiquer /kritike/ *v.t.* criticize.
croasser /krɔase/ *v.i.* caw.
croc /kro/ *n.m.* (*dent*) fang; (*crochet*) hook.
croc-en-jambe (*pl.* **crocs-en-jambe**) /krɔkɑ̃ʒɑ̃b/ *n.m.* = **croche-pied.**
croche /krɔʃ/ *n.f.* quaver. **double ~,** semiquaver.
croche-pied /krɔʃpje/ *n.m.* **faire un ~ à,** trip up.
crochet /krɔʃɛ/ *n.m.* hook; (*détour*) detour; (*signe*) (square) bracket; (*tricot*) crochet. **faire au ~,** crochet.
crochu /krɔʃy/ *a.* hooked.
crocodile /krɔkɔdil/ *n.m.* crocodile.
crocus /krɔkys/ *n.m.* crocus.

croire† /krwar/ *v.t./i.* believe (**à, en,** in); (*estimer*) think, believe (**que,** that).

croisade /krwazad/ *n.f.* crusade.

croisé /krwaze/ *a.* (*veston*) double-breasted. ● *n.m.* crusader.

croisée /krwaze/ *n.f.* window. **~ des chemins,** crossroads.

crois|er[1] /krwaze/ *v.t.,* **se ~er** *v. pr.* cross; (*passant, véhicule*) pass (each other). **(se) ~er les bras,** fold one's arms. **(se) ~er les jambes,** cross one's legs. **~ement** *n.m.* crossing; passing; (*carrefour*) crossroads.

crois|er[2] /krwaze/ *v.i.* (*bateau*) cruise. **~eur** *n.m.* cruiser. **~ière** *n.f.* cruise.

croissan|t[1], **~te** /krwasɑ̃, -t/ *a.* growing. **~ce** *n.f.* growth.

croissant[2] /krwasɑ̃/ *n.m.* crescent; (*pâtisserie*) croissant.

croître† /krwatr/ *v.i.* grow; (*lune*) wax.

croix /krwa/ *n.f.* cross. **~ gammée,** swastika. **C~-Rouge,** Red Cross.

croque-monsieur /krɔkməsjø/ *n.m. invar.* toasted ham and cheese sandwich.

croque-mort /krɔkmɔr/ *n.m.* (*fam.*) undertaker's assistant.

croqu|er /krɔke/ *v.t./i.* crunch; (*dessiner*) sketch. **chocolat à ~er,** plain chocolate. **~ant, ~ante** *a.* crunchy.

croquet /krɔkɛ/ *n.m.* croquet.

croquette /krɔkɛt/ *n.f.* croquette.

croquis /krɔki/ *n.m.* sketch.

crosse /krɔs/ *n.f.* (*de fusil*) butt; (*d'évêque*) crook.

crotte /krɔt/ *n.f.* droppings.

crotté /krɔte/ *a.* muddy.

crottin /krɔtɛ̃/ *n.m.* (horse) dung.

crouler /krule/ *v.i.* collapse; (*être en ruines*) crumble.

croupe /krup/ *n.f.* rump; (*de colline*) brow. **en ~,** pillion.

croupier /krupje/ *n.m.* croupier.

croupir /krupir/ *v.i.* stagnate.

croustill|er /krustije/ *v.i.* be crusty. **~ant, ~ante** *a.* crusty; (*fig.*) spicy.

croûte /krut/ *n.f.* crust; (*de fromage*) rind; (*de plaie*) scab. **en ~,** (*culin.*) en croûte.

croûton /krutɔ̃/ *n.m.* (*bout de pain*) crust; (*avec potage*) croûton.

croyable /krwajabl/ *a.* credible.

croyan|t, ~te /krwajɑ̃, -t/ *n.m., f.* believer. **~ce** *n.f.* belief.

CRS *abrév.* (*Compagnies républicaines de sécurité*) French state security police.

cru[1] /kry/ *voir* croire.

cru[2] /kry/ *a.* raw; (*lumière*) harsh; (*propos*) crude. ● *n.m.* vineyard; (*vin*) wine.

crû /kry/ *voir* croître.

cruauté /kryote/ *n.f.* cruelty.

cruche /kryʃ/ *n.f.* pitcher.

cruc|ial (*m. pl.* **~iaux**) /krysjal, -jo/ *a.* crucial.

crucif|ier /krysifje/ *v.t.* crucify. **~ixion** *n.f.* crucifixion.

crucifix /krysifi/ *n.m.* crucifix.

crudité /krydite/ *n.f.* (*de langage*) crudeness. **~s,** (*culin.*) raw vegetables.

crue /kry/ *n.f.* rise in water level. **en ~,** in spate.

cruel, ~le /kryɛl/ *a.* cruel.

crûment /krymɑ̃/ *adv.* crudely.

crustacés /krystase/ *n.m. pl.* shellfish.

crypte /kript/ *n.f.* crypt.

Cuba /kyba/ *n.m.* Cuba.

cubain, ~e /kybɛ̃, -ɛn/ *a.* & *n.m., f.* Cuban.

cub|e /kyb/ *n.m.* cube. ● *a.* (*mètre etc.*) cubic. **~ique** *a.* cubic.

cueill|ir† /kœjir/ *v.t.* pick, gather; (*personne*: *fam.*) pick up. **~ette** *n.f.* picking, gathering.

cuill|er, ~ère /kɥijɛr/ *n.f.* spoon. **~er à soupe,** soup-spoon; (*mesure*) tablespoonful. **~erée** *n.f.* spoonful.

cuir /kɥir/ *n.m.* leather. **~ chevelu,** scalp.

cuirassé /kɥirase/ *n.m.* battleship.

cuire /kɥir/ *v.t./i.* cook; (*picoter*) smart. **~ (au four),** bake. **faire ~,** cook.

cuisine /kɥizin/ *n.f.* kitchen; (*art*) cookery, cooking; (*aliments*) cooking. **faire la ~,** cook.

cuisin|er /kɥizine/ *v.t./i.* cook; (*interroger*: *fam.*) grill. **~ier, ~ière** *n.m., f.* cook; *n.f.* (*appareil*) cooker, stove.

cuisse /kɥis/ *n.f.* thigh; (*de poulet, mouton*) leg.

cuisson /kɥisɔ̃/ *n.m.* cooking.

cuit, ~e /kɥi, -t/ *a.* cooked. **bien ~,** well done *ou* cooked. **trop ~,** overdone.

cuivr|e /kɥivr/ *n.m.* copper. **~e (jaune),** brass. **~es,** (*mus.*) brass. **~é** *a.* coppery.

cul /ky/ *n.m.* (*derrière: fam.*) backside, bum.
culasse /kylas/ *n.f.* (*auto.*) cylinder head; (*arme*) breech.
culbut|e /kylbyt/ *n.f.* somersault; (*chute*) tumble. **~er** *v.i.* tumble; *v.t.* knock over.
cul-de-sac (*pl.* **culs-de-sac**) /kydsak/ *n.m.* cul-de-sac.
culinaire /kylinɛr/ *a.* culinary; (*recette*) cooking.
culminer /kylmine/ *v.i.* reach the highest point.
culot[1] /kylo/ *n.m.* (*audace: fam.*) nerve, cheek.
culot[2] /kylo/ *n.m.* (*fond: techn.*) base.
culotte /kylɔt/ *n.f.* (*de femme*) knickers; (*Amer.*) panties. **~ (de cheval),** (riding) breeches. **~ courte,** short trousers.
culpabilité /kylpabilite/ *n.f.* guilt.
culte /kylt/ *n.m.* cult, worship; (*religion*) religion; (*protestant*) service.
cultivé /kyltive/ *a.* cultured.
cultiv|er /kyltive/ *v.t.* cultivate; (*plantes*) grow. **~ateur, ~atrice** *n.m., f.* farmer.
culture /kyltyr/ *n.f.* cultivation; (*de plantes*) growing; (*agriculture*) farming; (*éducation*) culture. **~s,** (*terrains*) lands under cultivation. **~ physique,** physical training.
culturel, ~le /kyltyrɛl/ *a.* cultural.
cumuler /kymyle/ *v.t.* (*fonctions*) hold simultaneously.
cupide /kypid/ *a.* grasping.
cure /kyr/ *n.f.* (course of) treatment, cure.
curé /kyre/ *n.m.* (parish) priest.
cur|er /kyre/ *v.t.* clean. **se ~er les dents/ongles,** clean one's teeth/ nails. **~e-dent** *n.m.* toothpick. **~e-pipe** *n.m.* pipe-cleaner.
curieu|x, ~se /kyrjø, -z/ *a.* curious. ● *n.m., f.* (*badaud*) onlooker. **~sement** *adv.* curiously.
curiosité /kyrjozite/ *n.f.* curiosity; (*objet*) curio; (*spectacle*) unusual sight.
curriculum vitae /kyrikylɔm vite/ *n.m. invar.* curriculum vitae.
curseur /kyrsœr/ *n.m.* cursor.
cutané /kytane/ *a.* skin.
cuve /kyv/ *n.f.* tank.
cuvée /kyve/ *n.f.* (*de vin*) vintage.
cuvette /kyvɛt/ *n.f.* bowl; (*de lavabo*) (wash-)basin; (*des cabinets*) pan, bowl.
CV /seve/ *n.m.* CV.
cyanure /sjanyr/ *n.m.* cyanide.
cybernétique /sibɛrnetik/ *n.f.* cybernetics.
cycl|e /sikl/ *n.m.* cycle. **~ique** *a.* cyclic(al).
cyclis|te /siklist/ *n.m./f.* cyclist. ● *a.* cycle. **~me** *n.m.* cycling.
cyclomoteur /syklɔmɔtœr/ *n.m.* moped.
cyclone /siklon/ *n.m.* cyclone.
cygne /siɲ/ *n.m.* swan.
cylindr|e /silɛ̃dr/ *n.m.* cylinder. **~ique** *a.* cylindrical.
cylindrée /silɛ̃dre/ *n.f.* (*de moteur*) capacity.
cymbale /sɛ̃bal/ *n.f.* cymbal.
cystite /sistit/ *n.f.* cystitis.
cyni|que /sinik/ *a.* cynical. ● *n.m.* cynic. **~sme** *n.m.* cynicism.
cyprès /siprɛ/ *n.m.* cypress.
cypriote /siprijɔt/ *a.* & *n.m./f.* Cypriot.

D

d' /d/ *voir* de.
d'abord /dabɔr/ *adv.* first; (*au début*) at first.
dactylo /daktilo/ *n.f.* typist. **~(graphie)** *n.f.* typing. **~graphe** *n.f.* typist. **~graphier** *v.t.* type.
dada /dada/ *n.m.* hobby-horse.
dahlia /dalja/ *n.m.* dahlia.
daigner /deɲe/ *v.t.* deign.
daim /dɛ̃/ *n.m.* (fallow) deer; (*cuir*) suede.
dall|e /dal/ *n.f.* paving stone, slab. **~age** *n.m.* paving.
daltonien, ~ne /daltɔnjɛ̃, -jɛn/ *a.* colour-blind.
dame /dam/ *n.f.* lady; (*cartes, échecs*) queen. **~s,** (*jeu*) draughts; (*jeu: Amer.*) checkers.
damier /damje/ *n.m.* draught-board; (*Amer.*) checker-board. **à ~,** chequered.
damn|er /dɑne/ *v.t.* damn. **~ation** *n.f.* damnation.
dancing /dɑ̃siŋ/ *n.m.* dance-hall.
dandiner (se) /(sə)dɑ̃dine/ *v. pr.* waddle.
Danemark /danmark/ *n.m.* Denmark.
danger /dɑ̃ʒe/ *n.m.* danger. **en ~,** in danger. **mettre en ~,** endanger.

dangereu|x, ~se /dɑ̃ʒrø, -z/ *a.* dangerous.
danois, ~e /danwa, -z/ *a.* Danish. ● *n.m., f.* Dane. ● *n.m.* (*lang.*) Danish.
dans /dɑ̃/ *prép.* in; (*mouvement*) into; (*à l'intérieur de*) inside, in; (*approximation*) about. **~ dix jours,** in ten days' time. **prendre/boire/***etc.* **~,** take/ drink/*etc.* out of *ou* from.
dans|e /dɑ̃s/ *n.f.* dance; (*art*) dancing. **~er** *v.t./i.* dance. **~eur, ~euse** *n.m., f.* dancer.
dard /dar/ *n.m.* (*d'animal*) sting.
darne /darn/ *n.f.* steak (*of fish*).
dat|e /dat/ *n.f.* date. **~e limite,** deadline; **~e limite de vente,** sell-by date; **~e de péremption,** expiry date. **~er** *v.t./i.* date. **à ~er de,** as from.
datt|e /dat/ *n.f.* (*fruit*) date. **~ier** *n.m.* date-palm.
daube /dob/ *n.f.* casserole.
dauphin /dofɛ̃/ *n.m.* (*animal*) dolphin.
davantage /davɑ̃taʒ/ *adv.* more; (*plus longtemps*) longer. **~ de,** more. **~ que,** more than; longer than.
de, d'* /də, d/ *prép.* (*de + le = du, de + les = des*) of; (*provenance*) from; (*moyen, manière*) with; (*agent*) by. ● *article* some; (*interrogation*) any, some. **le livre de mon ami,** my friend's book. **un pont de fer,** an iron bridge. **dix mètres de haut,** ten metres high. **du pain,** (some) bread; **une tranche de pain,** a slice of bread. **des fleurs,** (some) flowers.
dé /de/ *n.m.* (*à jouer*) dice; (*à coudre*) thimble. **dés,** (*jeu*) dice.
dealer /dilər/ *n.m.* (*drug*) dealer.
débâcle /debɑkl/ *n.f.* (*mil.*) rout.
déball|er /debale/ *v.t.* unpack; (*montrer, péj.*) spill out. **~age** *n.m.* unpacking.
débarbouiller /debarbuje/ *v.t.* wash the face of. **se ~** *v. pr.* wash one's face.
débarcadère /debarkadɛr/ *n.m.* landing-stage.
débardeur /debardœr/ *n.m.* docker; (*vêtement*) tank top.
débarqu|er /debarke/ *v.t./i.* disembark, land; (*arriver: fam.*) turn up. **~ement** *n.m.* disembarkation.
débarras /debara/ *n.m.* junk room. **bon ~!,** good riddance!
débarrasser /debarase/ *v.t.* clear (**de,** of). **~ qn. de,** take from s.o.; (*défaut, ennemi*) rid s.o. of. **se ~ de,** get rid of, rid o.s. of.
débat /deba/ *n.m.* debate.
débattre† [1] /debatr/ *v.t.* debate. ● *v.i.* **~ de,** discuss.
débattre† [2] **(se)** /(sə)debatr/ *v. pr.* struggle (to get free).
débauch|e /deboʃ/ *n.f.* debauchery; (*fig.*) profusion. **~er** [1] *v.t.* debauch.
débaucher [2] /deboʃe/ *v.t.* (*licencier*) lay off.
débile /debil/ *a.* weak; (*fam.*) stupid. ● *n.m./f.* moron.
débit /debi/ *n.m.* (rate of) flow; (*de magasin*) turnover; (*élocution*) delivery; (*de compte*) debit. **~ de tabac,** tobacconist's shop; **~ de boissons,** licensed premises.
débi|ter /debite/ *v.t.* cut up; (*fournir*) produce; (*vendre*) sell; (*dire: péj.*) spout; (*compte*) debit. **~teur, ~trice** *n.m., f.* debtor; *a.* (*compte*) in debit.
débl|ayer /debleje/ *v.t.* clear. **~aiement, ~ayage** *n.m.* clearing.
déblo|quer /deblɔke/ *v.t.* (*prix, salaires*) free. **~cage** *n.m.* freeing.
déboires /debwar/ *n.m. pl.* disappointments.
déboiser /debwaze/ *v.t.* clear (of trees).
déboîter /debwate/ *v.i.* (*véhicule*) pull out. ● *v.t.* (*membre*) dislocate.
débord|er /debɔrde/ *v.i.* overflow. ● *v.t.* (*dépasser*) extend beyond. **~er de,** (*joie etc.*) be overflowing with. **~é** *a.* snowed under (**de,** with). **~ement** *n.m.* overflowing.
débouché /debuʃe/ *n.m.* opening; (*carrière*) prospect; (*comm.*) outlet; (*sortie*) end, exit.
déboucher /debuʃe/ *v.t.* (*bouteille*) uncork; (*évier*) unblock. ● *v.i.* emerge (**de,** from). **~ sur,** (*rue*) lead into.
débourser /deburse/ *v.t.* pay out.
déboussolé /debusɔle/ *a.* (*fam.*) disorientated, disoriented.
debout /dəbu/ *adv.* standing; (*levé, éveillé*) up. **être ~, se tenir ~,** be standing, stand. **se mettre ~,** stand up.
déboutonner /debutɔne/ *v.t.* unbutton. **se ~** *v. pr.* unbutton o.s.; (*vêtement*) come undone.
débraillé /debrɑje/ *a.* slovenly.
débrancher /debrɑ̃ʃe/ *v.t.* unplug, disconnect.

débray|er /debreje/ *v.i.* (*auto.*) declutch; (*faire grève*) stop work. **~age** /debrɛjaʒ/ *n.m.* (*pédale*) clutch; (*grève*) stoppage.

débris /debri/ *n.m. pl.* fragments; (*détritus*) rubbish, debris.

débrouill|er /debruje/ *v.t.* disentangle; (*problème*) sort out. **se ~er** *v. pr.* manage. **~ard, ~arde** *a.* (*fam.*) resourceful.

débroussailler /debrusaje/ *v.t.* clear (of brushwood).

début /deby/ *n.m.* beginning. **faire ses ~s,** (*en public*) make one's début.

début|er /debyte/ *v.i.* begin; (*dans un métier etc.*) start out. **~ant, ~ante** *n.m., f.* beginner.

déca /deka/ *n.m.* decaffeinated coffee.

décafeiné /dekafeine/ *a.* decaffeinated. ● *n.m.* **du ~,** decaffeinated coffee.

deçà (en) /(ɑ̃)dəsa/ *adv.* this side. ● *prép.* **en ~ de,** this side of.

décacheter /dekaʃte/ *v.t.* open.

décade /dekad/ *n.f.* ten days; (*décennie*) decade.

décaden|t, ~te /dekadɑ̃, -t/ *a.* decadent. **~ce** *n.f.* decadence.

décalcomanie /dekalkɔmani/ *n.f.* transfer; (*Amer.*) decal.

décal|er /dekale/ *v.t.* shift. **~age** *n.m.* (*écart*) gap. **~age horaire,** time difference.

décalquer /dekalke/ *v.t.* trace.

décamper /dekɑ̃pe/ *v.i.* clear off.

décanter /dekɑ̃te/ *v.t.* allow to settle. **se ~** *v. pr.* settle.

décap|er /dekape/ *v.t.* scrape down; (*surface peinte*) strip. **~ant** *n.m.* chemical agent; (*pour peinture*) paint stripper.

décapotable /dekapɔtabl/ *a.* convertible.

décapsul|er /dekapsyle/ *v.t.* take the cap off. **~eur** *n.m.* bottle- opener.

décarcasser (se) /(sə)dekarkase/ *v. pr.* (*fam.*) work o.s. to death.

décathlon /dekatlɔ̃/ *n.m.* decathlon.

décéd|er /desede/ *v.i.* die. **~é** *a.* deceased.

décel|er /desle/ *v.t.* detect; (*démontrer*) reveal. **~able** *a.* detectable.

décembre /desɑ̃br/ *n.m.* December.

décennie /deseni/ *n.f.* decade.

déc|ent, ~ente /desɑ̃, -t/ *a.* decent. **~emment** /-amɑ̃/ *adv.* decently. **~ence** *n.f.* decency.

décentralis|er /desɑ̃tralize/ *v.t.* decentralize. **~ation** *n.f.* decentralization.

déception /desɛpsjɔ̃/ *n.f.* disappointment.

décerner /desɛrne/ *v.t.* award.

décès /desɛ/ *n.m.* death.

décev|oir† /dɛsvwar/ *v.t.* disappoint. **~ant, ~ante** *a.* disappointing.

déchaîn|er /deʃene/ *v.t.* (*violence etc.*) unleash; (*enthousiasme*) arouse a good deal of. **se ~er** *v. pr.* erupt. **~ement** /-ɛnmɑ̃/ *n.m.* (*de passions*) outburst.

décharge /deʃarʒ/ *n.f.* (*salve*) volley of shots. **~ (électrique),** electrical discharge. **~ (publique),** rubbish tip.

décharg|er /deʃarʒe/ *v.t.* unload; (*arme, accusé*) discharge. **~er de,** release from. **se ~er** *v. pr.* (*batterie, pile*) go flat. **~ement** *n.m.* unloading.

décharné /deʃarne/ *a.* bony.

déchausser (se) /(sə)deʃose/ *v. pr.* take off one's shoes; (*dent*) work loose.

dèche /dɛʃ/ *n.f.* (*fam.*) **dans la ~,** broke.

déchéance /deʃeɑ̃s/ *n.f.* decay.

déchet /deʃɛ/ *n.m.* (*reste*) scrap; (*perte*) waste. **~s,** (*ordures*) refuse.

déchiffrer /deʃifre/ *v.t.* decipher.

déchiqueter /deʃikte/ *v.t.* tear to shreds.

déchir|ant, ~ante /deʃirɑ̃, -t/ *a.* heart-breaking. **~ement** *n.m.* heart-break; (*conflit*) split.

déchir|er /deʃire/ *v.t.* tear; (*lacérer*) tear up; (*arracher*) tear off *ou* out; (*diviser*) tear apart; (*oreilles: fig.*) split. **se ~er** *v. pr.* tear. **~ure** *n.f.* tear.

déch|oir /deʃwar/ *v.i.* demean o.s. **~oir de,** (*rang*) lose, fall from. **~u** *a.* fallen.

décibel /desibɛl/ *n.m.* decibel.

décid|er /deside/ *v.t.* decide on; (*persuader*) persuade. **~er que/de,** decide that/to. ● *v.i.* decide. **~er de qch.,** decide on sth. **se ~er** *v. pr.* make up one's mind (**à,** to). **~é** *a.* (*résolu*) determined; (*fixé, marqué*) decided. **~ément** *adv.* really.

décim|al, ~ale (*m. pl.* **~aux**) /desimal, -o/ *a.* & *n.f.* decimal.

décimètre /desimɛtr/ *n.m.* decimetre.

décisi|f, ~ve /desizif, -v/ *a.* decisive.

décision /desizjɔ̃/ *n.f.* decision.

déclar|er /deklare/ *v.t.* declare; (*naissance*) register. **se ~er** *v. pr.* (*feu*) break out. **~er forfait,** (*sport*) withdraw. **~ation** *n.f.* declaration; (*commentaire politique*) statement. **~ation d'impôts,** tax return.

déclasser /deklɑse/ *v.t.* (*coureur*) relegate; (*hôtel*) downgrade.

déclench|er /deklɑ̃ʃe/ *v.t.* (*techn.*) release, set off; (*lancer*) launch; (*provoquer*) trigger off. **se ~er** *v. pr.* (*techn.*) go off. **~eur** *n.m.* (*photo.*) trigger.

déclic /deklik/ *n.m.* click; (*techn.*) trigger mechanism.

déclin /deklɛ̃/ *n.m.* decline.

déclin|er[1] /dekline/ *v.i.* decline. **~aison** *n.f.* (*lang.*) declension.

décliner[2] /dekline/ *v.t.* (*refuser*) decline; (*dire*) state.

déclivité /deklivite/ *n.f.* slope.

décocher /dekɔʃe/ *v.t.* (*coup*) fling; (*regard*) shoot.

décoder /dekɔde/ *v.t.* decode.

décoiffer /dekwafe/ *v.t.* (*ébouriffer*) disarrange the hair of.

décoincer /dekwɛ̃se/ *v.t.* free.

décoll|er[1] /dekɔle/ *v.i.* (*avion*) take off. **~age** *n.m.* take-off.

décoller[2] /dekɔle/ *v.t.* unstick.

décolleté /dekɔlte/ *a.* low-cut. ● *n.m.* low neckline.

décolor|er /dekɔlɔre/ *v.t.* fade; (*cheveux*) bleach. **se ~er** *v. pr.* fade. **~ation** *n.f.* bleaching.

décombres /dekɔ̃br/ *n.m. pl.* rubble.

décommander /dekɔmɑ̃de/ *v.t.* cancel.

décompos|er /dekɔ̃poze/ *v.t.* break up; (*substance*) decompose; (*visage*) contort. **se ~er** *v. pr.* (*pourrir*) decompose. **~ition** *n.f.* decomposition.

décompt|e /dekɔ̃t/ *n.m.* deduction; (*détail*) breakdown. **~er** *v.t.* deduct.

déconcerter /dekɔ̃sɛrte/ *v.t.* disconcert.

décongel|er /dekɔ̃ʒle/ *v.t.* thaw. **~ation** *n.f.* thawing.

décongestionner /dekɔ̃ʒɛstjɔne/ *v.t.* relieve congestion in.

déconseill|er /dekɔ̃seje/ *v.t.* **~er qch. à qn.,** advise s.o. against sth. **~é** *a.* not advisable, inadvisable.

décontenancer /dekɔ̃tnɑ̃se/ *v.t.* disconcert.

décontract|er /dekɔ̃trakte/ *v.t.*, **se ~** *v. pr.* relax. **~é** *a.* relaxed.

déconvenue /dekɔ̃vny/ *n.f.* disappointment.

décor /dekɔr/ *n.m.* (*paysage, théâtre*) scenery; (*cinéma*) set; (*cadre*) setting; (*de maison*) décor.

décorati|f, ~ve /dekɔratif, -v/ *a.* decorative.

décor|er /dekɔre/ *v.t.* decorate. **~ateur, ~atrice** *n.m., f.* (interior) decorator. **~ation** *n.f.* decoration.

décortiquer /dekɔrtike/ *v.t.* shell; (*fig.*) dissect.

découdre (se) /(sə)dekudr/ *v. pr.* come unstitched.

découler /dekule/ *v.i.* **~ de,** follow from.

découp|er /dekupe/ *v.t.* cut up; (*viande*) carve; (*détacher*) cut out. **se ~er sur,** stand out against. **~age** *n.m.* (*image*) cut-out.

décourag|er /dekuraʒe/ *v.t.* discourage. **se ~er** *v. pr.* become discouraged. **~ement** *n.m.* discouragement. **~é** *a.* discouraged.

décousu /dekuzy/ *a.* (*vêtement*) falling apart; (*idées etc.*) disjointed.

découvert, ~e /dekuvɛr, -t/ *a.* (*tête etc.*) bare; (*terrain*) open. ● *n.m.* (*de compte*) overdraft. ● *n.f.* discovery. **à ~,** exposed; (*fig.*) openly. **à la ~e de,** in search of.

découvrir† /dekuvrir/ *v.t.* discover; (*enlever ce qui couvre*) uncover; (*voir*) see; (*montrer*) reveal. **se ~** *v. pr.* uncover o.s.; (*se décoiffer*) take one's hat off; (*ciel*) clear.

décrasser /dekrase/ *v.t.* clean.

décrépit, ~e /dekrepi, -t/ *a.* decrepit. **~ude** *n.f.* decay.

décret /dekrɛ/ *n.m.* decree. **~er** /-ete/ *v.t.* decree.

décrié /dekrije/ *v.t.* decried.

décrire† /dekrir/ *v.t.* describe.

décrisp|er (se) /(sə)dekrispe/ *v. pr.* become less tense. **~ation** *n.f.* lessening of tension.

décroch|er /dekrɔʃe/ *v.t.* unhook; (*obtenir: fam.*) get. ● *v.i.* (*abandonner: fam.*) give up. **~er (le téléphone),** pick up the phone. **~é** *a.* (*téléphone*) off the hook.

décroître /dekrwatr/ *v.i.* decrease.

décrue /dekry/ *n.f.* going down (of river water).

déçu /desy/ *a.* disappointed.

décupl|e /dekypl/ *n.m.* **au ~e,** tenfold. **le ~e de,** ten times. **~er** *v.t./i.* increase tenfold.

dédaign|er /dedeɲe/ *v.t.* scorn. **~er de faire,** consider it beneath one to do. **~eux, ~euse** /dedɛɲø, -z/ *a.* scornful.

dédain /dedɛ̃/ *n.m.* scorn.

dédale /dedal/ *n.m.* maze.

dedans /dədɑ̃/ *adv.* & *n.m.* inside. **au ~ (de),** inside. **en ~,** on the inside.

dédicac|e /dedikas/ *n.f.* dedication, inscription. **~er** *v.t.* dedicate, inscribe.

dédier /dedje/ *v.t.* dedicate.

dédommag|er /dedɔmaʒe/ *v.t.* compensate (**de,** for). **~ement** *n.m.* compensation.

dédouaner /dedwane/ *v.t.* clear through customs.

dédoubler /deduble/ *v.t.* split into two. **~ un train,** put on a relief train.

déd|uire† /dedɥir/ *v.t.* deduct; (*conclure*) deduce. **~uction** *n.f.* deduction; **~uction d'impôts** tax deduction.

déesse /deɛs/ *n.f.* goddess.

défaillance /defajɑ̃s/ *n.f.* weakness; (*évanouissement*) black-out; (*panne*) failure.

défaill|ir /defajir/ *v.i.* faint; (*forces etc.*) fail. **~ant, ~ante** *a.* (*personne*) faint; (*candidat*) defaulting.

défaire† /defɛr/ *v.t.* undo; (*valise*) unpack; (*démonter*) take down; (*débarrasser*) rid. **se ~** *v. pr.* come undone. **se ~ de,** rid o.s. of.

défait, ~e[1] /defɛ, -t/ *a.* (*cheveux*) ruffled; (*visage*) haggard.

défaite[2] /defɛt/ *n.f.* defeat.

défaitisme /defetizm/ *n.m.* defeatism.

défaitiste /defetist/ *a.* & *n.m./f.* defeatist.

défalquer /defalke/ *v.t.* (*somme*) deduct.

défaut /defo/ *n.m.* fault, defect; (*d'un verre, diamant, etc.*) flaw; (*carence*) lack; (*pénurie*) shortage. **à ~ de,** for lack of. **en ~,** at fault. **faire ~,** (*argent etc.*) be lacking. **par ~,** (*jurid.*) in one's absence.

défav|eur /defavœr/ *n.f.* disfavour. **~orable** *a.* unfavourable.

défavoriser /defavɔrize/ *v.t.* put at a disadvantage.

défection /defɛksjɔ̃/ *n.f.* desertion. **faire ~,** desert.

défect|ueux, ~ueuse /defɛktɥø, -z/ *a.* faulty, defective. **~uosité** *n.f.* faultiness; (*défaut*) fault.

défendre /defɑ̃dr/ *v.t.* defend; (*interdire*) forbid. **~ à qn. de,** forbid s.o. to. **se ~** *v. pr.* defend o.s.; (*se débrouiller*) manage; (*se protéger*) protect o.s. **se ~ de,** (*refuser*) refrain from.

défense /defɑ̃s/ *n.f.* defence; (*d'éléphant*) tusk. **~ de fumer**/*etc.*, no smoking/*etc.*

défenseur /defɑ̃sœr/ *n.m.* defender.

défensi|f, ~ve /defɑ̃sif, -v/ *a.* & *n.f.* defensive.

déféren|t, ~te /deferɑ̃, -t/ *a.* deferential. **~ce** *n.f.* deference.

déférer /defere/ *v.t.* (*jurid.*) refer. ● *v.i.* **~ à,** (*avis etc.*) defer to.

déferler /defɛrle/ *v.i.* (*vagues*) break; (*violence etc.*) erupt.

défi /defi/ *n.m.* challenge; (*refus*) defiance. **mettre au ~,** challenge.

déficeler /defisle/ *v.t.* untie.

déficience /defisjɑ̃s/ *n.f.* deficiency.

déficient /defisjɑ̃/ *a.* deficient.

déficit /defisit/ *n.m.* deficit. **~aire** *a.* in deficit.

défier /defje/ *v.t.* challenge; (*braver*) defy. **se ~ de,** mistrust.

défilé[1] /defile/ *n.m.* procession; (*mil.*) parade; (*fig.*) (continual) stream. **~ de mode,** fashion parade.

défilé[2] /defile/ *n.m.* (*géog.*) gorge.

défiler /defile/ *v.i.* march (past); (*visiteurs*) stream; (*images*) flash by. **se ~** *v. pr.* (*fam.*) sneak off.

défini /defini/ *a.* definite.

définir /definir/ *v.t.* define.

définissable /definisabl/ *a.* definable.

définiti|f, ~ve /definitif, -v/ *a.* final; (*permanent*) definitive. **en ~ve,** in the final analysis. **~vement** *adv.* definitively, permanently.

définition /definisjɔ̃/ *n.f.* definition; (*de mots croisés*) clue.

déflagration /deflagrɑsjɔ̃/ *n.f.* explosion.

déflation /deflɑsjɔ̃/ *n.f.* deflation. **~niste** /-jɔnist/ *a.* deflationary.

défoncer /defɔ̃se/ *v.t.* (*porte etc.*) break down; (*route, terrain*) dig up; (*lit*) break the springs of. **se ~** *v. pr.* (*fam.*) work like mad; (*drogué*) get high.

déform|er /defɔrme/ *v.t.* put out of shape; (*membre*) deform; (*faits, pensée*) distort. **~ation** *n.f.* loss of shape; deformation; distortion.

défouler (se) /(sə)defule/ *v. pr.* let off steam.

défraîchir (se) /(sə)defreʃir/ *v. pr.* become faded.
défrayer /defreje/ *v.t.* (*payer*) pay the expenses of.
défricher /defriʃe/ *v.t.* clear (for cultivation).
défroisser /defrwase/ *v.t.* smooth out.
défunt, ~e /defœ̃, -t/ *a.* (*mort*) late. ● *n.m., f.* deceased.
dégagé /degaʒe/ *a.* clear; (*ton*) free and easy.
dégag|er /degaʒe/ *v.t.* (*exhaler*) give off; (*désencombrer*) clear; (*délivrer*) free; (*faire ressortir*) bring out. ● *v.i.* (*football*) kick the ball (down the pitch *ou* field). **se ~er** *v. pr.* free o.s.; (*ciel, rue*) clear; (*odeur etc.*) emanate. **~ement** *n.m.* giving off; clearing; freeing; (*espace*) clearing; (*football*) clearance.
dégainer /degene/ *v.t./i.* draw.
dégarnir /degarnir/ *v.t.* clear, empty. **se ~** *v. pr.* clear, empty; (*crâne*) go bald.
dégâts /degɑ/ *n.m. pl.* damage.
dégel /deʒɛl/ *n.m.* thaw. **~er** /deʒle/ *v.t./i.* thaw (out). **(faire) ~er,** (*culin.*) thaw.
dégénér|er /deʒenere/ *v.i.* degenerate. **~é, ~ée** *a. & n.m., f.* degenerate.
dégingandé /deʒɛ̃gɑ̃de/ *a.* gangling.
dégivrer /deʒivre/ *v.t.* (*auto.*) de-ice; (*réfrigérateur*) defrost.
déglacer /deglase/ *v.t.* (*culin.*) deglaze.
déglingu|er /deglɛ̃ge/ (*fam.*) *v.t.* knock about. **se ~er** *v. pr.* fall to bits. **~é** *adj.* falling to bits.
dégonfl|er /degɔ̃fle/ *v.t.* let down, deflate. **se ~er** *v. pr.* (*fam.*) get cold feet. **~é** *a.* (*pneu*) flat; (*lâche*: *fam.*) yellow.
dégorger /degɔrʒe/ *v.i.* **faire ~,** (*culin.*) soak.
dégouliner /deguline/ *v.i.* trickle.
dégourdi /degurdi/ *a.* smart.
dégourdir /degurdir/ *v.t.* (*membre, liquide*) warm up. **se ~ les jambes,** stretch one's legs.
dégoût /degu/ *n.m.* disgust.
dégoût|er /degute/ *v.t.* disgust. **~er qn. de qch.,** put s.o. off sth. **~ant, ~ante** *a.* disgusting. **~é** *a.* disgusted. **~é de,** sick of. **faire le ~é,** look disgusted.
dégradant /degradɑ̃/ *a.* degrading.
dégrader /degrade/ *v.t.* degrade; (*abîmer*) damage. **se ~** *v. pr.* (*se détériorer*) deteriorate.
dégrafer /degrafe/ *v.t.* unhook.
degré /dəgre/ *n.m.* degree; (*d'escalier*) step.
dégressi|f, ~ve /degresif, -v/ *a.* gradually lower.
dégrèvement /degrɛvmɑ̃/ *n.m.* **~ fiscal** *ou* **d'impôts**, tax reduction.
dégrever /degrəve/ *v.t.* reduce the tax on.
dégringol|er /degrɛ̃gɔle/ *v.i.* tumble (down). ● *v.t.* rush down. **~ade** *n.f.* tumble.
dégrossir /degrɔsir/ *v.t.* (*bois*) trim; (*projet*) rough out.
déguerpir /degɛrpir/ *v.i.* clear off.
dégueulasse /degœlas/ *a.* (*argot*) disgusting, lousy.
dégueuler /degœle/ *v.t.* (*argot*) throw up.
déguis|er /degize/ *v.t.* disguise. **se ~er** *v. pr.* disguise o.s.; (*au carnaval etc.*) dress up. **~ement** *n.m.* disguise; (*de carnaval etc.*) fancy dress.
dégust|er /degyste/ *v.t.* taste, sample; (*savourer*) enjoy. **~ation** *n.f.* tasting, sampling.
déhancher (se) /(sə)deɑ̃ʃe/ *v. pr.* sway one's hips.
dehors /dəɔr/ *adv. & n.m.* outside. ● *n.m. pl.* (*aspect de qn.*) exterior. **au ~ (de),** outside. **en ~ de,** outside; (*hormis*) apart from. **jeter/mettre/***etc.* **~,** throw/put/*etc.* out.
déjà /deʒa/ *adv.* already; (*avant*) before, already.
déjà-vu /deʒavy/ *n.m. inv.* déjà vu.
déjeuner /deʒœne/ *v.i.* (have) lunch; (*le matin*) (have) breakfast. ● *n.m.* lunch. **(petit) ~,** breakfast.
déjouer /deʒwe/ *v.t.* thwart.
delà /dəla/ *adv. & prép.* **au ~ (de), en ~ (de), par ~,** beyond.
délabrer (se) /(sə)delɑbre/ *v. pr.* become dilapidated.
délacer /delase/ *v.t.* undo.
délai /delɛ/ *n.m.* time-limit; (*attente*) wait; (*sursis*) extension (of time). **sans ~,** without delay. **dans les plus brefs ~s,** as soon as possible.
délaisser /delese/ *v.t.* desert.
délass|er /delɑse/ *v.t.,* **se ~er** *v. pr.* relax. **~ement** *n.m.* relaxation.
délation /delɑsjɔ̃/ *n.f.* informing.
délavé /delave/ *a.* faded.

délayer /deleje/ *v.t.* mix (with liquid); (*idée*) drag out.
delco /dɛlkɔ/ *n.m.* (P., *auto.*) distributor.
délecter (se) /(sə)delɛkte/ *v. pr.* **se ~ de,** delight in.
délégation /delegɑsjɔ̃/ *n.f.* delegation.
délégu|er /delege/ *v.t.* delegate. **~é, ~ée** *n.m., f.* delegate.
délibéré /delibere/ *a.* deliberate; (*résolu*) determined. **~ment** *adv.* deliberately.
délibér|er /delibere/ *v.i.* deliberate. **~ation** *n.f.* deliberation.
délicat, ~e /delika, -t/ *a.* delicate; (*plein de tact*) tactful; (*exigeant*) particular. **~ement** /-tmɑ̃/ *adv.* delicately; tactfully. **~esse** /-tɛs/ *n.f.* delicacy; tact. **~esses** /-tɛs/ *n.f. pl.* (kind) attentions.
délice /delis/ *n.m.* delight. **~s** *n.f. pl.* delights.
délicieu|x, ~se /delisjø, -z/ *a.* (*au goût*) delicious; (*charmant*) delightful.
délié /delje/ *a.* fine, slender; (*agile*) nimble.
délier /delje/ *v.t.* untie; (*délivrer*) free. **se ~** *v. pr.* come untied.
délimit|er /delimite/ *v.t.* determine, demarcate. **~ation** *n.f.* demarcation.
délinquan|t, ~te /delɛ̃kɑ̃, -t/ *a.* & *n.m., f.* delinquent. **~ce** *n.f.* delinquency.
délire /delir/ *n.m.* delirium; (*fig.*) frenzy.
délir|er /delire/ *v.i.* be delirious (**de,** with); (*déraisonner*) rave. **~ant, ~ante** *a.* delirious; (*frénétique*) frenzied; (*fam.*) wild.
délit /deli/ *n.m.* offence, crime.
délivr|er /delivre/ *v.t.* free, release; (*pays*) deliver; (*remettre*) issue. **~ance** *n.f.* release; deliverance; issue.
déloger /delɔʒe/ *v.t.* force out.
déloy|al (*m. pl.* **~aux**) /delwajal, -jo/ *a.* disloyal; (*procédé*) unfair.
delta /dɛlta/ *n.m.* delta.
deltaplane /dɛltaplan/ *n.m.* hang glider.
déluge /delyʒ/ *n.m.* flood; (*pluie*) downpour.
démagogie /demagɔʒi/ *n.m.* demagogy.
démagogue /demagɔg/ *n.m./f.* demagogue.
demain /dmɛ̃/ *adv.* tomorrow.
demande /dmɑ̃d/ *n.f.* request; (*d'emploi*) application; (*exigence*) demand. **~ en mariage,** proposal (of marriage).
demandé /dmɑ̃de/ *a.* in demand.
demander /dmɑ̃de/ *v.t.* ask for; (*chemin, heure*) ask; (*emploi*) apply for; (*nécessiter*) require. **~ que/si,** ask that/if. **~ qch. à qn.,** ask s.o. for sth. **~ à qn. de,** ask s.o. to. **~ en mariage,** propose to. **se ~ si/où/** *etc.*, wonder if/where/*etc.*
demandeu|r, ~se /dmɑ̃dœr, -øz/ *n.m., f.* **les ~rs d'emploi** job seekers.
démang|er /demɑ̃ʒe/ *v.t./i.* itch. **~eaison** *n.f.* itch(ing).
démanteler /demɑ̃tle/ *v.t.* break up.
démaquill|er (se) /(sə)demakije/ *v. pr.* remove one's make-up. **~ant** *n.m.* make-up remover.
démarcation /demarkɑsjɔ̃/ *n.f.* demarcation.
démarchage /demarʃaʒ/ *n.m.* door-to-door selling.
démarche /demarʃ/ *n.f.* walk, gait; (*procédé*) step. **faire des ~s auprès de,** make approaches to.
démarcheu|r, ~se /demarʃœr, -øz/ *n.m., f.* (door-to-door) canvasser.
démarr|er /demare/ *v.i.* (*moteur*) start (up); (*partir*) move off; (*fig.*) get moving. ● *v.t.* (*fam.*) get moving. **~age** *n.m.* start. **~eur** *n.m.* starter.
démasquer /demaske/ *v.t.* unmask.
démêlant /demelɑ̃/ *n.m.* conditioner.
démêler /demele/ *v.t.* disentangle.
démêlés /demele/ *n.m. pl.* trouble.
déménag|er /demenaʒe/ *v.i.* move (house). ● *v.t.* (*meubles*) remove. **~ement** *n.m.* move; (*de meubles*) removal. **~eur** *n.m.* removal man; (*Amer.*) furniture mover.
démener (se) /(sə)demne/ *v. pr.* move about wildly; (*fig.*) exert o.s.
démen|t, ~te /demɑ̃, -t/ *a.* insane. ● *n.m., f.* lunatic. **~ce** *n.f.* insanity.
démenti /demɑ̃ti/ *n.m.* denial.
démentir /demɑ̃tir/ *v.t.* refute; (*ne pas être conforme à*) belie. **~ que,** deny that.
démerder (se) /(sə)demɛrde/ (*fam.*) manage.
démesuré /deməzyre/ *a.* inordinate.
démettre /demɛtr/ *v.t.* (*poignet etc.*) dislocate. **~ qn. de,** dismiss s.o. from. **se ~** *v. pr.* resign (**de,** from).

demeure /dəmœr/ *n.f.* residence. **mettre en ~ de,** order to.
demeurer /dəmœre/ *v.i.* live; (*rester*) remain.
demi, ~e /dmi/ *a.* half(-). ● *n.m., f.* half. ● *n.m.* (*bière*) (half-pint) glass of beer; (*football*) half-back. ● *n.f.* (*à l'horloge*) half-hour. ● *adv.* **à ~,** half; (*ouvrir, fermer*) half-way. **à la ~e,** at half-past. **une heure et ~e,** an hour and a half; (*à l'horloge*) half past one. **une ~-journée/-livre/***etc.*, half a day/pound/*etc.*, a half-day/-pound/*etc.* **~-cercle** *n.m.* semicircle. **~-finale** *n.f.* semifinal. **~-frère** *n.m.* stepbrother. **~-heure** *n.f.* half-hour, half an hour. **~-jour** *n.m.* half-light. **~-mesure** *n.f.* half-measure. **à ~-mot** *adv.* without having to express every word. **~-pension** *n.f.* half-board. **~-pensionnaire** *n.m./f.* day-boarder. **~-sel** *a. invar.* slightly salted. **~-sœur** *n.f.* stepsister. **~-tarif** *n.m.* half-fare. **~-tour** *n.m.* about turn; (*auto.*) U-turn. **faire ~-tour,** turn back.
démis, ~e /demi, -z/ *a.* dislocated. **~ de ses fonctions,** removed from his post.
démission /demisjɔ̃/ *n.f.* resignation. **~ner** /-jɔne/ *v.i.* resign.
démobiliser /demɔbilize/ *v.t.* demobilize.
démocrate /demɔkrat/ *n.m./f.* democrat. ● *a.* democratic.
démocrat|ie /demɔkrasi/ *n.f.* democracy. **~ique** /-atik/ *a.* democratic.
démodé /demɔde/ *a.* old-fashioned.
démographi|e /demɔgrafi/ *n.f.* demography. **~que** *a.* demographic.
demoiselle /dəmwazɛl/ *n.f.* young lady; (*célibataire*) spinster. **~ d'honneur,** bridesmaid.
démol|ir /demɔlir/ *v.t.* demolish. **~ition** *n.f.* demolition.
démon /demɔ̃/ *n.m.* demon. **le D~,** the Devil.
démoniaque /demɔnjak/ *a.* fiendish.
démonstra|teur, ~trice /demɔ̃stratœr, -tris/ *n.m., f.* demonstrator. **~tion** /-ɑsjɔ̃/ *n.f.* demonstration; (*de force*) show.
démonstrati|f, ~ve /demɔ̃stratif, -v/ *a.* demonstrative.
démonter /demɔ̃te/ *v.t.* take apart, dismantle; (*installation*) take down; (*fig.*) disconcert. **se ~** *v. pr.* come apart.
démontrer /demɔ̃tre/ *v.t.* show, demonstrate.
démoraliser /demɔralize/ *v.t.* demoralize.
démuni /demyni/ *a.* impoverished. **~ de,** without.
démunir /demynir/ *v.t.* **~ de,** deprive of. **se ~ de,** part with.
démystifier /demistifje/ *v.t.* enlighten.
dénaturer /denatyre/ *v.t.* (*faits etc.*) distort.
dénégation /denegɑsjɔ̃/ *n.f.* denial.
dénicher /deniʃe/ *v.t.* (*trouver*) dig up; (*faire sortir*) flush out.
dénigr|er /denigre/ *v.t.* denigrate. **~ement** *n.m.* denigration.
dénivellation /denivɛlɑsjɔ̃/ *n.f.* (*pente*) slope.
dénombrer /denɔ̃bre/ *v.t.* count; (*énumérer*) enumerate.
dénomination /denɔminɑsjɔ̃/ *n.f.* designation.
dénommé, ~e /denɔme/ *n. m., f.* **le ~ X,** the said X.
dénonc|er /denɔ̃se/ *v.t.* denounce; (*scol.*) tell on. **se ~er** *v. pr.* give o.s. up. **~iateur, ~iatrice** *n.m., f.* informer; (*scol.*) tell-tale. **~iation** *n.f.* denunciation.
dénoter /denɔte/ *v.t.* denote.
dénouement /denumɑ̃/ *n.m.* outcome; (*théâtre*) dénouement.
dénouer /denwe/ *v.t.* unknot, undo. **se ~** *v. pr.* (*nœud*) come undone.
dénoyauter /denwajote/ *v.t.* stone; (*Amer.*) pit.
denrée /dɑ̃re/ *n.f.* foodstuff.
dens|e /dɑ̃s/ *a.* dense. **~ité** *n.f.* density.
dent /dɑ̃/ *n.f.* tooth; (*de roue*) cog. **faire ses ~s,** teethe. **~aire** /-tɛr/ *a.* dental.
dentelé /dɑ̃tle/ *a.* jagged.
dentelle /dɑ̃tɛl/ *n.f.* lace.
dentier /dɑ̃tje/ *n.m.* denture.
dentifrice /dɑ̃tifris/ *n.m.* toothpaste.
dentiste /dɑ̃tist/ *n.m./f.* dentist.
dentition /dɑ̃tisjɔ̃/ *n.f.* teeth.
dénud|er /denyde/ *v.t.* bare. **~é** *a.* bare.
dénué /denɥe/ *a.* **~ de,** devoid of.
dénuement /denymɑ̃/ *n.m.* destitution.
déodorant /deɔdɔrɑ̃/ *a.m.* & *n.m.* **(produit) ~,** deodorant.
déontologi|e /deɔ̃tɔlɔʒi/ *n.f.* code of practice. **~que** *a.* ethical.

dépann|er /depane/ *v.t.* repair; (*fig.*) help out. **~age** *n.m.* repair. **de ~age,** (*service etc.*) breakdown. **~euse** *n.f.* breakdown lorry; (*Amer.*) wrecker.

dépareillé /depareje/ *a.* odd, not matching.

départ /depar/ *n.m.* departure; (*sport*) start. **au ~,** at the outset.

départager /departaʒe/ *v.t.* settle the matter between.

département /departəmɑ̃/ *n.m.* department.

dépassé /depɑse/ *a.* outdated.

dépass|er /depɑse/ *v.t.* go past, pass; (*véhicule*) overtake; (*excéder*) exceed; (*rival*) surpass; (*dérouter: fam.*) be beyond. ● *v.i.* stick out; (*véhicule*) overtake. **~ement** *n.m.* overtaking.

dépays|er /depeize/ *v.t.* disorientate, disorient. **~ant, ~e** *a.* disorientating. **~ement** *n.m.* disorientation; (*changement*) change of scenery.

dépêch|e /depɛʃ/ *n.f.* dispatch. **~er**[1] /-eʃe/ *v.t.* dispatch.

dépêcher[2] **(se)** /(sə)depeʃe/ *v. pr.* hurry (up).

dépeindre /depɛ̃dr/ *v.t.* depict.

dépendance /depɑ̃dɑ̃s/ *n.f.* dependence; (*bâtiment*) outbuilding.

dépendre /depɑ̃dr/ *v.t.* take down. ● *v.i.* depend **(de,** on). **~ de,** (*appartenir à*) belong to.

dépens (aux) /(o)depɑ̃/ *prép.* **aux ~ de,** at the expense of.

dépens|e /depɑ̃s/ *n.f.* expense; expenditure. **~er** *v.t./i.* spend; (*énergie etc.*) expend. **se ~er** *v. pr.* exert o.s.

dépens|ier, ~ière /depɑ̃sje, -jɛr/ *a.* **être ~ier,** be a spendthrift.

dépérir /deperir/ *v.i.* wither.

dépêtrer (se) /(sə) depetre/ *v. pr.* get o.s. out **(de,** of).

dépeupler /depœple/ *v.t.* depopulate. **se ~** *v. pr.* become depopulated.

déphasé /defɑze/ *a.* (*fam.*) out of touch.

dépilatoire /depilatwar/ *a.* & *n.m.* depilatory.

dépist|er /depiste/ *v.t.* detect; (*criminel*) track down; (*poursuivant*) throw off the scent. **~age** *n.m.* detection.

dépit /depi/ *n.m.* resentment. **en ~ de,** despite. **en ~ du bon sens,** against all common sense. **~é** /-te/ *a.* vexed.

déplacé /deplase/ *a.* out of place.

déplac|er /deplase/ *v.t.* move. **se ~er** *v. pr.* move; (*voyager*) travel. **~ement** *n.m.* moving; travel(-ling).

déplaire /deplɛr/ *v.i.* **~ à,** (*irriter*) displease. **ça me déplaît,** I dislike that.

déplaisant, ~e /deplɛzɑ̃, -t/ *a.* unpleasant, disagreeable.

déplaisir /deplezir/ *n.m.* displeasure.

dépliant /deplijɑ̃/ *n.m.* leaflet.

déplier /deplije/ *v.t.* unfold.

déplor|er /deplɔre/ *v.t.* (*trouver regrettable*) deplore; (*mort*) lament. **~able** *a.* deplorable.

dépl|oyer /deplwaje/ *v.t.* (*ailes, carte*) spread; (*courage*) display; (*armée*) deploy. **~oiement** *n.m.* display; deployment.

déport|er /depɔrte/ *v.t.* (*exiler*) deport; (*dévier*) carry off course. **~ation** *n.f.* deportation.

déposer /depoze/ *v.t.* put down; (*laisser*) leave; (*passager*) drop; (*argent*) deposit; (*installation*) dismantle; (*plainte*) lodge; (*armes*) lay down; (*roi*) depose. ● *v.i.* (*jurid.*) testify. **se ~** *v. pr.* settle.

dépositaire /depozitɛr/ *n.m./f.* (*comm.*) agent.

déposition /depozisjɔ̃/ *n.f.* (*jurid.*) statement.

dépôt /depo/ *n.m.* (*garantie, lie*) deposit; (*entrepôt*) warehouse; (*d'autobus*) depot; (*d'ordures*) dump. **laisser en ~,** give for safe keeping.

dépotoir /depɔtwar/ *n.m.* rubbish dump.

dépouille /depuj/ *n.f.* skin, hide. **~ (mortelle),** mortal remains. **~s,** (*butin*) spoils.

dépouiller /depuje/ *v.t.* go through; (*votes*) count; (*écorcher*) skin. **~ de,** strip of.

dépourvu /depurvy/ *a.* **~ de,** devoid of. **prendre au ~,** catch unawares.

dépréc|ier /depresje/ *v.t.,* **se ~ier** *v. pr.* depreciate. **~iation** *n.f.* depreciation.

déprédations /depredɑsjɔ̃/ *n.f. pl.* damage.

dépr|imer /deprime/ *v.t.* depress. **~ession** *n.f.* depression. **~ession nerveuse,** nervous breakdown.

depuis /dəpɥi/ *prép.* since; (*durée*) for; (*à partir de*) from. ● *adv.* (ever) since. **~ que,** since. **~ quand attendez-vous?,** how long have you been waiting?

députation /depytasjɔ̃/ *n.f.* deputation.

député, ~e /depyte/ *n.m., f.* Member of Parliament.

déraciné, ~e /derasine/ *a. & n.m., f.* rootless (person).

déraciner /derasine/ *v.t.* uproot.

déraill|er /deraje/ *v.i.* be derailed; (*fig., fam.*) be talking nonsense. **faire ~er,** derail. **~ement** *n.m.* derailment. **~eur** *n.m.* (*de vélo*) gear mechanism, *dérailleur*.

déraisonnable /derɛzɔnabl/ *a.* unreasonable.

dérang|er /derɑ̃ʒe/ *v.t.* (*gêner*) bother, disturb; (*dérégler*) upset, disrupt. **se ~er** *v. pr.* put o.s. out. **ça vous ~e si . . .?,** do you mind if . . .? **~ement** *n.m.* bother; (*désordre*) disorder, upset. **en ~ement,** out of order.

dérap|er /derape/ *v.i.* skid; (*fig.*) get out of control. **~age** *n.m.* skid.

déréglé /deregle/ *a.* (*vie*) dissolute; (*estomac*) upset; (*pendule*) (that is) not running properly.

dérégler /deregle/ *v.t.* put out of order. **se ~** *v. pr.* go wrong.

dérision /derizjɔ̃/ *n.f.* mockery. **par ~,** derisively. **tourner en ~,** mock.

dérisoire /derizwar/ *a.* derisory.

dérivatif /derivatif/ *n.m.* distraction.

dériv|e /deriv/ *n.f.* **aller à la ~e,** drift. **~er**[1] *v.i.* (*bateau*) drift; *v.t.* (*détourner*) divert.

dériv|er[2] /derive/ *v.i.* **~er de,** derive from. **~é** *a.* derived; *n.m.* derivative; (*techn.*) by-product.

dermatolo|gie /dɛrmatɔlɔʒi/ *n.f.* dermatology. **~gue** /-g/ *n.m./f.* dermatologist.

dern|ier, ~ière /dɛrnje, -jɛr/ *a.* last; (*nouvelles, mode*) latest; (*étage*) top. ● *n.m., f.* last (one). **ce ~ier,** the latter. **en ~ier,** last. **le ~ier cri,** the latest fashion.

dernièrement /dɛrnjɛrmɑ̃/ *adv.* recently.

dérobé /derɔbe/ *a.* hidden. **à la ~e,** stealthily.

dérober /derɔbe/ *v.t.* steal; (*cacher*) hide (**à,** from). **se ~** *v. pr.* slip away. **se ~ à,** (*obligation*) shy away from; (*se cacher à*) hide from.

dérogation /derɔgasjɔ̃/ *n.f.* exemption.

déroger /derɔʒe/ *v.i.* **~ à,** go against.

dérouiller (se) /(sə)deruje/ *v. pr.* **se ~ les jambes** to stretch one's legs.

déroul|er /derule/ *v.t.* (*fil etc.*) unwind. **se ~er** *v. pr.* unwind; (*avoir lieu*) take place; (*récit, paysage*) unfold. **~ement** *n.m.* (*d'une action*) development.

déroute /derut/ *n.f.* (*mil.*) rout.

dérouter /derute/ *v.t.* disconcert.

derrière /dɛrjɛr/ *prép. & adv.* behind. ● *n.m.* back, rear; (*postérieur*) behind. **de ~,** back, rear; (*pattes*) hind. **par ~,** (from) behind, at the back *ou* rear.

des /de/ *voir* de.

dès /dɛ/ *prép.* (right) from, from the time of. **~ lors,** from then on. **~ que,** as soon as.

désabusé /dezabyze/ *a.* disillusioned.

désaccord /dezakɔr/ *n.m.* disagreement. **~é** /-de/ *a.* out of tune.

désaffecté /dezafɛkte/ *a.* disused.

désaffection /dezafɛksjɔ̃/ *n.f.* alienation (**pour,** from).

désagréable /dezagreabl/ *a.* unpleasant.

désagréger (se) /(sə)dezagreʒe/ *v. pr.* disintegrate.

désagrément /dezagremɑ̃/ *n.m.* annoyance.

désaltérant /dezalterɑ̃/ *a.* thirst-quenching, refreshing.

désaltérer /dezaltere/ *v.i.*, **se ~** *v. pr.* quench one's thirst.

désamorcer /dezamɔrse/ *v.t.* (*situation, obus*) defuse.

désappr|ouver /dezapruve/ *v.t.* disapprove of. **~obation** *n.f.* disapproval.

désarçonner /dezarsɔne/ *v.t.* disconcert, throw; (*jockey*) unseat, throw.

désarmant /dezarmɑ̃/ *a.* disarming.

désarm|er /dezarme/ *v.t./i.* disarm. **~ement** *n.m.* (*pol.*) disarmament.

désarroi /dezarwa/ *n.m.* confusion.

désarticulé /dezartikyle/ *a.* dislocated.

désastr|e /dezastr/ *n.m.* disaster. **~eux, ~euse** *a.* disastrous.

désavantag|e /dezavɑ̃taʒ/ *n.m.* disadvantage. **~er** *v.t.* put at a disadvantage. **~eux, ~euse** *a.* disadvantageous.

désaveu (*pl.* **~x**) /dezavø/ *n.m.* repudiation.

désavouer /dezavwe/ *v.t.* repudiate.

désaxé, ~e /dezakse/ *a. & n.m., f.* unbalanced (person).

descendan|t, ~te /desɑ̃dɑ̃, -t/ *n.m., f.* descendant. **~ce** *n.f.* descent; (*enfants*) descendants.

descendre /desɑ̃dr/ *v.i.* (*aux. être*) go down; (*venir*) come down; (*passager*) get off *ou* out; (*nuit*) fall. **~ de,** (*être issu de*) be descended from. **~ à l'hôtel,** go to a hotel. ● *v.t.* (*aux. avoir*) (*escalier etc.*) go *ou* come down; (*objet*) take down; (*abattre, fam.*) shoot down.

descente /desɑ̃t/ *n.f.* descent; (*pente*) (downward) slope; (*raid*) raid. **~ de lit,** bedside rug.

descripti|f, ~ve /dɛskriptif, -v/ *a.* descriptive.

description /dɛskripsjɔ̃/ *n.f.* description.

désemparé /dezɑ̃pare/ *a.* distraught.

désemplir /dezɑ̃plir/ *v.i.* **ne pas ~,** be always crowded.

désendettement /dezɑ̃dɛtmɑ̃/ *n.m.* getting out of debt.

désenfler /dezɑ̃fle/ *v.i.* go down.

déséquilibre /dezekilibr/ *n.m.* imbalance. **en ~,** unsteady.

déséquilibr|er /dezekilibre/ *v.t.* throw off balance. **~é, ~ée** *a. & n.m., f.* unbalanced (person).

désert[1] **~e** /dezɛr, -t/ *a.* deserted.

désert[2] /dezɛr/ *n.m.* desert. **~ique** /-tik/ *a.* desert.

déserter /dezɛrte/ *v.t./i.* desert. **~eur** *n.m.* deserter. **~ion** /-ɛrsjɔ̃/ *n.f.* desertion.

désespér|er /dezɛspere/ *v.i.*, **se ~er** *v. pr.* despair. **~er de,** despair of. **~ant, ~ante** *a.* utterly disheartening. **~é** *a.* in despair; (*état, cas*) hopeless; (*effort*) desperate. **~ément** *adv.* desperately.

désespoir /dezɛspwar/ *n.m.* despair. **au ~,** in despair. **en ~ de cause,** as a last resort.

déshabill|er /dezabije/ *v.t.* **se ~er** *v. pr.* undress, get undressed. **~é** *a.* undressed; *n.m.* négligée.

déshabituer (se) /(sə)dezabitɥe/ *v. pr.* **se ~ de,** get out of the habit of.

désherb|er /dezɛrbe/ *v.t.* weed. **~ant** *n.m.* weed-killer.

déshérit|er /dezerite/ *v.t.* disinherit. **~é** *a.* (*région*) deprived. **les ~és** *n.m. pl.* the underprivileged.

déshonneur /dezɔnœr/ *n.m.* dishonour.

déshonor|er /dezɔnɔre/ *v.t.* dishonour. **~ant, ~ante** *a.* dishonourable.

déshydrater /dezidrate/ *v.t.*, **se ~** *v. pr.* dehydrate.

désigner /deziɲe/ *v.t.* (*montrer*) point to *ou* out; (*élire*) appoint; (*signifier*) indicate.

désillusion /dezilyzjɔ̃/ *n.f.* disillusionment.

désincrust|er /dezɛ̃kryste/ *v. pr.* (*chaudière*) descale; (*peau*) exfoliate. **~ant** *a.* **produit ~ant,** (skin) scrub.

désinence /dezinɑ̃s/ *n.f.* (*gram.*) ending.

désinfect|er /dezɛ̃fɛkte/ *v.t.* disinfect. **~ant** *n.m.* disinfectant.

désinfection /dezɛ̃fɛksjɔ̃/ *n.f.* disinfection.

désintégrer /dezɛ̃tegre/ *v.t.*, **se ~** *v. pr.* disintegrate.

désintéressé /dezɛ̃terese/ *a.* disinterested.

désintéresser (se) /(sə)dezɛ̃terese/ *v. pr.* **se ~ de,** lose interest in.

désintoxication /dezɛ̃tɔksikasjɔ̃/ *n.f.* detoxification. **cure de ~,** detoxification course.

désintoxiquer /dezɛ̃tɔksike/ *v.t.* cure of an addiction; (*régime*) purify.

désinvolt|e /dezɛ̃vɔlt/ *a.* casual. **~ure** *n.f.* casualness.

désir /dezir/ *n.m.* wish, desire; (*convoitise*) desire.

désirer /dezire/ *v.t.* want; (*convoiter*) desire. **~ faire,** want *ou* wish to do.

désireu|x, ~se /dezirø, -z/ *a.* **~x de,** anxious to.

désist|er (se) /(sə)deziste/ *v. pr.* withdraw. **~ement** *n.m.* withdrawal.

désobéir /dezɔbeir/ *v.i.* **~ (à),** disobey.

désobéissan|t, ~te /dezɔbeisɑ̃, -t/ *a.* disobedient. **~ce** *n.f.* disobedience.

désobligeant, ~e /dezɔbliʒɑ̃, -t/ *a.* disagreeable, unkind.

désodé /desɔde/ *a.* sodium-free.

désodorisant /dezɔdɔrizɑ̃/ *n.m.* air freshener.

désœuvr|é /dezœvre/ *a.* idle. **~ement** *n.m.* idleness.

désolé /dezɔle/ *a.* (*région*) desolate.

désol|er /dezɔle/ *v.t.* distress. **être ~é,** (*regretter*) be sorry. **~ation** *n.f.* distress.

désopilant, ~e /dezɔpilɑ̃, -t/ *a.* hilarious.
désordonné /dezɔrdɔne/ *a.* untidy; (*mouvements*) uncoordinated.
désordre /dezɔrdr/ *n.m.* disorder; (*de vêtements, cheveux*) untidiness. **mettre en ~,** make untidy.
désorganiser /dezɔrganize/ *v.t.* disorganize.
désorienté /dezɔrjɑ̃te/ *a.* disorientated.
désorienter /dezɔrjɑ̃te/ *v.t.* disorientate, disorient.
désormais /dezɔrmɛ/ *adv.* from now on.
désosser /dezɔse/ *v.t.* bone.
despote /dɛspɔt/ *n.m.* despot.
desquels, desquelles /dekɛl/ *voir* lequel.
dessécher /deseʃe/ *v.t.*, **se ~** *v. pr.* dry out *ou* up.
dessein /desɛ̃/ *n.m.* intention. **à ~,** intentionally.
desserrer /desere/ *v.t.* loosen. **sans ~ les dents,** without opening his/her mouth. **se ~** *v. pr.* come loose.
dessert /desɛr/ *n.m.* dessert.
desserte /desɛrt/ *n.f.* (*transports*) service, servicing.
desservir /desɛrvir/ *v.t./i.* clear away; (*autobus*) provide a service to, serve.
dessin /desɛ̃/ *n.m.* drawing; (*motif*) design; (*contour*) outline. **~ animé,** (*cinéma*) cartoon. **~ humoristique,** cartoon.
dessin|er /desine/ *v.t./i.* draw; (*fig.*) outline. **se ~er** *v. pr.* appear, take shape. **~ateur, ~atrice** *n.m., f.* artist; (*industriel*) draughtsman.
dessoûler /desule/ *v.t./i.* sober up.
dessous /dsu/ *adv.* underneath. ● *n.m.* under-side, underneath. ● *n.m. pl.* underclothes. **du ~,** bottom; (*voisins*) downstairs. **en ~, par ~,** underneath. **~-de-plat** *n.m. invar.* (heat-resistant) table-mat. **~-de-table** *n.m. invar.* backhander.
dessus /dsy/ *adv.* on top (of it), on it. ● *n.m.* top. **du ~,** top; (*voisins*) upstairs. **en ~,** above. **par ~,** over (it). **avoir le ~,** get the upper hand. **~-de-lit** *n.m. invar.* bedspread.
destabilis|er /destabilize/ *v.t.* destabilize. **~ation** *n.f.* destabilization.
destin /dɛstɛ̃/ *n.m.* (*sort*) fate; (*avenir*) destiny.
destinataire /dɛstinatɛr/ *n.m./f.* addressee.
destination /dɛstinɑsjɔ̃/ *n.f.* destination; (*emploi*) purpose. **à ~ de,** (going) to.
destinée /dɛstine/ *n.f.* (*sort*) fate; (*avenir*) destiny.
destin|er /dɛstine/ *v.t.* **~er à,** intend for; (*vouer*) destine for; (*affecter*) earmark for. **être ~é à faire,** be intended to do; (*condamné, obligé*) be destined to do. **se ~er à,** (*carrière*) intend to take up.
destit|uer /dɛstitɥe/ *v.t.* dismiss (from office). **~ution** *n.f.* dismissal.
destruc|teur, ~trice /dɛstryktœr, -tris/ *a.* destructive.
destruction /dɛstryksjɔ̃/ *n.f.* destruction.
dés|uet, ~uète /dezɥɛ, -t/ *a.* outdated.
désunir /dezynir/ *v.t.* divide.
détachant /detaʃɑ̃/ *n.m.* stain-remover.
détach|é /detaʃe/ *a.* detached. **~ement** *n.m.* detachment.
détacher /detaʃe/ *v.t.* untie; (*ôter*) remove, detach; (*déléguer*) send (on assignment *ou* secondment). **se ~** *v. pr.* come off, break away; (*nœud etc.*) come undone; (*ressortir*) stand out.
détail /detaj/ *n.m.* detail; (*de compte*) breakdown; (*comm.*) retail. **au ~,** (*vendre etc.*) retail. **de ~,** (*prix etc.*) retail. **en ~,** in detail.
détaillé /detaje/ *a.* detailed.
détaill|er /detaje/ *v.t.* (*articles*) sell in small quantities, split up. **~ant, ~ante** *n.m., f.* retailer.
détaler /detale/ *v.i.* (*fam.*) make tracks, run off.
détartrant /detartrɑ̃/ *n.m.* descaler.
détaxer /detakse/ *v.t.* reduce the tax on.
détect|er /detɛkte/ *v.t.* detect. **~eur** *n.m.* detector. **~ion** /-ksjɔ̃/ *n.f.* detection.
détective /detɛktiv/ *n.m.* detective.
déteindre /detɛ̃dr/ *v.i.* (*couleur*) run (**sur,** on to). **~ sur,** (*fig.*) rub off on.
détend|re /detɑ̃dr/ *v.t.* slacken; (*ressort*) release; (*personne*) relax. **se ~re** *v. pr.* become slack, slacken; be released; relax. **~u** *a.* (*calme*) relaxed.
détenir† /detnir/ *v.t.* hold; (*secret, fortune*) possess.

détente /detɑ̃t/ *n.f.* relaxation; (*pol.*) détente; (*saut*) spring; (*gâchette*) trigger; (*relâchement*) release.
déten|teur, ~trice /detɑ̃tœr, -tris/ *n.m., f.* holder.
détention /detɑ̃sjɔ̃/ *n.f.* **~ préventive,** custody.
détenu, ~e /detny/ *n.m., f.* prisoner.
détergent /detɛrʒɑ̃/ *n.m.* detergent.
détérior|er /deterjɔre/ *v.t.* damage. **se ~er** *v. pr.* deteriorate. **~ation** *n.f.* damaging; deterioration.
détermin|er /detɛrmine/ *v.t.* determine. **se ~er** *v. pr.* make up one's mind (**à,** to). **~ation** *n.f.* determination. **~é** *a.* (*résolu*) determined; (*précis*) definite.
déterrer /detere/ *v.t.* dig up.
détersif /detɛrsif/ *n.m.* detergent.
détestable /detɛstabl/ *a.* foul.
détester /detɛste/ *v.t.* hate. **se ~** *v. pr.* hate each other.
déton|er /detɔne/ *v.i.* explode, detonate. **~ateur** *n.m.* detonator. **~ation** *n.f.* explosion, detonation.
détonner /detɔne/ *v.i.* clash.
détour /detur/ *n.m.* bend; (*crochet*) detour; (*fig.*) roundabout means.
détourné /deturne/ *a.* roundabout.
détourn|er /deturne/ *v.t.* divert; (*tête, yeux*) turn away; (*avion*) hijack; (*argent*) embezzle. **se ~er de,** stray from. **~ement** *n.m.* hijack(ing); embezzlement.
détrac|teur, ~trice /detraktœr, -tris/ *n.m., f.* critic.
détraquer /detrake/ *v.t.* break, put out of order; (*estomac*) upset. **se ~** *v. pr.* (*machine*) go wrong.
détresse /detrɛs/ *n.f.* distress.
détriment /detrimɑ̃/ *n.m.* detriment.
détritus /detrity(s)/ *n.m. pl.* rubbish.
détroit /detrwa/ *n.m.* strait.
détromper /detrɔ̃pe/ *v.t.* undeceive, enlighten.
détruire† /detrɥir/ *v.t.* destroy.
dette /dɛt/ *n.f.* debt.
deuil /dœj/ *n.m.* mourning; (*perte*) bereavement. **porter le ~,** be in mourning.
deux /dø/ *a.* & *n.m.* two. **~ fois,** twice. **tous (les) ~,** both. **~- pièces** *n.m. invar.* (*vêtement*) two-piece; (*logement*) two-room flat *or* apartment. **~-points** *n.m. invar.* (*gram.*) colon. **~-roues** *n.m. invar.* two-wheeled vehicle.
deuxième /døzjɛm/ *a.* & *n.m./f.* second. **~ment** *adv.* secondly.
dévaler /devale/ *v.t./i.* hurtle down.
dévaliser /devalize/ *v.t.* rob, clean out.
dévaloriser /devalɔrize/ *v.t.*, **se ~** *v. pr.* reduce in value.
dévalorisant, ~e /devalɔrizɑ̃, -t/ *a.* demeaning.
déval|uer /devalɥe/ *v.t.*, **se ~uer** *v. pr.* devalue. **~uation** *n.f.* devaluation.
devancer /dəvɑ̃se/ *v.t.* be *ou* go ahead of; (*arriver*) arrive ahead of; (*prévenir*) anticipate.
devant /dvɑ̃/ *prép.* in front of; (*distance*) ahead of; (*avec mouvement*) past; (*en présence de*) before; (*face à*) in the face of. • *adv.* in front; (*à distance*) ahead. • *n.m.* front. **prendre les ~s,** take the initiative. **de ~,** front. **par ~,** at *ou* from the front, in front. **aller au ~ de qn.,** go to meet sb. **aller au ~ des désirs de qn.,** anticipate sb.'s wishes.
devanture /dvɑ̃tyr/ *n.f.* shop front; (*étalage*) shop-window.
dévaster /devaste/ *v.t.* devastate.
déveine /devɛn/ *n.f.* bad luck.
développ|er /devlɔpe/ *v.t.*, **se ~er** *v. pr.* develop. **~ement** *n.m.* development; (*de photos*) developing.
devenir† /dəvnir/ *v.i.* (*aux. être*) become. **qu'est-il devenu?,** what has become of him?
dévergondé /devɛrgɔ̃de/ *a.* shameless.
déverser /devɛrse/ *v.t.*, **se ~** *v. pr.* empty out, pour out.
dévêtir /devetir/ *v.t.*, **se ~** *v. pr.* undress.
déviation /devjɑsjɔ̃/ *n.f.* diversion.
dévier /devje/ *v.t.* divert; (*coup*) deflect. • *v.i.* (*ballon, balle*) veer; (*personne*) deviate.
devin /dəvɛ̃/ *n.m.* fortune-teller.
deviner /dvine/ *v.t.* guess; (*apercevoir*) distinguish.
devinette /dvinɛt/ *n.f.* riddle.
devis /dvi/ *n.m.* estimate.
dévisager /devizaʒe/ *v.t.* stare at.
devise /dviz/ *n.f.* motto. **~s,** (*monnaie*) (foreign) currency.
dévisser /devise/ *v.t.* unscrew.
dévitaliser /devitalize/ *v.t.* (*dent*) kill the nerve in.
dévoiler /devwale/ *v.t.* reveal.
devoir[1] /dvwar/ *n.m.* duty; (*scol.*) homework; (*fait en classe*) exercise.

devoir†[2] /dvwar/ *v.t.* owe. ● *v. aux.* **~ faire,** (*nécessité*) must do, have (got) to do; (*intention*) be due to do. **~ être,** (*probabilité*) must be. **vous devriez,** you should. **il aurait dû,** he should have.

dévolu /devɔly/ *n.m.* **jeter son ~ sur,** set one's heart on. ● *a.* **~ à,** allotted to.

dévorer /devɔre/ *v.t.* devour.

dévot, ~e /devo, -ɔt/ *a.* devout.

dévotion /devosjɔ̃/ *n.f.* (*relig.*) devotion.

dévou|er (se) /(sə)devwe/ *v. pr.* devote o.s. (**à,** to); (*se sacrifier*) sacrifice o.s. **~é** *a.* devoted. **~ement** /-vumɑ̃/ *n.m.* devotion.

dextérité /dɛksterite/ *n.f.* skill.

diab|ète /djabɛt/ *n.m.* diabetes. **~étique** *a.* & *n.m./f.* diabetic.

diab|le /djɑbl/ *n.m.* devil. **~olique** *a.* diabolical.

diagnosti|c /djagnɔstik/ *n.m.* diagnosis. **~quer** *v.t.* diagnose.

diagon|al, ~ale (*m. pl.* **~aux**) /djagɔnal, -o/ *a.* & *n.f.* diagonal. **en ~ale,** diagonally.

diagramme /djagram/ *n.m.* diagram; (*graphique*) graph.

dialecte /djalɛkt/ *n.m.* dialect.

dialogu|e /djalɔg/ *n.m.* dialogue. **~er** *v.i.* (*pol.*) have a dialogue.

diamant /djamɑ̃/ *n.m.* diamond.

diamètre /djamɛtr/ *n.m.* diameter.

diapason /djapazɔ̃/ *n.m.* tuning fork.

diaphragme /djafragm/ *n.m.* diaphragm.

diapo /djapo/ *n.f.* (colour) slide.

diapositive /djapozitiv/ *n.f.* (colour) slide.

diarrhée /djare/ *n.f.* diarrhoea.

dictat|eur /diktatœr/ *n.m.* dictator. **~ure** *n.f.* dictatorship.

dict|er /dikte/ *v.t.* dictate. **~ée** *n.f.* dictation.

diction /diksjɔ̃/ *n.f.* diction.

dictionnaire /diksjɔnɛr/ *n.m.* dictionary.

dicton /diktɔ̃/ *n.m.* saying.

dièse /djɛz/ *n.m.* (*mus.*) sharp.

diesel /djezɛl/ *n.m.* & *a. invar.* diesel.

diète /djɛt/ *n.f.* (*régime*) diet.

diététicien, ~ne /djetetisjɛ̃, -jɛn/ *n.m., f.* dietician.

diététique /djetetik/ *n.f.* dietetics. ● *a.* **produit** *ou* **aliment ~,** dietary product.

dieu (*pl.* **~x**) /djø/ *n.m.* god. **D~,** God.

diffamatoire /difamatwar/ *a.* defamatory.

diffam|er /difame/ *v.t.* slander; (*par écrit*) libel. **~ation** *n.f.* slander; libel.

différé (en) /(ɑ̃)difere/ *adv.* (*émission*) recorded.

différemment /diferamɑ̃/ *adv.* differently.

différence /diferɑ̃s/ *n.f.* difference. **à la ~ de,** unlike.

différencier /diferɑ̃sje/ *v.t.* differentiate. **se ~ de,** (*différer de*) differ from.

différend /diferɑ̃/ *n.m.* difference (of opinion).

différent, ~e /diferɑ̃, -t/ *a.* different (**de,** from).

différentiel, ~le /diferɑ̃sjɛl/ *a.* & *n.m.* differential.

différer[1] /difere/ *v.t.* postpone.

différer[2] /difere/ *v.i.* differ (**de,** from).

difficile /difisil/ *a.* difficult. **~ment** *adv.* with difficulty.

difficulté /difikylte/ *n.f.* difficulty.

difform|e /difɔrm/ *a.* deformed. **~ité** *n.f.* deformity.

diffus, ~e /dify, -z/ *a.* diffuse.

diffus|er /difyze/ *v.t.* broadcast; (*lumière, chaleur*) diffuse. **~ion** *n.f.* broadcasting; diffusion.

dig|érer /diʒere/ *v.t.* digest; (*endurer: fam.*) stomach. **~este, ~estible** *adjs.* digestible. **~estion** *n.f.* digestion.

digesti|f, ~ve /diʒɛstif, -v/ *a.* digestive. ● *n.m.* after-dinner liqueur.

digit|al (*m. pl.* **~aux**) /diʒital, -o/ *a.* digital.

digne /diɲ/ *a.* (*noble*) dignified; (*honnête*) worthy. **~ de,** worthy of. **~ de foi,** trustworthy.

dignité /diɲite/ *n.f.* dignity.

digression /digresjɔ̃/ *n.f.* digression.

digue /dig/ *n.f.* dike.

diktat /diktat/ *n.m.* diktat.

dilapider /dilapide/ *v.t.* squander.

dilat|er /dilate/ *v.t.*, **se ~er** *v. pr.* dilate. **~ation** /-ɑsjɔ̃/ *n.f.* dilation.

dilemme /dilɛm/ *n.m.* dilemma.

dilettante /diletɑ̃t/ *n.m., f.* amateur.

diluant /dilɥɑ̃/ *n.m.* thinner.

diluer /dilɥe/ *v.t.* dilute.

diluvien, ~ne /dilyvjɛ̃, -ɛn/ *a.* (*pluie*) torrential.

dimanche /dimɑ̃ʃ/ *n.m.* Sunday.

dimension /dimɑ̃sjɔ̃/ *n.f.* (*taille*) size; (*mesure*) dimension.

dimin|uer /diminɥe/ *v.t.* reduce, decrease; (*plaisir, courage, etc.*) lessen; (*dénigrer*) lessen. ● *v.i.* decrease. **~ution** *n.f.* decrease (**de**, in).

diminutif /diminytif/ *n.m.* diminutive; (*surnom*) pet name *ou* form.

dinde /dɛ̃d/ *n.f.* turkey.

dindon /dɛ̃dɔ̃/ *n.m.* turkey.

dîn|er /dine/ *n.m.* dinner. ● *v.i.* have dinner. **~eur, ~euse** *n.m., f.* diner.

dingue /dɛ̃g/ *a.* (*fam.*) crazy.

dinosaure /dinozɔr/ *n.m.* dinosaur.

diocèse /djɔsɛz/ *n.m.* diocese.

diphtérie /difteri/ *n.f.* diphtheria.

diphtongue /diftɔ̃g/ *n.f.* diphthong.

diplomate /diplɔmat/ *n.m.* diplomat. ● *a.* diplomatic.

diplomat|ie /diplɔmasi/ *n.f.* diplomacy. **~ique** /-atik/ *a.* diplomatic.

diplôm|e /diplom/ *n.m.* certificate, diploma; (*univ.*) degree. **~é** *a.* qualified.

dire† /dir/ *v.t.* say; (*secret, vérité, heure*) tell; (*penser*) think. **~ que,** say that. **~ à qn. que/de,** tell s.o. that/to. **se ~** *v. pr.* (*mot*) be said; (*fatigué etc.*) say that one is. **ça me/vous/***etc.* **dit de faire,** I/you/*etc.* feel like doing. **on dirait que,** it would seem that, it seems that. **dis/dites donc!,** hey! ● *n.m.* **au ~ de, selon les ~s de,** according to.

direct /dirɛkt/ *a.* direct. **en ~,** (*émission*) live. **~ement** *adv.* directly.

direc|teur, ~trice /dirɛktœr, -tris/ *n.m., f.* director; (*chef de service*) manager, manageress; (*d'école*) headmaster, headmistress.

direction /dirɛksjɔ̃/ *n.f.* (*sens*) direction; (*de société etc.*) management; (*auto.*) steering. **en ~ de,** (going) to.

directive /dirɛktiv/ *n.f.* instruction.

dirigeant, ~e /diriʒɑ̃, -t/ *n.m., f.* (*pol.*) leader; (*comm.*) manager. ● *a.* (*classe*) ruling.

diriger /diriʒe/ *v.t.* run, manage, direct; (*véhicule*) steer; (*orchestre*) conduct; (*braquer*) aim; (*tourner*) turn. **se ~** *v. pr.* guide o.s. **se ~ vers,** make one's way to.

dirigis|me /diriʒism/ *n.m.* interventionism. **~te** /-ist/ *a.* & *n.m./f.* interventionist.

dis /di/ *voir* dire.

discern|er /disɛrne/ *v.t.* discern. **~ement** *n.m.* discernment.

disciple /disipl/ *n.m.* disciple.

disciplin|e /disiplin/ *n.f.* discipline. **~aire** *a.* disciplinary. **~er** *v.t.* discipline.

discontinu /diskɔ̃tiny/ *a.* intermittent.

discontinuer /diskɔ̃tinɥe/ *v.i.* **sans ~,** without stopping.

discordant, ~e /diskɔrdɑ̃, -t/ *a.* discordant.

discorde /diskɔrd/ *n.f.* discord.

discothèque /diskɔtɛk/ *n.f.* record library; (*club*) disco(thèque).

discount /diskunt/ *n.m.* discount.

discourir /diskurir/ *v.i.* (*péj.*) hold forth, ramble on.

discours /diskur/ *n.m.* speech.

discréditer /diskredite/ *v.t.* discredit.

discr|et, ~ète /diskrɛ, -t/ *a.* discreet. **~ètement** *adv.* discreetly.

discrétion /diskresjɔ̃/ *n.f.* discretion. **à ~,** as much as one desires.

discrimination /diskriminɑsjɔ̃/ *n.f.* discrimination.

discriminatoire /diskriminatwar/ *a.* discriminatory.

disculper /diskylpe/ *v.t.* exonerate. **se ~** *v. pr.* prove o.s. innocent.

discussion /diskysjɔ̃/ *n.f.* discussion; (*querelle*) argument.

discuté /diskyte/ *a.* controversial.

discut|er /diskyte/ *v.t.* discuss; (*contester*) question. ● *v.i.* (*parler*) talk; (*répliquer*) argue. **~er de,** discuss. **~able** *a.* debatable.

disette /dizɛt/ *n.f.* (food) shortage.

diseuse /dizøz/ *n.f.* **~ de bonne aventure,** fortune-teller.

disgrâce /disgrɑs/ *n.f.* disgrace.

disgracieu|x, ~se /disgrasjø, -z/ *a.* ungainly.

disjoindre /disʒwɛ̃dr/ *v.t.* take apart. **se ~** *v. pr.* come apart.

disloquer /dislɔke/ *v.t.* (*membre*) dislocate; (*machine etc.*) break (apart). **se ~quer** *v. pr.* (*parti, cortège*) break up; (*meuble*) come apart. **~cation** *n.f.* (*anat.*) dislocation.

dispar|aître† /disparɛtr/ *v.i.* disappear; (*mourir*) die. **faire ~aître,** get rid of. **~ition** *n.f.* disappearance; (*mort*) death. **~u, ~ue** *a.* (*soldat etc.*) missing; *n.m., f.* missing person; (*mort*) dead person.

disparate /disparat/ *a.* ill-assorted.

disparité /disparite/ *n.f.* disparity.

dispensaire /dispɑ̃sɛr/ *n.m.* clinic.

dispense /dispɑ̃s/ *n.f.* exemption.

dispenser /dispɑ̃se/ *v.t.* exempt **(de,** from). **se ~ de (faire),** avoid (doing).
disperser /dispɛrse/ *v.t.* (*éparpiller*) scatter; (*répartir*) disperse. **se ~** *v. pr.* disperse.
disponib|le /disponibl/ *a.* available. **~ilité** *n.f.* availability.
dispos, ~e /dispo, -z/ *a.* **frais et ~,** fresh and alert.
disposé /dispoze/ *a.* **bien/mal ~,** in a good/bad mood. **~ à,** prepared to. **~ envers,** disposed towards.
disposer /dispoze/ *v.t.* arrange. **~ à,** (*engager à*) incline to. ● *v.i.* **~ de,** have at one's disposal. **se ~ à,** prepare to.
dispositif /dispozitif/ *n.m.* device; (*plan*) plan of action. **~ anti-parasite,** suppressor.
disposition /dispozisjɔ̃/ *n.f.* arrangement; (*humeur*) mood; (*tendance*) tendency. **~s,** (*préparatifs*) arrangements; (*aptitude*) aptitude. **à la ~ de,** at the disposal of.
disproportionné /disproporsjone/ *a.* disproportionate.
dispute /dispyt/ *n.f.* quarrel.
disputer /dispyte/ *v.t.* (*match*) play; (*course*) run in; (*prix*) fight for; (*gronder: fam.*) tell off. **se ~** *v. pr.* quarrel; (*se battre pour*) fight over; (*match*) be played.
disquaire /diskɛr/ *n.m./f.* record dealer.
disqualif|ier /diskalifje/ *v.t.* disqualify. **~ication** *n.f.* disqualification.
disque /disk/ *n.m.* (*mus.*) record; (*sport*) discus; (*cercle*) disc, disk. **~ dur,** hard disk.
disquette /diskɛt/ *n.f.* (floppy) disk.
dissection /disɛksjɔ̃/ *n.f.* dissection.
dissemblable /disɑ̃blabl/ *a.* dissimilar.
disséminer /disemine/ *v.t.* scatter.
disséquer /diseke/ *v.t.* dissect.
dissertation /disɛrtɑsjɔ̃/ *n.f.* (*scol.*) essay.
disserter /disɛrte/ *v.i.* **~ sur,** comment upon.
dissiden|t, ~te /disidɑ̃, -t/ *a.* & *n.m., f.* dissident. **~ce** *n.f.* dissidence.
dissimul|er /disimyle/ *v.t.* conceal **(à,** from). **se ~er** *v. pr.* conceal o.s. **~ation** *n.f.* concealment; (*fig.*) deceit.
dissipé /disipe/ *a.* (*élève*) unruly.
dissip|er /disipe/ *v.t.* (*fumée, crainte*) dispel; (*fortune*) squander; (*personne*) lead into bad ways. **se ~er** *v. pr.* disappear. **~ation** *n.f.* squandering; (*indiscipline*) misbehaviour.
dissolution /disolysjɔ̃/ *n.f.* dissolution.
dissolvant /disolvɑ̃/ *n.m.* solvent; (*pour ongles*) nail polish remover.
dissonant, ~e /disonɑ̃, -t/ *a.* discordant.
dissoudre† /disudr/ *v.t.*, **se ~** *v. pr.* dissolve.
dissua|der /disɥade/ *v.t.* dissuade **(de,** from). **~sion** /-ɥazjɔ̃/ *n.f.* dissuasion. **force de ~sion,** deterrent force.
dissuasi|f, ~ve /disɥazif, -v/ *a.* dissuasive.
distance /distɑ̃s/ *n.f.* distance; (*écart*) gap. **à ~,** at *ou* from a distance.
distancer /distɑ̃se/ *v.t.* leave behind.
distant, ~e /distɑ̃, -t/ *a.* distant.
distendre /distɑ̃dr/ *v.t.*, **se ~** *v. pr.* distend.
distill|er /distile/ *v.t.* distil. **~ation** *n.f.* distillation.
distillerie /distilri/ *n.f.* distillery.
distinct, ~e /distɛ̃(kt), -ɛ̃kt/ *a.* distinct. **~ement** /-ɛ̃ktəmɑ̃/ *adv.* distinctly.
distincti|f, ~ve /distɛ̃ktif, -v/ *a.* distinctive.
distinction /distɛ̃ksjɔ̃/ *n.f.* distinction.
distingué /distɛ̃ge/ *a.* distinguished.
distinguer /distɛ̃ge/ *v.t.* distinguish.
distraction /distraksjɔ̃/ *n.f.* absentmindedness; (*oubli*) lapse; (*passe-temps*) distraction.
distraire† /distrɛr/ *v.t.* amuse; (*rendre inattentif*) distract. **se ~** *v. pr.* amuse o.s.
distrait, ~e /distrɛ, -t/ *a.* absent-minded. **~ement** *a.* absent-mindedly.
distrayant, ~e /distrɛjɑ̃, -t/ *a.* entertaining.
distrib|uer /distribɥe/ *v.t.* hand out, distribute; (*répartir, amener*) distribute; (*courrier*) deliver. **~uteur** *n.m.* (*auto., comm.*) distributor. **~uteur (automatique),** vending-machine; (*de billets*) (cash) dispenser. **~ution** *n.f.* distribution; (*du courrier*) delivery; (*acteurs*) cast.
district /distrikt/ *n.m.* district.

dit[1]**, dites** /di, dit/ *voir* dire.
dit[2]**, ~e** /di, dit/ *a.* (*décidé*) agreed; (*surnommé*) called.
diurétique /djyretik/ *a. & n.m.* diuretic.
diurne /djyrn/ *a.* diurnal.
divag|uer /divage/ *v.i.* rave. **~ations** *n.f. pl.* ravings.
divan /divɑ̃/ *n.m.* divan.
divergen|t, ~te /divɛrʒɑ̃, -t/ *a.* divergent. **~ce** *n.f.* divergence.
diverger /divɛrʒe/ *v.i.* diverge.
divers, ~e /divɛr, -s/ *a.* (*varié*) diverse; (*différent*) various. **~ement** /-səmɑ̃/ *adv.* variously.
diversifier /divɛrsifje/ *v.t.* diversify.
diversion /divɛrsjɔ̃/ *n.f.* diversion.
diversité /divɛrsite/ *n.f.* diversity.
divert|ir /divɛrtir/ *v.t.* amuse. **se ~ir** *v. pr.* amuse o.s. **~issement** *n.m.* amusement.
dividende /dividɑ̃d/ *n.m.* dividend.
divin, ~e /divɛ̃, -in/ *a.* divine.
divinité /divinite/ *n.f.* divinity.
divis|er /divize/ *v.t.*, **se ~er** *v. pr.* divide. **~ion** *n.f.* division.
divorc|e /divɔrs/ *n.m.* divorce. **~é ~ée** *a.* divorced; *n.m., f.* divorcee. **~er** *v.i.* **~er (d'avec),** divorce.
divulguer /divylge/ *v.t.* divulge.
dix /dis/ (/di/ *before consonant*, /diz/ *before vowel*) *a. & n.m.* ten. **~ième** /dizjɛm/ *a. & n.m./f.* tenth.
dix-huit /dizɥit/ *a. & n.m.* eighteen. **~ième** *a. & n.m./f.* eighteenth.
dix-neu|f /diznœf/ *a. & n.m.* nineteen. **~vième** *a. & n.m./f.* nineteenth.
dix-sept /disɛt/ *a. & n.m.* seventeen. **~ième** *a. & n.m./f.* seventeenth.
dizaine /dizɛn/ *n.f.* (about) ten.
docile /dɔsil/ *a.* docile.
docilité /dɔsilite/ *n.f.* docility.
dock /dɔk/ *n.m.* dock.
docker /dɔkɛr/ *n.m.* docker.
doct|eur /dɔktœr/ *n.m.* doctor. **~oresse** *n.f.* (*fam.*) lady doctor.
doctorat /dɔktɔra/ *n.m.* doctorate.
doctrin|e /dɔktrin/ *n.f.* doctrine. **~aire** *a.* doctrinaire.
document /dɔkymɑ̃/ *n.m.* document. **~aire** /-tɛr/ *a. & n.m.* documentary.
documentaliste /dɔkymɑ̃talist/ *n.m./f.* information officer.
document|er /dɔkymɑ̃te/ *v.t.* document. **se ~er** *v. pr.* collect information. **~ation** *n.f.* information, literature. **~é** *a.* well-documented.
dodo /dodo/ *n.m.* **faire ~,** (*langage enfantin*) go to byebyes.
dodu /dɔdy/ *a.* plump.
dogm|e /dɔgm/ *n.m.* dogma. **~atique** *a.* dogmatic.
doigt /dwa/ *n.m.* finger. **un ~ de,** a drop of. **à deux ~s de,** a hair's breadth away from. **~ de pied,** toe.
doigté /dwate/ *n.m.* (*mus.*) fingering, touch; (*adresse*) tact.
dois, doit /dwa/ *voir* devoir[2].
Dolby /dɔlbi/ *n.m. & a.* (P.) Dolby (P.).
doléances /dɔleɑ̃s/ *n.f. pl.* grievances.
dollar /dɔlar/ *n.m.* dollar.
domaine /dɔmɛn/ *n.m.* estate, domain; (*fig.*) domain.
dôme /dom/ *n.m.* dome.
domestique /dɔmɛstik/ *a.* domestic. ● *n.m./f.* servant.
domestiquer /dɔmɛstike/ *v.t.* domesticate.
domicile /dɔmisil/ *n.m.* home. **à ~,** at home; (*livrer*) to the home.
domicilié /dɔmisilje/ *a.* resident.
domin|er /dɔmine/ *v.t./i.* dominate; (*surplomber*) tower over, dominate; (*équipe*) dictate the game (to). **~ant, ~ante** *a.* dominant; *n.f.* dominant feature. **~ation** *n.f.* domination.
domino /dɔmino/ *n.m.* domino.
dommage /dɔmaʒ/ *n.m.* (*tort*) harm. **~(s),** (*dégâts*) damage. **c'est ~,** it's a pity. **quel ~,** what a shame. **~s-intérêts** *n.m. pl.* (*jurid.*) damages.
dompt|er /dɔ̃te/ *v.t.* tame. **~eur, ~euse** *n.m., f.* tamer.
don /dɔ̃/ *n.m.* (*cadeau, aptitude*) gift.
dona|teur, ~trice /dɔnatœr, -tris/ *n.m., f.* donor.
donation /dɔnɑsjɔ̃/ *n.f.* donation.
donc /dɔ̃k/ *conj.* so, then; (*par conséquent*) so, therefore.
donjon /dɔ̃ʒɔ̃/ *n.m.* (*tour*) keep.
donné /dɔne/ *a.* (*fixé*) given; (*pas cher: fam.*) dirt cheap. **étant ~ que,** given that.
données /dɔne/ *n.f. pl.* (*de science*) data; (*de problème*) facts.
donner /dɔne/ *v.t.* give; (*vieilles affaires*) give away; (*distribuer*) give out; (*récolte etc.*) produce; (*film*) show; (*pièce*) put on. ● *v.i.* **~ sur,** look out on to. **~ dans,** (*piège*) fall into. **ça donne soif/faim,** it makes one thirsty/ hungry. **~ à réparer/** *etc.*, take to be repaired/*etc.* **~ lieu à,** give rise to. **se ~ à,** devote o.s. to. **se**

~ du mal, go to a lot of trouble (**pour faire,** to do).

donneu|r, ~se /dɔnœr, -øz/ *n.m., f.* (*de sang*) donor.

dont /dɔ̃/ *pron. rel.* (*chose*) whose, of which; (*personne*) whose; (*partie d'un tout*) of whom; (*chose*) of which; (*provenance*) from which; (*manière*) in which. **le père ~ la fille,** the father whose daughter. **ce ~,** what. **~ il a besoin,** which he needs. **l'enfant ~ il est fier,** the child he is proud of. **trois enfants ~ deux sont jumeaux,** three children, two of whom are twins.

dopage /dɔpaʒ/ *n.m.* doping.

doper /dɔpe/ *v.t.* dope. **se ~** *v. pr.* take dope.

doré /dɔre/ *a.* (*couleur d'or*) golden; (*avec dorure*) gold. **la bourgeoisie ~e** the affluent middle class.

dorénavant /dɔrenavɑ̃/ *adv.* henceforth.

dorer /dɔre/ *v.t.* gild; (*culin.*) brown.

dorloter /dɔrlɔte/ *v.t.* pamper.

dorm|ir† /dɔrmir/ *v.i.* sleep; (*être endormi*) be asleep. **~eur, ~euse** *n.m., f.* sleeper. **il dort debout,** he can't keep awake. **une histoire à ~ir debout,** a cock-and-bull story.

dortoir /dɔrtwar/ *n.m.* dormitory.

dorure /dɔryr/ *n.f.* gilding.

dos /do/ *n.m.* back; (*de livre*) spine. **à ~ de,** riding on. **de ~,** from behind. **~ crawlé,** backstroke.

dos|e /doz/ *n.f.* dose. **~age** *n.m.* (*mélange*) mixture. **faire le ~age de,** measure out; balance. **~er** *v.t.* measure out; (*équilibrer*) balance.

dossard /dɔsar/ *n.m.* (*sport*) number.

dossier /dɔsje/ *n.m.* (*documents*) file; (*de chaise*) back.

dot /dɔt/ *n.f.* dowry.

doter /dɔte/ *v.t.* **~ de,** equip with.

douan|e /dwan/ *n.f.* customs. **~ier, ~ière** *a.* customs; *n.m., f.* customs officer.

doubl|e /dubl/ *a. & adv.* double. ● *n.m.* (*copie*) duplicate; (*sosie*) double. **le ~e (de),** twice as much *ou* as many (as). **le ~e messieurs,** the men's doubles. **~e décimètre,** ruler. **~ement**[1] *adv.* doubly.

doubl|er /duble/ *v.t./i.* double; (*dépasser*) overtake; (*vêtement*) line; (*film*) dub; (*classe*) repeat; (*cap*) round. **~ement**[2] *n.m.* doubling. **~ure** *n.f.* (*étoffe*) lining; (*acteur*) understudy.

douce /dus/ *voir* doux.

douceâtre /dusɑtr/ *a.* sickly sweet.

doucement /dusmɑ̃/ *adv.* gently.

douceur /dusœr/ *n.f.* (*mollesse*) softness; (*de climat*) mildness; (*de personne*) gentleness; (*joie, plaisir*) sweetness. **~s,** (*friandises*) sweet things. **en ~,** smoothly.

douch|e /duʃ/ *n.f.* shower. **~er** *v.t.* give a shower to. **se ~er** *v. pr.* have *ou* take a shower.

doudoune /dudun/ *n.f.* (*fam.*) anorak.

doué /dwe/ *a.* gifted. **~ de,** endowed with.

douille /duj/ *n.f.* (*électr.*) socket.

douillet, ~te /dujɛ, -t/ *a.* cosy, comfortable; (*personne*: *péj.*) soft.

doul|eur /dulœr/ *n.f.* pain; (*chagrin*) grief. **~oureux, ~oureuse** *a.* painful. **la ~oureuse** *n.f.* the bill.

doute /dut/ *n.m.* doubt. **sans ~,** no doubt. **sans aucun ~,** without doubt.

douter /dute/ *v.i.* **~ de,** doubt. **se ~ de,** suspect.

douteu|x, ~se /dutø, -z/ *a.* doubtful.

Douvres /duvr/ *n.m./f.* Dover.

doux, douce /du, dus/ *a.* (*moelleux*) soft; (*sucré*) sweet; (*clément, pas fort*) mild; (*pas brusque, bienveillant*) gentle.

douzaine /duzɛn/ *n.f.* about twelve; (*douze*) dozen. **une ~ d'œufs**/*etc.*, a dozen eggs/*etc.*

douz|e /duz/ *a. & n.m.* twelve. **~ième** *a. & n.m./f.* twelfth.

doyen, ~ne /dwajɛ̃, -jɛn/ *n.m., f.* dean; (*en âge*) most senior person.

dragée /draʒe/ *n.f.* sugared almond.

dragon /dragɔ̃/ *n.m.* dragon.

dragu|e /drag/ *n.f.* (*bateau*) dredger. **~er** *v.t.* (*rivière*) dredge; (*filles*: *fam.*) chat up, try to pick up.

drain /drɛ̃/ *n.m.* drain.

drainer /drene/ *v.t.* drain.

dramatique /dramatik/ *a.* dramatic; (*tragique*) tragic. ● *n.f.* (television) drama.

dramatiser /dramatize/ *v.t.* dramatize.

dramaturge /dramatyrʒ/ *n.m./f.* dramatist.

drame /dram/ *n.m.* drama.

drap /dra/ *n.m.* sheet; (*tissu*) (woollen) cloth. **~-housse** /draus/ *n.m.* fitted sheet.

drapeau (*pl.* **~x**) /drapo/ *n.m.* flag.

draper /drape/ *v.t.* drape.

dress|er /drese/ *v.t.* put up, erect; (*tête*) raise; (*animal*) train; (*liste*) draw up. **se ~er** *v. pr.* (*bâtiment etc.*) stand; (*personne*) draw o.s. up. **~er l'oreille,** prick up one's ears. **~age** /drɛsaʒ/ *n.m.* training. **~eur, ~euse** /drɛsœr, -øz/ *n.m., f.* trainer.

dribbler /drible/ *v.t./i.* (*sport*) dribble.

drille /drij/ *n.m.* **un joyeux ~,** a cheery character.

drive /drajv/ *n.m.* (*comput.*) drive.

drogue /drɔg/ *n.f.* drug. **la ~,** drugs.

drogu|er /drɔge/ *v.t.* (*malade*) drug heavily, dose up; (*victime*) drug. **se ~er** *v. pr.* take drugs. **~é, ~ée** *n.m., f.* drug addict.

drogu|erie /drɔgri/ *n.f.* hardware and chemist's shop; (*Amer.*) drugstore. **~iste** *n.m./f.* owner of a *droguerie.*

droit[1], **~e** /drwa, -t/ *a.* (*non courbe*) straight; (*loyal*) upright; (*angle*) right. ● *adv.* straight. ● *n.f.* straight line.

droit[2], **~e** /drwa, -t/ *a.* (*contraire de gauche*) right. **à ~e,** on the right; (*direction*) (to the) right. **la ~e,** the right (side); (*pol.*) the right (wing). **~ier, ~ière** /-tje, -tjɛr/ *a. & n.m., f.* right-handed (person).

droit[3] /drwa/ *n.m.* right. **~(s),** (*taxe*) duty; (*d'inscription*) fee(s). **le ~,** (*jurid.*) law. **avoir ~ à,** be entitled to. **avoir le ~ de,** be allowed to. **être dans son ~,** be in the right. **~ d'auteur,** copyright. **~s d'auteur,** royalties.

drôle /drol/ *a.* funny. **~ d'air,** funny look. **~ment** *adv.* funnily; (*extrêmement: fam.*) dreadfully.

dromadaire /drɔmadɛr/ *n.m.* dromedary.

dru /dry/ *a.* thick. **tomber ~,** fall thick and fast.

drugstore /drœgstɔr/ *n.m.* drugstore.

du /dy/ *voir* de.

dû, due /dy/ *voir* devoir[2]. ● *a.* due. ● *n.m.* due; (*argent*) dues. **~ à,** due to.

duc, duchesse /dyk, dyʃɛs/ *n.m., f.* duke, duchess.

duel /dɥɛl/ *n.m.* duel.

dune /dyn/ *n.f.* dune.

duo /dɥo/ *n.m.* (*mus.*) duet; (*fig.*) duo.

dup|e /dyp/ *n.f.* dupe. **~er** *v.t.* dupe.

duplex /dyplɛks/ *n.m.* split-level apartment; (*Amer.*) duplex; (*émission*) link-up.

duplicata /dyplikata/ *n.m. invar.* duplicate.

duplicité /dyplisite/ *n.f.* duplicity.

duquel /dykɛl/ *voir* lequel.

dur /dyr/ *a.* hard; (*sévère*) harsh, hard; (*viande*) tough, hard; (*col, brosse*) stiff. ● *adv.* hard. ● *n.m.* tough guy. **~ d'oreille,** hard of hearing.

durable /dyrabl/ *a.* lasting.

durant /dyrɑ̃/ *prép.* during; (*mesure de temps*) for.

durc|ir /dyrsir/ *v.t./i.,* **se ~ir** *v. pr.* harden. **~issement** *n.m.* hardening.

dure /dyr/ *n.f.* **à la ~,** the hard way.

durée /dyre/ *n.f.* length; (*période*) duration.

durement /dyrmɑ̃/ *adv.* harshly.

durer /dyre/ *v.i.* last.

dureté /dyrte/ *n.f.* hardness; (*sévérité*) harshness.

duvet /dyvɛ/ *n.m.* down; (*sac*) (down-filled) sleeping-bag.

dynami|que /dinamik/ *a.* dynamic. **~sme** *n.m.* dynamism.

dynamit|e /dinamit/ *n.f.* dynamite. **~er** *v.t.* dynamite.

dynamo /dinamo/ *n.f.* dynamo.

dynastie /dinasti/ *n.f.* dynasty.

dysenterie /disɑ̃tri/ *n.f.* dysentery.

E

eau (*pl.* **~x**) /o/ *n.f.* water. **~ courante/dormante,** running/still water. **~ de Cologne,** eau-de-Cologne. **~ dentifrice,** mouthwash. **~ de toilette,** eau de toilette. **~-de-vie** (*pl.* **~x-de-vie**) *n.f.* brandy. **~ douce/salée,** fresh/salt water. **~-forte** (*pl.* **~x-fortes**) *n.f.* etching. **~ potable,** drinking water. **~ de Javel,** bleach. **~ minérale,** mineral water. **~ gazeuse,** fizzy water. **~ plate,** still water. **~x usées,** dirty water. **tomber à l'~** (*fig.*) fall through. **prendre l'~,** take in water.

ébahi /ebai/ *a.* dumbfounded.

ébattre (s') /(s)ebatr/ *v. pr.* frolic.

ébauch|e /eboʃ/ *n.f.* outline. **~er** *v.t.* outline. **s'~er** *v. pr.* form.

ébène /ebɛn/ *n.f.* ebony.

ébéniste /ebenist/ *n.m.* cabinet-maker.

éberlué /ebɛrlɥe/ *a.* flabbergasted.

éblou|ir /ebluir/ *v.t.* dazzle. **~issement** *n.m.* dazzle, dazzling; (*malaise*) dizzy turn.

éboueur /ebwœr/ *n.m.* dustman; (*Amer.*) garbage collector.

ébouillanter /ebujɑ̃te/ *v.t.* scald.

éboul|er (s') /(s)ebule/ *v. pr.* crumble, collapse. **~ement** *n.m.* landslide. **~is** *n.m. pl.* fallen rocks and earth.

ébouriffé /eburife/ *a.* dishevelled.

ébranler /ebrɑ̃le/ *v.t.* shake. **s'~** *v. pr.* move off.

ébrécher /ebreʃe/ *v.t.* chip.

ébriété /ebrijete/ *n.f.* intoxication.

ébrouer (s') /(s)ebrue/ *v. pr.* shake o.s.

ébruiter /ebrɥite/ *v.t.* spread about.

ébullition /ebylisjɔ̃/ *n.f.* boiling. **en ~,** boiling.

écaille /ekaj/ *n.f.* (*de poisson*) scale; (*de peinture, roc*) flake; (*matière*) tortoiseshell.

écailler /ekaje/ *v.t.* (*poisson*) scale. **s'~** *v. pr.* flake (off).

écarlate /ekarlat/ *a.* & *n.f.* scarlet.

écarquiller /ekarkije/ *v.t.* **~ les yeux,** open one's eyes wide.

écart /ekar/ *n.m.* gap; (*de prix etc.*) difference; (*embardée*) swerve; (*de conduite*) lapse (**de,** in). **à l'~,** out of the way. **tenir à l'~,** (*participant*) keep out of things. **à l'~ de,** away from.

écarté /ekarte/ *a.* (*lieu*) remote. **les jambes ~es,** (with) legs apart. **les bras ~s,** with one's arms out.

écartement /ekartəmɑ̃/ *n.m.* gap.

écarter /ekarte/ *v.t.* (*objets*) move apart; (*ouvrir*) open; (*éliminer*) dismiss. **~ qch. de,** move sth. away from. **~ qn. de,** keep s.o. away from. **s'~** *v. pr.* (*s'éloigner*) move away; (*quitter son chemin*) move aside. **s'~ de,** stray from.

ecchymose /ekimoz/ *n.f.* bruise.

ecclésiastique /eklezjastik/ *a.* ecclesiastical. ● *n.m.* clergyman.

écervelé, ~e /esɛrvəle/ *a.* scatter-brained. ● *n.m., f.* scatter-brain.

échafaud|age /eʃafodaʒ/ *n.m.* scaffolding; (*amas*) heap. **~er** *v.t.* (*projets*) construct.

échalote /eʃalɔt/ *n.f.* shallot.

échang|e /eʃɑ̃ʒ/ *n.m.* exchange. **en ~e (de),** in exchange (for). **~er** *v.t.* exchange (**contre,** for).

échangeur /eʃɑ̃ʒœr/ *n.m.* (*auto.*) interchange.

échantillon /eʃɑ̃tijɔ̃/ *n.m.* sample. **~nage** /-jɔnaʒ/ *n.m.* range of samples.

échappatoire /eʃapatwar/ *n.f.* (clever) way out.

échappée /eʃape/ *n.f.* (*sport*) breakaway.

échappement /eʃapmɑ̃/ *n.m.* exhaust.

échapper /eʃape/ *v.i.* **~ à,** escape; (*en fuyant*) escape (from). **s'~** *v. pr.* escape. **~ des mains de** *ou* **à,** slip out of the hands of. **l'~ belle,** have a narrow *ou* lucky escape.

écharde /eʃard/ *n.f.* splinter.

écharpe /eʃarp/ *n.f.* scarf; (*de maire*) sash. **en ~,** (*bras*) in a sling.

échasse /eʃɑs/ *n.f.* stilt.

échassier /eʃasje/ *n.m.* wader.

échaud|er /eʃode/ *v.t.* **se faire ~er, être ~é,** get one's fingers burnt.

échauffer /eʃofe/ *v.t.* heat; (*fig.*) excite. **s'~** *v. pr.* warm up.

échauffourée /eʃofure/ *n.f.* (*mil.*) skirmish; (*bagarre*) scuffle.

échéance /eʃeɑ̃s/ *n.f.* due date (for payment); (*délai*) deadline; (*obligation*) (financial) commitment.

échéant (le cas) /(ləkɑz)eʃeɑ̃/ *adv.* if the occasion arises, possibly.

échec /eʃɛk/ *n.m.* failure. **~s,** (*jeu*) chess. **~ et mat,** checkmate. **en ~,** in check.

échelle /eʃɛl/ *n.f.* ladder; (*dimension*) scale.

échelon /eʃlɔ/ *n.m.* rung; (*de fonctionnaire*) grade; (*niveau*) level.

échelonner /eʃlɔne/ *v.t.* spread out, space out.

échevelé /eʃəvle/ *a.* dishevelled.

échine /eʃin/ *n.f.* backbone.

échiquier /eʃikje/ *n.m.* chessboard.

écho /eko/ *n.m.* echo. **~s,** (*dans la presse*) gossip.

échographie /ekɔgrafi/ *n.f.* ultrasound (scan).

échoir /eʃwar/ *v.i.* (*dette*) fall due; (*délai*) expire.

échoppe /eʃɔp/ *n.f.* stall.

échouer[1] /eʃwe/ *v.i.* fail.

échouer[2] /eʃwe/ *v.t.* (*bateau*) ground. ● *v.i.*, **s'~** *v. pr.* run aground.

échu /eʃy/ *a.* (*délai*) expired.

éclabouss|er /eklabuse/ *v.t.* splash. **~ure** *n.f.* splash.

éclair /eklɛr/ *n.m.* (flash of) lightning; (*fig.*) flash; (*gâteau*) éclair. ● *a. invar.* lightning.

éclairag|e /eklɛraʒ/ *n.m.* lighting; (*point de vue*) light. **~iste** /-aʒist/ *n.m.* lighting technician.
éclaircie /eklɛrsi/ *n.f.* sunny interval.
éclairc|ir /eklɛrsir/ *v.t.* make lighter; (*mystère*) clear up. **s'~ir** *v. pr.* (*ciel*) clear; (*mystère*) become clearer. **~issement** *n.m.* clarification.
éclairer /eklere/ *v.t.* light (up); (*personne*) give some light to; (*fig.*) enlighten; (*situation*) throw light on. ● *v.i.* give light. **s'~** *v. pr.* become clearer. **s'~ à la bougie,** use candle-light.
éclaireu|r, ~se /eklɛrœr, -øz/ *n.m., f.* (boy) scout, (girl) guide. ● *n.m.* (*mil.*) scout.
éclat /ekla/ *n.m.* fragment; (*de lumière*) brightness; (*de rire*) (out)-burst; (*splendeur*) brilliance.
éclatant, ~e /eklatɑ̃, -t/ *a.* brilliant.
éclat|er /eklate/ *v.i.* burst; (*exploser*) go off; (*verre*) shatter; (*guerre*) break out; (*groupe*) split up. **~er de rire,** burst out laughing. **~ement** *n.m.* bursting; (*de bombe*) explosion; (*scission*) split.
éclipse /eklips/ *n.f.* eclipse.
éclipser /eklipse/ *v.t.* eclipse. **s'~** *v. pr.* slip away.
écl|ore /eklɔr/ *v.i.* (*œuf*) hatch; (*fleur*) open. **~osion** *n.f.* hatching; opening.
écluse /eklyz/ *n.f.* (*de canal*) lock.
écœurant, ~e /ekœrɑ̃, -t/ *a.* (*gâteau*) sickly; (*fig.*) disgusting.
écœurer /ekœre/ *v.t.* sicken.
école /ekɔl/ *n.f.* school. **~ maternelle/primaire/secondaire,** nursery/primary/secondary school. **~ normale,** teachers' training college.
écol|ier, ~ière /ekɔlje, -jɛr/ *n.m., f.* schoolboy, schoolgirl.
écolo /ekɔlo/ *a.* & *n.m./f.* (*fam.*) green.
ecolog|ie /ekɔlɔʒi/ *n.f.* ecology. **~ique** *a.* ecological, green.
écologiste /ekɔlɔʒist/ *n.m./f.* ecologist.
econduire /ekɔ̃dɥir/ *v.t.* dismiss.
économat /ekɔnɔma/ *n.m.* bursary.
économe /ekɔnɔm/ *a.* thrifty. ● *n.m./f.* bursar.
économ|ie /ekɔnɔmi/ *n.f.* economy. **~ies,** (*argent*) savings. **une ~ie de,** (*gain*) a saving of. **~ie politique,** economics. **~ique** *a.* (*pol.*) economic; (*bon marché*) economical. **~iser** *v.t./i.* save. **~iste** *n.m./f.* economist.
écoper /ekɔpe/ *v.t.* bail out. **~ (de),** (*fam.*) get.
écorce /ekɔrs/ *n.f.* bark; (*de fruit*) peel.
écorch|er /ekɔrʃe/ *v.t.* graze; (*animal*) skin. **s'~er** *v. pr.* graze o.s. **~ure** *n.f.* graze.
écossais, ~e /ekɔsɛ, -z/ *a.* Scottish. ● *n.m., f.* Scot.
Écosse /ekɔs/ *n.f.* Scotland.
écosser /ekɔse/ *v.t.* shell.
écosystème /ekɔsistɛm/ *n.m.* ecosystem.
écouler[1] /ekule/ *v.t.* dispose of, sell.
écoul|er[2] **(s')** /(s)ekule/ *v. pr.* flow (out), run (off); (*temps*) pass. **~ement** *n.m.* flow.
écourter /ekurte/ *v.t.* shorten.
écoute /ekut/ *n.f.* listening. **à l'~ (de),** listening in (to). **aux ~s,** attentive. **heures de grande ~,** peak time. **~s téléphoniques,** phone tapping.
écout|er /ekute/ *v.t.* listen to; (*radio*) listen (in) to. ● *v.i.* listen. **~eur** *n.m.* earphones; (*de téléphone*) receiver.
écran /ekrɑ̃/ *n.m.* screen. **~ total,** sun-block.
écrasant, ~e /ekrɑzɑ̃, -t/ *a.* overwhelming.
écraser /ekrɑze/ *v.t.* crush; (*piéton*) run over. **s'~** *v. pr.* crash **(contre,** into).
écrémé /ekreme/ *a.* **lait ~,** skimmed milk. **lait demi-~,** semi-skimmed milk.
écrevisse /ekrəvis/ *n.f.* crayfish.
écrier (s') /(s)ekrije/ *v. pr.* exclaim.
écrin /ekrɛ̃/ *n.m.* case.
écrire† /ekrir/ *v.t./i.* write; (*orthographier*) spell. **s'~** *v. pr.* (*mot*) be spelt.
écrit /ekri/ *n.m.* document; (*examen*) written paper. **par ~,** in writing.
écriteau (*pl.* **~x**) /ekrito/ *n.m.* notice.
écriture /ekrityr/ *n.f.* writing. **~s,** (*comm.*) accounts. **l'É~ (sainte),** the Scriptures.
écrivain /ekrivɛ̃/ *n.m.* writer.
écrou /ekru/ *n.m.* nut.
écrouer /ekrue/ *v.t.* imprison.
écrouler (s') /(s)ekrule/ *v. pr.* collapse.
écru /ekry/ *a.* (*couleur*) natural; (*tissu*) raw.
Écu /eky/ *n.m. invar.* ecu.

écueil /ekœj/ *n.m.* reef; (*fig.*) danger.
éculé /ekyle/ *a.* (*soulier*) worn at the heel; (*fig.*) well-worn.
écume /ekym/ *n.f.* foam; (*culin.*) scum.
écum|er /ekyme/ *v.t.* skim; (*piller*) plunder. • *v.i.* foam. **~oire** *n.f.* skimmer.
écureuil /ekyrœj/ *n.m.* squirrel.
écurie /ekyri/ *n.f.* stable.
écuy|er, ~ère /ekɥije, -jɛr/ *n.m., f.* (horse) rider.
eczéma /ɛgzema/ *n.m.* eczema.
édenté /edɑ̃te/ *a.* toothless.
édifice /edifis/ *n.m.* building.
édif|ier /edifje/ *v.t.* construct; (*porter à la vertu, éclairer*) edify. **~ication** *n.f.* construction; edification.
édit /edi/ *n.m.* edict.
édi|ter /edite/ *v.t.* publish; (*annoter*) edit. **~teur, ~trice** *n.m., f.* publisher; editor.
édition /edisjɔ̃/ *n.f.* edition; (*industrie*) publishing.
éditor|ial (*pl.* **~iaux**) /editɔrjal, -jo/ *n.m.* editorial.
édredon /edrədɔ̃/ *n.m.* eiderdown.
éducateur, ~trice /edykatœr, -tris/ *n.m., f.* teacher.
éducati|f, ~ve /edykatif, -v/ *a.* educational.
éducation /edykɑsjɔ̃/ *n.f.* education; (*dans la famille*) upbringing; (*manières*) manners. **~ physique,** physical education.
édulcorant /edylkɔrɑ̃/ *n.m.* & *a.* **(produit) ~,** sweetener.
éduquer /edyke/ *v.t.* educate; (*à la maison*) bring up.
effac|é /efase/ *a.* (*modeste*) unassuming. **~ement** *n.m.* unassuming manner; (*suppression*) erasure.
effacer /efase/ *v.t.* (*gommer*) rub out; (*par lavage*) wash out; (*souvenir etc.*) erase. **s'~** *v. pr.* fade; (*s'écarter*) step aside.
effar|er /efare/ *v.t.* alarm. **~ement** *n.m.* alarm.
effaroucher /efaruʃe/ *v.t.* scare away.
effecti|f[1]**, ~ve** /efɛktif, -v/ *a.* effective. **~vement** *adv.* effectively; (*en effet*) indeed.
effectif[2] /efɛktif/ *n.m.* size, strength. **~s,** numbers.
effectuer /efɛktɥe/ *v.t.* carry out, make.
efféminé /efemine/ *a.* effeminate.
effervescen|t, ~te /efɛrvesɑ̃, -t/ *a.* **comprimé ~t,** effervescent tablet. **~ce** *n.f.* excitement.
effet /efɛ/ *n.m.* effect; (*impression*) impression. **~s,** (*habits*) clothes, things. **en ~,** indeed. **faire de l'~,** have an effect, be effective. **faire bon/mauvais ~,** make a good/bad impression.
efficac|e /efikas/ *a.* effective; (*personne*) efficient. **~ité** *n.f.* effectiveness; efficiency.
effigie /efiʒi/ *n.f.* effigy.
effilocher (s') /(s)efilɔʃe/ *v. pr.* fray.
efflanqué /eflɑ̃ke/ *a.* emaciated.
effleurer /eflœre/ *v.t.* touch lightly; (*sujet*) touch on; (*se présenter à*) occur to.
effluves /eflyv/ *n.m. pl.* exhalations.
effondr|er (s') /(s)efɔ̃dre/ *v. pr.* collapse. **~ement** *n.m.* collapse.
efforcer (s') /(s)efɔrse/ *v. pr.* try (hard) (**de,** to).
effort /efɔr/ *n.m.* effort.
effraction /efraksjɔ̃/ *n.f.* **entrer par ~,** break in.
effray|er /efreje/ *v.t.* frighten; (*décourager*) put off. **s'~er** *v. pr.* be frightened. **~ant, ~ante** *a.* frightening; (*fig.*) frightful.
effréné /efrene/ *a.* wild.
effriter (s') /(s)efrite/ *v. pr.* crumble.
effroi /efrwa/ *n.m.* dread.
effronté /efrɔ̃te/ *a.* impudent.
effroyable /efrwajabl/ *a.* dreadful.
effusion /efyzjɔ̃/ *n.f.* **~ de sang,** bloodshed.
ég|al, ~ale (*m. pl.* **~aux**) /egal, -o/ *a.* equal; (*surface, vitesse*) even. • *n. m., f.* equal. **ça m'est/lui est ~al,** it is all the same to me/him. **sans égal,** matchless. **d'~ à égal,** between equals.
également /egalmɑ̃/ *adv.* equally; (*aussi*) as well.
égaler /egale/ *v.t.* equal.
égaliser /egalize/ *v.t./i.* (*sport*) equalize; (*niveler*) level out; (*cheveux*) trim.
égalit|é /egalite/ *n.f.* equality; (*de surface, d'humeur*) evenness. **à ~é (de points),** equal. **~aire** *a.* egalitarian.
égard /egar/ *n.m.* regard. **~s,** consideration. **à cet ~,** in this respect. **à l'~ de,** with regard to; (*envers*) towards. **eu ~ à,** in view of.
égar|er /egare/ *v.t.* mislay; (*tromper*) lead astray. **s'~er** *v. pr.* get lost; (*se*

tromper) go astray. **~ement** *n.m.* loss; (*affolement*) confusion.

égayer /egeje/ *v.t.* (*personne*) cheer up; (*pièce*) brighten up.

égide /eʒid/ *n.f.* aegis.

églantier /eglɑ̃tje/ *n.m.* wild rose (-bush).

églefin /egləfɛ̃/ *n.m.* haddock.

église /egliz/ *n.f.* church.

égoïs|te /egɔist/ *a.* selfish. ● *n.m./f.* egoist. **~me** *n.m.* selfishness, egoism.

égorger /egɔrʒe/ *v.t.* slit the throat of.

égosiller (s') /(s)egozije/ *v. pr.* shout one's head off.

égout /egu/ *n.m.* sewer.

égoutt|er /egute/ *v.t./i.*, **s'~er** *v. pr.* (*vaisselle*) drain. **~oir** *n.m.* draining-board; (*panier*) dish drainer.

égratign|er /egratiɲe/ *v.t.* scratch. **~ure** *n.f.* scratch.

égrener /egrəne/ *v.t.* (*raisins*) pick off; (*notes*) sound one by one.

Égypte /eʒipt/ *n.f.* Egypt.

égyptien, ~ne /eʒipsjɛ̃, -jɛn/ *a.* & *n.m.*, *f.* Egyptian.

eh /e/ *int.* hey. **eh bien,** well.

éjacul|er /eʒakyle/ *v.i.* ejaculate. **~ation** *n.f.* ejaculation.

éjectable *a.* **siège ~,** ejector seat.

éjecter /eʒɛkte/ *v.t.* eject.

élabor|er /elabɔre/ *v.t.* elaborate. **~ation** *n.f.* elaboration.

élaguer /elage/ *v.t.* prune.

élan [1] /elɑ̃/ *n.m.* (*sport*) run-up; (*vitesse*) momentum; (*fig.*) surge.

élan [2] /elɑ̃/ *n.m.* (*animal*) moose.

élancé /elɑ̃se/ *a.* slender.

élancement /elɑ̃smɑ̃/ *n.m.* twinge.

élancer (s') /(s)elɑ̃se/ *v. pr.* leap forward, dash; (*se dresser*) soar.

élarg|ir /elarʒir/ *v.t.*, **s'~ir** *v. pr.* widen. **~issement** *n.m.* widening.

élasti|que /elastik/ *a.* elastic. ● *n.m.* elastic band; (*tissu*) elastic. **~cité** *n.f.* elasticity.

élec|teur, ~trice /elɛktœr, -tris/ *n.m.*, *f.* voter, elector.

élection /elɛksjɔ̃/ *n.f.* election.

élector|al (*m. pl.* **~aux**) /elɛktɔral, -o/ *a.* (*réunion etc.*) election; (*collège*) electoral.

électorat /elɛktɔra/ *n.m.* electorate, voters.

électricien /elɛktrisjɛ̃/ *n.m.* electrician.

électricité /elɛktrisite/ *n.f.* electricity.

électrifier /elɛktrifje/ *v.t.* electrify.

électrique /elɛktrik/ *a.* electric (al).

électrocuter /elɛktrɔkyte/ *v.t.* electrocute.

électroménager /elɛktrɔmenaʒe/ *n.m.* **l'~,** household appliances.

électron /elɛktrɔ̃/ *n.m.* electron.

électronique /elɛktrɔnik/ *a.* electronic. ● *n.f.* electronics.

électrophone /elɛktrɔfɔn/ *n.m.* record-player.

élég|ant, ~ante /elegɑ̃, -t/ *a.* elegant. **~amment** *adv.* elegantly. **~ance** *n.f.* elegance.

élément /elemɑ̃/ *n.m.* element; (*meuble*) unit. **~aire** /-tɛr/ *a.* elementary.

éléphant /elefɑ̃/ *n.m.* elephant.

élevage /ɛlvaʒ/ *n.m.* (stock-)breeding.

élévation /elevɑsjɔ̃/ *n.f.* raising; (*hausse*) rise; (*plan*) elevation.

élève /elɛv/ *n.m./f.* pupil.

élevé /ɛlve/ *a.* high; (*noble*) elevated. **bien ~,** well-mannered.

élever /ɛlve/ *v.t.* raise; (*enfants*) bring up, raise; (*animal*) breed. **s'~** *v. pr.* rise; (*dans le ciel*) soar up. **s'~ à,** amount to.

éleveu|r, ~se /ɛlvœr, -øz/ *n.m.*, *f.* (stock-)breeder.

éligible /eliʒibl/ *a.* eligible.

élimé /elime/ *a.* worn thin.

élimin|er /elimine/ *v.t.* eliminate. **~ation** *n.f.* elimination. **~atoire** *a.* eliminating; *n.f.* (*sport*) heat.

élire† /elir/ *v.t.* elect.

élite /elit/ *n.f.* élite.

elle /ɛl/ *pron.* she; (*complément*) her; (*chose*) it. **~-même** *pron.* herself; itself.

elles /ɛl/ *pron.* they; (*complément*) them. **~-mêmes** *pron.* themselves.

ellip|se /elips/ *n.f.* ellipse. **~tique** *a.* elliptical.

élocution /elɔkysjɔ̃/ *n.f.* diction.

élog|e /elɔʒ/ *n.m.* praise. **faire l'~e de,** praise. **~ieux, ~ieuse** *a.* laudatory.

éloigné /elwaɲe/ *a.* distant. **~ de,** far away from. **parent ~,** distant relative.

éloign|er /elwaɲe/ *v.t.* take away *ou* remove (**de,** from); (*personne aimée*) estrange (**de,** from); (*danger*) ward off; (*visite*) put off. **s'~er** *v. pr.* go *ou* move away (**de,** from); (*affectivement*) become estranged (**de,** from). **~ement** *n.m.* removal; (*distance*) distance; (*oubli*) estrangement.

élongation /elɔ̃gasjɔ̃/ *n.f.* strained muscle.

éloquen|t, ~te /elɔkɑ̃, -t/ *a.* eloquent. **~ce** *n.f.* eloquence.

élu, ~e /ely/ *a.* elected. ● *n.m., f.* (*pol.*) elected representative.

élucider /elyside/ *v.t.* elucidate.

éluder /elyde/ *v.t.* elude.

émacié /emasje/ *a.* emaciated.

ém|ail (*pl.* **~aux**) /emaj, -o/ *n.m.* enamel.

émaillé /emaje/ *a.* enamelled. **~ de,** studded with.

émancip|er /emɑ̃sipe/ *v.t.* emancipate. **s'~er** *v. pr.* become emancipated. **~ation** *n.f.* emancipation.

éman|er /emane/ *v.i.* emanate. **~ation** *n.f.* emanation.

émarger /emarʒe/ *v.t.* initial.

emball|er /ɑ̃bale/ *v.t.* pack, wrap; (*personne*: *fam.*) enthuse. **s'~er** *v. pr.* (*moteur*) race; (*cheval*) bolt; (*personne*) get carried away. **~age** *n.m.* package, wrapping.

embarcadère /ɑ̃barkadɛr/ *n.m.* landing-stage.

embarcation /ɑ̃barkɑsjɔ̃/ *n.f.* boat.

embardée /ɑ̃barde/ *n.f.* swerve.

embargo /ɑ̃bargo/ *n.m.* embargo.

embarqu|er /ɑ̃barke/ *v.t.* embark; (*charger*) load; (*emporter*: *fam.*) cart off. ● *v.i.*, **s'~er** *v. pr.* board, embark. **s'~er dans,** embark upon. **~ement** *n.m.* embarkation; loading.

embarras /ɑ̃bara/ *n.m.* obstacle, (*gêne*) embarrassment; (*difficulté*) difficulty.

embarrasser /ɑ̃barɑse/ *v.t.* clutter (up); (*gêner dans les mouvements*) hinder; (*fig.*) embarrass. **s'~ de,** burden o.s. with.

embauch|e /ɑ̃boʃ/ *n.f.* hiring; (*emploi*) employment. **~er** *v.t.* hire, take on.

embauchoir /ɑ̃boʃwar/ *n.m.* shoe tree.

embaumer /ɑ̃bome/ *v.t./i.* (make) smell fragrant; (*cadavre*) embalm.

embellir /ɑ̃belir/ *v.t.* brighten up; (*récit*) embellish.

embêt|er /ɑ̃bete/ *v.t.* (*fam.*) annoy. **s'~er** *v. pr.* (*fam.*) get bored. **~ant, ~ante** *a.* (*fam.*) annoying. **~ement** /ɑ̃bɛtmɑ̃/ *n.m.* (*fam.*) annoyance.

emblée (d') /(d)ɑ̃ble/ *adv.* right away.

emblème /ɑ̃blɛm/ *n.m.* emblem.

embobiner /ɑ̃bɔbine/ *v.t.* (*fam.*) get round.

emboîter /ɑ̃bwate/ *v.t.*, **s'~** *v. pr.* fit together. **(s')~ dans,** fit into. **~ le pas à qn.,** (*imiter*) follow suit.

embonpoint /ɑ̃bɔ̃pwɛ̃/ *n.m.* stoutness.

embouchure /ɑ̃buʃyr/ *n.f.* (*de fleuve*) mouth; (*mus.*) mouthpiece.

embourber (s') /(s)ɑ̃burbe/ *v. pr.* get bogged down.

embourgeoiser (s') /(s)ɑ̃burʒwaze/ *v. pr.* become middle-class.

embout /ɑ̃bu/ *n.m.* tip.

embouteillage /ɑ̃butɛjaʒ/ *n.m.* traffic jam.

emboutir /ɑ̃butir/ *v.t.* (*heurter*) crash into.

embranchement /ɑ̃brɑ̃ʃmɑ̃/ *n.m.* (*de routes*) junction.

embraser /ɑ̃brɑze/ *v.t.* set on fire, fire. **s'~** *v. pr.* flare up.

embrass|er /ɑ̃brase/ *v.t.* kiss; (*adopter, contenir*) embrace. **s'~er** *v. pr.* kiss. **~ades** *n.f. pl.* kissing.

embrasure /ɑ̃brɑzyr/ *n.f.* opening.

embray|er /ɑ̃breje/ *v.i.* let in the clutch. **~age** /ɑ̃brɛjaʒ/ *n.m.* clutch.

embrigader /ɑ̃brigade/ *v.t.* enrol.

embrocher /ɑ̃brɔʃe/ *v.t.* (*viande*) spit.

embrouiller /ɑ̃bruje/ *v.t.* mix up; (*fils*) tangle. **s'~** *v. pr.* get mixed up.

embroussaillé /ɑ̃brusɑje/ *a.* (*poils, chemin*) bushy.

embryon /ɑ̃brijɔ/ *n.m.* embryo. **~naire** /-jɔnɛr/ *a.* embryonic.

embûches /ɑ̃byʃ/ *n.f. pl.* traps.

embuer /ɑ̃bɥe/ *v.t.* mist up.

embuscade /ɑ̃byskad/ *n.f.* ambush.

embusquer (s') /(s)ɑ̃byske/ *v. pr.* lie in ambush.

éméché /emeʃe/ *a.* tipsy.

émeraude /ɛmrod/ *n.f.* emerald.

émerger /emɛrʒe/ *v.i.* emerge; (*fig.*) stand out.

émeri /ɛmri/ *n.m.* emery.

émerveill|er /emɛrveje/ *v.t.* amaze. **s'~er de,** marvel at, be amazed at. **~ement** /-vɛjmɑ̃/ *n.m.* amazement, wonder.

émett|re† /emɛtr/ *v.t.* give out; (*message*) transmit; (*timbre, billet*) issue; (*opinion*) express. **~eur** *n.m.* transmitter.

émeut|e /emøt/ *n.f.* riot. **~ier, ~ière** *n.m., f.* rioter.

émietter /emjete/ *v.t.*, **s'~** *v. pr.* crumble.

émigrant, ~e /emigrɑ̃, -t/ *n.m., f.* emigrant.

émigr|er /emigre/ *v.i.* emigrate. **~ation** *n.f.* emigration.

émincer /emɛ̃se/ *v.t.* cut into thin slices.

émin|ent, ~ente /eminɑ̃, -t/ *a.* eminent. **~emment** /-amɑ̃/ *adv.* eminently. **~ence** *n.f.* eminence; (*colline*) hill. **~ence grise,** éminence grise.

émissaire /emisɛr/ *n.m.* emissary.

émission /emisjɔ̃/ *n.f.* emission; (*de message*) transmission; (*de timbre*) issue; (*programme*) bro adcast.

emmagasiner /ɑ̃magazine/ *v.t.* store.

emmanchure /ɑ̃mɑ̃ʃyr/ *n.f.* armhole.

emmêler /ɑ̃mele/ *v.t.* tangle. **s'~** *v. pr.* get mixed up.

emménager /ɑ̃menaʒe/ *v.i.* move in. **~ dans,** move into.

emmener /ɑ̃mne/ *v.t.* take; (*comme prisonnier*) take away.

emmerder /ɑ̃mɛrde/ *v.t.* (*argot*) bother. **s'~** *v. pr.* (*argot*) get bored.

emmitoufier /ɑ̃mitufle/ *v.t.*, **s'~** *v. pr.* wrap up (warmly).

émoi /emwa/ *n.m.* excitement.

émoluments /emɔlymɑ̃/ *n.m. pl.* remuneration.

émonder /emɔ̃de/ *v.t.* prune.

émoti|f, ~ve /emɔtif, -v/ *a.* emotional.

émotion /emosjɔ̃/ *n.f.* emotion; (*peur*) fright. **~nel, ~nelle** /-jɔnɛl/ *a.* emotional.

émousser /emuse/ *v.t.* blunt.

émouv|oir /emuvwar/ *v.t.* move. **s'~oir** *v. pr.* be moved. **~ant, ~ante** *a.* moving.

empailler /ɑ̃paje/ *v.t.* stuff.

empaqueter /ɑ̃pakte/ *v.t.* package.

emparer (s') /(s)ɑ̃pare/ *v. pr.* **s'~ de,** seize.

empâter (s') /(s)ɑ̃pɑte/ *v. pr.* fill out, grow fatter.

empêchement /ɑ̃pɛʃmɑ̃/ *n.m.* hitch, difficulty.

empêcher /ɑ̃peʃe/ *v.t.* prevent. **~ de faire,** prevent *ou* stop (from) doing. **il ne peut pas s'~ de penser,** he cannot help thinking. **(il) n'empêche que,** still.

empêch|eur, ~euse /ɑ̃peʃœr, -øz/ *n.m., f.* **~eur de tourner en rond,** spoilsport.

empeigne /ɑ̃pɛɲ/ *n.f.* upper.

empereur /ɑ̃prœr/ *n.m.* emperor.

empeser /ɑ̃pəze/ *v.t.* starch.

empester /ɑ̃pɛste/ *v.t.* make stink, stink out; (*essence etc.*) stink of. ● *v.i.* stink.

empêtrer (s') /(s)ɑ̃petre/ *v. pr.* become entangled.

emphase /ɑ̃fɑz/ *n.f.* pomposity.

empiéter /ɑ̃pjete/ *v.i.* **~ sur,** encroach upon.

empiffrer (s') /(s)ɑ̃pifre/ *v. pr.* (*fam.*) gorge o.s.

empiler /ɑ̃pile/ *v.t.*, **s'~** *v. pr.* pile (up).

empire /ɑ̃pir/ *n.m.* empire; (*fig.*) control.

empirer /ɑ̃pire/ *v.i.* worsen.

empirique /ɑ̃pirik/ *a.* empirical.

emplacement /ɑ̃plasmɑ̃/ *n.m.* site.

emplâtre /ɑ̃plɑtr/ *n.m.* (*méd.*) plaster.

emplettes /ɑ̃plɛt/ *n.f. pl.* purchase. **faire des ~,** do one's shopping.

emplir /ɑ̃plir/ *v.t.*, **s'~** *v. pr.* fill.

emploi /ɑ̃plwa/ *n.m.* use; (*travail*) job. **~ du temps,** timetable. **l'~,** (*pol.*) employment.

employ|er /ɑ̃plwaje/ *v.t.* use; (*personne*) employ. **s'~er** *v. pr.* be used. **s'~er à,** devote o.s. to. **~é, ~ée** *n.m., f.* employee. **~eur, ~euse** *n.m., f.* employer.

empocher /ɑ̃pɔʃe/ *v.t.* pocket.

empoigner /ɑ̃pwaɲe/ *v.t.* grab. **s'~** *v. pr.* come to blows.

empoisonn|er /ɑ̃pwazɔne/ *v.t.* poison; (*empuantir*) stink out; (*embêter*: *fam.*) annoy. **~ement** *n.m.* poisoning.

emport|é /ɑ̃pɔrte/ *a.* quicktempered. **~ement** *n.m.* anger.

emporter /ɑ̃pɔrte/ *v.t.* take (away); (*entraîner*) carry away; (*prix*) carry off; (*arracher*) tear off. **~ un chapeau**/*etc.*, (*vent*) blow off a hat/*etc.* **s'~** *v. pr.* lose one's temper. **l'~,** get the upper hand (**sur,** of). **plat à ~,** take-away.

empoté /ɑ̃pɔte/ *a.* silly.

empourpré /ɑ̃purpre/ *a.* crimson.

empreint, ~e /ɑ̃prɛ̃, -t/ *a.* **~ de,** marked with. ● *n.f.* mark. **~e (digitale),** fingerprint. **~e de pas,** footprint.

empress|er (s') /(s)ɑ̃prese/ *v. pr.* **s'~er auprès de,** be attentive to. **s'~er de,** hasten to. **~é** *a.* eager, attentive. **~ement** /ɑ̃prɛsmɑ̃/ *n.m.* eagerness.

emprise /ɑ̃priz/ *n.f.* influence.

emprisonn|er /ɑ̃prizɔne/ *v.t.* imprison. **~ement** *n.m.* imprisonment.
emprunt /ɑ̃prœ̃/ *n.m.* loan. **faire un ~,** take out a loan.
emprunté /ɑ̃prœ̃te/ *a.* awkward.
emprunt|er /ɑ̃prœ̃te/ *v.t.* borrow (**à,** from); (*route*) take; (*fig.*) assume. **~eur, ~euse** *n.m., f.* borrower.
ému /emy/ *a.* moved; (*apeuré*) nervous; (*joyeux*) excited.
émulation /emylɑsjɔ̃/ *n.f.* emulation.
émule /emyl/ *n.m./f.* imitator.
émulsion /emylsjɔ̃/ *n.f.* emulsion.
en[1] /ɑ̃/ *prép.* in; (*avec direction*) to; (*manière, état*) in, on; (*moyen de transport*) by; (*composition*) made of. **en cadeau/médecin/***etc.*, as a present/doctor/*etc.* **en guerre,** at war. **en faisant,** by *ou* on *ou* while doing.
en[2] /ɑ̃/ *pron.* of it, of them; (*moyen*) with it; (*cause*) from it; (*lieu*) from there. **en avoir/vouloir/***etc.*, have/want/*etc.* some. **ne pas en avoir/vouloir/***etc.*, not have/want/*etc.* any. **où en êtes-vous?,** where are you up to?, how far have you got? **j'en ai assez,** I've had enough. **en êtes-vous sûr?,** are you sure?
encadr|er /ɑ̃kɑdre/ *v.t.* frame; (*entourer d'un trait*) circle; (*entourer*) surround. **~ement** *n.m.* framing; (*de porte*) frame.
encaiss|er /ɑ̃kese/ *v.t.* (*argent*) collect; (*chèque*) cash; (*coups: fam.*) take. **~eur** /ɑ̃kɛsœr/ *n.m.* debt-collector.
encart /ɑ̃kar/ *n.m.* **~ publicitaire,** (advertising) insert.
en-cas /ɑ̃kɑ/ *n.m.* (stand-by) snack.
encastré /ɑ̃kastre/ *a.* built-in.
encaustiqu|e /ɑ̃kɔstik/ *n.f.* wax polish. **~er** *v.t.* wax.
enceinte[1] /ɑ̃sɛ̃t/ *a.f.* pregnant. **~ de 3 mois,** 3 months pregnant.
enceinte[2] /ɑ̃sɛ̃t/ *n.f.* enclosure. **~ (acoustique),** loudspeaker.
encens /ɑ̃sɑ̃/ *n.m.* incense.
encercler /ɑ̃sɛrkle/ *v.t.* surround.
enchaîn|er /ɑ̃ʃene/ *v.t.* chain (up); (*coordonner*) link (up). ● *v.i.* continue. **s'~er** *v. pr.* be linked (up). **~ement** /ɑ̃ʃɛnmɑ̃/ *n.m.* (*suite*) chain; (*liaison*) link(ing).
enchant|er /ɑ̃ʃɑ̃te/ *v.t.* delight; (*ensorceler*) enchant. **~é** *a.* (*ravi*) delighted. **~ement** *n.m.* delight; (*magie*) enchantment.
enchâsser /ɑ̃ʃɑse/ *v.t.* set.
enchère /ɑ̃ʃɛr/ *n.f.* bid. **mettre** *ou* **vendre aux ~s,** sell by auction.
enchevêtrer /ɑ̃ʃvetre/ *v.t.* tangle. **s'~** *v. pr.* become tangled.
enclave /ɑ̃klav/ *n.f.* enclave.
enclencher /ɑ̃klɑ̃ʃe/ *v.t.* engage.
enclin, ~e /ɑ̃klɛ̃, -in/ *a.* **~ à,** inclined to.
enclore /ɑ̃klɔr/ *v.t.* enclose.
enclos /ɑ̃klo/ *n.m.* enclosure.
enclume /ɑ̃klym/ *n.f.* anvil.
encoche /ɑ̃kɔʃ/ *n.f.* notch.
encoignure /ɑ̃kɔɲyr/ *n.f.* corner.
encoller /ɑ̃kɔle/ *v.t.* paste.
encolure /ɑ̃kɔlyr/ *n.f.* neck.
encombre /ɑ̃kɔ̃br/ *n.m.* **sans ~,** without any problems.
encombr|er /ɑ̃kɔ̃bre/ *v.t.* clutter (up); (*gêner*) hamper. **s'~er de,** burden o.s. with. **~ant, ~ante** *a.* cumbersome. **~ement** *n.m.* congestion; (*auto.*) traffic jam; (*volume*) bulk.
encontre de (à l') /(al)ɑ̃kɔ̃trədə/ *prép.* against.
encore /ɑ̃kɔr/ *adv.* (*toujours*) still; (*de nouveau*) again; (*de plus*) more; (*aussi*) also. **~ mieux/plus grand/***etc.*, even better/larger/*etc.* **~ une heure/un café/***etc.*, another hour/coffee/ *etc.* **pas ~,** not yet. **si ~,** if only.
encourag|er /ɑ̃kuraʒe/ *v.t.* encourage. **~ement** *n.m.* encouragement.
encourir /ɑ̃kurir/ *v.t.* incur.
encrasser /ɑ̃krase/ *v.t.* clog up (with dirt).
encr|e /ɑ̃kr/ *n.f.* ink. **~er** *v.t.* ink.
encrier /ɑ̃krije/ *n.m.* ink-well.
encroûter (s') /(s)ɑ̃krute/ *v. pr.* become doggedly set in one's ways. **s'~ dans,** sink into.
encyclopéd|ie /ɑ̃siklɔpedi/ *n.f.* encyclopaedia. **~ique** *a.* encyclopaedic.
endetter /ɑ̃dete/ *v.t.*, **s'~** *v. pr.* get into debt.
endeuiller /ɑ̃dœje/ *v.t.* plunge into mourning.
endiablé /ɑ̃djɑble/ *a.* wild.
endiguer /ɑ̃dige/ *v.t.* dam; (*fig.*) check.
endimanché /ɑ̃dimɑ̃ʃe/ *a.* in one's Sunday best.
endive /ɑ̃div/ *n.f.* chicory.

endocrinolo|gie /ɑ̃dɔkrinɔlɔʒi/ *n.f.* endocrinology. **~gue** *n.m./f.* endocrinologist.

endoctrin|er /ɑ̃dɔktrine/ *v.t.* indoctrinate. **~ement** *n.m.* indoctrination.

endommager /ɑ̃dɔmaʒe/ *v.t.* damage.

endorm|ir /ɑ̃dɔrmir/ *v.t.* send to sleep; (*atténuer*) allay. **s'~ir** *v. pr.* fall asleep. **~i** *a.* asleep; (*apathique*) sleepy.

endosser /ɑ̃dɔse/ *v.t.* (*vêtement*) put on; (*assumer*) assume; (*comm.*) endorse.

endroit /ɑ̃drwa/ *n.m.* place; (*de tissu*) right side. **à l'~,** the right way round, right side out.

end|uire /ɑ̃dɥir/ *v.t.* coat. **~uit** *n.m.* coating.

endurance /ɑ̃dyrɑ̃s/ *n.f.* endurance.

endurant, ~e /ɑ̃dyrɑ̃, -t/ *a.* tough.

endurci /ɑ̃dyrsi/ *a.* **célibataire ~,** confirmed bachelor.

endurcir /ɑ̃dyrsir/ *v.t.* harden. **s'~** *v. pr.* become hard(ened).

endurer /ɑ̃dyre/ *v.t.* endure.

énerg|ie /enɛrʒi/ *n.f.* energy; (*techn.*) power. **~étique** *a.* energy. **~ique** *a.* energetic.

énervant, ~e /enɛrvɑ̃, -t/ *a.* irritating, annoying.

énerver /enɛrve/ *v.t.* irritate. **s'~** *v. pr.* get worked up.

enfance /ɑ̃fɑ̃s/ *n.f.* childhood. **la petite ~,** infancy.

enfant /ɑ̃fɑ̃/ *n.m./f.* child. **~ en bas âge,** infant. **~illage** /-tijaʒ/ *n.m.* childishness. **~in, ~ine** /-tɛ̃, -tin/ *a.* childlike; (*puéril*) childish; (*jeu, langage*) children's.

enfanter /ɑ̃fɑ̃te/ *v.t./i.* give birth (to).

enfer /ɑ̃fɛr/ *n.m.* hell.

enfermer /ɑ̃fɛrme/ *v.t.* shut up. **s'~** *v. pr.* shut o.s. up.

enferrer (s') /(s)ɑ̃fere/ *v. pr.* become entangled.

enfiévré /ɑ̃fjevre/ *a.* feverish.

enfilade /ɑ̃filad/ *n.f.* string, row.

enfiler /ɑ̃file/ *v.t.* (*aiguille*) thread; (*anneaux*) string; (*vêtement*) slip on; (*rue*) take; (*insérer*) insert.

enfin /ɑ̃fɛ̃/ *adv.* at last, finally; (*en dernier lieu*) finally; (*somme toute*) after all; (*résignation, conclusion*) well.

enflammer /ɑ̃flame/ *v.t.* set fire to; (*méd.*) inflame. **s'~** *v. pr.* catch fire.

enfl|er /ɑ̃fle/ *v.t./i.*, **s'~er** *v. pr.* swell. **~é** *a.* swollen. **~ure** *n.f.* swelling.

enfoncer /ɑ̃fɔ̃se/ *v.t.* (*épingle etc.*) push *ou* drive in; (*chapeau*) push down; (*porte*) break down; (*mettre*) thrust, put. ● *v.i.*, **s'~** *v. pr.* sink (**dans,** into).

enfouir /ɑ̃fwir/ *v.t.* bury.

enfourcher /ɑ̃furʃe/ *v.t.* mount.

enfourner /ɑ̃furne/ *v.t.* put in the oven.

enfreindre /ɑ̃frɛ̃dr/ *v.t.* infringe.

enfuir† (s') /(s)ɑ̃fɥir/ *v. pr.* run off.

enfumer /ɑ̃fyme/ *v.t.* fill with smoke.

engagé /ɑ̃gaʒe/ *a.* committed.

engageant, ~e /ɑ̃gaʒɑ̃, -t/ *a.* attractive.

engag|er /ɑ̃gaʒe/ *v.t.* (*lier*) bind, commit; (*embaucher*) take on; (*commencer*) start; (*introduire*) insert; (*entraîner*) involve; (*encourager*) urge; (*investir*) invest. **s'~er** *v. pr.* (*promettre*) commit o.s.; (*commencer*) start; (*soldat*) enlist; (*concurrent*) enter. **s'~er à faire,** undertake to do. **s'~er dans,** (*voie*) enter. **~ement** *n.m.* (*promesse*) promise; (*pol., comm.*) commitment; (*début*) start; (*inscription: sport*) entry.

engelure /ɑ̃ʒlyr/ *n.f.* chilblain.

engendrer /ɑ̃ʒɑ̃dre/ *v.t.* beget; (*causer*) generate.

engin /ɑ̃ʒɛ̃/ *n.m.* machine; (*outil*) instrument; (*projectile*) missile. **~ explosif,** explosive device.

englober /ɑ̃glɔbe/ *v.t.* include.

engloutir /ɑ̃glutir/ *v.t.* swallow (up). **s'~** *v. pr.* (*navire*) be engulfed.

engorger /ɑ̃gɔrʒe/ *v.t.* block.

engou|er (s') /(s)ɑ̃gwe/ *v. pr.* **s'~er de,** become infatuated with. **~ement** /-umɑ̃/ *n.m.* infatuation.

engouffrer /ɑ̃gufre/ *v.t.* devour. **s'~ dans,** rush into (with force).

engourd|ir /ɑ̃gurdir/ *v.t.* numb. **s'~ir** *v. pr.* go numb. **~i** *a.* numb.

engrais /ɑ̃grɛ/ *n.m.* manure; (*chimique*) fertilizer.

engraisser /ɑ̃grese/ *v.t.* fatten. **s'~** *v. pr.* get fat.

engrenage /ɑ̃grənaʒ/ *n.m.* gears; (*fig.*) chain (of events).

engueuler /ɑ̃gœle/ *v.t.* (*argot*) curse, swear at, hurl abuse at.

enhardir (s') /(s)ɑ̃ardir/ *v. pr.* become bolder.

énième /ɛnjɛm/ *a.* (*fam.*) umpteenth.

énigm|e /enigm/ *n.f.* riddle, enigma. **~atique** *a.* enigmatic.

enivrer /ɑ̃nivre/ *v.t.* intoxicate. **s'~** *v. pr.* get drunk.
enjamb|er /ɑ̃ʒɑ̃be/ *v.t.* step over; (*pont*) span. **~ée** *n.f.* stride.
enjeu (*pl.* **~x**) /ɑ̃ʒø/ *n.m.* stake(s).
enjôler /ɑ̃ʒole/ *v.t.* wheedle.
enjoliver /ɑ̃ʒɔlive/ *v.t.* embellish.
enjoliveur /ɑ̃ʒɔlivœr/ *n.m.* hub-cap.
enjoué /ɑ̃ʒwe/ *a.* cheerful.
enlacer /ɑ̃lase/ *v.t.* entwine.
enlaidir /ɑ̃ledir/ *v.t.* make ugly. ● *v.i.* grow ugly.
enlèvement /ɑ̃lɛvmɑ̃/ *n.m.* removal; (*rapt*) kidnapping.
enlever /ɑ̃lve/ *v.t.* (*emporter*) take (away), remove (**à**, from); (*vêtement*) take off, remove; (*tache*, *organe*) take out, remove; (*kidnapper*) kidnap; (*gagner*) win.
enliser (s') /(s)ɑ̃lize/ *v. pr.* get bogged down.
enluminure /ɑ̃lyminyr/ *n.f.* illumination.
enneig|é /ɑ̃neʒe/ *a.* snow-covered. **~ement** /ɑ̃nɛʒmɑ̃/ *n.m.* snow conditions.
ennemi /ɛnmi/ *n.m.* & *a.* enemy. **~ de,** (*fig.*) hostile to. **l'~ public numéro un,** public enemy number one.
ennui /ɑ̃nɥi/ *n.m.* boredom; (*tracas*) trouble, worry. **il a des ~s,** he's got problems.
ennuyer /ɑ̃nɥije/ *v.t.* bore; (*irriter*) annoy; (*préoccuper*) worry. **s'~** *v. pr.* get bored.
ennuyeu|x, ~se /ɑ̃nɥijø, -z/ *a.* boring; (*fâcheux*) annoying.
énoncé /enɔ̃se/ *n.m.* wording, text; (*gram.*) utterance.
énoncer /enɔ̃se/ *v.t.* express, state.
enorgueillir (s') /(s)ɑ̃nɔrgœjir/ *v. pr.* **s'~ de,** pride o.s. on.
énorm|e /enɔrm/ *a.* enormous. **~ément** *adv.* enormously. **~ément de,** an enormous amount of. **~ité** *n.f.* enormous size; (*atrocité*) enormity; (*bévue*) enormous blunder.
enquérir (s') /(s)ɑ̃kerir/ *v. pr.* **s'~ de,** enquire about.
enquêt|e /ɑ̃kɛt/ *n.f.* investigation; (*jurid.*) inquiry; (*sondage*) survey. **mener l'~e,** lead the inquiry. **~er** /-ete/ *v.i.* **~er (sur),** investigate. **~eur, ~euse** *n.m., f.* investigator.
enquiquin|er /ɑ̃kikine/ *v.t.* (*fam.*) bother. **~ant, ~ante** *a.* irritating. **c'est ~ant,** it's a nuisance.
enraciné /ɑ̃rasine/ *a.* deep-rooted.
enrag|er /ɑ̃raʒe/ *v.i.* be furious. **faire ~er,** annoy. **~é** *a.* furious; (*chien*) mad; (*fig.*) fanatical. **~eant, ~eante** *a.* infuriating.
enrayer /ɑ̃reje/ *v.t.* check.
enregistr|er /ɑ̃rʒistre/ *v.t.* note, record; (*mus.*) record. **(faire) ~er,** (*bagages*) register, check in. **~ement** *n.m.* recording; (*des bagages*) registration.
enrhumer (s') /(s)ɑ̃ryme/ *v. pr.* catch a cold.
enrich|ir /ɑ̃riʃir/ *v.t.* enrich. **s'~ir** *v. pr.* grow rich(er). **~issement** *n.m.* enrichment.
enrober /ɑ̃rɔbe/ *v.t.* coat (**de,** with).
enrôler /ɑ̃role/ *v.t.*, **s'~** *v. pr.* enlist, enrol.
enrou|er (s') /(s)ɑ̃rwe/ *v. pr.* become hoarse. **~é** *a.* hoarse.
enrouler /ɑ̃rule/ *v.t.*, **s'~** *v. pr.* wind. **s'~ dans une couverture,** roll o.s. up in a blanket.
ensabler /ɑ̃sɑble/ *v.t.*, **s'~** *v. pr.* (*port*) silt up.
ensanglanté /ɑ̃sɑ̃glɑ̃te/ *a.* bloodstained.
enseignant, ~e /ɑ̃sɛɲɑ̃, -t/ *n.m., f.* teacher. ● *a.* teaching.
enseigne /ɑ̃sɛɲ/ *n.f.* sign.
enseignement /ɑ̃sɛɲmɑ̃/ *n.m.* teaching; (*instruction*) education.
enseigner /ɑ̃seɲe/ *v.t./i.* teach. **~ qch. à qn.,** teach s.o. sth.
ensemble /ɑ̃sɑ̃bl/ *adv.* together. ● *n.m.* unity; (*d'objets*) set; (*mus.*) ensemble; (*vêtements*) outfit. **dans l'~,** on the whole. **d'~,** (*idée etc.*) general. **l'~ de,** (*totalité*) all of, the whole of.
ensemencer /ɑ̃smɑ̃se/ *v.t.* sow.
enserrer /ɑ̃sere/ *v.t.* grip (tightly).
ensevelir /ɑ̃səvlir/ *v.t.* bury.
ensoleill|é /ɑ̃sɔleje/ *a.* sunny. **~ement** /ɑ̃sɔlɛjmɑ̃/ *n.m.* (period of) sunshine.
ensommeillé /ɑ̃sɔmeje/ *a.* sleepy.
ensorceler /ɑ̃sɔrsəle/ *v.t.* bewitch.
ensuite /ɑ̃sɥit/ *adv.* next, then; (*plus tard*) later.
ensuivre (s') /(s)ɑ̃sɥivr/ *v. pr.* follow. **et tout ce qui s'ensuit,** and so on.
entaill|e /ɑ̃tɑj/ *n.f.* notch; (*blessure*) gash. **~er** *v.t.* notch; gash.
entamer /ɑ̃tame/ *v.t.* start; (*inciser*) cut into; (*ébranler*) shake.
entass|er /ɑ̃tɑse/ *v.t.*, **s'~er** *v. pr.* pile up. **(s')~er dans,** cram (together) into. **~ement** *n.m.* (*tas*) pile.

entendement /ãtãdmã/ *n.m.* understanding. **ça dépasse l'~,** it defies one's understanding.

entendre /ãtãdr/ *v.t.* hear; (*comprendre*) understand; (*vouloir*) intend, mean; (*vouloir dire*) mean. **s'~** *v. pr.* (*être d'accord*) agree. **~ dire que,** hear that. **~ parler de,** hear of. **s'~ (bien),** get on (**avec,** with). **(cela) s'entend,** of course.

entendu /ãtãdy/ *a.* (*convenu*) agreed; (*sourire, air*) knowing. **bien ~,** of course. **(c'est) ~!,** all right!

entente /ãtãt/ *n.f.* understanding. **à double ~,** with a double meaning.

entériner /ãterine/ *v.t.* ratify.

enterr|er /ãtere/ *v.t.* bury. **~ement** /ãtɛrmã/ *n.m.* burial, funeral.

entêtant, ~e /ãtɛtã, -t/ *a.* heady.

en-tête /ãtɛt/ *n.m.* heading. **à ~,** headed.

entêt|é /ãtete/ *a.* stubborn. **~ement** /ãtɛtmã/ *n.m.* stubbornness.

entêter (s') /(s)ãtete/ *v. pr.* persist (**à, dans,** in).

enthousias|me /ãtuzjasm/ *n.m.* enthusiasm. **~mer** *v.t.* enthuse. **s'~mer pour,** enthuse over. **~te** *a.* enthusiastic.

enticher (s') /(s)ãtiʃe/ *v. pr.* **s'~ de,** become infatuated with.

ent|ier, ~ière /ãtje, -jɛr/ *a.* whole; (*absolu*) absolute; (*entêté*) unyielding. ● *n.m.* whole. **en ~ier,** entirely. **~ièrement** *adv.* entirely.

entité /ãtite/ *n.f.* entity.

entonner /ãtɔne/ *v.t.* start singing.

entonnoir /ãtɔnwar/ *n.m.* funnel; (*trou*) crater.

entorse /ãtɔrs/ *n.f.* sprain. **~ à,** (*loi*) infringement of.

entortiller /ãtɔrtije/ *v.t.* wrap (up); (*enrouler*) wind, wrap; (*duper*) deceive.

entourage /ãturaʒ/ *n.m.* circle of family and friends; (*bordure*) surround.

entourer /ãture/ *v.t.* surround (**de,** with); (*réconforter*) rally round. **~ de,** (*écharpe etc.*) wrap round.

entracte /ãtrakt/ *n.m.* interval.

entraide /ãtrɛd/ *n.f.* mutual aid.

entraider (s') /(s)ãtrede/ *v. pr.* help each other.

entrailles /ãtraj/ *n.f. pl.* entrails.

entrain /ãtrɛ̃/ *n.m.* zest, spirit.

entraînant, ~e /ãtrɛnã, -t/ *a.* rousing.

entraînement /ãtrɛnmã/ *n.m.* (*sport*) training.

entraîn|er /ãtrene/ *v.t.* carry away *ou* along; (*emmener, influencer*) lead; (*impliquer*) entail; (*sport*) train; (*roue*) drive. **~eur** /ãtrɛnœr/ *n.m.* trainer.

entrav|e /ãtrav/ *n.f.* hindrance. **~er** *v.t.* hinder.

entre /ãtr(ə)/ *prép.* between; (*parmi*) among(st). **~ autres,** among other things. **l'un d'~ nous/vous/eux,** one of us/you/them.

entrebâillé /ãtrəbɑje/ *a.* ajar.

entrechoquer (s') /(s)ãtrəʃɔke/ *v. pr.* knock against each other.

entrecôte /ãtrəkot/ *n.f.* rib steak.

entrecouper /ãtrəkupe/ *v.t.* **~ de,** intersperse with.

entrecroiser (s') /(s)ãtrəkrwaze/ *v. pr.* (*routes*) intersect.

entrée /ãtre/ *n.f.* entrance; (*accès*) admission, entry; (*billet*) ticket; (*culin.*) first course; (*de données: techn.*) input. **~ interdite,** no entry.

entrefaites (sur ces) /(syrsez)ãtrəfɛt/ *adv.* at that moment.

entrefilet /ãtrəfilɛ/ *n.m.* paragraph.

entrejambe /ãtrəʒãb/ *n.m.* crotch.

entrelacer /ãtrəlase/ *v.t.*, **s'~** *v. pr.* intertwine.

entremêler /ãtrəmele/ *v.t.*, **s'~** *v. pr.* (inter)mingle.

entremets /ãtrəmɛ/ *n.m.* dessert.

entremetteu|r, ~se /ãtrəmɛtœr, -øz/ *n.m., f.* (*péj.*) go-between.

entre|mettre (s') /(s)ãtrəmɛtr/ *v. pr.* intervene. **~mise** *n.f.* intervention. **par l'~mise de,** through.

entreposer /ãtrəpoze/ *v.t.* store.

entrepôt /ãtrəpo/ *n.m.* warehouse.

entreprenant, ~e /ãtrəprənã, -t/ *a.* (*actif*) enterprising; (*séducteur*) forward.

entreprendre† /ãtrəprãdr/ *v.t.* start on; (*personne*) buttonhole. **~ de faire,** undertake to do.

entrepreneur /ãtrəprənœr/ *n.m.* **~ (de bâtiments),** (building) contractor.

entreprise /ãtrəpriz/ *n.f.* undertaking; (*société*) firm.

entrer /ãtre/ *v.i.* (*aux. être*) go in, enter; (*venir*) come in, enter. **~ dans,** go *ou* come into, enter; (*club*) join. **~ en collision,** collide (**avec,** with). **faire ~,** (*personne*) show in. **laisser ~,** let in.

entresol /ãtrəsɔl/ *n.m.* mezzanine.

entre-temps /ɑ̃trətɑ̃/ *adv.* meanwhile.

entretenir† /ɑ̃trətnir/ *v.t.* maintain; (*faire durer*) keep alive. **~ qn. de,** converse with s.o. about. **s'~** *v. pr.* speak (**de,** about; **avec,** to).

entretien /ɑ̃trətjɛ̃/ *n.m.* maintenance; (*discussion*) talk; (*audience pour un emploi*) interview.

entrevoir /ɑ̃trəvwar/ *v.t.* make out; (*brièvement*) glimpse.

entrevue /ɑ̃trəvy/ *n.f.* interview.

entrouvrir /ɑ̃truvrir/ *v.t.* half-open.

énumér|er /enymere/ *v.t.* enumerate. **~ation** *n.f.* enumeration.

envah|ir /ɑ̃vair/ *v.t.* invade, overrun; (*douleur, peur*) overcome. **~isseur** *n.m.* invader.

enveloppe /ɑ̃vlɔp/ *n.f.* envelope; (*emballage*) covering; (*techn.*) casing.

envelopper /ɑ̃vlɔpe/ *v.t.* wrap (up); (*fig.*) envelop.

envenimer /ɑ̃vnime/ *v.t.* embitter. **s'~** *v. pr.* become embittered.

envergure /ɑ̃vɛrgyr/ *n.f.* wing-span; (*importance*) scope; (*qualité*) calibre.

envers /ɑ̃vɛr/ *prép.* toward(s), to. ● *n.m.* (*de tissu*) wrong side. **à l'~,** upside down; (*pantalon*) back to front; (*chaussette*) inside out.

enviable /ɑ̃vjabl/ *a.* enviable. **peu ~,** unenviable.

envie /ɑ̃vi/ *n.f.* desire, wish; (*jalousie*) envy. **avoir ~ de,** want, feel like. **avoir ~ de faire,** want to do, feel like doing.

envier /ɑ̃vje/ *v.t.* envy.

envieu|x, ~se /ɑ̃vjø, -z/ *a. & n.m., f.* envious (person).

environ /ɑ̃virɔ̃/ *adv.* (round) about. **~s** *n.m. pl.* surroundings. **aux ~s de,** round about.

environnement /ɑ̃virɔnmɑ̃/ *n.m.* environment.

environn|er /ɑ̃virɔne/ *v.t.* surround. **~ant, ~ante** *a.* surrounding.

envisager /ɑ̃vizaʒe/ *v.t.* consider. **~ de faire,** consider doing.

envoi /ɑ̃vwa/ *n.m.* dispatch; (*paquet*) consignment.

envol /ɑ̃vɔl/ *n.m.* flight; (*d'avion*) take-off.

envoler (s') /(s)ɑ̃vɔle/ *v. pr.* fly away; (*avion*) take off; (*papiers*) blow away.

envoûter /ɑ̃vute/ *v.t.* bewitch.

envoyé, ~e /ɑ̃vwaje/ *n.m., f.* envoy; (*de journal*) correspondent.

envoyer† /ɑ̃vwaje/ *v.t.* send; (*lancer*) throw. **~ promener qn.,** give s.o. the brush-off.

enzyme /ɑ̃zim/ *n.m.* enzyme.

épagneul, ~e /epaɲœl/ *n.m., f.* spaniel.

épais, ~se /epɛ, -s/ *a.* thick. **~seur** /-sœr/ *n.f.* thickness.

épaissir /epesir/ *v.t./i.,* **s'~** *v. pr.* thicken.

épanch|er (s') /(s)epɑ̃ʃe/ *v. pr.* pour out one's feelings; (*liquide*) pour out. **~ement** *n.m.* outpouring.

épanoui /epanwi/ *a.* (*joyeux*) beaming, radiant.

épan|ouir (s') /(s)epanwir/ *v. pr.* (*fleur*) open out; (*visage*) beam; (*personne*) blossom. **~ouissement** *n.m.* (*éclat*) blossoming, full bloom.

épargne /eparɲ/ *n.f.* saving; (*somme*) savings. **caisse d'~,** savings bank.

épargn|er /eparɲe/ *v.t./i.* save; (*ne pas tuer*) spare. **~er qch. à qn.,** spare s.o. sth. **~ant, ~ante** *n.m., f.* saver.

éparpiller /eparpije/ *v.t.* scatter. **s'~** *v. pr.* scatter; (*fig.*) dissipate one's efforts.

épars, ~e /epar, -s/ *a.* scattered.

épat|er /epate/ *v.t.* (*fam.*) amaze. **~ant, ~ante** *a.* (*fam.*) amazing.

épaule /epol/ *n.f.* shoulder.

épauler /epole/ *v.t.* (*arme*) raise; (*aider*) support.

épave /epav/ *n.f.* wreck.

épée /epe/ *n.f.* sword.

épeler /ɛple/ *v.t.* spell.

éperdu /epɛrdy/ *a.* wild, frantic. **~ment** *adv.* wildly, frantically.

éperon /eprɔ̃/ *n.m.* spur. **~ner** /-ɔne/ *v.t.* spur (on).

épervier /epɛrvje/ *n.m.* sparrowhawk.

éphémère /efemɛr/ *a.* ephemeral.

éphéméride /efemerid/ *n.f.* tear-off calendar.

épi /epi/ *n.m.* (*de blé*) ear. **~ de cheveux,** tuft of hair.

épic|e /epis/ *n.f.* spice. **~é** *a.* spicy. **~er** *v.t.* spice.

épic|ier, ~ière /episje, -jɛr/ *n.m., f.* grocer. **~erie** *n.f.* grocery shop; (*produits*) groceries.

épidémie /epidemi/ *n.f.* epidemic.

épiderme /epidɛrm/ *n.m.* skin.

épier /epje/ *v.t.* spy on.

épilep|sie /epilɛpsi/ *n.f.* epilepsy. **~tique** *a.* & *n.m./f.* epileptic.

épiler /epile/ *v.t.* remove unwanted hair from; (*sourcils*) pluck.

épilogue /epilɔg/ *n.m.* epilogue; (*fig.*) outcome.

épinard /epinar/ *n.m.* (*plante*) spinach. **~s**, (*nourriture*) spinach.

épin|e /epin/ *n.f.* thorn, prickle; (*d'animal*) prickle, spine. **~e dorsale**, backbone. **~eux, ~euse** *a.* thorny.

épingl|e /epɛ̃gl/ *n.f.* pin. **~e de nourrice, ~e de sûreté**, safety-pin. **~er** *v.t.* pin; (*arrêter*: *fam.*) nab.

épique /epik/ *a.* epic.

épisod|e /epizɔd/ *n.m.* episode. **à ~es**, serialized. **~ique** *a.* occasional.

épitaphe /epitaf/ *n.f.* epitaph.

épithète /epitɛt/ *n.f.* epithet.

épître /epitr/ *n.f.* epistle.

éploré /eplɔre/ *a.* tearful.

épluche-légumes /eplyʃlegym/ *n.m. invar.* (potato) peeler.

épluch|er /eplyʃe/ *v.t.* peel; (*examiner*: *fig.*) scrutinize. **~age** *n.m.* peeling; (*fig.*) scrutiny. **~ure** *n.f.* piece of peel *ou* peeling. **~ures** *n.f. pl.* peelings.

époong|e /epɔ̃ʒ/ *n.f.* sponge. **~er** *v.t.* (*liquide*) sponge up; (*surface*) sponge (down); (*front*) mop; (*dettes*) wipe out.

épopée /epɔpe/ *n.f.* epic.

époque /epɔk/ *n.f.* time, period. **à l'~**, at the time. **d'~**, period.

épouse /epuz/ *n.f.* wife.

épouser[1] /epuze/ *v.t.* marry.

épouser[2] /epuze/ *v.t.* (*forme*, *idée*) assume, embrace, adopt.

épousseter /epuste/ *v.t.* dust.

époustouflant, ~e /epustuflɑ̃, -t/ *a.* (*fam.*) staggering.

épouvantable /epuvɑ̃tabl/ *a.* appalling.

épouvantail /epuvɑ̃taj/ *n.m.* scarecrow.

épouvant|e /epuvɑ̃t/ *n.f.* terror. **~er** *v.t.* terrify.

époux /epu/ *n.m.* husband. **les ~**, the married couple.

éprendre (s') /(s)eprɑ̃dr/ *v. pr.* **s'~ de**, fall in love with.

épreuve /eprœv/ *n.f.* test; (*sport*) event; (*malheur*) ordeal; (*photo.*) print; (*d'imprimerie*) proof. **mettre à l'~**, put to the test.

éprouvé /epruve/ *a.* (well-)proven.

éprouv|er /epruve/ *v.t.* test; (*ressentir*) experience; (*affliger*) distress. **~ant, ~ante** *a.* testing.

éprouvette /epruvɛt/ *n.f.* test-tube. **bébé-~**, test-tube baby.

épuis|er /epɥize/ *v.t.* (*fatiguer*, *user*) exhaust. **s'~er** *v. pr.* become exhausted. **~é** *a.* exhausted; (*livre*) out of print. **~ement** *n.m.* exhaustion.

épuisette /epɥizɛt/ *n.f.* fishing-net.

épur|er /epyre/ *v.t.* purify; (*pol.*) purge. **~ation** *n.f.* purification; (*pol.*) purge.

équat|eur /ekwatœr/ *n.m.* equator. **~orial** (*m. pl.* **~oriaux**) *a.* equatorial.

équation /ekwɑsjɔ̃/ *n.f.* equation.

équerre /ekɛr/ *n.f.* (set) square. **d'~**, square.

équilibr|e /ekilibr/ *n.m.* balance. **être** *ou* **se tenir en ~e**, (*personne*) balance; (*objet*) be balanced. **~é** *a.* well-balanced. **~er** *v.t.* balance. **s'~er** *v. pr.* (*forces etc.*) counterbalance each other.

équilibriste /ekilibrist/ *n.m./f.* tightrope walker.

équinoxe /ekinɔks/ *n.m.* equinox.

équipage /ekipaʒ/ *n.m.* crew.

équipe /ekip/ *n.f.* team. **~ de nuit/jour**, night/day shift.

équipé /ekipe/ *a.* **bien/mal ~**, well/poorly equipped.

équipée /ekipe/ *n.f.* escapade.

équipement /ekipmɑ̃/ *n.m.* equipment. **~s**, (*installations*) amenities, facilities.

équiper /ekipe/ *v.t.* equip (**de**, with). **s'~** *v. pr.* equip o.s.

équip|ier, ~ière /ekipje, -jɛr/ *n.m., f.* team member.

équitable /ekitabl/ *a.* fair. **~ment** /-əmɑ̃/ *adv.* fairly.

équitation /ekitɑsjɔ̃/ *n.f.* (horse-)riding.

équité /ekite/ *n.f.* equity.

équivalen|t, ~te /ekivalɑ̃, -t/ *a.* equivalent. **~ce** *n.f.* equivalence.

équivaloir /ekivalwar/ *v.i.* **~ à**, be equivalent to.

équivoque /ekivɔk/ *a.* equivocal; (*louche*) questionable. ● *n.f.* ambiguity.

érable /erabl/ *n.m.* maple.

érafl|er /erafle/ *v.t.* scratch. **~ure** *n.f.* scratch.

éraillé /erɑje/ *a.* (*voix*) raucous.

ère /ɛr/ *n.f.* era.

érection /erɛksjɔ̃/ *n.f.* erection.
éreinter /erɛ̃te/ *v.t.* exhaust; (*fig.*) criticize severely.
ergoter /ɛrgɔte/ *v.i.* quibble.
ériger /eriʒe/ *v.t.* erect. **(s')~ en,** set (o.s.) up as.
ermite /ɛrmit/ *n.m.* hermit.
éroder /erɔde/ *v.t.* erode.
érosion /erozjɔ̃/ *n.f.* erosion.
éroti|que /erɔtik/ *a.* erotic. **~sme** *n.m.* eroticism.
errer /ɛre/ *v.i.* wander.
erreur /ɛrœr/ *n.f.* mistake, error. **dans l'~,** mistaken. **par ~,** by mistake. **~ judiciaire,** miscarriage of justice.
erroné /ɛrɔne/ *a.* erroneous.
ersatz /ɛrzats/ *n.m.* ersatz.
érudit, ~e /erydi, -t/ *a.* scholarly. ● *n.m., f.* scholar. **~ion** /-sjɔ̃/ *n.f.* scholarship.
éruption /erypsjɔ̃/ *n.f.* eruption; (*méd.*) rash.
es /ɛ/ *voir* être.
escabeau (*pl.* **~x**) /ɛskabo/ *n.m.* step-ladder; (*tabouret*) stool.
escadre /ɛskadr/ *n.f.* (*naut.*) squadron.
escadrille /ɛskadrij/ *n.f.* (*aviat.*) flight, squadron.
escadron /ɛskadrɔ̃/ *n.m.* (*mil.*) squadron.
escalad|e /ɛskalad/ *n.f.* climbing; (*pol., comm.*) escalation. **~er** *v.t.* climb.
escalator /ɛskalatɔr/ *n.m.* (P.) escalator.
escale /ɛskal/ *n.f.* (*d'avion*) stopover; (*port*) port of call. **faire ~ à,** (*avion, passager*) stop over at; (*navire, passager*) put in at.
escalier /ɛskalje/ *n.m.* stairs. **~ mécanique** *ou* **roulant,** escalator.
escalope /ɛskalɔp/ *n.f.* escalope.
escamotable /ɛskamɔtabl/ *a.* (*techn.*) retractable.
escamoter /ɛskamɔte/ *v.t.* make vanish; (*éviter*) dodge.
escargot /ɛskargo/ *n.m.* snail.
escarmouche /ɛskarmuʃ/ *n.f.* skirmish.
escarpé /ɛskarpe/ *a.* steep.
escarpin /ɛskarpɛ̃/ *n.m.* pump.
escient /esjɑ̃/ *n.m.* **à bon ~,** with good reason.
esclaffer (s') /(s)ɛsklafe/ *v. pr.* guffaw, burst out laughing.
esclandre /ɛsklɑ̃dr/ *n.m.* scene.
esclav|e /ɛsklav/ *n.m./f.* slave. **~age** *n.m.* slavery.
escompte /ɛskɔ̃t/ *n.m.* discount.
escompter /ɛskɔ̃te/ *v.t.* expect; (*comm.*) discount.
escort|e /ɛskɔrt/ *n.f.* escort. **~er** *v.t.* escort. **~eur** *n.m.* escort (ship).
escouade /ɛskwad/ *n.f.* squad.
escrim|e /ɛskrim/ *n.f.* fencing. **~eur, ~euse** *n.m., f.* fencer.
escrimer (s') /(s)ɛskrime/ *v. pr.* struggle.
escroc /ɛskro/ *n.m.* swindler.
escroqu|er /ɛskrɔke/ *v.t.* swindle. **~er qch. à qn.,** swindle s.o. out of sth. **~erie** *n.f.* swindle.
espace /ɛspas/ *n.m.* space. **~s verts,** gardens, parks.
espacer /ɛspase/ *v.t.* space out. **s'~** *v. pr.* become less frequent.
espadrille /ɛspadrij/ *n.f.* rope sandals.
Espagne /ɛspaɲ/ *n.f.* Spain.
espagnol, ~e /ɛspaɲɔl/ *a.* Spanish. ● *n.m., f.* Spaniard. ● *n.m.* (*lang.*) Spanish.
espagnolette /ɛspaɲɔlɛt/ *n.f.* (window) catch.
espèce /ɛspɛs/ *n.f.* kind, sort; (*race*) species. **~s,** (*argent*) cash. **~ d'idiot/de brute/***etc.***!,** you idiot/ brute/*etc.*!
espérance /ɛsperɑ̃s/ *n.f.* hope.
espérer /ɛspere/ *v.t.* hope for. **~ faire/que,** hope to do/that. ● *v.i.* hope. **~ en,** have faith in.
espiègle /ɛspjɛgl/ *a.* mischievous.
espion, ~ne /ɛspjɔ̃, -jɔn/ *n.m., f.* spy.
espionn|er /ɛspjɔne/ *v.t./i.* spy (on). **~age** *n.m.* espionage, spying.
esplanade /ɛsplanad/ *n.f.* esplanade.
espoir /ɛspwar/ *n.m.* hope.
esprit /ɛspri/ *n.m.* spirit; (*intellect*) mind; (*humour*) wit. **perdre l'~,** lose one's mind. **reprendre ses ~s,** come to. **vouloir faire de l'~,** try to be witty.
Esquimau, ~de (*m. pl.* **~x**) /ɛskimo, -d/ *n.m., f.* Eskimo.
esquinter /ɛskɛ̃te/ *v.t.* (*fam.*) ruin.
esquiss|e /ɛskis/ *n.f.* sketch; (*fig.*) suggestion. **~er** *v.t.* sketch; (*geste etc.*) make an attempt at.
esquiv|e /ɛskiv/ *n.f.* (*sport*) dodge. **~er** *v.t.* dodge. **s'~er** *v. pr.* slip away.
essai /esɛ/ *n.m.* testing; (*épreuve*) test, trial; (*tentative*) try; (*article*) essay. **à l'~,** on trial.

essaim /esɛ̃/ *n.m.* swarm. **~er** /eseme/ *v.i.* swarm; (*fig.*) spread.
essayage /esɛjaʒ/ *n.m.* (*de vêtement*) fitting. **salon d'~,** fitting room.
essayer /eseje/ *v.t./i.* try; (*vêtement*) try (on); (*voiture etc.*) try (out). **~ de faire,** try to do.
essence[1] /esɑ̃s/ *n.f.* (*carburant*) petrol; (*Amer.*) gas.
essence[2] /esɑ̃s/ *n.f.* (*nature, extrait*) essence.
essentiel, ~le /esɑ̃sjɛl/ *a.* essential. ● *n.m.* **l'~,** the main thing; (*quantité*) the main part. **~lement** *adv.* essentially.
essieu (*pl.* **~x**) /esjø/ *n.m.* axle.
essor /esɔr/ *n.m.* expansion. **prendre son ~,** expand.
essor|er /esɔre/ *v.t.* (*linge*) spin-dry; (*en tordant*) wring. **~euse** *n.f.* spin-drier.
essouffler *v.t.* make breathless. **s'~** *v. pr.* get out of breath.
ess|uyer[1] /esɥije/ *v.t.* wipe. **s'~uyer** *v. pr.* dry *ou* wipe o.s. **~uie-glace** *n.m. invar.* windscreen wiper; (*Amer.*) windshield wiper. **~uie-mains** *n.m. invar.* hand-towel.
essuyer[2] /esɥije/ *v.t.* (*subir*) suffer.
est[1] /ɛ/ *voir* être.
est[2] /ɛst/ *n.m.* east. ● *a. invar.* east; (*partie*) eastern; (*direction*) easterly.
estampe /ɛstɑ̃p/ *n.f.* print.
estampille /ɛstɑ̃pij/ *n.f.* stamp.
esthète /ɛstɛt/ *n.m./f.* aesthete.
esthéticienne /ɛstetisjɛn/ *n.f.* beautician.
esthétique /ɛstetik/ *a.* aesthetic.
estimable /ɛstimabl/ *a.* worthy.
estimation /ɛstimasjɔ̃/ *n.f.* valuation.
estime /ɛstim/ *n.f.* esteem.
estim|er /ɛstime/ *v.t.* (*objet*) value; (*calculer*) estimate; (*respecter*) esteem; (*considérer*) consider. **~ation** *n.f.* valuation; (*calcul*) estimation.
estiv|al (*m. pl.* **~aux**) /ɛstival, -o/ *a.* summer. **~ant, ~ante** *n.m., f.* summer visitor, holiday-maker.
estomac /ɛstɔma/ *n.m.* stomach.
estomaqué /ɛstɔmake/ *a.* (*fam.*) stunned.
estomper (s') /(s)ɛstɔ̃pe/ *v. pr.* become blurred.
estrade /ɛstrad/ *n.f.* platform.
estragon /ɛstragɔ̃/ *n.m.* tarragon.
estrop|ier /ɛstrɔpje/ *v.t.* cripple; (*fig.*) mangle. **~ié, ~iée** *n.m., f.* cripple.
estuaire /ɛstɥɛr/ *n.m.* estuary.
estudiantin, ~e /ɛstydjɑ̃tɛ̃, -in/ *a.* student.
esturgeon /ɛstyrʒɔ̃/ *n.m.* sturgeon.
et /e/ *conj.* and. **et moi/lui/***etc.***?,** what about me/him/*etc.*?
étable /etabl/ *n.f.* cow-shed.
établi[1] /etabli/ *a.* established. **un fait bien ~,** a well-established fact.
établi[2] /etabli/ *n.m.* work-bench.
établir /etablir/ *v.t.* establish; (*liste, facture*) draw up; (*personne, camp, record*) set up. **s'~** *v. pr.* (*personne*) establish o.s. **s'~ épicier/***etc.*, set (o.s.) up as a grocer/*etc.* **s'~ à son compte,** set up on one's own.
établissement /etablismɑ̃/ *n.m.* (*bâtiment, institution*) establishment.
étage /etaʒ/ *n.m.* floor, storey; (*de fusée*) stage. **à l'~,** upstairs. **au premier ~,** on the first floor.
étager (s') /(s)etaʒe/ *v. pr.* rise at different levels.
étagère /etaʒɛr/ *n.f.* shelf; (*meuble*) shelving unit.
étai /etɛ/ *n.m.* prop, buttress.
étain /etɛ̃/ *n.m.* pewter.
étais, était /etɛ/ *voir* être.
étal (*pl.* **~s**) /etal/ *n.m.* stall.
étalag|e /etalaʒ/ *n.m.* display; (*vitrine*) shop-window. **faire ~e de,** show off **~iste** *n.m./f.* window-dresser.
étaler /etale/ *v.t.* spread; (*journal*) spread (out); (*vacances*) stagger; (*exposer*) display. **s'~** *v. pr.* (*s'étendre*) stretch out; (*tomber: fam.*) fall flat. **s'~ sur,** (*paiement*) be spread over.
étalon /etalɔ̃/ *n.m.* (*cheval*) stallion; (*modèle*) standard.
étanche /etɑ̃ʃ/ *a.* watertight; (*montre*) waterproof.
étancher /etɑ̃ʃe/ *v.t.* (*soif*) quench; (*sang*) stem.
étang /etɑ̃/ *n.m.* pond.
étant /etɑ̃/ *voir* être.
étape /etap/ *n.f.* stage; (*lieu d'arrêt*) stopover.
état /eta/ *n.m.* state; (*liste*) statement; (*métier*) profession; (*nation*) State. **en bon/mauvais ~,** in good/bad condition. **en ~ de,** in a position to. **hors d'~ de,** not in a position to. **en ~ de marche,** in working order. **~ civil,** civil status. **~-major** (*pl.* **~s-majors**) *n.m.* (*officiers*) staff.

faire ~ de, (*citer*) mention. **être dans tous ses ~s,** be in a state. **~ des lieux,** inventory.

étatisé /etatize/ *a.* State-controlled.

États-Unis /etazyni/ *n.m. pl.* **~ (d'Amérique),** United States (of America).

étau (*pl.* **~x**) /eto/ *n.m.* vice.

étayer /eteje/ *v.t.* prop up.

été[1] /ete/ *voir* être.

été[2] /ete/ *n.m.* summer.

étein|dre† /etɛ̃dr/ *v.t.* put out, extinguish; (*lumière, radio*) turn off. **s'~dre** *v. pr.* (*feu*) go out; (*mourir*) die. **~t, ~te** /etɛ̃, -t/ *a.* (*feu*) out; (*volcan*) extinct.

étendard /etɑ̃dar/ *n.m.* standard.

étendre /etɑ̃dr/ *v.t.* spread; (*journal, nappe*) spread out; (*bras, jambes*) stretch (out); (*linge*) hang out; (*agrandir*) extend. **s'~** *v. pr.* (*s'allonger*) stretch out; (*se propager*) spread; (*plaine etc.*) stretch. **s'~ sur,** (*sujet*) dwell on.

étendu, ~e /etɑ̃dy/ *a.* extensive. ● *n.f.* area; (*d'eau*) stretch; (*importance*) extent.

éternel, ~le /etɛrnɛl/ *a.* eternal. **~lement** *adv.* eternally.

éterniser (s') /(s)etɛrnize/ *v. pr.* (*durer*) drag on.

éternité /etɛrnite/ *n.f.* eternity.

étern|uer /etɛrnɥe/ *v.i.* sneeze. **~uement** /-ymɑ̃/ *n.m.* sneeze.

êtes /ɛt/ *voir* être.

éthique /etik/ *a.* ethical. ● *n.f.* ethics.

ethn|ie /ɛtni/ *n.f.* ethnic group. **~ique** *a.* ethnic.

éthylisme /etilism/ *n.m.* alcoholism.

étinceler /etɛ̃sle/ *v.i.* sparkle.

étincelle /etɛ̃sɛl/ *n.f.* spark.

étioler (s') /(s)etjɔle/ *v. pr.* wilt.

étiqueter /etikte/ *v.t.* label.

étiquette /etikɛt/ *n.f.* label; (*protocole*) etiquette.

étirer /etire/ *v.t.*, **s'~** *v. pr.* stretch.

étoffe /etɔf/ *n.f.* fabric.

étoffer /etɔfe/ *v.t.*, **s'~** *v. pr.* fill out.

étoil|e /etwal/ *n.f.* star. **à la belle ~e,** in the open. **~e de mer,** starfish. **~é** *a.* starry.

étonn|er /etɔne/ *v.t.* amaze. **s'~er** *v. pr.* be amazed (**de,** at). **~ant, ~ante** *a.* amazing. **~ement** *n.m.* amazement.

étouffée /etufe/ *n.f.* **cuire à l'~,** braise.

étouff|er /etufe/ *v.t./i.* suffocate; (*sentiment, révolte*) stifle; (*feu*) smother; (*bruit*) muffle. **on ~e,** it is stifling. **s'~er** *v. pr.* suffocate; (*en mangeant*) choke. **~ant, ~ante** *a.* stifling.

étourd|i, ~ie /eturdi/ *a.* unthinking, scatter-brained. ● *n.m., f.* scatter-brain. **~erie** *n.f.* thoughtlessness; (*acte*) thoughtless act.

étourd|ir /eturdir/ *v.t.* stun; (*griser*) make dizzy. **~issant, ~issante** *a.* stunning. **~issement** *n.m.* (*syncope*) dizzy spell.

étourneau (*pl.* **~x**) /eturno/ *n.m.* starling.

étrange /etrɑ̃ʒ/ *a.* strange. **~ment** *adv.* strangely. **~té** *n.f.* strangeness.

étrang|er, ~ère /etrɑ̃ʒe, -ɛr/ *a.* strange, unfamiliar; (*d'un autre pays*) foreign. ● *n.m., f.* foreigner; (*inconnu*) stranger. **à l'~er,** abroad. **de l'~er,** from abroad.

étrangler /etrɑ̃gle/ *v.t.* strangle; (*col*) stifle. **s'~** *v. pr.* choke.

être† /ɛtr/ *v.i.* be. ● *v. aux.* (*avec aller, sortir, etc.*) have. **~ donné/fait par,** (*passif*) be given/done by. ● *n.m.* (*personne, créature*) being. **~ humain,** human being **~ médecin/tailleur/***etc.*, be a doctor/a tailor/*etc.* **~ à qn.,** be s.o.'s. **c'est à faire,** it needs to be *ou* should be done. **est-ce qu'il travaille?,** is he working?, does he work? **vous travaillez, n'est-ce pas?,** you are working, aren't you?, you work, don't you? **il est deux heures/***etc.*, it is two o'clock/*etc.* **nous sommes le six mai,** it is the sixth of May.

étrein|dre /etrɛ̃dr/ *v.t.* grasp; (*ami*) embrace. **~te** /-ɛ̃t/ *n.f.* grasp; embrace.

étrenner /etrene/ *v.t.* use for the first time.

étrennes /etrɛn/ *n.f. pl.* (*cadeau*) New Year's gift.

étrier /etrije/ *n.m.* stirrup.

étriqué /etrike/ *a.* tight; (*fig.*) small-minded.

étroit, ~e /etrwa, -t/ *a.* narrow; (*vêtement*) tight; (*liens, surveillance*) close. **à l'~,** cramped. **~ement** /-tmɑ̃/ *adv.* closely. **~esse** /-tɛs/ *n.f.* narrowness.

étude /etyd/ *n.f.* study; (*bureau*) office. **(salle d')~,** (*scol.*) prep room; (*scol., Amer.*) study hall. **à l'~,**

under consideration. **faire des ~s (de),** study.

étudiant, ~e /etydjɑ̃, -t/ *n.m., f.* student.

étudier /etydje/ *v.t./i.* study.

étui /etɥi/ *n.m.* case.

étuve /etyv/ *n.f.* steamroom. **quelle ~!,** it's like a hothouse in here.

étuvée /etyve/ *n.f.* **cuire à l'~,** braise.

etymologie /etimɔlɔʒi/ *n.f.* etymology.

eu, eue /y/ *voir* avoir.

eucalyptus /økaliptys/ *n.m.* eucalyptus.

euphémisme /øfemism/ *n.m.* euphemism.

euphorie /øfɔri/ *n.f.* euphoria.

Europe /ørɔp/ *n.f.* Europe.

européen, ~ne /ørɔpeɛ̃, -eɛn/ *a. & n.m., f.* European.

euthanasie /øtanazi/ *n.f.* euthanasia.

eux /ø/ *pron.* they; (*complément*) them. **~-mêmes** *pron.* themselves.

évac|uer /evakɥe/ *v.t.* evacuate. **~uation** *n.f.* evacuation.

évad|er (s') /(s)evade/ *v. pr.* escape. **~é, ~ée** *a.* escaped; *n.m., f.* escaped prisoner.

éval|uer /evalɥe/ *v.t.* assess. **~uation** *n.f.* assessment.

évang|ile /evɑ̃ʒil/ *n.m.* gospel. **l'Évangile,** the Gospel. **~élique** *a.* evangelical.

évan|ouir (s') /(s)evanwir/ *v. pr.* faint; (*disparaître*) vanish. **~ouissement** *n.m.* (*syncope*) fainting fit.

évapor|er /evapɔre/ *v.t.*, **s'~er** *v. pr.* evaporate. **~ation** *n.f.* evaporation.

évasi|f, ~ve /evazif, -v/ *a.* evasive.

évasion /evazjɔ̃/ *n.f.* escape; (*par le rêve etc.*) escapism.

éveil /evɛj/ *n.m.* awakening. **donner l'~ à,** arouse the suspicions of. **en ~,** alert.

éveill|er /eveje/ *v.t.* awake(n); (*susciter*) arouse. **s'~er** *v. pr.* awake(n); be aroused. **~é** *a.* awake; (*intelligent*) alert.

événement /evɛnmɑ̃/ *n.m.* event.

éventail /evɑ̃taj/ *n.m.* fan; (*gamme*) range.

éventaire /evɑ̃tɛr/ *n.m.* stall, stand.

éventé /evɑ̃te/ *a.* (*gâté*) stale.

éventrer /evɑ̃tre/ *v.t.* (*sac etc.*) rip open.

éventualité /evɑ̃tɥalite/ *n.f.* possibility. **dans cette ~,** in that event.

éventuel, ~le /evɑ̃tɥɛl/ *a.* possible. **~lement** *adv.* possibly.

évêque /evɛk/ *n.m.* bishop.

évertuer (s') /(s)evɛrtɥe/ *v. pr.* **s'~ à,** struggle hard to.

éviction /eviksjɔ̃/ *n.f.* eviction.

évidemment /evidamɑ̃/ *adv.* obviously; (*bien sûr*) of course.

évidence /evidɑ̃s/ *n.f.* obviousness; (*fait*) obvious fact. **être en ~,** be conspicuous. **mettre en ~,** (*fait*) highlight.

évident, ~e /evidɑ̃, -t/ *a.* obvious, evident.

évider /evide/ *v.t.* hollow out.

évier /evje/ *n.m.* sink.

évincer /evɛ̃se/ *v.t.* oust.

éviter /evite/ *v.t.* avoid (**de faire,** doing). **~ à qn.,** (*dérangement etc.*) spare s.o.

évoca|teur ~trice /evɔkatœr, -tris/ *a.* evocative.

évocation /evɔkɑsjɔ̃/ *n.f.* evocation.

évolué /evɔlɥe/ *a.* highly developed.

évol|uer /evɔlɥe/ *v.i.* develop; (*se déplacer*) move, manœuvre; (*Amer.*) maneuver. **~ution** *n.f.* development; (*d'une espèce*) evolution; (*déplacement*) movement.

évoquer /evɔke/ *v.t.* call to mind, evoke.

ex- /ɛks/ *préf.* ex-.

exacerber /ɛgzasɛrbe/ *v.t.* exacerbate.

exact, ~e /ɛgza(kt), -akt/ *a.* exact, accurate; (*correct*) correct; (*personne*) punctual. **~ement** /-ktəmɑ̃/ *adv.* exactly. **~itude** /-ktityd/ *n.f.* exactness; punctuality.

ex aequo /ɛgzeko/ *adv.* (*classer*) equal. **être ~,** be equally placed.

exagéré /ɛgzaʒere/ *a.* excessive.

exagér|er /ɛgzaʒere/ *v.t./i.* exaggerate; (*abuser*) go too far. **~ation** *n.f.* exaggeration.

exaltation /ɛgzaltɑsjɔ̃/ *n.f.* elation.

exalté, ~e /ɛgzalte/ *n.m., f.* fanatic.

exalter /ɛgzalte/ *v.t.* excite; (*glorifier*) exalt.

examen /ɛgzamɛ̃/ *n.m.* examination; (*scol.*) exam(ination).

examin|er /ɛgzamine/ *v.t.* examine. **~ateur, ~atrice** *n.m., f.* examiner.

exaspér|er /ɛgzaspere/ *v.t.* exasperate. **~ation** *n.f.* exasperation.

exaucer /ɛgzose/ *v.t.* grant; (*personne*) grant the wish(es) of.
excavateur /ɛkskavatœr/ *n.m.* digger.
excavation /ɛkskavɑsjɔ̃/ *n.f.* excavation.
excédent /ɛksedɑ̃/ *n.m.* surplus. **~ de bagages,** excess luggage. **~ de la balance commerciale,** trade surplus. **~aire** /-tɛr/ *a.* excess, surplus.
excéder[1] /ɛksede/ *v.t.* (*dépasser*) exceed.
excéder[2] /ɛksede/ *v.t.* (*agacer*) irritate.
excellen|t, ~te /ɛksɛlɑ̃, -t/ *a.* excellent. **~ce** *n.f.* excellence.
exceller /ɛksele/ *v.i.* excel (**dans,** in).
excentri|que /ɛksɑ̃trik/ *a. & n.m./f.* eccentric. **~cité** *n.f.* eccentricity.
excepté /ɛksɛpte/ *a. & prép.* except.
excepter /ɛksɛpte/ *v.t.* except.
exception /ɛksɛpsjɔ̃/ *n.f.* exception. **à l'~ de,** except for. **d'~,** exceptional. **faire ~,** be an exception. **~nel, ~nelle** /-jɔnɛl/ *a.* exceptional. **~nellement** /-jɔnɛlmɑ̃/ *adv.* exceptionally.
excès /ɛksɛ/ *n.m.* excess. **~ de vitesse,** speeding.
excessi|f, ~ve /ɛksesif, -v/ *a.* excessive. **~vement** *adv.* excessively.
excitant /ɛksitɑ̃/ *n.m.* stimulant.
excit|er /ɛksite/ *v.t.* excite; (*encourager*) exhort (**à,** to); (*irriter: fam.*) annoy. **~ation** *n.f.* excitement.
exclam|er (s') /(s)ɛksklame/ *v. pr.* exclaim. **~ation** *n.f.* exclamation.
exclu|re† /ɛksklyr/ *v.t.* exclude; (*expulser*) expel; (*empêcher*) preclude. **~sion** *n.f.* exclusion.
exclusi|f, ~ve /ɛksklyzif, -v/ *a.* exclusive. **~vement** *adv.* exclusively. **~vité** *n.f.* (*comm.*) exclusive rights. **en ~vité à,** (*film*) (showing) exclusively at.
excrément(s) /ɛkskremɑ̃/ *n.m.* (*pl.*). excrement.
excroissance /ɛkskrwasɑ̃s/ *n.f.* (out)growth, excrescence.
excursion /ɛkskyrsjɔ̃/ *n.f.* excursion; (*à pied*) hike.
excuse /ɛkskyz/ *n.f.* excuse. **~s,** apology. **faire des ~s,** apologize.
excuser /ɛkskyze/ *v.t.* excuse. **s'~** *v. pr.* apologize (**de,** for). **je m'excuse,** (*fam.*) excuse me.
exécrable /ɛgzekrabl/ *a.* abominable.
exécrer /ɛgzekre/ *v.t.* loathe.
exécut|er /ɛgzekyte/ *v.t.* carry out, execute; (*mus.*) perform; (*tuer*) execute. **~ion** /-sjɔ̃/ *n.f.* execution; (*mus.*) performance.
exécuti|f, ~ve /ɛgzekytif, -v/ *a. & n.m.* (*pol.*) executive.
exemplaire /ɛgzɑ̃plɛr/ *a.* exemplary. ● *n.m.* copy.
exemple /ɛgzɑ̃pl/ *n.m.* example. **par ~,** for example. **donner l'~,** set an example.
exempt, ~e /ɛgzɑ̃, -t/ *a.* **~ de,** exempt from.
exempt|er /ɛgzɑ̃te/ *v.t.* exempt (**de,** from). **~ion** /-psjɔ̃/ *n.f.* exemption.
exercer /ɛgzɛrse/ *v.t.* exercise; (*influence, contrôle*) exert; (*métier*) work at; (*former*) train, exercise. **s'~ (à),** practise.
exercice /ɛgzɛrsis/ *n.m.* exercise; (*mil.*) drill; (*de métier*) practice. **en ~,** in office; (*médecin*) in practice.
exhaler /ɛgzale/ *v.t.* emit.
exhausti|f, ~ve /ɛgzostif, -v/ *a.* exhaustive.
exhiber /ɛgzibe/ *v.t.* exhibit.
exhibitionniste /ɛgzibisjɔnist/ *n.m./f.* exhibitionist.
exhorter /ɛgzɔrte/ *v.t.* exhort (**à,** to).
exigence /ɛgziʒɑ̃s/ *n.f.* demand.
exig|er /ɛgziʒe/ *v.t.* demand. **~eant, ~eante** *a.* demanding.
exigu, ~ë /ɛgzigy/ *a.* tiny.
exil /ɛgzil/ *n.m.* exile. **~é, ~ée** *n.m., f.* exile. **~er** *v.t.* exile. **s'~er** *v. pr.* go into exile.
existence /ɛgzistɑ̃s/ *n.f.* existence.
exist|er /ɛgziste/ *v.i.* exist. **~ant, ~ante** *a.* existing.
exode /ɛgzɔd/ *n.m.* exodus.
exonér|er /ɛgzɔnere/ *v.t.* exempt (**de,** from). **~ation** *n.f.* exemption.
exorbitant, ~e /ɛgzɔrbitɑ̃, -t/ *a.* exorbitant.
exorciser /ɛgzɔrsize/ *v.t.* exorcize.
exotique /ɛgzɔtik/ *a.* exotic.
expansi|f, ~ve /ɛkspɑ̃sif, -v/ *a.* expansive.
expansion /ɛkspɑ̃sjɔ̃/ *n.f.* expansion.
expatr|ier (s') /(s)ɛkspatrije/ *v. pr.* leave one's country. **~ié, ~iée** *n.m., f.* expatriate.
expectative /ɛkspɛktativ/ *n.f.* **dans l'~,** still waiting.
expédient, ~e /ɛkspedjɑ̃, -t/ *a. & n.m.* expedient. **vivre d'~s,** live by one's wits. **user d'~s,** resort to expedients.

expéd|ier /ɛkspedje/ *v.t.* send, dispatch; (*tâche*: *péj.*) dispatch. **~iteur, ~itrice** *n.m.*, *f.* sender. **~ition** *n.f.* dispatch; (*voyage*) expedition.

expéditi|f, ~ve /ɛkspeditif, -v/ *a.* quick.

expérience /ɛksperjɑ̃s/ *n.f.* experience; (*scientifique*) experiment.

expérimenté /ɛksperimɑ̃te/ *a.* experienced.

expériment|er /ɛksperimɑ̃te/ *v.t.* test, experiment with. **~al** (*m. pl.* **~aux**) *a.* experimental. **~ation** *n.f.* experimentation.

expert, ~e /ɛkspɛr, -t/ *a.* expert. ● *n.m.* expert; (*d'assurances*) valuer; (*Amer.*) appraiser. **~-comptable** (*pl.* **~s-comptables**) *n.m.* accountant.

expertis|e /ɛkspɛrtiz/ *n.f.* expert appraisal. **~er** *v.t.* appraise.

expier /ɛkspje/ *v.t.* atone for.

expir|er /ɛkspire/ *v.i.* breathe out; (*finir*, *mourir*) expire. **~ation** *n.f.* expiry.

explicati|f, ~ve /ɛksplikatif, -v/ *a.* explanatory.

explication /ɛksplikɑsjɔ̃/ *n.f.* explanation; (*fig.*) discussion; (*scol.*) commentary. **~ de texte,** (*scol.*) literary commentary.

explicite /ɛksplisit/ *a.* explicit.

expliquer /ɛksplike/ *v.t.* explain. **s'~** *v. pr.* explain o.s.; (*discuter*) discuss things; (*être compréhensible*) be understandable.

exploit /ɛksplwa/ *n.m.* exploit.

exploitant /ɛksplwatɑ̃/ *n.m.* **~ (agricole),** farmer.

exploit|er /ɛksplwate/ *v.t.* (*personne*) exploit; (*ferme*) run; (*champs*) work. **~ation** *n.f.* exploitation; running; working; (*affaire*) concern. **~eur, ~euse** *n.m.*, *f.* exploiter.

explor|er /ɛksplɔre/ *v.t.* explore. **~ateur, ~atrice** *n.m.*, *f.* explorer. **~ation** *n.f.* exploration.

explos|er /ɛksploze/ *v.i.* explode. **faire ~er,** explode; (*bâtiment*) blow up. **~ion** *n.f.* explosion.

explosi|f, ~ve /ɛksplozif, -v/ *a.* & *n.m.* explosive.

export|er /ɛkspɔrte/ *v.t.* export. **~ateur, ~atrice** *n.m.*, *f.* exporter; *a.* exporting. **~ation** *n.f.* export.

exposant, ~e /ɛkspozɑ̃, -t/ *n.m.*, *f.* exhibitor.

exposé /ɛkspoze/ *n.m.* talk (**sur,** on); (*d'une action*) account. **faire l'~ de la situation,** give an account of the situation.

expos|er /ɛkspoze/ *v.t.* display, show; (*expliquer*) explain; (*soumettre*, *mettre en danger*) expose (**à,** to); (*vie*) endanger. **~é au nord**/*etc.*, facing north/*etc.* **s'~er à,** expose o.s. to.

exposition /ɛkspozisjɔ̃/ *n.f.* display; (*salon*) exhibition. **~ à,** exposure to.

exprès[1] /ɛksprɛ/ *adv.* specially; (*délibérément*) on purpose.

expr|ès[2]**, ~esse** /ɛksprɛs/ *a.* express. **~essément** *adv.* expressly.

exprès[3] /ɛksprɛs/ *a. invar.* & *n.m.* **lettre ~,** express letter. **(par) ~,** sent special delivery.

express /ɛksprɛs/ *a.* & *n.m. invar.* **(café) ~,** espresso. **(train) ~,** fast train.

expressi|f, ~ve /ɛkspresif, -v/ *a.* expressive.

expression /ɛksprɛsjɔ̃/ *n.f.* expression. **~ corporelle,** physical expression.

exprimer /ɛksprime/ *v.t.* express. **s'~** *v. pr.* express o.s.

expuls|er /ɛkspylse/ *v.t.* expel; (*locataire*) evict; (*joueur*) send off. **~ion** *n.f.* expulsion; eviction.

expurger /ɛkspyrʒe/ *v.t.* expurgate.

exquis, ~e /ɛkski, -z/ *a.* exquisite.

extase /ɛkstɑz/ *n.f.* ecstasy.

extasier (s') /(s)ɛkstɑzje/ *v. pr.* **s'~ sur,** be ecstatic about.

extensible /ɛkstɑ̃sibl/ *a.* expandable, extendible. **tissu ~,** stretch fabric.

extensi|f, ~ve /ɛkstɑ̃sif, -v/ *a.* extensive.

extension /ɛkstɑ̃sjɔ̃/ *n.f.* extension; (*expansion*) expansion.

exténuer /ɛkstenɥe/ *v.t.* exhaust.

extérieur /ɛksterjœr/ *a.* outside; (*signe*, *gaieté*) outward; (*politique*) foreign. ● *n.m.* outside, exterior; (*de personne*) exterior. **à l'~ (de),** outside. **~ement** *adv.* outwardly.

extérioriser /ɛksterjɔrize/ *v.t.* show, externalize.

extermin|er /ɛkstɛrmine/ *v.t.* exterminate. **~ation** *n.f.* extermination.

externe /ɛkstɛrn/ *a.* external. ● *n.m.*/*f.* (*scol.*) day pupil.

extincteur /ɛkstɛ̃ktœr/ *n.m.* fire extinguisher.

extinction /ɛkstɛ̃ksjɔ̃/ *n.f.* extinction. **~ de voix,** loss of voice.

extirper /ɛkstirpe/ *v.t.* eradicate.

extor|quer /ɛkstɔrke/ *v.t.* extort. **~sion** *n.f.* extortion.
extra /ɛkstra/ *a. invar.* first-rate. ● *n.m. invar.* (*repas*) (special) treat.
extra- /ɛkstra/ *préf.* extra-.
extrad|er /ɛkstrade/ *v.t.* extradite. **~ition** *n.f.* extradition.
extr|aire† /ɛkstrɛr/ *v.t.* extract. **~action** *n.f.* extraction.
extrait /ɛkstrɛ/ *n.m.* extract.
extraordinaire /ɛkstraɔrdinɛr/ *a.* extraordinary.
extravagan|t, ~te /ɛkstravagɑ̃, -t/ *a.* extravagant. **~ce** *n.f.* extravagance.
extraverti, ~e /ɛkstravɛrti/ *n.m., f.* extrovert.
extrême /ɛkstrɛm/ *a.* & *n.m.* extreme. **E~-Orient** *n.m.* Far East. **~ment** *adv.* extremely.
extrémiste /ɛkstremist/ *n.m., f.* extremist.
extrémité /ɛkstremite/ *n.f.* extremity, end; (*misère*) dire straits. **~s,** (*excès*) extremes.
exubéran|t, ~te /ɛgzyberɑ̃, -t/ *a.* exuberant. **~ce** *n.f.* exuberance.
exulter /ɛgzylte/ *v.i.* exult.
exutoire /ɛgzytwar/ *n.m.* outlet.

F

F *abrév.* (*franc, francs*) franc, francs.
fable /fɑbl/ *n.f.* fable.
fabrique /fabrik/ *n.f.* factory.
fabri|quer /fabrike/ *v.t.* make; (*industriellement*) manufacture; (*fig.*) make up. **~cant, ~cante** *n.m., f.* manufacturer. **~cation** *n.f.* making; manufacture.
fabul|er /fabyle/ *v.i.* fantasize. **~ation** *n.f.* fantasizing.
fabuleu|x, ~se /fabylø, -z/ *a.* fabulous.
fac /fak/ *n.f.* (*fam.*) university.
façade /fasad/ *n.f.* front; (*fig.*) façade.
face /fas/ *n.f.* face; (*d'un objet*) side. **en ~ (de), d'en ~,** opposite. **en ~ de,** (*fig.*) faced with. **~ à,** facing; (*fig.*) faced with. **faire ~ à,** face.
facétie /fasesi/ *n.f.* joke.
facette /fasɛt/ *n.f.* facet.
fâch|er /fɑʃe/ *v.t.* anger. **se ~er** *v. pr.* get angry; (*se brouiller*) fall out. **~é** *a.* angry; (*désolé*) sorry.
fâcheu|x, ~se /fɑʃø, -z/ *a.* unfortunate.
facil|e /fasil/ *a.* easy; (*caractère*) easygoing. **~ement** *adv.* easily. **~ité** *n.f.* easiness; (*aisance*) ease; (*aptitude*) ability; (*possibilité*) facility. **~ités de paiement,** easy terms.
faciliter /fasilite/ *v.t.* facilitate.
façon /fasɔ̃/ *n.f.* way; (*de vêtement*) cut. **~s,** (*chichis*) fuss. **de cette ~,** in this way. **de ~ à,** so as to. **de toute ~,** anyway.
façonner /fasɔne/ *v.t.* shape; (*faire*) make.
facteur[1] /faktœr/ *n.m.* postman.
facteur[2] /faktœr/ *n.m.* (*élément*) factor.
factice /faktis/ *a.* artificial.
faction /faksjɔ̃/ *n.f.* faction. **de ~,** (*mil.*) on guard.
factur|e /faktyr/ *n.f.* bill; (*comm.*) invoice. **~er** *v.t.* invoice.
facultati|f, ~ve /fakyltatif, -v/ *a.* optional.
faculté /fakylte/ *n.f.* faculty; (*possibilité*) power; (*univ.*) faculty.
fade /fad/ *a.* insipid.
fagot /fago/ *n.m.* bundle of firewood.
fagoter /fagɔte/ *v.t.* (*fam.*) rig out.
faibl|e /fɛbl/ *a.* weak; (*espoir, quantité, écart*) slight; (*revenu, intensité*) low. ● *n.m.* weakling; (*penchant, défaut*) weakness. **~e d'esprit,** feeble-minded. **~esse** *n.f.* weakness. **~ir** *v.i* weaken.
faïence /fajɑ̃s/ *n.f.* earthenware.
faille /faj/ *n.f.* (*géog.*) fault; (*fig.*) flaw.
faillir /fajir/ *v.i.* **j'ai failli acheter/** *etc.*, I almost bought/*etc.*
faillite /fajit/ *n.f.* bankruptcy; (*fig.*) collapse.
faim /fɛ̃/ *n.f.* hunger. **avoir ~,** be hungry.
fainéant, ~e /feneɑ̃, -t/ *a.* idle. ● *n.m., f.* idler.
faire† /fɛr/ *v.t.* make; (*activité*) do; (*rêve, chute, etc.*) have; (*dire*) say. **ça fait 20 F,** that's 20 F. **ça fait 3 ans,** it's been 3 years. ● *v.i.* do; (*paraître*) look. **se ~,** *v. pr.* (*petit etc.*) make o.s.; (*amis, argent*) make; (*illusions*) have; (*devenir*) become. **~ du rugby/du violon/***etc.*, play rugby/the violin/*etc.* **~ construire/punir/***etc.*, have *ou* get built/punished/*etc.*, **~ pleurer/tomber/** *etc.*, make cry/fall/*etc.* **se ~ tuer/***etc.*, get

killed/*etc.* **se ~ couper les cheveux,** have one's hair cut. **il fait beau/chaud/***etc.*, it is fine/hot/*etc.* **~ l'idiot,** play the fool. **ne ~ que pleurer/***etc.*, (*faire continuellement*) do nothing but cry/*etc.* **ça ne fait rien,** it doesn't matter. **se ~ à,** get used to. **s'en ~,** worry. **ça se fait,** that is done. **~-part** *n.m. invar.* announcement.

fais, fait[1] /fɛ/ *voir* faire.

faisable /fəzabl/ *a.* feasible.

faisan /fəzɑ̃/ *n.m.* pheasant.

faisandé /fəzɑ̃de/ *a.* high.

faisceau (*pl.* **~x**) /fɛso/ *n.m.* (*rayon*) beam; (*fagot*) bundle.

fait[2], **~e** /fɛ, fɛt/ *a.* done; (*fromage*) ripe. **~ pour,** made for. **tout ~,** ready made. **c'est bien ~ pour toi,** it serves you right.

fait[3] /fɛ/ *n.m.* fact; (*événement*) event. **au ~ (de),** informed (of). **de ce ~,** therefore. **du ~ de,** on account of. **~ divers,** (trivial) news item. **~ nouveau,** new development. **sur le ~,** in the act.

faîte /fɛt/ *n.m.* top; (*fig.*) peak.

faites /fɛt/ *voir* faire.

faitout /fɛtu/ *n.m.* stew-pot.

falaise /falɛz/ *n.f.* cliff.

falloir† /falwar/ *v.i.* **il faut qch./qn.,** we, you, *etc.* need sth./so. **il lui faut du pain,** he needs bread. **il faut rester,** we, you, *etc.* have to *ou* must stay. **il faut que j'y aille,** I have to *ou* must go. **il faudrait que tu partes,** you should leave. **il aurait fallu le faire,** we, you, *etc.* should have done it. **il s'en faut de beaucoup que je sois,** I am far from being. **comme il faut,** properly; *a.* proper.

falot, ~e /falo, -ɔt/ *a.* grey.

falsifier /falsifje/ *v.t.* falsify.

famélique /famelik/ *a.* starving.

fameu|x, ~se /famø, -z/ *a.* famous; (*excellent*: *fam.*) first-rate. **~sement** *adv.* (*fam.*) extremely.

famil|ial (*m. pl.* **~iaux**) /familjal, -jo/ *a.* family.

familiar|iser /familjarize/ *v.t.* familiarize (**avec,** with). **se ~iser** *v. pr.* familiarize o.s. **~isé** *a.* familiar. **~ité** *n.f.* familiarity.

famil|ier, ~ière /familje, -jɛr/ *a.* familiar; (*amical*) informal. ● *n.m.* regular visitor. **~ièrement** *adv.* informally.

famille /famij/ *n.f.* family. **en ~,** with one's family.

famine /famin/ *n.f.* famine.

fanati|que /fanatik/ *a.* fanatical. ● *n.m./f.* fanatic. **~sme** *n.m.* fanaticism.

faner (se) /(sə)fane/ *v. pr.* fade.

fanfare /fɑ̃far/ *n.f.* brass band; (*musique*) fanfare.

fanfaron, ~ne /fɑ̃farɔ̃, -ɔn/ *a.* boastful. ● *n.m., f.* boaster.

fanion /fanjɔ̃/ *n.m.* pennant.

fantaisie /fɑ̃tezi/ *n.f.* imagination, fantasy; (*caprice*) whim. **(de) ~,** (*boutons etc.*) fancy.

fantaisiste /fɑ̃tezist/ *a.* unorthodox.

fantasme /fɑ̃tasm/ *n.m.* fantasy.

fantasque /fɑ̃task/ *a.* whimsical.

fantastique /fɑ̃tastik/ *a.* fantastic.

fantoche /fɑ̃tɔʃ/ *a.* puppet.

fantôme /fɑ̃tom/ *n.m.* ghost. ● *a.* (*péj.*) bogus.

faon /fɑ̃/ *n.m.* fawn.

faramineu|x, ~se /faraminø, -z/ *a.* astronomical.

farc|e[1] /fars/ *n.f.* (practical) joke; (*théâtre*) farce. **~eur, ~euse** *n.m., f.* joker.

farc|e[2] /fars/ *n.f.* (*hachis*) stuffing. **~ir** *v.t.* stuff.

fard /far/ *n.m.* make-up. **piquer un ~,** blush. **~er** /-de/ *v.t.*, **se ~er** *v. pr.* make up.

fardeau (*pl.* **~x**) /fardo/ *n.m.* burden.

farfelu, ~e /farfəly/ *a. & n.m., f.* eccentric.

farin|e /farin/ *n.f.* flour. **~eux, ~euse** *a.* floury. **les ~eux** *n.m. pl.* starchy food.

farouche /faruʃ/ *a.* shy; (*peu sociable*) unsociable; (*violent*) fierce. **~ment** *adv.* fiercely.

fascicule /fasikyl/ *n.m.* volume.

fascin|er /fasine/ *v.t.* fascinate. **~ation** *n.f.* fascination.

fascis|te /faʃist/ *a. & n.m./f.* fascist. **~me** *n.m.* fascism.

fasse /fas/ *voir* faire.

faste /fast/ *n.m.* splendour.

fast-food /fastfud/ *n.m.* fast-food place.

fastidieu|x, ~se /fastidjø, -z/ *a.* tedious.

fat|al (*m. pl.* **~als**) /fatal/ *a.* inevitable; (*mortel*) fatal. **~alement** *adv.* inevitably. **~alité** *n.f.* (*destin*) fate.

fataliste /fatalist/ *n.m./f.* fatalist.

fatidique /fatidik/ *a.* fateful.

fatigant, ~e /fatigɑ̃, -t/ *a.* tiring; (*ennuyeux*) tiresome.

fatigue /fatig/ *n.f.* fatigue, tiredness.

fatigu|er /fatige/ *v.t.* tire; (*yeux, moteur*) strain. ● *v.i.* (*moteur*) labour. **se ~er** *v. pr.* get tired, tire (**de,** of). **~é** *a.* tired.

fatras /fatra/ *n.m.* jumble.

faubourg /fobur/ *n.m.* suburb.

fauché /foʃe/ *a.* (*fam.*) broke.

faucher /foʃe/ *v.t.* (*herbe*) mow; (*voler: fam.*) pinch. **~ qn.,** (*véhicule, tir*) mow s.o. down.

faucille /fosij/ *n.f.* sickle.

faucon /fokɔ̃/ *n.m.* falcon, hawk.

faudra, faudrait /fodra, fodrɛ/ *voir* falloir.

faufiler (se) /(sə)fofile/ *v. pr.* edge one's way.

faune /fon/ *n.f.* wildlife, fauna.

faussaire /fosɛr/ *n.m.* forger.

fausse /fos/ *voir* faux[2].

faussement /fosmɑ̃/ *adv.* falsely, wrongly.

fausser /fose/ *v.t.* buckle; (*fig.*) distort. **~ compagnie à,** sneak away from.

fausseté /foste/ *n.f.* falseness.

faut /fo/ *voir* falloir.

faute /fot/ *n.f.* mistake; (*responsabilité*) fault; (*délit*) offence; (*péché*) sin. **en ~,** at fault. **~ de,** for want of. **~ de quoi,** failing which. **sans faute,** without fail. **~ de frappe,** typing error. **~ de goût,** bad taste. **~ professionelle,** professional misconduct.

fauteuil /fotœj/ *n.m.* armchair; (*de président*) chair; (*théâtre*) seat. **~ roulant,** wheelchair.

fauti|f, ~ve /fotif, -v/ *a.* guilty; (*faux*) faulty. ● *n.m., f.* guilty party.

fauve /fov/ *a.* (*couleur*) fawn. ● *n.m.* wild cat.

faux[1] /fo/ *n.f.* scythe.

faux[2]**, fausse** /fo, fos/ *a.* false; (*falsifié*) fake, forged; (*numéro, calcul*) wrong; (*voix*) out of tune. **c'est ~!,** that is wrong! **~ témoignage,** perjury. **faire ~ bond à qn.,** stand s.o. up. ● *adv.* (*chanter*) out of tune. ● *n.m.* forgery. **fausse alerte,** false alarm. **fausse couche,** miscarriage. **~-filet** *n.m.* sirloin. **~ frais,** *n.m. pl.* incidental expenses. **~-monnayeur** *n.m.* forger.

faveur /favœr/ *n.f.* favour. **de ~,** (*régime*) preferential. **en ~ de,** in favour of.

favorable /favɔrabl/ *a.* favourable.

favori, ~te /favɔri, -t/ *a.* & *n.m., f.* favourite. **~tisme** *n.m.* favouritism.

favoriser /favɔrize/ *v.t.* favour.

fax /faks/ *n.m.* fax. **~er** *v.t.* fax.

fébrile /febril/ *a.* feverish.

fécond, ~e /fekɔ̃, -d/ *a.* fertile. **~er** /-de/ *v.t.* fertilize. **~ité** /-dite/ *n.f.* fertility.

fédér|al (*m. pl.* **~aux**) /federal, -o/ *a.* federal.

fédération /federɑsjɔ̃/ *n.f.* federation.

fée /fe/ *n.f.* fairy.

féer|ie /fe(e)ri/ *n.f.* magical spectacle. **~ique** *a.* magical.

feindre† /fɛ̃dr/ *v.t.* feign. **~ de,** pretend to.

feinte /fɛ̃t/ *n.f.* feint.

fêler /fele/ *v.t.*, **se ~** *v. pr.* crack.

félicit|er /felisite/ *v.t.* congratulate (**de,** on). **~ations** *n.f. pl.* congratulations (**pour,** on).

félin, ~e /felɛ̃, -in/ *a.* & *n.m.* feline.

fêlure /felyr/ *n.f.* crack.

femelle /fəmɛl/ *a.* & *n.f.* female.

fémin|in, ~ine /feminɛ̃, -in/ *a.* feminine; (*sexe*) female; (*mode, équipe*) women's. ● *n.m.* feminine. **~ité** *n.f.* femininity.

féministe /feminist/ *n.m./f.* feminist.

femme /fam/ *n.f.* woman; (*épouse*) wife. **~ au foyer,** housewife. **~ de chambre,** chambermaid. **~ de ménage,** cleaning lady.

fémur /femyr/ *n.m.* thigh-bone.

fendiller /fɑ̃dije/ *v.t.*, **se ~** *v. pr.* crack.

fendre /fɑ̃dr/ *v.t.* (*couper*) split, (*fissurer*) crack; (*foule*) push through. **se ~** *v. pr.* crack.

fenêtre /fənɛtr/ *n.f.* window.

fenouil /fənuj/ *n.m.* fennel.

fente /fɑ̃t/ *n.f.* (*ouverture*) slit, slot; (*fissure*) crack.

féod|al (*m. pl.* **~aux**) /feɔdal, -o/ *a.* feudal.

fer /fɛr/ *n.m.* iron. **~ (à repasser),** iron. **~ à cheval,** horseshoe. **~-blanc** (*pl.* **~s-blancs**) *n.m.* tinplate. **~ de lance,** spearhead. **~ forgé,** wrought iron.

fera, ferait /fəra, fərɛ/ *voir* faire.

férié /ferje/ *a.* **jour ~,** public holiday.

ferme[1] /fɛrm/ *a.* firm. ● *adv.* (*travailler*) hard. **~ment** /-əmɑ̃/ *adv.* firmly.

ferme[2] /fɛrm/ *n.f.* farm; (*maison*) farm(house).

fermé /fɛrme/ *a.* closed; (*gaz, radio, etc.*) off.
ferment /fɛrmɑ̃/ *n.m.* ferment.
ferment|er /fɛrmɑ̃te/ *v.i.* ferment. **~ation** *n.f.* fermentation.
fermer /fɛrme/ *v.t./i.* close, shut; (*cesser d'exploiter*) close *ou* shut down; (*gaz, robinet*) turn off. **se ~** *v. pr.* close, shut.
fermeté /fɛrməte/ *n.f.* firmness.
fermeture /fɛrmətyr/ *n.f.* closing; (*dispositif*) catch. **~ annuelle,** annual closure. **~ éclair,** (P.) zip (-fastener); (*Amer.*) zipper.
ferm|ier, ~ière /fɛrmje, -jɛr/ *n.m.* farmer. ● *n.f.* farmer's wife. ● *a.* farm.
fermoir /fɛrmwar/ *n.m.* clasp.
féroc|e /ferɔs/ *a.* ferocious. **~ité** *n.f.* ferocity.
ferraille /fɛrɑj/ *n.f.* scrap-iron.
ferré /fɛre/ *a.* (*canne*) steel-tipped.
ferrer /fɛre/ *v.t.* (*cheval*) shoe.
ferronnerie /fɛrɔnri/ *n.f.* ironwork.
ferroviaire /fɛrɔvjɛr/ *a.* rail(way).
ferry(-boat) /fɛri(bot)/ *n.m.* ferry.
fertil|e /fɛrtil/ *a.* fertile. **~e en,** (*fig.*) rich in. **~iser** *v.t.* fertilize. **~ité** *n.f.* fertility.
féru, ~e /fery/ *a.* **~ de,** passionate about.
ferv|ent, ~ente /fɛrvɑ̃, -t/ *a.* fervent. ● *n.m., f.* enthusiast (**de,** of). **~eur** *n.f.* fervour.
fesse /fɛs/ *n.f.* buttock.
fessée /fese/ *n.f.* spanking.
festin /fɛstɛ̃/ *n.m.* feast.
festival (*pl.* **~s**) /fɛstival/ *n.m.* festival.
festivités /fɛstivite/ *n.f. pl.* festivities.
festoyer /fɛstwaje/ *v.i.* feast.
fêtard /fɛtar/ *n.m.* merry-maker.
fête /fɛt/ *n.f.* holiday; (*religieuse*) feast; (*du nom*) name-day; (*réception*) party; (*en famille*) celebration; (*foire*) fair; (*folklorique*) festival. **~ des Mères,** Mother's Day. **~ foraine,** fun-fair. **faire la ~,** make merry. **les ~s (de fin d'année),** the Christmas season.
fêter /fete/ *v.t.* celebrate; (*personne*) give a celebration for.
fétiche /fetiʃ/ *n.m.* fetish; (*fig.*) mascot.
fétide /fetid/ *a.* fetid.
feu[1] (*pl.* **~x**) /fø/ *n.m.* fire; (*lumière*) light; (*de réchaud*) burner. **~x (rouges),** (traffic) lights. **à ~ doux/vif,** on a low/high heat. **du ~,** (*pour cigarette*) a light. **au ~!,** fire! **~ d'artifice,** firework display. **~ de joie,** bonfire. **~ rouge/vert/orange,** red/green/amber *ou* yellow (*Amer.*). **~ de position,** sidelight. **mettre le ~ à,** set fire to. **prendre ~,** catch fire. **jouer avec le ~,** play with fire. **ne pas faire long ~,** not last.
feu[2] /fø/ *a- invar.* (*mort*) late.
feuillage /fœjaʒ/ *n.m.* foliage.
feuille /fœj/ *n.f.* leaf; (*de papier, bois, etc.*) sheet; (*formulaire*) form.
feuillet /fœjɛ/ *n.m.* leaf.
feuilleter /fœjte/ *v.t.* leaf through.
feuilleton /fœjtɔ̃/ *n.m.* (*à suivre*) serial; (*histoire complète*) series.
feuillu /fœjy/ *a.* leafy.
feutre /føtr/ *n.m.* felt; (*chapeau*) felt hat; (*crayon*) felt-tip (pen).
feutré /føtre/ *a.* (*bruit*) muffled.
fève /fɛv/ *n.f.* broad bean.
février /fevrije/ *n.m.* February.
fiable /fjabl/ *a.* reliable.
fiançailles /fjɑ̃saj/ *n.f. pl.* engagement.
fianc|er (se) /(sə)fjɑ̃se/ *v. pr.* become engaged (**avec,** to). **~é, ~ée** *a.* engaged; *n.m.* fiancé; *n.f.* fiancée.
fiasco /fjasko/ *n.m.* fiasco.
fibre /fibr/ *n.f.* fibre. **~ de verre,** fibreglass.
ficeler /fisle/ *v.t.* tie up.
ficelle /fisɛl/ *n.f.* string.
fiche /fiʃ/ *n.f.* (index) card; (*formulaire*) form, slip; (*électr.*) plug.
ficher[1] /fiʃe/ *v.t.* (*enfoncer*) drive (**dans,** into).
ficher[2] /fiʃe/ *v.t.* (*faire*: *fam.*) do; (*donner*: *fam.*) give; (*mettre*: *fam.*) put. **se ~ de,** (*fam.*) make fun of. **~ le camp,** (*fam.*) clear off. **il s'en fiche,** (*fam.*) he couldn't care less.
fichier /fiʃje/ *n.m.* file.
fichu /fiʃy/ *a.* (*mauvais*: *fam.*) rotten; (*raté*: *fam.*) done for. **mal ~,** (*fam.*) terrible.
ficti|f, ~ve /fiktif, -v/ *a.* fictitious.
fiction /fiksjɔ̃/ *n.f.* fiction.
fidèle /fidɛl/ *a.* faithful. ● *n.m./f.* (*client*) regular; (*relig.*) believer. **~s,** (*à l'église*) congregation. **~ment** *adv.* faithfully.
fidélité /fidelite/ *n.f.* fidelity.
fier[1], **fière** /fjɛr/ *a.* proud (**de,** of). **fièrement** *adv.* proudly. **~té** *n.f.* pride.
fier[2] **(se)** /(sə)fje/ *v. pr.* **se ~ à,** trust.
fièvre /fjɛvr/ *n.f.* fever.

fiévreu|x, ~se /fjevrø, -z/ *a.* feverish.
figé /fiʒe/ *a.* fixed, set; (*manières*) stiff.
figer /fiʒe/ *v.t./i.*, **se ~** *v. pr.* congeal. **~ sur place,** petrify.
fignoler /fiɲɔle/ *v.t.* refine (upon), finish off meticulously.
figu|e /fig/ *n.f.* fig. **~ier** *n.m.* fig-tree.
figurant, ~e /figyrɑ̃, -t/ *n.m., f.* (*cinéma*) extra.
figure /figyr/ *n.f.* face; (*forme, personnage*) figure; (*illustration*) picture.
figuré /figyre/ *a.* (*sens*) figurative. **au ~,** figuratively.
figurer /figyre/ *v.i.* appear. ● *v.t.* represent. **se ~** *v. pr.* imagine.
fil /fil/ *n.m.* thread; (*métallique, électrique*) wire; (*de couteau*) edge; (*à coudre*) cotton. **au ~ de,** with the passing of. **au ~ de l'eau,** with the current. **~ de fer,** wire. **au bout du ~,** on the phone.
filament /filamɑ̃/ *n.m.* filament.
filature /filatyr/ *n.f.* (textile) mill; (*surveillance*) shadowing.
file /fil/ *n.f.* line; (*voie: auto.*) lane. **~ (d'attente),** queue; (*Amer.*) line. **en ~ indienne,** in single file. **se mettre en ~,** line up.
filer /file/ *v.t.* spin; (*suivre*) shadow. **~ qch. à qn.,** (*fam.*) slip s.o. sth. ● *v.i.* (*bas*) ladder, run; (*liquide*) run; (*aller vite: fam.*) speed along, fly by; (*partir: fam.*) dash off. **~ doux,** do as one's told. **~ à l'anglaise,** take French leave.
filet /filɛ/ *n.m.* net; (*d'eau*) trickle; (*de viande*) fillet. **~ (à bagages),** (luggage) rack. **~ à provisions,** string bag (*for shopping*).
fil|ial, ~iale (*m. pl.* **~iaux**) /filjal, -jo/ *a.* filial. ● *n.f.* subsidiary (company).
filière /filjɛr/ *n.f.* (official) channels; (*de trafiquants*) network. **passer par** *ou* **suivre la ~,** (*employé*) work one's way up.
filigrane /filigran/ *n.m.* watermark. **en ~,** between the lines.
filin /filɛ̃/ *n.m.* rope.
fille /fij/ *n.f.* girl; (*opposé à fils*) daughter. **~-mère** (*pl.* **~s-mères**) *n.f.* (*péj.*) unmarried mother.
fillette /fijɛt/ *n.f.* little girl.
filleul /fijœl/ *n.m* godson. **~e** *n.f.* god-daughter.
film /film/ *n.m.* film. **~ d'épouvante/muet/parlant,** horror/silent/talking film. **~ dramatique,** drama. **~er** *v.t.* film.
filon /filɔ̃/ *n.m.* (*géol.*) seam; (*situation*) source of wealth.
filou /filu/ *n.m.* crook.
fils /fis/ *n.m.* son.
filtr|e /filtr/ *n.m.* filter. **~er** *v.t./i.* filter; (*personne*) screen.
fin [1] /fɛ̃/ *n.f.* end. **à la ~,** finally. **en ~ de compte,** all things considered. **~ de semaine,** weekend. **mettre ~ à,** put an end to. **prendre ~,** come to an end.
fin [2], fine /fɛ̃, fin/ *a.* fine; (*tranche, couche*) thin; (*taille*) slim; (*plat*) exquisite; (*esprit, vue*) sharp. ● *adv.* (*couper*) finely. **~es herbes,** herbs.
fin|al, ~ale (*m. pl.* **~aux** *ou* **~als**) /final, -o/ *a.* final. ● *n.f.* (*sport*) final; (*gram.*) final syllable. ● *n.m.* (*pl.* **~aux** *ou* **~als**) (*mus.*) finale. **~alement** *adv.* finally; (*somme toute*) after all.
finaliste /finalist/ *n.m./f.* finalist.
financ|e /finɑ̃s/ *n.f.* finance. **~er** *v.t.* finance. **~ier, ~ière** *a.* financial; *n.m.* financier.
finesse /finɛs/ *n.f.* fineness; (*de taille*) slimness; (*acuité*) sharpness. **~s,** (*de langue*) niceties.
fini /fini/ *a.* finished; (*espace*) finite. ● *n.m.* finish.
finir /finir/ *v.t./i.* finish, end; (*arrêter*) stop; (*manger*) finish (up). **en ~ avec,** have done with. **~ par faire,** end up doing. **ça va mal ~,** it will turn out badly.
finition /finisjɔ̃/ *n.f.* finish.
finlandais, ~e /fɛ̃lɑ̃dɛ, -z/ *a.* Finnish. ● *n.m., f.* Finn.
finlande /fɛ̃lɑ̃d/ *n.f.* Finland.
finnois, ~e /finwa, -z/ *a.* Finnish. ● *n.m.* (*lang.*) Finnish.
fiole /fjɔl/ *n.f.* phial.
firme /firm/ *n.f.* firm.
fisc /fisk/ *n.m.* tax authorities. **~al** (*m. pl.* **~aux**) *a.* tax, fiscal. **~alité** *n.f.* tax system.
fission /fisjɔ̃/ *n.f.* fission.
fissur|e /fisyr/ *n.f.* crack. **~er** *v.t.*, **se ~er** *v. pr.* crack.
fiston /fistɔ̃/ *n.m.* (*fam.*) son.
fixation /fiksɑsjɔ̃/ *n.f.* fixing; (*complexe*) fixation.
fixe /fiks/ *a.* fixed; (*stable*) steady. **à heure ~,** at a set time. **menu à prix ~,** set menu.

fix|er /fikse/ *v.t.* fix. **~er (du regard),** stare at. **se ~er** *v. pr.* (*s'installer*) settle down. **être ~é,** (*personne*) have made up one's mind.
flacon /flakɔ̃/ *n.m.* bottle.
flageolet /flaʒɔlɛ/ *n.m.* (*haricot*) (dwarf) kidney bean.
flagrant, ~e /flagrɑ̃, -t/ *a.* flagrant. **en ~ délit,** in the act.
flair /flɛr/ *n.m.* (sense of) smell; (*fig.*) intuition. **~er** /flere/ *v.t.* sniff at; (*fig.*) sense.
flamand, ~e /flamɑ̃, -d/ *a.* Flemish. ● *n.m.* (*lang.*) Flemish. ● *n.m., f.* Fleming.
flamant /flamɑ̃/ *n.m.* flamingo.
flambant /flɑ̃bɑ̃/ *adv.* **~ neuf,** brand-new.
flambé, ~e /flɑ̃be/ *a.* (*culin.*) flambé.
flambeau (*pl.* **~x**) /flɑ̃bo/ *n.m.* torch.
flambée /flɑ̃be/ *n.f.* blaze; (*fig.*) explosion.
flamber /flɑ̃be/ *v.i.* blaze; (*prix*) shoot up. ● *v.t.* (*aiguille*) sterilize; (*volaille*) singe.
flamboyer /flɑ̃bwaje/ *v.i.* blaze.
flamme /flam/ *n.f.* flame; (*fig.*) ardour. **en ~s,** ablaze.
flan /flɑ̃/ *n.m.* custard-pie.
flanc /flɑ̃/ *n.m.* side; (*d'animal, d'armée*) flank.
flancher /flɑ̃ʃe/ *v.i.* (*fam.*) give in.
Flandre(s) /flɑ̃dr/ *n.f.* (*pl.*) Flanders.
flanelle /flanɛl/ *n.f.* flannel.
flân|er /flɑne/ *v.i.* stroll. **~erie** *n.f.* stroll.
flanquer /flɑ̃ke/ *v.t.* flank; (*jeter: fam.*) chuck; (*donner: fam.*) give. **~ à la porte,** kick out.
flaque /flak/ *n.f.* (*d'eau*) puddle; (*de sang*) pool.
flash (*pl.* **~es**) /flaʃ/ *n.m.* (*photo.*) flash; (*information*) news flash.
flasque /flask/ *a.* flabby.
flatt|er /flate/ *v.t.* flatter. **se ~er de,** pride o.s. on. **~erie** *n.f.* flattery. **~eur, ~euse** *a.* flattering; *n.m., f.* flatterer.
fléau (*pl.* **~x**) /fleo/ *n.m.* (*désastre*) scourge; (*personne*) bane.
flèche /flɛʃ/ *n.f.* arrow; (*de clocher*) spire. **monter en ~,** spiral. **partir en ~,** shoot off.
flécher /fleʃe/ *v.t.* mark *ou* signpost (with arrows).
fléchette /fleʃɛt/ *n.f.* dart.
fléchir /fleʃir/ *v.t.* bend; (*personne*) move. ● *v.i.* (*faiblir*) weaken; (*poutre*) sag, bend.
flegmatique /flɛgmatik/ *a.* phlegmatic.
flemm|e /flɛm/ *n.f.* (*fam.*) laziness. **j'ai la ~e de faire,** I can't be bothered doing. **~ard, ~arde** *a.* (*fam.*) lazy; *n.m., f.* (*fam.*) lazy-bones.
flétrir /fletrir/ *v.t.*, **se ~** *v. pr.* wither.
fleur /flœr/ *n.f.* flower. **à ~ de terre/d'eau,** just above the ground/water. **à ~s,** flowery. **~ de l'âge,** prime of life. **en ~s,** in flower.
fleur|ir /flœrir/ *v.i.* flower; (*arbre*) blossom; (*fig.*) flourish. ● *v.t.* adorn with flowers. **~i** *a.* flowery.
fleuriste /flœrist/ *n.m./f.* florist.
fleuve /flœv/ *n.m.* river.
flexible /flɛksibl/ *a.* flexible.
flexion /flɛksjɔ̃/ *n.f.* (*anat.*) flexing.
flic /flik/ *n.m.* (*fam.*) cop.
flipper /flipœr/ *n.m.* pinball (machine).
flirter /flœrte/ *v.i.* flirt.
flocon /flɔkɔ̃/ *n.m.* flake.
flopée /flɔpe/ *n.f.* (*fam.*) **une ~ de,** masses of.
floraison /flɔrɛzɔ̃/ *n.f.* flowering.
flore /flɔr/ *n.f.* flora.
florissant, ~e /flɔrisɑ̃, -t/ *a.* flourishing.
flot /flo/ *n.m.* flood, stream. **être à ~,** be afloat. **les ~s,** the waves.
flottant, ~e /flɔtɑ̃, -t/ *a.* (*vêtement*) loose; (*indécis*) indecisive.
flotte /flɔt/ *n.f.* fleet; (*pluie: fam.*) rain; (*eau: fam.*) water.
flottement /flɔtmɑ̃/ *n.m.* (*incertitude*) indecision.
flott|er /flɔte/ *v.i.* float; (*drapeau*) flutter; (*nuage, parfum, pensées*) drift; (*pleuvoir: fam.*) rain. **~eur** *n.m.* float.
flou /flu/ *a.* out of focus; (*fig.*) vague.
fluct|uer /flyktɥe/ *v.i.* fluctuate. **~uation** *n.f.* fluctuation.
fluet, ~te /flyɛ, -t/ *a.* thin.
fluid|e /flɥid/ *a.* & *n.m.* fluid. **~ité** *n.f.* fluidity.
fluor /flyɔr/ *n.m.* (*pour les dents*) fluoride.
fluorescent, ~e /flyɔresɑ̃, -t/ *a.* fluorescent.
flût|e /flyt/ *n.f.* flute; (*verre*) champagne glass. **~iste** *n.m./f.* flautist; (*Amer.*) flutist.

fluv|ial (*m. pl.* **~iaux**) /flyvjal, -jo/ *a.* river.

flux /fly/ *n.m.* flow. **~ et reflux,** ebb and flow.

FM /ɛfɛm/ *abrév. f.* FM.

foc /fɔk/ *n.m.* jib.

fœtus /fetys/ *n.m.* foetus.

foi /fwa/ *n.f.* faith. **être de bonne/ mauvaise ~,** be acting in good/bad faith. **ma ~!,** well (indeed)! **digne de ~,** reliable.

foie /fwa/ *n.m.* liver. **~ gras,** foie gras.

foin /fwɛ̃/ *n.m.* hay. **faire tout un ~,** (*fam.*) make a fuss.

foire /fwar/ *n.f.* fair. **faire la ~,** (*fam.*) make merry.

fois /fwa/ *n.f.* time. **une ~,** once. **deux ~,** twice. **à la ~,** at the same time. **des ~,** (*parfois*) sometimes. **une ~ pour toutes,** once and for all.

foison /fwazɔ̃/ *n.f.* abundance. **à ~,** in abundance. **~ner** /-ɔne/ *v.i.* abound (**de,** in).

fol /fɔl/ *voir* fou.

folâtrer /fɔlɑtre/ *v.i.* frolic.

folichon, ~ne /fɔliʃɔ̃, -ɔn/ *a.* **pas ~,** (*fam.*) not much fun.

folie /fɔli/ *n.f.* madness; (*bêtise*) foolish thing, folly.

folklor|e /fɔlklɔr/ *n.m.* folklore. **~ique** *a.* folk; (*fam.*) picturesque.

folle /fɔl/ *voir* fou.

follement /fɔlmɑ̃/ *adv.* madly.

fomenter /fɔmɑ̃te/ *v.t.* foment.

fonc|er [1] /fɔ̃se/ *v.t./i.* darken. **~é** *a.* dark.

foncer [2] /fɔ̃se/ *v.i.* (*fam.*) dash along. **~ sur,** (*fam.*) charge at.

fonc|ier, ~ière /fɔ̃sje, -jɛr/ *a.* fundamental; (*comm.*) real estate. **~ièrement** *adv.* fundamentally.

fonction /fɔ̃ksjɔ̃/ *n.f.* function; (*emploi*) position. **~s,** (*obligations*) duties. **en ~ de,** according to. **~ publique,** civil service. **voiture de ~,** company car.

fonctionnaire /fɔ̃ksjɔnɛr/ *n.m./f.* civil servant.

fonctionnel, ~le /fɔ̃ksjɔnɛl/ *a.* functional.

fonctionn|er /fɔ̃ksjɔne/ *v.i.* work. **faire ~er,** work. **~ement** *n.m.* working.

fond /fɔ̃/ *n.m.* bottom; (*de salle, magasin, etc.*) back; (*essentiel*) basis; (*contenu*) content; (*plan*) background. **à ~,** thoroughly. **au ~,** basically. **de ~,** (*bruit*) background; (*sport*) long-distance. **de ~ en comble,** from top to bottom. **au** *ou* **dans le ~,** really.

fondament|al (*m. pl.* **~aux**) /fɔ̃damɑ̃tal, -o/ *a.* fundamental.

fondation /fɔ̃dɑsjɔ̃/ *n.f.* foundation.

fond|er /fɔ̃de/ *v.t.* found; (*baser*) base (**sur,** on). **(bien) ~é,** well-founded. **~é à,** justified in. **se ~er sur,** be guided by, place one's reliance on. **~ateur, ~atrice** *n.m., f.* founder.

fonderie /fɔ̃dri/ *n.f.* foundry.

fondre /fɔ̃dr/ *v.t./i.* melt; (*dans l'eau*) dissolve; (*mélanger*) merge. **se ~** *v. pr.* merge. **faire ~,** melt; dissolve. **~ en larmes,** burst into tears. **~ sur,** swoop on.

fondrière /fɔ̃drijɛr/ *n.f.* pot-hole.

fonds /fɔ̃/ *n.m.* fund. ● *n.m. pl.* (*capitaux*) funds. **~ de commerce,** business.

fondu /fɔ̃dy/ *a.* melted; (*métal*) molten.

font /fɔ̃/ *voir* faire.

fontaine /fɔ̃tɛn/ *n.f.* fountain; (*source*) spring.

fonte /fɔ̃t/ *n.f.* melting; (*fer*) cast iron. **~ des neiges,** thaw.

foot /fut/ *n.m.* (*fam.*) football.

football /futbol/ *n.m.* football. **~eur** *n.m.* footballer.

footing /futiŋ/ *n.m.* fast walking.

forage /fɔraʒ/ *n.m.* drilling.

forain /fɔrɛ̃/ *n.m.* fairground entertainer. **(marchand) ~,** stallholder (*at a fair or market*).

forçat /fɔrsa/ *n.m.* convict.

force /fɔrs/ *n.f.* force; (*physique*) strength; (*hydraulique etc.*) power. **~s,** (*physiques*) strength. **à ~ de,** by sheer force of. **de ~, par la ~,** by force. **~ de dissuasion,** deterrent. **~ de frappe,** strike force, deterrent. **~ de l'âge,** prime of life. **~s de l'ordre,** police (force).

forcé /fɔrse/ *a.* forced; (*inévitable*) inevitable.

forcément /fɔrsemɑ̃/ *adv.* necessarily; (*évidemment*) obviously.

forcené, ~e /fɔrsəne/ *a.* frenzied. ● *n.m., f.* maniac.

forceps /fɔrsɛps/ *n.m.* forceps.

forcer /fɔrse/ *v.t.* force (**à faire,** to do); (*voix*) strain. ● *v.i.* (*exagérer*) overdo it. **se ~** *v. pr.* force o.s.

forcir /fɔrsir/ *v.i.* fill out.

forer /fɔre/ *v.t.* drill.

forest|ier, ~ière /fɔrɛstje, -jɛr/ *a.* forest.

foret /fɔrɛ/ *n.m.* drill.
forêt /fɔrɛ/ *n.f.* forest.
forfait /fɔrfɛ/ *n.m.* (*comm.*) inclusive price. **~aire** /-tɛr/ *a.* (*prix*) inclusive.
forge /fɔrʒ/ *n.f.* forge.
forger /fɔrʒe/ *v.t.* forge; (*inventer*) make up.
forgeron /fɔrʒərɔ̃/ *n.m.* blacksmith.
formaliser (se) /(sə)fɔrmalize/ *v. pr.* take offence (**de,** at).
formalité /fɔrmalite/ *n.f.* formality.
format /fɔrma/ *n.m.* format.
formater /fɔrmate/ *v.t.* (*comput.*) format.
formation /fɔrmɑsjɔ̃/ *n.f.* formation; (*de médecin etc.*) training; (*culture*) education. **~ permanente** *ou* **continue,** continuing education. **~ professionnelle,** professional training.
forme /fɔrm/ *n.f.* form; (*contour*) shape, form. **~s,** (*de femme*) figure. **en ~,** (*sport*) in good shape, on form. **en ~ de,** in the shape of. **en bonne et due ~,** in due form.
formel, ~le /fɔrmɛl/ *a.* formal; (*catégorique*) positive. **~lement** *adv.* positively.
former /fɔrme/ *v.t.* form; (*instruire*) train. **se ~** *v. pr.* form.
formidable /fɔrmidabl/ *a.* fantastic.
formulaire /fɔrmylɛr/ *n.m.* form.
formul|e /fɔrmyl/ *n.f.* formula; (*expression*) expression; (*feuille*) form. **~e de politesse,** polite phrase, letter ending. **~er** *v.t.* formulate.
fort[1], **~e** /fɔr, -t/ *a.* strong; (*grand*) big; (*pluie*) heavy; (*bruit*) loud; (*pente*) steep; (*élève*) clever. ● *adv.* (*frapper*) hard; (*parler*) loud; (*très*) very; (*beaucoup*) very much. ● *n.m.* strong point. **au plus ~ de,** at the height of. **c'est une ~e tête,** she/he's headstrong.
fort[2] /fɔr/ *n.m.* (*mil.*) fort.
forteresse /fɔrtərɛs/ *n.f.* fortress.
fortifiant /fɔrtifjɑ̃/ *n.m.* tonic.
fortif|ier /fɔrtifje/ *v.t.* fortify. **~ication** *n.f.* fortification.
fortiori /fɔrsjɔri/ **a ~,** even more so.
fortuit, ~e /fɔrtɥi, -t/ *a.* fortuitous.
fortune /fɔrtyn/ *n.f.* fortune. **de ~,** (*improvisé*) makeshift. **faire ~,** make one's fortune.
fortuné /fɔrtyne/ *a.* wealthy.
fosse /fos/ *n.f.* pit; (*tombe*) grave. **~ d'aisances,** cesspool. **~ d'orchestre,** orchestral pit. **~ septique,** septic tank.
fossé /fose/ *n.m.* ditch; (*fig.*) gulf.
fossette /fosɛt/ *n.f.* dimple.
fossile /fosil/ *n.m.* fossil.
fossoyeur /foswajœr/ *n.m.* gravedigger.
fou *ou* **fol*, folle** /fu, fɔl/ *a.* mad; (*course, regard*) wild; (*énorme: fam.*) tremendous. **~ de,** crazy about. ● *n.m.* madman; (*bouffon*) jester. ● *n.f.* madwoman; (*fam.*) gay. **le ~ rire,** the giggles.
foudre /fudr/ *n.f.* lightning.
foudroy|er /fudrwaje/ *v.t.* strike by lightning; (*maladie etc.*) strike down; (*atterrer*) stagger. **~ant, ~ante** *a.* staggering; (*mort, maladie*) violent.
fouet /fwɛ/ *n.m.* whip; (*culin.*) whisk.
fouetter /fwete/ *v.t.* whip; (*crème etc.*) whisk.
fougère /fuʒɛr/ *n.f.* fern.
fougu|e /fug/ *n.f.* ardour. **~eux, ~euse** *a.* ardent.
fouill|e /fuj/ *n.f.* search; (*archéol.*) excavation. **~er** *v.t./i.* search; (*creuser*) dig. **~er dans,** (*tiroir*) rummage through.
fouillis /fuji/ *n.m.* jumble.
fouine /fwin/ *n.f.* beech-marten.
fouiner /fwine/ *v.i.* nose about.
foulard /fular/ *n.m.* scarf.
foule /ful/ *n.f.* crowd. **une ~ de,** (*fig.*) a mass of.
foulée /fule/ *n.f.* stride. **il l'a fait dans la ~,** he did it while he was at it.
fouler /fule/ *v.t.* press; (*sol*) tread. **se ~ le poignet/le pied** sprain one's wrist/foot. **ne pas se ~,** (*fam.*) not strain o.s.
foulure /fulyr/ *n.f.* sprain.
four /fur/ *n.m.* oven; (*de potier*) kiln; (*théâtre*) flop. **~ à micro-ondes,** microwave oven. **~ crématoire,** crematorium.
fourbe /furb/ *a.* deceitful.
fourbu /furby/ *a.* exhausted.
fourche /furʃ/ *n.f.* fork; (*à foin*) pitchfork.
fourchette /furʃɛt/ *n.f.* fork; (*comm.*) margin.
fourchu /furʃy/ *a.* forked.
fourgon /furgɔ̃/ *n.m.* van; (*wagon*) wagon. **~ mortuaire,** hearse.
fourgonnette /furgɔnɛt/ *n.f.* (small) van.
fourmi /furmi/ *n.f.* ant. **avoir des ~s,** have pins and needles.

fourmiller /furmije/ *v.i.* swarm (**de,** with).

fournaise /furnɛz/ *n.f.* (*feu, endroit*) furnace.

fourneau (*pl.* **~x**) /furno/ *n.m.* stove.

fournée /furne/ *n.f.* batch.

fourni /furni/ *a.* (*épais*) thick.

fourn|ir /furnir/ *v.t.* supply, provide; (*client*) supply; (*effort*) put in. **~ir à qn.,** supply s.o. with. **se ~ir chez,** shop at. **~isseur** *n.m.* supplier. **~iture** *n.f.* supply.

fourrage /furaʒ/ *n.m.* fodder.

fourré [1] /fure/ *n.m.* thicket.

fourré [2] /fure/ *a.* (*vêtement*) fur-lined; (*gâteau etc.*) filled (*with jam, cream, etc.*).

fourreau (*pl.* **~x**) /furo/ *n.m.* sheath.

fourr|er /fure/ *v.t.* (*mettre: fam.*) stick. **~e-tout** *n.m. invar.* (*sac*) holdall.

fourreur /furœr/ *n.m.* furrier.

fourrière /furjɛr/ *n.f.* (*lieu*) pound.

fourrure /furyr/ *n.f.* fur.

fourvoyer (se) /(sə)furvwaje/ *v. pr.* go astray.

foutaise /futɛz/ *n.f.* (*argot*) rubbish.

foutre /futr/ *v.t.* (*argot*) = **ficher** [2].

foutu, ~e /futy/ *a.* (*argot*) = **fichu.**

foyer /fwaje/ *n.m.* home; (*âtre*) hearth; (*club*) club; (*d'étudiants*) hostel; (*théâtre*) foyer; (*photo.*) focus; (*centre*) centre.

fracas /fraka/ *n.m.* din; (*de train*) roar; (*d'objet qui tombe*) crash.

fracass|er /frakase/ *v.t.,* **se ~er** *v. pr.* smash. **~ant, ~ante** *a.* (*bruyant, violent*) shattering.

fraction /fraksjɔ̃/ *n.f.* fraction. **~ner** /-jɔne/ *v.t.,* **se ~ner** *v. pr.* split (up).

fractur|e /fraktyr/ *n.f.* fracture. **~er** *v.t.* (*os*) fracture; (*porte etc.*) break open.

fragil|e /fraʒil/ *a.* fragile. **~ité** *n.f.* fragility.

fragment /fragmɑ̃/ *n.m.* bit, fragment. **~aire** /-tɛr/ *a.* fragmentary. **~er** /-te/ *v.t.* split, fragment.

fraîche /frɛʃ/ *voir* frais [1].

fraîchement /frɛʃmɑ̃/ *adv.* (*récemment*) freshly; (*avec froideur*) coolly.

fraîcheur /frɛʃœr/ *n.f.* coolness; (*nouveauté*) freshness.

fraîchir /freʃir/ *v.i.* freshen.

frais [1]**, fraîche** /frɛ, -ʃ/ *a.* fresh; (*temps, accueil*) cool; (*peinture*) wet. ● *adv.* (*récemment*) newly. ● *n.m.* **mettre au ~,** put in a cool place. **prendre le ~,** take a breath of cool air. **~ et dispos,** fresh. **il fait ~,** it is cool.

frais [2] /frɛ/ *n.m. pl.* expenses; (*droits*) fees. **~ généraux,** (*comm.*) overheads, running expenses. **~ de scolarité,** school fees.

frais|e /frɛz/ *n.f.* strawberry. **~ier** *n.m.* strawberry plant.

frambois|e /frɑ̃bwaz/ *n.f.* raspberry. **~ier** *n.m.* raspberry bush.

fran|c [1]**, ~che** /frɑ̃, -ʃ/ *a.* frank; (*regard*) open; (*net*) clear; (*cassure*) clean; (*libre*) free; (*véritable*) downright. **~c-maçon** (*pl.* **~cs-maçons**) *n.m.* Freemason. **~c-maçonnerie** *n.f.* Freemasonry. **~-parler** *n.m. inv.* outspokenness.

franc [2] /frɑ̃/ *n.m.* franc.

français, ~e /frɑ̃sɛ, -z/ *a.* French. ● *n.m., f.* Frenchman, Frenchwoman. ● *n.m.* (*lang.*) French.

France /frɑ̃s/ *n.f.* France.

franche /frɑ̃ʃ/ *voir* franc [1].

franchement /frɑ̃ʃmɑ̃/ *adv.* frankly; (*nettement*) clearly; (*tout à fait*) really.

franchir /frɑ̃ʃir/ *v.t.* (*obstacle*) get over; (*traverser*) cross; (*distance*) cover; (*limite*) exceed.

franchise /frɑ̃ʃiz/ *n.f.* frankness; (*douanière*) exemption (from duties).

franco /frɑ̃ko/ *adv.* postage paid.

franco- /frɑ̃ko/ *préf.* Franco-.

francophone /frɑ̃kɔfɔn/ *a.* French-speaking. ● *n.m./f.* French speaker.

frange /frɑ̃ʒ/ *n.f.* fringe.

franquette (à la bonne) /(alabɔn)frɑ̃kɛt/ *adv.* informally.

frappant, ~e /frapɑ̃, -t/ *a.* striking.

frappe /frap/ *n.f.* (*de courrier etc.*) typing; (*de dactylo*) touch.

frappé, ~e /frape/ *a.* chilled.

frapp|er /frape/ *v.t./i.* strike; (*battre*) hit, strike; (*monnaie*) mint; (*à la porte*) knock, bang. **~é de panique,** panic-stricken.

frasque /frask/ *n.f.* escapade.

fratern|el, ~elle /fratɛrnɛl/ *a.* brotherly. **~iser** *v.i.* fraternize. **~ité** *n.f.* brotherhood.

fraude /frod/ *n.f.* fraud; (*à un examen*) cheating.

frauder /frode/ *v.t./i.* cheat.

frauduleu|x, ~se /frodylø, -z/ *a.* fraudulent.

frayer /freje/ *v.t.* open up. **se ~ un passage,** force one's way (**dans,** through).
frayeur /frɛjœr/ *n.f.* fright.
fredonner /frədɔne/ *v.t.* hum.
free-lance /frilɑ̃s/ *a.* & *n.m./f.* free-lance.
freezer /frizœr/ *n.m.* freezer.
frégate /fregat/ *n.f.* frigate.
frein /frɛ̃/ *n.m.* brake. **mettre un ~ à,** curb. **~ à main,** hand brake.
frein|er /frene/ *v.t.* slow down; (*modérer, enrayer*) curb. ● *v.i.* (*auto.*) brake. **~age** /frɛnaʒ/ *n.m.* braking.
frelaté /frəlate/ *a.* adulterated.
frêle /frɛl/ *a.* frail.
frelon /frəlɔ̃/ *n.m.* hornet.
freluquet /frəlyke/ *n.m.* (*fam.*) weed.
frémir /fremir/ *v.i.* shudder, shake; (*feuille, eau*) quiver.
frêne /frɛn/ *n.m.* ash.
frénésie /frenezi/ *n.f.* frenzy. **~tique** *a.* frenzied.
fréqu|ent, ~ente /frekɑ̃ -t/ *a.* frequent. **~emment** /-amɑ̃/ *adv.* frequently. **~ence** *n.f.* frequency.
fréquenté /frekɑ̃te/ *a.* crowded.
fréquent|er /frekɑ̃te/ *v.t.* frequent; (*école*) attend; (*personne*) see. **~ation** *n.f.* frequenting. **~ations** *n.f. pl.* acquaintances.
frère /frɛr/ *n.m.* brother.
fresque /frɛsk/ *n.f.* fresco.
fret /frɛt/ *n.m.* freight.
frétiller /fretije/ *v.i.* wriggle.
fretin /frətɛ̃/ *n.m.* **menu ~,** small fry.
friable /frijabl/ *a.* crumbly.
friand, ~e /frijɑ̃, -d/ *a.* **~ de,** fond of.
friandise /frijɑ̃diz/ *n.f.* sweet; (*Amer.*) candy; (*gâteau*) cake.
fric /frik/ *n.m.* (*fam.*) money.
fricassée /frikase/ *n.f.* casserole.
friche (en) /(ɑ̃)friʃ/ *adv.* fallow. **être en ~,** lie fallow.
friction /friksjɔ̃/ *n.f.* friction; (*massage*) rub-down. **~ner** /-jɔne/ *v.t.* rub (down).
frigidaire /friʒidɛr/ *n.m.* (P.) refrigerator.
frigid|e /friʒid/ *a.* frigid. **~ité** *n.f.* frigidity.
frigo /frigo/ *n.m.* (*fam.*) fridge.
frigorif|ier /frigɔrifje/ *v.t.* refrigerate. **~ique** *a.* (*vitrine etc.*) refrigerated.
frileu|x, ~se /frilø, -z/ *a.* sensitive to cold.
frime /frim/ *n.f.* (*fam.*) show off. **~r** *v.i.* (*fam.*) putting on a show.
frimousse /frimus/ *n.f.* (sweet) face.
fringale /frɛ̃gal/ *n.f.* (*fam.*) ravenous appetite.
fringant, ~e /frɛ̃gɑ̃, -t/ *a.* dashing.
fringues /frɛ̃g/ *n.f. pl.* (*fam.*) togs.
friper /fripe/ *v.t.*, **se ~** *v. pr.* crumple.
fripon, ~ne /fripɔ̃, -ɔn/ *n.m., f.* rascal. ● *a.* rascally.
fripouille /fripuj/ *n.f.* rogue.
frire /frir/ *v.t./i.* fry. **faire ~,** fry.
frise /friz/ *n.f.* frieze.
fris|er /frize/ *v.t./i.* (*cheveux*) curl; (*personne*) curl the hair of. **~é** *a.* curly.
frisquet /friskɛ/ *a.m.* (*fam.*) chilly.
frisson /frisɔ̃/ *n.m.* (*de froid*) shiver; (*de peur*) shudder. **~ner** /-ɔne/ *v.i.* shiver; shudder.
frit, ~e /fri, -t/ *a.* fried. ● *n.f.* chip. **avoir la ~e,** (*fam.*) feel good.
friteuse /fritøz/ *n.f.* (deep)fryer.
friture /frityr/ *n.f.* fried fish; (*huile*) (frying) oil *ou* fat.
frivol|e /frivɔl/ *a.* frivolous. **~ité** *n.f.* frivolity.
froid, ~e /frwa, -d/ *a.* & *n.m.* cold. **avoir/prendre ~,** be/catch cold. **il fait ~,** it is cold. **~ement** /-dmɑ̃/ *adv.* coldly; (*calculer*) coolly. **~eur** /-dœr/ *n.f.* coldness.
froisser /frwase/ *v.t.* crumple; (*fig.*) offend. **se ~** *v. pr.* crumple; (*fig.*) take offence. **se ~ un muscle,** strain a muscle.
frôler /frole/ *v.t.* brush against, skim; (*fig.*) come close to.
fromag|e /frɔmaʒ/ *n.m.* cheese. **~er, ~ère** *a.* cheese; *n.m., f.* cheese maker; (*marchand*) cheesemonger.
froment /frɔmɑ̃/ *n.m.* wheat.
froncer /frɔ̃se/ *v.t.* gather. **~ les sourcils,** frown.
fronde /frɔ̃d/ *n.f.* sling; (*fig.*) revolt.
front /frɔ̃/ *n.m.* forehead; (*mil., pol.*) front. **de ~,** at the same time; (*de face*) head-on; (*côte à côte*) abreast. **faire ~ à,** face up to. **~al** (*m. pl.* **~aux**) /-tal, -to/ *a.* frontal.
frontali|er, ère /frɔ̃talje, -ɛr/ *a.* border. **(travailleur) ~er,** commuter from across the border.
frontière /frɔ̃tjɛr/ *n.f.* border, frontier.
frott|er /frɔte/ *v.t./i.* rub; (*allumette*) strike. **~ement** *n.m.* rubbing.
frottis /frɔti/ *n.m.* **~ vaginal,** smear test.

frouss|e /frus/ *n.f.* (*fam.*) fear. **avoir la ~e,** (*fam.*) be scared. **~ard, ~arde** *n.m., f.* (*fam.*) coward.
fructifier /fryktifje/ *v.i.* **faire ~,** put to work.
fructueu|x, ~se /fryktɥø, -z/ *a.* fruitful.
frug|al (*m. pl.* **~aux**) /frygal, -o/ *a.* frugal. **~alité** *n.f.* frugality.
fruit /frɥi/ *n.m.* fruit. **des ~s,** (some) fruit. **~s de mer,** seafood. **~é** /-te/ *a.* fruity. **~ier, ~ière** /-tje, -tjɛr/ *a.* fruit; *n.m., f.* fruiterer.
fruste /fryst/ *a.* coarse.
frustr|er /frystre/ *v.t.* frustrate. **~ant, ~ante** *a.* frustrating. **~ation** *n.f.* frustration.
fuel /fjul/ *n.m.* fuel oil.
fugiti|f, ~ve /fyʒitif, -v/ *a.* (*passager*) fleeting. ● *n.m., f.* fugitive.
fugue /fyg/ *n.f.* (*mus.*) fugue. **faire une ~,** run away.
fuir† /fɥir/ *v.i.* flee, run away; (*eau, robinet, etc.*) leak. ● *v.t.* (*éviter*) shun.
fuite /fɥit/ *n.f.* flight; (*de liquide, d'une nouvelle*) leak. **en ~,** on the run. **mettre en ~,** put to flight. **prendre la ~,** take (to) flight.
fulgurant, ~e /fylgyrɑ̃, -t/ *a.* (*vitesse*) lightning.
fumée /fyme/ *n.f.* smoke; (*vapeur*) steam.
fum|er /fyme/ *v.t./i.* smoke. **~e-cigarette** *n.m. invar.* cigarette-holder. **~é** *a.* (*poisson, verre*) smoked. **~eur, ~euse** *n.m., f.* smoker.
fumet /fymɛ/ *n.m.* aroma.
fumeu|x, ~se /fymø, -z/ *a.* (*confus*) hazy.
fumier /fymje/ *n.m.* manure.
fumiste /fymist/ *n.m./f.* (*fam.*) shirker.
funambule /fynɑ̃byl/ *n.m./f.* tightrope walker.
funèbre /fynɛbr/ *a.* funeral; (*fig.*) gloomy.
funérailles /fyneraj/ *n.f. pl.* funeral.
funéraire /fynerɛr/ *a.* funeral.
funeste /fynɛst/ *a.* fatal.
funiculaire /fynikylɛr/ *n.m.* funicular.
fur /fyr/ *n.m.* **au ~ et à mesure,** as one goes along, progressively. **au ~ et à mesure que,** as.
furet /fyrɛ/ *n.m.* ferret.
fureter /fyrte/ *v.i.* nose (about).
fureur /fyrœr/ *n.f.* fury; (*passion*) passion. **avec ~,** furiously; passionately. **mettre en ~,** infuriate. **faire ~,** be all the rage.
furibond, ~e /furibɔ̃, -d/ *a.* furious.
furie /fyri/ *n.f.* fury; (*femme*) shrew.
furieu|x, ~se /fyrjø, -z/ *a.* furious.
furoncle /fyrɔ̃kl/ *n.m.* boil.
furti|f, ~ve /fyrtif, -v/ *a.* furtive.
fusain /fyzɛ̃/ *n.m.* (*crayon*) charcoal; (*arbre*) spindle-tree.
fuseau (*pl.* **~x**) /fyzo/ *n.m.* ski trousers; (*pour filer*) spindle. **~ horaire,** time zone.
fusée /fyze/ *n.f.* rocket.
fuselage /fyzlaʒ/ *n.m.* fuselage.
fuselé /fyzle/ *a.* slender.
fusible /fyzibl/ *n.m.* fuse.
fuser /fyze/ *v.i.* issue forth.
fusil /fyzi/ *n.m.* rifle, gun; (*de chasse*) shotgun. **~ mitrailleur,** machine-gun.
fusill|er /fyzije/ *v.t.* shoot. **~ade** *n.f.* shooting.
fusion /fyzjɔ̃/ *n.f.* fusion; (*comm.*) merger. **~ner** /-jɔne/ *v.t./i.* merge.
fut /fy/ *voir* être.
fût /fy/ *n.m.* (*tonneau*) barrel; (*d'arbre*) trunk.
futé /fyte/ *a.* cunning.
futil|e /fytil/ *a.* futile. **~ité** *n.f.* futility.
futur /fytyr/ *a.* & *n.m.* future. **~e femme/maman,** wife-/mother-to-be.
fuyant, ~e /fɥijɑ̃, -t/ *a.* (*front, ligne*) receding; (*personne*) evasive.
fuyard, ~e /fɥijar, -d/ *n.m., f.* runaway.

G

gabardine /gabardin/ *n.f.* gabardine; raincoat.
gabarit /gabari/ *n.m.* dimension; (*patron*) template; (*fig.*) calibre.
gâcher /gɑʃe/ *v.t.* (*gâter*) spoil; (*gaspiller*) waste.
gâchette /gɑʃɛt/ *n.f.* trigger.
gâchis /gɑʃi/ *n.m.* waste.
gadoue /gadu/ *n.f.* sludge.
gaff|e /gaf/ *n.f.* blunder. **faire ~e,** (*fam.*) be careful (**à,** of). **~er** *v.i.* blunder.
gag /gag/ *n.m.* gag.
gage /gaʒ/ *n.m.* pledge; (*de jeu*) forfeit. **~s,** (*salaire*) wages. **en ~**

de, as a token of. **mettre en ~,** pawn.

gageure /gaʒyr/ *n.f.* wager (against all the odds).

gagn|er /gaɲe/ *v.t.* (*match, prix, etc.*) win; (*argent, pain*) earn; (*temps, terrain*) gain; (*atteindre*) reach; (*convaincre*) win over. ● *v.i.* win; (*fig.*) gain. **~er sa vie,** earn one's living. **~ant, ~ante,** *a.* winning; *n.m., f.* winner. **~e-pain** *n.m. invar.* job.

gai /ge/ *a.* cheerful; (*ivre*) merry. **~ement** *adv.* cheerfully. **~eté** *n.f.* cheerfulness. **~etés** *n.f. pl.* delights.

gaillard, ~e /gajar, -d/ *a.* hale and hearty; (*grivois*) coarse. ● *n.m.* hale and hearty fellow; (*type*: *fam.*) fellow.

gain /gɛ̃/ *n.m.* (*salaire*) earnings; (*avantage*) gain; (*économie*) saving. **~s,** (*comm.*) profits; (*au jeu*) winnings.

gaine /gɛn/ *n.f.* (*corset*) girdle; (*étui*) sheath.

gala /gala/ *n.m.* gala.

galant, ~e /galɑ̃, -t/ *a.* courteous; (*scène, humeur*) romantic.

galaxie /galaksi/ *n.f.* galaxy.

galb|e /galb/ *n.m.* curve. **~é** *a.* shapely.

gale /gal/ *n.f.* (*de chat etc.*) mange.

galéjade /galeʒad/ *n.f.* (*fam.*) tall tale.

galère /galɛr/ *n.f.* (*navire*) galley. **c'est la ~!,** (*fam.*) what an ordeal!

galérer /galere/ *v.i.* (*fam.*) have a hard time.

galerie /galri/ *n.f.* gallery; (*théâtre*) circle; (*de voiture*) roof- rack.

galet /galɛ/ *n.m.* pebble.

galette /galɛt/ *n.f.* flat cake.

galeu|x, ~se /galø, -z/ *a.* (*animal*) mangy.

galipette /galipɛt/ *n.f.* somersault.

Galles /gal/ *n.f. pl.* **le pays de ~,** Wales.

gallois, ~e /galwa, -z/ *a.* Welsh. ● *n.m., f.* Welshman, Welshwoman. ● *n.m.* (*lang.*) Welsh.

galon /galɔ̃/ *n.m.* braid; (*mil.*) stripe. **prendre du ~,** bc promoted.

galop /galo/ *n.m.* gallop. **aller au ~,** gallop. **~ d'essai,** trial run. **~er** /-ɔpe/ *v.i.* (*cheval*) gallop; (*personne*) run.

galopade /galɔpad/ *n.f.* wild rush.

galopin /galɔpɛ̃/ *n.m.* (*fam.*) rascal.

galvaudé /galvode/ *a.* worthless.

gambad|e /gɑ̃bad/ *n.f.* leap. **~er** *v.i.* leap about.

gamelle /gamɛl/ *n.f.* (*de soldat*) mess bowl *ou* tin; (*d'ouvrier*) food-box.

gamin, ~e /gamɛ̃, -in/ *a.* playful. ● *n.m., f.* (*fam.*) kid.

gamme /gam/ *n.f.* (*mus.*) scale; (*série*) range. **haut de ~,** up-market, top of the range. **bas de ~,** down-market, bottom of the range.

gang /gɑ̃g/ *n.m.* gang.

ganglion /gɑ̃glijɔ̃/ *n.m.* swelling.

gangrène /gɑ̃grɛn/ *n.f.* gangrene.

gangster /gɑ̃gstɛr/ *n.m.* gangster; (*escroc*) crook.

gant /gɑ̃/ *n.m.* glove. **~ de toilette,** face-flannel, face-cloth. **~é** /gɑ̃te/ *a.* (*personne*) wearing gloves.

garag|e /garaʒ/ *n.m.* garage. **~iste** *n.m.* garage owner; (*employé*) garage mechanic.

garant, ~e /garɑ̃, -t/ *n.m., f.* guarantor. ● *n.m.* guarantee. **se porter ~ de,** guarantee, vouch for.

garant|ie /garɑ̃ti/ *n.f.* guarantee; (*protection*) safeguard. **~ies,** (*de police d'assurance*) cover. **~ir** *v.t.* guarantee; (*protéger*) protect (**de,** from).

garce /gars/ *n.f.* (*fam.*) bitch.

garçon /garsɔ̃/ *n.m.* boy; (*célibataire*) bachelor. **~ (de café),** waiter. **~ d'honneur,** best man.

garçonnière /garsɔnjɛr/ *n.f.* bachelor flat.

garde[1] /gard/ *n.f.* guard; (*d'enfants, de bagages*) care; (*service*) guard (duty); (*infirmière*) nurse. **de ~,** on duty. **~ à vue,** (police) custody. **mettre en ~,** warn. **prendre ~,** be careful (**à,** of). **(droit de) ~,** custody (**de,** of).

garde[2] /gard/ *n.m.* (*personne*) guard; (*de propriété, parc*) warden. **~ champêtre,** village policeman. **~ du corps,** bodyguard.

gard|er /garde/ *v.t.* (*conserver, maintenir*) keep; (*vêtement*) keep on; (*surveiller*) look after; (*défendre*) guard. **se ~er** *v. pr.* (*denrée*) keep. **~er le lit,** stay in bed. **se ~er de faire,** be careful not to do. **~e-à-vous** *int.* (*mil.*) attention. **~e-boue** *n.m. invar.* mudguard. **~e-chasse** (*pl.* **~es-chasses**) *n.m.* gamekeeper. **~e-fou** *n.m.* railing. **~e-manger** *n.m. invar.* (food) safe; (*placard*) larder. **~e-robe** *n.f.* wardrobe.

garderie /gardəri/ *n.f.* crèche.

gardien, ~ne /gardjɛ̃, -jɛn/ *n.m., f.* (*de prison, réserve*) warden; (*d'immeuble*) caretaker; (*de musée*) attendant; (*garde*) guard. **~ de but,** goalkeeper. **~ de la paix,** policeman. **~ de nuit,** night watchman. **~ne d'enfants,** childminder.

gare[1] /gar/ *n.f.* (*rail.*) station. **~ routière,** coach station; (*Amer.*) bus station.

gare[2] /gar/ *int.* **~ (à toi),** watch out!

garer /gare/ *v.t.*, **se ~** *v. pr.* park.

gargariser (se) /(sə)gargarize/ *v. pr.* gargle.

gargarisme /gargarism/ *n.m.* gargle.

gargouille /garguj/ *n.f.* (water)-spout; (*sculptée*) gargoyle.

gargouiller /garguje/ *v.i.* gurgle.

garnement /garnəmɑ̃/ *n.m.* rascal.

garn|ir /garnir/ *v.t.* fill; (*décorer*) decorate; (*couvrir*) cover; (*doubler*) line; (*culin.*) garnish. **~i** *a.* (*plat*) served with vegetables. **bien ~i,** (*rempli*) well-filled.

garnison /garnizɔ̃/ *n.f.* garrison.

garniture /garnityr/ *n.f.* (*légumes*) vegetables; (*ornement*) trimming; (*de voiture*) trim.

garrot /garo/ *n.m.* (*méd.*) tourniquet.

gars /gɑ/ *n.m.* (*fam.*) fellow.

gas-oil /gɑzɔjl/ *n.m.* diesel oil.

gaspill|er /gaspije/ *v.t.* waste. **~age** *n.m.* waste.

gastrique /gastrik/ *a.* gastric.

gastronom|e /gastrɔnɔm/ *n.m./f.* gourmet. **~ie** *n.f.* gastronomy.

gâteau (*pl.* **~x**) /gɑto/ *n.m.* cake. **~ sec,** biscuit; (*Amer.*) cookie. **un papa ~,** a doting dad.

gâter /gɑte/ *v.t.* spoil. **se ~** *v. pr.* (*dent, viande*) go bad; (*temps*) get worse.

gâterie /gɑtri/ *n.f.* little treat.

gâteu|x, ~se /gɑtø, -z/ *a.* senile.

gauch|e[1] /goʃ/ *a.* left. **à ~e,** on the left; (*direction*) (to the) left. **la ~e,** the left (side); (*pol.*) the left (wing). **~er, ~ère** *a. & n.m., f.* left-handed (person). **~iste** *a. & n.m./f.* (*pol.*) leftist.

gauche[2] /goʃ/ *a.* (*maladroit*) awkward. **~rie** *n.f.* awkwardness.

gaufre /gofr/ *n.f.* waffle.

gaufrette /gofrɛt/ *n.f.* wafer.

gaulois, ~e /golwa, -z/ *a.* Gallic; (*fig.*) bawdy. ● *n.m., f.* Gaul.

gausser (se) /(sə)gose/ *v. pr.* **se ~ de,** deride, scoff at.

gaver /gave/ *v.t.* force-feed; (*fig.*) cram. **se ~ de,** gorge o.s. with.

gaz /gɑz/ *n.m. invar.* gas. **~ lacrymogène,** tear-gas.

gaze /gɑz/ *n.f.* gauze.

gazelle /gazɛl/ *n.f.* gazelle.

gaz|er /gɑze/ *v.i.* (*fam.*) **ça ~e,** it's going all right.

gazette /gazɛt/ *n.f.* newspaper.

gazeu|x, ~se /gɑzø, -z/ *a.* (*boisson*) fizzy.

gazoduc /gaʒɔdyk/ *n.m.* gas pipeline.

gazomètre /gɑzɔmɛtr/ *n.m.* gasometer.

gazon /gɑzɔ̃/ *n.m.* lawn, grass.

gazouiller /gazuje/ *v.i.* (*oiseau*) chirp; (*bébé*) babble.

geai /ʒɛ/ *n.m.* jay.

géant, ~e /ʒeɑ̃, -t/ *a. & n.m., f.* giant.

geindre /ʒɛ̃dr/ *v.i.* groan.

gel /ʒɛl/ *n.m.* frost; (*pâte*) gel; (*comm.*) freezing.

gélatine /ʒelatin/ *n.f.* gelatine.

gel|er /ʒəle/ *v.t./i.* freeze. **on gèle,** it's freezing. **~é** *a.* frozen; (*membre abîmé*) frost-bitten. **~ée** *n.f.* frost; (*culin.*) jelly. **~ée blanche,** hoar-frost.

gélule /ʒelyl/ *n.f.* (*méd.*) capsule.

Gémeaux /ʒemo/ *n.m. pl.* Gemini.

gém|ir /ʒemir/ *v.i.* groan. **~issement** *n.m.* groan(ing).

gênant, ~e /ʒɛnɑ̃, -t/ *a.* embarrassing; (*irritant*) annoying.

gencive /ʒɑ̃siv/ *n.f.* gum.

gendarme /ʒɑ̃darm/ *n.m.* policeman, gendarme. **~rie** /-əri/ *n.f.* police force; (*local*) police station.

gendre /ʒɑ̃dr/ *n.m.* son-in-law.

gène /ʒɛn/ *n.m.* gene.

gêne /ʒɛn/ *n.f.* discomfort; (*confusion*) embarrassment; (*dérangement*) trouble. **dans la ~,** in financial straits.

généalogie /ʒenealɔʒi/ *n.f.* genealogy.

gên|er /ʒene/ *v.t.* bother, disturb; (*troubler*) embarrass; (*encombrer*) hamper; (*bloquer*) block. **~é** *a.* embarrassed.

génér|al (*m. pl.* **~aux**) /ʒeneral, -o/ *a.* general. ● *n.m.* (*pl.* **~aux**) general. **en ~al,** in general. **~alement** *adv.* generally.

généralis|er /ʒeneralize/ *v.t./i.* generalize. **se ~er** *v. pr.* become general. **~ation** *n.f.* generalization.

généraliste /ʒeneralist/ *n.m./f.* general practitioner, GP.

généralité /ʒeneralite/ *n.f.* majority. **~s,** general points.
génération /ʒenerɑsjɔ̃/ *n.f.* generation.
génératrice /ʒeneratris/ *n.f.* generator.
généreu|x, ~se /ʒenerø, -z/ *a.* generous. **~sement** *adv.* generously.
générique /ʒenerik/ *n.m.* (*cinéma*) credits. ● *a.* generic.
générosité /ʒenerozite/ *n.f.* generosity.
genêt /ʒənɛ/ *n.m.* (*plante*) broom.
génétique /ʒenetik/ *a.* genetic. ● *n.f.* genetics.
Genève /ʒənɛv/ *n.m./f.* Geneva.
gén|ial (*m. pl.* **~iaux**) /ʒenjal, -jo/ *a.* brilliant; (*fam.*) fantastic.
génie /ʒeni/ *n.m.* genius. **~ civil,** civil engineering.
genièvre /ʒənjɛvr/ *n.m.* juniper.
génisse /ʒenis/ *n.f.* heifer.
génit|al (*m. pl.* **~aux**) /ʒenital, -o/ *a.* genital.
génocide /ʒenɔsid/ *n.m.* genocide.
génoise /ʒenwaz/ *n.f.* sponge (cake).
genou (*pl.* **~x**) /ʒnu/ *n.m.* knee. **à ~x,** kneeling. **se mettre à ~x,** kneel.
genre /ʒɑ̃r/ *n.m.* sort, kind; (*attitude*) manner; (*gram.*) gender. **~ de vie,** life-style.
gens /ʒɑ̃/ *n.m./f. pl.* people
genti|l, ~lle /ʒɑ̃ti, -j/ *a.* kind, nice; (*agréable*) nice; (*sage*) good. **~llesse** /-jɛs/ *n.f.* kindness. **~ment** *adv.* kindly.
géograph|ie /ʒeɔgrafi/ *n.f.* geography. **~e** *n.m./f.* geographer. **~ique** *a.* geographical.
geôl|ier, ~ière /ʒolje, -jɛr/ *n.m., f.* gaoler, jailer.
géolo|gie /ʒeɔlɔʒi/ *n.f.* geology. **~gique** *a.* geological. **~gue** *n.m./f.* geologist.
géomètre /ʒeɔmɛtr/ *n.m.* surveyor.
géométr|ie /ʒeɔmetri/ *n.f.* geometry. **~ique** *a.* geometric.
géranium /ʒeranjɔm/ *n.m.* geranium.
géran|t, ~te /ʒerɑ̃, -t/ *n.m., f.* manager, manageress. **~t d'immeuble,** landlord's agent. **~ce** *n.f.* management.
gerbe /ʒɛrb/ *n.f.* (*de fleurs, d'eau*) spray; (*de blé*) sheaf.
gercé /ʒɛrse/ *a.* chapped.
ger|cer /ʒɛrse/ *v.t./i.*, **se ~cer** *v. pr.* chap. **~çure** *n.f.* chap.
gérer /ʒere/ *v.t.* manage.
germain, ~e /ʒɛrmɛ̃, -ɛn/ *a.* **cousin ~,** first cousin.
germanique /ʒɛrmanik/ *a.* Germanic.
germ|e /ʒɛrm/ *n.m.* germ. **~er** *v.i.* germinate.
gésier /ʒezje/ *n.m.* gizzard.
gestation /ʒɛstɑsjɔ̃/ *n.f.* gestation.
geste /ʒɛst/ *n.m.* gesture.
gesticul|er /ʒɛstikyle/ *v.i.* gesticulate. **~ation** *n.f.* gesticulation.
gestion /ʒɛstjɔ̃/ *n.f.* management.
geyser /ʒɛzɛr/ *n.m.* geyser.
ghetto /gɛto/ *n.m.* ghetto.
gibecière /ʒibsjɛr/ *n.f.* shoulder-bag.
gibet /ʒibɛ/ *n.m.* gallows.
gibier /ʒibje/ *n.m.* (*animaux*) game.
giboulée /ʒibule/ *n.f.* shower.
gicl|er /ʒikle/ *v.i.* squirt. **faire ~er,** squirt. **~ée** *n.f.* squirt.
gifl|e /ʒifl/ *n.f.* slap (in the face). **~er** *v.t.* slap.
gigantesque /ʒigɑ̃tɛsk/ *a.* gigantic.
gigot /ʒigo/ *n.m.* leg (of lamb).
gigoter /ʒigɔte/ *v.i.* (*fam.*) wriggle.
gilet /ʒilɛ/ *n.m.* waistcoat; (*cardigan*) cardigan. **~ de sauvetage,** life-jacket.
gin /dʒin/ *n.m.* gin.
gingembre /ʒɛ̃ʒɑ̃br/ *n.m.* ginger.
gingivite /ʒɛ̃ʒivit/ *n.f.* gum infection.
girafe /ʒiraf/ *n.f.* giraffe.
giratoire /ʒiratwar/ *a.* **sens ~,** roundabout.
giroflée /ʒirɔfle/ *n.f.* wallflower.
girouette /ʒirwɛt/ *n.f.* weathercock, weather-vane.
gisement /ʒizmɑ̃/ *n.m.* deposit.
gitan, ~e /ʒitɑ̃, -an/ *n.m., f.* gypsy.
gîte /ʒit/ *n.m.* (*maison*) home; (*abri*) shelter. **~ rural,** holiday cottage.
givr|e /ʒivr/ *n.m.* (hoar-)frost. **~er** *v.t.*, **se ~er** *v. pr.* frost (up).
givré /ʒivre/ *a.* (*fam.*) nuts.
glace /glas/ *n.f.* ice; (*crème*) ice-cream; (*vitre*) window; (*miroir*) mirror; (*verre*) glass.
glac|er /glase/ *v.t.* freeze; (*gâteau, boisson*) ice; (*papier*) glaze; (*pétrifier*) chill. **se ~er** *v. pr.* freeze. **~é** *a.* (*vent, accueil*) icy.
glac|ial (*m. pl.* **~iaux**) /glasjal, -jo/ *a.* icy.
glacier /glasje/ *n.m.* (*géog.*) glacier; (*vendeur*) ice-cream man.

glacière /glasjɛr/ *n.f.* icebox.
glaçon /glasɔ̃/ *n.m.* (*pour boisson*) ice-cube; (*péj.*) cold fish.
glaïeul /glajœl/ *n.m.* gladiolus.
glaise /glɛz/ *n.f.* clay.
gland /glɑ̃/ *n.m.* acorn; (*ornement*) tassel.
glande /glɑ̃d/ *n.f.* gland.
glander /glɑ̃de/ *v.i.* (*fam.*) laze around.
glaner /glane/ *v.t.* glean.
glapir /glapir/ *v.i.* yelp.
glas /glɑ/ *n.m.* knell.
glauque /glok/ *a.* (*fig.*) gloomy.
glissant, ~e /glisɑ̃, -t/ *a.* slippery.
gliss|er /glise/ *v.i.* slide; (*sur l'eau*) glide; (*déraper*) slip; (*véhicule*) skid. ● *v.t.*, **se ~er** *v. pr.* slip (**dans,** into). **~ade** *n.f.* sliding; (*endroit*) slide. **~ement** *n.m.* sliding; gliding; (*fig.*) shift. **~ement de terrain,** landslide.
glissière /glisjɛr/ *n.f.* groove. **à ~,** (*porte, système*) sliding.
glob|al (*m. pl.* **~aux**) /glɔbal, -o/ *a.* (*entier, général*) overall. **~alement** *adv.* as a whole.
globe /glɔb/ *n.m.* globe. **~ oculaire,** eyeball. **~ terrestre,** globe.
globule /glɔbyl/ *n.m.* (*du sang*) corpuscle.
gloire /glwar/ *n.f.* glory.
glorieu|x, ~se /glɔrjø, -z/ *a.* glorious. **~sement** *adv.* gloriously.
glorifier /glɔrifje/ *v.t.* glorify.
glose /gloz/ *n.f.* gloss.
glossaire /glɔsɛr/ *n.m.* glossary.
glouss|er /gluse/ *v.i.* chuckle; (*poule*) cluck. **~ement** *n.m.* chuckle; cluck.
glouton, ~ne /glutɔ̃, -ɔn/ *a.* gluttonous. ● *n.m., f.* glutton.
gluant, ~e /glyɑ̃, -t/ *a.* sticky.
glucose /glykoz/ *n.m.* glucose.
glycérine /gliserin/ *n.f.* glycerine.
glycine /glisin/ *n.f.* wisteria.
gnome /gnom/ *n.m.* gnome.
go /go/ **tout de go,** straight out.
GO (*abrév. grandes ondes*) long wave.
goal /gol/ *n.m.* goalkeeper.
gobelet /gɔblɛ/ *n.m.* tumbler, mug.
gober /gɔbe/ *v.t.* swallow (whole). **je ne peux pas le ~,** (*fam.*) I can't stand him.
godasse /gɔdas/ *n.f.* (*fam.*) shoe.
godet /gɔdɛ/ *n.m.* (small) pot.
goéland /gɔelɑ̃/ *n.m.* (sea)gull.
goélette /gɔelɛt/ *n.f.* schooner.
gogo (à) /(a)gɔgo/ *adv.* (*fam.*) galore, in abundance.
goguenard, ~e /gɔgnar, -d/ *a.* mocking.
goguette (en) /(ɑ̃)gɔgɛt/ *adv.* (*fam.*) having a binge *ou* spree.
goinfr|e /gwɛ̃fr/ *n.m.* (*glouton: fam.*) pig. **se ~er** *v. pr.* (*fam.*) stuff o.s. like a pig (**de,** with).
golf /gɔlf/ *n.m.* golf; golf course.
golfe /gɔlf/ *n.m.* gulf.
gomm|e /gɔm/ *n.f.* rubber; (*Amer.*) eraser; (*résine*) gum. **~er** *v.t.* rub out.
gond /gɔ̃/ *n.m.* hinge. **sortir de ses ~s,** go mad.
gondol|e /gɔ̃dɔl/ *n.f.* gondola. **~ier** *n.m.* gondolier.
gondoler (se) /(sə)gɔ̃dɔle/ *v. pr.* warp; (*rire: fam.*) split one's sides.
gonfl|er /gɔ̃fle/ *v.t./i.* swell; (*ballon, pneu*) pump up, blow up; (*exagérer*) inflate. **se ~er** *v. pr.* swell. **~é** *a.* swollen. **il est ~é,** (*fam.*) he's got a nerve. **~ement** *n.m.* swelling.
gorge /gɔrʒ/ *n.f.* throat; (*poitrine*) breast; (*vallée*) gorge.
gorgée /gɔrʒe/ *n.f.* sip, gulp.
gorg|er /gɔrʒe/ *v.t.* fill (**de,** with). **se ~er** *v. pr.* gorge o.s. (**de,** with). **~é de,** full of.
gorille /gɔrij/ *n.m.* gorilla; (*garde: fam.*) bodyguard.
gosier /gozje/ *n.m.* throat.
gosse /gɔs/ *n.m./f.* (*fam.*) kid.
gothique /gɔtik/ *a.* Gothic.
goudron /gudrɔ̃/ *n.m.* tar. **~ner** /-ɔne/ *v.t.* tar; (*route*) surface. **à faible teneur en ~,** low tar.
gouffre /gufr/ *n.m.* gulf, abyss.
goujat /guʒa/ *n.m.* lout, boor.
goulot /gulo/ *n.m.* neck. **boire au ~,** drink from the bottle.
goulu, ~e /guly/ *a.* gluttonous. ● *n.m., f.* glutton.
gourde /gurd/ *n.f.* (*à eau*) flask; (*idiot: fam.*) chump.
gourdin /gurdɛ̃/ *n.m.* club, cudgel.
gourer (se) /(sə)gure/ *v. pr.* (*fam.*) make a mistake.
gourmand, ~e /gurmɑ̃, -d/ *a.* greedy. ● *n.m., f.* glutton. **~ise** /-diz/ *n.f.* greed; (*mets*) delicacy.
gourmet /gurmɛ/ *n.m.* gourmet.
gourmette /gurmɛt/ *n.f.* chain bracelet.
gousse /gus/ *n.f.* **~ d'ail,** clove of garlic.
goût /gu/ *n.m.* taste.

goûter /gute/ *v.t.* taste; (*apprécier*) enjoy. ● *v.i.* have tea. ● *n.m.* tea, snack. **~ à** *ou* **de,** taste.
goutt|e /gut/ *n.f.* drop; (*méd.*) gout. **~er** *v.i.* drip.
goutte-à-goutte /gutagut/ *n.m.* drip.
gouttelette /gutlɛt/ *n.f.* droplet.
gouttière /gutjɛr/ *n.f.* gutter.
gouvernail /guvɛrnaj/ *n.m.* rudder; (*barre*) helm.
gouvernante /guvɛrnɑ̃t/ *n.f.* governess.
gouvernement /guvɛrnəmɑ̃/ *n.m.* government. **~al** (*m. pl.* **~aux**) /-tal, -to/ *a.* government.
gouvern|er /guvɛrne/ *v.t./i.* govern. **~eur** *n.m.* governor.
grâce /grɑs/ *n.f.* (*charme*) grace; (*faveur*) favour; (*jurid.*) pardon; (*relig.*) grace. **~ à,** thanks to.
gracier /grasje/ *v.t.* pardon.
gracieu|x, ~se /grasjø, -z/ *a.* graceful; (*gratuit*) free. **~sement** *adv.* gracefully; free (of charge).
gradation /gradɑsjɔ̃/ *n.f.* gradation.
grade /grad/ *n.m.* rank. **monter en ~,** be promoted.
gradé /grade/ *n.m.* non-commissioned officer.
gradin /gradɛ̃/ *n.m.* tier, step. **en ~s,** terraced.
gradué /gradɥe/ *a.* graded, graduated.
graduel, ~le /gradɥɛl/ *a.* gradual.
grad|uer /gradɥe/ *v.t.* increase gradually. **~uation** *n.f.* graduation.
graffiti /grafiti/ *n.m. pl.* graffiti.
grain /grɛ̃/ *n.m.* grain; (*naut.*) squall; (*de café*) bean; (*de poivre*) pepper corn. **~ de beauté,** beauty spot. **~ de raisin,** grape.
graine /grɛn/ *n.f.* seed.
graissage /grɛsaʒ/ *n.m.* lubrication.
graiss|e /grɛs/ *n.f.* fat; (*lubrifiant*) grease. **~er** *v.t.* grease. **~eux, ~euse** *a.* greasy.
gramm|aire /gramɛr/ *n.f.* grammar. **~atical** (*m. pl.* **~aticaux**) *a.* grammatical.
gramme /gram/ *n.m.* gram.
grand, ~e /grɑ̃, -d/ *a.* big, large; (*haut*) tall; (*mérite, distance, ami*) great; (*bruit*) loud; (*plus âgé*) big. ● *adv.* (*ouvrir*) wide. **~ ouvert,** wide open. **voir ~,** think big. ● *n.m., f.* (*adulte*) grown-up; (*enfant*) older child. **au ~ air,** in the open air. **au ~ jour,** in broad daylight; (*fig.*) in the open. **de ~e envergure,** large-scale. **en ~e partie,** largely. **~-angle,** *n.m.* wide angle. **~e banlieue,** outer suburbs. **G~e-Bretagne** *n.f.* Great Britain. **pas ~-chose,** not much. **~ ensemble,** housing estate. **~es lignes,** (*rail.*) main lines. **~ magasin,** department store. **~-mère** (*pl.* **~s-mères**) *n.f.* grandmother. **~s-parents** *n.m. pl.* grandparents. **~-père** (*pl.* **~s-pères**) *n.m.* grandfather. **~e personne,** grown-up. **~ public,** general public. **~-rue** *n.f.* high street. **~e surface,** hypermarket. **~es vacances,** summer holidays.
grandeur /grɑ̃dœr/ *n.f.* greatness; (*dimension*) size. **folie des ~s,** delusions of grandeur.
grandiose /grɑ̃djoz/ *a.* grandiose.
grandir /grɑ̃dir/ *v.i.* grow; (*bruit*) grow louder. ● *v.t.* make taller.
grange /grɑ̃ʒ/ *n.f.* barn.
granit /granit/ *n.m.* granite.
granulé /granyle/ *n.m.* granule.
graphique /grafik/ *a.* graphic. ● *n.m.* graph.
graphologie /grafɔlɔʒi/ *n.f.* graphology.
grappe /grap/ *n.f.* cluster. **~ de raisin,** bunch of grapes.
grappin /grapɛ̃/ *n.m.* **mettre le ~ sur,** get one's claws into.
gras, ~se /grɑ, -s/ *a.* fat; (*aliment*) fatty; (*surface*) greasy; (*épais*) thick; (*caractères*) bold. ● *n.m.* (*culin.*) fat. **faire la ~se matinée,** sleep late. **~sement payé,** highly paid.
gratification /gratifikɑsjɔ̃/ *n.f.* bonus, satisfaction.
gratifi|er /gratifje/ *v.t.* favour, reward (**de,** with). **~ant, ~ante** *a.* rewarding.
gratin /gratɛ̃/ *n.m.* baked dish with cheese topping; (*élite*: *fam.*) upper crust.
gratis /gratis/ *adv.* free.
gratitude /gratityd/ *n.f.* gratitude.
gratt|er /grate/ *v.t./i.* scratch; (*avec un outil*) scrape. **se ~er** *v. pr.* scratch o.s. **ça me ~e,** (*fam.*) it itches. **~e-ciel** *n.m. invar.* skyscraper. **~-papier** *n.m. invar.* (*péj.*) pen pusher.
gratuit, ~e /gratɥi, -t/ *a.* free; (*acte*) gratuitous. **~ement** /-tmɑ̃/ *adv.* free (of charge).
gravats /gravɑ/ *n.m. pl.* rubble.

grave /grav/ *a.* serious; (*solennel*) grave; (*voix*) deep; (*accent*) grave. **~ment** *adv.* seriously; gravely.

grav|er /grave/ *v.t.* engrave; (*sur bois*) carve. **~eur** *n.m.* engraver.

gravier /gravje/ *n.m.* gravel.

gravir /gravir/ *v.t.* climb.

gravitation /gravitɑsjɔ̃/ *n.f.* gravitation.

gravité /gravite/ *n.f.* gravity.

graviter /gravite/ *v.i.* revolve.

gravure /gravyr/ *n.f.* engraving; (*de tableau, photo*) print, plate.

gré /gre/ *n.m.* (*volonté*) will; (*goût*) taste. **à son ~,** (*agir*) as one likes. **de bon ~,** willingly. **bon ~ mal gré,** like it or not. **je vous en saurais ~,** I'll be grateful for that.

grec, ~que /grɛk/ *a.* & *n.m., f.* Greek. ● *n.m.* (*lang.*) Greek.

Grèce /grɛs/ *n.f.* Greece.

greff|e /grɛf/ *n.f.* graft, (*d'organe*) transplant. **~er** /grefe/ *v.t.* graft; transplant.

greffier /grefje/ *n.m.* clerk of the court.

grégaire /gregɛr/ *a.* gregarious.

grêle[1] /grɛl/ *a.* (*maigre*) spindly; (*voix*) shrill.

grêl|e[2] /grɛl/ *n.f.* hail. **~er** /grele/ *v.i.* hail. **~on** *n.m.* hailstone.

grelot /grəlo/ *n.m.* (little) bell.

grelotter /grəlɔte/ *v.i.* shiver.

grenade[1] /grənad/ *n.f.* (*fruit*) pomegranate.

grenade[2] /grənad/ *n.f.* (*explosif*) grenade.

grenat /grəna/ *a. invar.* dark red.

grenier /grənje/ *n.m.* attic; (*pour grain*) loft.

grenouille /grənuj/ *n.f.* frog.

grès /grɛ/ *n.m.* sandstone; (*poterie*) stoneware.

grésiller /grezije/ *v.i.* sizzle; (*radio*) crackle.

grève[1] /grɛv/ *n.f.* strike. **se mettre en ~,** go on strike. **~ du zèle,** work-to-rule; (*Amer.*) rule-book slowdown. **~ de la faim,** hunger strike. **~ sauvage,** wildcat strike.

grève[2] /grɛv/ *n.f.* (*rivage*) shore.

gréviste /grevist/ *n.m./f.* striker.

gribouill|er /gribuje/ *v.t./i.* scribble. **~is** /-ji/ *n.m.* scribble.

grief /grijɛf/ *n.m.* grievance.

grièvement /grijɛvmɑ̃/ *adv.* seriously.

griff|e /grif/ *n.f.* claw; (*de couturier*) label. **~er** *v.t.* scratch, claw.

griffonner /grifɔne/ *v.t./i.* scrawl.

grignoter /griɲɔte/ *v.t./i.* nibble.

gril /gril/ *n.m.* grill, grid(iron).

grillade /grijad/ *n.f.* (*viande*) grill.

grillage /grijaʒ/ *n.m.* wire netting.

grille /grij/ *n.f.* railings; (*portail*) (metal) gate; (*de fenêtre*) bars; (*de cheminée*) grate; (*fig.*) grid.

grill|er /grije/ *v.t./i.* burn; (*ampoule*) blow; (*feu rouge*) go through. **(faire) ~er,** (*pain*) toast; (*viande*) grill; (*café*) roast. **~e-pain** *n.m. invar.* toaster.

grillon /grijɔ̃/ *n.m.* cricket.

grimace /grimas/ *n.f.* (funny) face; (*de douleur, dégoût*) grimace.

grimer /grime/ *v.t.,* **se ~** *v. pr.* make up.

grimper /grɛ̃pe/ *v.t./i.* climb.

grinc|er /grɛ̃se/ *v.i.* creak. **~er des dents,** grind one's teeth. **~ement** *n.m.* creak(ing).

grincheu|x, ~se /grɛ̃ʃø, -z/ *a.* grumpy.

gripp|e /grip/ *n.f.* influenza, flu. **être ~é,** have (the) flu; (*mécanisme*) be seized up *ou* jammed.

gris, ~e /gri, -z/ *a.* grey; (*saoul*) tipsy.

grisaille /grizɑj/ *n.f.* greyness, gloom.

grisonner /grizɔne/ *v.i.* go grey.

grisou /grizu/ *n.m.* **coup de ~,** firedamp explosion.

grive /griv/ *n.f.* (*oiseau*) thrush.

grivois, ~e /grivwa, -z/ *a.* bawdy.

grog /grɔg/ *n.m.* grog.

grogn|er /grɔɲe/ *v.i.* growl; (*fig.*) grumble. **~ement** *n.m.* growl; grumble.

grognon, ~ne /grɔɲɔ̃, -ɔn/ *a.* grumpy.

groin /grwɛ̃/ *n.m.* snout.

grommeler /grɔmle/ *v.t./i.* mutter.

grond|er /grɔ̃de/ *v.i.* rumble; (*chien*) growl; (*conflit etc.*) be brewing. ● *v.t.* scold. **~ement** *n.m.* rumbling; growling.

groom /grum/ *n.m.* page(-boy).

gros, ~se /gro, -s/ *a.* big, large; (*gras*) fat; (*important*) great; (*épais*) thick; (*lourd*) heavy. ● *n.m., f.* fat man, fat woman. ● *n.m.* **le ~ de,** the bulk of. **de ~,** (*comm.*) wholesale. **en ~,** roughly; (*comm.*) wholesale. **~ bonnet,** (*fam.*) bigwig. **~ lot,** jackpot. **~ mot,** rude word. **~ plan,** close-up. **~ titre,** headline. **~se caisse,** big drum.

groseille /grozɛj/ *n.f.* (red *ou* white) currant. **~ à maquereau,** gooseberry.

grosse /gros/ *voir* gros.

grossesse /grosɛs/ *n.f.* pregnancy.

grosseur /grosœr/ *n.f.* (*volume*) size; (*enflure*) lump.

gross|ier, ~ière /grosje, -jɛr/ *a.* coarse, rough; (*imitation, instrument*) crude; (*vulgaire*) coarse; (*insolent*) rude; (*erreur*) gross. **~ièrement** *adv.* (*sommairement*) roughly; (*vulgairement*) coarsely. **~ièreté** *n.f.* coarseness; crudeness; rudeness; (*mot*) rude word.

grossir /grosir/ *v.t./i.* swell; (*personne*) put on weight; (*au microscope*) magnify; (*augmenter*) grow; (*exagérer*) magnify.

grossiste /grosist/ *n.m./f.* wholesaler.

grosso modo /grosomɔdo/ *adv.* roughly.

grotesque /grɔtɛsk/ *a.* grotesque; (*ridicule*) ludicrous.

grotte /grɔt/ *n.f.* cave, grotto.

grouill|er /gruje/ *v.i.* be swarming (**de,** with). **~ant, ~ante** *a.* swarming.

groupe /grup/ *n.m.* group; (*mus.*) band. **~ électrogène,** generating set. **~ scolaire,** school block.

group|er /grupe/ *v.t.,* **se ~er** *v. pr.* group (together). **~ement** *n.m.* grouping.

grue /gry/ *n.f.* (*machine, oiseau*) crane.

grumeau (*pl.* **~x**) /grymo/ *n.m.* lump.

gruyère /gryjɛr/ *n.m.* gruyère (cheese).

gué /ge/ *n.m.* ford. **passer** *ou* **traverser à ~,** ford.

guenon /gənɔ̃/ *n.f.* female monkey.

guépard /gepar/ *n.m.* cheetah.

guêp|e /gɛp/ *n.f.* wasp. **~ier** /gepje/ *n.m.* wasp's nest; (*fig.*) trap.

guère /gɛr/ *adv.* **(ne) ~,** hardly. **il n'y a ~ d'espoir,** there is no hope.

guéridon /geridɔ̃/ *n.m.* pedestal table.

guérill|a /gerija/ *n.f.* guerrilla warfare. **~ero** /-jero/ *n.m.* guerrilla.

guér|ir /gerir/ *v.t.* (*personne, maladie, mal*) cure (**de,** of); (*plaie, membre*) heal. ● *v.i.* get better; (*blessure*) heal. **~ir de,** recover from. **~ison** *n.f.* curing; healing; (*de personne*) recovery. **~isseur, ~isseuse** *n.m., f.* healer.

guérite /gerit/ *n.f.* (*mil.*) sentry-box.

guerre /gɛr/ *n.f.* war. **en ~,** at war. **faire la ~,** wage war (**à,** against). **~ civile,** civil war. **~ d'usure,** war of attrition.

guerr|ier, ~ière /gɛrje, -jɛr/ *a.* warlike. ● *n.m., f.* warrior.

guet /gɛ/ *n.m.* watch. **faire le ~,** be on the watch. **~-apens** /gɛtapɑ̃/ *n.m. invar.* ambush.

guetter /gete/ *v.t.* watch; (*attendre*) watch out for.

gueule /gœl/ *n.f.* mouth; (*figure: fam.*) face. **ta ~!,** (*fam.*) shut up!

gueuler /gœle/ *v.i.* (*fam.*) bawl.

gueuleton /gœltɔ̃/ *n.m.* (*repas: fam.*) blow-out, slap-up meal.

gui /gi/ *n.m.* mistletoe.

guichet /giʃɛ/ *n.m.* window, counter; (*de gare*) ticket-office (window); (*de théâtre*) box-office (window).

guide /gid/ *n.m.* guide. ● *n.f.* (*fille scout*) girl guide. **~s** *n.f. pl.* (*rênes*) reins.

guider /gide/ *v.t.* guide.

guidon /gidɔ̃/ *n.m.* handlebars.

guignol /giɲɔl/ *n.m.* puppet; (*personne*) clown; (*spectacle*) puppet-show.

guili-guili /giligili/ *n.m.* (*fam.*) tickle. **faire ~ à,** tickle.

guillemets /gijmɛ/ *n.m. pl.* quotation marks, inverted commas. **entre ~,** in inverted commas.

guilleret, ~te /gijrɛ, -t/ *a.* sprightly, jaunty.

guillotin|e /gijɔtin/ *n.f.* guillotine. **~er** *v.t.* guillotine.

guimauve /gimov/ *n.f.* marshmallow. **c'est de la ~,** (*fam.*) it's mush.

guindé /gɛ̃de/ *a.* stilted.

guirlande /girlɑ̃d/ *n.f.* garland.

guise /giz/ *n.f.* **à sa ~,** as one pleases. **en ~ de,** by way of.

guitar|e /gitar/ *n.f.* guitar. **~iste** *n.m./f.* guitarist.

gus /gys/ *n.m.* (*fam.*) bloke.

guttur|al (*m. pl.* **~aux**) /gytyral, -o/ *a.* guttural.

gym /ʒim/ *n.f.* gym.

gymnas|e /ʒimnɑz/ *n.m.* gym(nasium). **~te** /-ast/ *n.m./f.* gymnast. **~tique** /-astik/ *n.f.* gymnastics.

gynécolo|gie /ʒinekɔlɔʒi/ *n.f.* gynaecology. **~gique** *a.* gynaeco-

logical. **~gue** *n.m./f.* gynaecologist.
gypse /ʒips/ *n.m.* gypsum.

H

habile /abil/ *a.* skilful, clever. **~té** *n.f.* skill.
habilité /abilite/ *a.* **~ à faire,** entitled to do.
habill|er /abije/ *v.t.* dress (**de,** in); (*équiper*) clothe; (*recouvrir*) cover (**de,** with). **s'~er** *v. pr.* dress (o.s.), get dressed; (*se déguiser*) dress up. **~é** *a.* (*costume*) dressy. **~ement** *n.m.* clothing.
habit /abi/ *n.m.* dress, outfit; (*de cérémonie*) tails. **~s,** clothes.
habitable /abitabl/ *a.* (in)habitable.
habitant, ~e /abitɑ̃, -t/ *n.m., f.* (*de maison*) occupant; (*de pays*) inhabitant.
habitat /abita/ *n.m.* housing conditions; (*d'animal*) habitat.
habitation /abitɑsjɔ̃/ *n.f.* living; (*logement*) house.
habit|er /abite/ *v.i.* live. ● *v.t.* live in; (*planète, zone*) inhabit. **~é** *a.* (*terre*) inhabited.
habitude /abityd/ *n.f.* habit. **avoir l'~ de faire,** be used to doing. **d'~,** usually. **comme d'~,** as usual.
habitué, ~e /abitɥe/ *n.m., f.* regular visitor; (*client*) regular.
habituel, ~le /abitɥɛl/ *a.* usual. **~lement** *adv.* usually.
habituer /abitɥe/ *v.t.* **~ à,** accustom to. **s'~ à,** get used to.
hache /'aʃ/ *n.f.* axe.
haché /'aʃe/ *a.* (*viande*) minced; (*phrases*) jerky.
hacher /'aʃe/ *v.t.* mince; (*au couteau*) chop.
hachette /'aʃɛt/ *n.f.* hatchet.
hachis /'aʃi/ *n.m.* minced meat; (*Amer.*) ground meat.
hachisch /'aʃiʃ/ *n.m.* hashish.
hachoir /'aʃwar/ *n.m.* (*appareil*) mincer; (*couteau*) chopper; (*planche*) chopping board.
hagard, ~e /'agar, -d/ *a.* wild(-looking).
haie /'ɛ/ *n.f.* hedge; (*rangée*) row. **course de ~s,** hurdle race.
haillon /'ɑjɔ̃/ *n.m.* rag.
hain|e /'ɛn/ *n.f.* hatred. **~eux, ~euse** *a.* full of hatred.
haïr /'air/ *v.t.* hate.
hâl|e /'ɑl/ *n.m.* (sun-)tan. **~é** *a.* (sun-)tanned.
haleine /alɛn/ *n.f.* breath. **hors d'~,** out of breath. **travail de longue ~,** long job.
hal|er /'ale/ *v.t.* tow. **~age** *n.m.* towing.
haleter /'alte/ *v.i.* pant.
hall /'ol/ *n.m.* hall; (*de gare*) concourse.
halle /'al/ *n.f.* (covered) market. **~s,** (main) food market.
hallucination /alysinɑsjɔ̃/ *n.f.* hallucination.
halo /'alo/ *n.m.* halo.
halte /'alt/ *n.f.* stop; (*repos*) break; (*escale*) stopping place. ● *int.* stop; (*mil.*) halt. **faire ~,** stop.
halt|ère /altɛr/ *n.m.* dumb-bell. **~érophilie** *n.f.* weight-lifting.
hamac /'amak/ *n.m.* hammock.
hamburger /ɑ̃burgœr/ *n.m.* hamburger.
hameau (*pl.* **~x**) /'amo/ *n.m.* hamlet.
hameçon /amsɔ̃/ *n.m.* (fish-)hook.
hanche /'ɑ̃ʃ/ *n.f.* hip.
hand-ball /'ɑ̃dbal/ *n.m.* handball.
handicap /'ɑ̃dikap/ *n.m.* handicap. **~é, ~ée** *a.* & *n.m., f.* handicapped (person). **~er** *v.t.* handicap.
hangar /'ɑ̃gar/ *n.m.* shed; (*pour avions*) hangar.
hanneton /'antɔ̃/ *n.m.* May-bug.
hanter /'ɑ̃te/ *v.t.* haunt.
hantise /'ɑ̃tiz/ *n.f.* obsession (**de,** with).
happer /'ape/ *v.t.* snatch, catch.
haras /'ara/ *n.m.* stud-farm.
harasser /'arase/ *v.t.* exhaust.
harcèlement /'arsɛlmɑ̃/ *n.m.* **~ sexuel,** sexual harassment.
harceler /'arsəle/ *v.t.* harass.
hardi /'ardi/ *a.* bold. **~esse** /-djɛs/ *n.f.* boldness. **~ment** *adv.* boldly.
hareng /'arɑ̃/ *n.m.* herring.
hargn|e /'arɲ/ *n.f.* (aggressive) bad temper. **~eux, ~euse** *a.* bad-tempered.
haricot /'ariko/ *n.m.* bean. **~ vert,** French *ou* string bean; (*Amer.*) green bean.
harmonica /armɔnika/ *n.m.* harmonica.
harmon|ie /armɔni/ *n.f.* harmony. **~ieux, ~ieuse** *a.* harmonious.

harmoniser /armɔnize/ *v.t.*, **s'~** *v. pr.* harmonize.

harnacher /'arnaʃe/ *v.t.* harness.

harnais /'arnɛ/ *n.m.* harness.

harp|e /'arp/ *n.f.* harp. **~iste** *n.m./f.* harpist.

harpon /'arpɔ̃/ *n.m.* harpoon. **~ner** /-ɔne/ *v.t.* harpoon; (*arrêter: fam.*) detain.

hasard /'azar/ *n.m.* chance; (*coïncidence*) coincidence. **~s,** (*risques*) hazards. **au ~,** (*choisir etc.*) at random; (*flâner*) aimlessly. **~eux, ~euse** /-dø, -z/ *a.* risky.

hasarder /'azarde/ *v.t.* risk; (*remarque*) venture. **se ~ dans,** risk going into. **se ~ à faire,** risk doing.

hâte /'ɑt/ *n.f.* haste. **à la ~, en ~,** hurriedly. **avoir ~ de,** be eager to.

hâter /'ɑte/ *v.t.* hasten. **se ~** *v. pr.* hurry (**de,** to).

hâti|f, ~ve /'ɑtif, -v/ *a.* hasty; (*précoce*) early.

hauss|e /'os/ *n.f.* rise (**de,** in). **~e des prix,** price rises. **en ~e,** rising. **~er** *v.t.* raise; (*épaules*) shrug. **se ~er** *v. pr.* stand up, raise o.s. up.

haut, ~e /'o, 'ot/ *a.* high; (*de taille*) tall. ● *adv.* high; (*parler*) loud(ly); (*lire*) aloud. ● *n.m.* top. **à ~e voix,** aloud. **des ~s et des bas,** ups and downs. **en ~,** (*regarder, jeter*) up; (*dans une maison*) upstairs. **en ~ (de),** at the top (of). **~ en couleur,** colourful. **plus ~,** further up, higher up; (*dans un texte*) above. **en ~ lieu,** in high places. **~-de-forme** (*pl.* **~s-de-forme**) *n.m.* top hat. **~-fourneau** (*pl.* **~s-fourneaux**) *n.m.* blast-furnace. **~-le-cœur** *n.m. invar.* nausea. **~-parleur** *n.m.* loudspeaker.

hautain, ~e /'otɛ̃, -ɛn/ *a.* haughty.

hautbois /'obwɑ/ *n.m.* oboe.

hautement /'otmɑ̃/ *adv.* highly.

hauteur /'otœr/ *n.f.* height; (*colline*) hill; (*arrogance*) haughtiness. **à la ~,** (*fam.*) up to it. **à la ~ de,** level with; (*tâche, situation*) equal to.

hâve /'ɑv/ *a.* gaunt.

havre /'ɑvr/ *n.m.* haven.

Haye (La) /(la)'ɛ/ *n.f.* The Hague.

hayon /'ɑjɔ̃/ *n.m.* (*auto.*) rear opening, tail-gate.

hebdo /ɛbdɔ/ *n.m.* (*fam.*) weekly.

hebdomadaire /ɛbdɔmadɛr/ *a.* & *n.m.* weekly.

héberg|er /ebɛrʒe/ *v.t.* accommodate, take in. **~ement** *n.m.* accommodation.

hébété /ebete/ *a.* dazed.

hébraïque /ebraik/ *a.* Hebrew.

hébreu (*pl.* **~x**) /ebrø/ *a.m.* Hebrew. ● *n.m.* (*lang.*) Hebrew. **c'est de l'~!,** it's double Dutch.

hécatombe /ekatɔ̃b/ *n.f.* slaughter.

hectare /ɛktar/ *n.m.* hectare (*=10,000 square metres*).

hégémonie /eʒemɔni/ *n.f.* hegemony.

hein /'ɛ̃/ *int.* (*fam.*) eh.

hélas /'elɑs/ *int.* alas. ● *adv.* sadly.

héler /'ele/ *v.t.* hail.

hélice /elis/ *n.f.* propeller.

hélicoptère /elikɔptɛr/ *n.m.* helicopter.

helvétique /ɛlvetik/ *a.* Swiss.

hématome /ematom/ *n.m.* bruise.

hémisphère /emisfɛr/ *n.m.* hemisphere.

hémorragie /emɔraʒi/ *n.f.* haemorrhage.

hémorroïdes /emɔrɔid/ *n.f. pl.* piles, haemorrhoids.

henn|ir /'enir/ *v.i.* neigh. **~issement** *n.m.* neigh.

hépatite /epatit/ *n.f.* hepatitis.

herbage /ɛrbaʒ/ *n.m.* pasture.

herb|e /ɛrb/ *n.f.* grass; (*méd., culin.*) herb. **en ~e,** green; (*fig.*) budding. **~eux, ~euse** *a.* grassy.

herbicide /ɛrbisid/ *n.m.* weed-killer.

hérédit|é /eredite/ *n.f.* heredity. **~aire** *a.* hereditary.

héré|sie /erezi/ *n.f.* heresy. **~tique** *a.* heretical; *n.m./f.* heretic.

hériss|er /'erise/ *v.t.*, **se ~er** *v. pr.* bristle. **~er qn.,** ruffle s.o. **~é** *a.* bristling (**de,** with).

hérisson /'erisɔ̃/ *n.m.* hedgehog.

héritage /eritaʒ/ *n.m.* inheritance; (*spirituel etc.*) heritage.

hérit|er /erite/ *v.t./i.* inherit (**de,** from). **~er de qch.,** inherit sth. **~ier, ~ière** *n.m., f.* heir, heiress.

hermétique /ɛrmetik/ *a.* airtight; (*fig.*) unfathomable. **~ment** *adv.* hermetically.

hermine /ɛrmin/ *n.f.* ermine.

hernie /'ɛrni/ *n.f.* hernia.

héroïne[1] /erɔin/ *n.f.* (*femme*) heroine.

héroïne[2] /erɔin/ *n.f.* (*drogue*) heroin.

héroï|que /erɔik/ *a.* heroic. **~sme** *n.m.* heroism.

héron /'erɔ̃/ *n.m.* heron.
héros /'ero/ *n.m.* hero.
hésit|er /ezite/ *v.i.* hesitate (**à**, to). **en ~ant,** hesitantly. **~ant, ~ante** *a.* hesitant. **~ation** *n.f.* hesitation.
hétéro /eterɔ/ *n.m.* & *a.* (*fam.*) straight.
hétéroclite /eterɔklit/ *a.* heterogeneous.
hétérogène /eterɔʒɛn/ *a.* heterogeneous.
hétérosexuel, ~le /eterɔseksyɛl/ *n.m., f.* & *a.* heterosexual.
hêtre /'ɛtr/ *n.m.* beech.
heure /œr/ *n.f.* time; (*mesure de durée*) hour; (*scol.*) period. **quelle ~ est-il?,** what time is it? **il est dix/***etc.* **~s,** it is ten/*etc.* o'clock. **à l'~,** (*venir, être*) on time. **d'~ en heure,** hourly. **~ avancée,** late hour. **~ d'affluence, ~ de pointe,** rush-hour. **~ indue,** ungodly hour. **~s creuses,** off-peak periods. **~s supplémentaires,** overtime.
heureusement /œrøzmɑ̃/ *adv.* fortunately, luckily.
heureu|x, ~se /œrø, -z/ *a.* happy; (*chanceux*) lucky, fortunate.
heurt /'œr/ *n.m.* collision; (*conflit*) clash.
heurter /'œrte/ *v.t.* (*cogner*) hit; (*mur etc.*) bump into, hit; (*choquer*) offend. **se ~ à,** bump into, hit; (*fig.*) come up against.
hexagone /ɛgzagɔn/ *n.m.* hexagon. **l'~,** France.
hiberner /iberne/ *v.i.* hibernate.
hibou (*pl.* **~x**) /'ibu/ *n.m.* owl.
hideu|x, ~se /'idø, -z/ *a.* hideous.
hier /jɛr/ *adv.* yesterday. **~ soir,** last night, yesterday evening.
hiérarch|ie /'jerarʃi/ *n.f.* hierarchy. **~ique** *a.* hierarchical.
hi-fi† /'ifi/ *a. invar.* & *n.f.* (*fam.*) hi-fi.
hilare /ilar/ *a.* merry.
hilarité /ilarite/ *n.f.* laughter.
hindou, ~e /ɛ̃du/ *a.* & *n.m., f.* Hindu.
hippi|que /ipik/ *a.* horse, equestrian. **~sme** *n.m.* horse-riding.
hippodrome /ipɔdrom/ *n.m.* racecourse.
hippopotame /ipɔpɔtam/ *n.m.* hippopotamus.
hirondelle /irɔ̃dɛl/ *n.f.* swallow.
hirsute /irsyt/ *a.* shaggy.
hisser /'ise/ *v.t.* hoist, haul. **se ~** *v. pr.* raise o.s.
histoire /istwar/ *n.f.* (*récit, mensonge*) story; (*étude*) history; (*affaire*) business. **~(s),** (*chichis*) fuss. **~s,** (*ennuis*) trouble.
historien, ~ne /istɔrjɛ̃, -jɛn/ *n.m., f.* historian.
historique /istɔrik/ *a.* historical.
hiver /ivɛr/ *n.m.* winter. **~nal** (*m. pl.* **~naux**) *a.* winter; (*glacial*) wintry. **~ner** *v.i.* winter.
H.L.M. /'aʃɛlɛm/ *n.m./f.* (=*habitation à loyer modéré*) block of council flats; (*Amer.*) (government-sponsored) low-cost apartment building.
hocher /'ɔʃe/ *v.t.* **~ la tête,** (*pour dire oui*) nod; (*pour dire non*) shake one's head.
hochet /'ɔʃɛ/ *n.m.* rattle.
hockey /'ɔkɛ/ *n.m.* hockey. **~ sur glace,** ice hockey.
hold-up /'ɔldœp/ *n.m. invar.* (*attaque*) hold-up.
hollandais, ~e /'ɔlɑ̃dɛ, -z/ *a.* Dutch. • *n.m., f.* Dutchman, Dutchwoman. • *n.m.* (*lang.*) Dutch.
Hollande /'ɔlɑ̃d/ *n.f.* Holland.
hologramme /ɔlɔgram/ *n.m.* hologram.
homard /'ɔmar/ *n.m.* lobster.
homéopathie /ɔmeɔpati/ *n.f.* homoeopathy.
homicide /ɔmisid/ *n.m.* homicide. **~ involontaire,** manslaughter.
hommage /ɔmaʒ/ *n.m.* tribute. **~s,** (*salutations*) respects. **rendre ~ à,** pay tribute.
homme /ɔm/ *n.m.* man; (*espèce*) man(kind). **~ d'affaires,** businessman. **~ de la rue,** man in the street. **~ d'État,** statesman. **~ de paille,** stooge. **~-grenouille** (*pl.* **~s-grenouilles**) *n.m.* frogman. **~ politique,** politician.
homog|ène /ɔmɔʒɛn/ *a.* homogeneous. **~énéité** *n.f.* homogeneity.
homologue /ɔmɔlɔg/ *n.m./f.* counterpart.
homologué /ɔmɔlɔge/ *a.* (*record*) officially recognized; (*tarif*) official.
homologuer /ɔmɔlɔge/ *v.t.* recognize (officially), validate.
homonyme /ɔmɔnim/ *n.m.* (*personne*) namesake.
homosex|uel, ~uelle /ɔmɔsɛksɥɛl/ *a.* & *n.m., f.* homosexual. **~ualité** *n.f.* homosexuality.
Hongrie /'ɔ̃gri/ *n.f.* Hungary.

hongrois, ~e /'ɔ̃grwa, -z/ *a. & n.m., f.* Hungarian.

honnête /ɔnɛt/ *a.* honest; (*satisfaisant*) fair. **~ment** *adv.* honestly; fairly. **~té** *n.f.* honesty.

honneur /ɔnœr/ *n.m.* honour; (*mérite*) credit. **d'~,** (*invité, place*) of honour; (*membre*) honorary. **en l'~ de,** in honour of. **en quel ~?,** (*fam.*) why? **faire ~ à,** (*équipe, famille*) bring credit to.

honorable /ɔnɔrabl/ *a.* honourable; (*convenable*) respectable. **~ment** /-əmɑ̃/ *adv.* honourably; respectably.

honoraire /ɔnɔrɛr/ *a.* honorary. **~s** *n.m. pl.* fees.

honorer /ɔnɔre/ *v.t.* honour; (*faire honneur à*) do credit to. **s'~ de,** pride o.s. on.

honorifique /ɔnɔrifik/ *a.* honorary.

hont|e /'ɔ̃t/ *n.f.* shame. **avoir ~e,** be ashamed (**de,** of). **faire ~e à,** make ashamed. **~eux, ~euse** *a.* (*personne*) ashamed (**de,** of); (*action*) shameful. **~eusement** *adv.* shamefully.

hôpit|al (*pl.* **~aux**) /ɔpital, -o/ *n.m.* hospital.

hoquet /'ɔkɛ/ *n.m.* hiccup. **le ~,** (the) hiccups.

horaire /ɔrɛr/ *a.* hourly. ● *n.m.* timetable. **~ flexible,** flexitime.

horizon /ɔrizɔ̃/ *n.m.* horizon; (*perspective*) view.

horizont|al (*m. pl.* **~aux**) /ɔrizɔ̃tal, -o/ *a.* horizontal. **~alement** *adv.* horizontally.

horloge /ɔrlɔʒ/ *n.f.* clock.

horlog|er, ~ère /ɔrlɔʒe, -ɛr/ *n.m., f.* watchmaker.

hormis /'ɔrmi/ *prép.* save.

hormon|al (*m. pl.* **~aux**) /ɔrmɔnal, -no/ *a.* hormonal, hormone.

hormone /ɔrmɔn/ *n.f.* hormone.

horoscope /ɔrɔskɔp/ *n.m.* horoscope.

horreur /ɔrœr/ *n.f.* horror. **avoir ~ de,** detest.

horrible /ɔribl/ *a.* horrible. **~ment** /-əmɑ̃/ *adv.* horribly.

horrifier /ɔrifje/ *v.t.* horrify.

hors /'ɔr/ *prép.* **~ de,** out of; (*à l'extérieur de*) outside. **~-bord** *n.m. invar.* speedboat. **~ d'atteinte,** out of reach. **~ d'haleine,** out of breath. **~-d'œuvre** *n.m. invar.* hors-d'œuvre. **~ de prix,** exorbitant. **~ de soi,** beside o.s. **~-jeu** *a. invar.* offside. **~-la-loi** *n.m. invar.* outlaw. **~ pair,** outstanding. **~-taxe** *a. invar.* duty-free.

hortensia /ɔrtɑ̃sja/ *n.m.* hydrangea.

horticulture /ɔrtikyltyr/ *n.f.* horticulture.

hospice /ɔspis/ *n.m.* home.

hospital|ier, ~ière [1] /ɔspitalje, -jɛr/ *a.* hospitable. **~ité** *n.f.* hospitality.

hospital|ier, ~ière [2] /ɔspitalje, -jɛr/ *a.* (*méd.*) hospital. **~iser** *v.t.* take to hospital.

hostie /ɔsti/ *n.f.* (*relig.*) host.

hostil|e /ɔstil/ *a.* hostile. **~ité** *n.f.* hostility.

hosto /ɔsto/ *n.m.* (*fam.*) hospital.

hôte /ot/ *n.m.* (*maître*) host; (*invité*) guest.

hôtel /otɛl/ *n.m.* hotel. **~ (particulier),** (private) mansion. **~ de ville,** town hall. **~ier, ~ière** /otəlje, -jɛr/ *a.* hotel; *n.m., f.* hotelier. **~lerie** *n.f.* hotel business; (*auberge*) country hotel.

hôtesse /otɛs/ *n.f.* hostess. **~ de l'air,** air hostess.

hotte /'ɔt/ *n.f.* basket; (*de cuisinière*) hood.

houblon /'ublɔ̃/ *n.m.* **le ~,** hops.

houill|e /'uj/ *n.f.* coal. **~e blanche,** hydroelectric power. **~er, ~ère** *a.* coal; *n.f.* coalmine.

houl|e /'ul/ *n.f.* (*de mer*) swell. **~eux, ~euse** *a.* stormy.

houligan /uligan/ *n.m.* hooligan.

houppette /'upɛt/ *n.f.* powder-puff.

hourra /'ura/ *n.m. & int.* hurrah.

housse /'us/ *n.f.* dust-cover.

houx /'u/ *n.m.* holly.

hovercraft /ɔvɛrkraft/ *n.m.* hovercraft.

hublot /'yblo/ *n.m.* porthole.

huche /'yʃ/ *n.f.* **~ à pain,** breadbin.

huer /'ɥe/ *v.t.* boo. **huées** *n.f. pl.* boos.

huil|e /ɥil/ *n.f.* oil; (*personne: fam.*) bigwig. **~er** *v.t.* oil. **~eux, ~euse** *a.* oily.

huis /'ɥi/ *n.m.* **à ~ clos,** in camera.

huissier /ɥisje/ *n.m.* (*appariteur*) usher; (*jurid.*) bailiff.

huit /'ɥi(t)/ *a.* eight. ● *n.m.* eight. **~ jours,** a week. **lundi en ~,** a week on Monday. **~aine** /'ɥitɛn/ *n.f.* (*semaine*) week. **~ième** /'ɥitjɛm/ *a. & n.m./f.* eighth.

huître /ɥitr/ *n.f.* oyster.

humain, ~e /ymɛ̃, ymɛn/ *a.* human; (*compatissant*) humane. **~ement** /ymɛnmɑ̃/ *adv.* humanly; humanely.

humanitaire /ymanitɛr/ *a.* humanitarian.
humanité /ymanite/ *n.f.* humanity.
humble /œ̃bl/ *a.* humble.
humecter /ymɛkte/ *v.t.* moisten.
humer /'yme/ *v.t.* smell.
humeur /ymœr/ *n.f.* mood; (*tempérament*) temper. **de bonne/mauvaise ~,** in a good/bad mood.
humid|e /ymid/ *a.* damp; (*chaleur, climat*) humid; (*lèvres, yeux*) moist. **~ité** *n.f.* humidity.
humil|ier /ymilje/ *v.t.* humiliate. **~iation** *n.f.* humiliation.
humilité /ymilite/ *n.f.* humility.
humorist|e /ymɔrist/ *n.m./f.* humorist. **~ique** *a.* humorous.
humour /ymur/ *n.m.* humour; (*sens*) sense of humour.
huppé /'ype/ *a.* (*fam.*) high-class.
hurl|er /'yrle/ *v.t./i.* howl. **~ement** *n.m.* howl(ing).
hurluberlu /yrlybɛrly/ *n.m.* scatterbrain.
hutte /'yt/ *n.f.* hut.
hybride /ibrid/ *a.* & *n.m.* hybrid.
hydratant, ~e /idratɑ̃, -t/ *a.* (*lotion*) moisturizing.
hydrate /idrat/ *n.m.* **~ de carbone,** carbohydrate.
hydraulique /idrolik/ *a.* hydraulic.
hydravion /idravjɔ̃/ *n.m.* seaplane.
hydro-electrique /idrɔelɛktrik/ *a.* hydroelectric.
hydrogène /idrɔʒɛn/ *n.m.* hydrogen.
hyène /'jɛn/ *n.f.* hyena.
hyg|iène /iʒjɛn/ *n.f.* hygiene. **~iénique** /iʒjenik/ *a.* hygienic.
hymne /imn/ *n.m.* hymn. **~ national,** national anthem.
hyper- /ipɛr/ *préf.* hyper-.
hypermarché /ipɛrmarʃe/ *n.m.* (*supermarché*) hypermarket.
hypermétrope /ipɛrmetrɔp/ *a.* longsighted.
hypertension /ipɛrtɑ̃sjɔ̃/ *n.f.* high blood-pressure.
hypno|se /ipnoz/ *n.f.* hypnosis. **~tique** /-ɔtik/ *a.* hypnotic. **~tisme** /-ɔtism/ *n.m.* hypnotism.
hypnotis|er /ipnɔtize/ *v.t.* hypnotize. **~eur** *n.m.* hypnotist.
hypocrisie /ipɔkrizi/ *n.f.* hypocrisy.
hypocrite /ipɔkrit/ *a.* hypocritical. ● *n.m./f.* hypocrite.
hypoth|èque /ipɔtɛk/ *n.f.* mortgage. **~équer** *v.t.* mortgage.
hypoth|èse /ipɔtɛz/ *n.f.* hypothesis. **~étique** *a.* hypothetical.
hystér|ie /isteri/ *n.f.* hysteria. **~ique** *a.* hysterical.

I

iceberg /isbɛrg/ *n.m.* iceberg.
ici /isi/ *adv.* (*espace*) here; (*temps*) now. **d'~ demain,** by tomorrow. **d'~ là,** in the meantime. **d'~ peu,** shortly. **~ même,** in this very place.
icône /ikon/ *n.f.* icon.
idé|al (*m. pl.* **~aux**) /ideal, -o/ *a.* ideal. ● *n.m.* (*pl.* **~aux**) ideal. **~aliser** *v.t.* idealize.
idéalis|te /idealist/ *a.* idealistic. ● *n.m./f.* idealist. **~me** *n.m.* idealism.
idée /ide/ *n.f.* idea; (*esprit*) mind. **~ fixe,** obsession. **~ reçue,** conventional opinion.
identif|ier /idɑ̃tifje/ *v.t.,* **s'~ier** *v. pr.* identify (**à,** with). **~ication** *n.f.* identification.
identique /idɑ̃tik/ *a.* identical.
identité /idɑ̃tite/ *n.f.* identity.
idéolog|ie /ideɔlɔʒi/ *n.f.* ideology. **~ique** *a.* ideological.
idiom|e /idjom/ *n.m.* idiom. **~atique** /idjɔmatik/ *a.* idiomatic.
idiot, ~e /idjo, idjɔt/ *a.* idiotic. ● *n.m., f.* idiot. **~ie** /idjɔsi/ *n.f.* idiocy; (*acte, parole*) idiotic thing.
idiotisme /idjɔtism/ *n.m.* idiom.
idolâtrer /idɔlatre/ *v.t.* idolize.
idole /idɔl/ *n.f.* idol.
idyll|e /idil/ *n.f.* idyll. **~ique** *a.* idyllic.
if /if/ *n.m.* (*arbre*) yew.
igloo /iglu/ *n.m.* igloo.
ignare /iɲar/ *a.* ignorant. ● *n.m./f.* ignoramus.
ignifugé /iɲifyʒe/ *a.* fireproof.
ignoble /iɲɔbl/ *a.* vile.
ignoran|t, ~te /iɲɔrɑ̃, -t/ *a.* ignorant. ● *n.m., f.* ignoramus. **~ce** *n.f.* ignorance.
ignorer /iɲɔre/ *v.t.* not know; (*personne*) ignore.
il /il/ *pron.* he; (*chose*) it. **il est vrai/** *etc.* **que,** it is true/*etc.* that. **il neige/ pleut/***etc.*, it is snowing/raining/*etc.* **il y a,** there is; (*pluriel*) there are; (*temps*) ago; (*durée*) for. **il y a 2 ans,** 2 years ago. **il y a plus d'une heure que j'attends,** I've been waiting for over an hour.

île /il/ *n.f.* island. **~ déserte,** desert island. **~s anglo-normandes,** Channel Islands. **~s Britanniques,** British Isles.

illég|al (*m. pl.* **~aux**) /ilegal, -o/ *a.* illegal. **~alité** *n.f.* illegality.

illégitim|e /ileʒitim/ *a.* illegitimate. **~ité** *n.f.* illegitimacy.

illettré, ~e /iletre/ *a.* & *n.m., f.* illiterate.

illicite /ilisit/ *a.* illicit.

illimité /ilimite/ *a.* unlimited.

illisible /ilizibl/ *a.* illegible; (*livre*) unreadable.

illogique /ilɔʒik/ *a.* illogical.

illumin|er /ilymine/ *v.t.*, **s'~er** *v. pr.* light up. **~ation** *n.f.* illumination. **~é** *a.* (*monument*) floodlit.

illusion /ilyzjɔ̃/ *n.f.* illusion. **se faire des ~s,** delude o.s. **~ner** /-jɔne/ *v.t.* delude. **~niste** /-jɔnist/ *n.m./f.* conjuror.

illusoire /ilyzwar/ *a.* illusory.

illustre /ilystr/ *a.* illustrious.

illustr|er /ilystre/ *v.t.* illustrate. **s'~er** *v. pr.* become famous. **~ation** *n.f.* illustration. **~é** *a.* illustrated; *n.m.* illustrated magazine.

îlot /ilo/ *n.m.* island; (*de maisons*) block.

ils /il/ *pron.* they.

imag|e /imaʒ/ *n.f.* picture; (*métaphore*) image; (*reflet*) reflection. **~é** *a.* full of imagery.

imaginaire /imaʒinɛr/ *a.* imaginary.

imaginati|f, ~ve /imaʒinatif, -v/ *a.* imaginative.

imagin|er /imaʒine/ *v.t.* imagine; (*inventer*) think up. **s'~er** *v. pr.* imagine (**que,** that). **~ation** *n.f.* imagination.

imbattable /ɛ̃batabl/ *a.* unbeatable.

imbécil|e /ɛ̃besil/ *a.* idiotic. ● *n.m./f.* idiot. **~lité** *n.f.* idiocy; (*action*) idiotic thing.

imbib|er /ɛ̃bibe/ *v.t.* soak (**de,** with). **être ~é,** (*fam.*) be sozzled. **s'~er** *v. pr.* become soaked.

imbriqué /ɛ̃brike/ *a.* (*lié*) linked.

imbroglio /ɛ̃brɔglio/ *n.m.* imbroglio.

imbu /ɛ̃by/ *a.* **~ de,** full of.

imbuvable /ɛ̃byvabl/ *a.* undrinkable; (*personne*: *fam.*) insufferable.

imit|er /imite/ *v.t.* imitate; (*personnage*) impersonate; (*faire comme*) do the same as; (*document*) copy. **~ateur, ~atrice** *n.m., f.* imitator; impersonator. **~ation** *n.f.* imitation; impersonation.

immaculé /imakyle/ *a.* spotless.

immangeable /ɛ̃mɑ̃ʒabl/ *a.* inedible.

immatricul|er /imatrikyle/ *v.t.* register. **(se) faire ~er,** register. **~ation** *n.f.* registration.

immature /imatyr/ *a.* immature.

immédiat, ~e /imedja, -t/ *a.* immediate. ● *n.m.* **dans l'~,** for the moment. **~ement** /-tmɑ̃/ *adv.* immediately.

immens|e /imɑ̃s/ *a.* immense. **~ément** *adv.* immensely. **~ité** *n.f.* immensity.

immer|ger /imɛrʒe/ *v.t.* immerse. **s'~ger** *v. pr.* submerge. **~sion** *n.f.* immersion.

immeuble /imœbl/ *n.m.* block of flats, building. **~ (de bureaux),** (office) building *ou* block.

immigr|er /imigre/ *v.i.* immigrate. **~ant, ~ante** *a.* & *n.m., f.* immigrant. **~ation** *n.f.* immigration. **~é, ~ée** *a.* & *n.m., f.* immigrant.

imminen|t, ~te /iminɑ̃, -t/ *a.* imminent. **~ce** *n.f.* imminence.

immiscer (s') /(s)imise/ *v. pr.* interfere (**dans,** in).

immobil|e /imɔbil/ *a.* still, motionless. **~ité** *n.f.* stillness; (*inaction*) immobility.

immobil|ier, ~ière /imɔbilje, -jɛr/ *a.* property. **agence ~ière,** estate agent's office; (*Amer.*) real estate office. **agent ~ier,** estate agent; (*Amer.*) real estate agent. **l'~ier,** property; (*Amer.*) real estate.

immobilis|er /imɔbilize/ *v.t.* immobilize; (*stopper*) stop. **s'~er** *v. pr.* stop. **~ation** *n.f.* immobilization.

immodéré /imɔdere/ *a.* immoderate.

immoler /imɔle/ *v.t.* sacrifice.

immonde /imɔ̃d/ *a.* filthy.

immondices /imɔ̃dis/ *n.f. pl.* refuse.

immor|al (*m. pl.* **~aux**) /imɔral, -o/ *a.* immoral. **~alité** *n.f.* immorality.

immortaliser /imɔrtalize/ *v.t.* immortalize.

immort|el, ~elle /imɔrtɛl/ *a.* immortal. **~alité** *n.f.* immortality.

immuable /imɥabl/ *a.* unchanging.

immunis|er /imynize/ *v.t.* immunize. **~é contre,** (*à l'abri de*) immune to.

immunité /imynite/ *n.f.* immunity.

impact /ɛ̃pakt/ *n.m.* impact.

impair[1] /ɛ̃pɛr/ *a.* (*numéro*) odd.

impair[2] /ɛ̃pɛr/ *n.m.* blunder.

impardonnable /ɛ̃pardɔnabl/ *a.* unforgivable.

imparfait, ~e /ɛ̃parfɛ, -t/ *a. & n.m.* imperfect.

impart|ial (*m. pl.* **~iaux**) /ɛ̃parsjal, -jo/ *a.* impartial. **~ialité** *n.f.* impartiality.

impasse /ɛ̃pɑs/ *n.f.* (*rue*) dead end; (*situation*) deadlock.

impassible /ɛ̃pasibl/ *a.* impassive.

impat|ient, ~iente /ɛ̃pasjɑ̃, -t/ *a.* impatient. **~iemment** /-jamɑ̃/ *adv.* impatiently. **~ience** *n.f.* impatience.

impatienter /ɛ̃pasjɑ̃te/ *v.t.* annoy. **s'~** *v. pr.* lose patience (**contre,** with).

impayable /ɛ̃pɛjabl/ *a.* (killingly) funny, hilarious.

impayé /ɛ̃peje/ *a.* unpaid.

impeccable /ɛ̃pekabl/ *a.* impeccable.

impénétrable /ɛ̃penetrabl/ *a.* impenetrable.

impensable /ɛ̃pɑ̃sabl/ *a.* unthinkable.

impérati|f, ~ve /ɛ̃peratif, -v/ *a.* imperative. ● *n.m.* requirement; (*gram.*) imperative.

impératrice /ɛ̃peratris/ *n.f.* empress.

imperceptible /ɛ̃pɛrsɛptibl/ *a.* imperceptible.

imperfection /ɛ̃pɛrfɛksjɔ̃/ *n.f.* imperfection.

impér|ial (*m. pl.* **~iaux**) /ɛ̃perjal, -jo/ *a.* imperial. **~ialisme** *n.m.* imperialism.

impériale /ɛ̃perjal/ *n.f.* upper deck.

impérieu|x, ~se /ɛ̃perjø, -z/ *a.* imperious; (*pressant*) pressing.

impérissable /ɛ̃perisabl/ *a.* undying.

imperméable /ɛ̃pɛrmeabl/ *a.* impervious (**à,** to); (*manteau, tissu*) waterproof. ● *n.m.* raincoat.

impersonnel, ~le /ɛ̃pɛrsɔnɛl/ *a.* impersonal.

impertinen|t, ~te /ɛ̃pɛrtinɑ̃, -t/ *a.* impertinent. **~ce** *n.f.* impertinence.

imperturbable /ɛ̃pɛrtyrbabl/ *a.* unshakeable.

impét|ueux, ~ueuse /ɛ̃petɥø, -z/ *a.* impetuous. **~uosité** *n.f.* impetuosity.

impitoyable /ɛ̃pitwajabl/ *a.* merciless.

implacable /ɛ̃plakabl/ *a.* implacable.

implant /ɛ̃plɑ̃/ *n.m.* implant.

implant|er /ɛ̃plɑ̃te/ *v.t.* establish. **s'~er** *v. pr.* become established. **~ation** *n.f.* establishment.

implication /ɛ̃plikɑsjɔ̃/ *n.f.* implication.

implicite /ɛ̃plisit/ *a.* implicit.

impliquer /ɛ̃plike/ *v.t.* imply (**que,** that). **~ dans,** implicate in.

implorer /ɛ̃plɔre/ *v.t.* implore.

impoli /ɛ̃pɔli/ *a.* impolite. **~tesse** *n.f.* impoliteness; (*remarque*) impolite remark.

impondérable /ɛ̃pɔ̃derabl/ *a. & n.m.* imponderable.

impopulaire /ɛ̃pɔpylɛr/ *a.* unpopular.

importance /ɛ̃pɔrtɑ̃s/ *n.f.* importance; (*taille*) size; (*ampleur*) extent. **sans ~,** unimportant.

important, ~e /ɛ̃pɔrtɑ̃, -t/ *a.* important; (*en quantité*) considerable, sizeable, big. ● *n.m.* **l'~,** the important thing.

import|er[1] /ɛ̃pɔrte/ *v.t.* (*comm.*) import. **~ateur, ~atrice** *n.m., f.* importer; *a.* importing. **~ation** *n.f.* import.

import|er[2] /ɛ̃pɔrte/ *v.i.* matter, be important (**à,** to). **il ~e que,** it is important that. **n'~e, peu ~e,** it does not matter. **n'~e comment,** anyhow. **n'~e où,** anywhere. **n'~e qui,** anybody. **n'~e quoi,** anything.

importun, ~e /ɛ̃pɔrtœ̃, -yn/ *a.* troublesome. ● *n.m., f.* nuisance. **~er** /-yne/ *v.t.* trouble.

imposant, ~e /ɛ̃pozɑ̃, -t/ *a.* imposing.

imposer /ɛ̃poze/ *v.t.* impose (**à,** on); (*taxer*) tax. **s'~** *v. pr.* (*action*) be essential; (*se faire reconnaître*) stand out. **en ~ à qn.,** impress s.o.

imposition /ɛ̃pozisjɔ̃/ *n.f.* taxation. **~ des mains,** laying on of hands.

impossibilité /ɛ̃pɔsibilite/ *n.f.* impossibility. **dans l'~ de,** unable to.

impossible /ɛ̃pɔsibl/ *a. & n.m.* impossible. **faire l'~,** do the impossible.

impost|eur /ɛ̃pɔstœr/ *n.m.* impostor. **~ure** *n.f.* imposture.

impôt /ɛ̃po/ *n.m.* tax. **~s,** (*contributions*) tax(ation), taxes. **~ sur le revenu,** income tax.

impotent, ~e /ɛ̃pɔtɑ̃, -t/ *a.* crippled. ● *n.m., f.* cripple.

impraticable /ɛ̃pratikabl/ *a.* (*route*) impassable.

imprécis, ~e /ɛ̃presi, -z/ *a.* imprecise. **~ion** /-zjɔ̃/ *n.f.* imprecision.

imprégner /ɛ̃preɲe/ *v.t.* fill (**de,** with); (*imbiber*) impregnate (**de,** with). **s' ~ de,** become filled with;

(*s'imbiber*) become impregnated with.

imprenable /ɛ̃prənabl/ *a.* impregnable.

impresario /ɛ̃presarjo/ *n.m.* manager.

impression /ɛ̃presjɔ̃/ *n.f.* impression; (*de livre*) printing.

impressionn|er /ɛ̃presjɔne/ *v.t.* impress. **~able** *a.* impressionable. **~ant, ~ante** *a.* impressive.

imprévisible /ɛ̃previzibl/ *a.* unpredictable.

imprévoyant, ~e /ɛ̃prevwajɑ̃, -t/ *a.* improvident.

imprévu /ɛ̃prevy/ *a.* unexpected. ● *n.m.* unexpected incident.

imprim|er /ɛ̃prime/ *v.t.* print; (*marquer*) imprint; (*transmettre*) impart. **~ante** *n.f.* (*d'un ordinateur*) printer. **~é** *a.* printed; *n.m.* (*formulaire*) printed form. **~erie** *n.f.* (*art*) printing; (*lieu*) printing works. **~eur** *n.m.* printer.

improbable /ɛ̃prɔbabl/ *a.* unlikely, improbable.

impromptu /ɛ̃prɔ̃pty/ *a.* & *adv.* impromptu.

impropr|e /ɛ̃prɔpr/ *a.* incorrect. **~e à,** unfit for. **~iété,** *n.f.* incorrectness; (*erreur*) error.

improvis|er /ɛ̃prɔvize/ *v.t./i.* improvise. **~ation** *n.f.* improvisation.

improviste (à l') /(al)ɛ̃prɔvist/ *adv.* unexpectedly.

imprud|ent, ~ente /ɛ̃prydɑ̃, -t/ *a.* careless. **il est ~ent de,** it is unwise to. **~emment** /-amɑ̃/ *adv.* carelessly. **~ence** *n.f.* carelessness; (*acte*) careless action.

impuden|t, ~te /ɛ̃pydɑ̃, -t/ *a.* impudent. **~ce** *n.f.* impudence.

impudique /ɛ̃pydik/ *a.* immodest.

impuissan|t, ~te /ɛ̃pɥisɑ̃, -t/ *a.* helpless; (*méd.*) impotent. **~t à,** powerless to. **~ce** *n.f.* helplessness; (*méd.*) impotence.

impulsi|f, ~ve /ɛ̃pylsif, -v/ *a.* impulsive.

impulsion /ɛ̃pylsjɔ̃/ *n.f.* (*poussée, influence*) impetus; (*instinct, mouvement*) impulse.

impunément /ɛ̃pynemɑ̃/ *adv.* with impunity.

impuni /ɛ̃pyni/ *a.* unpunished.

impunité /ɛ̃pynite/ *n.f.* impunity.

impur /ɛ̃pyr/ *a.* impure. **~eté** *n.f.* impurity.

imput|er /ɛ̃pyte/ *v.t.* **~er à,** impute to. **~able** *a.* ascribable (**à,** to).

inabordable /inabɔrdabl/ *a.* (*prix*) prohibitive.

inacceptable /inaksɛptabl/ *a.* unacceptable; (*scandaleux*) outrageous.

inaccessible /inaksesibl/ *a.* inaccessible.

inaccoutumé /inakutyme/ *a.* unaccustomed.

inachevé /inaʃve/ *a.* unfinished.

inacti|f, ~ve /inaktif, -v/ *a.* inactive.

inaction /inaksjɔ̃/ *n.f.* inactivity.

inadapté, ~e /inadapte/ *n.m., f.* (*psych.*) maladjusted person.

inadéquat, ~e /inadekwa, -t/ *a.* inadequate.

inadmissible /inadmisibl/ *a.* unacceptable.

inadvertance /inadvɛrtɑ̃s/ *n.f.* **par ~,** by mistake.

inaltérable /inalterabl/ *a.* stable, that does not deteriorate; (*sentiment*) unfailing.

inanimé /inanime/ *a.* (*évanoui*) unconscious; (*mort*) lifeless; (*matière*) inanimate.

inaperçu /inapɛrsy/ *a.* unnoticed.

inappréciable /inapresjabl/ *a.* invaluable.

inapte /inapt/ *a.* unsuited (**à,** to). **~ à faire,** incapable of doing.

inarticulé /inartikyle/ *a.* inarticulate.

inassouvi /inasuvi/ *a.* unsatisfied.

inattendu /inatɑ̃dy/ *a.* unexpected.

inattenti|f, ~ve /inatɑ̃tif, -v/ *a.* inattentive (**à,** to).

inattention /inatɑ̃sjɔ̃/ *n.f.* inattention.

inaugur|er /inɔgyre/ *v.t.* inaugurate. **~ation** *n.f.* inauguration.

inaugur|al (*m. pl.* **~aux**) /inɔgyral, -o/ *a.* inaugural.

incalculable /ɛ̃kalkylabl/ *a.* incalculable.

incapable /ɛ̃kapabl/ *a.* incapable (**de qch.,** of sth.). **~ de faire,** unable to do, incapable of doing. ● *n.m./f.* incompetent.

incapacité /ɛ̃kapasite/ *n.f.* incapacity. **dans l' ~ de,** unable to.

incarcérer /ɛ̃karsere/ *v.t.* incarcerate.

incarn|er /ɛ̃karne/ *v.t.* embody. **~ation** *n.f.* embodiment, incarnation. **~é** *a.* (*ongle*) ingrowing.

incartade /ɛ̃kartad/ *n.f.* indiscretion, misdeed, prank.

incassable /ɛ̃kɑsabl/ *a.* unbreakable.

incendiaire /ɛ̃sɑ̃djɛr/ *a.* incendiary, (*propos*) inflammatory. ● *n.m./f.* arsonist.

incend|ie /ɛ̃sɑ̃di/ *n.m.* fire. **~ie criminel,** arson. **~ier** *v.t.* set fire to.

incert|ain, ~aine /ɛ̃sɛrtɛ̃, -ɛn/ *a.* uncertain; (*contour*) vague. **~itude** *n.f.* uncertainty.

incessamment /ɛ̃sɛsamɑ̃/ *adv.* shortly.

incessant, ~e /ɛ̃sɛsɑ̃, -t/ *a.* incessant.

incest|e /ɛ̃sɛst/ *n.m.* incest. **~ueux, ~ueuse** *a.* incestuous.

inchangé /ɛ̃ʃɑ̃ʒe/ *a.* unchanged.

incidence /ɛ̃sidɑ̃s/ *n.f.* effect.

incident /ɛ̃sidɑ̃/ *n.m.* incident. **~ technique,** technical hitch.

incinér|er /ɛ̃sinere/ *v.t.* incinerate; (*mort*) cremate. **~ateur** *n.m.* incinerator.

incis|er /ɛ̃size/ *v.t.* (*abcès etc.*) lance. **~ion** *n.f.* lancing; (*entaille*) incision.

incisi|f, ~ve /ɛ̃sizif, -v/ *a.* incisive.

incit|er /ɛ̃site/ *v.t.* incite (**à,** to). **~ation** *n.f.* incitement.

inclinaison /ɛ̃klinɛzɔ̃/ *n.f.* incline; (*de la tête*) tilt.

inclination[1] /ɛ̃klinɑsjɔ̃/ *n.f.* (*penchant*) inclination.

inclin|er /ɛ̃kline/ *v.t.* tilt, lean; (*courber*) bend; (*inciter*) encourage (**à,** to). ● *v.i.* **~er à,** be inclined to. **s'~er** *v. pr.* (*se courber*) bow down; (*céder*) give in; (*chemin*) slope. **~er la tête,** (*approuver*) nod; (*révérence*) bow. **~ation**[2] *n.f.* (*de la tête*) nod; (*du buste*) bow.

incl|ure /ɛ̃klyr/ *v.t.* include; (*enfermer*) enclose. **jusqu'au lundi ~us,** up to and including Monday. **~usion** *n.f.* inclusion.

incognito /ɛ̃kɔɲito/ *adv.* incognito.

incohéren|t, ~te /ɛ̃kɔerɑ̃, -t/ *a.* incoherent. **~ce** *n.f.* incoherence.

incollable /ɛ̃kɔlabl/ *a.* **il est ~,** he can't be stumped.

incolore /ɛ̃kɔlɔr/ *a.* colourless; (*crème, verre*) clear.

incomber /ɛ̃kɔ̃be/ *v.i.* **il vous/***etc.* **incombe de,** it is your/*etc.* responsibility to.

incombustible /ɛ̃kɔ̃bystibl/ *a.* incombustible.

incommode /ɛ̃kɔmɔd/ *a.* awkward.

incommoder /ɛ̃kɔmɔde/ *v.t.* inconvenience.

incomparable /ɛ̃kɔ̃parabl/ *a.* incomparable.

incompatib|le /ɛ̃kɔ̃patibl/ *a.* incompatible. **~ilité** *n.f.* incompatibility.

incompéten|t, ~te /ɛ̃kɔ̃petɑ̃, -t/ *a.* incompetent. **~ce** *n.f.* incompetence.

incompl|et, ~ète /ɛ̃kɔ̃plɛ, -t/ *a.* incomplete.

incompréhensible /ɛ̃kɔ̃preɑ̃sibl/ *a.* incomprehensible.

incompréhension /ɛ̃kɔ̃preɑ̃sjɔ̃/ *n.f.* lack of understanding.

incompris, ~e /ɛ̃kɔ̃pri, -z/ *a.* misunderstood.

inconcevable /ɛ̃kɔ̃svabl/ *a.* inconceivable.

inconciliable /ɛ̃kɔ̃siljabl/ *a.* irreconcilable.

inconditionnel, ~le /ɛ̃kɔ̃disjɔnɛl/ *a.* unconditional.

inconduite /ɛ̃kɔ̃dɥit/ *n.f.* loose behaviour.

inconfort /ɛ̃kɔ̃fɔr/ *n.m.* discomfort. **~able** /-tabl/ *a.* uncomfortable.

incongru /ɛ̃kɔ̃gry/ *a.* unseemly.

inconnu, ~e /ɛ̃kɔny/ *a.* unknown (**à,** to). ● *n.m., f.* stranger. ● *n.m.* **l'~,** the unknown. ● *n.f.* unknown (quantity).

inconsc|ient, ~iente /ɛ̃kɔ̃sjɑ̃, -t/ *a.* unconscious (**de,** of); (*fou*) mad. ● *n.m.* (*psych.*) subconscious. **~iemment** /-jamɑ̃/ *adv.* unconsciously. **~ience** *n.f.* unconsciousness; (*folie*) madness.

inconsidéré /ɛ̃kɔ̃sidere/ *a.* thoughtless.

inconsistant, ~e /ɛ̃kɔ̃sistɑ̃, -t/ *a.* (*fig.*) flimsy.

inconsolable /ɛ̃kɔ̃sɔlabl/ *a.* inconsolable.

inconstan|t, ~te /ɛ̃kɔ̃stɑ̃, -t/ *a.* fickle. **~ce** *n.f.* fickleness.

incontest|able /ɛ̃kɔ̃tɛstabl/ *a.* indisputable. **~é** *a.* undisputed.

incontinen|t, ~te /ɛ̃kɔ̃tinɑ̃, -t/ *a.* incontinent. **~ce** *n.f.* incontinence.

incontrôlable /ɛ̃kɔ̃trolabl/ *a.* unverifiable.

inconvenan|t, ~te /ɛ̃kɔ̃vnɑ̃, -t/ *a.* improper. **~ce** *n.f.* impropriety.

inconvénient /ɛ̃kɔ̃venjɑ̃/ *n.m.* disadvantage; (*risque*) risk; (*objection*) objection.

incorpor|er /ɛ̃kɔrpɔre/ *v.t.* incorporate; (*mil.*) enlist. **~ation** *n.f.* incorporation; (*mil.*) enlistment.

incorrect /ɛ̃kɔrɛkt/ *a.* (*faux*) incorrect; (*malséant*) improper; (*impoli*) impolite.

incorrigible /ɛ̃kɔriʒibl/ *a.* incorrigible.

incrédul|e /ɛ̃kredyl/ *a.* incredulous. **~ité** *n.f.* incredulity.

increvable /ɛ̃krəvabl/ *a.* (*fam.*) tireless.

incriminer /ɛ̃krimine/ *v.t.* incriminate.

incroyable /ɛ̃krwajabl/ *a.* incredible.

incroyant, ~e /ɛ̃krwajɑ̃, -t/ *n.m., f.* non-believer.

incrust|er /ɛ̃kryste/ *v.t.* (*décorer*) inlay (**de**, with). **s'~er** (*invité: péj.*) take root. **~ation** *n.f.* inlay.

incubateur /ɛ̃kybatœr/ *n.m.* incubator.

inculp|er /ɛ̃kylpe/ *v.t.* charge (**de**, with). **~ation** *n.f.* charge. **~é, ~ée** *n.m., f.* accused.

inculquer /ɛ̃kylke/ *v.t.* instil (**à**, into).

inculte /ɛ̃kylt/ *a.* uncultivated; (*personne*) uneducated.

incurable /ɛ̃kyrabl/ *a.* incurable.

incursion /ɛ̃kyrsjɔ̃/ *n.f.* incursion.

incurver /ɛ̃kyrve/ *v.t.*, **s'~** *v. pr.* curve.

Inde /ɛ̃d/ *n.f.* India.

indécen|t, ~te /ɛ̃desɑ̃, -t/ *a.* indecent. **~ce** *n.f.* indecency.

indéchiffrable /ɛ̃deʃifrabl/ *a.* indecipherable.

indécis, ~e /ɛ̃desi, -z/ *a.* indecisive; (*qui n'a pas encore pris de décision*) undecided. **~ion** /-izjɔ̃/ *n.f.* indecision.

indéfendable /ɛ̃defɑ̃dabl/ *a.* indefensible.

indéfini /ɛ̃defini/ *a.* indefinite; (*vague*) undefined. **~ment** *adv.* indefinitely. **~ssable** *a.* indefinable.

indélébile /ɛ̃delebil/ *a.* indelible.

indélicat, ~e /ɛ̃delika, -t/ *a.* (*malhonnête*) unscrupulous.

indemne /ɛ̃dɛmn/ *a.* unharmed.

indemniser /ɛ̃dɛmnize/ *v.t.* compensate (**de**, for).

indemnité /ɛ̃dɛmnite/ *n.f.* indemnity; (*allocation*) allowance. **~s de licenciement,** redundancy payment.

indéniable /ɛ̃denjabl/ *a.* undeniable.

indépend|ant, ~ante /ɛ̃depɑ̃dɑ̃, -t/ *a.* independent. **~amment** *adv.* independently. **~amment de,** apart from. **~ance** *n.f.* independence.

indescriptible /ɛ̃dɛskriptibl/ *a.* indescribable.

indésirable /ɛ̃dezirabl/ *a.* & *n.m./f.* undesirable.

indestructible /ɛ̃dɛstryktibl/ *a.* indestructible.

indétermination /ɛ̃detɛrminɑsjɔ̃/ *n.f.* indecision.

indéterminé /ɛ̃detɛrmine/ *a.* unspecified.

index /ɛ̃dɛks/ *n.m.* forefinger; (*liste*) index. **~er** *v.t.* index.

indic /ɛ̃dik/ (*fam.*) grass.

indica|teur, ~trice /ɛ̃dikatœr, -tris/ *n.m., f.* (police) informer. ● *n.m.* (*livre*) guide; (*techn.*) indicator. **~teur des chemins de fer,** railway timetable. **~teur des rues,** street directory.

indicati|f, ~ve /ɛ̃dikatif, -v/ *a.* indicative (**de**, of). ● *n.m.* (*radio*) signature tune; (*téléphonique*) dialling code; (*gram.*) indicative.

indication /ɛ̃dikɑsjɔ̃/ *n.f.* indication; (*renseignement*) information; (*directive*) instruction.

indice /ɛ̃dis/ *n.m.* sign; (*dans une enquête*) clue; (*des prix*) index; (*de salaire*) rating.

indien, ~ne /ɛ̃djɛ̃, -jɛn/ *a.* & *n.m., f.* Indian.

indifféremment /ɛ̃diferamɑ̃/ *adv.* equally.

indifféren|t, ~te /ɛ̃diferɑ̃, -t/ *a.* indifferent (**à**, to). **ça m'est ~t,** it makes no difference to me. **~ce** *n.f.* indifference.

indigène /ɛ̃diʒɛn/ *a.* & *n.m./f.* native.

indigen|t, ~te /ɛ̃diʒɑ̃, -t/ *a.* poor **~ce** *n.f.* poverty.

indigest|e /ɛ̃diʒɛst/ *a.* indigestible. **~ion** *n.f.* indigestion.

indignation /ɛ̃diɲɑsjɔ̃/ *n.f.* indignation.

indign|e /ɛ̃diɲ/ *a.* unworthy (**de**, of); (*acte*) vile. **~ité** *n.f.* unworthiness; (*acte*) vile act.

indigner /ɛ̃diɲe/ **s'~** *v. pr.* become indignant (**de**, at).

indiqu|er /ɛ̃dike/ *v.t.* show, indicate; (*renseigner sur*) point out, tell; (*déterminer*) give, state, appoint. **~er du doigt,** point to *ou* out *ou* at. **~é** *a.* (*heure*) appointed; (*opportun*) appropriate; (*conseillé*) recommended.

indirect /ɛ̃dirɛkt/ *a.* indirect.

indiscipliné /ɛ̃disipline/ *a.* unruly.

indiscr|et, ~ète /ɛ̃diskrɛ, -t/ *a.* inquisitive. **~étion** *n.f.* indiscretion; inquisitiveness.
indiscutable /ɛ̃diskytabl/ *a.* unquestionable.
indispensable /ɛ̃dispɑ̃sabl/ *a.* indispensable. **il est ~ qu'il vienne,** it is essential that he comes.
indispos|er /ɛ̃dispoze/ *v.t.* make unwell. **~er** (*mécontenter*) antagonize. **~é** *a.* unwell. **~ition** *n.f.* indisposition.
indistinct, ~e /ɛ̃distɛ̃(kt), -ɛ̃kt/ *a.* indistinct. **~ement** /-ɛ̃ktəmɑ̃/ *adv.* indistinctly; (*également*) without distinction.
individ|u /ɛ̃dividy/ *n.m.* individual. **~ualiste** *n.m./f.* individualist.
individuel, ~le /ɛ̃dividɥɛl/ *a.* individual; (*opinion*) personal. **chambre ~le,** single room. **maison ~le,** private house. **~lement** *adv.* individually.
indivisible /ɛ̃divizibl/ *a.* indivisible.
indolen|t, ~te /ɛ̃dɔlɑ̃, -t/ *a.* indolent. **~ce** *n.f.* indolence.
indolore /ɛ̃dɔlɔr/ *a.* painless.
Indonésie /ɛ̃dɔnezi/ *n.f.* Indonesia.
Indonésien, ~ne /ɛ̃dɔnezjɛ̃, -jɛn/ *a.* & *n.m., f.* Indonesian.
indu, ~e /ɛ̃dy/ *a.* **à une heure ~e,** at some ungodly hour.
induire /ɛ̃dɥir/ *v.t.* infer (**de,** from). **~ en erreur,** mislead.
indulgen|t, ~te /ɛ̃dylʒɑ̃, -t/ *a.* indulgent; (*clément*) lenient. **~ce** *n.f.* indulgence; leniency.
industr|ie /ɛ̃dystri/ *n.f.* industry. **~ialisé** *a.* industrialized.
industriel, ~le /ɛ̃dystrijɛl/ *a.* industrial. ● *n.m.* industrialist. **~lement** *adv.* industrially.
inébranlable /inebrɑ̃labl/ *a.* unshakeable.
inédit, ~e /inedi, -t/ *a.* unpublished; (*fig.*) original.
inefficace /inefikas/ *a.* ineffective.
inég|al (*m. pl.* **~aux**) /inegal, -o/ *a.* unequal; (*irrégulier*) uneven. **~alé** *a.* unequalled. **~alable** *a.* matchless. **~alité** *n.f.* (*injustice*) inequality; (*irrégularité*) unevenness; (*différence*) difference (**de,** between).
inéluctable /inelyktabl/ *a.* inescapable.
inept|e /inɛpt/ *a.* inept, absurd. **~ie** /inɛpsi/ *n.f.* ineptitude.
inépuisable /inepɥizabl/ *a.* inexhaustible.
inert|e /inɛrt/ *a.* inert; (*mort*) lifeless. **~ie** /inɛrsi/ *n.f.* inertia.
inespéré /inɛspere/ *a.* unhoped for.
inestimable /inɛstimabl/ *a.* priceless.
inévitable /inevitabl/ *a.* inevitable.
inexact, ~e /inɛgza(kt), -akt/ *a.* (*imprécis*) inaccurate; (*incorrect*) incorrect.
inexcusable /inɛkskyzabl/ *a.* unforgivable.
inexistant, ~e /inɛgzistɑ̃, -t/ *a.* non-existent.
inexorable /inɛgzɔrabl/ *a.* inexorable.
inexpérience /inɛksperjɑ̃s/ *n.f.* inexperience.
inexpli|cable /inɛksplikabl/ *a.* inexplicable. **~qué** *a.* unexplained.
in extremis /inɛkstremis/ *adv.* & *a.* (*par nécessité*) (taken/done etc.) as a last resort; (*au dernier moment*) (at the) last minute.
inextricable /inɛkstrikabl/ *a.* inextricable.
infaillible /ɛ̃fajibl/ *a.* infallible.
infâme /ɛ̃fɑm/ *a.* vile.
infamie /ɛ̃fami/ *n.f.* infamy; (*action*) vile action.
infanterie /ɛ̃fɑ̃tri/ *n.f.* infantry.
infantile /ɛ̃fɑ̃til/ *a.* infantile.
infantilisme /ɛ̃fɑ̃tilism/ *n.m.* infantilism. **faire de l'~,** be childish.
infarctus /ɛ̃farktys/ *n.m.* coronary (thrombosis).
infatigable /ɛ̃fatigabl/ *a.* tireless.
infatué /ɛ̃fatɥe/ *a.* **~ de sa personne,** full of himself.
infect /ɛ̃fɛkt/ *a.* revolting.
infect|er /ɛ̃fɛkte/ *v.t.* infect. **s'~er** *v. pr.* become infected. **~ion** /-ksjɔ̃/ *n.f.* infection.
infectieu|x, ~se /ɛ̃fɛksjø, -z/ *a.* infectious.
inférieur, ~e /ɛ̃ferjœr/ *a.* (*plus bas*) lower; (*moins bon*) inferior (**à,** to). ● *n.m., f.* inferior. **~ à,** (*plus petit que*) smaller than.
infériorité /ɛ̃ferjɔrite/ *n.f.* inferiority.
infern|al (*m. pl.* **~aux**) /ɛ̃fɛrnal, -o/ *a.* infernal.
infester /ɛ̃fɛste/ *v.t.* infest.
infid|èle /ɛ̃fidɛl/ *a.* unfaithful. **~élité** *n.f.* unfaithfulness; (*acte*) infidelity.
infiltr|er (s') /(s)ɛ̃filtre/ *v. pr.* **s'~er (dans),** (*personnes, idées, etc.*) infil-

trate; (*liquide*) percolate. **~ation** *n.f.* infiltration.

infime /ɛ̃fim/ *a.* tiny, minute.

infini /ɛ̃fini/ *a.* infinite. ● *n.m.* infinity. **à l'~,** endlessly. **~ment** *adv.* infinitely.

infinité /ɛ̃finite/ *n.f.* **une ~ de,** an infinite amount of.

infinitésimal /ɛ̃finitezimal/ *a.* infinitesimal.

infinitif /ɛ̃finitif/ *n.m.* infinitive.

infirm|e /ɛ̃firm/ *a.* & *n.m./f.* disabled (person). **~ité** *n.f.* disability.

infirmer /ɛ̃firme/ *v.t.* invalidate.

infirm|erie /ɛ̃firməri/ *n.f.* sickbay, infirmary. **~ier** *n.m.* (male) nurse. **~ière** *n.f.* nurse. **~ière-chef,** sister.

inflammable /ɛ̃flamabl/ *a.* (in)flammable.

inflammation /ɛ̃flamɑsjɔ̃/ *n.f.* inflammation.

inflation /ɛ̃flɑsjɔ̃/ *n.f.* inflation.

inflexible /ɛ̃flɛksibl/ *a.* inflexible.

inflexion /ɛ̃flɛksjɔ̃/ *n.f.* inflexion.

infliger /ɛ̃fliʒe/ *v.t.* inflict; (*sanction*) impose.

influen|ce /ɛ̃flyɑ̃s/ *n.f.* influence. **~çable** *a.* easily influenced. **~cer** *v.t.* influence.

influent, ~e /ɛ̃flyɑ̃, -t/ *a.* influential.

influer /ɛ̃flye/ *v.i.* **~ sur,** influence.

info /ɛ̃fo/ *n.f.* (some) news. **les ~s,** the news.

informa|teur, ~trice /ɛ̃fɔrmatœr, -tris/ *n.m., f.* informant.

informaticien, ~ne /ɛ̃fɔrmatisjɛ̃, -jɛn/ *n.m., f.* computer scientist.

information /ɛ̃fɔrmɑsjɔ̃/ *n.f.* information; (*jurid.*) inquiry. **une ~,** (some) information; (*nouvelle*) (some) news. **les ~s,** the news.

informati|que /ɛ̃fɔrmatik/ *n.f.* computer science; (*techniques*) data processing. **~ser** *v.t.* computerize.

informe /ɛ̃fɔrm/ *a.* shapeless.

informer /ɛ̃fɔrme/ *v.t.* inform (**de,** about, of). **s'~** *v. pr.* enquire (**de,** about).

infortune /ɛ̃fɔrtyn/ *n.f.* misfortune.

infraction /ɛ̃fraksjɔ̃/ *n.f.* offence. **~ à,** breach of.

infranchissable /ɛ̃frɑ̃ʃisabl/ *a.* impassable; (*fig.*) insuperable.

infrarouge /ɛ̃fraruʒ/ *a.* infra-red.

infrastructure /ɛ̃frastryktyr/ *n.f.* infrastructure.

infructueu|x, ~se /ɛ̃fryktɥø, -z/ *a.* fruitless.

infus|er /ɛ̃fyze/ *v.t./i.* infuse, brew. **~ion** *n.f.* herb-tea, infusion.

ingénier (s') /(s)ɛ̃ʒenje/ *v. pr.* **s'~ à,** strive to.

ingénieur /ɛ̃ʒenjœr/ *n.m.* engineer.

ingén|ieux, ~ieuse /ɛ̃ʒenjø, -z/ *a.* ingenious. **~iosité** *n.f.* ingenuity.

ingénu /ɛ̃ʒeny/ *a.* naïve.

ingér|er (s') /(s)ɛ̃ʒere/ *v. pr.* **s'~er dans,** interfere in. **~ence** *n.f.* interference.

ingrat, ~e /ɛ̃gra, -t/ *a.* ungrateful; (*pénible*) thankless; (*disgracieux*) unattractive. **~itude** /-tityd/ *n.f.* ingratitude.

ingrédient /ɛ̃gredjɑ̃/ *n.m.* ingredient.

ingurgiter /ɛ̃gyrʒite/ *v.t.* swallow.

inhabité /inabite/ *a.* uninhabited.

inhabituel, ~le /inabitɥɛl/ *a.* unusual.

inhalation /inalɑsjɔ̃/ *n.f.* inhaling.

inhérent, ~e /inerɑ̃, -t/ *a.* inherent (**à,** in).

inhibition /inibisjɔ̃/ *n.f.* inhibition.

inhospital|ier, ~ière /inɔspitalje, -jɛr/ *a.* inhospitable.

inhumain, ~e /inymɛ̃, -ɛn/ *a.* inhuman.

inhum|er /inyme/ *v.t.* bury. **~ation** *n.f.* burial.

inimaginable /inimaʒinabl/ *a.* unimaginable.

inimitié /inimitje/ *n.f.* enmity.

ininterrompu /inɛ̃tɛrɔ̃py/ *a.* continuous, uninterrupted.

iniqu|e /inik/ *a.* iniquitous. **~ité** *n.f.* iniquity.

init|ial (*m. pl.* **~iaux**) /inisjal, -jo/ *a.* initial. **~ialement** *adv.* initially.

initiale /inisjal/ *n.f.* initial.

initialis|er /inisjalize/ (*comput.*) format. **~ation** *n.f.* formatting.

initiative /inisjativ/ *n.f.* initiative.

init|ier /inisje/ *v.t.* initiate (**à,** into). **s'~ier** *v. pr.* become initiated (**à,** into). **~iateur, ~iatrice** *n.m., f.* initiator. **~iation** *n.f.* initiation.

inject|er /ɛ̃ʒɛkte/ *v.t.* inject. **~é de sang,** bloodshot. **~ion** /-ksjɔ̃/ *n.f.* injection.

injur|e /ɛ̃ʒyr/ *n.f.* insult. **~ier** *v.t.* insult. **~ieux, ~ieuse** *a.* insulting.

injust|e /ɛ̃ʒyst/ *a.* unjust, unfair. **~ice** *n.f.* injustice.

inlassable /ɛ̃lɑsabl/ *a.* tireless.

inné /ine/ *a.* innate, inborn.

innocen|t, ~te /inɔsɑ̃, -t/ *a.* & *n.m., f.* innocent. **~ce** *n.f.* innocence.

innocenter /inɔsɑ̃te/ *v.t.* (*disculper*) clear, prove innocent.
innombrable /inɔ̃brabl/ *a.* countless.
innov|er /inɔve/ *v.i.* innovate. **~ateur, ~atrice** *n.m., f.* innovator. **~ation** *n.f.* innovation.
inoccupé /inɔkype/ *a.* unoccupied.
inoculer /inɔkyle/ *v.t.* inoculate.
inodore /inɔdɔr/ *a.* odourless.
inoffensi|f, ~ve /inɔfɑ̃sif, -v/ *a.* harmless.
inond|er /inɔ̃de/ *v.t.* flood; (*mouiller*) soak; (*envahir*) inundate (**de,** with). **~é de soleil,** bathed in sunlight. **~ation** *n.f.* flood; (*action*) flooding.
inopérant, ~e /inɔperɑ̃, -t/ *a.* inoperative.
inopiné /inɔpine/ *a.* unexpected.
inopportun, ~e /inɔpɔrtœ̃, -yn/ *a.* inopportune.
inoubliable /inublijabl/ *a.* unforgettable.
inouï /inwi/ *a.* incredible.
inox /inɔks/ *n.m.* (P.) stainless steel.
inoxydable /inɔksidabl/ *a.* **acier ~,** stainless steel.
inqualifiable /ɛ̃kalifjabl/ *a.* unspeakable.
inqu|iet, ~iète /ɛ̃kjɛ, -jɛt/ *a.* worried. ● *n.m., f.* worrier.
inquiét|er /ɛ̃kjete/ *v.t.* worry. **s'~er** worry (**de,** about). **~ant, ~ante** *a.* worrying.
inquiétude /ɛ̃kjetyd/ *n.f.* anxiety, worry.
inquisition /ɛ̃kizisjɔ̃/ *n.f.* inquisition.
insaisissable /ɛ̃sezisabl/ *a.* indefinable.
insalubre /ɛ̃salybr/ *a.* unhealthy.
insanité /ɛ̃sanite/ *n.f.* insanity.
insatiable /ɛ̃sasjabl/ *a.* insatiable.
insatisfaisant, ~e /ɛ̃satisfəzɑ̃, -t/ *a.* unsatisfactory.
insatisfait, ~e /ɛ̃satisfɛ, -t/ *a.* (*mécontent*) dissatisfied; (*frustré*) unfulfilled.
inscription /ɛ̃skripsjɔ̃/ *n.f.* inscription; (*immatriculation*) enrolment.
inscrire† /ɛ̃skrir/ *v.t.* write (down); (*graver, tracer*) inscribe; (*personne*) enrol; (*sur une liste*) put down. **s'~** *v. pr.* put one's name down. **s'~ à,** (*école*) enrol at; (*club, parti*) join; (*examen*) enter for. **s'~ dans le cadre de,** come within the framework of.
insecte /ɛ̃sɛkt/ *n.m.* insect.
insecticide /ɛ̃sɛktisid/ *n.m.* insecticide.
insécurité /ɛ̃sekyrite/ *n.f.* insecurity.
insensé /ɛ̃sɑ̃se/ *a.* mad.
insensib|le /ɛ̃sɑ̃sibl/ *a.* insensitive (**à,** to); (*graduel*) imperceptible. **~ilité** *n.f.* insensitivity.
inséparable /ɛ̃separabl/ *a.* inseparable.
insérer /ɛ̃sere/ *v.t.* insert. **s'~ dans,** be part of.
insidieu|x, ~se /ɛ̃sidjø, -z/ *a.* insidious.
insigne /ɛ̃siɲ/ *n.m.* badge. **~(s),** (*d'une fonction*) insignia.
insignifian|t, ~te /ɛ̃siɲifjɑ̃, -t/ *a.* insignificant. **~ce** *n.f.* insignificance.
insinuation /ɛ̃sinɥasjɔ̃/ *n.f.* insinuation.
insinuer /ɛ̃sinɥe/ *v.t.* insinuate. **s'~ dans,** penetrate.
insipide /ɛ̃sipid/ *a.* insipid.
insistan|t, ~te /ɛ̃sistɑ̃, -t/ *a.* insistent. **~ce** *n.f.* insistence.
insister /ɛ̃siste/ *v.i.* insist (**pour faire,** on doing). **~ sur,** stress.
insolation /ɛ̃sɔlasjɔ̃/ *n.f.* (*méd.*) sunstroke.
insolen|t, ~te /ɛ̃sɔlɑ̃, -t/ *a.* insolent. **~ce** *n.f.* insolence.
insolite /ɛ̃sɔlit/ *a.* unusual.
insoluble /ɛ̃sɔlybl/ *a.* insoluble.
insolvable /ɛ̃sɔlvabl/ *a.* insolvent.
insomnie /ɛ̃sɔmni/ *n.f.* insomnia.
insonoriser /ɛ̃sɔnɔrize/ *v.t.* soundproof.
insoucian|t, ~te /ɛ̃susjɑ̃, -t/ *a.* carefree. **~ce** *n.f.* unconcern.
insoumission /ɛ̃sumisjɔ̃/ *n.f.* rebelliousness.
insoupçonnable /ɛ̃supsɔnabl/ *a.* undetectable.
insoutenable /ɛ̃sutnabl/ *a.* unbearable; (*argument*) untenable.
inspec|ter /ɛ̃spɛkte/ *v.t.* inspect. **~teur, ~trice** *n.m., f.* inspector. **~tion** /-ksjɔ̃/ *n.f.* inspection.
inspir|er /ɛ̃spire/ *v.t.* inspire. ● *v.i.* breathe in. **~er à qn.,** inspire s.o. with. **s'~er de,** be inspired by. **~ation** *n.f.* inspiration; (*respiration*) breath.
instab|le /ɛ̃stabl/ *a.* unstable; (*temps*) unsettled; (*meuble, équilibre*) unsteady. **~ilité** *n.f.* instability; unsteadiness.
install|er /ɛ̃stale/ *v.t.* install; (*gaz, meuble*) put in; (*étagère*) put up;

(*équiper*) fit out. **s'~er** *v. pr.* settle (down); (*emménager*) settle in. **s'~er comme,** set o.s. up as. **~ation** *n.f.* installation; (*de local*) fitting out; (*de locataire*) settling in. **~ations** *n.f. pl.* (*appareils*) fittings.

instance /ɛ̃stɑ̃s/ *n.f.* authority; (*prière*) entreaty. **avec ~,** with insistence. **en ~,** pending. **en ~ de,** in the course of, on the point of.

instant /ɛ̃stɑ̃/ *n.m.* moment, instant. **à l'~,** this instant.

instantané /ɛ̃stɑ̃tane/ *a.* instantaneous; (*café*) instant.

instar /ɛ̃star/ *n.m.* **à l'~ de,** like.

instaur|er /ɛ̃store/ *v.t.* institute. **~ation** *n.f.* institution.

instiga|teur, ~trice /ɛ̃stigatœr, -tris/ *n.m., f.* instigator. **~tion** /-ɑsjɔ̃/ *n.f.* instigation.

instinct /ɛ̃stɛ̃/ *n.m.* instinct. **d'~,** instinctively.

instincti|f, ~ve /ɛ̃stɛ̃ktif, -v/ *a.* instinctive. **~vement** *adv.* instinctively.

instit /ɛ̃stit/ *n.m./f.* (*fam.*) teacher.

instituer /ɛ̃stitɥe/ *v.t.* establish.

institut /ɛ̃stity/ *n.m.* institute. **~ de beauté,** beauty parlour. **~ universitaire de technologie,** polytechnic, technical college.

institu|teur, ~trice /ɛ̃stitytœr, -tris/ *n.m., f.* primary-school teacher.

institution /ɛ̃stitysjɔ̃/ *n.f.* institution; (*école*) private school.

instructi|f, ~ve /ɛ̃stryktif, -v/ *a.* instructive.

instruction /ɛ̃stryksjɔ̃/ *n.f.* education; (*document*) directive. **~s,** (*ordres, mode d'emploi*) instructions.

instruire† /ɛ̃strɥir/ *v.t.* teach, educate. **~ de,** inform of. **s'~** *v. pr.* educate o.s. **s'~ de,** enquire about.

instruit, ~e /ɛ̃strɥi, -t/ *a.* educated.

instrument /ɛ̃strymɑ̃/ *n.m.* instrument; (*outil*) implement.

insu /ɛ̃sy/ *n.m.* **à l'~ de,** without the knowledge of.

insubordination /ɛ̃sybɔrdinɑsjɔ̃/ *n.f.* insubordination.

insuffisan|t, ~te /ɛ̃syfizɑ̃, -t/ *a.* inadequate; (*en nombre*) insufficient. **~ce** *n.f.* inadequacy.

insulaire /ɛ̃sylɛr/ *a.* island. ● *n.m./f.* islander.

insuline /ɛ̃sylin/ *n.f.* insulin.

insult|e /ɛ̃sylt/ *n.f.* insult. **~er** *v.t.* insult.

insupportable /ɛ̃sypɔrtabl/ *a.* unbearable.

insurg|er (s') /(s)ɛ̃syrʒe/ *v. pr.* rebel. **~é, ~ée** *a.* & *n.m., f.* rebel.

insurmontable /ɛ̃syrmɔ̃tabl/ *a.* insurmountable.

insurrection /ɛ̃syrɛksjɔ̃/ *n.f.* insurrection.

intact /ɛ̃takt/ *a.* intact.

intangible /ɛ̃tɑ̃ʒibl/ *a.* intangible.

intarissable /ɛ̃tarisabl/ *a.* inexhaustible.

intégr|al (*m. pl.* **~aux**) /ɛ̃tegral, -o/ *a.* complete; (*édition*) unabridged. **~alement** *adv.* in full. **~alité** *n.f.* whole. **dans son ~alité,** in full.

intégrant, ~e /ɛ̃tɛgrɑ̃, -t/ *a.* **faire partie ~e de,** be part and parcel of.

intègre /ɛ̃tɛgr/ *a.* upright.

intégr|er /ɛ̃tegre/ *v.t.,* **s'~er** *v. pr.* integrate. **~ation** *n.f.* integration.

intégri|ste /ɛ̃tɛgrist/ *a.* fundamentalist. **~sme** /-sm/ *n.m.* fundamentalism.

intégrité /ɛ̃tegrite/ *n.f.* integrity.

intellect /ɛ̃telɛkt/ *n.m.* intellect. **~uel, ~uelle** *a.* & *n.m., f.* intellectual.

intelligence /ɛ̃teliʒɑ̃s/ *n.f.* intelligence; (*compréhension*) understanding; (*complicité*) complicity.

intellig|ent, ~ente /ɛ̃teliʒɑ̃, -t/ *a.* intelligent. **~emment** /-amɑ̃/ *adv.* intelligently.

intelligible /ɛ̃teliʒibl/ *a.* intelligible.

intempéries /ɛ̃tɑ̃peri/ *n.f. pl.* severe weather.

intempesti|f, ~ve /ɛ̃tɑ̃pɛstif, -v/ *a.* untimely.

intenable /ɛ̃tnabl/ *a.* unbearable; (*enfant*) impossible.

intendan|t, ~te /ɛ̃tɑ̃dɑ̃, -t/ *n.m.* (*mil.*) quartermaster. ● *n.m., f.* (*scol.*) bursar. **~ce** *n.f.* (*scol.*) bursar's office.

intens|e /ɛ̃tɑ̃s/ *a.* intense; (*circulation*) heavy. **~ément** *adv.* intensely. **~ifier** *v.t.,* **s'~ifier** *v. pr.* intensify. **~ité** *n.f.* intensity.

intensi|f, ~ve /ɛ̃tɑ̃sif, -v/ *a.* intensive.

intenter /ɛ̃tɑ̃te/ *v.t.* **~ un procès** *ou* **une action,** institute proceedings (**à, contre,** against).

intention /ɛ̃tɑ̃sjɔ̃/ *n.f.* intention (**de faire,** of doing). **à l'~ de qn.,** for s.o. **~né** /-jɔne/ *a.* **bien/mal ~né,** well-/ill-intentioned.

intentionnel, ~le /ɛ̃tɑ̃sjɔnɛl/ *a.* intentional.

inter- /ɛ̃tɛr/ *préf.* inter-.

interaction /ɛ̃tɛraksjɔ̃/ *n.f.* interaction.

intercaler /ɛ̃tɛrkale/ *v.t.* insert.

intercéder /ɛ̃tɛrsede/ *v.i.* intercede (**en faveur de,** on behalf of).

intercept|er /ɛ̃tɛrsɛpte/ *v.t.* intercept. **~ion** /-psjɔ̃/ *n.f.* interception.

interchangeable /ɛ̃tɛrʃɑ̃ʒabl/ *a.* interchangeable.

interdiction /ɛ̃tɛrdiksjɔ̃/ *n.f.* ban. **~ de fumer,** no smoking.

interdire† /ɛ̃tɛrdir/ *v.t.* forbid; (*officiellement*) ban, prohibit. **~ à qn. de faire,** forbid s.o. to do.

interdit, ~e /ɛ̃tɛrdi, -t/ *a.* (*étonné*) nonplussed.

intéressant, ~e /ɛ̃terɛsɑ̃, -t/ *a.* interesting; (*avantageux*) attractive.

intéressé, ~e /ɛ̃terese/ *a.* (*en cause*) concerned; (*pour profiter*) self-interested. ● *n.m., f.* person concerned.

intéresser /ɛ̃terese/ *v.t.* interest; (*concerner*) concern. **s'~ à,** be interested in.

intérêt /ɛ̃terɛ/ *n.m.* interest; (*égoïsme*) self-interest. **~(s),** (*comm.*) interest. **vous avez ~ à,** it is in your interest to.

interférence /ɛ̃tɛrferɑ̃s/ *n.f.* interference.

intérieur /ɛ̃terjœr/ *a.* inner, inside; (*vol, politique*) domestic; (*vie, calme*) inner. ● *n.m.* interior; (*de boîte, tiroir*) inside. **à l'~ (de),** inside; (*fig.*) within. **~ement** *adv.* inwardly.

intérim /ɛ̃terim/ *n.m.* interim. **assurer l'~,** deputize (**de,** for). **par ~,** acting. **faire de l'~,** temp. **~aire** *a.* temporary, interim.

interjection /ɛ̃tɛrʒɛksjɔ̃/ *n.f.* interjection.

interlocu|teur, ~trice /ɛ̃tɛrlɔkytœr, -tris/ *n.m., f.* **son ~teur,** the person one is speaking to.

interloqué /ɛ̃tɛrlɔke/ *a.* **être ~,** be taken aback.

intermède /ɛ̃tɛrmɛd/ *n.m.* interlude.

intermédiaire /ɛ̃tɛrmedjɛr/ *a.* intermediate. ● *n.m./f.* intermediary.

interminable /ɛ̃tɛrminabl/ *a.* endless.

intermittence /ɛ̃tɛrmitɑ̃s/ *n.f.* **par ~,** intermittently.

intermittent, ~e /ɛ̃tɛrmitɑ̃, -t/ *a.* intermittent.

internat /ɛ̃tɛrna/ *n.m.* boarding-school.

internation|al (*m. pl.* **~aux**) /ɛ̃tɛrnasjɔnal, -o/ *a.* international.

interne /ɛ̃tɛrn/ *a.* internal. ● *n.m./f.* (*scol.*) boarder.

intern|er /ɛ̃tɛrne/ *v.t.* (*pol.*) intern; (*méd.*) confine. **~ement** *n.m.* (*pol.*) internment.

interpell|er /ɛ̃tɛrpəle/ *v.t.* shout to; (*apostropher*) shout at; (*interroger*) question. **~ation** *n.f.* (*pol.*) questioning.

interphone /ɛ̃tɛrfɔn/ *n.m.* intercom.

interposer (s') /(s)ɛ̃tɛrpoze/ *v. pr.* intervene.

interpr|ète /ɛ̃tɛrprɛt/ *n.m./f.* interpreter; (*artiste*) performer. **~étariat** *n.m.* interpreting.

interprét|er /ɛ̃tɛrprete/ *v.t.* interpret; (*jouer*) play; (*chanter*) sing. **~ation** *n.f.* interpretation; (*d'artiste*) performance.

interroga|teur, ~trice /ɛ̃tɛrɔgatœr, -tris/ *a.* questioning.

interrogati|f, ~ve /ɛ̃tɛrɔgatif, -v/ *a.* interrogative.

interrogatoire /ɛ̃terɔgatwar/ *n.m.* interrogation.

interro|ger /ɛ̃terɔʒe/ *v.t.* question; (*élève*) test. **~gateur, ~gatrice** *a.* questioning. **~gation** *n.f.* question; (*action*) questioning; (*épreuve*) test.

interr|ompre† /ɛ̃terɔ̃pr/ *v.t.* break off, interrupt; (*personne*) interrupt. **s'~ompre** *v. pr.* break off. **~upteur** *n.m.* switch. **~uption** *n.f.* interruption; (*arrêt*) break.

intersection /ɛ̃tɛrsɛksjɔ̃/ *n.f.* intersection.

interstice /ɛ̃tɛrstis/ *n.m.* crack.

interurbain /ɛ̃tɛryrbɛ̃/ *n.m.* long-distance telephone service.

intervalle /ɛ̃tɛrval/ *n.m.* space; (*temps*) interval. **dans l'~,** in the meantime.

interven|ir† /ɛ̃tɛrvənir/ *v.i.* intervene; (*survenir*) occur; (*méd.*) operate. **~tion** /-vɑ̃sjɔ̃/ *n.f.* intervention; (*méd.*) operation.

intervertir /ɛ̃tɛrvɛrtir/ *v.t.* invert.

interview /ɛ̃tɛrvju/ *n.f.* interview. **~er** /-ve/ *v.t.* interview.

intestin /ɛ̃tɛstɛ̃/ *n.m.* intestine.

intim|e /ɛ̃tim/ *a.* intimate; (*fête, vie*) private; (*dîner*) quiet. ● *n.m./f.* intimate friend. **~ement** *adv.*

intimately. **~ité** *n.f.* intimacy; (*vie privée*) privacy.
intimid|er /ɛ̃timide/ *v.t.* intimidate. **~ation** *n.f.* intimidation.
intituler /ɛ̃tityle/ *v.t.* entitle. **s'~** *v. pr.* be entitled.
intolérable /ɛ̃tɔlerabl/ *a.* intolerable.
intoléran|t, ~te /ɛ̃tɔlerɑ̃, -t/ *a.* intolerant. **~ce** *n.f.* intolerance.
intonation /ɛ̃tɔnɑsjɔ̃/ *n.f.* intonation.
intox /ɛ̃tɔks/ *n.f.* (*fam.*) brainwashing.
intoxi|quer /ɛ̃tɔsike/ *v.t.* poison; (*pol.*) brainwash. **~cation** *n.f.* poisoning; (*pol.*) brainwashing.
intraduisible /ɛ̃tradɥizibl/ *a.* untranslatable.
intraitable /ɛ̃trɛtabl/ *a.* inflexible.
intransigean|t, ~te /ɛ̃trɑ̃siʒɑ̃, -t/ *a.* intransigent. **~ce** *n.f.* intransigence.
intransiti|f, ~ve /ɛ̃trɑ̃zitif, -v/ *a.* intransitive.
intraveineu|x, ~se /ɛ̃travɛnø, -z/ *a.* intravenous.
intrépide /ɛ̃trepid/ *a.* fearless.
intrigu|e /ɛ̃trig/ *n.f.* intrigue; (*théâtre*) plot. **~er** *v.t./i.* intrigue.
intrinsèque /ɛ̃trɛ̃sɛk/ *a.* intrinsic.
introduction /ɛ̃trɔdyksjɔ̃/ *n.f.* introduction.
introduire† /ɛ̃trɔdɥir/ *v.t.* introduce, bring in; (*insérer*) put in, insert. **~ qn.**, show s.o. in. **s'~ dans**, get into, enter.
introspecti|f, ~ve /ɛ̃trɔspɛktif, -v/ *a.* introspective.
introuvable /ɛ̃truvabl/ *a.* that cannot be found.
introverti, ~e /ɛ̃trɔvɛrti/ *n.m., f.* introvert. ● *a.* introverted.
intrus, ~e /ɛ̃try, -z/ *n.m., f.* intruder. **~ion** /-zjɔ̃/ *n.f.* intrusion.
intuiti|f, ~ve /ɛ̃tɥitif, -v/ *a.* intuitive.
intuition /ɛ̃tɥisjɔ̃/ *n.f.* intuition.
inusable /inyzabl/ *a.* hard-wearing.
inusité /inyzite/ *a.* little used.
inutil|e /inytil/ *a.* useless; (*vain*) needless. **~ement** *adv.* needlessly. **~ité** *n.f.* uselessness.
inutilisable /inytilizabl/ *a.* unusable.
invalid|e /ɛ̃valid/ *a.* & *n.m./f.* disabled (person). **~ité** *n.f.* disablement.
invariable /ɛ̃varjabl/ *a.* invariable.
invasion /ɛ̃vɑzjɔ̃/ *n.f.* invasion.
invectiv|e /ɛ̃vɛktiv/ *n.f.* invective. **~er** *v.t.* abuse.
invend|able /ɛ̃vɑ̃dabl/ *a.* unsaleable. **~u** *a.* unsold.
inventaire /ɛ̃vɑ̃tɛr/ *n.m.* inventory. **faire l'~ de,** take stock of.
invent|er /ɛ̃vɑ̃te/ *v.t.* invent. **~eur** *n.m.* inventor. **~ion** /ɛ̃vɑ̃sjɔ̃/ *n.f.* invention.
inventi|f, ~ve /ɛ̃vɑ̃tif, -v/ *a.* inventive.
inverse /ɛ̃vɛrs/ *a.* opposite; (*ordre*) reverse. ● *n.m.* reverse. **~ment** /-əmɑ̃/ *adv.* conversely.
invers|er /ɛ̃vɛrse/ *v.t.* reverse, invert. **~ion** *n.f.* inversion.
investigation /ɛ̃vɛstigɑsjɔ̃/ *n.f.* investigation.
invest|ir /ɛ̃vɛstir/ *v.t.* invest. **~issement** *n.m.* (*comm.*) investment.
investiture /ɛ̃vɛstityr/ *n.f.* nomination.
invétéré /ɛ̃vetere/ *a.* inveterate.
invincible /ɛ̃vɛ̃sibl/ *a.* invincible.
invisible /ɛ̃vizibl/ *a.* invisible.
invit|er /ɛ̃vite/ *v.t.* invite (**à,** to). **~ation** *n.f.* invitation. **~é, ~ée** *n.m., f.* guest.
invivable /ɛ̃vivabl/ *a.* unbearable.
involontaire /ɛ̃vɔlɔ̃tɛr/ *a.* involuntary.
invoquer /ɛ̃vɔke/ *v.t.* call upon, invoke; (*alléguer*) plead.
invraisembl|able /ɛ̃vrɛsɑ̃blabl/ *a.* improbable; (*incroyable*) incredible. **~ance** *n.f.* improbability.
invulnérable /ɛ̃vylnerabl/ *a.* invulnerable.
iode /jɔd/ *n.m.* iodine.
ion /jɔ̃/ *n.m.* ion.
ira, irait /ira, irɛ/ *voir* aller[1].
Irak /irak/ *n.m.* Iraq. **~ien, ~ienne** *a.* & *n.m., f.* Iraqi.
Iran /irɑ̃/ *n.m.* Iran. **~ien, ~ienne** /iranjɛ̃, -jɛn/ *a.* & *n.m., f.* Iranian.
irascible /irasibl/ *a.* irascible.
iris /iris/ *n.m.* iris.
irlandais, ~e /irlɑ̃dɛ, -z/ *a.* Irish. ● *n.m., f.* Irishman, Irishwoman.
Irlande /irlɑ̃d/ *n.f.* Ireland.
iron|ie /irɔni/ *n.f.* irony. **~ique** *a.* ironic(al).
irraisonné /irɛzɔne/ *a.* irrational.
irrationnel, ~le /irasjɔnɛl/ *a.* irrational.
irréalisable /irealizabl/ *a.* (*projet*) unworkable.
irrécupérable /irekyperabl/ *a.* irretrievable, beyond recall.
irréel, ~le /ireɛl/ *a.* unreal.

irréfléchi /irefleʃi/ *a.* thoughtless.
irréfutable /irefytabl/ *a.* irrefutable.
irrégul|ier, ~ière /iregylje, -jɛr/ *a.* irregular. **~arité** *n.f.* irregularity.
irrémédiable /iremedjabl/ *a.* irreparable.
irremplaçable /irɑ̃plasabl/ *a.* irreplaceable.
irréparable /ireparabl/ *a.* beyond repair.
irréprochable /ireprɔʃabl/ *a.* flawless.
irrésistible /irezistibl/ *a.* irresistible; (*drôle*) hilarious.
irrésolu /irezɔly/ *a.* indecisive.
irrespirable /irɛspirabl/ *a.* stifling.
irresponsable /irɛspɔ̃sabl/ *a.* irresponsible.
irréversible /ireversibl/ *a.* irreversible.
irrévocable /irevɔkabl/ *a.* irrevocable.
irrigation /irigɑsjɔ̃/ *n.f.* irrigation.
irriguer /irige/ *v.t.* irrigate.
irrit|er /irite/ *v.t.* irritate. **s'~er de,** be annoyed at. **~able** *a.* irritable. **~ation** *n.f.* irritation.
irruption /irypsjɔ̃/ *n.f.* **faire ~ dans,** burst into.
Islam /islam/ *n.m.* Islam.
islamique /islamik/ *a.* Islamic.
islandais, ~e /islɑ̃dɛ, -z/ *a.* Icelandic. ● *n.m., f.* Icelander. ● *n.m.* (*lang.*) Icelandic.
Islande /islɑ̃d/ *n.f.* Iceland.
isolé /izɔle/ *a.* isolated. **~ment** *adv.* in isolation.
isol|er /izɔle/ *v.t.* isolate; (*électr.*) insulate. **s'~er** *v. pr.* isolate o.s. **~ant** *n.m.* insulating material. **~ation** *n.f.* insulation. **~ement** *n.m.* isolation.
isoloir /izɔlwar/ *n.m.* polling booth.
Isorel /izɔrɛl/ *n.m.* (P.) hardboard.
isotope /izɔtɔp/ *n.m.* isotope.
Israël /israɛl/ *n.m.* Israel.
israélien, ~ne /israeljɛ̃, -jɛn/ *a.* & *n.m., f.* Israeli.
israélite /israelit/ *a.* Jewish. ● *n.m./f.* Jew, Jewess.
issu /isy/ *a.* **être ~ de,** come from.
issue /isy/ *n.f.* exit; (*résultat*) outcome; (*fig.*) solution. **à l'~ de,** at the conclusion of. **rue** *ou* **voie sans ~,** dead end.
isthme /ism/ *n.m.* isthmus.
Italie /itali/ *n.f.* Italy.
italien, ~ne /italjɛ̃, -jɛn/ *a.* & *n.m., f.* Italian. ● *n.m.* (*lang.*) Italian.
italique /italik/ *n.m.* italics.
itinéraire /itinerɛr/ *n.m.* itinerary, route.
itinérant, ~e /itinerɑ̃, -t/ *a.* itinerant.
I.U.T. /iyte/ *n.m.* (*abrév.*) polytechnic.
I.V.G. /iveʒe/ *n.f.* (*abrév.*) abortion.
ivoire /ivwar/ *n.m.* ivory.
ivr|e /ivr/ *a.* drunk. **~esse** *n.f.* drunkenness. **~ogne** *n.m.* drunk(ard).

J

j' /ʒ/ *voir* je.
jacasser /ʒakase/ *v.i.* chatter.
jachère (en) /(ɑ̃)ʒaʃɛr/ *adv.* fallow.
jacinthe /ʒasɛ̃t/ *n.f.* hyacinth.
jade /ʒad/ *n.m.* jade.
jadis /ʒadis/ *adv.* long ago.
jaillir /ʒajir/ *v.i.* (*liquide*) spurt (out); (*lumière*) stream out; (*apparaître, fuser*) burst forth.
jais /ʒɛ/ *n.m.* **(noir) de ~,** jet-black.
jalon /ʒalɔ̃/ *n.m.* (*piquet*) marker. **~ner** /-ɔne/ *v.t.* mark (out).
jalou|x, ~se /ʒalu, -z/ *a.* jealous. **~ser** *v.t.* be jealous of. **~sie** *n.f.* jealousy; (*store*) (venetian) blind.
jamais /ʒamɛ/ *adv.* ever. **(ne) ~,** never. **il ne boit ~,** he never drinks. **à ~,** for ever. **si ~,** if ever.
jambe /ʒɑ̃b/ *n.f.* leg.
jambon /ʒɑ̃bɔ̃/ *n.m.* ham. **~neau** (*pl.* **~neaux**) /-ɔno/ *n.m.* knuckle of ham.
jante /ʒɑ̃t/ *n.f.* rim.
janvier /ʒɑ̃vje/ *n.m.* January.
Japon /ʒapɔ̃/ *n.m.* Japan.
japonais, ~e /ʒapɔnɛ, -z/ *a.* & *n.m., f.* Japanese. ● *n.m.* (*lang.*) Japanese.
japper /ʒape/ *v.i.* yelp.
jaquette /ʒakɛt/ *n.f.* (*de livre, femme*) jacket; (*d'homme*) morning coat.
jardin /ʒardɛ̃/ *n.m.* garden. **~ d'enfants,** nursery (school). **~ public,** public park.
jardin|er /ʒardine/ *v.i.* garden. **~age** *n.m.* gardening. **~ier, ~ière** *n.m., f.* gardener; *n.f.* (*meuble*) plant-stand. **~ière de légumes,** mixed vegetables.
jargon /ʒargɔ̃/ *n.m.* jargon.
jarret /ʒarɛ/ *n.m.* back of the knee.

jarretelle /ʒartɛl/ *n.f.* suspender; (*Amer.*) garter.
jarretière /ʒartjɛr/ *n.f.* garter.
jaser /ʒaze/ *v.i.* jabber.
jasmin /ʒasmɛ̃/ *n.m.* jasmine.
jatte /ʒat/ *n.f.* bowl.
jaug|e /ʒoʒ/ *n.f.* capacity; (*de navire*) tonnage; (*compteur*) gauge. **~er** *v.t.* gauge.
jaun|e /ʒon/ *a.* & *n.m.* yellow; (*péj.*) scab. **~e d'œuf,** (egg) yolk. **rire ~e,** laugh on the other side of one's face. **~ir** *v.t./i.* turn yellow.
jaunisse /ʒonis/ *n.f.* jaundice.
javelot /ʒavlo/ *n.m.* javelin.
jazz /dʒaz/ *n.m.* jazz.
J.C. /ʒezykri/ *n.m.* (*abrév.*) **500 avant/après ~,** 500 B.C./A.D.
je, j'* /ʒə, ʒ/ *pron.* I.
jean /dʒin/ *n.m.* jeans.
jeep /(d)ʒip/ *n.f.* jeep.
jerrycan /ʒerikan/ *n.m.* jerrycan.
jersey /ʒɛrzɛ/ *n.m.* jersey.
Jersey /ʒɛrzɛ/ *n.f.* Jersey.
Jésus /ʒezy/ *n.m.* Jesus.
jet[1] /ʒɛ/ *n.m.* throw; (*de liquide, vapeur*) jet. **~ d'eau,** fountain.
jet[2] /dʒɛt/ *n.m.* (*avion*) jet.
jetable /ʒətabl/ *a.* disposable.
jetée /ʒte/ *n.f.* pier.
jeter /ʒte/ *v.t.* throw; (*au rebut*) throw away; (*regard, ancre, lumière*) cast; (*cri*) utter; (*bases*) lay. **~ un coup d'œil,** have *ou* take a look (**à,** at). **se ~ contre,** (*heurter*) bash into. **se ~ dans,** (*fleuve*) flow into. **se ~ sur,** (*se ruer sur*) rush at.
jeton /ʒtɔ̃/ *n.m.* token; (*pour compter*) counter.
jeu (*pl.* **~x**) /ʒø/ *n.m.* game; (*amusement*) play; (*au casino etc.*) gambling; (*théâtre*) acting; (*série*) set; (*de lumière, ressort*) play. **en ~,** (*honneur*) at stake; (*forces*) at work. **~ de cartes,** (*paquet*) pack of cards. **~ d'échecs,** (*boîte*) chess set. **~ de mots,** pun. **~ télévisé,** television quiz.
jeudi /ʒødi/ *n.m.* Thursday.
jeun (à) /(a)ʒœ̃/ *adv.* **être/rester à ~,** be/stay without food; **comprimé à prendre à ~,** tablet to be taken on an empty stomach.
jeune /ʒœn/ *a.* young. ● *n.m./f.* young person. **~ fille,** girl. **~s mariés,** newlyweds. **les ~s,** young people.
jeûn|e /ʒøn/ *n.m.* fast. **~er** *v.i.* fast.
jeunesse /ʒœnɛs/ *n.f.* youth; (*apparence*) youthfulness. **la ~,** (*jeunes*) the young.
joaill|ier, ~ière /ʒɔɑlje, -jɛr/ *n.m., f.* jeweller. **~erie** *n.f.* jewellery; (*magasin*) jeweller's shop.
job /dʒɔb/ *n.m.* (*fam.*) job.
jockey /ʒɔkɛ/ *n.m.* jockey.
joie /ʒwa/ *n.f.* joy.
joindre† /ʒwɛ̃dr/ *v.t.* join (**à,** to); (*contacter*) contact; (*mains, pieds*) put together; (*efforts*) combine; (*dans une enveloppe*) enclose. **se ~ à,** join.
joint, ~e /ʒwɛ̃, -t/ *a.* (*efforts*) joint; (*pieds*) together. ● *n.m.* joint; (*ligne*) join; (*de robinet*) washer. **~ure** /-tyr/ *n.f.* joint; (*ligne*) join.
joker /ʒɔkɛr/ *n.m.* (*carte*) joker.
joli /ʒɔli/ *a.* pretty, nice; (*somme, profit*) nice. **c'est du ~!,** (*ironique*) charming! **c'est bien ~ mais,** that is all very well but. **~ment** *adv.* prettily; (*très: fam.*) awfully.
jonc /ʒɔ̃/ *n.m.* (bul)rush.
jonch|er /ʒɔ̃ʃe/ *v.t.*, **~é de,** littered with.
jonction /ʒɔ̃ksjɔ̃/ *n.f.* junction.
jongl|er /ʒɔ̃gle/ *v.i.* juggle. **~eur, ~euse** *n.m., f.* juggler.
jonquille /ʒɔ̃kij/ *n.f.* daffodil.
Jordanie /ʒɔrdani/ *n.f.* Jordan.
joue /ʒu/ *n.f.* cheek.
jou|er /ʒwe/ *v.t./i.* play; (*théâtre*) act; (*au casino etc.*) gamble; (*fonctionner*) work; (*film, pièce*) put on; (*cheval*) back; (*être important*) count. **~er à *ou* de,** play. **~er la comédie,** put on an act. **bien ~é!,** well done!
jouet /ʒwɛ/ *n.m.* toy; (*personne, fig.*) plaything; (*victime*) victim.
joueu|r, ~se /ʒwœr, -øz/ *n.m., f.* player; (*parieur*) gambler.
joufflu /ʒufly/ *a.* chubby-cheeked; (*visage*) chubby.
joug /ʒu/ *n.m.* yoke.
jouir /ʒwir/ *v.i.* (*sexe*) come. **~ de,** enjoy.
jouissance /ʒwisɑ̃s/ *n.f.* pleasure; (*usage*) use (**de qch.,** of sth.).
joujou (*pl.* **~x**) /ʒuʒu/ *n.m.* (*fam.*) toy.
jour /ʒur/ *n.m.* day; (*opposé à nuit*) day(time); (*lumière*) daylight; (*aspect*) light; (*ouverture*) gap. **de nos ~s,** nowadays. **du ~ au lendemain,** overnight. **il fait ~,** it is (day)light. **~ chômé *ou* férié,** public holiday. **~ de fête,** holiday. **~ ouvrable, ~**

de travail, working day. **mettre à ~,** update. **mettre au ~,** uncover. **au grand ~,** in the open. **donner le ~,** give birth. **voir le ~,** be born. **vivre au ~ le jour,** live from day to day.
journ|al (*pl.* **~aux**) /ʒurnal, -o/ *n.m.* (news)paper; (*spécialisé*) journal; (*intime*) diary; (*radio*) news. **~al de bord,** log-book.
journal|ier, ~ière /ʒurnalje, -jɛr/ *a.* daily.
journalis|te /ʒurnalist/ *n.m./f.* journalist. **~me** *n.m.* journalism.
journée /ʒurne/ *n.f.* day.
journellement /ʒurnɛlmɑ̃/ *adv.* daily.
jov|ial (*m. pl.* **~iaux**) /ʒɔvjal, -jo/ *a.* jovial.
joyau (*pl.* **~x**) /ʒwajo/ *n.m.* gem.
joyeu|x, ~se /ʒwajø, -z/ *a.* merry, joyful. **~x anniversaire,** happy birthday. **~sement** *adv.* merrily.
jubilé /ʒybile/ *n.m.* jubilee.
jubil|er /ʒybile/ *v.i.* be jubilant. **~ation** *n.f.* jubilation.
jucher /ʒyʃe/ *v.t.*, **se ~** *v. pr.* perch.
judaï|que /ʒydaik/ *a.* Jewish. **~sme** *n.m.* Judaism.
judas /ʒyda/ *n.m.* peep-hole.
judiciaire /ʒydisjɛr/ *a.* judicial.
judicieu|x, ~se /ʒydisjø, -z/ *a.* judicious.
judo /ʒydo/ *n.m.* judo.
juge /ʒyʒ/ *n.m.* judge; (*arbitre*) referee. **~ de paix,** Justice of the Peace. **~ de touche,** linesman.
jugé (au) /(o)ʒyʒe/ *adv.* by guesswork.
jugement /ʒyʒmɑ̃/ *n.m.* judgement; (*criminel*) sentence.
jugeote /ʒyʒɔt/ *n.f.* (*fam.*) gumption, common sense.
juger /ʒyʒe/ *v.t./i.* judge; (*estimer*) consider (**que,** that). **~ de,** judge.
juguler /ʒygyle/ *v.t.* stifle, check.
jui|f, ~ve /ʒɥif, -v/ *a.* Jewish. ● *n.m., f.* Jew, Jewess.
juillet /ʒɥijɛ/ *n.m.* July.
juin /ʒɥɛ̃/ *n.m.* June.
jules /ʒyl/ *n.m.* (*fam.*) guy.
jum|eau, ~elle (*m. pl.* **~eaux**) /ʒymo, -ɛl/ *a. & n.m., f.* twin. **~elage** *n.m.* twinning. **~eler** *v.t.* (*villes*) twin.
jumelles /ʒymɛl/ *n.f. pl.* binoculars.
jument /ʒymɑ̃/ *n.f.* mare.
jungle /ʒœ̃gl/ *n.f.* jungle.
junior /ʒynjɔr/ *n.m./f. & a.* junior.
junte /ʒœ̃t/ *n.f.* junta.
jupe /ʒyp/ *n.f.* skirt.
jupon /ʒypɔ̃/ *n.m.* slip, petticoat.
juré, ~e /ʒyre/ *n.m., f.* juror. ● *a.* sworn.
jurer /ʒyre/ *v.t.* swear (**que,** that). ● *v.i.* (*pester*) swear; (*contraster*) clash (**avec,** with). **~ de qch./de faire,** swear to sth./to do.
juridiction /ʒyridiksjɔ̃/ *n.f.* jurisdiction; (*tribunal*) court of law.
juridique /ʒyridik/ *a.* legal.
juriste /ʒyrist/ *n.m./f.* legal expert.
juron /ʒyrɔ̃/ *n.m.* swear-word.
jury /ʒyri/ *n.m.* jury.
jus /ʒy/ *n.m.* juice; (*de viande*) gravy. **~ de fruit,** fruit juice.
jusque /ʒysk(ə)/ *prép.* **jusqu'à,** (up) to, as far as; (*temps*) until, till; (*limite*) up to; (*y compris*) even. **jusqu'à ce que,** until. **jusqu'à présent,** until now. **jusqu'en,** until. **jusqu'où?,** how far? **~ dans, ~ sur,** as far as.
juste /ʒyst/ *a.* fair, just; (*légitime*) just; (*correct, exact*) right; (*vrai*) true; (*vêtement*) tight; (*quantité*) on the short side. **le ~ milieu,** the happy medium. ● *adv.* rightly, correctly; (*chanter*) in tune; (*seulement, exactement*) just. **(un peu) ~,** (*calculer, mesurer*) a bit fine *ou* close. **au ~,** exactly. **c'était ~,** (*presque raté*) it was a close thing.
justement /ʒystəmɑ̃/ *adv.* just; (*avec justice ou justesse*) justly.
justesse /ʒystɛs/ *n.f.* accuracy. **de ~,** just, narrowly.
justice /ʒystis/ *n.f.* justice; (*autorités*) law; (*tribunal*) court.
justif|ier /ʒystifje/ *v.t.* justify. ● *v.i.* **~ier de,** prove. **se ~ier** *v. pr.* justify o.s. **~iable** *a.* justifiable. **~ication** *n.f.* justification.
juteu|x, ~se /ʒytø, -z/ *a.* juicy.
juvénile /ʒyvenil/ *a.* youthful.
juxtaposer /ʒykstapoze/ *v.t.* juxtapose.

K

kaki /kaki/ *a. invar. & n.m.* khaki.
kaléidoscope /kaleidɔskɔp/ *n.m.* kaleidoscope.
kangourou /kɑ̃guru/ *n.m.* kangaroo.
karaté /karate/ *n.m.* karate.

kart /kart/ *n.m.* go-cart.
kascher /kaʃɛr/ *a. invar.* kosher.
képi /kepi/ *n.m.* kepi.
kermesse /kɛrmɛs/ *n.f.* fair; (*de charité*) fête.
kérosène /kerozɛn/ *n.m.* kerosene, aviation fuel.
kibboutz /kibuts/ *n.m.* kibbutz.
kidnapp|er /kidnape/ *v.t.* kidnap. **~eur, ~euse** *n.m., f.* kidnapper.
kilo /kilo/ *n.m.* kilo.
kilogramme /kilɔgram/ *n.m.* kilogram.
kilohertz /kilɔɛrts/ *n.m.* kilohertz.
kilom|ètre /kilɔmɛtr/ *n.m.* kilometre. **~étrage** *n.m.* (*approx.*) mileage.
kilowatt /kilɔwat/ *n.m.* kilowatt.
kinésithérapie /kineziterapi/ *n.f.* physiotherapy.
kiosque /kjɔsk/ *n.m.* kiosk. **~ à musique,** bandstand.
kit /kit/ *n.m.* **meubles en ~,** flat-pack furniture.
kiwi /kiwi/ *n.m.* (*fruit, bird*) kiwi.
klaxon /klaksɔn/ *n.m.* (P.) (*auto.*) horn. **~ner** /-e/ *v.i.* sound one's horn.
knock-out /nɔkaut/ *n.m.* knock-out.
ko /kao/ *n.m.* (*comput.*) k.
K.O. /kao/ *a. invar.* (knocked) out.
k-way /kawe/ *n.m. invar.* (P.) cagoule.
kyste /kist/ *n.m.* cyst.

L

l', la /l, la/ *voir* le.
là /la/ *adv.* there; (*ici*) here; (*chez soi*) in; (*temps*) then. **c'est là que,** this is where. **là où,** where. **là-bas** *adv.* over there. **là-dedans** *adv.* inside, in there. **là-dessous** *adv.* underneath, under there. **là-dessus** *adv.* on there. **là-haut** *adv.* up there; (*à l'étage*) upstairs.
-là /la/ *adv.* (*après un nom précédé de ce, cette, etc.*) **cet homme-là,** that man. **ces maisons-là,** those houses.
label /labɛl/ *n.m.* (*comm.*) seal.
labeur /labœr/ *n.m.* toil.
labo /labo/ *n.m.* (*fam.*) lab.
laboratoire /labɔratwar/ *n.m.* laboratory.
laborieu|x, ~se /labɔrjø, -z/ *a.* laborious; (*personne*) industrious; (*dur*) heavy going. **classes/masses ~ses,** working classes/masses.
labour /labur/ *n.m.* ploughing; (*Amer.*) plowing. **~er** *v.t./i.* plough; (*Amer.*) plow; (*déchirer*) rip at. **~eur** *n.m.* ploughman; (*Amer.*) plowman.
labyrinthe /labirɛ̃t/ *n.m.* maze.
lac /lak/ *n.m.* lake.
lacer /lase/ *v.t.* lace up.
lacérer /lasere/ *v.t.* tear (up).
lacet /lasɛ/ *n.m.* (shoe-)lace; (*de route*) sharp bend, zigzag.
lâche /lɑʃ/ *a.* cowardly; (*détendu*) loose. • *n.m./f.* coward. **~ment** *adv.* in a cowardly way.
lâcher /lɑʃe/ *v.t.* let go of; (*abandonner*) give up; (*laisser*) leave; (*libérer*) release; (*parole*) utter; (*desserrer*) loosen. • *v.i.* give way. **~ prise,** let go.
lâcheté /lɑʃte/ *n.f.* cowardice.
laconique /lakɔnik/ *a.* laconic.
lacrymogène /lakrimɔʒɛn/ *a.* **gaz ~,** tear gas. **grenade ~,** tear gas grenade.
lacté /lakte/ *a.* milk.
lacune /lakyn/ *n.f.* gap.
ladite /ladit/ *voir* ledit.
lagune /lagyn/ *n.f.* lagoon.
laïc /laik/ *n.m.* layman.
laid, ~e /lɛ, lɛd/ *a.* ugly; (*action*) vile. **~eur** /lɛdœr/ *n.f.* ugliness.
lain|e /lɛn/ *n.f.* wool. **de ~e,** woollen. **~age** *n.m.* woollen garment.
laïque /laik/ *a.* secular; (*habit, personne*) lay. • *n.m./f.* layman, laywoman.
laisse /lɛs/ *n.f.* lead, leash.
laisser /lese/ *v.t.* leave. **~ qn. faire,** let s.o. do. **~ qch. à qn.,** let s.o. have sth., leave s.o. sth. **~ tomber,** drop. **se ~ aller,** let o.s. go. **~-aller** *n.m. invar.* carelessness. **laissez-passer** *n.m. invar.* pass.
lait /lɛ/ *n.m.* milk. **frère/sœur de ~,** foster-brother/-sister. **~age** /lɛtaʒ/ *n.m.* milk product. **~eux, ~euse** /lɛtø, -z/ *a.* milky.
lait|ier, ~ière /letje, lɛtjɛr/ *a.* dairy. • *n.m., f.* dairyman, dairywoman. • *n.m.* (*livreur*) milkman. **~erie** /lɛtri/ *n.f.* dairy.
laiton /lɛtɔ̃/ *n.m.* brass.
laitue /lety/ *n.f.* lettuce.
laïus /lajys/ *n.m.* (*péj.*) big speech.
lama /lama/ *n.m.* llama.
lambeau (*pl.* **~x**) /lɑ̃bo/ *n.m.* shred. **en ~x,** in shreds.
lambris /lɑ̃bri/ *n.m.* panelling.

lame /lam/ *n.f.* blade; (*lamelle*) strip; (*vague*) wave. **~ de fond,** ground swell.

lamelle /lamɛl/ *n.f.* (thin) strip.

lamentable /lamɑ̃tabl/ *a.* deplorable.

lament|er (se) /(sə)lamɑ̃te/ *v. pr.* moan. **~ation(s)** *n.f.* (*pl.*) moaning.

laminé /lamine/ *a.* laminated.

lampadaire /lɑ̃padɛr/ *n.m.* standard lamp; (*de rue*) street lamp.

lampe /lɑ̃p/ *n.f.* lamp; (*de radio*) valve; (*Amer.*) vacuum tube. **~ (de poche),** torch; (*Amer.*) flashlight. **~ de chevet,** bedside lamp.

lampion /lɑ̃pjɔ̃/ *n.m.* (Chinese) lantern.

lance /lɑ̃s/ *n.f.* spear; (*de tournoi*) lance; (*tuyau*) hose. **~ d'incendie,** fire hose.

lancée /lɑ̃se/ *n.f.* **continuer sur sa ~,** keep going.

lanc|er /lɑ̃se/ *v.t.* throw; (*avec force*) hurl; (*navire, idée, personne*) launch; (*émettre*) give out; (*regard*) cast; (*moteur*) start. **se ~er** *v. pr.* (*sport*) gain momentum; (*se précipiter*) rush. **se ~er dans,** launch into. ● *n.m.* throw; (*action*) throwing. **~ement** *n.m.* throwing; (*de navire*) launching. **~e-missiles** *n.m. invar.* missile launcher. **~e-pierres** *n.m. invar.* catapult.

lancinant, ~e /lɑ̃sinɑ̃, -t/ *a.* haunting; (*douleur*) throbbing.

landau /lɑ̃do/ *n.m.* pram; (*Amer.*) baby carriage.

lande /lɑ̃d/ *n.f.* heath, moor.

langage /lɑ̃gaʒ/ *n.m.* language.

langoureu|x, ~se /lɑ̃gurø, -z/ *a.* languid.

langoust|e /lɑgust/ *n.f.* (spiny) lobster. **~ine** *n.f.* (Norway) lobster.

langue /lɑ̃g/ *n.f.* tongue; (*idiome*) language. **il m'a tiré la ~,** he stuck out his tongue out at me. **de ~ anglaise/française,** English-/French-speaking. **~ maternelle,** mother tongue.

languette /lɑ̃gɛt/ *n.f.* tongue.

langueur /lɑ̃gœr/ *n.f.* languor.

langu|ir /lɑ̃gir/ *v.i.* languish; (*conversation*) flag. **faire ~ir qn.,** keep s.o. waiting. **se ~ir de,** miss. **~issant, ~issante** *a.* languid.

lanière /lanjɛr/ *n.f.* strap.

lanterne /lɑ̃tɛrn/ *n.f.* lantern; (*électrique*) lamp; (*de voiture*) sidelight.

laper /lape/ *v.t./i.* lap.

lapider /lapide/ *v.t.* stone.

lapin /lapɛ̃/ *n.m.* rabbit. **poser un ~ à qn.,** stand s.o. up.

laps /laps/ *n.m.* **~ de temps,** lapse of time.

lapsus /lapsys/ *n.m.* slip (of the tongue).

laquais /lakɛ/ *n.m.* lackey.

laqu|e /lak/ *n.f.* lacquer. **~er** *v.t.* lacquer.

laquelle /lakɛl/ *voir* lequel.

larcin /larsɛ̃/ *n.m.* theft.

lard /lar/ *n.m.* (pig's) fat; (*viande*) bacon.

large /larʒ/ *a.* wide, broad; (*grand*) large; (*non borné*) broad; (*généreux*) generous. ● *adv.* (*mesurer*) broadly; (*voir*) big. ● *n.m.* **de ~,** (*mesure*) wide. **le ~,** (*mer*) the open sea. **au ~ de,** (*en face de*: *naut.*) off. **~ d'esprit,** broad-minded. **~ment** /-əmɑ̃/ *adv.* widely; (*ouvrir*) wide; (*amplement*) amply; (*généreusement*) generously; (*au moins*) easily.

largesse /larʒɛs/ *n.f.* generosity.

largeur /larʒœr/ *n.f.* width, breadth; (*fig.*) breadth.

larguer /large/ *v.t.* drop. **~ les amarres,** cast off.

larme /larm/ *n.f.* tear; (*goutte*: *fam.*) drop.

larmoyant, ~e /larmwajɑ̃, -t/ *a.* tearful.

larron /larɔ̃/ *n.m.* thief.

larve /larv/ *n.f.* larva.

larvé /larve/ *a.* latent.

laryngite /larɛ̃ʒit/ *n.f.* laryngitis.

larynx /larɛ̃ks/ *n.m.* larynx.

las, ~se /lɑ, lɑs/ *a.* weary.

lasagnes /lazaɲ/ *n.f. pl.* lasagne.

lasci|f, ~ve /lasif, -v/ *a.* lascivious.

laser /lazɛr/ *n.m.* laser.

lasse /lɑs/ *voir* las.

lasser /lɑse/ *v.t.* weary. **se ~** *v. pr.* weary (**de,** of).

lassitude /lɑsityd/ *n.f.* weariness.

lasso /laso/ *n.m.* lasso.

latent, ~e /latɑ̃, -t/ *a.* latent.

latér|al (*m. pl.* **~aux**) /lateral, -o/ *a.* lateral.

latex /latɛks/ *n.m.* latex.

latin, ~e /latɛ̃, -in/ *a.* & *n.m., f.* Latin. ● *n.m.* (*lang.*) Latin.

latitude /latityd/ *n.f.* latitude.

latrines /latrin/ *n.f. pl.* latrine(s).

latte /lat/ *n.f.* lath; (*de plancher*) board.

lauréat, ~e /lɔrea, -t/ *a.* prize-winning. ● *n.m., f.* prize-winner.

laurier /lɔrje/ *n.m.* laurel; (*culin.*) bay-leaves.
lavable /lavabl/ *a.* washable.
lavabo /lavabo/ *n.m.* wash-basin. **~s,** toilet(s).
lavage /lavaʒ/ *n.m.* washing. **~ de cerveau,** brainwashing.
lavande /lavɑ̃d/ *n.f.* lavender.
lave /lav/ *n.f.* lava.
lav|er /lave/ *v.t.* wash; (*injure etc.*) avenge. **se ~er** *v. pr.* wash (o.s.). **(se) ~er de,** clear (o.s.) of. **~e-glace** *n.m.* windscreen washer. **~eur de carreaux,** window-cleaner. **~e-vaisselle** *n.m. invar.* dishwasher.
laverie /lavri/ *n.f.* **~ (automatique),** launderette; (*Amer.*) laundromat.
lavette /lavɛt/ *n.f.* dishcloth; (*péj.*) wimp.
lavoir /lavwar/ *n.m.* wash-house.
laxati|f, ~ve /laksatif, -v/ *a. & n.m.* laxative.
laxisme /laksism/ *n.m.* laxity.
layette /lɛjɛt/ *n.f.* baby clothes.
le *ou* **l'*, la** *ou* **l'*** (*pl.* **les**) /lə, l/, /la, le/ *article* the; (*mesure*) a, per. ● *pron.* (*homme*) him; (*femme*) her; (*chose, animal*) it. **les** *pron.* them. **aimer le thé/la France,** like tea/France. **le matin,** in the morning. **il sort le mardi,** he goes out on Tuesdays. **levez le bras,** raise your arm. **je le connais,** I know him. **je le sais,** I know (it).
lécher /leʃe/ *v.t.* lick.
lèche-vitrines /lɛʃvitrin/ *n.m.* **faire du ~,** go window-shopping.
leçon /ləsɔ̃/ *n.f.* lesson. **faire la ~ à,** lecture.
lec|teur, ~trice /lɛktœr, -tris/ *n.m., f.* reader; (*univ.*) foreign language assistant. **~teur de cassettes,** cassette player. **~teur de disquettes,** (disk) drive.
lecture /lɛktyr/ *n.f.* reading.
ledit, ladite (*pl.* **lesdit(e)s**) /lədi, ladit, ledi(t)/ *a.* the aforesaid.
lég|al (*m. pl.* **~aux**) /legal, -o/ *a.* legal. **~alement** *adv.* legally. **~aliser** *v.t.* legalize. **~alité** *n.f.* legality; (*loi*) law.
légation /legɑsjɔ̃/ *n.f.* legation.
légend|e /leʒɑ̃d/ *n.f.* (*histoire, inscription*) legend. **~aire** *a.* legendary.
lég|er, ~ère /leʒe, -ɛr/ *a.* light; (*bruit, faute, maladie*) slight; (*café, argument*) weak; (*imprudent*) thoughtless; (*frivole*) fickle. **à la ~ère,** thoughtlessly. **~èrement** /-ɛrmɑ̃/ *adv.* lightly; (*agir*) thoughtlessly; (*un peu*) slightly. **~èreté** /-ɛrte/ *n.f.* lightness; thoughtlessness.
légion /leʒjɔ̃/ *n.f.* legion. **une ~ de,** a crowd of. **~naire** /-jɔnɛr/ *n.m.* (*mil.*) legionnaire.
législati|f, ~ve /leʒislatif, -v/ *a.* legislative.
législation /leʒislɑsjɔ̃/ *n.f.* legislation.
legislature /leʒislatyr/ *n.f.* term of office.
légitim|e /leʒitim/ *a.* legitimate. **en état de ~e défense,** acting in self-defence. **~ité** *n.f.* legitimacy.
legs /lɛg/ *n.m.* legacy.
léguer /lege/ *v.t.* bequeath.
légume /legym/ *n.m.* vegetable.
lendemain /lɑ̃dmɛ̃/ *n.m.* **le ~,** the next day, the day after; (*fig.*) the future. **le ~ de,** the day after. **le ~ matin/soir,** the next morning/evening.
lent, ~e /lɑ̃, lɑ̃t/ *a.* slow. **~ement** /lɑ̃tmɑ̃/ *adv.* slowly. **~eur** /lɑ̃tœr/ *n.f.* slowness.
lentille [1] /lɑ̃tij/ *n.f.* (*plante*) lentil.
lentille [2] /lɑ̃tij/ *n.f.* (*verre*) lens; **~s de contact,** (contact) lenses.
léopard /leɔpar/ *n.m.* leopard.
lèpre /lɛpr/ *n.f.* leprosy.
lequel, laquelle (*pl.* **lesquel(le)s**) /ləkɛl, lakɛl, lekɛl/ *pron.* (*à + lequel = auquel, à + lesquel(le)s = auxquel(le)s; de + lequel = duquel, de + lesquel(le)s = desquel(le)s*) which; (*interrogatif*) which (one); (*personne*) who; (*complément indirect*) whom.
les /le/ *voir* le.
lesbienne /lɛsbjɛn/ *n.f.* lesbian.
léser /leze/ *v.t.* wrong.
lésiner /lezine/ *v.i.* **ne pas ~ sur,** not stint on.
lésion /lezjɔ̃/ *n.f.* lesion.
lesquels, lesquelles /lekɛl/ *voir* lequel.
lessive /lesiv/ *n.f.* washing-powder; (*linge, action*) washing.
lest /lɛst/ *n.m.* ballast. **jeter du ~,** (*fig.*) climb down. **~er** *v.t.* ballast.
leste /lɛst/ *a.* nimble; (*grivois*) coarse.
létharg|ie /letarʒi/ *n.f.* lethargy. **~ique** *a.* lethargic.
lettre /lɛtr/ *n.f.* letter. **à la ~,** literally. **en toutes ~s,** in full. **~**

exprès, express letter. **les ~s,** (*univ.*) (the) arts.

lettré /letre/ *a.* well-read.

leucémie /løsemi/ *n.f.* leukaemia.

leur /lœr/ *a.* (*f. invar.*) their. ● *pron.* (to) them. **le ~, la ~, les ~s,** theirs.

leurr|e /lœr/ *n.m.* illusion; (*duperie*) deception. **~er** *v.t.* delude.

levain /ləvɛ̃/ *n.m.* leaven.

levé /ləve/ *a.* (*debout*) up.

levée /ləve/ *n.f.* lifting; (*de courrier*) collection; (*de troupes, d'impôts*) levying.

lever /ləve/ *v.t.* lift (up), raise; (*interdiction*) lift; (*séance*) close; (*armée, impôts*) levy. ● *v.i.* (*pâte*) rise. **se ~** *v. pr.* get up; (*soleil, rideau*) rise; (*jour*) break. ● *n.m.* **au ~,** on getting up. **~ du jour,** daybreak. **~ du rideau,** (*théâtre*) curtain (up). **~ du soleil,** sunrise.

levier /ləvje/ *n.m.* lever.

lèvre /lɛvr/ *n.f.* lip.

lévrier /levrije/ *n.m.* greyhound.

levure /ləvyr/ *n.f.* yeast. **~ alsacienne** *ou* **chimique,** baking powder.

lexicographie /lɛksikɔgrafi/ *n.f.* lexicography.

lexique /lɛksik/ *n.m.* vocabulary; (*glossaire*) lexicon.

lézard /lezar/ *n.m.* lizard.

lézard|e /lezard/ *n.f.* crack. **se ~er** *v. pr.* crack.

liaison /ljɛzɔ̃/ *n.f.* connection; (*transport*) link; (*contact*) contact; (*gram., mil.*) liaison; (*amoureuse*) affair.

liane /ljan/ *n.f.* creeper.

liasse /ljas/ *n.f.* bundle, wad.

Liban /libɑ̃/ *n.m.* Lebanon.

libanais, ~e /libanɛ, -z/ *a. & n.m., f.* Lebanese.

libell|er /libele/ *v.t.* (*chèque*) write; (*lettre*) draw up. **~é à l'ordre de,** made out to.

libellule /libelyl/ *n.f.* dragonfly.

libér|al (*m. pl.* **~aux**) /liberal, -o/ *a.* liberal. **les professions ~ales** the professions. **~alement** *adv.* liberally. **~alisme** *n.m.* liberalism. **~alité** *n.f.* liberality.

libér|er /libere/ *v.t.* (*personne*) free, release; (*pays*) liberate, free. **se ~er** *v. pr.* free o.s. **~ateur, ~atrice** *a.* liberating; *n.m., f.* liberator. **~ation** *n.f.* release; (*de pays*) liberation.

liberté /libɛrte/ *n.f.* freedom, liberty; (*loisir*) free time. **en ~ provisoire,** on bail. **être/mettre en ~,** be/set free.

libertin, ~e /libɛrtɛ̃, -in/ *a. & n.m., f.* libertine.

librair|e /librɛr/ *n.m./f.* bookseller. **~ie** /-eri/ *n.f.* bookshop.

libre /libr/ *a.* free; (*place, pièce*) vacant, free; (*passage*) clear; (*école*) private (*usually religious*). **~ de qch./de faire,** free from sth./to do. **~-échange** *n.m.* free trade. **~ment** /-əmɑ̃/ *adv.* freely. **~-service** (*pl.* **~s-services**) *n.m.* self-service.

Libye /libi/ *n.f.* Libya.

libyen, ~ne /libjɛ̃, -jɛn/ *a. & n.m., f.* Libyan.

licence /lisɑ̃s/ *n.f.* licence; (*univ.*) degree.

licencié, ~e /lisɑ̃sje/ *n.m., f.* **~ ès lettres/sciences,** Bachelor of Arts/Science.

licenc|ier /lisɑ̃sje/ *v.t.* make redundant, (*pour faute*) dismiss. **~iements** *n.m. pl.* redundancies.

licencieu|x, ~se /lisɑ̃sjø, -z/ *a.* licentious, lascivious.

lichen /likɛn/ *n.m.* lichen.

licite /lisit/ *a.* lawful.

licorne /likɔrn/ *n.f.* unicorn.

lie /li/ *n.f.* dregs.

liège /ljɛʒ/ *n.m.* cork.

lien /ljɛ̃/ *n.m.* (*rapport*) link; (*attache*) bond, tie; (*corde*) rope.

lier /lje/ *v.t.* tie (up), bind; (*relier*) link; (*engager, unir*) bind. **~ conversation,** strike up a conversation. **se ~ avec,** make friends with. **ils sont très liés,** they are very close.

lierre /ljɛr/ *n.m.* ivy.

lieu (*pl.* **~x**) /ljø/ *n.m.* place. **~x,** (*locaux*) premises; (*d'un accident*) scene. **au ~ de,** instead of. **avoir ~,** take place. **tenir ~ de,** serve as. **en premier ~,** firstly. **en dernier ~,** lastly. **~ commun,** commonplace.

lieutenant /ljøtnɑ̃/ *n.m.* lieutenant.

lièvre /ljɛvr/ *n.m.* hare.

ligament /ligamɑ̃/ *n.m.* ligament.

ligne /liɲ/ *n.f.* line; (*trajet*) route; (*formes*) lines; (*de femme*) figure. **en ~,** (*joueurs etc.*) lined up; (*personne au téléphone*) on the phone.

lignée /liɲe/ *n.f.* ancestry, line.

ligoter /ligɔte/ *v.t.* tie up.

ligu|e /lig/ *n.f.* league. **se ~er** *v. pr.* form a league (**contre,** against).

lilas /lilɑ/ *n.m. & a. invar.* lilac.

limace /limas/ *n.f.* slug.

limande /limɑ̃d/ *n.f.* (*poisson*) dab.

lim|e /lim/ *n.f.* file. **~e à ongles,** nail file. **~er** *v.t.* file.
limier /limje/ *n.m.* bloodhound; (*policier*) sleuth.
limitation /limitɑsjɔ̃/ *n.f.* limitation. **~ de vitesse,** speed limit.
limit|e /limit/ *n.f.* limit; (*de jardin, champ*) boundary. ● *a.* (*vitesse, âge*) maximum. **cas ~e,** borderline case. **date ~e,** deadline. **~er** *v.t.* limit; (*délimiter*) form the border of.
limoger /limɔʒe/ *v.t.* dismiss.
limon /limɔ̃/ *n.m.* stilt.
limonade /limɔnad/ *n.f.* lemonade.
limpid|e /lɛ̃pid/ *a.* limpid, clear. **~ité** *n.f.* clearness.
lin /lɛ̃/ *n.m.* (*tissu*) linen.
linceul /lɛ̃sœl/ *n.m.* shroud.
linéaire /lineɛr/ *a.* linear.
linge /lɛ̃ʒ/ *n.m.* linen; (*lessive*) washing; (*torchon*) cloth. **~ (de corps),** underwear. **~rie** *n.f.* underwear.
lingot /lɛ̃go/ *n.m.* ingot.
linguiste /lɛ̃gɥist/ *n.m./f.* linguist.
linguistique /lɛ̃gɥistik/ *a.* linguistic. ● *n.f.* linguistics.
lino /lino/ *n.m.* lino.
linoléum /linɔleɔm/ *n.m.* linoleum.
lion, ~ne /ljɔ̃, ljɔn/ *n.m., f.* lion, lioness. **le L~,** leo.
lionceau (*pl.* **~x**) /ljɔ̃so/ *n.m.* lion cub.
liquéfier /likefje/ *v.t.,* **se ~** *v. pr.* liquefy.
liqueur /likœr/ *n.f.* liquour.
liquide /likid/ *a.* & *n.m.* liquid. **(argent) ~,** ready money. **payer en ~,** pay cash.
liquid|er /likide/ *v.t.* liquidate; (*vendre*) sell. **~ation** *n.f.* liquidation; (*vente*) (clearance) sale.
lire† [1] /lir/ *v.t./i.* read.
lire [2] /lir/ *n.f.* lira.
lis [1] /li/ *voir* lire[1].
lis [2] /lis/ *n.m.* (*fleur*) lily.
lisible /lizibl/ *a.* legible; (*roman etc.*) readable.
lisière /lizjɛr/ *n.f.* edge.
liss|e /lis/ *a.* smooth. **~er** *v.t.* smooth.
liste /list/ *n.f.* list. **~ électorale,** register of voters.
listing /listiŋ/ *n.m.* printout.
lit [1] /li/ *voir* lire[1].
lit [2] /li/ *n.m.* (*de personne, fleuve*) bed. **se mettre au ~,** get into bed. **~ de camp,** camp-bed. **~ d'enfant,** cot. **~ d'une personne,** single bed.
litanie /litani/ *n.f.* litany.
litchi /litʃi/ *n.m.* litchi.
literie /litri/ *n.f.* bedding.
litière /litjɛr/ *n.f.* (*paille*) litter.
litige /litiʒ/ *n.m.* dispute.
litre /litr/ *n.m.* litre.
littéraire /literɛr/ *a.* literary.
littér|al (*m. pl.* **~aux**) /literal, -o/ *a.* literal. **~alement** *adv.* literally.
littérature /literatyr/ *n.f.* literature.
littor|al (*pl.* **~aux**) /litɔral, -o/ *n.m.* coast.
liturg|ie /lityrʒi/ *n.f.* liturgy. **~ique** *a.* liturgical.
livide /livid/ *a.* (*blême*) pallid.
livraison /livrɛzɔ̃/ *n.f.* delivery.
livre [1] /livr/ *n.m.* book. **~ de bord,** log-book. **~ de compte,** books. **~ de poche,** paperback.
livre [2] /livr/ *n.f.* (*monnaie, poids*) pound.
livrée /livre/ *n.f.* livery.
livr|er /livre/ *v.t.* deliver; (*abandonner*) give over (**à,** to); (*secret*) give away. **~é à soi-même,** left to o.s. **se ~er à,** give o.s. over to; (*actes, boisson*) indulge in; (*se confier à*) confide in; (*effectuer*) carry out.
livret /livrɛ/ *n.m.* book; (*mus.*) libretto. **~ scolaire,** school report (book).
livreu|r, ~se /livrœr, -øz/ *n.m., f.* delivery boy *ou* girl.
lobe /lɔb/ *n.m.* lobe.
loc|al [1] (*m. pl.* **~aux**) /lɔkal, -o/ *a.* local. **~alement** *adv.* locally.
loc|al [2] (*pl.* **~aux**) /lɔkal, -o/ *n.m.* premises. **~aux,** premises.
localisé /lɔkalize/ *a.* localized.
localité /lɔkalite/ *n.f.* locality.
locataire /lɔkatɛr/ *n.m./f.* tenant; (*de chambre, d'hôtel*) lodger.
location /lɔkɑsjɔ̃/ *n.f.* (*de maison*) renting; (*de voiture*) hiring, renting; (*de place*) booking, reservation; (*guichet*) booking office; (*théâtre*) box office; (*par propriétaire*) renting out; hiring out. **en ~,** (*voiture*) on hire, rented.
lock-out /lɔkaut/ *n.m. invar.* lockout.
locomotion /lɔkɔmosjɔ̃/ *n.f.* locomotion.
locomotive /lɔkɔmɔtiv/ *n.f.* engine, locomotive.
locution /lɔkysjɔ̃/ *n.f.* phrase.
logarithme /lɔgaritm/ *n.m.* logarithm.
loge /lɔʒ/ *n.f.* (*de concierge*) lodge; (*d'acteur*) dressing-room; (*de spectateur*) box.

logement /lɔʒmɑ̃/ *n.m.* accommodation; (*appartement*) flat; (*habitat*) housing.
log|er /lɔʒe/ *v.t.* accommodate. ● *v.i.*, **se ~er** *v. pr.* live. **trouver à se ~er,** find accommodation. **être ~é,** live. **se ~er dans,** (*balle*) lodge itself in.
logeu|r, ~se /lɔʒœr, -øz/ *n.m., f.* landlord, landlady.
logiciel /lɔʒisjɛl/ *n.m.* software.
logique /lɔʒik/ *a.* logical. ● *n.f.* logic. **~ment** *adv.* logically.
logis /lɔʒi/ *n.m.* dwelling.
logistique /lɔʒistik/ *n.f.* logistics.
logo /lɔgo/ *n.m.* logo.
loi /lwa/ *n.f.* law.
loin /lwɛ̃/ *adv.* far (away). **au ~,** far away. **de ~,** from far away; (*de beaucoup*) by far. **~ de là,** far from it. **plus ~,** further. **il revient de ~,** (*fig.*) he had a close shave.
lointain, ~e /lwɛ̃tɛ̃, -ɛn/ *a.* distant. ● *n.m.* distance.
loir /lwar/ *n.m.* dormouse.
loisir /lwazir/ *n.m.* (spare) time. **~s,** spare time; (*distractions*) spare time activities. **à ~,** at one's leisure.
londonien, ~ne /lɔ̃dɔnjɛ̃, -jɛn/ *a.* London. ● *n.m., f.* Londoner.
Londres /lɔ̃dr/ *n.m./f.* London.
long, ~ue /lɔ̃, lɔ̃g/ *a.* long. ● *n.m.* **de ~,** (*mesure*) long. **à la ~ue,** in the end. **à ~ terme,** long-term. **de ~ en large,** back and forth. **~ à faire,** a long time doing. **(tout) le ~ de,** (all) along.
longer /lɔ̃ʒe/ *v.t.* go along; (*limiter*) border.
longévité /lɔ̃ʒevite/ *n.f.* longevity.
longiligne /lɔ̃ʒiliɲ/ *a.* tall and slender.
longitude /lɔ̃ʒityd/ *n.f.* longitude.
longtemps /lɔ̃tɑ̃/ *adv.* a long time. **avant ~,** before long. **trop ~,** too long. **ça prendra ~,** it will take a long time.
longue /lɔ̃g/ *voir* long.
longuement /lɔ̃gmɑ̃/ *adv.* at length.
longueur /lɔ̃gœr/ *n.f.* length. **~s,** (*de texte etc.*) over-long parts. **à ~ de journée,** all day long. **~ d'onde,** wavelength.
longue-vue /lɔ̃gvy/ *n.f.* telescope.
look /luk/ *n.m.* (*fam.*) look, image.
lopin /lɔpɛ̃/ *n.m.* **~ de terre,** patch of land.
loquace /lɔkas/ *a.* talkative.
loque /lɔk/ *n.f.* **~s,** rags. **~ (humaine),** (human) wreck.
loquet /lɔkɛ/ *n.m.* latch.
lorgner /lɔrɲe/ *v.t.* eye.
lors de /lɔrdə/ *prép.* at the time of.
lorsque /lɔrsk(ə)/ *conj.* when.
losange /lɔzɑ̃ʒ/ *n.m.* diamond.
lot /lo/ *n.m.* prize; (*portion, destin*) lot.
loterie /lɔtri/ *n.f.* lottery.
lotion /losjɔ̃/ *n.f.* lotion.
lotissement /lɔtismɑ̃/ *n.m.* (*à construire*) building plot; (*construit*) (housing) development.
louable /lwabl/ *a.* praiseworthy.
louange /lwɑ̃ʒ/ *n.f.* praise.
louche[1] /luʃ/ *a.* shady, dubious.
louche[2] /luʃ/ *n.f.* ladle.
loucher /luʃe/ *v.i.* squint.
louer[1] /lwe/ *v.t.* (*maison*) rent; (*voiture*) hire, rent; (*place*) book, reserve; (*propriétaire*) rent out; hire out. **à ~,** to let, for rent (*Amer.*).
louer[2] /lwe/ *v.t.* (*approuver*) praise (**de,** for). **se ~ de,** congratulate o.s. on.
loufoque /lufɔk/ *a.* (*fam.*) crazy.
loup /lu/ *n.m.* wolf.
loupe /lup/ *n.f.* magnifying glass.
louper /lupe/ *v.t.* (*fam.*) miss.
lourd, ~e /lur, -d/ *a.* heavy; (*chaleur*) close; (*faute*) gross. **~ de conséquences,** with dire consequences. **~ement** /-dəmɑ̃/ *adv.* heavily. **~eur** /-dœr/ *n.f.* heaviness.
lourdaud, ~e /lurdo, -d/ *a.* loutish. ● *n.m., f.* lout, oaf.
loutre /lutr/ *n.f.* otter.
louve /luv/ *n.f.* she-wolf.
louveteau (*pl.* **~x**) /luvto/ *n.m.* wolf cub; (*scout*) Cub (Scout).
louvoyer /luvwaje/ *v.i.* (*fig.*) sidestep the issue; (*naut.*) tack.
loy|al (*m. pl.* **~aux**) /lwajal, -o/ *a.* loyal; (*honnête*) fair. **~alement** *adv.* loyally; fairly. **~auté** *n.f.* loyalty; fairness.
loyer /lwaje/ *n.m.* rent.
lu /ly/ *voir* lire[1].
lubie /lybi/ *n.f.* whim.
lubrif|ier /lybrifje/ *v.t.* lubricate. **~iant** *n.m.* lubricant.
lubrique /lybrik/ *a.* lewd.
lucarne /lykarn/ *n.f.* skylight.
lucid|e /lysid/ *a.* lucid. **~ité** *n.f.* lucidity.
lucrati|f, ~ve /lykratif, -v/ *a.* lucrative. **à but non ~f,** non-profit-making.

lueur /lɥœr/ *n.f.* (faint) light, glimmer; (*fig.*) glimmer, gleam.
luge /lyʒ/ *n.f.* toboggan.
lugubre /lygybr/ *a.* gloomy.
lui /lɥi/ *pron.* him; (*sujet*) he; (*chose*) it; (*objet indirect*) (to) him; (*femme*) (to) her; (*chose*) (to) it. **~-même** *pron.* himself; itself.
luire† /lɥir/ *v.i.* shine; (*reflet humide*) glisten; (*reflet chaud, faible*) glow.
lumbago /lɔ̃bago/ *n.m.* lumbago.
lumière /lymjɛr/ *n.f.* light. **~s,** (*connaissances*) knowledge. **faire (toute) la ~ sur,** clear up.
luminaire /luminɛr/ *n.m.* lamp.
lumineu|x, ~se /lyminø, -z/ *a.* luminous; (*éclairé*) illuminated; (*source, rayon*) (of) light; (*vif*) bright.
lunaire /lynɛr/ *a.* lunar.
lunatique /lynatik/ *a.* temperamental.
lunch /lœnʃ/ *n.m.* buffet lunch.
lundi /lœ̃di/ *n.m.* Monday.
lune /lyn/ *n.f.* moon. **~ de miel,** honeymoon.
lunette /lynɛt/ *n.f.* **~s,** glasses; (*de protection*) goggles. **~ arrière,** (*auto.*) rear window. **~s de soleil,** sun-glasses.
luron /lyrɔ̃/ *n.m.* **gai** *ou* **joyeux ~,** (*fam.*) quite a lad.
lustre /lystr/ *n.m.* (*éclat*) lustre; (*objet*) chandelier.
lustré /lystre/ *a.* shiny.
luth /lyt/ *n.m.* lute.
lutin /lytɛ̃/ *n.m.* goblin.
lutrin /lytrɛ̃/ *n.m.* lectern.
lutt|e /lyt/ *n.f.* fight, struggle; (*sport*) wrestling. **~er** *v.i.* fight, struggle; (*sport*) wrestle. **~eur, ~euse** *n.m., f.* fighter; (*sport*) wrestler.
luxe /lyks/ *n.m.* luxury. **de ~,** luxury; (*produit*) de luxe.
Luxembourg /lyksɑ̃bur/ *n.m.* Luxemburg.
lux|er /lykse/ *v.t.* **se ~er le genou,** dislocate one's knee. **~ation** *n.f.* dislocation.
luxueu|x, ~se /lyksɥø, -z/ *a.* luxurious.
luxure /lyksyr/ *n.f.* lust.
luxuriant, ~e /lyksyrjɑ̃, -t/ *a.* luxuriant.
luzerne /lyzɛrn/ *n.f.* (*plante*) lucerne, alfalfa.
lycée /lise/ *n.m.* (secondary) school. **~n, ~nne** /-ɛ̃, -ɛn/ *n.m., f.* pupil (at secondary school).
lynch|er /lɛ̃ʃe/ *v.t.* lynch. **~age** *n.m.* lynching.
lynx /lɛ̃ks/ *n.m.* lynx.
lyophilis|er /ljɔfilize/ *v.t.* freeze-dry. **~é** *a.* freeze-dried.
lyre /lir/ *n.f.* lyre.
lyri|que /lirik/ *a.* (*poésie*) lyric; (*passionné*) lyrical. **artiste/théâtre ~que,** opera singer/-house. **~sme** *n.m.* lyricism.
lys /lis/ *n.m.* lily.

M

m' /m/ *voir* me.
ma /ma/ *voir* mon.
maboul /mabul/ *a.* (*fam.*) mad.
macabre /makabr/ *a.* gruesome, macabre.
macadam /makadam/ *n.m.* (*goudronné*) Tarmac (P.).
macaron /makarɔ̃/ *n.m.* (*gâteau*) macaroon; (*insigne*) badge.
macaronis /makarɔni/ *n.m. pl.* macaroni.
macédoine /masedwan/ *n.f.* mixed vegetables. **~ de fruits,** fruit salad.
macérer /masere/ *v.t./i.* soak; (*dans du vinaigre*) pickle.
mâchefer /mɑʃfɛr/ *n.m.* clinker.
mâcher /mɑʃe/ *v.t.* chew. **ne pas ~ ses mots,** not mince one's words.
machiavélique /makjavelik/ *a.* machiavellian.
machin /maʃɛ̃/ *n.m.* (*chose: fam.*) thing; (*personne: fam.*) what's-his-name.
machin|al (*m. pl.* **~aux**) /maʃinal, -o/ *a.* automatic. **~alement** *adv.* automatically.
machinations /maʃinɑsjɔ̃/ *n.f. pl.* machinations.
machine /maʃin/ *n.f.* machine; (*d'un train, navire*) engine. **~ à écrire,** typewriter. **~ à laver/coudre,** washing-/sewing-machine. **~ à sous,** fruit machine; (*Amer.*) slot-machine. **~-outil** (*pl.* **~s-outils**) *n.f.* machine tool. **~rie** *n.f.* machinery.
machiner /maʃine/ *v.t.* plot.
machiniste /maʃinist/ *n.m.* (*théâtre*) stage-hand; (*conducteur*) driver.
macho /ma(t)ʃo/ *n.m.* (*fam.*) macho.
mâchoire /mɑʃwar/ *n.f.* jaw.
mâchonner /mɑʃɔne/ *v.t.* chew at.

maçon /masɔ̃/ *n.m.* builder; (*poseur de briques*) bricklayer. **~nerie** /-ɔnri/ *n.f.* brickwork; (*pierres*) stonework, masonry.

maçonnique /masɔnik/ *a.* Masonic.

macrobiotique /makrɔbjɔtik/ *a.* macrobiotic.

maculer /makyle/ *v.t.* stain.

Madagascar /madagaskar/ *n.f.* Madagascar.

madame (*pl.* **mesdames**) /madam, medam/ *n.f.* madam. **M~** *ou* **Mme Dupont,** Mrs Dupont. **bonsoir, mesdames,** good evening, ladies.

madeleine /madlɛn/ *n.f.* madeleine (*small shell-shaped sponge-cake*).

mademoiselle (*pl.* **mesdemoiselles**) /madmwazɛl, medmwazɛl/ *n.f.* miss. **M~** *ou* **Mlle Dupont,** Miss Dupont. **bonsoir, mesdemoiselles,** good evening, ladies.

madère /madɛr/ *n.m.* (*vin*) Madeira.

madone /madɔn/ *n.f.* madonna.

madrig|al (*pl.* **~aux**) /madrigal, -o/ *n.m.* madrigal.

maestro /maɛstro/ *n.m.* maestro.

maf(f)ia /mafja/ *n.f.* Mafia.

magasin /magazɛ̃/ *n.m.* shop, store; (*entrepôt*) warehouse; (*d'une arme etc.*) magazine.

magazine /magazin/ *n.m.* magazine; (*émission*) programme.

Maghreb /magrɛb/ *n.m.* North Africa. **~in, ~ine** *a.* & *n.m., f.* North African.

magicien, ~ne /maʒisjɛ̃, -jɛn/ *n.m., f.* magician.

magie /maʒi/ *n.f.* magic.

magique /maʒik/ *a.* magic; (*mystérieux*) magical.

magistr|al (*m. pl.* **~aux**) /maʒistral, -o/ *a.* masterly; (*grand*: *hum.*) colossal. **~alement** *adv.* in a masterly fashion.

magistrat /maʒistra/ *n.m.* magistrate.

magistrature /maʒistratyr/ *n.f.* judiciary.

magnanim|e /maɲanim/ *a.* magnanimous. **~ité** *n.f.* magnanimity.

magnat /magna/ *n.m.* tycoon, magnate.

magner (se) /(sə)maɲe/ *v. pr.* (*argot*) hurry.

magnésie /maɲezi/ *n.f.* magnesia.

magnéti|que /maɲetik/ *a.* magnetic. **~ser** *v.t.* magnetize. **~sme** *n.m.* magnetism.

magnétophone /maɲetɔfɔn/ *n.m.* tape recorder. **~ à cassettes,** cassette recorder.

magnétoscope /maɲetɔskɔp/ *n.m.* video-recorder.

magnifi|que /maɲifik/ *a.* magnificent. **~cence** *n.f.* magnificence.

magnolia /maɲɔlja/ *n.m.* magnolia.

magot /mago/ *n.m.* (*fam.*) hoard (of money).

magouill|er /maguje/ *v.i.* (*fam.*) scheming. **~eur, ~euse** *n.m., f.* (*fam.*) schemer. **~e** *n.f.* (*fam.*) scheming.

magret /magrɛ/ *n.m.* **~ de canard,** steaklet of duck.

mai /mɛ/ *n.m.* May.

maigr|e /mɛgr/ *a.* thin; (*viande*) lean; (*yaourt*) low fat; (*fig.*) poor, meagre. **faire ~e,** abstain from meat. **~ement** *adv.* poorly. **~eur** *n.f.* thinness; leanness; (*fig.*) meagreness.

maigrir /megrir/ *v.i.* get thin(ner); (*en suivant un régime*) slim. ● *v.t.* make thin(ner).

maille /mɑj/ *n.f.* stitch; (*de filet*) mesh. **~ filée,** ladder, run.

maillet /majɛ/ *n.m.* mallet.

maillon /mɑjɔ̃/ *n.m.* link.

maillot /majo/ *n.m.* (*de sport*) jersey. **~ (de corps),** vest. **~ (de bain),** (swimming) costume.

main /mɛ̃/ *n.f.* hand. **avoir la ~ heureuse,** be lucky. **donner la ~ à qn.,** hold s.o.'s hand. **en ~s propres,** in person. **en bonnes ~,** in good hands. **~ courante,** handrail. **~-d'œuvre** (*pl.* **~s- d'œuvre**) *n.f.* labour; (*ensemble d'ouvriers*) labour force. **~-forte** *n.f. invar.* assistance. **se faire la ~,** get the hang of it. **perdre la ~,** lose one's touch. **sous la ~,** to hand. **vol/attaque à ~ armée,** armed robbery/attack.

mainmise /mɛ̃miz/ *n.f.* **~ sur,** complete hold on.

maint, ~e /mɛ̃, mɛ̃t/ *a.* many a. **~s,** many. **à ~es reprises,** on many occasions.

maintenant /mɛ̃tnɑ̃/ *adv.* now; (*de nos jours*) nowadays.

maintenir† /mɛ̃tnir/ *v.t.* keep, maintain; (*soutenir*) hold up; (*affirmer*) maintain. **se ~** *v. pr.* (*continuer*) persist; (*rester*) remain.

maintien /mɛ̃tjɛ̃/ *n.m.* (*attitude*) bearing; (*conservation*) maintenance.
maire /mɛr/ *n.m.* mayor.
mairie /meri/ *n.f.* town hall; (*administration*) town council.
mais /mɛ/ *conj.* but. **~ oui, ~ si,** of course. **~ non,** definitely not.
maïs /mais/ *n.m.* (*à cultiver*) maize; (*culin.*) sweetcorn; (*Amer.*) corn.
maison /mɛzɔ̃/ *n.f.* house; (*foyer*) home; (*immeuble*) building. **~ (de commerce),** firm. ● *a. invar.* (*culin.*) home-made. **à la ~,** at home. **rentrer** *ou* **aller à la ~,** go home. **~ des jeunes,** youth centre. **~ de repos, ~ de convalescence,** convalescent home. **~ de retraite,** old people's home. **~ mère,** parent company.
maisonnée /mɛzɔne/ *n.f.* household.
maisonnette /mɛzɔnɛt/ *n.f.* small house, cottage.
maître /mɛtr/ *n.m.* master. **~ (d'école),** schoolmaster. **~ de,** in control of. **se rendre ~ de,** gain control of; (*incendie*) bring under control. **~ assistant/de conférences,** junior/senior lecturer. **~ chanteur,** blackmailer. **~ d'hôtel,** head waiter; (*domestique*) butler. **~ nageur,** swimming instructor.
maîtresse /mɛtrɛs/ *n.f.* mistress. **~ (d'école),** schoolmistress. ● *a.f.* (*idée, poutre, qualité*) main. **~ de,** in control of.
maîtris|e /metriz/ *n.f.* mastery; (*univ.*) master's degree. **~e (de soi),** self-control. **~er** *v.t.* master; (*incendie*) control; (*personne*) subdue. **se ~er** *v. pr.* control o.s.
maïzena /maizena/ *n.f.* (P.) cornflour.
majesté /maʒɛste/ *n.f.* majesty.
majestueu|x, ~se /maʒɛstɥø, -z/ *a.* majestic. **~sement** *adv.* majestically.
majeur /maʒœr/ *a.* major; (*jurid.*) of age. ● *n.m.* middle finger. **en ~e partie,** mostly. **la ~e partie de,** most of.
major|er /maʒɔre/ *v.t.* increase. **~ation** *n.f.* increase (**de,** in).
majorit|é /maʒɔrite/ *n.f.* majority. **en ~é,** chiefly. **~aire** *a.* majority. **être ~aire,** be in the majority.
Majorque /majɔrk/ *n.f.* Majorca.
majuscule /maʒyskyl/ *a.* capital. ● *n.f.* capital letter.

mal[1] /mal/ *adv.* badly; (*incorrectement*) wrong(ly). **~ (à l'aise),** uncomfortable. **aller ~,** (*malade*) be bad. **c'est ~ de,** it is wrong *ou* bad to. **~ entendre/comprendre,** not hear/understand properly. **~ famé,** of ill repute. **~ fichu,** (*personne*: *fam.*) feeling lousy. **~ en point,** in a bad state. **pas ~,** not bad; quite a lot.
mal[2] (*pl.* **maux**) /mal, mo/ *n.m.* evil; (*douleur*) pain, ache; (*maladie*) disease; (*effort*) trouble; (*dommage*) harm; (*malheur*) misfortune. **avoir ~ à la tête/aux dents/à la gorge,** have a headache/a toothache/a sore throat. **avoir le ~ de mer/du pays,** be seasick/homesick. **faire du ~ à,** hurt, harm. **se donner du ~ pour faire qch.,** go to a lot of trouble to do sth.
malade /malad/ *a.* sick, ill; (*bras, gorge*) bad; (*plante*) diseased. **tu es complètement ~!,** (*fam.*) you're mad. ● *n.m./f.* sick person; (*d'un médecin*) patient.
maladie /maladi/ *n.f.* illness, disease.
maladi|f, ~ve /maladif, -v/ *a.* sickly; (*peur*) morbid.
maladresse /maladrɛs/ *n.f.* clumsiness; (*erreur*) blunder.
maladroit, ~e /maladrwa, -t/ *a.* & *n.m., f.* clumsy (person).
malais, ~e[1] /malɛ, -z/ *a.* & *n.m., f.* Malay.
malaise[2] /malɛz/ *n.m.* feeling of faintness *ou* dizziness; (*fig.*) uneasiness, malaise.
malaisé /maleze/ *a.* difficult.
malaria /malarja/ *n.f.* malaria.
Malaysia /malɛzja/ *n.f.* Malaysia.
malaxer /malakse/ *v.t.* (*pétrir*) knead; (*mêler*) mix.
malchanc|e /malʃɑ̃s/ *n.f.* misfortune. **~eux, ~euse** *a.* unlucky.
malcommode /malkɔmɔd/ *a.* awkward.
mâle /mɑl/ *a.* male; (*viril*) manly. ● *n.m.* male.
malédiction /malediksjɔ̃/ *n.f.* curse.
maléfice /malefis/ *n.m.* evil spell.
maléfique /malefik/ *a.* evil.
malencontreu|x, ~se /malɑ̃kɔ̃trø, -z/ *a.* unfortunate.
malentendant, ~e *a.* & *n.m., f.* hard of hearing.
malentendu /malɑ̃tɑ̃dy/ *n.m.* misunderstanding.
malfaçon /malfasɔ̃/ *n.f.* fault.

malfaisant, ~e /malfəzɑ̃, -t/ *a.* harmful.
malfaiteur /malfɛtœr/ *n.m.* criminal.
malformation /malfɔrmɑsjɔ̃/ *n.f.* malformation.
malgache /malgaʃ/ *a.* & *n.m./f.* Malagasy.
malgré /malgre/ *prép.* in spite of, despite. **~ tout,** after all.
malhabile /malabil/ *a.* clumsy.
malheur /malœr/ *n.m.* misfortune; (*accident*) accident. **faire un ~,** be a big hit.
malheureu|x, ~se /malœrø, -z/ *a.* unhappy; (*regrettable*) unfortunate; (*sans succès*) unlucky; (*insignifiant*) wretched. ● *n.m., f.* (poor) wretch. **~sement** *adv.* unfortunately.
malhonnête /malɔnɛt/ *a.* dishonest. **~té** *n.f.* dishonesty; (*action*) dishonest action.
malic|e /malis/ *n.f.* mischievousness; (*méchanceté*) malice. **~ieux, ~ieuse** *a.* mischievous.
mal|in, ~igne /malɛ̃, -iɲ/ *a.* clever, smart; (*méchant*) malicious; (*tumeur*) malignant; (*difficile: fam.*) difficult. **~ignité** *n.f.* malignancy.
malingre /malɛ̃gr/ *a.* puny.
malintentionné /malɛ̃tɑ̃sjɔne/ *a.* malicious.
malle /mal/ *n.f.* (*valise*) trunk; (*auto.*) boot; (*auto., Amer.*) trunk.
malléable /maleabl/ *a.* malleable.
mallette /malɛt/ *n.f.* (small) suitcase.
malmener /malməne/ *v.t.* manhandle, handle roughly.
malnutrition /malnytrisjɔ̃/ *n.f.* malnutrition.
malodorant, ~e /malɔdɔrɑ̃, -t/ *a.* smelly, foul-smelling.
malotru /malɔtry/ *n.m.* boor.
malpoli /malpɔli/ *a.* impolite.
malpropre /malprɔpr/ *a.* dirty. **~té** /-əte/ *n.f.* dirtiness.
malsain, ~e /malsɛ̃, -ɛn/ *a.* unhealthy.
malt /malt/ *n.m.* malt.
maltais, ~e /maltɛ, -z/ *a.* & *n.m., f.* Maltese.
Malte /malt/ *n.f.* Malta.
maltraiter /maltrete/ *v.t.* ill-treat.
malveillan|t, ~te /malvɛjɑ̃, -t/ *a.* malevolent. **~ce** *n.f.* malevolence.
maman /mamɑ̃/ *n.f.* mum(my), mother.
mamelle /mamɛl/ *n.f.* teat.
mamelon /mamlɔ̃/ *n.m.* (*anat.*) nipple; (*colline*) hillock.
mamie /mami/ *n.f.* (*fam.*) granny.
mammifère /mamifɛr/ *n.m.* mammal.
mammouth /mamut/ *n.m.* mammoth.
manche[1] /mɑ̃ʃ/ *n.f.* sleeve; (*sport, pol.*) round. **la M~,** the Channel.
manche[2] /mɑ̃ʃ/ *n.m.* (*d'un instrument*) handle. **~ à balai,** broomstick.
manchette /mɑ̃ʃɛt/ *n.f.* cuff; (*de journal*) headline.
manchot[1]**, ~e** /mɑ̃ʃo, -ɔt/ *a.* & *n.m., f.* one-armed (person); (*sans bras*) armless (person).
manchot[2] /mɑ̃ʃo/ *n.m.* (*oiseau*) penguin.
mandarin /mɑ̃darɛ̃/ *n.m.* (*fonctionnaire*) mandarin.
mandarine /mɑ̃darin/ *n.f.* tangerine, mandarin (orange).
mandat /mɑ̃da/ *n.m.* (*postal*) money order; (*pol.*) mandate; (*procuration*) proxy; (*de police*) warrant. **~aire** /-tɛr/ *n.m.* (*représentant*) representative. **~er** /-te/ *v.t.* (*pol.*) delegate.
manège /manɛʒ/ *n.m.* riding-school; (*à la foire*) merry-go-round; (*manœuvre*) wiles, ploy.
manette /manɛt/ *n.f.* lever; (*comput.*) joystick.
mangeable /mɑ̃ʒabl/ *a.* edible.
mangeoire /mɑ̃ʒwar/ *n.f.* trough.
mang|er /mɑ̃ʒe/ *v.t./i.* eat; (*fortune*) go through; (*ronger*) eat into. ● *n.m.* food. **donner à ~er à,** feed. **~eur, ~euse** *n.m., f.* eater.
mangue /mɑ̃g/ *n.f.* mango.
maniable /manjabl/ *a.* easy to handle.
maniaque /manjak/ *a.* fussy. ● *n.m./f.* fuss-pot; (*fou*) maniac. **un ~ de,** a maniac for.
manie /mani/ *n.f.* habit; obsession.
man|ier /manje/ *v.t.* handle. **~iement** *n.m.* handling.
manière /manjɛr/ *n.f.* way, manner. **~s,** (*politesse*) manners; (*chichis*) fuss. **de cette ~,** in this way. **de ~ à,** so as to. **de toute ~,** anyway, in any case.
maniéré /manjere/ *a.* affected.
manif /manif/ *n.f.* (*fam.*) demo.
manifestant, ~e /manifɛstɑ̃, -t/ *n.m., f.* demonstrator.
manifeste /manifɛst/ *a.* obvious. ● *n.m.* manifesto.

manifest|er[1] /manifɛste/ *v.t.* show, manifest. **se ~er** *v. pr.* (*sentiment*) show itself; (*apparaître*) appear. **~ation**[1] *n.f.* expression, demonstration, manifestation; (*de maladie*) appearance.

manifest|er[2] /manifɛste/ *v.i.* (*pol.*) demonstrate. **~ation**[2] *n.f.* (*pol.*) demonstration; (*événement*) event.

manigan|ce /manigɑ̃s/ *n.f.* little plot. **~er** *v.t.* plot.

manipul|er /manipyle/ *v.t.* handle; (*péj.*) manipulate. **~ation** *n.f.* handling; (*péj.*) manipulation.

manivelle /manivɛl/ *n.f.* crank.

manne /man/ *n.f.* (*aubaine*) godsend.

mannequin /mankɛ̃/ *n.m.* (*personne*) model; (*statue*) dummy.

manœuvr|e[1] /manœvr/ *n.f.* manœuvre. **~er** *v.t./i.* manœuvre; (*machine*) operate.

manœuvre[2] /manœvr/ *n.m.* (*ouvrier*) labourer.

manoir /manwar/ *n.m.* manor.

manque /mɑ̃k/ *n.m.* lack (**de,** of); (*vide*) gap. **~s,** (*défauts*) faults. **~ à gagner,** loss of profit. **en (état de) ~,** having withdrawal symptoms.

manqué /mɑ̃ke/ *a.* (*écrivain etc.*) failed. **garçon ~,** tomboy.

manquement /mɑ̃kmɑ̃/ *n.m.* **~ à,** breach of.

manquer /mɑ̃ke/ *v.t.* miss; (*gâcher*) spoil; (*examen*) fail. ● *v.i.* be short *ou* lacking; (*absent*) be absent; (*en moins, disparu*) be missing; (*échouer*) fail. **~ à,** (*devoir*) fail in. **~ de,** be short of, lack. **il/ça lui manque,** he misses him/it. **~ (de) faire,** (*faillir*) nearly do. **ne pas ~ de,** not fail to.

mansarde /mɑ̃sard/ *n.f.* attic.

manteau (*pl.* **~x**) /mɑ̃to/ *n.m.* coat.

manucur|e /manykyr/ *n.m./f.* manicurist. **~er** *v.t.* manicure.

manuel, ~le /manɥɛl/ *a.* manual. ● *n.m.* (*livre*) manual. **~lement** *adv.* manually.

manufactur|e /manyfaktyr/ *n.f.* factory. **~é** *a.* manufactured.

manuscrit, ~e /manyskri, -t/ *a.* handwritten. ● *n.m.* manuscript.

manutention /manytɑ̃sjɔ̃/ *n.f.* handling.

mappemonde /mapmɔ̃d/ *n.f.* world map; (*sphère*) globe.

maquereau (*pl.* **~x**) /makro/ *n.m.* (*poisson*) mackerel; (*fam.*) pimp.

maquette /makɛt/ *n.f.* (scale) model; (*mise en page*) paste-up.

maquill|er /makije/ *v.t.* make up; (*truquer*) fake. **se ~er** *v. pr.* make (o.s.) up. **~age** *n.m.* make-up.

maquis /maki/ *n.m.* (*paysage*) scrub; (*mil.*) Maquis, underground.

maraîch|er, ~ère /mareʃe, -ɛʃɛr/ *n.m., f.* market gardener; (*Amer.*) truck farmer. **cultures ~ères,** market gardening.

marais /marɛ/ *n.m.* marsh.

marasme /marasm/ *n.m.* slump.

marathon /maratɔ̃/ *n.m.* marathon.

marbre /marbr/ *n.m.* marble.

marc /mar/ *n.m.* (*eau-de-vie*) marc. **~ de café,** coffee-grounds.

marchand, ~e /marʃɑ̃, -d/ *n.m., f.* trader; (*de charbon, vins*) merchant. ● *a.* (*valeur*) market. **~ de couleurs,** ironmonger; (*Amer.*) hardware merchant. **~ de journaux,** newsagent. **~ de légumes,** greengrocer. **~ de poissons,** fishmonger.

marchand|er /marʃɑ̃de/ *v.t.* haggle over. ● *v.i.* haggle. **~age** *n.m.* haggling.

marchandise /marʃɑ̃diz/ *n.f.* goods.

marche /marʃ/ *n.f.* (*démarche, trajet*) walk; (*rythme*) pace; (*mil., mus.*) march; (*d'escalier*) step; (*sport*) walking; (*de machine*) working; (*de véhicule*) running. **en ~,** (*train etc.*) moving. **faire ~ arrière,** (*véhicule*) reverse. **mettre en ~,** start (up). **se mettre en ~,** start moving.

marché /marʃe/ *n.m.* market; (*contrat*) deal. **faire son ~,** do one's shopping. **~ aux puces,** flea market. **M~ commun,** Common Market. **~ noir,** black market.

marchepied /marʃəpje/ *n.m.* (*de train, camion*) step.

march|er /marʃe/ *v.i.* walk; (*aller*) go; (*fonctionner*) work, run; (*prospérer*) go well; (*consentir: fam.*) agree. **~er (au pas),** (*mil.*) march. **faire ~er qn.,** pull s.o.'s leg. **~eur, ~euse** *n.m., f.* walker.

mardi /mardi/ *n.m.* Tuesday. **M~ gras,** Shrove Tuesday.

mare /mar/ *n.f.* (*étang*) pond; (*flaque*) pool.

marécag|e /marekaʒ/ *n.m.* marsh. **~eux, ~euse** *a.* marshy.

maréch|al (*pl.* **~aux**) /mareʃal, -o/ *n.m.* marshal. **~al-ferrant** (*pl.* **~aux-ferrants**) blacksmith.

marée /mare/ *n.f.* tide; (*poissons*) fresh fish. **~ haute/basse,** high/low tide. **~ noire,** oil-slick.
marelle /marɛl/ *n.f.* hopscotch.
margarine /margarin/ *n.f.* margarine.
marge /marʒ/ *n.f.* margin. **en ~ de,** (*à l'écart de*) on the fringe(s) of. **~ bénéficiaire,** profit margin.
margin|al, ~ale (*m. pl.* **~aux**) /marʒinal, -o/ *a.* marginal. ● *n.m., f.* drop-out.
marguerite /margərit/ *n.f.* daisy; (*qui imprime*) daisy-wheel.
mari /mari/ *n.m.* husband.
mariage /marjaʒ/ *n.m.* marriage; (*cérémonie*) wedding.
marié, ~e /marje/ *a.* married. ● *n.m.* (bride)groom. ● *n.f.* bride. **les ~s,** the bride and groom.
marier /marje/ *v.t.* marry. **se ~** *v. pr.* get married, marry. **se ~ avec,** marry, get married to.
marin, ~e /marɛ̃, -in/ *a.* sea. ● *n.m.* sailor. ● *n.f.* navy. **~e marchande,** merchant navy.
mariner /marine/ *v.t./i.* marinate. **faire ~,** (*fam.*) keep hanging around.
marionnette /marjɔnɛt/ *n.f.* puppet; (*à fils*) marionette.
maritalement /maritalmɑ̃/ *adv.* as husband and wife.
maritime /maritim/ *a.* maritime, coastal; (*droit, agent*) shipping.
mark /mark/ *n.m.* mark.
marmaille /marmaj/ *n.f.* (*enfants: fam.*) brats.
marmelade /marməlad/ *n.f.* stewed fruit. **~ (d'oranges),** marmelade.
marmite /marmit/ *n.f.* (cooking-)pot.
marmonner /marmɔne/ *v.t./i.* mumble.
marmot /marmo/ *n.m.* (*fam.*) kid.
marmotter /marmɔte/ *v.t./i.* mumble.
Maroc /marɔk/ *n.m.* Morocco.
marocain, ~e /marɔkɛ̃, -ɛn/ *a.* & *n.m., f.* Moroccan.
maroquinerie /marɔkinri/ *n.f.* (*magasin*) leather goods shop.
marotte /marɔt/ *n.f.* fad, craze.
marquant, ~e /markɑ̃, -t/ *a.* (*remarquable*) outstanding; (*qu'on n'oublie pas*) significant.
marque /mark/ *n.f.* mark; (*de produits*) brand, make. **à vos ~s!,** (*sport*) on your marks! **de ~,** (*comm.*) brand-name; (*fig.*) important. **~ de fabrique,** trade mark. **~ déposée,** registered trade mark.
marqué /marke/ *a.* marked.
marquer /marke/ *v.t.* mark; (*indiquer*) show; (*écrire*) note down; (*point, but*) score; (*joueur*) mark; (*animal*) brand. ● *v.i.* (*trace*) leave a mark; (*événement*) stand out.
marqueterie /markɛtri/ *n.f.* marquetry.
marquis, ~e[1] /marki, -z/ *n.m., f.* marquis, marchioness.
marquise[2] /markiz/ *n.f.* (*auvent*) glass awning.
marraine /marɛn/ *n.f.* godmother.
marrant, ~e /marɑ̃, -t/ *a.* (*fam.*) funny.
marre /mar/ *adv.* **en avoir ~,** (*fam.*) be fed up (**de,** with).
marrer (se) /(sə)mare/ *v. pr.* (*fam.*) laugh, have a (good) laugh.
marron /marɔ̃/ *n.m.* chestnut; (*couleur*) brown; (*coup: fam.*) thump. ● *a. invar.* brown. **~ d'Inde,** horse-chestnut.
mars /mars/ *n.m.* March.
marsouin /marswɛ̃/ *n.m.* porpoise.
marteau (*pl.* **~x**) /marto/ *n.m.* hammer. **~ (de porte),** (door) knocker. **~ piqueur** *ou* **pneumatique,** pneumatic drill. **être ~,** (*fam.*) mad.
marteler /martəle/ *v.t.* hammer.
mart|ial (*m. pl.* **~iaux**) /marsjal, -jo/ *a.* martial.
martien, ~ne /marsjɛ̃, -jɛn/ *a.* & *n.m., f.* Martian.
martyr, ~e[1] /martir/ *n.m., f.* martyr. ● *a.* martyred. **~iser** *v.t.* martyr; (*fig.*) batter.
martyre[2] /martir/ *n.m.* (*souffrance*) martyrdom.
marxis|te /marksist/ *a.* & *n.m./f.* Marxist. **~me** *n.m.* Marxism.
mascara /maskara/ *n.m.* mascara.
mascarade /maskarad/ *n.f.* masquerade.
mascotte /maskɔt/ *n.f.* mascot.
masculin, ~e /maskylɛ̃, -in/ *a.* masculine; (*sexe*) male; (*mode, équipe*) men's. ● *n.m.* masculine. **~ité** /-inite/ *n.f.* masculinity.
maso /mazo/ *n.m./f.* (*fam.*) masochist. ● *a. invar.* masochistic.
masochis|te /mazɔʃist/ *n.m./f.* masochist. ● *a.* masochistic. **~me** *n.m.* masochism.

masqu|e /mask/ *n.m.* mask. **~er** *v.t.* (*cacher*) hide, conceal (**à**, from); (*lumière*) block (off).

massacr|e /masakr/ *n.m.* massacre. **~er** *v.t.* massacre; (*abîmer: fam.*) spoil.

massage /masaʒ/ *n.m.* massage.

masse /mas/ *n.f.* (*volume*) mass; (*gros morceau*) lump, mass; (*outil*) sledge-hammer. **en ~,** (*vendre*) in bulk; (*venir*) in force; (*production*) mass. **la ~,** (*foule*) the masses. **une ~ de,** (*fam.*) masses of.

masser[1] /mase/ *v.t.*, **se ~** *v. pr.* (*gens, foule*) mass.

mass|er[2] /mase/ *v.t.* (*pétrir*) massage. **~eur, ~euse** *n.m., f.* masseur, masseuse.

massi|f, ~ve /masif, -v/ *a.* massive; (*or, argent*) solid. ● *n.m.* (*de fleurs*) clump; (*géog.*) massif. **~vement** *adv.* (*en masse*) in large numbers.

massue /masy/ *n.f.* club, bludgeon.

mastic /mastik/ *n.m.* putty.

mastiquer /mastike/ *v.t.* (*mâcher*) chew.

masturb|er (se) /(sə)mastyrbe/ *v. pr.* masturbate. **~ation** *n.f.* masturbation.

masure /mazyr/ *n.f.* hovel.

mat /mat/ *a.* (*couleur*) matt; (*bruit*) dull. **être ~,** (*aux échecs*) be checkmate.

mât /mɑ/ *n.m.* mast; (*pylône*) pole.

match /matʃ/ *n.m.* match; (*Amer.*) game. **(faire) ~ nul,** tie, draw. **~ aller,** first leg. **~ retour,** return match.

matelas /matla/ *n.m.* mattress. **~ pneumatique,** air mattress.

matelassé /matlase/ *a.* padded; (*tissu*) quilted.

matelot /matlo/ *n.m.* sailor.

mater /mate/ *v.t.* (*personne*) subdue; (*réprimer*) stifle.

matérialiser (se) /(sə)materjalize/ *v. pr.* materialize.

matérialiste /materjalist/ *a.* materialistic. ● *n.m./f.* materialist.

matériaux /materjo/ *n.m. pl.* materials.

matériel, ~le /materjɛl/ *a.* material. ● *n.m.* equipment, materials; (*d'un ordinateur*) hardware.

maternel, ~le /matɛrnɛl/ *a.* motherly, maternal; (*rapport de parenté*) maternal. ● *n.f.* nursery school.

maternité /matɛrnite/ *n.f.* maternity hospital; (*état de mère*) motherhood.

mathémati|que /matematik/ *a.* mathematical. ● *n.f. pl.* mathematics. **~cien, ~cienne** *n.m., f.* mathematician.

maths /mat/ *n.f. pl.* (*fam.*) maths.

matière /matjɛr/ *n.f.* matter; (*produit*) material; (*sujet*) subject. **en ~ de,** as regards. **~ plastique,** plastic. **~s grasses,** fat. **à 0% de ~s grasses,** fat free. **~s premières,** raw materials.

matin /matɛ̃/ *n.m.* morning. **de bon ~,** early in the morning.

matin|al (*m. pl.* **~aux**) /matinal, -o/ *a.* morning; (*de bonne heure*) early. **être ~,** be up early.

matinée /matine/ *n.f.* morning; (*spectacle*) matinée.

matou /matu/ *n.m.* tom-cat.

matraqu|e /matrak/ *n.f.* (*de police*) truncheon; (*Amer.*) billy (club). **~er** *v.t.* club, beat; (*message*) plug.

matrice /matris/ *n.f.* (*techn.*) matrix.

matrimon|ial (*m. pl.* **~iaux**) /matrimɔnjal, -jo/ *a.* matrimonial.

maturité /matyrite/ *n.f.* maturity.

maudire† /modir/ *v.t.* curse.

maudit, ~e /modi, -t/ *a.* (*fam.*) damned.

maugréer /mogree/ *v.i.* grumble.

mausolée /mozɔle/ *n.m.* mausoleum.

maussade /mosad/ *a.* gloomy.

mauvais, ~e /mɔvɛ, -z/ *a.* bad; (*erroné*) wrong; (*malveillant*) evil; (*désagréable*) nasty, bad; (*mer*) rough. ● *n.m.* **il fait ~,** the weather is bad. **le ~ moment,** the wrong time. **~e herbe,** weed. **~e langue,** gossip. **~e passe,** tight spot. **~ traitements,** ill-treatment.

mauve /mov/ *a.* & *n.m.* mauve.

mauviette /movjɛt/ *n.f.* weakling.

maux /mo/ *voir* mal[2].

maxim|al (*m. pl.* **~aux**) /maksimal, -o/ *a.* maximum.

maxime /maksim/ *n.f.* maxim.

maximum /maksimɔm/ *a.* & *n.m.* maximum. **au ~,** as much as possible; (*tout au plus*) at most.

mayonnaise /majɔnɛz/ *n.f.* mayonnaise.

mazout /mazut/ *n.m.* (fuel) oil.

me, m'* /mə, m/ *pron.* me; (*indirect*) (to) me; (*réfléchi*) myself.

méandre /meɑ̃dr/ *n.m.* meander.

mec /mek/ *n.m.* (*fam.*) bloke, guy.

mécanicien /mekanisjɛ̃/ *n.m.* mechanic; (*rail.*) train driver.

mécani|que /mekanik/ *a.* mechanical; (*jouet*) clockwork. **problème ~que,** engine trouble. ● *n.f.* mechanics; (*mécanisme*) mechanism. **~ser** *v.t.* mechanize.

mécanisme /mekanism/ *n.m.* mechanism.

méch|ant, ~ante /meʃɑ̃, -t/ *a.* (*cruel*) wicked; (*désagréable*) nasty; (*enfant*) naughty; (*chien*) vicious; (*sensationnel: fam.*) terrific. ● *n.m., f.* (*enfant*) naughty child. **~amment** *adv.* wickedly. **~anceté** *n.f.* wickedness; (*action*) wicked action.

mèche /mɛʃ/ *n.f.* (*de cheveux*) lock; (*de bougie*) wick; (*d'explosif*) fuse. **de ~ avec,** in league with.

méconnaissable /mekɔnɛsabl/ *a.* unrecognizable.

méconn|aître /mekɔnɛtr/ *v.t.* be ignorant of; (*mésestimer*) underestimate. **~aissance** *n.f.* ignorance. **~u** *a.* unrecognized.

mécontent, ~e /mekɔ̃tɑ̃, -t/ *a.* dissatisfied (**de,** with); (*irrité*) annoyed (**de,** at, with). **~ement** /-tmɑ̃/ *n.m.* dissatisfaction; annoyance. **~er** /-te/ *v.t.* dissatisfy; (*irriter*) annoy.

médaill|e /medaj/ *n.f.* medal; (*insigne*) badge; (*bijou*) medallion. **~é, ~ée** *n.m., f.* medal holder.

médaillon /medajɔ̃/ *n.m.* medallion; (*bijou*) locket.

médecin /mɛdsɛ̃/ *n.m.* doctor.

médecine /mɛdsin/ *n.f.* medicine.

média /medja/ *n.m.* medium. **les ~s,** the media.

média|teur, ~trice /medjatœr, -tris/ *n.m., f.* mediator.

médiation /medjɑsjɔ̃/ *n.f.* mediation.

médiatique /medjatik/ *a.* **événement/personnalité ~,** media event/personality.

médic|al (*m. pl.* **~aux**) /medikal, -o/ *a.* medical.

médicament /medikamɑ̃/ *n.m.* medicine.

médicin|al (*m. pl.* **~aux**) /medisinal, -o/ *a.* medicinal.

médico-lég|al (*m. pl.* **~aux**) /medikɔlegal, -o/ *a.* forensic.

médiév|al (*m. pl.* **~aux**) /medjeval, -o/ *a.* medieval.

médiocr|e /medjɔkr/ *a.* mediocre, poor. **~ement** *adv.* (*peu*) not very; (*mal*) in a mediocre way. **~ité** *n.f.* mediocrity.

médire /medir/ *v.i.* **~ de,** speak ill of.

médisance /medizɑ̃s/ *n.f.* **~(s),** malicious gossip.

méditati|f, ~ve /meditatif, -v/ *a.* (*pensif*) thoughtful.

médit|er /medite/ *v.t./i.* meditate. **~er de,** plan to. **~ation** *n.f.* meditation.

Méditerranée /mediterane/ *n.f.* **la ~,** the Mediterranean.

méditerranéen, ~ne /mediteraneɛ̃, -ɛn/ *a.* Mediterranean.

médium /medjɔm/ *n.m.* (*personne*) medium.

méduse /medyz/ *n.f.* jellyfish.

meeting /mitiŋ/ *n.m.* meeting.

méfait /mefɛ/ *n.m.* misdeed. **les ~s de,** (*conséquences*) the ravages of.

méfian|t, ~te /mefjɑ̃, -t/ *a.* distrustful. **~ce** *n.f.* distrust.

méfier (se) /(sə)mefje/ *v. pr.* be wary *ou* careful. **se ~ de,** distrust, be wary of.

mégarde (par) /(par)megard/ *adv.* by accident, accidentally.

mégère /meʒɛr/ *n.f.* (*femme*) shrew.

mégot /mego/ *n.m.* (*fam.*) cigarette-end.

meilleur, ~e /mɛjœr/ *a.* & *adv.* better (**que,** than). **le ~ livre/***etc.*, the best book/*etc.* **mon ~ ami/***etc.*, my best friend/*etc.* **~ marché,** cheaper. ● *n.m., f.* **le ~/la ~e,** the best (one).

mélancol|ie /melɑ̃kɔli/ *n.f.* melancholy. **~ique** *a.* melancholy.

mélang|e /melɑ̃ʒ/ *n.m.* mixture, blend. **~er** *v.t.*, **se ~er** *v. pr.* mix, blend; (*embrouiller*) mix up.

mélasse /melas/ *n.f.* treacle; (*Amer.*) molasses.

mêlée /mele/ *n.f.* scuffle; (*rugby*) scrum.

mêler /mele/ *v.t.* mix (**à,** with); (*qualités*) combine; (*embrouiller*) mix up. **~ à,** (*impliquer dans*) involve in. **se ~** *v. pr.* mix; combine. **se ~ à,** (*se joindre à*) join. **se ~ de,** meddle in. **mêle-toi de ce qui te regarde,** mind your own business.

méli-mélo /melimelo/ *n.m.* (*pl.* **mélis-mélos**) jumble.

mélo /melo/ (*fam.*) *n.m.* melodrama. ● *a. invar.* melodramatic.

mélod|ie /melɔdi/ *n.f.* melody. **~ieux, ~ieuse** *a.* melodious. **~ique** *a.* melodic.

mélodram|e /melɔdram/ *n.m.* melodrama. **~atique** *a.* melodramatic.

mélomane /melɔman/ *n.m./f.* music lover.

melon /mlɔ̃/ *n.m.* melon. **(chapeau) ~,** bowler (hat).

membrane /mɑ̃bran/ *n.f.* membrane.

membre[1] /mɑ̃br/ *n.m.* limb.

membre[2] /mɑ̃br/ *n.m.* (*adhérent*) member.

même /mɛm/ *a.* same. **ce livre/***etc.* **~,** this very book/*etc.* **la bonté/***etc.* **~,** kindness/*etc.* itself. ● *pron.* **le ~/la ~,** the same (one). ● *adv.* even. **à ~,** (*sur*) directly on. **à ~ de,** in a position to. **de ~,** (*aussi*) too; (*de la même façon*) likewise. **de ~ que,** just as. **en ~ temps,** at the same time.

mémé /meme/ *n.f.* (*fam.*) granny.

mémo /memo/ *n.m.* memo.

mémoire /memwar/ *n.f.* memory. ● *n.m.* (*requête*) memorandum; (*univ.*) dissertation. **~s,** (*souvenirs écrits*) memoirs. **à la ~ de,** to the memory of. **de ~,** from memory. **~ morte/vive,** (*comput.*) ROM/RAM.

mémorable /memɔrabl/ *a.* memorable.

mémorandum /memɔrɑ̃dɔm/ *n.m.* memorandum.

menac|e /mənas/ *n.f.* threat. **~er** *v.t.* threaten (**de faire,** to do).

ménage /menaʒ/ *n.m.* (married) couple; (*travail*) housework. **se mettre en ~,** set up house. **scène de ~,** scene. **dépenses du ~,** household expenditure.

ménagement /menaʒmɑ̃/ *n.m.* care and consideration.

ménag|er[1]**, ~ère** /menaʒe, -ɛr/ *a.* household, domestic. **travaux ~ers,** housework. ● *n.f.* housewife.

ménager[2] /menaʒe/ *v.t.* treat with tact; (*utiliser*) be sparing in the use of; (*organiser*) prepare (carefully).

ménagerie /menaʒri/ *n.f.* menagerie.

mendiant, ~e /mɑ̃djɑ̃, -t/ *n.m., f.* beggar.

mendicité /mɑ̃disite/ *n.f.* begging.

mendier /mɑ̃dje/ *v.t.* beg for. ● *v.i.* beg.

menées /məne/ *n.f. pl.* schemings.

mener /məne/ *v.t.* lead; (*entreprise, pays*) run. ● *v.i.* lead. **~ à,** (*accompagner à*) take to. **~ à bien,** see through.

meneur /mənœr/ *n.m.* (*chef*) (ring)leader. **~ de jeu,** compère; (*Amer.*) master of ceremonies.

méningite /menɛ̃ʒit/ *n.f.* meningitis.

ménopause /menɔpoz/ *n.f.* menopause.

menotte /mənɔt/ *n.f.* (*fam.*) hand. **~s,** handcuffs.

mensong|e /mɑ̃sɔ̃ʒ/ *n.m.* lie; (*action*) lying. **~er, ~ère** *a.* untrue.

menstruation /mɑ̃stryɑsjɔ̃/ *n.f.* menstruation.

mensualité /mɑ̃sɥalite/ *n.f.* monthly payment.

mensuel, ~le /mɑ̃sɥɛl/ *a.* & *n.m.* monthly. **~lement** *adv.* monthly.

mensurations /mɑ̃syrɑsjɔ̃/ *n.f. pl.* measurements.

ment|al (*m. pl.* **~aux**) /mɑ̃tal, -o/ *a.* mental.

mentalité /mɑ̃talite/ *n.f.* mentality.

menteu|r, ~se /mɑ̃tœr, -øz/ *n.m., f.* liar. ● *a.* untruthful.

menthe /mɑ̃t/ *n.f.* mint.

mention /mɑ̃sjɔ̃/ *n.f.* mention; (*annotation*) note; (*scol.*) grade. **~ bien,** (*scol.*) distinction. **~ner** /-jɔne/ *v.t.* mention.

mentir† /mɑ̃tir/ *v.i.* lie.

menton /mɑ̃tɔ̃/ *n.m.* chin.

mentor /mɛ̃tɔr/ *n.m.* mentor.

menu[1] /məny/ *n.m.* (*carte*) menu; (*repas*) meal.

menu[2] /məny/ *a.* (*petit*) tiny; (*fin*) fine; (*insignifiant*) minor. ● *adv.* (*couper*) fine.

menuis|ier /mənɥizje/ *n.m.* carpenter, joiner. **~erie** *n.f.* carpentry, joinery.

méprendre (se) /(sə)meprɑ̃dr/ *v. pr.* **se ~ sur,** be mistaken about.

mépris /mepri/ *n.m.* contempt, scorn (**de,** for). **au ~ de,** in defiance of.

méprisable /meprizabl/ *a.* despicable.

méprise /mepriz/ *n.f.* mistake.

mépris|er /meprize/ *v.t.* scorn, despise. **~ant, ~ante** *a.* scornful.

mer /mɛr/ *n.f.* sea; (*marée*) tide. **en haute ~,** on the open sea.

mercenaire /mɛrsənɛr/ *n.m.* & *a.* mercenary.

merci /mɛrsi/ *int.* thank you, thanks (**de, pour,** for). ● *n.f.* mercy. **~ beaucoup, ~ bien,** thank you very much.

merc|ier, ~ière /mɛrsje, -jɛr/ *n.m., f.* haberdasher; (*Amer.*) notions merchant. **~erie** *n.f.* haberdashery; (*Amer.*) notions store.

mercredi /mɛrkrədi/ *n.m.* Wednesday. **~ des Cendres,** Ash Wednesday.

mercure /mɛrkyr/ *n.m.* mercury.

merde /mɛrd/ *n.f.* (*fam.*) shit. **être dans la ~,** be in a mess.

mère /mɛr/ *n.f.* mother. **~ de famille,** mother.

méridien /meridjɛ̃/ *n.m.* meridian.

méridion|al, ~ale (*m. pl.* **~aux**) /meridjɔnal, -o/ *a.* southern. ● *n.m., f.* southerner.

meringue /mərɛ̃g/ *n.f.* meringue.

mérite /merit/ *n.m.* merit. **il n'a aucun ~,** that's as it should be. **il a du ~,** it's very much to his credit.

mérit|er /merite/ *v.t.* deserve. **~ant, ~ante** *a.* deserving.

méritoire /meritwar/ *a.* commendable.

merlan /mɛrlɑ̃/ *n.m.* whiting.

merle /mɛrl/ *n.m.* blackbird.

merveille /mɛrvɛj/ *n.f.* wonder, marvel. **à ~,** wonderfully. **faire des ~s,** work wonders.

merveilleu|x, ~se /mɛrvɛjø, -z/ *a.* wonderful, marvellous. **~sement** *adv.* wonderfully.

mes /me/ *voir* mon.

mésange /mezɑ̃ʒ/ *n.f.* tit(mouse).

mésaventure /mezavɑ̃tyr/ *n.f.* misadventure.

mesdames /medam/ *voir* madame.

mesdemoiselles /medmwazɛl/ *voir* mademoiselle.

mésentente /mezɑ̃tɑ̃t/ *n.f.* disagreement.

mesquin, ~e /mɛskɛ̃, -in/ *a.* mean. **~erie** /-inri/ *n.f.* meanness.

mess /mɛs/ *n.m.* (*mil.*) mess.

messag|e /mesaʒ/ *n.m.* message. **~er, ~ère** *n.m., f.* messenger.

messe /mɛs/ *n.f.* (*relig.*) mass.

Messie /mesi/ *n.m.* Messiah.

messieurs /mesjø/ *voir* monsieur.

mesure /məzyr/ *n.f.* measurement; (*quantité, étalon*) measure; (*disposition*) measure, step; (*cadence*) time; (*modération*) moderation. **à ~ que,** as. **dans la ~ où,** in so far as. **dans une certaine ~,** to some extent. **en ~ de,** in a position to.

mesuré /məzyre/ *a.* measured; (*personne*) moderate.

mesurer /məzyre/ *v.t.* measure; (*juger*) assess; (*argent, temps*) ration. **se ~ avec,** pit o.s. against.

met /mɛ/ *voir* mettre.

métabolisme /metabɔlism/ *n.m.* metabolism.

mét|al (*pl.* **~aux**) /metal, -o/ *n.m.* metal. **~allique** *a.* (*objet*) metal; (*éclat etc.*) metallic.

métallurg|ie /metalyrʒi/ *n.f.* (*industrie*) steel *ou* metal industry. **~iste** *n.m.* steel *ou* metal worker.

métamorphos|e /metamɔrfoz/ *n.f.* metamorphosis. **~er** *v.t.*, **se ~er** *v. pr.* transform.

métaphor|e /metafɔr/ *n.f.* metaphor. **~ique** *a.* metaphorical.

météo /meteo/ *n.f.* (*bulletin*) weather forecast.

météore /meteɔr/ *n.m.* meteor.

météorolog|ie /meteɔrɔlɔʒi/ *n.f.* meteorology; (*service*) weather bureau. **~ique** *a.* weather; (*études etc.*) meteorological.

méthod|e /metɔd/ *n.f.* method; (*ouvrage*) course, manual. **~ique** *a.* methodical.

méticuleu|x, ~se /metikylø, -z/ *a.* meticulous.

métier /metje/ *n.m.* job; (*manuel*) trade; (*intellectuel*) profession; (*expérience*) skill. **~ (à tisser),** loom. **remettre sur le ~,** keep going back to the drawing-board.

métis, ~se /metis/ *a.* & *n.m., f.* half-caste.

métrage /metraʒ/ *n.m.* length. **court ~,** short film. **long ~,** full-length film.

mètre /mɛtr/ *n.m.* metre; (*règle*) rule. **~ ruban,** tape-measure.

métreur /metrœr/ *n.m.* quantity surveyor.

métrique /metrik/ *a.* metric.

métro /metro/ *n.m.* underground; (*à Paris*) Métro.

métropol|e /metrɔpɔl/ *n.f.* metropolis; (*pays*) mother country. **~itain, ~itaine** *a.* metropolitan.

mets[1] /mɛ/ *n.m.* dish.

mets[2] /mɛ/ *voir* mettre.

mettable /mɛtabl/ *a.* wearable.

metteur /mɛtœr/ *n.m.* **~ en scène,** (*théâtre*) producer; (*cinéma*) director.

mettre† /mɛtr/ *v.t.* put; (*vêtement*) put on; (*radio, chauffage, etc.*) put *ou* switch on; (*table*) lay; (*pendule*) set; (*temps*) take; (*installer*) put in; (*supposer*) suppose. **se ~** *v. pr.* put o.s.; (*objet*) go; (*porter*) wear. **~ bas,** give birth. **~ qn. en boîte,** pull s.o.'s leg. **~ en cause** *ou* **en question,** question. **~ en colère,** make angry. **~ en valeur,** highlight. (*un bien*) exploit. **se ~ à,** (*entrer dans*) get *ou* go into. **se ~ à faire,** start doing. **se ~ à l'aise,** make o.s. comfortable. **se ~ à table,** sit down at the table. **se ~ au travail,** set to work. **(se) ~ en ligne,** line up. **se ~ dans tous ses états,** get into a state. **se ~ du sable dans les yeux,** get sand in one's eyes.

meuble /mœbl/ *n.m.* piece of furniture. **~s,** furniture.

meublé /møble/ *n.m.* furnished flatlet.

meubler /møble/ *v.t.* furnish; (*fig.*) fill. **se ~** *v. pr.* buy furniture.

meugl|er /møgle/ *v.i.* moo. **~ement(s)** *n.m.* (*pl.*) mooing.

meule /møl/ *n.f.* (*de foin*) haystack; (*à moudre*) millstone.

meun|ier, ~ière /mønje, -jɛr/ *n.m.*, *f.* miller.

meurs, meurt /mœr/ *voir* mourir.

meurtr|e /mœrtr/ *n.m.* murder. **~ier, ~ière** *a.* deadly; *n.m.* murderer; *n.f.* murderess.

meurtr|ir /mœrtrir/ *v.t.* bruise. **~issure** *n.f.* bruise.

meute /møt/ *n.f.* (*troupe*) pack.

mexicain, ~e /mɛksikɛ̃, -ɛn/ *a.* & *n.m.*, *f.* Mexican.

Mexique /mɛksik/ *n.m.* Mexico.

mi- /mi/ *préf.* mid-, half-. **à mi-chemin,** half-way. **à mi-côte,** half-way up the hill. **la mi-juin**/*etc.*, mid-June/*etc.*

miaou /mjau/ *n.m.* mew.

miaul|er /mjole/ *v.i.* mew. **~ement** *n.m.* mew.

miche /miʃ/ *n.f.* round loaf.

micro /mikro/ *n.m.* microphone, mike; (*comput.*) micro.

micro- /mikro/ *préf.* micro-.

microbe /mikrɔb/ *n.m.* germ.

microfilm /mikrɔfilm/ *n.m.* microfilm.

micro-onde /mikrɔɔ̃d/ *n.f.* microwave. **un (four à) ~s,** microwave (oven).

microphone /mikrɔfɔn/ *n.m.* microphone.

microplaquette /mikrɔplakɛt/ *n.f.* (micro)chip.

microprocesseur /mikrɔprɔsɛsœr/ *n.m.* microprocess.

microscop|e /mikrɔskɔp/ *n.m.* microscope. **~ique** *a.* microscopic.

microsillon /mikrɔsijɔ̃/ *n.m.* long-playing record.

midi /midi/ *n.m.* twelve o'clock, midday, noon; (*déjeuner*) lunch-time; (*sud*) south. **le M~,** the South of France.

mie /mi/ *n.f.* soft part (of the loaf). **un pain de ~,** a sandwich loaf.

miel /mjɛl/ *n.m.* honey.

mielleu|x, ~se /mjɛlø, -z/ *a.* unctuous.

mien, ~ne /mjɛ̃, mjɛn/ *pron.* **le ~, la ~ne, les ~(ne)s,** mine.

miette /mjɛt/ *n.f.* crumb; (*fig.*) scrap. **en ~s,** in pieces.

mieux /mjø/ *adv.* & *a. invar.* better **(que,** than). **le** *ou* **la** *ou* **les ~,** (the) best. ● *n.m.* best; (*progrès*) improvement. **faire de son ~,** do one's best. **tu ferais ~ de faire,** you would be better off doing. **le ~ serait de,** the best thing would be to.

mièvre /mjɛvr/ *a.* genteel and insipid.

mignon, ~ne /miɲɔ̃, -ɔn/ *a.* pretty.

migraine /migrɛn/ *n.f.* headache.

migration /migrɑsjɔ̃/ *n.f.* migration.

mijoter /miʒɔte/ *v.t./i.* simmer; (*tramer*: *fam.*) cook up.

mil /mil/ *n.m.* a thousand.

milic|e /milis/ *n.f.* militia. **~ien** *n.m.* militiaman.

milieu (*pl.* **~x**) /miljø/ *n.m.* middle; (*environnement*) environment; (*groupe*) circle; (*voie*) middle way; (*criminel*) underworld. **au ~ de,** in the middle of. **en plein** *ou* **au beau ~ de,** right in the middle (of).

militaire /militɛr/ *a.* military. ● *n.m.* soldier.

milit|er /milite/ *v.i.* be a militant. **~er pour,** militate in favour of. **~ant, ~ante** *n.m.*, *f.* militant.

milk-shake /milkʃɛk/ *n.m.* milk shake.

mille[1] /mil/ *a.* & *n.m. invar.* a thousand. **deux ~,** two thousand. **dans le ~,** bang on target.

mille[2] /mil/ *n.m.* **~ (marin),** (nautical) mile.

millénaire /milenɛr/ *n.m.* millennium.

mille-pattes /milpat/ *n.m. invar.* centipede.

millésime /milezim/ *n.m.* year.

millésimé /milezime/ *a.* **vin ~,** vintage wine.

millet /mijɛ/ *n.m.* millet.

milliard /miljar/ *n.m.* thousand million, billion. **~aire** /-dɛr/ *n.m./f.* multimillionaire.
millier /milje/ *n.m.* thousand. **un ~ (de),** about a thousand.
millimètre /milimɛtr/ *n.m.* millimetre.
million /miljɔ̃/ *n.m.* million. **deux ~s (de),** two million. **~naire** /-jɔnɛr/ *n.m./f.* millionaire.
mim|e /mim/ *n.m./f.* (*personne*) mime. ● *n.m.* (*art*) mime. **~er** *v.t.* mime; (*singer*) mimic.
mimique /mimik/ *n.f.* (expressive) gestures.
mimosa /mimoza/ *n.m.* mimosa.
minable /minabl/ *a.* shabby.
minaret /minarɛ/ *n.m.* minaret.
minauder /minode/ *v.i.* simper.
minc|e /mɛ̃s/ *a.* thin; (*svelte, insignifiant*) slim. ● *int.* dash (it). **~ir** *v.i.* get slimmer. **ça te ~it,** it makes you look slimmer. **~eur** *n.f.* thinness; slimness.
mine[1] /min/ *n.f.* expression; (*allure*) appearance. **avoir bonne ~,** look well. **faire ~ de,** make as if to.
mine[2] /min/ *n.f.* (*exploitation, explosif*) mine; (*de crayon*) lead. **~ de charbon,** coal-mine.
miner /mine/ *v.t.* (*saper*) undermine; (*garnir d'explosifs*) mine.
minerai /minrɛ/ *n.m.* ore.
minér|al (*m. pl.* **~aux**) /mineral, -o/ *a.* mineral. ● *n.m.* (*pl.* **~aux**) mineral.
minéralogique /mineralɔʒik/ *a.* **plaque ~,** number/license (*Amer.*) plate.
minet, ~te /minɛ, -t/ *n.m., f.* (*chat: fam.*) puss(y).
mineur[1]**, ~e** /minœr/ *a.* minor; (*jurid.*) under age. ● *n.m., f.* (*jurid.*) minor.
mineur[2] /minœr/ *n.m.* (*ouvrier*) miner.
mini- /mini/ *préf.* mini-.
miniature /minjatyr/ *n.f.* & *a.* miniature.
minibus /minibys/ *n.m.* minibus.
min|ier, ~ière /minje, -jɛr/ *a.* mining.
minim|al (*m. pl.* **~aux**) /minimal, -o/ *a.* minimum.
minime /minim/ *a.* minor. ● *n.m./f.* (*sport*) junior.
minimiser /minimize/ *v.t.* minimize.
minimum /minimɔm/ *a.* & *n.m.* minimum. **au ~,** (*pour le moins*) at the very least.
mini-ordinateur /miniɔrdinatœr/ *n.m.* minicomputer.
minist|ère /ministɛr/ *n.m.* ministry; (*gouvernement*) government. **~ère de l'Intérieur,** Home Office; (*Amer.*) Department of the Interior. **~ériel, ~érielle** *a.* ministerial, government.
ministre /ministr/ *n.m.* minister. **~ de l'Intérieur,** Home Secretary; (*Amer.*) Secretary of the Interior.
Minitel /minitɛl/ *n.m.* (P.) Minitel (*telephone videotext system*).
minorer /minɔre/ *v.t.* reduce.
minorit|é /minɔrite/ *n.f.* minority. **~aire** *a.* minority. **être ~aire,** be in the minority.
minuit /minɥi/ *n.m.* midnight.
minuscule /minyskyl/ *a.* minute. ● *n.f.* **(lettre) ~,** small letter.
minut|e /minyt/ *n.f.* minute. **~er** *v.t.* time (to the minute).
minuterie /minytri/ *n.f.* time-switch.
minutie /minysi/ *n.f.* meticulousness.
minutieu|x, ~se /minysjø, -z/ *a.* meticulous. **~sement** *adv.* meticulously.
mioche /mjɔʃ/ *n.m., f.* (*fam.*) youngster, kid.
mirabelle /mirabɛl/ *n.f.* (mirabelle) plum.
miracle /mirɑkl/ *n.m.* miracle.
miraculeu|x, ~se /mirakylø, -z/ *a.* miraculous. **~sement** *adv.* miraculously.
mirage /mirɑʒ/ *n.m.* mirage.
mire /mir/ *n.f.* (*fig.*) centre of attraction; (TV) test card.
miro /miro/ *a. invar.* (*fam.*) short-sighted.
mirobolant, ~e /mirɔbɔlɑ̃, -t/ *a.* (*fam.*) marvellous.
miroir /mirwar/ *n.m.* mirror.
miroiter /mirwate/ *v.i.* gleam, shimmer.
mis, ~e[1] /mi, miz/ *voir* mettre. ● *a.* **bien ~,** well-dressed.
misanthrope /mizɑ̃trɔp/ *n.m.* misanthropist. ● *a.* misanthropic.
mise[2] /miz/ *n.f.* (*argent*) stake; (*tenue*) attire. **~ à feu,** blast-off. **~ au point,** adjustment; (*fig.*) clarification. **~ de fonds,** capital outlay. **~ en garde,** warning. **~ en scène,** (*théâtre*) production; (*cinéma*) direction.

miser /mize/ *v.t.* (*argent*) bet, stake (**sur,** on). **~ sur,** (*compter sur*: *fam.*) bank on.

misérable /mizerabl/ *a.* miserable, wretched; (*indigent*) poverty-stricken; (*minable*) seedy. ● *n.m./f.* wretch.

mis|ère /mizɛr/ *n.f.* (grinding) poverty; (*malheur*) misery. **~éreux, ~éreuse** *n.m., f.* pauper.

miséricorde /mizerikɔrd/ *n.f.* mercy.

missel /misɛl/ *n.m.* missal.

missile /misil/ *n.m.* missile.

mission /misjɔ̃/ *n.m.* mission. **~naire** /-jɔnɛr/ *n.m./f.* missionary.

missive /misiv/ *n.f.* missive.

mistral /mistral/ *n.m. invar.* (*vent*) mistral.

mitaine /mitɛn/ *n.f.* mitten.

mit|e /mit/ *n.f.* (clothes-)moth. **~é** *a.* moth-eaten.

mi-temps /mitɑ̃/ *n.f. invar.* (*repos*: *sport*) half-time; (*période*: *sport*) half. **à ~,** part time.

miteu|x, ~se /mitø, -z/ *a.* shabby.

mitigé /mitiʒe/ *a.* (*modéré*) lukewarm.

mitonner /mitɔne/ *v.t.* cook slowly with care; (*fig.*) cook up.

mitoyen, ~ne /mitwajɛ̃, -ɛn/ *a.* **mur ~,** party wall.

mitrailler /mitrɑje/ *v.t.* machine-gun; (*fig.*) bombard.

mitraill|ette /mitrɑjɛt/ *n.f.* sub-machine-gun. **~euse** *n.f.* machine-gun.

mi-voix (à) /(a)mivwa/ *adv.* in an undertone.

mixeur /miksœr/ *n.m.* liquidizer, blender.

mixte /mikst/ *a.* mixed; (*usage*) dual; (*tribunal*) joint; (*école*) co-educational.

mixture /mikstyr/ *n.f.* (*péj.*) mixture.

mobile[1] /mɔbil/ *a.* mobile; (*pièce*) moving; (*feuillet*) loose. ● *n.m.* (*art*) mobile.

mobile[2] /mɔbil/ *n.m.* (*raison*) motive.

mobilier /mɔbilje/ *n.m.* furniture.

mobilis|er /mɔbilize/ *v.t.* mobilize. **~ation** *n.f.* mobilization.

mobilité /mɔbilite/ *n.f.* mobility.

mobylette /mɔbilɛt/ *n.f.* (P.) moped.

mocassin /mɔkasɛ̃/ *n.m.* moccasin.

moche /mɔʃ/ *a.* (*laid*: *fam.*) ugly; (*mauvais*: *fam.*) lousy.

modalité /mɔdalite/ *n.f.* mode.

mode[1] /mɔd/ *n.f.* fashion; (*coutume*) custom. **à la ~,** fashionable.

mode[2] /mɔd/ *n.m.* method, mode; (*genre*) way. **~ d'emploi,** directions (for use).

modèle /mɔdɛl/ *n.m.* & *a.* model. **~ réduit,** (small-scale) model.

modeler /mɔdle/ *v.t.* model (**sur,** on). **se ~ sur,** model o.s. on.

modem /mɔdɛm/ *n.m.* modem.

modéré, ~e /mɔdere/ *a.* & *n.m., f.* moderate. **~ment** *adv.* moderately.

modér|er /mɔdere/ *v.t.* moderate. **se ~er** *v. pr.* restrain o.s. **~ateur, ~atrice** *a.* moderating. **~ation** *n.f.* moderation.

modern|e /mɔdɛrn/ *a.* modern. ● *n.m.* modern style. **~iser** *v.t.* modernize.

modest|e /mɔdɛst/ *a.* modest. **~ement** *adv.* modestly. **~ie** *n.f.* modesty.

modif|ier /mɔdifje/ *v.t.* modify. **se ~ier** *v. pr.* alter. **~ication** *n.f.* modification.

modique /mɔdik/ *a.* low.

modiste /mɔdist/ *n.f.* milliner.

module /mɔdyl/ *n.m.* module.

modul|er /mɔdyle/ *v.t./i.* modulate. **~ation** *n.f.* modulation.

moelle /mwal/ *n.f.* marrow. **~ épinière,** spinal cord.

moelleu|x, ~se /mwalø, -z/ *a.* soft; (*onctueux*) smooth.

mœurs /mœr(s)/ *n.f. pl.* (*morale*) morals; (*habitudes*) customs; (*manières*) ways.

moi /mwa/ *pron.* me; (*indirect*) (to) me; (*sujet*) I. ● *n.m.* self. **~-même** *pron.* myself.

moignon /mwaɲɔ̃/ *n.m.* stump.

moindre /mwɛ̃dr/ *a.* (*moins grand*) less(er). **le** *ou* **la ~, les ~s,** the slightest, the least.

moine /mwan/ *n.m.* monk.

moineau (*pl.* **~x**) /mwano/ *n.m.* sparrow.

moins /mwɛ̃/ *adv.* less (**que,** than). ● *prép.* (*soustraction*) minus. **~ de,** (*quantité*) less, not so much (**que,** as); (*objets, personnes*) fewer, not so many (**que,** as). **~ de dix francs/d'une livre**/*etc.*, less than ten francs/one pound/*etc.* **le** *ou* **la** *ou* **les ~,** the least. **le ~ grand/haut,** the smallest/lowest. **au ~, du ~,** at least. **de ~,** less. **en ~,** less; (*manquant*) missing. **une heure ~ dix,** ten to one. **à ~ que,** unless. **de ~ en moins,** less and less.

mois /mwa/ *n.m.* month.

moïse /mɔiz/ *n.m.* moses basket.

mois|i /mwazi/ *a.* mouldy. ● *n.m.* mould. **de ~i,** (*odeur, goût*) musty. **~ir** *v.i.* go mouldy. **~issure** *n.f.* mould.

moisson /mwasɔ̃/ *n.f.* harvest.

moissonn|er /mwasɔne/ *v.t.* harvest, reap. **~eur, ~euse** *n.m., f.* harvester. **~euse-batteuse** (*pl.* **~euses-batteuses**) *n.f.* combine harvester.

moit|e /mwat/ *a.* sticky, clammy. **~eur** *n.f.* stickiness.

moitié /mwatje/ *n.f.* half; (*milieu*) half-way mark. **à ~,** half-way. **à ~ vide/fermé/***etc.*, half empty/closed/*etc.* **à ~ prix,** (at) half-price. **la ~ de,** half (of). **~ moitié,** half-and-half.

moka /mɔka/ *n.m.* (*gâteau*) coffee cream cake.

mol /mɔl/ *voir* mou.

molaire /mɔlɛr/ *n.f.* molar.

molécule /mɔlekyl/ *n.f.* molecule.

molester /mɔlɛste/ *v.t.* manhandle, rough up.

molle /mɔl/ *voir* mou.

moll|ement /mɔlmɑ̃/ *adv.* softly; (*faiblement*) feebly. **~esse** *n.f.* softness; (*faiblesse, indolence*) feebleness.

mollet /mɔlɛ/ *n.m.* (*de jambe*) calf.

molletonné /mɔltɔne/ *a.* (fleece-) lined.

mollir /mɔlir/ *v.i.* soften; (*céder*) yield.

mollusque /mɔlysk/ *n.m.* mollusc.

môme /mom/ *n.m./f.* (*fam.*) kid.

moment /mɔmɑ̃/ *n.m.* moment; (*période*) time. **(petit) ~,** short while. **au ~ où,** when. **par ~s,** now and then. **du ~ où** *ou* **que,** seeing that. **en ce ~,** at the moment.

momentané /mɔmɑ̃tane/ *a.* momentary. **~ment** *adv.* momentarily; (*en ce moment*) at present.

momie /mɔmi/ *n.f.* mummy.

mon, ma *ou* **mon*** (*pl.* **mes**) /mɔ̃, ma, mɔ̃n, me/ *a.* my.

Monaco /mɔnako/ *n.f.* Monaco.

monarchie /mɔnarʃi/ *n.f.* monarchy.

monarque /mɔnark/ *n.m.* monarque.

monastère /mɔnastɛr/ *n.m.* monastery.

monceau (*pl.* **~x**) /mɔ̃so/ *n.m.* heap, pile.

mondain, ~e /mɔ̃dɛ̃, -ɛn/ *a.* society, social.

monde /mɔ̃d/ *n.m.* world. **du ~,** (a lot of) people; (*quelqu'un*) somebody. **le (grand) ~,** (high) society. **se faire un ~ de qch.,** make a great deal of fuss about sth.

mond|ial (*m. pl.* **~iaux**) /mɔ̃djal, -jo/ *a.* world; (*influence*) worldwide. **~ialement** *adv.* the world over.

monégasque /mɔnegask/ *a. & n.m./f.* Monegasque.

monétaire /mɔnetɛr/ *a.* monetary.

moni|teur, ~trice /mɔnitœr, -tris/ *n.m., f.* instructor, instructress; (*de colonie de vacances*) supervisor; (*Amer.*) (camp) counselor.

monnaie /mɔnɛ/ *n.f.* currency; (*pièce*) coin; (*appoint*) change. **faire la ~ de,** get change for. **faire à qn. la ~ de,** give s.o. change for. **menue** *ou* **petite ~,** small change.

monnayer /mɔneje/ *v.t.* convert into cash.

mono /mɔno/ *a. invar.* mono.

monocle /mɔnɔkl/ *n.m.* monocle.

monocorde /mɔnɔkɔrd/ *a.* monotonous.

monogramme /mɔnɔgram/ *n.m.* monogram.

monologue /mɔnɔlɔg/ *n.m.* monologue.

monopol|e /mɔnɔpɔl/ *n.m.* monopoly. **~iser** *v.t.* monopolize.

monosyllabe /mɔnɔsilab/ *n.m.* monosyllable.

monoton|e /mɔnɔtɔn/ *a.* monotonous. **~ie** *n.f.* monotony.

monseigneur /mɔ̃sɛɲœr/ *n.m.* Your *ou* His Grace.

monsieur (*pl.* **messieurs**) /məsjø, mesjø/ *n.m.* gentleman. **M~** *ou* **M. Dupont,** Mr Dupont. **Messieurs** *ou* **MM. Dupont,** Messrs Dupont. **oui ~,** yes; (*avec déférence*) yes, sir.

monstre /mɔ̃str/ *n.m.* monster. ● *a.* (*fam.*) colossal.

monstr|ueux, ~ueuse /mɔ̃stryø, -z/ *a.* monstrous. **~uosité** *n.f.* monstrosity.

mont /mɔ̃/ *n.m.* mount. **par ~s et par vaux,** up hill and down dale.

montage /mɔ̃taʒ/ *n.m.* (*assemblage*) assembly; (*cinéma*) editing.

montagn|e /mɔ̃taɲ/ *n.f.* mountain; (*région*) mountains. **~es russes,** roller-coaster. **~ard, ~arde** *n.m., f.* mountain dweller. **~eux, ~euse** *a.* mountainous.

montant[1]**, ~e** /mɔ̃tɑ̃, -t/ *a.* rising; (*col*) high-necked.

montant[2] /mɔ̃tɑ̃/ *n.m.* amount; (*pièce de bois*) upright.

mont-de-piété (*pl.* **monts-de-piété**) /mɔ̃dpjete/ *n.m.* pawnshop.

monte-charge /mɔ̃tʃarʒ/ *n.m. invar.* service lift; (*Amer.*) dumb waiter.

montée /mɔ̃te/ *n.f.* ascent, climb; (*de prix*) rise; (*côte*) hill. **au milieu de la ~,** halfway up. **à la ~ de lait,** when the milk comes.

monter /mɔ̃te/ *v.i.* (*aux. être*) go *ou* come up; (*grimper*) climb; (*prix, mer*) rise. **~ à,** (*cheval*) mount. **~ dans,** (*train, avion*) get on to; (*voiture*) get into. **~ sur,** (*colline*) climb up; (*trône*) ascend. ● *v.t.* (*aux. avoir*) go *ou* come up; (*objet*) take *ou* bring up; (*cheval, garde*) mount; (*société*) start up. **~ à cheval,** (*sport*) ride. **~ en flèche,** soar. **~ en graine,** go to seed.

monteu|r, ~se /mɔ̃tœr, -øz/ *n.m., f.* (*techn.*) fitter; (*cinéma*) editor.

monticule /mɔ̃tikyl/ *n.m.* mound.

montre /mɔ̃tr/ *n.f.* watch. **~-bracelet** (*pl.* **~s-bracelets**) *n.f.* wristwatch. **faire ~ de,** show.

montrer /mɔ̃tre/ *v.t.* show (**à,** to). **se ~** *v. pr.* show o.s.; (*être*) be; (*s'avérer*) prove to be. **~ du doigt,** point to.

monture /mɔ̃tyr/ *n.f.* (*cheval*) mount; (*de lunettes*) frame; (*de bijou*) setting.

monument /mɔnymɑ̃/ *n.m.* monument. **~ aux morts,** war memorial. **~al** (*m. pl.* **~aux**) /-tal, -to/ *a.* monumental.

moqu|er (se) /(sə)mɔke/ *v. pr.* **se ~er de,** make fun of. **je m'en ~e,** (*fam.*) I couldn't care less. **~erie** *n.f.* mockery. **~eur, ~euse** *a.* mocking.

moquette /mɔkɛt/ *n.f.* fitted carpet; (*Amer.*) wall-to-wall carpeting.

mor|al, ~ale (*m. pl.* **~aux**) /mɔral, -o/ *a.* moral. ● *n.m.* (*pl.* **~aux**) morale. ● *n.f.* moral code; (*mœurs*) morals; (*de fable*) moral. **avoir le ~al,** be on form. **ça m'a remonté le ~al,** it gave me a boost. **faire la ~ale à,** lecture. **~alement** *adv.* morally. **~alité** *n.f.* morality; (*de fable*) moral.

moralisa|teur, ~trice /mɔralizatœr, -tris/ *a.* moralizing.

morbide /mɔrbid/ *a.* morbid.

morceau (*pl.* **~x**) /mɔrso/ *n.m.* piece, bit; (*de sucre*) lump; (*de viande*) cut; (*passage*) passage. **manger un ~,** have a bite to eat. **mettre en ~x,** smash *ou* tear *etc.* to bits.

morceler /mɔrsəle/ *v.t.* fragment.

mordant, ~e /mɔrdɑ̃, -t/ *a.* scathing; (*froid*) biting. ● *n.m.* (*énergie*) vigour, punch.

mordiller /mɔrdije/ *v.t.* nibble at.

mord|re /mɔrdr/ *v.t./i.* bite. **~re sur,** overlap into. **~re à l'hameçon,** bite. **~u, ~ue** *n.m., f.* (*fam.*) fan; *a.* bitten. **~u de,** (*fam.*) crazy about.

morfondre (se) /(sə)mɔrfɔ̃dr/ *v. pr.* mope, wait anxiously.

morgue[1] /mɔrg/ *n.f.* morgue, mortuary.

morgue[2] /mɔrg/ *n.f.* (*attitude*) haughtiness.

moribond, ~e /mɔribɔ̃, -d/ *a.* dying.

morne /mɔrn/ *a.* dull.

morose /mɔroz/ *a.* morose.

morphine /mɔrfin/ *n.f.* morphine.

mors /mɔr/ *n.m.* (*de cheval*) bit.

morse[1] /mɔrs/ *n.m.* walrus.

morse[2] /mɔrs/ *n.m.* (*code*) Morse code.

morsure /mɔrsyr/ *n.f.* bite.

mort[1] /mɔr/ *n.f.* death.

mort[2]**, ~e** /mɔr, -t/ *a.* dead. ● *n.m., f.* dead man, dead woman. **les ~s,** the dead. **~ de fatigue,** dead tired. **~-né** *a.* stillborn.

mortadelle /mɔrtadɛl/ *n.f.* mortadella.

mortalité /mɔrtalite/ *n.f.* death rate.

mortel, ~le /mɔrtɛl/ *a.* mortal; (*accident*) fatal; (*poison, silence*) deadly. ● *n.m., f.* mortal. **~lement** *adv.* mortally.

mortier /mɔrtje/ *n.m.* mortar.

mortifié /mɔrtifje/ *a.* mortified.

mortuaire /mɔrtɥɛr/ *a.* (*cérémonie*) funeral; (*avis*) death.

morue /mɔry/ *n.f.* cod.

mosaïque /mɔzaik/ *n.f.* mosaic.

Moscou /mɔsku/ *n.m./f.* Moscow.

mosquée /mɔske/ *n.f.* mosque.

mot /mo/ *n.m.* word; (*lettre, message*) line, note. **~ d'ordre,** watchword. **~ de passe,** password. **~s croisés,** crossword (puzzle).

motard /mɔtar/ *n.m.* biker; (*policier*) police motorcyclist.

motel /mɔtɛl/ *n.m.* motel.

moteur[1] /mɔtœr/ *n.m.* engine, motor. **barque à ~,** motor launch.

mo|teur[2]**, ~trice** /mɔtœr, -tris/ *a.* (*nerf*) motor; (*force*) driving. **à 4 roues motrices,** 4-wheel drive.

motif /mɔtif/ *n.m.* reason; (*jurid.*) motive; (*dessin*) pattern.

motion /mosjɔ̃/ *n.f.* motion.

motiv|er /mɔtive/ *v.t.* motivate; (*justifier*) justify. **~ation** *n.f.* motivation.
moto /mɔto/ *n.f.* motor cycle. **~cycliste** *n.m./f.* motorcyclist.
motorisé /mɔtɔrize/ *a.* motorized.
motrice /mɔtris/ *voir* moteur².
motte /mɔt/ *n.f.* lump; (*de beurre*) slab; (*de terre*) clod. **~ de gazon,** turf.
mou *ou* **mol*, molle** /mu, mɔl/ *a.* soft; (*péj.*) flabby; (*faible, indolent*) feeble. ● *n.m.* **du ~,** slack. **avoir du ~,** be slack.
mouchard, ~e /muʃar, -d/ *n.m., f.* informer; (*scol.*) sneak. **~er** /-de/ *v.t.* (*fam.*) inform on.
mouche /muʃ/ *n.f.* fly.
moucher (se) /(sə)muʃe/ *v. pr.* blow one's nose.
moucheron /muʃrɔ̃/ *n.m.* midge.
moucheté /muʃte/ *a.* speckled.
mouchoir /muʃwar/ *n.m.* hanky; handkerchief; (*en papier*) tissue.
moudre /mudr/ *v.t.* grind.
moue /mu/ *n.f.* long face. **faire la ~,** pull a long face.
mouette /mwɛt/ *n.f.* (sea)gull.
moufle /mufl/ *n.f.* (*gant*) mitten.
mouill|er /muje/ *v.t.* wet, make wet. **se ~er** *v. pr.* get (o.s.) wet. **~er (l'ancre),** anchor. **~é** *a.* wet.
moulage /mulaʒ/ *n.m.* cast.
moul|e¹ /mul/ *n.m.* mould. **~er** *v.t.* mould; (*statue*) cast. **~e à gâteau,** cake tin. **~e à tarte,** flan dish.
moule² /mul/ *n.f.* (*coquillage*) mussel.
moulin /mulɛ̃/ *n.m.* mill; (*moteur: fam.*) engine. **~ à vent,** windmill.
moulinet /mulinɛ/ *n.m.* (*de canne à pêche*) reel. **faire des ~s avec qch.,** twirl sth. around.
moulinette /mulinɛt/ *n.f.* (P.) purée maker.
moulu /muly/ *a.* ground; (*fatigué: fam.*) dead beat.
moulure /mulyr/ *n.f.* moulding.
mourant, ~e /murɑ̃, -t/ *a.* dying. ● *n.m., f.* dying person.
mourir† /murir/ *v.i.* (*aux. être*) die. **~ d'envie de,** be dying to. **~ de faim,** be starving. **~ d'ennui,** be dead bored.
mousquetaire /muskətɛr/ *n.m.* musketeer.
mousse¹ /mus/ *n.f.* moss; (*écume*) froth, foam; (*de savon*) lather; (*dessert*) mousse. **~ à raser,** shaving cream.
mousse² /mus/ *n.m.* ship's boy.
mousseline /muslin/ *n.f.* muslin; (*de soie*) chiffon.
mousser /muse/ *v.i.* froth, foam; (*savon*) lather.
mousseu|x, ~se /musø, -z/ *a.* frothy. ● *n.m.* sparkling wine.
mousson /musɔ̃/ *n.f.* monsoon.
moustach|e /mustaʃ/ *n.f.* moustache. **~es,** (*d'animal*) whiskers. **~u** *a.* wearing a moustache.
moustiquaire /mustikɛr/ *n.f.* mosquito-net.
moustique /mustik/ *n.m.* mosquito.
moutarde /mutard/ *n.f.* mustard.
mouton /mutɔ̃/ *n.m.* sheep; (*peau*) sheepskin; (*viande*) mutton.
mouvant, ~e /muvɑ̃, -t/ *a.* changing; (*terrain*) shifting.
mouvement /muvmɑ̃/ *n.m.* movement; (*agitation*) bustle; (*en gymnastique*) exercise; (*impulsion*) impulse; (*tendance*) tendency. **en ~,** in motion.
mouvementé /muvmɑ̃te/ *a.* eventful.
mouvoir† /muvwar/ *v.t.* (*membre*) move. **se ~** *v. pr.* move.
moyen¹, ~ne /mwajɛ̃, -jɛn/ *a.* average; (*médiocre*) poor. ● *n.f.* average; (*scol.*) pass-mark. **de taille ~ne,** medium-sized. **~ âge,** Middle Ages. **~ne d'âge,** average age. **M~-Orient** *n.m.* Middle East. **~nement** /-jɛnmɑ̃/ *adv.* moderately.
moyen² /mwajɛ̃/ *n.m.* means, way. **~s,** means; (*dons*) abilities. **au ~ de,** by means of. **il n'y a pas ~ de,** it is not possible to.
moyennant /mwajɛnɑ̃/ *prép.* (*pour*) for; (*grâce à*) with.
moyeu (*pl.* **~x**) /mwajø/ *n.m.* hub.
mû, mue¹ /my/ *a.* driven (**par,** by).
mucoviscidose /mykɔvisidoz/ *n.f.* cystic fibrosis.
mue² /my/ *n.f.* moulting; (*de voix*) breaking of the voice.
muer /mɥe/ *v.i.* moult; (*voix*) break. **se ~ en,** change into.
muesli /mysli/ *n.m.* muesli.
muet, ~te /mɥɛ, -t/ *a.* (*personne*) dumb; (*fig.*) speechless (**de,** with); (*silencieux*) silent. ● *n.m., f.* dumb person.
mufle /myfl/ *n.m.* nose, muzzle; (*personne: fam.*) boor, lout.

mugir /myʒir/ *v.i.* (*vache*) moo; (*bœuf*) bellow; (*fig.*) howl.
muguet /mygɛ/ *n.m.* lily of the valley.
mule /myl/ *n.f.* (she-)mule; (*pantoufle*) mule.
mulet /mylɛ/ *n.m.* (he-)mule.
multi- /mylti/ *préf.* multi-.
multicolore /myltikɔlɔr/ *a.* multicoloured.
multination|al, ~ale (*m. pl.* **~aux**) /myltinasjɔnal, -o/ *a.* & *n.f.* multinational.
multiple /myltipl/ *a.* & *n.m.* multiple.
multiplicité /myltiplisite/ *n.f.* multiplicity, abundance.
multipl|ier /myltiplije/ *v.t.*, **se ~ier** *v. pr.* multiply. **~ication** *n.f.* multiplication.
multitude /myltityd/ *n.f.* multitude, mass.
municip|al (*m. pl.* **~aux**) /mynisipal, -o/ *a.* municipal; (*conseil*) town. **~alité** *n.f.* (*ville*) municipality; (*conseil*) town council.
munir /mynir/ *v.t.* **~ de,** provide with. **se ~ de,** provide o.s. with.
munitions /mynisjɔ̃/ *n.f. pl.* ammunition.
mur /myr/ *n.m.* wall. **~ du son,** sound barrier.
mûr /myr/ *a.* ripe; (*personne*) mature.
muraille /myrɑj/ *n.f.* (high) wall.
mur|al (*m. pl.* **~aux**) /myral, -o/ *a.* wall; (*tableau*) mural.
mûre /myr/ *n.f.* blackberry.
muret /myrɛ/ *n.m.* low wall.
mûrir /myrir/ *v.t./i.* ripen; (*abcès*) come to a head; (*personne, projet*) mature.
murmur|e /myrmyr/ *n.m.* murmur. **~er** *v.t./i.* murmur.
musc /mysk/ *n.m.* musk.
muscade /myskad/ *n.f.* **noix (de) ~,** nutmeg.
muscl|e /myskl/ *n.m.* muscle. **~é** *a.* muscular, brawny.
muscul|aire /myskylɛr/ *a.* muscular. **~ature** *n.f.* muscles.
museau (*pl.* **~x**) /myzo/ *n.m.* muzzle; (*de porc*) snout.
musée /myze/ *n.m.* museum; (*de peinture*) art gallery.
museler /myzle/ *v.t.* muzzle.
muselière /myzəljɛr/ *n.f.* muzzle.
musette /myzɛt/ *n.f.* haversack.
muséum /myzeɔm/ *n.m.* (natural history) museum.
music|al (*m. pl.* **~aux**) /myzikal, -o/ *a.* musical.
music-hall /myzikol/ *n.m.* variety theatre.
musicien, ~ne /myzisjɛ̃, -jɛn/ *a.* musical. ● *n.m., f.* musician.
musique /myzik/ *n.f.* music; (*orchestre*) band.
musulman, ~e /myzylmɑ̃, -an/ *a.* & *n.m., f.* Muslim.
mutation /mytɑsjɔ̃/ *n.f.* change; (*biologique*) mutation.
muter /myte/ *v.t.* transfer.
mutil|er /mytile/ *v.t.* mutilate. **~ation** *n.f.* mutilation. **~é, ée** *a.* & *n.m., f.* disabled (person).
mutin, ~e /mytɛ̃, -in/ *a.* saucy. ● *n.m., f.* rebel.
mutin|er (se) /(sə)mytine/ *v. pr.* mutiny. **~é** *a.* mutinous. **~erie** *n.f.* mutiny.
mutisme /mytism/ *n.m.* silence.
mutuel, ~le /mytɥɛl/ *a.* mutual. ● *n.f.* Friendly Society; (*Amer.*) benefit society. **~lement** *adv.* mutually; (*l'un l'autre*) each other.
myop|e /mjɔp/ *a.* short-sighted. **~ie** *n.f.* short-sightedness.
myosotis /mjozɔtis/ *n.m.* forget-me-not.
myriade /mirjad/ *n.f.* myriad.
myrtille /mirtij/ *n.f.* bilberry; (*Amer.*) blueberry.
mystère /mistɛr/ *n.m.* mystery.
mystérieu|x, ~se /misterjø, -z/ *a.* mysterious.
mystif|ier /mistifje/ *v.t.* deceive, hoax. **~ication** *n.f.* hoax.
mysti|que /mistik/ *a.* mystic(al). ● *n.m./f.* mystic. ● *n.f.* (*puissance*) mystique. **~cisme** *n.m.* mysticism.
myth|e /mit/ *n.m.* myth. **~ique** *a.* mythical.
mytholog|ie /mitɔlɔʒi/ *n.f.* mythology. **~ique** *a.* mythological.
mythomane /mitɔman/ *n.m./f.* compulsive liar (and fantasizer).

N

n' /n/ *voir* ne.
nacr|e /nakr/ *n.f.* mother-of-pearl. **~é** *a.* pearly.
nage /naʒ/ *n.f.* swimming; (*manière*) (swimming) stroke. **à la ~,** by

swimming. **traverser à la ~,** swim across. **en ~,** sweating.

nageoire /naʒwar/ *n.f.* fin.

nag|er /naʒe/ *v.t./i.* swim. **~eur, ~euse** *n.m., f.* swimmer.

naguère /nagɛr/ *adv.* some time ago.

naï|f, ~ve /naif, -v/ *a.* naïve.

nain, ~e /nɛ̃, nɛn/ *n.m., f. & a.* dwarf.

naissance /nɛsɑ̃s/ *n.f.* birth. **donner ~ à,** give birth to, (*fig.*) give rise to.

naître† /nɛtr/ *v.i.* be born; (*résulter*) arise (**de,** from). **faire ~,** (*susciter*) give rise to.

naïveté /naivte/ *n.f.* naïvety.

nana /nana/ *n.f.* (*fam.*) girl.

nanti /nɑ̃ti/ *n.m.* **les ~s,** the affluent.

nantir /nɑ̃tir/ *v.t.* **~ de,** provide with.

naphtaline /naftalin/ *n.f.* mothballs.

nappe /nap/ *n.f.* table-cloth; (*de pétrole, gaz*) layer. **~ phréatique,** ground water.

napperon /naprɔ̃/ *n.m.* (cloth) table-mat.

narcotique /narkɔtik/ *a. & n.m.* narcotic.

narguer /narge/ *v.t.* mock.

narine /narin/ *n.f.* nostril.

narquois, ~e /narkwa, -z/ *a.* derisive.

narr|er /nare/ *v.t.* narrate. **~ateur, ~atrice** *n.m., f.* narrator. **~ation** *n.f.* narrative; (*action*) narration; (*scol.*) composition.

nas|al (*m. pl.* **~aux**) /nazal, -o/ *a.* nasal.

naseau (*pl.* **~x**) /nazo/ *n.m.* nostril.

nasiller /nazije/ *v.i.* have a nasal twang.

nat|al (*m. pl.* **~als**) /natal/ *a.* native.

natalité /natalite/ *n.f.* birth rate.

natation /natɑsjɔ̃/ *n.f.* swimming.

nati|f, ~ve /natif, -v/ *a.* native.

nation /nɑsjɔ̃/ *n.f.* nation.

nation|al, ~ale (*m. pl.* **~aux**) /nasjɔnal, -o/ *a.* national. ● *n.f.* A road; (*Amer.*) highway. **~aliser** *v.t.* nationalize. **~alisme** *n.m.* nationalism.

nationalité /nasjɔnalite/ *n.f.* nationality.

Nativité /nativite/ *n.f.* **la ~,** the Nativity.

natte /nat/ *n.f.* (*de cheveux*) plait; (*tapis de paille*) mat.

naturaliser /natyralize/ *v.t.* naturalize.

nature /natyr/ *n.f.* nature. ● *a. invar.* (*eau, omelette, etc.*) plain. **de ~ à,** likely to. **payer en ~,** pay in kind. **~ morte,** still life.

naturel, ~le /natyrɛl/ *a.* natural. ● *n.m.* nature; (*simplicité*) naturalness. **~lement** *adv.* naturally.

naufrag|e /nofraʒ/ *n.m.* (ship-)wreck. **faire ~e,** be shipwrecked; (*bateau*) be wrecked. **~é, ~ée** *a. & n.m., f.* shipwrecked (person).

nauséabond, ~e /nozeabɔ̃, -d/ *a.* nauseating.

nausée /noze/ *n.f.* nausea.

nautique /notik/ *a.* nautical; (*sports*) aquatic.

naval (*m. pl.* **~s**) /naval/ *a.* naval.

navet /navɛ/ *n.m.* turnip; (*film, tableau*) dud.

navette /navɛt/ *n.f.* shuttle (service). **faire la ~,** shuttle back and forth.

navigable /navigabl/ *a.* navigable.

navig|uer /navige/ *v.i.* sail; (*piloter*) navigate. **~ateur** *n.m.* seafarer; (*d'avion*) navigator. **~ation** *n.f.* navigation; (*trafic*) shipping.

navire /navir/ *n.m.* ship.

navré /navre/ *a.* sorry (**de,** to).

navrer /navre/ *v.t.* upset.

ne, n'* /nə, n/ *adv.* **ne pas,** not. **ne jamais,** never. **ne plus,** (*temps*) no longer, not any more. **ne que,** only. **je crains qu'il ne parte,** (*sans valeur négative*) I am afraid he will leave.

né, née /ne/ *voir* naître. ● *a. & n.m., f.* born. **il est né,** he was born. **premier-/dernier-né,** first-/last-born. **née Martin,** née Martin.

néanmoins /neɑ̃mwɛ̃/ *adv.* nevertheless.

néant /neɑ̃/ *n.m.* nothingness; (*aucun*) none.

nébuleu|x, ~se /nebylø, -z/ *a.* nebulous.

nécessaire /nesesɛr/ *a.* necessary. ● *n.m.* (*sac*) bag; (*trousse*) kit. **le ~,** (*l'indispensable*) the necessities. **faire le ~,** do what is necessary. **~ment** *adv.* necessarily.

nécessité /nesesite/ *n.f.* necessity.

nécessiter /nesesite/ *v.t.* necessitate.

nécrologie /nekrɔlɔʒi/ *n.f.* obituary.

néerlandais, ~e /neɛrlɑ̃dɛ, -z/ *a.* Dutch. ● *n.m., f.* Dutchman, Dutchwoman. ● *n.m.* (*lang.*) Dutch.

nef /nɛf/ *n.f.* nave.

néfaste /nefast/ *a.* harmful (**à,** to); (*funeste*) ill-fated.

négati|f, ~ve /negatif, -v/ *a. & n.m., f.* negative.
négation /negɑsjɔ̃/ *n.f.* negation.
négligé /neɡliʒe/ *a.* (*tenue, travail*) slovenly. ● *n.m.* (*tenue*) négligé.
négligeable /neɡliʒabl/ *a.* negligible, insignificant.
négligen|t, ~te /neɡliʒɑ̃, -t/ *a.* careless, negligent. **~ce** *n.f.* carelessness, negligence; (*erreur*) omission.
négliger /neɡliʒe/ *v.t.* neglect; (*ne pas tenir compte de*) disregard. **se ~** *v. pr.* neglect o.s.
négoc|e /neɡɔs/ *n.m.* business. **~iant, ~iante** *n.m., f.* merchant.
négoc|ier /neɡɔsje/ *v.t./i.* negotiate. **~iable** *a.* negotiable. **~iateur, ~iatrice** *n.m., f.* negotiator. **~iation** *n.f.* negotiation.
nègre[1] /nɛɡr/ *a.* (*musique etc.*) Negro.
nègre[2] /nɛɡr/ *n.m.* (*écrivain*) ghost writer.
neig|e /nɛʒ/ *n.f.* snow. **~eux, ~euse** *a.* snowy.
neiger /neʒe/ *v.i.* snow.
nénuphar /nenyfar/ *n.m.* waterlily.
néologisme /neɔlɔʒism/ *n.m.* neologism.
néon /neɔ̃/ *n.m.* neon.
néo-zélandais, ~e /neɔzelɑ̃dɛ, -z/ *a.* New Zealand. ● *n.m., f.* New Zealander.
nerf /nɛr/ *n.m.* nerve; (*vigueur: fam.*) stamina.
nerv|eux, ~euse /nɛrvø, -z/ *a.* nervous; (*irritable*) nervy; (*centre, cellule*) nerve-; (*voiture*) responsive. **~eusement** *adv.* nervously. **~osité** *n.f.* nervousness; (*irritabilité*) touchiness.
nervure /nɛrvyr/ *n.f.* (*bot.*) vein.
net, ~te /nɛt/ *a.* (*clair, distinct*) clear; (*propre*) clean; (*soigné*) neat; (*prix, poids*) net. ● *adv.* (*s'arrêter*) dead; (*refuser*) flatly; (*parler*) plainly; (*se casser*) clean. **~tement** *adv.* clearly; (*certainement*) definitely.
netteté /nɛtte/ *n.f.* clearness.
nettoy|er /nɛtwaje/ *v.t.* clean. **~age** *n.m.* cleaning. **~age à sec,** dry-cleaning.
neuf[1] /nœf/ (/nœv/ *before heures, ans*) *a. & n.m.* nine.
neu|f[2]**, ~ve** /nœf, -v/ *a. & n.m.* new. **remettre à ~f,** brighten up. **du ~f,** (*fait nouveau*) some new development.
neutr|e /nøtr/ *a.* neutral; (*gram.*) neuter. ● *n.m.* (*gram.*) neuter. **~alité** *n.f.* neutrality.
neutron /nøtrɔ̃/ *n.m.* neutron.
neuve /nœv/ *voir* neuf[2].
neuvième /nœvjɛm/ *a. & n.m./f.* ninth.
neveu (*pl.* **~x**) /nəvø/ *n.m.* nephew.
névros|e /nevroz/ *n.f.* neurosis. **~é, ~ée** *a. & n.m., f.* neurotic.
nez /ne/ *n.m.* nose. **~ à nez,** face to face. **~ épaté,** flat nose. **~ retroussé,** turned-up nose. **avoir du ~,** have flair.
ni /ni/ *conj.* neither, nor. **ni grand ni petit,** neither big nor small. **ni l'un ni l'autre ne fument,** neither (one nor the other) smokes.
niais, ~e /njɛ, -z/ *a.* silly. ● *n.m., f.* simpleton. **~erie** /-zri/ *n.f.* silliness.
niche /niʃ/ *n.f.* (*de chien*) kennel; (*cavité*) niche; (*farce*) trick.
nichée /niʃe/ *n.f.* brood.
nicher /niʃe/ *v.i.* nest. **se ~** *v. pr.* nest; (*se cacher*) hide.
nickel /nikɛl/ *n.m.* nickel. **c'est ~!,** (*fam.*) it's spotless.
nicotine /nikɔtin/ *n.f.* nicotine.
nid /ni/ *n.m.* nest. **~ de poule,** pothole.
nièce /njɛs/ *n.f.* niece.
nier /nje/ *v.t.* deny.
nigaud, ~e /niɡo, -d/ *a.* silly. ● *n.m., f.* silly idiot.
nippon, ~e /nipɔ̃, -ɔn/ *a. & n.m., f.* Japanese.
niveau (*pl.* **~x**) /nivo/ *n.m.* level; (*compétence*) standard. **au ~,** up to standard. **~ à bulle,** spirit-level. **~ de vie,** standard of living.
nivel|er /nivle/ *v.t.* level. **~lement** /-ɛlmɑ̃/ *n.m.* levelling.
noble /nɔbl/ *a.* noble. ● *n.m./f.* nobleman, noblewoman.
noblesse /nɔblɛs/ *n.f.* nobility.
noce /nɔs/ *n.f.* wedding; (*personnes*) wedding guests. **~s,** wedding. **faire la ~,** (*fam.*) make merry.
noci|f, ~ve /nɔsif, -v/ *a.* harmful.
noctambule /nɔktɑ̃byl/ *n.m./f.* night-owl, late-night reveller.
nocturne /nɔktyrn/ *a.* nocturnal.
Noël /nɔɛl/ *n.m.* Christmas.
nœud[1] /nø/ *n.m.* knot; (*ornemental*) bow. **~s,** (*fig.*) ties. **~ coulant,** noose. **~ papillon,** bow-tie.
nœud[2] /nø/ *n.m.* (*naut.*) knot.
noir, ~e /nwar/ *a.* black; (*obscur, sombre*) dark; (*triste*) gloomy.

● *n.m.* black; (*obscurité*) dark. **travail au ~,** moonlighting. ● *n.m., f.* (*personne*) Black. ● *n.f.* (*mus.*) crotchet. **~ceur** *n.f.* blackness; (*indignité*) vileness.

noircir /nwarsir/ *v.t./i.*, **se ~** *v. pr.* blacken.

nois|ette /nwazɛt/ *n.f.* hazel-nut; (*de beurre*) knob. **~etier** *n.m.* hazel tree.

noix /nwa/ *n.f.* nut; (*du noyer*) walnut; (*de beurre*) knob. **~ de cajou,** cashew nut. **~ de coco,** coconut. **à la ~,** (*fam.*) useless.

nom /nɔ̃/ *n.m.* name; (*gram.*) noun. **au ~ de,** on behalf of. **~ de famille,** surname. **~ de jeune fille,** maiden name. **~ propre,** proper noun.

nomade /nɔmad/ *a.* nomadic. ● *n.m./f.* nomad.

no man's land /nomanslɑ̃d/ *n.m. invar.* no man's land.

nombre /nɔ̃br/ *n.m.* number. **au ~ de,** (*parmi*) among; (*l'un de*) one of. **en (grand) ~,** in large numbers.

nombreu|x, ~se /nɔ̃brø, -z/ *a.* numerous; (*important*) large.

nombril /nɔ̃bri/ *n.m.* navel.

nomin|al (*m. pl.* **~aux**) /nɔminal, -o/ *a.* nominal.

nomination /nɔminɑsjɔ̃/ *n.f.* appointment.

nommément /nɔmemɑ̃/ *adv.* by name.

nommer /nɔme/ *v.t.* name; (*élire*) appoint. **se ~** *v. pr.* (*s'appeler*) be called.

non /nɔ̃/ *adv.* no; (*pas*) not. ● *n.m. invar.* no. **~ (pas) que,** not that. **il vient, ~?,** he is coming, isn't he? **moi ~ plus,** neither am, do, can, *etc.* I.

non- /nɔ̃/ *préf.* non-. **~-fumeur,** non-smoker.

nonante /nɔnɑ̃t/ *a. & n.m.* ninety.

nonchalance /nɔ̃ʃalɑ̃s/ *n.f.* nonchalance.

non-sens /nɔ̃sɑ̃s/ *n.m.* absurdity.

non-stop /nɔnstɔp/ *a. invar.* non-stop.

nord /nɔr/ *n.m.* north. ● *a. invar.* north; (*partie*) northern; (*direction*) northerly. **au ~ de,** to the north of. **~-africain, ~-africaine** *a. & n.m., f.* North African. **~-est** *n.m.* north-east. **~-ouest** *n.m.* north-west.

nordique /nɔrdik/ *a. & n.m./f.* Scandinavian.

norm|al, ~ale (*m. pl.* **~aux**) /nɔrmal, -o/ *a.* normal. ● *n.f.* normality; (*norme*) norm; (*moyenne*) average. **~alement** *adv.* normally.

normand, ~e /nɔrmɑ̃, -d/ *a. & n.m., f.* Norman.

Normandie /nɔrmɑ̃di/ *n.f.* Normandy.

norme /nɔrm/ *n.f.* norm; (*de production*) standard.

Norvège /nɔrvɛʒ/ *n.f.* Norway.

norvégien, ~ne /nɔrveʒjɛ̃, -jɛn/ *a. & n.m., f.* Norwegian.

nos /no/ *voir* notre.

nostalg|ie /nɔstalʒi/ *n.f.* nostalgia. **~ique** *a.* nostalgic.

notable /nɔtabl/ *a. & n.m.* notable.

notaire /nɔtɛr/ *n.m.* notary.

notamment /nɔtamɑ̃/ *adv.* notably.

notation /nɔtɑsjɔ̃/ *n.f.* notation; (*remarque*) remark.

note /nɔt/ *n.f.* (*remarque*) note; (*chiffrée*) mark; (*facture*) bill; (*mus.*) note. **~ (de service),** memorandum. **prendre ~ de,** take note of.

not|er /nɔte/ *v.t.* note, notice; (*écrire*) note (down); (*devoir*) mark. **bien/mal ~é,** (*employé etc.*) highly/poorly rated.

notice /nɔtis/ *n.f.* note; (*mode d'emploi*) directions.

notif|ier /nɔtifje/ *v.t.* notify (**à,** to). **~ication** *n.f.* notification.

notion /nosjɔ̃/ *n.f.* notion.

notoire /nɔtwar/ *a.* well-known; (*criminel*) notorious.

notre (*pl.* **nos**) /nɔtr, no/ *a.* our.

nôtre /notr/ *pron.* **le** *ou* **la ~, les ~s,** ours.

nouer /nwe/ *v.t.* tie, knot; (*relations*) strike up.

noueu|x, ~se /nwø, -z/ *a.* gnarled.

nougat /nuga/ *n.m.* nougat.

nouille /nuj/ *n.f.* (*idiot: fam.*) idiot.

nouilles /nuj/ *n.f. pl.* noodles.

nounours /nunurs/ *n.m.* teddy bear.

nourri /nuri/ *a.* (*fig.*) intense. **logé ~,** bed and board. **~ au sein,** breastfed.

nourrice /nuris/ *n.f.* child-minder; (*qui allaite*) wet-nurse.

nourr|ir /nurir/ *v.t.* feed; (*faire vivre*) feed, provide for; (*sentiment: fig.*) nourish. ● *v.i.* be nourishing. **se ~ir** *v. pr.* eat. **se ~ir de,** feed on. **~issant, ~issante** *a.* nourishing.

nourrisson /nurisɔ̃/ *n.m.* infant.

nourriture /nurityr/ *n.f.* food.

nous /nu/ *pron.* we; (*complément*) us; (*indirect*) (to) us; (*réfléchi*) ourselves; (*l'un l'autre*) each other. **~-mêmes** *pron.* ourselves.
nouveau *ou* **nouvel***, **nouvelle**[1] (*m. pl.* **~x**) /nuvo, nuvɛl/ *a.* & *n.m.* new. ● *n.m.*, *f.* (*élève*) new boy, new girl. **de ~, à ~,** again. **du ~,** (*fait nouveau*) some new development. **nouvel an,** new year. **~x mariés,** newly-weds. **~-né, ~-née** *a.* newborn; *n.m.*, *f.* newborn baby. **~ venu, nouvelle venue,** newcomer. **Nouvelle Zélande,** New Zealand.
nouveauté /nuvote/ *n.f.* novelty; (*chose*) new thing.
nouvelle[2] /nuvɛl/ *n.f.* (piece of) news; (*récit*) short story. **~s,** news.
nouvellement /nuvɛlmɑ̃/ *adv.* newly, recently.
novembre /nɔvɑ̃br/ *n.m.* November.
novice /nɔvis/ *a.* inexperienced. ● *n.m./f.* novice.
noyade /nwajad/ *n.f.* drowning.
noyau (*pl.* **~x**) /nwajo/ *n.m.* (*de fruit*) stone; (*de cellule*) nucleus; (*groupe*) group; (*centre*: *fig.*) core.
noyauter /nwajote/ *v.t.* (*organisation*) infiltrate.
noy|er[1] /nwaje/ *v.t.* drown; (*inonder*) flood. **se ~er** *v. pr.* drown; (*volontairement*) drown o.s. **se ~er dans un verre d'eau,** make a mountain out of a molehill. **~é, ~ée** *n.m.*, *f.* drowning person; (*mort*) drowned person.
noyer[2] /nwaje/ *n.m.* (*arbre*) walnut-tree.
nu /ny/ *a.* naked; (*mains, mur, fil*) bare. ● *n.m.* nude. **se mettre à nu,** (*fig.*) bare one's heart. **mettre à nu,** lay bare. **nu-pieds** *adv.* barefoot; *n.m. pl.* beach shoes. **nu-tête** *adv.* bareheaded. **à l'œil nu,** to the naked eye.
nuag|e /nyaʒ/ *n.m.* cloud. **~eux, ~euse** *a.* cloudy.
nuance /nyɑ̃s/ *n.f.* shade; (*de sens*) nuance; (*différence*) difference.
nuancer /nyɑ̃se/ *v.t.* (*opinion*) qualify.
nucléaire /nykleɛr/ *a.* nuclear.
nudis|te /nydist/ *n.m./f.* nudist. **~me** *n.m.* nudism.
nudité /nydite/ *n.f.* (*de personne*) nudity; (*de chambre etc.*) bareness.
nuée /nɥe/ *n.f.* (*foule*) host.
nues /ny/ *n.f. pl.* **tomber des ~,** be amazed. **porter aux ~,** extol.
nuire† /nɥir/ *v.i.* **~ à,** harm.
nuisible /nɥizibl/ *a.* harmful.
nuit /nɥi/ *n.f.* night. **cette ~,** tonight; (*hier*) last night. **il fait ~,** it is dark. **~ blanche,** sleepless night. **la ~, de ~,** at night. **~ de noces,** wedding night.
nul, ~le /nyl/ *a.* (*aucun*) no; (*zéro*) nil; (*qui ne vaut rien*) useless; (*non valable*) null. **match ~,** draw. **~ en,** no good at. ● *pron.* no one. **~ autre,** no one else. **~le part,** nowhere. **~lement** *adv.* not at all. **~lité** *n.f.* uselessness; (*personne*) useless person.
numéraire /nymerɛr/ *n.m.* cash.
numér|al (*pl.* **~aux**) /nymeral, -o/ *n.m.* numeral.
numérique /nymerik/ *a.* numerical; (*montre, horloge*) digital.
numéro /nymero/ *n.m.* number; (*de journal*) issue; (*spectacle*) act. **~ter** /-ɔte/ *v.t.* number.
nuque /nyk/ *n.f.* nape (of the neck).
nurse /nœrs/ *n.f.* (children's) nurse.
nutriti|f, ~ve /nytritif, -v/ *a.* nutritious; (*valeur*) nutritional.
nutrition /nytrisjɔ̃/ *n.f.* nutrition.
nylon /nilɔ̃/ *n.m.* nylon.
nymphe /nɛ̃f/ *n.f.* nymph.

O

oasis /ɔazis/ *n.f.* oasis.
obéir /ɔbeir/ *v.i.* obey. **~ à,** obey. **être obéi,** be obeyed.
obéissan|t, ~te /ɔbeisɑ̃, -t/ *a.* obedient. **~ce** *n.f.* obedience.
obèse /ɔbɛz/ *a.* obese.
obésité /ɔbezite/ *n.f.* obesity.
object|er /ɔbʒɛkte/ *v.t.* put forward (as an excuse). **~er que,** object that. **~ion** /-ksjɔ̃/ *n.f.* objection.
objecteur /ɔbʒɛktœr/ *n.m.* **~ de conscience,** conscientious objector.
objecti|f, ~ve /ɔbʒɛktif, -v/ *a.* objective. ● *n.m.* objective; (*photo.*) lens. **~vement** *adv.* objectively. **~vité** *n.f.* objectivity.
objet /ɔbʒɛ/ *n.m.* object; (*sujet*) subject. **être** *ou* **faire l'~ de,** be the subject of; (*recevoir*) receive. **~ d'art,** objet d'art. **~s de toilette,** toilet requisites. **~s trouvés,** lost property; (*Amer.*) lost and found.

obligation /ɔbligɑsjɔ̃/ *n.f.* obligation; (*comm.*) bond. **être dans l'~ de,** be under obligation to.
obligatoire /ɔbligatwar/ *a.* compulsory. **~ment** *adv.* of necessity; (*fam.*) inevitably.
obligean|t, ~te /ɔbliʒɑ̃, -t/ *a.* obliging, kind. **~ce** *n.f.* kindness.
oblig|er /ɔbliʒe/ *v.t.* compel, oblige (**à faire,** to do); (*aider*) oblige. **être ~é de,** have to. **~é à qn.,** obliged to s.o. (**de,** for).
oblique /ɔblik/ *a.* oblique. **regard ~,** sidelong glance. **en ~,** at an angle.
obliquer /ɔblike/ *v.i.* turn off (**vers,** towards).
oblitérer /ɔblitere/ *v.t.* (*timbre*) cancel.
oblong, ~ue /ɔblɔ̃, -g/ *a.* oblong.
obnubilé, ~e /ɔbnybile/ *a.* obsessed.
obsc|ène /ɔpsɛn/ *a.* obscene. **~énité** *n.f.* obscenity.
obscur /ɔpskyr/ *a.* dark; (*confus, humble*) obscure.
obscurantisme /ɔpskyrɑ̃tism/ *n.m.* obscurantism.
obscurcir /ɔpskyrsir/ *v.t.* darken; (*fig.*) obscure. **s'~** *v. pr.* (*ciel etc.*) darken.
obscurité /ɔpskyrite/ *n.f.* dark(-ness); (*passage, situation*) obscurity.
obséd|er /ɔpsede/ *v.t.* obsess. **~ant, ~ante** *a.* obsessive. **~é, ~ée** *n.m., f.* maniac.
obsèques /ɔpsɛk/ *n.f. pl.* funeral.
observation /ɔpsɛrvɑsjɔ̃/ *n.f.* observation; (*reproche*) criticism; (*obéissance*) observance. **en ~,** under observation.
observatoire /ɔpsɛrvatwar/ *n.m.* observatory; (*mil.*) observation post.
observ|er /ɔpsɛrve/ *v.t.* observe; (*surveiller*) watch, observe. **faire ~er qch.,** point sth. out (**à,** to). **~ateur, ~atrice** *a.* observant; *n.m., f.* observer.
obsession /ɔpsesjɔ̃/ *n.f.* obsession.
obstacle /ɔpstakl/ *n.m.* obstacle; (*cheval*) jump; (*athlète*) hurdle. **faire ~ à,** stand in the way of.
obstétrique /ɔpstetrik/ *n.f.* obstetrics.
obstin|é /ɔpstine/ *a.* obstinate. **~ation** *n.f.* obstinacy.
obstiner (s') /(s)ɔpstine/ *v. pr.* persist (**à,** in).
obstruction /ɔpstryksjɔ̃/ *n.f.* obstruction. **faire de l'~,** obstruct.
obstruer /ɔpstrye/ *v.t.* obstruct.
obten|ir† /ɔptənir/ *v.t.* get, obtain. **~tion** /-ɑ̃sjɔ̃/ *n.f.* obtaining.
obturateur /ɔptyratœr/ *n.m.* (*photo.*) shutter.
obtus, ~e /ɔpty, -z/ *a.* obtuse.
obus /ɔby/ *n.m.* shell.
occasion /ɔkazjɔ̃/ *n.f.* opportunity (**de faire,** of doing); (*circonstance*) occasion; (*achat*) bargain; (*article non neuf*) second-hand buy. **à l'~,** sometimes. **d'~,** second-hand. **~nel, ~nelle** /-jɔnɛl/ *a.* occasional.
occasionner /ɔkazjɔne/ *v.t.* cause.
occident /ɔksidɑ̃/ *n.m.* west. **~al, ~ale** (*m. pl.* **~aux**) /-tal, -to/ *a.* western. • *n.m., f.* westerner.
occulte /ɔkylt/ *a.* occult.
occupant, ~e /ɔkypɑ̃, -t/ *n.m., f.* occupant. • *n.m.* (*mil.*) forces of occupation.
occupation /ɔkypɑsjɔ̃/ *n.f.* occupation.
occupé /ɔkype/ *a.* busy; (*place, pays*) occupied; (*téléphone*) engaged; (*Amer.*) busy.
occuper /ɔkype/ *v.t.* occupy; (*poste*) hold. **s'~** *v. pr.* (*s'affairer*) keep busy (**à faire,** doing). **s'~ de,** (*personne, problème*) take care of; (*bureau, firme*) be in charge of.
occurrence (en l') /(ɑ̃l)ɔkyrɑ̃s/ *adv.* in this case.
océan /ɔseɑ̃/ *n.m.* ocean.
ocre /ɔkr/ *a. invar.* ochre.
octane /ɔktan/ *n.m.* octane.
octante /ɔktɑ̃t/ *a.* (*régional*) eighty.
octave /ɔktav/ *n.f.* (*mus.*) octave.
octet /ɔktɛ/ *n.m.* byte.
octobre /ɔktɔbr/ *n.m.* October.
octogone /ɔktɔgɔn/ *n.m.* octagon.
octroyer /ɔktrwaje/ *v.t.* grant.
oculaire /ɔkylɛr/ *a.* ocular.
oculiste /ɔkylist/ *n.m./f.* eye-specialist.
ode /ɔd/ *n.f.* ode.
odeur /ɔdœr/ *n.f.* smell.
odieu|x, ~se /ɔdjø, -z/ *a.* odious.
odorant, ~e /ɔdɔrɑ̃, -t/ *a.* sweet-smelling.
odorat /ɔdɔra/ *n.m.* (sense of) smell.
œcuménique /ekymenik/ *a.* ecumenical.
œil (*pl.* **yeux**) /œj, jø/ *n.m.* eye. **à l'~,** (*fam.*) free. **à mes yeux,** in my view. **faire de l'~ à,** make eyes at. **faire les gros yeux à,** scowl at. **ouvrir l'~,** keep one's eye open. **fermer l'~,** shut one's eyes. **~ poché,** black eye. **yeux bridés,** slit eyes.

œillade /œjad/ *n.f.* wink.
œillères /œjɛr/ *n.f. pl.* blinkers.
œillet /œjɛ/ *n.m.* (*plante*) carnation; (*trou*) eyelet.
œuf (*pl.* **~s**) /œf, ø/ *n.m.* egg. **~ à la coque/dur/sur le plat,** boiled/hard-boiled/fried egg.
œuvre /œvr/ *n.f.* (*ouvrage, travail*) work. **~ d'art,** work of art. **~ (de bienfaisance),** charity. **être à l'~,** be at work. **mettre en ~,** (*moyens*) implement.
œuvrer /œvre/ *v.i.* work.
off /ɔf/ *a. invar.* **voix ~,** voice off.
offense /ɔfɑ̃s/ *n.f.* insult; (*péché*) offence.
offens|er /ɔfɑ̃se/ *v.t.* offend. **s'~er de,** take offence at. **~ant, ~ante** *a.* offensive.
offensi|f, ~ve /ɔfɑ̃sif, -v/ *a. & n.f.* offensive.
offert, ~e /ɔfɛr, -t/ *voir* offrir.
office /ɔfis/ *n.m.* office; (*relig.*) service; (*de cuisine*) pantry. **d'~,** automatically.
officiel, ~le /ɔfisjɛl/ *a. & n.m., f.* official. **~lement** *adv.* officially.
officier[1] /ɔfisje/ *n.m.* officer.
officier[2] /ɔfisje/ *v.i.* (*relig.*) officiate.
officieu|x, ~se /ɔfisjø, -z/ *a.* unofficial. **~sement** *adv.* unofficially.
offrande /ɔfrɑ̃d/ *n.f.* offering.
offrant /ɔfrɑ̃/ *n.m.* **au plus ~,** to the highest bidder.
offre /ɔfr/ *n.f.* offer; (*aux enchères*) bid. **l'~ et la demande,** supply and demand. **~s d'emploi,** jobs advertised, (*rubrique*) situations vacant.
offrir† /ɔfrir/ *v.t.* offer (**de faire,** to do); (*cadeau*) give; (*acheter*) buy. **s'~** *v. pr.* offer o.s. (**comme,** as); (*spectacle*) present itself; (*s'acheter*) treat o.s. to. **~ à boire à,** (*chez soi*) give a drink to; (*au café*) buy a drink for.
offusquer /ɔfyske/ *v.t.* offend.
ogive /ɔʒiv/ *n.f.* (*atomique etc.*) warhead.
ogre /ɔgr/ *n.m.* ogre.
oh /o/ *int.* oh.
oie /wa/ *n.f.* goose.
oignon /ɔɲɔ̃/ *n.m.* (*légume*) onion; (*de tulipe etc.*) bulb.
oiseau (*pl.* **~x**) /wazo/ *n.m.* bird.
oisi|f, ~ve /wazif, -v/ *a.* idle. **~veté** *n.f.* idleness.
O.K. /ɔke/ *int.* O.K.
oléoduc /ɔleɔdyk/ *n.m.* oil pipeline.
oliv|e /ɔliv/ *n.f. & a. invar.* olive. **~ier** *n.m.* olive-tree.
olympique /ɔlɛ̃pik/ *a.* Olympic.
ombrag|e /ɔ̃braʒ/ *n.m.* shade. **prendre ~e de,** take offence at. **~é** *a.* shady. **~eux, ~euse** *a.* easily offended.
ombre /ɔ̃br/ *n.f.* (*pénombre*) shade; (*contour*) shadow; (*soupçon: fig.*) hint, shadow. **dans l'~,** (*secret*) in the dark. **faire de l'~ à qn.,** be in s.o.'s light.
ombrelle /ɔ̃brɛl/ *n.f.* parasol.
omelette /ɔmlɛt/ *n.f.* omelette.
omettre† /ɔmɛtr/ *v.t.* omit.
omission /ɔmisjɔ̃/ *n.f.* omission.
omnibus /ɔmnibys/ *n.m.* stopping train.
omoplate /ɔmɔplat/ *n.f.* shoulder-blade.
on /ɔ̃/ *pron.* we, you, one; (*les gens*) people, they; (*quelqu'un*) someone. **on dit,** people say, they say, it is said (**que,** that).
once /ɔ̃s/ *n.f.* ounce.
oncle /ɔ̃kl/ *n.m.* uncle.
onctueu|x, ~se /ɔ̃ktɥø, -z/ *a.* smooth.
onde /ɔ̃d/ *n.f.* wave. **~s courtes/longues,** short/long wave. **sur les ~s,** on the radio.
ondée /ɔ̃de/ *n.f.* shower.
on-dit /ɔ̃di/ *n.m. invar.* **les ~,** rumour.
ondul|er /ɔ̃dyle/ *v.i.* undulate; (*cheveux*) be wavy. **~ation** *n.f.* wave, undulation. **~é** *a.* (*chevelure*) wavy.
onéreu|x, ~se /ɔnerø, -z/ *a.* costly.
ongle /ɔ̃gl/ *n.m.* (finger-)nail. **se faire les ~s,** do one's nails.
ont /ɔ̃/ *voir* avoir.
ONU *abrév.* (*Organisation des nations unies*) UN.
onyx /ɔniks/ *n.m.* onyx.
onz|e /ɔ̃z/ *a. & n.m.* eleven. **~ième** *a. & n.m./f.* eleventh.
opale /ɔpal/ *n.f.* opal.
opa|que /ɔpak/ *a.* opaque. **~cité** *n.f.* opaqueness.
open /ɔpɛn/ *n.m.* open (championship).
opéra /ɔpera/ *n.m.* opera; (*édifice*) opera-house. **~-comique** (*pl.* **~s-comiques**) *n.m.* light opera.
opérateur /ɔperatœr/ *n.m.* (*caméraman*) cameraman.
opération /ɔperɑsjɔ̃/ *n.f.* operation; (*comm.*) deal.

opérationnel, ~le /ɔperasjɔnɛl/ *a.* operational.

opératoire /ɔperatwar/ *a.* (*méd.*) surgical. **bloc ~,** operating suite.

opérer /ɔpere/ *v.t.* (*personne*) operate on; (*kyste etc.*) remove; (*exécuter*) carry out, make. **se faire ~,** have an operation. ● *v.i.* (*méd.*) operate; (*faire effet*) work. **s'~** *v. pr.* (*se produire*) occur.

opérette /ɔperɛt/ *n.f.* operetta.

opiner /ɔpine/ *v.i.* nod.

opiniâtre /ɔpinjatr/ *a.* obstinate.

opinion /ɔpinjɔ̃/ *n.f.* opinion.

opium /ɔpjɔm/ *n.m.* opium.

opportun, ~e /ɔpɔrtœ̃, -yn/ *a.* opportune. **~ité** /-ynite/ *n.f.* opportuneness.

opposant, ~e /ɔpozɑ̃, -t/ *n.m., f.* opponent.

opposé /ɔpoze/ *a.* (*sens, angle, etc.*) opposite; (*factions*) opposing; (*intérêts*) conflicting. ● *n.m.* opposite. **à l'~,** (*opinion etc.*) contrary (**de,** to). **être ~ à,** be opposed to.

opposer /ɔpoze/ *v.t.* (*objets*) place opposite each other; (*personnes*) oppose; (*contraster*) contrast; (*résistance, argument*) put up. **s'~** *v. pr.* (*personnes*) confront each other; (*styles*) contrast. **s'~ à,** oppose.

opposition /ɔpozisjɔ̃/ *n.f.* opposition. **par ~ à,** in contrast with. **entrer en ~ avec,** come into conflict with. **faire ~ à un chèque,** stop a cheque.

oppress|er /ɔprese/ *v.t.* oppress. **~ant, ~ante** *a.* oppressive. **~eur** *n.m.* oppressor. **~ion** *n.f.* oppression.

opprimer /ɔprime/ *v.t.* oppress.

opter /ɔpte/ *v.i.* **~ pour,** opt for.

opticien, ~ne /ɔptisjɛ̃, -jɛn/ *n.m., f.* optician.

optimis|te /ɔptimist/ *n.m./f.* optimist. ● *a.* optimistic. **~me** *n.m.* optimism.

optimum /ɔptimɔm/ *a.* & *n.m.* optimum.

option /ɔpsjɔ̃/ *n.f.* option.

optique /ɔptik/ *a.* (*verre*) optical. ● *n.f.* (*perspective*) perspective.

opulen|t, ~te /ɔpylɑ̃, -t/ *a.* opulent. **~ce** *n.f.* opulence.

or[1] /ɔr/ *n.m.* gold. **d'~,** golden. **en ~,** gold; (*occasion*) golden.

or[2] /ɔr/ *conj.* now, well.

oracle /ɔrɑkl/ *n.m.* oracle.

orag|e /ɔraʒ/ *n.m.* (thunder)storm. **~eux, ~euse** *a.* stormy.

oraison /ɔrɛzɔ̃/ *n.f.* prayer.

or|al (*m. pl.* **~aux**) /ɔral, -o/ *a.* oral. ● *n.m.* (*pl.* **~aux**) oral.

orang|e /ɔrɑ̃ʒ/ *n.f.* & *a. invar.* orange. **~é** *a.* orange-coloured. **~er** *n.m.* orange-tree.

orangeade /ɔrɑ̃ʒad/ *n.f.* orangeade.

orateur /ɔratœr/ *n.m.* speaker.

oratorio /ɔratɔrjo/ *n.m.* oratorio.

orbite /ɔrbit/ *n.f.* orbit; (*d'œil*) socket.

orchestr|e /ɔrkɛstr/ *n.m.* orchestra; (*de jazz*) band; (*parterre*) stalls. **~er** *v.t.* orchestrate.

orchidée /ɔrkide/ *n.f.* orchid.

ordinaire /ɔrdinɛr/ *a.* ordinary; (*habituel*) usual; (*qualité*) standard. ● *n.m.* **l'~,** the ordinary; (*nourriture*) the standard fare. **d'~, à l'~,** usually. **~ment** *adv.* usually.

ordinateur /ɔrdinatœr/ *n.m.* computer.

ordination /ɔrdinɑsjɔ̃/ *n.f.* (*relig.*) ordination.

ordonnance /ɔrdɔnɑ̃s/ *n.f.* (*ordre, décret*) order; (*de médecin*) prescription; (*soldat*) orderly.

ordonné /ɔrdɔne/ *a.* tidy.

ordonner /ɔrdɔne/ *v.t.* order (**à qn. de,** s.o. to); (*agencer*) arrange; (*méd.*) prescribe; (*prêtre*) ordain.

ordre /ɔrdr/ *n.m.* order; (*propreté*) tidiness. **aux ~s de qn.,** at s.o.'s disposal. **avoir de l'~,** be tidy. **de premier ~,** first-rate. **l'~ du jour,** (*programme*) agenda. **mettre en ~,** tidy (up). **de premier ~,** first rate. **jusqu'à nouvel ~,** until further notice. **un ~ de grandeur,** an approximate idea.

ordure /ɔrdyr/ *n.f.* filth. **~s,** (*détritus*) rubbish; (*Amer.*) garbage. **~s ménagères,** household refuse.

oreille /ɔrɛj/ *n.f.* ear.

oreiller /ɔreje/ *n.m.* pillow.

oreillons /ɔrɛjɔ̃/ *n.m. pl.* mumps.

orfèvr|e /ɔrfɛvr/ *n.m.* goldsmith, silversmith. **~erie** *n.f.* goldsmith's *ou* silversmith's trade.

organe /ɔrgan/ *n.m.* organ; (*porteparole*) mouthpiece.

organigramme /ɔrganigram/ *n.m.* flow chart.

organique /ɔrganik/ *a.* organic.

organisation /ɔrganizɑsjɔ̃/ *n.f.* organization.

organis|er /ɔrganize/ *v.t.* organize. **s'~er** *v. pr.* organize o.s. **~ateur, ~atrice** *n.m., f.* organizer.

organisme /ɔrganism/ *n.m.* body, organism.

organiste /ɔrganist/ *n.m./f.* organist.

orgasme /ɔrgasm/ *n.m.* orgasm.

orge /ɔrʒ/ *n.f.* barley.

orgelet /ɔrʒəlɛ/ *n.m.* (*furoncle*) sty.

orgie /ɔrʒi/ *n.f.* orgy.

orgue /ɔrg/ *n.m.* organ. **~s** *n.f. pl.* organ. **~ de Barbarie,** barrel-organ.

orgueil /ɔrgœj/ *n.m.* pride.

orgueilleu|x, ~se /ɔrgœjø, -z/ *a.* proud.

Orient /ɔrjɑ̃/ *n.m.* **l'~,** the Orient.

orientable /ɔrjɑ̃tabl/ *a.* adjustable.

orient|al, ~ale (*m. pl.* **~aux**) /ɔrjɑ̃tal, -o/ *a.* eastern; (*de l'Orient*) oriental. ● *n.m., f.* Oriental.

orientation /ɔrjɑ̃tɑsjɔ̃/ *n.f.* direction; (*d'une politique*) course; (*de maison*) aspect. **~ professionnelle,** careers advisory service.

orienté /ɔrjɑ̃te/ *a.* (*partial*) slanted, tendentious.

orienter /ɔrjɑ̃te/ *v.t.* position; (*personne*) direct. **s'~** *v. pr.* (*se repérer*) find one's bearings. **s'~ vers,** turn towards.

orifice /ɔrifis/ *n.m.* orifice.

origan /ɔrigɑ̃/ *n.m.* oregano.

originaire /ɔriʒinɛr/ *a.* **être ~ de,** be a native of.

origin|al, ~ale (*m. pl.* **~aux**) /ɔriʒinal, -o/ *a.* original; (*curieux*) eccentric. ● *n.m.* original. ● *n.m., f.* eccentric. **~alité** *n.f.* originality; eccentricity.

origine /ɔriʒin/ *n.f.* origin. **à l'~,** originally. **d'~,** (*pièce, pneu*) original.

originel, ~le /ɔriʒinɛl/ *a.* original.

orme /ɔrm/ *n.m.* elm.

ornement /ɔrnəmɑ̃/ *n.m.* ornament. **~al** (*m. pl.* **~aux**) /-tal, -to/ *a.* ornamental.

orner /ɔrne/ *v.t.* decorate.

ornière /ɔrnjɛr/ *n.f.* rut.

ornithologie /ɔrnitɔlɔʒi/ *n.f.* ornithology.

orphelin, ~e /ɔrfəlɛ̃, -in/ *n.m., f.* orphan. ● *a.* orphaned. **~at** /-ina/ *n.m.* orphanage.

orteil /ɔrtɛj/ *n.m.* toe.

orthodox|e /ɔrtɔdɔks/ *a.* orthodox. **~ie** *n.f.* orthodoxy.

orthograph|e /ɔrtɔgraf/ *n.f.* spelling. **~ier** *v.t.* spell.

orthopédique /ɔrtɔpedik/ *a.* orthopaedic.

ortie /ɔrti/ *n.f.* nettle.

os (*pl.* **os**) /ɔs, o/ *n.m.* bone.

OS *abrév. voir* ouvrier spécialisé.

oscar /ɔskar/ *n.m.* award; (*au cinéma*) oscar.

oscill|er /ɔsile/ *v.i.* sway; (*techn.*) oscillate; (*hésiter*) waver, fluctuate. **~ation** *n.f.* (*techn.*) oscillation; (*variation*) fluctuation.

oseille /ozɛj/ *n.f.* (*plante*) sorrel.

os|er /oze/ *v.t./i.* dare. **~é** *a.* daring.

osier /ozje/ *n.m.* wicker.

ossature /ɔsatyr/ *n.f.* frame.

ossements /ɔsmɑ̃/ *n.m. pl.* bones.

osseu|x, ~se /ɔsø, -z/ *a.* bony; (*tissu*) bone.

ostensible /ɔstɑ̃sibl/ *a.* conspicuous, obvious.

ostentation /ɔstɑ̃tɑsjɔ̃/ *n.f.* ostentation.

ostéopathe /ɔsteɔpat/ *n.m./f.* osteopath.

otage /ɔtaʒ/ *n.m.* hostage.

otarie /ɔtari/ *n.f.* sea-lion.

ôter /ote/ *v.t.* remove (**à qn.,** from s.o.); (*déduire*) take away.

otite /ɔtit/ *n.f.* ear infection.

ou /u/ *conj.* or. **ou bien,** or else. **vous ou moi,** either you or me.

où /u/ *adv. & pron.* where; (*dans lequel*) in which; (*sur lequel*) on which; (*auquel*) at which. **d'où,** from which; (*pour cette raison*) hence. **d'où?,** from where? **par où,** through which. **par où?,** which way? **où qu'il soit,** wherever he may be. **au prix où c'est,** at those prices. **le jour où,** the day when.

ouate /wat/ *n.f.* cotton wool; (*Amer.*) absorbent cotton.

oubli /ubli/ *n.m.* forgetfulness; (*trou de mémoire*) lapse of memory; (*négligence*) oversight. **l'~,** (*tomber dans, sauver de*) oblivion.

oublier /ublije/ *v.t.* forget. **s'~** *v. pr.* forget o.s.; (*chose*) be forgotten.

oublieu|x, ~se /ublijø, -z/ *a.* forgetful (**de,** of).

ouest /wɛst/ *n.m.* west. ● *a. invar.* west; (*partie*) western; (*direction*) westerly.

ouf /uf/ *int.* phew.

oui /wi/ *adv.* yes.

ouï-dire (par) /(par)widir/ *adv.* by hearsay.

ouïe /wi/ *n.f.* hearing.

ouïes /wi/ *n.f. pl.* gills.

ouille /uj/ *int.* ouch.
ouïr /wir/ *v.t.* hear.
ouragan /uragɑ̃/ *n.m.* hurricane.
ourler /urle/ *v.t.* hem.
ourlet /urlɛ/ *n.m.* hem.
ours /urs/ *n.m.* bear. **~ blanc,** polar bear. **~ en peluche,** teddy bear. **~ mal léché,** boor.
ouste /ust/ *int. (fam.)* scram.
outil /uti/ *n.m.* tool.
outillage /utijaʒ/ *n.m.* tools; (*d'une usine*) equipment.
outiller /utije/ *v.t.* equip.
outrage /utraʒ/ *n.m.* (grave) insult.
outrag|er /utraʒe/ *v.t.* offend. **~eant, ~eante** *a.* offensive.
outranc|e /utrɑ̃s/ *n.f.* excess. **à ~e,** to excess; (*guerre*) all-out. **~ier, ~ière** *a.* excessive.
outre /utr/ *prép.* besides. **en ~,** besides. **~-mer** *adv.* overseas. **~ mesure,** excessively.
outrepasser /utrəpɑse/ *v.t.* exceed.
outrer /utre/ *v.t.* exaggerate; (*indigner*) incense.
outsider /utsajdœr/ *n.m.* outsider.
ouvert, ~e /uvɛr, -t/ *voir* ouvrir. ● *a.* open; (*gaz, radio, etc.*) on. **~ement** /-təmɑ̃/ *adv.* openly.
ouverture /uvɛrtyr/ *n.f.* opening; (*mus.*) overture; (*photo.*) aperture. **~s,** (*offres*) overtures. **~ d'esprit,** open-mindedness.
ouvrable /uvrabl/ *a.* **jour ~,** working day.
ouvrag|e /uvraʒ/ *n.m.* (*travail, livre*) work; (*couture*) needlework. **~é** *a.* finely worked.
ouvreuse /uvrøz/ *n.f.* usherette.
ouvr|ier, ~ière /uvrije, -jɛr/ *n.m., f.* worker. ● *a.* working-class; (*conflit*) industrial; (*syndicat*) workers'. **~ier qualifié/spécialisé,** skilled/unskilled worker.
ouvr|ir† /uvrir/ *v.t.* open (up); (*gaz, robinet, etc.*) turn *ou* switch on. ● *v.i.* open (up). **s'~ir** *v. pr.* open (up). **s'~ir à qn.,** open one's heart to s.o. **~e-boîte(s)** *n.m.* tin-opener. **~e-bouteille(s)** *n.m.* bottle-opener.
ovaire /ɔvɛr/ *n.m.* ovary.
ovale /ɔval/ *a. & n.m.* oval.
ovation /ɔvɑsjɔ̃/ *n.f.* ovation.
overdose /ɔvɛrdoz/ *n.f.* overdose.
ovni /ɔvni/ *n.m.* (*abrév.*) UFO.
ovule /ɔvyl/ *n.m.* (*à féconder*) egg; (*gynécologique*) pessary.
oxyder (s') /(s)ɔkside/ *v. pr.* become oxidized.
oxygène /ɔksiʒɛn/ *n.m.* oxygen.
oxygéner (s') /(s)ɔksiʒene/ *v. pr.* (*fam.*) get some fresh air.
ozone /ozon/ *n.f.* ozone. **la couche d'~,** the ozone layer.

P

pacemaker /pesmekœr/ *n.m.* pacemaker.
pachyderme /paʃidɛrm/ *n.m.* elephant.
pacifier /pasifje/ *v.t.* pacify.
pacifique /pasifik/ *a.* peaceful; (*personne*) peaceable; (*géog.*) Pacific. ● *n.m.* **P~,** Pacific (Ocean).
pacifiste /pasifist/ *n.m./f.* pacifist.
pacotille /pakɔtij/ *n.f.* trash.
pacte /pakt/ *n.m.* pact.
pactiser /paktize/ *v.i.* **~ avec,** be in league *ou* agreement with.
paddock /padɔk/ *n.m.* paddock.
pag|aie /pagɛ/ *n.f.* paddle. **~ayer** *v.i.* paddle.
pagaille /pagaj/ *n.f.* mess, shambles.
page /paʒ/ *n.f.* page. **être à la ~,** be up to date.
pagode /pagɔd/ *n.f.* pagoda.
paie /pɛ/ *n.f.* pay.
paiement /pɛmɑ̃/ *n.m.* payment.
païen, ~ne /pajɛ̃, -jɛn/ *a. & n.m., f.* pagan.
paillasse /pajas/ *n.f.* straw mattress; (*dans un laboratoire*) draining-board.
paillasson /pajasɔ̃/ *n.m.* doormat.
paille /pɑj/ *n.f.* straw; (*défaut*) flaw.
paillette /pajɛt/ *n.f.* (*sur robe*) sequin; (*de savon*) flake. **~s d'or,** gold-dust.
pain /pɛ̃/ *n.m.* bread: (*unité*) loaf (of bread); (*de savon etc.*) bar. **~ d'épice,** gingerbread. **~ grillé,** toast.
pair[1] /pɛr/ *a.* (*nombre*) even.
pair[2] /pɛr/ *n.m.* (*personne*) peer. **au ~,** (*jeune fille etc.*) au pair. **aller de ~,** go together (**avec,** with).
paire /pɛr/ *n.f.* pair.
paisible /pezibl/ *a.* peaceful.
paître /pɛtr/ *v.i.* (*brouter*) graze.
paix /pɛ/ *n.f.* peace; (*traité*) peace treaty.
Pakistan /pakistɑ̃/ *n.m.* Pakistan.
pakistanais, ~e /pakistanɛ, -z/ *a. & n.m., f.* Pakistani.

palace /palas/ *n.m.* luxury hotel.
palais[1] /palɛ/ *n.m.* palace. **P~ de Justice,** Law Courts. **~ des sports,** sports stadium.
palais[2] /palɛ/ *n.m.* (*anat.*) palate.
palan /palɑ̃/ *n.m.* hoist.
pâle /pɑl/ *a.* pale.
Palestine /palɛstin/ *n.f.* Palestine.
palestinien, ~ne /palɛstinjɛ̃, -jɛn/ *a.* & *n.m., f.* Palestinian.
palet /palɛ/ *n.m.* (*hockey*) puck.
paletot /palto/ *n.m.* thick jacket.
palette /palɛt/ *n.f.* palette.
pâleur /pɑlœr/ *n.f.* paleness.
palier /palje/ *n.m.* (*d'escalier*) landing; (*étape*) stage; (*de route*) level stretch.
pâlir /pɑlir/ *v.t./i.* (turn) pale.
palissade /palisad/ *n.f.* fence.
pallier /palje/ *v.t.* alleviate.
palmarès /palmarɛs/ *n.m.* list of prize-winners.
palm|e /palm/ *n.f.* palm leaf; (*symbole*) palm; (*de nageur*) flipper. **~ier** *n.m.* palm(-tree).
palmé /palme/ *a.* (*patte*) webbed.
pâlot, ~te /pɑlo, -ɔt/ *a.* pale.
palourde /palurd/ *n.f.* clam.
palper /palpe/ *v.t.* feel.
palpit|er /palpite/ *v.i.* (*battre*) pound, palpitate; (*frémir*) quiver. **~ations** *n.f. pl.* palpitations. **~ant, ~ante** *a.* thrilling.
paludisme /palydism/ *n.m.* malaria.
pâmer (se) /(sə)pɑme/ *v. pr.* swoon.
pamphlet /pɑ̃flɛ/ *n.m.* satirical pamphlet.
pamplemousse /pɑ̃pləmus/ *n.m.* grapefruit.
pan[1] /pɑ̃/ *n.m.* piece; (*de chemise*) tail.
pan[2] /pɑ̃/ *int.* bang.
panacée /panase/ *n.f.* panacea.
panache /panaʃ/ *n.m.* plume; (*bravoure*) gallantry; (*allure*) panache.
panaché /panaʃe/ *a.* (*bariolé, mélangé*) motley. **glace ~e,** mixed-flavour ice cream. ● *n.m.* shandy. **bière ~e, demi ~,** shandy.
pancarte /pɑ̃kart/ *n.f.* sign; (*de manifestant*) placard.
pancréas /pɑ̃kreɑs/ *n.m.* pancreas.
pané /pane/ *a.* breaded.
panier /panje/ *n.m.* basket. **~ à provisions,** shopping basket. **~ à salade,** (*fam.*) police van.
paniqu|e /panik/ *n.f.* panic. (*fam.*) **~er** *v.i.* panic.
panne /pan/ *n.f.* breakdown. **être en ~,** have broken down. **être en ~ sèche,** have run out of petrol *ou* gas (*Amer.*). **~ d'électricité** *ou* **de courant,** power failure.
panneau (*pl.* **~x**) /pano/ *n.m.* sign; (*publicitaire*) hoarding; (*de porte etc.*) panel. **~ (d'affichage),** notice-board. **~ (de signalisation),** road sign.
panoplie /panɔpli/ *n.f.* (*jouet*) outfit; (*gamme*) range.
panoram|a /panɔrama/ *n.m.* panorama. **~ique** *a.* panoramic.
panse /pɑ̃s/ *n.f.* paunch.
pans|er /pɑ̃se/ *v.t.* (*plaie*) dress; (*personne*) dress the wound(s) of; (*cheval*) groom. **~ement** *n.m.* dressing. **~ement adhésif,** sticking-plaster.
pantalon /pɑ̃talɔ̃/ *n.m.* (pair of) trousers. **~s,** trousers.
panthère /pɑ̃tɛr/ *n.f.* panther.
pantin /pɑ̃tɛ̃/ *n.m.* puppet.
pantomime /pɑ̃tɔmim/ *n.f.* mime; (*spectacle*) mime show.
pantoufle /pɑ̃tufl/ *n.f.* slipper.
paon /pɑ̃/ *n.m.* peacock.
papa /papa/ *n.m.* dad(dy). **de ~,** (*fam.*) old-time.
papauté /papote/ *n.f.* papacy.
pape /pap/ *n.m.* pope.
paperass|e /papras/ *n.f.* **~e(s),** (*péj.*) papers. **~erie** *n.f.* (*péj.*) papers; (*tracasserie*) red tape.
papet|ier, ~ière /paptje, -jɛr/ *n.m., f.* stationer. **~erie** /papetri/ *n.f.* (*magasin*) stationer's shop.
papier /papje/ *n.m.* paper; (*formulaire*) form. **~s (d'identité),** (identity) papers. **~ à lettres,** writing-paper. **~ aluminium,** tin foil. **~ buvard,** blotting-paper. **~ calque,** tracing-paper. **~ carbone,** carbon paper. **~ collant,** sticky paper. **~ de verre,** sandpaper. **~ hygiénique,** toilet-paper. **~ journal,** newspaper. **~ mâché,** papier mâché. **~ peint,** wallpaper.
papillon /papijɔ̃/ *n.m.* butterfly; (*contravention*) parking-ticket. **~ (de nuit),** moth.
papot|er /papɔte/ *v.i.* prattle. **~age** *n.m.* prattle.
paprika /paprika/ *n.m.* paprika.
Pâque /pɑk/ *n.f.* Passover.
paquebot /pakbo/ *n.m.* liner.
pâquerette /pɑkrɛt/ *n.f.* daisy.
Pâques /pɑk/ *n.f. pl.* & *n.m.* Easter.

paquet /pakɛ/ *n.m.* packet; (*de cartes*) pack; (*colis*) parcel. **un ~ de,** (*tas*) a mass of.

par /par/ *prép.* by; (*à travers*) through; (*motif*) out of, from; (*provenance*) from. **commencer/finir ~ qch.,** begin/end with sth. **commencer/finir ~ faire,** begin by/end up (by) doing. **~ an/mois/*etc.*,** a *ou* per year/month/*etc.* **~ avion,** (*lettre*) (by) airmail. **~-ci, par-là,** here and there. **~ contre,** on the other hand. **~ hasard,** by chance. **~ ici/là,** this/that way. **~ inadvertance,** inadvertently **~ intermittence,** intermittently. **~ l'intermédiaire de,** through. **~ jour,** a day. **~ malheur** *ou* **malchance,** unfortunately. **~ miracle,** miraculously. **~ moments,** at times. **~ opposition à,** as opposed to. **~ personne,** each, per person.

parabole /parabɔl/ *n.f.* (*relig.*) parable; (*maths*) parabola.

paracétamol /parasetamɔl/ *n.m.* paracetamol.

parachever /paraʃve/ *v.t.* perfect.

parachut|e /paraʃyt/ *n.m.* parachute. **~er** *v.t.* parachute. **~iste** *n.m./f.* parachutist; (*mil.*) paratrooper.

parad|e /parad/ *n.f.* parade; (*sport*) parry; (*réplique*) reply. **~er** *v.i.* show off.

paradis /paradi/ *n.m.* paradise. **~ fiscal,** tax haven.

paradox|e /paradɔks/ *n.m.* paradox. **~al** (*m. pl.* **~aux**) *a.* paradoxical.

paraffine /parafin/ *n.f.* paraffin wax.

parages /paraʒ/ *n.m. pl.* area, vicinity.

paragraphe /paragraf/ *n.m.* paragraph.

paraître† /parɛtr/ *v.i.* appear; (*sembler*) seem, appear; (*ouvrage*) be published, come out. **faire ~,** (*ouvrage*) bring out.

parallèle /paralɛl/ *a.* parallel; (*illégal*) unofficial. ● *n.m.* parallel. **faire un ~ entre,** draw a parallel between. **faire le ~,** make a connection. ● *n.f.* parallel (line). **~ment** *adv.* parallel (à, to).

paraly|ser /paralize/ *v.t.* paralyse. **~sie** *n.f.* paralysis. **~tique** *a.* & *n.m./f.* paralytic.

paramètre /paramɛtr/ *n.m.* parameter.

paranoïa /paranɔja/ *n.f.* paranoia.

parapet /parapɛ/ *n.m.* parapet.

paraphe /paraf/ *n.m.* signature.

paraphrase /parafraz/ *n.f.* paraphrase.

parapluie /paraplɥi/ *n.m.* umbrella.

parasite /parazit/ *n.m.* parasite. **~s,** (*radio*) interference.

parasol /parasɔl/ *n.m.* sunshade.

paratonnerre /paratɔnɛr/ *n.m.* lightning-conductor *ou* -rod.

paravent /paravɑ̃/ *n.m.* screen.

parc /park/ *n.m.* park; (*de bétail*) pen; (*de bébé*) play-pen; (*entrepôt*) depot. **~ de stationnement,** car- park.

parcelle /parsɛl/ *n.f.* fragment; (*de terre*) plot.

parce que /parsk(ə)/ *conj.* because.

parchemin /parʃəmɛ̃/ *n.m.* parchment.

parcimon|ie /parsimɔni/ *n.f.* **avec ~ie,** parsimoniously. **~ieux, ~ieuse** *a.* parsimonious.

parcmètre /parkmɛtr/ *n.m.* parking-meter.

parcourir† /parkurir/ *v.t.* travel *ou* go through; (*distance*) travel; (*des yeux*) glance at *ou* over.

parcours /parkur/ *n.m.* route; (*voyage*) journey.

par-delà /pardəla/ *prép.* & *adv.* beyond.

par-derrière /pardɛrjɛr/ *prép.* & *adv.* behind, at the back *ou* rear (of).

par-dessous /pardsu/ *prép.* & *adv.* under(neath).

pardessus /pardəsy/ *n.m.* overcoat.

par-dessus /pardsy/ *prép.* & *adv.* over. **~ bord,** overboard. **~ le marché,** into the bargain. **~ tout,** above all.

par-devant /pardəvɑ̃/ *adv.* at *ou* from the front, in front.

pardon /pardɔ̃/ *n.m.* forgiveness. **(je vous demande) ~!,** (I am) sorry!; (*pour demander qch.*) excuse me!

pardonn|er /pardɔne/ *v.t.* forgive. **~er qch. à qn.,** forgive s.o. for sth. **~able** *a.* forgivable.

paré /pare/ *a.* ready.

pare-balles /parbal/ *a. invar.* bulletproof.

pare-brise /parbriz/ *n.m. invar.* windscreen; (*Amer.*) windshield.

pare-chocs /parʃɔk/ *n.m. invar.* bumper.

pareil, ~le /parɛj/ *a.* similar (à to); (*tel*) such (a). ● *n.m., f.* equal. ● *adv.* (*fam.*) the same. **c'est ~,** it is the same. **vos ~s,** (*péj.*) those of your type, those like you. **~lement** *adv.* the same.

parement /parmɑ̃/ *n.m.* facing.

parent, ~e /parɑ̃, -t/ *a.* related (**de,** to). ● *n.m., f.* relative, relation. **~s** (*père et mère*) *n.m. pl.* parents. **~ seul,** single parent.

parenté /parɑ̃te/ *n.f.* relationship.

parenthèse /parɑ̃tɛz/ *n.f.* bracket, parenthesis; (*fig.*) digression.

parer[1] /pare/ *v.t.* (*coup*) parry. ● *v.i.* **~ à,** deal with. **~ au plus pressé,** tackle the most urgent things first.

parer[2] /pare/ *v.t.* (*orner*) adorn.

paress|e /parɛs/ *n.f.* laziness. **~er** /-ese/ *v.i.* laze (about). **~eux, ~euse** *a.* lazy; *n.m., f.* lazybones.

parfaire /parfɛr/ *v.t.* perfect.

parfait, ~e /parfɛ, -t/ *a.* perfect. **~ement** /-tmɑ̃/ *adv.* perfectly; (*bien sûr*) certainly.

parfois /parfwa/ *adv.* sometimes.

parfum /parfœ̃/ *n.m.* scent; (*substance*) perfume, scent; (*goût*) flavour.

parfum|er /parfyme/ *v.t.* perfume; (*gâteau*) flavour. **se ~er** *v. pr.* put on one's perfume. **~é** *a.* fragrant; (*savon*) scented. **~erie** *n.f.* (*produits*) perfumes; (*boutique*) perfume shop.

pari /pari/ *n.m.* bet.

par|ier /parje/ *v.t.* bet. **~ieur, ~ieuse** *n.m., f.* punter, better.

Paris /pari/ *n.m./f.* Paris.

parisien, ~ne /parizjɛ̃, -jɛn/ *a.* Paris, Parisian. ● *n.m., f.* Parisian.

parit|é /parite/ *n.f.* parity. **~aire** *a.* (*commission*) joint.

parjur|e /parʒyr/ *n.m.* perjury. ● *n.m./f.* perjurer. **se ~er** *v. pr.* perjure o.s.

parking /parkiŋ/ *n.m.* car-park; (*Amer.*) parking-lot; (*stationnement*) parking.

parlement /parləmɑ̃/ *n.m.* parliament. **~aire** /-tɛr/ *a.* parliamentary; *n.m./f.* Member of Parliament; (*fig.*) negotiator. **~er** /-te/ *v.i.* negotiate.

parl|er /parle/ *v.i.* talk, speak (**à,** to). ● *v.t.* (*langue*) speak; (*politique, affaires, etc.*) talk. **se ~er** *v. pr.* (*langue*) be spoken. ● *n.m.* speech; (*dialecte*) dialect. **~ant, ~ante** *a.* (*film*) talking; (*fig.*) eloquent. **~eur, ~euse** *n.m., f.* talker.

parloir /parlwar/ *n.m.* visiting room.

parmi /parmi/ *prép.* among(st).

parod|ie /parɔdi/ *n.f.* parody. **~ier** *v.t.* parody.

paroi /parwa/ *n.f.* wall; (*cloison*) partition (wall). **~ rocheuse,** rock face.

paroiss|e /parwas/ *n.f.* parish. **~ial** (*m. pl.* **~iaux**) *a.* parish. **~ien, ~ienne** *n.m., f.* parishioner.

parole /parɔl/ *n.f.* (*mot, promesse*) word; (*langage*) speech. **demander la ~,** ask to speak. **prendre la ~,** (begin to) speak. **tenir ~,** keep one's word. **croire qn. sur ~,** take s.o.'s word for it.

paroxysme /parɔksism/ *n.m.* height, highest point.

parquer /parke/ *v.t.,* **se ~** *v. pr.* (*auto.*) park. **~ des réfugiés,** pen up refugees.

parquet /parkɛ/ *n.m.* floor; (*jurid.*) public prosecutor's department.

parrain /parɛ̃/ *n.m.* godfather; (*fig.*) sponsor. **~er** /-ene/ *v.t.* sponsor.

pars, part[1] /par/ *voir* partir.

parsemer /parsəme/ *v.t.* strew (**de,** with).

part[2] /par/ *n.f.* share, part. **à ~,** (*de côté*) aside; (*séparément*) apart; (*excepté*) apart from. **d'autre ~,** on the other hand; (*de plus*) moreover. **de la ~ de,** from. **de toutes ~s,** from all sides. **de ~ et d'autre,** on both sides. **d'une ~,** on the one hand. **faire ~ à qn.,** inform s.o. (**de,** of). **faire la ~ des choses,** make allowances. **prendre ~ à,** take part in; (*joie, douleur*) share. **pour ma ~,** as for me.

partag|e /partaʒ/ *n.m.* dividing; sharing out; (*part*) share. **~er** *v.t.* divide; (*distribuer*) share out; (*avoir en commun*) share. **se ~er qch.,** share sth.

partance (en) /(ɑ̃)partɑ̃s/ *adv.* about to depart.

partant /partɑ̃/ *n.m.* (*sport*) starter.

partenaire /partənɛr/ *n.m./f.* partner.

parterre /partɛr/ *n.m.* flower-bed; (*théâtre*) stalls.

parti /parti/ *n.m.* (*pol.*) party; (*en mariage*) match; (*décision*) decision. **~ pris,** prejudice. **prendre ~ pour,** side with. **j'en prends mon ~,** I've come to terms with that.

part|ial (*m. pl.* **~iaux**) /parsjal, -jo/ *a.* biased. **~ialité** *n.f.* bias.

participe /partisip/ *n.m.* (*gram.*) participle.

particip|er /partisipe/ *v.i.* **~er à,** take part in, participate in; (*profits, frais*) share; (*spectacle*) appear in. **~ant, ~ante** *n.m., f.* participant (**à,** in); (*à un concours*) entrant. **~ation** *n.f.* participation; sharing; (*comm.*) interest. (*d'un artiste*) appearance.

particularité /partikylarite/ *n.f.* particularity.

particule /partikyl/ *n.f.* particle.

particul|ier, ~ière /partikylje, -jɛr/ *a.* (*spécifique*) particular; (*bizarre*) peculiar; (*privé*) private. ● *n.m.* private individual. **en ~ier,** in particular; (*en privé*) in private. **~ier à,** peculiar to. **~ièrement** *adv.* particularly.

partie /parti/ *n.f.* part; (*cartes, sport*) game; (*jurid.*) party; (*sortie*) outing, party. **une ~ de pêche,** a fishing trip. **en ~,** partly. **faire ~ de,** be part of; (*adhérer à*) belong to. **en grande ~,** largely. **~ intégrante,** integral part.

partiel, ~le /parsjɛl/ *a.* partial. ● *n.m.* (*univ.*) class examination. **~lement** *adv.* partially, partly.

partir† /partir/ *v.i.* (*aux. être*) go; (*quitter un lieu*) leave, go; (*tache*) come out; (*bouton*) come off; (*coup de feu*) go off; (*commencer*) start. **à ~ de,** from.

partisan, ~e /partizɑ̃, -an/ *n.m., f.* supporter. ● *n.m.* (*mil.*) partisan. **être ~ de,** be in favour of.

partition /partisjɔ̃/ *n.f.* (*mus.*) score.

partout /partu/ *adv.* everywhere. **~ où,** wherever.

paru /pary/ *voir* paraître.

parure /paryr/ *n.f.* adornment; (*bijoux*) jewellery; (*de draps*) set.

parution /parysjɔ̃/ *n.f.* publication.

parvenir† /parvənir/ *v.i.* (*aux. être*) **~ à,** reach; (*résultat*) achieve. **~ à faire,** manage to do. **faire ~,** send.

parvenu, ~e /parvəny/ *n.m., f.* upstart.

parvis /parvi/ *n.m.* (*place*) square.

pas[1] /pɑ/ *adv.* not. **(ne) ~,** not. **je ne sais ~,** I do not know. **~ de sucre/ livres/***etc.*, no sugar/books/*etc.* **~ du tout,** not at all. **~ encore,** not yet. **~ mal,** not bad; (*beaucoup*) quite a lot (**de,** of). **~ vrai?,** (*fam.*) isn't that so?

pas[2] /pɑ/ *n.m.* step; (*bruit*) footstep; (*trace*) footprint; (*vitesse*) pace; (*de vis*) thread. **à deux ~ (de),** close by. **au ~,** at a walking pace; (*véhicule*) very slowly. **au ~ (cadencé),** in step. **à ~ de loup,** stealthily. **faire les cent ~,** walk up and down. **faire les premiers ~,** take the first steps. **sur le ~ de la porte,** on the doorstep.

passable /pɑsabl/ *a.* tolerable. **mention ~,** pass mark.

passage /pɑsaʒ/ *n.m.* passing, passage; (*traversée*) crossing; (*visite*) visit; (*chemin*) way, passage; (*d'une œuvre*) passage. **de ~,** (*voyageur*) visiting; (*amant*) casual. **~ à niveau,** level crossing. **~ clouté,** pedestrian crossing. **~ interdit,** (*panneau*) no thoroughfare. **~ souterrain,** subway; (*Amer.*) underpass.

passag|er, ~ère /pɑsaʒe, -ɛr/ *a.* temporary. ● *n.m., f.* passenger. **~er clandestin,** stowaway.

passant, ~e /pɑsɑ̃, -t/ *a.* (*rue*) busy. ● *n.m., f.* passer-by. ● *n.m.* (*anneau*) loop.

passe /pɑs/ *n.f.* pass. **bonne/mauvaise ~,** good/bad patch. **en ~ de,** on the road to. **~-droit,** *n.m.* special privilege. **~-montagne** *n.m.* Balaclava. **~-partout** *n.m. invar.* master-key; *a. invar.* for all occasions. **~-temps** *n.m. invar.* pastime.

passé /pɑse/ *a.* (*révolu*) past; (*dernier*) last; (*fini*) over; (*fané*) faded. ● *prép.* after. ● *n.m.* past. **~ de mode,** out of fashion.

passeport /pɑspɔr/ *n.m.* passport.

passer /pɑse/ *v.i.* (*aux. être ou avoir*) pass; (*aller*) go; (*venir*) come; (*temps*) pass (by), go by; (*film*) be shown; (*couleur*) fade. ● *v.t.* (*aux. avoir*) pass, cross; (*donner*) pass, hand; (*mettre*) put; (*oublier*) overlook; (*enfiler*) slip on; (*dépasser*) go beyond; (*temps*) spend, pass; (*film*) show; (*examen*) take; (*commande*) place; (*soupe*) strain. **se ~** *v. pr.* happen, take place. **laisser ~,** let through; (*occasion*) miss. **~ à tabac,** (*fam.*) beat up. **~ devant,** (*édifice*) go past. **~ en fraude,** smuggle. **~ outre,** take no notice (**à,** of). **~ par,** go through. **~ pour,** (*riche etc.*) be taken to be. **~ sur,** (*détail*) pass over. **~ l'aspirateur,** hoover, vacuum. **~ un coup de fil à qn.,** give s.o. a ring. **je vous passe Mme X,** (*par le standard*) I'm putting you through to Mrs X; (*en donnant *l'appareil*) I'll hand you over to Mrs X. **se ~ de,** go *ou* do without.

passerelle /pɑsrɛl/ *n.f.* footbridge; (*pour accéder à un avion, à un navire*) gangway.

pass|eur, ~euse /pasœr, œz/ *n.m., f.* smuggler.

passible /pasibl/ *a.* **~ de,** liable to.

passi|f, ~ve /pasif, -v/ *a.* passive. ● *n.m.* (*comm.*) liabilities. **~vité** *n.f.* passiveness.

passion /pɑsjɔ̃/ *n.f.* passion.

passionn|er /pɑsjɔne/ *v.t.* fascinate. **se ~er pour,** have a passion for. **~é** *a.* passionate. **être ~é de,** have a passion for. **~ément** *adv.* passionately.

passoire /pɑswar/ *n.f.* (*à thé*) strainer; (*à légumes*) colander.

pastel /pastɛl/ *n.m.* & *a. invar.* pastel.

pastèque /pastɛk/ *n.f.* watermelon.

pasteur /pastœr/ *n.m.* (*relig.*) minister.

pasteurisé /pastœrize/ *a.* pasteurized.

pastiche /pastiʃ/ *n.m.* pastiche.

pastille /pastij/ *n.f.* (*bonbon*) pastille, lozenge.

pastis /pastis/ *n.m.* aniseed liqueur.

patate /patat/ *n.f.* (*fam.*) potato. **~ (douce),** sweet potato.

patauger /patoʒe/ *v.i.* splash about.

pâte /pɑt/ *n.f.* paste; (*farine*) dough; (*à tarte*) pastry; (*à frire*) batter. **~s (alimentaires),** pasta. **~ à modeler,** Plasticine (P.). **~ dentifrice,** toothpaste.

pâté /pɑte/ *n.m.* (*culin.*) pâté; (*d'encre*) ink-blot. **~ de maisons,** block of houses; (*de sable*) sand-pie. **~ en croûte,** meat pie.

pâtée /pɑte/ *n.f.* feed, mash.

patelin /patlɛ̃/ *n.m.* (*fam.*) village.

patent, ~e[1] /patɑ̃, -t/ *a.* patent.

patent|e[2] /patɑ̃t/ *n.f.* trade licence. **~é** *a.* licensed.

patère /patɛr/ *n.f.* (coat) peg.

patern|el, ~elle /patɛrnɛl/ *a.* paternal. **~ité** *n.f.* paternity.

pâteu|x, ~se /pɑtø, -z/ *a.* pasty; (*langue*) coated.

pathétique /patetik/ *a.* moving. ● *n.m.* pathos.

patholog|ie /patɔlɔʒi/ *n.f.* pathology. **~ique** *a.* pathological.

pat|ient, ~iente /pasjɑ̃, -t/ *a.* & *n.m., f.* patient. **~iemment** /-jamɑ̃/ *adv.* patiently. **~ience** *n.f.* patience.

patienter /pasjɑ̃te/ *v.i.* wait.

patin /patɛ̃/ *n.m.* skate. **~ à roulettes,** roller-skate.

patin|er /patine/ *v.i.* skate; (*voiture*) spin. **~age** *n.m.* skating. **~eur, ~euse** *n.m., f.* skater.

patinoire /patinwar/ *n.f.* skating-rink.

pâtir /pɑtir/ *v.i.* suffer (**de,** from).

pâtiss|ier, ~ière /pɑtisje, -jɛr/ *n.m., f.* pastry-cook, cake shop owner. **~erie** *n.f.* cake shop; (*gâteau*) pastry; (*art*) cake making.

patois /patwa/ *n.m.* patois.

patraque /patrak/ *a.* (*fam.*) peaky, out of sorts.

patrie /patri/ *n.f.* homeland.

patrimoine /patrimwan/ *n.m.* heritage.

patriot|e /patrijɔt/ *a.* patriotic. ● *n.m./f.* patriot. **~ique** *a.* patriotic. **~isme** *n.m.* patriotism.

patron[1]**, ~ne** /patrɔ̃, -ɔn/ *n.m., f.* employer, boss; (*propriétaire*) owner, boss; (*saint*) patron saint. **~al** (*m. pl.* **~aux**) /-ɔnal, -o/ *a.* employers'. **~at** /-ɔna/ *n.m.* employers.

patron[2] /patrɔ̃/ *n.m.* (*couture*) pattern.

patronage /patrɔnaʒ/ *n.m.* patronage; (*foyer*) youth club.

patronner /patrɔne/ *v.t.* support.

patrouill|e /patruj/ *n.f.* patrol. **~er** *v.i.* patrol.

patte /pat/ *n.f.* leg; (*pied*) foot; (*de chat*) paw. **~s,** (*favoris*) sideburns.

pâturage /pɑtyraʒ/ *n.m.* pasture.

pâture /pɑtyr/ *n.f.* food.

paume /pom/ *n.f.* (*de main*) palm.

paumé, ~e /pome/ *n.m., f.* (*fam.*) wretch, loser.

paumer /pome/ *v.t.* (*fam.*) lose.

paupière /popjɛr/ *n.f.* eyelid.

pause /poz/ *n.f.* pause; (*halte*) break.

pauvre /povr/ *a.* poor. ● *n.m./f.* poor man, poor woman. **~ment** /-əmɑ̃/ *adv.* poorly. **~té** /-əte/ *n.f.* poverty.

pavaner (se) /(sə)pavane/ *v. pr.* strut.

pav|er /pave/ *v.t.* pave; (*chaussée*) cobble. **~é** *n.m.* paving-stone; cobble(-stone).

pavillon[1] /pavijɔ̃/ *n.m.* house; (*de gardien*) lodge.

pavillon[2] /pavijɔ̃/ *n.m.* (*drapeau*) flag.

pavoiser /pavwaze/ *v.t.* deck with flags. ● *v.i.* put out the flags.

pavot /pavo/ *n.m.* poppy.

payant, ~e /pɛjɑ̃, -t/ *a.* (*billet*) for which a charge is made; (*spectateur*) (fee-)paying; (*rentable*) profitable.

payer /peje/ *v.t./i.* pay; (*service, travail, etc.*) pay for; (*acheter*) buy (**à,** for). **se ~** *v. pr.* (*s'acheter*) buy o.s. **faire ~ à qn.,** (*cent francs etc.*) charge s.o. (**pour,** for). **se ~ la tête de,** make fun of. **il me le paiera!,** he'll pay for this.

pays /pei/ *n.m.* country; (*région*) region; (*village*) village. **du ~,** local. **les P~-Bas,** the Netherlands. **le ~ de Galles,** Wales.

paysage /peizaʒ/ *n.m.* landscape.

paysan, ~ne /peizɑ̃, -an/ *n.m., f.* farmer, country person; (*péj.*) peasant. ● *a.* (*agricole*) farming; (*rural*) country.

PCV (en) /(ɑ̃)peseve/ *adv.* **appeler** *ou* **téléphoner en ~,** reverse the charges; (*Amer.*) call collect.

PDG *abrév. voir* président directeur général.

péage /peaʒ/ *n.m.* toll; (*lieu*) toll-gate.

peau (*pl.* **~x**) /po/ *n.f.* skin; (*cuir*) hide. **~ de chamois,** chamois (-leather). **~ de mouton,** sheepskin. **être bien/mal dans sa ~,** be/not be at ease with oneself.

pêche[1] /pɛʃ/ *n.f.* peach.

pêche[2] /pɛʃ/ *n.f.* (*activité*) fishing; (*poissons*) catch. **~ à la ligne,** angling.

péché /peʃe/ *n.m.* sin.

péch|er /peʃe/ *v.i.* sin. **~er par timidité/etc.,** be too timid/etc. **~eur, ~eresse** *n.m., f.* sinner.

pêch|er /peʃe/ *v.t.* (*poisson*) catch; (*dénicher: fam.*) dig up. ● *v.i.* fish. **~eur** *n.m.* fisherman; (*à la ligne*) angler.

pécule /pekyl/ *n.m.* (*économies*) savings.

pécuniaire /pekynjɛr/ *a.* financial.

pédago|gie /pedagɔʒi/ *n.f.* education. **~gique** *a.* educational. **~gue** *n.m./f.* teacher.

pédal|e /pedal/ *n.f.* pedal. **~er** *v.i.* pedal.

pédalo /pedalo/ *n.m.* pedal boat.

pédant, ~e /pedɑ̃, -t/ *a.* pedantic.

pédé /pede/ *n.m.* (*argot*) queer, fag (*Amer.*).

pédestre /pedɛstr/ *a.* **faire de la randonnée ~,** go walking *ou* hiking.

pédiatre /pedjatr/ *n.m./f.* paediatrician.

pédicure /pedikyr/ *n.m./f.* chiropodist.

pedigree /pedigre/ *n.m.* pedigree.

pègre /pɛgr/ *n.f.* underworld.

peign|e /pɛɲ/ *n.m.* comb. **~er** /peɲe/ *v.t.* comb; (*personne*) comb the hair of. **se ~er** *v. pr.* comb one's hair.

peignoir /pɛɲwar/ *n.m.* dressing-gown.

peindre† /pɛ̃dr/ *v.t.* paint.

peine /pɛn/ *n.f.* sadness, sorrow; (*effort, difficulté*) trouble; (*punition*) punishment; (*jurid.*) sentence. **avoir de la ~,** feel sad. **faire de la ~ à,** hurt. **ce n'est pas la ~ de faire,** it is not worth (while) doing. **se donner** *ou* **prendre la ~ de faire,** go to the trouble of doing. **~ de mort** death penalty.

peine (à) /(a)pɛn/ *adv.* hardly.

peiner /pene/ *v.i.* struggle. ● *v.t.* sadden.

peintre /pɛ̃tr/ *n.m.* painter. **~ en bâtiment,** house painter.

peinture /pɛ̃tyr/ *n.f.* painting; (*matière*) paint. **~ à l'huile,** oil-painting.

péjorati|f, ~ve /peʒɔratif, -v/ *a.* pejorative.

pelage /pəlaʒ/ *n.m.* coat, fur.

pêle-mêle /pɛlmɛl/ *adv.* in a jumble.

peler /pəle/ *v.t./i.* peel.

pèlerin /pɛlrɛ̃/ *n.m.* pilgrim. **~age** /-inaʒ/ *n.m.* pilgrimage.

pèlerine /pɛlrin/ *n.f.* cape.

pélican /pelikɑ̃/ *n.m.* pelican.

pelle /pɛl/ *n.f.* shovel; (*d'enfant*) spade. **~tée** *n.f.* shovelful.

pellicule /pelikyl/ *n.f.* film. **~s,** (*cheveux*) dandruff.

pelote /pəlɔt/ *n.f.* ball; (*d'épingles*) pincushion.

peloton /plɔtɔ̃/ *n.m.* troop, squad; (*sport*) pack. **~ d'exécution,** firing-squad.

pelotonner (se) /(sə)plɔtɔne/ *v. pr.* curl up.

pelouse /pluz/ *n.f.* lawn.

peluche /plyʃ/ *n.f.* (*tissu*) plush; (*jouet*) cuddly toy. **en ~,** (*lapin, chien*) fluffy, furry.

pelure /plyr/ *n.f.* peeling.

pén|al (*m. pl.* **~aux**) /penal, -o/ *a.* penal. **~aliser** *v.t.* penalize. **~alité** *n.f.* penalty.

penalt|y (*pl.* **~ies**) /penalti/ *n.m.* penalty (kick).

penaud, ~e /pəno, -d/ *a.* sheepish.

penchant /pãʃã/ *n.m.* inclination; (*goût*) liking (**pour,** for).
pench|er /pãʃe/ *v.t.* tilt. ● *v.i.* lean (over), tilt. **se ~er** *v. pr.* lean (forward). **~er pour,** favour. **se ~er sur,** (*problème etc.*) examine.
pendaison /pãdɛzɔ̃/ *n.f.* hanging.
pendant[1] /pãdã/ *prép.* (*au cours de*) during; (*durée*) for. **~ que,** while.
pendant[2]**, ~e** /pãdã, -t/ *a.* hanging; (*question etc.*) pending. ● *n.m.* (*contrepartie*) matching piece (**de,** to). **faire ~ à,** match. **~ d'oreille,** drop ear-ring.
pendentif /pãdãtif/ *n.m.* pendant.
penderie /pãdri/ *n.f.* wardrobe.
pend|re /pãdr/ *v.t./i.* hang. **se ~re** *v. pr.* hang (**à,** from); (*se tuer*) hang o.s. **~re la crémaillère,** have a house-warming. **~u, ~ue** *a.* hanging (**à,** from); *n.m., f.* hanged man, hanged woman.
pendul|e /pãdyl/ *n.f.* clock. ● *n.m.* pendulum. **~ette** *n.f.* (travelling) clock.
pénétr|er /penetre/ *v.i.* **~er (dans),** enter. ● *v.t.* penetrate. **se ~er de,** become convinced of. **~ant, ~ante** *a.* penetrating.
pénible /penibl/ *a.* difficult; (*douloureux*) painful; (*fatigant*) tiresome. **~ment** /-əmã/ *adv.* with difficulty; (*cruellement*) painfully.
péniche /peniʃ/ *n.f.* barge.
pénicilline /penisilin/ *n.f.* penicillin.
péninsule /penɛ̃syl/ *n.f.* peninsula.
pénis /penis/ *n.m.* penis.
pénitence /penitãs/ *n.f.* (*peine*) penance; (*regret*) penitence; (*fig.*) punishment. **faire ~,** repent.
péniten|cier /penitãsje/ *n.m.* penitentiary. **~tiaire** /-sjɛr/ *a.* prison.
pénombre /penɔ̃br/ *n.f.* half-light.
pensée[1] /pãse/ *n.f.* thought.
pensée[2] /pãse/ *n.f.* (*fleur*) pansy.
pens|er /pãse/ *v.t./i.* think. **~er à,** (*réfléchir à*) think about; (*se souvenir de, prévoir*) think of. **~er faire,** think of doing. **faire ~er à,** remind one of. **~eur** *n.m.* thinker.
pensi|f, ~ve /pãsif, -v/ *a.* pensive.
pension /pãsjɔ̃/ *n.f.* (*scol.*) boarding-school; (*repas, somme*) board; (*allocation*) pension. **~ (de famille),** guest-house. **~ alimentaire,** (*jurid.*) alimony. **~naire** /-jɔnɛr/ *n.m./f.* boarder; (*d'hôtel*) guest. **~nat** /-jɔna/ *n.m.* boarding-school.
pente /pãt/ *n.f.* slope. **en ~,** sloping.
Pentecôte /pãtkot/ *n.f.* **la ~,** Whitsun.
pénurie /penyri/ *n.f.* shortage.
pépé /pepe/ *n.m.* (*fam.*) grandad.
pépier /pepje/ *v.i.* chirp.
pépin /pepɛ̃/ *n.m.* (*graine*) pip; (*ennui: fam.*) hitch; (*parapluie: fam.*) brolly.
pépinière /pepinjɛr/ *n.f.* (tree) nursery.
perçant, ~e /pɛrsã, -t/ *a.* (*froid*) piercing; (*regard*) keen.
percée /pɛrse/ *n.f.* opening; (*attaque*) breakthrough.
perce-neige /pɛrsənɛʒ/ *n.m./f. invar.* snowdrop.
percepteur /pɛrsɛptœr/ *n.m.* tax-collector.
perceptible /pɛrsɛptibl/ *a.* perceptible.
perception /pɛrsɛpsjɔ̃/ *n.f.* perception; (*d'impôts*) collection.
percer /pɛrse/ *v.t.* pierce; (*avec perceuse*) drill; (*mystère*) penetrate. ● *v.i.* break through; (*dent*) come through.
perceuse /pɛrsøz/ *n.f.* drill.
percevoir† /pɛrsəvwar/ *v.t.* perceive; (*impôt*) collect.
perche /pɛrʃ/ *n.f.* (*bâton*) pole.
perch|er /pɛrʃe/ *v.t.*, **se ~er** *v. pr.* perch. **~oir** *n.m.* perch.
percolateur /pɛrkɔlatœr/ *n.m.* percolator.
percussion /pɛrkysjɔ̃/ *n.f.* percussion.
percuter /pɛrkyte/ *v.t.* strike; (*véhicule*) crash into.
perd|re /pɛrdr/ *v.t./i.* lose; (*gaspiller*) waste; (*ruiner*) ruin. **se ~re** *v. pr.* get lost; (*rester inutilisé*) go to waste. **~ant, ~ante** *a.* losing; *n.m., f.* loser. **~u** *a.* (*endroit*) isolated; (*moments*) spare; (*malade*) finished.
perdreau (*pl.* **~x**) /pɛrdro/ *n.m.* (young) partridge.
perdrix /pɛrdri/ *n.f.* partridge.
père /pɛr/ *n.m.* father. **~ de famille,** father, family man. **~ spirituel,** father figure. **le ~ Noël,** Father Christmas, Santa Claus.
péremptoire /perãptwar/ *a.* peremptory.
perfection /pɛrfɛksjɔ̃/ *n.f.* perfection.
perfectionn|er /pɛrfɛksjɔne/ *v.t.* improve. **se ~er en anglais**/*etc.*, improve one's English/*etc.* **~é** *a.*

sophisticated. **~ement** *n.m.* improvement.

perfectionniste /pɛrfɛksjɔnist/ *n.m./f.* perfectionist.

perfid|e /pɛrfid/ *a.* perfidious, treacherous. **~ie** *n.f.* perfidy.

perfor|er /pɛrfɔre/ *v.t.* perforate; (*billet, bande*) punch. **~ateur** *n.m.* (*appareil*) punch. **~ation** *n.f.* perforation; (*trou*) hole.

performan|ce /pɛrfɔrmɑ̃s/ *n.f.* performance. **~t, ~te** *a.* high-performance, successful.

perfusion /pɛrfysjɔ̃/ *n.f.* drip. **mettre qn. sous ~,** put s.o. on a drip.

péricliter /periklite/ *v.i.* decline, be in rapid decline.

péridural /peridyral/ *a.* **(anesthésie) ~e,** epidural.

péril /peril/ *n.m.* peril.

périlleu|x, ~se /perijø, -z/ *a.* perilous.

périmé /perime/ *a.* expired; (*désuet*) outdated.

périmètre /perimɛtr/ *n.m.* perimeter.

périod|e /perjɔd/ *n.f.* period. **~ique** *a.* periodic(al); *n.m.* (*journal*) periodical.

péripétie /peripesi/ *n.f.* (unexpected) event, adventure.

périphér|ie /periferi/ *n.f.* periphery; (*banlieue*) outskirts. **~ique** *a.* peripheral; *n.m.* **(boulevard) ~ique,** ring road.

périple /peripl/ *n.m.* journey.

pér|ir /perir/ *v.i.* perish, die. **~issable** *a.* perishable.

périscope /periskɔp/ *n.m.* periscope.

perle /pɛrl/ *n.f.* (*bijou*) pearl; (*boule, de sueur*) bead.

permanence /pɛrmanɑ̃s/ *n.f.* permanence; (*bureau*) duty office; (*scol.*) study room. **de ~,** on duty. **en ~,** permanently. **assurer une ~,** keep the office open.

permanent, ~e /pɛrmanɑ̃, -t/ *a.* permanent; (*spectacle*) continuous; (*comité*) standing. ● *n.f.* (*coiffure*) perm.

perméable /pɛrmeabl/ *a.* permeable; (*personne*) susceptible (**à,** to).

permettre† /pɛrmɛtr/ *v.t.* allow, permit. **~ à qn. de,** allow *ou* permit s.o. to. **se ~ de,** take the liberty to.

permis, ~e /pɛrmi, -z/ *a.* allowed. ● *n.m.* licence, permit. **~ (de conduire),** driving-licence.

permission /pɛrmisjɔ̃/ *n.f.* permission. **en ~,** (*mil.*) on leave.

permut|er /pɛrmyte/ *v.t.* change round. **~ation** *n.f.* permutation.

pernicieu|x, ~se /pɛrnisjø, -z/ *a.* pernicious.

Pérou /peru/ *n.m.* Peru.

perpendiculaire /pɛrpɑ̃dikylɛr/ *a.* & *n.f.* perpendicular.

perpétrer /pɛrpetre/ *v.t.* perpetrate.

perpétuel, ~le /pɛrpetɥɛl/ *a.* perpetual.

perpétuer /pɛrpetɥe/ *v.t.* perpetuate.

perpétuité (à) /(a)pɛrpetɥite/ *adv.* for life.

perplex|e /pɛrplɛks/ *a.* perplexed. **~ité** *n.f.* perplexity.

perquisition /pɛrkizisjɔ̃/ *n.f.* (police) search. **~ner** /-jɔne/ *v.t./i.* search.

perron /pɛrɔ̃/ *n.m.* (front) steps.

perroquet /pɛrɔkɛ/ *n.m.* parrot.

perruche /peryʃ/ *n.f.* budgerigar.

perruque /peryk/ *n.f.* wig.

persan, ~e /pɛrsɑ̃, -an/ *a.* & *n.m.* (*lang.*) Persian.

persécut|er /pɛrsekyte/ *v.t.* persecute. **~ion** /-ysjɔ̃/ *n.f.* persecution.

persévér|er /pɛrsevere/ *v.i.* persevere. **~ance** *n.f.* perseverance.

persienne /pɛrsjɛn/ *n.f.* (outside) shutter.

persil /pɛrsi/ *n.m.* parsley.

persistan|t, ~te /pɛrsistɑ̃, -t/ *a.* persistent; (*feuillage*) evergreen. **~ce** *n.f.* persistence.

persister /pɛrsiste/ *v.i.* persist (**à faire,** in doing).

personnage /pɛrsɔnaʒ/ *n.m.* character; (*important*) personality.

personnalité /pɛrsɔnalite/ *n.f.* personality.

personne /pɛrsɔn/ *n.f.* person. **~s,** people. ● *pron.* (*quelqu'un*) anybody. **(ne) ~,** nobody.

personnel, ~le /pɛrsɔnɛl/ *a.* personal; (*égoïste*) selfish. ● *n.m.* staff. **~lement** *adv.* personally.

personnifier /pɛrsɔnifje/ *v.t.* personify.

perspective /pɛrspɛktiv/ *n.f.* (*art*) perspective; (*vue*) view; (*possibilité*) prospect; (*point de vue*) viewpoint, perspective.

perspicac|e /pɛrspikas/ *a.* shrewd. **~ité** *n.f.* shrewdness.

persua|der /pɛrsɥade/ *v.t.* persuade (**de faire,** to do). **~sion** /-ɥazjɔ̃/ *n.f.* persuasion.

persuasi|f, ~ve /pɛrsɥazif, -v/ *a.* persuasive.

perte /pɛrt/ *n.f.* loss; (*ruine*) ruin. **à ~ de vue,** as far as the eye can see. **~ de,** (*temps, argent*) waste of. **~ sèche,** total loss. **~s,** (*méd.*) discharge.

pertinen|t, ~te /pɛrtinɑ̃, -t/ *a.* pertinent; (*esprit*) judicious. **~ce** *n.f.* pertinence.

perturb|er /pɛrtyrbe/ *v.t.* disrupt; (*personne*) perturb. **~ateur, ~atrice** *a.* disruptive; *n.m., f.* disruptive element. **~ation** *n.f.* disruption.

pervenche /pɛrvɑ̃ʃ/ *n.f.* periwinkle; (*fam.*) traffic warden.

pervers, ~e /pɛrvɛr, -s/ *a.* perverse; (*dépravé*) perverted. **~ion** /-sjɔ̃/ *n.f.* perversion.

pervert|ir /pɛrvɛrtir/ *v.t.* pervert. **~i, ~ie** *n.m., f.* pervert.

pes|ant, ~ante /pəzɑ̃, -t/ *a.* heavy. **~amment** *adv.* heavily. **~anteur** *n.f.* heaviness. **la ~anteur,** (*force*) gravity.

pèse-personne /pɛzpɛrsɔn/ *n.m.* (bathroom) scales.

pes|er /pəze/ *v.t./i.* weigh. **~er sur,** bear upon. **~ée** *n.f.* weighing; (*effort*) pressure.

peseta /pezeta/ *n.f.* peseta.

pessimis|te /pesimist/ *a.* pessimistic. ● *n.m.* pessimist. **~me** *n.m.* pessimism.

peste /pɛst/ *n.f.* plague; (*personne*) pest.

pester /pɛste/ *v.i.* **~ (contre),** curse.

pestilentiel, ~le /pɛstilɑ̃sjɛl/ *a.* fetid, stinking.

pet /pɛ/ *n.m.* fart.

pétale /petal/ *n.m.* petal.

pétanque /petɑ̃k/ *n.f.* bowls.

pétarader /petarade/ *v.i.* backfire.

pétard /petar/ *n.m.* banger.

péter /pete/ *v.i.* fart; (*fam.*) go bang; (*casser: fam.*) snap.

pétill|er /petije/ *v.i.* (*feu*) crackle; (*champagne, yeux*) sparkle. **~er d'intelligence,** sparkle with intelligence. **~ant, ~ante** *a.* (*gazeux*) fizzy.

petit, ~e /pti, -t/ *a.* small; (*avec nuance affective*) little; (*jeune*) young, small; (*faible*) slight; (*mesquin*) petty. ● *n.m., f.* little child; (*scol.*) junior. **~s,** (*de chat*) kittens; (*de chien*) pups. **en ~,** in miniature. **~ ami,** boy-friend. **~e amie,** girl-friend. **~ à petit,** little by little. **~es annonces,** small ads. **~e cuiller,** teaspoon. **~ déjeuner,** breakfast. **le ~ écran,** the small screen, television. **~-enfant** (*pl.* **~s-enfants**) *n.m.* grandchild. **~e-fille** (*pl.* **~es-filles**) *n.f.* granddaughter. **~-fils** (*pl.* **~s-fils**) *n.m.* grandson. **~ pain,** roll. **~-pois** (*pl.* **~s-pois**) *n.m.* garden pea.

petitesse /ptitɛs/ *n.f.* smallness; (*péj.*) meanness.

pétition /petisjɔ̃/ *n.f.* petition.

pétrifier /petrifje/ *v.t.* petrify.

pétrin /petrɛ̃/ *n.m.* (*situation: fam.*) **dans le ~,** in a fix.

pétrir /petrir/ *v.t.* knead.

pétrol|e /petrɔl/ *n.m.* (*brut*) oil; (*pour lampe etc.*) paraffin. **lampe à ~e,** oil lamp. **~ier, ~ière** *a.* oil; *n.m.* (*navire*) oil-tanker.

pétulant, ~e /petylɑ̃, -t/ *a.* exuberant, full of high spirits.

peu /pø/ *adv.* **~ (de),** (*quantité*) little, not much; (*nombre*) few, not many. **~ intéressant/*etc.*,** not very interesting/*etc.* ● *pron.* few. ● *n.m.* little. **un ~ (de),** a little. **à ~ près,** more or less. **de ~,** only just. **~ à peu,** gradually. **~ après/avant,** shortly after/before. **~ de chose,** not much. **~ nombreux,** few. **~ souvent,** seldom. **pour ~ que,** as long as.

peuplade /pœplad/ *n.f.* tribe.

peuple /pœpl/ *n.m.* people.

peupler /pœple/ *v.t.* populate.

peuplier /pøplije/ *n.m.* poplar.

peur /pœr/ *n.f.* fear. **avoir ~,** be afraid (**de,** of). **de ~ de,** for fear of. **faire ~ à,** frighten. **~eux, ~euse** *a.* fearful, timid.

peut /pø/ *voir* pouvoir[1].

peut-être /pøtɛtr/ *adv.* perhaps, maybe. **~ que,** perhaps, maybe.

peux /pø/ *voir* pouvoir[1].

pèze /pɛz/ *n.m.* (*fam.*) **du ~,** money, dough.

phallique /falik/ *a.* phallic.

phantasme /fɑ̃tasm/ *n.m.* fantasy.

phare /far/ *n.m.* (*tour*) lighthouse; (*de véhicule*) headlight. **~ anti-brouillard,** fog lamp.

pharmaceutique /farmasøtik/ *a.* pharmaceutical.

pharmac|ie /farmasi/ *n.f.* (*magasin*) chemist's (shop); (*Amer.*) pharmacy; (*science*) pharmacy; (*armoire*) medicine cabinet. **~ien, ~ienne** *n.m., f.* chemist, pharmacist.

pharyngite /farɛ̃ʒit/ *n.f.* pharyngitis.

phase /fɑz/ *n.f.* phase.

phénomène /fenɔmɛn/ *n.m.* phenomenon; (*original*: *fam.*) eccentric.

philanthrop|e /filɑ̃trɔp/ *n.m./f.* philanthropist. **~ique** *a.* philanthropic.

philatél|ie /filateli/ *n.f.* philately. **~iste** *n.m./f.* philatelist.

philharmonique /filarmɔnik/ *a.* philharmonic.

Philippines /filipin/ *n.f. pl.* **les ~,** the Philippines.

philosoph|e /filɔzɔf/ *n.m./f.* philosopher. ● *a.* philosophical. **~ie** *n.f.* philosophy. **~ique** *a.* philosophical.

phobie /fɔbi/ *n.f.* phobia.

phonétique /fɔnetik/ *a.* phonetic.

phoque /fɔk/ *n.m.* (*animal*) seal.

phosphate /fɔsfat/ *n.m.* phosphate.

phosphore /fɔsfɔr/ *n.m.* phosphorus.

photo /fɔto/ *n.f.* photo; (*art*) photography. **prendre en ~,** take a photo of. **~ d'identité,** passport photograph.

photocop|ie /fɔtɔkɔpi/ *n.f.* photocopy. **~ier** *v.t.* photocopy. **~ieuse** *n.f.* photocopier.

photogénique /fɔtɔʒenik/ *a.* photogenic.

photograph|e /fɔtɔgraf/ *n.m./f.* photographer. **~ie** *n.f.* photograph; (*art*) photography. **~ier** *v.t.* take a photo of. **~ique** *a.* photographic.

phrase /frɑz/ *n.f.* sentence.

physicien, ~ne /fizisjɛ̃, -jɛn/ *n.m., f.* physicist.

physiologie /fizjɔlɔʒi/ *n.f.* physiology.

physionomie /fizjɔnɔmi/ *n.f.* face.

physique[1] /fizik/ *a.* physical. ● *n.m.* physique. **au ~,** physically. **~ment** *adv.* physically.

physique[2] /fizik/ *n.f.* physics.

piailler /pjɑje/ *v.i.* squeal, squawk.

pian|o /pjano/ *n.m.* piano. **~iste** *n.m./f.* pianist.

pianoter /pjanɔte/ *v.t.* (*air*) tap out. ● *v.i.* (**sur,** on) (*ordinateur*) tap away; (*table*) tap one's fingers.

pic /pik/ *n.m.* (*outil*) pickaxe; (*sommet*) peak; (*oiseau*) woodpecker. **à ~,** (*verticalement*) sheer; (*couler*) straight to the bottom; (*arriver*) just at the right time.

pichenette /piʃnɛt/ *n.f.* flick.

pichet /piʃɛ/ *n.m.* jug.

pickpocket /pikpɔkɛt/ *n.m.* pickpocket.

pick-up /pikœp/ *n.m. invar.* record-player.

picorer /pikɔre/ *v.t./i.* peck.

picot|er /pikɔte/ *v.t.* prick; (*yeux*) make smart. **~ement** *n.m.* pricking; smarting.

pie /pi/ *n.f.* magpie.

pièce /pjɛs/ *n.f.* piece; (*chambre*) room; (*pour raccommoder*) patch; (*écrit*) document. **~ (de monnaie),** coin. **~ (de théâtre),** play. **dix francs/*etc.* (la) ~,** ten francs/*etc.* each. **~ de rechange,** spare part. **~ détachée,** part. **~ d'identité,** identity paper. **~ montée,** tiered cake. **~s justificatives,** supporting documents. **deux/trois *etc.* ~s,** two-/three-/*etc.* room flat *ou* apartment (*Amer.*).

pied /pje/ *n.m.* foot; (*de meuble*) leg; (*de lampe*) base; (*de salade*) plant. **à ~,** on foot. **au ~ de la lettre,** literally. **avoir ~,** have a footing. **avoir les ~s plats,** have flat feet. **comme un ~,** (*fam.*) terribly. **mettre sur ~,** set up. **~ bot,** club-foot. **sur un ~ d'égalité,** on an equal footing. **mettre les ~s dans le plat,** put one's foot in it. **c'est le ~!,** (*fam.*) it's great!

piédest|al (*pl.* **~aux**) /pjedɛstal, -o/ *n.m.* pedestal.

piège /pjɛʒ/ *n.m.* trap.

piég|er /pjeʒe/ *v.t.* trap; (*avec explosifs*) booby-trap. **lettre/voiture ~ée,** letter-/car-bomb.

pierr|e /pjɛr/ *n.f.* stone. **~e d'achoppement,** stumbling-block. **~e de touche,** touchstone. **~e précieuse,** precious stone. **~e tombale,** tombstone. **~eux, ~euse** *a.* stony.

piété /pjete/ *n.f.* piety.

piétiner /pjetine/ *v.i.* stamp one's feet; (*ne pas avancer*: *fig.*) mark time. ● *v.t.* trample (on).

piéton /pjetɔ̃/ *n.m.* pedestrian. **~nier, ~nière** /-ɔnje, -jɛr/ *a.* pedestrian.

piètre /pjɛtr/ *a.* wretched.

pieu (*pl.* **~x**) /pjø/ *n.m.* post, stake.

pieuvre /pjœvr/ *n.f.* octopus.

pieu|x, ~se /pjø, -z/ *a.* pious.

pif /pif/ *n.m.* (*fam.*) nose.

pigeon /piʒɔ̃/ *n.m.* pigeon.

piger /piʒe/ *v.t./i.* (*fam.*) understand, get (it).

pigment /pigmɑ̃/ *n.m.* pigment.

pignon /piɲɔ̃/ *n.m.* (*de maison*) gable.

pile /pil/ *n.f.* (*tas, pilier*) pile; (*électr.*) battery; (*atomique*) pile. ● *adv.* (*s'arrêter: fam.*) dead. **à dix heures ~,** (*fam.*) at ten on the dot. **~ ou face?,** heads or tails?

piler /pile/ *v.t.* pound.

pilier /pilje/ *n.m.* pillar.

pill|er /pije/ *v.t.* loot. **~age** *n.m.* looting. **~ard, ~arde** *n.m., f.* looter.

pilonner /pilɔne/ *v.t.* pound.

pilori /pilɔri/ *n.m.* **mettre** *ou* **clouer au ~,** pillory.

pilot|e /pilɔt/ *n.m.* pilot; (*auto.*) driver. ● *a.* pilot. **~er** *v.t.* (*aviat., naut.*) pilot; (*auto.*) drive; (*fig.*) guide.

pilule /pilyl/ *n.f.* pill. **la ~,** the pill.

piment /pimɑ̃/ *n.m.* pepper, pimento; (*fig.*) spice. **~é** /-te/ *a.* spicy.

pimpant, ~e /pɛ̃pɑ̃, -t/ *a.* spruce.

pin /pɛ̃/ *n.m.* pine.

pinard /pinar/ *n.m.* (*vin: fam.*) plonk, cheap wine.

pince /pɛ̃s/ *n.f.* (*outil*) pliers; (*levier*) crowbar; (*de crabe*) pincer; (*à sucre*) tongs. **~ (à épiler),** tweezers. **~ (à linge),** (clothes-)peg.

pinceau (*pl.* **~x**) /pɛ̃so/ *n.m.* paintbrush.

pinc|er /pɛ̃se/ *v.t.* pinch; (*arrêter: fam.*) pinch. **se ~er le doigt,** catch one's finger. **~é** *a.* (*ton, air*) stiff. **~ée** *n.f.* pinch (**de,** of).

pince-sans-rire /pɛ̃sɑ̃rir/ *a. invar.* po-faced. **c'est un ~,** he's po-faced.

pincettes /pɛ̃sɛt/ *n.f. pl.* (fire) tongs.

pinède /pinɛd/ *n.f.* pine forest.

pingouin /pɛ̃gwɛ̃/ *n.m.* penguin.

ping-pong /piŋpɔ̃g/ *n.m.* table tennis, ping-pong.

pingre /pɛ̃gr/ *a.* miserly.

pinson /pɛ̃sɔ̃/ *n.m.* chaffinch.

pintade /pɛ̃tad/ *n.f.* guinea-fowl.

pioch|e /pjɔʃ/ *n.f.* pick(axe). **~er** *v.t./i.* dig; (*étudier: fam.*) study hard, slog away (at).

pion /pjɔ̃/ *n.m.* (*de jeu*) piece; (*échecs*) pawn; (*scol., fam.*) supervisor.

pionnier /pjɔnje/ *n.m.* pioneer.

pipe /pip/ *n.f.* pipe. **fumer la ~,** smoke a pipe.

pipe-line /piplin/ *n.m.* pipeline.

piquant, ~e /pikɑ̃, -t/ *a.* (*barbe etc.*) prickly; (*goût*) pungent; (*détail etc.*) spicy. ● *n.m.* prickle; (*de hérisson*) spine, prickle; (*fig.*) piquancy.

pique[1] /pik/ *n.f.* (*arme*) pike.

pique[2] /pik/ *n.m.* (*cartes*) spades.

pique-niqu|e /piknik/ *n.m.* picnic. **~er** *v.i.* picnic.

piquer /pike/ *v.t.* prick; (*langue*) burn, sting; (*abeille etc.*) sting; (*serpent etc.*) bite; (*enfoncer*) stick; (*coudre*) (machine-)stitch; (*curiosité*) excite; (*crise*) have; (*voler: fam.*) pinch. ● *v.i.* (*avion*) dive; (*goût*) be hot. **~ une tête,** plunge headlong. **se ~ de,** pride o.s. on.

piquet /pikɛ/ *n.m.* stake; (*de tente*) peg. **au ~,** (*scol.*) in the corner. **~ de grève,** (strike) picket.

piqûre /pikyr/ *n.f.* prick; (*d'abeille etc.*) sting; (*de serpent etc.*) bite; (*point*) stitch; (*méd.*) injection, shot (*Amer.*) **faire une ~ à qn.,** give s.o. an injection.

pirate /pirat/ *n.m.* pirate. **~ de l'air,** hijacker. **~rie** *n.f.* piracy.

pire /pir/ *a.* worse (**que,** than). **le ~ livre**/*etc.*, the worst book/*etc.* ● *n.m.* **le ~,** the worst (thing). **au ~,** at worst.

pirogue /pirɔg/ *n.f.* canoe, dug-out.

pirouette /pirwɛt/ *n.f.* pirouette.

pis[1] /pi/ *n.m.* (*de vache*) udder.

pis[2] /pi/ *a. invar. & adv.* worse. **aller de mal en ~,** go from bad to worse.

pis-aller /pizale/ *n.m. invar.* stopgap, temporary expedient.

piscine /pisin/ *n.f.* swimming-pool. **~ couverte,** indoor swimming-pool.

pissenlit /pisɑ̃li/ *n.m.* dandelion.

pistache /pistaʃ/ *n.f.* pistachio.

piste /pist/ *n.f.* track; (*de personne, d'animal*) track, trail; (*aviat.*) runway; (*de cirque*) ring; (*de ski*) run; (*de patinage*) rink; (*de danse*) floor; (*sport*) race-track. **~ cyclable,** cycle-track; (*Amer.*) bicycle path.

pistolet /pistɔlɛ/ *n.m.* gun, pistol; (*de peintre*) spray-gun.

piston /pistɔ̃/ *n.m.* (*techn.*) piston. **il a un ~,** (*fam.*) somebody is pulling strings for him.

pistonner /pistɔne/ *v.t.* (*fam.*) recommend, pull strings for.

piteu|x, ~se /pitø, -z/ *a.* pitiful.

pitié /pitje/ *n.f.* pity. **il me fait ~, j'ai ~ de lui,** I pity him.

piton /pitɔ̃/ *n.m.* (*à crochet*) hook; (*sommet pointu*) peak.

pitoyable /pitwajabl/ *a.* pitiful.

pitre /pitr/ *n.m.* clown. **faire le ~,** clown around.

pittoresque /pitɔrɛsk/ *a.* picturesque.
pivot /pivo/ *n.m.* pivot. **~er** /-ɔte/ *v.i.* revolve; (*personne*) swing round.
pizza /pidza/ *n.f.* pizza.
placage /plakaʒ/ *n.m.* (*en bois*) veneer; (*sur un mur*) facing.
placard /plakar/ *n.m.* cupboard; (*affiche*) poster. **~er** /-de/ *v.t.* (*affiche*) post up; (*mur*) cover with posters.
place /plas/ *n.f.* place; (*espace libre*) room, space; (*siège*) seat, place; (*prix d'un trajet*) fare; (*esplanade*) square; (*emploi*) position; (*de parking*) space. **à la ~ de,** instead of. **en ~, à sa ~,** in its place. **faire ~ à,** give way to. **sur ~,** on the spot. **remettre qn. à sa ~,** put s.o. in his place. **ça prend de la ~,** it takes up a lot of room. **se mettre à la ~ de qn.** put oneself in s.o.'s shoes *ou* place.
placebo /plasebo/ *n.m.* placebo.
placenta /plasɛ̃ta/ *n.m.* placenta.
plac|er /plase/ *v.t.* place; (*invité, spectateur*) seat; (*argent*) invest. **se ~er** *v. pr.* (*personne*) take up a position; (*troisième etc.*: *sport*) come (in); (*à un endroit*) to go and stand (**à,** in). **~é** *a.* (*sport*) placed. **bien ~é pour,** in a position to. **~ement** *n.m.* (*d'argent*) investment.
placide /plasid/ *a.* placid.
plafond /plafɔ̃/ *n.m.* ceiling.
plage /plaʒ/ *n.f.* beach; (*station*) (seaside) resort; (*aire*) area.
plagiat /plaʒja/ *n.m.* plagiarism.
plaid /plɛd/ *n.m.* travelling-rug.
plaider /plede/ *v.t./i.* plead.
plaid|oirie /plɛdwari/ *n.f.* (defence) speech. **~oyer** *n.m.* plea.
plaie /plɛ/ *n.f.* wound; (*personne*: *fam.*) nuisance.
plaignant, ~e /plɛɲɑ̃, -t/ *n.m., f.* plaintiff.
plaindre† /plɛ̃dr/ *v.t.* pity. **se ~** *v. pr.* complain (**de,** about). **se ~ de,** (*souffrir de*) complain of.
plaine /plɛn/ *n.f.* plain.
plaint|e /plɛ̃t/ *n.f.* complaint; (*gémissement*) groan. **~if, ~ive** *a.* plaintive.
plaire† /plɛr/ *v.i.* **~ à,** please. **ça lui plaît,** he likes it. **elle lui plaît,** he likes her. **ça me plaît de faire,** I like *ou* enjoy doing. **s'il vous plaît,** please. **se ~** *v. pr.* (*à Londres etc.*) like *ou* enjoy it.
plaisance /plɛzɑ̃s/ *n.f.* **la (navigation de) ~,** yachting.
plaisant, ~e /plɛzɑ̃, -t/ *a.* pleasant; (*drôle*) amusing.
plaisant|er /plɛzɑ̃te/ *v.i.* joke. **~erie** *n.f.* joke. **~in** *n.m.* joker.
plaisir /plezir/ *n.m.* pleasure. **faire ~ à,** please. **pour le ~,** for fun *ou* pleasure.
plan[1] /plɑ̃/ *n.m.* plan; (*de ville*) map; (*surface, niveau*) plane. **~ d'eau,** expanse of water. **premier ~,** foreground. **dernier ~,** background.
plan[2]**, ~e** /plɑ̃, -an/ *a.* flat.
planche /plɑ̃ʃ/ *n.f.* board, plank; (*gravure*) plate; (*de potager*) bed. **~ à repasser,** ironing-board. **~ à voile,** sailboard; (*sport*) windsurfing.
plancher /plɑ̃ʃe/ *n.m.* floor.
plancton /plɑ̃ktɔ̃/ *n.m.* plankton.
plan|er /plane/ *v.i.* glide. **~er sur,** (*mystère, danger*) hang over. **~eur** *n.m.* (*avion*) glider.
planète /planɛt/ *n.f.* planet.
planif|ier /planifje/ *v.t.* plan. **~ication** *n.f.* planning.
planqu|e /plɑ̃k/ *n.f.* (*fam.*) hideout; (*emploi*: *fam.*) cushy job. **~er** *v.t.*, **se ~er** *v. pr.* hide.
plant /plɑ̃/ *n.m.* seedling; (*de légumes*) bed.
plante /plɑ̃t/ *n.f.* plant. **~ des pieds,** sole (of the foot).
plant|er /plɑ̃te/ *v.t.* (*plante etc.*) plant; (*enfoncer*) drive in; (*installer*) put up; (*mettre*) put. **rester ~é,** stand still, remain standing. **~ation** *n.f.* planting; (*de tabac etc.*) plantation.
plantureu|x, ~se /plɑ̃tyrø, -z/ *a.* abundant; (*femme*) buxom.
plaque /plak/ *n.f.* plate; (*de marbre*) slab; (*insigne*) badge; (*commémorative*) plaque. **~ chauffante,** hotplate. **~ minéralogique,** number-plate.
plaqu|er /plake/ *v.t.* (*bois*) veneer; (*aplatir*) flatten; (*rugby*) tackle; (*abandonner*: *fam.*) ditch. **~er qch. sur *ou* contre,** make sth. stick to. **~age** *n.m.* (*rugby*) tackle.
plasma /plasma/ *n.m.* plasma.
plastic /plastik/ *n.m.* plastic explosive.
plastique /plastik/ *a.* & *n.m.* plastic. **en ~,** plastic.
plastiquer /plastike/ *v.t.* blow up.

plat[1], **~e** /pla, -t/ *a.* flat. ● *n.m.* (*de la main*) flat. **à ~** *adv.* (*poser*) flat; *a.* (*batterie, pneu*) flat. **à ~ ventre,** flat on one's face.
plat[2] /pla/ *n.m.* (*culin.*) dish; (*partie de repas*) course.
platane /platan/ *n.m.* plane(-tree).
plateau (*pl.* **~x**) /plato/ *n.m.* tray; (*d'électrophone*) turntable, deck; (*de balance*) pan; (*géog.*) plateau. **~ de fromages,** cheeseboard.
plateau-repas (*pl.* **plateaux-repas**) *n.m.* tray meal.
plate-bande (*pl.* **plates-bandes**) /platbɑ̃d/ *n.f.* flower-bed.
plate-forme (*pl.* **plates-formes**) /platfɔrm/ *n.f.* platform.
platine[1] /platin/ *n.m.* platinum.
platine[2] /platin/ *n.f.* (*de tourne-disque*) turntable.
platitude /platityd/ *n.f.* platitude.
platonique /platɔnik/ *a.* platonic.
plâtr|e /plɑtr/ *n.m.* plaster; (*méd.*) (plaster) cast. **~er** *v.t.* plaster; (*membre*) put in plaster.
plausible /plozibl/ *a.* plausible.
plébiscite /plebisit/ *n.m.* plebiscite.
plein, ~e /plɛ̃, plɛn/ *a.* full (**de,** of); (*total*) complete. ● *n.m.* **faire le ~ (d'essence),** fill up (the tank). **à ~,** to the full. **à ~ temps,** full-time. **en ~ air,** in the open air. **en ~ milieu/visage,** right in the middle/the face. **en ~e nuit**/*etc.*, in the middle of the night/*etc.* **~ les mains,** all over one's hands.
pleinement /plɛnmɑ̃/ *adv.* fully.
pléthore /pletɔr/ *n.f.* over-abundance, plethora.
pleurer /plœre/ *v.i.* cry, weep (**sur,** over); (*yeux*) water. ● *v.t.* mourn.
pleurésie /plœrezi/ *n.f.* pleurisy.
pleurnicher /plœrniʃe/ *v.i.* (*fam.*) snivel.
pleurs (en) /(ɑ̃)plœr/ *adv.* in tears.
pleuvoir† /pløvwar/ *v.i.* rain; (*fig.*) rain *ou* shower down. **il pleut,** it is raining. **il pleut à verse** *ou* **à torrents,** it is pouring.
pli /pli/ *n.m.* fold; (*de jupe*) pleat; (*de pantalon*) crease; (*enveloppe*) cover; (*habitude*) habit. **(faux) ~,** crease.
pliant, ~e /plijɑ̃, -t/ *a.* folding; (*parapluie*) telescopic. ● *n.m.* folding stool, camp-stool.
plier /plije/ *v.t.* fold; (*courber*) bend; (*personne*) submit (**à,** to). ● *v.i.* bend; (*personne*) submit. **se ~** *v. pr.* fold. **se ~ à,** submit to.
plinthe /plɛ̃t/ *n.f.* skirting-board; (*Amer.*) baseboard.
plisser /plise/ *v.t.* crease; (*yeux*) screw up; (*jupe*) pleat.
plomb /plɔ̃/ *n.m.* lead; (*fusible*) fuse. **~s,** (*de chasse*) lead shot. **de** *ou* **en ~,** lead. **de ~,** (*ciel*) leaden.
plomb|er /plɔ̃be/ *v.t.* (*dent*) fill. **~age** *n.m.* filling.
plomb|ier /plɔ̃bje/ *n.m.* plumber. **~erie** *n.f.* plumbing.
plongeant, ~e /plɔ̃ʒɑ̃, -t/ *a.* (*vue*) from above; (*décolleté*) plunging.
plongeoir /plɔ̃ʒwar/ *n.m.* diving-board.
plongeon /plɔ̃ʒɔ̃/ *n.m.* dive.
plong|er /plɔ̃ʒe/ *v.i.* dive; (*route*) plunge. ● *v.t.* plunge. **se ~er** *v. pr.* plunge (**dans,** into). **~é dans,** (*lecture*) immersed in. **~ée** *n.f.* diving. **en ~ée** (*sous-marin*) submerged. **~eur, ~euse** *n.m., f.* diver; (*employé*) dishwasher.
plouf /pluf/ *n.m.* & *int.* splash.
ployer /plwaje/ *v.t./i.* bend.
plu /ply/ *voir* plaire, pleuvoir.
pluie /plɥi/ *n.f.* rain; (*averse*) shower. **~ battante/diluvienne,** driving/torrential rain.
plumage /plymaʒ/ *n.m.* plumage.
plume /plym/ *n.f.* feather; (*stylo*) pen; (*pointe*) nib.
plumeau (*pl.* **~x**) /plymo/ *n.m.* feather duster.
plumer /plyme/ *v.t.* pluck.
plumier /plymje/ *n.m.* pencil box.
plupart /plypar/ *n.f.* most. **la ~ des,** (*gens, cas, etc.*) most. **la ~ du temps,** most of the time. **pour la ~,** for the most part.
pluriel, ~le /plyrjɛl/ *a.* & *n.m.* plural. **au ~,** (*nom*) plural.
plus[1] /ply/ *adv. de négation.* **(ne) ~,** (*temps*) no longer, not any more. **(ne) ~ de,** (*quantité*) no more. **je n'y vais ~,** I do not go there any longer *ou* any more. **(il n'y a) ~ de pain,** (there is) no more bread.
plus[2] /ply/ (/plyz/ *before vowel,* /plys/ *in final position*) *adv.* more (**que,** than). **~ âgé/tard**/*etc.*, older/later/*etc.* **~ beau**/*etc.*, more beautiful/*etc.* **le ~,** the most. **le ~ beau**/*etc.*, the most beautiful; (*de deux*) the more beautiful. **le ~ de,** (*gens etc.*) most. **~ de,** (*pain etc.*) more; (*dix jours etc.*) more than. **il est ~ de huit heures**/*etc.* it is after eight/*etc.* o'clock. **de ~,** more (**que,** than);

(*en outre*) moreover. **(âgés) de ~ de** (*huit ans etc.*) over, more than. **de ~ en plus,** more and more. **en ~,** extra. **en ~ de,** in addition to. **~ ou moins,** more or less.
plus[3] /plys/ *conj.* plus.
plusieurs /plyzjœr/ *a. & pron.* several.
plus-value /plyvaly/ *n.f.* (*bénéfice*) profit.
plutôt /plyto/ *adv.* rather **(que,** than).
pluvieu|x, ~se /plyvjø, -z/ *a.* rainy.
pneu (*pl.* **~s**) /pnø/ *n.m.* tyre; (*lettre*) express letter. **~matique** *a.* inflatable.
pneumonie /pnømɔni/ *n.f.* pneumonia.
poche /pɔʃ/ *n.f.* pocket; (*sac*) bag. **~s,** (*sous les yeux*) bags.
pocher /pɔʃe/ *v.t.* (*œuf*) poach.
pochette /pɔʃɛt/ *n.f.* pack(et), envelope; (*sac*) bag, pouch; (*d'allumettes*) book; (*de disque*) sleeve; (*mouchoir*) pocket handkerchief. **~ surprise,** lucky bag.
podium /pɔdjɔm/ *n.m.* rostrum.
poêle[1] /pwal/ *n.f.* **~ (à frire),** frying-pan.
poêle[2] /pwal/ *n.m.* stove.
poème /pɔɛm/ *n.m.* poem.
poésie /pɔezi/ *n.f.* poetry; (*poème*) poem.
poète /pɔɛt/ *n.m.* poet.
poétique /pɔetik/ *a.* poetic.
poids /pwa/ *n.m.* weight. **~ coq/lourd/plume,** bantam weight/heavyweight/featherweight. **~ lourd,** (*camion*) lorry, juggernaut; (*Amer.*) truck.
poignant, ~e /pwaɲɑ̃, -t/ *a.* poignant.
poignard /pwaɲar/ *n.m.* dagger. **~er** /-de/ *v.t.* stab.
poigne /pwaɲ/ *n.f.* grip. **avoir de la ~,** have an iron fist.
poignée /pwaɲe/ *n.f.* handle; (*quantité*) handful. **~ de main,** handshake.
poignet /pwaɲɛ/ *n.m.* wrist; (*de chemise*) cuff.
poil /pwal/ *n.m.* hair; (*pelage*) fur; (*de brosse*) bristle. **~s,** (*de tapis*) pile. **à ~,** (*fam.*) naked. **~u** *a.* hairy.
poinçon /pwɛ̃sɔ̃/ *n.m.* awl; (*marque*) hallmark. **~ner** /-ɔne/ *v.t.* (*billet*) punch. **~neuse** /-ɔnøz/ *n.f.* punch.
poing /pwɛ̃/ *n.m.* fist.
point[1] /pwɛ̃/ *n.m.* point; (*note: scol.*) mark; (*tache*) spot, dot; (*de couture*) stitch. **~ (final),** full stop, period. **à ~,** (*culin.*) medium; (*arriver*) at the right time. **faire le ~,** take stock. **mettre au ~,** (*photo.*) focus; (*technique*) perfect; (*fig.*) clear up. **deux ~s,** colon. **~ culminant,** peak. **~ de repère,** landmark. **~s de suspension,** suspension points. **~ de suture,** (*méd.*) stitch. **~ de vente,** retail outlet. **~ de vue,** point of view. **~ d'interrogation/d'exclamation,** question/exclamation mark. **~ du jour,** daybreak. **~ mort,** (*auto.*) neutral. **~ virgule,** semicolon. **sur le ~ de,** about to.
point[2] /pwɛ̃/ *adv.* **(ne) ~,** not.
pointe /pwɛ̃t/ *n.f.* point, tip; (*clou*) tack; (*de grille*) spike; (*fig.*) touch (**de,** of). **de ~,** (*industrie*) highly advanced. **en ~,** pointed. **heure de ~,** peak hour. **sur la ~ des pieds,** on tiptoe.
pointer[1] /pwɛ̃te/ *v.t.* (*cocher*) tick off. ● *v.i.* (*employé*) clock in *ou* out. **se ~** *v. pr.* (*fam.*) turn up.
pointer[2] /pwɛ̃te/ *v.t.* (*diriger*) point, aim.
pointillé /pwɛ̃tije/ *n.m.* dotted line. ● *a.* dotted.
pointilleu|x, ~se /pwɛ̃tijø, -z/ *a.* fastidious, particular.
pointu /pwɛ̃ty/ *a.* pointed; (*aiguisé*) sharp.
pointure /pwɛ̃tyr/ *n.f.* size.
poire /pwar/ *n.f.* pear.
poireau (*pl.* **~x**) /pwaro/ *n.m.* leek.
poireauter /pwarote/ *v.i.* (*fam.*) hang about.
poirier /pwarje/ *n.m.* pear-tree.
pois /pwa/ *n.m.* pea; (*dessin*) dot.
poison /pwazɔ̃/ *n.m.* poison.
poisseu|x, ~se /pwasø, -z/ *a.* sticky.
poisson /pwasɔ̃/ *n.m.* fish. **~ rouge,** goldfish. **~ d'avril,** April fool. **les P~s,** Pisces.
poissonn|ier, ~ière /pwasɔnje, -jɛr/ *n.m., f.* fishmonger. **~erie** *n.f.* fish shop.
poitrail /pwatraj/ *n.m.* breast.
poitrine /pwatrin/ *n.f.* chest; (*seins*) bosom; (*culin.*) breast.
poivr|e /pwavr/ *n.m.* pepper. **~é** *a.* peppery. **~ière** *n.f.* pepper-pot.
poivron /pwavrɔ̃/ *n.m.* pepper, capsicum.

poivrot, ~e /pwavro, -ɔt/ *n.m., f.* (*fam.*) drunkard.
poker /pɔkɛr/ *n.m.* poker.
polaire /pɔlɛr/ *a.* polar.
polariser /pɔlarize/ *v.t.* polarize.
polaroïd /pɔlarɔid/ *n.m.* (P.) Polaroid (P.).
pôle /pol/ *n.m.* pole.
polémique /pɔlemik/ *n.f.* argument. ● *a.* controversial.
poli /pɔli/ *a.* (*personne*) polite. **~ment** *adv.* politely.
polic|e[1] /pɔlis/ *n.f.* police; (*discipline*) (law and) order. **~ier, ~ière** *a.* police; (*roman*) detective; *n.m.* policeman.
police[2] /pɔlis/ *n.f.* (*d'assurance*) policy.
polio(myélite) /pɔljɔ(mjelit)/ *n.f.* polio(myelitis).
polir /pɔlir/ *v.t.* polish.
polisson, ~ne /pɔlisɔ̃, -ɔn/ *a.* naughty. ● *n.m., f.* rascal.
politesse /pɔlitɛs/ *n.f.* politeness; (*parole*) polite remark.
politicien, ~ne /pɔlitisjɛ̃, -jɛn/ *n.m., f.* (*péj.*) politician.
politi|que /pɔlitik/ *a.* political. ● *n.f.* politics; (*ligne de conduite*) policy. **~ser** *v.t.* politicize.
pollen /pɔlɛn/ *n.m.* pollen.
polluant, ~e /pɔlɥɑ̃, -t/ *a.* polluting. ● *n.m.* pollutant.
poll|uer /pɔlɥe/ *v.t.* pollute. **~ution** *n.f.* pollution.
polo /pɔlo/ *n.m.* polo; (*vêtement*) sports shirt, tennis shirt.
Pologne /pɔlɔɲ/ *n.f.* Poland.
polonais, ~e /pɔlɔnɛ, -z/ *a.* Polish. ● *n.m., f.* Pole. ● *n.m.* (*lang.*) Polish.
poltron, ~ne /pɔltrɔ̃, -ɔn/ *a.* cowardly. ● *n.m., f.* coward.
polycopier /pɔlikɔpje/ *v.t.* duplicate, stencil.
polygamie /pɔligami/ *n.f.* polygamy.
polyglotte /pɔliglɔt/ *n.m./f.* polyglot.
polyvalent, ~e /pɔlivalɑ̃, -t/ *a.* varied; (*personne*) versatile.
pommade /pɔmad/ *n.f.* ointment.
pomme /pɔm/ *n.f.* apple; (*d'arrosoir*) rose. **~ d'Adam,** Adam's apple. **~ de pin,** pine cone. **~ de terre,** potato. **~s frites,** chips; (*Amer.*) French fries. **tomber dans les ~s,** (*fam.*) pass out.
pommeau (*pl.* **~x**) /pɔmo/ *n.m.* (*de canne*) knob.
pommette /pɔmɛt/ *n.f.* cheek-bone.
pommier /pɔmje/ *n.m.* apple-tree.
pompe /pɔ̃p/ *n.f.* pump; (*splendeur*) pomp. **~ à incendie,** fire-engine. **~s funèbres,** undertaker's.
pomper /pɔ̃pe/ *v.t.* pump; (*copier: fam.*) copy, crib. **~ l'air à qn.,** (*fam.*) get on s.o.'s nerves.
pompeu|x, ~se /pɔ̃pø, -z/ *a.* pompous.
pompier /pɔ̃pje/ *n.m.* fireman.
pompiste /pɔ̃pist/ *n.m./f.* petrol pump attendant; (*Amer.*) gas station attendant.
pompon /pɔ̃pɔ̃/ *n.m.* pompon.
pomponner /pɔ̃pɔne/ *v.t.* deck out.
poncer /pɔ̃se/ *v.t.* rub down.
ponctuation /pɔ̃ktɥɑsjɔ̃/ *n.f.* punctuation.
ponct|uel, ~uelle /pɔ̃ktɥɛl/ *a.* punctual. **~ualité** *n.f.* punctuality.
ponctuer /pɔ̃ktɥe/ *v.t.* punctuate.
pondéré /pɔ̃dere/ *a.* level-headed.
pondre /pɔ̃dr/ *v.t./i.* lay.
poney /pɔnɛ/ *n.m.* pony.
pont /pɔ̃/ *n.m.* bridge; (*de navire*) deck; (*de graissage*) ramp. **faire le ~,** take the extra day(s) off (*between holidays*). **~ aérien,** airlift. **~-levis** (*pl.* **~s-levis**) *n.m.* drawbridge.
ponte /pɔ̃t/ *n.f.* laying (of eggs).
pontife /pɔ̃tif/ *n.m.* **(souverain) ~,** pope.
pontific|al (*m. pl.* **~aux**) /pɔ̃tifikal, -o/ *a.* papal.
pop /pɔp/ *n.m. & a. invar.* (*mus.*) pop.
popote /pɔpɔt/ *n.f.* (*fam.*) cooking.
populace /pɔpylas/ *n.f.* (*péj.*) rabble.
popul|aire /pɔpylɛr/ *a.* popular; (*expression*) colloquial; (*quartier, origine*) working-class. **~arité** *n.f.* popularity.
population /pɔpylɑsjɔ̃/ *n.f.* population.
populeu|x, ~se /pɔpylø, -z/ *a.* populous.
porc /pɔr/ *n.m.* pig; (*viande*) pork.
porcelaine /pɔrsəlɛn/ *n.f.* china, porcelain.
porc-épic (*pl.* **porcs-épics**) /pɔrkepik/ *n.m.* porcupine.
porche /pɔrʃ/ *n.m.* porch.
porcherie /pɔrʃəri/ *n.f.* pigsty.
por|e /pɔr/ *n.m.* pore. **~eux, ~euse** *a.* porous.
pornograph|ie /pɔrnɔgrafi/ *n.f.* pornography. **~ique** *a.* pornographic.
port[1] /pɔr/ *n.m.* port, harbour. **à bon ~,** safely. **~ maritime,** seaport.

port[2] /pɔr/ *n.m.* (*transport*) carriage; (*d'armes*) carrying; (*de barbe*) wearing.

portail /pɔrtaj/ *n.m.* portal.

portant, ~e /pɔrtɑ̃, -t/ *a.* **bien/mal ~,** in good/bad health.

portati|f, ~ve /pɔrtatif, -v/ *a.* portable.

porte /pɔrt/ *n.f.* door; (*passage*) doorway; (*de jardin, d'embarquement*) gate. **mettre à la ~,** throw out. **~ d'entrée,** front door. **~-fenêtre** (*pl.* **~s-fenêtres**) *n.f.* French window.

porté /pɔrte/ *a.* **~ à,** inclined to. **~ sur,** fond of.

portée /pɔrte/ *n.f.* (*d'une arme*) range; (*de voûte*) span; (*d'animaux*) litter; (*impact*) significance; (*mus.*) stave. **à ~ de,** within reach of. **à ~ de (la) main,** within (arm's) reach. **hors de ~ (de),** out of reach (of). **à la ~ de qn.** at s.o.'s level.

portefeuille /pɔrtəfœj/ *n.m.* wallet; (*de ministre*) portfolio.

portemanteau (*pl.* **~x**) /pɔrtmɑ̃to/ *n.m.* coat *ou* hat stand.

port|er /pɔrte/ *v.t.* carry; (*vêtement, bague*) wear; (*fruits, responsabilité, nom*) bear; (*coup*) strike; (*amener*) bring; (*inscrire*) enter. ● *v.i.* (*bruit*) carry; (*coup*) hit home. **~er sur,** rest on; (*concerner*) bear on. **se ~er bien,** be *ou* feel well. **se ~er candidat,** stand as a candidate. **~er aux nues,** praise to the skies. **~e-avions** *n.m. invar.* aircraft-carrier. **~e-bagages** *n.m. invar.* luggage rack. **~e-bonheur** *n.m. invar.* (*objet*) charm. **~e-clefs** *n.m. invar.* key-ring. **~e-documents** *n.m. invar.* attaché case, document wallet. **~e-monnaie** *n.m. invar.* purse. **~e-parole** *n.m. invar.* spokesman. **~e-voix** *n.m. invar.* megaphone.

porteu|r, ~se /pɔrtœr, -øz/ *n.m., f.* (*de nouvelles*) bearer; (*méd.*) carrier. ● *n.m.* (*rail.*) porter.

portier /pɔrtje/ *n.m.* door-man.

portière /pɔrtjɛr/ *n.f.* door.

portillon /pɔrtijɔ̃/ *n.m.* gate.

portion /pɔrsjɔ̃/ *n.f.* portion.

portique /pɔrtik/ *n.m.* portico; (*sport*) crossbar.

porto /pɔrto/ *n.m.* port (wine).

portrait /pɔrtrɛ/ *n.m.* portrait. **~-robot** (*pl.* **~s-robots**) *n.m.* identikit, photofit.

portuaire /pɔrtɥɛr/ *a.* port.

portugais, ~e /pɔrtygɛ, -z/ *a.* & *n.m., f.* Portuguese. ● *n.m.* (*lang.*) Portuguese.

Portugal /pɔrtygal/ *n.m.* Portugal.

pose /poz/ *n.f.* installation; (*attitude*) pose; (*photo.*) exposure.

posé /poze/ *a.* calm, serious.

poser /poze/ *v.t.* put (down); (*installer*) install, put in; (*fondations*) lay; (*question*) ask; (*problème*) pose. ● *v.i.* (*modèle*) pose. **se ~** *v. pr.* (*avion, oiseau*) land; (*regard*) alight; (*se présenter*) arise. **~ sa candidature,** apply (**à,** for).

positi|f, ~ve /pozitif, -v/ *a.* positive.

position /pozisjɔ̃/ *n.f.* position; (*banque*) balance (of account). **prendre ~,** take a stand.

posologie /pozɔlɔʒi/ *n.f.* directions for use.

poss|éder /pɔsede/ *v.t.* possess; (*propriété*) own, possess. **~esseur** *n.m.* possessor; owner.

possessi|f, ~ve /pɔsesif, -v/ *a.* possessive.

possession /pɔsesjɔ̃/ *n.f.* possession. **prendre ~ de,** take possession of.

possibilité /pɔsibilite/ *n.f.* possibility.

possible /pɔsibl/ *a.* possible. ● *n.m.* **le ~,** what is possible. **dès que ~,** as soon as possible. **faire son ~,** do one's utmost. **le plus tard/***etc.* **~,** as late/*etc.* as possible. **pas ~,** impossible; (*int.*) really!

post- /pɔst/ *préf.* post- .

post|al (*m. pl.* **~aux**) /pɔstal, -o/ *a.* postal.

poste[1] /pɔst/ *n.f.* (*service*) post; (*bureau*) post office. **~ aérienne,** airmail. **mettre à la ~,** post. **~ restante,** poste restante.

poste[2] /pɔst/ *n.m.* (*lieu, emploi*) post; (*de radio, télévision*) set; (*téléphone*) extension (number). **~ d'essence,** petrol *ou* gas (*Amer.*) station. **~ d'incendie,** fire point. **~ de pilotage,** cockpit. **~ de police,** police station. **~ de secours,** first-aid post.

poster[1] /pɔste/ *v.t.* (*lettre, personne*) post.

poster[2] /pɔstɛr/ *n.m.* poster.

postérieur /pɔsterjœr/ *a.* later; (*partie*) back. **~ à,** after. ● *n.m.* (*fam.*) posterior.

postérité /pɔsterite/ *n.f.* posterity.

posthume /pɔstym/ *a.* posthumous.

postiche /pɔstiʃ/ *a.* false.

post|ier, ~ière /pɔstje, -jɛr/ *n.m., f.* postal worker.
post-scriptum /pɔstskriptɔm/ *n.m. invar.* postscript.
postul|er /pɔstyle/ *v.t./i.* apply (**à** *ou* **pour,** for); (*principe*) postulate. **~ant, ~ante** *n.m., f.* applicant.
posture /pɔstyr/ *n.f.* posture.
pot /po/ *n.m.* pot; (*en carton*) carton; (*en verre*) jar; (*chance: fam.*) luck; (*boisson: fam.*) drink. **~-au-feu** /pɔtofø/ *n.m. invar.* (*plat*) stew. **~ d'échappement,** exhaust-pipe. **~-de-vin** (*pl.* **~s-de-vin**) *n.m.* bribe. **~-pourri,** (*pl.* **~s-pourris**) *n.m.* pot pourri.
potable /pɔtabl/ *a.* drinkable. **eau ~,** drinking water.
potage /pɔtaʒ/ *n.m.* soup.
potag|er, ~ère /pɔtaʒe, -ɛr/ *a.* vegetable. ● *n.m.* vegetable garden.
pote /pɔt/ *n.m.* (*fam.*) chum.
poteau (*pl.* **~x**) /pɔto/ *n.m.* post; (*télégraphique*) pole. **~ indicateur,** signpost.
potelé /pɔtle/ *a.* plump.
potence /pɔtɑ̃s/ *n.f.* gallows.
potentiel, ~le /pɔtɑ̃sjɛl/ *a. & n.m.* potential.
pot|erie /pɔtri/ *n.f.* pottery; (*objet*) piece of pottery. **~ier** *n.m.* potter.
potins /pɔtɛ̃/ *n.m. pl.* gossip.
potion /posjɔ̃/ *n.f.* potion.
potiron /pɔtirɔ̃/ *n.m.* pumpkin.
pou (*pl.* **~x**) /pu/ *n.m.* louse.
poubelle /pubɛl/ *n.f.* dustbin; (*Amer.*) garbage can.
pouce /pus/ *n.m.* thumb; (*de pied*) big toe; (*mesure*) inch.
poudr|e /pudr/ *n.f.* powder. **~e (à canon),** gunpowder. **en ~e,** (*lait*) powdered; (*chocolat*) drinking. **~er** *v.t.* powder. **~eux, ~euse** *a.* powdery.
poudrier /pudrije/ *n.m.* (powder) compact.
poudrière /pudrijɛr/ *n.f.* (*région: fig.*) powder-keg.
pouf /puf/ *n.m.* pouffe.
pouffer /pufe/ *v.i.* guffaw.
pouilleu|x, ~se /pujø, -z/ *a.* filthy.
poulailler /pulɑje/ *n.m.* (hen-)coop.
poulain /pulɛ̃/ *n.m.* foal; (*protégé*) protégé.
poule /pul/ *n.f.* hen; (*culin.*) fowl; (*femme: fam.*) tart; (*rugby*) group.
poulet /pulɛ/ *n.m.* chicken.
pouliche /puliʃ/ *n.f.* filly.
poulie /puli/ *n.f.* pulley.
pouls /pu/ *n.m.* pulse.
poumon /pumɔ̃/ *n.m.* lung.
poupe /pup/ *n.f.* stern.
poupée /pupe/ *n.f.* doll.
poupon /pupɔ̃/ *n.m.* baby. **~nière** /-ɔnjɛr/ *n.f.* crèche, day nursery.
pour /pur/ *prép.* for; (*envers*) to; (*à la place de*) on behalf of; (*comme*) as. **~ cela,** for that reason. **~ cent,** per cent. **~ de bon,** for good. **~ faire,** (in order) to do. **~ que,** so that. **~ moi,** as for me. **~ petit/***etc.* **qu'il soit,** however small/*etc.* he may be. **trop poli/***etc.* **~,** too polite/*etc.* to. **le ~ et le contre,** the pros and cons. **~ ce qui est de,** as for.
pourboire /purbwar/ *n.m.* tip.
pourcentage /pursɑ̃taʒ/ *n.m.* percentage.
pourchasser /purʃase/ *v.t.* pursue.
pourparlers /purparle/ *n.m. pl.* talks.
pourpre /purpr/ *a. & n.m.* crimson; (*violet*) purple.
pourquoi /purkwa/ *conj. & adv.* why. ● *n.m. invar.* reason.
pourra, pourrait /pura, purɛ/ *voir* pouvoir[1].
pourr|ir /purir/ *v.t./i.* rot. **~i** *a.* rotten. **~iture** *n.f.* rot.
poursuite /pursɥit/ *n.f.* pursuit (**de,** of). **~s,** (*jurid.*) legal action.
poursuiv|re† /pursɥivr/ *v.t.* pursue; (*continuer*) continue (with). **~re (en justice),** (*au criminel*) prosecute; (*au civil*) sue. ● *v.i.,* **se ~re** *v. pr.* continue. **~ant, ~ante** *n.m., f.* pursuer.
pourtant /purtɑ̃/ *adv.* yet.
pourtour /purtur/ *n.m.* perimeter.
pourv|oir† /purvwar/ *v.t.* **~oir de,** provide with. ● *v.i.* **~oir à,** provide for. **~u de,** supplied with. ● *v. pr.* **se ~oir de** (*argent*) provide o.s. with. **~oyeur, ~oyeuse** *n.m., f.* supplier.
pourvu que /purvyk(ə)/ *conj.* (*condition*) provided (that); (*souhait*) let us hope (that). **pourvu qu'il ne soit rien arrivé,** I hope nothing's happened.
pousse /pus/ *n.f.* growth; (*bourgeon*) shoot.
poussé /puse/ *a.* (*études*) advanced.
poussée /puse/ *n.f.* pressure; (*coup*) push; (*de prix*) upsurge; (*méd.*) outbreak.
pousser /puse/ *v.t.* push; (*du coude*) nudge; (*cri*) let out; (*soupir*) heave; (*continuer*) continue; (*exhorter*)

urge (**à**, to); (*forcer*) drive (**à**, to); (*amener*) bring (**à**, to). ● *v.i.* push; (*grandir*) grow. **faire ~** (*cheveux*) let grow; (*plante*) grow. **se ~** *v. pr.* move over *ou* up.

poussette /pusɛt/ *n.f.* push-chair; (*Amer.*) (baby) stroller.

pouss|ière /pusjɛr/ *n.f.* dust. **~iéreux, ~iéreuse** *a.* dusty.

poussi|f, ~ve /pusif, -v/ *a.* short-winded, wheezing.

poussin /pusɛ̃/ *n.m.* chick.

poutre /putr/ *n.f.* beam: (*en métal*) girder.

pouvoir[1]† /puvwar/ *v. aux.* (*possibilité*) can, be able; (*permission, éventualité*) may, can. **il peut/pouvait/pourrait venir,** he can/could/might come. **je n'ai pas pu,** I could not. **j'ai pu faire,** (*réussi à*) I managed to do. **je n'en peux plus,** I am exhausted. **il se peut que,** it may be that.

pouvoir[2] /puvwar/ *n.m.* power; (*gouvernement*) government. **au ~,** in power. **~s publics,** authorities.

prairie /preri/ *n.f.* meadow.

praline /pralin/ *n.f.* sugared almond.

praticable /pratikabl/ *a.* practicable.

praticien, ~ne /pratisjɛ̃, -jɛn/ *n.m., f.* practitioner.

pratiquant, ~e /pratikɑ̃, -t/ *a.* practising. ● *n.m., f.* churchgoer.

pratique /pratik/ *a.* practical. ● *n.f.* practice, (*expérience*) experience. **la ~ du golf/du cheval,** golfing/riding. **~ment** *adv.* in practice; (*presque*) practically.

pratiquer /pratike/ *v.t./i.* practise; (*sport*) play; (*faire*) make.

pré /pre/ *n.m.* meadow.

pré- /pre/ *préf.* pre-.

préalable /prealabl/ *a.* preliminary, prior. ● *n.m.* precondition. **au ~,** first.

préambule /preɑ̃byl/ *n.m.* preamble.

préau (*pl.* **~x**) /preo/ *n.m.* (*scol.*) playground shelter.

préavis /preavi/ *n.m.* (advance) notice.

précaire /prekɛr/ *a.* precarious.

précaution /prekosjɔ̃/ *n.f.* (*mesure*) precaution; (*prudence*) caution.

précéd|ent, ~ente /presedɑ̃, -t/ *a.* previous. ● *n.m.* precedent. **~emment** /-amɑ̃/ *adv.* previously.

précéder /presede/ *v.t./i.* precede.

précepte /presɛpt/ *n.m.* precept.

précep|teur, ~trice /presɛptœr, -tris/ *n.m., f.* tutor.

prêcher /preʃe/ *v.t./i.* preach.

précieu|x, ~se /presjø, -z/ *a.* precious.

précipice /presipis/ *n.m.* abyss, chasm.

précipit|é /presipite/ *a.* hasty. **~amment** *adv.* hastily. **~ation** *n.f.* haste.

précipiter /presipite/ *v.t.* throw, precipitate; (*hâter*) hasten. **se ~** *v. pr.* rush (**sur**, at, on to); (*se jeter*) throw o.s; (*s'accélérer*) speed up.

précis, ~e /presi, -z/ *a.* precise; (*mécanisme*) accurate. ● *n.m.* summary. **dix heures/***etc.* **~es,** ten o'clock/*etc.* sharp. **~ément** /-zemɑ̃/ *adv.* precisely.

préciser /presize/ *v.t./i.* specify; (*pensée*) be more specific about. **se ~** *v. pr.* become clear(er).

précision /presizjɔ̃/ *n.f.* precision; (*détail*) detail.

précoc|e /prekɔs/ *a.* early; (*enfant*) precocious. **~ité** *n.f.* earliness; precociousness.

préconçu /prekɔ̃sy/ *a.* preconceived.

préconiser /prekɔnize/ *v.t.* advocate.

précurseur /prekyrsœr/ *n.m.* forerunner.

prédécesseur /predesesœr/ *n.m.* predecessor.

prédicateur /predikatœr/ *n.m.* preacher.

prédilection /predilɛksjɔ̃/ *n.f.* preference.

préd|ire† /predir/ *v.t.* predict. **~iction** *n.f.* prediction.

prédisposer /predispoze/ *v.t.* predispose.

prédominant, ~e /predɔminɑ̃, -t/ *a.* predominant.

prédominer /predɔmine/ *v.i.* predominate.

préfabriqué /prefabrike/ *a.* prefabricated.

préface /prefas/ *n.f.* preface.

préfecture /prefɛktyr/ *n.f.* prefecture. **~ de police,** police headquarters.

préférence /preferɑ̃s/ *n.f.* preference. **de ~,** preferably. **de ~ à,** in preference to.

préférentiel, ~le /preferɑ̃sjɛl/ *a.* preferential.

préfér|er /prefere/ *v.t.* prefer (**à**, to). **je ne préfère pas,** I'd rather not. **~er faire,** prefer to do. **~able** *a.* preferable. **~é, ~ée** *a. & n.m., f.* favourite.

préfet /prefɛ/ *n.m.* prefect. **~ de police,** prefect *ou* chief of police.

préfixe /prefiks/ *n.m.* prefix.

préhistorique /preistɔrik/ *a.* prehistoric.

préjudic|e /preʒydis/ *n.m.* harm, prejudice. **porter ~e à,** harm. **~iable** *a.* harmful.

préjugé /preʒyʒe/ *n.m.* prejudice. **avoir un ~ contre,** be prejudiced against. **sans ~s,** without prejudices.

préjuger /preʒyʒe/ *v.i.* **~ de,** prejudge.

prélasser (se) /(sə)prelɑse/ *v. pr.* loll (about).

prél|ever /prelve/ *v.t.* deduct (**sur,** from); (*sang*) take. **~èvement** *n.m.* deduction. **~èvement de sang,** blood sample.

préliminaire /preliminɛr/ *a.* & *n.m.* preliminary. **~s,** (*sexuels*) foreplay.

prélude /prelyd/ *n.m.* prelude.

prématuré /prematyre/ *a.* premature. ● *n.m.* premature baby.

prémédit|er /premedite/ *v.t.* premeditate. **~ation** *n.f.* premeditation.

prem|ier, ~ière /prəmje, -jɛr/ *a.* first; (*rang*) front, first; (*enfance*) early; (*nécessité, souci*) prime; (*qualité*) top, prime; (*état*) original. ● *n.m., f.* first (one). ● *n.m.* (*date*) first; (*étage*) first floor. ● *n.f.* (*rail.*) first class; (*exploit jamais vu*) first; (*cinéma, théâtre*) première. **de ~ier ordre,** first-rate. **en ~ier,** first. **~ier jet,** first draft. **~ier ministre,** Prime Minister.

premièrement /prəmjɛrmɑ̃/ *adv.* firstly.

prémisse /premis/ *n.f.* premiss.

prémonition /premɔnisjɔ̃/ *n.f.* premonition.

prémunir /premynir/ *v.t.* protect (**contre,** against).

prenant, ~e /prənɑ̃, -t/ *a.* (*activité*) engrossing; (*enfant*) demanding.

prénatal (*m. pl.* **~s**) /prenatal/ *a.* antenatal; (*Amer.*) prenatal.

prendre† /prɑ̃dr/ *v.t.* take; (*attraper*) catch, get; (*acheter*) get; (*repas*) have; (*engager, adopter*) take on; (*poids*) put on; (*chercher*) pick up; (*panique, colère*) take hold of. ● *v.i.* (*liquide*) set; (*feu*) catch; (*vaccin*) take. **se ~ pour,** think one is. **s'en ~ à,** attack; (*rendre responsable*) blame. **s'y ~,** set about (it).

preneu|r, ~se /prənœr, -øz/ *n.m., f.* buyer. **être ~r,** be willing to buy. **trouver ~r,** find a buyer.

prénom /prenɔ̃/ *n.m.* first name. **~mer** /-ɔme/ *v.t.* call. **se ~mer** *v. pr.* be called.

préoccup|er /preɔkype/ *v.t.* worry; (*absorber*) preoccupy. **se ~er de,** be worried about; be preoccupied about. **~ation** *n.f.* worry; (*idée fixe*) preoccupation.

préparatifs /preparatif/ *n.m. pl.* preparations.

préparatoire /preparatwar/ *a.* preparatory.

prépar|er /prepare/ *v.t.* prepare; (*repas, café*) make. **se ~er** *v. pr.* prepare o.s.; (*être proche*) be brewing. **~er à qn.,** (*surprise*) have (got) in store for s.o. **~ation** *n.f.* preparation.

prépondéran|t, ~te /prepɔ̃derɑ̃, -t/ *a.* dominant. **~ce** *n.f.* dominance.

prépos|er /prepoze/ *v.t.* put in charge (**à,** of). **~é, ~ée** *n.m., f.* employee; (*des postes*) postman, postwoman.

préposition /prepozisjɔ̃/ *n.f.* preposition.

préretraite /prerətrɛt/ *n.f.* early retirement.

prérogative /prerɔgativ/ *n.f.* prerogative.

près /prɛ/ *adv.* near, close. **~ de,** near (to), close to; (*presque*) nearly. **à cela ~,** apart from that. **de ~,** closely.

présag|e /prezaʒ/ *n.m.* foreboding, omen. **~er** *v.t.* forebode.

presbyte /prɛsbit/ *a.* long-sighted, far-sighted.

presbytère /prɛsbitɛr/ *n.m.* presbytery.

prescr|ire† /prɛskrir/ *v.t.* prescribe. **~iption** *n.f.* prescription.

préséance /preseɑ̃s/ *n.f.* precedence.

présence /prezɑ̃s/ *n.f.* presence; (*scol.*) attendance.

présent, ~e /prezɑ̃, -t/ *a.* present. ● *n.m.* (*temps, cadeau*) present. **à ~,** now.

présent|er /prezɑ̃te/ *v.t.* present; (*personne*) introduce (**à,** to); (*montrer*) show. **se ~er** *v. pr.* introduce o.s. (**à,** to); (*aller*) go; (*apparaître*) appear; (*candidat*) come forward; (*occasion etc.*) arise. **~er bien,** have a pleasing appearance. **se ~er à,** (*examen*) sit for; (*élection*) stand for. **se ~er bien,** look good. **~able** *a.* presentable. **~ateur, ~atrice** *n.m.,*

f. presenter. **~ation** *n.f.* presentation; introduction.
préservatif /prezɛrvatif/ *n.m.* condom.
préserv|er /prezɛrve/ *v.t.* protect. **~ation** *n.f.* protection, preservation.
présiden|t, ~te /prezidɑ̃, -t/ *n.m., f.* president; (*de firme, comité*) chairman, chairwoman. **~t directeur général,** managing director. **~ce** *n.f.* presidency; chairmanship.
présidentiel, ~le /prezidɑ̃sjɛl/ *a.* presidential.
présider /prezide/ *v.t.* preside over. ● *v.i.* preside.
présomption /prezɔ̃psjɔ̃/ *n.f.* presumption.
présomptueu|x, ~se /prezɔ̃ptɥø, -z/ *a.* presumptuous.
presque /prɛsk(ə)/ *adv.* almost, nearly. **~ jamais,** hardly ever. **~ rien,** hardly anything. **~ pas (de),** hardly any.
presqu'île /prɛskil/ *n.f.* peninsula.
pressant, ~e /prɛsɑ̃, -t/ *a.* pressing, urgent.
presse /prɛs/ *n.f.* (*journaux, appareil*) press.
pressent|ir /presɑ̃tir/ *v.t.* sense. **~iment** *n.m.* presentiment.
press|er /prese/ *v.t.* squeeze, press; (*appuyer sur, harceler*) press; (*hâter*) hasten; (*inciter*) urge (**de,** to). ● *v.i.* (*temps*) press; (*affaire*) be pressing. **se ~er** *v. pr.* (*se hâter*) hurry; (*se grouper*) crowd. **~é** *a.* in a hurry; (*orange, citron*) freshly squeezed. **~e-papiers** *n.m. invar.* paperweight.
pressing /presiŋ/ *n.m.* (*magasin*) dry-cleaner's.
pression /prɛsjɔ̃/ *n.f.* pressure. ● *n.m./f.* (*bouton*) press-stud; (*Amer.*) snap.
pressoir /prɛswar/ *n.m.* press.
pressuriser /presyrize/ *v.t.* pressurize.
prestance /prɛstɑ̃s/ *n.f.* (imposing) presence.
prestation /prɛstɑsjɔ̃/ *n.f.* allowance; (*d'artiste etc.*) performance.
prestidigita|teur, ~trice /prɛstidiʒitatœr, -tris/ *n.m., f.* conjuror. **~tion** /-ɑsjɔ̃/ *n.f.* conjuring.
prestig|e /prɛstiʒ/ *n.m.* prestige. **~ieux, ~ieuse** *a.* prestigious.
présumer /prezyme/ *v.t.* presume. **~ que,** assume that. **~ de,** overrate.
prêt[1]**, ~e** /prɛ, -t/ *a.* ready (**à qch.,** for sth., **à faire,** to do). **~-à-porter** /prɛ(t)apɔrte/ *n.m. invar.* ready-to-wear clothes.
prêt[2] /prɛ/ *n.m.* loan.
prétendant /pretɑ̃dɑ̃/ *n.m.* (*amoureux*) suitor.
prétend|re /pretɑ̃dr/ *v.t.* claim (**que,** that); (*vouloir*) intend. **~re qn. riche/***etc.*, claim that s.o. is rich/*etc.* **~u** *a.* so-called. **~ument** *adv.* supposedly, allegedly.
prétent|ieux, ~ieuse /pretɑ̃sjø, -z/ *a.* pretentious. **~ion** *n.f.* pretentiousness; (*exigence*) claim.
prêt|er /prete/ *v.t.* lend (**à,** to); (*attribuer*) attribute. ● *v.i.* **~er à,** lead to. **~er attention,** pay attention. **~er serment,** take an oath. **~eur, ~euse** /prɛtœr, -øz/ *n.m., f.* (money-)lender. **~eur sur gages,** pawnbroker.
prétext|e /pretɛkst/ *n.m.* pretext, excuse. **~er** *v.t.* plead.
prêtre /prɛtr/ *n.m.* priest.
prêtrise /pretriz/ *n.f.* priesthood.
preuve /prœv/ *n.f.* proof. **faire ~ de,** show. **faire ses ~s,** prove one's *ou* its worth.
prévaloir /prevalwar/ *v.i.* prevail.
prévenan|t, ~te /prɛvnɑ̃, -t/ *a.* thoughtful. **~ce(s)** *n.f.* (*pl.*) thoughtfulness.
prévenir† /prɛvnir/ *v.t.* (*menacer*) warn; (*informer*) tell; (*éviter, anticiper*) forestall.
préventi|f, ~ve /prevɑ̃tif, -v/ *a.* preventive.
prévention /prevɑ̃sjɔ̃/ *n.f.* prevention; (*préjugé*) prejudice. **~ routière,** road safety.
prévenu, ~e /prɛvny/ *n.m., f.* defendant.
prév|oir† /prevwar/ *v.t.* foresee; (*temps*) forecast; (*organiser*) plan (for), provide for; (*envisager*) allow (for). **~u pour,** (*jouet etc.*) designed for. **~isible** *a.* foreseeable. **~ision** *n.f.* prediction; (*météorologique*) forecast.
prévoyan|t, ~te /prevwajɑ, -t/ *a.* showing foresight. **~ce** *n.f.* foresight.
prier /prije/ *v.i.* pray. ● *v.t.* pray to; (*implorer*) beg (**de,** to); (*demander à*) ask (**de,** to). **je vous en prie,**

please; (*il n'y a pas de quoi*) don't mention it.

prière /prijɛr/ *n.f.* prayer; (*demande*) request. **~ de,** (*vous êtes prié de*) will you please.

primaire /primɛr/ *a.* primary.

primauté /primote/ *n.f.* primacy.

prime /prim/ *n.f.* free gift; (*d'employé*) bonus; (*subvention*) subsidy; (*d'assurance*) premium.

primé /prime/ *a.* prize-winning.

primer /prime/ *v.t./i.* excel.

primeurs /primœr/ *n.f. pl.* early fruit and vegetables.

primevère /primvɛr/ *n.f.* primrose.

primiti|f, ~ve /primitif, -v/ *a.* primitive; (*originel*) original. ● *n.m., f.* primitive.

primord|ial (*m. pl.* **~iaux**) /primɔrdjal, -jo/ *a.* essential.

princ|e /prɛ̃s/ *n.m.* prince. **~esse** *n.f.* princess. **~ier, ~ière** *a.* princely.

princip|al (*m. pl.* **~aux**) /prɛ̃sipal, -o/ *a.* main, principal. ● *n.m.* (*pl.* **~aux**) headmaster; (*chose*) main thing. **~alement** *adv.* mainly.

principauté /prɛ̃sipote/ *n.f.* principality.

principe /prɛ̃sip/ *n.m.* principle. **en ~,** theoretically; (*d'habitude*) as a rule.

printan|ier, ~ière /prɛ̃tanje, -jɛr/ *a.* spring(-like).

printemps /prɛ̃tɑ̃/ *n.m.* spring.

priorit|é /prijɔrite/ *n.f.* priority; (*auto.*) right of way. **~aire** *a.* priority. **être ~aire,** have priority.

pris, ~e [1] /pri, -z/ *voir* prendre. ● *a.* (*place*) taken; (*personne, journée*) busy; (*gorge*) infected. **~ de,** (*peur, fièvre, etc.*) stricken with. **~ de panique,** panic-stricken.

prise [2] /priz/ *n.f.* hold, grip; (*animal etc. attrapé*) catch; (*mil.*) capture. **~ (de courant),** (*mâle*) plug; (*femelle*) socket. **aux ~s avec,** at grips with. **~ de conscience,** awareness. **~ de contact,** first contact, initial meeting. **~ de position,** stand. **~ de sang,** blood test.

priser /prize/ *v.t.* (*estimer*) prize.

prisme /prism/ *n.m.* prism.

prison /prizɔ̃/ *n.f.* prison, gaol, jail; (*réclusion*) imprisonment. **~nier, ~nière** /-ɔnje, -jɛr/ *n.m., f.* prisoner.

privé /prive/ *a.* private. ● *n.m.* (*comm.*) private sector. **en ~, dans le ~,** in private.

priv|er /prive/ *v.t.* **~er de,** deprive of. **se ~er de,** go without. **~ation** *n.f.* deprivation; (*sacrifice*) hardship.

privil|ège /privilɛʒ/ *n.m.* privilege. **~égié, ~égiée** *a. & n.m., f.* privileged (person).

prix /pri/ *n.m.* price; (*récompense*) prize. **à tout ~,** at all costs. **au ~ de,** (*fig.*) at the expense of. **~ coûtant, ~ de revient,** cost price. **à ~ fixe,** set price.

pro- /pro/ *préf.* pro-.

probab|le /prɔbabl/ *a.* probable, likely. **~ilité** *n.f.* probability. **~lement** *adv.* probably.

probant, ~e /prɔbɑ̃, -t/ *a.* convincing, conclusive.

probité /prɔbite/ *n.f.* integrity.

problème /prɔblɛm/ *n.m.* problem.

procéd|er /prɔsede/ *v.i.* proceed. **~er à,** carry out. **~é** *n.m.* process; (*conduite*) behaviour.

procédure /prɔsedyr/ *n.f.* procedure.

procès /prɔsɛ/ *n.m.* (*criminel*) trial; (*civil*) lawsuit, proceedings. **~-verbal** (*pl.* **~-verbaux**) *n.m.* report; (*contravention*) ticket.

procession /prɔsesjɔ̃/ *n.f.* procession.

processus /prɔsesys/ *n.m.* process.

prochain, ~e /prɔʃɛ̃, -ɛn/ *a.* (*suivant*) next; (*proche*) imminent; (*avenir*) near. **je descends à la ~e,** I'm getting off at the next stop. ● *n.m.* fellow. **~ement** /-ɛnmɑ̃/ *adv.* soon.

proche /prɔʃ/ *a.* near, close; (*avoisinant*) neighbouring; (*parent, ami*) close. **~ de,** close *ou* near to. **de ~ en proche,** gradually. **dans un ~ avenir,** in the near future. **être ~,** (*imminent*) be approaching. **~s** *n.m. pl.* close relations. **P~-Orient** *n.m.* Near East.

proclam|er /prɔklame/ *v.t.* declare, proclaim. **~ation** *n.f.* declaration, proclamation.

procréation /prɔkreɑsjɔ̃/ *n.f.* procreation.

procuration /prɔkyrɑsjɔ̃/ *n.f.* proxy.

procurer /prɔkyre/ *v.t.* bring (**à,** to). **se ~** *v. pr.* obtain.

procureur /prɔkyrœr/ *n.m.* public prosecutor.

prodig|e /prɔdiʒ/ *n.m.* marvel; (*personne*) prodigy. **enfant/musicien ~e,** child/musical prodigy. **~ieux, ~ieuse** *a.* tremendous, prodigious.

prodigu|e /prɔdig/ *a.* wasteful. **fils ~e,** prodigal son. **~er** *v.t.* **~er à,** lavish on.

producti|f, ~ve /prɔdyktif, -v/ *a.* productive. **~vité** *n.f.* productivity.

prod|uire† /prɔdɥir/ *v.t.* produce. **se ~uire** *v. pr.* (*survenir*) happen; (*acteur*) perform. **~ucteur, ~uctrice** *a.* producing; *n.m., f.* producer. **~uction** *n.f.* production; (*produit*) product.

produit /prɔdɥi/ *n.m.* product. **~s,** (*de la terre*) produce. **~ chimique,** chemical. **~s alimentaires,** foodstuffs. **~ de consommation,** consumer goods. **~ national brut,** gross national product.

proéminent, ~e /prɔeminɑ̃, -t/ *a.* prominent.

prof /prɔf/ *n.m.* (*fam.*) teacher.

profane /prɔfan/ *a.* secular. ● *n.m./f.* lay person.

profaner /prɔfane/ *v.t.* desecrate.

proférer /prɔfere/ *v.t.* utter.

professer[1] /prɔfese/ *v.t.* (*déclarer*) profess.

professer[2] /prɔfese/ *v.t./i.* (*enseigner*) teach.

professeur /prɔfɛsœr/ *n.m.* teacher; (*univ.*) lecturer; (*avec chaire*) professor.

profession /prɔfɛsjɔ̃/ *n.f.* occupation; (*intellectuelle*) profession. **~nel, ~nelle** /-jɔnɛl/ *a.* professional; (*école*) vocational; *n.m., f.* professional.

professorat /prɔfɛsɔra/ *n.m.* teaching.

profil /prɔfil/ *n.m.* profile.

profiler (se) /(sə)prɔfile/ *v. pr.* be outlined.

profit /prɔfi/ *n.m.* profit. **au ~ de,** in aid of. **~able** /-tabl/ *a.* profitable.

profiter /prɔfite/ *v.i.* **~ à,** benefit. **~ de,** take advantage of.

profond, ~e /prɔfɔ̃, -d/ *a.* deep; (*sentiment, intérêt*) profound; (*causes*) underlying. **au plus ~ de,** in the depths of. **~ément** /-demɑ̃/ *adv.* deeply; (*différent, triste*) profoundly; (*dormir*) soundly. **~eur** /-dœr/ *n.f.* depth.

profusion /prɔfyzjɔ̃/ *n.f.* profusion.

progéniture /prɔʒenityr/ *n.f.* offspring.

programmation /prɔgramɑsjɔ̃/ *n.f.* programming.

programm|e /prɔgram/ *n.m.* programme; (*matières: scol.*) syllabus; (*informatique*) program. **~e (d'études),** curriculum. **~er** *v.t.* (*ordinateur, appareil*) program; (*émission*) schedule. **~eur, ~euse** *n.m., f.* computer programmer.

progrès /prɔgrɛ/ *n.m. & n.m. pl.* progress. **faire des ~,** make progress.

progress|er /prɔgrese/ *v.i.* progress. **~ion** /-ɛsjɔ̃/ *n.f.* progression.

progressi|f, ~ve /prɔgresif, -v/ *a.* progressive. **~vement** *adv.* progressively.

progressiste /prɔgresist/ *a.* progressive.

prohib|er /prɔibe/ *v.t.* prohibit. **~ition** *n.f.* prohibition.

prohibiti|f, ~ve /prɔibitif, -v/ *a.* prohibitive.

proie /prwa/ *n.f.* prey. **en ~ à,** tormented by.

projecteur /prɔʒɛktœr/ *n.m.* floodlight; (*mil.*) searchlight; (*cinéma*) projector.

projectile /prɔʒɛktil/ *n.m.* missile.

projection /prɔʒɛksjɔ̃/ *n.f.* projection; (*séance*) show.

projet /prɔʒɛ/ *n.m.* plan; (*ébauche*) draft. **~ de loi,** bill.

projeter /prɔʒte/ *v.t.* plan (**de,** to); (*film*) project, show; (*jeter*) hurl, project.

prolét|aire /prɔletɛr/ *n.m./f.* proletarian. **~ariat** *n.m.* proletariat. **~arien, ~arienne** *a.* proletarian.

prolifér|er /prɔlifere/ *v.i.* proliferate. **~ation** *n.f.* proliferation.

prolifique /prɔlifik/ *a.* prolific.

prologue /prɔlɔg/ *n.m.* prologue.

prolongation /prɔlɔ̃gɑsjɔ̃/ *n.f.* extension. **~s,** (*football*) extra time.

prolong|er /prɔlɔ̃ʒe/ *v.t.* prolong. **se ~er** *v. pr.* continue, extend. **~é** *a.* prolonged. **~ement** *n.m.* extension.

promenade /prɔmnad/ *n.f.* walk; (*à bicyclette, à cheval*) ride; (*en auto*) drive, ride. **faire une ~,** go for a walk.

promen|er /prɔmne/ *v.t.* take for a walk. **~er sur qch.,** (*main, regard*) run over sth. **se ~er** *v. pr.* walk. **(aller) se ~er,** go for a walk. **~eur, ~euse** *n.m., f.* walker.

promesse /prɔmɛs/ *n.f.* promise.

promett|re† /prɔmɛtr/ *v.t./i.* promise. **~re (beaucoup),** be promising. **se ~re de,** resolve to. **~eur, ~euse** *a.* promising.

promontoire /prɔmɔ̃twar/ *n.m.* headland.

promoteur /prɔmɔtœr/ *n.m.* (*immobilier*) property developer.

prom|ouvoir /prɔmuvwar/ *v.t.* promote. **être ~u,** be promoted. **~otion** *n.f.* promotion; (*univ.*) year; (*comm.*) special offer.

prompt, ~e /prɔ̃, -t/ *a.* swift.

prôner /prone/ *v.t.* extol; (*préconiser*) preach, advocate.

pronom /prɔnɔ̃/ *n.m.* pronoun. **~inal** (*m. pl.* **~inaux**) /-ɔminal, -o/ *a.* pronominal.

prononc|er /prɔnɔ̃se/ *v.t.* pronounce; (*discours*) make. **se ~er** *v. pr.* (*mot*) be pronounced; (*personne*) make a decision (**pour,** in favour of). **~é** *a.* pronounced. **~iation** *n.f.* pronunciation.

pronosti|c /prɔnɔstik/ *n.m.* forecast; (*méd.*) prognosis. **~quer** *v.t.* forecast.

propagande /prɔpagɑ̃d/ *n.f.* propaganda.

propag|er /prɔpaʒe/ *v.t.*, **se ~er** *v. pr.* spread. **~ation** /-gasjɔ̃/ *n.f.* spread (-ing).

proph|ète /prɔfɛt/ *n.m.* prophet. **~étie** /-esi/ *n.f.* prophecy. **~étique** *a.* prophetic. **~étiser** *v.t./i.* prophesy.

propice /prɔpis/ *a.* favourable.

proportion /prɔpɔrsjɔ̃/ *n.f.* proportion; (*en mathématiques*) ratio. **toutes ~s gardées,** making appropriate allowances. **~né** /-jɔne/ *a.* proportionate (**à,** to). **~nel, ~nelle** /-jɔnɛl/ *a.* proportional. **~ner** /-jɔne/ *v.t.* proportion.

propos /prɔpo/ *n.m.* intention; (*sujet*) subject. ● *n.m. pl.* (*paroles*) remarks. **à ~,** at the right time; (*dans un dialogue*) by the way. **à ~ de,** about. **à tout ~,** at every possible occasion.

propos|er /prɔpoze/ *v.t.* propose; (*offrir*) offer. **se ~er** *v. pr.* volunteer (**pour,** to); (*but*) set o.s. **se ~er de faire,** propose to do. **~ition** *n.f.* proposal; (*affirmation*) proposition; (*gram.*) clause.

propre[1] /prɔpr/ *a.* clean; (*soigné*) neat; (*honnête*) decent. **mettre au ~,** write out again neatly. **c'est du ~!** (*ironique*) well done! **~ment**[1] /-əmɑ̃/ *adv.* cleanly; neatly; decently.

propre[2] /prɔpr/ *a.* (*à soi*) own; (*sens*) literal. **~ à,** (*qui convient*) suited to; (*spécifique*) peculiar to. **~-à-rien** *n.m./f.* good-for-nothing. **~ment**[2] /-əmɑ̃/ *adv.* strictly. **le bureau/etc. ~ment dit,** the office/*etc.* itself.

propreté /prɔprəte/ *n.f.* cleanliness; (*netteté*) neatness.

propriétaire /prɔprijetɛr/ *n.m./f.* owner; (*comm.*) proprietor; (*qui loue*) landlord, landlady.

propriété /prɔprijete/ *n.f.* property; (*droit*) ownership.

propuls|er /prɔpylse/ *v.t.* propel. **~ion** *n.f.* propulsion.

prorata /prɔrata/ *n.m. invar.* **au ~ de,** in proportion to.

proroger /prɔrɔʒe/ *v.t.* (*contrat*) defer; (*passeport*) extend.

prosaïque /prozaik/ *a.* prosaic.

proscr|ire /prɔskrir/ *v.t.* proscribe. **~it, ~ite** *a.* proscribed; *n.m., f.* (*exilé*) exile.

prose /proz/ *n.f.* prose.

prospec|ter /prɔspɛkte/ *v.t.* prospect. **~teur, ~trice** *n.m., f.* prospector. **~tion** /-ksjɔ̃/ *n.f.* prospecting.

prospectus /prɔspɛktys/ *n.m.* leaflet.

prosp|ère /prɔspɛr/ *a.* flourishing, thriving. **~érer** *v.i.* thrive, prosper. **~érité** *n.f.* prosperity.

prostern|er (se) /(sə)prɔstɛrne/ *v. pr.* bow down. **~é** *a.* prostrate.

prostit|uée /prɔstitɥe/ *n.f.* prostitute. **~ution** *n.f.* prostitution.

prostré /prɔstre/ *a.* prostrate.

protagoniste /prɔtagɔnist/ *n.m.* protagonist.

protec|teur, ~trice /prɔtɛktœr, -tris/ *n.m., f.* protector. ● *a.* protective.

protection /prɔtɛksjɔ̃/ *n.f.* protection; (*fig.*) patronage.

protég|er /prɔteʒe/ *v.t.* protect; (*fig.*) patronize. **se ~er** *v. pr.* protect o.s. **~é** *n.m.* protégé. **~ée** *n.f.* protégée.

protéine /prɔtein/ *n.f.* protein.

protestant, ~e /prɔtɛstɑ̃, -t/ *a.* & *n.m., f.* Protestant.

protest|er /prɔtɛste/ *v.t./i.* protest. **~ation** *n.f.* protest.

protocole /prɔtɔkɔl/ *n.m.* protocol.

prototype /prɔtɔtip/ *n.m.* prototype.

protubéran|t, ~te /prɔtyberɑ̃, -t/ *a.* bulging. **~ce,** *n.f.* protuberance.

proue /pru/ *n.f.* bow, prow.

prouesse /pruɛs/ *n.f.* feat, exploit.

prouver /pruve/ *v.t.* prove.

provenance /prɔvnɑ̃s/ *n.f.* origin. **en ~ de,** from.

provenç|al, ~ale (*m. pl.* **~aux**) /prɔvɑ̃sal, -o/ *a.* & *n.m., f.* Provençal.

Provence /prɔvɑ̃s/ *n.f.* Provence.

provenir† /prɔvnir/ *v.i.* **~ de,** come from.

proverb|e /prɔvɛrb/ *n.m.* proverb. **~ial** (*m. pl.* **~iaux**) *a.* proverbial.

providence /prɔvidɑ̃s/ *n.f.* providence.

provinc|e /prɔvɛ̃s/ *n.f.* province. **de ~e,** provincial. **la ~e,** the provinces. **~ial, ~iale** (*m. pl.* **~iaux**) *a.* & *n.m., f.* provincial.

proviseur /prɔvizœr/ *n.m.* headmaster, principal.

provision /prɔvizjɔ̃/ *n.f.* supply, store; (*dans un compte*) funds; (*acompte*) deposit. **~s,** (*vivres*) provisions. **panier à ~s,** shopping basket.

provisoire /prɔvizwar/ *a.* temporary. **~ment** *adv.* temporarily.

provo|quer /prɔvɔke/ *v.t.* cause; (*exciter*) arouse; (*défier*) provoke. **~cant, ~cante** *a.* provocative. **~cation** *n.f.* provocation.

proximité /prɔksimite/ *n.f.* proximity. **à ~ de,** close to.

prude /pryd/ *a.* prudish. ● *n.f.* prude.

prud|ent, ~ente /prydɑ̃, -t/ *a.* cautious; (*sage*) wise. **soyez ~ent,** be careful. **~emment** /-amɑ̃/ *adv.* cautiously; wisely. **~ence** *n.f.* caution; wisdom.

prune /pryn/ *n.f.* plum.

pruneau (*pl.* **~x**) /pryno/ *n.m.* prune.

prunelle[1] /prynɛl/ *n.f.* (*pupille*) pupil.

prunelle[2] /prynɛl/ *n.f.* (*fruit*) sloe.

psaume /psom/ *n.m.* psalm.

pseudo- /psødɔ/ *préf.* pseudo-.

pseudonyme /psødɔnim/ *n.m.* pseudonym.

psychanalys|e /psikanaliz/ *n.f.* psychoanalysis. **~er** *v.t.* psychoanalyse. **~te** /-st/ *n.m./f.* psychoanalyst.

psychiatr|e /psikjatr/ *n.m./f.* psychiatrist. **~ie** *n.f.* psychiatry. **~ique** *a.* psychiatric.

psychique /psiʃik/ *a.* mental, psychological.

psycholo|gie /psikɔlɔʒi/ *n.f.* psychology. **~gique** *a.* psychological. **~gue** *n.m./f.* psychologist.

psychosomatique /psikɔsɔmatik/ *a.* psychosomatic.

psychothérapie /psikɔterapi/ *n.f.* psychotherapy.

PTT *abrév.* (*Postes, Télécommunications et Télédiffusion*) Post Office.

pu /py/ *voir* pouvoir[1].

puant, ~e /pɥɑ̃, -t/ *a.* stinking. **~eur** /-tœr/ *n.f.* stink.

pub /pyb/ *n.f.* **la ~,** advertising. **une ~,** an advert.

puberté /pybɛrte/ *n.f.* puberty.

publi|c, ~que /pyblik/ *a.* public. ● *n.m.* public; (*assistance*) audience. **en ~c,** in public.

publicit|é /pyblisite/ *n.f.* publicity, advertising; (*annonce*) advertisement. **~aire** *a.* publicity.

publ|ier /pyblije/ *v.t.* publish. **~ication** *n.f.* publication.

publiquement /pyblikmɑ̃/ *adv.* publicly.

puce[1] /pys/ *n.f.* flea. **marché aux ~s,** flea market.

puce[2] /pys/ *n.f.* (*électronique*) chip.

pud|eur /pydœr/ *n.f.* modesty. **~ique** *a.* modest.

pudibond, ~e /pydibɔ̃, -d/ *a.* prudish.

puer /pɥe/ *v.i.* stink. ● *v.t.* stink of.

puéricultrice /pɥerikyltris/ *n.f.* children's nurse.

puéril /pɥeril/ *a.* puerile.

pugilat /pyʒila/ *n.m.* fight.

puis /pɥi/ *adv.* then.

puiser /pɥize/ *v.t.* draw (**qch. dans,** sth. from). ● *v.i.* **~ dans qch.,** dip into sth.

puisque /pɥisk(ə)/ *conj.* since, as.

puissance /pɥisɑ̃s/ *n.f.* power. **en ~** *a.* potential; *adv.* potentially.

puiss|ant, ~ante /pɥisɑ̃, -t/ *a.* powerful. **~amment** *adv.* powerfully.

puits /pɥi/ *n.m.* well; (*de mine*) shaft.

pull(-over) /pyl(ɔvɛr)/ *n.m.* pullover, jumper.

pulpe /pylp/ *n.f.* pulp.

pulsation /pylsɑsjɔ̃/ *n.f.* (heart-)beat.

pulvéris|er /pylverize/ *v.t.* pulverize; (*liquide*) spray. **~ateur** *n.m.* spray.

punaise /pynɛz/ *n.f.* (*insecte*) bug; (*clou*) drawing-pin; (*Amer.*) thumbtack.

punch[1] /pɔ̃ʃ/ *n.m.* punch.

punch[2] /pœnʃ/ *n.m.* **avoir du ~,** have drive.

pun|ir /pynir/ *v.t.* punish. **~ition** *n.f.* punishment.

punk /pœnk/ *a. invar.* punk.

pupille[1] /pypij/ *n.f.* (*de l'œil*) pupil.

pupille[2] /pypij/ *n.m./f.* (*enfant*) ward.

pupitre /pypitr/ *n.m.* (*scol.*) desk. **~ à musique,** music stand.
pur /pyr/ *a.* pure; (*whisky*) neat. **~ement** *adv.* purely. **~eté** *n.f.* purity. **~-sang** *n.m. invar.* (*cheval*) thoroughbred.
purée /pyre/ *n.f.* purée; (*de pommes de terre*) mashed potatoes.
purgatoire /pyrgatwar/ *n.m.* purgatory.
purg|e /pyrʒ/ *n.f.* purge. **~er** *v.t.* (*pol.*, *méd.*) purge; (*peine*: *jurid.*) serve.
purif|ier /pyrifje/ *v.t.* purify. **~ication** *n.f.* purification.
purin /pyrɛ̃/ *n.m.* (liquid) manure.
puritain, ~e /pyritɛ̃, -ɛn/ *n.m.*, *f.* puritan. ● *a.* puritanical.
pus /py/ *n.m.* pus.
pustule /pystyl/ *n.f.* pimple.
putain /pytɛ̃/ *n.f.* (*fam.*) whore.
putréfier (se) /(sə)pytrefje/ *v. pr.* putrefy.
putsch /putʃ/ *n.m.* putsch.
puzzle /pœzl/ *n.m.* jigsaw (puzzle).
P-V *abrév.* (*procès-verbal*) ticket, traffic fine.
pygmée /pigme/ *n.m.* pygmy.
pyjama /piʒama/ *n.m.* pyjamas. **un ~,** a pair of pyjamas.
pylône /pilon/ *n.m.* pylon.
pyramide /piramid/ *n.f.* pyramid.
Pyrénées /pirene/ *n.f. pl.* **les ~,** the Pyrenees.
pyromane /pirɔman/ *n.m./f.* arsonist.

Q

QG *abrév.* (quartier général) HQ.
QI *abrév.* (*quotient intellectuel*) IQ.
qu' /k/ *voir* que.
quadrill|er /kadrije/ *v.t.* (*zone*) comb, control. **~age** *n.m.* (*mil.*) control. **~é** *a.* (*papier*) squared.
quadrupède /kadrypɛd/ *n.m.* quadruped.
quadrupl|e /kadrypl/ *a.* & *n.m.* quadruple. **~er** *v.t./i.* quadruple. **~és, ~ées** *n.m.*, *f. pl.* quadruplets.
quai /ke/ *n.m.* (*de gare*) platform; (*de port*) quay; (*de rivière*) embankment.
qualificatif /kalifikatif/ *n.m.* (*épithète*) term.
qualif|ier /kalifje/ *v.t.* qualify; (*décrire*) describe (**de,** as). **se ~ier** *v. pr.* qualify (**pour,** for). **~ication** *n.f.* qualification; description. **~ié** *a.* qualified; (*main d'œuvre*) skilled.
qualit|é /kalite/ *n.f.* quality; (*titre*) occupation. **en ~é de,** in one's capacity as. **~atif, ~ative** *a.* qualitative.
quand /kɑ̃/ *conj.* & *adv.* when. **~ même,** all the same. **~ (bien) même,** even if.
quant (à) /kɑ̃t(a)/ *prép.* as for.
quant-à-soi /kɑ̃taswa/ *n.m.* **rester sur son ~,** stand aloof.
quantit|é /kɑ̃tite/ *n.f.* quantity. **une ~é de,** a lot of. **des ~és,** masses. **~atif, ~ative** *a.* quantitative.
quarantaine /karɑ̃tɛn/ *n.f.* (*méd.*) quarantine. **une ~ (de),** about forty.
quarant|e /karɑ̃t/ *a.* & *n.m.* forty. **~ième** *a.* & *n.m./f.* fortieth.
quart /kar/ *n.m.* quarter; (*naut.*) watch. **~ (de litre),** quarter litre. **~ de finale,** quarter-final. **~ d'heure,** quarter of an hour.
quartier /kartje/ *n.m.* neighbourhood, district; (*de lune, bœuf*) quarter; (*de fruit*) segment. **~s,** (*mil.*) quarters. **de ~, du ~,** local. **~ général,** headquarters. **avoir ~ libre,** be free.
quartz /kwarts/ *n.m.* quartz.
quasi- /kazi/ *préf.* quasi-.
quasiment /kazimɑ̃/ *adv.* almost.
quatorz|e /katɔrz/ *a.* & *n.m.* fourteen. **~ième** *a.* & *n.m./f.* fourteenth.
quatre /katr(ə)/ *a.* & *n.m.* four. **~-vingt(s)** *a.* & *n.m.* eighty. **~-vingt-dix** *a.* & *n.m.* ninety.
quatrième /katrijɛm/ *a.* & *n.m./f.* fourth. **~ment** *adv.* fourthly.
quatuor /kwatɥɔr/ *n.m.* quartet.
que, qu'* /kə, k/ *conj.* that; (*comparaison*) than. **qu'il vienne,** let him come. **qu'il vienne ou non,** whether he comes or not. **ne faire ~ demander**/*etc.*, only ask/*etc.* ● *adv.* **(ce) ~ tu es bête, qu'est-ce ~ tu es bête,** how silly you are. **~ de,** what a lot of. ● *pron. rel.* (*personne*) that, whom; (*chose*) that, which; (*temps, moment*) when; (*interrogatif*) what. **un jour**/*etc.* **~,** one day/*etc.* when. **~ faites-vous?, qu'est-ce ~ vous faites?,** what are you doing?
Québec /kebɛk/ *n.m.* Quebec.
quel, ~le /kɛl/ *a.* what; (*interrogatif*) which, what; (*qui*) who. ● *pron.*

which. **~ dommage,** what a pity. **~ qu'il soit,** (*chose*) whatever *ou* whichever it may be; (*personne*) whoever he may be.

quelconque /kɛlkɔ̃k/ *a.* any, some; (*banal*) ordinary; (*médiocre*) poor.

quelque /kɛlkə/ *a.* some. **~s,** a few, some. ● *adv.* (*environ*) some. **et ~,** (*fam.*) and a bit. **~ chose,** something; (*interrogation*) anything. **~ part,** somewhere. **~ peu,** somewhat.

quelquefois /kɛlkəfwa/ *adv.* sometimes.

quelques|-uns, ~-unes /kɛlkəzœ̃, -yn/ *pron.* some, a few.

quelqu'un /kɛlkœ̃/ *pron.* someone, somebody; (*interrogation*) anyone, anybody.

quémander /kemɑ̃de/ *v.t.* beg for.

qu'en-dira-t-on /kɑ̃diratɔ̃/ *n.m. invar.* **le ~,** gossip.

querell|e /kərɛl/ *n.f.* quarrel. **~eur, ~euse** *a.* quarrelsome.

quereller (se) /(sə)kərele/ *v. pr.* quarrel.

question /kɛstjɔ̃/ *n.f.* question; (*affaire*) matter, question. **en ~,** in question; (*en jeu*) at stake. **il est ~ de,** (*cela concerne*) it is about; (*on parle de*) there is talk of. **il n'en est pas ~,** it is out of the question. **~ner** /-jɔne/ *v.t.* question.

questionnaire /kɛstjɔnɛr/ *n.m.* questionnaire.

quêt|e /kɛt/ *n.f.* (*relig.*) collection. **en ~e de,** in search of. **~er** /kete/ *v.i.* collect money; *v.t.* seek.

quetsche /kwɛtʃ/ *n.f.* (sort of dark red) plum.

queue /kø/ *n.f.* tail; (*de poêle*) handle; (*de fruit*) stalk; (*de fleur*) stem; (*file*) queue; (*file: Amer.*) line; (*de train*) rear. **faire la ~,** queue (up); (*Amer.*) line up. **~ de cheval,** pony-tail.

qui /ki/ *pron. rel.* (*personne*) who; (*chose*) which, that; (*interrogatif*) who; (*après prép.*) whom; (*quiconque*) whoever. **à ~ est ce stylo**/*etc.*?, whose pen/*etc.* is this? **qu'est-ce ~?,** what? **~ est-ce qui?,** who? **~ que ce soit,** anyone.

quiche /kiʃ/ *n.f.* quiche.

quiconque /kikɔ̃k/ *pron.* whoever; (*n'importe qui*) anyone.

quiétude /kjetyd/ *n.f.* quiet.

quignon /kiɲɔ̃/ *n.m.* **~ de pain,** chunk of bread.

quille [1] /kij/ *n.f.* (*de bateau*) keel.

quille [2] /kij/ *n.f.* (*jouet*) skittle.

quincaill|ier, ~ière /kɛ̃kɑje, -jɛr/ *n.m., f.* hardware dealer. **~erie** *n.f.* hardware; (*magasin*) hardware shop.

quinine /kinin/ *n.f.* quinine.

quinquenn|al (*m. pl.* **~aux**) /kɛ̃kenal, -o/ *a.* five-year.

quint|al (*pl.* **~aux**) /kɛ̃tal, -o/ *n.m.* quintal (= *100 kg.*).

quinte /kɛ̃t/ *n.f.* **~ de toux,** coughing fit.

quintette /kɛ̃tɛt/ *n.m.* quintet.

quintupl|e /kɛ̃typl/ *a.* fivefold. ● *n.m.* quintuple. **~er** *v.t./i.* increase fivefold. **~és, ~ées,** *n.m., f. pl.* quintuplets.

quinzaine /kɛ̃zɛn/ *n.f.* **une ~ (de),** about fifteen.

quinz|e /kɛ̃z/ *a.* & *n.m.* fifteen. **~e jours,** two weeks. **~ième** *a.* & *n.m./f.* fifteenth.

quiproquo /kiprɔko/ *n.m.* misunderstanding.

quittance /kitɑ̃s/ *n.f.* receipt.

quitte /kit/ *a.* quits (**envers,** with). **~ à faire,** even if it means doing.

quitter /kite/ *v.t.* leave; (*vêtement*) take off. **se ~** *v. pr.* part.

quoi /kwa/ *pron.* what; (*après prép.*) which. **de ~ vivre/manger**/*etc.*, (*assez*) enough to live on/to eat/*etc.* **de ~ écrire,** sth. to write with, what is necessary to write with. **~ que,** whatever. **~ que ce soit,** anything.

quoique /kwak(ə)/ *conj.* (al)though.

quolibet /kɔlibɛ/ *n.m.* gibe.

quorum /kɔrɔm/ *n.m.* quorum.

quota /kɔta/ *n.m.* quota.

quote-part (*pl.* **quotes-parts**) /kɔtpar/ *n.f.* share.

quotidien, ~ne /kɔtidjɛ̃, -jɛn/ *a.* daily; (*banal*) everyday. ● *n.m.* daily (paper). **~nement** /-jɛnmɑ̃/ *adv.* daily.

quotient /kɔsjɑ̃/ *n.m.* quotient.

R

rab /rab/ *n.m.* (*fam.*) extra. **il y en a en ~,** there's some over.

rabâcher /rabɑʃe/ *v.t.* keep repeating.

rabais /rabɛ/ *n.m.* (price) reduction.

rabaisser /rabese/ *v.t.* (*déprécier*) belittle; (*réduire*) reduce.

rabat /raba/ *n.m.* flap. **~-joie** *n.m. invar.* killjoy.
rabattre /rabatr/ *v.t.* pull *ou* put down; (*diminuer*) reduce; (*déduire*) take off. **se ~** *v. pr.* (*se refermer*) close; (*véhicule*) cut in, turn sharply. **se ~ sur,** fall back on.
rabbin /rabɛ̃/ *n.m.* rabbi.
rabibocher /rabibɔʃe/ *v.t.* (*fam.*) reconcile.
rabiot /rabjo/ *n.m.* (*fam.*) = **rab.**
râblé /rɑble/ *a.* stocky, sturdy.
rabot /rabo/ *n.m.* plane. **~er** /-ɔte/ *v.t.* plane.
raboteu|x, ~se /rabɔtø, -z/ *a.* uneven.
rabougri /rabugri/ *a.* stunted.
rabrouer /rabrue/ *v.t.* snub.
racaille /rakɑj/ *n.f.* rabble.
raccommoder /rakɔmɔde/ *v.t.* mend; (*personnes*: *fam.*) reconcile.
raccompagner /rakɔ̃paɲe/ *v.t.* see *ou* take back (home).
raccord /rakɔr/ *n.m.* link; (*de papier peint*) join. **~ (de peinture),** touch-up.
raccord|er /rakɔrde/ *v.t.* connect, join. **~ement** *n.m.* connection.
raccourci /rakursi/ *n.m.* short cut. **en ~,** in brief.
raccourcir /rakursir/ *v.t.* shorten. ● *v.i.* get shorter.
raccrocher /rakrɔʃe/ *v.t.* hang back up; (*personne*) grab hold of; (*relier*) connect. **~ (le récepteur),** hang up. **se ~ à,** cling to; (*se relier à*) be connected to *ou* with.
rac|e /ras/ *n.f.* race; (*animale*) breed. **de ~e,** pure-bred. **~ial** (*m. pl.* **~iaux**) *a.* racial.
rachat /raʃa/ *n.m.* buying (back); (*de pécheur*) redemption.
racheter /raʃte/ *v.t.* buy (back); (*davantage*) buy more; (*nouvel objet*) buy another; (*pécheur*) redeem. **se ~** *v. pr.* make amends.
racine /rasin/ *n.f.* root. **~ carrée/cubique,** square/cube root.
racis|te /rasist/ *a.* & *n.m./f.* racist. **~me** *n.m.* racism.
racket /rakɛt/ *n.m.* racketeering.
raclée /rɑkle/ *n.f.* (*fam.*) thrashing.
racler /rɑkle/ *v.t.* scrape. **se ~ la gorge,** clear one's throat.
racol|er /rakɔle/ *v.t.* solicit; (*marchand, parti*) drum up. **~age** *n.m.* soliciting.
racontars /rakɔ̃tar/ *n.m. pl.* (*fam.*) gossip, stories.
raconter /rakɔ̃te/ *v.t.* (*histoire*) tell, relate; (*vacances etc.*) tell about. **~ à qn. que,** tell s.o. that, say to s.o. that.
racorni /rakɔrni/ *a.* hard(ened).
radar /radar/ *n.m.* radar.
rade /rad/ *n.f.* harbour. **en ~,** (*personne*: *fam.*) stranded, behind.
radeau (*pl.* **~x**) /rado/ *n.m.* raft.
radiateur /radjatœr/ *n.m.* radiator; (*électrique*) heater.
radiation /radjɑsjɔ̃/ *n.f.* (*énergie*) radiation.
radic|al (*m. pl.* **~aux**) /radikal, -o/ *a.* radical. ● *n.m.* (*pl.* **~aux**) radical.
radier /radje/ *v.t.* cross off.
radieu|x, ~se /radjø, -z/ *a.* radiant.
radin, ~e /radɛ̃, -in/ *a.* (*fam.*) stingy.
radio /radjo/ *n.f.* radio; (*radiographie*) X-ray.
radioacti|f, ~ve /radjɔaktif, -v/ *a.* radioactive. **~vité** *n.f.* radioactivity.
radiocassette /radjɔkasɛt/ *n.f.* radio-cassette-player.
radiodiffus|er /radjɔdifyze/ *v.t.* broadcast. **~ion** *n.f.* broadcasting.
radiograph|ie /radjɔgrafi/ *n.f.* (*photographie*) X-ray. **~ier** *v.t.* X-ray. **~ique** *a.* X-ray.
radiologue /radjɔlɔg/ *n.m./f.* radiographer.
radiophonique /radjɔfɔnik/ *a.* radio.
radis /radi/ *n.m.* radish. **ne pas avoir un ~,** be broke.
radoter /radɔte/ *v.i.* (*fam.*) talk drivel.
radoucir (se) /(sə)radusir/ *v. pr.* calm down; (*temps*) become milder.
rafale /rafal/ *n.f.* (*de vent*) gust; (*tir*) burst of gunfire.
raffermir /rafɛrmir/ *v.t.* strengthen. **se ~** *v. pr.* become stronger.
raffin|é /rafine/ *a.* refined. **~ement** *n.m.* refinement.
raffin|er /rafine/ *v.t.* refine. **~age** *n.m.* refining. **~erie** *n.f.* refinery.
raffoler /rafɔle/ *v.i.* **~ de,** be extremely fond of.
raffut /rafy/ *n.m.* (*fam.*) din.
rafiot /rafjo/ *n.m.* (*fam.*) boat.
rafistoler /rafistɔle/ *v.t.* (*fam.*) patch up.
rafle /rɑfl/ *n.f.* (police) raid.
rafler /rɑfle/ *v.t.* grab, swipe.
rafraîch|ir /rafreʃir/ *v.t.* cool (down); (*raviver*) brighten up; (*personne, mémoire*) refresh. **se ~ir** *v. pr.* (*se laver*) freshen up; (*boire*) refresh

o.s.; (*temps*) get cooler. **~issant, ~issante** *a.* refreshing.

rafraîchissement /rafreʃismɑ̃/ *n.m.* (*boisson*) cold drink. **~s,** (*fruits etc.*) refreshments.

ragaillardir /ragajardir/ *v.t.* (*fam.*) buck up. **se ~** *v. pr.* buck up.

rag|e /raʒ/ *n.f.* rage; (*maladie*) rabies. **faire ~e,** rage. **~e de dents,** raging toothache. **~er** *v.i.* rage. **~eur, ~euse** *a.* ill-tempered. **~eant, ~eante** *a.* maddening.

ragot(s) /rago/ *n.m.* (*pl.*) (*fam.*) gossip.

ragoût /ragu/ *n.m.* stew.

raid /rɛd/ *n.m.* (*mil.*) raid; (*sport*) rally.

raid|e /rɛd/ *a.* stiff; (*côte*) steep; (*corde*) tight; (*cheveux*) straight. ● *adv.* (*en pente*) steeply. **~eur** *n.f.* stiffness; steepness.

raidir /redir/ *v.t.*, **se ~** *v. pr.* stiffen; (*position*) harden; (*corde*) tighten.

raie[1] /rɛ/ *n.f.* line; (*bande*) strip; (*de cheveux*) parting.

raie[2] /rɛ/ *n.f.* (*poisson*) skate.

raifort /rɛfɔr/ *n.m.* horse-radish.

rail /rɑj/ *n.m.* (*barre*) rail. **le ~,** (*transport*) rail.

raill|er /rɑje/ *v.t.* mock (at). **~erie** *n.f.* mocking remark. **~eur, ~euse** *a.* mocking.

rainure /renyr/ *n.f.* groove.

raisin /rɛzɛ̃/ *n.m.* **~(s),** grapes. **~ sec,** raisin.

raison /rɛzɔ̃/ *n.f.* reason. **à ~ de,** at the rate of. **avec ~,** rightly. **avoir ~,** be right (**de faire,** to do). **avoir ~ de qn.,** get the better of s.o. **donner ~ à,** prove right. **en ~ de,** (*cause*) because of. **~ de plus,** all the more reason. **perdre la ~,** lose one's mind.

raisonnable /rɛzɔnabl/ *a.* reasonable, sensible.

raisonn|er /rɛzɔne/ *v.i.* reason. ● *v.t.* (*personne*) reason with. **~ement** *n.m.* reasoning; (*propositions*) argument.

rajeunir /raʒœnir/ *v.t.* make (look) younger; (*moderniser*) modernize; (*méd.*) rejuvenate. ● *v.i.* look younger.

rajout /raʒu/ *n.m.* addition. **~er** /-te/ *v.t.* add.

rajust|er /raʒyste/ *v.t.* straighten; (*salaires*) (re)adjust. **~ement** *n.m.* (re)adjustment.

râl|e /rɑl/ *n.m.* (*de blessé*) groan. **~er** *v.i.* groan; (*protester*: *fam.*) moan.

ralent|ir /ralɑ̃tir/ *v.t./i.*, **se ~ir** *v. pr.* slow down. **~i** *a.* slow; *n.m.* (*cinéma*) slow motion. **être** *ou* **tourner au ~i,** tick over, idle.

rall|ier /ralje/ *v.t.* rally; (*rejoindre*) rejoin. **se ~ier** *v. pr.* rally. **se ~ier à,** (*avis*) come over to. **~iement** *n.m.* rallying.

rallonge /ralɔ̃ʒ/ *n.f.* (*de table*) extension. **~ de,** (*supplément de*) extra.

rallonger /ralɔ̃ʒe/ *v.t.* lengthen.

rallumer /ralyme/ *v.t.* light (up) again; (*lampe*) switch on again; (*ranimer*: *fig.*) revive.

rallye /rali/ *n.m.* rally.

ramadan /ramadɑ̃/ *n.m.* Ramadan.

ramassé /ramɑse/ *a.* squat; (*concis*) concise.

ramass|er /ramɑse/ *v.t.* pick up; (*récolter*) gather; (*recueillir*) collect. **se ~er** *v. pr.* draw o.s. together, curl up. **~age** *n.m.* (*cueillette*) gathering. **~age scolaire,** school bus service.

rambarde /rɑ̃bard/ *n.f.* guardrail.

rame /ram/ *n.f.* (*aviron*) oar; (*train*) train; (*perche*) stake.

rameau (*pl.* **~x**) /ramo/ *n.m.* branch.

ramener /ramne/ *v.t.* bring back. **~ à,** (*réduire à*) reduce to. **se ~** *v. pr.* (*fam.*) turn up. **se ~ à,** (*problème*) come down to.

ram|er /rame/ *v.i.* row. **~eur, ~euse** *n.m., f.* rower.

ramif|ier (se) /(sə)ramifje/ *v. pr.* ramify. **~ication** *n.f.* ramification.

ramollir /ramɔlir/ *v.t.*, **se ~** *v. pr.* soften.

ramon|er /ramɔne/ *v.t.* sweep. **~eur** *n.m.* (chimney-)sweep.

rampe /rɑ̃p/ *n.f.* banisters; (*pente*) ramp. **~ de lancement,** launching pad.

ramper /rɑ̃pe/ *v.i.* crawl.

rancard /rɑ̃kar/ *n.m.* (*fam.*) appointment.

rancart /rɑ̃kar/ *n.m.* **mettre** *ou* **jeter au ~,** (*fam.*) scrap.

ranc|e /rɑ̃s/ *a.* rancid. **~ir** *v.i.* go *ou* turn rancid.

rancœur /rɑ̃kœr/ *n.f.* resentment.

rançon /rɑ̃sɔ̃/ *n.f.* ransom. **~ner** /-ɔne/ *v.t.* hold to ransom.

rancun|e /rɑ̃kyn/ *n.f.* grudge. **sans ~!,** no hard feelings. **~ier, ~ière** *a.* vindictive.

randonnée /rɑ̃dɔne/ *n.f.* walk; (*en auto, vélo*) ride.

rang /rɑ̃/ *n.m.* row; (*hiérarchie, condition*) rank. **se mettre en ~,** line up. **au premier ~,** in the first row; (*fig.*) at the forefront. **de second ~,** (*péj.*) second-rate.

rangée /rɑ̃ʒe/ *n.f.* row.

rang|er /rɑʒe/ *v.t.* put away; (*chambre etc.*) tidy (up); (*disposer*) place; (*véhicule*) park. **se ~er** *v. pr.* (*véhicule*) park; (*s'écarter*) stand aside; (*s'assagir*) settle down. **se ~er à,** (*avis*) accept. **~ement** *n.m.* (*de chambre*) tidying (up); (*espace*) storage space.

ranimer /ranime/ *v.t.*, **se ~** *v. pr.* revive.

rapace[1] /rapas/ *n.m.* bird of prey.

rapace[2] /rapas/ *a.* grasping.

rapatr|ier /rapatrije/ *v.t.* repatriate. **~iement** *n.m.* repatriation.

râp|e /rɑp/ *n.f.* (*culin.*) grater; (*lime*) rasp. **~er** *v.t.* grate; (*bois*) rasp.

râpé /rɑpe/ *a.* threadbare. **c'est ~!,** (*fam.*) that's right out!

rapetisser /raptise/ *v.t.* make smaller. ● *v.i.* get smaller.

râpeu|x, ~se /rɑpø, -z/ *a.* rough.

rapid|e /rapid/ *a.* fast, rapid. ● *n.m.* (*train*) express (train); (*cours d'eau*) rapids *pl.* **~ement** *adv.* fast, rapidly. **~ité** *n.f.* speed.

rapiécer /rapjese/ *v.t.* patch.

rappel /rapɛl/ *n.m.* recall; (*deuxième avis*) reminder; (*de salaire*) back pay; (*méd.*) booster.

rappeler /raple/ *v.t.* call back; (*diplomate, réserviste*) recall; (*évoquer*) remind, recall. **~ qch. à qn.,** (*redire*) remind s.o. of sth. **se ~** *v. pr.* remember, recall.

rapport /rapɔr/ *n.m.* connection; (*compte rendu*) report; (*profit*) yield. **~s,** (*relations*) relations. **en ~ avec,** (*accord*) in keeping with. **mettre/se mettre en ~ avec,** put/get in touch with. **par ~ à,** in relation to. **~s (sexuels),** intercourse.

rapport|er /rapɔrte/ *v.t.* bring back; (*profit*) bring in; (*dire, répéter*) report. ● *v.i.* (*comm.*) bring in a good return; (*mouchard*: *fam.*) tell. **se ~er à,** relate to. **s'en ~er à,** rely on. **~eur, ~euse** *n.m., f.* (*mouchard*) tell-tale; *n.m.* (*instrument*) protractor.

rapproch|er /raprɔʃe/ *v.t.* bring closer (**de,** to); (*réconcilier*) bring together; (*comparer*) compare. **se ~er** *v. pr.* get *ou* come closer (**de,** to); (*personnes, pays*) come together; (*s'apparenter*) be close (**de,** to). **~é** *a.* close. **~ement** *n.m.* reconciliation; (*rapport*) connection; (*comparaison*) parallel.

rapt /rapt/ *n.m.* abduction.

raquette /rakɛt/ *n.f.* (*de tennis*) racket; (*de ping-pong*) bat.

rare /rar/ *a.* rare; (*insuffisant*) scarce. **~ment** *adv.* rarely, seldom. **~té** *n.f.* rarity; scarcity; (*objet*) rarity.

raréfier (se) /(sə)rarefje/ *v. pr.* (*nourriture etc.*) become scarce.

ras, ~e /rɑ, rɑz/ *a.* (*herbe, poil*) short. **à ~ de,** very close to. **en avoir ~ le bol,** (*fam.*) be really fed up. **~e campagne,** open country. **coupé à ~,** cut short. **à ~ bord,** to the brim. **pull ~ du cou,** round-neck pull-over. **~-le-bol** *n.m.* (*fam.*) anger.

ras|er /rɑze/ *v.t.* shave; (*cheveux, barbe*) shave off; (*frôler*) skim; (*abattre*) raze; (*ennuyer*: *fam.*) bore. **se ~er** *v. pr.* shave. **~age** *n.m.* shaving. **~eur, ~euse** *n.m., f.* (*fam.*) bore.

rasoir /rɑzwar/ *n.m.* razor.

rassas|ier /rasazje/ *v.t.* satisfy. **être ~ié de,** have had enough of.

rassembl|er /rasɑ̃ble/ *v.t.* gather; (*courage*) muster. **se ~er** *v. pr.* gather. **~ement** *n.m.* gathering.

rasseoir (se) /(sə)raswar/ *v. pr.* sit down again.

rass|is, ~ise *ou* **~ie** /rasi, -z/ *a.* (*pain*) stale.

rassurer /rasyre/ *v.t.* reassure.

rat /ra/ *n.m.* rat.

ratatiner (se) /(sə)ratatine/ *v. pr.* shrivel up.

rate /rat/ *n.f.* spleen.

râteau (*pl.* **~x**) /rɑto/ *n.m.* rake.

râtelier /rɑtəlje/ *n.m.* (stable-)rack; (*fam.*) dentures.

rat|er /rate/ *v.t./i.* miss; (*gâcher*) spoil; (*échouer*) fail. **c'est ~é,** that's right out. **~é, ~ée** *n.m., f.* (*personne*) failure. **avoir des ~és,** (*auto.*) backfire.

ratif|ier /ratifje/ *v.t.* ratify. **~ication** *n.f.* ratification.

ratio /rasjo/ *n.m.* ratio.

ration /rɑsjɔ̃/ *n.f.* ration.

rationaliser /rasjɔnalize/ *v.t.* rationalize.
rationnel, ~le /rasjɔnɛl/ *a.* rational.
rationn|er /rasjɔne/ *v.t.* ration. **~ement** *n.m.* rationing.
ratisser /ratise/ *v.t.* rake; (*fouiller*) comb.
rattacher /rataʃe/ *v.t.* tie up again; (*relier*) link; (*incorporer*) join.
rattrapage /ratrapaʒ/ *n.m.* **~ scolaire,** remedial classes.
rattraper /ratrape/ *v.t.* catch; (*rejoindre*) catch up with; (*retard, erreur*) make up for. **se ~** *v. pr.* catch up; (*se dédommager*) make up for it. **se ~ à,** catch hold of.
ratur|e /ratyr/ *n.f.* deletion. **~er** *v.t.* delete.
rauque /rok/ *a.* raucous, harsh.
ravager /ravaʒe/ *v.t.* devastate, ravage.
ravages /ravaʒ/ *n.m. pl.* **faire des ~,** wreak havoc.
raval|er /ravale/ *v.t.* (*façade etc.*) clean; (*humilier*) lower (**à,** down to). **~ement** *n.m.* cleaning.
ravi /ravi/ *a.* delighted (**que,** that).
ravier /ravje/ *n.m.* hors-d'œuvre dish.
ravigoter /ravigɔte/ *v.t.* (*fam.*) buck up.
ravin /ravɛ̃/ *n.m.* ravine.
ravioli /ravjɔli/ *n.m. pl.* ravioli.
ravir /ravir/ *v.t.* delight. **~ à qn.,** (*enlever*) rob s.o. of.
raviser (se) /(sə)ravize/ *v. pr.* change one's mind.
ravissant, ~e /ravisɑ̃, -t/ *a.* beautiful.
ravisseu|r, ~se /ravisœr, -øz/ *n.m., f.* kidnapper.
ravitaill|er /ravitaje/ *v.t.* provide with supplies; (*avion*) refuel. **se ~er** *v. pr.* stock up. **~ement** *n.m.* provision of supplies (**de,** to), refuelling; (*denrées*) supplies.
raviver /ravive/ *v.t.* revive.
rayé /reje/ *a.* striped.
rayer /reje/ *v.t.* scratch; (*biffer*) cross out.
rayon /rɛjɔ̃/ *n.m.* ray; (*planche*) shelf; (*de magasin*) department; (*de roue*) spoke; (*de cercle*) radius. **~ d'action,** range. **~ de miel,** honeycomb. **~ X,** X-ray. **en connaître un ~,** (*fam.*) know one's stuff.
rayonn|er /rɛjɔne/ *v.i.* radiate; (*de joie*) beam; (*se déplacer*) tour around (*from a central point*). **~ement** *n.m.* (*éclat*) radiance; (*influence*) influence; (*radiations*) radiation.
rayure /rejyr/ *n.f.* scratch; (*dessin*) stripe. **à ~s,** striped.
raz-de-marée /rɑdmare/ *n.m. invar.* tidal wave. **~ électoral,** landslide.
re- /rə/ *préf.* re-.
ré- /re/ *préf.* re-.
réacteur /reaktœr/ *n.m.* jet engine; (*nucléaire*) reactor.
réaction /reaksjɔ̃/ *n.f.* reaction. **~ en chaîne,** chain reaction. **~naire** /-jɔnɛr/ *a. & n.m./f.* reactionary.
réadapter /readapte/ *v.t.,* **se ~** *v. pr.* readjust (**à,** to).
réaffirmer /reafirme/ *v.t.* reaffirm.
réagir /reaʒir/ *v.i.* react.
réalis|er /realize/ *v.t.* carry out; (*effort, bénéfice, achat*) make; (*rêve*) fulfil; (*film*) produce, direct; (*capital*) realize; (*se rendre compte de*) realize. **se ~er** *v. pr.* materialize. **~ateur, ~atrice** *n.m., f.* (*cinéma*) director; (*TV*) producer. **~ation** *n.f.* realization; (*œuvre*) achievement.
réalis|te /realist/ *a.* realistic. ● *n.m./f.* realist. **~me** *n.m.* realism.
réalité /realite/ *n.f.* reality.
réanim|er /reanime/ *v.t.* resuscitate. **~ation** *n.f.* resuscitation. **service de ~ation,** intensive care.
réapparaître /reaparɛtr/ *v.i.* reappear.
réarm|er (se) /(sə)rearme/ *v. pr.* rearm. **~ement** *n.m.* rearmament.
rébarbati|f, ~ve /rebarbatif, -v/ *a.* forbidding, off-putting.
rebâtir /rəbɑtir/ *v.t.* rebuild.
rebelle /rəbɛl/ *a.* rebellious; (*soldat*) rebel. ● *n.m./f.* rebel.
rebeller (se) /(sə)rəbele/ *v. pr.* rebel, hit back defiantly.
rébellion /rebeljɔ̃/ *n.f.* rebellion.
rebiffer (se) /(sə)rəbife/ *v. pr.* (*fam.*) rebel.
rebond /rəbɔ̃/ *n.m.* bounce; (*par ricochet*) rebound. **~ir** /-ɔ̃dir/ *v.i.* bounce; rebound.
rebondi /rəbɔ̃di/ *a.* chubby.
rebondissement /rəbɔ̃dismɑ̃/ *n.m.* (new) development.
rebord /rəbɔr/ *n.m.* edge. **~ de la fenêtre,** window-ledge.
rebours (à) /(a)rəbur/ *adv.* the wrong way.
rebrousse-poil (à) /(a)rəbruspwal/ *adv.* (*fig.*) **prendre qn. ~,** rub s.o. up the wrong way.

rebrousser /rəbruse/ *v.t.* **~ chemin,** turn back.

rebuffade /rəbyfad/ *n.f.* rebuff.

rébus /rebys/ *n.m.* rebus.

rebut /rəby/ *n.m.* **mettre** *ou* **jeter au ~,** scrap.

rebut|er /rəbyte/ *v.t.* put off. **~ant, ~ante** *a.* off-putting.

récalcitrant, ~e /rekalsitrɑ̃, -t/ *a.* stubborn.

recal|er /rəkale/ *v.t.* (*fam.*) fail. **se faire ~er** *ou* **être ~é,** fail.

récapitul|er /rekapityle/ *v.t./i.* recapitulate. **~ation** *n.f.* recapitulation.

recel /rəsɛl/ *n.m.* receiving. **~er** /rəs(ə)le/ *v.t.* (*objet volé*) receive; (*cacher*) conceal.

récemment /resamɑ̃/ *adv.* recently.

recens|er /rəsɑ̃se/ *v.t.* (*population*) take a census of; (*objets*) list. **~ement** *n.m.* census; list.

récent, ~e /resɑ̃, -t/ *a.* recent.

récépissé /resepise/ *n.m.* receipt.

récepteur /resɛptœr/ *n.m.* receiver.

récepti|f, ~ve /resɛptif, -v/ *a.* receptive.

réception /resɛpsjɔ̃/ *n.f.* reception. **~ de,** (*lettre etc.*) receipt of. **~niste** /-jɔnist/ *n.m./f.* receptionist.

récession /resesjɔ̃/ *n.f.* recession.

recette /rəsɛt/ *n.f.* (*culin.*) recipe; (*argent*) takings. **~s,** (*comm.*) receipts.

receveu|r, ~se /rəsvœr, -øz/ *n.m., f.* (*des impôts*) tax collector.

recevoir† /rəsvwar/ *v.t.* receive; (*client, malade*) see; (*obtenir*) get, receive. **être reçu (à),** pass. ● *v.i.* (*médecin*) receive patients. **se ~** *v. pr.* (*tomber*) land.

rechange (de) /(də)rəʃɑ̃ʒ/ *a.* (*roue, vêtements, etc.*) spare; (*solution etc.*) alternative.

réchapper /reʃape/ *v.i.* **~ de** *ou* **à,** come through, survive.

recharg|e /rəʃarʒ/ *n.f.* (*de stylo*) refill. **~er** *v.t.* refill; (*batterie*) recharge.

réchaud /reʃo/ *n.m.* stove.

réchauff|er /reʃofe/ *v.t.* warm up. **se ~er** *v. pr.* warm o.s. up; (*temps*) get warmer. **~ement** *n.m.* (*de température*) rise (**de,** in).

rêche /rɛʃ/ *a.* rough.

recherche /rəʃɛrʃ/ *n.f.* search (**de,** for); (*raffinement*) elegance. **~(s),** (*univ.*) research. **~s,** (*enquête*) investigations.

recherch|er /rəʃɛrʃe/ *v.t.* search for. **~é** *a.* in great demand; (*élégant*) elegant. **~é pour meurtre,** wanted for murder.

rechigner /rəʃiɲe/ *v.i.* **~ à,** balk at.

rechut|e /rəʃyt/ *n.f.* (*méd.*) relapse. **~er** *v.i.* relapse.

récidiv|e /residiv/ *n.f.* second offence. **~er** *v.i.* commit a second offence.

récif /resif/ *n.m.* reef.

récipient /resipjɑ̃/ *n.m.* container.

réciproque /resiprɔk/ *a.* mutual, reciprocal. **~ment** *adv.* each other; (*inversement*) conversely.

récit /resi/ *n.m.* (*compte rendu*) account, story; (*histoire*) story.

récital (*pl.* **~s**) /resital/ *n.m.* recital.

récit|er /resite/ *v.t.* recite. **~ation** *n.f.* recitation.

réclame /reklam/ *n.f.* **faire de la ~,** advertise. **en ~,** on offer.

réclam|er /reklame/ *v.t.* call for, demand; (*revendiquer*) claim. ● *v.i.* complain. **~ation** *n.f.* complaint.

reclus, ~e /rəkly, -z/ *n.m., f.* recluse. ● *a.* cloistered.

réclusion /reklyzjɔ̃/ *n.f.* imprisonment.

recoin /rəkwɛ̃/ *n.m.* nook.

récolt|e /rekɔlt/ *n.f.* (*action*) harvest; (*produits*) crop, harvest; (*fig.*) crop. **~er** *v.t.* harvest, gather; (*fig.*) collect.

recommand|er /rəkɔmɑ̃de/ *v.t.* recommend; (*lettre*) register. **envoyer en ~é,** send registered. **~ation** *n.f.* recommendation.

recommencer /rəkɔmɑ̃se/ *v.t./i.* (*reprendre*) begin *ou* start again; (*refaire*) repeat. **ne recommence pas,** don't do it again.

récompens|e /rekɔ̃pɑ̃s/ *n.f.* reward; (*prix*) award. **~er** *v.t.* reward (**de,** for).

réconcil|ier /rekɔ̃silje/ *v.t.* reconcile. **se ~ier** *v. pr.* become reconciled (**avec,** with). **~iation** *n.f.* reconciliation.

reconduire† /rəkɔ̃dɥir/ *v.t.* see home; (*à la porte*) show out; (*renouveler*) renew.

réconfort /rekɔ̃fɔr/ *n.m.* comfort. **~er** /-te/ *v.t.* comfort.

reconnaissable /rəkɔnɛsabl/ *a.* recognizable.

reconnaissan|t, ~te /rəkɔnɛsɑ̃, -t/ *a.* grateful (**de,** for). **~ce** *n.f.* gratitude; (*fait de reconnaître*) recognition; (*mil.*) reconnaissance.

reconnaître† /rəkɔnɛtr/ *v.t.* recognize; (*admettre*) admit (**que,** that); (*mil.*) reconnoitre; (*enfant, tort*) acknowledge.
reconstituant /rəkɔ̃stitɥɑ̃/ *n.m.* tonic.
reconstituer /rəkɔ̃stitɥe/ *v.t.* reconstitute; (*crime*) reconstruct.
reconstr|uire† /rəkɔ̃strɥir/ *v.t.* rebuild. **~uction** *n.f.* rebuilding.
reconversion /rəkɔ̃vɛrsjɔ̃/ *n.f.* (*de main-d'œuvre*) redeployment.
recopier /rəkɔpje/ *v.t.* copy out.
record /rəkɔr/ *n.m.* & *a. invar.* record.
recoupe|r /rəkupe/ *v.t.* confirm. **se ~** *v. pr.* check, tally, match up. **par ~ment,** by making connections.
recourbé /rəkurbe/ *a.* curved; (*nez*) hooked.
recourir /rəkurir/ *v.i.* **~ à,** resort to.
recours /rəkur/ *n.m.* resort. **avoir ~ à,** have recourse to, resort to.
recouvrer /rəkuvre/ *v.t.* recover.
recouvrir† /rəkuvrir/ *v.t.* cover.
récréation /rekreɑsjɔ̃/ *n.f.* recreation; (*scol.*) playtime.
récrier (se) /(sə)rekrije/ *v. pr.* cry out.
récrimination /rekriminɑsjɔ̃/ *n.f.* recrimination.
recroqueviller (se) /(sə)rəkrɔkvije/ *v. pr.* curl up.
recrudescence /rəkrydesɑ̃s/ *n.f.* new outbreak.
recrue /rəkry/ *n.f.* recruit.
recrut|er /rəkryte/ *v.t.* recruit. **~ement** *n.m.* recruitment.
rectang|le /rɛktɑ̃gl/ *n.m.* rectangle. **~ulaire** *a.* rectangular.
rectif|ier /rɛktifje/ *v.t.* correct, rectify. **~ication** *n.f.* correction.
recto /rɛkto/ *n.m.* front of the page.
reçu /rəsy/ *voir* recevoir. ● *n.m.* receipt. ● *a.* accepted; (*candidat*) successful.
recueil /rəkœj/ *n.m.* collection.
recueill|ir† /rəkœjir/ *v.t.* collect; (*prendre chez soi*) take in. **se ~ir** *v. pr.* meditate. **~ement** *n.m.* meditation. **~i** *a.* meditative.
recul /rəkyl/ *n.m.* retreat; (*éloignement*) distance; (*déclin*) decline. **(mouvement de) ~,** backward movement. **~ade** *n.f.* retreat.
reculé /rəkyle/ *a.* (*région*) remote.
reculer /rəkyle/ *v.t./i.* move back; (*véhicule*) reverse; (*armée*) retreat; (*diminuer*) decline; (*différer*) postpone. **~ devant,** (*fig.*) shrink from.
reculons (à) /(a)rəkylɔ̃/ *adv.* backwards.
récupér|er /rekypere/ *v.t./i.* recover; (*vieux objets*) salvage. **~ation** *n.f.* recovery; salvage.
récurer /rekyre/ *v.t.* scour. **poudre à ~,** scouring powder.
récuser /rekyze/ *v.t.* challenge. **se ~** *v. pr.* state that one is not qualified to judge.
recycl|er /rəsikle/ *v.t.* (*personne*) retrain; (*chose*) recycle. **se ~er** *v. pr.* retrain. **~age** *n.m.* retraining; recycling.
rédac|teur, ~trice /redaktœr, -tris/ *n.m., f.* writer, editor. **le ~teur en chef,** the editor (in chief).
rédaction /redaksjɔ̃/ *n.f.* writing; (*scol.*) composition; (*personnel*) editorial staff.
reddition /redisjɔ̃/ *n.f.* surrender.
redemander /rədmɑ̃de/ *v.t.* ask again for; ask for more of.
redevable /rədvabl/ *a.* **être ~ à qn. de,** (*argent*) owe sb; (*fig.*) be indebted to s.o. for.
redevance /rədvɑ̃s/ *n.f.* (*de télévision*) licence fee.
rédiger /rediʒe/ *v.t.* write; (*contrat*) draw up.
redire† /rədir/ *v.t.* repeat. **avoir** *ou* **trouver à ~ à,** find fault with.
redondant, ~e /rədɔ̃dɑ̃, -t/ *a.* superfluous.
redonner /rədɔne/ *v.t.* give back; (*davantage*) give more.
redoubl|er /rəduble/ *v.t./i.* increase; (*classe: scol.*) repeat. **~er de prudence/*etc.*,** be more careful/*etc.* **~ement** *n.m.* (*accroissement*) increase (**de,** in).
redout|er /rədute/ *v.t.* dread. **~able** *a.* formidable.
redoux /rədu/ *n.m.* milder weather.
redress|er /rədrese/ *v.t.* straighten (out *ou* up); (*situation*) right, redress. **se ~er** *v. pr.* (*personne*) straighten (o.s.) up; (*se remettre debout*) stand up; (*pays, économie*) recover. **~ement** /rədrɛsmɑ̃/ *n.m.* (*relèvement*) recovery.
réduction /redyksjɔ̃/ *n.f.* reduction.
réduire† /redɥir/ *v.t.* reduce (**à,** to). **se ~ à,** (*revenir à*) come down to.
réduit[1]**, ~e** /redɥi, -t/ *a.* (*objet*) small-scale; (*limité*) limited.
réduit[2] /redɥi/ *n.m.* recess.

réédu|quer /reedyke/ *v.t.* (*personne*) rehabilitate; (*membre*) re-educate. **~cation** *n.f.* rehabilitation; re-education.

réel, ~le /reɛl/ *a.* real. ● *n.m.* reality. **~lement** *adv.* really.

réexpédier /reɛkspedje/ *v.t.* forward; (*retourner*) send back.

refaire† /rəfɛr/ *v.t.* do again; (*erreur, voyage*) make again; (*réparer*) do up, redo.

réfection /refɛksjɔ̃/ *n.f.* repair.

réfectoire /refɛktwar/ *n.m.* refectory.

référence /referɑ̃s/ *n.f.* reference.

référendum /referɛ̃dɔm/ *n.m.* referendum.

référer /refere/ *v.i.* **en ~ à,** refer the matter to. **se ~ à,** refer to.

refermer /rəfɛrme/ *v.t.*, **se ~,** *v. pr.* close (again).

refiler /rəfile/ *v.t.* (*fam.*) palm off (**à,** on).

réfléch|ir /refleʃir/ *v.i.* think (**à,** about). ● *v.t.* reflect. **se ~ir** *v. pr.* be reflected. **~i** *a.* (*personne*) thoughtful; (*verbe*) reflexive.

refl|et /rəflɛ/ *n.m.* reflection; (*lumière*) light. **~éter** /-ete/ *v.t.* reflect. **se ~éter** *v. pr.* be reflected.

réflexe /reflɛks/ *a.* & *n.m.* reflex.

réflexion /reflɛksjɔ̃/ *n.f.* reflection; (*pensée*) thought, reflection. **à la ~,** on second thoughts.

refluer /rəflye/ *v.i.* flow back; (*foule*) retreat.

reflux /rəfly/ *n.m.* (*de marée*) ebb.

refondre /rəfɔ̃dr/ *v.t.* recast.

réform|e /refɔrm/ *n.f.* reform. **~ateur, ~atrice** *n.m., f.* reformer. **~er** *v.t.* reform; (*soldat*) invalid (out of the army).

refoul|er /rəfule/ *v.t.* (*larmes*) force back; (*désir*) repress. **~é** *a.* repressed. **~ement** *n.m.* repression.

réfractaire /refraktɛr/ *a.* **être ~ à,** resist.

refrain /rəfrɛ̃/ *n.m.* chorus. **le même ~,** the same old story.

refréner /rəfrene/ *v.t.* curb, check.

réfrigér|er /refriʒere/ *v.t.* refrigerate. **~ateur** *n.m.* refrigerator.

refroid|ir /rəfrwadir/ *v.t./i.* cool (down). **se ~ir** *v. pr.* (*personne, temps*) get cold; (*ardeur*) cool (off). **~issement** *n.m.* cooling; (*rhume*) chill.

refuge /rəfyʒ/ *n.m.* refuge; (*chalet*) mountain hut.

réfug|ier (se) /(sə)refyʒje/ *v. pr.* take refuge. **~ié, ~iée** *n.m., f.* refugee.

refus /rəfy/ *n.m.* refusal. **ce n'est pas de ~,** I wouldn't say no. **~er** /-ze/ *v.t.* refuse (**de,** to); (*recaler*) fail. **se ~er à,** (*évidence etc.*) reject.

réfuter /refyte/ *v.t.* refute.

regagner /rəgɑɲe/ *v.t.* regain; (*revenir à*) get back to.

regain /rəgɛ̃/ *n.m.* **~ de,** renewal of.

régal (*pl.* **~s**) /regal/ *n.m.* treat. **~er** *v.t.* treat (**de,** to). **se ~er** *v. pr.* treat o.s. (**de,** to).

regard /rəgar/ *n.m.* (*expression, coup d'œil*) look; (*fixe*) stare; (*vue, œil*) eye. **au ~ de,** in regard to. **en ~ de,** compared with.

regardant, ~e /rəgardɑ̃, -t/ *a.* careful (with money). **peu ~ (sur),** not fussy (about).

regarder /rəgarde/ *v.t.* look at; (*observer*) watch; (*considérer*) consider; (*concerner*) concern. **~ (fixement),** stare at. ● *v.i.* look. **~ à,** (*qualité etc.*) pay attention to. **~ vers,** (*maison*) face. **se ~** *v. pr.* (*personnes*) look at each other.

régates /regat/ *n.f. pl.* regatta.

régénérer /reʒenere/ *v.t.* regenerate.

régen|t, ~te /reʒɑ̃, -t/ *n.m., f.* regent. **~ce** *n.f.* regency.

régenter /reʒɑ̃te/ *v.t.* rule.

reggae /rege/ *n.m.* reggae.

régie /reʒi/ *n.f.* (*entreprise*) public corporation; (*radio, TV*) control room; (*cinéma, théâtre*) production.

regimber /rəʒɛ̃be/ *v.i.* balk.

régime /reʒim/ *n.m.* (*organisation*) system; (*pol.*) regime; (*méd.*) diet; (*de moteur*) speed; (*de bananes*) bunch. **se mettre au ~,** go on a diet.

régiment /reʒimɑ̃/ *n.m.* regiment.

région /reʒjɔ̃/ *n.f.* region. **~al** (*m. pl.* **~aux**) /-jɔnal, -o/ *a.* regional.

régir /reʒir/ *v.t.* govern.

régisseur /reʒisœr/ *n.m.* (*théâtre*) stage-manager; (*cinéma, TV*) assistant director.

registre /rəʒistr/ *n.m.* register.

réglage /reglaʒ/ *n.m.* adjustment.

règle /rɛgl/ *n.f.* rule; (*instrument*) ruler. **~s,** (*de femme*) period. **en ~,** in order. **~ à calculer,** slide-rule.

réglé /regle/ *a.* (*vie*) ordered; (*arrangé*) settled.

règlement /rɛgləmɑ̃/ *n.m.* regulation; (*règles*) regulations; (*solution, paiement*) settlement. **~aire** /-tɛr/ *a.* (*uniforme*) regulation.

réglement|er /rɛgləmɑ̃te/ *v.t.* regulate. **~ation** *n.f.* regulation.
régler /regle/ *v.t.* settle; (*machine*) adjust; (*programmer*) set; (*facture*) settle; (*personne*) settle up with; (*papier*) rule. **~ son compte à,** settle a score with.
réglisse /reglis/ *n.f.* liquorice.
règne /rɛɲ/ *n.m.* reign; (*végétal, animal, minéral*) kingdom.
régner /reɲe/ *v.i.* reign.
regorger /rəgɔrʒe/ *v.i.* **~ de,** be overflowing with.
regret /rəgrɛ/ *n.m.* regret. **à ~,** with regret.
regrett|er /rəgrete/ *v.t.* regret; (*personne*) miss. **~able** *a.* regrettable.
regrouper /rəgrupe/ *v.t.*, group together. **se ~** *v. pr.* gather (together).
régulariser /regylarize/ *v.t.* regularize.
régulation /regylɑsjɔ̃/ *n.f.* regulation.
régul|ier, ~ière /regylje, -jɛr/ *a.* regular; (*qualité, vitesse*) steady, even; (*ligne, paysage*) even; (*légal*) legal; (*honnête*) honest. **~arité** *n.f.* regularity; steadiness; evenness. **~ièrement** *adv.* regularly; (*d'ordinaire*) normally.
réhabilit|er /reabilite/ *n.f.* rehabilitate. **~ation** *n.f.* rehabilitation.
rehausser /rəose/ *v.t.* raise; (*faire valoir*) enhance.
rein /rɛ̃/ *n.m.* kidney. **~s,** (*dos*) back.
réincarnation /reɛ̃karnasjɔ̃/ *n.f.* reincarnation.
reine /rɛn/ *n.f.* queen. **~-claude** *n.f.* greengage.
réinsertion /reɛ̃sɛrsjɔ̃/ *n.f.* reintegration, rehabilitation.
réintégrer /reɛ̃tegre/ *v.t.* (*lieu*) return to; (*jurid.*) reinstate.
réitérer /reitere/ *v.t.* repeat.
rejaillir /rəʒajir/ *v.i.* **~ sur,** rebound on.
rejet /rəʒɛ/ *n.m.* rejection.
rejeter /rəʒte/ *v.t.* throw back; (*refuser*) reject; (*vomir*) bring up; (*déverser*) discharge. **~ une faute/*etc.* sur qn.,** shift the blame for a mistake/*etc.* on to s.o.
rejeton(s) /rəʒtɔ̃/ *n.m.* (*pl.*) (*fam.*) offspring.
rejoindre† /rəʒwɛ̃dr/ *v.t.* go back to, rejoin; (*rattraper*) catch up with; (*rencontrer*) join, meet. **se ~** *v. pr.* (*personnes*) meet; (*routes*) join, meet.
réjoui /reʒwi/ *a.* joyful.
réjou|ir /reʒwir/ *v.t.* delight. **se ~ir** *v. pr.* be delighted (**de qch.,** at sth.). **~issances** *n.f. pl.* festivities. **~issant, ~issante** *a.* cheering.
relâche /rəlɑʃ/ *n.m.* (*repos*) respite. **faire ~,** (*théâtre*) close.
relâché /rəlɑʃe/ *a.* lax.
relâch|er /rəlɑʃe/ *v.t.* slacken; (*personne*) release; (*discipline*) relax. **se ~er** *v. pr.* slacken. **~ement** *n.m.* slackening.
relais /rəlɛ/ *n.m.* relay. **~ (routier),** roadside café.
relanc|e /rəlɑ̃s/ *n.f.* boost. **~er** *v.t.* boost, revive; (*renvoyer*) throw back.
relati|f, ~ve /rəlatif, -v/ *a.* relative.
relation /rəlɑsjɔ̃/ *n.f.* relation(ship); (*ami*) acquaintance; (*récit*) account. **~s,** relation. **en ~ avec qn.,** in touch with s.o.
relativement /rəlativmɑ̃/ *adv.* relatively. **~ à,** in relation to.
relativité /rəlativite/ *n.f.* relativity.
relax|er (se) /(sə)rəlakse/ *v. pr.* relax. **~ation** *n.f.* relaxation. **~e** *a.* (*fam.*) laid-back.
relayer /rəleje/ *v.t.* relieve; (*émission*) relay. **se ~** *v. pr.* take over from one another.
reléguer /rəlege/ *v.t.* relegate.
relent /rəlɑ̃/ *n.m.* stink.
relève /rəlɛv/ *n.f.* relief. **prendre** *ou* **assurer la ~,** take over (**de,** from).
relevé /rəlve/ *n.m.* list; (*de compte*) statement; (*de compteur*) reading. ● *a.* spicy.
relever /rəlve/ *v.t.* pick up; (*personne tombée*) help up; (*remonter*) raise; (*col*) turn up; (*manches*) roll up; (*sauce*) season; (*goût*) bring out; (*compteur*) read; (*défi*) accept; (*relayer*) relieve; (*remarquer, noter*) note; (*rebâtir*) rebuild. ● *v.i.* **~ de,** (*dépendre de*) be the concern of; (*méd.*) recover from. **se ~** *v. pr.* (*personne*) get up (again); (*pays, économie*) recover.
relief /rəljɛf/ *n.m.* relief. **mettre en ~,** highlight.
relier /rəlje/ *v.t.* link (**à,** to); (*ensemble*) link together; (*livre*) bind.
religieu|x, ~se /rəliʒjø, -z/ *a.* religious. ● *n.m.* monk. ● *n.f.* nun; (*culin.*) choux bun.
religion /rəliʒjɔ̃/ *n.f.* religion.

reliquat /rəlika/ *n.m.* residue.
relique /rəlik/ *n.f.* relic.
reliure /rəljyr/ *n.f.* binding.
reluire /rəlɥir/ *v.i.* shine. **faire ~,** shine.
reluisant, ~e /rəlɥizɑ̃, -t/ *a.* **peu** *ou* **pas ~,** not brilliant.
reman|ier /rəmanje/ *v.t.* revise; (*ministère*) reshuffle. **~iement** *n.m.* revision; reshuffle.
remarier (se) /(sə)rəmarje/ *v. pr.* remarry.
remarquable /rəmarkabl/ *a.* remarkable.
remarque /rəmark/ *n.f.* remark; (*par écrit*) note.
remarquer /rəmarke/ *v.t.* notice; (*dire*) say. **faire ~,** point out (**à,** to). **se faire ~,** attract attention. **remarque(z),** mind you.
remblai /rɑ̃blɛ/ *n.m.* embankment.
rembourrer /rɑ̃bure/ *v.t.* pad.
rembours|er /rɑ̃burse/ *v.t.* repay; (*billet, frais*) refund. **~ement** *n.m.* repayment; refund.
remède /rəmɛd/ *n.m.* remedy; (*médicament*) medicine.
remédier /rəmedje/ *v.i.* **~ à,** remedy.
remémorer (se) /(sə)rəmemɔre/ *v. pr.* recall.
remerc|ier /rəmɛrsje/ *v.t.* thank (**de,** for); (*licencier*) dismiss. **~iements** *n.m. pl.* thanks.
remettre† /rəmɛtr/ *v.t.* put back; (*vêtement*) put back on; (*donner*) hand (over); (*devoir, démission*) hand in; (*restituer*) give back; (*différer*) put off; (*ajouter*) add; (*se rappeler*) remember; (*peine*) remit. **se ~** *v. pr.* (*guérir*) recover. **se ~ à,** go back to. **se ~ à faire,** start doing again. **s'en ~ à,** leave it to. **~ en cause** *ou* **en question,** call into question.
réminiscence /reminisɑ̃s/ *n.f.* reminiscence.
remise[1] /rəmiz/ *n.f.* (*abri*) shed.
remise[2] /rəmiz/ *n.f.* (*rabais*) discount; (*livraison*) delivery; (*ajournement*) postponement. **~ en cause** *ou* **en question,** calling into question.
remiser /rəmize/ *v.t.* put away.
rémission /remisjɔ̃/ *n.f.* remission.
remontant /rəmɔ̃tɑ̃/ *n.m.* tonic.
remontée /rəmɔ̃te/ *n.f.* ascent; (*d'eau, de prix*) rise. **~ mécanique,** ski-lift.
remont|er /rəmɔ̃te/ *v.i.* go *ou* come (back) up; (*prix, niveau*) rise (again); (*revenir*) go back. ● *v.t.* (*rue etc.*) go *ou* come (back) up; (*relever*) raise; (*montre*) wind up; (*objet démonté*) put together again; (*personne*) buck up. **~e-pente** *n.m.* ski-lift.
remontoir /rəmɔ̃twar/ *n.m.* winder.
remontrer /rəmɔ̃tre/ *v.t.* show again. **en ~ à qn.,** go one up on s.o.
remords /rəmɔr/ *n.m.* remorse. **avoir un** *ou* **des ~,** feel remorse.
remorqu|e /rəmɔrk/ *n.f.* (*véhicule*) trailer. **en ~e,** on tow. **~er** *v.t.* tow.
remorqueur /rəmɔrkœr/ *n.m.* tug.
remous /rəmu/ *n.m.* eddy; (*de bateau*) backwash; (*fig.*) turmoil.
rempart /rɑ̃par/ *n.m.* rampart.
remplaçant, ~e /rɑ̃plasɑ̃, -t/ *n.m., f.* replacement; (*joueur*) reserve.
remplac|er /rɑ̃plase/ *v.t.* replace. **~ement** *n.m.* replacement.
rempli /rɑ̃pli/ *a.* full (**de,** of).
rempl|ir /rɑ̃plir/ *v.t.* fill (up); (*formulaire*) fill (in *ou* out); (*tâche, condition*) fulfil. **se ~ir** *v. pr.* fill (up). **~issage** *n.m.* filling; (*de texte*) padding.
remporter /rɑ̃pɔrte/ *v.t.* take back; (*victoire*) win.
remuant, ~e /rəmɥɑ̃, -t/ *a.* restless.
remue-ménage /rəmymenaʒ/ *n.m. invar.* commotion, bustle.
remuer /rəmɥe/ *v.t./i.* move; (*thé, café*) stir; (*gigoter*) fidget. **se ~** *v. pr.* move.
rémunér|er /remynere/ *v.t.* pay. **~ation** *n.f.* payment.
renâcler /rənɑkle/ *v.i.* snort. **~ à,** balk at, jib at.
ren|aître /rənɛtr/ *v.i.* be reborn; (*sentiment*) be revived. **~aissance** *n.f.* rebirth.
renard /rənar/ *n.m.* fox.
renchérir /rɑ̃ʃerir/ *v.i.* become dearer. **~ sur,** go one better than.
rencontr|e /rɑ̃kɔ̃tr/ *n.f.* meeting; (*de routes*) junction; (*mil.*) encounter; (*match*) match; (*Amer.*) game. **~er** *v.t.* meet; (*heurter*) strike; (*trouver*) find. **se ~er** *v. pr.* meet.
rendement /rɑ̃dmɑ̃/ *n.m.* yield; (*travail*) output.
rendez-vous /rɑ̃devu/ *n.m.* appointment; (*d'amoureux*) date; (*lieu*) meeting-place. **prendre ~ (avec),** make an appointment (with).
rendormir (se) /(sə)rɑ̃dɔrmir/ *v. pr.* go back to sleep.

rendre /rɑ̃dr/ *v.t.* give back, return; (*donner en retour*) return; (*monnaie*) give; (*hommage*) pay; (*justice*) dispense; (*jugement*) pronounce. **~ heureux/possible/***etc.*, make happy/possible/ *etc.* ● *v.i.* (*terres*) yield; (*vomir*) vomit. **se ~** *v. pr.* (*capituler*) surrender; (*aller*) go (**à,** to); (*ridicule, utile, etc.*) make o.s. **~ compte de,** report on. **~ des comptes à,** be accountable to. **~ justice à qn.,** do s.o. justice. **~ service (à),** help. **~ visite à,** visit. **se ~ compte de,** realize.

rendu /rɑ̃dy/ *a.* **être ~,** (*arrivé*) have arrived.

rêne /rɛn/ *n.f.* rein.

renégat, ~e /rənega, -t/ *n.m., f.* renegade.

renfermé /rɑ̃fɛrme/ *n.m.* stale smell. **sentir le ~,** smell stale. ● *a.* withdrawn.

renfermer /rɑ̃fɛrme/ *v.t.* contain. **se ~ (en soi-même),** withdraw (into o.s.).

renfl|é /rɑ̃fle/ *a.* bulging. **~ement** *n.m.* bulge.

renflouer /rɑ̃flue/ *v.t.* refloat.

renfoncement /rɑ̃fɔ̃smɑ̃/ *n.m.* recess.

renforcer /rɑ̃fɔrse/ *v.t.* reinforce.

renfort /rɑ̃fɔr/ *n.m.* reinforcement. **de ~,** (*armée, personnel*) back-up. **à grand ~ de,** with a great deal of.

renfrogn|er (se) /(sə)rɑ̃frɔɲe/ *v. pr.* scowl. **~é** *a.* surly, sullen.

rengaine /rɑ̃gɛn/ *n.f.* (*péj.*) **la même ~,** the same old story.

renier /rənje/ *v.t.* (*personne, pays*) disown, deny; (*foi*) renounce.

renifler /rənifle/ *v.t./i.* sniff.

renne /rɛn/ *n.m.* reindeer.

renom /rənɔ̃/ *n.m.* renown; (*réputation*) reputation. **~mé** /-ɔme/ *a.* famous. **~mée** /-ɔme/ *n.f.* fame; reputation.

renonc|er /rənɔ̃se/ *v.i.* **~er à,** (*habitude, ami, etc.*) give up, renounce. **~er à faire,** give up (all thought of) doing. **~ement** *n.m.*, **~iation** *n.f.* renunciation.

renouer /rənwe/ *v.t.* tie up (again); (*reprendre*) renew. ● *v.i.* **~ avec,** start up again with.

renouveau (*pl.* **~x**) /rənuvo/ *n.m.* revival.

renouvel|er /rənuvle/ *v.t.* renew; (*réitérer*) repeat. **se ~er** *v. pr.* be renewed; be repeated. **~lement** /-vɛlmɑ̃/ *n.m.* renewal.

rénov|er /renɔve/ *v.t.* (*édifice*) renovate; (*institution*) reform. **~ation** *n.f.* renovation; reform.

renseignement /rɑ̃sɛɲmɑ̃/ *n.m.* **~(s),** information. **(bureau des) ~s,** information desk.

renseigner /rɑ̃seɲe/ *v.t.* inform, give information to. **se ~** *v. pr.* enquire, make enquiries, find out.

rentab|le /rɑ̃tabl/ *a.* profitable. **~ilité** *n.f.* profitability.

rent|e /rɑ̃t/ *n.f.* (private) income; (*pension*) pension, annuity. **~ier, ~ière** *n.m., f.* person of private means.

rentrée /rɑ̃tre/ *n.f.* return; **la ~ parlementaire,** the reopening of Parliament; (*scol.*) start of the new year.

rentrer /rɑ̃tre/ (*aux. être*) *v.i.* go *ou* come back home, return home; (*entrer*) go *ou* come in; (*entrer à nouveau*) go *ou* come back in; (*revenu*) come in; (*élèves*) go back. **~ dans,** (*heurter*) smash into. ● *v.t.* (*aux. avoir*) bring in; (*griffes*) draw in; (*vêtement*) tuck in **~ dans l'ordre,** be back to normal. **~ dans ses frais,** break even.

renverse (à la) /(ala)rɑ̃vɛrs/ *adv.* backwards.

renvers|er /rɑ̃vɛrse/ *v.t.* knock over *ou* down; (*piéton*) knock down; (*liquide*) upset, spill; (*mettre à l'envers*) turn upside down; (*gouvernement*) overturn; (*inverser*) reverse. **se ~er** *v. pr.* (*véhicule*) overturn; (*verre, vase*) fall over. **~ement** *n.m.* (*pol.*) overthrow.

renv|oi /rɑ̃vwa/ *n.m.* return; dismissal; expulsion; postponement; reference; (*rot*) belch. **~oyer**† *v.t.* send back, return; (*employé*) dismiss; (*élève*) expel; (*ajourner*) 1postpone; (*référer*) refer; (*réfléchir*) reflect.

réorganiser /reɔrganize/ *v.t.* reorganize.

réouverture /reuvɛrtyr/ *n.f.* reopening.

repaire /rəpɛr/ *n.m.* den.

répandre /repɑ̃dr/ *v.t.* (*liquide*) spill; (*étendre, diffuser*) spread; (*lumière, sang*) shed; (*odeur*) give off. **se ~** *v. pr.* spread; (*liquide*) spill. **se ~ en,** (*injures etc.*) pour forth, launch forth into.

répandu /repɑ̃dy/ *a.* (*courant*) widespread.

répar|er /repare/ *v.t.* repair, mend; (*faute*) make amends for; (*remédier à*) put right. **~ateur** *n.m.* repairer. **~ation** *n.f.* repair; (*compensation*) compensation.

repartie /rəparti/ *n.f.* retort. **avoir (le sens) de la ~,** be good at repartee.

repartir† /rəpartir/ *v.i.* start (up) again; (*voyageur*) set off again; (*s'en retourner*) go back.

répart|ir /repartir/ *v.t.* distribute; (*partager*) share out; (*étaler*) spread. **~ition** *n.f.* distribution.

repas /rəpɑ/ *n.m.* meal.

repass|er /rəpɑse/ *v.i.* come *ou* go back. ● *v.t.* (*linge*) iron; (*leçon*) go over; (*examen*) retake, (*film*) show again. **~age** *n.m.* ironing.

repêcher /rəpeʃe/ *v.t.* fish out; (*candidat*) allow to pass.

repentir /rəpɑ̃tir/ *n.m.* repentance. **se ~** *v. pr.* (*relig.*) repent (**de,** of). **se ~ de,** (*regretter*) regret.

répercu|ter /reperkyte/ *v.t.* (*bruit*) echo. **se ~ter** *v. pr.* echo. **se ~ter sur,** have repercussions on. **~ssion** *n.f.* repercussion.

repère /rəpɛr/ *n.m.* mark; (*jalon*) marker; (*fig.*) landmark.

repérer /rəpere/ *v.t.* locate, spot. **se ~** *v. pr.* find one's bearings.

répert|oire /repɛrtwar/ *n.m.* index; (*artistique*) repertoire. **~orier** *v.t.* index.

répéter /repete/ *v.t.* repeat. ● *v.t./i.* (*théâtre*) rehearse. **se ~** *v. pr.* be repeated; (*personne*) repeat o.s.

répétition /repetisjɔ̃/ *n.f.* repetition; (*théâtre*) rehearsal.

repiquer /rəpike/ *v.t.* (*plante*) plant out.

répit /repi/ *n.m.* rest, respite.

replacer /rəplase/ *v.t.* replace.

repl|i /rəpli/ *n.m.* fold; (*retrait*) withdrawal. **~ier** *v.t.* fold (up); (*ailes, jambes*) tuck in. **se ~ier** *v. pr.* withdraw (**sur soi-même,** into o.s.).

répliqu|e /replik/ *n.f.* reply; (*riposte*) retort; (*discussion*) objection; (*théâtre*) line(s); (*copie*) replica. **~er** *v.t./i.* reply; (*riposter*) retort; (*objecter*) answer back.

répondant, ~e /repɔ̃dɑ̃, -t/ *n.m., f.* guarantor. **avoir du ~,** have money behind one.

répondeur /repɔ̃dœr/ *n.m.* answering machine.

répondre /repɔ̃dr/ *v.t.* (*remarque etc.*) reply with. **~ que,** answer *ou* reply that. ● *v.i.* answer, reply; (*être insolent*) answer back; (*réagir*) respond (**à,** to). **~ à,** answer. **~ de,** answer for.

réponse /repɔ̃s/ *n.f.* answer, reply; (*fig.*) response.

report /rəpɔr/ *n.m.* (*transcription*) transfer; (*renvoi*) postponement.

reportage /rəpɔrtaʒ/ *n.m.* report; (*en direct*) commentary, (*par écrit*) article.

reporter[1] /rəpɔrte/ *v.t.* take back; (*ajourner*) put off; (*transcrire*) transfer. **se ~ à,** refer to.

reporter[2] /rəpɔrtɛr/ *n.m.* reporter.

repos /rəpo/ *n.m.* rest; (*paix*) peace; (*tranquillité*) peace and quiet; (*moral*) peace of mind.

repos|er /rəpoze/ *v.t.* put down again; (*délasser*) rest. ● *v.i.* rest (**sur,** on). **se ~er** *v. pr.* rest. **se ~er sur,** rely on. **~ant, ~ante** *a.* restful. **laisser ~er,** (*pâte*) leave to stand.

repoussant, ~e /rəpusɑ̃, -t/ *a.* repulsive.

repousser /rəpuse/ *v.t.* push back; (*écarter*) push away; (*dégoûter*) repel; (*décliner*) reject; (*ajourner*) put back. ● *v.i.* grow again.

répréhensible /repreɑ̃sibl/ *a.* blameworthy.

reprendre† /rəprɑ̃dr/ *v.t.* take back; (*retrouver*) regain; (*souffle*) get back; (*évadé*) recapture; (*recommencer*) resume; (*redire*) repeat; (*modifier*) alter; (*blâmer*) reprimand. **~ du pain/***etc.*, take some more bread/*etc.* ● *v.i.* (*recommencer*) resume; (*affaires*) pick up. **se ~** *v. pr.* (*se ressaisir*) pull o.s. together; (*se corriger*) correct o.s. **on ne m'y reprendra pas,** I won't be caught out again.

représailles /rəprezɑj/ *n.f. pl.* reprisals.

représentati|f, ~ve /rəprezɑ̃tatif, -v/ *a.* representative.

représent|er /rəprezɑ̃te/ *v.t.* represent; (*théâtre*) perform. **se ~er** *v. pr.* (*s'imaginer*) imagine. **~ant, ~ante** *n.m., f.* representative. **~ation** *n.f.* representation; (*théâtre*) performance.

réprimand|e /reprimɑ̃d/ *n.f.* reprimand. **~er** *v.t.* reprimand.

répr|imer /reprime/ *v.t.* (*peuple*) repress (*sentiment*) suppress. **~ession** *n.f.* repression.

repris /rəpri/ *n.m.* **~ de justice,** ex-convict.

reprise /rəpriz/ *n.f.* resumption; (*théâtre*) revival; (*télévision*) repeat; (*de tissu*) darn, mend; (*essor*) recovery; (*comm.*) part-exchange, trade-in. **à plusieurs ~s,** on several occasions.

repriser /rəprize/ *v.t.* darn, mend.

réprobation /reprɔbɑsjɔ̃/ *n.f.* condemnation.

reproch|e /rəprɔʃ/ *n.m.* reproach, blame. **~er** *v.t.* **~er qch. à qn.,** reproach *ou* blame s.o. for sth.

reprod|uire† /rəprɔdɥir/ *v.t.* reproduce. **se ~uire** *v. pr.* reproduce; (*arriver*) recur. **~ucteur, ~uctrice** *a.* reproductive. **~uction** *n.f.* reproduction.

réprouver /repruve/ *v.t.* condemn.

reptile /rɛptil/ *n.m.* reptile.

repu /rəpy/ *a.* satiated.

républi|que /repyblik/ *n.f.* republic. **~que populaire,** people's republic. **~cain, ~caine** *a.* & *n.m., f.* republican.

répudier /repydje/ *v.t.* repudiate.

répugnance /repyɲɑ̃s/ *n.f.* repugnance; (*hésitation*) reluctance.

répugn|er /repyɲe/ *v.i.* **~er à,** be repugnant to. **~er à faire,** be reluctant to do. **~ant, ~ante** *a.* repulsive.

répulsion /repylsjɔ̃/ *n.f.* repulsion.

réputation /repytɑsjɔ̃/ *n.f.* reputation.

réputé /repyte/ *a.* renowned (**pour,** for). **~ pour être,** reputed to be.

requérir /rəkerir/ *v.t.* require, demand.

requête /rəkɛt/ *n.f.* request; (*jurid.*) petition.

requiem /rekɥijɛm/ *n.m. invar.* requiem.

requin /rəkɛ̃/ *n.m.* shark.

requis, ~e /rəki, -z/ *a.* required.

réquisition /rekizisjɔ̃/ *n.f.* requisition. **~ner** /-jɔne/ *v.t.* requisition.

rescapé, ~e /rɛskape/ *n.m., f.* survivor. ● *a.* surviving.

rescousse /rɛskus/ *n.f.* **à la ~,** to the rescue.

réseau (*pl.* **~x**) /rezo/ *n.m.* network.

réservation /rezɛrvɑsjɔ̃/ *n.f.* reservation. **bureau de ~,** booking office.

réserve /rezɛrv/ *n.f.* reserve; (*restriction*) reservation, reserve; (*indienne*) reservation; (*entrepôt*) store-room. **en ~,** in reserve. **les ~s,** (*mil.*) the reserves.

réserv|er /rezɛrve/ *v.t.* reserve; (*place*) book, reserve. **se ~er le droit de,** reserve the right to. **~é** *a.* (*personne, place*) reserved.

réserviste /rezɛrvist/ *n.m.* reservist.

réservoir /rezɛrvwar/ *n.m.* tank; (*lac*) reservoir.

résidence /rezidɑ̃s/ *n.f.* residence.

résident, ~e /rezidɑ̃, -t/ *n.m., f.* resident foreigner. **~iel, ~ielle** /-sjɛl/ *a.* residential.

résider /rezide/ *v.i.* reside.

résidu /rezidy/ *n.m.* residue.

résign|er (se) /(sə)reziɲe/ *v. pr.* **se ~er à faire,** resign o.s. to doing. **~ation** *n.f.* resignation.

résilier /rezilje/ *v.t.* terminate.

résille /rezij/ *n.f.* (hair-)net.

résine /rezin/ *n.f.* resin.

résistance /rezistɑ̃s/ *n.f.* resistance; (*fil électrique*) element.

résistant, ~e /rezistɑ̃, -t/ *a.* tough.

résister /reziste/ *v.i.* resist. **~ à,** resist; (*examen, chaleur*) stand up to.

résolu /rezɔly/ *voir* **résoudre.** ● *a.* resolute. **~ à,** resolved to. **~ment** *adv.* resolutely.

résolution /rezɔlysjɔ̃/ *n.f.* (*fermeté*) resolution; (*d'un problème*) solving.

résonance /rezɔnɑ̃s/ *n.f.* resonance.

résonner /rezɔne/ *v.i.* resound.

résor|ber /rezɔrbe/ *v.t.* reduce. **se ~ber** *v. pr.* be reduced. **~ption** *n.f.* reduction.

résoudre† /rezudr/ *v.t.* solve; (*décider*) decide on. **se ~ à,** resolve to.

respect /rɛspɛ/ *n.m.* respect.

respectab|le /rɛspɛktabl/ *a.* respectable. **~ilité** *n.f.* respectability.

respecter /rɛspɛkte/ *v.t.* respect. **faire ~,** (*loi, décision*) enforce.

respecti|f, ~ve /rɛspɛktif, -v/ *a.* respective. **~vement** *adv.* respectively.

respectueu|x, ~se /rɛspɛktɥø, -z/ *a.* respectful.

respir|er /rɛspire/ *v.i.* breathe; (*se reposer*) get one's breath. ● *v.t.* breathe; (*exprimer*) radiate.

~ation *n.f.* breathing; (*haleine*) breath. **~atoire** *a.* breathing.

resplend|ir /rɛsplɑ̃dir/ *v.i.* shine (**de,** with). **~issant, ~issante** *a.* radiant.

responsabilité /rɛspɔ̃sabilite/ *n.f.* responsibility; (*légale*) liability.

responsable /rɛspɔ̃sabl/ *a.* responsible (**de,** for). **~ de,** (*chargé de*) in charge of. ● *n.m./f.* person in charge; (*coupable*) person responsible.

resquiller /rɛskije/ *v.i.* (*fam.*) get in without paying; (*dans la queue*) jump the queue.

ressaisir (se) /(sə)rəsezir/ *v. pr.* pull o.s. together.

ressasser /rəsase/ *v.t.* keep going over.

ressembl|er /rəsɑ̃ble/ *v.i.* **~er à,** resemble, look like. **se ~er** *v. pr.* look alike. **~ance** *n.f.* resemblance. **~ant, ~ante** *a.* (*portrait*) true to life; (*pareil*) alike.

ressemeler /rəsəmle/ *v.t.* sole.

ressentiment /rəsɑ̃timɑ̃/ *n.m.* resentment.

ressentir /rəsɑ̃tir/ *v.t.* feel. **se ~ de,** feel the effects of.

resserre /rəsɛr/ *n.f.* shed.

resserrer /rəsere/ *v.t.* tighten; (*contracter*) contract. **se ~** *v. pr.* tighten; contract; (*route etc.*) narrow.

resservir /rəsɛrvir/ *v.i.* come in useful (again).

ressort /rəsɔr/ *n.m.* (*objet*) spring; (*fig.*) energy. **du ~ de,** within the jurisdiction *ou* scope of. **en dernier ~,** in the last resort.

ressortir† /rəsɔrtir/ *v.i.* go *ou* come back out; (*se voir*) stand out. **faire ~,** bring out. **~ de,** (*résulter*) result *ou* emerge from.

ressortissant, ~e /rəsɔrtisɑ̃, -t/ *n.m., f.* national.

ressource /rəsurs/ *n.f.* resource. **~s,** resources.

ressusciter /resysite/ *v.i.* come back to life.

restant, ~e /rɛstɑ̃, -t/ *a.* remaining. ● *n.m.* remainder.

restaur|ant /rɛstɔrɑ̃/ *n.m.* restaurant. **~ateur, ~atrice** *n.m., f.* restaurant owner.

restaur|er /rɛstɔre/ *v.t.* restore. **se ~er** *v. pr.* eat. **~ation** *n.f.* restoration; (*hôtellerie*) catering.

reste /rɛst/ *n.m.* rest; (*d'une soustraction*) remainder. **~s,** remains (**de,** of); (*nourriture*) leftovers. **un ~ de pain/***etc.*, some left-over bread/*etc.* **au ~, du ~,** moreover, besides.

rest|er /rɛste/ *v.i.* (*aux. être*) stay, remain; (*subsister*) be left, remain. **il ~e du pain/***etc.*, there is some bread/*etc.* left (over). **il me ~e du pain,** I have some bread left (over). **il me ~e à,** it remains for me to. **en ~er à,** go no further than. **en ~er là,** stop there.

restit|uer /rɛstitɥe/ *v.t.* (*rendre*) return, restore; (*son*) reproduce. **~ution** *n.f.* return.

restreindre† /rɛstrɛ̃dr/ *v.t.* restrict. **se ~** *v. pr.* (*dans les dépenses*) cut down.

restricti|f, ~ve /rɛstriktif, -v/ *a.* restrictive.

restriction /rɛstriksjɔ̃/ *n.f.* restriction.

résultat /rezylta/ *n.m.* result.

résulter /rezylte/ *v.i.* **~ de,** result from.

résum|er /rezyme/ *v.t.*, **se ~er** *v. pr.* summarize. **~é** *n.m.* summary. **en ~é,** in short.

résurrection /rezyrɛksjɔ̃/ *n.f.* resurrection; (*renouveau*) revival.

rétabl|ir /retablir/ *v.t.* restore; (*personne*) restore to health. **se ~ir** *v. pr.* be restored; (*guérir*) recover. **~issement** *n.m.* restoring; (*méd.*) recovery.

retaper /rətape/ *v.t.* (*maison etc.*) do up. **se ~** *v. pr.* (*guérir*) get back on one's feet.

retard /rətar/ *n.m.* lateness; (*sur un programme*) delay; (*infériorité*) backwardness. **avoir du ~,** be late; (*montre*) be slow. **en ~,** late; (*retardé*) backward. **en ~ sur,** behind. **rattraper** *ou* **combler son ~,** catch up.

retardataire /rətardatɛr/ *n.m./f.* latecomer. ● *a.* (*arrivant*) late.

retardé /rətarde/ *a.* backward.

retardement (à) /(a)rətardəmɑ̃/ *a.* (*bombe etc.*) delayed-action.

retarder /rətarde/ *v.t.* delay; (*sur un programme*) set back; (*montre*) put back. ● *v.i.* (*montre*) be slow; (*fam.*) be out of touch.

retenir† /rətnir/ *v.t.* hold back; (*souffle, attention, prisonnier*) hold; (*eau, chaleur*) retain, hold; (*larmes*) hold back; (*garder*) keep; (*retarder*) detain; (*réserver*) book; (*se rappeler*) remember; (*déduire*) deduct; (*accepter*) accept. **se ~** *v. pr.* (*se contenir*)

restrain o.s. **se ~ à,** hold on to. **se ~ de,** stop o.s. from.
rétention /retɑ̃sjɔ̃/ *n.f.* retention.
retent|ir /rətɑ̃tir/ *v.i.* ring out (**de,** with). **~issant, ~issante** *a.* resounding. **~issement** *n.m.* (*effet, répercussion*) effect.
retenue /rətny/ *n.f.* restraint; (*somme*) deduction; (*scol.*) detention.
réticen|t, ~te /retisɑ̃, -t/ *a.* (*hésitant*) reluctant; (*réservé*) reticent. **~ce** *n.f.* reluctance; reticence.
rétif, ~ve /retif, -v/ *a.* restive, recalcitrant.
rétine /retin/ *n.f.* retina.
retiré /rətire/ *a.* (*vie*) secluded; (*lieu*) remote.
retirer /rətire/ *v.t.* (*sortir*) take out; (*ôter*) take off; (*argent, candidature*) withdraw; (*avantage*) derive. **~ à qn.,** take away from s.o. **se ~** *v. pr.* withdraw, retire.
retombées /rətɔ̃be/ *n.f. pl.* fall-out.
retomber /rətɔ̃be/ *v.i.* fall; (*à nouveau*) fall again. **~ dans,** (*erreur etc.*) fall back into.
rétorquer /retɔrke/ *v.t.* retort.
rétorsion /retɔrsjɔ̃/ *n.f.* **mesures de ~,** retaliation.
retouch|e /rətuʃ/ *n.f.* touch-up; alteration. **~er** *v.t.* touch up; (*vêtement*) alter.
retour /rətur/ *n.m.* return. **être de ~,** be back (**de,** from). **~ en arrière,** flashback. **par ~ du courrier,** by return of post. **en ~,** in return.
retourner /rəturne/ *v.t.* (*aux. avoir*) turn over; (*vêtement*) turn inside out; (*lettre, compliment*) return; (*émouvoir: fam.*) upset. ● *v.i.* (*aux. être*) go back, return. **se ~** *v. pr.* turn round; (*dans son lit*) twist and turn. **s'en ~,** go back. **se ~ contre,** turn against.
retracer /rətrase/ *v.t.* retrace.
rétracter /retrakte/ *v.t.*, **se ~** *v. pr.* retract.
retrait /rətrɛ/ *n.m.* withdrawal; (*des eaux*) ebb, receding. **être (situé) en ~,** be set back.
retraite /rətrɛt/ *n.f.* retirement; (*pension*) (retirement) pension; (*fuite, refuge*) retreat. **mettre à la ~,** pension off. **prendre sa ~,** retire.
retraité, ~e /rətrete/ *a.* retired. ● *n.m., f.* (old-age) pensioner, senior citizen.
retrancher /rətrɑ̃ʃe/ *v.t.* remove; (*soustraire*) deduct. **se ~** *v. pr.* (*mil.*) entrench o.s. **se ~ derrière/dans,** take refuge behind/in.
retransm|ettre /rətrɑ̃smɛtr/ *v.t.* broadcast. **~ission** *n.f.* broadcast.
rétrécir /retresir/ *v.t.* narrow; (*vêtement*) take in. ● *v.i.* (*tissu*) shrink. **se ~,** (*rue*) narrow.
rétrib|uer /retribɥe/ *v.t.* pay. **~ution** *n.f.* payment.
rétroacti|f, ~ve /retrɔaktif, -v/ *a.* retrospective. **augmentation à effet ~f,** backdated pay rise.
rétrograd|e /retrɔgrad/ *a.* retrograde. **~er** *v.i.* (*reculer*) fall back, recede; *v.t.* demote.
rétrospectivement /retrɔspɛktivmɑ̃/ *adv.* in retrospect.
retrousser /rətruse/ *v.t.* pull up.
retrouvailles /rətruvɑj/ *n.f. pl.* reunion.
retrouver /rətruve/ *v.t.* find (again); (*rejoindre*) meet (again); (*forces, calme*) regain; (*se rappeler*) remember. **se ~** *v. pr.* find o.s. (back); (*se réunir*) meet (again). **s'y ~,** (*s'orienter, comprendre*) find one's way; (*rentrer dans ses frais*) break even.
rétroviseur /retrɔvizœr/ *n.m.* (*auto.*) (rear-view) mirror.
réunion /reynjɔ̃/ *n.f.* meeting; (*d'objets*) collection.
réunir /reynir/ *v.t.* gather, collect; (*rapprocher*) bring together; (*convoquer*) call together; (*raccorder*) join; (*qualités*) combine. **se ~** *v. pr.* meet.
réussi /reysi/ *a.* successful.
réussir /reysir/ *v.i.* succeed, be successful (**à faire,** in doing). **~ à qn.,** work well for s.o.; (*climat etc.*) agree with s.o. ● *v.t.* make a success of.
réussite /reysit/ *n.f.* success; (*jeu*) patience.
revaloir /rəvalwar/ *v.t.* **je vous revaudrai cela,** (*en mal*) I'll pay you back for this; (*en bien*) I'll repay you some day.
revaloriser /rəvalɔrize/ *v.t.* (*monnaie*) revalue; (*salaires*) raise.
revanche /rəvɑ̃ʃ/ *n.f.* revenge; (*sport*) return *ou* revenge match. **en ~,** on the other hand.
rêvasser /rɛvase/ *v.i.* day-dream.
rêve /rɛv/ *n.m.* dream. **faire un ~,** have a dream.
revêche /rəvɛʃ/ *a.* ill-tempered.

réveil /revɛj/ *n.m.* waking up, (*fig.*) awakening; (*pendule*) alarm-clock.

réveill|er /reveje/ *v.t.*, **se ~er** *v. pr.* wake (up); (*fig.*) awaken. **~é** *a.* awake. **~e-matin** *n.m. invar.* alarm-clock.

réveillon /revɛjɔ̃/ *n.m.* (*Noël*) Christmas Eve; (*nouvel an*) New Year's Eve. **~ner** /-jɔne/ *v.i.* celebrate the *réveillon.*

révél|er /revele/ *v.t.* reveal. **se ~er** *v. pr.* be revealed. **se ~er facile**/*etc.*, prove easy/*etc.* **~ateur, ~atrice** *a.* revealing. ● *n.m.* (*photo*) developer. **~ation** *n.f.* revelation.

revenant /rəvnɑ̃/ *n.m.* ghost.

revendi|quer /rəvɑ̃dike/ *v.t.* claim. **~catif, ~cative** *a.* (*mouvement etc.*) in support of one's claims. **~cation** *n.f.* claim; (*action*) claiming.

revend|re /rəvɑ̃dr/ *v.t.* sell (again). **~eur, ~euse** *n.m., f.* dealer.

revenir† /rəvnir/ *v.i.* (*aux. être*) come back, return (**à,** to). **~ à,** (*activité*) go back to; (*se résumer à*) come down to; (*échoir à*) fall to; (*coûter*) cost. **~ de,** (*maladie, surprise*) get over. **~ sur ses pas,** retrace one's steps. **faire ~,** (*culin.*) brown. **ça me revient,** it comes back to me.

revente /rəvɑ̃t/ *n.f.* resale.

revenu /rəvny/ *n.m.* income; (*d'un état*) revenue.

rêver /reve/ *v.t./i.* dream (**à** *ou* **de,** of).

réverbération /revɛrberɑsjɔ̃/ *n.f.* reflection, reverberation.

réverbère /revɛrbɛr/ *n.m.* street lamp.

révérenc|e /reverɑ̃s/ *n.f.* reverence; (*salut d'homme*) bow; (*salut de femme*) curtsy. **~ieux, ~ieuse** *a.* reverent.

révérend, ~e /reverɑ̃, -d/ *a. & n.m.* reverend.

rêverie /rɛvri/ *n.f.* day-dream; (*activité*) day-dreaming.

revers /rəvɛr/ *n.m.* reverse; (*de main*) back; (*d'étoffe*) wrong side; (*de veste*) lapel; (*tennis*) backhand; (*fig.*) set-back.

réversible /revɛrsibl/ *a.* reversible.

revêt|ir /rəvetir/ *v.t.* cover; (*habit*) put on; (*prendre, avoir*) assume. **~ement** /-vɛtmɑ̃/ *n.m.* covering; (*de route*) surface.

rêveu|r, ~se /rɛvœr, -øz/ *a.* dreamy. ● *n.m., f.* dreamer.

revigorer /rəvigɔre/ *v.t.* revive.

revirement /rəvirmɑ̃/ *n.m.* sudden change.

révis|er /revize/ *v.t.* revise; (*véhicule*) overhaul. **~ion** *n.f.* revision; overhaul.

revivre† /rəvivr/ *v.i.* live again. ● *v.t.* relive. **faire ~,** revive.

révocation /revɔkɑsjɔ̃/ *n.f.* repeal; (*d'un fonctionnaire*) dismissal.

revoir† /rəvwar/ *v.t.* see (again); (*réviser*) revise. **au ~,** goodbye.

révolte /revɔlt/ *n.f.* revolt.

révolt|er /revɔlte/ *v.t.*, **se ~er** *v. pr.* revolt. **~ant, ~ante** *a.* revolting. **~é, ~ée** *n.m., f.* rebel.

révolu /revɔly/ *a.* past.

révolution /revɔlysjɔ̃/ *n.f.* revolution. **~naire** /-jɔnɛr/ *a. & n.m./f.* revolutionary. **~ner** /- jɔne/ *v.t.* revolutionize.

revolver /revɔlvɛr/ *n.m.* revolver, gun.

révoquer /revɔke/ *v.t.* repeal; (*fonctionnaire*) dismiss.

revue /rəvy/ *n.f.* (*examen, défilé*) review; (*magazine*) magazine; (*spectacle*) variety show.

rez-de-chaussée /redʃose/ *n.m. invar.* ground floor; (*Amer.*) first floor.

RF *abrév.* (*République Française*) French Republic.

rhabiller (se) /(sə)rabije/ *v. pr.* get dressed (again), dress (again).

rhapsodie /rapsɔdi/ *n.f.* rhapsody.

rhétorique /retɔrik/ *n.f.* rhetoric. ● *a.* rhetorical.

rhinocéros /rinɔserɔs/ *n.m.* rhinoceros.

rhubarbe /rybarb/ *n.f.* rhubarb.

rhum /rɔm/ *n.m.* rum.

rhumatis|me /rymatism/ *n.m.* rheumatism. **~ant, ~ante** /-zɑ̃, -t/ *a.* rheumatic.

rhume /rym/ *n.m.* cold. **~ des foins,** hay fever.

ri /ri/ *voir* rire.

riant, ~e /rjɑ̃, -t/ *a.* cheerful.

ricaner /rikane/ *v.i.* snigger, giggle.

riche /riʃ/ *a.* rich (**en,** in). ● *n.m./f.* rich person. **~ment** *adv.* richly.

richesse /riʃɛs/ *n.f.* wealth; (*de sol, décor*) richness. **~s,** wealth.

ricoch|er /rikɔʃe/ *v.i.* rebound, ricochet. **~et** *n.m.* rebound, ricochet. **par ~er,** indirectly.

rictus /riktys/ *n.m.* grin, grimace.

rid|e /rid/ *n.f.* wrinkle; (*sur l'eau*) ripple. **~er** *v.t.* wrinkle; (*eau*) ripple.

rideau (*pl.* **~x**) /rido/ *n.m.* curtain; (*métallique*) shutter; (*fig.*) screen. **~ de fer,** (*pol.*) Iron Curtain.

ridicul|e /ridikyl/ *a.* ridiculous. ● *n.m.* absurdity. **le ~e,** ridicule. **~iser** *v.t.* ridicule.

rien /rjɛ̃/ *pron.* **(ne) ~,** nothing. ● *n.m.* trifle. **de ~!,** don't mention it! **~ d'autre/de plus,** nothing else/more. **~ du tout,** nothing at all. **~ que,** just, only. **trois fois ~,** next to nothing. **il n'y est pour ~,** he has nothing to do with it. **en un ~ de temps,** in next to no time. **~ à faire,** it's no good!

rieu|r, ~se /rijœr, rijøz/ *a.* merry.

rigid|e /riʒid/ *a.* rigid; (*muscle*) stiff. **~ité** *n.f.* rigidity; stiffness.

rigole /rigɔl/ *n.f.* channel.

rigol|er /rigɔle/ *v.i.* laugh; (*s'amuser*) have some fun; (*plaisanter*) joke. **~ade** *n.f.* fun.

rigolo, ~te /rigɔlo, -ɔt/ *a.* (*fam.*) funny. ● *n.m., f.* (*fam.*) joker.

rigoureu|x, ~se /rigurø, -z/ *a.* rigorous; (*hiver*) harsh. **~sement** *adv.* rigorously.

rigueur /rigœr/ *n.f.* rigour. **à la ~,** at a pinch. **être de ~,** be the rule. **tenir ~ à qn. de qch.,** hold sth. against s.o.

rim|e /rim/ *n.f.* rhyme. **~er** *v.i.* rhyme **(avec,** with). **cela ne ~e à rien,** it makes no sense.

rin|cer /rɛ̃se/ *v.t.* rinse. **~çage** *n.m.* rinse; (*action*) rinsing. **~ce-doigts** *n.m. invar.* finger-bowl.

ring /riŋ/ *n.m.* boxing ring.

ripost|e /ripɔst/ *n.f.* retort; (*mil.*) reprisal. **~er** *v.i.* retaliate; *v.t.* retort **(que,** that). **~er à,** (*attaque*) counter; (*insulte etc.*) reply to.

rire† /rir/ *v.i.* laugh **(de,** at); (*plaisanter*) joke; (*s'amuser*) have fun. **c'était pour ~,** it was a joke. ● *n.m.* laugh. **~s, le ~,** laughter.

risée /rize/ *n.f.* **la ~ de,** the laughing-stock of.

risible /rizibl/ *a.* laughable.

risqu|e /risk/ *n.m.* risk. **~é** *a.* risky; (*osé*) daring. **~er** *v.t.* risk. **~er de faire,** stand a good chance of doing. **se ~er à/dans,** venture to/into.

rissoler /risɔle/ *v.t./i.* brown. **(faire) ~,** brown.

ristourne /risturn/ *n.f.* discount.

rite /rit/ *n.m.* rite; (*habitude*) ritual.

rituel, ~le /ritɥɛl/ *a.* & *n.m.* ritual.

rivage /rivaʒ/ *n.m.* shore.

riv|al, ~ale (*m. pl.* **~aux**) /rival, -o/ *n.m., f.* rival. ● *a.* rival. **~aliser** *v.i.* compete **(avec,** with). **~alité** *n.f.* rivalry.

rive /riv/ *n.f.* (*de fleuve*) bank; (*de lac*) shore.

riv|er /rive/ *v.t.* rivet. **~er son clou à qn.,** shut s.o. up. **~et** *n.m.* rivet.

riverain, ~e /rivrɛ̃, -ɛn/ *a.* riverside. ● *n.m., f.* riverside resident; (*d'une rue*) resident.

rivière /rivjɛr/ *n.f.* river.

rixe /riks/ *n.f.* brawl.

riz /ri/ *n.m.* rice. **~ière** /rizjɛr/ *n.f.* paddy(-field), rice field.

robe /rɔb/ *n.f.* (*de femme*) dress; (*de juge*) robe; (*de cheval*) coat. **~ de chambre,** dressing-gown.

robinet /rɔbinɛ/ *n.m.* tap; (*Amer.*) faucet.

robot /rɔbo/ *n.m.* robot.

robuste /rɔbyst/ *a.* robust. **~sse** /-ɛs/ *n.f.* robustness.

roc /rɔk/ *n.m.* rock.

rocaill|e /rɔkaj/ *n.f.* rocky ground; (*de jardin*) rockery. **~eux, ~euse** *a.* (*terrain*) rocky.

roch|e /rɔʃ/ *n.f.* rock. **~eux, ~euse** *a.* rocky.

rocher /rɔʃe/ *n.m.* rock.

rock /rɔk/ *n.m.* (*mus.*) rock.

rod|er /rɔde/ *v.t.* (*auto.*) run in; (*auto., Amer.*) break in. **être ~é,** (*personne*) be broken in. **~age** *n.m.* running in; breaking in.

rôd|er /rode/ *v.i.* roam; (*suspect*) prowl. **~eur, ~euse** *n.m., f.* prowler.

rogne /rɔɲ/ *n.f.* (*fam.*) anger.

rogner /rɔɲe/ *v.t.* trim; (*réduire*) cut. **~ sur,** cut down on.

rognon /rɔɲɔ̃/ *n.m.* (*culin.*) kidney.

rognures /rɔɲyr/ *n.f. pl.* scraps.

roi /rwa/ *n.m.* king. **les Rois mages,** the Magi. **la fête des Rois,** Twelfth Night.

roitelet /rwatlɛ/ *n.m.* wren.

rôle /rol/ *n.m.* role, part.

romain, ~e /rɔmɛ̃, -ɛn/ *a.* & *n.m., f.* Roman. ● *n.f.* (*laitue*) cos.

roman /rɔmɑ̃/ *n.m.* novel; (*fig.*) story; (*genre*) fiction.

romance /rɔmɑ̃s/ *n.f.* sentimental ballad.

romanc|ier, ~ière /rɔmɑ̃sje, -jɛr/ *n.m., f.* novelist.

romanesque /rɔmanɛsk/ *a.* romantic; (*fantastique*) fantastic. **œuvres ~s,** novels, fiction.

romanichel, ~le /rɔmaniʃɛl/ *n.m., f.* gypsy.
romanti|que /rɔmɑ̃tik/ *a. & n.m./f.* romantic. **~sme** *n.m.* romanticism.
rompre† /rɔ̃pr/ *v.t./i.* break; (*relations*) break off; (*fiancés*) break it off. **se ~** *v. pr.* break.
rompu /rɔ̃py/ *a.* (*exténué*) exhausted.
ronces /rɔ̃s/ *n.f. pl.* brambles.
ronchonner /rɔ̃ʃɔne/ *v.i.* (*fam.*) grumble.
rond, ~e[1] /rɔ̃, rɔ̃d/ *a.* round; (*gras*) plump; (*ivre*: *fam.*) tight. ● *n.m.* (*cercle*) ring; (*tranche*) slice. **il n'a pas un ~,** (*fam.*) he hasn't got a penny. **en ~,** in a circle. **~ement** /rɔ̃dmɑ̃/ *adv.* briskly; (*franchement*) straight. **~eur** /rɔ̃dœr/ *n.f.* roundness; (*franchise*) frankness; (*embonpoint*) plumpness. **~-point** (*pl.* **~s-points**) *n.m.* roundabout; (*Amer.*) traffic circle.
ronde[2] /rɔ̃d/ *n.f.* round(s); (*de policier*) beat; (*mus.*) semibreve.
rondelet, ~te /rɔ̃dlɛ, -t/ *a.* chubby.
rondelle /rɔ̃dɛl/ *n.f.* (*techn.*) washer; (*tranche*) slice.
rondin /rɔ̃dɛ̃/ *n.m.* log.
ronfl|er /rɔ̃fle/ *v.i.* snore; (*moteur*) hum. **~ement(s)** *n.m.* (*pl.*) snoring; humming.
rong|er /rɔ̃ʒe/ *v.t.* gnaw (at); (*vers, acide*) eat into; (*personne*: *fig.*) consume. **se ~er les ongles,** bite one's nails. **~eur** *n.m.* rodent.
ronronn|er /rɔ̃rɔne/ *v.i.* purr. **~ement** *n.m.* purr(ing).
roquette /rɔkɛt/ *n.f.* rocket.
rosace /rɔzas/ *n.f.* (*d'église*) rose window.
rosaire /rozɛr/ *n.m.* rosary.
rosbif /rɔsbif/ *n.m.* roast beef.
rose /roz/ *n.f.* rose. ● *a.* pink; (*situation, teint*) rosy. ● *n.m.* pink.
rosé /roze/ *a.* pinkish; (*vin*) *rosé.* ● *n.m. rosé.*
roseau (*pl.* **~x**) /rozo/ *n.m.* reed.
rosée /roze/ *n.f.* dew.
roseraie /rozrɛ/ *n.f.* rose garden.
rosette /rozɛt/ *n.f.* rosette.
rosier /rozje/ *n.m.* rose-bush, rose tree.
rosse /rɔs/ *a.* (*fam.*) nasty.
rosser /rɔse/ *v.t.* thrash.
rossignol /rɔsiɲɔl/ *n.m.* nightingale.
rot /ro/ *n.m.* (*fam.*) burp.
rotati|f, ~ve /rɔtatif, -v/ *a.* rotary.
rotation /rɔtɑsjɔ̃/ *n.f.* rotation.
roter /rɔte/ *v.i.* (*fam.*) burp.
rotin /rɔtɛ̃/ *n.m.* (rattan) cane.
rôt|ir /rotir/ *v.t./i.*, **se ~ir** *v. pr.* roast. **~i** *n.m.* roasting meat; (*cuit*) roast. **~i de porc,** roast pork.
rôtisserie /rotisri/ *n.f.* grill-room.
rôtissoire /rotiswar/ *n.f.* (roasting) spit.
rotule /rɔtyl/ *n.f.* kneecap.
roturi|er, ère /rɔtyrje, -ɛr/ *n.m., f.* commoner.
rouage /rwaʒ/ *n.m.* (*techn.*) (working) part. **~s,** (*d'une organisation*: *fig.*) wheels.
roucouler /rukule/ *v.i.* coo.
roue /ru/ *n.f.* wheel. **~ (dentée),** cog(-wheel). **~ de secours,** spare wheel.
roué /rwe/ *a.* wily, calculating.
rouer /rwe/ *v.t.* **~ de coups,** thrash.
rouet /rwɛ/ *n.m.* spinning-wheel.
rouge /ruʒ/ *a.* red; (*fer*) red-hot. ● *n.m.* red; (*vin*) red wine; (*fard*) rouge. **~ (à lèvres),** lipstick. ● *n.m./f.* (*pol.*) red. **~-gorge** (*pl.* **~s-gorges**) *n.m.* robin.
rougeole /ruʒɔl/ *n.f.* measles.
rougeoyer /ruʒwaje/ *v.i.* glow (red).
rouget /ruʒɛ/ *n.m.* red mullet.
rougeur /ruʒœr/ *n.f.* redness; (*tache*) red blotch; (*gêne, honte*) red face.
rougir /ruʒir/ *v.t./i.* turn red; (*de honte*) blush.
rouill|e /ruj/ *n.f.* rust. **~é** *a.* rusty. **~er** *v.i.*, **se ~er** *v. pr.* get rusty, rust.
roulant, ~e /rulɑ̃, -t/ *a.* (*meuble*) on wheels; (*escalier*) moving.
rouleau (*pl.* **~x**) /rulo/ *n.m.* roll; (*outil, vague*) roller. **~ à pâtisserie,** rolling-pin. **~ compresseur,** steam-roller.
roulement /rulmɑ̃/ *n.m.* rotation; (*bruit*) rumble; (*succession de personnes*) turnover; (*de tambour*) roll. **~ à billes,** ball-bearing. **par ~,** in rotation.
rouler /rule/ *v.t./i.* roll; (*ficelle, manches*) roll up; (*duper*: *fam.*) cheat; (*véhicule, train*) go, travel; (*conducteur*) drive. **se ~ dans** *v. pr.* roll (over) in.
roulette /rulɛt/ *n.f.* (*de meuble*) castor; (*de dentiste*) drill; (*jeu*) roulette. **comme sur des ~s,** very smoothly.
roulis /ruli/ *n.m.* rolling.
roulotte /rulɔt/ *n.f.* caravan.
roumain, ~e /rumɛ̃, -ɛn/ *a. & n.m., f.* Romanian.
Roumanie /rumani/ *n.f.* Romania.
roupiller /rupije/ *v.i.* (*fam.*) sleep.

rouquin, ~e /rukɛ̃, -in/ *a.* (*fam.*) redhaired. ● *n.m., f.* (*fam.*) redhead.
rouspéter /ruspete/ *v.i.* (*fam.*) grumble, moan, complain.
rousse /rus/ *voir* roux.
roussir /rusir/ *v.t.* scorch. ● *v.i.* turn brown.
route /rut/ *n.f.* road; (*naut., aviat.*) route; (*direction*) way; (*voyage*) journey; (*chemin*: *fig.*) path. **en ~,** on the way. **en ~!,** let's go! **mettre en ~,** start. **~ nationale,** trunk road, main road. **se mettre en ~,** set out.
rout|ier, ~ière /rutje, -jɛr/ *a.* road. ● *n.m.* long-distance lorry driver *ou* truck driver (*Amer.*); (*restaurant*) roadside café.
routine /rutin/ *n.f.* routine.
rouvrir /ruvrir/ *v.t.*, **se ~ir** *v. pr.* reopen, open again.
rou|x, ~sse /ru, rus/ *a.* red, reddish-brown; (*personne*) red-haired. ● *n.m., f.* redhead.
roy|al (*m. pl.* **~aux**) /rwajal, jo/ *a.* royal; (*total*: *fam.*) thorough. **~alement** *adv.* royally.
royaume /rwajom/ *n.m.* kingdom. **R~-Uni** *n.m.* United Kingdom.
royauté /rwajote/ *n.f.* royalty.
ruade /ryad, rɥad/ *n.f.* kick.
ruban /rybɑ̃/ *n.m.* ribbon; (*de magnétophone*) tape; (*de chapeau*) band. **~ adhésif,** sticky tape.
rubéole /rybeɔl/ *n.f.* German measles.
rubis /rybi/ *n.m.* ruby; (*de montre*) jewel.
rubrique /rybrik/ *n.f.* heading; (*article*) column.
ruche /ryʃ/ *n.f.* beehive.
rude /ryd/ *a.* rough; (*pénible*) tough; (*grossier*) crude; (*fameux*: *fam.*) tremendous. **~ment** *adv.* (*frapper etc.*) hard; (*traiter*) harshly; (*très*: *fam.*) awfully.
rudiment|s /rydimɑ̃/ *n.m. pl.* rudiments. **~aire** /-tɛr/ *a.* rudimentary.
rudoyer /rydwaje/ *v.t.* treat harshly.
rue /ry/ *n.f.* street.
ruée /rɥe/ *n.f.* rush.
ruelle /rɥɛl/ *n.f.* alley.
ruer /rɥe/ *v.i.* (*cheval*) kick. **se ~ dans/vers,** rush into/towards. **se ~ sur,** pounce on.
rugby /rygbi/ *n.m.* Rugby.
rugby|man (*pl.* **~men**) /rygbiman, -mɛn/ *n.m.* Rugby player.
rug|ir /ryʒir/ *v.i.* roar. **~issement** *n.m.* roar.
rugueu|x, ~se /rygø, -z/ *a.* rough.
ruin|e /rɥin/ *n.f.* ruin. **en ~e(s),** in ruins. **~er** *v.t.* ruin.
ruineu|x, ~se /rɥinø, -z/ *a.* ruinous.
ruisseau (*pl.* **~x**) /rɥiso/ *n.m.* stream; (*rigole*) gutter.
ruisseler /rɥisle/ *v.i.* stream.
rumeur /rymœr/ *n.f.* (*nouvelle*) rumour; (*son*) murmur, hum; (*protestation*) rumblings.
ruminer /rymine/ *v.t./i.* (*herbe*) ruminate; (*méditer*) meditate.
rupture /ryptyr/ *n.f.* break; (*action*) breaking; (*de contrat*) breach; (*de pourparlers*) breakdown.
rur|al (*m. pl.* **~aux**) /ryral, -o/ *a.* rural.
rus|e /ryz/ *n.f.* cunning; (*perfidie*) trickery. **une ~e,** a trick, a ruse. **~é** *a.* cunning.
russe /rys/ *a.* & *n.m./f.* Russian. ● *n.m.* (*lang.*) Russian.
Russie /rysi/ *n.f.* Russia.
rustique /rystik/ *a.* rustic.
rustre /rystr/ *n.m.* lout, boor.
rutilant, ~e /rytilɑ̃, -t/ *a.* sparkling, gleaming.
rythm|e /ritm/ *n.m.* rhythm; (*vitesse*) rate; (*de la vie*) pace. **~é, ~ique** *adjs.* rhythmical.

S

s' /s/ *voir* se.
sa /sa/ *voir* son[1].
SA *abrév.* (*société anonyme*) PLC.
sabbat /saba/ *n.m.* sabbath. **~ique** *a.* **année ~ique,** sabbatical year.
sabl|e /sɑbl/ *n.m.* sand. **~es mouvants,** quicksands. **~er** *v.t.* sand. **~er le champagne,** drink champagne. **~eux, ~euse, ~onneux, ~onneuse** *adjs.* sandy.
sablier /sɑblije/ *n.m.* (*culin.*) eggtimer.
saborder /sabɔrde/ *v.t.* (*navire, projet*) scuttle.
sabot /sabo/ *n.m.* (*de cheval etc.*) hoof; (*chaussure*) clog; (*de frein*) shoe. **~ de Denver,** (wheel) clamp.
sabot|er /sabɔte/ *v.t.* sabotage; (*bâcler*) botch. **~age** *n.m.* sabotage; (*acte*) act of sabotage. **~eur, ~euse** *n.m., f.* saboteur.

sabre /sɑbr/ *n.m.* sabre.

sac /sak/ *n.m.* bag; (*grand, en toile*) sack. **mettre à ~,** (*maison*) ransack; (*ville*) sack. **~ à dos,** rucksack. **~ à main,** handbag. **~ de couchage,** sleeping-bag. **mettre dans le même ~,** lump together.

saccad|e /sakad/ *n.f.* jerk. **~é** *a.* jerky.

saccager /sakaʒe/ *v.t.* (*ville, pays*) sack; (*maison*) ransack; (*ravager*) wreck.

saccharine /sakarin/ *n.f.* saccharin.

sacerdoce /sasɛrdɔs/ *n.m.* priesthood; (*fig.*) vocation.

sachet /saʃɛ/ *n.m.* (small) bag; (*de médicament etc.*) sachet. **~ de thé,** tea-bag.

sacoche /sakɔʃ/ *n.f.* bag; (*d'élève*) satchel; (*de moto*) saddle-bag.

sacquer /sake/ *v.t.* (*fam.*) sack. **je ne peux pas le ~,** I can't stand him.

sacr|e /sakr/ *n.m.* (*de roi*) coronation; (*d'évêque*) consecration. **~er** *v.t.* crown; consecrate.

sacré /sakre/ *a.* sacred; (*maudit: fam.*) damned.

sacrement /sakrəmɑ̃/ *n.m.* sacrament.

sacrifice /sakrifis/ *n.m.* sacrifice.

sacrifier /sakrifje/ *v.t.* sacrifice. **~ à,** conform to. **se ~** *v. pr.* sacrifice o.s.

sacrilège /sakrilɛʒ/ *n.m.* sacrilege. ● *a.* sacrilegious.

sacristain /sakristɛ̃/ *n.m.* sexton.

sacristie /sakristi/ *n.f.* (*protestante*) vestry; (*catholique*) sacristy.

sacro-saint, ~e /sakrosɛ̃, -t/ *a.* sacrosanct.

sadi|que /sadik/ *a.* sadistic. ● *n.m./f.* sadist. **~sme** *n.m.* sadism.

safari /safari/ *n.m.* safari.

sagace /sagas/ *a.* shrewd.

sage /saʒ/ *a.* wise; (*docile*) good. ● *n.m.* wise man. **~-femme** (*pl.* **~s-femmes**) *n.f.* midwife. **~ment** *adv.* wisely; (*docilement*) quietly. **~sse** /-ɛs/ *n.f.* wisdom.

Sagittaire /saʒitɛr/ *n.m.* **le ~,** Sagittarius.

Sahara /saara/ *n.m.* **le ~,** the Sahara (desert).

saignant, ~e /sɛɲɑ̃, -t/ *a.* (*culin.*) rare.

saign|er /seɲe/ *v.t./i.* bleed. **~er du nez,** have a nosebleed. **~ée** *n.f.* bleeding. **~ement** *n.m.* bleeding. **~ement de nez,** nosebleed.

saill|ie /saji/ *n.f.* projection. **faire ~ie,** project. **~ant, ~ante** *a.* projecting; (*remarquable*) salient.

sain, ~e /sɛ̃, sɛn/ *a.* healthy; (*moralement*) sane. **~ et sauf,** safe and sound. **~ement** /sɛnmɑ̃/ *adv.* healthily; (*juger*) sanely.

saindoux /sɛ̃du/ *n.m.* lard.

saint, ~e /sɛ̃, sɛ̃t/ *a.* holy; (*bon, juste*) saintly. ● *n.m., f.* saint. **S~e-Esprit** *n.m.* Holy Spirit. **S~-Siège** *n.m.* Holy See. **S~-Sylvestre** *n.f.* New Year's Eve. **S~e Vierge,** Blessed Virgin.

sainteté /sɛ̃tte/ *n.f.* holiness; (*d'un lieu*) sanctity.

sais /sɛ/ *voir* savoir.

saisie /sezi/ *n.f.* (*jurid.*) seizure; (*comput.*) keyboarding. **~ de données,** data capture.

sais|ir /sezir/ *v.t.* grab (hold of), seize; (*occasion, biens*) seize; (*comprendre*) grasp; (*frapper*) strike; (*comput.*) keyboard, capture. **~i de,** (*peur*) stricken by, overcome by. **se ~ir de,** seize. **~issant, ~issante** *a.* (*spectacle*) gripping.

saison /sɛzɔ̃/ *n.f.* season. **la morte ~,** the off season. **~nier, ~nière** /-ɔnje, -jɛr/ *a.* seasonal.

sait /sɛ/ *voir* savoir.

salad|e /salad/ *n.f.* salad; (*laitue*) lettuce; (*désordre: fam.*) mess. **~ier** *n.m.* salad bowl.

salaire /salɛr/ *n.m.* wages, salary.

salami /salami/ *n.m.* salami.

salarié, ~e /salarje/ *a.* wage-earning. ● *n.m., f.* wage-earner.

salaud /salo/ *n.m.* (*argot*) bastard.

sale /sal/ *a.* dirty, filthy; (*mauvais*) nasty.

sal|er /sale/ *v.t.* salt. **~é** *a.* (*goût*) salty; (*plat*) salted; (*viande, poisson*) salt; (*grivois: fam.*) spicy; (*excessif: fam.*) steep.

saleté /salte/ *n.f.* dirtiness; (*crasse*) dirt; (*action*) dirty trick; (*obscénité*) obscenity. **~(s),** (*camelote*) rubbish. **~s,** (*détritus*) mess.

salière /saljɛr/ *n.f.* salt-cellar.

salin, ~e /salɛ̃, -in/ *a.* saline.

sal|ir /salir/ *v.t.* (make) dirty; (*réputation*) tarnish. **se ~ir** *v. pr.* get dirty. **~issant, ~issante** *a.* dirty; (*étoffe*) easily dirtied.

salive /saliv/ *n.f.* saliva.

salle /sal/ *n.f.* room; (*grande, publique*) hall; (*d'hôpital*) ward; (*théâtre, cinéma*) auditorium. **~ à manger,**

dining-room. **~ d'attente,** waiting-room. **~ de bains,** bathroom. **~ de séjour,** living-room. **~ de classe,** classroom. **~ d'embarquement,** departure lounge. **~ d'opération,** operating theatre. **~ des ventes,** saleroom.

salon /salɔ̃/ *n.m.* lounge; (*de coiffure, beauté*) salon; (*exposition*) show. **~ de thé,** tea-room.

salope /salɔp/ *n.f.* (*argot*) bitch.

saloperie /salɔpri/ *n.f.* (*fam.*) (*action*) dirty trick; (*chose de mauvaise qualité*) rubbish.

salopette /salɔpɛt/ *n.f.* dungarees; (*d'ouvrier*) overalls.

salsifis /salsifi/ *n.m.* salsify.

saltimbanque /saltɛ̃bɑ̃k/ *n.m./f.* (street *ou* fairground) acrobat.

salubre /salybr/ *a.* healthy.

saluer /salɥe/ *v.t.* greet; (*en partant*) take one's leave of; (*de la tête*) nod to; (*de la main*) wave to; (*mil.*) salute.

salut /saly/ *n.m.* greeting; (*de la tête*) nod; (*de la main*) wave; (*mil.*) salute; (*sauvegarde, rachat*) salvation. ● *int.* (*bonjour: fam.*) hallo; (*au revoir: fam.*) bye-bye.

salutaire /salytɛr/ *a.* salutary.

salutation /salytɑsjɔ̃/ *n.f.* greeting. **veuillez agréer, Monsieur, mes ~s distingués,** yours faithfully.

salve /salv/ *n.f.* salvo.

samedi /samdi/ *n.m.* Saturday.

sanatorium /sanatɔrjɔm/ *n.m.* sanatorium.

sanctifier /sɑ̃ktifje/ *v.t.* sanctify.

sanction /sɑ̃ksjɔ̃/ *n.f.* sanction. **~ner** /-jɔne/ *v.t.* sanction; (*punir*) punish.

sanctuaire /sɑ̃ktɥɛr/ *n.m.* sanctuary.

sandale /sɑ̃dal/ *n.f.* sandal.

sandwich /sɑ̃dwitʃ/ *n.m.* sandwich.

sang /sɑ̃/ *n.m.* blood. **~-froid** *n.m. invar.* calm, self-control. **se faire du mauvais ~** *ou* **un ~ d'encre** be worried stiff.

sanglant, ~e /sɑ̃glɑ̃, -t/ *a.* bloody.

sangl|e /sɑ̃gl/ *n.f.* strap. **~er** *v.t.* strap.

sanglier /sɑ̃glije/ *n.m.* wild boar.

sanglot /sɑ̃glo/ *n.m.* sob. **~er** /-ɔte/ *v.i.* sob.

sangsue /sɑ̃sy/ *n.f.* leech.

sanguin, ~e /sɑ̃gɛ̃, -in/ *a.* (*groupe etc.*) blood; (*caractère*) fiery.

sanguinaire /sɑ̃ginɛr/ *a.* bloodthirsty.

sanitaire /sanitɛr/ *a.* health; (*conditions*) sanitary; (*appareils, installations*) bathroom, sanitary. **~s** *n.m. pl.* bathroom.

sans /sɑ̃/ *prép.* without. **~ que vous le sachiez,** without your knowing. **~-abri** /sɑ̃zabri/ *n.m./f. invar.* homeless person. **~ ça, ~ quoi,** otherwise. **~ arrêt,** nonstop. **~ encombre/faute/ tarder,** without incident/fail/delay. **~ fin/goût/ limite,** endless/tasteless/limitless. **~-gêne** *a. invar.* inconsiderate, thoughtless; *n.m. invar.* thoughtlessness. **~ importance/pareil/ précédent/travail,** unimportant/ unparalleled/unprecedented/ unemployed. **~ plus,** but no more than that, but nothing more.

santé /sɑ̃te/ *n.f.* health. **à ta** *ou* **votre santé,** cheers!

saoul, ~e /su, sul/ *voir* soûl.

saper /sape/ *v.t.* undermine.

sapeur /sapœr/ *n.m.* (*mil.*) sapper. **~-pompier** (*pl.* **~s-pompiers**) *n.m.* fireman.

saphir /safir/ *n.m.* sapphire.

sapin /sapɛ̃/ *n.m.* fir(-tree). **~ de Noël,** Christmas tree.

sarbacane /sarbakan/ *n.f.* (*jouet*) pea-shooter.

sarcas|me /sarkasm/ *n.m.* sarcasm. **~tique** *a.* sarcastic.

sarcler /sarkle/ *v.t.* weed.

sardine /sardin/ *n.f.* sardine.

sardonique /sardɔnik/ *a.* sardonic.

sarment /sarmɑ̃/ *n.m.* vine shoot.

sas /sɑs/ *n.m.* (*naut., aviat.*) airlock.

satané /satane/ *a.* (*fam.*) blasted.

satanique /satanik/ *a.* satanic.

satellite /satelit/ *n.m.* satellite.

satin /satɛ̃/ *n.m.* satin.

satir|e /satir/ *n.f.* satire. **~ique** *a.* satirical.

satisfaction /satisfaksjɔ̃/ *n.f.* satisfaction.

satis|faire† /satisfɛr/ *v.t.* satisfy. ● *v.i.* **~faire à,** satisfy. **~faisant, ~faisante** *a.* (*acceptable*) satisfactory. **~fait, ~faite** *a.* satisfied (**de,** with).

satur|er /satyre/ *v.t.* saturate. **~ation** *n.f.* saturation.

sauc|e /sos/ *n.f.* sauce; (*jus de viande*) gravy. **~er** *v.t.* (*plat*) wipe. **se faire ~er** (*fam.*) get soaked. **~e tartare,** tartar sauce. **~ière** *n.f.* sauce-boat.

saucisse /sosis/ *n.f.* sausage.

saucisson /sosisɔ̃/ *n.m.* (slicing) sausage.

sauf[1] /sof/ *prép.* except. **~ erreur/imprévu,** barring error/the unforeseen. **~ avis contraire,** unless you hear otherwise.

sau|f[2], **~ve** /sof, sov/ *a.* safe, unharmed. **~f-conduit** *n.m.* safe conduct.

sauge /soʒ/ *n.f.* (*culin.*) sage.

saugrenu /sogrəny/ *a.* preposterous, ludicrous.

saule /sol/ *n.m.* willow. **~ pleureur,** weeping willow.

saumon /somɔ̃/ *n.m.* salmon. ● *a. invar.* salmon-pink.

saumure /somyr/ *n.f.* brine.

sauna /sona/ *n.m.* sauna.

saupoudrer /sopudre/ *v.t.* sprinkle (**de,** with).

saut /so/ *n.m.* jump, leap. **faire un ~ chez qn.,** pop round to s.o.'s (place). **le ~,** (*sport*) jumping. **~ en hauteur/longueur,** high/long jump. **~ périlleux,** somersault. **au ~ du lit,** on getting up.

sauté /sote/ *a.* & *n.m.* (*culin.*) sauté.

saut|er /sote/ *v.i.* jump, leap; (*exploser*) blow up; (*fusible*) blow; (*se détacher*) come off. ● *v.t.* jump (over); (*page, classe*) skip. **faire ~er,** (*détruire*) blow up; (*fusible*) blow; (*casser*) break; (*culin.*) sauté; (*renvoyer: fam.*) kick out. **~er à la corde,** skip. **~er aux yeux,** be obvious. **~e-mouton** *n.m.* leapfrog. **~er au cou de qn.,** fling one's arms round s.o. **~er sur une occasion,** jump at an opportunity.

sauterelle /sotrɛl/ *n.f.* grasshopper.

sautiller /sotije/ *v.i.* hop.

sauvage /sovaʒ/ *a.* wild; (*primitif, cruel*) savage; (*farouche*) unsociable; (*illégal*) unauthorized. ● *n.m./f.* unsociable person; (*brute*) savage. **~rie** *n.f.* savagery.

sauve /sov/ *voir* sauf[2].

sauvegard|e /sovgard/ *n.f.* safeguard; (*comput.*) backup. **~er** *v.t.* safeguard; (*comput.*) save.

sauv|er /sove/ *v.t.* save; (*d'un danger*) rescue, save; (*matériel*) salvage. **se ~er** *v. pr.* (*fuir*) run away; (*partir: fam.*) be off. **~e-qui-peut** *n.m. invar.* stampede. **~etage** *n.m.* rescue; salvage. **~eteur** *n.m.* rescuer. **~eur** *n.m.* saviour.

sauvette (à la) /(ala)sovɛt/ *adv.* hastily; (*vendre*) illicitly.

savamment /savamɑ̃/ *adv.* learnedly; (*avec habileté*) skilfully.

savan|t, ~e /savɑ̃, -t/ *a.* learned; (*habile*) skilful. ● *n.m.* scientist.

saveur /savœr/ *n.f.* flavour; (*fig.*) savour.

savoir† /savwar/ *v.t.* know; (*apprendre*) hear. **elle sait conduire/nager,** she can drive/swim. ● *n.m.* learning. **à ~,** namely. **faire ~ à qn. que,** inform s.o. that. **je ne saurais pas,** I could not, I cannot. **(pas) que je sache,** (not) as far as I know.

savon /savɔ̃/ *n.m.* soap. **passer un ~ à qn.,** (*fam.*) give s.o. a dressing down. **~ner** /-ɔne/ *v.t.* soap. **~nette** /-ɔnɛt/ *n.f.* bar of soap. **~neux, ~neuse** /-ɔnø, -z/ *a.* soapy.

savour|er /savure/ *v.t.* savour. **~eux, ~euse** *a.* tasty; (*fig.*) spicy.

saxo(phone) /saksɔ(fɔn)/ *n.m.* sax(ophone).

scabreu|x, ~se /skabrø, -z/ *a.* risky; (*indécent*) obscene.

scandal|e /skɑ̃dal/ *n.m.* scandal; (*tapage*) uproar; (*en public*) noisy scene. **faire ~e,** shock people. **faire un ~e,** make a scene. **~eux, ~euse** *a.* scandalous. **~iser** *v.t.* scandalize, shock.

scander /skɑ̃de/ *v.t.* (*vers*) scan; (*slogan*) chant.

scandinave /skɑ̃dinav/ *a.* & *n.m./f.* Scandinavian.

Scandinavie /skɑ̃dinavi/ *n.f.* Scandinavia.

scarabée /skarabe/ *n.m.* beetle.

scarlatine /skarlatin/ *n.f.* scarlet fever.

scarole /skarɔl/ *n.f.* endive.

sceau (*pl.* **~x**) /so/ *n.m.* seal.

scélérat /selera/ *n.m.* scoundrel.

scell|er /sele/ *v.t.* seal; (*fixer*) cement. **~és** *n.m. pl.* seals.

scénario /senarjo/ *n.m.* scenario.

scène /sɛn/ *n.f.* scene; (*estrade, art dramatique*) stage. **mettre en ~,** (*pièce*) stage. **~ de ménage,** domestic scene.

scepti|que /sɛptik/ *a.* sceptical. ● *n.m./f.* sceptic. **~cisme** *n.m.* scepticism.

sceptre /sɛptr/ *n.m.* sceptre.

schéma /ʃema/ *n.m.* diagram. **~tique** *a.* diagrammatic; (*sommaire*) sketchy.

schisme /ʃism/ *n.m.* schism.

schizophrène /skizɔfrɛn/ *a.* & *n.m./f.* schizophrenic.

sciatique /sjatik/ *n.f.* sciatica.
scie /si/ *n.f.* saw.
sciemment /sjamɑ̃/ *adv.* knowingly.
scien|ce /sjɑ̃s/ *n.f.* science; (*savoir*) knowledge. **~ce-fiction** *n.f.* science fiction. **~tifique** *a.* scientific; *n.m./f.* scientist.
scier /sje/ *v.t.* saw.
scinder /sɛ̃de/ *v.t.*, **se ~** *v. pr.* split.
scintill|er /sɛ̃tije/ *v.i.* glitter; (*étoile*) twinkle. **~ement** *n.m.* glittering; twinkling.
scission /sisjɔ̃/ *n.f.* split.
sciure /sjyr/ *n.f.* sawdust.
sclérose /skleroz/ *n.f.* sclerosis. **~ en plaques,** multiple sclerosis.
scol|aire /skɔlɛr/ *a.* school. **~arisation** *n.f.*, **~arité** *n.f.* schooling. **~arisé** *a.* provided with schooling.
scorbut /skɔrbyt/ *n.m.* scurvy.
score /skɔr/ *n.m.* score.
scories /skɔri/ *n.f. pl.* slag.
scorpion /skɔrpjɔ̃/ *n.m.* scorpion. **le S~,** Scorpio.
scotch [1] /skɔtʃ/ *n.m.* (*boisson*) Scotch (whisky).
scotch [2] /skɔtʃ/ *n.m.* (P.) Sellotape (P.); (*Amer.*) Scotch (tape) (P.).
scout, ~e /skut/ *n.m. & a.* scout.
script /skript/ *n.m.* (*cinéma*) script; (*écriture*) printing. **~-girl,** continuity girl.
scrupul|e /skrypyl/ *n.m.* scruple. **~eusement** *adv.* scrupulously. **~eux, ~euse** *a.* scrupulous.
scruter /skryte/ *v.t.* examine, scrutinize.
scrutin /skrytɛ̃/ *n.m.* (*vote*) ballot; (*opération électorale*) poll.
sculpt|er /skylte/ *v.t.* sculpture; (*bois*) carve (**dans,** out of). **~eur** *n.m.* sculptor. **~ure** *n.f.* sculpture.
se, s'* /sə, s/ *pron.* himself; (*femelle*) herself; (*indéfini*) oneself; (*non humain*) itself; (*pl.*) themselves; (*réciproque*) each other, one another. **se parler,** (*à soi-même*) talk to o.s.; (*réciproque*) talk to each other. **se faire,** (*passif*) be done. **se laver les mains,** (*possessif*) wash one's hands.
séance /seɑ̃s/ *n.f.* session; (*cinéma, théâtre*) show. **~ de pose,** sitting. **~ tenante,** forthwith.
seau (*pl.* **~x**) /so/ *n.m.* bucket, pail.
sec, sèche /sɛk, sɛʃ/ *a.* dry; (*fruits*) dried; (*coup, bruit*) sharp; (*cœur*) hard; (*whisky*) neat; (*Amer.*) straight. ● *n.m.* **à ~,** (*sans eau*) dry; (*sans argent*) broke. **au ~,** in a dry place. ● *n.f.* (*fam.*) (*cigarette*) fag.
sécateur /sekatœr/ *n.m.* (*pour les haies*) shears; (*petit*) secateurs.
sécession /sesesjɔ̃/ *n.f.* secession. **faire ~,** secede.
sèche /sɛʃ/ *voir* **sec. ~ment** *adv.* drily.
sèche-cheveux /sɛʃʃəvø/ *n.m. invar.* hair-drier.
sécher /seʃe/ *v.t./i.* dry; (*cours: fam.*) skip; (*ne pas savoir: fam.*) be stumped. **se ~** *v. pr.* dry o.s.
sécheresse /seʃrɛs/ *n.f.* dryness; (*temps sec*) drought.
séchoir /seʃwar/ *n.m.* drier.
second, ~e [1] /sgɔ̃, -d/ *a. & n.m., f.* second. ● *n.m.* (*adjoint*) second in command; (*étage*) second floor, (*Amer.*) third floor. ● *n.f.* (*transport*) second class.
secondaire /sgɔ̃dɛr/ *a.* secondary.
seconde [2] /sgɔ̃d/ *n.f.* (*instant*) second.
seconder /sgɔ̃de/ *v.t.* assist.
secouer /skwe/ *v.t.* shake; (*poussière, torpeur*) shake off. **se ~,** (*fam.*) (*se dépêcher*) get a move on; (*réagir*) shake o.s. up.
secour|ir /skurir/ *v.t.* assist, help. **~able** *a.* helpful. **~iste** *n.m./f.* first-aid worker.
secours /skur/ *n.m.* assistance, help. ● *n.m. pl.* (*méd.*) first aid. **au ~!,** help! **de ~,** emergency; (*équipe, opération*) rescue.
secousse /skus/ *n.f.* jolt, jerk; (*électrique*) shock; (*séisme*) tremor.
secr|et, ~ète /səkrɛ, t/ *a.* secret. ● *n.m.* secret; (*discrétion*) secrecy. **le ~et professionnel,** professional secrecy. **~et de Polichinelle,** open secret. **en ~et,** in secret, secretly.
secrétaire /skretɛr/ *n.m./f.* secretary. **~ de direction,** executive secretary. ● *n.m.* (*meuble*) writing-desk. **~ d'État,** junior minister.
secrétariat /skretarja/ *n.m.* secretarial work; (*bureau*) secretary's office; (*d'un organisme*) secretariat.
sécrét|er /sekrete/ *v.t.* secrete. **~ion** /-sjɔ̃/ *n.f.* secretion.
sect|e /sɛkt/ *n.f.* sect. **~aire** *a.* sectarian.
secteur /sɛktœr/ *n.m.* area; (*mil., comm.*) sector; (*circuit: électr.*) mains. **~ primaire/secondaire/ter-**

tiaire, primary/secondary/tertiary industry.

section /sɛksjɔ̃/ *n.f.* section; (*transports publics*) fare stage; (*mil.*) platoon. **~ner** /-jɔne/ *v.t.* sever.

sécu /seky/ *n.f.* (*fam.*) **la ~,** the social security services.

séculaire /sekylɛr/ *a.* age-old.

sécul|ier, ~ière /sekylje, -jɛr/ *a.* secular.

sécuriser /sekyrize/ *v.t.* reassure.

sécurité /sekyrite/ *n.f.* security; (*absence de danger*) safety. **en ~,** safe, secure. **S~ sociale,** social services, social security services.

sédatif /sedatif/ *n.m.* sedative.

sédentaire /sedɑ̃tɛr/ *a.* sedentary.

sédiment /sedimɑ̃/ *n.m.* sediment.

séditieu|x, ~se /sedisjø, -z/ *a.* seditious.

sédition /sedisjɔ̃/ *n.f.* sedition.

séd|uire† /sedɥir/ *v.t.* charm; (*plaire à*) appeal to; (*abuser de*) seduce. **~ucteur, ~uctrice** *a.* seductive; *n.m., f.* seducer. **~uction** *n.f.* seduction; (*charme*) charm. **~uisant, ~uisante** *a.* attractive.

segment /sɛgmɑ̃/ *n.m.* segment.

ségrégation /segregɑsjɔ̃/ *n.f.* segregation.

seigle /sɛgl/ *n.m.* rye.

seigneur /sɛɲœr/ *n.m.* lord. **le S~,** the Lord.

sein /sɛ̃/ *n.m.* breast; (*fig.*) bosom. **au ~ de,** in the midst of.

Seine /sɛn/ *n.f.* Seine.

séisme /seism/ *n.m.* earthquake.

seiz|e /sɛz/ *a.* & *n.m.* sixteen. **~ième** *a.* & *n.m./f.* sixteenth.

séjour /seʒur/ *n.m.* stay; (*pièce*) living-room. **~ner** *v.i.* stay.

sel /sɛl/ *n.m.* salt; (*piquant*) spice.

sélect /selɛkt/ *a.* select.

sélecti|f, ~ve /selɛktif, -v/ *a.* selective.

sélection /selɛksjɔ̃/ *n.f.* selection. **~ner** /-jɔne/ *v.t.* select.

self(-service) /sɛlf(sɛrvis)/ *n.m.* self-service.

selle /sɛl/ *n.f.* saddle.

seller /sele/ *v.t.* saddle.

sellette /sɛlɛt/ *n.f.* **sur la ~,** (*question*) under examination; (*personne*) in the hot seat.

selon /slɔ̃/ *prép.* according to (**que,** whether).

semaine /smɛn/ *n.f.* week. **en ~,** in the week.

sémantique /semɑ̃tik/ *a.* semantic. ● *n.f.* semantics.

sémaphore /semafɔr/ *n.m.* (*appareil*) semaphore.

semblable /sɑ̃blabl/ *a.* similar (**à,** to). **de ~s propos**/*etc.*, (*tels*) such remarks/*etc.* ● *n.m.* fellow (creature).

semblant /sɑ̃blɑ̃/ *n.m.* **faire ~ de,** pretend to. **un ~ de,** a semblance of.

sembl|er /sɑ̃ble/ *v.i.* seem (**à,** to; **que,** that). **il me ~e que,** it seems to me that.

semelle /smɛl/ *n.f.* sole.

semence /smɑ̃s/ *n.f.* seed; (*clou*) tack. **~s,** (*graines*) seed.

sem|er /sme/ *v.t.* sow; (*jeter, parsemer*) strew; (*répandre*) spread; (*personne*: *fam.*) lose. **~eur, ~euse** *n.m., f.* sower.

semestr|e /smɛstr/ *n.m.* half-year; (*univ.*) semester. **~iel, ~ielle** *a.* half-yearly.

semi- /səmi/ *préf.* semi-.

séminaire /seminɛr/ *n.m.* (*relig.*) seminary; (*univ.*) seminar.

semi-remorque /səmirəmɔrk/ *n.m.* articulated lorry; (*Amer.*) semi(-trailer).

semis /smi/ *n.m.* (*terrain*) seed-bed; (*plant*) seedling.

sémit|e /semit/ *a.* Semitic. ● *n.m./f.* Semite. **~ique** *a.* Semitic.

semonce /səmɔ̃s/ *n.f.* reprimand. **coup de ~,** warning shot.

semoule /smul/ *n.f.* semolina.

sénat /sena/ *n.m.* senate. **~eur** /-tœr/ *n.m.* senator.

sénil|e /senil/ *a.* senile. **~ité** *n.f.* senility.

sens /sɑ̃s/ *n.m.* sense; (*signification*) meaning, sense; (*direction*) direction. **à mon ~,** to my mind. **à ~ unique,** (*rue etc.*) one-way. **ça n'a pas de ~,** that does not make sense. **~ commun,** common sense. **~ giratoire,** roundabout; (*Amer.*) rotary. **~ interdit,** no entry; (*rue*) one-way street. **dans le ~ des aiguilles d'une montre,** clockwise. **~ dessus dessous,** upside down.

sensation /sɑ̃sɑsjɔ̃/ *n.f.* feeling, sensation. **faire ~,** create a sensation. **~nel, ~nelle** /-jɔnɛl/ *a.* sensational.

sensé /sɑ̃se/ *a.* sensible.

sensibiliser /sɑ̃sibilize/ *v.t.* **~ à,** make sensitive to.

sensib|le /sɑ̃sibl/ *a.* sensitive (**à,** to); (*appréciable*) noticeable. **~ilité** *n.f.*

sensitivity. **~lement** *adv.* noticeably; (*à peu près*) more or less.
sensoriel, ~le /sɑ̃sɔrjɛl/ *a.* sensory.
sens|uel, ~uelle /sɑ̃sɥɛl/ *a.* sensuous; (*sexuel*) sensual. **~ualité** *n.f.* sensuousness; sensuality.
sentenc|e /sɑ̃tɑ̃s/ *n.f.* sentence. **~ieux, ~ieuse** *a.* sententious.
senteur /sɑ̃tœr/ *n.f.* scent.
sentier /sɑ̃tje/ *n.m.* path.
sentiment /sɑ̃timɑ̃/ *n.m.* feeling. **avoir le ~ de,** be aware of.
sentiment|al (*m. pl.* **~aux**) /sɑ̃timɑ̃tal, -o/ *a.* sentimental. **~alité** *n.f.* sentimentality.
sentinelle /sɑ̃tinɛl/ *n.f.* sentry.
sentir† /sɑ̃tir/ *v.t.* feel; (*odeur*) smell; (*goût*) taste; (*pressentir*) sense. **~ la lavande**/*etc.*, smell of lavender/*etc.* ● *v.i.* smell. **je ne peux pas le ~,** (*fam.*) I can't stand him. **se ~ fier/mieux**/*etc.*, feel proud/better/*etc.*
séparatiste /separatist/ *a.* & *n.m./f.* separatist.
séparé /separe/ *a.* separate; (*conjoints*) separated. **~ment** *adv.* separately.
sépar|er /separe/ *v.t.* separate; (*en deux*) split. **se ~er** *v. pr.* separate, part (**de,** from); (*se détacher*) split. **se ~er de,** (*se défaire de*) part with. **~ation** *n.f.* separation.
sept /sɛt/ *a.* & *n.m.* seven.
septante /sɛptɑ̃t/ *a.* & *n.m.* (*en Belgique, Suisse*) seventy.
septembre /sɛptɑ̃br/ *n.m.* September.
septentrion|al (*m. pl.* **~aux**) /sɛptɑ̃trijɔnal, -o/ *a.* northern.
septième /sɛtjɛm/ *a.* & *n.m./f.* seventh.
sépulcre /sepylkr/ *n.m.* (*relig.*) sepulchre.
sépulture /sepyltyr/ *n.f.* burial; (*lieu*) burial place.
séquelles /sekɛl/ *n.f. pl.* (*maladie*) after-effects; (*fig.*) aftermath.
séquence /sekɑ̃s/ *n.f.* sequence.
séquestrer /sekɛstre/ *v.t.* confine (illegally); (*biens*) impound.
sera, serait /sra, srɛ/ *voir* être.
serein, ~e /sərɛ̃, -ɛn/ *a.* serene.
sérénade /serenad/ *n.f.* serenade.
sérénité /serenite/ *n.f.* serenity.
sergent /sɛrʒɑ̃/ *n.m.* sergeant.
série /seri/ *n.f.* series; (*d'objets*) set. **de ~,** (*véhicule etc.*) standard. **fabrication** *ou* **production en ~,** mass production.
sérieu|x, ~se /serjø, -z/ *a.* serious; (*digne de foi*) reliable; (*chances, raison*) good. ● *n.m.* seriousness. **garder/perdre son ~x,** keep/be unable to keep a straight face. **prendre au ~x,** take seriously. **~sement** *adv.* seriously.
serin /srɛ̃/ *n.m.* canary.
seringue /srɛ̃g/ *n.f.* syringe.
serment /sɛrmɑ̃/ *n.m.* oath; (*promesse*) pledge.
sermon /sɛrmɔ̃/ *n.m.* sermon. **~ner** /ɔne/ *v.t.* (*fam.*) lecture.
séropositi|f, ~ve /serɔpɔsitif, -v/ *a.* HIV-positive.
serpe /sɛrp/ *n.f.* bill(hook).
serpent /sɛrpɑ̃/ *n.m.* snake. **~ à sonnettes,** rattlesnake.
serpenter /sɛrpɑ̃te/ *v.i.* meander.
serpentin /sɛrpɑ̃tɛ̃/ *n.m.* streamer.
serpillière /sɛrpijɛr/ *n.f.* floor-cloth.
serre[1] /sɛr/ *n.f.* (*local*) greenhouse.
serre[2] /sɛr/ *n.f.* (*griffe*) claw.
serré /sere/ *a.* (*habit, nœud, programme*) tight; (*personnes*) packed, crowded; (*lutte, mailles*) close; (*cœur*) heavy.
serrer /sere/ *v.t.* (*saisir*) grip; (*presser*) squeeze; (*vis, corde, ceinture*) tighten; (*poing, dents*) clench; (*pieds*) pinch. **~ qn. dans ses bras,** hug. **~ les rangs,** close ranks. **~ qn.,** (*vêtement*) be tight on s.o. ● *v.i.* **~ à droite,** keep over to the right. **se ~** *v. pr.* (*se rapprocher*) squeeze (up) (**contre,** against). **~ de près,** follow closely. **~ la main à,** shake hands with.
serrur|e /seryr/ *n.f.* lock. **~ier** *n.m.* locksmith.
sertir /sɛrtir/ *v.t.* (*bijou*) set.
sérum /serɔm/ *n.m.* serum.
servante /sɛrvɑ̃t/ *n.f.* (maid)servant.
serveu|r, ~se /sɛrvœr, -øz/ *n.m., f.* waiter, waitress; (*au bar*) barman, barmaid.
serviable /sɛrvjabl/ *a.* helpful.
service /sɛrvis/ *n.m.* service; (*fonction, temps de travail*) duty; (*pourboire*) service (charge). **~ (non) compris,** service (not) included. **être de ~,** be on duty. **pendant le ~,** (when) on duty. **rendre un ~/mauvais ~ à qn.,** do s.o. a favour/disservice. **~ d'ordre,** (*policiers*) police. **~ après-vente,** after-sales service. **~ militaire,** military service.

serviette /sɛrvjɛt/ *n.f.* (*de toilette*) towel; (*sac*) briefcase. **~ (de table),** serviette; (*Amer.*) napkin. **~ hygiénique,** sanitary towel.
servile /sɛrvil/ *a.* servile.
servir† /sɛrvir/ *v.t./i.* serve; (*être utile*) be of use, serve. **~ qn. (à table),** wait on s.o. **ça sert à,** (*outil, récipient, etc.*) it is used for. **ça me sert à/de,** I use it for/as. **~ de,** serve as, be used as. **~ à qn. de guide/***etc.*, act as a guide/*etc.* for s.o. **se ~** *v. pr.* (*à table*) help o.s. (**de,** to). **se ~ de,** use.
serviteur /sɛrvitœr/ *n.m.* servant.
servitude /sɛrvityd/ *n.f.* servitude.
ses /se/ *voir* son[1].
session /sesjɔ̃/ *n.f.* session.
seuil /sœj/ *n.m.* doorstep; (*entrée*) doorway; (*fig.*) threshold.
seul, ~e /sœl/ *a.* alone, on one's own; (*unique*) only. **un ~ travail/***etc.*, only one job/*etc.* **pas un ~ ami/***etc.*, not a single friend/*etc.* **parler tout ~,** talk to o.s. **faire qch. tout ~,** do sth. on one's own. ● *n.m., f.* **le ~, la ~e,** the only one. **un ~, une ~e,** only one. **pas un ~,** not (a single) one.
seulement /sœlmɑ̃/ *adv.* only.
sève /sɛv/ *n.f.* sap.
sév|ère /sevɛr/ *a.* severe. **~èrement** *adv.* severely. **~érité** /-erite/ *n.f.* severity.
sévices /sevis/ *n.m. pl.* cruelty.
sévir /sevir/ *v.i.* (*fléau*) rage. **~ contre,** punish.
sevrer /səvre/ *v.t.* wean.
sex|e /sɛks/ *n.m.* sex; (*organes*) sex organs. **~isme** *n.m.* sexism. **~iste** *a.* sexist.
sex|uel, ~uelle /sɛksɥɛl/ *a.* sexual. **~ualité** *n.f.* sexuality.
seyant, ~e /sɛjɑ̃, -t/ *a.* becoming.
shampooing /ʃɑ̃pwɛ̃/ *n.m.* shampoo.
shérif /ʃerif/ *n.m.* sheriff.
short /ʃɔrt/ *n.m.* (pair of) shorts.
si[1] (**s'** *before il, ils*) /si, s/ *conj.* if; (*interrogation indirecte*) if, whether. **si on partait?,** (*suggestion*) what about going? **s'il vous** *ou* **te plaît,** please. **si oui,** if so. **si seulement,** if only.
si[2] /si/ *adv.* (*tellement*) so; (*oui*) yes. **un si bon repas,** such a good meal. **pas si riche que,** not as rich as. **si habile qu'il soit,** however skilful he may be. **si bien que,** with the result that.
siamois, ~e /sjamwa, -z/ *a.* Siamese.
Sicile /sisil/ *n.f.* Sicily.
sida /sida/ *n.m.* (*méd.*) AIDS.
sidéré /sidere/ *a.* staggered.
sidérurgie /sideryrʒi/ *n.f.* iron and steel industry.
siècle /sjɛkl/ *n.m.* century; (*époque*) age.
siège /sjɛʒ/ *n.m.* seat; (*mil.*) siege. **~ éjectable,** ejector seat. **~ social,** head office, headquarters.
siéger /sjeʒe/ *v.i.* (*assemblée*) sit.
sien, ~ne /sjɛ̃, sjɛn/ *pron.* **le ~, la ~ne, les ~(ne)s,** his; (*femme*) hers; (*chose*) its. **les ~s,** (*famille*) one's family.
sieste /sjɛst/ *n.f.* nap; (*en Espagne*) siesta. **faire la ~,** have an afternoon nap.
siffl|er /sifle/ *v.i.* whistle; (*avec un sifflet*) blow one's whistle; (*serpent, gaz*) hiss. ● *v.t.* (*air*) whistle; (*chien*) whistle to *ou* for; (*acteur*) hiss; (*signaler*) blow one's whistle for. **~ement** *n.m.* whistling. **un ~ement,** a whistle.
sifflet /siflɛ/ *n.m.* whistle. **~s,** (*huées*) boos.
siffloter /siflɔte/ *v.t./i.* whistle.
sigle /sigl/ *n.m.* abbreviation, acronym.
sign|al (*pl.* **~aux**) /siɲal, -o/ *n.m.* signal. **~aux lumineux,** (*auto.*) traffic signals.
signal|er /siɲale/ *v.t.* indicate; (*par une sonnerie, un écriteau*) signal; (*dénoncer, mentionner*) report; (*faire remarquer*) point out. **se ~er par,** distinguish o.s. by. **~ement** *n.m.* description.
signalisation /siɲalizɑsjɔ̃/ *n.f.* signalling, signposting; (*signaux*) signals.
signataire /siɲatɛr/ *n.m./f.* signatory.
signature /siɲatyr/ *n.f.* signature; (*action*) signing.
signe /siɲ/ *n.m.* sign; (*de ponctuation*) mark. **faire ~ à,** beckon (**de,** to); (*contacter*) contact. **faire ~ que non,** shake one's head. **faire ~ que oui,** nod.
signer /siɲe/ *v.t.* sign. **se ~** *v. pr.* (*relig.*) cross o.s.
signet /siɲɛ/ *m.* bookmark.
significati|f, ~ve /siɲifikatif, -v/ *a.* significant.
signification /siɲifikɑsjɔ̃/ *n.f.* meaning.

signifier /siɲifje/ *v.t.* mean, signify; (*faire connaître*) make known (**à,** to).

silenc|e /silɑ̃s/ *n.m.* silence; (*mus.*) rest. **garder le ~e,** keep silent. **~ieux, ~ieuse** *a.* silent; *n.m.* (*auto.*) silencer; (*auto., Amer.*) muffler.

silex /silɛks/ *n.m.* flint.

silhouette /silwɛt/ *n.f.* outline, silhouette.

silicium /silisjɔm/ *n.m.* silicon.

sillage /sijaʒ/ *n.m.* (*trace d'eau*) wake.

sillon /sijɔ̃/ *n.m.* furrow; (*de disque*) groove.

sillonner /sijɔne/ *v.t.* criss-cross.

silo /silo/ *n.m.* silo.

simagrées /simagre/ *n.f. pl.* fuss, pretence.

simil|aire /similɛr/ *a.* similar. **~itude** *n.f.* similarity.

simple /sɛ̃pl/ *a.* simple; (*non double*) single. ● *n.m.* (*tennis*) singles. **~ d'esprit** *n.m./f.* simpleton. **~ soldat,** private. **~ment** /-əmɑ̃/ *adv.* simply.

simplicité /sɛ̃plisite/ *n.f.* simplicity; (*naïveté*) simpleness.

simplif|ier /sɛ̃plifje/ *v.t.* simplify. **~ication** *n.f.* simplification.

simpliste /sɛ̃plist/ *a.* simplistic.

simulacre /simylakr/ *n.m.* pretence, sham.

simul|er /simyle/ *v.t.* simulate. **~ateur** *m.* (*appareil*) simulator. **~ation** *n.f.* simulation.

simultané /simyltane/ *a.* simultaneous. **~ment** *adv.* simultaneously.

sinc|ère /sɛ̃sɛr/ *a.* sincere. **~èrement** *adv.* sincerely. **~érité** *n.f.* sincerity.

singe /sɛ̃ʒ/ *n.m.* monkey, ape.

singer /sɛ̃ʒe/ *v.t.* mimic, ape.

singeries /sɛ̃ʒri/ *n.f. pl.* antics.

singulariser (se) /(sə)sɛ̃gylarize/ *v. pr.* make o.s. conspicuous.

singul|ier, ~ière /sɛ̃gylje, -jɛr/ *a.* peculiar, remarkable; (*gram.*) singular. ● *n.m.* (*gram.*) singular. **~arité** *n.f.* peculiarity. **~ièrement** *adv.* peculiarly; (*beaucoup*) remarkably.

sinistre[1] /sinistr/ *a.* sinister.

sinistr|e[2] /sinistr/ *n.m.* disaster; (*incendie*) blaze; (*dommages*) damage. **~é** *a.* disaster-stricken; *n.m., f.* disaster victim.

sinon /sinɔ̃/ *conj.* (*autrement*) otherwise; (*sauf*) except (**que,** that); (*si ce n'est*) if not.

sinueu|x, ~se /sinɥø, -z/ *a.* winding; (*fig.*) tortuous.

sinus /sinys/ *n.m.* (*anat.*) sinus.

sionisme /sjɔnism/ *n.m.* Zionism.

siphon /sifɔ̃/ *n.m.* siphon; (*de WC*) U-bend.

sirène[1] /sirɛn/ *n.f.* (*appareil*) siren.

sirène[2] /sirɛn/ *n.f.* (*femme*) mermaid.

sirop /siro/ *n.m.* syrup; (*boisson*) cordial.

siroter /sirɔte/ *v.t.* sip.

sirupeu|x, ~se /sirypø, -z/ *a.* syrupy.

sis, ~e /si, siz/ *a.* situated.

sismique /sismik/ *a.* seismic.

site /sit/ *n.m.* setting; (*pittoresque*) beauty spot; (*emplacement*) site; (*monument etc.*) place of interest.

sitôt /sito/ *adv.* **~ entré**/*etc.*, immediately after coming in/*etc.* **~ que,** as soon as. **pas de ~,** not for a while.

situation /sitɥasjɔ̃/ *n.f.* situation, position. **~ de famille,** marital status.

situ|er /sitɥe/ *v.t.* situate, locate. **se ~er** *v. pr.* (*se trouver*) be situated. **~é** *a.* situated.

six /sis/ (/si/ *before consonant,* /siz/ *before vowel*) *a. & n.m.* six. **~ième** /sizjɛm/ *a. & n.m./f.* sixth.

sketch (*pl.* **~es**) /skɛtʃ/ *n.m.* (*théâtre*) sketch.

ski /ski/ *n.m.* (*patin*) ski; (*sport*) skiing. **faire du ~,** ski. **~ de fond,** cross-country skiing. **~ nautique,** water-skiing.

sk|ier /skje/ *v.i.* ski. **~ieur, ~ieuse** *n.m., f.* skier.

slalom /slalɔm/ *n.m.* slalom.

slave /slav/ *a.* Slav; (*lang.*) Slavonic. ● *n.m./f.* Slav.

slip /slip/ *n.m.* (*d'homme*) (under)-pants; (*de femme*) knickers; (*Amer.*) panties. **~ de bain,** (swimming) trunks; (*du bikini*) briefs.

slogan /slɔgɑ̃/ *n.m.* slogan.

smoking /smɔkiŋ/ *n.m.* evening *ou* dinner suit, dinner-jacket.

snack(-bar) /snak(bar)/ *n.m.* snack-bar.

snob /snɔb/ *n.m./f.* snob. ● *a.* snobbish. **~isme** *n.m.* snobbery.

sobr|e /sɔbr/ *a.* sober. **~iété** *n.f.* sobriety.

sobriquet /sɔbrikɛ/ *n.m.* nickname.

sociable /sɔsjabl/ *a.* sociable.

soc|ial (*m. pl.* **~iaux**) /sɔsjal, -jo/ *a.* social.
socialis|te /sɔsjalist/ *n.m./f.* socialist. **~me** *n.m.* socialism.
société /sɔsjete/ *n.f.* society; (*compagnie, firme*) company.
sociolo|gie /sɔsjɔlɔʒi/ *n.f.* sociology. **~gique** *a.* sociological. **~gue** *n.m./f.* sociologist.
socle /sɔkl/ *n.m.* (*de colonne, statue*) plinth; (*de lampe*) base.
socquette /sɔkɛt/ *n.f.* ankle sock.
soda /sɔda/ *n.m.* (fizzy) drink.
sodium /sɔdjɔm/ *n.m.* sodium.
sœur /sœr/ *n.f.* sister.
sofa /sɔfa/ *n.m.* sofa.
soi /swa/ *pron.* oneself. **en ~,** in itself. **~-disant** *a. invar.* so-called; (*qui se veut tel*) self-styled; *adv.* supposedly.
soie /swa/ *n.f.* silk.
soif /swaf/ *n.f.* thirst. **avoir ~,** be thirsty. **donner ~ à,** make thirsty.
soigné /swaɲe/ *a.* tidy, neat; (*bien fait*) careful.
soigner /swaɲe/ *v.t.* look after, take care of; (*tenue, style*) take care over; (*maladie*) treat. **se ~** *v. pr.* look after o.s.
soigneu|x, ~se /swaɲø, -z/ *a.* careful (**de,** about); (*ordonné*) tidy. **~sement** *adv.* carefully.
soi-même /swamɛm/ *pron.* oneself.
soin /swɛ̃/ *n.m.* care; (*ordre*) tidiness. **~s,** care; (*méd.*) treatment. **avoir** *ou* **prendre ~ de qn./de faire,** take care of s.o./to do. **premiers ~s,** first aid.
soir /swar/ *n.m.* evening.
soirée /sware/ *n.f.* evening; (*réception*) party. **~ dansante,** dance.
soit /swa/ *voir* être. ● *conj.* (*à savoir*) that is to say. **~ . . . soit,** either . . . or.
soixantaine /swasɑ̃tɛn/ *n.f.* **une ~ (de),** about sixty.
soixant|e /swasɑ̃t/ *a.* & *n.m.* sixty. **~e-dix** *a.* & *n.m.* seventy. **~e-dixième** *a.* & *n.m./f.* seventieth. **~ième** *a.* & *n.m./f.* sixtieth.
soja /sɔʒa/ *n.m.* (*graines*) soya beans; (*plante*) soya.
sol /sɔl/ *n.m.* ground; (*de maison*) floor; (*terrain agricole*) soil.
solaire /sɔlɛr/ *a.* solar; (*huile, filtre*) sun. **les rayons ~s,** the sun's rays.
soldat /sɔlda/ *n.m.* soldier.
solde[1] /sɔld/ *n.f.* (*salaire*) pay.
solde[2] /sɔld/ *n.m.* (*comm.*) balance. **~s,** (*articles*) sale goods. **en ~,** (*acheter etc.*) at sale price. **les ~s,** the sales.
solder /sɔlde/ *v.t.* reduce; (*liquider*) sell off at sale price; (*compte*) settle. **se ~ par,** (*aboutir à*) end in.
sole /sɔl/ *n.f.* (*poisson*) sole.
soleil /sɔlɛj/ *n.m.* sun; (*chaleur*) sunshine; (*fleur*) sunflower. **il y a du ~,** it is sunny.
solennel, ~le /sɔlanɛl/ *a.* solemn.
solennité /sɔlanite/ *n.f.* solemnity.
solex /sɔlɛks/ *n.m.* (P.) moped.
solfège /sɔlfɛʒ/ *n.m.* elementary musical theory.
solid|aire /sɔlidɛr/ *a.* (*mécanismes*) interdependent; (*couple*) (mutually) supportive; (*ouvriers*) who show solidarity. **~arité** *n.f.* solidarity.
solidariser (se) /(sə)sɔlidarize/ *v. pr.* show solidarity (**avec,** with).
solid|e /sɔlid/ *a.* solid. ● *n.m.* (*objet*) solid; (*corps*) sturdy. **~ement** *adv.* solidly. **~ité** *n.f.* solidity.
solidifier /sɔlidifje/ *v.t.,* **se ~** *v. pr.* solidify.
soliste /sɔlist/ *n.m./f.* soloist.
solitaire /sɔlitɛr/ *a.* solitary. ● *n.m./f.* (*ermite*) hermit; (*personne insociable*) loner.
solitude /sɔlityd/ *n.f.* solitude.
solive /sɔliv/ *n.f.* joist.
sollicit|er /sɔlisite/ *v.t.* request; (*attirer, pousser*) prompt; (*tenter*) tempt; (*faire travailler*) make demands on. **~ation** *n.f.* earnest request.
sollicitude /sɔlisityd/ *n.f.* concern.
solo /sɔlo/ *n.m.* & *a. invar.* (*mus.*) solo.
solstice /sɔlstis/ *n.m.* solstice.
soluble /sɔlybl/ *a.* soluble.
solution /sɔlysjɔ̃/ *n.f.* solution.
solvable /sɔlvabl/ *a.* solvent.
solvant /sɔlvɑ̃/ *n.m.* solvent.
sombre /sɔ̃br/ *a.* dark; (*triste*) sombre.
sombrer /sɔ̃bre/ *v.i.* sink (**dans,** into).
sommaire /sɔmɛr/ *a.* summary; (*tenue, repas*) scant. ● *n.m.* summary.
sommation /sɔmasjɔ̃/ *n.f.* (*mil.*) warning; (*jurid.*) summons.
somme[1] /sɔm/ *n.f.* sum. **en ~, ~ toute,** in short. **faire la ~ de,** add (up), total (up).
somme[2] /sɔm/ *n.m.* (*sommeil*) nap.
sommeil /sɔmɛj/ *n.m.* sleep; (*besoin de dormir*) drowsiness. **avoir ~,** be

ou feel sleepy. **~ler** /-meje/ *v.i.* doze; (*fig.*) lie dormant.

sommelier /sɔməlje/ *n.m.* wine waiter.

sommer /sɔme/ *v.t.* summon.

sommes /sɔm/ *voir* être.

sommet /sɔmɛ/ *n.m.* top; (*de montagne*) summit; (*de triangle*) apex; (*gloire*) height.

sommier /sɔmje/ *n.m.* base (of bed).

somnambule /sɔmnɑ̃byl/ *n.m.* sleep-walker.

somnifère /sɔmnifɛr/ *n.m.* sleeping-pill.

somnolen|t, ~te /sɔmnɔlɑ̃, -t/ *a.* drowsy. **~ce** *n.f.* drowsiness.

somnoler /sɔmnɔle/ *v.i.* doze.

sompt|ueux, ~ueuse /sɔ̃ptɥø, -z/ *a.* sumptuous. **~uosité** *n.f.* sumptuousness.

son[1], **sa** *ou* **son*** (*pl.* **ses**) /sɔ̃, sa, sɔ̃n, se/ *a.* his; (*femme*) her; (*chose*) its; (*indéfini*) one's.

son[2] /sɔ̃/ *n.m.* (*bruit*) sound.

son[3] /sɔ̃/ *n.m.* (*de blé*) bran.

sonar /sonar/ *n.m.* Sonar.

sonate /sɔnat/ *n.f.* sonata.

sonde /sɔ̃d/ *n.f.* (*pour les forages*) drill; (*méd.*) probe.

sond|er /sɔ̃de/ *v.t.* sound; (*terrain*) drill; (*personne*) sound out. **~age** *n.m.* sounding; drilling. **~age (d'opinion),** (opinion) poll.

song|e /sɔ̃ʒ/ *n.m.* dream. **~er** *v.i.* dream; *v.t.* **~er que,** think that. **~er à,** think about. **~eur, ~euse** *a.* pensive.

sonnantes /sɔnɑ̃t/ *a.f. pl.* **à six**/*etc.* **heures ~,** on the stroke of six/*etc.*

sonné /sɔne/ *a.* (*fam.*) crazy; (*fatigué*) knocked out.

sonn|er /sɔne/ *v.t./i.* ring; (*clairon, glas*) sound; (*heure*) strike; (*domestique*) ring for. **midi ~é,** well past noon. **~er de,** (*clairon etc.*) sound, blow.

sonnerie /sɔnri/ *n.f.* ringing; (*de clairon*) sound; (*mécanisme*) bell.

sonnet /sɔnɛ/ *n.m.* sonnet.

sonnette /sɔnɛt/ *n.f.* bell.

sonor|e /sɔnɔr/ *a.* resonant; (*onde, effets, etc.*) sound. **~ité** *n.f.* resonance; (*d'un instrument*) tone.

sonoris|er /sɔnɔrize/ *v.t.* (*salle*) wire for sound. **~ation** *n.f.* (*matériel*) sound equipment.

sont /sɔ̃/ *voir* être.

sophistiqué /sɔfistike/ *a.* sophisticated.

soporifique /sɔpɔrifik/ *a.* soporific.

sorbet /sɔrbɛ/ *n.m.* sorbet.

sorcellerie /sɔrsɛlri/ *n.f.* witchcraft.

sorc|ier /sɔrsje/ *n.m.* sorcerer. **~ière** *n.f.* witch.

sordide /sɔrdid/ *a.* sordid; (*lieu*) squalid.

sort /sɔr/ *n.m.* (*destin, hasard*) fate; (*condition*) lot; (*maléfice*) spell. **tirer (qch.) au ~,** draw lots (for sth.).

sortant, ~e /sɔrtɑ̃, -t/ *a.* (*président etc.*) outgoing.

sorte /sɔrt/ *n.f.* sort, kind. **de ~ que,** so that. **en quelque ~,** in a way. **faire en ~ que,** see to it that.

sortie /sɔrti/ *n.f.* departure, exit; (*porte*) exit; (*promenade, dîner*) outing; (*invective*) outburst; (*parution*) appearance; (*de disque, gaz*) release; (*d'un ordinateur*) output. **~s,** (*argent*) outgoings.

sortilège /sɔrtilɛʒ/ *n.m.* (magic) spell.

sortir† /sɔrtir/ *v.i.* (*aux. être*) go out, leave; (*venir*) come out; (*aller au spectacle etc.*) go out; (*livre, film*) come out; (*plante*) come up. **~ de,** (*pièce*) leave; (*milieu social*) come from; (*limites*) go beyond. ● *v.t.* (*aux. avoir*) take out; (*livre, modèle*) bring out; (*dire: fam.*) come out with. **~ d'affaire, (s')en ~,** get out of an awkward situation. **~ du commun** *ou* **de l'ordinaire,** be out of the ordinary.

sosie /sɔzi/ *n.m.* double.

sot, ~te /so, sɔt/ *a.* foolish.

sottise /sɔtiz/ *n.f.* foolishness; (*action, remarque*) foolish thing.

sou /su/ *n.m.* **~s,** money. **pas un ~,** not a penny. **sans le ~,** without a penny. **près de ses ~s,** tight-fisted.

soubresaut /subrəso/ *n.m.* (sudden) start.

souche /suʃ/ *n.f.* (*d'arbre*) stump; (*de famille, vigne*) stock; (*de carnet*) counterfoil. **planté comme une ~,** standing like an idiot.

souci[1] /susi/ *n.m.* (*inquiétude*) worry; (*préoccupation*) concern. **se faire du ~,** worry.

souci[2] /susi/ *n.m.* (*plante*) marigold.

soucier (se) /(sə)susje/ *v. pr.* **se ~ de,** be concerned about.

soucieu|x, ~se /susjø, -z/ *a.* concerned (**de,** about).

soucoupe /sukup/ *n.f.* saucer. **~ volante,** flying saucer.

soudain, ~e /sudɛ̃, -ɛn/ *a.* sudden. ● *adv.* suddenly. **~ement** /-ɛnmɑ̃/

adv. suddenly. **~eté** /-ɛnte/ *n.f.* suddenness.

soude /sud/ *n.f.* soda.

soud|er /sude/ *v.t.* solder, (*à la flamme*) weld. **se ~er** *v. pr.* (*os*) knit (together). **~ure** *n.f.* soldering, welding; (*substance*) solder.

soudoyer /sudwaje/ *v.t.* bribe.

souffle /sufl/ *n.m.* blow, puff; (*haleine*) breath; (*respiration*) breathing; (*explosion*) blast; (*vent*) breath of air.

soufflé /sufle/ *n.m.* (*culin.*) soufflé.

souffl|er /sufle/ *v.i.* blow; (*haleter*) puff. ● *v.t.* (*bougie*) blow out; (*poussière, fumée*) blow; (*par explosion*) destroy; (*chuchoter*) whisper. **~er son rôle à,** prompt. **~eur, ~euse** *n.m., f.* (*théâtre*) prompter.

soufflet /suflɛ/ *n.m.* (*instrument*) bellows.

souffrance /sufrɑ̃s/ *n.f.* suffering. **en ~,** (*affaire*) pending.

souffr|ir† /sufrir/ *v.i.* suffer (**de,** from). ● *v.t.* (*endurer*) suffer; (*admettre*) admit of. **il ne peut pas le ~ir,** he cannot stand *ou* bear him. **~ant, ~ante** *a.* unwell.

soufre /sufr/ *n.m.* sulphur.

souhait /swɛ/ *n.m.* wish. **nos ~s de,** (*vœux*) good wishes for. **à vos ~s!,** bless you!

souhait|er /swete/ *v.t.* (*bonheur etc.*) wish for. **~er qch. à qn.,** wish s.o. sth. **~er que/faire,** hope that/to do. **~able** /swɛtabl/ *a.* desirable.

souiller /suje/ *v.t.* soil.

soûl, ~e /su, sul/ *a.* drunk. ● *n.m.* **tout son ~,** as much as one can.

soulag|er /sulaʒe/ *v.t.* relieve. **~ement** *n.m.* relief.

soûler /sule/ *v.t.* make drunk. **se ~** *v. pr.* get drunk.

soulèvement /sulɛvmɑ̃/ *n.m.* uprising.

soulever /sulve/ *v.t.* lift, raise; (*exciter*) stir; (*question, poussière*) raise. **se ~** *v. pr.* lift *ou* raise o.s. up; (*se révolter*) rise up.

soulier /sulje/ *n.m.* shoe.

souligner /suliɲe/ *v.t.* underline; (*taille, yeux*) emphasize.

soum|ettre† /sumɛtr/ *v.t.* (*dompter, assujettir*) subject (**à,** to); (*présenter*) submit (**à,** to). **se ~ettre** *v. pr.* submit (**à,** to). **~is, ~ise** *a.* submissive. **~ission** *n.f.* submission.

soupape /supap/ *n.f.* valve.

soupçon /supsɔ̃/ *n.m.* suspicion. **un ~ de,** (*fig.*) a touch of. **~ner** /-ɔne/ *v.t.* suspect. **~neux, ~neuse** /-ɔnø, -z/ *a.* suspicious.

soupe /sup/ *n.f.* soup.

souper /supe/ *n.m.* supper. ● *v.i.* have supper.

soupeser /supəze/ *v.t.* judge the weight of; (*fig.*) weigh up.

soupière /supjɛr/ *n.f.* (soup) tureen.

soupir /supir/ *n.m.* sigh. **pousser un ~,** heave a sigh. **~er** *v.i.* sigh.

soupir|ail (*pl.* **~aux**) /supiraj, -o/ *n.m.* small basement window.

soupirant /supirɑ̃/ *n.m.* suitor.

souple /supl/ *a.* supple; (*règlement, caractère*) flexible. **~sse** /-ɛs/ *n.f.* suppleness; flexibility.

source /surs/ *n.f.* source; (*eau*) spring. **de ~ sûre,** from a reliable source. **~ thermale,** hot springs.

sourcil /sursi/ *n.m.* eyebrow.

sourciller /sursije/ *v.i.* **sans ~,** without batting an eyelid.

sourd, ~e /sur, -d/ *a.* deaf; (*bruit, douleur*) dull; (*inquiétude, conflit*) silent, hidden. ● *n.m., f.* deaf person. **faire la ~e oreille,** turn a deaf ear. **~-muet** (*pl.* **~s-muets**), **~e-muette** (*pl.* **~es-muettes**) *a.* deaf and dumb; *n.m., f.* deaf mute.

sourdine /surdin/ *n.f.* (*mus.*) mute. **en ~,** quietly.

souricière /surisjɛr/ *n.f.* mousetrap; (*fig.*) trap.

sourire /surir/ *n.m.* smile. **garder le ~,** keep smiling. ● *v.i.* smile (**à,** at). **~ à,** (*fortune*) smile on.

souris /suri/ *n.f.* mouse.

sournois, ~e /surnwa, -z/ *a.* sly, underhand. **~ement** /-zmɑ̃/ *adv.* slyly.

sous /su/ *prép.* under, beneath. **~ la main,** handy. **~ la pluie,** in the rain. **~ peu,** shortly. **~ terre,** underground.

sous- /su/ *préf.* (*subordination*) sub-; (*insuffisance*) under-.

sous-alimenté /suzalimɑ̃te/ *a.* undernourished.

sous-bois /subwa/ *n.m. invar.* undergrowth.

souscr|ire /suskrir/ *v.i.* **~ire à,** subscribe to. **~iption** *n.f.* subscription.

sous-direct|eur, ~rice /sudirɛktœr, -ris/ *n.m., f.* assistant manager.

sous-entend|re /suzɑ̃tɑ̃dr/ *v.t.* imply. **~u** *n.m.* insinuation.

sous-estimer /suzɛstime/ *v.t.* underestimate.

sous-jacent, ~e /suʒasɑ̃, -t/ *a.* underlying.

sous-marin, ~e /sumarɛ̃, -in/ *a.* underwater. ● *n.m.* submarine.

sous-officier /suzɔfisje/ *n.m.* non-commissioned officer.

sous-préfecture /suprefɛktyr/ *n.f.* sub-prefecture.

sous-produit /suprɔdɥi/ *n.m.* by-product.

sous-programme /suprɔgram/ *n.m.* subroutine.

soussigné, ~e /susiɲe/ *a.* & *n.m., f.* undersigned.

sous-sol /susɔl/ *n.m.* (*cave*) basement.

sous-titr|e /sutitr/ *n.m.* subtitle. **~er** *v.t.* subtitle.

soustr|aire† /sustrɛr/ *v.t.* remove; (*déduire*) subtract. **se ~aire à,** escape from. **~action** *n.f.* (*déduction*) subtraction.

sous-trait|er /sutrete/ *v.t.* subcontract. **~ant** *n.m.* subcontractor.

sous-verre /suvɛr/ *n.m.* *invar.* picture frame, glass mount.

sous-vêtement /suvɛtmɑ̃/ *n.m.* undergarment. **~s,** underwear.

soutane /sutan/ *n.f.* cassock.

soute /sut/ *n.f.* (*de bateau*) hold. **~ à charbon,** coal-bunker.

soutenir† /sutnir/ *v.t.* support; (*fortifier, faire durer*) sustain; (*résister à*) withstand. **~ que,** maintain that. **se ~** *v. pr.* (*se tenir debout*) support o.s.

soutenu /sutny/ *a.* (*constant*) sustained; (*style*) lofty.

souterrain, ~e /sutɛrɛ̃, -ɛn/ *a.* underground. ● *n.m.* underground passage, subway.

soutien /sutjɛ̃/ *n.m.* support. **~-gorge** (*pl.* **~s-gorge**) *n.m.* bra.

soutirer /sutire/ *v.t.* **~ à qn.,** extract from s.o.

souvenir [1] /suvnir/ *n.m.* memory, recollection; (*objet*) memento; (*cadeau*) souvenir. **en ~ de,** in memory of.

souvenir [2]† **(se)** /(sə)suvnir/ *v. pr.* **se ~ de,** remember. **se ~ que,** remember that.

souvent /suvɑ̃/ *adv.* often.

souverain, ~e /suvrɛ̃, -ɛn/ *a.* sovereign; (*extrême: péj.*) supreme. ● *n.m., f.* sovereign. **~eté** /-ɛnte/ *n.f.* sovereignty.

soviétique /sɔvjetik/ *a.* Soviet. ● *n.m./f.* Soviet citizen.

soyeu|x, ~se /swajø, -z/ *a.* silky.

spacieu|x, ~se /spasjø, -z/ *a.* spacious.

spaghetti /spageti/ *n.m. pl.* spaghetti.

sparadrap /sparadra/ *n.m.* sticking-plaster; (*Amer.*) adhesive tape *ou* bandage.

spasm|e /spasm/ *n.m.* spasm. **~odique** *a.* spasmodic.

spat|ial (*m. pl.* **~iaux**) /spasjal, -jo/ *a.* space.

spatule /spatyl/ *n.f.* spatula.

speaker, ~ine /spikœr, -rin/ *n.m., f.* announcer.

spéc|ial (*m. pl.* **~iaux**) /spesjal, -jo/ *a.* special; (*singulier*) peculiar. **~ialement** *adv.* especially; (*exprès*) specially.

spécialis|er (se) /(sə)spesjalize/ *v. pr.* specialize (**dans,** in). **~ation** *n.f.* specialization.

spécialiste /spesjalist/ *n.m./f.* specialist.

spécialité /spesjalite/ *n.f.* speciality; (*Amer.*) specialty.

spécif|ier /spesifje/ *v.t.* specify. **~ication** *n.f.* specification.

spécifique /spesifik/ *a.* specific.

spécimen /spesimɛn/ *n.m.* specimen.

spectacle /spɛktakl/ *n.m.* sight, spectacle; (*représentation*) show.

spectaculaire /spɛktakylɛr/ *a.* spectacular.

specta|teur, ~trice /spɛktatœr, -tris/ *n.m., f.* onlooker; (*sport*) spectator. **les ~teurs,** (*théâtre*) the audience.

spectre /spɛktr/ *n.m.* (*revenant*) spectre; (*images*) spectrum.

spécul|er /spekyle/ *v.i.* speculate. **~ateur, ~atrice** *n.m., f.* speculator. **~ation** *n.f.* speculation.

spéléologie /speleɔlɔʒi/ *n.f.* cave exploration, pot-holing; (*Amer.*) spelunking.

sperme /spɛrm/ *n.m.* sperm.

sph|ère /sfɛr/ *n.f.* sphere. **~érique** *a.* spherical.

sphinx /sfɛ̃ks/ *n.m.* sphinx.

spirale /spiral/ *n.f.* spiral.

spirite /spirit/ *n.m./f.* spiritualist.

spirituel, ~le /spiritɥɛl/ *a.* spiritual; (*amusant*) witty.

spiritueux /spiritɥø/ *n.m.* (*alcool*) spirit.
splend|ide /splɑ̃did/ *a.* splendid. **~eur** *n.f.* splendour.
spongieu|x, ~se /spɔ̃ʒjø, -z/ *a.* spongy.
sponsor /spɔ̃sɔr/ *n.m.* sponsor. **~iser** *v.t.* sponsor.
spontané /spɔ̃tane/ *a.* spontaneous. **~ité** *n.f.* spontaneity. **~ment** *adv.* spontaneously.
sporadique /spɔradik/ *a.* sporadic.
sport /spɔr/ *n.m.* sport. ● *a. invar.* (*vêtements*) casual. **veste/voiture de ~,** sports jacket/car.
sporti|f, ~ve /spɔrtif, -v/ *a.* sporting; (*physique*) athletic; (*résultats*) sports. ● *n.m.* sportsman. ● *n.f.* sportswoman.
spot /spɔt/ *n.m.* spotlight; (*publicitaire*) ad.
spray /spre/ *n.m.* spray; (*méd.*) inhaler.
sprint /sprint/ *n.m.* sprint. **~er** *v.i.* sprint; *n.m.* /-œr/ sprinter.
square /skwar/ *n.m.* (public) garden.
squash /skwaʃ/ *n.m.* squash.
squatter /skwatœr/ *n.m.* squatter. **~iser** *v.t.* squat in.
squelett|e /skəlɛt/ *n.m.* skeleton. **~ique** /-etik/ *a.* skeletal; (*maigre*) all skin and bone.
stabiliser /stabilize/ *v.t.* stabilize.
stab|le /stabl/ *a.* stable. **~ilité** *n.f.* stability.
stade[1] /stad/ *n.m.* (*sport*) stadium.
stade[2] /stad/ *n.m.* (*phase*) stage.
stag|e /staʒ/ *n.m.* course. **~iaire** *a.* & *n.m./f.* course member; (*apprenti*) trainee.
stagn|er /stagne/ *v.i.* stagnate. **~ant, ~ante** *a.* stagnant. **~ation** *n.f.* stagnation.
stand /stɑ̃d/ *n.m.* stand, stall. **~ de tir,** (shooting-)range.
standard[1] /stɑ̃dar/ *n.m.* switchboard. **~iste** /-dist/ *n.m./f.* switchboard operator.
standard[2] /stɑ̃dar/ *a. invar.* standard. **~iser** /-dize/ *v.t.* standardize.
standing /stɑ̃diŋ/ *n.m.* status, standing. **de ~,** (*hôtel etc.*) luxury.
star /star/ *n.f.* (*actrice*) star.
starter /startɛr/ *n.m.* (*auto.*) choke.
station /stasjɔ̃/ *n.f.* station; (*halte*) stop. **~ balnéaire,** seaside resort. **~ debout,** standing position. **~ de taxis,** taxi rank; (*Amer.*) taxi stand. **~-service** (*pl.* **~s-service**) *n.f.* service station. **~ thermale,** spa.
stationnaire /stasjɔnɛr/ *a.* stationary.
stationn|er /stasjɔne/ *v.i.* park. **~ement** *n.m.* parking.
statique /statik/ *a.* static.
statistique /statistik/ *n.f.* statistic; (*science*) statistics. ● *a.* statistical.
statue /staty/ *n.f.* statue.
statuer /statɥe/ *v.i.* **~ sur,** rule on.
statu quo /statykwo/ *n.m.* status quo.
stature /statyr/ *n.f.* stature.
statut /staty/ *n.m.* status. **~s,** (*règles*) statutes. **~aire** /-tɛr/ *a.* statutory.
steak /stɛk/ *n.m.* steak.
stencil /stɛnsil/ *n.m.* stencil.
sténo /steno/ *n.f.* (*personne*) stenographer; (*sténographie*) shorthand.
sténodactylo /stenɔdaktilo/ *n.f.* shorthand typist; (*Amer.*) stenographer.
sténographie /stenɔgrafi/ *n.f.* shorthand.
stéréo /stereo/ *n.f.* & *a. invar.* stereo. **~phonique** /-eɔfɔnik/ *a.* stereophonic.
stéréotyp|e /stereɔtip/ *n.m.* stereotype. **~é** *a.* stereotyped.
stéril|e /steril/ *a.* sterile. **~ité** *n.f.* sterility.
stérilet /sterilɛ/ *n.m.* coil, IUD.
stérilis|er /sterilize/ *v.t.* sterilize. **~ation** *n.f.* sterilization.
stéroïde /sterɔid/ *a.* & *n.m.* steroid.
stéthoscope /stetɔskɔp/ *n.m.* stethoscope.
stigmat|e /stigmat/ *n.m.* mark, stigma. **~iser** *v.t.* stigmatize.
stimul|er /stimyle/ *v.t.* stimulate. **~ant** *n.m.* stimulus; (*médicament*) stimulant. **~ateur cardiaque,** pacemaker. **~ation** *n.f.* stimulation.
stipul|er /stipyle/ *v.t.* stipulate. **~ation** *n.f.* stipulation.
stock /stɔk/ *n.m.* stock. **~er** *v.t.* stock. **~iste** *n.m.* stockist; (*Amer.*) dealer.
stoïque /stɔik/ *a.* stoical. ● *n.m./f.* stoic.
stop /stɔp/ *int.* stop. ● *n.m.* stop sign; (*feu arrière*) brake light. **faire du ~,** (*fam.*) hitch-hike.
stopper /stɔpe/ *v.t./i.* stop; (*vêtement*) mend, reweave.
store /stɔr/ *n.m.* blind; (*Amer.*) shade; (*de magasin*) awning.
strabisme /strabism/ *n.m.* squint.

strapontin /strapɔ̃tɛ̃/ *n.m.* folding seat, jump seat.
stratagème /strataʒɛm/ *n.m.* stratagem.
stratég|ie /strateʒi/ *n.f.* strategy. **~ique** *a.* strategic.
stress /stres/ *n.* stress. **~ant** *a.* stressful. **~er** *v.t.* put under stress.
strict /strikt/ *a.* strict; (*tenue, vérité*) plain. **le ~ minimum,** the absolute minimum. **~ement** *adv.* strictly.
strident, ~e /stridɑ̃, -t/ *a.* shrill.
str|ie /stri/ *n.f.* streak. **~ier** *v.t.* streak.
strip-tease /striptiz/ *n.m.* strip-tease.
strophe /strɔf/ *n.f.* stanza, verse.
structur|e /stryktyr/ *n.f.* structure. **~al** (*m. pl.* **~aux**) *a.* structural. **~er** *v.t.* structure.
studieu|x, ~se /stydjø, -z/ *a.* studious; (*période*) devoted to study.
studio /stydjo/ *n.m.* (*d'artiste, de télévision, etc.*) studio; (*logement*) studio flat, bed-sitter.
stupéf|ait, ~aite /stypefɛ, -t/ *a.* amazed. **~action** *n.f.* amazement.
stupéf|ier /stypefje/ *v.t.* amaze. **~iant, ~iante** *a.* amazing; *n.m.* drug, narcotic.
stupeur /stypœr/ *n.f.* amazement; (*méd.*) stupor.
stupid|e /stypid/ *a.* stupid. **~ité** *n.f.* stupidity.
styl|e /stil/ *n.m.* style. **~isé** *a.* stylized.
stylé /stile/ *a.* well-trained.
styliste /stilist/ *n.m./f.* fashion designer.
stylo /stilo/ *n.m.* pen. **~ (à) bille,** ball-point pen. **~ (à) encre,** fountain-pen.
su /sy/ *voir* savoir.
suave /sɥav/ *a.* sweet.
subalterne /sybaltɛrn/ *a.* & *n.m./f.* subordinate.
subconscient, ~e /sypkɔ̃sjɑ̃, -t/ *a.* & *n.m.* subconscious.
subdiviser /sybdivize/ *v.t.* subdivide.
subir /sybir/ *v.t.* suffer; (*traitement, expériences*) undergo.
subit, ~e /sybi, -t/ *a.* sudden. **~ement** /-tmɑ̃/ *adv.* suddenly.
subjecti|f, ~ve /sybʒɛktif, -v/ *a.* subjective. **~vité** *n.f.* subjectivity.
subjonctif /sybʒɔ̃ktif/ *a.* & *n.m.* subjunctive.
subjuguer /sybʒyge/ *v.t.* (*charmer*) captivate.
sublime /syblim/ *a.* sublime.
submer|ger /sybmɛrʒe/ *v.t.* submerge; (*fig.*) overwhelm. **~sion** *n.f.* submersion.
subordonné, ~e /sybɔrdɔne/ *a.* & *n.m., f.* subordinate.
subord|onner /sybɔrdɔne/ *v.t.* subordinate (**à,** to). **~ination** *n.f.* subordination.
subreptice /sybrɛptis/ *a.* surreptitious.
subside /sybzid/ *n.m.* grant.
subsidiare /sypsidjɛr/ *a.* subsidiary.
subsist|er /sybziste/ *v.i.* subsist; (*durer, persister*) exist. **~ance** *n.f.* subsistence.
substance /sypstɑ̃s/ *n.f.* substance.
substantiel, ~le /sypstɑ̃sjɛl/ *a.* substantial.
substantif /sypstɑ̃tif/ *n.m.* noun.
substit|uer /sypstitɥe/ *v.t.* substitute (**à,** for). **se ~uer à,** (*remplacer*) substitute for; (*évincer*) take over from. **~ut** *n.m.* substitute; (*jurid.*) deputy public prosecutor. **~ution** *n.f.* substitution.
subterfuge /syptɛrfyʒ/ *n.m.* subterfuge.
subtil /syptil/ *a.* subtle. **~ité** *n.f.* subtlety.
subtiliser /syptilize/ *v.t.* **~ qch. (à qn.),** spirit sth. away (from s.o.).
subvenir /sybvənir/ *v.i.* **~ à,** provide for.
subvention /sybvɑ̃sjɔ̃/ *n.f.* subsidy. **~ner** /-jɔne/ *v.t.* subsidize.
subversi|f, ~ve /sybvɛrsif, -v/ *a.* subversive.
subversion /sybvɛrsjɔ̃/ *n.f.* subversion.
suc /syk/ *n.m.* juice.
succédané /syksedane/ *n.m.* substitute (**de,** for).
succéder /syksede/ *v.i.* **~ à,** succeed. **se ~** *v. pr.* succeed one another.
succès /syksɛ/ *n.m.* success. **à ~,** (*film, livre, etc.*) successful. **avoir du ~,** be a success.
successeur /syksesœr/ *n.m.* successor.
successi|f, ~ve /syksesif, -v/ *a.* successive. **~vement** *adv.* successively.
succession /syksesjɔ̃/ *n.f.* succession; (*jurid.*) inheritance.
succinct, ~e /syksɛ̃, -t/ *a.* succinct.
succomber /sykɔ̃be/ *v.i.* die. **~ à,** succumb to.
succulent, ~e /sykylɑ̃, -t/ *a.* succulent.

succursale /sykyrsal/ *n.f.* (*comm.*) branch.
sucer /syse/ *v.t.* suck.
sucette /sysɛt/ *n.f.* (*bonbon*) lollipop; (*tétine*) dummy; (*Amer.*) pacifier.
sucr|e /sykr/ *n.m.* sugar. **~e d'orge,** barley sugar. **~e en poudre,** caster sugar; (*Amer.*) finely ground sugar. **~e glace,** icing sugar. **~e roux,** brown sugar. **~ier, ~ière** *a.* sugar; *n.m.* (*récipient*) sugar-bowl.
sucr|er /sykre/ *v.t.* sugar, sweeten. **~é** *a.* sweet; (*additionné de sucre*) sweetened.
sucreries /sykrəri/ *n.f. pl.* sweets.
sud /syd/ *n.m.* south. ● *a. invar.* south; (*partie*) southern; (*direction*) southerly. **~-africain, ~-africaine** *a.* & *n.m., f.* South African. **~-est** *n.m.* south-east. **~-ouest** *n.m.* south-west.
Suède /sɥɛd/ *n.f.* Sweden.
suédois, ~e /sɥedwa, -z/ *a.* Swedish. ● *n.m., f.* Swede. ● *n.m.* (*lang.*) Swedish.
suer /sɥe/ *v.t./i.* sweat. **faire ~ qn.,** (*fam.*) get on s.o.'s nerves.
sueur /sɥœr/ *n.f.* sweat. **en ~,** sweating.
suff|ire† /syfir/ *v.i.* be enough (**à qn.,** for s.o.). **il ~it de faire,** one only has to do. **il ~it d'une goutte pour,** a drop is enough to. **~ire à,** (*besoin*) satisfy. **se ~ire à soi-même,** be self-sufficient.
suffis|ant, ~ante /syfizɑ̃, -t/ *a.* sufficient; (*vaniteux*) conceited. **~amment** *adv.* sufficiently. **~amment de,** sufficient. **~ance** *n.f.* (*vanité*) conceit.
suffixe /syfiks/ *n.m.* suffix.
suffoquer /syfɔke/ *v.t./i.* choke, suffocate.
suffrage /syfraʒ/ *n.m.* (*voix: pol.*) vote; (*modalité*) suffrage.
sugg|érer /sygʒere/ *v.t.* suggest. **~estion** /-ʒɛstjɔ̃/ *n.f.* suggestion.
suggesti|f, ~ve /sygʒɛstif, -v/ *a.* suggestive.
suicid|e /sɥisid/ *n.m.* suicide. **~aire** *a.* suicidal.
suicid|er (se) /(sə)sɥiside/ *v. pr.* commit suicide. **~é, ~ée** *n.m., f.* suicide.
suie /sɥi/ *n.f.* soot.
suint|er /sɥɛ̃te/ *v.i.* ooze. **~ement** *n.m.* oozing.
suis /sɥi/ *voir* être, suivre.
Suisse /sɥis/ *n.f.* Switzerland.
suisse /sɥis/ *a.* & *n.m.* Swiss. **~sse** /-ɛs/ *n.f.* Swiss (woman).
suite /sɥit/ *n.f.* continuation, rest; (*d'un film*) sequel; (*série*) series; (*appartement, escorte*) suite; (*résultat*) consequence; (*cohérence*) order. **~s,** (*de maladie*) after-effects. **à la ~, de ~,** (*successivement*) in succession. **à la ~ de,** (*derrière*) behind. **à la ~ de, par ~ de,** as a result of. **faire ~ (à),** follow. **par la ~,** afterwards. **~ à votre lettre du,** further to your letter of the.
suivant[1]**, ~e** /sɥivɑ̃, -t/ *a.* following, next. ● *n.m., f.* following *ou* next person.
suivant[2] /sɥivɑ̃/ *prép.* (*selon*) according to.
suivi /sɥivi/ *a.* steady, sustained; (*cohérent*) consistent. **peu/très ~,** (*cours*) poorly-/well-attended.
suivre† /sɥivr/ *v.t./i.* follow; (*comprendre*) keep up (with), follow. **se ~** *v. pr.* follow each other. **faire ~,** (*courrier etc.*) forward.
sujet[1]**, ~te** /syʒɛ, -t/ *a.* **~ à,** liable *ou* subject to. ● *n.m., f.* (*gouverné*) subject.
sujet[2] /syʒɛ/ *n.m.* (*matière, individu*) subject; (*motif*) cause; (*gram.*) subject. **au ~ de,** about.
sulfurique /sylfyrik/ *a.* sulphuric.
sultan /syltɑ̃/ *n.m.* sultan.
summum /sɔmɔm/ *n.m.* height.
super /sypɛr/ *n.m.* (*essence*) four-star, premium (*Amer.*). ● *a. invar.* (*fam.*) great. ● *adv.* (*fam.*) ultra, fantastically.
superbe /sypɛrb/ *a.* superb.
supercherie /sypɛrʃəri/ *n.f.* trickery.
supérette /syperɛt/ *n.f.* minimarket.
superficie /sypɛrfisi/ *n.f.* area.
superficiel, ~le /sypɛrfisjɛl/ *a.* superficial.
superflu /sypɛrfly/ *a.* superfluous. ● *n.m.* (*excédent*) surplus.
supérieur, ~e /syperjœr/ *a.* (*plus haut*) upper; (*quantité, nombre*) greater (**à,** than); (*études, principe*) higher (**à,** than); (*meilleur, hautain*) superior (**à,** to). ● *n.m., f.* superior.
supériorité /syperjɔrite/ *n.f.* superiority.
superlati|f, ~ve /sypɛrlatif, -v/ *a.* & *n.m.* superlative.
supermarché /sypɛrmarʃe/ *n.m.* supermarket.

superposer /sypɛrpoze/ *v.t.* superimpose.
superproduction /sypɛrprɔdyksjɔ̃/ *n.f.* (*film*) spectacular.
superpuissance /sypɛrpɥisɑ̃s/ *n.f.* superpower.
supersonique /sypɛrsɔnik/ *a.* supersonic.
superstit|ion /sypɛrstisjɔ̃/ *n.f.* superstition. **~ieux, ~ieuse** *a.* superstitious.
superviser /sypɛrvize/ *v.t.* supervise.
supplanter /syplɑ̃te/ *v.t.* supplant.
suppléan|t, ~te /sypleɑ̃, -t/ *n.m., f.* & *a.* **(professeur) ~t,** supply teacher; **(juge) ~t,** deputy (judge). **~ce** *n.f.* (*fonction*) temporary appointment.
suppléer /syplee/ *v.t.* (*remplacer*) replace; (*ajouter*) supply. ● *v.i.* **~ à,** (*compenser*) make up for.
supplément /syplemɑ̃/ *n.m.* (*argent*) extra charge; (*de frites, légumes*) extra portion. **en ~,** extra. **un ~ de,** (*travail etc.*) extra. **payer pour un ~ de bagages,** pay extra for excess luggage. **~aire** /-tɛr/ *a.* extra, additional.
supplic|e /syplis/ *n.m.* torture. **~ier** *v.t.* torture.
supplier /syplije/ *v.t.* beg, beseech (**de,** to).
support /sypɔr/ *n.m.* support; (*publicitaire: fig.*) medium.
support|er[1] /sypɔrte/ *v.t.* (*endurer*) bear; (*subir*) suffer; (*soutenir*) support; (*résister à*) withstand. **~able** *a.* bearable.
supporter[2] /sypɔrtɛr/ *n.m.* (*sport*) supporter.
suppos|er /sypoze/ *v.t.* suppose; (*impliquer*) imply. **à ~er que,** supposing that. **~ition** *n.f.* supposition.
suppositoire /sypɔzitwar/ *n.m.* suppository.
suppr|imer /syprime/ *v.t.* get rid of, remove; (*annuler*) cancel; (*mot*) delete. **~imer à qn.,** (*enlever*) take away from s.o. **~ession** *n.f.* removal; cancellation; deletion.
suprématie /sypremasi/ *n.f.* supremacy.
suprême /syprɛm/ *a.* supreme.
sur /syr/ *prép.* on, upon; (*par-dessus*) over; (*au sujet de*) about, on; (*proportion*) out of; (*mesure*) by. **aller/tourner/***etc.* **~,** go/turn/*etc.* towards. **mettre/jeter/***etc.* **~,** put/throw/*etc.* on to. **~-le-champ** *adv.* immediately. **~ le qui-vive,** on the alert. **~ mesure,** made to measure. **~ place,** on the spot. **~ ce,** hereupon.
sur- /syr/ *préf.* over-.
sûr /syr/ *a.* certain, sure; (*sans danger*) safe; (*digne de confiance*) reliable; (*main*) steady; (*jugement*) sound.
surabondance /syrabɔ̃dɑ̃s/ *n.f.* superabundance.
suranné /syrane/ *a.* outmoded.
surcharg|e /syrʃarʒ/ *n.f.* overloading; (*poids*) extra load. **~er** *v.t.* overload; (*texte*) alter.
surchauffer /syrʃofe/ *v.t.* overheat.
surchoix /syrʃwa/ *a. invar.* of finest quality.
surclasser /syrklɑse/ *v.t.* outclass.
surcroît /syrkrwa/ *n.m.* increase (**de,** in), additional amount (**de,** of). **de ~,** in addition.
surdité /syrdite/ *n.f.* deafness.
sureau (*pl.* **~x**) /syro/ *n.m.* (*arbre*) elder.
surélever /syrɛlve/ *v.t.* raise.
sûrement /syrmɑ̃/ *adv.* certainly; (*sans danger*) safely.
surench|ère /syrɑ̃ʃɛr/ *n.f.* higher bid. **~érir** *v.i.* bid higher (**sur,** than).
surestimer /syrɛstime/ *v.t.* overestimate.
sûreté /syrte/ *n.f.* safety; (*garantie*) surety; (*d'un geste*) steadiness. **être en ~,** be safe. **S~ (nationale),** *division of French Ministère de l'Intérieur in charge of police.*
surexcité /syrɛksite/ *a.* very excited.
surf /syrf/ *n.m.* surfing.
surface /syrfas/ *n.f.* surface. **faire ~,** (*sous-marin etc.*) surface. **en ~,** (*fig.*) superficially.
surfait, ~e /syrfɛ, -t/ *a.* overrated.
surgelé /syrʒəle/ *a.* (deep-)frozen. **(aliments) ~s,** frozen food.
surgir /syrʒir/ *v.i.* appear (suddenly); (*difficulté*) arise.
surhomme /syrɔm/ *n.m.* superman.
surhumain, ~e /syrymɛ̃, -ɛn/ *a.* superhuman.
surlendemain /syrlɑ̃dmɛ̃/ *n.m.* **le ~,** two days later. **le ~ de,** two days after.
surligneur /syrliɲœr/ *n.m.* highlighter (pen).
surmen|er /syrməne/ *v.t.,* **se ~er** *v. pr.* overwork. **~age** *n.m.* overworking; (*méd.*) overwork.

surmonter /syrmɔ̃te/ *v.t.* (*vaincre*) overcome, surmount; (*être au-dessus de*) surmount, top.

surnager /syrnaʒe/ *v.i.* float.

surnaturel, ~le /syrnatyrɛl/ *a.* supernatural.

surnom /syrnɔ̃/ *n.m.* nickname. **~mer** /-ɔme/ *v.t.* nickname.

surnombre (en) /(ɑ̃)syrnɔ̃br/ *adv.* too many. **il est en ~,** he is one too many.

surpasser /syrpɑse/ *v.t.* surpass.

surpeuplé /syrpœple/ *a.* overpopulated.

surplomb /syrplɔ̃/ *n.m.* **en ~,** overhanging. **~er** /-be/ *v.t./i.* overhang.

surplus /syrply/ *n.m.* surplus.

surpr|endre† /syrprɑ̃dr/ *v.t.* (*étonner*) surprise; (*prendre au dépourvu*) catch, surprise; (*entendre*) overhear. **~enant, ~enante** *a.* surprising. **~is, ~ise** *a.* surprised (**de,** at).

surprise /syrpriz/ *n.f.* surprise. **~-partie** (*pl.* **~s-parties**) *n.f.* party.

surréalisme /syrrealism/ *n.m.* surrealism.

sursaut /syrso/ *n.m.* start, jump. **en ~,** with a start. **~ de,** (*regain*) burst of. **~er** /-te/ *v.i.* start, jump.

sursis /syrsi/ *n.m.* reprieve; (*mil.*) deferment. **deux ans (de prison) avec ~,** a two-year suspended sentence.

surtaxe /syrtaks/ *n.f.* surcharge.

surtout /syrtu/ *adv.* especially, mainly; (*avant tout*) above all. **~ pas,** certainly not.

surveillant, ~e /syrvɛjɑ̃, -t/ *n.m., f.* (*de prison*) warder; (*au lycée*) supervisor (in charge of discipline).

surveill|er /syrveje/ *v.t.* watch; (*travaux, élèves*) supervise. **~ance** *n.f.* watch; supervision; (*de la police*) surveillance.

survenir /syrvənir/ *v.i.* occur, come about; (*personne*) turn up; (*événement*) take place.

survêtement /syrvɛtmɑ̃/ *n.m.* (*sport*) track suit.

survie /syrvi/ *n.f.* survival.

survivance /syrvivɑ̃s/ *n.f.* survival.

surviv|re† /syrvivr/ *v.i.* survive. **~re à,** (*conflit etc.*) survive; (*personne*) outlive. **~ant, ~ante,** *a.* surviving; *n.m., f.* survivor.

survol /syrvɔl/ *n.m.* **le ~ de,** flying over. **~er** *v.t.* fly over; (*livre*) skim through.

survolté /syrvɔlte/ *a.* (*surexcité*) worked up.

susceptib|le /sysɛptibl/ *a.* touchy. **~le de faire,** (*possibilité*) liable to do; (*capacité*) able to do. **~lité** n.f. susceptibility.

susciter /sysite/ *v.t.* (*éveiller*) arouse; (*occasionner*) create.

suspect, ~e /syspɛ, -ɛkt/ *a.* (*témoignage*) suspect; (*individu*) suspicious. **~ de,** suspected of. ● *n.m., f.* suspect. **~er** /-ɛkte/ *v.t.* suspect.

suspend|re /syspɑ̃dr/ *v.t.* (*arrêter, différer, destituer*) suspend; (*accrocher*) hang (up). **se ~re à,** hang from. **~u à,** hanging from.

suspens (en) /(ɑ̃)syspɑ̃/ *adv.* (*affaire*) in abeyance; (*dans l'indécision*) in suspense.

suspense /syspɛns/ *n.m.* suspense.

suspension /syspɑ̃sjɔ̃/ *n.f.* suspension; (*lustre*) chandelier.

suspicion /syspisjɔ̃/ *n.f.* suspicion.

susurrer /sysyre/ *v.t./i.* murmur.

suture /sytyr/ *n.f.* **point de ~,** stitch.

svelte /svɛlt/ *a.* slender.

S.V.P. *abrév. voir* s'il vous plaît.

sweat-shirt /switʃœrt/ *n.m.* sweatshirt.

syllabe /silab/ *n.f.* syllable.

symbol|e /sɛ̃bɔl/ *n.m.* symbol. **~ique** *a.* symbolic(al). **~iser** *v.t.* symbolize.

symétr|ie /simetri/ *n.f.* symmetry. **~ique** *a.* symmetrical.

sympa /sɛ̃pa/ *a. invar.* (*fam.*) nice. **sois ~,** be a pal.

sympath|ie /sɛ̃pati/ *n.f.* (*goût*) liking; (*affinité*) affinity; (*condoléances*) sympathy. **~ique** *a.* nice, pleasant.

sympathis|er /sɛ̃patize/ *v.i.* get on well (**avec,** with). **~ant, ~ante** *n.m., f.* sympathizer.

symphon|ie /sɛ̃fɔni/ *n.f.* symphony. **~ique** *a.* symphonic; (*orchestre*) symphony.

symposium /sɛ̃pozjɔm/ *n.m.* symposium.

sympt|ôme /sɛ̃ptom/ *n.m.* symptom. **~omatique** /-ɔmatik/ *a.* symptomatic.

synagogue /sinagɔg/ *n.f.* synagogue.

synchroniser /sɛ̃krɔnize/ *v.t.* synchronize.

syncope /sɛ̃kɔp/ *n.f.* (*méd.*) blackout.
syncoper /sɛ̃kɔpe/ *v.t.* syncopate.
syndic /sɛ̃dik/ *n.m.* **~ (d'immeuble),** managing agent.
syndic|at /sɛ̃dika/ *n.m.* (trade) union. **~at d'initiative,** tourist office. **~al** (*m. pl.* **~aux**) *a.* (trade-)union. **~aliste** *n.m./f.* trade-unionist; *a.* (trade-)union.
syndiqué, ~e /sɛ̃dike/ *n.m., f.* (trade-)union member.
syndrome /sɛ̃drom/ *n.m.* syndrome.
synonyme /sinɔnim/ *a.* synonymous. ● *n.m.* synonym.
syntaxe /sɛ̃taks/ *n.f.* syntax.
synthèse /sɛ̃tɛz/ *n.f.* synthesis.
synthétique /sɛ̃tetik/ *a.* synthetic.
synthé(tiseur) /sɛ̃te(tizœr)/ *n.m.* synthesizer.
syphilis /sifilis/ *n.f.* syphilis.
Syrie /siri/ *n.f.* Syria.
syrien, ~ne /sirjɛ̃, -jɛn/ *a.* & *n.m., f.* Syrian.
systématique /sistematik/ *a.* systematic. **~ment** *adv.* systematically.
système /sistɛm/ *n.m.* system. **le ~ D,** coping with problems.

T

t' /t/ *voir* te.
ta /ta/ *voir* ton[1].
tabac /taba/ *n.m.* tobacco; (*magasin*) tobacconist's shop. ● *a. invar.* buff. **~ à priser,** snuff.
tabasser /tabase/ *v.t.* (*fam.*) beat up.
table /tabl/ *n.f.* table. **à ~!,** come and eat! **faire ~ rase,** make a clean sweep (**de,** of). **~ de nuit,** bedside table. **~ des matières,** table of contents. **~ roulante,** (tea-)trolley; (*Amer.*) (serving) cart.
tableau (*pl.* **~x**) /tablo/ *n.m.* picture; (*peinture*) painting; (*panneau*) board; (*graphique*) chart; (*liste*) list. **~ (noir),** blackboard. **~ d'affichage,** notice-board. **~ de bord,** dashboard.
tabler /table/ *v.i.* **~ sur,** count on.
tablette /tablɛt/ *n.f.* shelf. **~ de chocolat,** bar of chocolate.
tablier /tablije/ *n.m.* apron; (*de pont*) platform; (*de magasin*) shutter.
tabloïd(e) /tablɔid/ *a.* & *n.m.* tabloid.
tabou /tabu/ *n.m.* & *a.* taboo.
tabouret /taburɛ/ *n.m.* stool.
tabulateur /tabylatœr/ *n.m.* tabulator.
tac /tak/ *n.m.* **du ~ au tac,** tit for tat.
tache /taʃ/ *n.f.* mark, spot; (*salissure*) stain. **faire ~ d'huile,** spread. **~ de rousseur,** freckle.
tâche /taʃ/ *n.f.* task, job.
tacher /taʃe/ *v.t.* stain. **se ~** *v. pr.* (*personne*) get stains on one's clothes.
tâcher /taʃe/ *v.i.* **~ de faire,** try to do.
tacheté /taʃte/ *a.* spotted.
tacite /tasit/ *a.* tacit.
taciturne /tasityrn/ *a.* taciturn.
tact /takt/ *n.m.* tact.
tactile /taktil/ *a.* tactile.
tactique /taktik/ *a.* tactical. ● *n.f.* tactics. **une ~,** a tactic.
taie /tɛ/ *n.f.* **~ d'oreiller,** pillowcase.
taillader /tɑjade/ *v.t.* gash, slash.
taille[1] /tɑj/ *n.f.* (*milieu du corps*) waist; (*hauteur*) height; (*grandeur*) size. **de ~,** sizeable. **être de ~ à faire,** be up to doing.
taill|e[2] /tɑj/ *n.f.* cutting; pruning; (*forme*) cut. **~er** *v.t.* cut; (*arbre*) prune; (*crayon*) sharpen; (*vêtement*) cut out. **se ~er** *v. pr.* (*argot*) clear off. **~e-crayon(s)** *n.m. invar.* pencil-sharpener.
tailleur /tɑjœr/ *n.m.* tailor; (*costume*) lady's suit. **en ~,** cross-legged.
taillis /taji/ *n.m.* copse.
taire† /tɛr/ *v.t.* say nothing about. **se ~** *v. pr.* be silent *ou* quiet; (*devenir silencieux*) fall silent. **faire ~,** silence.
talc /talk/ *n.m.* talcum powder.
talent /talɑ̃/ *n.m.* talent. **~ueux, ~ueuse** /-tɥø, -z/ *a.* talented.
taloche /talɔʃ/ *n.f.* (*fam.*) slap.
talon /talɔ̃/ *n.m.* heel; (*de chèque*) stub.
talonner /talɔne/ *v.t.* follow hard on the heels of.
talus /taly/ *n.m.* embankment.
tambour /tɑ̃bur/ *n.m.* drum; (*personne*) drummer; (*porte*) revolving door.
tambourin /tɑ̃burɛ̃/ *n.m.* tambourine.
tambouriner /tɑ̃burine/ *v.t./i.* drum (**sur,** on).
tamis /tami/ *n.m.* sieve. **~er** /-ze/ *v.t.* sieve.
Tamise /tamiz/ *n.f.* Thames.

tamisé /tamize/ *a.* (*lumière*) subdued.
tampon /tɑ̃pɔ̃/ *n.m.* (*pour boucher*) plug; (*ouate*) wad, pad; (*timbre*) stamp; (*de train*) buffer. **~ (hygiénique),** tampon.
tamponner /tɑ̃pɔne/ *v.t.* crash into; (*timbrer*) stamp; (*plaie*) dab; (*mur*) plug. **se ~** *v. pr.* (*véhicules*) crash into each other.
tandem /tɑ̃dɛm/ *n.m.* (*bicyclette*) tandem; (*personnes: fig.*) duo.
tandis que /tɑ̃dik(ə)/ *conj.* while.
tangage /tɑ̃gaʒ/ *n.m.* pitching.
tangente /tɑ̃ʒɑ̃t/ *n.f.* tangent.
tangible /tɑ̃ʒibl/ *a.* tangible.
tango /tɑ̃go/ *n.m.* tango.
tanguer /tɑ̃ge/ *v.i.* pitch.
tanière /tanjɛr/ *n.f.* den.
tank /tɑ̃k/ *n.m.* tank.
tann|er /tane/ *v.t.* tan. **~é** *a.* (*visage*) tanned, weather-beaten.
tant /tɑ̃/ *adv.* (*travailler, manger, etc.*) so much. **~ (de),** (*quantité*) so much; (*nombre*) so many. **~ que,** as long as; (*autant que*) as much as. **en ~ que,** (*comme*) as. **~ mieux!,** fine!, all the better! **~ pis!,** too bad!
tante /tɑ̃t/ *n.f.* aunt.
tantôt /tɑ̃to/ *adv.* sometimes; (*cet après-midi*) this afternoon.
tapag|e /tapaʒ/ *n.m.* din. **~eur, ~euse** *a.* rowdy; (*tape-à-l'œil*) flashy.
tapant, ~e /tapɑ̃, -t/ *a.* **à deux/trois/** *etc.* **heures ~es** at exactly two/three/*etc.* o'clock.
tape /tap/ *n.f.* slap. **~-à-l'œil** *a. invar.* flashy, tawdry.
taper /tape/ *v.t.* bang; (*enfant*) slap; (*emprunter: fam.*) touch for money. **~ (à la machine),** type. ● *v.i.* (*cogner*) bang; (*soleil*) beat down. **~ dans,** (*puiser dans*) dig into. **~ sur,** thump; (*critiquer: fam.*) knock. **se ~** *v. pr.* (*repas: fam.*) put away; (*corvée: fam.*) do.
tap|ir (se) /(sə)tapir/ *v. pr.* crouch. **~i** *a.* crouching.
tapis /tapi/ *n.m.* carpet; (*petit*) rug; (*aux cartes*) baize. **~ de bain,** bath mat. **~-brosse** *n.m.* doormat. **~ de sol,** groundsheet. **~ roulant,** (*pour objets*) conveyor belt.
tapiss|er /tapise/ *v.t.* (wall)paper; (*fig.*) cover (**de,** with). **~erie** *n.f.* tapestry; (*papier peint*) wallpaper. **~ier, ~ière** *n.m., f.* (*décorateur*) interior decorator; (*qui recouvre un siège*) upholsterer.
tapoter /tapɔte/ *v.t.* tap, pat.
taquin, ~e /takɛ̃, -in/ *a.* fond of teasing. ● *n.m., f.* tease(r). **~er** /-ine/ *v.t.* tease. **~erie(s)** /-inri/ *n.f.* (*pl.*) teasing.
tarabiscoté /tarabiskɔte/ *a.* overelaborate.
tard /tar/ *adv.* late. **au plus ~,** at the latest. **plus ~,** later. **sur le ~,** late in life.
tard|er /tarde/ *v.i.* (*être lent à venir*) be a long time coming. **~er (à faire),** take a long time (doing), delay (doing). **sans (plus) ~er,** without (further) delay. **il me tarde de,** I long to.
tardi|f, ~ve /tardif, -v/ *a.* late; (*regrets*) belated.
tare /tar/ *n.f.* (*défaut*) defect.
taré /tare/ *a.* cretin.
targette /tarʒɛt/ *n.f.* bolt.
targuer (se) /(sə)targe/ *v. pr.* **se ~ de,** boast about.
tarif /tarif/ *n.m.* tariff; (*de train, taxi*) fare. **~s postaux,** postage *ou* postal rates. **~aire** *a.* tariff.
tarir /tarir/ *v.t./i.*, **se ~** *v. pr.* dry up.
tartare /tartar/ *a.* (*culin.*) tartar.
tarte /tart/ *n.f.* tart; (*Amer.*) (open) pie. ● *a. invar.* (*sot: fam.*) stupid; (*laid: fam.*) ugly.
tartin|e /tartin/ *n.f.* slice of bread. **~e beurrée,** slice of bread and butter. **~er** *v.t.* spread.
tartre /tartr/ *n.m.* (*bouilloire*) fur, calcium deposit; (*dents*) tartar.
tas /tɑ/ *n.m.* pile, heap. **un** *ou* **des ~ de,** (*fam.*) lots of.
tasse /tɑs/ *n.f.* cup. **~ à thé,** teacup.
tasser /tɑse/ *v.t.* pack, squeeze; (*terre*) pack (down). **se ~** *v. pr.* (*terrain*) sink; (*se serrer*) squeeze up.
tâter /tɑte/ *v.t.* feel; (*fig.*) sound out. ● *v.i.* **~ de,** try out.
tatillon, ~ne /tatijɔ̃, -jɔn/ *a.* finicky.
tâtonn|er /tɑtɔne/ *v.i.* grope about. **~ements** *n.m. pl.* (*essais*) trial and error.
tâtons (à) /(a)tɑtɔ̃/ *adv.* **avancer** *ou* **marcher à ~,** grope one's way along.
tatou|er /tatwe/ *v.t.* tattoo. **~age** *n.m.* (*dessin*) tattoo.
taudis /todi/ *n.m.* hovel.
taule /tol/ *n.f.* (*fam.*) prison.
taup|e /top/ *n.f.* mole. **~inière** *n.f.* molehill.

taureau (*pl.* **~x**) /tɔro/ *n.m.* bull. **le T~,** Taurus.
taux /to/ *n.m.* rate.
taverne /tavɛrn/ *n.f.* tavern.
tax|e /taks/ *n.f.* tax. **~e sur la valeur ajoutée,** value added tax. **~er** *v.t.* tax; (*produit*) fix the price of. **~er qn. de,** accuse s.o. of.
taxi /taksi/ *n.m.* taxi(-cab); (*personne*: *fam.*) taxi-driver.
taxiphone /taksifɔn/ *n.m.* pay phone.
Tchécoslovaquie /tʃekɔslɔvaki/ *n.f.* Czechoslovakia.
tchèque /tʃɛk/ *a.* & *n.m./f.* Czech.
te, t'* /tə, t/ *pron.* you; (*indirect*) (to) you; (*réfléchi*) yourself.
technicien, ~ne /tɛknisjɛ̃, -jɛn/ *n.m., f.* technician.
technique /tɛknik/ *a.* technical. ● *n.f.* technique. **~ment** *adv.* technically.
technolog|ie /tɛknɔlɔʒi/ *n.f.* technology. **~ique** *a.* technological.
teck /tɛk/ *n.m.* teak.
tee-shirt /tiʃœrt/ *n.m.* tee-shirt.
teindre† /tɛ̃dr/ *v.t.* dye. **se ~ les cheveux** *v. pr.* dye one's hair.
teint /tɛ̃/ *n.m.* complexion.
teint|e /tɛ̃t/ *n.f.* shade, tint. **une ~e de,** (*fig.*) a tinge of. **~er** *v.t.* (*papier, verre, etc.*) tint; (*bois*) stain.
teintur|e /tɛ̃tyr/ *n.f.* dyeing; (*produit*) dye. **~erie** *n.f.* (*boutique*) dry-cleaner's. **~ier, ~ière** *n.m., f.* dry-cleaner.
tel, ~le /tɛl/ *a.* such. **un ~ livre**/*etc.*, such a book/*etc.* **un ~ chagrin**/*etc.*, such sorrow/*etc.* **~ que,** such as, like; (*ainsi que*) (just) as. **~ ou tel,** such-and-such. **~ quel,** (just) as it is.
télé /tele/ *n.f.* (*fam.*) TV.
télécommande /telekɔmɑ̃d/ *n.f.* remote control.
télécommunications /telekɔmynikɑsjɔ̃/ *n.f. pl.* telecommunications.
télécopi|e /telekɔpi/ *n.f.* tele(fax). **~eur** *n.m.* fax machine.
téléfilm /telefilm/ *n.m.* (tele)film.
télégramme /telegram/ *n.m.* telegram.
télégraph|e /telegraf/ *n.m.* telegraph. **~ier** *v.t./i.* **~ier (à),** cable. **~ique** *a.* telegraphic; (*fil, poteau*) telegraph.
téléguid|er /telegide/ *v.t.* control by radio. **~é** *a.* radio-controlled.
télématique /telematik/ *n.f.* computer communications.
télépathe /telepat/ *a.* & *n.m., f.* psychic.
télépathie /telepati/ *n.f.* telepathy.
téléphérique /teleferik/ *n.m.* cable-car.
téléphon|e /telefɔn/ *n.m.* (tele)-phone. **~e rouge,** (*pol.*) hot line. **~er** *v.t./i.* **~er (à),** (tele)phone. **~ique** *a.* (tele)phone. **~iste** *n.m./f.* operator.
télescop|e /telɛskɔp/ *n.m.* telescope. **~ique** *a.* telescopic.
télescoper /telɛskɔpe/ *v.t.* smash into. **se ~** *v. pr.* (*véhicules*) smash into each other.
télésiège /telesjɛʒ/ *n.m.* chair-lift.
téléski /teleski/ *n.m.* ski tow.
téléspecta|teur, ~trice /telespɛktatœr, -tris/ *n.m., f.* (television) viewer.
télévente /televɑ̃t/ *n.f.* telesales.
télévis|é /televize/ *a.* **émission ~ée,** television programme. **~eur** *n.m.* television set.
télévision /televizjɔ̃/ *n.f.* television.
télex /telɛks/ *n.m.* telex.
télexer /telɛkse/ *v.t.* telex.
telle /tɛl/ *voir* tel.
tellement /tɛlmɑ̃/ *adv.* (*tant*) so much; (*si*) so. **~ de,** (*quantité*) so much; (*nombre*) so many.
témér|aire /temerɛr/ *a.* rash. **~ité** *n.f.* rashness.
témoignage /temwaɲaʒ/ *n.m.* testimony, evidence; (*récit*) account. **~ de,** (*sentiment*) token of.
témoigner /temwaɲe/ *v.i.* testify (**de,** to). ● *v.t.* show. **~ que,** testify that.
témoin /temwɛ̃/ *n.m.* witness; (*sport*) baton. **être ~ de,** witness. **~ oculaire,** eyewitness.
tempe /tɑ̃p/ *n.f.* (*anat.*) temple.
tempérament /tɑ̃peramɑ̃/ *n.m.* temperament; (*physique*) constitution. **à ~,** (*acheter*) on hire-purchase; (*Amer.*) on the instalment plan.
température /tɑ̃peratyr/ *n.f.* temperature.
tempér|er /tɑ̃pere/ *v.t.* temper. **~é** *a.* (*climat*) temperate.
tempête /tɑ̃pɛt/ *n.f.* storm. **~ de neige,** snowstorm.
tempêter /tɑ̃pete/ *v.i.* (*crier*) rage.
temple /tɑ̃pl/ *n.m.* temple; (*protestant*) church.
temporaire /tɑ̃pɔrɛr/ *a.* temporary. **~ment** *adv.* temporarily.
temporel, ~le /tɑ̃pɔrɛl/ *a.* temporal.

temporiser /tɑ̃pɔrize/ *v.i.* play for time.

temps[1] /tɑ̃/ *n.m.* time; (*gram.*) tense; (*étape*) stage. **à ~ partiel/plein,** part-/full-time. **ces derniers ~,** lately. **dans le ~,** at one time. **dans quelque ~,** in a while. **de ~ en temps,** from time to time. **~ d'arrêt,** pause. **avoir tout son ~,** have plenty of time.

temps[2] /tɑ̃/ *n.m.* (*atmosphère*) weather. **~ de chien,** filthy weather. **quel ~ fait-il?,** what's the weather like?

tenace /tənas/ *a.* stubborn.

ténacité /tenasite/ *n.f.* stubbornness.

tenaille(s) /tənɑj/ *n.f.* (*pl.*) pincers.

tenanc|ier, ~ière /tənɑ̃sje, -jɛr/ *n.m., f.* keeper (**de,** of).

tenant /tənɑ̃/ *n.m.* (*partisan*) supporter; (*d'un titre*) holder.

tendance /tɑ̃dɑ̃s/ *n.f.* tendency; (*opinions*) leanings; (*évolution*) trend. **avoir ~ à,** have a tendency to, tend to.

tendon /tɑ̃dɔ̃/ *n.m.* tendon.

tendre[1] /tɑ̃dr/ *v.t.* stretch; (*piège*) set; (*bras*) stretch out; (*main*) hold out; (*cou*) crane; (*tapisserie*) hang. **~ à qn.,** hold out to s.o. ● *v.i.* **~ à,** tend to. **~ l'oreille,** prick up one's ears.

tendre[2] /tɑ̃dr/ *a.* tender; (*couleur, bois*) soft. **~ment** /-əmɑ̃/ *adv.* tenderly. **~sse** /-ɛs/ *n.f.* tenderness.

tendu /tɑ̃dy/ *a.* (*corde*) tight; (*personne, situation*) tense; (*main*) outstretched.

tén|èbres /tenɛbr/ *n.f. pl.* darkness. **~ébreux, ~ébreuse** *a.* dark.

teneur /tənœr/ *n.f.* content.

tenir† /tənir/ *v.t.* hold; (*pari, promesse, hôtel*) keep; (*place*) take up; (*propos*) utter; (*rôle*) play. **~ de,** (*avoir reçu de*) have got from. **~ pour,** regard as. **~ propre/chaud/** *etc.*, keep clean/warm/*etc.* ● *v.i.* hold. **~ à,** be attached to. **~ à faire,** be anxious to do. **~ dans,** fit into. **~ de qn.,** take after s.o. **se ~** *v. pr.* (*rester*) remain; (*debout*) stand; (*avoir lieu*) be held. **se ~ à,** hold on to. **se ~ bien,** behave o.s. **s'en ~ à,** (*se limiter à*) confine o.s. to. **~ bon,** stand firm. **~ compte de,** take into account. **~ le coup,** hold out. **~ tête à,** stand up to. **tiens!,** (*surprise*) hey!

tennis /tenis/ *n.m.* tennis; (*terrain*) tennis-court. ● *n.m. pl.* (*chaussures*) sneakers. **~ de table,** table tennis.

ténor /tenɔr/ *n.m.* tenor.

tension /tɑ̃sjɔ̃/ *n.f.* tension. **avoir de la ~,** have high blood-pressure.

tentacule /tɑ̃takyl/ *n.m.* tentacle.

tentative /tɑ̃tativ/ *n.f.* attempt.

tente /tɑ̃t/ *n.f.* tent.

tenter[1] /tɑ̃te/ *v.t.* try (**de faire,** to do).

tent|er[2] /tɑ̃te/ *v.t.* (*allécher*) tempt. **~é de,** tempted to. **~ation** *n.f.* temptation.

tenture /tɑ̃tyr/ *n.f.* (wall) hanging. **~s,** drapery.

tenu /təny/ *voir* **tenir**. ● *a.* **bien ~,** well-kept. **~ de,** obliged to.

ténu /teny/ *a.* (*fil etc.*) fine; (*cause, nuance*) tenuous.

tenue /təny/ *n.f.* (*habillement*) dress; (*de sport*) clothes; (*de maison*) upkeep; (*conduite*) (good) behaviour; (*maintien*) posture. **~ de soirée,** evening dress.

ter /tɛr/ *a. invar.* (*numéro*) B, b.

térébenthine /terebɑ̃tin/ *n.f.* turpentine.

tergiverser /tɛrʒivɛrse/ *v.i.* procrastinate.

terme /tɛrm/ *n.m.* (*mot*) term; (*date limite*) time-limit; (*fin*) end; (*date de loyer*) term. **à long/court ~,** long-/short-term. **en bons ~s,** on good terms (**avec,** with).

termin|al, ~ale (*m. pl.* **~aux**) /tɛrminal, -o/ *a.* terminal. **(classe) ~ale,** sixth form; (*Amer.*) twelfth grade. ● *n.m.* (*pl.* **~aux**) terminal.

termin|er /tɛrmine/ *v.t./i.* finish; (*soirée, débat*) end, finish. **se ~er** *v. pr.* end (**par,** with). **~aison** *n.f.* (*gram.*) ending.

terminologie /tɛrminɔlɔʒi/ *n.f.* terminology.

terminus /tɛrminys/ *n.m.* terminus.

terne /tɛrn/ *a.* dull, drab.

ternir /tɛrnir/ *v.t./i.*, **se ~** *v. pr.* tarnish.

terrain /tɛrɛ̃/ *n.m.* ground; (*parcelle*) piece of land; (*à bâtir*) plot. **~ d'aviation,** airfield. **~ de camping,** campsite. **~ de golf,** golf-course. **~ de jeu,** playground. **~ vague,** waste ground; (*Amer.*) vacant lot.

terrasse /tɛras/ *n.f.* terrace; (*de café*) pavement area.

terrassement /tɛrasmɑ̃/ *n.m.* excavation.

terrasser /tɛrase/ *v.t.* (*adversaire*) floor; (*maladie*) strike down.

terrassier /tɛrasje/ *n.m.* navvy, labourer, ditch-digger.

terre /tɛr/ *n.f.* (*planète, matière*) earth; (*étendue, pays*) land; (*sol*) ground; (*domaine*) estate. **à ~,** (*naut.*) ashore. **par ~,** (*tomber, jeter*) to the ground; (*s'asseoir, poser*) on the ground. **~ (cuite),** terracotta. **~-à-terre** *a. invar.* matter-of-fact, down-to-earth. **~-plein** *n.m.* platform, (*auto.*) central reservation. **la ~ ferme,** dry land. **~ glaise,** clay.

terreau (*m.pl.* **~x**) /tɛro/ *n.m.* compost.

terrer (se) /(sə)tɛre/ *v. pr.* hide o.s., dig o.s. in.

terrestre /tɛrɛstr/ *a.* land; (*de notre planète*) earth's; (*fig.*) earthly.

terreur /tɛrœr/ *n.f.* terror.

terreu|x, ~se /tɛrø, -z/ *a.* earthy; (*sale*) grubby.

terrible /tɛribl/ *a.* terrible; (*formidable: fam.*) terrific.

terrien, ~ne /tɛrjɛ̃, -jɛn/ *n.m., f.* earth-dweller.

terrier /tɛrje/ *n.m.* (*trou de lapin etc.*) burrow; (*chien*) terrier.

terrifier /tɛrifje/ *v.t.* terrify.

terrine /tɛrin/ *n.f.* (*culin.*) terrine.

territ|oire /tɛritwar/ *n.m.* territory. **~orial** (*m. pl.* **~oriaux**) *a.* territorial.

terroir /tɛrwar/ *n.m.* (*sol*) soil; (*région*) region. **du ~,** country.

terroriser /tɛrɔrize/ *v.t.* terrorize.

terroris|te /tɛrɔrist/ *n.m./f.* terrorist. **~me** *n.m.* terrorism.

tertre /tɛrtr/ *n.m.* mound.

tes /te/ *voir* ton[1].

tesson /tesɔ̃/ *n.m.* **~ de bouteille,** piece of broken bottle.

test /tɛst/ *n.m.* test. **~er** *v.t.* test.

testament /tɛstamɑ̃/ *n.m.* (*jurid.*) will; (*politique, artistique*) testament. **Ancien/Nouveau T~,** Old/New Testament.

testicule /tɛstikyl/ *n.m.* testicle.

tétanos /tetanos/ *n.m.* tetanus.

têtard /tɛtar/ *n.m.* tadpole.

tête /tɛt/ *n.f.* head; (*figure*) face; (*cheveux*) hair; (*cerveau*) brain. **à la ~ de,** at the head of. **à ~ reposée,** in a leisurely moment. **de ~,** (*calculer*) in one's head. **en ~,** (*sport*) in the lead. **faire la ~,** sulk. **faire une ~,** (*football*) head the ball. **tenir ~ à qn.,** stand up to s.o. **une forte ~,** a rebel. **la ~ la première,** head first. **il n'en fait qu'à sa ~,** he does just as he pleases. **de la ~ aux pieds,** from head to toe. **~-à-queue** *n.m. invar.* (*auto.*) spin. **~-à-tête** *n.m. invar.* tête-à-tête. **en ~-à-tête,** in private.

tétée /tete/ *n.f.* feed.

téter /tete/ *v.t./i.* suck.

tétine /tetin/ *n.f.* (*de biberon*) teat; (*sucette*) dummy; (*Amer.*) pacifier.

têtu /tety/ *a.* stubborn.

texte /tɛkst/ *n.m.* text; (*de leçon*) subject; (*morceau choisi*) passage.

textile /tɛkstil/ *n.m.* & *a.* textile.

textuel, ~le /tɛkstɥɛl/ *a.* literal.

texture /tɛkstyr/ *n.f.* texture.

thaïlandais, ~e /tailɑ̃dɛ, -z/ *a.* & *n.m., f.* Thai.

Thaïlande /tailɑ̃d/ *n.f.* Thailand.

thé /te/ *n.m.* tea.

théâtr|al (*m. pl.* **~aux**) /teɑtral, -o/ *a.* theatrical.

théâtre /teɑtr/ *n.m.* theatre; (*jeu forcé*) play-acting; (*d'un crime*) scene. **faire du ~,** act.

théière /tejɛr/ *n.f.* teapot.

thème /tɛm/ *n.m.* theme; (*traduction: scol.*) prose.

théolog|ie /teɔlɔʒi/ *n.f.* theology. **~ien** *n.m.* theologian. **~ique** *a.* theological.

théorème /teɔrɛm/ *n.m.* theorem.

théor|ie /teɔri/ *n.f.* theory. **~icien, ~icienne** *n.m., f.* theorist. **~ique** *a.* theoretical. **~iquement,** *adv.* theoretically.

thérap|ie /terapi/ *n.f.* therapy. **~eutique** *a.* therapeutic.

thermique /tɛrmik/ *a.* thermal.

thermomètre /tɛrmɔmɛtr/ *n.m.* thermometer.

thermonucléaire /tɛrmɔnykleɛr/ *a.* thermonuclear.

thermos /tɛrmos/ *n.m./f.* (P.) Thermos (P.) (flask).

thermostat /tɛrmɔsta/ *n.m.* thermostat.

thésauriser /tezɔrize/ *v.t./i.* hoard.

thèse /tɛz/ *n.f.* thesis.

thon /tɔ̃/ *n.m.* (*poisson*) tuna.

thrombose /trɔ̃boz/ *n.f.* thrombosis.

thym /tɛ̃/ *n.m.* thyme.

thyroïde /tirɔid/ *n.f.* thyroid.

tibia /tibja/ *n.m.* shin-bone.

tic /tik/ *n.m.* (*contraction*) twitch; (*manie*) mannerism.

ticket /tikɛ/ *n.m.* ticket.

tic-tac /tiktak/ *n.m. invar.* (*de pendule*) ticking. **faire ~,** go tick tock.

tiède /tjɛd/ *a.* lukewarm; (*atmosphère*) mild. **tiédeur** /tjedœr/ *n.f.* lukewarmness; mildness.

tiédir /tjedir/ *v.t./i.* **(faire) ~,** warm slightly.

tien, ~ne /tjɛ̃, tjɛn/ *pron.* **le ~, la ~ne, les ~(ne)s,** yours. **à la ~ ne!,** cheers!

tiens, tient /tjɛ̃/ *voir* tenir.

tiercé /tjɛrse/ *n.m.* place-betting.

tier|s, ~ce /tjɛr, -s/ *a.* third. ● *n.m.* (*fraction*) third; (*personne*) third party. **T~s-Monde** *n.m.* Third World.

tifs /tif/ *n.m. pl.* (*fam.*) hair.

tige /tiʒ/ *n.f.* (*bot.*) stem, stalk; (*en métal*) shaft.

tignasse /tiɲas/ *n.f.* mop of hair.

tigre /tigr/ *n.m.* tiger. **~sse** /-ɛs/ *n.f.* tigress.

tigré /tigre/ *a.* (*rayé*) striped; (*chat*) tabby.

tilleul /tijœl/ *n.m.* lime(-tree), linden (-tree); (*infusion*) lime tea.

timbale /tɛ̃bal/ *n.f.* (*gobelet*) (metal) tumbler.

timbr|e /tɛ̃br/ *n.m.* stamp; (*sonnette*) bell; (*de voix*) tone. **~e-poste** (*pl.* **~es-poste**) *n.m.* postage stamp. **~er** *v.t.* stamp.

timbré /tɛ̃bre/ *a.* (*fam.*) crazy.

timid|e /timid/ *a.* timid. **~ité** *n.f.* timidity.

timoré /timɔre/ *a.* timorous.

tintamarre /tɛ̃tamar/ *n.m.* din.

tint|er /tɛ̃te/ *v.i.* ring; (*clefs*) jingle. **~ement** *n.m.* ringing; jingling.

tique /tik/ *n.f.* (*insecte*) tick.

tir /tir/ *n.m.* (*sport*) shooting; (*action de tirer*) firing; (*feu, rafale*) fire. **~ à l'arc,** archery. **~ forain,** shooting-gallery.

tirade /tirad/ *n.f.* soliloquy.

tirage /tiraʒ/ *n.m.* (*de photo*) printing; (*de journal*) circulation; (*de livre*) edition; (*de loterie*) draw; (*de cheminée*) draught. **~ au sort,** drawing lots.

tiraill|er /tirɑje/ *v.t.* pull (away) at; (*harceler*) plague. **~é entre,** (*possibilités etc.*) torn between. **~ement** *n.m.* (*douleur*) gnawing pain; (*conflit*) conflict.

tiré /tire/ *a.* (*traits*) drawn.

tire-bouchon /tirbuʃɔ̃/ *n.m.* corkscrew.

tire-lait /tirlɛ/ *n.m.* breastpump.

tirelire /tirlir/ *n.f.* money-box; (*Amer.*) coin-bank.

tirer /tire/ *v.t.* pull; (*navire*) tow, tug; (*langue*) stick out; (*conclusion, trait, rideaux*) draw; (*coup de feu*) fire; (*gibier*) shoot; (*photo*) print. **~ de,** (*sortir*) take *ou* get out of; (*extraire*) extract from; (*plaisir, nom*) derive from. ● *v.i.* shoot, fire (**sur,** at). **~ sur,** (*couleur*) verge on; (*corde*) pull at. **se ~** *v. pr.* (*fam.*) clear off. **se ~ de,** get out of. **s'en ~,** (*en réchapper*) pull through; (*réussir: fam.*) cope. **~ à sa fin,** be drawing to a close. **~ au clair,** clarify. **~ au sort,** draw lots (for). **~ parti de,** take advantage of. **~ profit de,** profit from.

tiret /tirɛ/ *n.m.* dash.

tireur /tirœr/ *n.m.* gunman. **~ d'élite,** marksman. **~ isolé,** sniper.

tiroir /tirwar/ *n.m.* drawer. **~-caisse** (*pl.* **~s-caisses**) *n.m.* till.

tisane /tizan/ *n.f.* herb-tea.

tison /tizɔ̃/ *n.m.* ember.

tisonnier /tizɔnje/ *n.m.* poker.

tiss|er /tise/ *v.t.* weave. **~age** *n.m.* weaving. **~erand** /tisrɑ̃/ *n.m.* weaver.

tissu /tisy/ *n.m.* fabric, material; (*biologique*) tissue. **un ~ de,** (*fig.*) a web of. **~-éponge** (*pl.* **~s-éponge**) *n.m.* towelling.

titre /titr/ *n.m.* title; (*diplôme*) qualification; (*comm.*) bond. **~s,** (*droits*) claims. **(gros) ~s,** headlines. **à ce ~,** (*pour cette qualité*) as such. **à ~ d'exemple,** as an example. **à juste ~,** rightly. **à ~ privé,** in a private capacity. **~ de propriété,** title-deed.

titré /titre/ *a.* titled.

titrer /titre/ *v.t.* (*journal*) give as a headline.

tituber /titybe/ *v.i.* stagger.

titul|aire /titylɛr/ *a.* **être ~aire,** have tenure. **être ~aire de,** hold. ● *n.m./f.* (*de permis etc.*) holder. **~ariser** *v.t.* give tenure to.

toast /tost/ *n.m.* piece of toast; (*allocution*) toast.

toboggan /tɔbɔgɑ̃/ *n.m.* (*traîneau*) toboggan; (*glissière*) slide; (*auto.*) flyover; (*auto., Amer.*) overpass.

toc /tɔk/ *int.* **~ toc!** knock knock!

tocsin /tɔksɛ̃/ *n.m.* alarm (bell).

toge /tɔʒ/ *n.f.* (*de juge etc.*) gown.

tohu-bohu /tɔybɔy/ *n.m.* hubbub.

toi /twa/ *pron.* you; (*réfléchi*) yourself. **lève-~,** stand up.

toile /twal/ *n.f.* cloth; (*sac, tableau*) canvas; (*coton*) cotton. **~ d'arai-**

gnée, (spider's) web; (*délabrée*) cobweb. **~ de fond,** backdrop, backcloth.
toilette /twalɛt/ *n.f.* washing; (*habillement*) clothes, dress. **~s,** (*cabinets*) toilet(s). **de ~,** (*articles, savon, etc.*) toilet. **faire sa ~,** wash (and get ready).
toi-même /twamɛm/ *pron.* yourself.
toiser /twaze/ *v.t.* **~ qn.,** look s.o. up and down.
toison /twazɔ̃/ *n.f.* (*laine*) fleece.
toit /twa/ *n.m.* roof. **~ ouvrant,** (*auto.*) sun-roof.
toiture /twatyr/ *n.f.* roof.
tôle /tol/ *n.f.* (*plaque*) iron sheet. **~ ondulée,** corrugated iron.
tolérable /tɔlerabl/ *a.* tolerable.
toléran|t, ~te /tɔlerɑ̃, -t/ *a.* tolerant. **~ce** *n.f.* tolerance; (*importations: comm.*) allowance.
tolérer /tɔlere/ *v.t.* tolerate; (*importations: comm.*) allow.
tollé /tɔle/ *n.m.* hue and cry.
tomate /tɔmat/ *n.f.* tomato.
tombe /tɔ̃b/ *n.f.* grave; (*avec monument*) tomb.
tombeau (*pl.* **~x**) /tɔ̃bo/ *n.m.* tomb.
tombée /tɔ̃be/ *n.f.* **~ de la nuit,** nightfall.
tomber /tɔ̃be/ *v.i.* (*aux. être*) fall; (*fièvre, vent*) drop; (*enthousiasme*) die down. **faire ~,** knock over; (*gouvernement*) bring down. **laisser ~,** drop; (*abandonner*) let down. **laisse ~!,** forget it! **~ à l'eau,** (*projet*) fall through. **~ bien** *ou* **à point,** come at the right time. **~ en panne,** break down. **~ en syncope,** faint. **~ sur,** (*trouver*) run across.
tombola /tɔ̃bɔla/ *n.f.* tombola; (*Amer.*) lottery.
tome /tɔm/ *n.m.* volume.
ton [1], **ta** *ou* **ton*** (*pl.* **tes**) /tɔ̃, ta, tɔ̃n, te/ *a.* your.
ton [2] /tɔ̃/ *n.m.* tone; (*gamme: mus.*) key; (*hauteur de la voix*) pitch. **de bon ~,** in good taste.
tonalité /tɔnalite/ *n.f.* tone; (*téléphone*) dialling tone; (*téléphone: Amer.*) dial tone.
tond|re /tɔ̃dr/ *v.t.* (*herbe*) mow; (*mouton*) shear; (*cheveux*) clip. **~euse** *n.f.* shears; clippers. **~euse (à gazon),** (lawn-)mower.
tongs /tɔ̃g/ *n.f. pl.* flip-flops.
tonifier /tɔnifje/ *v.t.* tone up.
tonique /tɔnik/ *a.* & *n.m.* tonic.
tonne /tɔn/ *n.f.* ton(ne).
tonneau (*pl.* **~x**) /tɔno/ *n.m.* (*récipient*) barrel; (*naut.*) ton; (*culbute*) somersault.
tonnelle /tɔnɛl/ *n.f.* bower.
tonner /tɔne/ *v.i.* thunder.
tonnerre /tɔnɛr/ *n.m.* thunder.
tonte /tɔ̃t/ *n.f.* (*de gazon*) mowing; (*de moutons*) shearing.
tonton /tɔ̃tɔ̃/ *n.m.* (*fam.*) uncle.
tonus /tɔnys/ *n.m.* energy.
top /tɔp/ *n.m.* (*signal pour marquer un instant précis*) stroke.
topo /tɔpo/ *n.m.* (*fam.*) talk, oral report.
toquade /tɔkad/ *n.f.* craze; (*pour une personne*) infatuation.
toque /tɔk/ *n.f.* (fur) hat; (*de jockey*) cap; (*de cuisinier*) hat.
toqué /tɔke/ *a.* (*fam.*) crazy.
torche /tɔrʃ/ *n.f.* torch.
torcher /tɔrʃe/ *v.t.* (*fam.*) wipe.
torchon /tɔrʃɔ̃/ *n.m.* cloth, duster; (*pour la vaisselle*) tea-towel; (*Amer.*) dish-towel.
tordre /tɔrdr/ *v.t.* twist; (*linge*) wring. **se ~** *v. pr.* twist, bend; (*de douleur*) writhe. **se ~ (de rire),** split one's sides.
tordu /tɔrdy/ *a.* twisted, bent; (*esprit*) warped.
tornade /tɔrnad/ *n.f.* tornado.
torpeur /tɔrpœr/ *n.f.* lethargy.
torpill|e /tɔrpij/ *n.f.* torpedo. **~er** *v.t.* torpedo.
torréfier /tɔrefje/ *v.t.* roast.
torrent /tɔrɑ̃/ *n.m.* torrent. **~iel, ~ielle** /-sjɛl/ *a.* torrential.
torride /tɔrid/ *a.* torrid.
torsade /tɔrsad/ *n.f.* twist.
torse /tɔrs/ *n.m.* chest; (*sculpture*) torso.
tort /tɔr/ *n.m.* wrong. **à ~,** wrongly. **à ~ et à travers,** without thinking. **avoir ~,** be wrong (**de faire,** to do). **donner ~ à,** prove wrong. **être dans son ~,** be in the wrong. **faire (du) ~ à,** harm.
torticolis /tɔrtikɔli/ *n.m.* stiff neck.
tortiller /tɔrtije/ *v.t.* twist, twirl. **se ~** *v. pr.* wriggle, wiggle.
tortionnaire /tɔrsjɔnɛr/ *n.m.* torturer.
tortue /tɔrty/ *n.f.* tortoise; (*de mer*) turtle.
tortueu|x, ~se /tɔrtɥø, -z/ *a.* (*explication*) tortuous; (*chemin*) twisting.
tortur|e(s) /tɔrtyr/ *n.f.* (*pl.*) torture. **~er** *v.t.* torture.

tôt /to/ *adv.* early. **plus ~,** earlier. **au plus ~,** at the earliest. **le plus ~ possible,** as soon as possible. **~ ou tard,** sooner or later.

tot|al (*m. pl.* **~aux**) /tɔtal, -o/ *a.* total. ● *n.m.* (*pl.* **~aux**) total. ● *adv.* (*fam.*) to conclude, in short. **au ~al,** all in all. **~alement** *adv.* totally. **~aliser** *v.t.* total.

totalitaire /tɔtalitɛr/ *a.* totalitarian.

totalité /tɔtalite/ *n.f.* entirety. **la ~ de,** all of.

toubib /tubib/ *n.m.* (*fam.*) doctor.

touchant, ~e /tuʃɑ̃, -t/ *a.* (*émouvant*) touching.

touche /tuʃ/ *n.f.* (*de piano*) key; (*de peintre*) touch. **(ligne de) ~,** touch-line. **une ~ de,** a touch of.

toucher[1] /tuʃe/ *v.t.* touch; (*émouvoir*) move, touch; (*contacter*) get in touch with; (*cible*) hit; (*argent*) draw; (*chèque*) cash; (*concerner*) affect. ● *v.i.* **~ à,** touch; (*question*) touch on; (*fin, but*) approach. **je vais lui en ~ un mot,** I'll talk to him about it. **se ~** *v. pr.* (*lignes*) touch.

toucher[2] /tuʃe/ *n.m.* (*sens*) touch.

touffe /tuf/ *n.f.* (*de poils, d'herbe*) tuft; (*de plantes*) clump.

touffu /tufy/ *a.* thick, bushy; (*fig.*) complex.

toujours /tuʒur/ *adv.* always; (*encore*) still; (*en tout cas*) anyhow. **pour ~,** for ever.

toupet /tupɛ/ *n.m.* (*culot: fam.*) cheek, nerve.

toupie /tupi/ *n.f.* (*jouet*) top.

tour[1] /tur/ *n.f.* tower; (*immeuble*) tower block; (*échecs*) rook. **~ de contrôle,** control tower.

tour[2] /tur/ *n.m.* (*mouvement, succession, tournure*) turn; (*excursion*) trip; (*à pied*) walk; (*en auto*) drive; (*artifice*) trick; (*circonférence*) circumference; (*techn.*) lathe. **~ (de piste),** lap. **à ~ de rôle,** in turn. **à mon/***etc.* **~,** when it is my/*etc.* turn. **c'est mon/***etc.* **~ de,** it is my/*etc.* turn to. **faire le ~ de,** go round; (*question*) survey. **~ d'horizon,** survey. **~ de passe-passe,** sleight of hand. **~ de taille,** waist measurement; (*ligne*) waistline.

tourbe /turb/ *n.f.* peat.

tourbillon /turbijɔ̃/ *n.m.* whirlwind; (*d'eau*) whirlpool; (*fig.*) whirl, swirl. **~ner** /-jɔne/ *v.i.* whirl, swirl.

tourelle /turɛl/ *n.f.* turret.

tourisme /turism/ *n.m.* tourism. **faire du ~,** do some sightseeing.

tourist|e /turist/ *n.m./f.* tourist. **~ique** *a.* tourist; (*route*) scenic.

tourment /turmɑ̃/ *n.m.* torment. **~er** /-te/ *v.t.* torment. **se ~er** *v. pr.* worry.

tournage /turnaʒ/ *n.m.* (*cinéma*) shooting.

tournant[1]**, ~e** /turnɑ̃, -t/ *a.* (*qui pivote*) revolving.

tournant[2] /turnɑ̃/ *n.m.* bend; (*fig.*) turning-point.

tourne-disque /turnədisk/ *n.m.* record-player.

tournée /turne/ *n.f.* (*voyage, consommations*) round; (*théâtre*) tour. **faire la ~,** make the rounds (**de,** of). **je paye** *ou* **j'offre la ~,** I'll buy this round.

tourner /turne/ *v.t.* turn; (*film*) shoot, make. ● *v.i.* turn; (*toupie, tête*) spin; (*moteur, usine*) run. **se ~** *v. pr.* turn. **~ au froid,** turn cold. **~ autour de,** go round; (*personne, maison*) hang around; (*terre*) revolve round; (*question*) centre on. **~ de l'œil,** (*fam.*) faint. **~ en dérision,** mock. **~ en ridicule,** ridicule. **~ le dos à,** turn one's back on. **~ mal,** turn out badly.

tournesol /turnəsɔl/ *n.m.* sunflower.

tournevis /turnəvis/ *n.m.* screwdriver.

tourniquet /turnikɛ/ *n.m.* (*barrière*) turnstile.

tournoi /turnwa/ *n.m.* tournament.

tournoyer /turnwaje/ *v.i.* whirl.

tournure /turnyr/ *n.f.* turn; (*locution*) turn of phrase.

tourte /turt/ *n.f.* pie.

tourterelle /turtərɛl/ *n.f.* turtle-dove.

Toussaint /tusɛ̃/ *n.f.* **la ~,** All Saints' Day.

tousser /tuse/ *v.i.* cough.

tout[1]**, ~e** (*pl.* **tous, toutes** /tu, tut/) *a.* all; (*n'importe quel*) any; (*tout à fait*) entirely. **~ le pays/***etc.*, the whole country/*etc.*, all the country/*etc.* **~e la nuit/journée,** the whole night/day. **~ un paquet,** a whole pack. **tous les jours/mois/***etc.*, every day/month/*etc.* ● *pron.* everything, all. **tous** /tus/, **toutes,** all. **prendre ~,** take everything, take it all. **~ ce que,** all that. **~ le monde,** everyone. **tous les deux, toutes les deux,** both of them. **tous les trois,** all three (of them). ● *adv.*

(*très*) very; (*tout à fait*) quite. **~ au bout/début/***etc.*, right at the end/beginning/*etc.* **le ~ premier,** the very first. **~ en chantant/marchant/***etc.*, while singing/walking/*etc.* **~ à coup,** all of a sudden. **~ à fait,** quite, completely. **~ à l'heure,** in a moment; (*passé*) a moment ago. **~ au** *ou* **le long de,** throughout. **~ au plus/moins,** at most/least. **~ de même,** all the same. **~ de suite,** straight away. **~ entier,** whole. **~ le contraire,** quite the opposite. **~ neuf,** brand-new. **~ nu,** stark naked. **~ près,** nearby. **~-puissant, ~e-puissante** *a.* omnipotent. **~ seul,** alone. **~ terrain** *a. invar.* all terrain.

tout[2] /tu/ *n.m.* (*ensemble*) whole. **en ~,** in all. **pas du ~!,** not at all!

tout-à-l'égout /tutalegu/ *n.m.* main drainage.

toutefois /tutfwa/ *adv.* however.

toux /tu/ *n.f.* cough.

toxicomane /tɔksikɔman/ *n.m./f.* drug addict.

toxine /tɔksin/ *n.f.* toxin.

toxique /tɔksik/ *a.* toxic.

trac /trak/ *n.m.* **le ~,** nerves; (*théâtre*) stage fright.

tracas /traka/ *n.m.* worry. **~ser** /-se/ *v.t.*, **se ~ser** *v. pr.* worry.

trace /tras/ *n.f.* trace, mark; (*d'animal, de pneu*) tracks; (*vestige*) trace. **sur la ~ de,** on the track of **~s de pas,** footprints.

tracé /trase/ *n.m.* (*ligne*) line; (*plan*) layout.

tracer /trase/ *v.t.* draw, trace; (*écrire*) write; (*route*) mark out.

trachée(-artère) /traʃe(artɛr)/ *n.f.* windpipe.

tract /trakt/ *n.m.* leaflet.

tractations /traktɑsjɔ̃/ *n.f. pl.* dealings.

tracteur /traktœr/ *n.m.* tractor.

traction /traksjɔ̃/ *n.f.* (*sport*) press-up, push-up.

tradition /tradisjɔ̃/ *n.f.* tradition. **~nel, ~nelle** /-jɔnɛl/ *a.* traditional.

trad|uire† /tradɥir/ *v.t.* translate; (*sentiment*) express. **~uire en justice,** take to court. **~ucteur, ~uctrice** *n.m., f.* translator. **~uction** *n.f.* translation.

trafic /trafik/ *n.m.* (*commerce, circulation*) traffic.

trafiqu|er /trafike/ *v.i.* traffic. ● *v.t.* (*fam.*) (*vin*) doctor; (*moteur*) fiddle with. **~ant, ~ante** *n.m., f.* trafficker; (*d'armes, de drogues*) dealer.

tragédie /traʒedi/ *n.f.* tragedy.

tragique /traʒik/ *a.* tragic. **~ment** *adv.* tragically.

trah|ir /trair/ *v.t.* betray. **~ison** *n.f.* betrayal; (*crime*) treason.

train /trɛ̃/ *n.m.* (*rail.*) train; (*allure*) pace. **en ~,** (*en forme*) in shape. **en ~ de faire,** (busy) doing. **mettre en ~,** start up. **~ d'atterrissage,** undercarriage. **~ électrique,** (*jouet*) electric train set. **~ de vie,** lifestyle.

traînard, ~e /trɛnar, -d/ *n.m., f.* slowcoach; (*Amer.*) slowpoke; (*en marchant*) straggler.

traîne /trɛn/ *n.f.* (*de robe*) train. **à la ~,** lagging behind; (*en remorque*) in tow.

traîneau (*pl.* **~x**) /trɛno/ *n.m.* sledge.

traînée /trene/ *n.f.* (*trace*) trail; (*bande*) streak; (*femme: péj.*) slut.

traîner /trene/ *v.t.* drag (along); (*véhicule*) pull. ● *v.i.* (*pendre*) trail; (*rester en arrière*) trail behind; (*flâner*) hang about; (*papiers, affaires*) lie around. **~ (en longueur),** drag on. **se ~** *v. pr.* (*par terre*) crawl. **(faire) ~ en longueur,** drag out. **~ les pieds,** drag one's feet. **ça n'a pas traîné!,** that didn't take long.

train-train /trɛ̃trɛ̃/ *n.m.* routine.

traire† /trɛr/ *v.t.* milk.

trait /trɛ/ *n.m.* line; (*en dessinant*) stroke; (*caractéristique*) feature, trait; (*acte*) act. **~s,** (*du visage*) features. **avoir ~ à,** relate to. **d'un ~,** (*boire*) in one gulp. **~ d'union,** hyphen; (*fig.*) link.

traite /trɛt/ *n.f.* (*de vache*) milking; (*comm.*) draft. **d'une (seule) ~,** in one go, at a stretch.

traité /trete/ *n.m.* (*pacte*) treaty; (*ouvrage*) treatise.

traitement /trɛtmɑ̃/ *n.m.* treatment; (*salaire*) salary. **~ de données,** data processing. **~ de texte,** word processing.

traiter /trete/ *v.t.* treat; (*affaire*) deal with; (*données, produit*) process. **~ qn. de lâche/***etc.*, call s.o. a coward/*etc.* ● *v.i.* deal (**avec,** with). **~ de,** (*sujet*) deal with.

traiteur /trɛtœr/ *n.m.* caterer; (*boutique*) delicatessen.

traître, ~sse /trɛtr, -ɛs/ *a.* treacherous. ● *n.m./f.* traitor.

trajectoire /traʒɛktwar/ *n.f.* path.

trajet /traʒɛ/ *n.m.* (*à parcourir*) distance; (*voyage*) journey; (*itinéraire*) route.
trame /tram/ *n.f.* (*de tissu*) weft; (*de récit etc.*) framework. **usé jusqu'à la ~,** threadbare.
tramer /trame/ *v.t.* plot; (*complot*) hatch. **qu'est-ce qui se trame?,** what's brewing?
tramway /tramwɛ/ *n.m.* tram; (*Amer.*) streetcar.
tranchant, ~e /trɑ̃ʃɑ̃, -t/ *a.* sharp; (*fig.*) cutting. ● *n.m.* cutting edge. **à double ~,** two-edged.
tranche /trɑ̃ʃ/ *n.f.* (*rondelle*) slice; (*bord*) edge; (*partie*) portion.
tranchée /trɑ̃ʃe/ *n.f.* trench.
tranch|er[1] /trɑ̃ʃe/ *v.t.* cut; (*question*) decide. ● *v.i.* (*décider*) decide. **~é** *a.* (*net*) clear-cut.
trancher[2] /trɑ̃ʃe/ *v.i.* (*contraster*) contrast (**sur,** with).
tranquill|e /trɑ̃kil/ *a.* quiet; (*esprit*) at rest; (*conscience*) clear. **être/laisser ~e,** be/leave in peace. **~ement** *adv.* quietly. **~ité** *n.f.* (peace and) quiet; (*d'esprit*) peace of mind.
tranquillisant /trɑ̃kilizɑ̃/ *n.m.* tranquillizer.
tranquilliser /trɑ̃kilize/ *v.t.* reassure.
transaction /trɑ̃zaksjɔ̃/ *n.f.* transaction.
transat /trɑ̃zat/ *n.m.* (*fam.*) deckchair.
transatlantique /trɑ̃zatlɑ̃tik/ *n.m.* transatlantic liner. ● *a.* transatlantic.
transborder /trɑ̃sbɔrde/ *v.t.* transfer, transship.
transcend|er /trɑ̃sɑ̃de/ *v.t.* transcend. **~ant, ~ante** *a.* transcendent.
transcr|ire /trɑ̃skrir/ *v.t.* transcribe. **~iption** *n.f.* transcription; (*copie*) transcript.
transe /trɑ̃s/ *n.f.* **en ~,** in a trance; (*fig.*) very excited.
transférer /trɑ̃sfere/ *v.t.* transfer.
transfert /trɑ̃sfɛr/ *n.m.* transfer.
transform|er /trɑ̃sfɔrme/ *v.t.* change; (*radicalement*) transform; (*vêtement*) alter. **se ~er** *v. pr.* change; be transformed. **(se) ~er en,** turn into. **~ateur** *n.m.* transformer. **~ation** *n.f.* change; transformation.
transfuge /trɑ̃sfyʒ/ *n.m.* renegade.
transfusion /trɑ̃sfyzjɔ̃/ *n.f.* transfusion.
transgresser /trɑ̃sgrese/ *v.t.* disobey.
transiger /trɑ̃siʒe/ *v.i.* compromise. **ne pas ~ sur,** not compromise on.
transi /trɑ̃zi/ *a.* chilled to the bone.
transistor /trɑ̃zistɔr/ *n.m.* (*dispositif, poste de radio*) transistor.
transit /trɑ̃zit/ *n.m.* transit. **~er** *v.t./i.* pass in transit.
transiti|f, ~ve /trɑ̃zitif, -v/ *a.* transitive.
transi|tion /trɑ̃zisjɔ̃/ *n.f.* transition. **~toire** *a.* (*provisoire*) transitional.
translucide /trɑ̃slysid/ *a.* translucent.
transm|ettre† /trɑ̃smɛtr/ *v.t.* pass on; (*techn.*) transmit; (*radio*) broadcast. **~ission** *n.f.* transmission; (*radio*) broadcasting.
transparaître /trɑ̃sparɛtr/ *v.i.* show (through).
transparen|t, ~te /trɑ̃sparɑ̃, -t/ *a.* transparent. **~ce** *n.f.* transparency.
transpercer /trɑ̃spɛrse/ *v.t.* pierce.
transpir|er /trɑ̃spire/ *v.i.* perspire. **~ation** *n.f.* perspiration.
transplant|er /trɑ̃splɑ̃te/ *v.t.* (*bot., méd.*) transplant. **~ation** *n.f.* (*bot.*) transplantation; (*méd.*) transplant.
transport /trɑ̃spɔr/ *n.m.* transport(ation); (*sentiment*) rapture. **les ~s,** transport. **les ~s en commun,** public transport.
transport|er /trɑ̃spɔrte/ *v.t.* transport; (*à la main*) carry. **se ~er** *v. pr.* take o.s. (**à,** to). **~eur** *n.m.* haulier; (*Amer.*) trucker.
transposer /trɑ̃spoze/ *v.t.* transpose.
transvaser /trɑ̃svaze/ *v.t.* decant.
transvers|al (*m. pl.* **~aux**) /trɑ̃svɛrsal, -o/ *a.* cross, transverse.
trap|èze /trapɛz/ *n.m.* (*sport*) trapeze. **~éziste** /-ezist/ *n.m./f.* trapeze artist.
trappe /trap/ *n.f.* trapdoor.
trappeur /trapœr/ *n.m.* trapper.
trapu /trapy/ *a.* stocky.
traquenard /traknar/ *n.m.* trap.
traquer /trake/ *v.t.* track down.
traumatis|me /tromatism/ *n.m.* trauma. **~ant, ~ante** /-zɑ̃, -t/ *a.* traumatic. **~er** /-ze/ *v.t.* traumatize.
trav|ail (*pl.* **~aux**) /travaj, -o/ *n.m.* work; (*emploi, poste*) job; (*façonnage*) working. **~aux,** work. **en ~ail,** (*femme*) in labour. **~ail à la chaîne,** production line work. **~ail à la pièce** *ou* **à la tâche,** piece-work. **~ail au noir,** (*fam.*) moonlighting. **~aux forcés,** hard labour. **~aux**

manuels, handicrafts. **~aux ménagers,** housework.

travaill|er /travaje/ *v.i.* work; (*se déformer*) warp. **~er à,** (*livre etc.*) work on. ● *v.t.* (*façonner*) work; (*étudier*) work at *ou* on; (*tourmenter*) worry. **~eur, ~euse** *n.m., f.* worker; *a.* hardworking.

travailliste /travajist/ *a.* Labour. ● *n.m./f.* Labour party member.

travers /travɛr/ *n.m.* (*défaut*) failing. **à ~,** through. **au ~ (de),** through. **de ~,** (*chapeau, nez*) crooked; (*mal*) badly, the wrong way; (*regarder*) askance. **en ~ (de),** across.

traverse /travɛrs/ *n.f.* (*rail.*) sleeper; (*rail., Amer.*) tie.

traversée /travɛrse/ *n.f.* crossing.

traverser /travɛrse/ *v.t.* cross; (*transpercer*) go (right) through; (*période, forêt*) go *ou* pass through.

traversin /travɛrsɛ̃/ *n.m.* bolster.

travesti /travɛsti/ *n.m.* transvestite.

travestir /travɛstir/ *v.t.* disguise; (*vérité*) misrepresent.

trébucher /trebyʃe/ *v.i.* stumble, trip (over). **faire ~,** trip (up).

trèfle /trɛfl/ *n.m.* (*plante*) clover; (*cartes*) clubs.

treillage /trɛjaʒ/ *n.m.* trellis.

treillis[1] /treji/ *n.m.* trellis; (*en métal*) wire mesh.

treillis[2] /treji/ *n.m.* (*tenue militaire*) combat uniform.

treiz|e /trɛz/ *a.* & *n.m.* thirteen. **~ième** *a.* & *n.m./f.* thirteenth.

tréma /trema/ *n.m.* diaeresis.

trembl|er /trɑ̃ble/ *v.i.* shake, tremble; (*lumière, voix*) quiver. **~ement** *n.m.* shaking; (*frisson*) shiver. **~ement de terre,** earthquake.

trembloter /trɑ̃blɔte/ *v.i.* quiver.

trémousser (se) /(sə)tremuse/ *v. pr.* wriggle, wiggle.

trempe /trɑ̃p/ *n.f.* (*caractère*) calibre.

tremper /trɑ̃pe/ *v.t./i.* soak; (*plonger*) dip; (*acier*) temper. **mettre à ~** *ou* **faire ~,** soak. **~ dans,** (*fig.*) be involved in. **se ~** *v. pr.* (*se baigner*) have a dip.

trempette /trɑ̃pɛt/ *n.f.* **faire ~,** have a little dip.

tremplin /trɑ̃plɛ̃/ *n.m.* springboard.

trentaine /trɑ̃tɛn/ *n.f.* **une ~ (de),** about thirty. **il a la ~,** he's about thirty.

trent|e /trɑ̃t/ *a.* & *n.m.* thirty. **~ième** *a.* & *n.m./f.* thirtieth. **se mettre sur son ~e et un,** put on one's Sunday best. **tous les ~e-six du mois,** once in a blue moon.

trépider /trepide/ *v.i.* vibrate.

trépied /trepje/ *n.m.* tripod.

trépigner /trepiɲe/ *v.i.* stamp one's feet.

très /trɛ/ (/trɛz/ *before vowel*) *adv.* very. **~ aimé/estimé,** much liked/esteemed.

trésor /trezɔr/ *n.m.* treasure; (*ressources: comm.*) finances. **le T~,** the revenue department.

trésorerie /trezɔrri/ *n.f.* (*bureaux*) accounts department; (*du Trésor*) revenue office; (*argent*) finances; (*gestion*) accounts.

trésor|ier, ~ière /trezɔrje, -jɛr/ *n.m., f.* treasurer.

tressaill|ir /tresajir/ *v.i.* shake, quiver; (*sursauter*) start. **~ement** *n.m.* quiver; start.

tressauter /tresote/ *v.i.* (*sursauter*) start, jump.

tresse /trɛs/ *n.f.* braid, plait.

tresser /trese/ *v.t.* braid, plait.

tréteau (*pl.* **~x**) /treto/ *n.m.* trestle. **~x,** (*théâtre*) stage.

treuil /trœj/ *n.m.* winch.

trêve /trɛv/ *n.f.* truce; (*fig.*) respite. **~ de plaisanteries,** enough of this joking.

tri /tri/ *n.m.* (*classement*) sorting; (*sélection*) selection. **faire le ~ de,** sort; select. **~age** /-jaʒ/ *n.m.* sorting.

triang|le /trijɑ̃gl/ *n.m.* triangle. **~ulaire** *a.* triangular.

trib|al (*m. pl.* **~aux**) /tribal, -o/ *a.* tribal.

tribord /tribɔr/ *n.m.* starboard.

tribu /triby/ *n.f.* tribe.

tribulations /tribylasjɔ̃/ *n.f. pl.* tribulations.

tribun|al (*m. pl.* **~aux**) /tribynal, -o/ *n.m.* court. **~al d'instance,** magistrates' court.

tribune /tribyn/ *n.f.* (public) gallery; (*dans un stade*) grandstand; (*d'orateur*) rostrum; (*débat*) forum.

tribut /triby/ *n.m.* tribute.

tributaire /tribytɛr/ *a.* **~ de,** dependent on.

trich|er /triʃe/ *v.i.* cheat. **~erie** *n.f.* cheating. **une ~erie,** piece of trickery. **~eur, ~euse** *n.m., f.* cheat.

tricolore /trikɔlɔr/ *a.* three-coloured; (*français*) red, white and blue; (*français: fig.*) French.

tricot /triko/ *n.m.* knitting; (*pull*) sweater. **en ~,** knitted. **~ de corps,**

vest; (*Amer.*) undershirt. **~er** /-ɔte/ *v.t./i.* knit.

trictrac /triktrak/ *n.m.* backgammon.

tricycle /trisikl/ *n.m.* tricycle.

trier /trije/ *v.t.* (*classer*) sort; (*choisir*) select.

trilogie /trilɔʒi/ *n.f.* trilogy.

trimbaler /trɛ̃bale/ *v.t.*, **se ~** *v. pr.* (*fam.*) trail around.

trimer /trime/ *v.i.* (*fam.*) slave.

trimestr|e /trimɛstr/ *n.m.* quarter; (*scol.*) term. **~iel, ~ielle** *a.* quarterly; (*bulletin*) end-of-term.

tringle /trɛ̃gl/ *n.f.* rod.

Trinité /trinite/ *n.f.* **la ~,** (*dogme*) the Trinity; (*fête*) Trinity.

trinquer /trɛ̃ke/ *v.i.* clink glasses.

trio /trijo/ *n.m.* trio.

triomph|e /trijɔ̃f/ *n.m.* triumph. **~al** (*m. pl.* **~aux**) *a.* triumphant.

triomph|er /trijɔ̃fe/ *v.i.* triumph (**de,** over); (*jubiler*) be triumphant. **~ant, ~ante** *a.* triumphant.

trip|es /trip/ *n.f. pl.* (*mets*) tripe; (*entrailles: fam.*) guts.

triple /tripl/ *a.* triple, treble. ● *n.m.* **le ~,** three times as much (**de,** as). **~ment** /-əmɑ̃/ *adv.* trebly.

tripl|er /triple/ *v.t./i.* triple, treble. **~és, ~ées** *n.m., f. pl.* triplets.

tripot /tripo/ *n.m.* gambling den.

tripoter /tripɔte/ *v.t.* (*fam.*) fiddle with. ● *v.i.* (*fam.*) fiddle about.

trique /trik/ *n.f.* cudgel.

trisomique /trizɔmik/ *a.* **enfant ~,** Down's (syndrome) child.

triste /trist/ *a.* sad; (*rue, temps, couleur*) gloomy; (*lamentable*) wretched, dreadful. **~ment** /- əmɑ̃/ *adv.* sadly. **~sse** /-ɛs/ *n.f.* sadness; gloominess.

triv|ial (*m. pl.* **~iaux**) /trivjal, -jo/ *a.* coarse. **~ialité** *n.f.* coarseness.

troc /trɔk/ *n.m.* exchange; (*comm.*) barter.

troène /trɔɛn/ *n.m.* (*bot.*) privet.

trognon /trɔɲɔ̃/ *n.m.* (*de pomme*) core.

trois /trwɑ/ *a.* & *n.m.* three. **hôtel ~-étoiles,** three-star hotel. **~ième** /-zjɛm/ *a.* & *n.m./f.* third. **~ièmement** /-zjɛmmɑ̃/ *adv.* thirdly.

trombe /trɔ̃b/ *n.f.* **~ d'eau,** downpour.

trombone /trɔ̃bɔn/ *n.m.* (*mus.*) trombone; (*agrafe*) paper-clip.

trompe /trɔ̃p/ *n.f.* (*d'éléphant*) trunk; (*mus.*) horn.

tromp|er /trɔ̃pe/ *v.t.* deceive, mislead; (*déjouer*) elude. **se ~er** *v. pr.* be mistaken. **se ~er de route/train/*etc.*,** take the wrong road/train/*etc.* **~erie** *n.f.* deception. **~eur, ~euse** *a.* (*personne*) deceitful; (*chose*) deceptive.

trompette /trɔ̃pɛt/ *n.f.* trumpet.

tronc /trɔ̃/ *n.m.* trunk; (*boîte*) collection box.

tronçon /trɔ̃sɔ̃/ *n.m.* section. **~ner** /-ɔne/ *v.t.* cut into sections.

trôn|e /tron/ *n.m.* throne. **~er** *v.i.* occupy the place of honour.

tronquer /trɔ̃ke/ *v.t.* truncate.

trop /tro/ *adv.* (*grand, loin, etc.*) too; (*boire, marcher, etc.*) too much. **~ (de),** (*quantité*) too much; (*nombre*) too many. **c'est ~ chauffé,** it's overheated. **de ~, en ~,** too much; too many. **il a bu un verre de ~,** he's had one too many. **de ~,** (*intrus*) in the way. **~-plein** *n.m.* excess; (*dispositif*) overflow.

trophée /trɔfe/ *n.m.* trophy.

tropic|al (*m. pl.* **~aux**) /trɔpikal, -o/ *a.* tropical.

tropique /trɔpik/ *n.m.* tropic. **~s,** tropics.

troquer /trɔke/ *v.t.* exchange; (*comm.*) barter (**contre,** for).

trot /tro/ *n.m.* trot. **aller au ~,** trot. **au ~,** (*fam.*) on the double.

trotter /trɔte/ *v.i.* trot.

trotteuse /trɔtøz/ *n.f.* (*aiguille de montre*) second hand.

trottiner /trɔtine/ *v.i.* patter along.

trottinette /trɔtinɛt/ *n.f.* (*jouet*) scooter.

trottoir /trɔtwar/ *n.m.* pavement; (*Amer.*) sidewalk. **~ roulant,** moving walkway.

trou /tru/ *n.m.* hole; (*moment*) gap; (*lieu: péj.*) dump. **~ (de mémoire),** lapse (of memory). **~ de la serrure,** keyhole. **faire son ~,** carve one's niche.

trouble /trubl/ *a.* (*eau, image*) unclear; (*louche*) shady. ● *n.m.* agitation. **~s,** (*pol.*) disturbances; (*méd.*) trouble.

troubl|er /truble/ *v.t.* disturb; (*eau*) make cloudy; (*inquiéter*) trouble. **~ant, ~ante** *a.* disturbing. **se ~er** *v. pr.* (*personne*) become flustered. **~e-fête** *n.m./f. invar.* killjoy.

trouée /true/ *n.f.* gap, open space; (*mil.*) breach (**dans,** in).

trouer /true/ *v.t.* make a hole *ou* holes in. **mes chaussures se sont trouées,** my shoes have got holes in them.
trouille /truj/ *n.f.* **avoir la ~,** (*fam.*) be scared.
troupe /trup/ *n.f.* troop; (*d'acteurs*) troupe. **~s,** (*mil.*) troops.
troupeau (*pl.* **~x**) /trupo/ *n.m.* herd; (*de moutons*) flock.
trousse /trus/ *n.f.* case, bag; (*de réparations*) kit. **aux ~s de,** on the tail of. **~ de toilette,** toilet bag.
trousseau (*pl.* **~x**) /truso/ *n.m.* (*de clefs*) bunch; (*de mariée*) trousseau.
trouvaille /truvɑj/ *n.f.* find.
trouver /truve/ *v.t.* find; (*penser*) think. **aller/venir ~,** (*rendre visite à*) go/come and see. **se ~** *v. pr.* find o.s.; (*être*) be; (*se sentir*) feel. **il se trouve que,** it happens that. **se ~ mal,** faint.
truand /tryɑ̃/ *n.m.* gangster.
truc /tryk/ *n.m.* (*moyen*) way; (*artifice*) trick; (*chose*: *fam.*) thing. **~age** *n.m.* = **truquage.**
truchement /tryʃmɑ̃/ *n.m.* **par le ~ de,** through.
truculent, ~e /trykylɑ̃, -t/ *a.* colourful.
truelle /tryɛl/ *n.f.* trowel.
truffe /tryf/ *n.f.* (*champignon, chocolat*) truffle; (*nez*) nose.
truffer /tryfe/ *v.t.* (*fam.*) fill, pack (**de,** with).
truie /trɥi/ *n.f.* (*animal*) sow.
truite /trɥit/ *n.f.* trout.
truqu|er /tryke/ *v.t.* fix, rig; (*photo, texte*) fake. **~age** *n.m.* fixing; faking; (*cinéma*) special effect.
trust /trœst/ *n.m.* (*comm.*) trust.
tsar /tsar/ *n.m.* tsar, czar.
tsigane /tsigan/ *a.* & *n.m./f.* (Hungarian) gypsy.
tu[1] /ty/ *pron.* (*parent, ami, enfant, etc.*) you.
tu[2] /ty/ *voir* taire.
tuba /tyba/ *n.m.* (*mus.*) tuba; (*sport*) snorkel.
tube /tyb/ *n.m.* tube.
tubercul|eux, ~euse /tybɛrkylø, -z/ *a.* **être ~eux,** have tuberculosis. **~ose** *n.f.* tuberculosis.
tubulaire /tybylɛr/ *a.* tubular.
tubulure /tybylyr/ *n.f.* tubing.
tu|er /tɥe/ *v.t.* kill; (*d'une balle*) shoot, kill; (*épuiser*) exhaust. **se ~er** *v. pr.* kill o.s.; (*accident*) be killed. **~ant, ~ante,** *a.* exhausting. **~é, ~ée** *n.m., f.* person killed. **~eur, ~euse** *n.m., f.* killer.
tuerie /tyri/ *n.f.* slaughter.
tue-tête (à) /(a)tytɛt/ *adv.* at the top of one's voice.
tuile /tɥil/ *n.f.* tile; (*malchance*: *fam.*) (stroke of) bad luck.
tulipe /tylip/ *n.f.* tulip.
tuméfié /tymefje/ *a.* swollen.
tumeur /tymœr/ *n.f.* tumour.
tumult|e /tymylt/ *n.m.* commotion; (*désordre*) turmoil. **~ueux, ~ueuse** *a.* turbulent.
tunique /tynik/ *n.f.* tunic.
Tunisie /tynizi/ *n.f.* Tunisia.
tunisien, ~ne /tynizjɛ̃, -jɛn/ *a.* & *n.m., f.* Tunisian.
tunnel /tynɛl/ *n.m.* tunnel.
turban /tyrbɑ̃/ *n.m.* turban.
turbine /tyrbin/ *n.f.* turbine.
turbo /tyrbɔ/ *a.* turbo. *n.f.* (*voiture*) turbo.
turbulen|t, ~te /tyrbylɑ̃, -t/ *a.* boisterous, turbulent. **~ce** *n.f.* turbulence.
tur|c, ~que /tyrk/ *a.* Turkish. ● *n.m., f.* Turk. ● *n.m.* (*lang.*) Turkish.
turf /tyrf/ *n.m.* **le ~,** the turf. **~iste** *n.m./f.* racegoer.
Turquie /tyrki/ *n.f.* Turkey.
turquoise /tyrkwaz/ *a. invar.* turquoise.
tutelle /tytɛl/ *n.f.* (*jurid.*) guardianship; (*fig.*) protection.
tu|teur, ~trice /tytœr, -tris/ *n.m., f.* (*jurid.*) guardian. ● *n.m.* (*bâton*) stake.
tut|oyer /tytwaje/ *v.t.* address familiarly (using *tu*). **~oiement** *n.m.* use of (familiar) *tu*.
tuyau (*pl.* **~x**) /tɥijo/ *n.m.* pipe; (*conseil*: *fam.*) tip. **~ d'arrosage,** hose-pipe. **~ter** *v.t.* (*fam.*) give a tip to. **~terie** *n.f.* piping.
TVA *abrév.* (*taxe sur la valeur ajoutée*) VAT.
tympan /tɛ̃pɑ̃/ *n.m.* ear-drum.
type /tip/ *n.m.* (*modèle*) type; (*traits*) features; (*individu*: *fam.*) bloke, guy. ● *a. invar.* typical. **le ~ même de,** a classic example of.
typhoïde /tifɔid/ *n.f.* typhoid (fever).
typhon /tifɔ̃/ *n.m.* typhoon.
typhus /tifys/ *n.m.* typhus.
typique /tipik/ *a.* typical. **~ment** *adv.* typically.
tyran /tirɑ̃/ *n.m.* tyrant.

tyrann|ie /tirani/ *n.f.* tyranny. **~ique** *a.* tyrannical. **~iser** *v.t.* oppress, tyrannize.

U

ulcère /ylsɛr/ *n.m.* ulcer.
ulcérer /ylsere/ *v.t.* (*vexer*) embitter, gall.
ULM *abrév. m.* (*ultraléger motorisé*) microlight.
ultérieur /ylterjœr/ *a.*, **~ement** *adv.* later.
ultimatum /yltimatɔm/ *n.m.* ultimatum.
ultime /yltim/ *a.* final.
ultra /yltra/ *n.m./f.* hardliner.
ultra- /yltra/ *préf.* ultra-.
un, une /œ̃, yn/ *a.* one; (*indéfini*) a, an. **un enfant,** /œ̃nɑ̃fɑ̃/ a child. ● *pron. & n.m., f.* one. **l'un,** one. **les uns,** some. **l'un et l'autre,** both. **l'un l'autre, les uns les autres,** each other. **l'un ou l'autre,** either. **la une,** (*de journal*) front page. **un autre,** another. **un par un,** one by one.
unanim|e /ynanim/ *a.* unanimous. **~ité** *n.f.* unanimity. **à l'~ité,** unanimously.
uni /yni/ *a.* united; (*couple*) close; (*surface*) smooth; (*sans dessins*) plain.
unième /ynjɛm/ *a.* -first. **vingt et ~,** twenty-first. **cent ~,** one hundred and first.
unif|ier /ynifje/ *v.t.* unify. **~ication** *n.f.* unification.
uniform|e /ynifɔrm/ *n.m.* uniform. ● *a.* uniform. **~ément** *adv.* uniformly. **~iser** *v.t.* standardize. **~ité** *n.f.* uniformity.
unilatér|al (*m. pl.* **~aux**) /ynilateral, -o/ *a.* unilateral.
union /ynjɔ̃/ *n.f.* union. **l'U~ soviétique,** the Soviet Union.
unique /ynik/ *a.* (*seul*) only; (*prix, voie*) one; (*incomparable*) unique. **enfant ~,** only child. **sens ~,** one-way street. **~ment** *adv.* only, solely.
unir /ynir/ *v.t.*, **s'~** *v. pr.* unite, join.
unisson (à l') /(al)ynisɔ̃/ *adv.* in unison.
unité /ynite/ *n.f.* unit; (*harmonie*) unity.
univers /ynivɛr/ *n.m.* universe.
universel, ~le /ynivɛrsɛl/ *a.* universal.
universit|é /ynivɛrsite/ *n.f.* university. **~aire** *a.* university; *n.m./f.* academic.
uranium /yranjɔm/ *n.m.* uranium.
urbain, ~e /yrbɛ̃, -ɛn/ *a.* urban.
urbanisme /yrbanism/ *n.m.* town planning; (*Amer.*) city planning.
urgence /yrʒɑ̃s/ *n.f.* (*cas*) emergency; (*de situation, tâche, etc.*) urgency. **d'~** *a.* emergency; *adv.* urgently.
urgent, ~e /yrʒɑ̃, -t/ *a.* urgent.
urger /yrʒe/ *v.i.* **ça urge!,** (*fam.*) it's getting urgent.
urin|e /yrin/ *n.f.* urine. **~er** *v.i.* urinate.
urinoir /yrinwar/ *n.m.* urinal.
urne /yrn/ *n.f.* (*électorale*) ballot-box; (*vase*) urn. **aller aux ~s,** go to the polls.
URSS *abrév.* (*Union des Républiques Socialistes Soviétiques*) USSR.
urticaire /yrtikɛr/ *n.f.* **une crise d' ~,** nettle rash.
us /ys/ *n.m. pl.* **les us et coutumes,** habits and customs.
usage /yzaʒ/ *n.m.* use; (*coutume*) custom; (*de langage*) usage. **à l'~ de,** for. **d'~,** (*habituel*) customary. **faire ~ de,** make use of.
usagé /yzaʒe/ *a.* worn.
usager /yzaʒe/ *n.m.* user.
usé /yze/ *a.* worn (out); (*banal*) trite.
user /yze/ *v.t.* wear (out); (*consommer*) use (up). ● *v.i.* **~ de,** use. **s'~** *v. pr.* (*tissu etc.*) wear (out).
usine /yzin/ *n.f.* factory; (*de métallurgie*) works.
usité /yzite/ *a.* common.
ustensile /ystɑ̃sil/ *n.m.* utensil.
usuel, ~le /yzɥɛl/ *a.* ordinary, everyday.
usufruit /yzyfrɥi/ *n.m.* usufruct.
usure /yzyr/ *n.f.* (*détérioration*) wear (and tear).
usurper /yzyrpe/ *v.t.* usurp.
utérus /yterys/ *n.m.* womb, uterus.
utile /ytil/ *a.* useful. **~ment** *adv.* usefully.
utilis|er /ytilize/ *v.t.* use. **~able** *a.* usable. **~ation** *n.f.* use.
utilitaire /ytilitɛr/ *a.* utilitarian.
utilité /ytilite/ *n.f.* use(fulness).
utop|ie /ytɔpi/ *n.f.* Utopia; (*idée*) Utopian idea. **~ique** *a.* Utopian.
UV *abrév. f.* (*unité de valeur*) (*scol.*) credit.

V

va /va/ *voir* aller[1].

vacanc|e /vakɑ̃s/ *n.f.* (*poste*) vacancy. **~es,** holiday(s); (*Amer.*) vacation. **en ~es,** on holiday. **~ier, ~ière** *n.m., f.* holiday-maker; (*Amer.*) vacationer.

vacant, ~e /vakɑ̃, -t/ *a.* vacant.

vacarme /vakarm/ *n.m.* uproar.

vaccin /vaksɛ̃/ *n.m.* vaccine; (*inoculation*) vaccination.

vaccin|er /vaksine/ *v.t.* vaccinate. **~ation** *n.f.* vaccination.

vache /vaʃ/ *n.f.* cow. ● *a.* (*méchant: fam.*) nasty. **~ment** *adv.* (*très: fam.*) damned; (*pleuvoir, manger, etc.: fam.*) a hell of a lot. **~rie** *n.f.* (*fam.*) nastiness; (*chose: fam.*) nasty thing.

vacill|er /vasije/ *v.i.* sway, wobble; (*lumière*) flicker; (*fig.*) falter. **~ant, ~ante** *a.* (*mémoire, démarche*) shaky.

vadrouiller /vadruje/ *v.i.* (*fam.*) wander about.

va-et-vient /vaevjɛ̃/ *n.m. invar.* to and fro (motion); (*de personnes*) comings and goings.

vagabond, ~e /vagabɔ̃, -d/ *n.m., f.* (*péj.*) vagrant, vagabond. **~er** /-de/ *v.i.* wander.

vagin /vaʒɛ̃/ *n.m.* vagina.

vagir /vaʒir/ *v.i.* cry.

vague[1] /vag/ *a.* vague. ● *n.m.* vagueness. **il est resté dans le ~,** he was vague about it. **~ment** *adv.* vaguely.

vague[2] /vag/ *n.f.* wave. **~ de fond,** ground swell. **~ de froid,** cold spell. **~ de chaleur,** hot spell.

vaill|ant, ~ante /vajɑ̃, -t/ *a.* brave; (*vigoureux*) healthy. **~amment** /-amɑ̃/ *adv.* bravely.

vaille /vaj/ *voir* valoir.

vain, ~e /vɛ̃, vɛn/ *a.* vain. **en ~,** in vain. **~ement** /vɛnmɑ̃/ *adv.* vainly.

vain|cre† /vɛ̃kr/ *v.t.* defeat; (*surmonter*) overcome. **~cu, ~cue** *n.m., f.* (*sport*) loser. **~queur** *n.m.* victor; (*sport*) winner.

vais /vɛ/ *voir* aller[1].

vaisseau (*pl.* **~x**) /vɛso/ *n.m.* ship; (*veine*) vessel. **~ spatial,** space-ship.

vaisselle /vɛsɛl/ *n.f.* crockery; (*à laver*) dishes. **faire la ~,** do the washing-up, wash the dishes. **produit pour la ~,** washing-up liquid.

val (*pl.* **~s** *ou* **vaux**) /val, vo/ *n.m.* valley.

valable /valabl/ *a.* valid; (*de qualité*) worthwhile.

valet /valɛ/ *n.m.* (*cartes*) jack. **~ (de chambre),** manservant. **~ de ferme,** farm-hand.

valeur /valœr/ *n.f.* value; (*mérite*) worth, value. **~s,** (*comm.*) stocks and shares. **avoir de la ~,** be valuable.

valid|e /valid/ *a.* (*personne*) fit; (*billet*) valid. **~er** *v.t.* validate. **~ité** *n.f.* validity.

valise /valiz/ *n.f.* (suit)case. **faire ses ~s,** pack (one's bags).

vallée /vale/ *n.f.* valley.

vallon /valɔ̃/ *n.m.* (small) valley. **~né** /-ɔne/ *a.* undulating.

valoir† /valwar/ *v.i.* be worth; (*s'appliquer*) apply. **~ qch.,** be worth sth.; (*être aussi bon que*) be as good as sth. ● *v.t.* **~ qch. à qn.,** bring s.o. sth. **se ~** *v. pr.* (*être équivalents*) be as good as each other. **faire ~,** put forward to advantage; (*droit*) assert. **~ la peine, ~ le coup,** be worth it. **ça ne vaut rien,** it is no good. **il vaudrait mieux faire,** we'd better do. **ça ne me dit rien qui vaille,** I don't think much of it.

valoriser /valɔrize/ *v.t.* add value to. **se sentir valorisé,** feel valued.

vals|e /vals/ *n.f.* waltz. **~er** *v.i.* waltz.

valve /valv/ *n.f.* valve.

vampire /vɑ̃pir/ *n.m.* vampire.

van /vɑ̃/ *n.m.* van.

vandal|e /vɑ̃dal/ *n.m./f.* vandal. **~isme** *n.m.* vandalism.

vanille /vanij/ *n.f.* vanilla.

vanit|é /vanite/ *n.f.* vanity. **~eux, ~euse** *a.* vain, conceited.

vanne /van/ *n.f.* (*d'écluse*) sluice (-gate); (*fam.*) joke.

vant|ail (*pl.* **~aux**) /vɑ̃taj, -o/ *n.m.* door, flap.

vantard, ~e /vɑ̃tar, -d/ *a.* boastful; *n.m., f.* boaster. **~ise** /-diz/ *n.f.* boastfulness; (*acte*) boast.

vanter /vɑ̃te/ *v.t.* praise. **se ~** *v. pr.* boast (**de,** about).

va-nu-pieds /vanypje/ *n.m./f. invar.* vagabond, beggar.

vapeur[1] /vapœr/ *n.f.* (*eau*) steam; (*brume, émanation*) vapour.

vapeur[2] /vapœr/ *n.m.* (*bateau*) steamer.

vaporeu|x, ~se /vapɔrø, -z/ *a.* hazy; (*léger*) filmy, flimsy.
vaporis|er /vapɔrize/ *v.t.* spray. **~ateur** *n.m.* spray.
vaquer /vake/ *v.i.* **~ à,** attend to.
varappe /varap/ *n.f.* rock climbing.
vareuse /varøz/ *n.f.* (*d'uniforme*) tunic.
variable /varjabl/ *a.* variable; (*temps*) changeable.
variante /varjɑ̃t/ *n.f.* variant.
varicelle /varisɛl/ *n.f.* chicken-pox.
varices /varis/ *n.f. pl.* varicose veins.
var|ier /varje/ *v.t./i.* vary. **~iation** *n.f.* variation. **~ié** *a.* (*non monotone, étendu*) varied; (*divers*) various.
variété /varjete/ *n.f.* variety. **~s,** (*spectacle*) variety.
variole /varjɔl/ *n.f.* smallpox.
vase[1] /vɑz/ *n.m.* vase.
vase[2] /vɑz/ *n.f.* (*boue*) silt, mud.
vaseu|x, ~se /vɑzø, -z/ *a.* (*confus: fam.*) woolly, hazy.
vasistas /vazistɑs/ *n.m.* fanlight, hinged panel (*in door or window*).
vaste /vast/ *a.* vast, huge.
vaudeville /vodvil/ *n.m.* vaudeville, light comedy.
vau-l'eau (à) /(a)volo/ *adv.* downhill.
vaurien, ~ne /vorjɛ̃, -jɛn/ *n.m., f.* good-for-nothing.
vautour /votur/ *n.m.* vulture.
vautrer (se) /(sə)votre/ *v. pr.* sprawl. **se ~ dans,** (*vice, boue*) wallow in.
va-vite (à la) /(ala)vavit/ *adv.* (*fam.*) in a hurry.
veau (*pl.* **~x**) /vo/ *n.m.* calf; (*viande*) veal; (*cuir*) calfskin.
vécu /veky/ *voir* vivre. ● *a.* (*réel*) true, real.
vedette[1] /vədɛt/ *n.f.* (*artiste*) star. **en ~,** (*objet*) in a prominent position; (*personne*) in the limelight.
vedette[2] /vədɛt/ *n.f.* (*bateau*) launch.
végét|al (*m. pl.* **~aux**) /veʒetal, -o/ *a.* plant. ● *n.m.* (*pl.* **~aux**) plant.
végétalien, ~ne /veʒetaljɛ̃, -jɛn/ *a.* & *n.m., f.* vegan.
végétarien, ~ne /veʒetarjɛ̃, -jɛn/ *a.* & *n.m., f.* vegetarian.
végétation /veʒetɑsjɔ̃/ *n.f.* vegetation. **~s,** (*méd.*) adenoids.
végéter /veʒete/ *v.i.* vegetate.
véhémen|t, ~te /veemɑ̃, -t/ *a.* vehement. **~ce** *n.f.* vehemence.
véhicul|e /veikyl/ *n.m.* vehicle. **~er** *v.t.* convey.
veille[1] /vɛj/ *n.f.* **la ~ (de),** the day before. **la ~ de Noël,** Christmas Eve. **à la ~ de,** on the eve of.
veille[2] /vɛj/ *n.f.* (*état*) wakefulness.
veillée /veje/ *n.f.* evening (gathering); (*mortuaire*) vigil, wake.
veiller /veje/ *v.i.* stay up *ou* awake. **~ à,** attend to. **~ sur,** watch over. ● *v.t.* (*malade*) watch over.
veilleur /vɛjœr/ *n.m.* **~ de nuit,** night-watchman.
veilleuse /vɛjøz/ *n.f.* night-light; (*de véhicule*) sidelight; (*de réchaud*) pilot-light. **mettre qch. en ~,** put sth. on the back burner.
veinard, ~e /vɛnar, -d/ *n.m.,f.* (*fam.*) lucky devil.
veine[1] /vɛn/ *n.f.* (*anat.*) vein; (*nervure, filon*) vein.
veine[2] /vɛn/ *n.f.* (*chance: fam.*) luck. **avoir de la ~,** (*fam.*) be lucky.
velcro /vɛlkrɔ/ *n.m.* (P.) velcro.
véliplanchiste /veliplɑ̃ʃist/ *n.m./f.* windsurfer.
vélo /velo/ *n.m.* bicycle, bike; (*activité*) cycling.
vélodrome /velɔdrɔm/ *n.m.* velodrome, cycle-racing track.
vélomoteur /velɔmɔtœr/ *n.m.* moped.
velours /vlur/ *n.m.* velvet. **~ côtelé, ~ à côtes,** corduroy.
velouté /vəlute/ *a.* smooth. ● *n.m.* smoothness.
velu /vəly/ *a.* hairy.
venaison /vənɛzɔ̃/ *n.f.* venison.
vendang|es /vɑ̃dɑ̃ʒ/ *n.f. pl.* grape harvest. **~er** *v.i.* pick the grapes. **~eur, ~euse** *n.m., f.* grape-picker.
vendetta /vɑ̃deta/ *n.f.* vendetta.
vendeu|r, ~se /vɑ̃dœr, -øz/ *n.m., f.* shop assistant; (*marchand*) salesman, saleswoman; (*jurid.*) vendor, seller.
vendre /vɑ̃dr/ *v.t.*, **se ~** *v. pr.* sell. **à ~,** for sale.
vendredi /vɑ̃drədi/ *n.m.* Friday. **V~ saint,** Good Friday.
vénéneu|x, ~se /venenø, -z/ *a.* poisonous.
vénérable /venerabl/ *a.* venerable.
vénérer /venere/ *v.t.* revere.
vénérien, ~ne /venerjɛ̃, -jɛn/ *a.* venereal.
vengeance /vɑ̃ʒɑ̃s/ *n.f.* revenge, vengeance.
veng|er /vɑ̃ʒe/ *v.t.* avenge. **se ~er** *v. pr.* take (one's) revenge (**de,** for).

~eur, ~eresse *a.* vengeful; *n.m., f.* avenger.
ven|in /vənɛ̃/ *n.m.* venom. **~imeux, ~imeuse** *a.* poisonous, venomous.
venir† /vənir/ *v.i.* (*aux. être*) come (**de,** from). **~ faire,** come to do. **venez faire,** come and do. **~ de faire,** to have just done. **il vient/venait d'arriver,** he has/had just arrived. **en ~ à,** (*question, conclusion, etc.*) come to. **en ~ aux mains,** come to blows. **faire ~,** send for. **il m'est venu à l'esprit** *ou* **à l'idée que,** it occurred to me that.
vent /vɑ̃/ *n.m.* wind. **être dans le ~,** (*fam.*) be with it. **il fait du ~,** it is windy.
vente /vɑ̃t/ *n.f.* sale. **~ (aux enchères),** auction. **en ~,** on *ou* for sale. **~ de charité,** (charity) bazaar.
ventil|er /vɑ̃tile/ *v.t.* ventilate. **~ateur** *n.m.* fan, ventilator. **~ation** *n.f.* ventilation.
ventouse /vɑ̃tuz/ *n.f.* (*dispositif*) suction pad; (*pour déboucher l'évier etc.*) plunger.
ventre /vɑ̃tr/ *n.m.* belly, stomach; (*utérus*) womb. **avoir/prendre du ~,** have/develop a paunch.
ventriloque /vɑ̃trilɔk/ *n.m./f.* ventriloquist.
ventru /vɑ̃try/ *a.* pot-bellied.
venu /vəny/ *voir* venir. ● *a.* **bien ~,** (*à propos*) timely. **mal ~,** untimely. **être mal ~ de faire,** have no grounds for doing.
venue /vəny/ *n.f.* coming.
vêpres /vɛpr/ *n.f. pl.* vespers.
ver /vɛr/ *n.m.* worm; (*des fruits, de la viande*) maggot; (*du bois*) woodworm. **~ luisant,** glow-worm. **~ à sole,** silkworm. **~ solitaire,** tapeworm. **~ de terre,** earthworm.
véranda /verɑ̃da/ *n.f.* veranda.
verb|e /vɛrb/ *n.m.* (*gram.*) verb. **~al** (*m. pl.* **~aux**) *a.* verbal.
verdâtre /vɛrdɑtr/ *a.* greenish.
verdict /vɛrdikt/ *n.m.* verdict.
verdir /vɛrdir/ *v.i.* turn green.
verdoyant, ~e /vɛrdwajɑ̃, -t/ *a.* green, verdant.
verdure /vɛrdyr/ *n.f.* greenery.
véreu|x, ~se /verø, -z/ *a.* maggoty, wormy; (*malhonnête: fig.*) shady.
verger /vɛrʒe/ *n.m.* orchard.
vergla|s /vɛrgla/ *n.m.* (black) ice; (*Amer.*) sleet. **~cé** *a.* icy.
vergogne (sans) /(sɑ̃)vɛrgɔɲ/ *a.* shameless. ● *adv.* shamelessly.
véridique /veridik/ *a.* truthful.
vérif|ier /verifje/ *v.t.* check, verify; (*compte*) audit; (*confirmer*) confirm. **~ication** *n.f.* check(ing), verification.
véritable /veritabl/ *a.* true, real; (*authentique*) real. **~ment** /-əmɑ̃/ *adv.* really.
vérité /verite/ *n.f.* truth; (*de tableau, roman*) trueness to life. **en ~,** in fact.
vermeil, ~le /vɛrmɛj/ *a.* bright red.
vermicelle(s) /vɛrmisɛl/ *n.m.* (*pl.*) vermicelli.
vermine /vɛrmin/ *n.f.* vermin.
vermoulu /vɛrmuly/ *a.* wormeaten.
vermouth /vɛrmut/ *n.m.* (*apéritif*) vermouth.
verni /vɛrni/ *a.* (*fam.*) lucky. **chaussures ~es,** patent (leather) shoes.
vernir /vɛrnir/ *v.t.* varnish.
vernis /vɛrni/ *n.m.* varnish; (*de poterie*) glaze. **~ à ongles,** nail polish *ou* varnish.
vernissage /vɛrnisaʒ/ *n.m.* (*exposition*) preview.
vernisser /vɛrnise/ *v.t.* glaze.
verra, verrait /vɛra, vɛrɛ/ *voir* voir.
verre /vɛr/ *n.m.* glass. **prendre** *ou* **boire un ~,** have a drink. **~ de contact,** contact lens. **~ dépoli/grossissant,** frosted/magnifying glass. **~rie** *n.f.* (*objets*) glassware.
verrière /vɛrjɛr/ *n.f.* (*toit*) glass roof; (*paroi*) glass wall.
verrou /vɛru/ *n.m.* bolt. **sous les ~s,** behind bars.
verroulller /vɛruje/ *v.t.* bolt.
verrue /vɛry/ *n.f.* wart.
vers[1] /vɛr/ *prép.* towards; (*temps*) about.
vers[2] /vɛr/ *n.m.* (*ligne*) line. **les ~,** (*poésie*) verse.
versant /vɛrsɑ̃/ *n.m.* slope, side.
versatile /vɛrsatil/ *a.* fickle.
verse (à) /(a)vɛrs/ *adv.* in torrents.
versé /vɛrse/ *a.* **~ dans,** versed in.
Verseau /vɛrso/ *n.m.* **le ~,** Aquarius.
vers|er /vɛrse/ *v.t./i.* pour; (*larmes, sang*) shed; (*basculer*) overturn; (*payer*) pay. **~ement** *n.m.* payment.
verset /vɛrsɛ/ *n.m.* (*relig.*) verse.
version /vɛrsjɔ̃/ *n.f.* version; (*traduction*) translation.
verso /vɛrso/ *n.m.* back (of the page).
vert, ~e /vɛr, -t/ *a.* green; (*vieillard*) sprightly. ● *n.m.* green.
vertèbre /vɛrtɛbr/ *n.f.* vertebra.

vertement /vɛrtəmɑ̃/ *adv.* sharply.

vertic|al, ~ale (*m. pl.* **~aux**) /vɛrtikal, -o/ *a. & n.f.* vertical. **à la ~ale, ~alement** *adv.* vertically.

vertig|e /vɛrtiʒ/ *n.m.* dizziness. **~es,** dizzy spells. **avoir le** *ou* **un ~e,** feel dizzy. **~ineux, ~ineuse** *a.* dizzy; (*très grand*) staggering.

vertu /vɛrty/ *n.f.* virtue. **en ~ de,** by virtue of. **~eux, ~euse** /-tɥø, -z/ *a.* virtuous.

verve /vɛrv/ *n.f.* spirit, wit.

verveine /vɛrvɛn/ *n.f.* verbena.

vésicule /vezikyl/ *n.f.* **~ biliaire,** gall-bladder.

vessie /vesi/ *n.f.* bladder.

veste /vɛst/ *n.f.* jacket.

vestiaire /vɛstjɛr/ *n.m.* cloakroom; (*sport*) changing-room.

vestibule /vɛstibyl/ *n.m.* hall.

vestige /vɛstiʒ/ *n.m.* (*objet*) relic; (*trace*) vestige.

veston /vɛstɔ̃/ *n.m.* jacket.

vêtement /vɛtmɑ̃/ *n.m.* article of clothing. **~s,** clothes.

vétéran /veterɑ̃/ *n.m.* veteran.

vétérinaire /veterinɛr/ *n.m./f.* vet, veterinary surgeon, (*Amer.*) veterinarian.

vétille /vetij/ *n.f.* trifle.

vêt|ir /vetir/ *v.t.*, **se ~ir** *v. pr.* dress. **~u** *a.* dressed (**de,** in).

veto /veto/ *n.m. invar.* veto.

vétuste /vetyst/ *a.* dilapidated.

veu|f, ~ve /vœf, -v/ *a.* widowed. ● *n.m.* widower. ● *n.f.* widow.

veuille /vœj/ *voir* vouloir.

veule /vøl/ *a.* feeble.

veut, veux /vø/ *voir* vouloir.

vexation /vɛksɑsjɔ̃/ *n.f.* humiliation.

vex|er /vɛkse/ *v.t.* upset, hurt. **se ~er** *v. pr.* be upset, be hurt. **~ant, ~ante** *a.* upsetting.

via /vja/ *prép.* via.

viable /vjabl/ *a.* viable.

viaduc /vjadyk/ *n.m.* viaduct.

viande /vjɑ̃d/ *n.f.* meat.

vibr|er /vibre/ *v.i.* vibrate; (*être ému*) thrill. **~ant, ~ante** *a.* (*émouvant*) vibrant. **~ation** *n.f.* vibration.

vicaire /vikɛr/ *n.m.* curate.

vice /vis/ *n.m.* (*moral*) vice; (*défectuosité*) defect.

vice- /vis/ *préf.* vice-.

vice versa /vis(e)vɛrsa/ *adv.* vice versa.

vicier /visje/ *v.t.* taint.

vicieu|x, ~se /visjø, -z/ *a.* depraved. ● *n.m., f.* pervert.

vicin|al (*pl.* **~aux**) /visinal, -o/ *a.m.* **chemin ~al,** by-road, minor road.

vicomte /vikɔ̃t/ *n.m.* viscount.

victime /viktim/ *n.f.* victim; (*d'un accident*) casualty.

vict|oire /viktwar/ *n.f.* victory; (*sport*) win. **~orieux, ~orieuse** *a.* victorious; (*équipe*) winning.

victuailles /viktɥɑj/ *n.f. pl.* provisions.

vidang|e /vidɑ̃ʒ/ *n.f.* emptying; (*auto.*) oil change; (*dispositif*) waste pipe. **~er** *v.t.* empty.

vide /vid/ *a.* empty. ● *n.m.* emptiness, void; (*trou, manque*) gap; (*espace sans air*) vacuum. **à ~,** empty.

vidéo /video/ *a. invar.* video. **jeu ~,** video game. **~cassette** *n.f.* video(tape). **~thèque** *n.f.* video library.

vide-ordures /vidɔrdyr/ *n.m. invar.* (rubbish) chute.

vider /vide/ *v.t.* empty; (*poisson*) gut; (*expulser*: *fam.*) throw out. **~ les lieux,** vacate the premises. **se ~** *v. pr.* empty.

videur /vidœr/ *n.m.* bouncer.

vie /vi/ *n.f.* life; (*durée*) lifetime. **à ~, pour la ~,** for life. **donner la ~ à,** give birth to. **en ~,** alive. **~ chère,** high cost of living.

vieil /vjɛj/ *voir* vieux.

vieillard /vjɛjar/ *n.m.* old man.

vieille /vjɛj/ *voir* vieux.

vieillesse /vjɛjɛs/ *n.f.* old age.

vieill|ir /vjejir/ *v.i.* grow old, age; (*mot, idée*) become old-fashioned. ● *v.t.* age. **~issement** *n.m.* ageing.

viens, vient /vjɛ̃/ *voir* venir.

vierge /vjɛrʒ/ *n.f.* virgin. **la V~,** Virgo. ● *a.* virgin; (*feuille, film*) blank.

vieux *ou* **vieil*, vieille** (*m. pl.* **vieux**) /vjø, vjɛj/ *a.* old. ● *n.m.* old man. ● *n.f.* old woman. **les ~,** old people. **mon ~,** (*fam.*) old man *ou* boy. **ma vieille,** (*fam.*) old girl, dear. **vieille fille,** (*péj.*) spinster. **~ garçon,** bachelor. **~ jeu** *a. invar.* old-fashioned.

vif, vive /vif, viv/ *a.* lively; (*émotion, vent*) keen; (*froid*) biting; (*lumière*) bright; (*douleur, parole*) sharp; (*souvenir, style, teint*) vivid; (*succès, impatience*) great. **brûler/enterrer ~,** burn/bury alive. **de vive voix,**

personally. **avoir les nerfs à ~,** be on edge.
vigie /viʒi/ *n.f.* look-out.
vigilan|t, ~te /viʒilɑ̃, -t/ *a.* vigilant. **~ce** *n.f.* vigilance.
vigne /viɲ/ *n.f.* (*plante*) vine; (*vignoble*) vineyard.
vigneron, ~ne /viɲrɔ̃, -ɔn/ *n.m., f.* wine-grower.
vignette /viɲɛt/ *n.f.* (*étiquette*) label; (*auto.*) road tax sticker.
vignoble /viɲɔbl/ *n.m.* vineyard.
vigoureu|x, ~se /vigurø, -z/ *a.* vigorous, sturdy.
vigueur /vigœr/ *n.f.* vigour. **être/entrer en ~,** (*loi*) be/come into force. **en ~,** (*terme*) in use.
VIH *abrév.* (*virus d'immunodéficience humaine*) HIV.
vil /vil/ *a.* vile, base.
vilain, ~e /vilɛ̃, -ɛn/ *a.* (*mauvais*) nasty; (*laid*) ugly.
villa /villa/ *n.f.* (detached) house.
village /vilaʒ/ *n.m.* village.
villageois, ~e /vilaʒwa, -z/ *a.* village. ● *n.m., f.* villager.
ville /vil/ *n.f.* town; (*importante*) city. **~ d'eaux,** spa.
vin /vɛ̃/ *n.m.* wine. **~ d'honneur,** reception. **~ ordinaire,** table wine.
vinaigre /vinɛgr/ *n.m.* vinegar.
vinaigrette /vinɛgrɛt/ *n.f.* oil and vinegar dressing, vinaigrette.
vindicati|f, ~ve /vɛ̃dikatif, -v/ *a.* vindictive.
vingt /vɛ̃/ (/vɛ̃t/ *before vowel and in numbers 22-29*) *a.* & *n.m.* twenty. **~ième** *a.* & *n.m./f.* twentieth.
vingtaine /vɛ̃tɛn/ *n.f.* **une ~ (de),** about twenty.
vinicole /vinikɔl/ *a.* wine(-growing).
vinyle /vinil/ *n.m.* vinyl.
viol /vjɔl/ *n.m.* (*de femme*) rape; (*de lieu, loi*) violation.
violacé /vjɔlase/ *a.* purplish.
viol|ent, ~ente /vjɔlɑ̃, -t/ *a.* violent. **~emment** /-amɑ̃/ *adv.* violently. **~ence** *n.f.* violence; (*acte*) act of violence.
viol|er /vjɔle/ *v.t.* rape; (*lieu, loi*) violate. **~ation** *n.f.* violation.
violet, ~te /vjɔlɛ, -t/ *a.* & *n.m.* purple. ● *n.f.* violet.
violon /vjɔlɔ̃/ *n.m.* violin. **~iste** /-ɔnist/ *n.m./f.* violinist. **~ d'Ingres,** hobby.
violoncell|e /vjɔlɔ̃sɛl/ *n.m.* cello. **~iste** /-elist/ *n.m./f.* cellist.
vipère /vipɛr/ *n.f.* viper, adder.
virage /viraʒ/ *n.m.* bend; (*de véhicule*) turn; (*changement d'attitude: fig.*) change of course.
virée /vire/ *n.f.* (*fam.*) trip, outing.
vir|er /vire/ *v.i.* turn. **~er de bord,** tack. **~er au rouge/***etc.*, turn red/*etc.* ● *v.t.* (*argent*) transfer; (*expulser: fam.*) throw out. **~ement** *n.m.* (*comm.*) (credit) transfer.
virevolter /virvɔlte/ *v.i.* spin round, swing round.
virginité /virʒinite/ *n.f.* virginity.
virgule /virgyl/ *n.f.* comma; (*dans un nombre*) (decimal) point.
viril /viril/ *a.* manly, virile. **~ité** *n.f.* manliness, virility.
virtuel, ~le /virtɥɛl/ *a.* virtual. **~lement** *adv.* virtually.
virtuos|e /virtɥoz/ *n.m./f.* virtuoso. **~ité** *n.f.* virtuosity.
virulen|t, ~te /virylɑ̃, -t/ *a.* virulent. **~ce** *n.f.* virulence.
virus /virys/ *n.m.* virus.
vis [1] /vi/ *voir* vivre, voir.
vis [2] /vis/ *n.f.* screw.
visa /viza/ *n.m.* visa.
visage /vizaʒ/ *n.m.* face.
vis-à-vis /vizavi/ *adv.* face to face, opposite. **~ de,** opposite; (*à l'égard de*) with respect to. ● *n.m. invar.* (*personne*) person opposite.
viscères /visɛr/ *n.m. pl.* intestines.
visées /vize/ *n.f. pl.* aim. **avoir des ~ sur,** have designs on.
viser /vize/ *v.t.* aim at; (*concerner*) be aimed at; (*timbrer*) stamp. ● *v.i.* aim. **~ à,** aim at; (*mesure, propos*) be aimed at.
visib|le /vizibl/ *a.* visible. **~ilité** *n.f.* visibility. **~lement** *adv.* visibly.
visière /vizjɛr/ *n.f.* (*de casquette*) peak; (*de casque*) visor.
vision /vizjɔ̃/ *n.f.* vision.
visionnaire /vizjɔnɛr/ *a.* & *n.m./f.* visionary.
visionn|er /vizjɔne/ *v.t.* view. **~euse** *n.f.* (*appareil*) viewer.
visite /vizit/ *n.f.* visit; (*examen*) examination; (*personne*) visitor. **heures de ~,** visiting hours. **~ guidée,** guided tour. **rendre ~ à,** visit. **être en ~ (chez qn.),** be visiting (s.o.).
visit|er /vizite/ *v.t.* visit; (*examiner*) examine. **~eur, ~euse** *n.m., f.* visitor.
vison /vizɔ̃/ *n.m.* mink.
visqueu|x, ~se /viskø, -z/ *a.* viscous.

visser /vise/ *v.t.* screw (on).
visuel, ~le /vizɥɛl/ *a.* visual.
vit /vi/ *voir* vivre, voir.
vit|al (*m. pl.* **~aux**) /vital, -o/ *a.* vital. **~alité** *n.f.* vitality.
vitamine /vitamin/ *n.f.* vitamin.
vite /vit/ *adv.* fast, quickly; (*tôt*) soon. **~!**, quick! **faire ~**, be quick.
vitesse /vitɛs/ *n.f.* speed; (*régime*: *auto.*) gear. **à toute ~**, at top speed. **en ~**, in a hurry, quickly.
vitic|ole /vitikɔl/ *a.* wine. **~ulteur** *n.m.* wine-grower. **~ulture** *n.f.* wine-growing.
vitrage /vitraʒ/ *n.m.* (*vitres*) windows. **double-~**, double glazing.
vitr|ail (*pl.* **~aux**) /vitraj, -o/ *n.m.* stained-glass window.
vitr|e /vitr/ *n.f.* (window) pane; (*de véhicule*) window. **~é** *a.* glass, glazed. **~er** *v.t.* glaze.
vitrine /vitrin/ *n.f.* (shop) window; (*meuble*) display cabinet.
vivable /vivabl/ *a.* **ce n'est pas ~**, it's unbearable.
vivace /vivas/ *a.* (*plante, sentiment*) perennial.
vivacité /vivasite/ *n.f.* liveliness; (*agilité*) quickness; (*d'émotion, de l'air*) keenness; (*de souvenir, style, teint*) vividness.
vivant, ~e /vivɑ̃, -t/ *a.* (*doué de vie, en usage*) living; (*en vie*) alive, living; (*actif, vif*) lively. ● *n.m.* **un bon ~**, a bon viveur. **de son ~**, in one's lifetime. **les ~s**, the living.
vivats /viva/ *n.m. pl.* cheers.
vive [1] /viv/ *voir* vif.
vive [2] /viv/ *int.* **~ le roi/président/etc.!**, long live the king/president/etc.!
vivement /vivmɑ̃/ *adv.* (*vite, sèchement*) sharply; (*avec éclat*) vividly; (*beaucoup*) greatly. **~ la fin!**, roll on the end, I'll be glad when it's the end!
vivier /vivje/ *n.m.* fish-pond.
vivifier /vivifje/ *v.t.* invigorate.
vivisection /vivisɛksjɔ̃/ *n.f.* vivisection.
vivoter /vivɔte/ *v.i.* plod on, get by.
vivre† /vivr/ *v.i.* live. **~ de**, (*nourriture*) live on. ● *v.t.* (*vie*) live; (*période, aventure*) live through. **~s** *n.m. pl.* supplies. **faire ~**, (*famille etc.*) support. **~ encore**, be still alive.
vlan /vlɑ̃/ *int.* bang.
vocabulaire /vɔkabylɛr/ *n.m.* vocabulary.
voc|al (*m. pl.* **~aux**) /vɔkal, -o/ *a.* vocal.
vocalise /vɔkaliz/ *n.f.* voice exercise.
vocation /vɔkɑsjɔ̃/ *n.f.* vocation.
vociférer /vɔsifere/ *v.t./i.* scream.
vodka /vɔdka/ *n.f.* vodka.
vœu (*pl.* **~x**) /vø/ *n.m.* (*souhait*) wish; (*promesse*) vow.
vogue /vɔg/ *n.f.* fashion, vogue.
voguer /vɔge/ *v.i.* sail.
voici /vwasi/ *prép.* here is, this is; (*au pluriel*) here are, these are. **me ~**, here I am. **~ un an**, (*temps passé*) a year ago. **~ un an que**, it is a year since.
voie /vwa/ *n.f.* (*route*) road; (*chemin*) way; (*moyen*) means, way; (*partie de route*) lane; (*rails*) track; (*quai*) platform. **en ~ de**, in the process of. **en ~ de développement**, (*pays*) developing. **par la ~ des airs**, by air. **~ de dégagement**, slip-road. **~ ferrée**, railway; (*Amer.*) railroad. **~ lactée**, Milky Way. **~ navigable**, waterway. **~ publique**, public highway. **~ sans issue**, cul-de-sac, dead end. **sur la bonne ~**, (*fig.*) well under way. **mettre sur une ~ de garage**, (*fig.*) sideline.
voilà /vwala/ *prép.* there is, that is; (*au pluriel*) there are, those are; (*voici*) here is; here are. **le ~**, there he is. **~!**, right!; (*en offrant qch.*) there you are! **~ un an**, (*temps passé*) a year ago. **~ un an que**, it is a year since.
voilage /vwalaʒ/ *n.m.* net curtain.
voile [1] /vwal/ *n.f.* (*de bateau*) sail; (*sport*) sailing.
voile [2] /vwal/ *n.m.* veil; (*tissu léger et fin*) net.
voil|er [1] /vwale/ *v.t.* veil. **se ~er** *v. pr.* (*devenir flou*) become hazy. **~é** *a.* (*terme, femme*) veiled; (*flou*) hazy.
voiler [2] /vwale/ *v.t.*, **se ~** *v. pr.* (*roue etc.*) buckle.
voilier /vwalje/ *n.m.* sailing-ship.
voilure /vwalyr/ *n.f.* sails.
voir† /vwar/ *v.t./i.* see. **se ~** *v. pr.* (*être visible*) show; (*se produire*) be seen; (*se trouver*) find o.s.; (*se fréquenter*) see each other. **ça n'a rien à ~ avec**, that has nothing to do with. **faire ~, laisser ~**, show. **je ne peux pas le ~**, (*fam.*) I cannot stand him. **~ trouble**, have blurred vision. **voyons!**, (*irritation*) come on!
voire /vwar/ *adv.* indeed.

voirie /vwari/ *n.f.* (*service*) highway maintenance. **travaux de ~,** road-works.

voisin, ~e /vwazɛ̃, -in/ *a.* (*proche*) neighbouring; (*adjacent*) next (**de,** to); (*semblable*) similar (**de,** to). ● *n.m., f.* neighbour. **le ~,** the man next door.

voisinage /vwazinaʒ/ *n.m.* neighbourhood; (*proximité*) proximity.

voiture /vwatyr/ *n.f.* (motor) car; (*wagon*) coach, carriage. **en ~!,** all aboard! **~ à cheval,** horse-drawn carriage. **~ de course,** racing-car. **~ d'enfant,** pram; (*Amer.*) baby carriage. **~ de tourisme,** private car.

voix /vwa/ *n.f.* voice; (*suffrage*) vote. **à ~ basse,** in a whisper.

vol [1] /vɔl/ *n.m.* (*d'avion, d'oiseau*) flight; (*groupe d'oiseaux etc.*) flock, flight. **à ~ d'oiseau,** as the crow flies. **~ libre,** hang-gliding. **~ plané,** gliding.

vol [2] /vɔl/ *n.m.* (*délit*) theft; (*hold-up*) robbery. **~ à la tire,** pickpocketing.

volage /vɔlaʒ/ *a.* fickle.

volaille /vɔlɑj/ *n.f.* **la ~,** (*poules etc.*) poultry. **une ~,** a fowl.

volant /vɔlɑ̃/ *n.m.* (steering-)wheel; (*de jupe*) flounce.

volcan /vɔlkɑ̃/ *n.m.* volcano. **~ique** /-anik/ *a.* volcanic.

volée /vɔle/ *n.f.* flight; (*oiseaux*) flight, flock; (*de coups, d'obus*) volley. **à toute ~,** with full force. **de ~, à la ~,** in flight.

voler [1] /vɔle/ *v.i.* (*oiseau etc.*) fly.

vol|er [2] /vɔle/ *v.t./i.* steal (**à,** from). **il ne l'a pas ~é,** he deserved it. **~er qn.,** rob s.o. **~eur, ~euse** *n.m., f.* thief; *a.* thieving.

volet /vɔlɛ/ *n.m.* (*de fenêtre*) shutter; (*de document*) (folded *ou* tear-off) section. **trié sur le ~,** hand-picked.

voleter /vɔlte/ *v.i.* flutter.

volière /vɔljɛr/ *n.f.* aviary.

volontaire /vɔlɔ̃tɛr/ *a.* voluntary; (*personne*) determined. ● *n.m./f.* volunteer. **~ment** *adv.* voluntarily; (*exprès*) intentionally.

volonté /vɔlɔ̃te/ *n.f.* (*faculté, intention*) will; (*souhait*) wish; (*énergie*) will-power. **à ~,** (*à son gré*) at will. **bonne ~,** goodwill. **mauvaise ~,** ill will. **faire ses quatre ~s,** do exactly as one pleases.

volontiers /vɔlɔ̃tje/ *adv.* (*de bon gré*) with pleasure, willingly, gladly; (*ordinairement*) readily.

volt /vɔlt/ *n.m.* volt. **~age** *n.m.* voltage.

volte-face /vɔltəfas/ *n.f. invar.* about-face. **faire ~,** turn round.

voltige /vɔltiʒ/ *n.f.* acrobatics.

voltiger /vɔltiʒe/ *v.i.* flutter.

volubile /vɔlybil/ *a.* voluble.

volume /vɔlym/ *n.m.* volume.

volumineu|x, ~se /vɔlyminø, -z/ *a.* bulky.

volupt|é /vɔlypte/ *n.f.* sensual pleasure. **~ueux, ~ueuse** *a.* voluptuous.

vom|ir /vɔmir/ *v.t./i.* vomit. **~i** *n.m.* vomit. **~issement(s)** *n.m.* (*pl.*) vomiting.

vont /vɔ̃/ *voir* aller [1].

vorace /vɔras/ *a.* voracious.

vos /vo/ *voir* votre.

vote /vɔt/ *n.m.* (*action*) voting; (*d'une loi*) passing; (*suffrage*) vote.

vot|er /vɔte/ *v.i.* vote. ● *v.t.* vote for; (*adopter*) pass; (*crédits*) vote. **~ant, ~ante** *n.m., f.* voter.

votre (*pl.* **vos**) /vɔtr, vo/ *a.* your.

vôtre /votr/ *pron.* **le** *ou* **la ~, les ~s,** yours.

vou|er /vwe/ *v.t.* dedicate (**à,** to); (*promettre*) vow. **~é à l'échec,** doomed to failure.

vouloir† /vulwar/ *v.t.* want (**faire,** to do). **ça ne veut pas bouger**/*etc.*, it will not move/*etc.* **je voudrais/voudrais bien venir**/*etc.*, I should *ou* would like/really like to come/*etc.* **je veux bien venir**/*etc.*, I am happy to come/*etc.* **voulez-vous attendre**/*etc.***?**, will you wait/*etc.*? **veuillez attendre**/*etc.*, kindly wait/*etc.* **~ absolument faire,** insist on doing. **comme** *ou* **si vous voulez,** if you like *ou* wish. **en ~ à qn.,** have a grudge against s.o.; (*être en colère contre*) be annoyed with s.o. **qu'est-ce qu'il me veut?,** what does he want with me? **ne pas ~ de qch./qn.,** not want sth./s.o. **~ dire,** mean. **~ du bien à,** wish well.

voulu /vuly/ *a.* (*délibéré*) intentional; (*requis*) required.

vous /vu/ *pron.* (*sujet, complément*) you; (*indirect*) (to) you; (*réfléchi*) yourself; (*pl.*) yourselves; (*l'un l'autre*) each other. **~-même** *pron.* yourself. **~-mêmes** *pron.* yourselves.

voûte /vut/ *n.f.* (*plafond*) vault; (*porche*) archway.

voûté /vute/ *a.* bent, stooped. **il a le dos ~,** he's stooped.

vouv|oyer /vuvwaje/ *v.t.* address politely (using *vous*). **~oiement** *n.m.* use of (polite) *vous*.

voyage /vwajaʒ/ *n.m.* journey, trip; (*par mer*) voyage. **~(s),** (*action*) travelling. **~ d'affaires,** business trip. **~ de noces,** honeymoon. **~ organisé,** (package) tour.

voyag|er /vwajaʒe/ *v.i.* travel. **~eur, ~euse** *n.m., f.* traveller.

voyant[1]**, ~e** /vwajɑ̃, -t/ *a.* gaudy. ● *n.f.* (*femme*) clairvoyant.

voyant[2] /vwajɑ̃/ *n.m.* (*signal*) (warning) light.

voyelle /vwajɛl/ *n.f.* vowel.

voyeur /vwajœr/ *n.m.* voyeur.

voyou /vwaju/ *n.m.* hooligan.

vrac (en) /(ɑ̃)vrak/ *adv.* in disorder; (*sans emballage, au poids*) loose, in bulk.

vrai /vrɛ/ *a.* true; (*réel*) real. ● *n.m.* truth. **à ~ dire,** to tell the truth.

vraiment /vrɛmɑ̃/ *adv.* really.

vraisembl|able /vrɛsɑ̃blabl/ *a.* likely. **~ablement** *adv.* very likely. **~ance** *n.f.* likelihood, plausibility.

vrille /vrij/ *n.f.* (*aviat.*) spin.

vromb|ir /vrɔ̃bir/ *v.i.* hum. **~issement** *n.m.* humming.

VRP *abrév. m.* (*voyageur représentant placier*) rep.

vu /vy/ *voir* voir. ● *a.* **bien/mal ~,** well/not well thought of. ● *prép.* in view of. **~ que,** seeing that.

vue /vy/ *n.f.* (*spectacle*) sight; (*sens*) (eye)sight; (*panorama, idée*) view. **avoir en ~,** have in mind. **à ~,** (*tirer, payable*) at sight. **de ~,** by sight. **perdre de ~,** lose sight of. **en ~,** (*proche*) in sight; (*célèbre*) in the public eye. **en ~ de faire,** with a view to doing.

vulg|aire /vylgɛr/ *a.* (*grossier*) vulgar; (*ordinaire*) common. **~arité** *n.f.* vulgarity.

vulgariser /vylgarize/ *v.t.* popularize.

vulnérab|le /vylnerabl/ *a.* vulnerable. **~ilité** *n.f.* vulnerability.

vulve /vylv/ *n.f.* vulva.

W

wagon /vagɔ̃/ *n.m.* (*de voyageurs*) carriage; (*Amer.*) car; (*de marchandises*) wagon; (*Amer.*) freight car. **~-lit** (*pl.* **~s-lits**) *n.m.* sleeping-car, sleeper. **~-restaurant** (*pl.* **~s-restaurants**) *n.m.* dining-car.

walkman /wokman/ *n.m.* (P.) walkman.

wallon, ~ne /walɔ̃, -ɔn/ *a.* & *n.m., f.* Walloon.

waters /watɛr/ *n.m. pl.* toilet.

watt /wat/ *n.m.* watt.

w.-c. /(dublə)vese/ *n.m. pl.* toilet.

week-end /wikɛnd/ *n.m.* weekend.

western /wɛstɛrn/ *n.m.* western.

whisk|y (*pl.* **~ies**) /wiski/ *n.m.* whisky.

X

xénophob|e /ksenɔfɔb/ *a.* xenophobic. ● *n.m./f.* xenophobe. **~ie** *n.f.* xenophobia.

xérès /kserɛs/ *n.m.* sherry.

xylophone /ksilɔfɔn/ *n.m.* xylophone.

Y

y /i/ *adv.* & *pron.* there; (*dessus*) on it; (*pl.*) on them; (*dedans*) in it; (*pl.*) in them. **s'y habituer,** (*à cela*) get used to it. **s'y attendre,** expect it. **y penser,** think of it. **il y entra,** (*dans cela*) he entered it. **j'y vais,** I'm on my way. **ça y est,** that is it. **y être pour qch.,** have sth. to do with it.

yacht /jɔt/ *n.m.* yacht.

yaourt /jaur(t)/ *n.m.* yoghurt. **~ière** /-tjɛr/ *n.f.* yoghurt maker.

yeux /jø/ *voir* œil.

yiddish /(j)idiʃ/ *n.m.* Yiddish.

yoga /jɔga/ *n.m.* yoga.

yougoslave /jugɔslav/ *a.* & *n.m./f.* Yugoslav.

Yougoslavie /jugɔslavi/ *n.f.* Yugoslavia.

yo-yo /jojo/ *n.m. invar.* (P.) yo-yo (P.).

yuppie /jøpi/ *n.m./f.* yuppie.

Z

zèbre /zɛbr/ *n.m.* zebra.
zébré /zebre/ *a.* striped.
zèle /zɛl/ *n.m.* zeal.
zélé /zele/ *a.* zealous.
zénith /zenit/ *n.m.* zenith.
zéro /zero/ *n.m.* nought, zero; (*température*) zero; (*dans un numéro*) 0; (*football*) nil; (*football: Amer.*) zero; (*personne*) nonentity. **(re)partir de ~,** start from scratch.
zeste /zɛst/ *n.m.* peel. **un ~ de,** (*fig.*) a pinch of.
zézayer /zezeje/ *v.i.* lisp.
zigzag /zigzag/ *n.m.* zigzag. **en ~,** zigzag. **~uer** /-e/ *v.i.* zigzag.
zinc /zɛ̃g/ *n.m.* (*métal*) zinc; (*comptoir: fam.*) bar.
zizanie /zizani/ *n.f.* **semer la ~,** put the cat among the pigeons.
zizi /zizi/ *n.m.* (*fam.*) willy.
zodiaque /zɔdjak/ *n.m.* zodiac.
zona /zona/ *n.m.* (*méd.*) shingles.
zone /zon/ *n.f.* zone, area; (*faubourgs*) shanty town. **~ bleue,** restricted parking zone.
zoo /zo(o)/ *n.m.* zoo.
zoolog|ie /zɔɔlɔʒi/ *n.f.* zoology. **~ique** *a.* zoological. **~iste** *n.m./f.* zoologist.
zoom /zum/ *n.m.* zoom lens.
zut /zyt/ *int.* blast (it), (oh) hell.

TEST YOURSELF WITH WORD GAMES

This section contains a number of word games which will help you to use your dictionary more effectively and to build up your knowledge of French vocabulary and usage in a fun and entertaining way. You will find answers to all puzzles and games at the end of the section.

1. Madame Irma

Madame Irma is very good at predicting the future, but she is not very good at conjugating French verbs in the future tense. Help her to replace all the verbs in brackets with the correct future form.

Lion 23 juillet-22 août

Cette semaine, les Lions (être) à la fête. **Travail**: Il ne (falloir) pas vous laisser démoraliser par les problèmes et les discussions qui (pouvoir) surgir en début de semaine. Les 19 et 20 avril vous (offrir) la possibilité d'un changement radical dans votre carrière. Pourquoi ne pas saisir votre chance? **Santé**: Le stress ne vous (épargner) pas, surtout le 18. Attention! Pour décompresser, faites un peu de sport et tout (aller) bien. **Amitié**: Vous êtes très sociable et cette semaine, vous vous (faire) encore de nouveaux amis. **Côté cœur**: Vénus (veiller) sur vous. Une nouvelle rencontre (survenir) peut-être. Si vous avez un partenaire, votre relation (être) au beau fixe.

2 Power cut

Unfortunately, there was a power cut while Jean was writing a computer manual for his office staff. He had just began to label his diagram of a computer. Can you help Jean unscramble the letters and get on with his labelling.

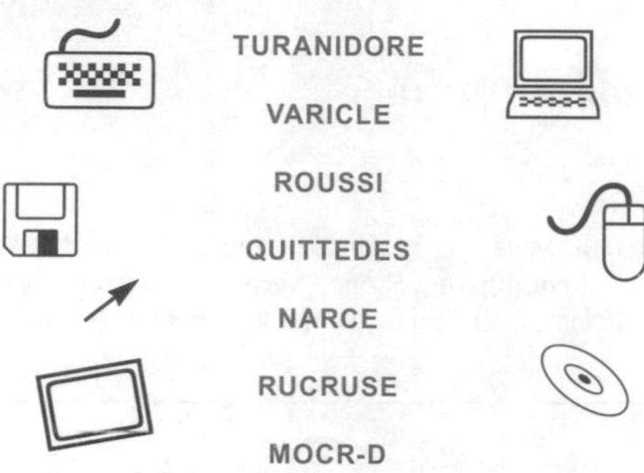

3 From one word to the other

By changing only one letter on each line, you can get from the first word to the last one. Try it!

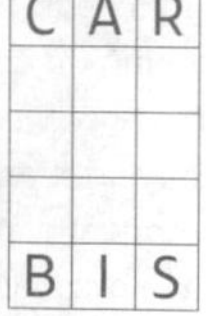

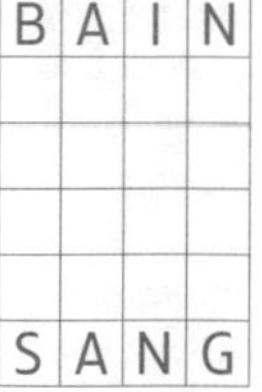

4 The odd meaning out

Watch out: one word can have different meanings. In the following exercise, only two of the suggested translations are correct. Use the dictionary to spot the odd one out, then find the correct French translation for it.

example:

blindé	❑	armoured
	☑	blind
	❑	immune

blind = aveugle

lentille	❑	lentil
	❑	lense
	❑	lent
porte	❑	door
	❑	carry
	❑	port
gauche	❑	left
	❑	gauge
	❑	awkward
broche	❑	broach
	❑	brooch
	❑	spit
duvet	❑	duvet
	❑	down
	❑	sleeping-bag
livret	❑	book
	❑	liver
	❑	libretto

5 Word magnets

Antoine's brother took all his magnets off the fridge door to wipe it clean. He put them back the wrong way round. Can you help Antoine rewrite the correct sentences?

heure	hier	suis	me	levé	bonne	de	je

____

dit	pourtant	je	fois	lui	plusieurs	ai	le

____

sur	sortant	table	les	prends	clés	en	la

____

ira	Portugal	elle	prochaine	au	vacances	l'année	en

____

film	voir	un	allés	cinéma	sommes	nous	au

____

voisine	de	là	frère	pas	le	la	n'est

____

6 What are they like?

Here are two lists of adjectives you can use to describe people's characteristics. Each word in the second column is the opposite of one of the adjectives in the first column. Can you link them?

1. grand	A. intelligent
2. blond	B. méchant
3. bête	C. gros
4. énervé	D. petit
5. gentil	E. sympathique
6. timide	F. brun
7. patient	G. calme
8. désagréable	H. extraverti
9. poli	I. impatient
10. maigre	J. malpoli

example: 1.D. *grand* est le contraire de *petit*.

7 Crossword

	A	B	C	D	E	F	G	H	I	J
1										
2										
3										
4										
5										
6										
7	A	N	T	A	N					
8										
9										

Across

1. the following day = le . . .
2. (a) a noun starting with the same three letters as 'émotion'
   (b) a yew
3. a day
4. toys
5. harmful
6. (a) my
   (b) a girl's name which sounds like the word Christmas in French

eg. 7. (a) (of) long ago = (d')ANTAN
   (b) an egg = un . . .

8. (a) (c) past participle of the verb meaning "to laugh"
   (b) and
9. (a) past participle of the verb meaning 'to grab'
   (b) present form of the verb meaning 'to be'= il . . .

down

A. (a) masculine article meaning 'the'
   (b) never

B. (a) short for knock-out (both in English and in French)
   (b) a year = un . . .

C. (a) masculine article meaning 'a'
   (b) the noun corresponding to the verb 'trier'

D. the verb meaning 'to have lunch' in the imperfect = je . . .

E. an emotion = une . . .

F. lather = la . . .

G. (a) a tune = un . . .
   (b) a small island (starting with the same two letters as 'île')

H. a nobleman = un . . .

I. (a) the present form of the verb meaning 'to deny' = je . . .
   (b) a possessive adjective. Ces livres sont à mes parents. Ce sont . . . livres.

J. (a) a broad bean = une . . .
   (b) perfect form of the verb meaning 'to do' = il . . .

8. The odd one out

In each of the following series, all the words but one are related. Find the odd one out and explain why. If there are words you don't know, use your dictionary to find out what they mean.

example: stylo, agenda, livre, carnet scolaire, brosse à dents

The odd one out is 'brosse à dents', because you wouldn't find it in a schoolbag.

1. voiture, avion, moteur, train, autocar

2. casserole, poêle, cafetière, cendrier, saladier

3. télévision, cassette, chaîne-hifi, magnétoscope, baladeur

4. ski nautique, natation, plongée, varappe, planche à voile

5. redoubler, courir, sauter, glisser, descendre, monter

6. chou, sou, caillou, genou, hibou, bijou

9 The shopping list

Paul has prepared a shopping list. When his friend sees the list, he realises that he needs exactly the same things. He asks Paul whether he would mind buying two of everything. Help Paul rewrite his list. Watch out: the plurals of compound nouns are irregular. If in doubt, look them up in your dictionary.

Acheter:	Acheter:
un taille-crayons	deux taille-crayons
un bloc-notes	....
un timbre-poste	....
un abat-jour	....
un couvre-lit	....
un cache-pot	....
un tire-bouchon	....
un ouvre-boîte	....
un réveille-matin	....
un chou-fleur	....

10 The vocabulary tree

Once you have found the correct translations for the following words, write them down on the tree. Some of the letters will be used for more than one word.

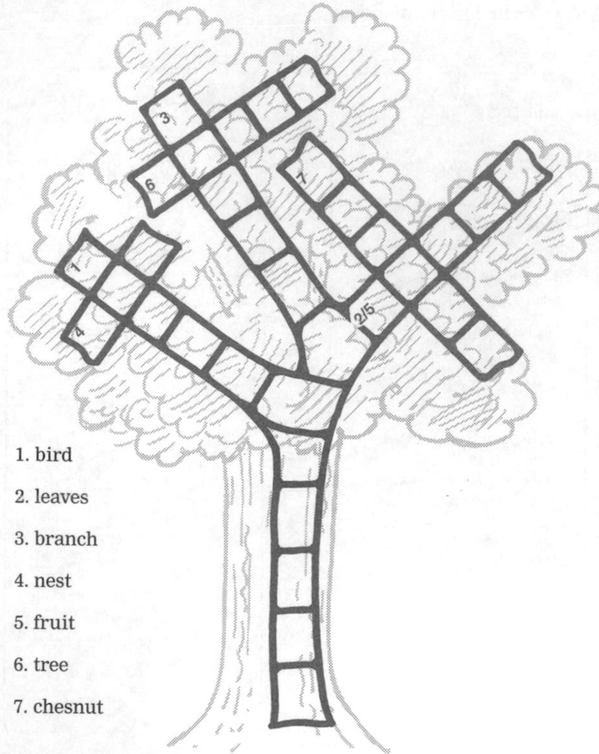

1. bird
2. leaves
3. branch
4. nest
5. fruit
6. tree
7. chesnut

11 The mystery word

To fill in the grid, find the French words for all the musical instruments illustrated below. Once you have completed the grid, you'll discover the name of a famous classical musician.

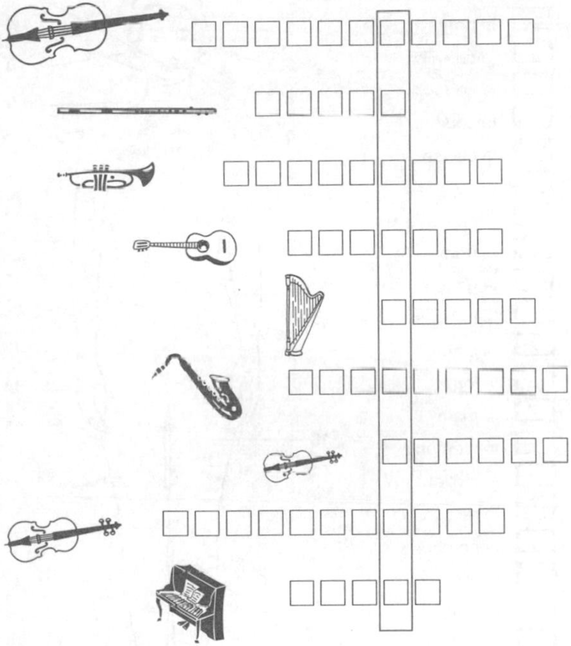

The musician is __________ .

12 Body parts

Can you put the right number in the boxes next to the French words in the list?

- ☐ la bouche
- ☐ le bras
- ☐ la cheville
- ☐ le cou
- ☐ le coude
- ☐ la cuisse
- ☐ le doigt
- ☐ l'épaule
- ☐ le front
- ☐ le genou
- ☐ la hanche
- ☐ la jambe
- ☐ la joue
- ☐ la main
- ☐ le menton
- ☐ le mollet
- ☐ le nez
- ☐ le nombril
- ☐ l'œil
- ☐ l'oreille
- ☐ l'orteil
- ☐ le pied
- ☐ le poignet
- ☐ la tête

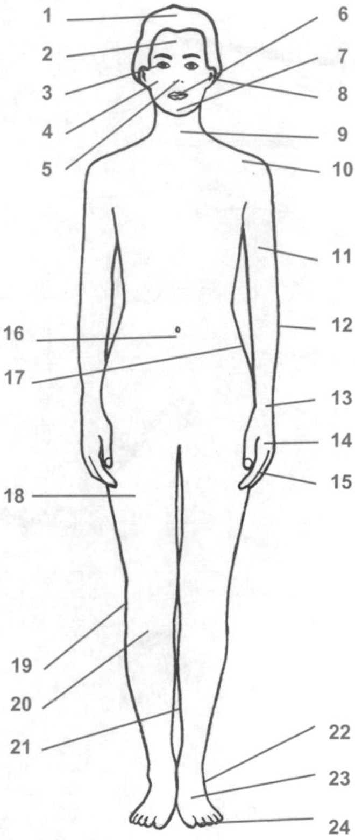

13 Liar liar!

Today, Sabine had a day-off. She tells her mother what she has been up to:

> “*Ce matin, je me suis levée juste après ton départ. J'ai bu du café au lait et j'ai mangé des tartines. Après avoir fait ma toilette et m'être habillée, je suis allée au parc. Il faisait très beau et j'avais envie de me promener. Je suis revenue à la maison pour chercher mon maillot de bain et je suis allée à la piscine découverte. J'y suis restée pendant deux heures. En sortant, j'avais très faim, alors je me suis installée dans un café. J'ai commandé un sandwich. Après ça, je suis allée au cinéma. Le film était super! Je suis rentrée à la maison un peu avant que tu arrives.*”

What she doesn't say is that her little brother, Adrien, skipped school to spend the day with her. Rewrite her statement.

> “*Ce matin, nous nous sommes levés juste après ton départ...*”

Answers

1

seronts
faudra
pourront
offriront
épargnera
ira
ferez
veillera
surviendra
sera

2

ordinateur
clavier
souris
disquette
écran
curseur
cd-rom

3

C	A	R
B	A	R
B	A	S
B	U	S
B	I	S

B	A	I	N
M	A	I	N
S	A	I	N
S	A	I	S
S	A	N	S
S	A	N	G

4

lent = prêté
port = porto
gauge = jauge
broach = entamer
duvet = couette
liver = foie

5

Hier, je me suis levé de bonne heure.
Pourtant, je le lui ai dit plusieurs fois.
Prends les clés sur la table en sortant.
L'année prochaine, elle ira en vacances au Portugal.
Nous sommes allés voir un film au cinéma.
Le frère de la voisine n'est pas là.

6

1.D. *grand* est le contraire de *petit*.
2.F. *blond* est le contraire de *brun*.
3.A. *bête* est le contraire d'*intelligent*.

4.G. *énervé* est le contraire de *calme*.
5.B. *gentil* est le contraire de *méchant*.
6.H. *timide* est le contraire d'*extraverti*.
7.I. *patient* est le contraire d'*impatient*.
8.E. *désagréable* est le contraire de *sympathique*.
9.J. *poli* est le contraire de *malpoli*.
10.C. *maigre* est le contraire de *gros*.

7

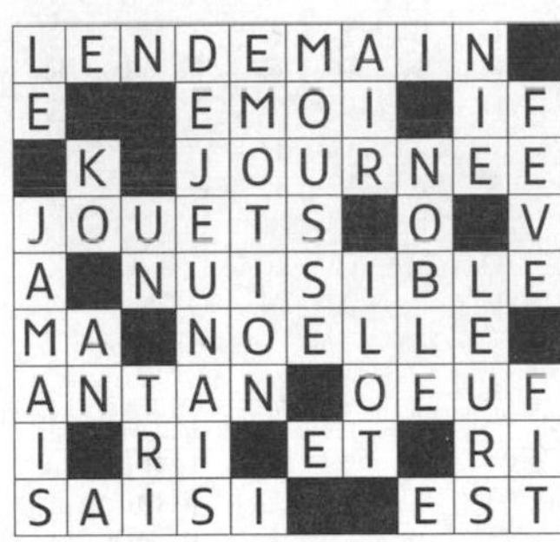

8

1. moteur - because it isn't a vehicle
2. cendrier - because it is not used for cooking
3. cassette - because it isn't an electrical device
4. varappe - because it is the only sport in the list which isn't a water-sport
5. redoubler - because it is the only verb in the list which doesn't describe a movement
6. sou - because it ends in "-s" in the plural, not in "-x" like the other five

9

deux taille–crayons
deux blocs–notes
deux timbres–poste
deux abat–jour
deux couvre–lits
deux cache–pots
deux tire–bouchons
deux ouvre–boîtes
deux réveille–matin
deux choux-fleurs

10

1. oiseau
2. feuilles
3. branche
4. nid
5. fruit
6. arbre
7. marron

11

```
  C O N T R E B A S S E
      F L U T E
    T R O M P E T T E
        G U I T A R E
              H A R P E
        S A X O P H O N E
              V I O L O N
V I O L O N C E L L E
        P I A N O
```

12

6. la bouche
11. le bras
22. la cheville
9. le cou
12. le coude
18. la cuisse
15. le doigt
10. l'épaule
2. le front
20. le genou
17. la hanche
19. la jambe
4. la joue
14. la main
7. le menton
21. le mollet
5. le nez
16. le nombril
3. l'œil
8. l'oreille
24. l'orteil
23. le pied
13. le poignet
1. la tête

13

"Ce matin, nous nous sommes levés juste après ton départ. Nous avons bu du café au lait et nous avons mangé des tartines. Après avoir fait notre toilette et nous être habillés, nous sommes allés au parc. Il faisait très beau et nous avions envie de nous promener. Nous sommes revenus à la maison pour chercher nos maillots de bain et nous sommes allés à la piscine découverte. Nous y sommes restés pendant deux heures. En sortant, nous avions très faim, alors nous nous sommes installés dans un café. Nous avons commandé des sandwichs. Après ça, nous sommes allés au cinéma. Le film était super! Nous sommes rentrés à la maison un peu avant que tu arrives."

Anglais-Français
English-French

A

a /eɪ, *unstressed* ə/ *a.* (*before vowel* **an** /æn, ən/) un(e). **I'm a painter,** je suis peintre. **ten pence a kilo,** dix pence le kilo. **once a year,** une fois par an.
aback /ə'bæk/ *adv.* **taken ~,** déconcerté, interdit.
abandon /ə'bændən/ *v.t.* abandonner. ● *n.* désinvolture *f.* **~ed** *a.* (*behaviour*) débauché. **~ment** *n.* abandon *m.*
abashed /ə'bæʃt/ *a.* confus.
abate /ə'beɪt/ *v.i.* se calmer. ● *v.t.* diminuer. **~ment** *n.* diminution *f.*
abattoir /'æbətwɑ:(r)/ *n.* abattoir *m.*
abbey /'æbɪ/ *n.* abbaye *f.*
abb|ot /'æbət/ *n.* abbé *m.* **~ess** *n.* abbesse *f.*
abbreviat|e /ə'bri:vɪeɪt/ *v.t.* abréger. **~ion** /-'eɪʃn/ *n.* abréviation *f.*
abdicat|e /'æbdɪkeɪt/ *v.t./i.* abdiquer. **~ion** /-'keɪʃn/ *n.* abdication *f.*
abdom|en /'æbdəmən/ *n.* abdomen *m.* **~inal** /-'dɒmɪnl/ *a.* abdominal.
abduct /æb'dʌkt/ *v.t.* enlever. **~ion** /-kʃn/ *n.* rapt *m.* **~or** *n.* ravisseu|r, -se *m., f.*
aberration /æbə'reɪʃn/ *n.* aberration *f.*
abet /ə'bet/ *v.t.* (*p.t.* **abetted**) (*jurid.*) encourager.
abeyance /ə'beɪəns/ *n.* **in ~,** (*matter*) en suspens; (*custom*) en désuétude.
abhor /əb'hɔ:(r)/ *v.t.* (*p.t.* **abhorred**) exécrer. **~rence** /-'hɒrəns/ *n.* horreur *f.* **~rent** /-'hɒrənt/ *a.* exécrable.
abide /ə'baɪd/ *v.t.* supporter. **~ by,** respecter.
abiding /ə'baɪdɪŋ/ *a.* éternel.
ability /ə'bɪlətɪ/ *n.* aptitude *f.* (**to do,** à faire); (*talent*) talent *m.*
abject /'æbdʒekt/ *a.* abject.
ablaze /ə'bleɪz/ *a.* en feu. **~ with,** (*anger etc.*: *fig.*) enflammé de.
abl|e /'eɪbl/ *a.* (**-er, -est**) capable (**to,** de). **be ~e,** pouvoir; (*know how to*) savoir. **~y** *adv.* habilement.
ablutions /ə'blu:ʃnz/ *n. pl.* ablutions *f. pl.*
abnormal /æb'nɔ:ml/ *a.* anormal. **~ity** /-'mælətɪ/ *n.* anomalie *f.* **~ly** *adv.* (*unusually*) exceptionnellement.
aboard /ə'bɔ:d/ *adv.* à bord. ● *prep.* à bord de.
abode /ə'bəʊd/ (*old use*) demeure *f.* **of no fixed ~,** sans domicile fixe.
aboli|sh /ə'bɒlɪʃ/ *v.t.* supprimer, abolir. **~tion** /æbə'lɪʃn/ *n.* suppression *f.*, abolition *f.*
abominable /ə'bɒmɪnəbl/ *a.* abominable.
abominat|e /ə'bɒmɪneɪt/ *v.t.* exécrer. **~ion** /-'neɪʃn/ *n.* abomination *f.*
aboriginal /æbə'rɪdʒənl/ *a.* & *n.* aborigène (*m.*).
aborigines /æbə'rɪdʒəni:z/ *n. pl.* aborigènes *m. pl.*
abort /ə'bɔ:t/ *v.t.* faire avorter. ● *v.i.* avorter. **~ive** *a.* (*attempt etc.*) manqué.
abortion /ə'bɔ:ʃn/ *n.* avortement *m.* **have an ~,** se faire avorter.
abound /ə'baʊnd/ *v.i.* abonder (**in,** en).
about /ə'baʊt/ *adv.* (*approximately*) environ; (*here and there*) çà et là; (*all round*) partout, autour; (*nearby*) dans les parages; (*of rumour*) en circulation. ● *prep.* au sujet de; (*round*) autour de; (*somewhere in*) dans. **~-face, ~-turn** *ns.* (*fig.*) volteface *f. invar.* **~ here,** par ici. **be ~ to do,** être sur le point de faire. **how** *or* **what ~ leaving,** si on partait. **what's the film ~?,** quel est le sujet du film? **talk ~,** parler de.
above /ə'bʌv/ *adv.* au-dessus; (*on page*) ci-dessus. ● *prep.* au-dessus de. **he is not ~ lying,** il n'est pas incapable de mentir. **~ all,** par-dessus tout. **~-board** *a.* honnête. **~-mentioned** *a.* mentionné ci-dessus.

abrasion /əˈbreɪʒn/ *n.* frottement *m.*; (*injury*) écorchure *f.*
abrasive /əˈbreɪsɪv/ *a.* abrasif; (*manner*) brusque. ● *n.* abrasif *m.*
abreast /əˈbrest/ *adv.* de front. **keep ~ of,** se tenir au courant de.
abridge /əˈbrɪdʒ/ *v.t.* abréger. **~ment** *n.* abrégement *m.*, réduction *f.*; (*abridged text*) abrégé *m.*
abroad /əˈbrɔːd/ *adv.* à l'étranger; (*far and wide*) de tous côtés.
abrupt /əˈbrʌpt/ *a.* (*sudden, curt*) brusque; (*steep*) abrupt. **~ly** *adv.* (*suddenly*) brusquement; (*curtly, rudely*) avec brusquerie. **~ness** *n.* brusquerie *f.*
abscess /ˈæbses/ *n.* abcès *m.*
abscond /əbˈskɒnd/ *v.i.* s'enfuir.
abseil /ˈæbseɪl/ *v.i.* descendre en rappel.
absen|t[1] /ˈæbsənt/ *a.* absent; (*look etc.*) distrait. **~ce** *n.* absence *f.*; (*lack*) manque *m.* **in the ~ce of,** à défaut de. **~tly** *adv.* distraitement. **~t-minded** *a.* distrait. **~t-mindedness** *n.* distraction *f.*
absent[2] /əbˈsent/ *v. pr.* **~ o.s.,** s'absenter.
absentee /æbsənˈtiː/ *n.* absent(e) *m.* (*f.*). **~ism** *n.* absentéisme *m.*
absolute /ˈæbsəluːt/ *a.* absolu; (*coward etc.*: *fam.*) véritable. **~ly** *adv.* absolument.
absolution /æbsəˈluːʃn/ *n.* absolution *f.*
absolve /əbˈzɒlv/ *v.t.* (*from sin*) absoudre (**from,** de); (*from vow etc.*) délier (**from,** de).
absor|b /əbˈsɔːb/ *v.t.* absorber. **~ption** *n.* absorption *f.*
absorbent /əbˈsɔːbənt/ *a.* absorbant. **~ cotton,** (*Amer.*) coton hydrophile *m.*
abst|ain /əbˈsteɪn/ *v.i.* s'abstenir (**from,** de). **~ention** /-ˈstenʃn/ *n.* abstention *f.*; (*from drink*) abstinence *f.*
abstemious /əbˈstiːmɪəs/ *a.* sobre.
abstinen|ce /ˈæbstɪnəns/ *n.* abstinence *f.* **~t** *a.* sobre.
abstract[1] /ˈæbstrækt/ *a.* abstrait. ● *n.* (*quality*) abstrait *m.*; (*summary*) résumé *m.*
abstract[2] /əbˈstrækt/ *v.t.* retirer, extraire. **~ion** /-kʃn/ *n.* extraction *f.*; (*idea*) abstraction *f.*
abstruse /əbˈstruːs/ *a.* obscur.
absurd /əbˈsɜːd/ *a.* absurde. **~ity** *n.* absurdité *f.*

abundan|t /əˈbʌndənt/ *a.* abondant. **~ce** *n.* abondance *f.* **~tly** *adv.* (*entirely*) tout à fait.
abuse[1] /əˈbjuːz/ *v.t.* (*misuse*) abuser de; (*ill-treat*) maltraiter; (*insult*) injurier.
abus|e[2] /əˈbjuːs/ *n.* (*misuse*) abus *m.* (**of,** de); (*insults*) injures *f. pl.* **~ive** *a.* injurieux. **get ~ive,** devenir grossier.
abut /əˈbʌt/ *v.i.* (*p.t.* **abutted**) être contigu (**on,** à).
abysmal /əˈbɪzməl/ *a.* (*great*) profond; (*bad*: *fam.*) exécrable.
abyss /əˈbɪs/ *n.* abîme *m.*
academic /ækəˈdemɪk/ *a.* universitaire; (*scholarly*) intellectuel; (*pej.*) théorique. ● *n.* universitaire *m./f.* **~ally** /-lɪ/ *adv.* intellectuellement.
academ|y /əˈkædəmɪ/ *n.* (*school*) école *f.* **A~y,** (*society*) Académie *f.* **~ician** /-ˈmɪʃn/ *n.* académicien(ne) *m.* (*f.*).
accede /əkˈsiːd/ *v.i.* **~ to,** (*request, post, throne*) accéder à.
accelerat|e /əkˈseləreɪt/ *v.t.* accélérer. ● *v.i.* (*speed up*) s'accélérer; (*auto.*) accélérer. **~ion** /-ˈreɪʃn/ *n.* accélération *f.*
accelerator /əkˈseləreɪtə(r)/ *n.* (*auto.*) accélérateur *m.*
accent[1] /ˈæksənt/ *n.* accent *m.*
accent[2] /ækˈsent/ *v.t.* accentuer.
accentuat|e /əkˈsentʃʊeɪt/ *v.t.* accentuer. **~ion** /-ˈeɪʃn/ *n.* accentuation *f.*
accept /əkˈsept/ *v.t.* accepter. **~able** *a.* acceptable. **~ance** *n.* acceptation *f.*; (*approval, favour*) approbation *f.*
access /ˈækses/ *n.* accès *m.* (**to sth.,** à qch.; **to s.o.,** auprès de qn.). **~ible** /əkˈsesəbl/ *a.* accessible. **~ road,** route d'accès *f.*
accession /ækˈseʃn/ *n.* accession *f.*; (*thing added*) nouvelle acquisition *f.*
accessory /əkˈsesərɪ/ *a.* accessoire. ● *n.* accessoire *m.*; (*person*: *jurid.*) complice *m./f.*
accident /ˈæksɪdənt/ *n.* accident *m.*; (*chance*) hasard *m.* **~al** /-ˈdentl/ *a.* accidentel, fortuit. **~ally** /-ˈdentəlɪ/ *adv.* involontairement. **~-prone,** qui attire les accidents.
acclaim /əˈkleɪm/ *v.t.* acclamer. ● *n.* acclamation(s) *f.* (*pl.*).
acclimat|e /ˈæklɪmeɪt/ *v.t./i.* (*Amer.*) (s')acclimater. **~ion** /-ˈmeɪʃn/ *n.* (*Amer.*) acclimatation *f.*

acclimatiz|e /ə'klaɪmətaɪz/ *v.t./i.* (s')acclimater. **~ation** /-'zeɪʃn/ *n.* acclimatation *f.*

accommodat|e /ə'kɒmədeɪt/ *v.t.* loger, avoir de la place pour; (*adapt*) adapter; (*supply*) fournir; (*oblige*) obliger. **~ing** *a.* obligeant. **~ion** /-'deɪʃn/ *n.* (*living premises*) logement *m.*; (*rented rooms*) chambres *f. pl.*

accompan|y /ə'kʌmpənɪ/ *v.t.* accompagner. **~iment** *n.* accompagnement *m.* **~ist** *n.* accompagna|teur, -trice *m., f.*

accomplice /ə'kʌmplɪs/ *n.* complice *m./f.*

accomplish /ə'kʌmplɪʃ/ *v.t.* (*perform*) accomplir; (*achieve*) réaliser. **~ed** *a.* accompli. **~ment** *n.* accomplissement *m.* **~ments** *n. pl.* (*abilities*) talents *m. pl.*

accord /ə'kɔ:d/ *v.i.* concorder. ● *v.t.* accorder. ● *n.* accord *m.* **of one's own ~,** de sa propre initiative. **~ance** *n.* **in ~ance with,** conformément à.

according /ə'kɔ:dɪŋ/ *adv.* **~ to,** selon, suivant. **~ly** *adv.* en conséquence.

accordion /ə'kɔ:dɪən/ *n.* accordéon *m.*

accost /ə'kɒst/ *v.t.* aborder.

account /ə'kaʊnt/ *n.* (*comm.*) compte *m.*; (*description*) compte rendu *m.*; (*importance*) importance *f.* ● *v.t.* considérer. **~ for,** rendre compte de, expliquer. **on ~ of,** à cause de. **on no ~,** en aucun cas. **take into ~,** tenir compte de. **~able** *a.* responsable (**for,** de; **to,** envers). **~ability** /-ə'bɪlətɪ/ *n.* responsabilité *f.*

accountan|t /ə'kaʊntənt/ *n.* comptable *m./f.*, expert-comptable *m.* **~cy** *n.* comptabilité *f.*

accredited /ə'kredɪtɪd/ *a.* accrédité.

accrue /ə'kru:/ *v.i.* s'accumuler. **~ to,** (*come to*) revenir à.

accumulat|e /ə'kju:mjʊleɪt/ *v.t./i.* (s')accumuler. **~ion** /-'leɪʃn/ *n.* accumulation *f.*

accumulator /ə'kju:mjʊleɪtə(r)/ *n.* (*battery*) accumulateur *m.*

accura|te /'ækjərət/ *a.* exact, précis. **~cy** *n.* exactitude *f.*, précision *f.* **~tely** *adv.* exactement, avec précision.

accus|e /ə'kju:z/ *v.t.* accuser. **the ~ed,** l'accusé(e) *m.(f.).* **~ation** /ækju:'zeɪʃn/ *n.* accusation *f.*

accustom /ə'kʌstəm/ *v.t.* accoutumer. **~ed** *a.* accoutumé. **become ~ed to,** s'accoutumer à.

ace /eɪs/ *n.* (*card, person*) as *m.*

ache /eɪk/ *n.* douleur *f.*, mal *m.* ● *v.i.* faire mal. **my leg ~s,** ma jambe me fait mal, j'ai mal à la jambe.

achieve /ə'tʃi:v/ *v.t.* réaliser, accomplir; (*success*) obtenir. **~ment** *n.* réalisation *f.* (**of,** de); (*feat*) exploit *m.*, réussite *f.*

acid /'æsɪd/ *a.* & *n.* acide (*m.*). **~ity** /ə'sɪdətɪ/ *n.* acidité *f.* **~ rain,** pluies acides *f. pl.*

acknowledge /ək'nɒlɪdʒ/ *v.t.* reconnaître. **~ (receipt of),** accuser réception de. **~ment** *n.* reconnaissance *f.*; accusé de réception *m.*

acme /'ækmɪ/ *n.* sommet *m.*

acne /'æknɪ/ *n.* acné *f.*

acorn /'eɪkɔ:n/ *n.* (*bot.*) gland *m.*

acoustic /ə'ku:stɪk/ *a.* acoustique. **~s** *n. pl.* acoustique *f.*

acquaint /ə'kweɪnt/ *v.t.* **~ s.o. with sth.,** mettre qn. au courant de qch. **be ~ed with,** (*person*) connaître; (*fact*) savoir. **~ance** *n.* (*knowledge, person*) connaissance *f.*

acquiesce /ækwɪ'es/ *v.i.* consentir. **~nce** *n.* consentement *m.*

acqui|re /ə'kwaɪə(r)/ *v.t.* acquérir; (*habit*) prendre. **~sition** /ækwɪ'zɪʃn/ *n.* acquisition *f.* **~sitive** /ə'kwɪzətɪv/ *a.* avide, âpre au gain.

acquit /ə'kwɪt/ *v.t.* (*p.t.* **acquitted**) acquitter. **~ o.s. well,** bien s'en tirer. **~tal** *n.* acquittement *m.*

acre /'eɪkə(r)/ *n.* (*approx.*) demi-hectare *m.* **~age** *n.* superficie *f.*

acrid /'ækrɪd/ *a.* âcre.

acrimon|ious /ækrɪ'məʊnɪəs/ *a.* acerbe, acrimonieux. **~y** /'ækrɪmənɪ/ *n.* acrimonie *f.*

acrobat /'ækrəbæt/ *n.* acrobate *m./f.* **~ic** /-'bætɪk/ *a.* acrobatique. **~ics** /-'bætɪks/ *n. pl.* acrobatie *f.*

acronym /'ækrənɪm/ *n.* sigle *m.*

across /ə'krɒs/ *adv.* & *prep.* (*side to side*) d'un côté à l'autre (de); (*on other side*) de l'autre côté (**from,** de); (*crosswise*) en travers (de), à travers. **go** *or* **walk ~,** traverser.

acrylic /ə'krɪlɪk/ *a.* & *n.* acrylique (*m.*).

act /ækt/ *n.* (*deed, theatre*) acte *m.*; (*in variety show*) numéro *m.*; (*decree*) loi *f.* ● *v.i.* agir; (*theatre*) jouer; (*function*) marcher; (*pretend*) jouer la comédie. ● *v.t.* (*part, role*) jouer. **~ as,** servir de. **~ing** *a.* (*temporary*) intérimaire; *n.* (*theatre*) jeu *m.*

action /'ækʃn/ *n.* action *f.*; (*mil.*) combat *m.* **out of ~,** hors service. **take ~,** agir.

activate /'æktɪveɪt/ *v.t.* (*machine*) actionner; (*reaction*) activer.

activ|e /'æktɪv/ *a.* actif; (*interest*) vif; (*volcano*) en activité. **~ism** *n.* activisme *m.* **~ist** *n.* activiste *m./f.* **~ity** /-'tɪvətɪ/ *n.* activité *f.*

ac|tor /'aektə(r)/ *n.* acteur *m.* **~tress** *n.* actrice *f.*

actual /'æktʃʊəl/ *a.* réel; (*example*) concret. **the ~ pen which,** le stylo même que. **in the ~ house,** (*the house itself*) dans la maison elle-même. **no ~ promise,** pas de promesse en tant que telle. **~ity** /-'ælətɪ/ *n.* réalité *f.* **~ly** *adv.* (*in fact*) en réalité, réellement.

actuary /'æktʃʊərɪ/ *n.* actuaire *m./f.*

acumen /'ækjʊmen, *Amer.* ə'kju:mən/ *n.* perspicacité *f.*

acupunctur|e /'ækjʊpʌŋktʃə(r)/ *n.* acupuncture *f.* **~ist** *n.* acupuncteur *m.*

acute /ə'kju:t/ *a.* aigu; (*mind*) pénétrant; (*emotion*) intense, vif; (*shortage*) grave. **~ly** *adv.* vivement. **~ness** *n.* intensité *f.*

ad /æd/ *n.* (*fam.*) annonce *f.*

AD *abbr.* après J.-C.

adamant /'ædəmənt/ *a.* inflexible.

Adam's apple /'ædəmz'æpl/ *n.* pomme d'Adam *f.*

adapt /ə'dæpt/ *v.t./i.* (s')adapter. **~ation** /-'teɪʃn/ *n.* adaptation *f.* **~or** *n.* (*electr.*) adaptateur *m.*; (*for two plugs*) prise multiple *f.*

adaptab|le /ə'dæptəbl/ *a.* souple; (*techn.*) adaptable. **~ility** /-'bɪlətɪ/ *n.* souplesse *f.*

add /æd/ *v.t./i.* ajouter. **~ (up),** (*total*) additionner. **~ up to,** (*total*) s'élever à. **~ing machine,** machine à calculer *f.*

adder /'ædə(r)/ *n.* vipère *f.*

addict /'ædɪkt/ *n.* intoxiqué(e) *m.* (*f.*); (*fig.*) fanatique *m./f.*

addict|ed /ə'dɪktɪd/ *a.* **~ed to,** (*drink*) adonné à. **be ~ed to,** (*fig.*) être un fanatique de. **~ion** /-kʃn/ *n.* (*med.*) dépendance *f.*; (*fig.*) manie *f.* **~ive** *a.* (*drug etc.*) qui crée une dépendance.

addition /ə'dɪʃn/ *n.* addition *f.* **in ~,** en outre. **~al** /-ʃənl/ *a.* supplémentaire.

additive /'ædɪtɪv/ *n.* additif *m.*

address /ə'dres/ *n.* adresse *f.*; (*speech*) allocution *f.* ● *v.t.* adresser; (*speak to*) s'adresser à. **~ee** /ædre'si:/ *n.* destinataire *m./f.*

adenoids /'ædɪnɔɪdz/ *n. pl.* végétations (adénoïdes) *f. pl.*

adept /'ædept, *Amer.* ə'dept/ *a. & n.* expert (**at,** en) (*m.*).

adequa|te /'ædɪkwət/ *a.* suffisant; (*satisfactory*) satisfaisant. **~cy** *n.* quantité suffisante *f.*; (*of person*) compétence *f.* **~tely** *adv.* suffisamment.

adhere /əd'hɪə(r)/ *v.i.* adhérer (**to,** à). **~ to,** (*fig.*) respecter. **~nce** /-rəns/ *n.* adhésion *f.*

adhesion /əd'hi:ʒn/ *n.* (*grip*) adhérence *f.*; (*support: fig.*) adhésion *f.*

adhesive /əd'hi:sɪv/ *a. & n.* adhésif (*m.*).

ad infinitum /ædɪnfɪ'naɪtəm/ *adv.* à l'infini.

adjacent /ə'dʒeɪsnt/ *a.* contigu (**to,** à).

adjective /'ædʒɪktɪv/ *n.* adjectif *m.*

adjoin /ə'dʒɔɪn/ *v.t.* être contigu à.

adjourn /ə'dʒɜ:n/ *v.t.* ajourner. ● *v.t./i.* **~ (the meeting),** suspendre la séance. **~ to,** (*go*) se retirer à.

adjudicate /ə'dʒu:dɪkeɪt/ *v.t./i.* juger.

adjust /ə'dʒʌst/ *v.t.* (*machine*) régler; (*prices*) (r)ajuster; (*arrange*) rajuster, arranger. ● *v.t./i.* **~ (o.s.) to,** s'adapter à. **~able** *a.* réglable. **~ment** *n.* (*techn.*) réglage *m.*; (*of person*) adaptation *f.*

ad lib /æd'lɪb/ *v.i.* (*p.t.* **ad libbed**) (*fam.*) improviser.

administer /ad'mɪnɪstə(r)/ *v.t.* administrer.

administration /ədmɪnɪ'streɪʃn/ *n.* administration *f.*

administrative /əd'mɪnɪstrətɪv/ *a.* administratif.

administrator /əd'mɪnɪstreɪtə(r)/ *n.* administra|teur, -trice *m., f.*

admirable /'ædmərəbl/ *a.* admirable.

admiral /'ædmərəl/ *n.* amiral *m.*

admir|e /əd'maɪə(r)/ *v.t.* admirer. **~ation** /ædmə'reɪʃn/ *n.* admiration *f.* **~er** *n.* admira|teur, -trice *m., f.*

admissible /əd'mɪsəbl/ *a.* admissible.

admission /əd'mɪʃn/ *n.* admission *f.*; (*to museum, theatre, etc.*) entrée *f.*; (*confession*) aveu *m.*

admit /əd'mɪt/ *v.t.* (*p.t.* **admitted**) laisser entrer; (*acknowledge*) reconnaître, admettre. **~ to,** avouer. **~tance** *n.* entrée *f.* **~tedly** *adv.* il est vrai (que).

admonish /əd'mɒnɪʃ/ *v.t.* réprimander.

ado /ə'du:/ *n.* **without more ~,** sans plus de cérémonies.

adolescen|t /ædə'lesnt/ *n.* & *a.* adolescent(e) (*m.* (*f.*)). **~ce** *n.* adolescence *f.*

adopt /ə'dɒpt/ *v.t.* adopter. **~ed** *a.* (*child*) adoptif. **~ion** /-pʃn/ *n.* adoption *f.*

adoptive /ə'dɒptɪv/ *a.* adoptif.

ador|e /ə'dɔ:(r)/ *v.t.* adorer. **~able** *a.* adorable. **~ation** /ædə'reɪʃn/ *n.* adoration *f.*

adorn /ə'dɔ:n/ *v.t.* orner. **~ment** *n.* ornement *m.*

adrift /ə'drɪft/ *a.* & *adv.* à la dérive.

adroit /ə'drɔɪt/ *a.* adroit.

adulation /ædjʊ'leɪʃn/ *n.* adulation *f.*

adult /'ædʌlt/ *a.* & *n.* adulte (*m./f.*). **~hood** *n.* condition d'adulte *f.*

adulterate /ə'dʌltəreɪt/ *v.t.* falsifier, frelater, altérer.

adulter|y /ə'dʌltərɪ/ *n.* adultère *m.* **~er, ~ess** *ns.* épou|x, -se adultère *m., f.* **~ous** *a.* adultère.

advance /əd'vɑ:ns/ *v.t.* avancer. ● *v.i.* (s')avancer; (*progress*) avancer. ● *n.* avance *f.* ● *a.* (*payment*) anticipé. **in ~,** à l'avance. **~d** *a.* avancé; (*studies*) supérieur. **~ment** *n.* avancement *m.*

advantage /əd'vɑ:ntɪdʒ/ *n.* avantage *m.* **take ~ of,** profiter de; (*person*) exploiter. **~ous** /ædvən'teɪdʒəs/ *a.* avantageux.

advent /'ædvənt/ *n.* arrivée *f.*

Advent /'ædvənt/ *n.* Avent *m.*

adventur|e /əd'ventʃə(r)/ *n.* aventure *f.* **~er** *n.* explora|teur, -trice *m., f.*; (*pej.*) aventur|ier, -ière *m., f.* **~ous** *a.* aventureux.

adverb /'ædvɜ:b/ *n.* adverbe *m.*

adversary /'ædvəsərɪ/ *n.* adversaire *m./f.*

advers|e /'ædvɜ:s/ *a.* défavorable. **~ity** /əd'vɜ:sətɪ/ *n.* adversité *f.*

advert /'ædvɜ:t/ *n.* (*fam.*) annonce *f.*; (*TV*) pub *f.*, publicité *f.* **~isement** /əd'vɜ:tɪsmənt/ *n.* publicité *f.*; (*in paper etc.*) annonce *f.*

advertis|e /'ædvətaɪz/ *v.t./i.* faire de la publicité (pour); (*sell*) mettre une annonce (pour vendre). **~ for,** (*seek*) chercher (par voie d'annonce). **~ing** *n.* publicité *f.* **~er** /-ə(r)/ *n.* annonceur *m.*

advice /əd'vaɪs/ *n.* conseil(s) *m.* (*pl.*); (*comm.*) avis *m.* **some ~, a piece of ~,** un conseil.

advis|e /əd'vaɪz/ *v.t.* conseiller; (*inform*) aviser. **~e against,** déconseiller. **~able** *a.* conseillé, prudent (**to,** de). **~er** *n.* conseill|er, -ère *m., f.* **~ory** *a.* consultatif.

advocate[1] /'ædvəkət/ *n.* (*jurid.*) avocat *m.* **~s of,** les défenseurs de.

advocate[2] /'ædvəkeɪt/ *v.t.* recommander.

aegis /'i:dʒɪs/ *n.* **under the ~ of,** sous l'égide de *f.*

aeon /'i:ən/ *n.* éternité *f.*

aerial /'eərɪəl/ *a.* aérien. ● *n.* antenne *f.*

aerobatics /eərə'bætɪks/ *n. pl.* acrobatie aérienne *f.*

aerobics /eə'rəʊbɪks/ *n.* aérobic *m.*

aerodrome /'eərədrəʊm/ *n.* aérodrome *m.*

aerodynamic /eərəʊdaɪ'næmɪk/ *a.* aérodynamique.

aeroplane /'eərəpleɪn/ *n.* avion *m.*

aerosol /'eərəsɒl/ *n.* atomiseur *m.*

aesthetic /i:s'θetɪk, *Amer.* es'θetɪk/ *a.* esthétique.

afar /ə'fɑ:(r)/ *adv.* **from ~,** de loin.

affable /'æfəbl/ *a.* affable.

affair /ə'feə(r)/ *n.* (*matter*) affaire *f.*; (*romance*) liaison *f.*

affect /ə'fekt/ *v.t.* affecter. **~ation** /æfek'teɪʃn/ *n.* affectation *f.* **~ed** *a.* affecté.

affection /ə'fekʃn/ *n.* affection *f.*

affectionate /ə'fekʃənət/ *a.* affectueux.

affiliat|e /ə'fɪlɪeɪt/ *v.t.* affilier. **~ed company,** filiale *f.* **~ion** /-'eɪʃn/ *n.* affiliation *f.*

affinity /ə'fɪnətɪ/ *n.* affinité *f.*

affirm /ə'fɜ:m/ *v.t.* affirmer. **~ation** /æfə'meɪʃn/ *n.* affirmation *f.*

affirmative /ə'fɜ:mətɪv/ *a.* affirmatif. ● *n.* affirmative *f.*

affix /ə'fɪks/ *v.t.* apposer.

afflict /ə'flɪkt/ *v.t.* affliger. **~ion** /-kʃn/ *n.* affliction *f.*, détresse *f.*

affluen|t /'æflʊənt/ *a.* riche. **~ce** *n.* richesse *f.*

afford /ə'fɔ:d/ *v.t.* avoir les moyens d'acheter; (*provide*) fournir. **~ to do,** avoir les moyens de faire; (*be able*) se permettre de faire. **can you ~ the time?,** avez-vous le temps?

affray /ə'freɪ/ *n.* rixe *f.*

affront /ə'frʌnt/ *n.* affront *m.* ● *v.t.* insulter.

afield /ə'fi:ld/ *adv.* **far ~,** loin.

afloat /ə'fləʊt/ *adv.* à flot.

afoot /ə'fʊt/ *adv.* **sth. is ~,** il se trame *or* se prépare qch.

aforesaid /ə'fɔ:sed/ *a.* susdit.

afraid /ə'freɪd/ *a.* **be ~,** avoir peur (**of, to,** de; **that,** que); (*be sorry*) regretter. **I am ~ that,** (*regret to say*) je regrette de dire que.

afresh /ə'freʃ/ *adv.* de nouveau.

Africa /'æfrɪkə/ *n.* Afrique *f.* **~n** *a.* & *n.* africain(e) (*m.* (*f.*)).

after /'ɑ:ftə(r)/ *adv.* & *prep.* après. ● *conj.* après que. **~ doing,** après avoir fait. **~ all** après tout. **~-effect** *n.* suite *f.* **~-sales service,** service après-vente *m.* **~ the manner of,** d'après. **be ~,** (*seek*) chercher.

aftermath /'ɑ:ftəmɑ:θ/ *n.* suites *f. pl.*

afternoon /ɑ:ftə'nu:n/ *n.* après-midi *m./f. invar.*

afters /'ɑ:ftəz/ *n. pl.* (*fam.*) dessert *m.*

aftershave /'ɑ:ftəʃeɪv/ *n.* lotion après-rasage *f.*

afterthought /'ɑ:ftəθɔ:t/ *n.* réflexion après coup *f.* **as an ~,** en y repensant.

afterwards /'ɑ:ftəwədz/ *adv.* après, par la suite.

again /ə'gen/ *adv.* de nouveau, encore une fois; (*besides*) en outre. **do ~, see ~**/*etc.*, refaire, revoir/*etc.*

against /ə'genst/ *prep.* contre. **~ the law,** illégal.

age /eɪdʒ/ *n.* âge *m.* ● *v.t./i.* (*pres. p.* **ageing**) vieillir. **~ group,** tranche d'âge *f.* **~ limit,** limite d'âge. **for ~s,** (*fam.*) une éternité. **of ~,** (*jurid.*) majeur. **ten years of ~,** âgé de dix ans. **~less** *a.* toujours jeune.

aged[1] /eɪdʒd/ *a.* **~ six,** âgé de six ans.

aged[2] /'eɪdʒɪd/ *a.* âgé, vieux.

agen|cy /'eɪdʒənsɪ/ *n.* agence *f.*; (*means*) entremise *f.* **~t** *n.* agent *m.*

agenda /ə'dʒendə/ *n.* ordre du jour *m.*

agglomeration /əglɒmə'reɪʃn/ *n.* agglomération *f.*

aggravat|e /'ægrəveɪt/ *v.t.* (*make worse*) aggraver; (*annoy*: *fam.*) exaspérer. **~ion** /-'veɪʃn/ *n.* aggravation *f.*; exaspération *f.*; (*trouble*: *fam.*) ennuis *m. pl.*

aggregate /'ægrɪgət/ *a.* & *n.* total (*m.*).

aggress|ive /ə'gresɪv/ *a.* agressif. **~ion** /-ʃn/ *n.* agression *f.* **~iveness** *n.* agressivité *f.* **~or** *n.* agresseur *m.*

aggrieved /ə'gri:vd/ *a.* peiné.

aghast /ə'gɑ:st/ *a.* horrifié.

agil|e /'ædʒaɪl, *Amer.* 'ædʒl/ *a.* agile. **~ity** /ə'dʒɪlətɪ/ *n.* agilité *f.*

agitat|e /'ædʒɪteɪt/ *v.t.* agiter. **~ion** /-'teɪʃn/ *n.* agitation *f.* **~or** *n.* agita|teur, -trice *m., f.*

agnostic /æg'nɒstɪk/ *a.* & *n.* agnostique (*m./f.*).

ago /ə'gəʊ/ *adv.* il y a. **a month ~,** il y a un mois. **long ~,** il y a longtemps. **how long ~?,** il y a combien de temps?

agog /ə'gɒg/ *a.* impatient, en émoi.

agon|y /'ægənɪ/ *n.* grande souffrance *f.*; (*mental*) angoisse *f.* **~ize** *v.i.* souffrir. **~ize over,** se torturer l'esprit pour. **~ized** *a.* angoissé. **~izing** *a.* angoissant.

agree /ə'gri:/ *v.i.* être *or* se mettre d'accord (**on,** sur); (*of figures*) concorder. ● *v.t.* (*date*) convenir de. **~ that,** reconnaître que. **~ to do,** accepter de faire. **~ to sth.,** accepter qch. **onions don't ~ with me,** je ne digère pas les oignons. **~d** *a.* (*time, place*) convenu. **be ~d,** être d'accord.

agreeable /ə'gri:əbl/ *a.* agréable. **be ~,** (*willing*) être d'accord.

agreement /ə'gri:mənt/ *n.* accord *m.* **in ~,** d'accord.

agricultur|e /'ægrɪkʌltʃə(r)/ *n.* agriculture *f.* **~al** /-'kʌltʃərəl/ *a.* agricole.

aground /ə'graʊnd/ *adv.* **run ~,** (*of ship*) (s')échouer.

ahead /ə'hed/ *adv.* (*in front*) en avant, devant; (*in advance*) à l'avance. **~ of s.o.,** devant qn.; en avance sur qn. **~ of time,** en avance. **straight ~,** tout droit.

aid /eɪd/ *v.t.* aider. ● *n.* aide *f.* **in ~ of,** au profit de.

aide /eɪd/ *n.* aide *m./f.*

AIDS /eɪdz/ *n.* (*med.*) sida *m.*

ail /eɪl/ *v.t.* **what ~s you?,** qu'avez-vous? **~ing** *a.* souffrant. **~ment** *n.* maladie *f.*

aim /eɪm/ *v.t.* diriger; (*gun*) braquer (**at,** sur); (*remark*) destiner. ● *v.i.* viser. ● *n.* but *m.* **~ at,** viser. **~ to,** avoir l'intention de. **take ~,** viser. **~less** *a.*, **~lessly** *adv.* sans but.

air /eə(r)/ *n.* air *m.* ● *v.t.* aérer; (*views*) exposer librement. ● *a.*

(*base etc.*) aérien. **~-bed** *n.* matelas pneumatique *m.* **~-conditioned** *a.* climatisé. **~-conditioning** *n.* climatisation *f.* **~ force/hostess,** armée/hôtesse de l'air *f.* **~ letter,** aérogramme *m.* **~mail,** poste aérienne *f.* **by ~mail,** par avion. **~ raid,** attaque aérienne *f.* **~ terminal,** aérogare *f.* **~ traffic controller,** aiguilleur du ciel *m.* **by ~,** par avion. **in the ~,** (*rumour*) répandu; (*plan*) incertain. **on the ~,** à l'antenne.

airborne /'eəbɔ:n/ *a.* en (cours de) vol; (*troops*) aéroporté.

aircraft /'eəkru:ft/ *n. invar.* avion *m.* **~-carrier** *n.* porte-avions *m. invar.*

airfield /'eəfi:ld/ *n.* terrain d'aviation *m.*

airgun /'eəgʌn/ *n.* carabine à air comprimé *f.*

airlift /'eəlɪft/ *n.* pont aérien *m.* ● *v.t.* transporter par pont aérien.

airline /'eəlaɪn/ *n.* ligne aérienne *f.* **~r** /-ə(r)/ *n.* avion de ligne *m.*

airlock /'eəlɒk/ *n.* (*in pipe*) bulle d'air *f.*; (*chamber: techn.*) sas *m.*

airman /'eəmən/ *n.* (*pl.* **-men**) aviateur *m.*

airplane /'eəpleɪn/ *n.* (*Amer.*) avion *m.*

airport /'eəpɔ:t/ *n.* aéroport *m.*

airsickness /'eəsɪknɪs/ *n.* mal de l'air *m.*

airtight /'eətaɪt/ *a.* hermétique.

airways /'eəweɪz/ *n. pl.* compagnie d'aviation *f.*

airworthy /'eəwɜ:ðɪ/ *a.* en état de navigation.

airy /'eərɪ/ *a.* (**-ier, -iest**) bien aéré; (*manner*) désinvolte.

aisle /aɪl/ *n.* (*of church*) nef latérale *f.*; (*gangway*) couloir *m.*

ajar /ə'dʒɑ:(r)/ *adv. & a.* entrouvert.

akin /ə'kɪn/ *a.* **~ to,** apparenté à.

alabaster /'æləbɑ:stə(r)/ *n.* albâtre *m.*

à la carte /ɑ:lɑ:'kɑ:t/ *adv. & a.* (*culin.*) à la carte.

alacrity /ə'lækrətɪ/ *n.* empressement *m.*

alarm /ə'lɑ:m/ *n.* alarme *f.*; (*clock*) réveil *m.* ● *v.t.* alarmer. **~-clock** *n.* réveil *m.*, réveille-matin *m. invar.* **~ist** *n.* alarmiste *m./f.*

alas /ə'læs/ *int.* hélas.

albatross /'ælbətrɒs/ *n.* albatros *m.*

album /'ælbəm/ *n.* album *m.*

alcohol /'ælkəhɒl/ *n.* alcool *m.* **~ic** /-'hɒlɪk/ *a.* alcoolique; (*drink*) alcoolisé; *n.* alcoolique *m./f.* **~ism** *n.* alcoolisme *m.*

alcove /'ælkəʊv/ *n.* alcôve *f.*

ale /eɪl/ *n.* bière *f.*

alert /ə'lɜ:t/ *a.* (*lively*) vif; (*watchful*) vigilant. ● *n.* alerte *f.* ● *v.t.* alerter. **~ s.o. to,** prévenir qn. de. **on the ~,** sur le qui-vive. **~ness** *n.* vivacité *f.*; vigilance *f.*

A-level /'eɪlevl/ *n.* baccalauréat *m.*

algebra /'ældʒɪbrə/ *n.* algèbre *f.* **~ic** /-'breɪɪk/ *a.* algébrique.

Algeria /æl'dʒɪərɪə/ *n.* Algérie *f.* **~n** *a. & n.* algérien(ne) (*m.* (*f.*)).

algorithm /'ælgərɪðm/ *n.* algorithme *m.*

alias /'eɪlɪəs/ *n.* (*pl.* **-ases**) faux nom *m.* ● *adv.* alias.

alibi /'ælɪbaɪ/ *n.* (*pl.* **-is**) alibi *m.*

alien /'eɪlɪən/ *n. & a.* étrang|er, -ère (*m., f.*) (**to,** à).

alienat|e /'eɪlɪəneɪt/ *v.t.* aliéner. **~e one's friends/***etc.*, s'aliéner ses amis/*etc.* **~ion** /-'neɪʃn/ *n.* aliénation *f.*

alight[1] /ə'laɪt/ *v.i.* (*person*) descendre; (*bird*) se poser.

alight[2] /ə'laɪt/ *a.* en feu, allumé.

align /ə'laɪn/ *v.t.* aligner. **~ment** *n.* alignement *m.*

alike /ə'laɪk/ *a.* semblable. ● *adv.* de la même façon. **look** *or* **be ~,** se ressembler.

alimony /'ælɪmənɪ, *Amer.* -məʊnɪ/ *n.* pension alimentaire *f.*

alive /ə'laɪv/ *a.* vivant. **~ to,** sensible à, sensibilisé à. **~ with,** grouillant de.

alkali /'ælkəlaɪ/ *n.* (*pl.* **-is**) alcali *m.*

all /ɔ:l/ *a.* tout(e), tous, toutes. ● *pron.* tous, toutes; (*everything*) tout. ● *adv.* tout. **~ (the) men,** tous les hommes. **~ of it,** (le) tout. **~ of us,** nous tous. **~ but,** presque. **~ for sth.,** à fond pour qch. **~ in,** (*exhausted*) épuisé. **~-in** *a.* tout compris. **~-in wrestling,** catch *m.* **~ out,** à fond. **~-out** *a.* (*effort*) maximum. **~ over,** partout (sur *or* dans); (*finished*) fini. **~ right,** bien; (*agreeing*) bon! **~ round,** dans tous les domaines; (*for all*) pour tous. **~-round** *a.* général. **~ there,** (*alert*) éveillé. **~ the better,** tant mieux. **~ the same,** tout de même. **the best of ~,** le meilleur.

allay /ə'leɪ/ *v.t.* calmer.

allegation /ælɪ'geɪʃn/ *n.* allégation *f.*

allege /ə'ledʒ/ *v.t.* prétendre. **~dly** /-ɪdlɪ/ *adv.* d'après ce qu'on dit.
allegiance /ə'li:dʒəns/ *n.* fidélité *f.*
allerg|y /'ælədʒɪ/ *n.* allergie *f.* **~ic** /ə'lɜ:dʒɪk/ *a.* allergique (**to,** à).
alleviate /ə'li:vɪeɪt/ *v.t.* alléger.
alley /'ælɪ/ *n.* (*street*) ruelle *f.*
alliance /ə'laɪəns/ *n.* alliance *f.*
allied /'ælaɪd/ *a.* allié.
alligator /'ælɪgeɪtə(r)/ *n.* alligator *m.*
allocat|e /'æləkeɪt/ *v.t.* (*assign*) attribuer; (*share out*) distribuer. **~ion** /-'keɪʃn/ *n.* allocation *f.*
allot /ə'lɒt/ *v.t.* (*p.t.* **allotted**) attribuer. **~ment** *n.* attribution *f.*; (*share*) partage *m.*; (*land*) parcelle de terre *f.* (*louée pour la culture*).
allow /ə'laʊ/ *v.t.* permettre; (*grant*) accorder; (*reckon on*) prévoir; (*agree*) reconnaître. **~ s.o. to,** permettre à qn. de. **~ for,** tenir compte de.
allowance /ə'laʊəns/ *n.* allocation *f.*, indemnité *f.* **make ~s for,** être indulgent envers; (*take into account*) tenir compte de.
alloy /'ælɔɪ/ *n.* alliage *m.*
allude /ə'lu:d/ *v.i.* **~ to,** faire allusion à.
allure /ə'lʊə(r)/ *v.t.* attirer.
allusion /ə'lu:ʒn/ *n.* allusion *f.*
ally[1] /'ælaɪ/ *n.* allié(e) *m.* (*f.*).
ally[2] /ə'laɪ/ *v.t.* allier. **~ o.s. with,** s'allier à *or* avec.
almanac /'ɔ:lmənæk/ *n.* almanach *m.*
almighty /ɔ:l'maɪtɪ/ *a.* tout-puissant; (*very great: fam.*) sacré, formidable.
almond /'ɑ:mənd/ *n.* amande *f.*
almost /'ɔ:lməʊst/ *adv.* presque.
alms /ɑ:mz/ *n.* aumône *f.*
alone /ə'ləʊn/ *a.* & *adv.* seul.
along /ə'lɒŋ/ *prep.* le long de. ● *adv.* **come ~,** venir. **go** *or* **walk ~,** passer. **all ~,** (*time*) tout le temps, depuis le début. **~ with,** avec.
alongside /əlɒŋ'saɪd/ *adv.* (*naut.*) bord à bord. **come ~,** accoster. ● *prep.* le long de.
aloof /ə'lu:f/ *adv.* à l'écart. ● *a.* distant. **~ness** *n.* réserve *f.*
aloud /ə'laʊd/ *adv.* à haute voix.
alphabet /'ælfəbet/ *n.* alphabet *m.* **~ical** /-'betɪkl/ *a.* alphabétique.
alpine /'ælpaɪn/ *a.* (*landscape*) alpestre; (*climate*) alpin.
Alpine /'ælpaɪn/ *a.* des Alpes.
Alps /ælps/ *n. pl.* **the ~,** les Alpes *f. pl.*
already /ɔ:l'redɪ/ *adv.* déjà.
alright /ɔ:l'raɪt/ *a.* & *adv.* = **all right.**
Alsatian /æl'seɪʃn/ *n.* (*dog*) berger allemand *m.*
also /'ɔ:lsəʊ/ *adv.* aussi.
altar /'ɔ:ltə(r)/ *n.* autel *m.*
alter /'ɔ:ltə(r)/ *v.t./i.* changer. **~ation** /-'reɪʃn/ *n.* changement *m.*; (*to garment*) retouche *f.*
alternate[1] /ɔ:l'tɜ:nət/ *a.* alterné, alternatif; (*Amer.*) = **alternative. on ~ days/***etc.*, (*first one then the other*) tous les deux jours/*etc.* **~ly** *adv.* tour à tour.
alternate[2] /'ɔ:ltəneɪt/ *v.i.* alterner. ● *v.t.* faire alterner.
alternative /ɔ:l'tɜ:nətɪv/ *a.* autre; (*policy*) de rechange. ● *n.* alternative *f.*, choix *m.* **~ly** *adv.* comme alternative. **or ~ly,** ou alors.
alternator /'ɔ:ltəneɪtə(r)/ *n.* alternateur *m.*
although /ɔ:l'ðəʊ/ *conj.* bien que.
altitude /'æltɪtju:d/ *n.* altitude *f.*
altogether /ɔ:ltə'geðə(r)/ *adv.* (*completely*) tout à fait; (*on the whole*) à tout prendre.
aluminium /æljʊ'mɪnɪəm/ (*Amer.* **aluminum** /ə'lu:mɪnəm/) *n.* aluminium *m.*
always /'ɔ:lweɪz/ *adv.* toujours.
am /æm/ *see* be.
a.m. /eɪ'em/ *adv.* du matin.
amalgamate /ə'mælgəmeɪt/ *v.t./i.* (s')amalgamer; (*comm.*) fusionner.
amass /ə'mæs/ *v.t.* amasser.
amateur /'æmətə(r)/ *n.* amateur *m.* ● *a.* (*musician etc.*) amateur *invar.* **~ish** *a.* (*pej.*) d'amateur. **~ishly** *adv.* en amateur.
amaz|e /ə'meɪz/ *v.t.* étonner. **~ed** *a.* étonné. **~ement** *n.* étonnement *m.* **~ingly** *adv.* étonnament.
ambassador /æm'bæsədə(r)/ *n.* ambassadeur *m.*
amber /'æmbə(r)/ *n.* ambre *m.*; (*auto.*) feu orange *m.*
ambigu|ous /æm'bɪgjʊəs/ *a.* ambigu. **~ity** /-'gju:ətɪ/ *n.* ambiguïté *f.*
ambiti|on /æm'bɪʃn/ *n.* ambition *f.* **~ous** *a.* ambitieux.
ambivalent /æm'bɪvələnt/ *a.* ambigu, ambivalent.
amble /'æmbl/ *v.i.* marcher sans se presser, s'avancer lentement.
ambulance /'æmbjʊləns/ *n.* ambulance *f.*
ambush /'æmbʊʃ/ *n.* embuscade *f.* ● *v.t.* tendre une embuscade à.

amenable /ə'mi:nəbl/ *a.* obligeant. **~ to,** (*responsive*) sensible à.
amend /ə'mend/ *v.t.* modifier, corriger. **~ment** *n.* (*to rule*) amendement *m.*
amends /ə'mendz/ *n. pl.* **make ~,** réparer son erreur.
amenities /ə'mi:nətɪz/ *n. pl.* (*pleasant features*) attraits *m. pl.*; (*facilities*) aménagements *m. pl.*
America /ə'merɪkə/ *n.* Amérique *f.* **~n** *a.* & *n.* américain(e) (*m.* (*f.*)).
amiable /'eɪmɪəbl/ *a.* aimable.
amicable /'æmɪkəbl/ *a.* amical.
amid(st) /ə'mɪd(st)/ *prep.* au milieu de.
amiss /ə'mɪs/ *a.* & *adv.* mal. **sth. ~,** qch. qui ne va pas. **take sth. ~,** être offensé par qch.
ammonia /ə'məʊnɪə/ *n.* (*gas*) ammoniac *m.*; (*water*) ammoniaque *f.*
ammunition /æmjʊ'nɪʃn/ *n.* munitions *f. pl.*
amnesia /æm'ni:zɪə/ *n.* amnésie *f.*
amnesty /'æmnəstɪ/ *n.* amnistie *f.*
amok /ə'mɒk/ *adv.* **run ~,** devenir fou furieux; (*crowd*) se déchaîner.
among(st) /ə'mʌŋ(st)/ *prep.* parmi, entre. **~ the crowd,** (*in the middle of*) parmi la foule. **~ the English**/*etc.*, (*race, group*) chez les Anglais/*etc.* **~ ourselves**/*etc.*, entre nous/*etc.*
amoral /eɪ'mɒrəl/ *a.* amoral.
amorous /'æmərəs/ *a.* amoureux.
amorphous /ə'mɔ:fəs/ *a.* amorphe.
amount /ə'maʊnt/ *n.* quantité *f.*; (*total*) montant *m.*; (*sum of money*) somme *f.* ● *v.i.* **~ to,** (*add up to*) s'élever à; (*be equivalent to*) revenir à.
amp /æmp/ *n.* (*fam.*) ampère *m.*
ampere /'æmpeə(r)/ *n.* ampère *m.*
amphibi|an /æm'fɪbɪən/ *n.* amphibie *m.* **~ous** *a.* amphibie.
ampl|e /'æmpl/ *a.* (**-er, -est**) (*enough*) (bien) assez de; (*large, roomy*) ample. **~y** *adv.* amplement.
amplif|y /'æmplɪfaɪ/ *v.t.* amplifier. **~ier** *n.* amplificateur *m.*
amputat|e /'æmpjʊteɪt/ *v.t.* amputer. **~ion** /-'teɪʃn/ *n.* amputation *f.*
amuck /ə'mʌk/ *see* amok.
amuse /ə'mju:z/ *v.t.* amuser. **~ment** *n.* amusement *m.*, divertissement *m.* **~ment arcade,** salle de jeux *f.*
an /æn, *unstressed* ən/ *see* a.
anachronism /ə'nækrənɪzəm/ *n.* anachronisme *m.*
anaem|ia /ə'ni:mɪə/ *n.* anémie *f.* **~ic** *a.* anémique.
anaesthetic /ænɪs'θetɪk/ *n.* anesthésique *m.* **give an ~,** faire une anesthésie (**to,** à).
analogue, analog /'ænəlɒg/ *a.* analogique.
analogy /ə'nælədʒɪ/ *n.* analogie *f.*
analys|e (*Amer.* **analyze**) /'ænəlaɪz/ *v.t.* analyser. **~t** /-ɪst/ *n.* analyste *m./f.*
analysis /ə'næləsɪs/ *n.* (*pl.* **-yses** /-əsi:z/) analyse *f.*
analytic(al) /ænə'lɪtɪk(l)/ *a.* analytique.
anarch|y /'ænəkɪ/ *n.* anarchie *f.* **~ist** *n.* anarchiste *m./f.*
anathema /ə'næθəmə/ *n.* **that is ~ to me,** j'ai cela en abomination.
anatom|y /ə'nætəmɪ/ *n.* anatomie *f.* **~ical** /ænə'tɒmɪkl/ *a.* anatomique.
ancest|or /'ænsestə(r)/ *n.* ancêtre *m.* **~ral** /-'sestrəl/ *a.* ancestral.
anchor /'æŋkə(r)/ *n.* ancre *f.* ● *v.t.* mettre à l'ancre. ● *v.i.* jeter l'ancre.
anchovy /'æntʃəvɪ/ *n.* anchois *m.*
ancient /'eɪnʃənt/ *a.* ancien.
ancillary /æn'sɪlərɪ/ *a.* auxiliaire.
and /ænd, *unstressed* ən(d)/ *conj.* et. **go ~ see him,** allez le voir. **richer ~ richer,** de plus en plus riche.
anecdote /'ænɪkdəʊt/ *n.* anecdote *f.*
anemia /ə'ni:mɪə/ *n.* (*Amer.*) = **anaemia.**
anesthetic /ænɪs'θetɪk/ (*Amer.*) = **anaesthetic.**
anew /ə'nju:/ *adv.* de *or* à nouveau.
angel /'eɪndʒl/ *n.* ange *m.* **~ic** /æn'dʒelɪk/ *a.* angélique.
anger /'æŋgə(r)/ *n.* colère *f.* ● *v.t.* mettre en colère, fâcher.
angle[1] /'æŋgl/ *n.* angle *m.*
angle[2] /'æŋgl/ *v.i.* pêcher (à la ligne). **~ for,** (*fig.*) quêter. **~r** /-ə(r)/ *n.* pêcheu|r, -se *m., f.*
Anglican /'æŋglɪkən/ *a.* & *n.* anglican(e) (*m.* (*f.*)).
Anglo- /'æŋgləʊ/ *pref.* anglo- .
Anglo-Saxon /'æŋgləʊ'sæksn/ *a.* & *n.* anglo-saxon(ne) (*m.* (*f.*)).
angr|y /'æŋgrɪ/ *a.* (**-ier, -iest**) fâché, en colère. **get ~y,** se fâcher, se mettre en colère (**with,** contre). **make s.o. ~y,** mettre qn. en colère. **~ily** *adv.* en colère.
anguish /'æŋgwɪʃ/ *n.* angoisse *f.*
angular /'æŋgjʊlə(r)/ *a.* (*features*) anguleux.
animal /'ænɪml/ *n.* & *a.* animal (*m.*).

animate[1] /'ænɪmət/ *a.* animé.

animat|e[2] /'ænɪmeɪt/ *v.t.* animer. **~ion** /-'meɪʃn/ *n.* animation *f.*

animosity /ænɪ'mɒsətɪ/ *n.* animosité *f.*

aniseed /'ænɪsi:d/ *n.* anis *m.*

ankle /'æŋkl/ *n.* cheville *f.* **~ sock,** socquette *f.*

annex /ə'neks/ *v.t.* annexer. **~ation** /ænek'seɪʃn/ *n.* annexion *f.*

annexe /'æneks/ *n.* annexe *f.*

annihilate /ə'naɪəleɪt/ *v.t.* anéantir.

anniversary /ænɪ'vɜ:sərɪ/ *n.* anniversaire *m.*

announce /ə'naʊns/ *v.t.* annoncer. **~ment** *n.* annonce *f.* **~r** /-ə(r)/ *n.* (*radio, TV*) speaker(ine) *m.* (*f.*).

annoy /ə'nɔɪ/ *v.t.* agacer, ennuyer. **~ance** *n.* contrariété *f.* **~ed** *a.* fâché (**with,** contre). **get ~ed,** se fâcher. **~ing** *a.* ennuyeux.

annual /'ænjʊəl/ *a.* annuel. ● *n.* publication annuelle *f.* **~ly** *adv.* annuellement.

annuity /ə'nju:ətɪ/ *n.* rente (viagère) *f.*

annul /ə'nʌl/ *v.t.* (*p.t.* **annulled**) annuler. **~ment** *n.* annulation *f.*

anomal|y /ə'nɒməlɪ/ *n.* anomalie *f.* **~ous** *a.* anormal.

anonym|ous /ə'nɒnɪməs/ *a.* anonyme. **~ity** /ænə'nɪmətɪ/ *n.* anonymat *m.*

anorak /'ænəræk/ *n.* anorak *m.*

another /ə'nʌðə(r)/ *a. & pron.* un(e) autre. **~ coffee,** (*one more*) encore un café. **~ ten minutes,** encore dix minutes, dix minutes de plus.

answer /'ɑ:nsə(r)/ *n.* réponse *f.*; (*solution*) solution *f.* ● *v.t.* répondre à; (*prayer*) exaucer. ● *v.i.* répondre. **~ the door,** ouvrir la porte. **~ back,** répondre. **~ for,** répondre de. **~ to,** (*superior*) dépendre de; (*description*) répondre à **~able** *a.* responsable (**for,** de; **to,** devant). **~ing machine,** répondeur *m.*

ant /ænt/ *n.* fourmi *f.*

antagonis|m /æn'tægənɪzəm/ *n.* antagonisme *m.* **~tic** /-'nɪstɪk/ *a.* antagoniste.

antagonize /æn'tægənaɪz/ *v.t.* provoquer l'hostilité de.

Antarctic /æn'tɑ:ktɪk/ *a. & n.* antarctique (*m.*).

ante- /'æntɪ/ *pref.* anti-, anté-.

antelope /'æntɪləʊp/ *n.* antilope *f.*

antenatal /'æntɪneɪtl/ *a.* prénatal.

antenna /æn'tenə/ *n.* (*pl.* **-ae** /-i:/) (*of insect*) antenne *f.*; (*pl.* **-as**; *aerial: Amer.*) antenne *f.*

anthem /'ænθəm/ *n.* (*relig.*) motet *m.*; (*of country*) hymne national *m.*

anthology /æn'θɒlədʒɪ/ *n.* anthologie *f.*

anthropolog|y /ænθrə'pɒlədʒɪ/ *n.* anthropologie *f.* **~ist** *n.* anthropologue *m./f.*

anti- /'æntɪ/ *pref.* anti-. **~-aircraft** *a.* antiaérien.

antibiotic /æntɪbaɪ'ɒtɪk/ *n.* antibiotique *m.*

antibody /'æntɪbɒdɪ/ *n.* anticorps *m.*

antic /'æntɪk/ *n.* bouffonnerie *f.*

anticipat|e /æn'tɪsɪpeɪt/ *v.t.* (*foresee, expect*) prévoir, s'attendre à; (*forestall*) devancer. **~ion** /-'peɪʃn/ *n.* attente *f.* **in ~ion of,** en prévision *or* attente de.

anticlimax /æntɪ'klaɪmæks/ *n.* (*letdown*) déception *f.* **it was an ~,** ça n'a pas répondu à l'attente.

anticlockwise /æntɪ'klɒkwaɪz/ *adv. & a.* dans le sens inverse des aiguilles d'une montre.

anticyclone /æntɪ'saɪkləʊn/ *n.* anticyclone *m.*

antidote /'æntɪdəʊt/ *n.* antidote *m.*

antifreeze /'æntɪfri:z/ *n.* antigel *m.*

antihistamine /æntɪ'hɪstəmi:n/ *n.* antihistaminique *m.*

antipathy /æn'tɪpəθɪ/ *n.* antipathie *f.*

antiquated /'æntɪkweɪtɪd/ *a.* vieillot, suranné.

antique /æn'ti:k/ *a.* (*old*) ancien; (*from antiquity*) antique. ● *n.* objet ancien *m.*, antiquité *f.* **~ dealer,** antiquaire *m./f.* **~ shop,** magasin d'antiquités *m.*

antiquity /æn'tɪkwətɪ/ *n.* antiquité *f.*

anti-Semiti|c /æntɪsɪ'mɪtɪk/ *a.* antisémite. **~sm** /-'semɪtɪzəm/ *n.* antisémitisme *m.*

antiseptic /æntɪ'septɪk/ *a. & n.* antiseptique (*m.*).

antisocial /æntɪ'səʊʃl/ *a.* asocial, antisocial; (*unsociable*) insociable.

antithesis /æn'tɪθəsɪs/ *n.* (*pl.* **-eses** /-əsi:z/) antithèse *f.*

antlers /'æntləz/ *n. pl.* bois *m. pl.*

anus /'eɪnəs/ *n.* anus *m.*

anvil /'ænvɪl/ *n.* enclume *f.*

anxiety /æŋ'zaɪətɪ/ *n.* (*worry*) anxiété *f.*; (*eagerness*) impatience *f.*

anxious /'æŋkʃəs/ *a.* (*troubled*) anxieux; (*eager*) impatient (**to,** de).

~ly *adv.* anxieusement; impatiemment.

any /'enɪ/ *a.* (*some*) du, de l', de la, des; (*after negative*) de, d'; (*every*) tout; (*no matter which*) n'importe quel. **at ~ moment,** à tout moment. **have you ~ water?,** avez-vous de l'eau? ● *pron.* (*no matter which one*) n'importe lequel; (*someone*) quelqu'un; (*any amount of it or them*) en. **I do not have ~,** je n'en ai pas. **did you see ~ of them?,** en avez-vous vu? ● *adv.* (*a little*) un peu. **do you have ~ more?,** en avez-vous encore? **do you have ~ more tea?,** avez-vous encore du thé? **not ~,** nullement. **I don't do it ~ more,** je ne le fais plus.

anybody /'enɪbɒdɪ/ *pron.* n'importe qui; (*somebody*) quelqu'un; (*after negative*) personne. **he did not see ~,** il n'a vu personne.

anyhow /'enɪhaʊ/ *adv.* de toute façon; (*badly*) n'importe comment.

anyone /'enɪwʌn/ *pron.* = **anybody**.

anything /'enɪθɪŋ/ *pron.* n'importe quoi; (*something*) quelque chose; (*after negative*) rien. **he did not see ~,** il n'a rien vu. **~ but,** (*cheap etc.*) nullement. **~ you do,** tout ce que tu fais.

anyway /'enɪweɪ/ *adv.* de toute façon.

anywhere /'enɪweə(r)/ *adv.* n'importe où; (*somewhere*) quelque part; (*after negative*) nulle part. **he does not go ~,** il ne va nulle part. **~ you go,** partout où tu vas, où que tu ailles. **~ else,** partout ailleurs.

apart /ə'pɑ:t/ *adv.* (*on or to one side*) à part; (*separated*) séparé; (*into pieces*) en pièces. **~ from,** à part, excepté. **ten metres ~,** (*distant*) à dix mètres l'un de l'autre. **come ~,** (*break*) tomber en morceaux; (*machine*) se démonter. **legs ~,** les jambes écartées. **keep ~,** séparer. **take ~,** démonter.

apartment /ə'pɑ:tmənt/ *n.* (*Amer.*) appartement *m.* **~s,** logement *m.*

apath|y /'æpəθɪ/ *n.* apathie *f.* **~etic** /-'θetɪk/ *a.* apathique.

ape /eɪp/ *n.* singe *m.* ● *v.t.* singer.

aperitif /ə'perətɪf/ *n.* apéritif *m.*

aperture /'æpətʃə(r)/ *n.* ouverture *f.*

apex /'eɪpeks/ *n.* sommet *m.*

apiece /ə'pi:s/ *adv.* chacun.

apologetic /əpɒlə'dʒetɪk/ *a.* (*tone etc.*) d'excuse. **be ~,** s'excuser. **~ally** /-lɪ/ *adv.* en s'excusant.

apologize /ə'pɒlədʒaɪz/ *v.i.* s'excuser (**for,** de; **to,** auprès de).

apology /ə'pɒlədʒɪ/ *n.* excuses *f. pl.*; (*defence of belief*) apologie *f.*

Apostle /ə'pɒsl/ *n.* apôtre *m.*

apostrophe /ə'pɒstrəfɪ/ *n.* apostrophe *f.*

appal /ə'pɔ:l/ *v.t.* (*p.t.* **appalled**) épouvanter. **~ling** *a.* épouvantable.

apparatus /æpə'reɪtəs/ *n.* (*machine & anat.*) appareil *m.*

apparel /ə'pærəl/ *n.* habillement *m.*

apparent /ə'pærənt/ *a.* apparent. **~ly** *adv.* apparemment.

appeal /ə'pi:l/ *n.* appel *m.*; (*attractiveness*) attrait *m.*, charme *m.* ● *v.i.* (*jurid.*) faire appel. **~ to s.o.,** (*beg*) faire appel à qn.; (*attract*) plaire à qn. **~ to s.o. for sth.,** demander qch. à qn. **~ing** *a.* (*attractive*) attirant.

appear /ə'pɪə(r)/ *v.i.* apparaître; (*arrive*) se présenter; (*seem, be published*) paraître; (*theatre*) jouer. **~ on TV,** passer à la télé. **~ance** *n.* apparition *f.*; (*aspect*) apparence *f.*

appease /ə'pi:z/ *v.t.* apaiser.

appendicitis /əpendɪ'saɪtɪs/ *n.* appendicite *f.*

appendix /ə'pendɪks/ *n.* (*pl.* **-ices** /-ɪsi:z/) appendice *m.*

appetite /'æpɪtaɪt/ *n.* appétit *m.*

appetizer /'æpɪtaɪzə(r)/ *n.* (*snack*) amuse-gueule *m. invar.*; (*drink*) apéritif *m.*

appetizing /'æpɪtaɪzɪŋ/ *a.* appétissant.

applau|d /ə'plɔ:d/ *v.t./i.* applaudir; (*decision*) applaudir à. **~se** *n.* applaudissements *m. pl.*

apple /'æpl/ *n.* pomme *f.* **~-tree** *n.* pommier *m.*

appliance /ə'plaɪəns/ *n.* appareil *m.*

applicable /'æplɪkəbl/ *a.* applicable.

applicant /'æplɪkənt/ *n.* candidat(e) *m.* (*f.*) (**for,** à).

application /æplɪ'keɪʃn/ *n.* application *f.*; (*request, form*) demande *f.*; (*for job*) candidature *f.*

apply /ə'plaɪ/ *v.t.* appliquer. ● *v.i.* **~ to,** (*refer*) s'appliquer à; (*ask*) s'adresser à. **~ for,** (*job*) postuler pour; (*grant*) demander. **~ o.s. to,** s'appliquer à. **applied** *a.* appliqué.

appoint /ə'pɔɪnt/ *v.t.* (*to post*) nommer; (*fix*) désigner. **well-~ed** *a.* bien équipé. **~ment** *n.* nomination *f.*; (*meeting*) rendez-vous *m. invar.*;

(*job*) poste *m.* **make an ~ment,** prendre rendez-vous (**with,** avec).
apportion /ə'pɔ:ʃn/ *v.t.* répartir.
apprais|e /ə'preɪz/ *v.t.* évaluer. **~al** *n.* évaluation *f.*
appreciable /ə'pri:ʃəbl/ *a.* appréciable.
appreciat|e /ə'pri:ʃɪeɪt/ *v.t.* (*like*) apprécier; (*understand*) comprendre; (*be grateful for*). être reconnaissant de. ● *v.i.* prendre de la valeur. **~ion** /-'eɪʃn/ *n.* appréciation *f.*; (*gratitude*) reconnaissance *f.*; (*rise*) augmentation *f.* **~ive** / ə'pri:ʃɪətɪv/ *a.* reconnaissant; (*audience*) enthousiaste.
apprehen|d /æprɪ'hend/ *v.t.* (*arrest, fear*) appréhender; (*understand*) comprendre. **~sion** *n.* appréhension *f.*
apprehensive /æprɪ'hensɪv/ *a.* inquiet. **be ~ of,** craindre.
apprentice /ə'prentɪs/ *n.* apprenti *m.* ● *v.t.* mettre en apprentissage. **~ship** *n.* apprentissage *m.*
approach /ə'prəʊtʃ/ *v.t.* (s')approcher de; (*accost*) aborder; (*with request*) s'adresser à. ● *v.i.* (s')approcher. ● *n.* approche *f.* **an ~ to,** (*problem*) une façon d'aborder; (*person*) une démarche auprès de. **~able** *a.* accessible; (*person*) abordable.
appropriate[1] /ə'prəʊprɪət/ *a.* approprié, propre. **~ly** *adv.* à propos.
appropriate[2] /ə'prəʊprɪeɪt/ *v.t.* s'approprier.
approval /ə'pru:vl/ *n.* approbation *f.* **on ~,** à *or* sous condition.
approv|e /ə'pru:v/ *v.t./i.* approuver. **~e of,** approuver. **~ingly** *adv.* d'un air *or* d'un ton approbateur.
approximate[1] /ə'prɒksɪmət/ *a.* approximatif. **~ly** *adv.* approximativement.
approximat|e[2] /ə'prɒksɪmeɪt/ *v.i.* **~e to,** se rapprocher de. **~ion** /-'meɪʃn/ *n.* approximation *f.*
apricot /'eɪprɪkɒt/ *n.* abricot *m.*
April /'eɪprəl/ *n.* avril *m.* **make an ~ fool of,** faire un poisson d'avril à.
apron /'eɪprən/ *n.* tablier *m.*
apse /æps/ *n.* (*of church*) abside *f.*
apt /æpt/ *a.* (*suitable*) approprié; (*pupil*) doué. **be ~ to,** avoir tendance à. **~ly** *adv.* à propos.
aptitude /'æptɪtju:d/ *n.* aptitude *f.*
aqualung /'ækwəlʌŋ/ *n.* scaphandre autonome *m.*
aquarium /ə'kweərɪəm/ *n.* (*pl.* **-ums**) aquarium *m.*
Aquarius /ə'kweərɪəs/ *n.* le Verseau.
aquatic /ə'kwætɪk/ *a.* aquatique; (*sport*) nautique.
aqueduct /'ækwɪdʌkt/ *n.* aqueduc *m.*
Arab /'ærəb/ *n.* & *a.* arabe (*m./f.*). **~ic** *a.* & *n.* (*lang.*) arabe (*m.*). **~ic numerals,** chiffres arabes *m. pl.*
Arabian /ə'reɪbɪən/ *a.* arabe.
arable /'ærəbl/ *a.* arable.
arbiter /'ɑ:bɪtə(r)/ *n.* arbitre *m.*
arbitrary /'ɑ:bɪtrərɪ/ *a.* arbitraire.
arbitrat|e /'ɑ:bɪtreɪt/ *v.i.* arbitrer. **~ion** /-'treɪʃn/ *n.* arbitrage *m.* **~or** *n.* arbitre *m.*
arc /ɑ:k/ *n.* arc *m.*
arcade /ɑ:'keɪd/ *n.* (*shops*) galerie *f.*; (*arches*) arcades *f. pl.*
arch[1] /ɑ:tʃ/ *n.* arche *f.*; (*in church etc.*) arc *m.*; (*of foot*) voûte plantaire *f.* ● *v.t./i.* (s')arquer.
arch[2] /ɑ:tʃ/ *a.* (*playful*) malicieux.
arch- /ɑ:tʃ/ *pref.* (*hypocrite etc.*) grand, achevé.
archaeolog|y /ɑ:kɪ'ɒlədʒɪ/ *n.* archéologie *f.* **~ical** /-ə'lɒdʒɪkl/ *a.* archéologique. **~ist** *n.* archéologue *m./f.*
archaic /ɑ:'keɪɪk/ *a.* archaïque.
archbishop /ɑ:tʃ'bɪʃəp/ *n.* archevêque *m.*
archeology /ɑ:kɪ'ɒlədʒɪ/ *n.* (*Amer.*) = **archaeology**.
archer /'ɑ:tʃə(r)/ *n.* archer *m.* **~y** *n.* tir à l'arc *m.*
archetype /'ɑ:kɪtaɪp/ *n.* archétype *m.*, modèle *m.*
archipelago /ɑ:kɪ'peləgəʊ/ *n.* (*pl.* **-os**) archipel *m.*
architect /'ɑ:kɪtekt/ *n.* architecte *m.*
architectur|e /'ɑ:kɪtektʃə(r)/ *n.* architecture *f.* **~al** /-'tektʃərəl/ *a.* architectural.
archiv|es /'ɑ:kaɪvz/ *n. pl.* archives *f. pl.* **~ist** /-ɪvɪst/ *n.* archiviste *m./f.*
archway /'ɑ:tʃweɪ/ *n.* voûte *f.*
Arctic /'ɑ:ktɪk/ *a.* & *n.* arctique (*m.*). **arctic** *a.* glacial.
ardent /'ɑ:dnt/ *a.* ardent. **~ly** *adv.* ardemment.
ardour /'ɑ:də(r)/ *n.* ardeur *f.*
arduous /'ɑ:djʊəs/ *a.* ardu.
are /ɑ:(r)/ *see* be.
area /'eərɪə/ *n.* (*surface*) superficie *f.*; (*region*) région *f.*; (*district*) quartier *m.*; (*fig.*) domaine *m.* **parking/picnic ~,** aire de parking/de pique-nique *f.*
arena /ə'ri:nə/ *n.* arène *f.*

aren't /ɑ:nt/ = **are not.**

Argentin|a /ɑ:dʒən'ti:nə/ *n.* Argentine *f.* **~e** /'ɑ:dʒəntaɪn/, **~ian** /-'tɪnɪən/ *a.* & *n.* argentin(e) (*m.* (*f.*)).

argu|e /'ɑ:gju:/ *v.i.* (*quarrel*) se disputer; (*reason*) argumenter. ● *v.t.* (*debate*) discuter. **~e that,** alléguer que. **~able** /-ʊəbl/ *a.* le cas selon certains. **~ably** *adv.* selon certains.

argument /'ɑ:gjʊmənt/ *n.* dispute *f.*; (*reasoning*) argument *m.*; (*discussion*) débat *m.* **~ative** /-'mentətɪv/ *a.* raisonneur, contrariant.

arid /'ærɪd/ *a.* aride.

Aries /'eəri:z/ *n.* le Bélier.

arise /ə'raɪz/ *v.i.* (*p.t.* **arose,** *p.p.* **arisen**) se présenter; (*old use*) se lever. **~ from,** résulter de.

aristocracy /ærɪ'stɒkrəsɪ/ *n.* aristocratie *f.*

aristocrat /'ærɪstəkræt, *Amer.* ə'rɪstəkræt/ *n.* aristocrate *m./f.* **~ic** /-'krætɪk/ *a.* aristocratique.

arithmetic /ə'rɪθmətɪk/ *n.* arithmétique *f.*

ark /ɑ:k/ *n.* (*relig.*) arche *f.*

arm[1] /ɑ:m/ *n.* bras *m.* **~ in arm,** bras dessus bras dessous. **~-band** *n.* brassard *m.*

arm[2] /ɑ:m/ *v.t.* armer. **~ed robbery,** vol à main armée *m.*

armament /'ɑ:məmənt/ *n.* armement *m.*

armchair /'ɑ:mtʃeə(r)/ *n.* fauteuil *m.*

armistice /'ɑ:mɪstɪs/ *n.* armistice *m.*

armour /'ɑ:mə(r)/ *n.* armure *f.*; (*on tanks etc.*) blindage *m.* **~-clad, ~ed** *adjs.* blindé.

armoury /'ɑ:mərɪ/ *n.* arsenal *m.*

armpit /'ɑ:mpɪt/ *n.* aisselle *f.*

arms /ɑ:mz/ *n. pl.* (*weapons*) armes *f. pl.* **~ dealer,** trafiquant d'armes *m.*

army /'ɑ:mɪ/ *n.* armée *f.*

aroma /ə'rəʊmə/ *n.* arôme *m.* **~tic** /ærə'mætɪk/ *a.* aromatique.

arose /ə'rəʊz/ *see* arise.

around /ə'raʊnd/ *adv.* (tout) autour; (*here and there*) çà et là. ● *prep.* autour de. **~ here,** par ici.

arouse /ə'raʊz/ *v.t.* (*awaken, cause*) éveiller; (*excite*) exciter.

arrange /ə'reɪndʒ/ *v.t.* arranger; (*time, date*) fixer. **~ to,** s'arranger pour. **~ment** *n.* arrangement *m.* **make ~ments,** prendre des dispositions.

array /ə'reɪ/ *v.t.* (*mil.*) déployer; (*dress*) vêtir. ● *n.* **an ~ of,** (*display*) un étalage impressionnant de.

arrears /ə'rɪəz/ *n. pl.* arriéré *m.* **in ~,** (*rent*) arriéré. **he is in ~,** il a des paiements en retard.

arrest /ə'rest/ *v.t.* arrêter; (*attention*) retenir. ● *n.* arrestation *f.* **under ~,** en état d'arrestation.

arrival /ə'raɪvl/ *n.* arrivée *f.* **new ~,** nouveau venu *m.*, nouvelle venue *f.*

arrive /ə'raɪv/ *v.i.* arriver.

arrogan|t /'ærəgənt/ *a.* arrogant. **~ce** *n.* arrogance *f.* **~tly** *adv.* avec arrogance.

arrow /'ærəʊ/ *n.* flèche *f.*

arse /ɑ:s/ *n.* (*sl.*) cul *m.* (*sl.*)

arsenal /'ɑ:sənl/ *n.* arsenal *m.*

arsenic /'ɑ:snɪk/ *n.* arsenic *m.*

arson /'ɑ:sn/ *n.* incendie criminel *m.* **~ist** *n.* incendiaire *m./f.*

art /ɑ:t/ *n.* art *m.*; (*fine arts*) beaux-arts *m. pl.* **~s,** (*univ.*) lettres *f. pl.* **~ gallery,** (*public*) musée (d'art) *m.*; (*private*) galerie (d'art) *f.* **~ school,** école des beaux-arts *f.*

artefact /'ɑ:tɪfækt/ *n.* objet fabriqué *m.*

arter|y /'ɑ:tərɪ/ *n.* artère *f.* **~ial** /-'tɪərɪəl/ *a.* artériel. **~ial road,** route principale *f.*

artful /'ɑ:tfl/ *a.* astucieux, rusé. **~ness** *n.* astuce *f.*

arthriti|s /ɑ:'θraɪtɪs/ *n.* arthrite *f.* **~c** /-ɪtɪk/ *a.* arthritique.

artichoke /'ɑ:tɪtʃəʊk/ *n.* artichaut *m.*

article /'ɑ:tɪkl/ *n.* article *m.* **~ of clothing,** vêtement *m.* **~d** *a.* (*jurid.*) en stage.

articulate[1] /ɑ:'tɪkjʊlət/ *a.* (*person*) capable de s'exprimer clairement; (*speech*) distinct.

articulat|e[2] /ɑ:'tɪkjʊleɪt/ *v.t./i.* articuler. **~ed lorry,** semi-remorque *m.* **~ion** /-'leɪʃn/ *n.* articulation *f.*

artifice /'ɑ:tɪfɪs/ *n.* artifice *m.*

artificial /ɑ:tɪ'fɪʃl/ *a.* artificiel. **~ity** /-ʃɪ'ælətɪ/ *n.* manque de naturel *m.*

artillery /ɑ:'tɪlərɪ/ *n.* artillerie *f.*

artisan /ɑ:tɪ'zæn/ *n.* artisan *m.*

artist /'ɑ:tɪst/ *n.* artiste *m./f.* **~ic** /-'tɪstɪk/ *a.* artistique. **~ry** *n.* art *m.*

artiste /ɑ:'ti:st/ *n.* (*entertainer*) artiste *m./f.*

artless /'ɑ:tlɪs/ *a.* ingénu, naïf.

artwork /'a:twɜ:k/ *n.* (*of book*) illustrations *f. pl.*

as /æz, *unstressed* əz/ *adv.* & *conj.* comme; (*while*) pendant que. **as you get older,** en vieillissant. **as she came in,** en entrant. **as a mother,** en tant que mère. **as a gift,** en cadeau.

as from Monday, à partir de lundi. **as tall as,** aussi grand que. **~ for, as to,** quant à. **~ if,** comme si. **you look as if you're tired,** vous avez l'air (d'être) fatigué. **as much, as many,** autant (**as**, que). **as soon as,** aussitôt que. **as well,** aussi (**as**, bien que). **as wide as possible,** aussi large que possible.

asbestos /æz'bestɒs/ *n.* amiante *f.*

ascend /ə'send/ *v.t.* gravir; (*throne*) monter sur. ● *v.i.* monter. **~ant** *n.* **be in the ~ant,** monter.

ascent /ə'sent/ *n.* (*climbing*) ascension *f.*; (*slope*) côte *f.*

ascertain /æsə'teɪn/ *v.t.* s'assurer de. **~ that,** s'assurer que.

ascetic /ə'setɪk/ *a.* ascétique. ● *n.* ascète *m./f.*

ascribe /ə'skraɪb/ *v.t.* attribuer.

ash[1] /æʃ/ *n.* **~(-tree),** frêne *m.*

ash[2] /æʃ/ *n.* cendre *f.* **Ash Wednesday,** Mercredi des Cendres *m.* **~en** *a.* cendreux.

ashamed /ə'ʃeɪmd/ *a.* **be ~,** avoir honte (**of**, de).

ashore /ə'ʃɔ:(r)/ *adv.* à terre.

ashtray /'æʃtreɪ/ *n.* cendrier *m.*

Asia /'eɪʃə, *Amer.* 'eɪʒə/ *n.* Asie *f.* **~n** *a.* & *n.* asiatique (*m./f.*). **the ~n community,** la communauté indo-pakistanaise. **~tic** /-ɪ'ætɪk/ *a.* asiatique.

aside /ə'saɪd/ *adv.* de côté. ● *n.* aparté *m.* **~ from,** à part.

ask /ɑ:sk/ *v.t./i.* demander; (*a question*) poser; (*invite*) inviter. **~ s.o. sth.,** demander qch. à qn. **~ s.o. to do,** demander à qn. de faire. **~ about,** (*thing*) se renseigner sur; (*person*) demander des nouvelles de. **~ for,** demander.

askance /ə'skæns/ *adv.* **look ~ at,** regarder avec méfiance.

askew /ə'skju:/ *adv.* & *a.* de travers.

asleep /ə'sli:p/ *a.* endormi; (*numb*) engourdi. ● *adv.* **fall ~,** s'endormir.

asparagus /ə'spærəgəs/ *n.* (*plant*) asperge *f.*; (*culin.*) asperges *f. pl.*

aspect /'æspekt/ *n.* aspect *m.*; (*direction*) orientation *f.*

aspersions /ə'spɜ:ʃnz/ *n. pl.* **cast ~ on,** calomnier.

asphalt /'æsfælt, *Amer.* 'æsfɔ:lt/ *n.* asphalte *m.* ● *v.t.* asphalter.

asphyxiat|e /əs'fɪksɪeɪt/ *v.t./i.* (s')asphyxier. **~ion** /-'eɪʃn/ *n.* asphyxie *f.*

aspir|e /əs'paɪə(r)/ *v.i.* **~e to,** aspirer à. **~ation** /æspə'reɪʃn/ *n.* aspiration *f.*

aspirin /'æsprɪn/ *n.* aspirine *f.*

ass /æs/ *n.* âne *m.*; (*person: fam.*) idiot(e) *m.* (*f.*).

assail /ə'seɪl/ *v.t.* assaillir. **~ant** *n.* agresseur *m.*

assassin /ə'sæsɪn/ *n.* assassin *m.*

assassinat|e /ə'sæsɪneɪt/ *v.t.* assassiner. **~ion** /-'neɪʃn/ *n.* assassinat *m.*

assault /ə'sɔ:lt/ *n.* (*mil.*) assaut *m.*; (*jurid.*) agression *f.* ● *v.t.* (*person: jurid.*) agresser.

assembl|e /ə'sembl/ *v.t.* (*things*) assembler; (*people*) rassembler. ● *v.i.* s'assembler, se rassembler. **~age** *n.* assemblage *m.*

assembly /ə'semblɪ/ *n.* assemblée *f.* **~ line,** chaîne de montage *f.*

assent /ə'sent/ *n.* assentiment *m.* ● *v.i.* consentir.

assert /ə'sɜ:t/ *v.t.* affirmer; (*one's rights*) revendiquer. **~ion** /-ʃn/ *n.* affirmation *f.* **~ive** *a.* affirmatif, péremptoire.

assess /ə'ses/ *v.t.* évaluer; (*payment*) déterminer le montant de. **~ment** *n.* évaluation *f.* **~or** *n.* (*valuer*) expert *m.*

asset /'æset/ *n.* (*advantage*) atout *m.* **~s,** (*comm.*) actif *m.*

assiduous /ə'sɪdjʊəs/ *a.* assidu.

assign /ə'saɪn/ *v.t.* (*allot*) assigner. **~ s.o. to,** (*appoint*) affecter qn. à.

assignment /ə'saɪnmənt/ *n.* (*task*) mission *f.*, tâche *f.*; (*schol.*) rapport *m.*

assimilat|e /ə'sɪməleɪt/ *v.t./i.* (s')assimiler. **~ion** /-'leɪʃn/ *n.* assimilation *f.*

assist /ə'sɪst/ *v.t./i.* aider. **~ance** *n.* aide *f.*

assistant /ə'sɪstənt/ *n.* aide *m./f.*; (*in shop*) vendeu|r, -se *m., f.* ● *a.* (*manager etc.*) adjoint.

associat|e[1] /ə'səʊʃɪeɪt/ *v.t.* associer. ● *v.i.* **~e with,** fréquenter. **~ion** /-'eɪʃn/ *n.* association *f.*

associate[2] /ə'səʊʃɪət/ *n.* & *a.* associé(e) (*m.* (*f.*)).

assort|ed /ə'sɔ:tɪd/ *a.* divers; (*foods*) assortis. **~ment** *n.* assortiment *m.* **an ~ment of guests**/*etc.*, des invités/*etc.* divers.

assume /ə'sju:m/ *v.t.* supposer, présumer; (*power, attitude*) prendre; (*role, burden*) assumer.

assumption /ə'sʌmpʃn/ *n.* (*sth. supposed*) supposition *f.*
assurance /ə'ʃʊərəns/ *n.* assurance *f.*
assure /ə'ʃʊə(r)/ *v.t.* assurer. **~d** *a.* assuré. **~dly** /-rɪdlɪ/ *adv.* assurément.
asterisk /'æstərɪsk/ *n.* astérisque *m.*
astern /ə'stɜ:n/ *adv.* à l'arrière.
asthma /'æsmə/ *n.* asthme *m.* **~tic** /-'mætɪk/ *a.* & *n.* asthmatique (*m./f.*).
astonish /ə'stɒnɪʃ/ *v.t.* étonner. **~ingly** *adv.* étonnamment. **~ment** *n.* étonnement *m.*
astound /ə'staʊnd/ *v.t.* stupéfier.
astray /ə'streɪ/ *adv.* & *a.* **go ~,** s'égarer. **lead ~,** égarer.
astride /ə'straɪd/ *adv.* & *prep.* à califourchon (sur).
astrolog|y /ə'strɒlədʒɪ/ *n.* astrologie *f.* **~er** *n.* astrologue *m.*
astronaut /'æstrənɔ:t/ *n.* astronaute *m./f.*
astronom|y /ə'strɒnəmɪ/ *n.* astronomie *f.* **~er** *n.* astronome *m.* **~ical** /æstrə'nɒmɪkl/ *a.* astronomique.
astute /ə'stju:t/ *a.* astucieux. **~ness** *n.* astuce *f.*
asylum /ə'saɪləm/ *n.* asile *m.*
at /æt, *unstressed* ət/ *prep.* à. **at the doctor's**/*etc.*, chez le médecin/*etc.* **surprised at,** (*cause*) étonné de. **angry at,** fâché contre. **not at all,** pas du tout. **no wind**/*etc.* **at all,** (*of any kind*) pas le moindre vent/*etc.* **at night,** la nuit. **at once,** tout de suite; (*simultaneously*) à la fois. **~ sea,** en mer. **at times,** parfois.
ate /et/ *see* eat.
atheis|t /'eɪθɪɪst/ *n.* athée *m./f.* **~m** /-zəm/ *n.* athéisme *m.*
athlet|e /'æθli:t/ *n.* athlète *m./f.* **~ic** /-'letɪk/ *a.* athlétique. **~ics** /-'letɪks/ *n. pl.* athlétisme *m.*
Atlantic /ət'læntɪk/ *a.* atlantique. ● *n.* **~ (Ocean),** Atlantique *m.*
atlas /'ætləs/ *n.* atlas *m.*
atmospher|e /'ætməsfɪə(r)/ *n.* atmosphère *f.* **~ic** /-'ferɪk/ *a.* atmosphérique.
atoll /'ætɒl/ *n.* atoll *m.*
atom /'ætəm/ *n.* atome *m.* **~ic** /ə'tɒmɪk/ *a.* atomique. **~(ic) bomb,** bombe atomique *f.*
atomize /'ætəmaɪz/ *v.t.* atomiser. **~r** /-ə(r)/ *n.* atomiseur *m.*
atone /ə'təʊn/ *v.i.* **~ for,** expier. **~ment** *n.* expiation *f.*
atrocious /ə'trəʊʃəs/ *a.* atroce.
atrocity /ə'trɒsətɪ/ *n.* atrocité *f.*
atrophy /'ætrəfi/ *n.* atrophie *f.* ● *v.t./i.* (s')atrophier.
attach /ə'tætʃ/ *v.t./i.* (s')attacher; (*letter*) joindre (**to,** à). **~ed** *a.* **be ~ed to,** (*like*) être attaché à. **the ~ed letter,** la lettre ci-jointe. **~ment** *n.* (*accessory*) accessoire *m.*; (*affection*) attachement *m.*
attaché /ə'tæʃeɪ/ *n.* (*pol.*) attaché(e) *m.* (*f.*). **~ case,** mallette *f.*
attack /ə'tæk/ *n.* attaque *f.*; (*med.*) crise *f.* ● *v.t.* attaquer. **~er** *n.* agresseur *m.*, attaquant(e) *m.* (*f.*).
attain /ə'teɪn/ *v.t.* atteindre (à); (*gain*) acquérir. **~able** *a.* accessible. **~ment** *n.* acquisition *f.* (**of,** de). **~ments,** réussites *f. pl.*
attempt /ə'tempt/ *v.t.* tenter. ● *n.* tentative *f.* **an ~ on s.o.'s life,** un attentat contre qn.
attend /ə'tend/ *v.t.* assister à; (*class*) suivre; (*school, church*) aller à; (*escort*) accompagner. ● *v.i.* assister. **~ (to),** (*look after*) s'occuper de. **~ance** *n.* présence *f.*; (*people*) assistance *f.*
attendant /ə'tendənt/ *n.* employé(e) *m.* (*f.*); (*servant*) serviteur *m.* ● *a.* concomitant.
attention /ə'tenʃn/ *n.* attention *f.*; **~!,** (*mil.*) garde-à-vous! **pay ~,** faire *or* prêter attention (**to,** à).
attentive /ə'tentɪv/ *a.* attentif; (*considerate*) attentionné. **~ly** *adv.* attentivement. **~ness** *n.* attention *f.*
attenuate /ə'tenjʊeɪt/ *v.t.* atténuer.
attest /ə'test/ *v.t./i.* **~ (to),** attester. **~ation** /æte'steɪʃn/ *n.* attestation *f.*
attic /'ætɪk/ *n.* grenier *m.*
attitude /'ætɪtju:d/ *n.* attitude *f.*
attorney /ə'tɜ:nɪ/ *n.* mandataire *m.*; (*Amer.*) avocat *m.*
attract /ə'trækt/ *v.t.* attirer. **~ion** /-kʃn/ *n.* attraction *f.*; (*charm*) attrait *m.*
attractive /ə'træktɪv/ *a.* attrayant, séduisant. **~ly** *adv.* agréablement. **~ness** *n.* attrait *m.*, beauté *f.*
attribute[1] /ə'trɪbju:t/ *v.t.* **~ to,** attribuer à.
attribute[2] /'ætrɪbju:t/ *n.* attribut *m.*
attrition /ə'trɪʃn/ *n.* **war of ~,** guerre d'usure *f.*
aubergine /'əʊbəʒi:n/ *n.* aubergine *f.*
auburn /'ɔ:bən/ *a.* châtain roux *invar.*
auction /'ɔ:kʃn/ *n.* vente aux enchères *f.* ● *v.t.* vendre aux

enchères. **~eer** /-ə'nɪə(r)/ *n.* commissaire-priseur *m.*
audaci|ous /ɔː'deɪʃəs/ *a.* audacieux. **~ty** /-æsətɪ/ *n.* audace *f.*
audible /'ɔːdəbl/ *a.* audible.
audience /'ɔːdɪəns/ *n.* auditoire *m.*; (*theatre, radio*) public *m.*; (*interview*) audience *f.*
audio typist /'ɔːdɪəʊ'taɪpɪst/ *n.* audiotypiste *m./f.*
audio-visual /ɔːdɪəʊ'vɪʒʊəl/ *a.* audiovisuel.
audit /'ɔːdɪt/ *n.* vérification des comptes *f.* ● *v.t.* vérifier.
audition /ɔː'dɪʃn/ *n.* audition *f.* ● *v.t./i.* auditionner.
auditor /'ɔːdɪtə(r)/ *n.* commissaire aux comptes *m.*
auditorium /ɔːdɪ'tɔːrɪəm/ *n.* (*of theatre etc.*) salle *f.*
augur /'ɔːgə(r)/ *v.i.* **~ well/ill,** être de bon/mauvais augure.
August /'ɔːgəst/ *n.* août *m.*
aunt /ɑːnt/ *n.* tante *f.*
au pair /əʊ'peə(r)/ *n.* jeune fille au pair *f.*
aura /'ɔːrə/ *n.* atmosphère *f.*
auspices /'ɔːspɪsɪz/ *n. pl.* auspices *m. pl.*, égide *f.*
auspicious /ɔː'spɪʃəs/ *a.* favorable.
auster|e /ɔː'stɪə(r)/ *a.* austère. **~ity** /-erətɪ/ *n.* austérité *f.*
Australia /ɒ'streɪlɪə/ *n.* Australie *f.* **~n** *a.* & *n.* australien(ne) (*m.* (*f.*)).
Austria /'ɒstrɪə/ *n.* Autriche *f.* **~n** *a.* & *n.* autrichien(ne) (*m.* (*f.*)).
authentic /ɔː'θentɪk/ *a.* authentique. **~ity** /-ən'tɪsətɪ/ *n.* authenticité *f.*
authenticate /ɔː'θentɪkeɪt/ *v.t.* authentifier.
author /'ɔːθə(r)/ *n.* auteur *m.* **~ship** *n.* (*origin*) paternité *f.*
authoritarian /ɔːθɒrɪ'teərɪən/ *a.* autoritaire.
authorit|y /ɔː'θɒrətɪ/ *n.* autorité *f.*; (*permission*) autorisation *f.* **~ative** /-ɪtətɪv/ *a.* (*credible*) qui fait autorité; (*trusted*) autorisé; (*manner*) autoritaire.
authoriz|e /'ɔːθəraɪz/ *v.t.* autoriser. **~ation** /-'zeɪʃn/ *n.* autorisation *f.*
autistic /ɔː'tɪstɪk/ *a.* autistique.
autobiography /ɔːtəbaɪ'ɒgrəfɪ/ *n.* autobiographie *f.*
autocrat /'ɔːtəkræt/ *n.* autocrate *m.* **~ic** /-'krætɪk/ *a.* autocratique.
autograph /'ɔːtəgrɑːf/ *n.* autographe *m.* ● *v.t.* signer, dédicacer.
auto-immune /ɔːtəʊɪ'mjuːn/ *a.* autoimmune.
automat|e /'ɔːtəmeɪt/ *v.t.* automatiser. **~ion** /-'meɪʃn/ *n.* automatisation *f.*
automatic /ɔːtə'mætɪk/ *a.* automatique. ● *n.* (*auto.*) voiture automatique. *f.* **~ally** /-klɪ/ *adv.* automatiquement.
automobile /'ɔːtəməbiːl/ *n.* (*Amer.*) auto(mobile) *f.*
autonom|y /ɔː'tɒnəmɪ/ *n.* autonomie *f.* **~ous** *a.* autonome.
autopsy /'ɔːtɒpsɪ/ *n.* autopsie *f.*
autumn /'ɔːtəm/ *n.* automne *m.* **~al** /-'tʌmnəl/ *a.* automnal.
auxiliary /ɔːg'zɪlɪərɪ/ *a.* & *n.* auxiliaire (*m./f.*) **~ (verb),** auxiliaire *m.*
avail /ə'veɪl/ *v.t.* **~ o.s. of,** profiter de. ● *n.* **of no ~,** inutile. **to no ~,** sans résultat.
availab|le /ə'veɪləbl/ *a.* disponible. **~ility** /-'bɪlətɪ/ *n.* disponibilité *f.*
avalanche /'ævəlɑːnʃ/ *n.* avalanche *f.*
avant-garde /ævɑ̃'gɑːd/ *a.* d'avant-garde.
avaric|e /'ævərɪs/ *n.* avarice *f.* **~ious** /-'rɪʃəs/ *a.* avare.
avenge /ə'vendʒ/ *v.t.* venger. **~ o.s.,** se venger (**on,** de).
avenue /'ævənjuː/ *n.* avenue *f.*; (*line of approach*: *fig.*) voie *f.*
average /'ævərɪdʒ/ *n.* moyenne *f.* ● *a.* moyen. ● *v.t./i.* faire la moyenne de; (*produce, do*) faire en moyenne. **on ~,** en moyenne.
avers|e /ə'vɜːs/ *a.* **be ~e to,** répugner à. **~ion** /-ʃn/ *n.* aversion *f.*
avert /ə'vɜːt/ *v.t.* (*turn away*) détourner; (*ward off*) éviter.
aviary /'eɪvɪərɪ/ *n.* volière *f.*
aviation /eɪvɪ'eɪʃn/ *n.* aviation *f.*
avid /'ævɪd/ *a.* avide.
avocado /ævə'kɑːdəʊ/ *n.* (*pl.* **-os**) avocat *m.*
avoid /ə'vɔɪd/ *v.t.* éviter. **~able** *a.* évitable. **~ance** *n.* **the ~ance of s.o./sth. is . . .,** éviter qn./qch., c'est . . .
await /ə'weɪt/ *v.t.* attendre.
awake /ə'weɪk/ *v.t./i.* (*p.t.* **awoke,** *p.p.* **awoken**) (s')éveiller. ● *a.* **be ~,** ne pas dormir, être (r)éveillé.
awaken /ə'weɪkən/ *v.t./i.* (s')éveiller.
award /ə'wɔːd/ *v.t.* attribuer. ● *n.* récompense *f.*, prix *m.*; (*scholarship*) bourse *f.* **pay ~,** augmentation (de salaire) *f.*

aware /ə'weə(r)/ *a.* averti. **be ~ of,** (*danger*) être conscient de; (*fact*) savoir. **become ~ of,** prendre conscience de. **~ness** *n.* conscience *f.*

awash /ə'wɒʃ/ *a.* inondé (**with,** de).

away /ə'weɪ/ *adv.* (*far*) (au) loin; (*absent*) absent, parti; (*persistently*) sans arrêt; (*entirely*) complètement. **~ from,** loin de. **move ~,** s'écarter; (*to new home*) déménager. **six kilometres ~,** à six kilomètres (de distance). **take ~,** emporter. ● *a. & n.* **~ (match),** match à l'extérieur *m.*

awe /ɔ:/ *n.* crainte (révérencielle) *f.* **~-inspiring, ~some** *adjs.* terrifiant; (*sight*) imposant. **~struck** *a.* terrifié.

awful /'ɔ:fl/ *a.* affreux. **~ly** /'ɔ:flɪ/ *adv.* (*badly*) affreusement; (*very: fam.*) rudement.

awhile /ə'waɪl/ *adv.* quelque temps.

awkward /'ɔ:kwəd/ *a.* difficile; (*inconvenient*) inopportun; (*clumsy*) maladroit; (*embarrassing*) gênant; (*embarrassed*) gêné. **~ly** *adv.* maladroitement; avec gêne. **~ness** *n.* maladresse *f.*; (*discomfort*) gêne *f.*

awning /'ɔ:nɪŋ/ *n.* auvent *m.*; (*of shop*) store *m.*

awoke, awoken /ə'wəʊk, ə'wəʊkən/ *see* awake.

awry /ə'raɪ/ *adv.* **go ~,** mal tourner. **sth. is ~,** qch. ne va pas.

axe, (*Amer.*) **ax** /æks/ *n.* hache *f.* ● *v.t.* (*pres. p.* **axing**) réduire; (*eliminate*) supprimer; (*employee*) renvoyer.

axiom /'æksɪəm/ *n.* axiome *m.*

axis /'æksɪs/ *n.* (*pl.* **axes** /-si:z/) axe *m.*

axle /'æksl/ *n.* essieu *m.*

ay(e) /aɪ/ *adv. & n.* oui (*m. invar.*).

B

BA *abbr. see* Bachelor of Arts.

babble /'bæbl/ *v.i.* babiller; (*stream*) gazouiller. ● *n.* babillage *m.*

baboon /bə'bu:n/ *n.* babouin *m.*

baby /'beɪbɪ/ *n.* bébé *m.* **~ carriage,** (*Amer.*) voiture d'enfant *f.* **~-sit** *v.i.* garder les enfants. **~-sitter** *n.* baby-sitter *m./f.*

babyish /'beɪbɪʃ/ *a.* enfantin.

bachelor /'bætʃələ(r)/ *n.* célibataire *m.* **B~ of Arts/Science,** licencié(e) ès lettres/sciences *m.* (*f.*).

back /bæk/ *n.* (*of person, hand, page, etc.*) dos *m.*; (*of house*) derrière *m.*; (*of vehicle*) arrière *m.*; (*of room*) fond *m.*; (*of chair*) dossier *m.*; (*football*) arrière *m.* ● *a.* de derrière, arrière *invar.*; (*taxes*) arriéré. ● *adv.* en arrière; (*returned*) de retour, rentré. ● *v.t.* (*support*) appuyer; (*bet on*) miser sur; (*vehicle*) faire reculer. ● *v.i.* (*of person, vehicle*) reculer. **at the ~ of beyond,** au diable. **at the ~ of the book,** à la fin du livre. **come ~,** revenir. **give ~,** rendre. **take ~,** reprendre. **I want it ~,** je veux le récupérer. **in ~ of,** (*Amer.*) derrière. **~-bencher** *n.* (*pol.*) membre sans portefeuille *m.* **~ down,** abandonner, se dégonfler. **~ number,** vieux numéro *m.* **~ out,** se dégager, se dégonfler; (*auto.*) sortir en reculant. **~-pedal** *v.i.* pédaler en arrière; (*fig.*) faire machine arrière (**on,** à propos de). **~ up,** (*support*) appuyer. **~-up** *n.* appui *m.*; (*Amer., fam.*) embouteillage *m.*; (*comput.*) sauvegarde *f.*; *a.* de réserve; (*comput.*) de sauvegarde.

backache /'bækeɪk/ *n.* mal de reins *m.*, mal aux reins *m.*

backbiting /'bækbaɪtɪŋ/ *n.* médisance *f.*

backbone /'bækbəʊn/ *n.* colonne vertébrale *f.*

backdate /bæk'deɪt/ *v.t.* antidater; (*arrangement*) rendre rétroactif.

backer /'bækə(r)/ *n.* partisan *m.*; (*comm.*) bailleur de fonds *m.*

backfire /bæk'faɪə(r)/ *v.i.* (*auto.*) pétarader; (*fig.*) mal tourner.

backgammon /bæk'gæmən/ *n.* trictrac *m.*

background /'bækgraʊnd/ *n.* fond *m.*, arrière-plan *m.*; (*context*) contexte *m.*; (*environment*) milieu *m.*; (*experience*) formation *f.* ● *a.* (*music, noise*) de fond.

backhand /'bækhænd/ *n.* revers *m.* **~ed** *a.* équivoque. **~ed stroke,** revers *m.* **~er** *n.* revers *m.*; (*bribe: sl.*) pot de vin *m.*

backing /'bækɪŋ/ *n.* appui *m.*

backlash /'bæklæʃ/ *n.* choc en retour *m.*, répercussions *f. pl.*

backlog /'bæklɒg/ *n.* accumulation (de travail) *f.*

backpack /'bækpæk/ *n.* sac à dos *m.*

backside /ˈbæksaɪd/ *n.* (*buttocks*: *fam.*) derrière *m.*
backstage /bækˈsteɪdʒ/ *a.* & *adv.* dans les coulisses.
backstroke /ˈbækstrəʊk/ *n.* dos crawlé *m.*
backtrack /ˈbæktræk/ *v.i.* rebrousser chemin; (*change one's opinion*) faire marche arrière.
backward /ˈbækwəd/ *a.* (*step etc.*) en arrière; (*retarded*) arriéré.
backwards /ˈbækwədz/ *adv.* en arrière; (*walk*) à reculons; (*read*) à l'envers; (*fall*) à la renverse. **go ~ and forwards,** aller et venir.
backwater /ˈbækwɔːtə(r)/ *n.* (*pej.*) trou perdu *m.*
bacon /ˈbeɪkən/ *n.* lard *m.*; (*in rashers*) bacon *m.*
bacteria /bækˈtɪərɪə/ *n. pl.* bactéries *f. pl.* **~l** *a.* bactérien.
bad /bæd/ *a.* (**worse, worst**) mauvais; (*wicked*) méchant; (*ill*) malade; (*accident*) grave; (*food*) gâté. **feel ~,** se sentir mal. **go ~,** se gâter. **~ language,** gros mots *m. pl.* **~-mannered** *a.* mal élevé. **~-tempered** *a.* grincheux. **~ly** *adv.* mal; (*hurt*) grièvement. **too ~!,** tant pis; (*I'm sorry*) dommage! **want ~ly,** avoir grande envie de.
badge /bædʒ/ *n.* insigne *m.*; (*of identity*) plaque *f.*
badger /ˈbædʒə(r)/ *n.* blaireau *m.* ● *v.t.* harceler.
badminton /ˈbædmɪntən/ *n.* badminton *m.*
baffle /ˈbæfl/ *v.t.* déconcerter.
bag /bæg/ *n.* sac *m.* **~s,** (*luggage*) bagages *m.pl.*; (*under eyes*) poches *f. pl.* ● *v.t.* (*p.t.* **bagged**) mettre en sac; (*take*: *fam.*) s'adjuger. **~s of,** (*fam.*) beaucoup de.
baggage /ˈbægɪdʒ/ *n.* bagages *m. pl.* **~ reclaim,** livraison des bagages *f.*
baggy /ˈbægɪ/ *a.* trop grand.
bagpipes /ˈbægpaɪps/ *n. pl.* cornemuse *f.*
Bahamas /bəˈhɑːməz/ *n. pl.* **the ~,** les Bahamas *f. pl.*
bail[1] /beɪl/ *n.* caution *f.* **on ~,** sous caution. ● *v.t.* mettre en liberté (provisoire) sous caution. **~ out,** (*fig.*) sortir d'affaire.
bail[2] /beɪl/ *n.* (*cricket*) bâtonnet *m.*
bail[3] /beɪl/ *v.t.* (*naut.*) écoper.
bailiff /ˈbeɪlɪf/ *n.* huissier *m.*
bait /beɪt/ *n.* appât *m.* ● *v.t.* appâter; (*fig.*) tourmenter.
bak|e /beɪk/ *v.t.* (faire) cuire (au four). ● *v.i.* cuire (au four); (*person*) faire du pain *or* des gâteaux. **~ed beans,** haricots blancs à la tomate *m.pl.* **~ed potato,** pomme de terre en robe des champs *f.* **~er** *n.* boulang|er, -ère *m., f.* **~ing** *n.* cuisson *f.* **~ing-powder** *n.* levure *f.*
bakery /ˈbeɪkərɪ/ *n.* boulangerie *f.*
Balaclava /bæləˈklɑːvə/ *n.* **~ (helmet),** passe-montagne *m.*
balance /ˈbæləns/ *n.* équilibre *m.*; (*scales*) balance *f.*; (*outstanding sum*: *comm.*) solde *m.*; (*of payments, of trade*) balance *f.*; (*remainder*) reste *m.*; (*money in account*) position *f.* ● *v.t.* tenir en équilibre; (*weigh up* & *comm.*) balancer; (*budget*) équilibrer; (*to compensate*) contrebalancer. ● *v. i.* être en équilibre. **~d** *a.* équilibré.
balcony /ˈbælkənɪ/ *n.* balcon *m.*
bald /bɔːld/ *a.* (**-er, -est**) chauve; (*tyre*) lisse; (*fig.*) simple. **~ing** *a.* **be ~ing,** perdre ses cheveux. **~ness** *n.* calvitie *f.*
bale[1] /beɪl/ *n.* (*of cotton*) balle *f.*; (*of straw*) botte *f.*
bale[2] /beɪl/ *v.i.* **~ out,** sauter en parachute.
baleful /ˈbeɪlfʊl/ *a.* sinistre.
balk /bɔːk/ *v.t.* contrecarrer. ● *v.i.* **~ at,** reculer devant.
ball[1] /bɔːl/ *n.* (*golf, tennis, etc.*) balle *f.*; (*football*) ballon *m.*; (*croquet, billiards, etc.*) boule *f.*; (*of wool*) pelote *f.*; (*sphere*) boule *f.* **~-bearing** *n.* roulement à billes *m.* **~-cock** *n.* robinet à flotteur *m.* **~-point** *n.* stylo à bille *m.*
ball[2] /bɔːl/ *n.* (*dance*) bal *m.*
ballad /ˈbæləd/ *n.* ballade *f.*
ballast /ˈbæləst/ *n.* lest *m.*
ballerina /bæləˈriːnə/ *n.* ballerine *f.*
ballet /ˈbæleɪ/ *n.* ballet *m.*
ballistic /bəˈlɪstɪk/ *a.* **~ missile,** engin balistique *m.*
balloon /bəˈluːn/ *n.* ballon *m.*
ballot /ˈbælət/ *n.* scrutin *m.* **~-(paper),** bulletin de vote *m.* **~-box** *n.* urne *f.* ● *v.i.* (*p.t.* **balloted**) (*pol.*) voter. ● *v.t.* (*members*) consulter par voie de scrutin.
ballroom /ˈbɔːlrʊm/ *n.* salle de bal *f.*
ballyhoo /bælɪˈhuː/ *n.* (*publicity*) battage *m.*; (*uproar*) tapage *m.*
balm /bɑːm/ *n.* baume *m.* **~y** *a.* (*fragrant*) embaumé; (*mild*) doux; (*crazy*: *sl.*) dingue.

baloney /bə'ləʊnɪ/ *n.* (*sl.*) idioties *f. pl.*, calembredaines *f. pl.*
balustrade /bælə'streɪd/ *n.* balustrade *f.*
bamboo /bæm'bu:/ *n.* bambou *m.*
ban /bæn/ *v.t.* (*p.t.* **banned**) interdire. **~ from,** exclure de. ● *n.* interdiction *f.*
banal /bə'nɑ:l, *Amer.* 'beɪnl/ *a.* banal. **~ity** /-ælətɪ/ *n.* banalité *f.*
banana /bə'nɑ:nə/ *n.* banane *f.*
band /bænd/ *n.* (*strip, group of people*) bande *f.*; (*mus.*) orchestre *m.*; (*pop group*) groupe *m.* (*mil.*) fanfare *f.* ● *v.i.* **~ together,** se liguer.
bandage /'bændɪdʒ/ *n.* pansement *m.* ● *v.t.* bander, panser.
bandit /'bændɪt/ *n.* bandit *m.*
bandstand /'bændstænd/ *n.* kiosque à musique *m.*
bandwagon /'bændwægən/ *n.* **climb on the ~,** prendre le train en marche.
bandy[1] /'bændɪ/ *v.t.* **~ about,** (*rumours, ideas, etc.*) faire circuler.
bandy[2] /'bændɪ/ *a.* (**-ier, -iest**) qui a les jambes arquées.
bang /bæŋ/ *n.* (*blow, noise*) coup (violent) *m.*; (*explosion*) détonation *f.*; (*of door*) claquement *m.* ● *v.t./i.* frapper; (*door*) claquer. ● *int.* vlan. ● *adv.* (*fam.*) exactement. **~ in the middle,** en plein milieu. **~ one's head,** se cogner la tête. **~s,** frange *f.*
banger /'bæŋə(r)/ *n.* (*firework*) pétard *m.*; (*culin., sl.*) saucisse *f.* **(old) ~,** (*car: sl.*) guimbarde *f.*
bangle /'bæŋgl/ *n.* bracelet *m.*
banish /'bænɪʃ/ *v.t.* bannir.
banisters /'bænɪstəz/ *n. pl.* rampe (d'escalier) *f.*
banjo /'bændʒəʊ/ (*pl.* **-os**) banjo *m.*
bank[1] /bæŋk/ *n.* (*of river*) rive *f.*; (*of earth*) talus *m.*; (*of sand*) banc *m.* ● *v.t.* (*earth*) amonceler; (*fire*) couvrir. ● *v.i.* (*aviat.*) virer.
bank[2] /bæŋk/ *n.* banque *f.* ● *v.t.* mettre en banque. ● *v.i.* **~ with,** avoir un compte à. **~ account,** compte en banque *m.* **~ card,** carte bancaire *f.* **~ holiday,** jour férié *m.* **~ on,** compter sur. **~ statement,** relevé de compte *m.*
bank|ing /'bæŋkɪŋ/ *n.* opérations bancaires *f. pl.*; (*as career*) la banque. **~er** *n.* banquier *m.*
banknote /'bæŋknəʊt/ *n.* billet de banque *m.*
bankrupt /'bæŋkrʌpt/ *a.* **be ~,** être en faillite. **go ~,** faire faillite. ● *n.* failli(e) *m.* (*f.*). ● *v.t.* mettre en faillite. **~cy** *n.* faillite *f.*
banner /'bænə(r)/ *n.* bannière *f.*
banns /bænz/ *n. pl.* bans *m. pl.*
banquet /'bæŋkwɪt/ *n.* banquet *m.*
banter /'bæntə(r)/ *n.* plaisanterie *f.* ● *v.i.* plaisanter.
bap /bæp/ *n.* petit pain *m.*
baptism /'bæptɪzəm/ *n.* baptême *m.*
Baptist /'bæptɪst/ *n.* baptiste *m./f.*
baptize /bæp'taɪz/ *v.t.* baptiser.
bar /bɑ:(r)/ *n.* (*of metal*) barre *f.*; (*on window & jurid.*) barreau *m.*; (*of chocolate*) tablette *f.*; (*pub*) bar *m.*; (*counter*) comptoir *m.*, bar *m.*; (*division: mus.*) mesure *f.*; (*fig.*) obstacle *m.* ● *v.t.* (*p.t.* **barred**) (*obstruct*) barrer; (*prohibit*) interdire; (*exclude*) exclure. ● *prep.* sauf. **~ code,** code-barres *m. invar.* **~ of soap,** savonnette *f.*
Barbados /bɑ:'beɪdɒs/ *n.* Barbade *f.*
barbarian /bɑ:'beərɪən/ *n.* barbare *m./f.*
barbari|c /bɑ:'bærɪk/ *a.* barbare. **~ty** /-ətɪ/ *n.* barbarie *f.*
barbarous /'bɑ:bərəs/ *a.* barbare.
barbecue /'bɑ:bɪkju:/ *n.* barbecue *m.* ● *v.t.* griller, rôtir (au barbecue).
barbed /bɑ:bd/ *a.* **~ wire,** fil de fer barbelé *m.*
barber /'bɑ:bə(r)/ *n.* coiffeur *m.* (*pour hommes*).
barbiturate /bɑ:'bɪtjʊrət/ *n.* barbiturique *m.*
bare /beə(r)/ *a.* (**-er, -est**) (*not covered or adorned*) nu; (*cupboard*) vide; (*mere*) simple. ● *v.t.* mettre à nu.
barefaced /'beəfeɪst/ *a.* éhonté.
barefoot /'beəfʊt/ *a.* nu-pieds *invar.*, pieds nus.
barely /'beəlɪ/ *adv.* à peine.
bargain /'bɑ:gɪn/ *n.* (*deal*) marché *m.*; (*cheap thing*) occasion *f.* ● *v.i.* négocier; (*haggle*) marchander. **not ~ for,** ne pas s'attendre à.
barge /bɑ:dʒ/ *n.* chaland *m.* ● *v.i.* **~ in,** interrompre; (*into room*) faire irruption.
baritone /'bærɪtəʊn/ *n.* baryton *m.*
bark[1] /bɑ:k/ *n.* (*of tree*) écorce *f.*
bark[2] /bɑ:k/ *n.* (*of dog*) aboiement *m.* ● *v.i.* aboyer.
barley /'bɑ:lɪ/ *n.* orge *f.* **~ sugar,** sucre d'orge *m.*

barmaid /'bɑ:meɪd/ *n.* serveuse *f.*

barman /'bɑ:mən/ *n.* (*pl.* **-men**) barman *m.*

barmy /'bɑ:mɪ/ *a.* (*sl.*) dingue.

barn /bɑ:n/ *n.* grange *f.*

barometer /bə'rɒmɪtə(r)/ *n.* baromètre *m.*

baron /'bærən/ *n.* baron *m.* **~ess** *n.* baronne *f.*

baroque /bə'rɒk, *Amer.* bə'rəʊk/ *a.* & *n.* baroque (*m.*).

barracks /'bærəks/ *n. pl.* caserne *f.*

barrage /'bærɑ:ʒ, *Amer.* bə'rɑ:ʒ/ *n.* (*barrier*) barrage *m.*; (*mil.*) tir de barrage *m.*; (*of complaints*) série *f.*

barrel /'bærəl/ *n.* tonneau *m.*; (*of oil*) baril *m.*; (*of gun*) canon *m.* **~-organ** *n.* orgue de Barbarie *m.*

barren /'bærən/ *a.* stérile.

barricade /bærɪ'keɪd/ *n.* barricade *f.* ● *v.t.* barricader.

barrier /'bærɪə(r)/ *n.* barrière *f.*

barring /'bɑ:rɪŋ/ *prep.* sauf.

barrister /'bærɪstə(r)/ *n.* avocat *m.*

barrow /'bærəʊ/ *n.* charrette à bras *f.*; (*wheelbarrow*) brouette *f.*

bartender /'bɑ:tendə(r)/ *n.* (*Amer.*) barman *m.*

barter /'bɑ:tə(r)/ *n.* troc *m.*, échange *m.* ● *v.t.* troquer, échanger (**for,** contre).

base /beɪs/ *n.* base *f.* ● *v.t.* baser (**on,** sur; **in,** à). ● *a.* bas, ignoble. **~less** *a.* sans fondement.

baseball /'beɪsbɔ:l/ *n.* base-ball *m.*

baseboard /'beɪsbɔ:d/ *n.* (*Amer.*) plinthe *f.*

basement /'beɪsmənt/ *n.* sous-sol *m.*

bash /bæʃ/ *v.t.* cogner. ● *n.* coup (violent) *m.* **have a ~ at,** (*sl.*) s'essayer à. **~ed in,** enfoncé.

bashful /'bæʃfl/ *a.* timide.

basic /'beɪsɪk/ *a.* fondamental, élémentaire. **the ~s,** les éléments de base *m. pl.* **~ally** /-klɪ/ *adv.* au fond.

basil /'bæzɪl, *Amer.* 'beɪzl/ *n.* basilic *m.*

basin /'beɪsn/ *n.* (*for liquids*) cuvette *f.*; (*for food*) bol *m.*; (*for washing*) lavabo *m.*; (*of river*) bassin *m.*

basis /'beɪsɪs/ *n.* (*pl.* **bases** /-si:z/) base *f.*

bask /bɑ:sk/ *v.i.* se chauffer.

basket /'bɑ:skɪt/ *n.* corbeille *f.*; (*with handle*) panier *m.*

basketball /'bɑ:skɪtbɔ:l/ *n.* basket (-ball) *m.*

Basque /bɑ:sk/ *a.* & *n.* basque (*m./f.*).

bass[1] /beɪs/ *a.* (*mus.*) bas, grave. ● *n.* (*pl.* **basses**) basse *f.*

bass[2] /bæs/ *n. invar.* (*freshwater fish*) perche *f.*; (*sea*) bar *m.*

bassoon /bə'su:n/ *n.* basson *m.*

bastard /'bɑ:stəd/ *n.* bâtard(e) *m.* (*f.*); (*sl.*) sal|aud, -ope *m.*, *f.*

baste[1] /beɪst/ *v.t.* (*sew*) bâtir.

baste[2] /beɪst/ *v.t.* (*culin.*) arroser.

bastion /'bæstɪən/ *n.* bastion *m.*

bat[1] /bæt/ *n.* (*cricket etc.*) batte *f.*; (*table tennis*) raquette *f.* ● *v.t.* (*p.t.* **batted**) (*ball*) frapper. **not ~ an eyelid,** ne pas sourciller.

bat[2] /bæt/ *n.* (*animal*) chauve-souris *f.*

batch /bætʃ/ *n.* (*of people*) fournée *f.*; (*of papers*) paquet *m.*; (*of goods*) lot *m.*

bated /'beɪtɪd/ *a.* **with ~ breath,** en retenant son souffle.

bath /bɑ:θ/ *n.* (*pl.* **-s** /bɑ:ðz/) bain *m.*; (*tub*) baignoire *f.* **(swimming) ~s,** piscine *f.* ● *v.t.* donner un bain à ● *a.* de bain. **have a ~,** prendre un bain. **~ mat,** tapis de bain *m.*

bathe /beɪð/ *v.t.* baigner. ● *v.i.* se baigner; (*Amer.*) prendre un bain. ● *n.* bain (de mer) *m.* **~r** /-ə(r)/ *n.* baigneu|r, -se *m.*, *f.*

bathing /'beɪðɪŋ/ *n.* baignade *f.* **~-costume** *n.* maillot de bain *m.*

bathrobe /'bæθrəʊb/ *m.* (*Amer.*) robe de chambre *f.*

bathroom /'bɑ:θrʊm/ *n.* salle de bains *f.*

baton /'bætən/ *n.* (*mil.*) bâton *m.*; (*mus.*) baguette *f.*

battalion /bə'tæljən/ *n.* bataillon *m.*

batter /'bætə(r)/ *v.t.* (*strike*) battre; (*ill-treat*) maltraiter. ● *n.* (*culin.*) pâte (à frire) *f.* **~ed** *a.* (*pan, car*) cabossé; (*face*) meurtri. **~ing** *n.* **take a ~ing,** subir des coups.

battery /'bætərɪ/ *n.* (*mil., auto.*) batterie *f.*; (*of torch, radio*) pile *f.*

battle /'bætl/ *n.* bataille *f.*; (*fig.*) lutte *f.* ● *v.i.* se battre.

battlefield /'bætlfi:ld/ *n.* champ de bataille *m.*

battlements /'bætlmənts/ *n. pl.* (*crenellations*) créneaux *m. pl.*; (*wall*) remparts *m. pl.*

battleship /'bætlʃɪp/ *n.* cuirassé *m.*

baulk /bɔ:k/ *v.t./i.* = **balk**.

bawd|y /'bɔ:dɪ/ *a.* (**-ier, -iest**) paillard. **~iness** *n.* paillardise *f.*

bawl /bɔ:l/ *v.t./i.* brailler.

bay[1] /beɪ/ *n.* (*bot.*) laurier *m.* **~-leaf** *n.* feuille de laurier *f.*

bay[2] /beɪ/ *n.* (*geog., archit.*) baie *f.*; (*area*) aire *f.* **~ window,** fenêtre en saillie *f.*

bay[3] /beɪ/ *n.* (*bark*) aboiement *m.* • *v.i.* aboyer. **at ~,** aux abois. **keep** *or* **hold at ~,** tenir à distance.

bayonet /ˈbeɪənɪt/ *n.* baïonnette *f.*

bazaar /bəˈzɑː(r)/ *n.* (*shop, market*) bazar *m.*; (*sale*) vente *f.*

BC *abbr.* (*before Christ*) avant J.-C.

be /biː/ *v.i.* (*present tense* **am, are, is;** *p.t.* **was, were**; *p.p.* **been**) être. **be hot/right/***etc.*, avoir chaud/ raison/ *etc.* **he is 30,** (*age*) il a 30 ans. **it is fine/cold/***etc.*, (*weather*) il fait beau/froid/*etc.* **I'm a painter** • je suis peintre • **how are you?,** (*health*) comment allez-vous? **he is to leave,** (*must*) il doit partir; (*will*) il va partir, il est prévu qu'il parte. **how much is it?,** (*cost*) ça fait *or* c'est combien? **be reading/walking/***etc.*, (*aux.*) lire/ marcher/*etc.* **the child was found,** l'enfant a été retrouvé, on a retrouvé l'enfant. **have been to,** avoir été à, être allé à.

beach /biːtʃ/ *n.* plage *f.*

beacon /ˈbiːkən/ *n.* (*lighthouse*) phare *m.*; (*marker*) balise *f.*

bead /biːd/ *n.* perle *f.*

beak /biːk/ *n.* bec *m.*

beaker /ˈbiːkə(r)/ *n.* gobelet *m.*

beam /biːm/ *n.* (*timber*) poutre *f.*; (*of light*) rayon *m.*; (*of torch*) faisceau *m.* • *v.i.* (*radiate*) rayonner. • *v.t.* (*broadcast*) diffuser. **~ing** *a.* radieux.

bean /biːn/ *n.* haricot *m.*; (*of coffee*) grain *m.*

bear[1] /beə(r)/ *n.* ours *m.*

bear[2] /beə(r)/ *v.t.* (*p.t.* **bore,** *p.p.* **borne**) (*carry, show, feel*) porter; (*endure, sustain*) supporter; (*child*) mettre au monde. • *v.i.* **~ left/***etc.*, (*go*) prendre à gauche/*etc.* **~ in mind,** tenir compte de. **~ on,** se rapporter à. **~ out,** corroborer. **~ up!,** courage! **~able** *a.* supportable. **~er** *n.* porteu|r, -se *m., f.*

beard /bɪəd/ *n.* barbe *f.* **~ed** *a.* barbu.

bearing /ˈbeərɪŋ/ *n.* (*behaviour*) maintien *m.*; (*relevance*) rapport *m.* **get one's ~s,** s'orienter.

beast /biːst/ *n.* bête *f.*; (*person*) brute *f.*

beastly /ˈbiːstlɪ/ *a.* (**-ier, -iest**) (*fam.*) détestable.

beat /biːt/ *v.t./i.* (*p.t.* **beat,** *p.p.* **beaten**) battre. • *n.* (*of drum, heart*) battement *m.*; (*mus.*) mesure *f.*; (*of policeman*) ronde *f.* **~ a retreat,** battre en retraite. **~ it!,** dégage! **~ s.o. down,** faire baisser son prix à qn. **~ off the competition,** éliminer la concurrence. **~ up,** tabasser. **it ~s me,** (*fam.*) ça me dépasse. **~er** *n.* batteur *m.* **~ing** *n.* raclée *f.*

beautician /bjuːˈtɪʃn/ *n.* esthéticien(ne) *m.* (*f.*).

beautiful /ˈbjuːtɪfl/ *a.* beau. **~ly** /-flɪ/ *adv.* merveilleusement.

beautify /ˈbjuːtɪfaɪ/ *v.t.* embellir.

beauty /ˈbjuːtɪ/ *n.* beauté *f.* **~ parlour,** institut de beauté *m.* **~ spot,** grain de beauté *m.*; (*fig.*) site pittoresque *m.*

beaver /ˈbiːvə(r)/ *n.* castor *m.*

became /bɪˈkeɪm/ *see* become.

because /bɪˈkɒz/ *conj.* parce que. **~ of,** à cause de.

beck /bek/ *n.* **at the ~ and call of,** aux ordres de.

beckon /ˈbekən/ *v.t./i.* **~ (to),** faire signe à.

become /bɪˈkʌm/ *v.t./i.* (*p.t.* **became,** *p.p.* **become**) devenir; (*befit*) convenir à. **what has ~ of her?,** qu'est-elle devenue?

becoming /bɪˈkʌmɪŋ/ *a.* (*seemly*) bienséant; (*clothes*) seyant.

bed /bed/ *n.* lit *m.*; (*layer*) couche *f.*; (*of sea*) fond *m.*; (*of flowers*) parterre *m.* **go to ~,** (aller) se coucher. • *v.i.* (*p.t.* **bedded**). **~ down,** se coucher. **~ding** *n.* literie *f.*

bedbug /ˈbedbʌg/ *n.* punaise *f.*

bedclothes /ˈbedkləʊðz/ *n. pl.* couvertures *f. pl.* et draps *m. pl.*

bedevil /bɪˈdevl/ *v.t.* (*p.t.* **bedevilled**) (*confuse*) embrouiller; (*plague*) tourmenter.

bedlam /ˈbedləm/ *n.* chahut *m.*

bedraggled /bɪˈdrægld/ *a.* (*untidy*) débraillé.

bedridden /ˈbedrɪdn/ *a.* cloué au lit.

bedroom /ˈbedrʊm/ *n.* chambre (à coucher) *f.*

bedside /ˈbedsaɪd/ *n.* chevet *m.* **~ book,** livre de chevet *m.*

bedsit, bedsitter /ˈbedsɪt, -ˈsɪtə(r)/ *ns.* (*fam.*) *n.* chambre meublée *f.*, studio *m.*

bedspread /ˈbedspred/ *n.* dessus-de-lit *m. invar.*

bedtime /ˈbedtaɪm/ *n.* heure du coucher *f.*

bee /bi:/ *n.* abeille *f.* **make a ~-line for,** aller tout droit vers.
beech /bi:tʃ/ *n.* hêtre *m.*
beef /bi:f/ *n.* bœuf *m.* ● *v.i.* (*grumble*: *sl.*) rouspéter.
beefburger /'bi:fbɜ:gə(r)/ *n.* hamburger *m.*
beefeater /'bi:fi:tə(r)/ *n.* hallebardier *m.*
beefy /'bi:fɪ/ *a.* (**-ier, -iest**) musclé.
beehive /'bi:haɪv/ *n.* ruche *f.*
been /bi:n/ *see* be.
beer /bɪə(r)/ *n.* bière *f.*
beet /bi:t/ *n.* (*plant*) betterave *f.*
beetle /'bi:tl/ *n.* scarabée *m.*
beetroot /'bi:tru:t/ *n. invar.* (*culin.*) betterave *f.*
befall /bɪ'fɔ:l/ *v.t.* (*p.t.* **befell,** *p.p.* **befallen**) arriver à.
befit /bɪ'fɪt/ (*v.t.* (*p.t.* **befitted**) convenir à, seoir à.
before /bɪ'fɔ:(r)/ *prep.* (*time*) avant; (*place*) devant. ● *adv.* avant; (*already*) déjà. ● *conj.* **~ leaving,** avant de partir. **~ he leaves,** avant qu'il (ne) parte. **the day ~,** la veille. **two days ~,** deux jours avant.
beforehand /bɪ'fɔ:hænd/ *adv.* à l'avance, avant.
befriend /bɪ'frend/ *v.t.* offrir son amitié à, aider.
beg /beg/ *v.t.* (*p.t.* **begged**) (*entreat*) supplier (**to do,** de faire). **~ (for),** (*money*, *food*) mendier; (*request*) solliciter, demander. ● *v.i.* **~ (for alms),** mendier. **it is going ~ging,** personne n'en veut.
began /bɪ'gæn/ *see* begin.
beggar /'begə(r)/ *n.* mendiant(e) *m.* (*f.*); (*sl.*) individu *m.*
begin /bɪ'gɪn/ *v.t./i.* (*p.t.* **began,** *p.p.* **begun,** *pres. p.* **beginning**) commencer (**to do,** à faire). **~ner** *n.* débutant(e) *m.* (*f.*). **~ning** *n.* commencement *m.*, début *m.*
begrudge /bɪ'grʌdʒ/ *v.t.* (*envy*) envier; (*give unwillingly*) donner à contrecœur. **~ doing,** faire à contrecœur.
beguile /bɪ'gaɪl/ *v.t.* tromper.
begun /bɪ'gʌn/ *see* begin.
behalf /bɪ'hɑ:f/ *n.* **on ~ of,** pour; (*as representative*) au nom de, pour (le compte de).
behave /bɪ'heɪv/ *v.i.* se conduire. **~ (o.s.),** se conduire bien.
behaviour, (*Amer.*) **behavior** /bɪ'heɪvjə(r)/ *n.* conduite *f.*, comportement *m.*
behead /bɪ'hed/ *v.t.* décapiter.
behind /bɪ'haɪnd/ *prep.* derrière; (*in time*) en retard sur. ● *adv.* derrière; (*late*) en retard. ● *n.* (*buttocks*) derrière *m.* **leave ~,** oublier.
behold /bɪ'həʊld/ *v.t.* (*p.t.* **beheld**) (*old use*) voir.
beige /beɪʒ/ *a.* & *n.* beige (*m.*).
being /'bi:ɪŋ/ *n.* (*person*) être *m.* **bring into ~,** créer. **come into ~,** prendre naissance.
belated /bɪ'leɪtɪd/ *a.* tardif.
belch /beltʃ/ *v.i.* faire un renvoi. ● *v.t.* **~ out,** (*smoke*) vomir. ● *n.* renvoi *m.*
belfry /'belfrɪ/ *n.* beffroi *m.*
Belgi|um /'beldʒəm/ *n.* Belgique *f.* **~an** *a.* & *n.* belge (*m./f.*).
belie /bɪ'laɪ/ *v.t.* démentir.
belief /bɪ'li:f/ *n.* croyance *f.*; (*trust*) confiance *f.*; (*faith*: *relig.*) foi *f.*
believ|e /bɪ'li:v/ *v.t./i.* croire. **~e in,** croire à; (*deity*) croire en. **~able** *a.* croyable. **~er** *n.* croyant(e) *m.* (*f.*).
belittle /bɪ'lɪtl/ *v.t.* déprécier.
bell /bel/ *n.* cloche *f.*; (*small*) clochette *f.*; (*on door*) sonnette *f.*; (*of phone*) sonnerie *f.*
belligerent /bɪ'lɪdʒərənt/ *a.* & *n.* belligérant(e) (*m.* (*f.*)).
bellow /'beləʊ/ *v.t./i.* beugler.
bellows /'beləʊz/ *n. pl.* soufflet *m.*
belly /'belɪ/ *n.* ventre *m.* **~-ache** *n.* mal au ventre *m.*
bellyful /'belɪfʊl/ *n.* **have a ~,** en avoir plein le dos.
belong /bɪ'lɒŋ/ *v.i.* **~ to,** appartenir à; (*club*) être membre de.
belongings /bɪ'lɒŋɪŋz/ *n. pl.* affaires *f. pl.*
beloved /bɪ'lʌvɪd/ *a.* & *n.* bien-aimé(e) (*m.* (*f.*)).
below /bɪ'ləʊ/ *prep.* au-dessous de; (*fig.*) indigne de. ● *adv.* en dessous; (*on page*) ci-dessous.
belt /belt/ *n.* ceinture *f.*; (*techn.*) courroie *f.*; (*fig.*) région *f.* ● *v.t.* (*hit*: *sl.*) rosser. ● *v.i.* (*rush*: *sl.*) filer à toute allure.
beltway /'beltweɪ/ *n.* (*Amer.*) périphérique *m.*
bemused /bɪ'mju:zd/ *a.* (*confused*) stupéfié; (*thoughtful*) pensif.
bench /bentʃ/ *n.* banc *m.*; (*working-table*) établi *m.* **the ~,** (*jurid.*) la magistrature (assise). **~-mark** *n.* repère *m.*
bend /bend/ *v.t./i.* (*p.t.* **bent**) (se) courber; (*arm*, *leg*) plier. ● *n.*

courbe *f.*; (*in road*) virage *m.*; (*of arm, knee*) pli *m.* **~ down** *or* **over,** se pencher.

beneath /bɪ'ni:θ/ *prep.* sous, au-dessous de; (*fig.*) indigne de. ● *adv.* (au-)dessous.

benefactor /'benɪfæktə(r)/ *n.* bienfai|teur, -trice *m., f.*

beneficial /benɪ'fɪʃl/ *a.* avantageux, favorable.

benefit /'benɪfɪt/ *n.* avantage *m.*; (*allowance*) allocation *f.* ● *v.t.* (*p.t.* **benefited,** *pres. p.* **benefiting**) (*be useful to*) profiter à; (*do good to*) faire du bien à. **~ from,** tirer profit de.

benevolen|t /bɪ'nevələnt/ *a.* bienveillant. **~ce** *n.* bienveillance *f.*

benign /bɪ'naɪn/ *a.* (*kindly*) bienveillant; (*med.*) bénin.

bent /bent/ *see* bend. ● *n.* (*talent*) aptitude *f.*; (*inclination*) penchant *m.* ● *a.* tordu; (*sl.*) corrompu. **~ on doing,** décidé à faire.

bequeath /bɪ'kwi:ð/ *v.t.* léguer.

bequest /bɪ'kwest/ *n.* legs *m.*

bereave|d /bɪ'ri:vd/ *a.* **the ~d wife/** *etc.*, la femme/*etc.* du disparu. **~ment** *n.* deuil *m.*

beret /'bereɪ/ *n.* béret *m.*

Bermuda /bə'mju:də/ *n.* Bermudes *f. pl.*

berry /'berɪ/ *n.* baie *f.*

berserk /bə'sɜ:k/ *a.* **go ~,** devenir fou furieux.

berth /bɜ:θ/ *n.* (*in train, ship*) couchette *f.*; (*anchorage*) mouillage *m.* ● *v.i.* mouiller. **give a wide ~ to,** éviter.

beseech /bɪ'si:tʃ/ *v.t.* (*p.t.* **besought**) implorer, supplier.

beset /bɪ'set/ *v.t.* (*p.t.* **beset,** *pres. p.* **besetting**) (*attack*) assaillir; (*surround*) entourer.

beside /bɪ'saɪd/ *prep.* à côté de. **~ o.s.,** hors de soi. **~ the point,** sans rapport.

besides /bɪ'saɪdz/ *prep.* en plus de; (*except*) excepté. ● *adv.* en plus.

besiege /bɪ'si:dʒ/ *v.t.* assiéger.

best /best/ *a.* meilleur. **the ~ book/** *etc.*, le meilleur livre/*etc.* ● *adv.* **(the) ~,** (*sing etc.*) le mieux. ● *n.* **the ~ (one),** le meilleur, la meilleure. **~ man,** garçon d'honneur *m.* **the ~ part of,** la plus grande partie de. **the ~ thing is to . . . ,** le mieux est de . . . **do one's ~,** faire de son mieux. **make the ~ of,** s'accommoder de.

bestow /bɪ'stəʊ/ *v.t.* accorder.

best-seller /best'selə(r)/ *n.* best-seller *m.*, succès de librairie *m.*

bet /bet/ *n.* pari *m.* ● *v.t./i.* (*p.t.* **bet** *or* **betted,** *pres. p.* **betting**) parier.

betray /bɪ'treɪ/ *v.t.* trahir. **~al** *n.* trahison *f.*

better /'betə(r)/ *a.* meilleur. ● *adv.* mieux. ● *v.t.* (*improve*) améliorer; (*do better than*) surpasser. ● *n.* **one's ~s,** ses supérieurs *m. pl.* **be ~ off,** (*financially*) avoir plus d'argent. **he's ~ off at home,** il est mieux chez lui. **I had ~ go,** je ferais mieux de partir. **the ~ part of,** la plus grande partie de. **get ~,** s'améliorer; (*recover*) se remettre. **get the ~ of,** l'emporter sur. **so much the ~,** tant mieux.

betting-shop /'betɪŋʃɒp/ *n.* bureau de P.M.U. *m.*

between /bɪ'twi:n/ *prep.* entre. ● *adv.* **in ~,** au milieu.

beverage /'bevərɪdʒ/ *n.* boisson *f.*

bevy /'bevɪ/ *n.* essaim *m.*

beware /bɪ'weə(r)/ *v.i.* prendre garde (**of,** à).

bewilder /bɪ'wɪldə(r)/ *v.t.* désorienter, embarrasser. **~ment** *n.* désorientation *f.*

bewitch /bɪ'wɪtʃ/ *v.t.* enchanter.

beyond /bɪ'jɒnd/ *prep.* au-delà de; (*doubt, reach*) hors de; (*besides*) excepté. ● *adv.* au-delà. **it is ~ me,** ça me dépasse.

bias /'baɪəs/ *n.* (*inclination*) penchant *m.*; (*prejudice*) préjugé *m.* ● *v.t.* (*p.t.* **biased**) influencer. **~ed** *a.* partial.

bib /bɪb/ *n.* bavoir *m.*

Bible /'baɪbl/ *n.* Bible *f.*

biblical /'bɪblɪkl/ *a.* biblique.

bicarbonate /baɪ'kɑ:bənət/ *n.* bicarbonate *m.*

biceps /'baɪseps/ *n.* biceps *m.*

bicker /'bɪkə(r)/ *v.i.* se chamailler.

bicycle /'baɪsɪkl/ *n.* bicyclette *f.* ● *v.i.* faire de la bicyclette.

bid[1] /bɪd/ *n.* (*at auction*) offre *f.*, enchère *f.*; (*attempt*) tentative *f.* ● *v.t./i.* (*p.t.* & *p.p.* **bid,** *pres. p.* **bidding**) (*offer*) faire une offre *or* une enchère (de). **the highest ~der,** le plus offrant.

bid[2] /bɪd/ *v.t.* (*p.t.* **bade** /bæd/, *p.p.* **bidden** *or* **bid,** *pres. p.* **bidding**) ordonner; (*say*) dire. **~ding** *n.* ordre *m.*

bide /baɪd/ *v.t.* **~ one's time,** attendre le bon moment.

biennial /baɪ'enɪəl/ *a.* biennal.

bifocals /baɪ'fəʊklz/ *n. pl.* lunettes bifocales *f. pl.*

big /bɪg/ *a.* (**bigger, biggest**) grand; (*in bulk*) gros; (*generous*: *sl.*) généreux: ● *adv.* (*fam.*) en grand; (*earn*: *fam.*) gros. **~ business,** les grandes affaires. **~-headed** *a.* prétentieux. **~ shot,** (*sl.*) huile *f.* **think ~,** (*fam.*) voir grand.

bigam|y /'bɪgəmɪ/ *n.* bigamie *f.* **~ist** *n.* bigame *m./f.* **~ous** *a.* bigame.

bigot /'bɪgət/ *n.* fanatique *m./f.* **~ed** *a.* fanatique. **~ry** *n.* fanatisme *m.*

bike /baɪk/ *n.* (*fam.*) vélo *m.*

bikini /bɪ'ki:nɪ/ *n.* (*pl.* **-is**) bikini *m.*

bilberry /'bɪlbərɪ/ *n.* myrtille *f.*

bile /baɪl/ *n.* bile *f.*

bilingual /baɪ'lɪŋgwəl/ *a.* bilingue.

bilious /'bɪlɪəs/ *a.* bilieux.

bill[1] /bɪl/ *n.* (*invoice*) facture *f.*; (*in hotel, for gas, etc.*) note *f.*; (*in restaurant*) addition *f.*; (*of sale*) acte *m.*; (*pol.*) projet de loi *m.*; (*banknote*: *Amer.*) billet de banque *m.* ● *v.t.* (*person*: *comm.*) envoyer la facture à. (*theatre*) **on the ~,** à l'affiche.

bill[2] /bɪl/ *n.* (*of bird*) bec *m.*

billboard /'bɪlbɔ:d/ *n.* panneau d'affichage *m.*

billet /'bɪlɪt/ *n.* cantonnement *m.* ● *v.t.* (*p.t.* **billeted**) cantonner (**on,** chez).

billfold /'bɪlfəʊld/ *n.* (*Amer.*) portefeuille *m.*

billiards /'bɪljədz/ *n.* billard *m.*

billion /'bɪljən/ *n.* billion *m.*; (*Amer.*) milliard *m.*

billy-goat /'bɪlɪgəʊt/ *n.* bouc *m.*

bin /bɪn/ *n.* (*for rubbish, litter*) boîte (à ordures) *f.*, poubelle *f.*; (*for bread*) huche *f.*, coffre *m.*

binary /'baɪnərɪ/ *a.* binaire.

bind /baɪnd/ *v.t.* (*p.t.* **bound**) lier; (*book*) relier; (*jurid.*) obliger. ● *n.* (*bore*: *sl.*) plaie *f.* **be ~ing on,** être obligatoire pour.

binding /'baɪndɪŋ/ *n.* reliure *f.*

binge /bɪndʒ/ *n.* **go on a ~,** (*spree*: *sl.*) faire la bringue.

bingo /'bɪŋgəʊ/ *n.* loto *m.*

binoculars /bɪ'nɒkjʊləz/ *n. pl.* jumelles *f. pl.*

biochemistry /baɪəʊ'kemɪstrɪ/ *n.* biochimie *f.*

biodegradable /baɪəʊdɪ'greɪdəbl/ *a.* biodégradable.

biograph|y /baɪ'ɒgrəfɪ/ *n.* biographie *f.* **~er** *n.* biographe *m./f.*

biolog|y /baɪ'ɒlədʒɪ/ *n.* biologie *f.* **~ical** /-ə'lɒdʒɪkl/ *a.* biologique. **~ist** *n.* biologiste *m./f.*

biorhythm /'baɪəʊrɪðəm/ *n.* biorythme *m.*

birch /bɜ:tʃ/ *n.* (*tree*) bouleau *m.*; (*whip*) verge *f.*, fouet *m.*

bird /bɜ:d/ *n.* oiseau *m.*; (*fam.*) individu *m.*; (*girl*: *sl.*) poule *f.*

Biro /'baɪərəʊ/ *n.* (*pl.* **-os**) (P.) stylo à bille *m.*, Bic *m.* (P.).

birth /bɜ:θ/ *n.* naissance *f.* **give ~,** accoucher. **~ certificate,** acte de naissance *m.* **~-control** *n.* contrôle des naissances *m.* **~-rate** *n.* natalité *f.*

birthday /'bɜ:θdeɪ/ *n.* anniversaire *m.*

birthmark /'bɜ:θmɑ:k/ *n.* tache de vin *f.*, envie *f.*

biscuit /'bɪskɪt/ *n.* biscuit *m.*; (*Amer.*) petit pain (au lait) *m.*

bisect /baɪ'sekt/ *v.t.* couper en deux.

bishop /'bɪʃəp/ *n.* évêque *m.*

bit[1] /bɪt/ *n.* morceau *m.*; (*of horse*) mors *m.*; (*of tool*) mèche *f.* **a ~,** (*a little*) un peu.

bit[2] /bɪt/ *see* bite.

bit[3] /bɪt/ *n.* (*comput.*) bit *m.*, élement binaire *m.*

bitch /bɪtʃ/ *n.* chienne *f.*; (*woman*: *fam.*) garce *f.* ● *v.i.* (*grumble*: *fam.*) râler. **~y** *a.* (*fam.*) vache.

bite /baɪt/ *v.t./i.* (*p.t.* **bit,** *p.p.* **bitten**) mordre. ● *n.* morsure *f.*; (*by insect*) piqûre *f.*; (*mouthful*) bouchée *f.* **~ one's nails,** se ronger les ongles. **have a ~,** manger un morceau.

biting /'baɪtɪŋ/ *a.* mordant.

bitter /'bɪtə(r)/ *a.* amer; (*weather*) glacial, âpre. ● *n.* bière anglaise *f.* **~ly** *adv.* amèrement. **it is ~ly cold,** il fait un temps glacial. **~ness** *n.* amertume *f.*

bitty /'bɪtɪ/ *a.* décousu.

bizarre /bɪ'zɑ:(r)/ *a.* bizarre.

blab /blæb/ *v.i.* (*p.t.* **blabbed**) jaser.

black /blæk/ *a.* (**-er, -est**) noir. ● *n.* (*colour*) noir *m.* **B~,** (*person*) Noir(e) *m.* (*f.*). ● *v.t.* noircir; (*goods*) boycotter. **~ and blue,** couvert de bleus. **~ eye,** œil poché *m.* **~ ice,** verglas *m.* **~ list,** liste noire *f.* **~ market,** marché noir *m.* **~ sheep,** brebis galeuse *f.* **~ spot,** point noir *m.*

blackberry /ˈblækbərɪ/ *n.* mûre *f.*
blackbird /ˈblækbɜːd/ *n.* merle *m.*
blackboard /ˈblækbɔːd/ *n.* tableau noir *m.*
blackcurrant /ˈblækkʌrənt/ *n.* cassis *m.*
blacken /ˈblækən/ *v.t./i.* noircir.
blackhead /ˈblækhed/ *n.* point noir *m.*
blackleg /ˈblækleg/ *n.* jaune *m.*
blacklist /ˈblæklɪst/ *v.t.* mettre sur la liste noire *or* à l'index.
blackmail /ˈblækmeɪl/ *n.* chantage *m.* ● *v.t.* faire chanter. **~er** *n.* maître-chanteur *m.*
blackout /ˈblækaʊt/ *n.* panne d'électricité *f.*; (*med.*) syncope *f.*
blacksmith /ˈblæksmɪθ/ *n.* forgeron *m.*
bladder /ˈblædə(r)/ *n.* vessie *f.*
blade /bleɪd/ *n.* (*of knife etc.*) lame *f.*; (*of propeller, oar*) pale *f.* **~ of grass,** brin d'herbe *m.*
blame /bleɪm/ *v.t.* accuser. ● *n.* faute *f.* **~ s.o. for sth.,** reprocher qch. à qn. **he is to ~,** il est responsable (**for,** de). **~less** *a.* irréprochable.
bland /blænd/ *a.* (**-er, -est**) (*gentle*) doux; (*insipid*) fade.
blank /blæŋk/ *a.* blanc; (*look*) vide; (*cheque*) en blanc. ● *n.* blanc *m.* **~ (cartridge),** cartouche à blanc *f.*
blanket /ˈblæŋkɪt/ *n.* couverture *f.*; (*layer: fig.*) couche *f.* ● *v.t.* (*p.t.* **blanketed**) recouvrir.
blare /bleə(r)/ *v.t./i.* beugler. ● *n.* vacarme *m.*, beuglement *m.*
blarney /ˈblɑːnɪ/ *n.* boniment *m.*
blasé /ˈblɑːzeɪ/ *a.* blasé.
blasphem|y /ˈblæsfəmɪ/ *n.* blasphème *m.* **~ous** *a.* blasphématoire; (*person*) blasphémateur.
blast /blɑːst/ *n.* explosion *f.*; (*wave of air*) souffle *m.*; (*of wind*) rafale *f.*; (*noise from siren etc.*) coup *m.* ● *v.t.* (*blow up*) faire sauter. **~ed** *a.* (*fam.*) maudit, fichu. **~-furnace** *n.* haut fourneau *m.* **~ off,** être mis à feu. **~-off** *n.* mise à feu *f.*
blatant /ˈbleɪtnt/ *a.* (*obvious*) flagrant; (*shameless*) éhonté.
blaze[1] /bleɪz/ *n.* flamme *f.*; (*conflagration*) incendie *m.*; (*fig.*) éclat *m.* ● *v.i.* (*fire*) flamber; (*sky, eyes, etc.*) flamboyer.
blaze[2] /bleɪz/ *v.t.* **~ a trail,** montrer *or* marquer la voie.
blazer /ˈbleɪzə(r)/ *n.* blazer *m.*
bleach /bliːtʃ/ *n.* décolorant *m.*; (*for domestic use*) eau de Javel *f.* ● *v.t./i.* blanchir; (*hair*) décolorer.
bleak /bliːk/ *a.* (**-er, -est**) morne.
bleary /ˈblɪərɪ/ *a.* (*eyes*) voilé.
bleat /bliːt/ *n.* bêlement *m.* ● *v.i.* bêler.
bleed /bliːd/ *v.t./i.* (*p.t.* **bled**) saigner.
bleep /bliːp/ *n.* bip *m.* **~er** *n.* bip *m.*
blemish /ˈblemɪʃ/ *n.* tare *f.*, défaut *m.*; (*on reputation*) tache *f.* ● *v.t.* entacher.
blend /blend/ *v.t./i.* (se) mélanger. ● *n.* mélange *m.* **~er** *n.* mixer *n.*
bless /bles/ *v.t.* bénir. **be ~ed with,** avoir le bonheur de posséder. **~ing** *n.* bénédiction *f.*; (*benefit*) avantage *m.*; (*stroke of luck*) chance *f.*
blessed /ˈblesɪd/ *a.* (*holy*) saint; (*damned: fam.*) sacré.
blew /bluː/ *see* blow[1].
blight /blaɪt/ *n.* (*disease: bot.*) rouille *f.*; (*fig.*) fléau *m.*
blind /blaɪnd/ *a.* aveugle. ● *v.t.* aveugler. ● *n.* (*on window*) store *m.*; (*deception*) feinte *f.* **be ~ to,** ne pas voir. **~ alley,** impasse *f.* **~ corner,** virage sans visibilité *m.* **~ man,** aveugle *m.* **~ spot,** (*auto.*) angle mort *m.* **~ers** *n. pl.* (*Amer.*) œillères *f. pl.* **~ly** *adv.* aveuglément. **~ness** *n.* cécité *f.*
blindfold /ˈblaɪndfəʊld/ *a. & adv.* les yeux bandés. ● *n.* bandeau *m.* ● *v.t.* bander les yeux à.
blink /blɪŋk/ *v.i.* cligner des yeux; (*of light*) clignoter.
blinkers /ˈblɪŋkəz/ *n. pl.* œillères *f. pl.*
bliss /blɪs/ *n.* félicité *f.* **~ful** *a.* bienheureux. **~fully** *adv.* joyeusement, merveilleusement.
blister /ˈblɪstə(r)/ *n.* ampoule *f.* (*on paint*) cloque *f.* ● *v.i.* se couvrir d'ampoules; cloquer.
blithe /blaɪð/ *a.* joyeux.
blitz /blɪts/ *n.* (*aviat.*) raid éclair *m.* ● *v.t.* bombarder.
blizzard /ˈblɪzəd/ *n.* tempête de neige *f.*
bloated /ˈbləʊtɪd/ *a.* gonflé.
bloater /ˈbləʊtə(r)/ *n.* hareng saur *m.*
blob /blɒb/ *n.* (*drop*) (grosse) goutte *f.*; (*stain*) tache *f.*
bloc /blɒk/ *n.* bloc *m.*
block /blɒk/ *n.* bloc *m.*; (*buildings*) pâté de maisons *m.*; (*in pipe*) obstruction *f.* **~ (of flats),** immeuble *m.* ● *v.t.* bloquer. **~ letters,** majus-

cules *f. pl.* **~age** *n.* obstruction *f.* **~-buster** *n.* gros succès *m.*

blockade /blɒ'keɪd/ *n.* blocus *m.* ● *v.t.* bloquer.

bloke /bləʊk/ *n.* (*fam.*) type *m.*

blond /blɒnd/ *a.* & *n.* blond (*m.*).

blonde /blɒnd/ *a.* & *n.* blonde (*f.*).

blood /blʌd/ *n.* sang *m.* ● *a.* (*donor, bath, etc.*) de sang; (*bank, poisoning, etc.*) du sang; (*group, vessel*) sanguin. **~-curdling** *a.* à tourner le sang. **~less** *a.* (*fig.*) pacifique. **~-pressure** *n.* tension artérielle *f.* **~test**, prise de sang *f.*

bloodhound /'blʌdhaʊnd/ *n.* limier *m.*

bloodshed /'blʌdʃed/ *n.* effusion de sang *f.*

bloodshot /'blʌdʃɒt/ *a.* injecté de sang.

bloodstream /'blʌdstri:m/ *n.* sang *m.*

bloodthirsty /'blʌdθɜ:stɪ/ *a.* sanguinaire.

bloody /'blʌdɪ/ *a.* (**-ier, -iest**) sanglant; (*sl.*) sacré. ● *adv.* (*sl.*) vachement. **~-minded** *a.* (*fam.*) hargneux, obstiné.

bloom /blu:m/ *n.* fleur *f.* ● *v.i.* fleurir; (*fig.*) s'épanouir.

bloomer /'blu:mə(r)/ *n.* (*sl.*) gaffe *f.*

blossom /'blɒsəm/ *n.* fleur(s) *f.* (*pl.*). ● *v.i.* fleurir; (*person: fig.*) s'épanouir.

blot /blɒt/ *n.* tache *f.* ● *v.t.* (*p.t.* **blotted**) tacher; (*dry*) sécher. **~ out**, effacer. **~ter, ~ting-paper** *ns.* buvard *m.*

blotch /blɒtʃ/ *n.* tache *f.* **~y** *a.* couvert de taches.

blouse /blaʊz/ *n.* chemisier *m.*

blow[1] /bləʊ/ *v.t./i.* (*p.t.* **blew**, *p.p.* **blown**) souffler; (*fuse*) (faire) sauter; (*squander: sl.*) claquer; (*opportunity*) rater. **~ one's nose**, se moucher. **~ a whistle**, siffler. **~ away** *or* **off**, emporter. **~-dry** *v.t.* sécher; *n.* brushing *m.* **~ out**, (*candle*) souffler. **~-out** *n.* (*of tyre*) éclatement *m.* **~ over**, passer. **~ up**, (faire) sauter; (*tyre*) gonfler; (*photo.*) agrandir.

blow[2] /bləʊ/ *n.* coup *m.*

blowlamp /'bləʊlæmp/ *n.* chalumeau *m.*

blown /bləʊn/ *see* blow[1].

blowtorch /'bləʊtɔ:tʃ/ *n.* (*Amer.*) chalumeau *m.*

blowy /'bləʊɪ/ *a.* **it is ~**, il y a du vent.

bludgeon /'blʌdʒən/ *n.* gourdin *m.* ● *v.t.* matraquer.

blue /blu:/ *a.* (**-er, -est**) bleu; (*film*) porno. ● *n.* bleu *m.* **come out of the ~**, être inattendu. **have the ~s**, avoir le cafard.

bluebell /'blu:bel/ *n.* jacinthe des bois *f.*

bluebottle /'blu:bɒtl/ *n.* mouche à viande *f.*

blueprint /'blu:prɪnt/ *n.* plan *m.*

bluff[1] /blʌf/ *v.t./i.* bluffer. ● *n.* bluff *m.* **call. s.o.'s ~**, dire chiche à qn.

bluff[2] /blʌf/ *a.* (*person*) brusque.

blunder /'blʌndə(r)/ *v.i.* faire une gaffe; (*move*) avancer à tâtons. ● *n.* gaffe *f.*

blunt /blʌnt/ *a.* (*knife*) émoussé; (*person*) brusque. ● *v.t.* émousser. **~ly** *adv.* carrément. **~ness** *n.* brusquerie *f.*

blur /blɜ:(r)/ *n.* tache floue *f.* ● *v.t.* (*p.t.* **blurred**) rendre flou.

blurb /blɜ:b/ *n.* résumé publicitaire *m.*

blurt /blɜ:t/ *v.t.* **~ out**, lâcher, dire.

blush /blʌʃ/ *v.i.* rougir. ● *n.* rougeur *f.* **~er** *n.* blush *m.*

bluster /'blʌstə(r)/ *v.i.* (*wind*) faire rage; (*swagger*) fanfaronner. **~y** *a.* à bourrasques.

boar /bɔ:(r)/ *n.* sanglier *m.*

board /bɔ:d/ *n.* planche *f.*; (*for notices*) tableau *m.*; (*food*) pension *f.*; (*committee*) conseil *m.* ● *v.t./i.* (*bus, train*) monter dans; (*naut.*) monter à bord (de). **~ of directors**, conseil d'administration *m.* **go by the ~**, passer à l'as. **full ~**, pension complète *f.* **half ~**, demi-pension *f.* **on ~**, à bord. **~ up**, boucher. **~ with**, être en pension chez. **~er** *n.* pensionnaire *m./f.* **~ing-house** *n.* pension (de famille) *f.* **~ing-school** *n.* pensionnat *m.*, pension *f.*

boast /bəʊst/ *v.i.* se vanter (**about**, de). ● *v.t.* s'enorgueillir de. ● *n.* vantardise *f.* **~er** *n.* vantard(e) *m.* (*f.*). **~ful** *a.* vantard. **~fully** *adv.* en se vantant.

boat /bəʊt/ *n.* bateau *m.*; (*small*) canot *m.* **in the same ~**, logé à la même enseigne. **~ing** *n.* canotage *m.*

boatswain /'bəʊsn/ *n.* maître d'équipage *m.*

bob[1] /bɒb/ *v.i.* (*p.t.* **bobbed**). **~ up and down**, monter et descendre.

bob[2] /bɒb/ *n. invar.* (*sl.*) shilling *m.*

bobby /'bɒbɪ/ *n.* (*fam.*) flic *m.*

bobsleigh /ˈbɒbsleɪ/ *n.* bob-(sleigh) *m.*

bode /bəʊd/ *v.i.* **~ well/ill,** être de bon/mauvais augure.

bodily /ˈbɒdɪlɪ/ *a.* physique, corporel. ● *adv.* physiquement; (*in person*) en personne.

body /ˈbɒdɪ/ *n.* corps *m.*; (*mass*) masse *f.*; (*organization*) organisme *m.* **~(work),** (*auto.*) carrosserie *f.* **the main ~ of,** le gros de. **~-builder** *n.* culturiste *m./f.* **~-building** *n.* culturisme *m.*

bodyguard /ˈbɒdɪgɑːd/ *n.* garde du corps *m.*

bog /bɒg/ *n.* marécage *m.* ● *v.t.* (*p.t.* **bogged**). **get ~ged down,** s'embourber.

boggle /ˈbɒgl/ *v.i.* **the mind ~s,** on est stupéfait.

bogus /ˈbəʊgəs/ *a.* faux.

bogy /ˈbəʊgɪ/ *n.* (*annoyance*) embêtement *m.* **~(man),** croquemitaine *m.*

boil[1] /bɔɪl/ *n.* furoncle *m.*

boil[2] /bɔɪl/ *v.t./i.* (faire) bouillir. **bring to the ~,** porter à ébullition. **~ down to,** se ramener à. **~ over,** déborder. **~ing hot,** bouillant. **~ing point,** point d'ébullition *m.* **~ed** *a.* (*egg*) à la coque; (*potatoes*) à l'eau.

boiler /ˈbɔɪlə(r)/ *n.* chaudière *f.* **~ suit,** bleu (de travail) *m.*

boisterous /ˈbɔɪstərəs/ *a.* tapageur.

bold /bəʊld/ *a.* (**-er, -est**) hardi; (*cheeky*) effronté; (*type*) gras. **~ness** *n.* hardiesse *f.*

Bolivia /bəˈlɪvɪə/ *n.* Bolivie *f.* **~n** *a.* & *n.* bolivien(ne) (*m.* (*f.*)).

bollard /ˈbɒləd/ *n.* (*on road*) borne *f.*

bolster /ˈbəʊlstə(r)/ *n.* traversin *m.* ● *v.t.* soutenir.

bolt /bəʊlt/ *n.* verrou *m.*; (*for nut*) boulon *m.*; (*lightning*) éclair *m.* ● *v.t.* (*door etc.*) verrouiller; (*food*) engouffrer. ● *v.i.* se sauver. **~ upright,** tout droit.

bomb /bɒm/ *n.* bombe *f.* ● *v.t.* bombarder. **~ scare,** alerte à la bombe *f.* **~er** *n.* (*aircraft*) bombardier *m.*; (*person*) plastiqueur *m.*

bombard /bɒmˈbɑːd/ *v.t.* bombarder.

bombastic /bɒmˈbæstɪk/ *a.* grandiloquent.

bombshell /ˈbɒmʃel/ *n.* **be a ~,** tomber comme une bombe.

bona fide /bəʊnəˈfaɪdɪ/ *a.* de bonne foi.

bond /bɒnd/ *n.* (*agreement*) engagement *m.*; (*link*) lien *m.*; (*comm.*) obligation *f.*, bon *m.* **in ~,** (entreposé) en douane.

bondage /ˈbɒndɪdʒ/ *n.* esclavage *m.*

bone /bəʊn/ *n.* os *m.*; (*of fish*) arête *f.* ● *v.t.* désosser. **~-dry** *a.* tout à fait sec. **~ idle,** paresseux comme une couleuvre.

bonfire /ˈbɒnfaɪə(r)/ *n.* feu *m.*; (*for celebration*) feu de joie *m.*

bonnet /ˈbɒnɪt/ *n.* (*hat*) bonnet *m.*; (*of vehicle*) capot *m.*

bonus /ˈbəʊnəs/ *n.* prime *f.*

bony /ˈbəʊnɪ/ *a.* (**-ier, -iest**) (*thin*) osseux; (*meat*) plein d'os; (*fish*) plein d'arêtes.

boo /buː/ *int.* hou. ● *v.t./i.* huer. ● *n.* huée *f.*

boob /buːb/ *n.* (*blunder*: *sl.*) gaffe *f.* ● *v.i.* (*sl.*) gaffer.

booby-trap /ˈbuːbɪtræp/ *n.* engin piégé *m.* ● *v.t.* (*p.t.* **-trapped**) piéger.

book /bʊk/ *n.* livre *m.*; (*of tickets etc.*) carnet *m.* **~s,** (*comm.*) comptes *m. pl.* ● *v.t.* (*reserve*) réserver; (*driver*) dresser un P.V. à; (*player*) prendre le nom de; (*write down*) inscrire. ● *v.i.* retenir des places. **~able** *a.* qu'on peut retenir. **(fully) ~ed,** complet. **~ing office,** guichet *m.*

bookcase /ˈbʊkkeɪs/ *n.* bibliothèque *f.*

bookkeeping /ˈbʊkkiːpɪŋ/ *n.* comptabilité *f.*

booklet /ˈbʊklɪt/ *n.* brochure *f.*

bookmaker /ˈbʊkmeɪkə(r)/ *n.* bookmaker *m.*

bookseller /ˈbʊkselə(r)/ *n.* libraire *m./f.*

bookshop /ˈbʊkʃɒp/ *n.* librairie *f.*

bookstall /ˈbʊkstɔːl/ *n.* kiosque (à journaux) *m.*

boom /buːm/ *v.i.* (*gun, wind, etc.*) gronder; (*trade*) prospérer. ● *n.* grondement *m.*; (*comm.*) boom *m.*, prospérité *f.*

boon /buːn/ *n.* (*benefit*) aubaine *f.*

boost /buːst/ *v.t.* stimuler; (*morale*) 1remonter; (*price*) augmenter; (*publicize*) faire de la réclame pour. ● *n.* **give a ~ to,** = **boost.**

boot /buːt/ *n.* (*knee-length*); botte *f.*; (*ankle-length*) chaussure (montante) *f.*; (*for walking*) chaussure de marche *f.*; (*sport*) chaussure de sport *f.*; (*of vehicle*) coffre *m.*

● *v.t./i.* **~ up,** (*comput.*) démarrer, lancer (le programme). **get the ~,** (*sl.*) être mis à la porte.

booth /bu:ð/ *n.* (*for telephone*) cabine *f.*; (*at fair*) baraque *f.*

booty /'bu:tɪ/ *n.* butin *m.*

booze /bu:z/ *v.i.* (*fam.*) boire (beaucoup). ● *n.* (*fam.*) alcool *m.*; (*spree*) beuverie *f.*

border /'bɔ:də(r)/ *n.* (*edge*) bord *m.*; (*frontier*) frontière *f.*; (*in garden*) bordure *f.* ● *v.i.* **~ on,** (*be next to, come close to*) être voisin de, avoisiner.

borderline /'bɔ:dəlaɪn/ *n.* ligne de démarcation *f.* **~ case,** cas limite *m.*

bore[1] /bɔ:(r)/ *see* bear[2].

bore[2] /bɔ:(r)/ *v.t./i.* (*techn.*) forer.

bore[3] /bɔ:(r)/ *v.t.* ennuyer. ● *n.* raseu|r, -se *m., f.*; (*thing*) ennui *m.* **be ~d,** s'ennuyer. **~dom** *n.* ennui *m.* **boring** *a.* ennuyeux.

born /bɔ:n/ *a.* né. **be ~,** naître.

borne /bɔ:n/ *see* bear[2].

borough /'bʌrə/ *n.* municipalité *f.*

borrow /'bɒrəʊ/ *v.t.* emprunter (**from,** à). **~ing** *n.* emprunt *m.*

bosom /'bʊzəm/ *n.* sein *m.* **~ friend,** ami(e) intime *m.* (*f.*).

boss /bɒs/ *n.* (*fam.*) patron(ne) *m.* (*f.*) ● *v.t.* **~ (about),** (*fam.*) donner des ordres à, régenter.

bossy /'bɒsɪ/ *a.* autoritaire.

botan|y /'bɒtənɪ/ *n.* botanique *f.* **~ical** /bə'tænɪkl/ *a.* botanique. **~ist** *n.* botaniste *m./f.*

botch /bɒtʃ/ *v.t.* bâcler, saboter.

both /bəʊθ/ *a.* les deux. ● *pron.* tous *or* toutes (les) deux, l'un(e) et l'autre. ● *adv.* à la fois. **~ the books,** les deux livres. **we ~ agree,** nous sommes tous les deux d'accord. **I bought ~ (of them),** j'ai acheté les deux. **I saw ~ of you,** je vous ai vus tous les deux. **~ Paul and Anne,** (et) Paul et Anne.

bother /'bɒðə(r)/ *v.t.* (*annoy, worry*) ennuyer; (*disturb*) déranger. ● *v.i.* se déranger. ● *n.* ennui *m.*; (*effort*) peine *f.* **don't ~ (calling),** ce n'est pas la peine (d'appeler). **don't ~ about us,** ne t'inquiète pas pour nous. **I can't be ~ed,** j'ai la flemme. **it's no ~,** ce n'est rien.

bottle /'bɒtl/ *n.* bouteille *f.*; (*for baby*) biberon *m.* ● *v.t.* mettre en bouteille(s). **~ bank,** collecteur (de verre usagé) *m.* **~-opener** *n.* ouvre-bouteille(s) *m.* **~ up,** contenir.

bottleneck /'bɒtlnek/ *n.* (*traffic jam*) bouchon *m.*

bottom /'bɒtəm/ *n.* fond *m.*; (*of hill, page, etc.*) bas *m.*; (*buttocks*) derrière *m.* ● *a.* inférieur, du bas. **~less** *a.* insondable.

bough /baʊ/ *n.* rameau *m.*

bought /bɔ:t/ *see* buy.

boulder /'bəʊldə(r)/ *n.* rocher *m.*

boulevard /'bu:ləvɑ:d/ *n.* boulevard *m.*

bounce /baʊns/ *v.i.* rebondir; (*person*) faire des bonds, bondir; (*cheques*: *sl.*) être refusé. ● *v.t.* faire rebondir. ● *n.* rebond *m.*

bouncer /'baʊnsə(r)/ *n.* videur *m.*

bound[1] /baʊnd/ *v.i.* (*leap*) bondir. ● *n.* bond *m.*

bound[2] /baʊnd/ *see* bind. ● *a.* **be ~ for,** être en route pour, aller. vers. **~ to,** (*obliged*) obligé de; (*certain*) sûr de.

boundary /'baʊndrɪ/ *n.* limite *f.*

bound|s /baʊndz/ *n. pl.* limites *f. pl.* **out of ~s,** interdit. **~ed by,** limité par. **~less** *a.* sans bornes.

bouquet /bʊ'keɪ/ *n.* bouquet *m.*

bout /baʊt/ *n.* période *f.*; (*med.*) accès *m.*; (*boxing*) combat *m.*

boutique /bu:'ti:k/ *n.* boutique (de mode) *f.*

bow[1] /bəʊ/ *n.* (*weapon*) arc *m.*; (*mus.*) archet *m.*; (*knot*) nœud *m.* **~-legged** *a.* aux jambes arquées. **~-tie** *n.* nœud papillon *m.*

bow[2] /baʊ/ *n.* (*with head*) salut *m.*; (*with body*) révérence *f.* ● *v.t./i.* (s')incliner.

bow[3] /baʊ/ *n.* (*naut.*) proue *f.*

bowels /'baʊəlz/ *n. pl.* intestins *m. pl.*; (*fig.*) entrailles *f. pl.*

bowl[1] /bəʊl/ *n.* cuvette *f.*; (*for food*) bol *m.*; (*for soup etc.*) assiette creuse *f.*

bowl[2] /bəʊl/ *n.* (*ball*) boule *f.* ● *v.t./i.* (*cricket*) lancer. **~ over,** bouleverser. **~ing** *n.* jeu de boules *m.* **~ing-alley** *n.* bowling *m.*

bowler[1] /'bəʊlə(r)/ *n.* (*cricket*) lanceur *m.*

bowler[2] /'bəʊlə(r)/ *n.* **~ (hat),** (chapeau) melon *m.*

box[1] /bɒks/ *n.* boîte *f.*; (*cardboard*) carton *m.* (*theatre*) loge *f.* ● *v.t.* mettre en boîte. **the ~,** (*fam.*) la télé. **~ in,** enfermer. **~-office** *n.* bureau de location *m.* **Boxing Day,** le lendemain de Noël.

box[2] /bɒks/ *v.t./i.* (*sport*) boxer. **~ s.o.'s ears,** gifler qn. **~ing** *n.* boxe *f.*; *a.* de boxe.

boy /bɔɪ/ *n.* garçon *m.* **~-friend** *n.* (petit) ami *m.* **~hood** *n.* enfance *f.* **~ish** *a.* enfantin, de garçon.

boycott /ˈbɔɪkɒt/ *v.t.* boycotter. ● *n.* boycottage *m.*

bra /brɑː/ *n.* soutien-gorge *m.*

brace /breɪs/ *n.* (*fastener*) attache *f.*; (*dental*) appareil *m.*; (*for bit*) vilbrequin *m.* **~s,** (*for trousers*) bretelles *f. pl.* ● *v.t.* soutenir. **~ o.s.,** rassembler ses forces.

bracelet /ˈbreɪslɪt/ *n.* bracelet *m.*

bracing /ˈbreɪsɪŋ/ *a.* vivifiant.

bracken /ˈbrækən/ *n.* fougère *f.*

bracket /ˈbrækɪt/ *n.* (*for shelf etc.*) tasseau *m.*, support *m.*; (*group*) tranche *f.* **(round) ~,** (*printing sign*) parenthèse *f.* **(square) ~,** crochet *m.* ● *v.t.* (*p.t.* **bracketed**) mettre entre parenthèses *or* crochets.

brag /bræg/ *v.i.* (*p.t.* **bragged**) se vanter.

braid /breɪd/ *n.* (*trimming*) galon *m.*; (*of hair*) tresse *f.*

Braille /breɪl/ *n.* braille *m.*

brain /breɪn/ *n.* cerveau *m.* **~s,** (*fig.*) intelligence *f.* ● *v.t.* assommer. **~-child** *n.* invention personnelle *f.* **~-drain** *n.* exode des cerveaux *m.* **~less** *a.* stupide.

brainwash /ˈbreɪnwɒʃ/ *v.t.* faire un lavage de cerveau à.

brainwave /ˈbreɪnweɪv/ *n.* idée géniale *f.*, trouvaille *f.*

brainy /ˈbreɪnɪ/ *a.* (**-ier, -iest**) intelligent.

braise /breɪz/ *v.t.* braiser.

brake /breɪk/ *n.* (*auto & fig.*) frein *m.* ● *v.t./i.* freiner. **~ fluid,** liquide de frein *m.* **~ light,** feu de stop *m.* **~ lining,** garniture de frein *f.*

bramble /ˈbræmbl/ *n.* ronce *f.*

bran /bræn/ *n.* (*husks*) son *m.*

branch /brɑːntʃ/ *n.* branche *f.*; (*of road*) embranchement *m.*; (*comm.*) succursale *f.*; (*of bank*) agence *f.* ● *v.i.* **~ (off),** bifurquer.

brand /brænd/ *n.* marque *f.* ● *v.t.* **~ s.o. as,** donner à qn. la réputation de. **~-new** *a.* tout neuf.

brandish /ˈbrændɪʃ/ *v.t.* brandir.

brandy /ˈbrændɪ/ *n.* cognac *m.*

brash /bræʃ/ *a.* effronté.

brass /brɑːs/ *n.* cuivre *m.* **get down to ~ tacks,** en venir aux choses sérieuses. **the ~,** (*mus.*) les cuivres *m. pl.* **top ~,** (*sl.*) gros bonnets *m. pl.*

brassière /ˈbræsɪə(r), *Amer.* brəˈzɪər/ *n.* soutien-gorge *m.*

brat /bræt/ *n.* (*child: pej.*) môme *m./f.*; (*ill-behaved*) garnement *m.*

bravado /brəˈvɑːdəʊ/ *n.* bravade *f.*

brave /breɪv/ *a.* (**-er, -est**) courageux, brave. ● *n.* (*American Indian*) brave *m.* ● *v.t.* braver. **~ry** /-ərɪ/ *n.* courage *m.*

bravo /ˈbrɑːvəʊ/ *int.* bravo.

brawl /brɔːl/ *n.* bagarre *f.* ● *v.i.* se bagarrer.

brawn /brɔːn/ *n.* muscles *m. pl.* **~y** *a.* musclé.

bray /breɪ/ *n.* braiment *m.* ● *v.i.* braire.

brazen /ˈbreɪzn/ *a.* effronté.

brazier /ˈbreɪzɪə(r)/ *n.* brasero *m.*

Brazil /brəˈzɪl/ *n.* Brésil *m.* **~ian** *a.* & *n.* brésilien(ne) (*m.* (*f.*)).

breach /briːtʃ/ *n.* violation *f.*; (*of contract*) rupture *f.*; (*gap*) brèche *f.* ● *v.t.* ouvrir une brèche dans.

bread /bred/ *n.* pain *m.* **~ and butter,** tartine *f.* **~-bin,** (*Amer.*) **~-box** *ns.* boîte à pain *f.* **~-winner** *n.* soutien de famille *m.*

breadcrumbs /ˈbredkrʌmz/ *n. pl.* (*culin.*) chapelure *f.*

breadline /ˈbredlaɪn/ *n.* **on the ~,** dans l'indigence.

breadth /bretθ/ *n.* largeur *f.*

break /breɪk/ *v.t.* (*p.t.* **broke,** *p.p.* **broken**) casser; (*smash into pieces*) briser; (*vow, silence, rank, etc.*) rompre; (*law*) violer; (*a record*) battre; (*news*) révéler; (*journey*) interrompre; (*heart, strike, ice*) briser. ● *v.i.* (se) casser; se briser. ● *n.* cassure *f.*, rupture *f.*; (*in relationship, continuity*) rupture *f.*; (*interval*) interruption *f.*; (*at school*) récréation *f.*, récré *f.*; (*for coffee*) pause *f.*; (*luck: fam.*) chance *f.* **~ one's arm,** se casser le bras. **~ away from,** quitter. **~ down** *v.i.* (*collapse*) s'effondrer; (*fail*) échouer; (*machine*) tomber en panne; *v.t.* (*door*) enfoncer; (*analyse*) analyser. **~ even,** rentrer dans ses frais. **~-in** *n.* cambriolage *m.* **~ into,** cambrioler. **~ off,** (se) détacher; (*suspend*) rompre; (*stop talking*) s'interrompre. **~ out,** (*fire, war, etc.*) éclater. **~ up,** (*end*) (faire) cesser; (*couple*) rompre; (*marriage*) (se) briser; (*crowd*) (se) disperser; (*schools*) entrer en vacances. **~able** *a.* cassable. **~age** *n.* casse *f.*

breakdown /'breɪkdaʊn/ *n.* (*techn.*) panne *f.*; (*med.*) dépression *f.*; (*of figures*) analyse *f.* ● *a.* (*auto.*) de dépannage.

breaker /'breɪkə(r)/ *n.* (*wave*) brisant *m.*

breakfast /'brekfəst/ *n.* petit déjeuner *m.*

breakthrough /'breɪkθru:/ *n.* percée *f.*

breakwater /'breɪkwɔ:tə(r)/ *n.* brise-lames *m. invar.*

breast /brest/ *n.* sein *m.*; (*chest*) poitrine *f.* **~-feed** *v.t.* (*p.t.* **-fed**) allaiter. **~-stroke** *n.* brasse *f.*

breath /breθ/ *n.* souffle *m.*, haleine *f.* **out of ~,** essoufflé. **under one's ~,** tout bas. **~less** *a.* essouflé.

breathalyser /'breθəlaɪzə(r)/ *n.* alcootest *m.*

breath|e /bri:ð/ *v.t./i.* respirer. **~ in,** inspirer. **~ out,** expirer. **~ing** *n.* respiration *f.*

breather /'bri:ðə(r)/ *n.* moment de repos *m.*

breathtaking /'breθteɪkɪŋ/ *a.* à vous couper le souffle.

bred /bred/ *see* breed.

breeches /'brɪtʃɪz/ *n. pl.* culotte *f.*

breed /bri:d/ *v.t.* (*p.t.* **bred**) élever; (*give rise to*) engendrer. ● *v.i.* se reproduire. ● *n.* race *f.* **~er** *n.* éleveur *m.* **~ing** *n.* élevage *m.*; (*fig.*) éducation *f.*

breez|e /bri:z/ *n.* brise *f.* **~y** *a.* (*weather*) frais; (*cheerful*) jovial; (*casual*) désinvolte.

Breton /'bretn/ *a.* & *n.* breton(ne) (*m.* (*f.*)).

brevity /'brevətɪ/ *n.* brièveté *f.*

brew /bru:/ *v.t.* (*beer*) brasser; (*tea*) faire infuser. ● *v.i.* fermenter; infuser; (*fig.*) se préparer. ● *n.* décoction *f.* **~er** *n.* brasseur *m.* **~ery** *n.* brasserie *f.*

bribe /braɪb/ *n.* pot-de-vin *m.* ● *v.t.* soudoyer, acheter. **~ry** /-ərɪ/ *n.* corruption *f.*

brick /brɪk/ *n.* brique *f.*

bricklayer /'brɪkleɪə(r)/ *n.* maçon *m.*

bridal /'braɪdl/ *a.* nuptial.

bride /braɪd/ *n.* mariée *f.*

bridegroom /'braɪdgrʊm/ *n.* marié *m.*

bridesmaid /'braɪdzmeɪd/ *n.* demoiselle d'honneur *f.*

bridge[1] /brɪdʒ/ *n.* pont *m.*; (*naut.*) passerelle *f.*; (*of nose*) arête *f.* ● *v.t.* **~ a gap,** combler une lacune.

bridge[2] /brɪdʒ/ *n.* (*cards*) bridge *m.*

bridle /'braɪdl/ *n.* bride *f.* ● *v.t.* brider. **~-path** *n.* allée cavalière *f.*

brief[1] /bri:f/ *a.* (**-er, -est**) bref. **~ly** *adv.* brièvement. **~ness** *n.* brièveté *f.*

brief[2] /bri:f/ *n.* instructions *f. pl.*; (*jurid.*) dossier *m.* ● *v.t.* donner des instructions à. **~ing** *n.* briefing *m.*

briefcase /'bri:fkeɪs/ *n.* serviette *f.*

briefs /bri:fs/ *n. pl.* slip *m.*

brigad|e /brɪ'geɪd/ *n.* brigade *f.* **~ier** /-ə'dɪə(r)/ *n.* général de brigade *m.*

bright /braɪt/ *a.* (**-er, -est**) brillant, vif; (*day, room*) clair; (*cheerful*) gai; (*clever*) intelligent. **~ly** *adv.* brillamment. **~ness** *n.* éclat *m.*

brighten /'braɪtn/ *v.t.* égayer. ● *v.i.* (*weather*) s'éclaircir; (*of face*) s'éclairer.

brillian|t /'brɪljənt/ *a.* brillant; (*light*) éclatant; (*very good*: *fam.*) super. **~ce** *n.* éclat *m.*

brim /brɪm/ *n.* bord *m.* ● *v.i.* (*p.t.* **brimmed**). **~ over,** déborder.

brine /braɪn/ *n.* saumure *f.*

bring /brɪŋ/ *v.t.* (*p.t.* **brought**) (*thing*) apporter; (*person, vehicle*) amener. **~ about,** provoquer. **~ back,** rapporter; ramener. **~ down,** faire tomber; (*shoot down, knock down*) abattre. **~ forward,** avancer. **~ off,** réussir. **~ out,** (*take out*) sortir; (*show*) faire ressortir; (*book*) publier. **~ round** *or* **to,** ranimer. **~ to bear,** (*pressure etc.*) exercer. **~ up,** élever; (*med.*) vomir; (*question*) soulever.

brink /brɪŋk/ *n.* bord *m.*

brisk /brɪsk/ *a.* (**-er, -est**) vif. **~ness** *n.* vivacité *f.*

bristl|e /'brɪsl/ *n.* poil *m.* ● *v.i.* se hérisser. **~ing with,** hérissé de.

Britain /'brɪtn/ *n.* Grande-Bretagne *f.*

British /'brɪtɪʃ/ *a.* britannique. **the ~,** les Britanniques *m. pl.*

Briton /'brɪtn/ *n.* Britannique *m./f.*

Brittany /'brɪtənɪ/ *n.* Bretagne *f.*

brittle /'brɪtl/ *a.* fragile.

broach /brəʊtʃ/ *v.t.* entamer.

broad /brɔ:d/ *a.* (**-er, -est**) large; (*daylight, outline*) grand. **~ bean,** fève *f.* **~-minded** *a.* large d'esprit. **~ly** *adv.* en gros.

broadcast /'brɔ:dkɑ:st/ *v.t./i.* (*p.t.* **broadcast**) diffuser; (*person*) parler

à la télévision *or* à la radio. ● *n.* émission *f.*
broaden /ˈbrɔ:dn/ *v.t./i.* (s')élargir.
broccoli /ˈbrɒkəlɪ/ *n. invar.* brocoli *m.*
brochure /ˈbrəʊʃə(r)/ *n.* brochure *f.*
broke /brəʊk/ *see* break. ● *a.* (*penniless*: *sl.*) fauché.
broken /ˈbrəʊkən/ *see* break. ● *a.* ~ **English,** mauvais anglais *m.* ~-**hearted** *a.* au cœur brisé.
broker /ˈbrəʊkə(r)/ *n.* courtier *m.*
brolly /ˈbrɒlɪ/ *n.* (*fam.*) pépin *m.*
bronchitis /brɒŋˈkaɪtɪs/ *n.* bronchite *f.*
bronze /brɒnz/ *n.* bronze *m.* ● *v.t./i.* (se) bronzer.
brooch /brəʊtʃ/ *n.* broche *f.*
brood /bru:d/ *n.* nichée *f.*, couvée *f.* ● *v.i.* couver; (*fig.*) méditer tristement. ~**y** *a.* mélancolique.
brook[1] /brʊk/ *n.* ruisseau *m.*
brook[2] /brʊk/ *v.t.* souffrir.
broom /bru:m/ *n.* balai *m.*
broomstick /ˈbru:mstɪk/ *n.* manche à balai *m.*
broth /brɒθ/ *n.* bouillon *m.*
brothel /ˈbrɒθl/ *n.* maison close *f.*
brother /ˈbrʌðə(r)/ *n.* frère *m.* ~**hood** *n.* fraternité *f.* ~-**in-law** *n.* (*pl.* ~**s-in-law**) beau-frère *m.* ~**ly** *a.* fraternel.
brought /brɔ:t/ *see* bring.
brow /braʊ/ *n.* front *m.*; (*of hill*) sommet *m.*
browbeat /ˈbraʊbi:t/ *v.t.* (*p.t.* **-beat,** *p.p.* **-beaten**) intimider.
brown /braʊn/ *a.* (**-er, -est**) marron (*invar.*); (*cheveux*) brun. ● *n.* marron *m.*; brun *m.* ● *v.t./i.* brunir; (*culin.*) (faire) dorer. **be** ~**ed off,** (*sl.*) en avoir ras le bol. ~ **bread,** pain bis *m.* ~ **sugar,** cassonade *f.*
Brownie /ˈbraʊnɪ/ *n.* jeannette *f.*
browse /braʊz/ *v.i.* feuilleter; (*animal*) brouter.
bruise /bru:z/ *n.* bleu *m.* ● *v.t.* (*hurt*) faire un bleu à; (*fruit*) abîmer. ~**d** *a.* couvert de bleus.
brunch /brʌntʃ/ *n.* petit déjeuner copieux *m.* (*pris comme déjeuner*).
brunette /bru:ˈnet/ *n.* brunette *f.*
brunt /brʌnt/ *n.* **the** ~ **of,** le plus fort de.
brush /brʌʃ/ *n.* brosse *f.*; (*skirmish*) accrochage *m.*; (*bushes*) broussailles *f. pl.* ● *v.t.* brosser. ~ **against,** effleurer. ~ **aside,** écarter. **give s.o. the** ~-**off,** (*reject*: *fam.*) envoyer promener qn. ~ **up (on),** se remettre à.
Brussels /ˈbrʌslz/ *n.* Bruxelles *m./f.* ~ **sprouts,** choux de Bruxelles *m. pl.*
brutal /ˈbru:tl/ *a.* brutal. ~**ity** /-ˈtælətɪ/ *n.* brutalité *f.*
brute /bru:t/ *n.* brute *f.* **by** ~ **force,** par la force.
B.Sc. *abbr. see* Bachelor of Science.
bubble /ˈbʌbl/ *n.* bulle *f.* ● *v.i.* bouillonner. ~ **bath,** bain moussant *m.* ~ **over,** déborder.
buck[1] /bʌk/ *n.* mâle *m.* ● *v.i.* ruer. ~ **up,** (*sl.*) prendre courage; (*hurry*: *sl.*) se grouiller.
buck[2] /bʌk/ *n.* (*Amer., sl.*) dollar *m.*
buck[3] /bʌk/ *n.* **pass the** ~**,** rejeter la responsabilité (**to,** sur).
bucket /ˈbʌkɪt/ *n.* seau *m.* ~ **shop,** agence de charters *f.*
buckle /ˈbʌkl/ *n.* boucle *f.* ● *v.t./i.* (*fasten*) (se) boucler; (*bend*) voiler. ~ **down to,** s'atteler à.
bud /bʌd/ *n.* bourgeon *m.* ● *v.i.* (*p.t.* **budded**) bourgeonner.
Buddhis|t /ˈbʊdɪst/ *a. & n.* bouddhiste (*m./f.*) ~**m** /-ɪzəm/ *n.* bouddhisme *m.*
budding /ˈbʌdɪŋ/ *a.* (*talent etc.*) naissant; (*film star etc.*) en herbe.
buddy /ˈbʌdɪ/ *n.* (*fam.*) copain *m.*
budge /bʌdʒ/ *v.t./i.* (faire) bouger.
budgerigar /ˈbʌdʒərɪgɑ:(r)/ *n.* perruche *f.*
budget /ˈbʌdʒɪt/ *n.* budget *m.* ● *v.i.* (*p.t.* **budgeted**). ~ **for,** prévoir (dans son budget).
buff /bʌf/ *n.* (*colour*) chamois *m.*; (*fam.*) fanatique *m./f.*
buffalo /ˈbʌfələʊ/ *n.* (*pl.* **-oes** *or* **-o**) buffle *m.*; (*Amer.*) bison *m.*
buffer /ˈbʌfə(r)/ *n.* tampon *m.* ~ **zone,** zone tampon *f.*
buffet[1] /ˈbʊfeɪ/ *n.* (*meal, counter*) buffet *m.* ~ **car,** buffet *m.*
buffet[2] /ˈbʌfɪt/ *n.* (*blow*) soufflet *m.* ● *v.t.* (*p.t.* **buffeted**) souffleter.
buffoon /bəˈfu:n/ *n.* bouffon *m.*
bug /bʌg/ *n.* (*insect*) punaise *f.*; (*any small insect*) bestiole *f.*; (*germ*: *sl.*) microbe *m.*; (*device*: *sl.*) micro *m.*; (*defect*: *sl.*) défaut *m.* ● *v.t.* (*p.t.* **bugged**) mettre des micros dans; (*Amer., sl.*) embêter.
buggy /ˈbʌgɪ/ *n.* (*child's*) poussette *f.*
bugle /ˈbju:gl/ *n.* clairon *m.*
build /bɪld/ *v.t./i.* (*p.t.* **built**) bâtir, construire. ● *n.* carrure *f.* ~ **up,** (*increase*) augmenter, monter; (*ac-*

cumulate) (s')accumuler. **~-up** *n.* accumulation *f.*; (*fig.*) publicité *f.* **~er** *n.* entrepreneur *m.*; (*workman*) ouvrier *m.*

building /'bɪldɪŋ/ *n.* bâtiment *m.*; (*dwelling*) immeuble *m.* **~ society,** caisse d'épargne-logement *f.*

built /bɪlt/ *see* build. **~-in** *a.* encastré. **~-up area,** agglomération *f.*, zone urbanisée *f.*

bulb /bʌlb/ *n.* oignon *m.*; (*electr.*) ampoule *f.* **~ous** *a.* bulbeux.

Bulgaria /bʌl'geərɪə/ *n.* Bulgarie *f.* **~n** *a.* & *n.* bulgare (*m./f.*).

bulg|e /bʌldʒ/ *n.* renflement *m.* ● *v.i.* se renfler, être renflé. **be ~ing with,** être gonflé *or* bourré de.

bulimia /bju:'lɪmɪə/ *n.* boulimie *f.*

bulk /bʌlk/ *n.* grosseur *f.* **in ~,** en gros; (*loose*) en vrac. **the ~ of,** la majeure partie de. **~y** *a.* gros.

bull /bʊl/ *n.* taureau *m.* **~'s-eye** *n.* centre (de la cible) *m.*

bulldog /'bʊldɒg/ *n.* bouledogue *m.*

bulldoze /'bʊldəʊz/ *v.t.* raser au bulldozer. **~r** /-ə(r)/ *n.* bulldozer *m.*

bullet /'bʊlɪt/ *n.* balle *f.* **~-proof** *a.* pare-balles *invar.*; (*vehicle*) blindé.

bulletin /'bʊlətɪn/ *n.* bulletin *m.*

bullfight /'bʊlfaɪt/ *n.* corrida *f.* **~er** *n.* torero *m.*

bullion /'bʊljən/ *n.* or *or* argent en lingots *m.*

bullring /'bʊlrɪŋ/ *n.* arène *f.*

bully /'bʊlɪ/ *n.* brute *f.*; tyran *m.* ● *v.t.* (*treat badly*) brutaliser; (*persecute*) tyranniser; (*coerce*) forcer (**into,** à).

bum[1] /bʌm/ *n.* (*sl.*) derrière *m.*

bum[2] /bʌm/ *n.* (*Amer., sl.*) vagabond(e) *m.* (*f.*).

bumble-bee /'bʌmblbi:/ *n.* bourdon *m.*

bump /bʌmp/ *n.* choc *m.*; (*swelling*) bosse *f.* ● *v.t./i.* cogner, heurter. **~ along,** cahoter. **~ into,** (*hit*) rentrer dans; (*meet*) tomber sur. **~y** *a.* cahoteux.

bumper /'bʌmpə(r)/ *n.* pare-chocs *m. invar.* ● *a.* exceptionnel.

bumptious /'bʌmpʃəs/ *a.* prétentieux.

bun /bʌn/ *n.* (*cake*) petit pain au lait *m.*; (*hair*) chignon *m.*

bunch /bʌntʃ/ *n.* (*of flowers*) bouquet *m.*; (*of keys*) trousseau *m.*; (*of people*) groupe *m.*; (*of bananas*) régime *m.* **~ of grapes,** grappe de raisin *f.*

bundle /'bʌndl/ *n.* paquet *m.* ● *v.t.* mettre en paquet; (*push*) pousser.

bung /bʌŋ/ *n.* bonde *f.* ● *v.t.* boucher; (*throw*: *sl.*) flanquer.

bungalow /'bʌŋgələʊ/ *n.* bungalow *m.*

bungle /'bʌŋgl/ *v.t.* gâcher.

bunion /'bʌnjən/ *n.* (*med.*) oignon *m.*

bunk[1] /bʌŋk/ *n.* couchette *f.* **~-beds** *n. pl.* lits superposés *m. pl.*

bunk[2] /bʌŋk/ *n.* (*nonsense*: *sl.*) foutaise(s) *f.* (*pl.*).

bunker /'bʌŋkə(r)/ *n.* (*mil.*) bunker *m.*

bunny /'bʌnɪ/ *n.* (*children's use*) (Jeannot) lapin *m.*

buoy /bɔɪ/ *n.* bouée *f.* ● *v.t.* **~ up,** (*hearten*) soutenir, encourager.

buoyan|t /'bɔɪənt/ *a.* (*cheerful*) gai. **~cy** *n.* gaieté *f.*

burden /'bɜ:dn/ *n.* fardeau *m.* ● *v.t.* accabler. **~some** *a.* lourd.

bureau /'bjʊərəʊ/ *n.* (*pl.* **-eaux** /-əʊz/) bureau *m.*

bureaucracy /bjʊə'rɒkrəsɪ/ *n.* bureaucratie *f.*

bureaucrat /'bjʊərəkræt/ *n.* bureaucrate *m./f.* **~ic** /-'krætɪk/ *a.* bureaucratique.

burglar /'bɜ:glə(r)/ *n.* cambrioleur *m.* **~ize** *v.t.* (*Amer.*) cambrioler. **~ alarm,** alarme *f.* **~y** *n.* cambriolage *m.*

burgle /'bɜ:gl/ *v.t.* cambrioler.

Burgundy /'bɜ:gəndɪ/ *n.* (*wine*) bourgogne *m.*

burial /'berɪəl/ *n.* enterrement *m.*

burlesque /bɜ:'lesk/ *n.* (*imitation*) parodie *f.*

burly /'bɜ:lɪ/ *a.* (**-ier, -iest**) costaud, solidement charpenté.

Burm|a /'bɜ:mə/ *n.* Birmanie *f.* **~ese** /-'mi:z/ *a.* & *n.* birman(e) (*m.* (*f.*)).

burn /bɜ:n/ *v.t./i.* (*p.t.* **burned** *or* **burnt**) brûler. ● *n.* brûlure *f.* **~ down** *or* **be ~ed down,** être réduit en cendres. **~er** *n.* brûleur *m.* **~ing** *a.* (*fig.*) brûlant.

burnish /'bɜ:nɪʃ/ *v.t.* polir.

burnt /bɜ:nt/ *see* burn.

burp /bɜ:p/ *n.* (*fam.*) rot *m.* ● *v.i.* (*fam.*) roter.

burrow /'bʌrəʊ/ *n.* terrier *m.* ● *v.t.* creuser.

bursar /'bɜ:sə(r)/ *n.* économe *m./f.*

bursary /'bɜ:sərɪ/ *n.* bourse *f.*

burst /bɜ:st/ *v.t./i.* (*p.t.* **burst**) crever, (faire) éclater. ● *n.* explosion *f.*; (*of laughter*) éclat *m.*; (*surge*) élan *m.*

be ~ing with, déborder de. **~ into,** faire irruption dans. **~ into tears,** fondre en larmes. **~ out laughing,** éclater de rire. **~ pipe,** conduite qui a éclaté *f.*

bury /'berɪ/ *v.t.* (*person etc.*) enterrer; (*hide, cover*) enfouir; (*engross, thrust*) plonger.

bus /bʌs/ *n.* (*pl.* **buses**) (auto)bus *m.* ● *v.t.* transporter en bus. ● *v.i.* (*p.t.* **bussed**) prendre l'autobus. **~-stop** *n.* arrêt d'autobus *m.*

bush /bʊʃ/ *n.* buisson *m.*; (*land*) brousse *f.* **~y** *a.* broussailleux.

business /'bɪznɪs/ *n.* (*task, concern*) affaire *f.*; (*commerce*) affaires *f. pl.*; (*line of work*) métier *m.*; (*shop*) commerce *m.* **he has no ~ to,** il n'a pas le droit de. **mean ~,** être sérieux. **that's none of your ~!,** ça ne vous regarde pas! **~man,** homme d'affaires *m.*

businesslike /'bɪznɪslaɪk/ *a.* sérieux.

busker /'bʌskə(r)/ *n.* musicien(ne) des rues *m.* (*f.*).

bust[1] /bʌst/ *n.* buste *m.*; (*bosom*) poitrine *f.*

bust[2] /bʌst/ *v.t./i.* (*p.t.* **busted** *or* **bust**) (*burst*: *sl.*) crever; (*break*: *sl.*) (se) casser. ● *a.* (*broken, finished*: *sl.*) fichu. **~-up** *n.* (*sl.*) engueulade *f.* **go ~,** (*sl.*) faire faillite.

bustl|e /'bʌsl/ *v.i.* s'affairer. ● *n.* affairement *m.*, remue-ménage *m.* **~ing** *a.* (*place*) bruyant, animé.

bus|y /'bɪzɪ/ *a.* (**-ier, -iest**) occupé; (*street*) animé; (*day*) chargé. ● *v.t.* **~y o.s. with,** s'occuper à. **~ily** *adv.* activement.

busybody /'bɪzɪbɒdɪ/ *n.* **be a ~,** faire la mouche du coche.

but /bʌt, *unstressed* bət/ *conj.* mais. ● *prep.* sauf. ● *adv.* (*only*) seulement. **~ for,** sans. **nobody ~,** personne d'autre que. **nothing ~,** rien que.

butane /'bju:teɪn/ *n.* butane *m.*

butcher /'bʊtʃə(r)/ *n.* boucher *m.* ● *v.t.* massacrer. **~y** *n.* boucherie *f.*, massacre *m.*

butler /'bʌtlə(r)/ *n.* maître d'hôtel *m.*

butt /bʌt/ *n.* (*of gun*) crosse *f.*; (*of cigarette*) mégot *m.*; (*target*) cible *f.*; (*barrel*) tonneau; (*Amer., fam.*) derrière *m.* ● *v.i.* **~ in,** interrompre.

butter /'bʌtə(r)/ *n.* beurre *m.* ● *v.t.* beurrer. **~-bean** *n.* haricot blanc *m.* **~-fingers** *n.* maladroit(e) *m.* (*f.*).

buttercup /'bʌtəkʌp/ *n.* bouton-d'or *m.*

butterfly /'bʌtəflaɪ/ *n.* papillon *m.*

buttock /'bʌtək/ *n.* fesse *f.*

button /'bʌtn/ *n.* bouton *m.* ● *v.t./i.* **~ (up),** (se) boutonner.

buttonhole /'bʌtnhəʊl/ *n.* boutonnière *f.* ● *v.t.* accrocher.

buttress /'bʌtrɪs/ *n.* contrefort *m.* ● *v.t.* soutenir.

buxom /'bʌksəm/ *a.* bien en chair.

buy /baɪ/ *v.t.* (*p.t.* **bought**) acheter (**from,** à); (*believe*: *sl.*) croire, avaler. ● *n.* achat *m.* **~ sth for s.o.** acheter qch. à qn., prendre qch. pour qn. **~er** *n.* acheteu|r, -se *m., f.*

buzz /bʌz/ *n.* bourdonnement *m.* ● *v.i.* bourdonner. **~ off,** (*sl.*) ficher le camp. **~er** *n.* sonnerie *f.*

by /baɪ/ *prep.* par, de; (*near*) à côté de; (*before*) avant; (*means*) en, à, par. **by bike,** à vélo. **by car,** en auto. **by day,** de jour. **by the kilo,** au kilo. **by running**/*etc.*, en courant/*etc.* **by sea,** par mer. **by that time,** à ce moment-là. **~ the way,** à propos. ● *adv.* (*near*) tout près. **by and large,** dans l'ensemble. **by-election** *n.* élection partielle *f.* **~-law** *n.* arrêté *m.*; (*of club etc.*) statut *m.* **by o.s.,** tout seul. **~-product** *n.* sous-produit *m.*; (*fig.*) conséquence *f.* **by-road** *n.* chemin de traverse *m.*

bye(-bye) /baɪ('baɪ)/ *int.* (*fam.*) au revoir, salut.

bypass /'baɪpɑ:s/ *n.* (*auto.*) route qui contourne *f.*; (*med.*) pontage *m.* ● *v.t.* contourner.

bystander /'baɪstændə(r)/ *n.* specta|teur, -trice *m., f.*

byte /baɪt/ *n.* octet *m.*

byword /'baɪwɜ:d/ *n.* **be a ~ for,** être connu pour.

C

cab /kæb/ *n.* taxi *m.*; (*of lorry, train*) cabine *f.*

cabaret /'kæbəreɪ/ *n.* spectacle (de cabaret) *m.*

cabbage /'kæbɪdʒ/ *n.* chou *m.*

cabin /'kæbɪn/ *n.* (*hut*) cabane *f.*; (*in ship, aircraft*) cabine *f.*

cabinet /'kæbɪnɪt/ *n.* (petite) armoire *f.*, meuble de rangement *m.*; (*for* *filing*) classeur *m.* **C~,** (*pol.*) cabinet *m.* **~-maker** *n.* ébéniste *m.*

cable /'keɪbl/ *n.* câble *m.* ● *v.t.* câbler. **~-car** *n.* téléphérique *m.* **~ railway,** funiculaire *m.*

caboose /kə'bu:s/ *n.* (*rail., Amer.*) fourgon *m.*

cache /kæʃ/ *n.* (*place*) cachette *f.* **a ~ of arms,** des armes cachées.

cackle /'kækl/ *n.* caquet *m.* ● *v.i.* caqueter.

cactus /'kæktəs/ *n.* (*pl.* **-ti** /-taɪ/ *or* **-tuses**) cactus *m.*

caddie /'kædɪ/ *n.* (*golf*) caddie *m.*

caddy /'kædɪ/ *n.* boîte à thé *f.*

cadence /'keɪdns/ *n.* cadence *f.*

cadet /kə'det/ *n.* élève officier *m.*

cadge /kædʒ/ *v.t.* se fairer payer, écornifler. ● *v.i.* quémander. **~ money from,** taper. **~r** /-ə(r)/ *n.* écornifleu|r, -se *m., f.*

Caesarean /sɪ'zeərɪən/ *a.* **~ (section),** césarienne *f.*

café /'kæfeɪ/ *n.* café(-restaurant) *m.*

cafeteria /kæfɪ'tɪərɪə/ *n.* cafétéria *f.*

caffeine /'kæfi:n/ *n.* caféine *f.*

cage /keɪdʒ/ *n.* cage *f.* ● *v.t.* mettre en cage.

cagey /'keɪdʒɪ/ *a.* (*secretive: fam.*) peu communicatif.

cagoule /kə'gu:l/ *n.* K-way *n.* (P.).

Cairo /'kaɪərəʊ/ *n.* le Caire *m.*

cajole /kə'dʒəʊl/ *v.t.* **~ s.o. into doing,** faire l'enjoleur pour que qn. fasse.

cake /keɪk/ *n.* gâteau *m.* **~d** *a.* durci. **~d with,** raidi par.

calamit|y /kə'læmətɪ/ *n.* calamité *f.* **~ous** *a.* désastreux.

calcium /'kælsɪəm/ *n.* calcium *m.*

calculat|e /'kælkjʊleɪt/ *v.t./i.* calculer; (*Amer.*) supposer. **~ed** *a.* (*action*) délibéré. **~ing** *a.* calculateur. **~ion** /-'leɪʃn/ *n.* calcul *m.* **~or** *n.* calculatrice *f.*

calculus /'kælkjʊləs/ *n.* (*pl.* **-li** /-laɪ/ *or* **-luses**) calcul *m.*

calendar /'kælɪndə(r)/ *n.* calendrier *m.*

calf[1] /kɑ:f/ *n.* (*pl.* **calves**) (*young cow or bull*) veau *m.*

calf[2] /kɑ:f/ *n.* (*pl.* **calves**) (*of leg*) mollet *m.*

calibre /'kælɪbə(r)/ *n.* calibre *m.*

calico /'kælɪkəʊ/ *n.* calicot *m.*

call /kɔ:l/ *v.t./i.* appeler. **~ (in *or* round),** (*visit*) passer. ● *n.* appel *m.*; (*of bird*) cri *m.*; visite *f.* **be ~ed,** (*named*) s'appeler. **be on ~,** être de garde. **~ back,** rappeler; (*visit*) repasser. **~-box** *n.* cabine téléphonique *f.* **~ for,** (*require*) demander; (*fetch*) passer prendre. **~-girl** *n.* call-girl *f.* **~ off,** annuler. **~ out (to),** appeler. **~ on,** (*visit*) passer chez; (*appeal to*) faire appel à. **~ up,** appeler (au téléphone); (*mil.*) mobiliser, appeler. **~er** *n.* visiteu|r, -se *m., f.*; (*on phone*) personne qui appelle *f.* **~ing** *n.* vocation *f.*

callous /'kæləs/ *a.*, **~ly** *adv.* sans pitié. **~ness** *n.* manque de pitié *m.*

callow /'kæləʊ/ *a.* (**-er, -est**) inexpérimenté.

calm /kɑ:m/ *a.* (**-er, -est**) calme. ● *n.* calme *m.* ● *v.t./i.* **~ (down),** (se) calmer. **~ness** *n.* calme *m.*

calorie /'kælərɪ/ *n.* calorie *f.*

camber /'kæmbə(r)/ *n.* (*of road*) bombement *m.*

camcorder /'kæmkɔ:də(r)/ *n.* caméscope *m.*

came /keɪm/ *see* come.

camel /'kæml/ *n.* chameau *m.*

cameo /'kæmɪəʊ/ *n.* (*pl.* **-os**) camée *m.*

camera /'kæmərə/ *n.* appareil (-photo) *m.*; (*for moving pictures*) caméra *f.* **in ~,** à huis clos. **~man** *n.* (*pl.* **-men**) caméraman *m.*

camouflage /'kæməflɑ:ʒ/ *n.* camouflage *m.* ● *v.t.* camoufler.

camp[1] /kæmp/ *n.* camp *m.* ● *v.i.* camper. **~-bed** *n.* lit de camp *m.* **~er** *n.* campeu|r, -se *m., f.* **~er (-van),** camping-car *m.* **~ing** *n.* camping *m.*

camp[2] /kæmp/ *a.* (*mannered*) affecté; (*vulgar*) de mauvais goût.

campaign /kæm'peɪn/ *n.* campagne *f.* ● *v.i.* faire campagne.

campsite /'kæmpsaɪt/ *n.* (*for holidaymakers*) camping *m.*

campus /'kæmpəs/ *n.* (*pl.* **-puses**) campus *m.*

can[1] /kæn/ *n.* bidon *m.*; (*sealed container for food*) boîte *f.* ● *v.t.* (*p.t.* **canned**) mettre en boîte. **~ it!,** (*Amer., sl.*) ferme-la! **~ned music,** musique de fond enregistrée *f.* **~-opener** *n.* ouvre-boîte(s) *m.*

can[2] /kæn, *unstressed* kən/ *v. aux.* (*be able to*) pouvoir; (*know how to*) savoir.

Canad|a /'kænədə/ *n.* Canada *m.* **~ian** /kə'neɪdɪən/ *a. & n.* canadien(ne) (*m.* (*f.*)).

canal /kə'næl/ *n.* canal *m.*

canary /kə'neərɪ/ *n.* canari *m.*

cancel /'kænsl/ *v.t./i.* (*p.t.* **cancelled**) (*call off, revoke*) annuler; (*cross out*) barrer; (*a stamp*) oblitérer. **~ out,** (se) neutraliser. **~lation** /-ə'leɪʃn/ *n.* annulation *f.*; oblitération *f.*

cancer /'kænsə(r)/ *n.* cancer *m.* **~ous** *a.* cancéreux.

Cancer /'kænsə(r)/ *n.* le Cancer.

candid /'kændɪd/ *a.* franc. **~ness** *n.* franchise *f.*

candida|te /'kændɪdeɪt/ *n.* candidat(e) *m.* (*f.*). **~cy** /-əsɪ/ *n.* candidature *f.*

candle /'kændl/ *n.* bougie *f.*, chandelle *f.*; (*in church*) cierge *m.*

candlestick /'kændlstɪk/ *n.* bougeoir *m.*, chandelier *m.*

candour, (*Amer.*) **candor** /'kændə(r)/ *n.* franchise *f.*

candy /'kændɪ/ *n.* (*Amer.*) bonbon(s) *m.* (*pl.*) **~-floss** *n.* barbe à papa *f.*

cane /keɪn/ *n.* canne *f.*; (*for baskets*) rotin *m.*; (*for punishment: schol.*) baguette *f.*, bâton *m.* ● *v.t.* donner des coups de baguette *or* de bâton à, fustiger.

canine /'keɪnaɪn/ *a.* canin.

canister /'kænɪstə(r)/ *n.* boîte *f.*

cannabis /'kænəbɪs/ *n.* cannabis *m.*

cannibal /'kænɪbl/ *n.* cannibale *m./f.* **~ism** *n.* cannibalisme *m.*

cannon /'kænən/ *n.* (*pl.* **~** *or* **~s**) canon *m.* **~-ball** *n.* boulet de canon *m.*

cannot /'kænət/ = **can not.**

canny /'kænɪ/ *a.* rusé, madré.

canoe /kə'nu:/ *n.* (*sport*) canoë *m.*, kayak *m.* ● *v.i.* faire du canoë *or* du kayak. **~ist** *n.* canoéiste *m./f.*

canon /'kænən/ *n.* (*clergyman*) chanoine *m.*; (*rule*) canon *m.*

canonize /'kænənaɪz/ *v.t.* canoniser.

canopy /'kænəpɪ/ *n.* dais *m.*; (*over doorway*) marquise *f.*

can't /kɑ:nt/ = **can not.**

cantankerous /kæn'tæŋkərəs/ *a.* acariâtre, grincheux.

canteen /kæn'ti:n/ *n.* (*restaurant*) cantine *f.*; (*flask*) bidon *m.*

canter /'kæntə(r)/ *n.* petit galop *m.* ● *v.i.* aller au petit galop.

canvas /'kænvəs/ *n.* toile *f.*

canvass /'kænvəs/ *v.t./i.* (*comm., pol.*) solliciter des commandes *or* des voix (de). **~ing** *n.* (*comm.*) démarchage *m.*; (*pol.*) démarchage électoral *m.* **~ opinion,** sonder l'opinion.

canyon /'kænjən/ *n.* cañon *m.*

cap /kæp/ *n.* (*hat*) casquette *f.*; (*of bottle, tube*) bouchon *m.*; (*of beer or milk bottle*) capsule *f.*; (*of pen*) capuchon *m.*; (*for toy gun*) amorce *f.* ● *v.t.* (*p.t.* **capped**) (*bottle*) capsuler; (*outdo*) surpasser. **~ped with,** coiffé de.

capab|le /'keɪpəbl/ *a.* (*person*) capable (**of,** de), compétent. **be ~le of,** (*of situation, text, etc.*) être susceptible de. **~ility** /-'bɪlətɪ/ *n.* capacité *f.* **~ly** *adv.* avec compétence.

capacity /kə'pæsətɪ/ *n.* capacité *f.* **in one's ~ as,** en sa qualité de.

cape [1] /keɪp/ *n.* (*cloak*) cape *f.*

cape [2] /keɪp/ *n.* (*geog.*) cap *m.*

caper [1] /'keɪpə(r)/ *v.i.* gambader. ● *n.* (*prank*) farce *f.*; (*activity: sl.*) affaire *f.*

caper [2] /'keɪpə(r)/ *n.* (*culin.*) câpre *f.*

capital /'kæpɪtl/ *a.* capital. ● *n.* (*town*) capitale *f.*; (*money*) capital *m.* **~ (letter),** majuscule *f.*

capitalis|t /'kæpɪtəlɪst/ *a.* & *n.* capitaliste (*m./f.*). **~m** /-zəm/ *n.* capitalisme *m.*

capitalize /'kæpɪtəlaɪz/ *v.i.* **~ on,** tirer profit de.

capitulat|e /kə'pɪtʃʊleɪt/ *v.i.* capituler. **~ion** /-'leɪʃn/ *n.* capitulation *f.*

capricious /kə'prɪʃəs/ *a.* capricieux.

Capricorn /'kæprɪkɔ:n/ *n.* le Capricorne.

capsize /kæp'saɪz/ *v.t./i.* (faire) chavirer.

capsule /'kæpsju:l/ *n.* capsule *f.*

captain /'kæptɪn/ *n.* capitaine *m.*

caption /'kæpʃn/ *n.* (*for illustration*) légende *f.*; (*heading*) sous-titre *m.*

captivate /'kæptɪveɪt/ *v.t.* captiver.

captiv|e /'kæptɪv/ *a.* & *n.* capti|f, -ve (*m., f.*). **~ity** /-'tɪvətɪ/ *n.* captivité *f.*

capture /'kæptʃə(r)/ *v.t.* (*person, animal*) prendre, capturer; (*attention*) retenir. ● *n.* capture *f.*

car /kɑ:(r)/ *n.* voiture *f.* **~ ferry,** ferry *m.* **~-park** *n.* parking *m.* **~ phone,** téléphone de voiture *m.* **~-wash** *n.* station de lavage *f.*, lave-auto *m.*

carafe /kə'ræf/ *n.* carafe *f.*

caramel /'kærəmel/ *n.* caramel *m.*

carat /'kærət/ *n.* carat *m.*

caravan /'kærəvæn/ *n.* caravane *f.*

carbohydrate /kɑ:bəʊ'haɪdreɪt/ *n.* hydrate de carbone *m.*

carbon /'kɑ:bən/ *n.* carbone *m.* **~ copy, ~ paper,** carbone *m.*

carburettor, (*Amer.*) **carburetor** /kɑ:bjʊ'retə(r)/ *n.* carburateur *m.*
carcass /'kɑ:kəs/ *n.* carcasse *f.*
card /kɑ:d/ *n.* carte *f.* **~-index** *n.* fichier *m.*
cardboard /'kɑ:dbɔ:d/ *n.* carton *m.*
cardiac /'kɑ:dɪæk/ *a.* cardiaque.
cardigan /'kɑ:dɪgən/ *n.* cardigan *m.*
cardinal /'kɑ:dɪnl/ *a.* cardinal. ● *n.* (*relig.*) cardinal *m.*
care /keə(r)/ *n.* (*attention*) soin *m.*, attention *f.*; (*worry*) souci *m.*; (*protection*) garde *f.* ● *v.i.* **~ about,** s'intéresser à. **~ for,** s'occuper de; (*invalid*) soigner. **~ to** *or* **for,** aimer, vouloir. **I don't ~,** ça m'est égal. **take ~ of,** s'occuper de. **take ~ (of yourself),** prends soin de toi. **take ~ to do sth.,** faire bien attention à faire qch.
career /kə'rɪə(r)/ *n.* carrière *f.* ● *v.i.* aller à toute vitesse.
carefree /'keəfri:/ *a.* insouciant.
careful /'keəfl/ *a.* soigneux; (*cautious*) prudent. (**be**) **~!,** (fais) attention! **~ly** *adv.* avec soin.
careless /'keəlɪs/ *a.* négligent; (*work*) peu soigné. **~ about,** peu soucieux de. **~ly** *adv.* négligemment. **~ness** *n.* négligence *f.*
caress /kə'res/ *n.* caresse *f.* ● *v.t.* caresser.
caretaker /'keəteɪkə(r)/ *n.* gardien(ne) *m.* (*f.*). ● *a.* (*president*) par intérim.
cargo /'kɑ:gəʊ/ *n.* (*pl.* **-oes**) cargaison *f.* **~ boat,** cargo *m.*
Caribbean /kærɪ'bi:ən/ *a.* caraïbe. ● *n.* **the ~,** (*sea*) la mer des Caraïbes; (*islands*) les Antilles *f. pl.*
caricature /'kærɪkətjʊə(r)/ *n.* caricature *f.* ● *v.t.* caricaturer.
caring /'keərɪŋ/ *a.* (*mother, son, etc.*) aimant. ● *n.* affection *f.*
carnage /'kɑ:nɪdʒ/ *n.* carnage *m.*
carnal /'kɑ:nl/ *a.* charnel.
carnation /kɑ:'neɪʃn/ *n.* œillet *m.*
carnival /'kɑ:nɪvl/ *n.* carnaval *m.*
carol /'kærəl/ *n.* chant (de Noël) *m.*
carp [1] /kɑ:p/ *n. invar.* carpe *f.*
carp [2] /kɑ:p/ *v.i.* **~ (at),** critiquer.
carpent|er /'kɑ:pɪntə(r)/ *n.* charpentier *m.*; (*for light woodwork, furniture*) menuisier *m.* **~ry** *n.* charpenterie *f.*; menuiserie *f.*
carpet /'kɑ:pɪt/ *n.* tapis *m.* ● *v.t.* (*p.t.* **carpeted**) recouvrir d'un tapis. **~-sweeper** *n.* balai mécanique *m.* **on the ~,** (*fam.*) sur la sellette.
carriage /'kærɪdʒ/ *n.* (*rail & horse-drawn*) voiture *f.*; (*of goods*) transport *m.*; (*cost*) port *m.*
carriageway /'kærɪdʒweɪ/ *n.* chaussée *f.*
carrier /'kærɪə(r)/ *n.* transporteur *m.*; (*med.*) porteu|r, -se *m., f.* **~ (bag),** sac en plastique *m.*
carrot /'kærət/ *n.* carotte *f.*
carry /'kærɪ/ *v.t./i.* porter; (*goods*) transporter; (*involve*) comporter; (*motion*) voter. **be carried away,** s'emballer. **~-cot** *n.* porte-bébé *m.* **~ off,** enlever; (*prize*) remporter. **~ on,** continuer; (*behave*: *fam.*) se conduire (mal). **~ out,** (*an order, plan*) exécuter; (*duty*) accomplir; (*task*) effectuer.
cart /kɑ:t/ *n.* charrette *f.* ● *v.t.* transporter; (*heavy object*: *sl.*) trimballer.
cartilage /'kɑ:tɪlɪdʒ/ *n.* cartilage *m.*
carton /'kɑ:tn/ *n.* (*box*) carton *m.*; (*of yoghurt, cream*) pot *m.*; (*of cigarettes*) cartouche *f.*
cartoon /kɑ:'tu:n/ *n.* dessin (humoristique) *m.*; (*cinema*) dessin animé *m.* **~ist** *n.* dessina|teur, -trice *m., f.*
cartridge /'kɑ:trɪdʒ/ *n.* cartouche *f.*
carve /kɑ:v/ *v.t.* tailler; (*meat*) découper.
cascade /kæs'keɪd/ *n.* cascade *f.* ● *v.i.* tomber en cascade.
case [1] /keɪs/ *n.* cas *m.*; (*jurid.*) affaire *f.*; (*phil.*) arguments *m. pl.* **in ~ he comes,** au cas où il viendrait. **in ~ of fire,** en cas d'incendie. **in ~ of any problems,** au cas où il y aurait un problème. **in that ~,** à ce moment-là.
case [2] /keɪs/ *n.* (*crate*) caisse *f.*; (*for camera, cigarettes, spectacles, etc.*) étui *m.*; (*suitcase*) valise *f.*
cash /kæʃ/ *n.* argent *m.* ● *a.* (*price etc.*) (au) comptant. ● *v.t.* encaisser. **~ a cheque,** (*person*) encaisser un chèque; (*bank*) payer un chèque. **pay ~,** payer comptant. **in ~,** en espèces. **~ desk,** caisse *f.* **~ dispenser,** distributeur de billets *m.* **~-flow** *n.* cash-flow *m.* **~ in (on),** profiter (de). **~ register,** caisse enregistreuse *f.*
cashew /'kæʃu:/ *n.* noix de cajou *f.*
cashier /kæ'ʃɪə(r)/ *n.* caiss|ier, -ière *m., f.*
cashmere /'kæʃmɪə(r)/ *n.* cachemire *m.*
casino /kə'si:nəʊ/ *n.* (*pl.* **-os**) casino *m.*

cask /kɑ:sk/ *n.* tonneau *m.*
casket /'kɑ:skɪt/ *n.* (*box*) coffret *m.*; (*coffin*: *Amer.*) cercueil *m.*
casserole /'kæsərəʊl/ *n.* (*utensil*) cocotte *f.*; (*stew*) daube *f.*
cassette /kə'set/ *n.* cassette *f.*
cast /kɑ:st/ *v.t.* (*p.t.* **cast**) (*throw*) jeter; (*glance, look*) jeter; (*shadow*) projeter; (*vote*) donner; (*metal*) couler. **~ (off)**, (*shed*) se dépouiller de. ● *n.* (*theatre*) distribution *f.*; (*of dice*) coup *m.*; (*mould*) moule *m.*; (*med.*) plâtre *m.* **~ iron**, fonte *f.* **~-iron** *a.* de fonte; (*fig.*) solide. **~-offs** *n. pl.* vieux vêtements *m. pl.*
castanets /kæstə'nets/ *n. pl.* castagnettes *f. pl.*
castaway /'kɑ:stəweɪ/ *n.* naufragé(e) *m.* (*f.*).
caste /kɑ:st/ *n.* caste *f.*
castle /'kɑ:sl/ *n.* château *m.*; (*chess*) tour *f.*
castor /'kɑ:stə(r)/ *n.* (*wheel*) roulette *f.* **~ sugar**, sucre en poudre *m.*
castrat|e /kæ'streɪt/ *v.t.* châtrer. **~ion** /-ʃn/ *n.* castration *f.*
casual /'kæʒʊəl/ *a.* (*remark*) fait au hasard; (*meeting*) fortuit; (*attitude*) désinvolte; (*work*) temporaire; (*clothes*) sport *invar.* **~ly** *adv.* par hasard; (*carelessly*) avec désinvolture.
casualty /'kæʒʊəltɪ/ *n.* (*dead*) mort(e) *m.* (*f.*); (*injured*) blessé(e) *m.* (*f.*); (*accident victim*) accidenté(e) *m.* (*f.*).
cat /kæt/ *n.* chat *m.* **C~'s-eyes** *n. pl.* (P.) catadioptres *m. pl.*
catalogue /'kætəlɒg/ *n.* catalogue *m.* ● *v.t.* cataloguer.
catalyst /'kætəlɪst/ *n.* catalyseur *m.*
catapult /'kætəpʌlt/ *n.* lance-pierres *m. invar.* ● *v.t.* catapulter.
cataract /'kætərækt/ *n.* (*waterfall & med.*) cataracte *f.*
catarrh /kə'tɑ:(r)/ *n.* rhume *m.*, catarrhe *m.*
catastroph|e /kə'tæstrəfɪ/ *n.* catastrophe *f.* **~ic** /kætə'strɒfɪk/ *a.* catastrophique.
catch /kætʃ/ *v.t.* (*p.t.* **caught**) attraper; (*grab*) prendre, saisir; (*catch unawares*) surprendre; (*jam, trap*) prendre; (*understand*) saisir. ● *v.i.* prendre; (*get stuck*) se prendre (**in**, dans). ● *n.* capture *f.*, prise *f.*; (*on door*) loquet *m.*; (*fig.*) piège *m.* **~ fire**, prendre feu. **~ on**, (*fam.*) prendre, devenir populaire. **~ out**, prendre en faute. **~-phrase** *n.* slogan *m.* **~ sight of**, apercevoir. **~ s.o.'s eye**, attirer l'attention de qn. **~ up**, se rattraper. **~ up (with)**, rattraper.
catching /'kætʃɪŋ/ *a.* contagieux.
catchment /'kætʃmənt/ *n.* **~ area**, région desservie *f.*
catchy /'kætʃɪ/ *a.* facile à retenir.
categorical /kætɪ'gɒrɪkl/ *a.* catégorique.
category /'kætɪgərɪ/ *n.* catégorie *f.*
cater /'keɪtə(r)/ *v.i.* s'occuper de la nourriture. **~ for**, (*pander to*) satisfaire; (*of magazine etc.*) s'adresser à. **~er** *n.* traiteur *m.*
caterpillar /'kætəpɪlə(r)/ *n.* chenille *f.*
cathedral /kə'θi:drəl/ *n.* cathédrale *f.*
catholic /'kæθəlɪk/ *a.* universel. **C~** *a.* & *n.* catholique (*m./f.*). **C~ism** /kə'θɒlɪsɪzəm/ *n.* catholicisme *m.*
cattle /'kætl/ *n. pl.* bétail *m.*
catty /'kætɪ/ *a.* méchant.
caucus /'kɔ:kəs/ *n.* comité électoral *m.*
caught /kɔ:t/ *see* catch.
cauliflower /'kɒlɪflaʊə(r)/ *n.* chou-fleur *m.*
cause /kɔ:z/ *n.* cause *f.*; (*reason*) raison *f.*, motif *m.* ● *v.t.* causer. **~ sth. to grow/move/***etc.*, faire pousser/bouger/*etc.* qch.
causeway /'kɔ:zweɪ/ *n.* chaussée *f.*
cauti|on /'kɔ:ʃn/ *n.* prudence *f.*; (*warning*) avertissement *m.* ● *v.t.* avertir. **~ous** *a.* prudent. **~ously** *adv.* prudemment.
cavalier /kævə'lɪə(r)/ *a.* cavalier.
cavalry /'kævəlrɪ/ *n.* cavalerie *f.*
cave /keɪv/ *n.* caverne *f.*, grotte *f.* ● *v.i.* **~ in**, s'effondrer; (*agree*) céder.
caveman /'keɪvmæn/ *n.* (*pl.* **-men**) homme des cavernes *m.*
cavern /'kævən/ *n.* caverne *f.*
caviare, *Amer.* **caviar** /'kævɪɑ:(r)/ *n.* caviar *m.*
caving /'keɪvɪŋ/ *n.* spéléologie *f.*
cavity /'kævətɪ/ *n.* cavité *f.*
cavort /kə'vɔ:t/ *v.i.* gambader.
CD /si:'di:/ *n.* compact disc *m.*
cease /si:s/ *v.t./i.* cesser. **~-fire** *n.* cessez-le-feu *m. invar.* **~less** *a.* incessant.
cedar /'si:də(r)/ *n.* cèdre *m.*
cede /si:d/ *v.t.* céder.
cedilla /sɪ'dɪlə/ *n.* cédille *f.*
ceiling /'si:lɪŋ/ *n.* plafond *m.*
celebrat|e /'selɪbreɪt/ *v.t.* (*perform, glorify*) célébrer; (*event*) fêter,

célébrer. ● *v.i.* **we shall ~e,** on va fêter ça. **~ion** /-'breɪʃn/ *n.* fête *f.*
celebrated /'selɪbreɪtɪd/ *a.* célèbre.
celebrity /sɪ'lebrətɪ/ *n.* célébrité *f.*
celery /'selərɪ/ *n.* céleri *m.*
cell /sel/ *n.* cellule *f.*; (*electr.*) élément *m.*
cellar /'selə(r)/ *n.* cave *f.*
cell|o /'tʃeləʊ/ *n.* (*pl.* **-os**) violoncelle *m.* **~ist** *n.* violoncelliste *m./f.*
Cellophane /'seləfeɪn/ *n.* (P.) cellophane *f.* (P.).
Celt /kelt/ *n.* Celte *m./f.* **~ic** *a.* celtique, celte.
cement /sɪ'ment/ *n.* ciment *m.* ● *v.t.* cimenter. **~-mixer** *n.* bétonnière *f.*
cemetery /'semətrɪ/ *n.* cimetière *m.*
censor /'sensə(r)/ *n.* censeur *m.* ● *v.t.* censurer. **the ~,** la censure. **~ship** *n.* censure *f.*
censure /'senʃə(r)/ *n.* blâme *m.* ● *v.t.* blâmer.
census /'sensəs/ *n.* recensement *m.*
cent /sent/ *n.* (*coin*) cent *m.*
centenary /sen'ti:nərɪ, *Amer.* 'sentənərɪ/ *n.* centenaire *m.*
centigrade /'sentɪgreɪd/ *a.* centigrade.
centilitre, *Amer.* **centiliter** /'sentɪli:tə(r)/ *n.* centilitre *m.*
centimetre, *Amer.* **centimeter** /'sentɪmi:tə(r)/ *n.* centimètre *m.*
centipede /'sentɪpi:d/ *n.* millepattes *m. invar.*
central /'sentrəl/ *a.* central. **~ heating,** chauffage central *m.* **~ize** *v.t.* centraliser. **~ly** *adv.* (*situated*) au centre.
centre /'sentə(r)/ *n.* centre *m.* ● *v.t.* (*p.t.* **centred**) centrer. ● *v.i.* **~ on,** tourner autour de.
centrifugal /sen'trɪfjʊgl/ *a.* centrifuge.
century /'sentʃərɪ/ *n.* siècle *m.*
ceramic /sɪ'ræmɪk/ *a.* (*art*) céramique; (*object*) en céramique.
cereal /'sɪərɪəl/ *n.* céréale *f.*
cerebral /'serɪbrəl, *Amer.* sə'ri:brəl/ *a.* cérébral.
ceremonial /serɪ'məʊnɪəl/ *a.* de cérémonie. ● *n.* cérémonial *m.*
ceremon|y /'serɪmənɪ/ *n.* cérémonie *f.* **~ious** /-'məʊnɪəs/ *a.* solennel.
certain /'sɜ:tn/ *a.* certain. **for ~,** avec certitude. **make ~ of,** s'assurer de. **~ly** *adv.* certainement. **~ty** *n.* certitude *f.*
certificate /sə'tɪfɪkət/ *n.* certificat *m.*
certify /'sɜ:tɪfaɪ/ *v.t.* certifier.
cervical /sɜ:'vaɪkl/ *a.* cervical.
cessation /se'seɪʃn/ *n.* cessation *f.*
cesspit, cesspool /'sespɪt, 'sespu:l/ *ns.* fosse d'aisances *f.*
chafe /tʃeɪf/ *v.t.* frotter (contre).
chaff /tʃɑ:f/ *v.t.* taquiner.
chaffinch /'tʃæfɪntʃ/ *n.* pinson *m.*
chagrin /'ʃægrɪn/ *n.* vif dépit *m.*
chain /tʃeɪn/ *n.* chaîne *f.* ● *v.t.* enchaîner. **~ reaction,** réaction en chaîne *f.* **~-smoke** *v.i.* fumer de manière ininterrompue. **~ store,** magasin à succursales multiples *m.*
chair /tʃeə(r)/ *n.* chaise *f.*; (*armchair*) fauteuil *m.*; (*univ.*) chaire *f.* ● *v.t.* (*preside over*) présider.
chairman /'tʃeəmən/ *n.* (*pl.* **-men**) président(e) *m.* (*f.*).
chalet /'ʃæleɪ/ *n.* chalet *m.*
chalk /tʃɔ:k/ *n.* craie *f.* **~y** *a.* crayeux.
challeng|e /'tʃælɪndʒ/ *n.* défi *m.*; (*task*) gageure *f.* ● *v.t.* (*summon*) défier (**to do,** de faire); (*question truth of*) contester. **~er** *n.* (*sport*) challenger *m.* **~ing** *a.* stimulant.
chamber /'tʃeɪmbə(r)/ *n.* (*old use*) chambre *f.* **~ music,** musique de chambre *f.* **~-pot** *n.* pot de chambre *m.*
chambermaid /'tʃeɪmbəmeɪd/ *n.* femme de chambre *f.*
chamois /'ʃæmɪ/ *n.* **~(-leather),** peau de chamois *f.*
champagne /ʃæm'peɪn/ *n.* champagne *m.*
champion /'tʃæmpɪən/ *n.* champion(ne) *m.* (*f.*). ● *v.t.* défendre. **~ship** *n.* championnat *m.*
chance /tʃɑ:ns/ *n.* (*luck*) hasard *m.*; (*opportunity*) occasion *f.*; (*likelihood*) chances *f. pl.*; (*risk*) risque *m.* ● *a.* fortuit. ● *v.t.* **~ doing,** prendre le risque de faire. **~ it,** risquer le coup. **by ~,** par hasard. **by any ~,** par hasard. **~s are that,** il est probable que.
chancellor /'tʃɑ:nsələ(r)/ *n.* chancelier *m.* **C~ of the Exchequer,** Chancelier de l'Échiquier.
chancy /'tʃɑ:nsɪ/ *a.* risqué.
chandelier /ʃændə'lɪə(r)/ *n.* lustre *m.*
change /tʃeɪndʒ/ *v.t.* (*alter*) changer; (*exchange*) échanger (**for,** contre); (*money*) changer. **~ trains/one's dress/***etc.*, (*by substitution*) changer de train/de robe/*etc.* ● *v.i.* changer; (*change clothes*) se changer. ● *n.* changement *m.*; (*money*) monnaie *f.* **a ~ for the better,** une

amélioration. **a ~ for the worse,** un changement en pire. **~ into,** se transformer en; (*clothes*) mettre. **a ~ of clothes,** des vêtements de rechange. **~ one's mind,** changer d'avis. **~ over,** passer (**to,** à). **for a ~,** pour changer. **~-over** *n.* passage *m.* **~able** *a.* changeant; (*weather*) variable. **~ing** *a.* changeant. **~-ing room,** (*in shop*) cabine d'essayage *f.*; (*sport.*) vestiaire *m.*

channel /'tʃænl/ *n.* chenal *m.*; (*TV*) chaîne *f.*; (*medium, agency*) canal *m.*; (*groove*) rainure *f.* ● *v.t.* (*p.t.* **channelled**) (*direct*) canaliser. **the (English) C~,** la Manche. **the C~ Islands,** les îles anglo-normandes *f. pl.*

chant /tʃɑ:nt/ *n.* (*relig.*) psalmodie *f.*; (*of demonstrators*) chant (scandé) *m.* ● *v.t./i.* psalmodier; scander (des slogans).

chao|s /'keɪɒs/ *n.* chaos *m.* **~tic** /-'ɒtɪk/ *a.* chaotique.

chap /tʃæp/ *n.* (*man*: *fam.*) type *m.*

chapel /'tʃæpl/ *n.* chapelle *f.*; (*Nonconformist*) église (non-conformiste) *f.*

chaperon /'ʃæpərəʊn/ *n.* chaperon *m.* ● *v.t.* chaperonner.

chaplain /'tʃæplɪn/ *n.* aumônier *m.*

chapped /tʃæpt/ *a.* gercé.

chapter /'tʃæptə(r)/ *n.* chapitre *m.*

char[1] /tʃɑ:(r)/ *n.* (*fam.*) femme de ménage *f.*

char[2] /tʃɑ:(r)/ *v.t.* (*p.t.* **charred**) carboniser.

character /'kærəktə(r)/ *n.* caractère *m.*; (*in novel, play*) personnage *m.* **of good ~,** de bonne réputation. **~ize** *v.t.* caractériser.

characteristic /kærəktə'rɪstɪk/ *a.* & *n.* caractéristique (*f.*). **~ally** *adv.* typiquement.

charade /ʃə'rɑ:d/ *n.* charade *f.*

charcoal /'tʃɑ:kəʊl/ *n.* charbon (de bois) *m.*

charge /tʃɑ:dʒ/ *n.* prix *m.*; (*mil.*) charge *f.*; (*jurid.*) inculpation *f.*, accusation *f.*; (*task, custody*) charge *f.* **~s,** frais *m. pl.* ● *v.t.* faire payer; (*ask*) demander (**for,** pour); (*enemy, gun*) charger; (*jurid.*) inculper, accuser (**with,** de). ● *v.i.* foncer, se précipiter. **~ card,** carte d'achat *f.* **~ it to my account,** mettez-le sur mon compte. **in ~ of,** responsable de. **take ~ of,** prendre en charge, se charger de. **~able to,** (*comm.*) aux frais de.

charisma /kə'rɪzmə/ *n.* magnétisme *m.* **~tic** /kærɪz'mætɪk/ *a.* charismatique.

charit|y /'tʃærətɪ/ *n.* charité *f.*; (*society*) fondation charitable *f.* **~able** *a.* charitable.

charlatan /'ʃɑ:lətən/ *n.* charlatan *m.*

charm /tʃɑ:m/ *n.* charme *m.*; (*trinket*) amulette *f.* ● *v.t.* charmer. **~ing** *a.* charmant.

chart /tʃɑ:t/ *n.* (*naut.*) carte (marine) *f.*; (*table*) tableau *m.*, graphique *m.* ● *v.t.* (*route*) porter sur la carte.

charter /'tʃɑ:tə(r)/ *n.* charte *f.* **~ (flight),** charter *m.* ● *v.t.* affréter. **~ed accountant,** expert-comptable *m.*

charwoman /'tʃɑ:wʊmən/ *n.* (*pl.* **-women**) femme de ménage *f.*

chase /tʃeɪs/ *v.t.* poursuivre. ● *v.i.* courir (**after,** après). ● *n.* chasse *f.* **~ away** *or* **off,** chasser.

chasm /'kæzəm/ *n.* abîme *m.*

chassis /'ʃæsɪ/ *n.* châssis *m.*

chaste /tʃeɪst/ *a.* chaste.

chastise /tʃæ'staɪz/ *v.t.* châtier.

chastity /'tʃæstətɪ/ *n.* chasteté *f.*

chat /tʃæt/ *n.* causette *f.* ● *v.i.* (*p.t.* **chatted**) bavarder. **have a ~,** bavarder. **~ show,** talk-show *m.* **~ up,** (*fam.*) draguer. **~ty** *a.* bavard.

chatter /'tʃætə(r)/ *n.* bavardage *m.* ● *v.i.* bavarder. **his teeth are ~ing,** il claque des dents.

chatterbox /'tʃætəbɒks/ *n.* bavard(e) *m.* (*f.*).

chauffeur /'ʃəʊfə(r)/ *n.* chauffeur (de particulier) *m.*

chauvinis|t /'ʃəʊvɪnɪst/ *n.* chauvin(e) *m.* (*f.*). **male ~t,** (*pej.*) phallocrate *m.* **~m** /-zəm/ *n.* chauvinisme *m.*

cheap /tʃi:p/ *a.* (**-er, -est**) bon marché *invar.*; (*fare, rate*) réduit; (*worthless*) sans valeur. **~er,** meilleur marché *invar.* **~(ly)** *adv.* à bon marché. **~ness** *n.* bas prix *m.*

cheapen /'tʃi:pən/ *v.t.* déprécier.

cheat /'tʃi:t/ *v.i.* tricher; (*by fraud*) frauder. ● *v.t.* (*defraud*) frauder; (*deceive*) tromper. ● *n.* escroc *m.*

check[1] /tʃek/ *v.t./i.* vérifier; (*tickets*) contrôler; (*stop*) enrayer, arrêter; (*restrain*) contenir; (*rebuke*) réprimander; (*tick off*: *Amer.*) cocher. ● *n.* vérification *f.*; contrôle *m.*; (*curb*) frein *m.*; (*chess*) échec *m.*; (*bill*: *Amer.*) addition *f.*; (*cheque*:

Amer.) chèque *m.* **~ in,** signer le registre; (*at airport*) passer à l'enregistrement. **~-in** *n.* enregistrement *m.* **~-list** *n.* liste récapitulative *f.* **~ out,** régler sa note. **~-out** *n.* caisse *f.* **~-point** *n.* contrôle *m.* **~ up,** vérifier. **~ up on,** (*detail*) vérifier; (*situation*) s'informer sur. **~-up** *n.* examen médical *m.*

check[2] /tʃek/ *n.* (*pattern*) carreaux *m. pl.* **~ed** *a.* à carreaux.

checking /'tʃekɪŋ/ *a.* **~ account,** (*Amer.*) compte courant *m.*

checkmate /'tʃekmeɪt/ *n.* échec et mat *m.*

checkroom /'tʃekrʊm/ *n.* (*Amer.*) vestiaire *m.*

cheek /tʃi:k/ *n.* joue *f.*; (*impudence*) culot *m.* **~y** *a.* effronté.

cheer /tʃɪə(r)/ *n.* gaieté *f.* **~s,** acclamations *f. pl.*; (*when drinking*) à votre santé. ● *v.t.* acclamer, applaudir. **~ (up),** (*gladden*) remonter le moral à. **~ up,** prendre courage. **~ful** à gai. **~fulness** *n.* gaieté *f.*

cheerio /tʃɪərɪ'əʊ/ *int.* (*fam.*) salut.

cheese /tʃi:z/ *n.* fromage *m.*

cheetah /'tʃi:tə/ *n.* guépard *m.*

chef /ʃef/ *n.* (*cook*) chef *m.*

chemical /'kemɪkl/ *a.* chimique. ● *n.* produit chimique *m.*

chemist /'kemɪst/ *n.* pharmacien(ne) *m.* (*f.*); (*scientist*) chimiste *m./f.* **~'s shop,** pharmacie *f.* **~ry** *n.* chimie *f.*

cheque /tʃek/ *n.* chèque *m.* **~-book** *n.* chéquier *m.* **~ card,** carte bancaire *f.*

chequered /'tʃekəd/ *a.* (*pattern*) à carreaux; (*fig.*) mouvementé.

cherish /'tʃerɪʃ/ *v.t.* chérir; (*hope*) nourrir, caresser.

cherry /'tʃerɪ/ *n.* cerise *f.*

chess /tʃes/ *n.* échecs *m. pl.* **~-board** *n.* échiquier *m.*

chest /tʃest/ *n.* (*anat.*) poitrine *f.*; (*box*) coffre *m.* **~ of drawers,** commode *f.*

chestnut /'tʃesnʌt/ *n.* châtaigne *f.*; (*edible*) marron *m.*, châtaigne *f.*

chew /tʃu:/ *v.t.* mâcher. **~ing-gum** *n.* chewing-gum *m.*

chic /ʃi:k/ *a.* chic *invar.*

chick /tʃɪk/ *n.* poussin *m.*

chicken /'tʃɪkɪn/ *n.* poulet *m.* ● *a.* (*sl.*) froussard. ● *v.i.* **~ out,** (*sl.*) se dégonfler. **~-pox** *n.* varicelle *f.*

chick-pea /'tʃɪkpi:/ *n.* pois chiche *m.*

chicory /'tʃɪkərɪ/ *n.* (*for salad*) endive *f.*; (*in coffee*) chicorée *f.*

chief /tʃi:f/ *n.* chef *m.* ● *a.* principal. **~ly** *adv.* principalement.

chilblain /'tʃɪlbleɪn/ *n.* engelure *f.*

child /tʃaɪld/ *n.* (*pl.* **children** /'tʃɪldrən/) enfant *m./f.* **~hood** *n.* enfance *f.* **~ish** *a.* enfantin. **~less** *a.* sans enfants. **~like** *a.* innocent, candide. **~-minder** *n.* nourrice *f.*

childbirth /'tʃaɪldbɜ:θ/ *n.* accouchement *m.*

Chile /'tʃɪlɪ/ *n.* Chili *m.* **~an** *a.* & *n.* chilien(ne) (*m.* (*f.*)).

chill /tʃɪl/ *n.* froid *m.*; (*med.*) refroidissement *m.* ● *a.* froid. ● *v.t.* (*person*) donner froid à; (*wine*) rafraîchir; (*food*) mettre au frais. **~y** *a.* froid; (*sensitive to cold*) frileux. **be** *or* **feel ~y,** avoir froid.

chilli /'tʃɪlɪ/ *n.* (*pl.* **-ies**) piment *m.*

chime /tʃaɪm/ *n.* carillon *m.* ● *v.t./i.* carillonner.

chimney /'tʃɪmnɪ/ *n.* cheminée *f.* **~-sweep** *n.* ramoneur *m.*

chimpanzee /tʃɪmpæn'zi:/ *n.* chimpanzé *m.*

chin /tʃɪn/ *n.* menton *m.*

china /'tʃaɪnə/ *n.* porcelaine *f.*

Chin|a /'tʃaɪnə/ *n.* Chine *f.* **~ese** /-'ni:z/ *a.* & *n.* chinois(e) (*m.* (*f.*)).

chink[1] /tʃɪŋk/ *n.* (*slit*) fente *f.*

chink[2] /tʃɪŋk/ *n.* tintement *m.* ● *v.t./i.* (faire) tinter.

chip /tʃɪp/ *n.* (*on plate etc.*) ébréchure *f.*; (*piece*) éclat *m.*; (*of wood*) copeau *m.*; (*culin.*) frite *f.*; (*microchip*) microplaquette *f.*, puce *f.* ● *v.t./i.* (*p.t.* **chipped**) (s')ébrécher. **~ in,** (*fam.*) dire son mot; (*with money*: *fam.*) contribuer. **(potato) ~s,** (*Amer.*) chips *f. pl.*

chipboard /'tʃɪpbɔ:d/ *n.* aggloméré *m.*

chiropodist /kɪ'rɒpədɪst/ *n.* pédicure *m./f.*

chirp /tʃɜ:p/ *n.* pépiement *m.* ● *v.i.* pépier.

chirpy /'tʃɜ:pɪ/ *a.* gai.

chisel /'tʃɪzl/ *n.* ciseau *m.* ● *v.t.* (*p.t.* **chiselled**) ciseler.

chit /tʃɪt/ *n.* note *f.*, mot *m.*

chit-chat /'tʃɪttʃæt/ *n.* bavardage *m.*

chivalr|y /'ʃɪvlrɪ/ *n.* galanterie *f.* **~ous** *a.* chevaleresque.

chives /tʃaɪvz/ *n. pl.* ciboulette *f.*

chlorine /'klɔ:ri:n/ *n.* chlore *m.*

choc-ice /'tʃɒkaɪs/ *n.* esquimau *m.*

chock /tʃɒk/ *n.* cale *f.* **~-a-block, ~-full** *adjs.* archiplein.
chocolate /'tʃɒklət/ *n.* chocolat *m.*
choice /tʃɔɪs/ *n.* choix *m.* ● *a.* de choix.
choir /'kwaɪə(r)/ *n.* chœur *m.*
choirboy /'kwaɪəbɔɪ/ *n.* jeune choriste *m.*
choke /tʃəʊk/ *v.t./i.* (s')étrangler. ● *n.* starter *m.* **~ (up),** boucher.
cholera /'kɒlərə/ *n.* choléra *m.*
cholesterol /kə'lestərɒl/ *n.* cholestérol *m.*
choose /tʃu:z/ *v.t./i.* (*p.t.* **chose,** *p.p.* **chosen**) choisir. **~ to do,** décider de faire.
choosy /'tʃu:zɪ/ *a.* (*fam.*) exigeant.
chop /tʃɒp/ *v.t./i.* (*p.t.* **chopped**) (*wood*) couper (à la hache); (*food*) hacher. ● *n.* (*meat*) côtelette *f.* **~ down,** abattre. **~per** *n.* hachoir *m.*; (*sl.*) hélicoptère *m.* **~ping-board** *n.* planche à découper *f.*
choppy /'tʃɒpɪ/ *a.* (*sea*) agité.
chopstick /'tʃɒpstɪk/ *n.* baguette *f.*
choral /'kɔ:rəl/ *a.* choral.
chord /kɔ:d/ *n.* (*mus.*) accord *m.*
chore /tʃɔ:(r)/ *n.* travail (routinier) *m.*; (*unpleasant task*) corvée *f.*
choreography /kɒrɪ'ɒgrəfɪ/ *n.* chorégraphie *f.*
chortle /'tʃɔ:tl/ *n.* gloussement *m.* ● *v.i.* glousser.
chorus /'kɔ:rəs/ *n.* chœur *m.*; (*of song*) refrain *m.*
chose, chosen /tʃəʊz, 'tʃəʊzn/ *see* choose.
Christ /kraɪst/ *n.* le Christ.
christen /'krɪsn/ *v.t.* baptiser. **~ing** *n.* baptême *m.*
Christian /'krɪstʃən/ *a.* & *n.* chrétien(ne) (*m.* (*f.*)). **~ name,** prénom *m.* **~ity** /-stɪ'ænətɪ/ *n.* christianisme *m.*
Christmas /'krɪsməs/ *n.* Noël *m.* ● *a.* (*card, tree, etc.*) de Noël. **~-box** *n.* étrennes *f. pl.* **~ Day/Eve,** le jour/la veille de Noël.
chrome /krəʊm/ *n.* chrome *m.*
chromium /'krəʊmɪəm/ *n.* chrome *m.*
chromosome /'krəʊməsəʊm/ *n.* chromosome *m.*
chronic /'krɒnɪk/ *a.* (*situation, disease*) chronique; (*bad: fam.*) affreux.
chronicle /'krɒnɪkl/ *n.* chronique *f.*
chronolog|y /krə'nɒlədʒɪ/ *n.* chronologie *f.* **~ical** /krɒnə'lɒdʒɪkl/ *a.* chronologique.
chrysanthemum /krɪ'sænθəməm/ *n.* chrysanthème *m.*
chubby /'tʃʌbɪ/ *a.* (**-ier, -iest**) dodu, potelé.
chuck /tʃʌk/ *v.t.* (*fam.*) lancer. **~ away** *or* **out,** (*fam.*) balancer.
chuckle /'tʃʌkl/ *n.* gloussement *m.* ● *v.i.* glousser, rire.
chuffed /tʃʌft/ *a.* (*sl.*) bien content.
chum /tʃʌm/ *n.* cop|ain, -ine *m.*, *f.* **~my** *a.* amical. **~my with,** copain avec.
chunk /tʃʌŋk/ *n.* (gros) morceau *m.*
chunky /'tʃʌŋkɪ/ *a.* trapu.
church /'tʃɜ:tʃ/ *n.* église *f.*
churchyard /'tʃɜ:tʃjɑ:d/ *n.* cimetière *m.*
churlish /'tʃɜ:lɪʃ/ *a.* grossier.
churn /'tʃɜ:n/ *n.* baratte *f.*; (*milk-can*) bidon *m.* ● *v.t.* baratter. **~ out,** produire (en série).
chute /ʃu:t/ *n.* glissière *f.*; (*for rubbish*) vide-ordures *m. invar.*
chutney /'tʃʌtnɪ/ *n.* condiment (de fruits) *m.*
cider /'saɪdə(r)/ *n.* cidre *m.*
cigar /sɪ'gɑ:(r)/ *n.* cigare *m.*
cigarette /sɪgə'ret/ *n.* cigarette *f.* **~ end,** mégot *m.* **~-holder** *n.* fume-cigarette *m. invar.*
cinder /'sɪndə(r)/ *n.* cendre *f.*
cine-camera /'sɪnɪkæmərə/ *n.* caméra *f.*
cinema /'sɪnəmə/ *n.* cinéma *m.*
cinnamon /'sɪnəmən/ *n.* cannelle *f.*
cipher /'saɪfə(r)/ *n.* (*numeral, code*) chiffre *m.*; (*person*) nullité *f.*
circle /'sɜ:kl/ *n.* cercle *m.*; (*theatre*) balcon *m.* ● *v.t.* (*go round*) faire le tour de; (*word, error, etc.*) entourer d'un cercle. ● *v.i.* décrire des cercles.
circuit /'sɜ:kɪt/ *n.* circuit *m.* **~-breaker** *n.* disjoncteur *m.*
circuitous /sɜ:'kju:ɪtəs/ *a.* indirect.
circular /'sɜ:kjʊlə(r)/ *a.* & *n.* circulaire (*f.*).
circulat|e /'sɜ:kjʊleɪt/ *v.t./i.* (faire) circuler. **~ion** /-'leɪʃn/ *n.* circulation *f.*; (*of newspaper*) tirage *m.*
circumcis|e /'sɜ:kəmsaɪz/ *v.t.* circonc. **~ion** /-'sɪʒn/ *n.* circoncision *f.*
circumference /sɜ:'kʌmfərəns/ *n.* circonférence *f.*
circumflex /'sɜ:kəmfleks/ *n.* circonflexe *m.*
circumspect /'sɜ:kəmspekt/ *a.* circonspect.

circumstance /'sɜ:kəmstəns/ *n.* circonstance *f.* **~s,** (*financial*) situation financière *f.*
circus /'sɜ:kəs/ *n.* cirque *m.*
cistern /'sɪstən/ *n.* réservoir *m.*
citadel /'sɪtədel/ *n.* citadelle *f.*
cit|e /saɪt/ *v.t.* citer. **~ation** /-'teɪʃn/ *n.* citation *f.*
citizen /'sɪtɪzn/ *n.* citoyen(ne) *m.* (*f.*); (*of town*) habitant(e) *m.* (*f.*). **~ship** *n.* citoyenneté *f.*
citrus /'sɪtrəs/ *a.* **~ fruit(s),** agrumes *m. pl.*
city /'sɪtɪ/ *n.* (grande) ville *f.* **the C~,** la Cité de Londres.
civic /'sɪvɪk/ *a.* civique. **~ centre,** centre administratif *m.* **~s** *n. pl.* instruction civique *f.*
civil /'sɪvl/ *a.* civil; (*rights*) civique; (*defence*) passif. **~ engineer,** ingénieur civil *m.* **C~ Servant,** fonctionnaire *m./f.* **C~ Service,** fonction publique *f.* **~ war,** guerre civile *f.* **~ity** /sɪ'vɪlətɪ/ *n.* civilité *f.*
civilian /sɪ'vɪlɪən/ *a.* & *n.* civil(e) (*m.* (*f.*)).
civiliz|e /'sɪvəlaɪz/ *v.t.* civiliser. **~ation** /-'zeɪʃn/ *n.* civilisation *f.*
civvies /'sɪvɪz/ *n. pl.* **in ~,** (*sl.*) en civil.
clad /klæd/ *a.* **~ in,** vêtu de.
claim /kleɪm/ *v.t.* revendiquer, réclamer; (*assert*) prétendre. ● *n.* revendication *f.*, prétention *f.*; (*assertion*) affirmation *f.*; (*for insurance*) réclamation *f.*; (*right*) droit *m.*
claimant /'kleɪmənt/ *n.* (*of social benefits*) demandeur *m.*
clairvoyant /kleə'vɔɪənt/ *n.* voyant(e) *m.* (*f.*).
clam /klæm/ *n.* palourde *f.*
clamber /'klæmbə(r)/ *v.i.* grimper.
clammy /'klæmɪ/ *a.* (**-ier, -iest**) moite.
clamour /'klæmə(r)/ *n.* clameur *f.*, cris *m. pl.* ● *v.i.* **~ for,** demander à grands cris.
clamp /klæmp/ *n.* agrafe *f.*; (*large*) crampon *m.*; (*for carpentry*) serre-joint(s) *m.*; (*for car*) sabot de Denver *m.* ● *v.t.* serrer; (*car*) mettre un sabot de Denver à. **~ down on,** sévir contre.
clan /klæn/ *n.* clan *m.*
clandestine /klæn'destɪn/ *a.* clandestin.
clang /klæŋ/ *n.* son métallique *m.*
clanger /'klæŋə(r)/ *n.* (*sl.*) bévue *f.*
clap /klæp/ *v.t./i.* (*p.t.* **clapped**) applaudir; (*put forcibly*) mettre. ● *n.* applaudissement *m.*; (*of thunder*) coup *m.* **~ one's hands,** battre des mains.
claptrap /'klæptræp/ *n.* baratin *m.*
claret /'klærət/ *n.* bordeaux rouge *m.*
clarif|y /'klærɪfaɪ/ *v.t./i.* (se) clarifier. **~ication** /-ɪ'keɪʃn/ *n.* clarification *f.*
clarinet /klærɪ'net/ *n.* clarinette *f.*
clarity /'klærətɪ/ *n.* clarté *f.*
clash /klæʃ/ *n.* choc *m.*; (*fig.*) conflit *m.* ● *v.i.* (*metal objects*) s'entrechoquer; (*fig.*) se heurter.
clasp /klɑ:sp/ *n.* (*fastener*) fermoir *m.*, agrafe *f.* ● *v.t.* serrer.
class /klɑ:s/ *n.* classe *f.* ● *v.t.* classer.
classic /'klæsɪk/ *a.* & *n.* classique (*m.*). **~s,** (*univ.*) les humanités *f. pl.* **~al** *a.* classique.
classif|y /'klæsɪfaɪ/ *v.t.* classifier. **~ication** /-ɪ'keɪʃn/ *n.* classification *f.* **~ied** *a.* (*information etc.*) secret. **~ied advertisement,** petite annonce *f.*
classroom /'klɑ:srʊm/ *n.* salle de classe *f.*
classy /'klɑ:sɪ/ *a.* (*sl.*) chic *invar.*
clatter /'klætə(r)/ *n.* cliquetis *m.* ● *v.i.* cliqueter.
clause /klɔ:z/ *n.* clause *f.*; (*gram.*) proposition *f.*
claustrophob|ia /klɔ:strə'fəʊbɪə/ *n.* claustrophobie *f.* **~ic** *a.* & *n.* claustrophobe (*m./f.*).
claw /klɔ:/ *n.* (*of animal, small bird*) griffe *f.*; (*of bird of prey*) serre *f.*; (*of lobster*) pince *f.* ● *v.t.* griffer.
clay /kleɪ/ *n.* argile *f.*
clean /kli:n/ *a.* (**-er, -est**) propre; (*shape, stroke, etc.*) net. ● *adv.* complètement. ● *v.t.* nettoyer. ● *v.i.* **~ up,** faire le nettoyage. **~ one's teeth,** se brosser les dents. **~-shaven** *a.* glabre. **~er** *n.* (*at home*) femme de ménage *f.*; (*industrial*) agent de nettoyage *m./f.*; (*of clothes*) teintur|ier, -ière *m.*, *f.* **~ly** *adv.* proprement; (*sharply*) nettement.
cleanliness /'klenlɪnɪs/ *n.* propreté *f.*
cleans|e /klenz/ *v.t.* nettoyer; (*fig.*) purifier. **~ing cream,** crème démaquillante *f.*
clear /klɪə(r)/ *a.* (**-er, -est**) clair; (*glass*) transparent; (*profit*) net; (*road*) dégagé. ● *adv.* complètement. ● *v.t.* (*free*) dégager (**of,** de); (*table*) débarrasser; (*building*) évacuer; (*cheque*) encaisser; (*jump over*) franchir; (*debt*) liquider; (*jurid.*) disculper. **~ (away** *or*

off), (*remove*) enlever. ● *v.i.* (*fog*) se dissiper. ~ **of**, (*away from*) à l'écart de. ~ **off** *or* **out**, (*sl.*) décamper. ~ **out**, (*clean*) nettoyer. ~ **up**, (*tidy*) ranger; (*mystery*) éclaircir; (*of weather*) s'éclaircir. **make sth. ~**, être très clair sur qch. **~-cut** *a.* net. **~ly** *adv.* clairement.

clearance /'klıərəns/ *n.* (*permission*) autorisation *f.*; (*space*) dégagement *m.* ~ **sale**, liquidation *f.*

clearing /'klıərıŋ/ *n.* clairière *f.*

clearway /'klıəweı/ *n.* route à stationnement interdit *f.*

cleavage /'kli:vıdʒ/ *n.* clivage *m.*; (*breasts*) décolleté *m.*

clef /klef/ *n.* (*mus.*) clé *f.*

cleft /kleft/ *n.* fissure *f.*

clemen|t /'klemənt/ *a.* clément. **~cy** *n.* clémence *f.*

clench /klentʃ/ *v.t.* serrer.

clergy /'klɜ:dʒı/ *n.* clergé *m.* **~man** *n.* (*pl.* **-men**) ecclésiastique *m.*

cleric /'klerık/ *n.* clerc *m.* **~al** *a.* (*relig.*) clérical; (*of clerks*) de bureau, d'employé.

clerk /klɑ:k, *Amer.* klɜ:k/ *n.* employé(e) de bureau *m.* (*f.*). (*Amer.*) (**sales**) **~**, vendeu|r, -se *m.*, *f.*.

clever /'klevə(r)/ *a.* (**-er**, **-est**) intelligent; (*skilful*) habile. **~ly** *adv.* intelligemment; habilement. **~ness** *n.* intelligence *f.*

cliché /'kli:ʃeı/ *n.* cliché *m.*

click /klık/ *n.* déclic *m.* ● *v.i.* faire un déclic; (*people*: *sl.*) s'entendre, se plaire. ● *v.t.* (*heels, tongue*) faire claquer.

client /'klaıənt/ *n.* client(e) *m.* (*f.*).

clientele /kli:ən'tel/ *n.* clientèle *f.*

cliff /klıf/ *n.* falaise *f.*

climat|e /'klaımıt/ *n.* climat *m.* **~ic** /-'mætık/ *a.* climatique.

climax /'klaımæks/ *n.* point culminant *m.*; (*sexual*) orgasme *m.*

climb /klaım/ *v.t.* (*stairs*) monter, grimper; (*tree, ladder*) monter *or* grimper à; (*mountain*) faire l'ascension de. ● *v.i.* monter, grimper. ● *n.* montée *f.* ~ **down**, (*fig.*) reculer. **~-down**, *n.* recul *m.* **~er** *n.* (*sport*) alpiniste *m./f.*

clinch /klıntʃ/ *v.t.* (*a deal*) conclure.

cling /klıŋ/ *v.i.* (*p.t.* **clung**) se cramponner (**to**, à); (*stick*) coller. **~-film** *n.* (P.) film adhésif *m.*

clinic /'klınık/ *n.* centre médical *m.*; (*private*) clinique *f.*

clinical /'klınıkl/ *a.* clinique.

clink /klıŋk/ *n.* tintement *m.* ● *v.t./i.* (faire) tinter.

clinker /'klıŋkə(r)/ *n.* mâchefer *m.*

clip[1] /klıp/ *n.* (*for paper*) trombone *m.*; (*for hair*) barrette *f.*; (*for tube*) collier *m.* ● *v.t.* (*p.t.* **clipped**) attacher (**to**, à).

clip[2] /klıp/ *v.t.* (*p.t.* **clipped**) (*cut*) couper. ● *n.* coupe *f.*; (*of film*) extrait *m.*; (*blow*: *fam.*) taloche *f.* **~ping** *n.* coupure *f.*

clippers /'klıpəz/ *n. pl.* tondeuse *f.*; (*for nails*) coupe-ongles *m.*

clique /kli:k/ *n.* clique *f.*

cloak /kləʊk/ *n.* (grande) cape *f.*, manteau ample *m.*

cloakroom /'kləʊkrʊm/ *n.* vestiaire *m.*; (*toilet*) toilettes *f. pl.*

clobber /'klɒbə(r)/ *n.* (*sl.*) affaires *f. pl.* ● *v.t.* (*hit*: *sl.*) rosser.

clock /klɒk/ *n.* pendule *f.*; (*large*) horloge *f.* ● *v.i.* ~ **in** *or* **out**, pointer. ~ **up**, (*miles etc.*: *fam.*) faire. **~-tower** *n.* clocher *m.*

clockwise /'klɒkwaız/ *a.* & *adv.* dans le sens des aiguilles d'une montre.

clockwork /'klɒkwɜ:k/ *n.* mécanisme *m.* ● *a.* mécanique.

clog /klɒg/ *n.* sabot *m.* ● *v.t./i.* (*p.t.* **clogged**) (se) boucher.

cloister /'klɔıstə(r)/ *n.* cloître *m.*

close[1] /kləʊs/ *a.* (**-er**, **-est**) (*near*) proche (**to**, de); (*link, collaboration*) étroit; (*examination*) attentif; (*friend*) intime; (*order, match*) serré; (*weather*) lourd. ~ **together**, (*crowded*) serrés. ● *adv.* (tout) près. ● *n.* (*street*) impasse *f.* ~ **by**, ~ **at hand**, tout près. **~-up** *n.* gros plan *m.* **have a ~ shave**, l'échapper belle. **keep a ~ watch on**, surveiller de près. **~ly** *adv.* (*follow*) de près. **~ness** *n.* proximité *f.*

close[2] /kləʊz/ *v.t.* fermer. ● *v.i.* se fermer; (*of shop etc.*) fermer; (*end*) (se) terminer. ● *n.* fin *f.* **~d shop**, organisation qui exclut les travailleurs non syndiqués *f.*

closet /'klɒzıt/ *n.* (*Amer.*) placard *m.*

closure /'kləʊʒə(r)/ *n.* fermeture *f.*

clot /klɒt/ *n.* (*of blood*) caillot *m.*; (*in sauce*) grumeau *m.* ● *v.t./i.* (*p.t.* **clotted**) (se) coaguler.

cloth /klɒθ/ *n.* tissu *m.*; (*duster*) linge *m.*; (*table-cloth*) nappe *f.*

cloth|e /kləʊð/ *v.t.* vêtir. **~ing** *n.* vêtements *m. pl.*

clothes /kləʊðz/ *n. pl.* vêtements *m. pl.*, habits *m. pl.* **~-brush** *n.* brosse à habits *f.* **~-hanger** *n.* cintre *m.* **~-line** *n.* corde à linge *f.* **~-peg,** (*Amer.*) **~-pin** *ns.* pince à linge *f.*

cloud /klaʊd/ *n.* nuage *m.* ● *v.i.* se couvrir (de nuages); (*become gloomy*) s'assombrir. **~y** *a.* (*sky*) couvert; (*liquid*) trouble.

cloudburst /'klaʊdbɜ:st/ *n.* trombe d'eau *f.*

clout /klaʊt/ *n.* (*blow*) coup de poing *m.*; (*power*: *fam.*) pouvoir effectif *m.* ● *v.t.* frapper.

clove /kləʊv/ *n.* clou de girofle *m.* **~ of garlic,** gousse d'ail *f.*

clover /'kləʊvə(r)/ *n.* trèfle *m.*

clown /klaʊn/ *n.* clown *m.* ● *v.i.* faire le clown.

cloy /klɔɪ/ *v.t.* écœurer.

club /klʌb/ *n.* (*group*) club *m.*; (*weapon*) massue *f.* **~s,** (*cards*) trèfle *m.* ● *v.t./i.* (*p.t.* **clubbed**) matraquer. **(golf) ~,** club (de golf) *m.* **~ together,** (*share costs*) se cotiser.

cluck /klʌk/ *v.i.* glousser.

clue /klu:/ *n.* indice *m.*; (*in crossword*) définition *f.* **I haven't a ~,** (*fam.*) je n'en ai pas la moindre idée.

clump /klʌmp/ *n.* massif *m.*

clums|y /'klʌmzɪ/ *a.* (**-ier, -iest**) maladroit; (*tool*) peu commode. **~iness** *n.* maladresse *f.*

clung /klʌŋ/ *see* cling.

cluster /'klʌstə(r)/ *n.* (petit) groupe *m.* ● *v.i.* se grouper.

clutch /klʌtʃ/ *v.t.* (*hold*) serrer fort; (*grasp*) saisir. ● *v.i.* **~ at,** (*try to grasp*) essayer de saisir. ● *n.* étreinte *f.*; (*auto.*) embrayage *m.*

clutter /'klʌtə(r)/ *n.* désordre *m.*, fouillis *m.* ● *v.t.* encombrer.

coach /kəʊtʃ/ *n.* autocar *m.*; (*of train*) wagon *m.*; (*horse-drawn*) carrosse *m.*; (*sport*) entraîneu|r, -se *m., f.* ● *v.t.* donner des leçons (particulières) à; (*sport*) entraîner.

coagulate /kəʊ'ægjʊleɪt/ *v.t./i.* (se) coaguler.

coal /kəʊl/ *n.* charbon *m.* **~-mine** *n.* mine de charbon *f.*

coalfield /'kəʊlfi:ld/ *n.* bassin houiller *m.*

coalition /kəʊə'lɪʃn/ *n.* coalition *f.*

coarse /kɔ:s/ *a.* (**-er, -est**) grossier. **~ness** *n.* caractère grossier *m.*

coast /kəʊst/ *n.* côte *f.* ● *v.i.* (*car, bicycle*) descendre en roue libre. **~al** *a.* côtier.

coaster /'kəʊstə(r)/ *n.* (*ship*) caboteur *m.*; (*mat*) dessous de verre *m.*

coastguard /'kəʊstgɑ:d/ *n.* gardecôte *m.*

coastline /'kəʊstlaɪn/ *n.* littoral *m.*

coat /kəʊt/ *n.* manteau *m.*; (*of animal*) pelage *m.*; (*of paint*) couche *f.* ● *v.t.* enduire, couvrir; (*with chocolate*) enrober (**with,** de). **~-hanger** *n.* cintre *m.* **~ of arms,** armoiries *f. pl.* **~ing** *n.* couche *f.*

coax /kəʊks/ *v.t.* amadouer.

cob /kɒb/ *n.* (*of corn*) épi *m.*

cobble[1] /'kɒbl/ *n.* pavé *m.* **~-stone** *n.* pavé *m.*

cobble[2] /'kɒbl/ *v.t.* rapetasser.

cobbler /'kɒblə(r)/ *n.* (*old use*) cordonnier *m.*

cobweb /'kɒbweb/ *n.* toile d'araignée *f.*

cocaine /kəʊ'keɪn/ *n.* cocaïne *f.*

cock /kɒk/ *n.* (oiseau) mâle *m.*; (*rooster*) coq *m.* ● *v.t.* (*gun*) armer; (*ears*) dresser. **~-and-bull story,** histoire à dormir debout *f.* **~-eyed** *a.* (*askew*: *sl.*) de travers. **~-up** *n.* (*sl.*) pagaille *f.*

cockerel /'kɒkərəl/ *n.* jeune coq *m.*

cockle /'kɒkl/ *n.* (*culin.*) coque *f.*

cockney /'kɒknɪ/ *n.* Cockney *m./f.*

cockpit /'kɒkpɪt/ *n.* poste de pilotage *m.*

cockroach /'kɒkrəʊtʃ/ *n.* cafard *m.*

cocksure /kɒk'ʃʊə(r)/ *a.* sûr de soi.

cocktail /'kɒkteɪl/ *n.* cocktail *m.* **~ party,** cocktail *m.* **fruit ~,** macédoine (de fruits) *f.*

cocky /'kɒkɪ/ *a.* (**-ier, -iest**) trop sûr de soi, arrogant.

cocoa /'kəʊkəʊ/ *n.* cacao *m.*

coconut /'kəʊkənʌt/ *n.* noix de coco *f.*

cocoon /kə'ku:n/ *n.* cocon *m.*

COD *abbr.* (*cash on delivery*) paiement à la livraison *m.*

cod /kɒd/ *n. invar.* morue *f.* **~-liver oil,** huile de foie de morue *f.*

coddle /'kɒdl/ *v.t.* dorloter.

code /kəʊd/ *n.* code *m.* ● *v.t.* coder.

codify /'kəʊdɪfaɪ/ *v.t.* codifier.

coeducational /kəʊedʒʊ'keɪʃənl/ *a.* (*school, teaching*) mixte.

coerc|e /kəʊ'ɜ:s/ *v.t.* contraindre. **~ion** /-ʃn/ *n.* contrainte *f.*

coexist /kəʊɪg'zɪst/ *v.i.* coexister. **~ence** *n.* coexistence *f.*

coffee /'kɒfɪ/ *n.* café *m.* **~ bar,** café *m.*, cafétéria *f.* **~-pot** *n.* cafetière *f.* **~-table** *n.* table basse *f.*
coffer /'kɒfə(r)/ *n.* coffre *m.*
coffin /'kɒfɪn/ *n.* cercueil *m.*
cog /kɒg/ *n.* dent *f.*; (*fig.*) rouage *m.*
cogent /'kəʊdʒənt/ *a.* convaincant; (*relevant*) pertinent.
cognac /'kɒnjæk/ *n.* cognac *m.*
cohabit /kəʊ'hæbɪt/ *v.i.* vivre en concubinage.
coherent /kəʊ'hɪərənt/ *a.* cohérent.
coil /kɔɪl/ *v.t./i.* (s')enrouler. ● *n.* rouleau *m.*; (*one ring*) spire *f.*; (*contraceptive*) stérilet *m.*
coin /kɔɪn/ *n.* pièce (de monnaie) *f.* ● *v.t.* (*word*) inventer. **~age** *n.* monnaie *f.*; (*fig.*) invention *f.* **~-box** *n.* téléphone public *m.*
coincide /kəʊɪn'saɪd/ *v.i.* coïncider.
coinciden|ce /kəʊ'ɪnsɪdəns/ *n.* coïncidence *f.* **~tal** /-'dentl/ *a.* dû à une coïncidence.
coke /kəʊk/ *n.* coke *m.*
colander /'kʌləndə(r)/ *n.* passoire *f.*
cold /kəʊld/ *a.* (**-er, -est**) froid. **be** *or* **feel ~,** avoir froid. **it is ~,** il fait froid. ● *n.* froid *m.*; (*med.*) rhume *m.* **~-blooded** *a.* sans pitié. **~ cream,** crème de beauté *f.* **get ~ feet,** se dégonfler. **~-shoulder** *v.t.* snober. **~ sore,** bouton de fièvre *m.* **~ness** *n.* froideur *f.*
coleslaw /'kəʊlslɔː/ *n.* salade de chou cru *f.*
colic /'kɒlɪk/ *n.* coliques *f. pl.*
collaborat|e /kə'læbəreɪt/ *v.i.* collaborer. **~ion** /-'reɪʃn/ *n.* collaboration *f.* **~or** *n.* collabora|teur, -trice *m., f.*
collage /'kɒlɑːʒ/ *n.* collage *m.*
collapse /kə'læps/ *v.i.* s'effondrer; (*med.*) avoir un malaise. ● *n.* effondrement *m.*
collapsible /kə'læpsəbl/ *a.* pliant.
collar /'kɒlə(r)/ *n.* col *m.*; (*of dog*) collier *m.* ● *v.t.* (*take*: *sl.*) piquer. **~-bone** *n.* clavicule *f.*
collateral /kə'lætərəl/ *n.* nantissement *m.*
colleague /'kɒliːg/ *n.* collègue *m./f.*
collect /kə'lekt/ *v.t.* rassembler; (*pick up*) ramasser; (*call for*) passer prendre; (*money, rent*) encaisser; (*taxes*) percevoir; (*as hobby*) collectionner. ● *v.i.* se rassembler; (*dust*) s'amasser. ● *adv.* **call ~,** (*Amer.*) téléphoner en PCV. **~ion** /-kʃn/ *n.* collection *f.*; (*in church*) quête *f.*; (*of mail*) levée *f.* **~or** *n.* (*as hobby*) collectionneu|r, -se *m., f.*
collective /kə'lektɪv/ *a.* collectif.
college /'kɒlɪdʒ/ *n.* (*for higher education*) institut *m.*, école *f.*; (*within university*) collège *m.* **be at ~,** être en faculté.
collide /kə'laɪd/ *v.i.* entrer en collision (**with,** avec).
colliery /'kɒlɪərɪ/ *n.* houillère *f.*
collision /kə'lɪʒn/ *n.* collision *f.*
colloquial /kə'ləʊkwɪəl/ *a.* familier. **~ism** *n.* expression familière *f.*
collusion /kə'luːʒn/ *n.* collusion *f.*
colon /'kəʊlən/ *n.* (*gram.*) deux-points *m. invar.*; (*anat.*) côlon *m.*
colonel /'kɜːnl/ *n.* colonel *m.*
colonize /'kɒlənaɪz/ *v.t.* coloniser.
colon|y /'kɒlənɪ/ *n.* colonie *f.* **~ial** /kə'ləʊnɪəl/ *a.* & *n.* colonial(e) (*m.* (*f.*)).
colossal /kə'lɒsl/ *a.* colossal.
colour /'kʌlə(r)/ *n.* couleur *f.* ● *a.* (*photo etc.*) en couleur; (*TV set*) couleur *invar.* ● *v.t.* colorer; (*with crayon*) colorier. **~-blind** *a.* daltonien. **~-fast** *a.* grand teint. *invar.* **~ful** *a.* coloré; (*person*) haut en couleur. **~ing** *n.* (*of skin*) teint *m.*; (*in food*) colorant *m.*
coloured /'kʌləd/ *a.* (*person, pencil*) de couleur. ● *n.* personne de couleur *f.*
colt /kəʊlt/ *n.* poulain *m.*
column /'kɒləm/ *n.* colonne *f.*
columnist /'kɒləmnɪst/ *n.* journaliste chroniqueur *m.*
coma /'kəʊmə/ *n.* coma *m.*
comb /kəʊm/ *n.* peigne *m.* ● *v.t.* peigner; (*search*) ratisser. **~ one's hair,** se peigner.
combat /'kɒmbæt/ *n.* combat *m.* ● *v.t.* (*p.t.* **combated**) combattre. **~ant** /-ətənt/ *n.* combattant(e) *m.* (*f.*).
combination /kɒmbɪ'neɪʃn/ *n.* combinaison *f.*
combine[1] /kəm'baɪn/ *v.t./i.* (se) combiner, (s')unir.
combine[2] /'kɒmbaɪn/ *n.* (*comm.*) trust *m.*, cartel *m.* **~ harvester,** moissonneuse-batteuse *f.*
combustion /kəm'bʌstʃən/ *n.* combustion *f.*
come /kʌm/ *v.i.* (*p.t.* **came,** *p.p.* **come**) venir; (*occur*) arriver; (*sexually*) jouir. **~ about,** arriver. **~ across,** rencontrer *or* trouver par hasard. **~ away** *or* **off,** se détacher,

partir. **~ back,** revenir. **~-back** *n.* rentrée *f.*; (*retort*) réplique *f.* **~ by,** obtenir. **~ down,** descendre; (*price*) baisser. **~-down** *n.* humiliation *f.* **~ forward,** se présenter. **~ from,** être de. **~ in,** entrer. **~ in for,** recevoir. **~ into,** (*money*) hériter de. **~ off,** (*succeed*) réussir; (*fare*) s'en tirer. **~ on,** (*actor*) entrer en scène; (*light*) s'allumer; (*improve*) faire des progrès. **~ on!,** allez! **~ out,** sortir. **~ round** *or* **to,** revenir à soi. **~ through,** s'en tirer (indemne de). **~ to,** (*amount*) revenir à; (*decision, conclusion*) arriver à. **~ up,** monter; (*fig.*) se présenter. **~ up against,** rencontrer. **get one's ~-uppance** *n.* (*fam.*) finir par recevoir ce qu'on mérite. **~ up with,** (*find*) trouver; (*produce*) produire.

comedian /kə'mi:dɪən/ *n.* comique *m.*

comedy /'kɒmədɪ/ *n.* comédie *f.*

comely /'kʌmlɪ/ *a.* (**-ier, -iest**) (*old use*) avenant, beau.

comet /'kɒmɪt/ *n.* comète *f.*

comfort /'kʌmfət/ *n.* confort *m.*; (*consolation*) réconfort *m.* ● *v.t.* consoler. **one's ~s,** ses aises. **~able** *a.* (*chair, car, etc.*) confortable; (*person*) à l'aise, bien; (*wealthy*) aisé.

comforter /'kʌmfətə(r)/ *n.* (*baby's dummy*) sucette *f.*; (*quilt: Amer.*) édredon *m.*

comfy /'kʌmfɪ/ *a.* (*fam.*) = **comfortable**.

comic /'kɒmɪk/ *a.* comique. ● *n.* (*person*) comique *m.*; (*periodical*) comic *m.* **~ strip,** bande dessinée *f.* **~al** *a.* comique.

coming /'kʌmɪŋ/ *n.* arrivée *f.* ● *a.* à venir. **~s and goings,** allées et venues *f. pl.*

comma /'kɒmə/ *n.* virgule *f.*

command /kə'mɑ:nd/ *n.* (*authority*) commandement *m.*; (*order*) ordre *m.*; (*mastery*) maîtrise *f.* ● *v.t.* commander (**s.o. to,** à qn. de); (*be able to use*) disposer de; (*require*) nécessiter; (*respect*) inspirer. **~er** *n.* commandant *m.* **~ing** *a.* imposant.

commandeer /kɒmən'dɪə(r)/ *v.t.* réquisitionner.

commandment /kə'mɑ:ndmənt/ *n.* commandement *m.*

commando /kə'mɑ:ndəʊ/ *n.* (*pl.* **-os**) commando *m.*

commemorat|e /kə'meməreɪt/ *v.t.* commémorer. **~ion** /-'reɪʃn/ *n.* commémoration *f.* **~ive** /-ətɪv/ *a.* commémoratif.

commence /kə'mens/ *v.t./i.* commencer. **~ment** *n.* commencement *m.*; (*univ., Amer.*) cérémonie de distribution des diplômes *f.*

commend /kə'mend/ *v.t.* (*praise*) louer; (*entrust*) confier. **~able** *a.* louable. **~ation** /kɒmen'deɪʃn/ *n.* éloge *m.*

commensurate /kə'menʃərət/ *a.* proportionné.

comment /'kɒment/ *n.* commentaire *m.* ● *v.i.* faire des commentaires. **~ on,** commenter.

commentary /'kɒməntrɪ/ *n.* commentaire *m.*; (*radio, TV*) reportage *m.*

commentat|e /'kɒmənteɪt/ *v.i.* faire un reportage. **~or** *n.* commenta|teur, -trice *m., f.*

commerce /'kɒmɜ:s/ *n.* commerce *m.*

commercial /kə'mɜ:ʃl/ *a.* commercial; (*traveller*) de commerce. ● *n.* publicité *f.* **~ize** *v.t.* commercialiser.

commiserat|e /kə'mɪzəreɪt/ *v.i.* compatir (**with,** avec). **~ion** /-'reɪʃn/ *n.* commisération *f.*

commission /kə'mɪʃn/ *n.* commission *f.*; (*order for work*) commande *f.* ● *v.t.* (*order*) commander; (*mil.*) nommer officier. **~ to do,** charger de faire. **out of ~,** hors service. **~er** *n.* préfet (de police) *m.*; (*in E.C.*) commissaire *m.*

commissionaire /kəmɪʃə'neə(r)/ *n.* commissionnaire *m.*

commit /kə'mɪt/ *v.t.* (*p.t.* **committed**) commettre; (*entrust*) confier. **~ o.s.,** s'engager. **~ perjury,** se parjurer. **~ suicide,** se suicider. **~ to memory,** apprendre par cœur. **~ment** *n.* engagement *m.*

committee /kə'mɪtɪ/ *n.* comité *m.*

commodity /kə'mɒdətɪ/ *n.* produit *m.*, article *m.*

common /'kɒmən/ *a.* (**-er, -est**) (*shared by all*) commun; (*usual*) courant, commun; (*vulgar*) vulgaire, commun. ● *n.* terrain communal *m.* **~ law,** droit coutumier *m.* **C~ Market,** Marché Commun *m.* **~-room** *n.* (*schol.*) salle commune *f.* **~ sense,** bon sens *m.* **House of C~s,** Chambre des Communes *f.* **in ~,** en commun. **~ly** *adv.* communément.

commoner /ˈkɒmənə(r)/ *n.* rotur|ier, -ière *m., f.*

commonplace /ˈkɒmənpleɪs/ *a.* banal. ● *n.* banalité *f.*

Commonwealth /ˈkɒmənwelθ/ *n.* **the ~,** le Commonwealth *m.*

commotion /kəˈməʊʃn/ *n.* agitation *f.*, remue-ménage *m. invar.*

communal /ˈkɒmjʊnl/ *a.* (*shared*) commun; (*life*) collectif.

commune /ˈkɒmju:n/ *n.* (*group*) communauté *f.*

communicat|e /kəˈmju:nɪkeɪt/ *v.t./i.* communiquer. **~ion** /-ˈkeɪʃn/ *n.* communication *f.* **~ive** /-ətɪv/ *a.* communicatif.

communion /kəˈmju:nɪən/ *n.* communion *f.*

communiqué /kəˈmju:nɪkeɪ/ *n.* communiqué *m.*

Communis|t /ˈkɒmjʊnɪst/ *a.* & *n.* communiste (*m./f.*) **~m** /-zəm/ *n.* communisme *m.*

community /kəˈmju:nətɪ/ *n.* communauté *f.*

commutation /kɒmju:ˈteɪʃn/ *n.* **~ ticket,** carte d'abonnement *f.*

commute /kəˈmju:t/ *v.i.* faire la navette. ● *v.t.* (*jurid.*) commuer. **~r** /-ə(r)/ *n.* banlieusard(e) *m.* (*f.*).

compact[1] /kəmˈpækt/ *a.* compact. **~** /ˈkɒmpækt/ disc, (disque) compact *m.*

compact[2] /ˈkɒmpækt/ *n.* (*lady's case*) poudrier *m.*

companion /kəmˈpænjən/ *n.* comp|agnon, -agne *m., f.* **~ship** *n.* camaraderie *f.*

company /ˈkʌmpənɪ/ *n.* (*companionship, firm*) compagnie *f.*; (*guests*) invité(e)s *m.* (*f.*) *pl.*

comparable /ˈkɒmpərəbl/ *a.* comparable.

compar|e /kəmˈpeə(r)/ *v.t.* comparer (**with, to,** à). **~ed with** *or* **to,** en comparaison de. ● *v.i.* être comparable. **~ative** /-ˈpærətɪv/ *a.* (*study, form*) comparatif; (*comfort etc.*) relatif. **~atively** /-ˈpærətɪvlɪ/ *adv.* relativement.

comparison /kəmˈpærɪsn/ *n.* comparaison *f.*

compartment /kəmˈpɑ:tmənt/ *n.* compartiment *m.*

compass /ˈkʌmpəs/ *n.* (*for direction*) boussole *f.*; (*scope*) portée *f.* **~(es),** (*for drawing*) compas *m.*

compassion /kəmˈpæʃn/ *n.* compassion *f.* **~ate** *a.* compatissant.

compatib|le /kəmˈpætəbl/ *a.* compatible. **~ility** /-ˈbɪlətɪ/ *n.* compatibilité *f.*

compatriot /kəmˈpætrɪət/ *n.* compatriote *m./f.*

compel /kəmˈpel/ *v.t.* (*p.t.* **compelled**) contraindre. **~ling** *a.* irrésistible.

compendium /kəmˈpendɪəm/ *n.* abrégé *m.*, résumé *m.*

compensat|e /ˈkɒmpənseɪt/ *v.t./i.* (*financially*) dédommager (**for,** de). **~e for sth.,** compenser qch. **~ion** /-ˈseɪʃn/ *n.* compensation *f.*; (*financial*) dédommagement *m.*

compete /kəmˈpi:t/ *v.i.* concourir. **~ with,** rivaliser avec.

competen|t /ˈkɒmpɪtənt/ *a.* compétent. **~ce** *n.* compétence *f.*

competition /kɒmpəˈtɪʃn/ *n.* (*contest*) concours *m.*; (*sport*) compétition *f.*; (*comm.*) concurrence *f.*

competitive /kəmˈpetətɪv/ *a.* (*prices*) concurrentiel, compétitif. **~ examination,** concours *m.*

competitor /kəmˈpetɪtə(r)/ *n.* concurrent(e) *m.* (*f.*).

compile /kəmˈpaɪl/ *v.t.* (*list*) dresser; (*book*) rédiger. **~r** /-ə(r)/ *n.* rédac|teur, -trice *m., f.*

complacen|t /kəmˈpleɪsnt/ *a.* content de soi. **~cy** contentement de soi *m.*

complain /kəmˈpleɪn/ *v.i.* se plaindre (**about, of,** de).

complaint /kəmˈpleɪnt/ *n.* plainte *f.*; (*in shop etc.*) réclamation *f.*; (*illness*) maladie *f.*

complement /ˈkɒmplɪmənt/ *n.* complément *m.* ● *v.t.* compléter. **~ary** /-ˈmentrɪ/ *a.* complémentaire.

complet|e /kəmˈpli:t/ *a.* complet; (*finished*) achevé; (*downright*) parfait. ● *v.t.* achever; (*a form*) remplir. **~ely** *adv.* complètement. **~ion** /-ʃn/ *n.* achèvement *m.*

complex /ˈkɒmpleks/ *a.* complexe. ● *n.* (*psych., archit.*) complexe *m.* **~ity** /kəmˈpleksətɪ/ *n.* complexité *f.*

complexion /kəmˈplekʃn/ *n.* (*of face*) teint *m.*; (*fig.*) caractère *m.*

compliance /kəmˈplaɪəns/ *n.* (*agreement*) conformité *f.*

complicat|e /ˈkɒmplɪkeɪt/ *v.t.* compliquer. **~ed** *a.* compliqué. **~ion** /-ˈkeɪʃn/ *n.* complication *f.*

complicity /kəmˈplɪsətɪ/ *n.* complicité *f.*

compliment /'kɒmplɪmənt/ *n.* compliment *m.* ● *v.t.* /'kɒmplɪment/ complimenter.

complimentary /kɒmplɪ'mentrɪ/ *a.* (offert) à titre gracieux; (*praising*) flatteur.

comply /kəm'plaɪ/ *v.i.* **~ with,** se conformer à, obéir à.

component /kəm'pəʊnənt/ *n.* (*of machine etc.*) pièce *f.*; (*chemical substance*) composant *m.*; (*element: fig.*) composante *f.* ● *a.* constituant.

compose /kəm'pəʊz/ *v.t.* composer. **~ o.s.,** se calmer. **~d** *a.* calme. **~r** /-ə(r)/ *n.* (*mus.*) compositeur *m.*

composition /kɒmpə'zɪʃn/ *n.* composition *f.*

compost /'kɒmpɒst, *Amer.* 'kɒmpəʊst/ *n.* compost *m.*

composure /kəm'pəʊʒə(r)/ *n.* calme *m.*

compound[1] /'kɒmpaʊnd/ *n.* (*substance, word*) composé *m.*; (*enclosure*) enclos *m.* ● *a.* composé.

compound[2] /kəm'paʊnd/ *v.t.* (*problem etc.*) aggraver.

comprehen|d /kɒmprɪ'hend/ *v.t.* comprendre. **~sion** *n.* compréhension *f.*

comprehensive /kɒmprɪ'hensɪv/ *a.* étendu, complet; (*insurance*) tous risques *invar.* **~ school,** collège d'enseignement secondaire *m.*

compress /kəm'pres/ *v.t.* comprimer. **~ion** /-ʃn/ *n.* compression *f.*

comprise /kəm'praɪz/ *v.t.* comprendre, inclure.

compromise /'kɒmprəmaɪz/ *n.* compromis *m.* ● *v.t.* compromettre. ● *v.i.* transiger, trouver un compromis. **not ~ on,** ne pas transiger sur.

compulsion /kəm'pʌlʃn/ *n.* contrainte *f.*

compulsive /kəm'pʌlsɪv/ *a.* (*psych.*) compulsif; (*liar, smoker*) invétéré.

compulsory /kəm'pʌlsərɪ/ *a.* obligatoire.

compunction /kəm'pʌŋkʃn/ *n.* scrupule *m.*

computer /kəm'pju:tə(r)/ *n.* ordinateur *m.* **~ science,** informatique *f.* **~ize** *v.t.* informatiser.

comrade /'kɒmr(e)ɪd/ *n.* camarade *m./f.* **~ship** *n.* camaraderie *f.*

con[1] /kɒn/ *v.t.* (*p.t.* **conned**) (*sl.*) rouler, escroquer (**out of,** de). ● *n.* (*sl.*) escroquerie *f.* **~ s.o. into doing,** arnaquer qn. en lui faisant faire. **~ man,** (*sl.*) escroc *m.*

con[2] /kɒn/ *see* pro.

concave /'kɒŋkeɪv/ *a.* concave.

conceal /kən'si:l/ *v.t.* dissimuler. **~ment** *n.* dissimulation *f.*

concede /kən'si:d/ *v.t.* concéder. ● *v.i.* céder.

conceit /kən'si:t/ *n.* suffisance *f.* **~ed** *a.* suffisant.

conceivabl|e /kən'si:vəbl/ *a.* concevable. **~y** *adv.* **this may ~y be done,** il est concevable que cela puisse se faire.

conceive /kən'si:v/ *v.t./i.* concevoir. **~ of,** concevoir.

concentrat|e /'kɒnsntreɪt/ *v.t./i.* (se) concentrer. **~ion** /-'treɪʃn/ *n.* concentration *f.*

concept /'kɒnsept/ *n.* concept *m.* **~ual** /kən'septʃʊəl/ *a.* notionnel.

conception /kən'sepʃn/ *n.* conception *f.*

concern /kən'sɜ:n/ *n.* (*interest, business*) affaire *f.*; (*worry*) inquiétude *f.*; (*firm: comm.*) entreprise *f.*, affaire *f.* ● *v.t.* concerner. **~ o.s. with, be ~ed with,** s'occuper de. **~ing** *prep.* en ce qui concerne.

concerned /kən'sɜ:nd/ *a.* inquiet.

concert /'kɒnsət/ *n.* concert *m.* **in ~,** ensemble.

concerted /kən'sɜ:tɪd/ *a.* concerté.

concertina /kɒnsə'ti:nə/ *n.* concertina *m.*

concerto /kən'tʃeətəʊ/ *n.* (*pl.* **-os**) concerto *m.*

concession /kən'seʃn/ *n.* concession *f.*

conciliation /kənsɪlɪ'eɪʃn/ *n.* conciliation *f.*

concise /kən'saɪs/ *a.* concis. **~ly** *adv.* avec concision. **~ness** *n.* concision *f.*

conclu|de /kən'klu:d/ *v.t.* conclure. ● *v.i.* se terminer. **~ding** *a.* final. **~sion** *n.* conclusion *f.*

conclusive /kən'klu:sɪv/ *a.* concluant. **~ly** *adv.* de manière concluante.

concoct /kən'kɒkt/ *v.t.* confectionner; (*invent: fig.*) fabriquer. **~ion** /-kʃn/ *n.* mélange *m.*

concourse /'kɒŋkɔ:s/ *n.* (*rail.*) hall *m.*

concrete /'kɒŋkri:t/ *n.* béton *m.* ● *a.* concret. ● *v.t.* bétonner. **~-mixer** *n.* bétonnière *f.*

concur /kən'kɜ:(r)/ *v.i.* (*p.t.* **concurred**) être d'accord.

concurrently /kən'kʌrəntlɪ/ *adv.* simultanément.

concussion /kən'kʌʃn/ *n.* commotion (cérébrale) *f.*

condemn /kən'dem/ *v.t.* condamner. **~ation** /kɒndem'neɪʃn/ *n.* condamnation *f.*

condens|e /kən'dens/ *v.t./i.* (se) condenser. **~ation** /kɒnden'seɪʃn/ *n.* condensation *f.*; (*mist*) buée *f.*

condescend /kɒndɪ'send/ *v.i.* condescendre.

condiment /'kɒndɪmənt/ *n.* condiment *m.*

condition /kən'dɪʃn/ *n.* condition *f.* ● *v.t.* conditionner. **on ~ that,** à condition que. **~al** *a.* conditionnel. **be ~al upon,** dépendre de. **~er** *n.* après-shampooing *m.*

condolences /kən'dəʊlənsɪz/ *n. pl.* condoléances *f. pl.*

condom /'kɒndɒm/ *n.* préservatif *m.*

condominium /kɒndə'mɪnɪəm/ *n.* (*Amer.*) copropriété *f.*

condone /kən'dəʊn/ *v.t.* pardonner, fermer les yeux sur.

conducive /kən'dju:sɪv/ *a.* **~ to,** favorable à.

conduct[1] /kən'dʌkt/ *v.t.* conduire; (*orchestra*) diriger.

conduct[2] /'kɒndʌkt/ *n.* conduite *f.*

conduct|or /kən'dʌktə(r)/ *n.* chef d'orchestre *m.*; (*of bus*) receveur *m.*; (*on train*: *Amer.*) chef de train *m.*; (*electr.*) conducteur *m.* **~ress** *n.* receveuse *f.*

cone /kəʊn/ *n.* cône *m.*; (*of ice-cream*) cornet *m.*

confectioner /kən'fekʃənə(r)/ *n.* confiseu|r, -se *m., f.* **~y** *n.* confiserie *f.*

confederation /kənfedə'reɪʃn/ *n.* confédération *f.*

confer /kən'fɜ:(r)/ *v.t./i.* (*p.t.* **conferred**) conférer.

conference /'kɒnfərəns/ *n.* conférence *f.*

confess /kən'fes/ *v.t./i.* avouer; (*relig.*) (se) confesser. **~ion** /-ʃn/ *n.* confession *f.*; (*of crime*) aveu *m.*

confessional /kən'feʃənl/ *n.* confessionnal *m.*

confetti /kən'fetɪ/ *n.* confettis *m. pl.*

confide /kən'faɪd/ *v.t.* confier. ● *v.i.* **~ in,** se confier à.

confiden|t /'kɒnfɪdənt/ *a.* sûr. **~ce** *n.* (*trust*) confiance *f.*; (*boldness*) confiance en soi *f.*; (*secret*) confidence *f.* **~ce trick,** escroquerie *f.* **in ~ce,** en confidence.

confidential /kɒnfɪ'denʃl/ *a.* confidentiel.

configure /kən'fɪgə(r)/ *v.t.* (*comput.*) configurer.

confine /kən'faɪn/ *v.t.* enfermer; (*limit*) limiter. **~d space,** espace réduit *m.* **~d to,** limité à. **~ment** *n.* détention *f.*; (*med.*) couches *f. pl.*

confines /'kɒnfaɪnz/ *n. pl.* confins *m. pl.*

confirm /kən'fɜ:m/ *v.t.* confirmer. **~ation** /kɒnfə'meɪʃn/ *n.* confirmation *f.* **~ed** *a.* (*bachelor*) endurci; (*smoker*) invétéré.

confiscat|e /'kɒnfɪskeɪt/ *v.t.* confisquer. **~ion** /-'keɪʃn/ *n.* confiscation *f.*

conflagration /kɒnflə'greɪʃn/ *n.* incendie *m.*

conflict[1] /'kɒnflɪkt/ *n.* conflit *m.*

conflict[2] /kən'flɪkt/ *v.i.* (*statements, views*) être en contradiction (**with,** avec); (*appointments*) tomber en même temps (**with,** que). **~ing** *a.* contradictoire.

conform /kən'fɔ:m/ *v.t./i.* (se) conformer. **~ist** *n.* conformiste *m./f.*

confound /kən'faʊnd/ *v.t.* confondre. **~ed** *a.* (*fam.*) sacré.

confront /kən'frʌnt/ *v.t.* affronter. **~ with,** confronter avec. **~ation** /kɒnfrʌn'teɪʃn/ *n.* confrontation *f.*

confus|e /kən'fju:z/ *v.t.* embrouiller; (*mistake, confound*) confondre. **become ~ed,** s'embrouiller. **I am ~ed,** je m'y perds. **~ing** *a.* déroutant. **~ion** /-ʒn/ *n.* confusion *f.*

congeal /kən'dʒi:l/ *v.t./i.* (se) figer.

congenial /kən'dʒi:nɪəl/ *a.* sympathique.

congenital /kən'dʒenɪtl/ *a.* congénital.

congest|ed /kən'dʒestɪd/ *a.* encombré; (*med.*) congestionné. **~ion** /-stʃən/ *n.* (*traffic*) encombrement(s) *m.* (*pl.*); (*med.*) congestion *f.*

conglomerate /kən'glɒmərət/ *n.* (*comm.*) conglomérat *m.*

congratulat|e /kən'grætjʊleɪt/ *v.t.* féliciter (**on,** de). **~ions** /-'leɪʃnz/ *n. pl.* félicitations *f. pl.*

congregat|e /'kɒŋgrɪgeɪt/ *v.i.* se rassembler. **~ion** /-'geɪʃn/ *n.* assemblée *f.*

congress /'kɒŋgres/ *n.* congrès *m.* **C~,** (*Amer.*) le Congrès.

conic(al) /'kɒnɪk(l)/ *a.* conique.

conifer /'kɒnɪfə(r)/ *n.* conifère *m.*

conjecture /kən'dʒektʃə(r)/ *n.* conjecture *f.* ● *v.t./i.* conjecturer.

conjugal /'kɒndʒʊgl/ *a.* conjugal.

conjugat|e /'kɒndʒʊgeɪt/ *v.t.* conjuguer. **~ion** /-'geɪʃn/ *n.* conjugaison *f.*

conjunction /kən'dʒʌŋkʃn/ *n.* conjonction *f.* **in ~ with,** conjointement avec.

conjunctivitis /kɒndʒʌŋktɪ'vaɪtɪs/ *n.* conjonctivite *f.*

conjur|e /'kʌndʒə(r)/ *v.i.* faire des tours de passe-passe. ● *v.t.* **~e up,** faire apparaître. **~or** *n.* prestidigita|teur, -trice *m., f.*

conk /kɒŋk/ *v.i.* **~ out,** (*sl.*) tomber en panne.

conker /'kɒŋkə(r)/ *n.* (*horse-chestnut fruit*: *fam.*) marron *m.*

connect /kə'nekt/ *v.t./i.* (se) relier; (*in mind*) faire le rapport entre; (*install, wire up to mains*) brancher. **~ with,** (*of train*) assurer la correspondance avec. **~ed** *a.* lié. **be ~ed with,** avoir rapport à; (*deal with*) avoir des rapports avec.

connection /kə'nekʃn/ *n.* rapport *m.*; (*rail.*) correspondance *f.*; (*phone call*) communication *f.*; (*electr.*) contact *m.*; (*joining piece*) raccord *m.* **~s,** (*comm.*) relations *f. pl.*

conniv|e /kə'naɪv/ *v.i.* **~e at,** se faire le complice de. **~ance** *n.* connivence *f.*

connoisseur /kɒnə'sɜː(r)/ *n.* connaisseur *m.*

connot|e /kə'nəʊt/ *v.t.* connoter. **~ation** /kɒnə'teɪʃn/ *n.* connotation *f.*

conquer /'kɒŋkə(r)/ *v.t.* vaincre; (*country*) conquérir. **~or** *n.* conquérant *m.*

conquest /'kɒŋkwest/ *n.* conquête *f.*

conscience /'kɒnʃəns/ *n.* conscience *f.*

conscientious /kɒnʃɪ'enʃəs/ *a.* consciencieux.

conscious /'kɒnʃəs/ *a.* conscient; (*deliberate*) voulu. **~ly** *adv.* consciemment. **~ness** *n.* conscience *f.*; (*med.*) connaissance *f.*

conscript [1] /kən'skrɪpt/ *v.t.* recruter par conscription. **~ion** /-pʃn/ *n.* conscription *f.*

conscript [2] /'kɒnskrɪpt/ *n.* conscrit *m.*

consecrate /'kɒnsɪkreɪt/ *v.t.* consacrer.

consecutive /kən'sekjʊtɪv/ *a.* consécutif. **~ly** *adv.* consécutivement.

consensus /kən'sensəs/ *n.* consensus *m.*

consent /kən'sent/ *v.i.* consentir (**to,** à). ● *n.* consentement *m.*

consequence /'kɒnsɪkwəns/ *n.* conséquence *f.*

consequent /'kɒnsɪkwənt/ *a.* résultant. **~ly** *adv.* par conséquent.

conservation /kɒnsə'veɪʃn/ *n.* préservation *f.* **~ area,** zone classée *f.*

conservationist /kɒnsə'veɪʃənɪst/ *n.* défenseur de l'environnement *m.*

conservative /kən'sɜːvətɪv/ *a.* conservateur; (*estimate*) modeste. **C~** *a. & n.* conserva|teur, -trice (*m.* (*f.*)).

conservatory /kən'sɜːvətrɪ/ *n.* (*greenhouse*) serre *f.*; (*room*) véranda *f.*

conserve /kən'sɜːv/ *v.t.* conserver; (*energy*) économiser.

consider /kən'sɪdə(r)/ *v.t.* considérer; (*allow for*) tenir compte de; (*possibility*) envisager (**doing,** de faire). **~ation** /-'reɪʃn/ *n.* considération *f.*; (*respect*) égard(s) *m.* (*pl.*). **~ing** *prep.* compte tenu de.

considerabl|e /kən'sɪdərəbl/ *a.* considérable; (*much*) beaucoup de. **~y** *adv.* beaucoup, considérablement.

considerate /kən'sɪdərət/ *a.* prévenant, attentionné.

consign /kən'saɪn/ *v.t.* (*entrust*) confier; (*send*) expédier. **~ment** *n.* envoi *m.*

consist /kən'sɪst/ *v.i.* consister (**of,** en; **in doing,** à faire).

consisten|t /kən'sɪstənt/ *a.* cohérent. **~t with,** conforme à. **~cy** *n.* (*of liquids*) consistance *f.*; (*of argument*) cohérence *f.* **~tly** *adv.* régulièrement.

consol|e /kən'səʊl/ *v.t.* consoler. **~ation** /kɒnsə'leɪʃn/ *n.* consolation *f.*

consolidat|e /kən'sɒlɪdeɪt/ *v.t./i.* (se) consolider. **~ion** /-'deɪʃn/ *n.* consolidation *f.*

consonant /'kɒnsənənt/ *n.* consonne *f.*

consort [1] /'kɒnsɔːt/ *n.* époux *m.*, épouse *f.*

consort [2] /kən'sɔːt/ *v.i.* **~ with,** fréquenter.

consortium /kən'sɔːtɪəm/ *n.* (*pl.* **-tia**) consortium *m.*

conspicuous /kən'spɪkjʊəs/ *a.* (*easily seen*) en évidence; (*showy*) voyant; (*noteworthy*) remarquable.

conspiracy /kən'spɪrəsɪ/ *n.* conspiration *f.*

conspire /kən'spaɪə(r)/ *v.i.* (*person*) comploter (**to do,** de faire), conspirer; (*events*) conspirer (**to do,** à faire).

constable /'kʌnstəbl/ *n.* agent de police *m.*, gendarme *m.*

constant /'kɒnstənt/ *a.* incessant; (*unchanging*) constant; (*friend*) fidèle. ● *n.* constante *f.* **~ly** *adv.* constamment.

constellation /kɒnstə'leɪʃn/ *n.* constellation *f.*

consternation /kɒnstə'neɪʃn/ *n.* consternation *f.*

constipat|e /'kɒnstɪpeɪt/ *v.t.* constiper. **~ion** /-'peɪʃn/ *n.* constipation *f.*

constituency /kən'stɪtjʊənsɪ/ *n.* circonscription électorale *f.*

constituent /kən'stɪtjʊənt/ *a.* constitutif. ● *n.* élément constitutif *m.*; (*pol.*) élec|teur, -trice *m., f.*

constitut|e /'kɒnstɪtju:t/ *v.t.* constituer. **~ion** /-'tju:ʃn/ *n.* constitution *f.* **~ional** /-'tju:ʃənl/ *a.* constitutionnel; *n.* promenade *f.*

constrain /kən'streɪn/ *v.t.* contraindre.

constraint /kən'streɪnt/ *n.* contrainte *f.*

constrict /kən'strɪkt/ *v.t.* resserrer; (*movement*) gêner. **~ion** /-kʃn/ *n.* resserrement *m.*

construct /kən'strʌkt/ *v.t.* construire. **~ion** /-kʃn/ *n.* construction *f.* **~ion worker,** ouvrier du bâtiment *m.*

constructive /kən'strʌktɪv/ *a.* constructif.

construe /kən'stru:/ *v.t.* interpréter.

consul /'kɒnsl/ *n.* consul *m.* **~ar** /-jʊlə(r)/ *a.* consulaire.

consulate /'kɒnsjʊlət/ *n.* consulat *m.*

consult /kən'sʌlt/ *v.t.* consulter. ● *v.i.* **~ with,** conférer avec. **~ation** /kɒnsl'teɪʃn/ *n.* consultation *f.*

consultant /kən'sʌltənt/ *n.* conseil|ler, -ère *m., f.*; (*med.*) spécialiste *m./f.*

consume /kən'sju:m/ *v.t.* consommer; (*destroy*) consumer. **~r** /-ə(r)/ *n.* consomma|teur, -trice *m., f. a.* (*society*) de consommation.

consumerism /kən'sju:mərɪzəm/ *n.* protection des consommateurs *f.*

consummate /'kɒnsəmeɪt/ *v.t.* consommer.

consumption /kən'sʌmpʃn/ *n.* consommation *f.*; (*med.*) phtisie *f.*

contact /'kɒntækt/ *n.* contact *m.*; (*person*) relation *f.* ● *v.t.* contacter. **~ lenses,** lentilles (de contact) *f. pl.*

contagious /kən'teɪdʒəs/ *a.* contagieux.

contain /kən'teɪn/ *v.t.* contenir. **~ o.s.,** se contenir. **~er** *n.* récipient *m.*; (*for transport*) container *m.*

contaminat|e /kən'tæmɪneɪt/ *v.t.* contaminer. **~ion** /-'neɪʃn/ *n.* contamination *f.*

contemplat|e /'kɒntempleɪt/ *v.t.* (*gaze at*) contempler; (*think about*) envisager. **~ion** /-'pleɪʃn/ *n.* contemplation *f.*

contemporary /kən'temprərɪ/ *a.* & *n.* contemporain(e) (*m.* (*f.*)).

contempt /kən'tempt/ *n.* mépris *m.* **~ible** *a.* méprisable. **~uous** /-tʃʊəs/ *a.* méprisant.

contend /kən'tend/ *v.t.* soutenir. ● *v.i.* **~ with,** (*compete*) rivaliser avec; (*face*) faire face à. **~er** *n.* adversaire *m./f.*

content[1] /kən'tent/ *a.* satisfait. ● *v.t.* contenter. **~ed** *a.* satisfait. **~ment** *n.* contentement *m.*

content[2] /'kɒntent/ *n.* (*of letter*) contenu *m.*; (*amount*) teneur *f.* **~s,** contenu *m.*

contention /kən'tenʃn/ *n.* dispute *f.*; (*claim*) affirmation *f.*

contest[1] /'kɒntest/ *n.* (*competition*) concours *m.*; (*fight*) combat *m.*

contest[2] /kən'test/ *v.t.* contester; (*compete for or in*) disputer. **~ant** *n.* concurrent(e) *m.* (*f.*).

context /'kɒntekst/ *n.* contexte *m.*

continent /'kɒntɪnənt/ *n.* continent *m.* **the C~,** l'Europe (continentale) *f.* **~al** /-'nentl/ *a.* continental; européen. **~al quilt,** couette *f.*

contingen|t /kən'tɪndʒənt/ *a.* **be ~t upon,** dépendre de. ● *n.* (*mil.*) contingent *m.* **~cy** *n.* éventualité *f.* **~cy plan,** plan d'urgence *m.*

continual /kən'tɪnjʊəl/ *a.* continuel. **~ly** *adv.* continuellement.

continu|e /kən'tɪnju:/ *v.t./i.* continuer; (*resume*) reprendre. **~ance** *n.* continuation *f.* **~ation** /-ʊ'eɪʃn/ *n.* continuation *f.*; (*after interrup-*

tion) reprise *f.*; (*new episode*) suite *f.* **~ed** *a.* continu.

continuity /kɒntɪ'nju:ətɪ/ *n.* continuité *f.*

continuous /kən'tɪnjʊəs/ *a.* continu. **~ stationery,** papier continu *m.* **~ly** *adv.* sans interruption, continûment.

contort /kən'tɔ:t/ *v.t.* tordre. **~ o.s.,** se contorsionner. **~ion** /-ʃn/ *n.* torsion *f.*; contorsion *f.* **~ionist** /-ʃənɪst/ *n.* contorsionniste *m./f.*

contour /'kɒntʊə(r)/ *n.* contour *m.*

contraband /'kɒntrəbænd/ *n.* contrebande *f.*

contraception /kɒntrə'sepʃn/ *n.* contraception *f.*

contraceptive /kɒntrə'septɪv/ *a.* & *n.* contraceptif (*m.*).

contract[1] /'kɒntrækt/ *n.* contrat *m.*

contract[2] /kən'trækt/ *v.t./i.* (se) contracter. **~ion** /-kʃn/ *n.* contraction *f.*

contractor /kən'træktə(r)/ *n.* entrepreneur *m.*

contradict /kɒntrə'dɪkt/ *v.t.* contredire. **~ion** /-kʃn/ *n.* contradiction *f.* **~ory** *a.* contradictoire.

contralto /kən'træltəʊ/ *n.* (*pl.* **-os**) contralto *m.*

contraption /kən'træpʃn/ *n.* (*fam.*) engin *m.*, truc *m.*

contrary[1] /'kɒntrərɪ/ *a.* contraire (**to,** à). ● *n.* contraire *m.* ● *adv.* **~ to,** contrairement à. **on the ~,** au contraire.

contrary[2] /kən'treərɪ/ *a.* entêté.

contrast[1] /'kɒntrɑ:st/ *n.* contraste *m.*

contrast[2] /kən'trɑ:st/ *v.t./i.* contraster. **~ing** *a.* contrasté.

contraven|e /kɒntrə'vi:n/ *v.t.* enfreindre. **~tion** /-'venʃn/ *n.* infraction *f.*

contribut|e /kən'trɪbju:t/ *v.t.* donner. ● *v.i.* **~e to,** contribuer à; (*take part*) participer à; (*newspaper*) collaborer à. **~ion** /kɒntrɪ'bju:ʃn/ *n.* contribution *f.* **~or** *n.* collabora|teur, -trice *m., f.*

contrivance /kən'traɪvəns/ *n.* (*device*) appareil *m.*, truc *m.*

contrive /kən'traɪv/ *v.t.* imaginer. **~ to do,** trouver moyen de faire. **~d** *a.* tortueux.

control /kən'trəʊl/ *v.t.* (*p.t.* **controlled**) (*a firm etc.*) diriger; (*check*) contrôler; (*restrain*) maîtriser. ● *n.* contrôle *m.*; (*mastery*) maîtrise *f.* **~s,** commandes *f. pl.*; (*knobs*) boutons *m. pl.* **~ tower,** tour de contrôle *f.* **have under ~,** (*event*) avoir en main. **in ~ of,** maître de.

controversial /kɒntrə'vɜ:ʃl/ *a.* discutable, discuté.

controversy /'kɒntrəvɜ:sɪ/ *n.* controverse *f.*

conurbation /kɒnɜ:'beɪʃn/ *n.* agglomération *f.*, conurbation *f.*

convalesce /kɒnvə'les/ *v.i.* être en convalescence. **~nce** *n.* convalescence *f.* **~nt** *a.* & *n.* convalescent(e) (*m.* (*f.*)). **~nt home,** maison de convalescence *f.*

convector /kən'vektə(r)/ *n.* convecteur *m.*

convene /kən'vi:n/ *v.t.* convoquer. ● *v.i.* se réunir.

convenience /kən'vi:nɪəns/ *n.* commodité *f.* **~s,** toilettes *f. pl.* **all modern ~s,** tout le confort moderne. **at your ~,** quand cela vous conviendra, à votre convenance. **~ foods,** plats tout préparés *m. pl.*

convenient /kən'vi:nɪənt/ *a.* commode, pratique; (*time*) bien choisi. **be ~ for,** convenir à. **~ly** *adv.* (*arrive*) à propos. **~ly situated,** bien situé.

convent /'kɒnvənt/ *n.* couvent *m.*

convention /kən'venʃn/ *n.* (*assembly, agreement*) convention *f.*; (*custom*) usage *m.* **~al** *a.* conventionnel.

converge /kən'vɜ:dʒ/ *v.i.* converger.

conversant /kən'vɜ:snt/ *a.* **be ~ with,** connaître; (*fact*) savoir; (*machinery*) s'y connaître en.

conversation /kɒnvə'seɪʃn/ *n.* conversation *f.* **~al** *a.* (*tone etc.*) de la conversation; (*French etc.*) de tous les jours. **~alist** *n.* causeu|r, -se *m., f.*

converse[1] /kən'vɜ:s/ *v.i.* s'entretenir, converser (**with,** avec).

converse[2] /'kɒnvɜ:s/ *a.* & *n.* inverse (*m.*). **~ly** *adv.* inversement.

conver|t[1] /kən'vɜ:t/ *v.t.* convertir; (*house*) aménager. ● *v.i.* **~t into,** se transformer en. **~sion** /-ʃn/ *n.* conversion *f.* **~tible** *a.* convertible. ● *n.* (*car*) décapotable *f.*

convert[2] /'kɒnvɜ:t/ *n.* converti(e) *m.* (*f.*).

convex /'kɒnveks/ *a.* convexe.

convey /kən'veɪ/ *v.t.* (*wishes, order*) transmettre; (*goods, people*) transporter; (*idea, feeling*) communiquer.

~ance *n.* transport *m.* **~or belt,** tapis roulant *m.*

convict[1] /kən'vɪkt/ *v.t.* déclarer coupable. **~ion** /-kʃn/ *n.* condamnation *f.*; (*opinion*) conviction *f.*

convict[2] /'kɒnvɪkt/ *n.* prisonni|er, -ère *m., f.*

convinc|e /kən'vɪns/ *v.t.* convaincre. **~ing** *a.* convaincant.

convivial /kən'vɪvɪəl/ *a.* joyeux.

convoke /kən'vəʊk/ *v.t.* convoquer.

convoluted /'kɒnvəlu:tɪd/ *a.* (*argument etc.*) compliqué.

convoy /'kɒnvɔɪ/ *n.* convoi *m.*

convuls|e /kən'vʌls/ *v.t.* convulser; (*fig.*) bouleverser. **be ~ed with laughter,** se tordre de rire. **~ion** /-ʃn/ *n.* convulsion *f.*

coo /ku:/ *v.i.* roucouler.

cook /kʊk/ *v.t./i.* (faire) cuire; (*of person*) faire la cuisine. ● *n.* cuisin|ier, -ière *m., f.* **~ up,** (*fam.*) fabriquer. **~ing** *n.* cuisine *f.*; *a.* de cuisine.

cooker /'kʊkə(r)/ *n.* (*stove*) cuisinière *f.*; (*apple*) pomme à cuire *f.*

cookery /'kʊkərɪ/ *n.* cuisine *f.* **~ book,** livre de cuisine *m.*

cookie /'kʊkɪ/ *n.* (*Amer.*) biscuit *m.*

cool /ku:l/ *a.* (**-er, -est**) frais; (*calm*) calme; (*unfriendly*) froid. ● *n.* fraîcheur *f.*; (*calmness: sl.*) sang-froid *m.* ● *v.t./i.* rafraîchir. **in the ~,** au frais. **~ box,** glacière *f.* **~er** *n.* (*for food*) glacière *f.*; **~ly** *adv.* calmement; froidement. **~ness** *n.* fraîcheur *f.*; froideur *f.*

coop /ku:p/ *n.* poulailler *m.* ● *v.t.* **~ up,** enfermer.

co-operat|e /kəʊ'ɒpəreɪt/ *v.i.* coopérer. **~ion** /-'reɪʃn/ *n.* coopération *f.*

co-operative /kəʊ'ɒpərətɪv/ *a.* coopératif. ● *n.* coopérative *f.*

co-opt /kəʊ'ɒpt/ *v.t.* coopter.

co-ordinat|e /kəʊ'ɔ:dɪneɪt/ *v.t.* coordonner. **~ion** /-'neɪʃn/ *n.* coordination *f.*

cop /kɒp/ *v.t.* (*p.t.* **copped**) (*sl.*) piquer. ● *n.* (*policeman: sl.*) flic *m.* **~ out,** (*sl.*) se dérober. **~-out** *n.* (*sl.*) dérobade *f.*

cope /kəʊp/ *v.i.* assurer. **~ with,** s'en sortir avec.

copious /'kəʊpɪəs/ *a.* copieux.

copper[1] /'kɒpə(r)/ *n.* cuivre *m.*; (*coin*) sou *m.* ● *a.* de cuivre.

copper[2] /'kɒpə(r)/ *n.* (*sl.*) flic *m.*

coppice, copse /'kɒpɪs, kɒps/ *ns.* taillis *m.*

copulat|e /'kɒpjʊleɪt/ *v.i.* s'accoupler. **~ion** /-'leɪʃn/ *n.* copulation *f.*

copy /'kɒpɪ/ *n.* copie *f.*; (*of book, newspaper*) exemplaire *m.*; (*print: photo.*) épreuve *f.* ● *v.t./i.* copier. **~-writer** *n.* rédacteur-concepteur *m.*, rédactrice-conceptrice *f.*

copyright /'kɒpɪraɪt/ *n.* droit d'auteur *m.*, copyright *m.*

coral /'kɒrəl/ *n.* corail *m.*

cord /kɔ:d/ *n.* (petite) corde *f.*; (*of curtain, pyjamas, etc.*) cordon *m.*; (*electr.*) cordon électrique *m.*; (*fabric*) velours côtelé *m.*

cordial /'kɔ:dɪəl/ *a.* cordial. ● *n.* (*fruit-flavoured drink*) sirop *m.*

cordon /'kɔ:dn/ *n.* cordon *m.* ● *v.t.* **~ off,** mettre un cordon autour de.

corduroy /'kɔ:dərɔɪ/ *n.* velours côtelé *m.*, velours à côtes *m.*

core /kɔ:(r)/ *n.* (*of apple*) trognon *m.*; (*of problem*) cœur *m.*; (*techn.*) noyau *m.* ● *v.t.* vider.

cork /kɔ:k/ *n.* liège *m.*; (*for bottle*) bouchon *m.* ● *v.t.* boucher.

corkscrew /'kɔ:kskru:/ *n.* tire-bouchon *m.*

corn[1] /kɔ:n/ *n.* blé *m.*; (*maize: Amer.*) maïs *m.*; (*seed*) grain *m.* **~-cob** *n.* épi de maïs *m.*

corn[2] /kɔ:n/ *n.* (*hard skin*) cor *m.*

cornea /'kɔ:nɪə/ *n.* cornée *f.*

corned /kɔ:nd/ *a.* **~ beef,** corned-beef *m.*

corner /'kɔ:nə(r)/ *n.* coin *m.*; (*bend in road*) virage *m.*; (*football*) corner *m.* ● *v.t.* coincer, acculer; (*market*) accaparer. ● *v.i.* prendre un virage. **~-stone** *n.* pierre angulaire *f.*

cornet /'kɔ:nɪt/ *n.* cornet *m.*

cornflakes /'kɔ:nfleɪks/ *n. pl.* corn flakes *m. pl.*

cornflour /'kɔ:nflaʊə(r)/ *n.* farine de maïs *f.*

cornice /'kɔ:nɪs/ *n.* corniche *f.*

cornstarch /kɔ:nstɑ:tʃ/ *n. Amer.* = **cornflour.**

cornucopia /kɔ:njʊ'kəʊpɪə/ *n.* corne d'abondance *f.*

Corn|wall /'kɔ:nwəl/ *n.* Cornouailles *f.* **~ish** *a.* de Cornouailles.

corny /'kɔ:nɪ/ *a.* (**-ier, -iest**) (*trite: fam.*) rebattu; (*mawkish: fam.*) à l'eau de rose.

corollary /kə'rɒlərɪ, *Amer.* 'kɒrələrɪ/ *n.* corollaire *m.*

coronary /ˈkɒrənərɪ/ *n.* infarctus *m.*

coronation /kɒrəˈneɪʃn/ *n.* couronnement *m.*

coroner /ˈkɒrənə(r)/ *n.* coroner *m.*

corporal[1] /ˈkɔːpərəl/ *n.* caporal *m.*

corporal[2] /ˈkɔːpərəl/ *a.* **~ punishment,** châtiment corporel *m.*

corporate /ˈkɔːpərət/ *a.* en commun; (*body*) constitué.

corporation /kɔːpəˈreɪʃn/ *n.* (*comm.*) société *f.*; (*of town*) municipalité *f.*

corps /kɔː(r)/ *n.* (*pl.* **corps** /kɔːz/) corps *m.*

corpse /kɔːps/ *n.* cadavre *m.*

corpulent /ˈkɔːpjʊlənt/ *a.* corpulent.

corpuscle /ˈkɔːpʌsl/ *n.* globule *m.*

corral /kəˈrɑːl/ *n.* (*Amer.*) corral *m.*

correct /kəˈrekt/ *a.* (*right*) exact, juste, correct; (*proper*) correct. **you are ~,** vous avez raison. ● *v.t.* corriger. **~ion** /-kʃn/ *n.* correction *f.*

correlat|e /ˈkɒrəleɪt/ *v.t./i.* (faire) correspondre. **~ion** /-ˈleɪʃn/ *n.* corrélation *f.*

correspond /kɒrɪˈspɒnd/ *v.i.* correspondre. **~ence** *n.* correspondance *f.* **~ence course,** cours par correspondance *m.* **~ent** *n.* correspondant(e) *m.*(*f.*).

corridor /ˈkɒrɪdɔː(r)/ *n.* couloir *m.*

corroborate /kəˈrɒbəreɪt/ *v.t.* corroborer.

corro|de /kəˈrəʊd/ *v.t./i.* (se) corroder. **~sion** *n.* corrosion *f.*

corrosive /kəˈrəʊsɪv/ *a.* corrosif.

corrugated /ˈkɒrəgeɪtɪd/ *a.* ondulé. **~ iron,** tôle ondulée *f.*

corrupt /kəˈrʌpt/ *a.* corrompu. ● *v.t.* corrompre. **~ion** /-pʃn/ *n.* corruption *f.*

corset /ˈkɔːsɪt/ *n.* (*boned*) corset *m.*; (*elasticated*) gaine *f.*

Corsica /ˈkɔːsɪkə/ *n.* Corse *f.*

cortisone /ˈkɔːtɪzəʊn/ *n.* cortisone *f.*

cos /kɒs/ *n.* laitue romaine *f.*

cosh /kɒʃ/ *n.* matraque *f.* ● *v.t.* matraquer.

cosmetic /kɒzˈmetɪk/ *n.* produit de beauté *m.* ● *a.* cosmétique; (*fig.*, *pej.*) superficiel.

cosmic /ˈkɒzmɪk/ *a.* cosmique.

cosmonaut /ˈkɒzmənɔːt/ *n.* cosmonaute *m.*/*f.*

cosmopolitan /kɒzməˈpɒlɪt(ə)n/ *a.* & *n.* cosmopolite (*m.*/*f.*).

cosmos /ˈkɒzmɒs/ *n.* cosmos *m.*

Cossack /ˈkɒsæk/ *n.* cosaque *m.*

cosset /ˈkɒsɪt/ *v.t.* (*p.t.* **cosseted**) dorloter.

cost /kɒst/ *v.t.* (*p.t.* **cost**) coûter; (*p.t.* **costed**) établir le prix de. ● *n.* coût *m.* **~s,** (*jurid.*) dépens *m. pl.* **at all ~s,** à tout prix. **to one's ~,** à ses dépens. **~-effective** *a.* rentable. **~-effectiveness** *n.* rentabilité *f.* **~ price,** prix de revient *m.* **~ of living,** coût de la vie *m.*

co-star /ˈkəʊstɑː(r)/ *n.* partenaire *m.*/*f.*

costly /ˈkɒstlɪ/ *a.* (**-ier, -iest**) coûteux; (*valuable*) précieux.

costume /ˈkɒstjuːm/ *n.* costume *m.*; (*for swimming*) maillot *m.* **~ jewellery,** bijoux de fantaisie *m. pl.*

cos|y /ˈkəʊzɪ/ *a.* (**-ier, -iest**) confortable, intime. ● *n.* couvre-théière *m.* **~iness** *n.* confort *m.*

cot /kɒt/ *n.* lit d'enfant *m.*; (*camp-bed*: *Amer.*) lit de camp *m.*

cottage /ˈkɒtɪdʒ/ *n.* petite maison de campagne *f.*; (*thatched*) chaumière *f.* **~ cheese,** fromage blanc (maigre) *m.* **~ industry,** activité artisanale *f.* **~ pie,** hachis Parmentier *m.*

cotton /ˈkɒtn/ *n.* coton *m.*; (*for sewing*) fil (à coudre) *m.* ● *v.i.* **~ on,** (*sl.*) piger. **~ candy,** (*Amer.*) barbe à papa *f.* **~ wool,** coton hydrophile *m.*

couch /kaʊtʃ/ *n.* divan *m.* ● *v.t.* (*express*) formuler.

couchette /kuːˈʃet/ *n.* couchette *f.*

cough /kɒf/ *v.i.* tousser. ● *n.* toux *f.* **~ up,** (*sl.*) cracher, payer.

could /kʊd, *unstressed* kəd/ *p.t. of* **can**[2].

couldn't /ˈkʊdnt/ = **could not**.

council /ˈkaʊnsl/ *n.* conseil *m.* **~ house,** maison construite par la municipalité *f.*, (*approx.*) H.L.M. *m.*/*f.*

councillor /ˈkaʊnsələ(r)/ *n.* conseill|er, -ère municipal(e) *m.*, *f.*

counsel /ˈkaʊnsl/ *n.* conseil *m.* ● *n. invar.* (*jurid.*) avocat(e) *m.* (*f.*). **~lor** *n.* conseill|er, -ère *m.*, *f.*

count[1] /kaʊnt/ *v.t./i.* compter. ● *n.* compte *m.* **~ on,** compter sur.

count[2] /kaʊnt/ *n.* (*nobleman*) comte *m.*

countdown /ˈkaʊntdaʊn/ *n.* compte à rebours *m.*

countenance /ˈkaʊntɪnəns/ *n.* mine *f.* ● *v.t.* admettre, approuver.

counter[1] /ˈkaʊntə(r)/ *n.* comptoir *m.*; (*in bank etc.*) guichet *m.*; (*token*) jeton *m.*

counter[2] /'kaʊntə(r)/ *adv.* **~ to,** à l'encontre de. ● *a.* opposé. ● *v.t.* opposer; (*blow*) parer. ● *v.i.* riposter.
counter- /'kaʊntə(r)/ *pref.* contre-.
counteract /kaʊntər'ækt/ *v.t.* neutraliser.
counter-attack /'kaʊntərətæk/ *n.* contre-attaque *f.* ● *v.t./i.* contre-attaquer.
counterbalance /'kaʊntəbæləns/ *n.* contrepoids *m.* ● *v.t.* contrebalancer.
counter-clockwise /kaʊntə'klɒkwaɪz/ *a. & adv.* (*Amer.*) dans le sens inverse des aiguilles d'une montre.
counterfeit /'kaʊntəfɪt/ *a. & n.* faux (*m.*). ● *v.t.* contrefaire.
counterfoil /'kaʊntəfɔɪl/ *n.* souche *f.*
countermand /kaʊntə'mɑ:nd/ *v.t.* annuler.
counterpart /'kaʊntəpɑ:t/ *n.* équivalent *m.*; (*person*) homologue *m./f.*
counter-productive /kaʊntəprə'dʌktɪv/ *a.* (*measure*) qui produit l'effet contraire.
countersign /'kaʊntəsaɪn/ *v.t.* contresigner.
counter-tenor /'kaʊntətenə(r)/ *n.* haute-contre *m.*
countess /'kaʊntɪs/ *n.* comtesse *f.*
countless /'kaʊntlɪs/ *a.* innombrable.
countrified /'kʌntrɪfaɪd/ *a.* rustique.
country /'kʌntrɪ/ *n.* (*land, region*) pays *m.*; (*homeland*) patrie *f.*; (*countryside*) campagne *f.* **~ dance,** danse folklorique *f.*
countryman /'kʌntrɪmən/ *n.* (*pl.* **-men**) campagnard *m.*; (*fellow citizen*) compatriote *m.*
countryside /'kʌntrɪsaɪd/ *n.* campagne *f.*
county /'kaʊntɪ/ *n.* comté *m.*
coup /ku:/ *n.* (*achievement*) joli coup *m.*; (*pol.*) coup d'état *m.*
coupé /'ku:peɪ/ *n.* (*car*) coupé *m.*
couple /'kʌpl/ *n.* (*people, animals*) couple *m.* ● *v.t./i.* (s')accoupler. **a ~ (of),** (*two or three*) deux ou trois.
coupon /'ku:pɒn/ *n.* coupon *m.*; (*for shopping*) bon *or* coupon de réduction *m.*
courage /'kʌrɪdʒ/ *n.* courage *m.* **~ous** /kə'reɪdʒəs/ *a.* courageux.
courgette /kʊə'ʒet/ *n.* courgette *f.*
courier /'kʊrɪə(r)/ *n.* messag|er, -ère *m., f.*; (*for tourists*) guide *m.*
course /kɔ:s/ *n.* cours *m.*; (*for training*) stage *m.*; (*series*) série *f.*; (*culin.*) plat *m.*; (*for golf*) terrain *m.*; (*at sea*) itinéraire *m.* **change ~,** changer de cap. **~ (of action),** façon de faire *f.* **during the ~ of,** pendant. **in due ~,** en temps utile. **of ~,** bien sûr.
court /kɔ:t/ *n.* cour *f.*; (*tennis*) court *m.* ● *v.t.* faire la cour à; (*danger*) rechercher. **~ martial,** (*pl.* **courts martial**) conseil de guerre *m.* **~-martial** *v.t.* (*p.t.* **-martialled**) faire passer en conseil de guerre. **~-house** *n.* (*Amer.*) palais de justice *m.* **~ shoe,** escarpin *m.* **go to ~,** aller devant les tribunaux.
courteous /'kɜ:tɪəs/ *a.* courtois.
courtesy /'kɜ:təsɪ/ *n.* courtoisie *f.* **by ~ of,** avec la permission de.
courtier /'kɔ:tɪə(r)/ *n.* (*old use*) courtisan *m.*
courtroom /'kɔ:trʊm/ *n.* salle de tribunal *f.*
courtyard /'kɔ:tjɑ:d/ *n.* cour *f.*
cousin /'kʌzn/ *n.* cousin(e) *m.* (*f.*). **first ~,** cousin(e) germain(e) *m.* (*f.*).
cove /kəʊv/ *n.* anse *f.*, crique *f.*
covenant /'kʌvənənt/ *n.* convention *f.*
Coventry /'kɒvntrɪ/ *n.* **send to ~,** mettre en quarantaine.
cover /'kʌvə(r)/ *v.t.* couvrir. ● *n.* (*for bed, book, etc.*) couverture *f.*; (*lid*) couvercle *m.*; (*for furniture*) housse *f.*; (*shelter*) abri *m.* **~ charge,** couvert *m.* **~ up,** cacher; (*crime*) couvrir. **~ up for,** couvrir. **~-up** *n.* tentative pour cacher la vérité *f.* **take ~,** se mettre à l'abri. **~ing** *n.* enveloppe *f.* **~ing letter,** lettre *f.* (*jointe à un document*).
coverage /'kʌvərɪdʒ/ *n.* reportage *m.*
coveralls /'kʌvərɔ:lz/ (*Amer.*) bleu de travail *m.*
covert /'kʌvət, *Amer.* /'kəʊvɜ:rt/ *a.* (*activity*) secret; (*threat*) voilé (*look*) dérobé.
covet /'kʌvɪt/ *v.t.* convoiter.
cow /kaʊ/ *n.* vache *f.*
coward /'kaʊəd/ *n.* lâche *m./f.* **~ly** *a.* lâche.
cowardice /'kaʊədɪs/ *n.* lâcheté *f.*
cowboy /'kaʊbɔɪ/ *n.* cow-boy *m.*
cower /'kaʊə(r)/ *v.i.* se recroqueviller (sous l'effet de la peur).
cowshed /'kaʊʃed/ *n.* étable *f.*
cox /kɒks/ *n.* barreur *m.* ● *v.t.* barrer.

coxswain /'kɒksn/ *n.* barreur *m.*

coy /kɔɪ/ *a.* (**-er, -est**) (faussement) timide, qui fait le *or* la timide.

cozy /'kəʊzɪ/ *Amer.* = **cosy**.

crab /kræb/ *n.* crabe *m.* ● *v.i.* (*p.t.* **crabbed**) rouspéter. **~-apple** *n.* pomme sauvage *f.*

crack /kræk/ *n.* fente *f.*; (*in glass*) fêlure *f.*; (*noise*) craquement *m.*; (*joke: sl.*) plaisanterie *f.* ● *a.* (*fam.*) d'élite, ● *v.t./i.* (*break partially*) (se) fêler; (*split*) (se) fendre; (*nut*) casser; (*joke*) raconter; (*problem*) résoudre. **~ down on,** (*fam.*) sévir contre. **~ up,** (*fam.*) craquer. **get ~ing,** (*fam.*) s'y mettre.

cracked /krækt/ *a.* (*sl.*) cinglé.

cracker /'krækə(r)/ *n.* pétard *m.*; (*culin.*) biscuit (salé) *m.*

crackers /'krækəz/ *a.* (*sl.*) cinglé.

crackle /'krækl/ *v.i.* crépiter. ● *n.* crépitement *m.*

crackpot /'krækpɒt/ *n.* (*sl.*) cinglé(e) *m.* (*f.*).

cradle /'kreɪdl/ *n.* berceau *m.* ● *v.t.* bercer.

craft[1] /krɑ:ft/ *n.* métier artisanal *m.*; (*technique*) art *m.*; (*cunning*) ruse *f.*

craft[2] /krɑ:ft/ *n. invar.* (*boat*) bateau *m.*

craftsman /'krɑ:ftsmən/ *n.* (*pl.* **-men**) artisan *m.* **~ship** *n.* art *m.*

crafty /'krɑ:ftɪ/ *a.* (**-ier, -iest**) rusé.

crag /kræg/ *n.* rocher à pic *m.* **~gy** *a.* à pic; (*face*) rude.

cram /kræm/ *v.t./i.* (*p.t.* **crammed**). **~ (for an exam),** bachoter. **~ into,** (*pack*) (s')entasser dans. **~ with,** (*fill*) bourrer de.

cramp /kræmp/ *n.* crampe *f.*

cramped /kræmpt/ *a.* à l'étroit.

cranberry /'krænbərɪ/ *n.* canneberge *f.*

crane /kreɪn/ *n.* grue *f.* ● *v.t.* (*neck*) tendre.

crank[1] /kræŋk/ *n.* (*techn.*) manivelle *f.*

crank[2] /kræŋk/ *n.* excentrique *m./f.* **~y** *a.* excentrique; (*Amer.*) grincheux.

cranny /'krænɪ/ *n.* fissure *f.*

craps /kræps/ *n.* **shoot ~,** (*Amer.*) jouer aux dés.

crash /kræʃ/ *n.* accident *m.*; (*noise*) fracas *m.*; (*of thunder*) coup *m.*; (*of firm*) faillite *f.* ● *v.t./i.* avoir un accident (avec); (*of plane*) s'écraser; (*two vehicles*) se percuter. ● *a.* (*course*) intensif. **~-helmet** *n.* casque (anti-choc) *m.* **~ into,** rentrer dans. **~-land** *v.i.* atterrir en catastrophe.

crass /kræs/ *a.* grossier.

crate /kreɪt/ *n.* cageot *m.*

crater /'kreɪtə(r)/ *n.* cratère *m.*

cravat /krə'væt/ *n.* foulard *m.*

crav|e /kreɪv/ *v.t./i.* **~e (for),** désirer ardemment. **~ing** *n.* envie irrésistible *f.*

crawl /krɔ:l/ *v.i.* ramper; (*vehicle*) se traîner. ● *n.* (*pace*) pas *m.*; (*swimming*) crawl *m.* **be ~ing with,** grouiller de.

crayfish /'kreɪfɪʃ/ *n. invar.* écrevisse *f.*

crayon /'kreɪən/ *n.* crayon *m.*

craze /kreɪz/ *n.* engouement *m.*

crazed /kreɪzd/ *a.* affolé.

craz|y /'kreɪzɪ/ *a.* (**-ier, -iest**) fou. **~y about,** (*person*) fou de; (*thing*) fana *or* fou de. **~iness** *n.* folie *f.* **~y paving,** dallage irrégulier *m.*

creak /kri:k/ *n.* grincement *m.* ● *v.i.* grincer. **~y** *a.* grinçant.

cream /kri:m/ *n.* crème *f.* ● *a.* crème *invar.* ● *v.t.* écrémer. **~ cheese,** fromage frais *m.* **~ off,** se servir en prenant. **~y** *a.* crémeux.

crease /kri:s/ *n.* pli *m.* ● *v.t./i.* (se) froisser.

creat|e /kri:'eɪt/ *v.t.* créer. **~ion** /-ʃn/ *n.* création *f.* **~ive** *a.* créateur. **~or** *n.* créa|teur, -trice *m., f.*

creature /'kri:tʃə(r)/ *n.* créature *f.*

crèche /kreʃ/ *n.* garderie *f.*

credence /'kri:dns/ *n.* **give ~ to,** ajouter foi à.

credentials /krɪ'denʃlz/ *n. pl.* (*identity*) pièces d'identité *f. pl.*; (*competence*) références *f. pl.*

credib|le /'kredəbl/ *a.* (*excuse etc.*) croyable, plausible. **~ility** /-'bɪlətɪ/ *n.* crédibilité *f.*

credit /'kredɪt/ *n.* crédit *m.*; (*honour*) honneur *m.* **in ~,** créditeur. **~s,** (*cinema*) générique *m.* ● *a.* (*balance*) créditeur. ● *v.t.* (*p.t.* **credited**) croire; (*comm.*) créditer. **~ card,** carte de crédit *f.* **~ note,** avoir *m.* **~ s.o. with,** attribuer à qn. **~-worthy** *a.* solvable. **~or** *n.* créan|cier, -ière *m., f.*

creditable /'kredɪtəbl/ *a.* méritoire, honorable.

credulous /'kredjʊləs/ *a.* crédule.

creed /kri:d/ *n.* credo *m.*

creek /kri:k/ *n.* crique *f.*; (*Amer.*) ruisseau *m.* **up the ~,** (*sl.*) dans le pétrin.

creep /kri:p/ *v.i.* (*p.t.* **crept**) ramper; (*fig.*) se glisser. ● *n.* (*person*: *sl.*) pauvre type *m.* **give s.o. the ~s,** faire frissonner qn. **~er** *n.* liane *f.* **~y** *a.* qui fait frissonner.

cremat|e /krɪ'meɪt/ *v.t.* incinérer. **~ion** /-ʃn/ *n.* incinération *f.*

crematorium /kremə'tɔ:rɪəm/ *n.* (*pl.* **-ia**) crématorium *m.*

Creole /'kri:əʊl/ *n.* créole *m./f.*

crêpe /kreɪp/ *n.* crêpe *m.* **~ paper,** papier crêpon *m.*

crept /krept/ *see* creep.

crescendo /krɪ'ʃendəʊ/ *n.* (*pl.* **-os**) crescendo *m.*

crescent /'kresnt/ *n.* croissant *m.*; (*fig.*) rue en demi-lune *f.*

cress /kres/ *n.* cresson *m.*

crest /krest/ *n.* crête *f.*; (*coat of arms*) armoiries *f. pl.*

Crete /kri:t/ *n.* Crète *f.*

cretin /'kretɪn, *Amer.* 'kri:tn/ *n.* crétin(e) *m.* (*f.*). **~ous** *a.* crétin.

crevasse /krɪ'væs/ *n.* crevasse *f.*

crevice /'krevɪs/ *n.* fente *f.*

crew /kru:/ *n.* équipage *m.*; (*gang*) équipe *f.* **~ cut,** coupe en brosse *f.* **~ neck,** (col) ras du cou *m.*

crib[1] /krɪb/ *n.* lit d'enfant *m.*

crib[2] /krɪb/ *v.t./i.* (*p.t.* **cribbed**) copier. ● *n.* (*schol., fam.*) traduction *f.*, aide-mémoire *m. invar.*

crick /krɪk/ *n.* (*in neck*) torticolis *m.*

cricket[1] /'krɪkɪt/ *n.* (*sport*) cricket *m.* **~er** *n.* joueur de cricket *m.*

cricket[2] /'krɪkɪt/ *n.* (*insect*) grillon *m.*

crime /kraɪm/ *n.* crime *m.*; (*minor*) délit *m.*; (*acts*) criminalité *f.*

criminal /'krɪmɪnl/ *a.* & *n.* criminel(le) (*m.* (*f.*)).

crimp /krɪmp/ *v.t.* (*hair*) friser.

crimson /'krɪmzn/ *a.* & *n.* cramoisi (*m.*).

cring|e /krɪndʒ/ *v.i.* reculer; (*fig.*) s'humilier. **~ing** *a.* servile.

crinkle /'krɪŋkl/ *v.t./i.* (se) froisser. ● *n.* pli *m.*

cripple /'krɪpl/ *n.* infirme *m./f.* ● *v.t.* estropier; (*fig.*) paralyser.

crisis /'kraɪsɪs/ *n.* (*pl.* **crises** /-si:z/) crise *f.*

crisp /krɪsp/ *a.* (**-er, -est**) (*culin.*) croquant; (*air, reply*) vif. **~s** *n. pl.* chips *f. pl.*

criss-cross /'krɪskrɒs/ *a.* entrecroisé. ● *v.t./i.* (s')entrecroiser.

criterion /kraɪ'tɪərɪən/ *n.* (*pl.* **-ia**) critère *m.*

critic /'krɪtɪk/ *n.* critique *m.* **~al** *a.* critique. **~ally** *adv.* d'une manière critique; (*ill*) gravement.

criticism /'krɪtɪsɪzəm/ *n.* critique *f.*

criticize /'krɪtɪsaɪz/ *v.t./i.* critiquer.

croak /krəʊk/ *n.* (*bird*) croassement *m.*; (*frog*) coassement *m.* ● *v.i.* croasser; coasser.

crochet /'krəʊʃeɪ/ *n.* crochet *m.* ● *v.t.* faire au crochet.

crockery /'krɒkərɪ/ *n.* vaisselle *f.*

crocodile /'krɒkədaɪl/ *n.* crocodile *m.*

crocus /'krəʊkəs/ *n.* (*pl.* **-uses**) crocus *m.*

crony /'krəʊnɪ/ *n.* cop|ain, -ine *m., f.*

crook /krʊk/ *n.* (*criminal*: *fam.*) escroc *m.*; (*stick*) houlette *f.*

crooked /'krʊkɪd/ *a.* tordu; (*winding*) tortueux; (*askew*) de travers; (*dishonest*: *fig.*) malhonnête. **~ly** *adv.* de travers.

croon /kru:n/ *v.t./i.* chantonner.

crop /krɒp/ *n.* récolte *f.*; (*fig.*) quantité *f.* ● *v.t.* (*p.t.* **cropped**) couper. ● *v.i.* **~ up,** se présenter.

croquet /'krəʊkeɪ/ *n.* croquet *m.*

croquette /krəʊ'ket/ *n.* croquette *f.*

cross /krɒs/ *n.* croix *f.*; (*hybrid*) hybride *m.* ● *v.t./i.* traverser; (*legs, animals*) croiser; (*cheque*) barrer; (*paths*) se croiser. ● *a.* en colère, fâché (**with,** contre). **~-check** *v.t.* verifier (pour confirmer). **~-country (running),** cross *m.* **~ off** *or* **out,** rayer. **~ s.o.'s mind,** venir à l'esprit de qn. **talk at ~ purposes,** parler sans se comprendre. **~ly** *adv.* avec colère.

crossbar /'krɒsbɑ:(r)/ *n.* barre transversale *f.*

cross-examine /krɒsɪg'zæmɪn/ *v.t.* faire subir un contre-interrogatoire à.

cross-eyed /'krɒsaɪd/ *a.* **be ~,** loucher.

crossfire /'krɒsfaɪə(r)/ *n.* feux croisés *m. pl.*

crossing /'krɒsɪŋ/ *n.* (*by boat*) traversée *f.*; (*on road*) passage clouté *m.*

cross-reference /krɒs'refrəns/ *n.* renvoi *m.*

crossroads /'krɒsrəʊdz/ *n.* carrefour *m.*

cross-section /krɒs'sekʃn/ *n.* coupe transversale *f.*; (*sample*: *fig.*) échantillon *m.*

cross-wind /'krɒswɪnd/ *n.* vent de travers *m.*
crosswise /'krɒswaɪz/ *adv.* en travers.
crossword /'krɒswɜ:d/ *n.* mots croisés *m. pl.*
crotch /krɒtʃ/ *n.* (*of garment*) entrejambes *m. invar.*
crotchet /'krɒtʃɪt/ *n.* (*mus.*) noire *f.*
crotchety /'krɒtʃɪtɪ/ *a.* grincheux.
crouch /kraʊtʃ/ *v.i.* s'accroupir.
crow /krəʊ/ *n.* corbeau *m.* ● *v.i.* (*of cock*) (*p.t.* **crew**) chanter; (*fig.*) jubiler. **as the ~ flies,** à vol d'oiseau. **~'s feet,** pattes d'oie *f. pl.*
crowbar /'krəʊbɑ:(r)/ *n.* pied-de-biche *m.*
crowd /kraʊd/ *n.* foule *f.* ● *v.i.* affluer. ● *v.t.* remplir. **~ into,** (s')entasser dans. **~ed** *a.* plein.
crown /kraʊn/ *n.* couronne *f.*; (*top part*) sommet *m.* ● *v.t.* couronner. **C~ Court,** Cour d'assises *f.* **C~ prince,** prince héritier *m.*
crucial /'kru:ʃl/ *a.* crucial.
crucifix /'kru:sɪfɪks/ *n.* crucifix *m.*
crucif|y /'kru:sɪfaɪ/ *v.t.* crucifier. **~ixion** /-'fɪkʃn/ *n.* crucifixion *f.*
crude /kru:d/ *a.* (**-er, -est**) (*raw*) brut; (*rough, vulgar*) grossier.
cruel /krʊəl/ *a.* (**crueller, cruellest**) cruel. **~ty** *n.* cruauté *f.*
cruet /'kru:ɪt/ *n.* huilier *m.*
cruis|e /kru:z/ *n.* croisière *f.* ● *v.i.* (*ship*) croiser; (*tourists*) faire une croisière; (*vehicle*) rouler. **~er** *n.* croiseur *m.* **~ing speed,** vitesse de croisière *f.*
crumb /krʌm/ *n.* miette *f.*
crumble /'krʌmbl/ *v.t./i.* (s')effriter; (*bread*) (s')émietter; (*collapse*) s'écrouler.
crummy /'krʌmɪ/ *a.* (**-ier, -iest**) (*sl.*) moche, minable.
crumpet /'krʌmpɪt/ *n.* (*culin.*) petite crêpe (grillée) *f.*
crumple /'krʌmpl/ *v.t./i.* (se) froisser.
crunch /krʌntʃ/ *v.t.* croquer. ● *n.* (*event*) moment critique *m.* **when it comes to the ~,** quand ça devient sérieux.
crusade /kru:'seɪd/ *n.* croisade *f.* **~r** /-ə(r)/ *n.* (*knight*) croisé *m.*; (*fig.*) militant(e) *m.* (*f.*).
crush /krʌʃ/ *v.t.* écraser; (*clothes*) froisser. ● *n.* (*crowd*) presse *f.* **a ~ on,** (*sl.*) le béguin pour.
crust /krʌst/ *n.* croûte *f.* **~y** *a.* croustillant.
crutch /krʌtʃ/ *n.* béquille *f.*; (*crotch*) entrejambes *m. invar.*
crux /krʌks/ *n.* **the ~ of,** (*problem etc.*) le nœud de.
cry /kraɪ/ *n.* cri *m.* ● *v.i.* (*weep*) pleurer; (*call out*) crier. **~-baby** *n.* pleurnicheu|r, -se *m., f.* **~ off,** abandonner.
crying /'kraɪɪŋ/ *a.* (*evil etc.*) flagrant. **a ~ shame,** une vraie honte.
crypt /krɪpt/ *n.* crypte *f.*
cryptic /'krɪptɪk/ *a.* énigmatique.
crystal /'krɪstl/ *n.* cristal *m.* **~-clear** *a.* parfaitement clair. **~lize** *v.t./i.* (se) cristalliser.
cub /kʌb/ *n.* petit *m.* **Cub (Scout),** louveteau *m.*
Cuba /'kju:bə/ *n.* Cuba *m.* **~n** *a.* & *n.* cubain(e) (*m.* (*f.*)).
cubby-hole /'kʌbɪhəʊl/ *n.* cagibi *m.*
cub|e /kju:b/ *n.* cube *m.* **~ic** *a.* cubique; (*metre etc.*) cube.
cubicle /'kju:bɪkl/ *n.* (*in room, hospital, etc.*) box *m.*; (*at swimming-pool*) cabine *f.*
cuckoo /'kʊku:/ *n.* coucou *m.*
cucumber /'kju:kʌmbə(r)/ *n.* concombre *m.*
cuddl|e /'kʌdl/ *v.t.* câliner. ● *v.i.* (**kiss and**) **~e,** s'embrasser. ● *n.* caresse *f.* **~y** *a.* câlin, caressant.
cudgel /'kʌdʒl/ *n.* gourdin *m.*
cue[1] /kju:/ *n.* signal *m.*; (*theatre*) réplique *f.*
cue[2] /kju:/ *n.* (*billiards*) queue *f.*
cuff /kʌf/ *n.* manchette *f.*; (*Amer.*) revers *m.* ● *v.t.* gifler. **~-link** *n.* bouton de manchette *m.* **off the ~,** impromptu.
cul-de-sac /'kʌldəsæk/ *n.* (*pl.* **culs-de-sac**) impasse *f.*
culinary /'kʌlɪnərɪ/ *a.* culinaire.
cull /kʌl/ *v.t.* (*select*) choisir; (*kill*) abattre sélectivement.
culminat|e /'kʌlmɪneɪt/ *v.i.* **~e in,** se terminer par. **~ion** /-'neɪʃn/ *n.* point culminant *m.*
culprit /'kʌlprɪt/ *n.* coupable *m./f.*
cult /kʌlt/ *n.* culte *m.* **~ movie,** film culte.
cultivat|e /'kʌltɪveɪt/ *v.t.* cultiver. **~ion** /-'veɪʃn/ *n.* culture *f.*
cultural /'kʌltʃərəl/ *a.* culturel.
culture /'kʌltʃə(r)/ *n.* culture *f.* **~d** *a.* cultivé.
cumbersome /'kʌmbəsəm/ *a.* encombrant.
cumulative /'kju:mjʊlətɪv/ *a.* cumulatif.

cunning /'kʌnɪŋ/ *a.* rusé. ● *n.* astuce *f.*, ruse *f.*
cup /kʌp/ *n.* tasse *f.*; (*prize*) coupe *f.* **Cup final,** finale de la coupe *f.* **~ size,** profondeur de bonnet *f.* **~-tie** *n.* match de coupe *m.*
cupboard /'kʌbəd/ *n.* placard *m.*, armoire *f.*
cupful /'kʌpfʊl/ *n.* tasse *f.*
Cupid /'kju:pɪd/ *n.* Cupidon *m.*
curable /'kjʊərəbl/ *a.* guérissable.
curate /'kjʊərət/ *n.* vicaire *m.*
curator /kjʊə'reɪtə(r)/ *n.* (*of museum*) conservateur *m.*
curb[1] /kɜ:b/ *n.* (*restraint*) frein *m.* ● *v.t.* (*desires etc.*) refréner; (*price increase etc.*) freiner.
curb[2], (*Amer.*) **kerb** /kɜ:b/ *n.* bord du trottoir *m.*
curdle /'kɜ:dl/ *v.t./i.* (se) cailler.
curds /kɜ:dz/ *n. pl.* lait caillé *m.*
cure[1] /kjʊə(r)/ *v.t.* guérir; (*fig.*) éliminer. ● *n.* (*recovery*) guérison *f.*; (*remedy*) remède *m.*
cure[2] /kjʊə(r)/ *v.t.* (*culin.*) fumer; (*in brine*) saler.
curfew /'kɜ:fju:/ *n.* couvre-feu *m.*
curio /'kjʊərɪəʊ/ *n.* (*pl.* **-os**) curiosité *f.*, bibelot *m.*
curi|ous /'kjʊərɪəs/ *a.* curieux. **~osity** /-'ɒsətɪ/ *n.* curiosité *f.*
curl /kɜ:l/ *v.t./i.* (*hair*) boucler. ● *n.* boucle *f.* **~ up,** se pelotonner; (*shrivel*) se racornir.
curler /'kɜ:lə(r)/ *n.* bigoudi *m.*
curly /'kɜ:lɪ/ *a.* (**-ier, -iest**) bouclé.
currant /'kʌrənt/ *n.* raisin de Corinthe *m.*; (*berry*) groseille *f.*
currency /'kʌrənsɪ/ *n.* (*money*) monnaie *f.*; (*acceptance*) cours *m.* **foreign ~,** devises étrangères *f. pl.*
current /'kʌrənt/ *a.* (*common*) courant; (*topical*) actuel; (*year etc.*) en cours. ● *n.* courant *m.* **~ account,** compte courant *m.* **~ events,** l'actualité *f.* **~ly** *adv.* actuellement.
curriculum /kə'rɪkjʊləm/ *n.* (*pl.* **-la**) programme scolaire *m.* **~ vitae,** curriculum vitae *m.*
curry[1] /'kʌrɪ/ *n.* curry *m.*, cari *m.*
curry[2] /'kʌrɪ/ *v.t.* **~ favour with,** chercher les bonnes grâces de.
curse /kɜ:s/ *n.* malédiction *f.*; (*oath*) juron *m.* ● *v.t.* maudire. ● *v.i.* (*swear*) jurer.
cursor /'kɜ:sə(r)/ *n.* curseur *m.*
cursory /'kɜ:sərɪ/ *a.* (trop) rapide.
curt /kɜ:t/ *a.* brusque.
curtail /kɜ:'teɪl/ *v.t.* écourter, raccourcir; (*expenses etc.*) réduire.
curtain /'kɜ:tn/ *n.* rideau *m.*
curtsy /'kɜ:tsɪ/ *n.* révérence *f.* ● *v.i.* faire une révérence.
curve /kɜ:v/ *n.* courbe *f.* ● *v.t./i.* (se) courber; (*of road*) tourner.
cushion /'kʊʃn/ *n.* coussin *m.* ● *v.t.* (*a blow*) amortir; (*fig.*) protéger.
cushy /'kʊʃɪ/ *a.* (**-ier, -iest**) (*job etc.*: *fam.*) pépère.
custard /'kʌstəd/ *n.* crème anglaise *f.*; (*set*) crème renversée *f.*
custodian /kʌ'stəʊdɪən/ *n.* gardien(ne) *m.* (*f.*).
custody /'kʌstədɪ/ *n.* garde *f.*; (*jurid.*) détention préventive *f.*
custom /'kʌstəm/ *n.* coutume *f.*; (*patronage*: *comm.*) clientèle *f.* **~-built, ~-made** *adjs.* fait *etc.* sur commande. **~ary** *a.* d'usage.
customer /'kʌstəmə(r)/ *n.* client(e) *m.* (*f.*); (*fam.*) **an odd/a difficult ~,** un individu curieux/difficile.
customize /'kʌstəmaɪz/ *v.t.* personnaliser.
customs /'kʌstəmz/ *n. pl.* douane *f.* ● *a.* douanier. **~ officer,** douanier *m.*
cut /kʌt/ *v.t./i.* (*p.t.* **cut,** *pres. p.* **cutting**) couper; (*hedge, jewel*) tailler; (*prices etc.*) réduire. ● *n.* coupure *f.*; (*of clothes*) coupe *f.*; (*piece*) morceau *m.*; réduction *f.* **~ back** *or* **down (on),** réduire. **~-back** *n.* réduction *f.* **~ in,** (*auto.*) se rabattre. **~ off,** couper; (*fig.*) isoler. **~ out,** découper; (*leave out*) supprimer. **~-price** *a.* à prix réduit. **~ short,** (*visit*) écourter. **~ up,** couper; (*carve*) découper. **~ up about,** démoralisé par.
cute /kju:t/ *a.* (**-er, -est**) (*fam.*) astucieux; (*Amer.*) mignon.
cuticle /'kju:tɪkl/ *n.* petites peaux *f. pl.* (*de l'ongle*).
cutlery /'kʌtlərɪ/ *n.* couverts *m. pl.*
cutlet /'kʌtlɪt/ *n.* côtelette *f.*
cutting /'kʌtɪŋ/ *a.* cinglant. ● *n.* (*from newspaper*) coupure *f.*; (*plant*) bouture *f.* **~ edge,** tranchant *m.*
CV *abbr. see* curriculum vitae.
cyanide /'saɪənaɪd/ *n.* cyanure *m.*
cybernetics /saɪbə'netɪks/ *n.* cybernétique *f.*
cycl|e /'saɪkl/ *n.* cycle *m.*; (*bicycle*) vélo *m.* ● *v.i.* aller à vélo. **~ing** *n.* cyclisme *m.* **~ist** *n.* cycliste *m./f.*
cyclic(al) /'saɪklɪk(l)/ *a.* cyclique.

cyclone /'saɪkləʊn/ *n.* cyclone *m.*
cylind|er /'sɪlɪndə(r)/ *n.* cylindre *m.* **~rical** /-'lɪndrɪkl/ *a.* cylindrique.
cymbal /'sɪmbl/ *n.* cymbale *f.*
cynic /'sɪnɪk/ *n.* cynique *m./f.* **~al** *a.* cynique. **~ism** /-sɪzəm/ *n.* cynisme *m.*
cypress /'saɪprəs/ *n.* cyprès *m.*
Cypr|us /'saɪprəs/ *n.* Chypre *f.* **~iot** /'sɪprɪət/ *a.* & *n.* cypriote (*m./f.*).
cyst /sɪst/ *n.* kyste *m.* **~ic fibrosis,** mucoviscidose *f.*
cystitis /sɪst'aɪtɪs/ *n.* cystite *f.*
czar /zɑ:(r)/ *n.* tsar *m.*
Czech /tʃek/ *a.* & *n.* tchèque (*m./f.*).
Czechoslovak /tʃekə'sləʊvæk/ *a.* & *n.* tchécoslovaque (*m./f.*). **~ia** /-slə'vækɪə/ *n.* Tchécoslovaquie *f.*

D

dab /dæb/ *v.t.* (*p.t.* **dabbed**) tamponner. ● *n.* **a ~ of,** un petit coup de; (*fam.*) **be a ~ hand at,** avoir le coup de main pour. **~ sth. on,** appliquer qch. à petits coups sur.
dabble /'dæbl/ *v.i.* **~ in,** se mêler un peu de. **~r** /-ə(r)/ *n.* amateur *m.*
dad /dæd/ *n.* (*fam.*) papa *m.* **~dy** *n.* (*children's use*) papa *m.*
daffodil /'dæfədɪl/ *n.* jonquille *f.*
daft /dɑ:ft/ *a.* (**-er, -est**) idiot.
dagger /'dægə(r)/ *n.* poignard *m.*
dahlia /'deɪlɪə/ *n.* dahlia *m.*
daily /'deɪlɪ/ *a.* quotidien. ● *adv.* tous les jours. ● *n.* (*newspaper*) quotidien *m.*; (*charwoman: fam.*) femme de ménage *f.*
dainty /'deɪntɪ/ *a.* (**-ier, -iest**) délicat.
dairy /'deərɪ/ *n.* (*on farm*) laiterie *f.*; (*shop*) crémerie *f.* ● *a.* laitier.
daisy /'deɪzɪ/ *n.* pâquerette *f.* **~ wheel,** marguerite *f.*
dale /deɪl/ *n.* vallée *f.*
dam /dæm/ *n.* barrage *m.* ● *v.t.* (*p.t.* **dammed**) endiguer.
damag|e /'dæmɪdʒ/ *n.* dégâts *m. pl.*, dommages *m. pl.*; (*harm: fig.*) préjudice *m.* **~es,** (*jurid.*) dommages et intérêts *m. pl.* ● *v.t.* abîmer; (*fig.*) nuire à. **~ing** *a.* nuisible.
dame /deɪm/ *n.* (*old use*) dame *f.*; (*Amer., sl.*) fille *f.*
damn /dæm/ *v.t.* (*relig.*) damner; (*swear at*) maudire; (*condemn: fig.*) condamner. ● *int.* zut, merde. ● *n.* **not care a ~,** s'en foutre. ● *a.* sacré. ● *adv.* rudement. **~ation** /-'neɪʃn/ *n.* damnation *f.*
damp /dæmp/ *n.* humidité *f.* ● *a.* (**-er, -est**) humide. ● *v.t.* humecter; (*fig.*) refroidir. **~en** *v.t.* = **damp**. **~ness** *n.* humidité *f.*
dance /dɑ:ns/ *v.t./i.* danser. ● *n.* danse *f.*; (*gathering*) bal *m.* **~ hall,** dancing *m.*, salle de danse *f.* **~r** /-ə(r)/ *n.* danseu|r, -se *m., f.*
dandelion /'dændɪlaɪən/ *n.* pissenlit *m.*
dandruff /'dændrʌf/ *n.* pellicules *f. pl.*
dandy /'dændɪ/ *n.* dandy *m.*
Dane /deɪn/ *n.* Danois(e) *m.* (*f.*).
danger /'deɪndʒə(r)/ *n.* danger *m.*; (*risk*) risque *m.* **be in ~ of,** risquer de. **~ous** *a.* dangereux.
dangle /'dæŋgl/ *v.t./i.* (se) balancer, (laisser) pendre. **~ sth. in front of s.o.,** (*fig.*) faire miroiter qch. à qn.
Danish /'deɪnɪʃ/ *a.* danois. ● *n.* (*lang.*) danois *m.*
dank /dæŋk/ *a.* (**-er, -est**) humide et froid.
dapper /'dæpə(r)/ *a.* élégant.
dare /deə(r)/ *v.t.* **~ (to) do,** oser faire. **~ s.o. to do,** défier qn. de faire. ● *n.* défi *m.* **I ~ say,** je suppose (**that,** que).
daredevil /'deədevl/ *n.* casse-cou *m. invar.*
daring /'deərɪŋ/ *a.* audacieux.
dark /dɑ:k/ *a.* (**-er, -est**) obscur, sombre, noir; (*colour*) foncé, sombre; (*skin*) brun, foncé; (*gloomy*) sombre. ● *n.* noir *m.*; (*nightfall*) tombée de la nuit *f.* **~ horse,** individu aux talents inconnus *m.* **~-room** *n.* chambre noire *f.* **in the ~,** (*fig.*) dans l'ignorance (**about,** de). **~ness** *n.* obscurité *f.*
darken /'dɑ:kən/ *v.t./i.* (s')assombrir.
darling /'dɑ:lɪŋ/ *a.* & *n.* chéri(e) (*m.* (*f.*)).
darn /dɑ:n/ *v.t.* repriser.
dart /dɑ:t/ *n.* fléchette *f.* **~s,** (*game*) fléchettes *f. pl.* ● *v.i.* s'élancer.
dartboard /'dɑ:tbɔ:d/ *n.* cible *f.*
dash /dæʃ/ *v.i.* (*hurry*) se dépêcher; (*forward etc.*) se précipiter. ● *v.t.* jeter (avec violence); (*hopes*) briser. ● *n.* ruée *f.*; (*stroke*) tiret *m.* **a ~ of,** un peu de. **~ off,** (*leave*) partir en vitesse.
dashboard /'dæʃbɔ:d/ *n.* tableau de bord *m.*

dashing /ˈdæʃɪŋ/ *a.* fringant.

data /ˈdeɪtə/ *n. pl.* données *f. pl.* **~ processing**, traitement des données *m.*

database /ˈdeɪtəbeɪs/ *n.* base de données *f.*

date[1] /deɪt/ *n.* date *f.*; (*meeting: fam.*) rendez-vous *m.* ● *v.t./i.* dater; (*go out with: fam.*) sortir avec. **~ from**, dater de. **out of ~**, (*old-fashioned*) démodé; (*passport*) périmé. **to ~**, à ce jour. **up to ~**, (*modern*) moderne; (*list*) à jour. **~d** /-ɪd/ *a.* démodé.

date[2] /deɪt/ *n.* (*fruit*) datte *f.*

daub /dɔ:b/ *v.t.* barbouiller.

daughter /ˈdɔ:tə(r)/ *n.* fille *f.* **~-in-law** *n.* (*pl.* **~s-in-law**) belle-fille *f.*

daunt /dɔ:nt/ *v.t.* décourager.

dauntless /ˈdɔ:ntlɪs/ *a.* intrépide.

dawdle /ˈdɔ:dl/ *v.i.* lambiner. **~r** /-ə(r)/ *n.* lambin(e) *m.* (*f.*).

dawn /dɔ:n/ *n.* aube *f.* ● *v.i.* poindre; (*fig.*) naître. **it ~ed on me**, je m'en suis rendu compte.

day /deɪ/ *n.* jour *m.*; (*whole day*) journée *f.*; (*period*) époque *f.* **~-break** *n.* point du jour *m.* **~-dream** *n.* rêverie *f.*; *v.i.* rêvasser. **the ~ before**, la veille. **the following** *or* **next ~**, le lendemain.

daylight /ˈdeɪlaɪt/ *n.* jour *m.*

daytime /ˈdeɪtaɪm/ *n.* jour *m.*, journée *f.*

daze /deɪz/ *v.t.* étourdir; (*with drugs*) hébéter. ● *n.* **in a ~**, étourdi; hébété.

dazzle /ˈdæzl/ *v.t.* éblouir.

deacon /ˈdi:kən/ *n.* diacre *m.*

dead /ded/ *a.* mort; (*numb*) engourdi. ● *adv.* complètement. ● *n.* **in the ~ of**, au cœur de. **the ~**, les morts. **~ beat**, éreinté. **~ end**, impasse *f.* **~-end job**, travail sans avenir *m.* **a ~ loss**, (*thing*) une perte de temps; (*person*) une catastrophe. **~-pan** *a.* impassible. **in ~ centre**, au beau milieu. **stop ~**, s'arrêter net. **the race was a ~ heat**, ils ont été classés ex aequo.

deaden /ˈdedn/ *v.t.* (*sound, blow*) amortir; (*pain*) calmer.

deadline /ˈdedlaɪn/ *n.* date limite *f.*

deadlock /ˈdedlɒk/ *n.* impasse *f.*

deadly /ˈdedlɪ/ *a.* (**-ier, -iest**) mortel; (*weapon*) meurtrier.

deaf /def/ *a.* (**-er, -est**) sourd. **the ~ and dumb**, les sourds-muets. **~-aid** *n.* appareil acoustique *m.* **~ness** *n.* surdité *f.*

deafen /ˈdefn/ *v.t.* assourdir.

deal /di:l/ *v.t.* (*p.t.* **dealt**) donner; (*a blow*) porter. ● *v.i.* (*trade*) commercer. ● *n.* affaire *f.*; (*cards*) donne *f.* **a great** *or* **good ~**, beaucoup (**of**, de). **~ in**, faire le commerce de. **~ with**, (*handle, manage*) s'occuper de; (*be about*) traiter de. **~er** *n.* marchand(e) *m.* (*f.*); (*agent*) concessionnaire *m./f.*

dealings /ˈdi:lɪŋz/ *n. pl.* relations *f. pl.*

dean /di:n/ *n.* doyen *m.*

dear /dɪə(r)/ *a.* (**-er, -est**) cher. ● *n.* (**my**) **~**, mon cher, ma chère; (*darling*) (mon) chéri, (ma) chérie. ● *adv.* cher. ● *int.* **oh ~!**, oh mon Dieu! **~ly** *adv.* tendrement; (*pay*) cher.

dearth /dɜ:θ/ *n.* pénurie *f.*

death /deθ/ *n.* mort *f.* **~ certificate**, acte de décès *m.* **~ duty**, droits de succession *m. pl.* **~ penalty**, peine de mort *f.* **it is a ~-trap**, (*place, vehicle*) il y a danger de mort. **~ly** *a.* de mort, mortel.

debar /dɪˈbɑ:(r)/ *v.t.* (*p.t.* **debarred**) exclure.

debase /dɪˈbeɪs/ *v.t.* avilir.

debat|e /dɪˈbeɪt/ *n.* discussion *f.*, débat *m.* ● *v.t.* discuter. **~e whether**, se demander si. **~able** *a.* discutable.

debauch /dɪˈbɔ:tʃ/ *v.t.* débaucher. **~ery** *n.* débauche *f.*

debilitate /dɪˈbɪlɪteɪt/ *v.t.* débiliter.

debility /dɪˈbɪlətɪ/ *n.* débilité *f.*

debit /ˈdebɪt/ *n.* débit *m.* **in ~**, débiteur. ● *a.* (*balance*) débiteur. ● *v.t.* (*p.t.* **debited**) débiter.

debris /ˈdeɪbri:/ *n.* débris *m. pl.*

debt /det/ *n.* dette *f.* **in ~**, endetté. **~or** *n.* débi|teur, -trice *m., f.*

debunk /di:ˈbʌŋk/ *v.t.* (*fam.*) démythifier.

decade /ˈdekeɪd/ *n.* décennie *f.*

decaden|t /ˈdekədənt/ *a.* décadent. **~ce** *n.* décadence *f.*

decaffeinated /di:ˈkæfɪneɪtɪd/ *a.* décaféiné.

decanter /dɪˈkæntə(r)/ *n.* carafe *f.*

decathlon /dɪˈkæθlən/ *n.* décathlon *m.*

decay /dɪˈkeɪ/ *v.i.* se gâter, pourrir; (*fig.*) décliner. ● *n.* pourriture *f.*; (*of tooth*) carie *f.*; (*fig.*) déclin *m.*

deceased /dɪˈsi:st/ *a.* décédé. ● *n.* défunt(e) *m.* (*f.*).

deceit /dɪ'si:t/ *n.* tromperie *f.* **~ful** *a.* trompeur. **~fully** *adv.* d'une manière trompeuse.

deceive /dɪ'si:v/ *v.t.* tromper.

December /dɪ'sembə(r)/ *n.* décembre *m.*

decen|t /'di:snt/ *a.* décent, convenable; (*good*: *fam.*) (assez) bon; (*kind*: *fam.*) gentil. **~cy** *n.* décence *f.* **~tly** *adv.* décemment.

decentralize /di:'sentrəlaɪz/ *v.t.* décentraliser.

decept|ive /dɪ'septɪv/ *a.* trompeur. **~ion** /-pʃn/ *n.* tromperie *f.*

decibel /'desɪbel/ *n.* décibel *m.*

decide /dɪ'saɪd/ *v.t./i.* décider; (*question*) régler. **~ on,** se décider pour. **~ to do,** décider de faire. **~d** /-ɪd/ *a.* (*firm*) résolu; (*clear*) net. **~dly** /-ɪdlɪ/ *adv.* résolument; nettement.

deciduous /dɪ'sɪdjʊəs/ *a.* à feuillage caduc.

decimal /'desɪml/ *a.* décimal. ● *n.* décimale *f.* **~ point,** virgule *f.*

decimate /'desɪmeɪt/ *v.t.* décimer.

decipher /dɪ'saɪfə(r)/ *v.t.* déchiffrer.

decision /dɪ'sɪʒn/ *n.* décision *f.*

decisive /dɪ'saɪsɪv/ *a.* (*conclusive*) décisif; (*firm*) décidé. **~ly** *adv.* d'une façon décidée.

deck /dek/ *n.* pont *m.*; (*of cards*: *Amer.*) jeu *m.* **~-chair** *n.* chaise longue *f.* **top ~,** (*of bus*) impériale *f.*

declar|e /dɪ'kleə(r)/ *v.t.* déclarer. **~ation** /deklə'reɪʃn/ *n.* déclaration *f.*

decline /dɪ'klaɪn/ *v.t./i.* refuser (poliment); (*deteriorate*) décliner; (*fall*) baisser. ● *n.* déclin *m.*; baisse *f.*

decode /di:'kəʊd/ *v.t.* décoder.

decompos|e /di:kəm'pəʊz/ *v.t./i.* (se) décomposer. **~ition** /-ɒmpə'zɪʃn/ *n.* décomposition *f.*

décor /'deɪkɔ:(r)/ *n.* décor *m.*

decorat|e /'dekəreɪt/ *v.t.* décorer; (*room*) peindre *or* tapisser. **~ion** /-'reɪʃn/ *n.* décoration *f.* **~ive** /-ətɪv/ *a.* décoratif.

decorator /'dekəreɪtə(r)/ *n.* peintre en bâtiment *m.* **(interior) ~,** décora|teur, -trice d'appartements *m.*, *f.*

decorum /dɪ'kɔ:rəm/ *n.* décorum *m.*

decoy[1] /'di:kɔɪ/ *n.* (*bird*) appeau *m.*; (*trap*) piège *m.*, leurre *m.*

decoy[2] /dɪ'kɔɪ/ *v.t.* attirer, appâter.

decrease /dɪ'kri:s/ *v.t./i.* diminuer. ● *n.* /'di:kri:s/ diminution *f.*

decree /dɪ'kri:/ *n.* (*pol.*, *relig.*) décret *m.*; (*jurid.*) jugement *m.* ● *v.t.* (*p.t.* **decreed**) décréter.

decrepit /dɪ'krepɪt/ *a.* (*building*) délabré; (*person*) décrépit.

decry /dɪ'kraɪ/ *v.t.* dénigrer.

dedicat|e /'dedɪkeɪt/ *v.t.* dédier. **~e o.s. to,** se consacrer à. **~ed** *a.* dévoué. **~ion** /-'keɪʃn/ *n.* dévouement *m.*; (*in book*) dédicace *f.*

deduce /dɪ'dju:s/ *v.t.* déduire.

deduct /dɪ'dʌkt/ *v.t.* déduire; (*from wages*) retenir. **~ion** /-kʃn/ *n.* déduction *f.*; retenue *f.*

deed /di:d/ *n.* acte *m.*

deem /di:m/ *v.t.* juger.

deep /di:p/ *a.* (**-er, -est**) profond. ● *adv.* profondément. **~ in thought,** absorbé dans ses pensées. **~ into the night,** tard dans la nuit. **~-freeze** *n.* congélateur *m.*; *v.t.* congeler. **~-fry,** frire. **~ly** *adv.* profondément.

deepen /'di:pən/ *v.t.* approfondir. ● *v.i.* devenir plus profond; (*mystery*, *night*) s'épaissir.

deer /dɪə(r)/ *n. invar.* cerf *m.*; (*doe*) biche *f.*

deface /dɪ'feɪs/ *v.t.* dégrader.

defamation /defə'meɪʃn/ *n.* diffamation *f.*

default /dɪ'fɔ:lt/ *v.i.* (*jurid.*) faire défaut. ● *n.* **by ~,** (*jurid.*) par défaut. **win by ~,** gagner par forfait. ● *a.* (*comput.*) par défaut.

defeat /dɪ'fi:t/ *v.t.* vaincre; (*thwart*) faire échouer. ● *n.* défaite *f.*; (*of plan etc.*) échec *m.*

defect[1] /'di:fekt/ *n.* défaut *m.* **~ive** /dɪ'fektɪv/ *a.* défectueux.

defect[2] /dɪ'fekt/ *v.i.* faire défection. **~ to,** passer à. **~or** *n.* transfuge *m.*/*f.*

defence /dɪ'fens/ *n.* défense *f.* **~less** *a.* sans défense.

defend /dɪ'fend/ *v.t.* défendre. **~ant** *n.* (*jurid.*) accusé(e) *m.* (*f.*). **~er,** défenseur *m.*

defense /dɪ'fens/ *n. Amer.* =**defence**.

defensive /dɪ'fensɪv/ *a.* défensif. ● *n.* défensive *f.*

defer /dɪ'fɜ:(r)/ *v.t.* (*p.t.* **deferred**) (*postpone*) différer, remettre.

deferen|ce /'defərəns/ *n.* déférence *f.* **~tial** /-'renʃl/ *a.* déférent.

defian|ce /dɪ'faɪəns/ *n.* défi *m.* **in ~ce of,** au mépris de. **~t** *a.* de défi. **~tly** *adv.* d'un air de défi.

deficien|t /dɪˈfɪʃnt/ *a.* insuffisant. **be ~t in,** manquer de. **~cy** *n.* insuffisance *f.*; (*fault*) défaut *m.*
deficit /ˈdefɪsɪt/ *n.* déficit *m.*
defile /dɪˈfaɪl/ *v.t.* souiller.
define /dɪˈfaɪn/ *v.t.* définir.
definite /ˈdefɪnɪt/ *a.* précis; (*obvious*) net; (*firm*) catégorique; (*certain*) certain. **~ly** *adv.* certainement; (*clearly*) nettement.
definition /defɪˈnɪʃn/ *n.* définition *f.*
definitive /dɪˈfɪnətɪv/ *a.* définitif.
deflat|e /dɪˈfleɪt/ *v.t.* dégonfler. **~ion** /-ʃn/ *n.* dégonflement *m.*; (*comm.*) déflation *f.*
deflect /dɪˈflekt/ *v.t./i.* (faire) dévier.
deforestation /di:fɒrɪˈsteɪʃn/ *n.* déforestation.
deform /dɪˈfɔ:m/ *v.t.* déformer. **~ed** *a.* difforme. **~ity** *n.* difformité *f.*
defraud /dɪˈfrɔ:d/ *v.t.* (*state, customs*) frauder. **~ s.o. of sth.,** escroquer qch. à qn.
defray /dɪˈfreɪ/ *v.t.* payer.
defrost /di:ˈfrɒst/ *v.t.* dégivrer.
deft /deft/ *a.* **(-er, -est)** adroit. **~ness** *n.* adresse *f.*
defunct /dɪˈfʌŋkt/ *a.* défunt.
defuse /di:ˈfju:z/ *v.t.* désamorcer.
defy /dɪˈfaɪ/ *v.t.* défier; (*attempts*) résister à.
degenerate[1] /dɪˈdʒenəreɪt/ *v.i.* dégénérer (**into,** en).
degenerate[2] /dɪˈdʒenərət/ *a.* & *n.* dégénéré(e) (*m.* (*f.*)).
degrad|e /dɪˈgreɪd/ *v.t.* dégrader. **~ation** /degrəˈdeɪʃn/ *n.* dégradation *f.*; (*state*) déchéance *f.*
degree /dɪˈgri:/ *n.* degré *m.*; (*univ.*) diplôme universitaire *m.*; (*Bachelor's degree*) licence *f.* **higher ~,** (*univ.*) maîtrise *f.* *or* doctorat *m.* **to such a ~ that,** à tel point que.
dehydrate /di:ˈhaɪdreɪt/ *v.t./i.* (se) déshydrater.
de-ice /di:ˈaɪs/ *v.t.* dégivrer.
deign /deɪn/ *v.t.* **~ to do,** daigner faire.
deity /ˈdi:ɪtɪ/ *n.* divinité *f.*
deject|ed /dɪˈdʒektɪd/ *a.* abattu. **~ion** /-kʃn/ *n.* abattement *m.*
delay /dɪˈleɪ/ *v.t.* retarder. ● *v.i.* tarder. ● *n.* (*lateness, time overdue*) retard *m.*; (*waiting*) délai *m.* **~ doing,** attendre pour faire.
delectable /dɪˈlektəbl/ *a.* délectable, très agréable.
delegate[1] /ˈdelɪgət/ *n.* délégué(e) *m.* (*f.*).
delegat|e[2] /ˈdelɪgeɪt/ *v.t.* déléguer. **~ion** /-ˈgeɪʃn/ *n.* délégation *f.*
delet|e /dɪˈli:t/ *v.t.* effacer; (*with line*) barrer. **~ion** /-ʃn/ *n.* suppression *f.*; (*with line*) rature *f.*
deliberate[1] /dɪˈlɪbərət/ *a.* délibéré; (*steps, manner*) mesuré. **~ly** *adv.* exprès, délibérément.
deliberat|e[2] /dɪˈlɪbəreɪt/ *v.i.* délibérer. ● *v.t.* considérer. **~ion** /-ˈreɪʃn/ *n.* délibération *f.*
delica|te /ˈdelɪkət/ *a.* délicat. **~cy** *n.* délicatesse *f.*; (*food*) mets délicat *or* raffiné *m.*
delicatessen /delɪkəˈtesn/ *n.* épicerie fine *f.*, charcuterie *f.*
delicious /dɪˈlɪʃəs/ *a.* délicieux.
delight /dɪˈlaɪt/ *n.* grand plaisir *m.*, joie *f.*, délice *m.* (*f. in pl.*); (*thing*) délice *m.* (*f. in pl.*). ● *v.t.* réjouir. ● *v.i.* **~ in,** prendre plaisir à. **~ed** *a.* ravi. **~ful** *a.* charmant, très agréable.
delinquen|t /dɪˈlɪŋkwənt/ *a.* & *n.* délinquant(e) (*m.* (*f.*)) **~cy** *n.* délinquance *f.*
deliri|ous /dɪˈlɪrɪəs/ *a.* **be ~ous,** délirer. **~um** *n.* délire *m.*
deliver /dɪˈlɪvə(r)/ *v.t.* (*message*) remettre; (*goods*) livrer; (*letters*) distribuer; (*free*) délivrer; (*utter*) prononcer; (*med.*) accoucher; (*a blow*) porter. **~ance** *n.* délivrance *f.* **~y** *n.* livraison *f.*; distribution *f.*; accouchement *m.*
delta /ˈdeltə/ *n.* delta *m.*
delu|de /dɪˈlu:d/ *v.t.* tromper. **~de o.s.,** se faire des illusions. **~sion** /-ʒn/ *n.* illusion *f.*
deluge /ˈdelju:dʒ/ *n.* déluge *m.* ● *v.t.* inonder (**with,** de).
de luxe /dəˈlʌks/ *a.* de luxe.
delve /delv/ *v.i.* fouiller.
demagogue /ˈdeməgɒg/ *n.* démagogue *m./f.*
demand /dɪˈmɑ:nd/ *v.t.* exiger; (*in negotiations*) réclamer. ● *n.* exigence *f.*; (*claim*) revendication *f.*; (*comm.*) demande *f.* **in ~,** recherché. **on ~,** à la demande. **~ing** *a.* exigeant.
demarcation /di:mɑ:ˈkeɪʃn/ *n.* démarcation *f.*
demean /dɪˈmi:n/ *v.t.* **~ o.s.,** s'abaisser, s'avilir.
demeanour, (*Amer.*) **demeanor** /dɪˈmi:nə(r)/ *n.* comportement *m.*
demented /dɪˈmentɪd/ *a.* dément.

demerara /demə'reərə/ *n.* (*brown sugar*) cassonade *f.*
demise /dɪ'maɪz/ *n.* décès *m.*
demo /'deməʊ/ *n.* (*pl.* **-os**) (*demonstration: fam.*) manif *f.*
demobilize /diː'məʊbəlaɪz/ *v.t.* démobiliser.
democracy /dɪ'mɒkrəsɪ/ *n.* démocratie *f.*
democrat /'deməkræt/ *n.* démocrate *m./f.* **~ic** /-'krætɪk/ *a.* démocratique.
demoli|sh /dɪ'mɒlɪʃ/ *v.t.* démolir. **~tion** /demə'lɪʃn/ *n.* démolition *f.*
demon /'diːmən/ *n.* démon *m.*
demonstrat|e /'demənstreɪt/ *v.t.* démontrer. ● *v.i.* (*pol.*) manifester. **~ion** /-'streɪʃn/ *n.* démonstration *f.*; (*pol.*) manifestation *f.* **~or** *n.* manifestant(e) *m.* (*f.*).
demonstrative /dɪ'mɒnstrətɪv/ *a.* démonstratif.
demoralize /dɪ'mɒrəlaɪz/ *v.t.* démoraliser.
demote /dɪ'məʊt/ *v.t.* rétrograder.
demure /dɪ'mjʊə(r)/ *a.* modeste.
den /den/ *n.* antre *m.*
denial /dɪ'naɪəl/ *n.* dénégation *f.*; (*statement*) démenti *m.*
denigrate /'denɪgreɪt/ *v.t.* dénigrer.
denim /'denɪm/ *n.* toile de coton *f.* **~s**, (*jeans*) blue-jeans *m. pl.*
Denmark /'denmɑːk/ *n.* Danemark *m.*
denomination /dɪnɒmɪ'neɪʃn/ *n.* (*relig.*) confession *f.*; (*money*) valeur *f.*
denote /dɪ'nəʊt/ *v.t.* dénoter.
denounce /dɪ'naʊns/ *v.t.* dénoncer.
dens|e /dens/ *a.* (**-er, -est**) dense; (*person*) obtus. **~ely** *adv.* (*packed etc.*) très. **~ity** *n.* densité *f.*
dent /dent/ *n.* bosse *f.* ● *v.t.* cabosser. **there is a ~ in the car door,** la portière est cabossée.
dental /'dentl/ *a.* dentaire. **~ floss,** fil dentaire *m.* **~ surgeon,** dentiste *m./f.*
dentist /'dentɪst/ *n.* dentiste *m./f.* **~ry** *n.* art dentaire *m.*
dentures /'dentʃəz/ *n. pl.* dentier *m.*
denude /dɪ'njuːd/ *v.t.* dénuder.
denunciation /dɪnʌnsɪ'eɪʃn/ *n.* dénonciation *f.*
deny /dɪ'naɪ/ *v.t.* nier (**that,** que); (*rumour*) démentir; (*disown*) renier; (*refuse*) refuser.
deodorant /diː'əʊdərənt/ *n.* & *a.* déodorant (*m.*).
depart /dɪ'pɑːt/ *v.i.* partir. **~ from,** (*deviate*) s'écarter de.
department /dɪ'pɑːtmənt/ *n.* département *m.*; (*in shop*) rayon *m.*; (*in office*) service *m.* **D~ of Health,** ministère de la santé *m.* **~ store,** grand magasin *m.*
departure /dɪ'pɑːtʃə(r)/ *n.* départ *m.* **a ~ from,** (*custom, diet, etc.*) une entorse à.
depend /dɪ'pend/ *v.i.* dépendre (**on,** de). **it (all) ~s,** ça dépend. **~ on,** (*rely on*) compter sur. **~ing on the weather,** selon le temps qu'il fera. **~able** *a.* sûr. **~ence** *n.* dépendance *f.* **~ent** *a.* dépendant. **be ~ent on,** dépendre de.
dependant /dɪ'pendənt/ *n.* personne à charge *f.*
depict /dɪ'pɪkt/ *v.t.* (*describe*) dépeindre; (*in picture*) représenter.
deplete /dɪ'pliːt/ *v.t.* (*reduce*) réduire; (*use up*) épuiser.
deplor|e /dɪ'plɔː(r)/ *v.t.* déplorer. **~able** *a.* déplorable.
deploy /dɪ'plɔɪ/ *v.t.* déployer.
depopulate /diː'pɒpjʊleɪt/ *v.t.* dépeupler.
deport /dɪ'pɔːt/ *v.t.* expulser. **~ation** /diːpɔː'teɪʃn/ *n.* expulsion *f.*
depose /dɪ'pəʊz/ *v.t.* déposer.
deposit /dɪ'pɒzɪt/ *v.t.* (*p.t.* **deposited**) déposer. ● *n.* dépôt *m.*; (*of payment*) acompte *m.*; (*to reserve*) arrhes *f. pl.*; (*against damage*) caution *f.*; (*on bottle etc.*) consigne *f.*; (*of mineral*) gisement *m.* **~ account,** compte de dépôt *m.* **~or** *n.* (*comm.*) déposant(e) *m.* (*f.*), épargnant(e) *m.* (*f.*).
depot /'depəʊ, *Amer.* 'diːpəʊ/ *n.* dépôt *m.*; (*Amer.*) gare (routière) *f.*
deprav|e /dɪ'preɪv/ *v.t.* dépraver. **~ity** /-'prævətɪ/ *n.* dépravation *f.*
deprecate /'deprəkeɪt/ *v.t.* désapprouver.
depreciat|e /dɪ'priːʃɪeɪt/ *v.t./i.* (se) déprécier. **~ion** /-'eɪʃn/ *n.* dépréciation *f.*
depress /dɪ'pres/ *v.t.* (*sadden*) déprimer; (*push down*) appuyer sur. **become ~ed,** déprimer. **~ing** *a.* déprimant. **~ion** /-ʃn/ *n.* dépression *f.*
deprivation /deprɪ'veɪʃn/ *n.* privation *f.*
deprive /dɪ'praɪv/ *v.t.* **~ of,** priver de. **~d** *a.* (*child etc.*) déshérité.
depth /depθ/ *n.* profondeur *f.* **be out of one's ~,** perdre pied; (*fig.*) être perdu. **in the ~s of,** au plus profond de.

deputation /depjʊ'teɪʃn/ *n.* députation *f.*

deputize /'depjʊtaɪz/ *v.i.* assurer l'intérim (**for,** de). ● *v.t.* (*Amer.*) déléguer, nommer.

deputy /'depjʊtɪ/ *n.* suppléant(e) *m.* (*f.*) ● *a.* adjoint. **~ chairman,** vice-président *m.*

derail /dɪ'reɪl/ *v.t.* faire dérailler. **be ~ed,** dérailler. **~ment** *n.* déraillement *m.*

deranged /dɪ'reɪndʒd/ *a.* (*mind*) dérangé.

derelict /'derəlɪkt/ *a.* abandonné.

deri|de /dɪ'raɪd/ *v.t.* railler. **~sion** /-'rɪʒn/ *n.* dérision *f.* **~sive** *a.* (*laughter, person*) railleur.

derisory /dɪ'raɪsərɪ/ *a.* (*scoffing*) railleur; (*offer etc.*) dérisoire.

derivative /dɪ'rɪvətɪv/ *a.* & *n.* dérivé (*m.*).

deriv|e /dɪ'raɪv/ *v.t.* **~e from,** tirer de. ● *v.i.* **~e from,** dériver de. **~ation** /derɪ'veɪʃn/ *n.* dérivation *f.*

derogatory /dɪ'rɒgətrɪ/ *a.* (*word*) péjoratif; (*remark*) désobligeant.

derv /dɜ:v/ *n.* gas-oil *m.*, gazole *m.*

descend /dɪ'send/ *v.t./i.* descendre. **be ~ed from,** descendre de. **~ant** *n.* descendant(e) *m.* (*f.*).

descent /dɪ'sent/ *n.* descente *f.*; (*lineage*) origine *f.*

descri|be /dɪ'skraɪb/ *v.t.* décrire. **~ption** /-'skrɪpʃn/ *n.* description *f.* **~ptive** /-'skrɪptɪv/ *a.* descriptif.

desecrat|e /'desɪkreɪt/ *v.t.* profaner. **~ion** /-'kreɪʃn/ *n.* profanation *f.*

desert[1] /'dezət/ *n.* désert *m.* ● *a.* désertique. **~ island,** île déserte *f.*

desert[2] /dɪ'zɜ:t/ *v.t./i.* déserter. **~ed** *a.* désert. **~er** *n.* déserteur *m.* **~ion** /-ʃn/ *n.* désertion *f.*

deserts /dɪ'zɜ:ts/ *n. pl.* **one's ~,** ce qu'on mérite.

deserv|e /dɪ'zɜ:v/ *v.t.* mériter (**to,** de). **~edly** /-ɪdlɪ/ *adv.* à juste titre. **~ing** *a.* (*person*) méritant; (*action*) méritoire.

design /dɪ'zaɪn/ *n.* (*sketch*) dessin *m.*, plan *m.*; (*construction*) conception *f.*; (*pattern*) motif *m.*; (*style of dress*) modèle *m.*; (*aim*) dessein *m.* ● *v.t.* (*sketch*) dessiner; (*devise, intend*) concevoir. **~er** *n.* dessina|teur, -trice *m., f.*; (*of fashion*) styliste *m./f.*

designat|e /'dezɪgneɪt/ *v.t.* désigner. **~ion** /-'neɪʃn/ *n.* désignation *f.*

desir|e /dɪ'zaɪə(r)/ *n.* désir *m.* ● *v.t.* désirer. **~able** *a.* désirable. **~ability** /-ə'bɪlətɪ/ *n.* attrait *m.*

desk /desk/ *n.* bureau *m.*; (*of pupil*) pupitre *m.*; (*in hotel*) réception *f.*; (*in bank*) caisse *f.*

desolat|e /'desələt/ *a.* (*place*) désolé; (*bleak: fig.*) morne. **~ion** /-'leɪʃn/ *n.* désolation *f.*

despair /dɪ'speə(r)/ *n.* désespoir *m.* ● *v.i.* désespérer (**of,** de).

despatch /dɪ'spætʃ/ *v.t.* = **dispatch.**

desperate /'despərət/ *a.* désespéré; (*criminal*) prêt à tout. **be ~ for,** avoir une envie folle de. **~ly** *adv.* désespérément; (*worried*) terriblement; (*ill*) gravement.

desperation /despə'reɪʃn/ *n.* désespoir *m.* **in** *or* **out of ~,** en désespoir de cause.

despicable /dɪ'spɪkəbl/ *a.* méprisable, infâme.

despise /dɪ'spaɪz/ *v.t.* mépriser.

despite /dɪ'spaɪt/ *prep.* malgré.

desponden|t /dɪ'spɒndənt/ *a.* découragé. **~cy** *n.* découragement *m.*

despot /'despɒt/ *n.* despote *m.*

dessert /dɪ'zɜ:t/ *n.* dessert *m.* **~spoon** *n.* cuiller à dessert *f.* **~spoonful** *n.* cuillerée à soupe *f.*

destination /destɪ'neɪʃn/ *n.* destination *f.*

destine /'destɪn/ *v.t.* destiner.

destiny /'destɪnɪ/ *n.* destin *m.*

destitute /'destɪtju:t/ *a.* indigent. **~ of,** dénué de.

destr|oy /dɪ'strɔɪ/ *v.t.* détruire; (*animal*) abattre. **~uction** *n.* destruction *f.* **~uctive** *a.* destructeur.

destroyer /dɪ'strɔɪə(r)/ *n.* (*warship*) contre-torpilleur *m.*

detach /dɪ'tætʃ/ *v.t.* détacher. **~able** *a.* détachable. **~ed** *a.* détaché. **~ed house,** maison individuelle *f.*

detachment /dɪ'tætʃmənt/ *n.* détachement *m.*

detail /'di:teɪl/ *n.* détail *m.* ● *v.t.* exposer en détail; (*troops*) détacher. **go into ~,** entrer dans le détail. **~ed** *a.* détaillé.

detain /dɪ'teɪn/ *v.t.* retenir; (*in prison*) détenir. **~ee** /di:teɪ'ni:/ *n.* détenu(e) *m.* (*f.*).

detect /dɪ'tekt/ *v.t.* découvrir; (*perceive*) distinguer; (*tumour*) dépister; (*mine*) détecter. **~ion** /-kʃn/ *n.* découverte *f.*; dépistage *m.*; détection *f.* **~or** *n.* détecteur *m.*

detective /dɪ'tektɪv/ *n.* policier *m.*; (*private*) détective *m.*

detention /dɪ'tenʃn/ *n.* détention *f.*; (*schol.*) retenue *f.*

deter /dɪ'tɜ:(r)/ *v.t.* (*p.t.* **deterred**) dissuader (**from,** de).

detergent /dɪ'tɜ:dʒənt/ *a.* & *n.* détergent (*m.*).

deteriorat|e /dɪ'tɪərɪəreɪt/ *v.i.* se détériorer. **~ion** /-'reɪʃn/ *n.* détérioration *f.*

determin|e /dɪ'tɜ:mɪn/ *v.t.* déterminer. **~e to do,** décider de faire. **~ation** /-'neɪʃn/ *n.* détermination *f.* **~ed** *a.* déterminé. **~ed to do,** décidé à faire.

deterrent /dɪ'terənt, *Amer.* dɪ'tɜ:rənt/ *n.* force de dissuasion *f.*

detest /dɪ'test/ *v.t.* détester. **~able** *a.* détestable.

detonat|e /'detəneɪt/ *v.t./i.* (faire) détoner. **~ion** /-'neɪʃn/ *n.* détonation *f.* **~or** *n.* détonateur *m.*

detour /'di:tʊə(r)/ *n.* détour *m.*

detract /dɪ'trækt/ *v.i.* **~ from,** (*lessen*) diminuer.

detriment /'detrɪmənt/ *n.* détriment *m.* **~al** /-'mentl/ *a.* préjudiciable (**to,** à).

devalu|e /di:'vælju:/ *v.t.* dévaluer. **~ation** /-jʊ'eɪʃn/ *n.* dévaluation *f.*

devastat|e /'devəsteɪt/ *v.t.* dévaster; (*overwhelm*: *fig.*) accabler. **~ing** *a.* accablant.

develop /dɪ'veləp/ *v.t./i.* (*p.t.* **developed**) (se) développer; (*contract*) contracter; (*build on, transform*) exploiter, aménager; (*change*) évoluer; (*appear*) se manifester. **~ into,** devenir. **~ing country,** pays en voie de développement *m.* **~ment** *n.* développement *m.* **(housing) ~,** lotissement *m.* **(new) ~ment,** fait nouveau *m.*

deviant /'di:vɪənt/ *a.* anormal. ● *n.* (*psych.*) déviant *m.*

deviat|e /'di:vɪeɪt/ *v.i.* dévier. **~e from,** (*norm*) s'écarter de. **~ion** /-'eɪʃn/ *n.* déviation *f.*

device /dɪ'vaɪs/ *n.* appareil *m.*; (*scheme*) procédé *m.*

devil /'devl/ *n.* diable *m.* **~ish** *a.* diabolique.

devious /'di:vɪəs/ *a.* tortueux. **he is ~,** il a l'esprit tortueux.

devise /dɪ'vaɪz/ *v.t.* inventer; (*plan, means*) combiner, imaginer.

devoid /dɪ'vɔɪd/ *a.* **~ of,** dénué de.

devolution /di:və'lu:ʃn/ *n.* décentralisation *f.*; (*of authority, power*) délégation *f.* (**to,** à).

devot|e /dɪ'vəʊt/ *v.t.* consacrer. **~ed** *a.* dévoué. **~edly** *adv.* avec dévouement. **~ion** /-ʃn/ *n.* dévouement *m.*; (*relig.*) dévotion *f.* **~ions,** (*relig.*) dévotions *f. pl.*

devotee /devə'ti:/ *n.* **~ of,** passionné(e) de *m.* (*f.*).

devour /dɪ'vaʊə(r)/ *v.t.* dévorer.

devout /dɪ'vaʊt/ *a.* fervent.

dew /dju:/ *n.* rosée *f.*

dexterity /dek'sterətɪ/ *n.* dextérité *f.*

diabet|es /daɪə'bi:ti:z/ *n.* diabète *m.* **~ic** /-'betɪk/ *a.* & *n.* diabétique (*m./f.*).

diabolical /daɪə'bɒlɪkl/ *a.* diabolique; (*bad*: *fam.*) atroce.

diagnose /'daɪəgnəʊz/ *v.t.* diagnostiquer.

diagnosis /daɪəg'nəʊsɪs/ *n.* (*pl.* **-oses**) /-si:z/) diagnostic *m.*

diagonal /daɪ'ægənl/ *a.* diagonal. ● *n.* diagonale *f.* **~ly** *adv.* en diagonale.

diagram /'daɪəgræm/ *n.* schéma *m.*

dial /'daɪəl/ *n.* cadran *m.* ● *v.t.* (*p.t.* **dialled**) (*number*) faire; (*person*) appeler. **~ling code,** (*Amer.*) **~ code,** indicatif *m.* **~ling tone,** (*Amer.*) **~ tone,** tonalité *f.*

dialect /'daɪəlekt/ *n.* dialecte *m.*

dialogue /'daɪəlɒg/ *n.* dialogue *m.*

diameter /daɪ'æmɪtə(r)/ *n.* diamètre *m.*

diamond /'daɪəmənd/ *n.* diamant *m.*; (*shape*) losange *m.*; (*baseball*) terrain *m.* **~s,** (*cards*) carreau *m.*

diaper /'daɪəpə(r)/ *n.* (*baby's nappy*: *Amer.*) couche *f.*

diaphragm /'daɪəfræm/ *n.* diaphragme *m.*

diarrhoea, (*Amer.*) **diarrhea** /daɪə'rɪə/ *n.* diarrhée *f.*

diary /'daɪərɪ/ *n.* (*for appointments etc.*) agenda *m.*; (*appointments*) emploi du temps *m.* (*for private thoughts*) journal intime *m.*

dice /daɪs/ *n. invar.* dé *m.* ● *v.t.* (*food*) couper en dés.

dicey /'daɪsɪ/ *a.* (*fam.*) risqué.

dictat|e /dɪk'teɪt/ *v.t./i.* dicter. **~ion** /-ʃn/ *n.* dictée *f.*

dictates /'dɪkteɪts/ *n. pl.* préceptes *m. pl.*

dictator /dɪk'teɪtə(r)/ *n.* dictateur *m.* **~ship** *n.* dictature *f.*

dictatorial /dɪktəˈtɔːrɪəl/ *a.* dictatorial.
diction /ˈdɪkʃn/ *n.* diction *f.*
dictionary /ˈdɪkʃənrɪ/ *n.* dictionnaire *m.*
did /dɪd/ *see* do.
diddle /ˈdɪdl/ *v.t.* (*sl.*) escroquer.
didn't /ˈdɪdnt/ = **did not**.
die[1] /daɪ/ *v.i.* (*pres. p.* **dying**) mourir. ~ **down,** diminuer. ~ **out,** disparaître. **be dying to do/for,** mourir d'envie de faire/de.
die[2] /daɪ/ *n.* (*metal mould*) matrice *f.*, étampe *f.*
die-hard /ˈdaɪhɑːd/ *n.* réactionnaire *m./f.*
diesel /ˈdiːzl/ *n.* diesel *m.* ~ **engine,** moteur diesel *m.*
diet /ˈdaɪət/ *n.* (*habitual food*) alimentation *f.*; (*restricted*) régime *m.* • *v.i.* suivre un régime.
diet|etic /daɪəˈtetɪk/ *a.* diététique. **~ician** *n.* diététicien(ne) *m.* (*f.*).
differ /ˈdɪfə(r)/ *v.i.* différer (**from,** de); (*disagree*) ne pas être d'accord.
differen|t /ˈdɪfrənt/ *a.* différent. **~ce** *n.* différence *f.*; (*disagreement*) différend *m.* **~tly** *adv.* différemment (**from,** de).
differential /dɪfəˈrenʃl/ *a.* & *n.* différentiel (*m.*).
differentiate /dɪfəˈrenʃɪeɪt/ *v.t.* différencier. • *v.i.* faire la différence (**between,** entre).
difficult /ˈdɪfɪkəlt/ *a.* difficile. **~y** *n.* difficulté *f.*
diffiden|t /ˈdɪfɪdənt/ *a.* qui manque d'assurance. **~ce** *n.* manque d'assurance *m.*
diffuse[1] /dɪˈfjuːs/ *a.* diffus.
diffus|e[2] /dɪˈfjuːz/ *v.t.* diffuser. **~ion** /-ʒn/ *n.* diffusion *f.*
dig /dɪg/ *v.t./i.* (*p.t.* **dug,** *pres. p.* **digging**) creuser; (*thrust*) enfoncer. • *n.* (*poke*) coup de coude *m.*; (*remark*) coup de patte *m.*; (*archaeol.*) fouilles *f. pl.* **~s,** (*lodgings*: *fam.*) chambre meublée *f.* ~ **(over),** bêcher. ~ **up,** déterrer.
digest[1] /dɪˈdʒest/ *v.t./i.* digérer. **~ible** *a.* digestible. **~ion** /-stʃən/ *n.* digestion *f.*
digest[2] /ˈdaɪdʒest/ *n.* sommaire *m.*
digestive /dɪˈdʒestɪv/ *a.* digestif.
digger /ˈdɪgə(r)/ *n.* (*techn.*) pelleteuse *f.*, excavateur *m.*
digit /ˈdɪdʒɪt/ *n.* chiffre *m.*
digital /ˈdɪdʒɪtl/ *a.* (*clock*) numérique, à affichage numérique; (*recording*) numérique.
dignif|y /ˈdɪgnɪfaɪ/ *v.t.* donner de la dignité à. **~ied** *a.* digne.
dignitary /ˈdɪgnɪtərɪ/ *n.* dignitaire *m.*
dignity /ˈdɪgnɪtɪ/ *n.* dignité *f.*
digress /daɪˈgres/ *v.i.* faire une digression. ~ **from,** s'écarter de. **~ion** /-ʃn/ *n.* digression *f.*
dike /daɪk/ *n.* digue *f.*
dilapidated /dɪˈlæpɪdeɪtɪd/ *a.* délabré.
dilat|e /daɪˈleɪt/ *v.t./i.* (se) dilater. **~ion** /-ʃn/ *n.* dilatation *f.*
dilatory /ˈdɪlətərɪ/ *a.* dilatoire.
dilemma /dɪˈlemə/ *n.* dilemme *m.*
dilettante /dɪlɪˈtæntɪ/ *n.* dilettante *m./f.*
diligen|t /ˈdɪlɪdʒənt/ *a.* assidu. **~ce** *n.* assiduité *f.*
dilly-dally /ˈdɪlɪdælɪ/ *v.i.* (*fam.*) lanterner.
dilute /daɪˈljuːt/ *v.t.* diluer.
dim /dɪm/ *a.* (**dimmer, dimmest**) (*weak*) faible; (*dark*) sombre; (*indistinct*) vague; (*fam.*) stupide. • *v.t./i.* (*p.t.* **dimmed**) (*light*) (s')atténuer. **~ly** *adv.* (*shine*) faiblement; (*remember*) vaguement. **~mer** *n.* ~ **(switch),** variateur d'intensité *m.* **~ness** *n.* faiblesse *f.*; (*of room etc.*) obscurité *f.*
dime /daɪm/ *n.* (*in USA, Canada*) pièce de dix cents *f.*
dimension /daɪˈmenʃn/ *n.* dimension *f.*
diminish /dɪˈmɪnɪʃ/ *v.t./i.* diminuer.
diminutive /dɪˈmɪnjʊtɪv/ *a.* minuscule. • *n.* diminutif *m.*
dimple /ˈdɪmpl/ *n.* fossette *f.*
din /dɪn/ *n.* vacarme *m.*
dine /daɪn/ *v.i.* dîner. **~r** /-ə(r)/ *n.* dîneu|r, -se *m., f.*; (*rail.*) wagon-restaurant *m.*; (*Amer.*) restaurant à service rapide *m.*
dinghy /ˈdɪŋgɪ/ *n.* canot *m.*; (*inflatable*) canot pneumatique *m.*
ding|y /ˈdɪndʒɪ/ *a.* (**-ier, -iest**) miteux, minable. **~iness** *n.* aspect miteux *or* minable *m.*
dining-room /ˈdaɪnɪŋrʊm/ *n.* salle à manger *f.*
dinner /ˈdɪnə(r)/ *n.* (*evening meal*) dîner *m.*; (*lunch*) déjeuner *m.* **~-jacket** *n.* smoking *m.* ~ **party,** dîner *m.*
dinosaur /ˈdaɪnəsɔː(r)/ *n.* dinosaure *m.*

dint /dɪnt/ *n.* **by ~ of,** à force de.
diocese /'daɪəsɪs/ *n.* diocèse *m.*
dip /dɪp/ *v.t./i.* (*p.t.* **dipped**) plonger. ● *n.* (*slope*) déclivité *f.*; (*in sea*) bain rapide *m.* **~ into,** (*book*) feuilleter; (*savings*) puiser dans. **~ one's headlights,** se mettre en code.
diphtheria /dɪf'θɪərɪə/ *n.* diphtérie *f.*
diphthong /'dɪfθɒŋ/ *n.* diphtongue *f.*
diploma /dɪ'pləʊmə/ *n.* diplôme *m.*
diplomacy /dɪ'pləʊməsɪ/ *n.* diplomatie *f.*
diplomat /'dɪpləmæt/ *n.* diplomate *m./f.* **~ic** /-'mætɪk/ *a.* (*pol.*) diplomatique; (*tactful*) diplomate.
dire /daɪə(r)/ *a.* (**-er, -est**) affreux; (*need, poverty*) extrême.
direct /dɪ'rekt/ *a.* direct. ● *adv.* directement. ● *v.t.* diriger; (*letter, remark*) adresser; (*a play*) mettre en scène. **~ s.o. to,** indiquer à qn. le chemin de; (*order*) signifier à qn. de. **~ness** *n.* franchise *f.*
direction /dɪ'rekʃn/ *n.* direction *f.*; (*theatre*) mise en scène *f.* **~s,** indications *f. pl.* **ask ~s,** demander le chemin. **~s for use,** mode d'emploi *m.*
directly /dɪ'rektlɪ/ *adv.* directement; (*at once*) tout de suite. ● *conj.* dès que.
director /dɪ'rektə(r)/ *n.* direc|teur, -trice *m., f.*; (*theatre*) metteur en scène *m.*
directory /dɪ'rektərɪ/ *n.* (*phone book*) annuaire *m.*
dirt /dɜ:t/ *n.* saleté *f.*; (*earth*) terre *f.* **~ cheap,** (*sl.*) très bon marché *invar.* **~-track** *n.* (*sport*) cendrée *f.*
dirty /'dɜ:tɪ/ *a.* (**-ier, -iest**) sale; (*word*) grossier. **get ~,** se salir. ● *v.t./i.* (se) salir.
disability /dɪsə'bɪlətɪ/ *n.* handicap *m.*
disable /dɪs'eɪbl/ *v.t.* rendre infirme. **~d** *a.* handicapé.
disadvantage /dɪsəd'vɑ:ntɪdʒ/ *n.* désavantage *m.* **~d** *a.* déshérité.
disagree /dɪsə'gri:/ *v.i.* ne pas être d'accord (**with,** avec). **~ with s.o.,** (*food, climate*) ne pas convenir à qn. **~ment** *n.* désaccord *m.*; (*quarrel*) différend *m.*
disagreeable /dɪsə'gri:əbl/ *a.* désagréable.
disappear /dɪsə'pɪə(r)/ *v.i.* disparaître. **~ance** *n.* disparition *f.*
disappoint /dɪsə'pɔɪnt/ *v.t.* décevoir. **~ing** *a.* décevant. **~ed** *a.* déçu. **~ment** *n.* déception *f.*
disapprov|e /dɪsə'pru:v/ *v.i.* **~e (of),** désapprouver. **~al** *n.* désapprobation *f.*
disarm /dɪs'ɑ:m/ *v.t./i.* désarmer. **~ament** *n.* désarmement *m.*
disarray /dɪsə'reɪ/ *n.* désordre *m.*
disassociate /dɪsə'səʊʃɪeɪt/ *v.t.* = **dissociate.**
disast|er /dɪ'zɑ:stə(r)/ *n.* désastre *m.* **~rous** *a.* désastreux.
disband /dɪs'bænd/ *v.t./i.* (se) disperser.
disbelief /dɪsbɪ'li:f/ *n.* incrédulité *f.*
disc /dɪsk/ *n.* disque *m.*; (*comput.*) = **disk. ~ brake,** frein à disque *m.* **~ jockey,** disc-jockey *m.*, animateur *m.*
discard /dɪ'skɑ:d/ *v.t.* se débarrasser de; (*beliefs etc.*) abandonner.
discern /dɪ'sɜ:n/ *v.t.* discerner. **~ible** *a.* perceptible. **~ing** *a.* perspicace.
discharge[1] /dɪs'tʃɑ:dʒ/ *v.t.* (*unload*) décharger; (*liquid*) déverser; (*duty*) remplir; (*dismiss*) renvoyer; (*prisoner*) libérer. ● *v.i.* (*of pus*) s'écouler.
discharge[2] /'dɪstʃɑ:dʒ/ *n.* (*med.*) écoulement *m.*; (*dismissal*) renvoi *m.*; (*electr.*) décharge *m.*
disciple /dɪ'saɪpl/ *n.* disciple *m.*
disciplin|e /'dɪsɪplɪn/ *n.* discipline *f.* ● *v.t.* discipliner; (*punish*) punir. **~ary** *a.* disciplinaire.
disclaim /dɪs'kleɪm/ *v.t.* désavouer. **~er** *n.* correctif *m.*, précision *f.*
disclos|e /dɪs'kləʊz/ *v.t.* révéler. **~ure** /-ʒə(r)/ *n.* révélation *f.*
disco /'dɪskəʊ/ *n.* (*pl.* **-os**) (*club: fam.*) discothèque *f.*, disco *m.*
discol|our /dɪs'kʌlə(r)/ *v.t./i.* (se) décolorer. **~oration** /-'reɪʃn/ *n.* décoloration *f.*
discomfort /dɪs'kʌmfət/ *n.* gêne *f.*
disconcert /dɪskən'sɜ:t/ *v.t.* déconcerter.
disconnect /dɪskə'nekt/ *v.t.* détacher; (*unplug*) débrancher; (*cut off*) couper.
discontent /dɪskən'tent/ *n.* mécontentement *m.* **~ed** *a.* mécontent.
discontinue /dɪskən'tɪnju:/ *v.t.* interrompre, cesser.
discord /'dɪskɔ:d/ *n.* discorde *f.*; (*mus.*) dissonance *f.* **~ant** /-'skɔ:dənt/ *a.* discordant.
discothèque /'dɪskətek/ *n.* discothèque *f.*
discount[1] /'dɪskaʊnt/ *n.* rabais *m.*
discount[2] /dɪs'kaʊnt/ *v.t.* ne pas tenir compte de.

discourage /dɪ'skʌrɪdʒ/ *v.t.* décourager.
discourse /'dɪskɔ:s/ *n.* discours *m.*
discourteous /dɪs'kɜ:tɪəs/ *a.* impoli, peu courtois.
discover /di'skʌvə(r)/ *v.t.* découvrir. **~y** *n.* découverte *f.*
discredit /dɪs'kredɪt/ *v.t.* (*p.t.* **discredited**) discréditer. ● *n.* discrédit *m.*
discreet /dɪ'skri:t/ *a.* discret. **~ly** *adv.* discrètement.
discrepancy /dɪ'skrepənsɪ/ *n.* contradiction *f.*, incohérence *f.*
discretion /dɪ'skreʃn/ *n.* discrétion *f.*
discriminat|e /dɪ'skrɪmɪneɪt/ *v.t./i.* distinguer. **~e against,** faire de la discrimination contre. **~ing** *a.* (*person*) qui a du discernement. **~ion** /-'neɪʃn/ *n.* discernement *m.*; (*bias*) discrimination *f.*
discus /'dɪskəs/ *n.* disque *m.*
discuss /dɪ'skʌs/ *v.t.* (*talk about*) discuter de; (*argue about, examine critically*) discuter. **~ion** /-ʃn/ *n.* discussion *f.*
disdain /dɪs'deɪn/ *n.* dédain *m.* **~ful** *a.* dédaigneux.
disease /dɪ'zi:z/ *n.* maladie *f.* **~d** *a.* malade.
disembark /dɪsɪm'bɑ:k/ *v.t./i.* débarquer.
disembodied /dɪsɪm'bɒdɪd/ *a.* désincarné.
disenchant /dɪsɪn'tʃɑ:nt/ *v.t.* désenchanter. **~ment** *n.* desenchantement *m.*
disengage /dɪsɪn'geɪdʒ/ *v.t.* dégager; (*mil.*) retirer. ● *v.i.* (*mil.*) retirer; (*auto.*) débrayer. **~ment** *n.* dégagement *m.*
disentangle /dɪsɪn'tæŋgl/ *v.t.* démêler.
disfavour, (*Amer.*) **disfavor** /dɪs'feɪvə(r)/ *n.* défaveur *f.*
disfigure /dɪs'fɪgə(r)/ *v.t.* défigurer.
disgrace /dɪs'greɪs/ *n.* (*shame*) honte *f.*; (*disfavour*) disgrâce *f.* ● *v.t.* déshonorer. **~d** *a.* (*in disfavour*) disgracié. **~ful** *a.* honteux.
disgruntled /dɪs'grʌntld/ *a.* mécontent.
disguise /dɪs'gaɪz/ *v.t.* déguiser. ● *n.* déguisement *m.* **in ~,** déguisé.
disgust /dɪs'gʌst/ *n.* dégoût *m.* ● *v.t.* dégoûter. **~ing** *a.* dégoûtant.
dish /dɪʃ/ *n.* plat *m.* ● *v.t.* **~ out,** (*fam.*) distribuer. **~ up,** servir. **the ~es,** (*crockery*) la vaisselle.
dishcloth /'dɪʃklɒθ/ *n.* lavette *f.*; (*for drying*) torchon *m.*
dishearten /dɪs'hɑ:tn/ *v.t.* décourager.
dishevelled /dɪ'ʃevld/ *a.* échevelé.
dishonest /dɪs'ɒnɪst/ *a.* malhonnête. **~y** *n.* malhonnêteté *f.*
dishonour, (*Amer.*) **dishonor** /dɪs'ɒnə(r)/ *n.* déshonneur *m.* ● *v.t.* déshonorer. **~able** *a.* déshonorant. **~ably** *adv.* avec déshonneur.
dishwasher /'dɪʃwɒʃə(r)/ *n.* lave-vaisselle *m. invar.*
disillusion /dɪsɪ'lu:ʒn/ *v.t.* désillusionner. **~ment** *n.* désillusion *f.*
disincentive /dɪsɪn'sentɪv/ *n.* **be a ~ to,** décourager.
disinclined /dɪsɪn'klaɪnd/ *a.* **~ to,** peu disposé à.
disinfect /dɪsɪn'fekt/ *v.t.* désinfecter. **~ant** *n.* désinfectant *m.*
disinherit /dɪsɪn'herɪt/ *v.t.* déshériter.
disintegrate /dɪs'ɪntɪgreɪt/ *v.t./i.* (se) désintégrer.
disinterested /dɪs'ɪntrəstɪd/ *a.* désintéressé.
disjointed /dɪs'dʒɔɪntɪd/ *a.* (*talk*) décousu.
disk /dɪsk/ *n.* (*Amer.*) = **disc**; (*comput.*) disque *m.* **~ drive,** drive *m.*, lecteur de disquettes *m.*
diskette /dɪ'sket/ *n.* disquette *f.*
dislike /dɪs'laɪk/ *n.* aversion *f.* ● *v.t.* ne pas aimer.
dislocat|e /'dɪsləkeɪt/ *v.t.* (*limb*) disloquer. **~ion** /-'keɪʃn/ *n.* dislocation *f.*
dislodge /dɪs'lɒdʒ/ *v.t.* (*move*) déplacer; (*drive out*) déloger.
disloyal /dɪs'lɔɪəl/ *a.* déloyal. **~ty** *n.* déloyauté *f.*
dismal /'dɪzməl/ *a.* morne, triste.
dismantle /dɪs'mæntl/ *v.t.* démonter, défaire.
dismay /dɪs'meɪ/ *n.* consternation *f.* ● *v.t.* consterner.
dismiss /dɪs'mɪs/ *v.t.* renvoyer; (*appeal*) rejeter; (*from mind*) écarter. **~al** *n.* renvoi *m.*
dismount /dɪs'maʊnt/ *v.i.* descendre, mettre pied à terre.
disobedien|t /dɪsə'bi:dɪənt/ *a.* désobéissant. **~ce** *n.* désobéissance *f.*
disobey /dɪsə'beɪ/ *v.t.* désobéir à ● *v.i.* désobéir.

disorder /dɪs'ɔ:də(r)/ *n.* désordre *m.*; (*ailment*) trouble(s) *m.* (*pl.*). **~ly** *a.* désordonné.

disorganize /dɪs'ɔ:gənaɪz/ *v.t.* désorganiser.

disorientate /dɪs'ɔ:rɪənteɪt/ *v.t.* désorienter.

disown /dɪs'əʊn/ *v.t.* renier.

disparaging /dɪ'spærɪdʒɪŋ/ *a.* désobligeant. **~ly** *adv.* de façon désobligeante.

disparity /dɪ'spærətɪ/ *n.* disparité *f.*, écart *m.*

dispassionate /dɪ'spæʃənət/ *a.* impartial; (*unemotional*) calme.

dispatch /dɪ'spætʃ/ *v.t.* (*send, complete*) expédier; (*troops*) envoyer. ● *n.* expédition *f.*; envoi *m.*; (*report*) dépêche *f.* **~-rider** *n.* estafette *f.*

dispel /dɪ'spel/ *v.t.* (*p.t.* **dispelled**) dissiper.

dispensary /dɪ'spensərɪ/ *n.* pharmacie *f.*, officine *f.*

dispense /dɪ'spens/ *v.t.* distribuer; (*medicine*) préparer. ● *v.i.* **~ with,** se passer de. **~r** /-ə(r)/ *n.* (*container*) distributeur *m.*

dispers|e /dɪ'spɜ:s/ *v.t./i.* (se) disperser. **~al** *n.* dispersion *f.*

dispirited /dɪ'spɪrɪtɪd/ *a.* découragé, abattu.

displace /dɪs'pleɪs/ *v.t.* déplacer.

display /dɪ'spleɪ/ *v.t.* montrer, exposer; (*feelings*) manifester. ● *n.* exposition *f.*; manifestation *f.*; (*comm.*) étalage *m.*; (*of computer*) visuel *m.*

displeas|e /dɪs'pli:z/ *v.t.* déplaire à. **~ed with,** mécontent de. **~ure** /-'pleʒə(r)/ *n.* mécontentement *m.*

disposable /dɪ'spəʊzəbl/ *a.* à jeter.

dispos|e /dɪ'spəʊz/ *v.t.* disposer. ● *v.i.* **~e of,** se débarrasser de. **well ~ed to,** bien disposé envers. **~al** *n.* (*of waste*) évacuation *f.* **at s.o.'s ~al,** à la disposition de qn.

disposition /dɪspə'zɪʃn/ *n.* disposition *f.*; (*character*) naturel *m.*

disproportionate /dɪsprə'pɔ:ʃənət/ *a.* disproportionné.

disprove /dɪs'pru:v/ *v.t.* réfuter.

dispute /dɪ'spju:t/ *v.t.* contester. ● *n.* discussion *f.*; (*pol.*) conflit *m.* **in ~,** contesté.

disqualif|y /dɪs'kwɒlɪfaɪ/ *v.t.* rendre inapte; (*sport*) disqualifier. **~y from driving,** retirer le permis à. **~ication** /-ɪ'keɪʃn/ *n.* disqualification *f.*

disquiet /dɪs'kwaɪət/ *n.* inquiétude *f.* **~ing** *a.* inquiétant.

disregard /dɪsrɪ'gɑ:d/ *v.t.* ne pas tenir compte de. ● *n.* indifférence *f.* (**for,** à).

disrepair /dɪsrɪ'peə(r)/ *n.* mauvais état *m.*, délabrement *m.*

disreputable /dɪs'repjʊtəbl/ *a.* peu recommendable.

disrepute /dɪsrɪ'pju:t/ *n.* discrédit *m.*

disrespect /dɪsrɪ'spekt/ *n.* manque de respect *m.* **~ful** *a.* irrespectueux.

disrupt /dɪs'rʌpt/ *v.t.* (*disturb, break up*) perturber; (*plans*) déranger. **~ion** /-pʃn/ *n.* perturbation *f.* **~ive** *a.* perturbateur.

dissatisf|ied /dɪs'sætɪsfaɪd/ *a.* mécontent. **~action** /dɪsætɪs'fækʃn/ *n.* mécontentement *m.*

dissect /dɪ'sekt/ *v.t.* disséquer. **~ion** /-kʃn/ *n.* dissection *f.*

disseminate /dɪ'semmeɪt/ *v.t.* disséminer.

dissent /dɪ'sent/ *v.i.* différer (**from,** de). ● *n.* dissentiment *m.*

dissertation /dɪsə'teɪʃn/ *n.* (*univ.*) mémoire *m.*

disservice /dɪs'sɜ:vɪs/ *n.* mauvais service *m.*

dissident /'dɪsɪdənt/ *a.* & *n.* dissident(e) (*m.* (*f.*)).

dissimilar /dɪ'sɪmɪlə(r)/ *a.* dissemblable, différent.

dissipate /'dɪsɪpeɪt/ *v.t./i.* (se) dissiper; (*efforts*) gaspiller. **~d** /-ɪd/ *a.* (*person*) débauché.

dissociate /dɪ'səʊʃɪeɪt/ *v.t.* dissocier. **~ o.s. from,** se désolidariser de.

dissolute /'dɪsəlju:t/ *a.* dissolu.

dissolution /dɪsə'lu:ʃn/ *n.* dissolution *f.*

dissolve /dɪ'zɒlv/ *v.t./i.* (se) dissoudre.

dissuade /dɪ'sweɪd/ *v.t.* dissuader.

distance /'dɪstəns/ *n.* distance *f.* **from a ~,** de loin. **in the ~,** au loin.

distant /'dɪstənt/ *a.* éloigné, lointain; (*relative*) éloigné; (*aloof*) distant.

distaste /dɪs'teɪst/ *n.* dégoût *m.* **~ful** *a.* désagréable.

distemper /dɪ'stempə(r)/ *n.* (*paint*) badigeon *m.*; (*animal disease*) maladie *f.* ● *v.t.* badigeonner.

distend /dɪ'stend/ *v.t./i.* (se) distendre.

distil /dɪ'stɪl/ *v.t.* (*p.t.* **distilled**) distiller. **~lation** /-'leɪʃn/ *n.* distillation *f.*

distillery /dɪ'stɪlərɪ/ *n.* distillerie *f.*
distinct /dɪ'stɪŋkt/ *a.* distinct; (*marked*) net. **as ~ from,** par opposition à. **~ion** /-kʃn/ *n.* distinction *f.*; (*in exam*) mention très bien *f.* **~ive** *a.* distinctif. **~ly** *adv.* (*see*) distinctement; (*forbid*) expressément; (*markedly*) nettement.
distinguish /dɪ'stɪŋgwɪʃ/ *v.t./i.* distinguer. **~ed** *a.* distingué.
distort /dɪ'stɔ:t/ *v.t.* déformer. **~ion** /-ʃn/ *n.* distorsion *f.*; (*of facts*) déformation *f.*
distract /dɪ'strækt/ *v.t.* distraire. **~ed** *a.* (*distraught*) éperdu. **~ing** *a.* gênant. **~ion** /-kʃn/ *n.* (*lack of attention, entertainment*) distraction *f.*
distraught /dɪ'strɔ:t/ *a.* éperdu.
distress /dɪ'stres/ *n.* douleur *f.*; (*poverty, danger*) détresse *f.* ● *v.t.* peiner. **~ing** *a.* pénible.
distribut|e /dɪ'strɪbju:t/ *v.t.* distribuer. **~ion** /-'bju:ʃn/ *n.* distribution *f.* **~or** *n.* distributeur *m.*
district /'dɪstrɪkt/ *n.* région *f.*; (*of town*) quartier *m.*
distrust /dɪs'trʌst/ *n.* méfiance *f.* ● *v.t.* se méfier de.
disturb /dɪ'stɜ:b/ *v.t.* déranger; (*alarm, worry*) troubler. **~ance** *n.* dérangement *m.* (**of,** de); (*noise*) tapage *m.* **~ances** *n. pl.* (*pol.*) troubles *m. pl.* **~ed** *a.* troublé; (*psychologically*) perturbé. **~ing** *a.* troublant.
disused /dɪs'ju:zd/ *a.* désaffecté.
ditch /dɪtʃ/ *n.* fossé *m.* ● *v.t.* (*sl.*) abandonner.
dither /'dɪðə(r)/ *v.i.* hésiter.
ditto /'dɪtəʊ/ *adv.* idem.
divan /dɪ'væn/ *n.* divan *m.*
div|e /daɪv/ *v.i.* plonger; (*rush*) se précipiter. ● *n.* plongeon *m.*; (*of plane*) piqué *m.*; (*place: sl.*) bouge *m.* **~er** *n.* plongeu|r, -se *m., f.* **~ing-board** *n.* plongeoir *m.* **~ing-suit** *n.* tenue de plongée *f.*
diverge /daɪ'vɜ:dʒ/ *v.i.* diverger.
divergent /daɪ'vɜ:dʒənt/ *a.* divergent.
diverse /daɪ'vɜ:s/ *a.* divers.
diversify /daɪ'vɜ:sɪfaɪ/ *v.t.* diversifier.
diversity /daɪ'vɜ:sətɪ/ *n.* diversité *f.*
diver|t /daɪ'vɜ:t/ *v.t.* détourner; (*traffic*) dévier. **~sion** /-ʃn/ *n.* détournement *m.*; (*distraction*) diversion *f.*; (*of traffic*) déviation *f.*
divest /daɪ'vest/ *v.t.* **~ of,** (*strip of*) priver de, déposséder de.
divide /dɪ'vaɪd/ *v.t./i.* (se) diviser.
dividend /'dɪvɪdend/ *n.* dividende *m.*
divine /dɪ'vaɪn/ *a.* divin.
divinity /dɪ'vɪnətɪ/ *n.* divinité *f.*
division /dɪ'vɪʒn/ *n.* division *f.*
divorce /dɪ'vɔ:s/ *n.* divorce *m.* (**from,** d'avec). ● *v.t./i.* divorcer (d'avec). **~d** *a.* divorcé.
divorcee /dɪvɔ:'si:, *Amer.* dɪvɔ:'seɪ/ *n.* divorcé(e) *m.* (*f.*).
divulge /daɪ'vʌldʒ/ *v.t.* divulguer.
DIY *abbr. see* **do-it-yourself**.
dizz|y /'dɪzɪ/ *a.* (**-ier, -iest**) vertigineux. **be** *or* **feel ~y,** avoir le vertige. **~iness** *n.* vertige *m.*
do /du:/ *v.t./i.* (*3 sing. present tense* **does**; *p.t.* **did**; *p.p.*, **done**) faire; (*progress, be suitable*) aller; (*be enough*) suffire; (*swindle: sl.*) avoir. **do well/badly,** se débrouiller bien/mal. **do the house,** peindre *ou* nettoyer *etc.* la maison. **well done!,** bravo! **well done,** (*culin.*) bien cuit. **done for,** (*fam.*) fichu. ● *v. aux.* **do you see?,** voyez-vous? **do you live here?,** est-ce que vous habitez ici? **I do live here,** si, j'habite ici. **I do not smoke,** je ne fume pas. **don't you?, doesn't he?,** *etc.*, n'est-ce pas? ● *n.* (*pl.* **dos** *or* **do's**) soirée *f.*, fête *f.* **dos and don'ts,** choses à faire et à ne pas faire. **do away with,** supprimer. **do in,** (*sl.*) tuer. **do-it-yourself** *n.* bricolage *m.*; *a.* (*shop, book*) de bricolage. **do out,** (*clean*) nettoyer. **do up,** (*fasten*) fermer; (*house*) refaire. **it's to ~ with the house,** c'est à propos de la maison. **it's nothing to do with me,** ça n'a rien à voir avec moi. **I could do with a holiday,** j'aurais bien besoin de vacances. **~ without,** se passer de.
docile /'dəʊsaɪl/ *a.* docile.
dock[1] /dɒk/ *n.* dock *m.* ● *v.t./i.* (se) mettre à quai. **~er** *n.* docker *m.*
dock[2] /dɒk/ *n.* (*jurid.*) banc des accusés *m.*
dock[3] /dɒk/ *v.t.* (*money*) retrancher.
dockyard /'dɒkjɑ:d/ *n.* chantier naval *m.*
doctor /'dɒktə(r)/ *n.* médecin *m.*, docteur *m.*; (*univ.*) docteur *m.* ● *v.t.* (*cat*) châtrer; (*fig.*) altérer.
doctorate /'dɒktərət/ *n.* doctorat *m.*
doctrine /'dɒktrɪn/ *n.* doctrine *f.*
document /'dɒkjʊmənt/ *n.* document *m.* **~ary** /-'mentrɪ/ *a.* & *n.* documen-

taire (*m.*). **~ation** /-ˈeɪʃn/ *n.* documentation *f.*
doddering /ˈdɒdərɪŋ/ *a.* gâteux.
dodge /dɒdʒ/ *v.t.* esquiver. ● *v.i.* faire un saut de côté ● *n.* (*fam.*) truc *m.*
dodgems /ˈdɒdʒəmz/ *n. pl.* autos tamponneuses *f. pl.*
dodgy /ˈdɒdʒɪ/ *a.* (**-ier, -iest**) (*fam.*: *difficult*) épineux, délicat; (*dangerous*) douteux.
doe /dəʊ/ *n.* (*deer*) biche *f.*
does /dʌz/ *see* **do.**
doesn't /ˈdʌznt/ = **does not.**
dog /dɒg/ *n.* chien *m.* ● *v.t.* (*p.t.* **dogged**) poursuivre. **~-collar** *n.* (*fam.*) (faux) col d'ecclésiastique *m.* **~-eared** *a.* écorné.
dogged /ˈdɒgɪd/ *a.* obstiné.
dogma /ˈdɒgmə/ *n.* dogme *m.* **~tic** /-ˈmætɪk/ *a.* dogmatique.
dogsbody /ˈdɒgzbɒdɪ/ *n.* factotum *m.*, bonne à tout faire *f.*
doily /ˈdɔɪlɪ/ *n.* napperon *m.*
doings /ˈduːɪŋz/ *n. pl.* (*fam.*) activités *f. pl.*, occupations *f. pl.*
doldrums /ˈdɒldrəmz/ *n. pl.* **be in the ~,** (*person*) avoir le cafard.
dole /dəʊl/ *v.t.* **~ out,** distribuer. ● *n.* (*fam.*) indemnité de chômage *f.* **on the ~,** (*fam.*) au chômage.
doleful /ˈdəʊlfl/ *a.* triste, morne.
doll /dɒl/ *n.* poupée *f.* ● *v.t.* **~ up,** (*fam.*) bichonner.
dollar /ˈdɒlə(r)/ *n.* dollar *m.*
dollop /ˈdɒləp/ *n.* (*of food etc.*: *fam.*) gros morceau *m.*
dolphin /ˈdɒlfɪn/ *n.* dauphin *m.*
domain /dəˈmeɪn/ *n.* domaine *m.*
dome /dəʊm/ *n.* dôme *m.*
domestic /dəˈmestɪk/ *a.* familial; (*trade, flights, etc.*) intérieur; (*animal*) domestique. **~ science,** arts ménagers *m. pl.* **~ated** *a.* (*animal*) domestiqué.
domesticity /dɒmeˈstɪsətɪ/ *n.* vie de famille *f.*
dominant /ˈdɒmɪnənt/ *a.* dominant.
dominat|e /ˈdɒmɪneɪt/ *v.t./i.* dominer. **~ion** /-ˈneɪʃn/ *n.* domination *f.*
domineering /dɒmɪˈnɪərɪŋ/ *a.* dominateur, autoritaire.
dominion /dəˈmɪnjən/ *n.* (*British pol.*) dominion *m.*
domino /ˈdɒmɪnəʊ/ *n.* (*pl.* **-oes**) domino *m.* **~es,** (*game*) dominos *m. pl.*
don[1] /dɒn/ *v.t.* (*p.t.* **donned**) revêtir, endosser.
don[2] /dɒn/ *n.* professeur d'université *m.*
donat|e /dəʊˈneɪt/ *v.t.* faire don de. **~ion** /-ʃn/ *n.* don *m.*
done /dʌn/ *see* do.
donkey /ˈdɒŋkɪ/ *n.* âne *m.* the **~-work** le sale boulot.
donor /ˈdəʊnə(r)/ *n.* dona|teur, -trice *m., f.*; (*of blood*) donneu|r, -se *m., f.*
don't /dəʊnt/ = **do not.**
doodle /ˈduːdl/ *v.i.* griffonner.
doom /duːm/ *n.* (*ruin*) ruine *f.*; (*fate*) destin *m.* ● *v.t.* **be ~ed to,** être destiné *or* condamné à. **~ed (to failure),** voué à l'échec.
door /dɔː(r)/ *n.* porte *f.*; (*of vehicle*) portière *f.*, porte *f.*
doorbell /ˈdɔːbel/ *n.* sonnette *f.*
doorman /ˈdɔːmən/ *n.* (*pl.* **-men**) portier *m.*
doormat /ˈdɔːmæt/ *n.* paillasson *m.*
doorstep /ˈdɔːstep/ *n.* pas de (la) porte *m.*, seuil *m.*
doorway /ˈdɔːweɪ/ *n.* porte *f.*
dope /dəʊp/ *n.* (*fam.*) drogue *f.*; (*idiot*: *sl.*) imbécile *m./f.* ● *v.t.* doper. **~y** *a.* (*foolish*: *sl.*) imbécile.
dormant /ˈdɔːmənt/ *a.* en sommeil.
dormitory /ˈdɔːmɪtrɪ, *Amer.* ˈdɔːmɪtɔːrɪ/ *n.* dortoir *m.*; (*univ., Amer.*) résidence *f.*
dormouse /ˈdɔːmaʊs/ *n.* (*pl.* **-mice**) loir *m.*
dos|e /dəʊs/ *n.* dose *f.* **~age** *n.* dose *f.*; (*on label*) posologie *f.*
doss /dɒs/ *v.i.* (*sl.*) roupiller. **~-house** *n.* asile de nuit *m.*
dossier /ˈdɒsɪə(r)/ *n.* dossier *m.*
dot /dɒt/ *n.* point *m.* **on the ~,** (*fam.*) à l'heure pile. **~-matrix** *a.* (*printer*) matriciel.
dote /dəʊt/ *v.i.* **~ on,** être gaga de.
dotted /dɒtɪd/ *a.* (*fabric*) à pois. **~ line,** ligne en pointillés *f.* **~ with,** parsemé de.
dotty /ˈdɒtɪ/ *a.* (**-ier, -iest**) (*fam.*) cinglé, dingue.
double /ˈdʌbl/ *a.* double; (*room, bed*) pour deux personnes. ● *adv.* deux fois. ● *n.* double *m.*; (*stuntman*) doublure *f.* **~s,** (*tennis*) double *m.* ● *v.t./i.* doubler; (*fold*) plier en deux. **at** *or* **on the ~,** au pas de course. **~ the size,** deux fois plus grand: **pay ~,** payer le double. **~-bass** *n.* (*mus.*) contrebasse *f.* **~-breasted** *a.* croisé. **~-check** *v.t.* revérifier. **~ chin,** double menton *m.* **~-cross** *v.t.* tromper. **~-dealing** *n.* double jeu

m. **~-decker** *n.* autobus à impériale *m.* **~ Dutch,** de l'hébreu *m.*

doubly /'dʌblɪ/ *adv.* doublement.

doubt /daʊt/ *n.* doute *m.* ● *v.t.* douter de. **~ if** *or* **that,** douter que. **~ful** *a.* incertain, douteux; (*person*) qui a des doutes. **~less** *adv.* sans doute.

dough /dəʊ/ *n.* pâte *f.*; (*money*: *sl.*) fric *m.*

doughnut /'dəʊnʌt/ *n.* beignet *m.*

douse /daʊs/ *v.t.* arroser; (*light, fire*) éteindre.

dove /dʌv/ *n.* colombe *f.*

Dover /'dəʊvə(r)/ *n.* Douvres *m./f.*

dovetail /'dʌvteɪl/ *v.t./i.* (s')ajuster.

dowdy /'daʊdɪ/ *a.* (**-ier, -iest**) (*clothes*) sans chic, monotone.

down[1] /daʊn/ *n.* (*fluff*) duvet *m.*

down[2] /daʊn/ *adv.* en bas; (*of sun*) couché; (*lower*) plus bas. ● *prep.* en bas de; (*along*) le long de. ● *v.t.* (*knock down, shoot down*) abattre; (*drink*) vider. **come** *or* **go ~,** descendre. **go ~ to the post office,** aller à la poste. **~-and-out** *n.* clochard(e) *m.* (*f.*). **~-hearted** *a.* découragé. **~-market** *a.* bas de gamme. **~ payment,** acompte *m.* **~-to-earth** *a.* terre-à-terre *invar.* **~ under,** aux antipodes. **~ with,** à bas.

downcast /'daʊnkɑ:st/ *a.* démoralisé.

downfall /'daʊnfɔ:l/ *n.* chute *f.*

downgrade /daʊn'greɪd/ *v.t.* déclasser.

downhill /daʊn'hɪl/ *adv.* **go ~,** descendre; (*pej.*) baisser.

downpour /'daʊnpɔ:(r)/ *n.* grosse averse *f.*

downright /'daʊnraɪt/ *a.* (*utter*) véritable; (*honest*) franc. ● *adv.* carrément.

downs /daʊnz/ *n. pl.* région de collines *f.*

downstairs /daʊn'steəz/ *adv.* en bas. ● *a.* d'en bas.

downstream /'daʊnstri:m/ *adv.* en aval.

downtown /'daʊntaʊn/ *a.* (*Amer.*) du centre de la ville. **~ Boston**/*etc.*, le centre de Boston/*etc.*

downtrodden /'daʊntrɒdn/ *a.* opprimé.

downward /'daʊnwəd/ *a.* & *adv.*, **~s** *adv.* vers le bas.

dowry /'daʊərɪ/ *n.* dot *f.*

doze /dəʊz/ *v.i.* sommeiller. **~ off,** s'assoupir. ● *n.* somme *m.*

dozen /'dʌzn/ *n.* douzaine *f.* **a ~ eggs,** une douzaine d'œufs. **~s of,** (*fam.*) des dizaines de.

Dr *abbr.* (*Doctor*) Docteur.

drab /dræb/ *a.* terne.

draft[1] /drɑ:ft/ *n.* (*outline*) brouillon *m.*; (*comm.*) traite *f.* ● *v.t.* faire le brouillon de; (*draw up*) rédiger. **the ~,** (*mil., Amer.*) la conscription. **a ~ treaty,** un projet de traité.

draft[2] /drɑ:ft/ *n.* (*Amer.*) = **draught**.

drag /dræg/ *v.t./i.* (*p.t.* **dragged**) traîner; (*river*) draguer; (*pull away*) arracher. ● *n.* (*task*: *fam.*) corvée *f.*; (*person*: *fam.*) raseu|r, -se *m., f.* **in ~,** en travesti. **~ on,** s'éterniser.

dragon /'drægən/ *n.* dragon *m.*

dragon-fly /'drægənflaɪ/ *n.* libellule *f.*

drain /dreɪn/ *v.t.* (*land*) drainer; (*vegetables*) égoutter; (*tank, glass*) vider; (*use up*) épuiser. **~ (off),** (*liquid*) faire écouler. ● *v.i.* **~ (off),** (*of liquid*) s'écouler. ● *n.* (*sewer*) égout *m.* **~(-pipe),** tuyau d'écoulement *m.* **be a ~ on,** pomper. **~ing-board** *n.* égouttoir *m.*

drama /'drɑ:mə/ *n.* art dramatique *m.*, théâtre *m.*; (*play, event*) drame *m.* **~tic** /drə'mætɪk/ *a.* (*situation*) dramatique; (*increase*) spectaculaire. **~tist** /'dræmətɪst/ *n.* dramaturge *m.* **~tize** /'dræmətaɪz/ *v.t.* adapter pour la scène; (*fig.*) dramatiser.

drank /dræŋk/ *see* drink.

drape /dreɪp/ *v.t.* draper. **~s** *n. pl.* (*Amer.*) rideaux *m. pl.*

drastic /'dræstɪk/ *a.* sévère.

draught /drɑ:ft/ *n.* courant d'air *m.* **~s,** (*game*) dames *f. pl.* **~ beer,** bière (à la) pression *f.* **~y** *a.* plein de courants d'air.

draughtsman /'drɑ:ftsmən/ *n.* (*pl.* **-men**) dessina|teur, -trice industriel(le) *m., f.*

draw /drɔ:/ *v.t.* (*p.t.* **drew,** *p.p.* **drawn**) (*pull*) tirer; (*attract*) attirer; (*pass*) passer; (*picture*) dessiner; (*line*) tracer. ● *v.i.* dessiner; (*sport*) faire match nul; (*come, move*) venir. ● *n.* (*sport*) match nul *m.*; (*in lottery*) tirage au sort *m.* **~ back,** (*recoil*) reculer. **~ in,** (*days*) diminuer. **~ near,** (s')approcher (**to,** de). **~ out,** (*money*) retirer. **~ up** *v.i.* (*stop*) s'arrêter;

v.t. (*document*) dresser; (*chair*) approcher.
drawback /'drɔ:bæk/ *n.* inconvénient *m.*
drawbridge /'drɔ:brɪdʒ/ *n.* pont-levis *m.*
drawer /drɔ:(r)/ *n.* tiroir *m.*
drawers /drɔ:z/ *n. pl.* culotte *f.*
drawing /'drɔ:ɪŋ/ *n.* dessin *m.* **~-board** *n.* planche à dessin *f.* **~-pin** *n.* punaise *f.* **~-room** *n.* salon *m.*
drawl /drɔ:l/ *n.* voix traînante *f.*
drawn /drɔ:n/ *see* draw. ● *a.* (*features*) tiré; (*match*) nul.
dread /dred/ *n.* terreur *f.*, crainte *f.* ● *v.t.* redouter.
dreadful /'dredfl/ *a.* épouvantable, affreux. **~ly** *adv.* terriblement.
dream /dri:m/ *n.* rêve *m.* ● *v.t./i.* (*p.t.* **dreamed** *or* **dreamt**) rêver. ● *a.* (*ideal*) de ses rêves. **~ up,** imaginer. **~er** *n.* rêveu|r, -se *m., f.* **~y** *a.* rêveur.
drear|y /'drɪərɪ/ *a.* (**-ier, -iest**) triste; (*boring*) monotone. **~iness** *n.* tristesse *f.*; monotonie *f.*
dredge /dredʒ/ *n.* drague *f.* ● *v.t./i.* draguer. **~r** /-ə(r)/ *n.* dragueur *m.*
dregs /dregz/ *n. pl.* lie *f.*
drench /drentʃ/ *v.t.* tremper.
dress /dres/ *n.* robe *f.*; (*clothing*) tenue *f.* ● *v.t./i.* (s')habiller; (*food*) assaisonner; (*wound*) panser. **~ circle,** premier balcon *m.* **~ rehearsal,** répétition générale *f.* **~ up as,** se déguiser en. **get ~ed,** s'habiller.
dresser /'dresə(r)/ *n.* buffet *m.*; (*actor's*) habilleu|r, -se *m., f.*
dressing /'dresɪŋ/ *n.* (*sauce*) assaisonnement *m.*; (*bandage*) pansement *m.* **~-gown** *n.* robe de chambre *f.* **~-room** *n.* (*sport*) vestiaire *m.*; (*theatre*) loge *f.* **~-table** *n.* coiffeuse *f.*
dressmak|er /'dresmeɪkə(r)/ *n.* couturière *f.* **~ing** *n.* couture *f.*
dressy /'dresɪ/ *a.* (**-ier, -iest**) chic *invar.*
drew /dru:/ *see* draw.
dribble /'drɪbl/ *v.i.* couler goutte à goutte; (*person*) baver; (*football*) dribbler.
dribs and drabs /drɪbzn'dræbz/ *n. pl.* petites quantités *f. pl.*
dried /draɪd/ *a.* (*fruit etc.*) sec.
drier /'draɪə(r)/ *n.* séchoir *m.*
drift /drɪft/ *v.i.* aller à la dérive; (*pile up*) s'amonceler. ● *n.* dérive *f.*; amoncellement *m.*; (*of events*) tournure *f.*; (*meaning*) sens *m.* **~ towards,** glisser vers. **(snow) ~,** congère *f.* **~er** *n.* personne sans but dans la vie *f.*
driftwood /'drɪftwʊd/ *n.* bois flotté *m.*
drill /drɪl/ *n.* (*tool*) perceuse *f.*; (*for teeth*) roulette *f.*; (*training*) exercice *m.*; (*procedure: fam.*) marche à suivre *f.* **(pneumatic) ~,** marteau piqueur *m.* ● *v.t.* percer; (*train*) entraîner. ● *v.i.* être à l'exercice.
drily /'draɪlɪ/ *adv.* sèchement.
drink /drɪŋk/ *v.t./i.* (*p.t.* **drank,** *p.p.* **drunk**) boire. ● *n.* (*liquid*) boisson *f.*; (*glass of alcohol*) verre *m.* **a ~ of water,** un verre d'eau. **~able** *a.* (*not unhealthy*) potable; (*palatable*) buvable. **~er** *n.* buveu|r, -se *m., f.* **~ing water,** eau potable *f.*
drip /drɪp/ *v.i.* (*p.t.* **dripped**) (é)goutter; (*washing*) s'égoutter. ● *n.* goutte *f.*; (*person: sl.*) lavette *f.* **~-dry** *v.t.* laisser égoutter; *a.* sans repassage.
dripping /'drɪpɪŋ/ *n.* (*Amer.* **~s**) graisse de rôti *f.*
drive /draɪv/ *v.t.* (*p.t.* **drove,** *p.p.* **driven**) chasser, pousser; (*vehicle*) conduire; (*machine*) actionner. ● *v.i.* conduire. ● *n.* promenade en voiture *f.*; (*private road*) allée *f.*; (*fig.*) énergie *f.*; (*psych.*) instinct *m.*; (*pol.*) campagne *f.*; (*auto.*) traction *f.*; (*golf, comput.*) drive *m.* **it's a two-hour ~,** c'est deux heures en voiture. **~ at,** en venir à. **~ away,** (*of car*) partir. **~ in,** (*force in*) enfoncer. **~ mad,** rendre fou. **left-hand ~,** conduite à gauche *f.*
drivel /'drɪvl/ *n.* radotage *m.*
driver /'draɪvə(r)/ *n.* conduc|teur, -trice *m., f.*, chauffeur *m.* **~'s license** (*Amer.*), permis de conduire *m.*
driving /'draɪvɪŋ/ *n.* conduite *f.* **~ licence,** permis de conduire *m.* **~ rain,** pluie battante *f.* **~ school,** auto-école *f.* **take one's ~ test,** passer son permis.
drizzle /'drɪzl/ *n.* bruine *f.* ● *v.i.* bruiner.
dromedary /'drɒmədərɪ, (*Amer.*) 'drɒməderɪ/ *n.* dromadaire *m.*
drone /drəʊn/ *n.* (*noise*) bourdonnement *m.*; (*bee*) faux bourdon *m.* ● *v.i.* bourdonner; (*fig.*) parler d'une voix monotone.
drool /dru:l/ *v.i.* baver (**over,** sur).
droop /dru:p/ *v.i.* pencher, tomber.

drop /drɒp/ *n.* goutte *f.*; (*fall, lowering*) chute *f.* ● *v.t./i.* (*p.t.* **dropped**) (laisser) tomber; (*decrease, lower*) baisser. ~ **(off),** (*person from car*) déposer. ~ **a line,** écrire un mot (**to,** à). ~ **in,** passer (**on,** chez). ~ **off,** (*doze*) s'assoupir. ~ **out,** se retirer (**of,** de); (*of student*) abandonner. ~**-out** *n.* marginal(e) *m.* (*f.*), raté(e) *m.* (*f.*).

droppings /ˈdrɒpɪŋz/ *n. pl.* crottes *f. pl.*

dross /drɒs/ *n.* déchets *m. pl.*

drought /draʊt/ *n.* sécheresse *f.*

drove /drəʊv/ *see* drive.

droves /drəʊvz/ *n. pl.* foule(s) *f.* (*pl.*).

drown /draʊn/ *v.t./i.* (se) noyer.

drowsy /ˈdraʊzɪ/ *a.* somnolent. **be** *or* **feel** ~, avoir envie de dormir.

drudge /drʌdʒ/ *n.* esclave du travail *m.* ~**ry** /-ərɪ/ *n.* travail pénible et ingrat *m.*

drug /drʌg/ *n.* drogue *f.*; (*med.*) médicament *m.* ● *v.t.* (*p.t.* **drugged**) droguer. ~ **addict,** drogué(e) *m.* (*f.*). ~**gist** *n.* pharmacien (-ne) *m.* (*f.*).

drugstore /ˈdrʌgstɔ:(r)/ *n.* (*Amer.*) drugstore *m.*

drum /drʌm/ *n.* tambour *m.*; (*for oil*) bidon *m.* ~**s,** batterie *f.* ● *v.i.* (*p.t.* **drummed**) tambouriner. ● *v.t.* ~ **into s.o.,** répéter sans cesse à qn. ~ **up,** (*support*) susciter; (*business*) créer. ~**mer** *n.* tambour *m.*; (*in pop group*) batteur *m.*

drumstick /ˈdrʌmstɪk/ *n.* baguette de tambour *f.*; (*of chicken*) pilon *m.*

drunk /drʌŋk/ *see* drink. ● *a.* ivre. **get** ~, s'enivrer. ● *n.*, ~**ard** *n.* ivrogne(sse) *m.* (*f.*). ~**en** *a.* ivre; (*habitually*) ivrogne. ~**enness** *n.* ivresse *f.*

dry /draɪ/ *a.* (**drier, driest**) sec; (*day*) sans pluie. ● *v.t./i.* (faire) sécher. **be** *or* **feel** ~, avoir soif. ~**-clean** *v.t.* nettoyer à sec. ~**- cleaner** *n.* teinturier *m.* ~ **run,** galop d'essai *m.* ~ **up,** (*dry dishes*) essuyer la vaisselle; (*of supplies*) (se) tarir; (*be silent: fam.*) se taire. ~**ness** *n.* sécheresse *f.*

dual /ˈdju:əl/ *a.* double. ~ **carriageway,** route à quatre voies *f.* ~**-purpose** *a.* qui fait double emploi.

dub /dʌb/ *v.t.* (*p.t.* **dubbed**) (*film*) doubler; (*nickname*) surnommer.

dubious /ˈdju:bɪəs/ *a.* (*pej.*) douteux. **be** ~ **about sth.,** (*person*) avoir des doutes sur qch.

duchess /ˈdʌtʃɪs/ *n.* duchesse *f.*

duck /dʌk/ *n.* canard *m.* ● *v.i.* se baisser subitement. ● *v.t.* (*head*) baisser; (*person*) plonger dans l'eau. ~**ling** *n.* caneton *m.*

duct /dʌkt/ *n.* conduit *m.*

dud /dʌd/ *a.* (*tool etc.: sl.*) mal fichu; (*coin: sl.*) faux; (*cheque: sl.*) sans provision. ● *n.* **be a** ~, (*not work: sl.*) ne pas marcher.

dude /du:d/ *n.* (*Amer.*) dandy *m.*

due /dju:/ *a.* (*owing*) dû; (*expected*) attendu; (*proper*) qui convient. ● *adv.* ~ **east**/*etc.*, droit vers l'est/*etc.* ● *n.* dû *m.* ~**s,** droits *m. pl.*; (*of club*) cotisation *f.* ~ **to,** à cause de; (*caused by*) dû à. **she's** ~ **to leave now,** c'est prévu qu'elle parte maintenant. **in** ~ **course,** (*eventually*) avec le temps; (*at the right time*) en temps et lieu.

duel /ˈdju:əl/ *n.* duel *m.*

duet /dju:ˈet/ *n.* duo *m.*

duffle /ˈdʌfl/ *a.* ~ **bag,** sac de marin *m.* ~ **coat,** duffel-coat *m.*

dug /dʌg/ *see* dig.

duke /dju:k/ *n.* duc *m.*

dull /dʌl/ *a.* (**-er, -est**) ennuyeux; (*colour*) terne; (*weather*) morne; (*sound*) sourd; (*stupid*) bête; (*blunt*) émoussé. ● *v.t.* (*pain*) amortir; (*mind*) engourdir.

duly /ˈdju:lɪ/ *adv.* comme il convient; (*in due time*) en temps voulu.

dumb /dʌm/ *a.* (**-er, -est**) muet; (*stupid: fam.*) bête.

dumbfound /dʌmˈfaʊnd/ *v.t.* sidérer, ahurir.

dummy /ˈdʌmɪ/ *n.* (*comm.*) article factice *m.*; (*of tailor*) mannequin *m.*; (*of baby*) sucette *f.* ● *a.* factice. ~ **run,** galop d'essai *m.*

dump /dʌmp/ *v.t.* déposer; (*abandon: fam.*) se débarrasser de; (*comm.*) dumper. ● *n.* tas d'ordures *m.*; (*refuse tip*) décharge *f.*; (*mil.*) dépôt *m.*; (*dull place: fam.*) trou *m.* **be in the** ~**s,** (*fam.*) avoir le cafard.

dumpling /ˈdʌmplɪŋ/ *n.* boulette de pâte *f.*

dumpy /ˈdʌmpɪ/ *a.* (**-ier, -iest**) boulot, rondelet.

dunce /dʌns/ *n.* cancre *m.*, âne *m.*

dune /dju:n/ *n.* dune *f.*

dung /dʌŋ/ *n.* (*excrement*) bouse *f.*, crotte *f.*; (*manure*) fumier *m.*

dungarees /dʌŋgəˈri:z/ *n. pl.* (*overalls*) salopette *f.*; (*jeans: Amer.*) jean *m.*

dungeon /ˈdʌndʒən/ *n.* cachot *m.*
dunk /dʌŋk/ *v.t.* tremper.
dupe /dju:p/ *v.t.* duper. ● *n.* dupe *f.*
duplex /ˈdju:pleks/ *n.* duplex *m.*
duplicate[1] /ˈdju:plɪkət/ *n.* double *m.* ● *a.* identique.
duplicat|e[2] /ˈdju:plɪkeɪt/ *v.t.* faire un double de; (*on machine*) polycopier. **~or** *n.* duplicateur *m.*
duplicity /dju:ˈplɪsətɪ/ *n.* duplicité *f.*
durable /ˈdjʊərəbl/ *a.* (*tough*) résistant; (*enduring*) durable.
duration /djʊˈreɪʃn/ *n.* durée *f.*
duress /djʊˈres/ *n.* contrainte *f.*
during /ˈdjʊərɪŋ/ *prep.* pendant.
dusk /dʌsk/ *n.* crépuscule *m.*
dusky /ˈdʌskɪ/ *a.* (**-ier, -iest**) foncé.
dust /dʌst/ *n.* poussière *f.* ● *v.t.* épousseter; (*sprinkle*) saupoudrer (**with,** de). **~-jacket** *n.* jaquette *f.*
dustbin /ˈdʌstbɪn/ *n.* poubelle *f.*
duster /ˈdʌstə(r)/ *n.* chiffon *m.*
dustman /ˈdʌstmən/ *n.* (*pl.* **-men**) éboueur *m.*
dustpan /ˈdʌstpæn/ *n.* pelle à poussière *f.*
dusty /ˈdʌstɪ/ *a.* (**-ier, -iest**) poussiéreux.
Dutch /dʌtʃ/ *a.* hollandais. ● *n.* (*lang.*) hollandais *m.* **go ~,** partager les frais. **~man** *n.* Hollandais *m.* **~woman** *n.* Hollandaise *f.*
dutiful /ˈdju:tɪfl/ *a.* obéissant.
dut|y /ˈdju:tɪ/ *n.* devoir *m.*; (*tax*) droit *m.* **~ies,** (*of official etc.*) fonctions *f. pl.* **~y-free** *a.* hors-taxe. **on ~y,** de service.
duvet /ˈdu:veɪ/ *n.* couette *f.*
dwarf /dwɔ:f/ *n.* (*pl.* **-fs**) nain(e) *m.* (*f.*). ● *v.t.* rapetisser.
dwell /dwel/ *v.i.* (*p.t.* **dwelt**) demeurer. **~ on,** s'étendre sur. **~er** *n.* habitant(e) *m.* (*f.*). **~ing** *n.* habitation *f.*
dwindle /ˈdwɪndl/ *v.i.* diminuer.
dye /daɪ/ *v.t.* (*pres. p.* **dyeing**) teindre. ● *n.* teinture *f.*
dying /ˈdaɪɪŋ/ *a.* mourant; (*art*) qui se perd.
dynamic /daɪˈnæmɪk/ *a.* dynamique.
dynamism /ˈdaɪnəmɪzəm/ *n.* dynamisme *m.*
dynamite /ˈdaɪnəmaɪt/ *n.* dynamite *f.* ● *v.t.* dynamiter.
dynamo /ˈdaɪnəməʊ/ *n.* (*pl.* **-os**) dynamo *f.*
dynasty /ˈdɪnəstɪ, *Amer.* ˈdaɪnəstɪ/ *n.* dynastie *f.*
dysentery /ˈdɪsəntrɪ/ *n.* dysenterie *f.*
dyslexi|a /dɪsˈleksɪə/ *n.* dyslexie *f.* **~c** *a. & n.* dyslexique (*m./f.*).

E

each /i:tʃ/ *a.* chaque. ● *pron.* chacun(e). **~ one,** chacun(e). **~ other,** l'un(e) l'autre, les un(e)s les autres. **know ~ other,** se connaître. **love ~ other,** s'aimer. **a pound ~,** (*get*) une livre chacun; (*cost*) une livre chaque.
eager /ˈi:gə(r)/ *a.* impatient (**to,** de); (*supporter, desire*) ardent. **be ~ to,** (*want*) avoir envie de. **~ for,** avide de. **~ly** *adv.* avec impatience *or* ardeur. **~ness** *n.* impatience *f.*, désir *m.*, ardeur *f.*
eagle /ˈi:gl/ *n.* aigle *m.*
ear[1] /ɪə(r)/ *n.* oreille *f.* **~-drum** *n.* tympan *m.* **~-ring** *n.* boucle d'oreille *f.*
ear[2] /ɪə(r)/ *n.* (*of corn*) épi *m.*
earache /ˈɪəreɪk/ *n.* mal à l'oreille *m.*, mal d'oreille *m.*
earl /ɜ:l/ *n.* comte *m.*
earlier /ˈɜ:lɪə(r)/ *a.* (*in series*) précédent; (*in history*) plus ancien, antérieur; (*in future*) plus avancé. ● *adv.* précédemment; antérieurement; avant.
early /ˈɜ:lɪ/ (**-ier, -iest**) *adv.* tôt, de bonne heure; (*ahead of time*) en avance. ● *a.* premier; (*hour*) matinal; (*fruit*) précoce; (*retirement*) anticipé. **have an ~ dinner,** dîner tôt. **in ~ summer,** au début de l'été.
earmark /ˈɪəmɑ:k/ *v.t.* destiner, réserver (**for,** à).
earn /ɜ:n/ *v.t.* gagner; (*interest: comm.*) rapporter. **~ s.o. sth.,** (*bring*) valoir qch. à qn.
earnest /ˈɜ:nɪst/ *a.* sérieux. **in ~,** sérieusement.
earnings /ˈɜ:nɪŋz/ *n. pl.* salaire *m.*; (*profits*) bénéfices *m. pl.*
earphone /ˈɪəfəʊn/ *n.* écouteur *m.*
earshot /ˈɪəʃɒt/ *n.* **within ~,** à portée de voix.
earth /ɜ:θ/ *n.* terre *f.* ● *v.t.* (*electr.*) mettre à la terre. **why/how/where on ~ . . . ?,** pourquoi/comment/où diable . . . ? **~ly** *a.* terrestre.
earthenware /ˈɜ:θnweə(r)/ *n.* faïence *f.*

earthquake /ˈɜ:θkweɪk/ *n.* tremblement de terre *m.*

earthy /ˈɜ:θɪ/ *a.* (*of earth*) terreux; (*coarse*) grossier.

earwig /ˈɪəwɪg/ *n.* perce-oreille *m.*

ease /i:z/ *n.* aisance *f.*, facilité *f.*; (*comfort*) bien-être *m.* ● *v.t./i.* (se) calmer; (*relax*) (se) détendre; (*slow down*) ralentir; (*slide*) glisser. **at ~,** à l'aise; (*mil.*) au repos. **with ~,** aisément.

easel /ˈi:zl/ *n.* chevalet *m.*

east /i:st/ *n.* est *m.* ● *a.* d'est. ● *adv.* vers l'est. **the E~,** (*Orient*) l'Orient *m.* **~erly** *a.* d'est. **~ern** *a.* de l'est, oriental. **~ward** *a.* à l'est. **~wards** *adv.* vers l'est.

Easter /ˈi:stə(r)/ *n.* Pâques *f. pl.* (*or m. sing.*). **~ egg,** œuf de Pâques *m.*

easy /ˈi:zɪ/ *a.* (**-ier, -iest**) facile; (*relaxed*) aisé. **~ chair,** fauteuil *m.* **go ~ with,** (*fam.*) y aller doucement avec. **take it ~,** ne pas se fatiguer. **easily** *adv.* facilement.

easygoing /i:zɪˈgəʊɪŋ/ *a.* (*with people*) accommodant; (*relaxed*) décontracté.

eat /i:t/ *v.t./i.* (*p.t.* **ate,** *p.p.* **eaten**) manger. **~ into,** ronger. **~able** *a.* mangeable. **~er** *n.* mangeu|r, -se *m., f.*

eau-de-Cologne /əʊdəkəˈləʊn/ *n.* eau de Cologne *f.*

eaves /i:vz/ *n. pl.* avant-toit *m.*

eavesdrop /ˈi:vzdrɒp/ *v.i.* (*p.t.* **-dropped**). **~ (on),** écouter en cachette.

ebb /eb/ *n.* reflux *m.* ● *v.i.* refluer; (*fig.*) décliner.

ebony /ˈebənɪ/ *n.* ébène *f.*

ebullient /ɪˈbʌlɪənt/ *a.* exubérant.

EC *abbr.* (*European Community*) CE.

eccentric /ɪkˈsentrɪk/ *a.* & *n.* excentrique (*m./f.*). **~ity** /eksenˈtrɪsətɪ/ *n.* excentricité *f.*

ecclesiastical /ɪkli:zɪˈæstɪkl/ *a.* ecclésiastique.

echo /ˈekəʊ/ *n.* (*pl.* **-oes**) écho *m.* ● *v.t./i.* (*p.t.* **echoed,** *pres. p.* **echoing**) (se) répercuter; (*fig.*) répéter.

eclipse /ɪˈklɪps/ *n.* éclipse *f.* ● *v.t.* éclipser.

ecolog|y /i:ˈkɒlədʒɪ/ *n.* écologie *f.* **~ical** /i:kəˈlɒdʒɪkl/ *a.* écologique.

economic /i:kəˈnɒmɪk/ *a.* économique; (*profitable*) rentable. **~al** *a.* économique; (*person*) économe. **~s** *n.* économie politique *f.*

economist /ɪˈkɒnəmɪst/ *n.* économiste *m./f.*

econom|y /ɪˈkɒnəmɪ/ *n.* économie *f.* **~ize** *v.i.* **~ (on),** économiser.

ecosystem /ˈikəʊsɪstəm/ *n.* écosystème *m.*

ecstasy /ˈekstəsɪ/ *n.* extase *f.*

ECU /ˈeɪkju:/ *n.* ÉCU *m.*

eczema /ˈeksɪmə/ *n.* eczéma *m.*

eddy /ˈedɪ/ *n.* tourbillon *m.*

edge /edʒ/ *n.* bord *m.*; (*of town*) abords *m. pl.*; (*of knife*) tranchant *m.* ● *v.t.* border. ● *v.i.* (*move*) se glisser. **have the ~ on,** (*fam.*) l'emporter sur. **on ~,** énervé.

edgeways /ˈedʒweɪz/ *adv.* de côté. **I can't get a word in ~,** je ne peux pas placer un mot.

edging /ˈedʒɪŋ/ *n.* bordure *f.*

edgy /ˈedʒɪ/ *a.* énervé.

edible /ˈedɪbl/ *a.* mangeable; (*not poisonous*) comestible.

edict /ˈi:dɪkt/ *n.* décret *m.*

edifice /ˈedɪfɪs/ *n.* édifice *m.*

edify /ˈedɪfaɪ/ *v.t.* édifier.

edit /ˈedɪt/ *v.t.* (*p.t.* **edited**) (*newspaper*) diriger; (*prepare text of*) mettre au point, préparer; (*write*) rédiger; (*cut*) couper.

edition /ɪˈdɪʃn/ *n.* édition *f.*

editor /ˈedɪtə(r)/ *n.* (*writer*) rédac|teur, -trice *m., f.*; (*annotator*) édi|teur, -trice *m., f.* **the ~ (in chief),** le rédacteur en chef. **~ial** /-ˈtɔ:rɪəl/ *a.* de la rédaction; *n.* éditorial *m.*

educat|e /ˈedʒʊkeɪt/ *v.t.* instruire; (*mind, public*) éduquer. **~ed** *a.* instruit. **~ion** /-ˈkeɪʃn/ *n.* éducation *f.*; (*schooling*) enseignement *m.* **~ional** /-ˈkeɪʃənl/ *a.* pédagogique, éducatif.

EEC *abbr.* (*European Economic Community*) CEE *f.*

eel /i:l/ *n.* anguille *f.*

eerie /ˈɪərɪ/ *a.* (**-ier, -iest**) sinistre.

effect /ɪˈfekt/ *n.* effet *m.* ● *v.t.* effectuer. **come into ~,** entrer en vigueur. **in ~,** effectivement. **take ~,** agir.

effective /ɪˈfektɪv/ *a.* efficace; (*striking*) frappant; (*actual*) effectif. **~ly** *adv.* efficacement; de manière frappante; effectivement. **~ness** *n.* efficacité *f.*

effeminate /ɪˈfemɪnət/ *a.* efféminé.

effervescent /efəˈvesnt/ *a.* effervescent.

efficien|t /ɪ'fɪʃnt/ *a.* efficace; (*person*) compétent. **~cy** *n.* efficacité *f.*; compétence *f.* **~tly** *adv.* efficacement.
effigy /'efɪdʒɪ/ *n.* effigie *f.*
effort /'efət/ *n.* effort *m.* **~less** *a.* facile.
effrontery /ɪ'frʌntərɪ/ *n.* effronterie *f.*
effusive /ɪ'fju:sɪv/ *a.* expansif.
e.g. /i:'dʒi:/ *abbr.* par exemple.
egalitarian /ɪgælɪ'teərɪən/ *a.* égalitaire. ● *n.* égalitariste *m./f.*
egg[1] /eg/ *n.* œuf *m.* **~-cup** *n.* coquetier *m.* **~-plant** *n.* aubergine *f.*
egg[2] /eg/ *v.t.* **~ on,** (*fam.*) inciter.
eggshell /'egʃel/ *n.* coquille d'œuf *f.*
ego /'i:gəʊ/ *n.* (*pl.* **-os**) moi *m.* **~(t)ism** *n.* égoïsme *m.* **~(t)ist** *n.* égoïste *m./f.*
Egypt /'i:dʒɪpt/ *n.* Égypte *f.* **~ian** /ɪ'dʒɪpʃn/ *a.* & *n.* égyptien(ne) (*m.* (*f.*)).
eh /eɪ/ *int.* (*fam.*) hein.
eiderdown /'aɪdədaʊn/ *n.* édredon *m.*
eight /eɪt/ *a.* & *n.* huit (*m.*). **eighth** /eɪtθ/ *a.* & *n.* huitième (*m./f.*).
eighteen /eɪ'ti:n/ *a.* & *n.* dix-huit (*m.*). **~th** *a.* & *n.* dix-huitième (*m./f.*).
eight|y /'eɪtɪ/ *a.* & *n.* quatre-vingts (*m.*) **~ieth** *a.* & *n.* quatre-vingtième (*m./f.*).
either /'aɪðə(r)/ *a.* & *pron.* l'un(e) ou l'autre; (*with negative*) ni l'un(e) ni l'autre; (*each*) chaque. ● *adv.* non plus. ● *conj.* **~ . . . or,** ou (bien) . . . ou (bien); (*with negative*) ni . . . ni.
eject /ɪ'dʒekt/ *v.t.* éjecter. **~or seat,** siège éjectable *m.*
eke /i:k/ *v.t.* **~ out,** faire durer; (*living*) gagner difficilement.
elaborate[1] /ɪ'læbərət/ *a.* compliqué, recherché.
elaborate[2] /ɪ'læbəreɪt/ *v.t.* élaborer. ● *v.i.* préciser. **~ on,** s'étendre sur.
elapse /ɪ'læps/ *v.i.* s'écouler.
elastic /ɪ'læstɪk/ *a.* & *n.* élastique (*m.*). **~ band,** élastique *m.* **~ity** /elæ'stɪsətɪ/ *n.* élasticité *f.*
elated /ɪ'leɪtɪd/ *a.* fou de joie.
elbow /'elbəʊ/ *n.* coude *m.* **~ room,** possibilité de manœuvrer *f.*
elder[1] /'eldə(r)/ *a.* & *n.* aîné(e) (*m.* (*f.*)).
elder[2] /'eldə(r)/ *n.* (*tree*) sureau *m.*
elderly /'eldəlɪ/ *a.* (assez) âgé.
eldest /'eldɪst/ *a.* & *n.* aîné(e) (*m.* (*f.*)).
elect /ɪ'lekt/ *v.t.* élire. ● *a.* (*president etc.*) futur. **~ to do,** choisir de faire. **~ion** /-kʃn/ *n.* élection *f.*
elector /ɪ'lektə(r)/ *n.* élec|teur, -trice *m., f.* **~al** *a.* électoral. **~ate** *n.* électorat *m.*
electric /ɪ'lektrɪk/ *a.* électrique. **~ blanket,** couverture chauffante *f.* **~al** *a.* électrique.
electrician /ɪlek'trɪʃn/ *n.* électricien *m.*
electricity /ɪlek'trɪsətɪ/ *n.* électricité *f.*
electrify /ɪ'lektrɪfaɪ/ *v.t.* électrifier; (*excite*) électriser.
electrocute /ɪ'lektrəkju:t/ *v.t.* électrocuter.
electron /ɪ'lektrɒn/ *n.* électron *m.*
electronic /ɪlek'trɒnɪk/ *a.* électronique. **~s** *n.* électronique *f.*
elegan|t /'elɪgənt/ *a.* élégant. **~ce** *n.* élégance *f.* **~tly** *adv.* élégamment.
element /'elɪmənt/ *n.* élément *m.*; (*of heater etc.*) résistance *f.* **~ary** /-'mentrɪ/ *a.* élémentaire.
elephant /'elɪfənt/ *n.* éléphant *m.*
elevat|e /'elɪveɪt/ *v.t.* élever. **~ion** /-'veɪʃn/ *n.* élévation *f.*
elevator /'eləveɪtə(r)/ *n.* (*Amer.*) ascenseur *m.*
eleven /ɪ'levn/ *a.* & *n.* onze (*m.*). **~th** *a.* & *n.* onzième (*m./f.*).
elf /elf/ (*pl.* **elves**) lutin *m.*
elicit /ɪ'lɪsɪt/ *v.t.* obtenir (**from,** de).
eligible /'elɪdʒəbl/ *a.* admissible (**for,** à). **be ~ for,** (*entitled to*) avoir droit à.
eliminat|e /ɪ'lɪmɪneɪt/ *v.t.* éliminer. **~ion** /-'neɪʃn/ *n.* élimination *f.*
élit|e /eɪ'li:t/ *n.* élite *f.* **~ist** *a.* & *n.* élitiste (*m./f.*).
ellip|se /ɪ'lɪps/ *n.* ellipse *f.* **~tical** *a.* elliptique.
elm /elm/ *n.* orme *m.*
elocution /elə'kju:ʃn/ *n.* élocution *f.*
elongate /'i:lɒŋgeɪt/ *v.t.* allonger.
elope /ɪ'ləʊp/ *v.i.* s'enfuir. **~ment** *n.* fugue (amoureuse) *f.*
eloquen|t /'eləkwənt/ *a.* éloquent. **~ce** *n.* éloquence *f.* **~tly** *adv.* avec éloquence.
else /els/ *adv.* d'autre. **everybody ~,** tous les autres. **nobody ~,** personne d'autre. **nothing ~,** rien d'autre. **or ~,** ou bien. **somewhere ~,** autre part. **~where** *adv.* ailleurs.
elucidate /ɪ'lu:sɪdeɪt/ *v.t.* élucider.
elude /ɪ'lu:d/ *v.t.* échapper à; (*question*) éluder.

elusive /ɪ'lu:sɪv/ *a.* insaisissable.
emaciated /ɪ'meɪʃɪeɪtɪd/ *a.* émacié.
emanate /'eməneɪt/ *v.i.* émaner.
emancipat|e /ɪ'mænsɪpeɪt/ *v.t.* émanciper. **~ion** /-'peɪʃn/ *n.* émancipation *f.*
embalm /ɪm'bɑ:m/ *v.t.* embaumer.
embankment /ɪm'bæŋkmənt/ *n.* (*of river*) quai *m.*; (*of railway*) remblai *m.*, talus *m.*
embargo /ɪm'bɑ:gəʊ/ *n.* (*pl.* **-oes**) embargo *m.*
embark /ɪm'bɑ:k/ *v.t./i.* (s')embarquer. **~ on,** (*business etc.*) se lancer dans; (*journey*) commencer. **~ation** /embɑ:'keɪʃn/ *n.* embarquement *m.*
embarrass /ɪm'bærəs/ *v.t.* embarrasser, gêner. **~ment** *n.* embarras *m.*, gêne *f.*
embassy /'embəsɪ/ *n.* ambassade *f.*
embed /ɪm'bed/ *v.t.* (*p.t.* **embedded**) encastrer.
embellish /ɪm'belɪʃ/ *v.t.* embellir. **~ment** *n.* enjolivement *m.*
embers /'embəz/ *n. pl.* braise *f.*
embezzle /ɪm'bezl/ *v.t.* détourner. **~ment** *n.* détournement de fonds *m.* **~r** /-ə(r)/ *n.* escroc *m.*
embitter /ɪm'bɪtə(r)/ *v.t.* (*person*) aigrir; (*situation*) envenimer.
emblem /'embləm/ *n.* emblème *m.*
embod|y /ɪm'bɒdɪ/ *v.t.* incarner, exprimer; (*include*) contenir. **~iment** *n.* incarnation *f.*
emboss /ɪm'bɒs/ *v.t.* (*metal*) repousser; (*paper*) gaufrer.
embrace /ɪm'breɪs/ *v.t./i.* (s')embrasser. ● *n.* étreinte *f.*
embroider /ɪm'brɔɪdə(r)/ *v.t.* broder. **~y** *n.* broderie *f.*
embroil /ɪm'brɔɪl/ *v.t.* mêler (**in,** à).
embryo /'embrɪəʊ/ *n.* (*pl.* **-os**) embryon *m.* **~nic** /-'ɒnɪk/ *a.* embryonnaire.
emend /ɪ'mend/ *v.t.* corriger.
emerald /'emərəld/ *n.* émeraude *f.*
emerge /ɪ'mɜ:dʒ/ *v.i.* apparaître. **~nce** /-əns/ *n.* apparition *f.*
emergency /ɪ'mɜ:dʒənsɪ/ *n.* (*crisis*) crise *f.*; (*urgent case*: *med.*) urgence *f.* ● *a.* d'urgence. **~ exit,** sortie de secours *f.* **~ landing,** atterrissage forcé *m.* **in an ~,** en cas d'urgence.
emery /'emərɪ/ *n.* émeri *m.*
emigrant /'emɪgrənt/ *n.* émigrant(e) *m.* (*f.*).
emigrat|e /'emɪgreɪt/ *v.i.* émigrer. **~ion** /-'greɪʃn/ *n.* émigration *f.*
eminen|t /'emɪnənt/ *a.* éminent. **~ce** *n.* éminence *f.* **~tly** *adv.* éminemment, parfaitement.
emissary /'emɪsərɪ/ *n.* émissaire *m.*
emi|t /ɪ'mɪt/ *v.t.* (*p.t.* **emitted**) émettre. **~ssion** *n.* émission *f.*
emotion /ɪ'məʊʃn/ *n.* émotion *f.* **~al** *a.* (*person, shock*) émotif; (*speech, scene*) émouvant.
emotive /ɪ'məʊtɪv/ *a.* émotif.
emperor /'empərə(r)/ *n.* empereur *m.*
emphasis /'emfəsɪs/ *n.* (*on word*) accent *m.* **lay ~ on,** mettre l'accent sur.
emphasize /'emfəsaɪz/ *v.t.* souligner; (*syllable*) insister sur.
emphatic /ɪm'fætɪk/ *a.* catégorique; (*manner*) énergique.
empire /'empaɪə(r)/ *n.* empire *m.*
employ /ɪm'plɔɪ/ *v.t.* employer. **~er** *n.* employeu|r, -se *m., f.* **~ment** *n.* emploi *m.* **~ment agency,** agence de placement *f.*
employee /emplɔɪ'i:/ *n.* employé(e) *m.* (*f.*).
empower /ɪm'paʊə(r)/ *v.t.* autoriser (**to do,** à faire).
empress /'emprɪs/ *n.* impératrice *f.*
empt|y /'emptɪ/ *a.* (**-ier, -est**) vide; (*promise*) vain. ● *v.t./i.* (se) vider. **~y-handed** *a.* les mains vides. **on an ~y stomach,** à jeun. **~ies** *n. pl.* bouteilles vides *f. pl.* **~iness** *n.* vide *m.*
emulat|e /'emjʊleɪt/ *v.t.* imiter. **~ion** /-'leɪʃn/ *n.* (*comput.*) émulation *f.*
emulsion /ɪ'mʌlʃn/ *n.* émulsion *f.* **~ (paint),** peinture-émulsion *f.*
enable /ɪ'neɪbl/ *v.t.* **~ s.o. to,** permettre à qn. de.
enact /ɪ'nækt/ *v.t.* (*law*) promulguer; (*scene*) représenter.
enamel /ɪ'næml/ *n.* émail *m.* ● *v.t.* (*p.t.* **enamelled**) émailler.
enamoured /ɪ'næməd/ *a.* **be ~ of,** aimer beaucoup, être épris de.
encampment /ɪn'kæmpmənt/ *n.* campement *m.*
encase /ɪn'keɪs/ *v.t.* (*cover*) recouvrir (**in,** de); (*enclose*) enfermer (**in,** dans).
enchant /ɪn'tʃɑ:nt/ *v.t.* enchanter. **~ing** *a.* enchanteur. **~ment** *n.* enchantement *m.*
encircle /ɪn'sɜ:kl/ *v.t.* encercler.
enclave /'enkleɪv/ *n.* enclave *f.*
enclose /ɪn'kləʊz/ *v.t.* (*land*) clôturer; (*with letter*) joindre. **~d** *a.*

(*space*) clos; (*market*) couvert; (*with letter*) ci-joint.
enclosure /ɪn'kləʊʒə(r)/ *n.* enceinte *f.*; (*comm.*) pièce jointe *f.*
encompass /ɪn'kʌmpəs/ *v.t.* (*include*) inclure.
encore /'ɒŋkɔ:(r)/ *int.* & *n.* bis (*m.*).
encounter /ɪn'kaʊntə(r)/ *v.t.* rencontrer. ● *n.* rencontre *f.*
encourage /ɪn'kʌrɪdʒ/ *v.t.* encourager. **~ment** *n.* encouragement *m.*
encroach /ɪn'krəʊtʃ/ *v.i.* **~ upon,** empiéter sur.
encumber /ɪn'kʌmbə(r)/ *v.t.* encombrer.
encyclical /ɪn'sɪklɪkl/ *n.* encyclique *f.*
encyclopaed|ia, encycloped|ia /ɪnsaɪklə'pi:dɪə/ *n.* encyclopédie *f.* **~ic** *a.* encyclopédique.
end /end/ *n.* fin *f.*; (*farthest part*) bout *m.* ● *v.t./i.* (se) terminer. **~ up doing,** finir par faire. **come to an ~,** prendre fin. **~-product,** produit fini *m.* **in the ~,** finalement. **no ~ of,** (*fam.*) énormément de. **on ~,** (*upright*) debout; (*in a row*) de suite. **put an ~ to,** mettre fin à.
endanger /ɪn'deɪndʒə(r)/ *v.t.* mettre en danger.
endear|ing /ɪn'dɪərɪŋ/ *a.* attachant. **~ment** *n.* parole tendre *f.*
endeavour, (*Amer.*) **endeavor** /ɪn'devə(r)/ *n.* effort *m.* ● *v.i.* s'efforcer (**to,** de).
ending /'endɪŋ/ *n.* fin *f.*
endive /'endɪv/ *n.* chicorée *f.*
endless /'endlɪs/ *a.* interminable; (*times*) innombrable; (*patience*) infini.
endorse /ɪn'dɔ:s/ *v.t.* (*document*) endosser; (*action*) approuver. **~ment** *n.* (*auto.*) contravention *f.*
endow /ɪn'daʊ/ *v.t.* doter. **~ed with,** doté de. **~ment** *n.* dotation *f.* (**of,** de).
endur|e /ɪn'djʊə(r)/ *v.t.* supporter. ● *v.i.* durer. **~able** *a.* supportable. **~ance** *n.* endurance *f.* **~ing** *a.* durable.
enemy /'enəmɪ/ *n.* & *a.* ennemi(e) (*m.* (*f.*)).
energetic /enə'dʒetɪk/ *a.* énergique.
energy /'enədʒɪ/ *n.* énergie *f.*
enforce /ɪn'fɔ:s/ *v.t.* appliquer, faire respecter; (*impose*) imposer (**on,** à). **~d** *a.* forcé.
engage /ɪn'geɪdʒ/ *v.t.* engager. ● *v.i.* **~ in,** prendre part à. **~d** *a.* fiancé; (*busy*) occupé. **get ~d,** se fiancer. **~ment** *n.* fiançailles *f. pl.*; (*meeting*) rendez-vous *m.*; (*undertaking*) engagement *m.*
engaging /ɪn'geɪdʒɪŋ/ *a.* engageant, séduisant.
engender /ɪn'dʒendə(r)/ *v.t.* engendrer.
engine /'endʒɪn/ *n.* moteur *m.*; (*of train*) locomotive *f.*; (*of ship*) machine *f.* **~-driver** *n.* mécanicien *m.*
engineer /'endʒɪ'nɪə(r)/ *n.* ingénieur *m.*; (*appliance repairman*) dépanneur *m.* ● *v.t.* (*contrive: fam.*) machiner. **~ing** *n.* (*mechanical*) mécanique *f.*; (*road-building etc.*) génie *m.*
England /'ɪŋglənd/ *n.* Angleterre *f.*
English /'ɪŋglɪʃ/ *a.* anglais. ● *n.* (*lang.*) anglais *m.* **~-speaking** *a.* anglophone. **the ~,** les Anglais *m. pl.* **~man** *n.* Anglais *m.* **~woman** *n.* Anglaise *f.*
engrav|e /ɪn'greɪv/ *v.t.* graver. **~ing** *n.* gravure *f.*
engrossed /ɪn'grəʊst/ *a.* absorbé (**in,** par).
engulf /ɪn'gʌlf/ *v.t.* engouffrer.
enhance /ɪn'hɑ:ns/ *v.t.* rehausser; (*price, value*) augmenter.
enigma /ɪ'nɪgmə/ *n.* énigme *f.* **~tic** /enɪg'mætɪk/ *a.* énigmatique.
enjoy /ɪn'dʒɔɪ/ *v.t.* aimer (*doing,* faire); (*benefit from*) jouir de. **~ o.s.,** s'amuser. **~ your meal,** bon appétit! **~able** *a.* agréable. **~ment** *n.* plaisir *m.*
enlarge /ɪn'lɑ:dʒ/ *v.t./i.* (s')agrandir. **~ upon,** s'étendre sur. **~ment** *n.* agrandissement *m.*
enlighten /ɪn'laɪtn/ *v.t.* éclairer. **~ment** *n.* édification *f.*; (*information*) éclaircissements *m. pl.*
enlist /ɪn'lɪst/ *v.t.* (*person*) recruter; (*fig.*) obtenir. ● *v.i.* s'engager.
enliven /ɪn'laɪvn/ *v.t.* animer.
enmity /'enmətɪ/ *n.* inimitié *f.*
enormity /ɪ'nɔ:mətɪ/ *n.* énormité *f.*
enormous /ɪ'nɔ:məs/ *a.* énorme. **~ly** *adv.* énormément.
enough /ɪ'nʌf/ *adv.* & *n.* assez. ● *a.* assez de. **~ glasses/time/***etc.*, assez de verres/de temps/*etc.* **have ~ of,** en avoir assez de.
enquir|e /ɪn'kwaɪə(r)/ *v.t./i.* demander. **~e about,** se renseigner sur. **~y** *n.* demande de renseignements *f.*

enrage /ɪn'reɪdʒ/ *v.t.* mettre en rage, rendre furieux.
enrich /ɪn'rɪtʃ/ *v.t.* enrichir.
enrol, (*Amer.*) **enroll** /ɪn'rəʊl/ *v.t./i.* (*p.t.* **enrolled**) (s')inscrire. **~ment** *n.* inscription *f.*
ensconce /ɪn'skɒns/ *v.t.* **~ o.s.,** bien s'installer.
ensemble /ɒn'sɒmbl/ *n.* (*clothing & mus.*) ensemble *m.*
ensign /'ensən, 'ensaɪn/ *n.* (*flag*) pavillon *m.*
enslave /ɪn'sleɪv/ *v.t.* asservir.
ensue /ɪn'sju:/ *v.i.* s'ensuivre.
ensure /ɪn'ʃʊə(r)/ *v.t.* assurer. **~ that,** (*ascertain*) s'assurer que.
entail /ɪn'teɪl/ *v.t.* entraîner.
entangle /ɪn'tæŋgl/ *v.t.* emmêler.
enter /'entə(r)/ *v.t.* (*room, club, race, etc.*) entrer dans; (*note down, register*) inscrire; (*data*) entrer, saisir. ● *v.i.* entrer (**into,** dans). **~ for,** s'inscrire à.
enterprise /'entəpraɪz/ *n.* entreprise *f.*; (*boldness*) initiative *f.*
enterprising /'entəpraɪzɪŋ/ *a.* entreprenant.
entertain /entə'teɪn/ *v.t.* amuser, divertir; (*guests*) recevoir; (*ideas*) considérer. **~er** *n.* artiste *m./f.* **~ing** *a.* divertissant. **~ment** *n.* amusement *m.*, divertissement *m.*; (*performance*) spectacle *m.*
enthral, (*Amer.*) **enthrall** /ɪn'θrɔ:l/ *v.t.* (*p.t.* **enthralled**) captiver.
enthuse /ɪn'θju:z/ *v.i.* **~ over,** s'enthousiasmer pour.
enthusiasm /ɪn'θju:zɪæzəm/ *n.* enthousiasme *m.*
enthusiast /ɪn'θju:zɪæst/ *n.* fervent(e) *m.* (*f.*), passionné(e) *m.* (*f.*) (**for,** de). **~ic** /-'æstɪk/ *a.* (*supporter*) enthousiaste. **be ~ic about,** être enthusiasmé par. **~ically** *adv.* /-'æstɪklɪ/ *adv.* avec enthousiasme.
entice /ɪn'taɪs/ *v.t.* attirer. **~ to do,** entraîner à faire. **~ment** *n.* (*attraction*) attrait *m.*
entire /ɪn'taɪə(r)/ *a.* entier. **~ly** *adv.* entièrement.
entirety /ɪn'taɪərətɪ/ *n.* **in its ~,** en entier.
entitle /ɪn'taɪtl/ *v.t.* donner droit à (**to sth.,** à qch.; **to do,** de faire). **~d** *a.* (*book*) intitulé. **be ~d to sth.,** avoir droit à qch. **~ment** *n.* droit *m.*
entity /'entətɪ/ *n.* entité *f.*
entrails /'entreɪlz/ *n. pl.* entrailles *f. pl.*
entrance[1] /'entrəns/ *n.* (*entering, way in*) entrée *f.* (**to,** de); (*right to enter*) admission *f.* ● *a.* (*charge, exam*) d'entrée.
entrance[2] /ɪn'trɑ:ns/ *v.t.* transporter.
entrant /'entrənt/ *n.* (*sport*) concurrent(e) *m.* (*f.*); (*in exam*) candidat(e) *m.* (*f.*).
entreat /ɪn'tri:t/ *v.t.* supplier.
entrenched /ɪn'trentʃt/ *a.* ancré.
entrepreneur /ɒntrəprə'nɜ:(r)/ *n.* entrepreneur *m.*
entrust /ɪn'trʌst/ *v.t.* confier.
entry /'entrɪ/ *n.* (*entrance*) entrée *f.*; (*word on list*) mot inscrit *m.* **~ form,** feuille d'inscription *f.*
enumerate /ɪ'nju:məreɪt/ *v.t.* énumérer.
enunciate /ɪ'nʌnsɪeɪt/ *v.t.* (*word*) articuler; (*ideas*) énoncer.
envelop /ɪn'veləp/ *v.t.* (*p.t.* **enveloped**) envelopper.
envelope /'envələʊp/ *n.* enveloppe *f.*
enviable /'envɪəbl/ *a.* enviable.
envious /'envɪəs/ *a.* envieux (**of sth.,** de qch.). **~ of s.o.,** jaloux de qn. **~ly** *adv.* avec envie.
environment /ɪn'vaɪərənmənt/ *n.* milieu *m.*; (*ecological*) environnement *m.* **~al** /-'mentl/ *a.* du milieu; de l'environnement. **~alist** *n.* spécialiste de l'environnement *m./f.*
envisage /ɪn'vɪzɪdʒ/ *v.t.* envisager.
envoy /'envɔɪ/ *n.* envoyé(e) *m.* (*f.*).
envy /'envɪ/ *n.* envie *f.* ● *v.t.* envier.
enzyme /'enzaɪm/ *n.* enzyme *m.*
ephemeral /ɪ'femərəl/ *a.* éphémère.
epic /'epɪk/ *n.* épopée *f.* ● *a.* épique.
epidemic /epɪ'demɪk/ *n.* épidémie *f.*
epilep|sy /'epɪlepsɪ/ *n.* épilepsie *f.* **~tic** /-'leptɪk/ *a.* & *n.* épileptique (*m./f.*).
episode /'epɪsəʊd/ *n.* épisode *m.*
epistle /ɪ'pɪsl/ *n.* épître *f.*
epitaph /'epɪtɑ:f/ *n.* épitaphe *f.*
epithet /'epɪθet/ *n.* épithète *f.*
epitom|e /ɪ'pɪtəmɪ/ *n.* (*embodiment*) modèle *m.*; (*summary*) résumé *m.* **~ize** *v.t.* incarner.
epoch /'i:pɒk/ *n.* époque *f.* **~-making** *a.* qui fait époque.
equal /'i:kwəl/ *a.* & *n.* égal(e) (*m.f.*). ● *v.t.* (*p.t.* **equalled**) égaler. **~ opportunities/rights,** égalité des chances/droits *f.* **~ to,** (*task*) à la hauteur de. **~ity** /ɪ'kwɒlətɪ/ *n.* égalité *f.* **~ly** *adv.* également; (*just as*) tout aussi.

equalize /'i:kwəlaɪz/ *v.t./i.* égaliser. **~r** /-ə(r)/ *n.* (*goal*) but égalisateur *m.*

equanimity /ekwə'nɪmətɪ/ *n.* égalité d'humeur *f.*, calme *m.*

equate /ɪ'kweɪt/ *v.t.* assimiler, égaler (**with,** à).

equation /ɪ'kweɪʒn/ *n.* équation *f.*

equator /ɪ'kweɪtə(r)/ *n.* équateur *m.* **~ial** /ekwə'tɔ:rɪəl/ *a.* équatorial.

equilibrium /i:kwɪ'lɪbrɪəm/ *n.* équilibre *m.*

equinox /'i:kwɪnɒks/ *n.* équinoxe *m.*

equip /ɪ'kwɪp/ *v.t.* (*p.t.* **equipped**) équiper (**with,** de). **~ment** *n.* équipement *m.*

equitable /'ekwɪtəbl/ *a.* équitable.

equity /'ekwətɪ/ *n.* équité *f.*

equivalen|t /ɪ'kwɪvələnt/ *a.* & *n.* équivalent (*m.*). **~ce** *n.* équivalence *f.*

equivocal /ɪ'kwɪvəkl/ *a.* équivoque.

era /'ɪərə/ *n.* ère *f.*, époque *f.*

eradicate /ɪ'rædɪkeɪt/ *v.t.* supprimer, éliminer.

erase /ɪ'reɪz/ *v.t.* effacer. **~r**/-ə(r)/ *n.* (*rubber*) gomme *f.*

erect /ɪ'rekt/ *a.* droit. ● *v.t.* ériger. **~ion** /-kʃn/ *n.* érection *f.*

ermine /'ɜ:mɪn/ *n.* hermine *f.*

ero|de /ɪ'rəʊd/ *v.t.* ronger. **~sion** *n.* érosion *f.*

erotic /ɪ'rɒtɪk/ *a.* érotique. **~ism** /-sɪzəm/ *n.* érotisme *m.*

err /ɜ:(r)/ *v.i.* (*be mistaken*) se tromper; (*sin*) pécher.

errand /'erənd/ *n.* course *f.*

erratic /ɪ'rætɪk/ *a.* (*uneven*) irrégulier; (*person*) capricieux.

erroneous /ɪ'rəʊnɪəs/ *a.* erroné.

error /'erə(r)/ *n.* erreur *f.*

erudit|e /'eru:daɪt, *Amer.* 'erjʊdaɪt/ *a.* érudit. **~ion** /-'dɪʃn/ *n.* érudition *f.*

erupt /ɪ'rʌpt/ *v.i.* (*volcano*) entrer en éruption; (*fig.*) éclater. **~ion** /-pʃn/ *n.* éruption *f.*

escalat|e /'eskəleɪt/ *v.t./i.* (s')intensifier; (*of prices*) monter en flèche. **~ion** /-'leɪʃn/ *n.* escalade *f.*

escalator /'eskəleɪtə(r)/ *n.* escalier mécanique *m.*, escalator *m.*

escapade /eskə'peɪd/ *n.* fredaine *f.*

escape /ɪ'skeɪp/ *v.i.* s'échapper (**from a place,** d'un lieu); (*prisoner*) s'évader. ● *v.t.* échapper à. ● *n.* fuite *f.*, évasion *f.*; (*of gas etc.*) fuite *f.* **~ from s.o.,** échapper à qn. **~ to,** s'enfuir dans. **have a lucky** *or* **narrow ~,** l'échapper belle.

escapism /ɪ'skeɪpɪzəm/ *n.* évasion (de la réalité) *f.*

escort[1] /'eskɔ:t/ *n.* (*guard*) escorte *f.*; (*of lady*) cavalier *m.*

escort[2] /ɪ'skɔ:t/ *v.t.* escorter.

Eskimo /'eskɪməʊ/ *n.* (*pl.* **-os**) Esquimau(de) *m.* (*f.*).

especial /ɪ'speʃl/ *a.* particulier. **~ly** *adv.* particulièrement.

espionage /'espɪənɑ:ʒ/ *n.* espionnage *m.*

esplanade /esplə'neɪd/ *n.* esplanade *f.*

espresso /e'spresəʊ/ *n.* (*pl.* **-os**) (café) express *m.*

essay /'eseɪ/ *n.* essai *m.*; (*schol.*) rédaction *f.*; (*univ.*) dissertation *f.*

essence /'esns/ *n.* essence *f.*; (*main point*) essentiel *m.*

essential /ɪ'senʃl/ *a.* essentiel. ● *n. pl.* **the ~s,** l'essentiel *m.* **~ly** *adv.* essentiellement.

establish /ɪ'stæblɪʃ/ *v.t.* établir; (*business*, *state*) fonder. **~ment** *n.* établissement *m.*; fondation *f.* **the E~ment,** les pouvoirs établis *m.pl.*

estate /ɪ'steɪt/ *n.* (*land*) propriété *f.*; (*possessions*) biens *m. pl.*; (*inheritance*) succession *f.*; (*district*) cité *f.*, complexe *m.* **~ agent,** agent immobilier *m.* **~ car,** break *m.*

esteem /ɪ'sti:m/ *v.t.* estimer. ● *n.* estime *f.*

esthetic /es'θetik/ *a.* (*Amer.*) = **aesthetic.**

estimate[1] /'estɪmət/ *n.* (*calculation*) estimation *f.*; (*comm.*) devis *m.*

estimat|e[2] /'estɪmeɪt/ *v.t.* estimer. **~ion** /-'meɪʃn/ *n.* jugement *m.*; (*high regard*) estime *f.*

estuary /'estʃʊərɪ/ *n.* estuaire *m.*

etc. /ɛt'sɛtərə/ *adv.* etc.

etching /'etʃɪŋ/ *n.* eau-forte *f.*

eternal /ɪ'tɜ:nl/ *a.* éternel.

eternity /ɪ'tɜ:nətɪ/ *n.* éternité *f.*

ether /'i:θə(r)/ *n.* éther *m.*

ethic /'eθɪk/ *n.* éthique *f.* **~s,** moralité *f.* **~al** *a.* éthique.

ethnic /'eθnɪk/ *a.* ethnique.

ethos /'i:θɒs/ *n.* génie *m.*

etiquette /'etɪket/ *n.* étiquette *f.*

etymology /etɪ'mɒlədʒɪ/ *n.* étymologie *f.*

eucalyptus /ju:kə'lɪptəs/ *n.* (*pl.* **-tuses**) eucalyptus *m.*

eulogy /'ju:lədʒɪ/ *n.* éloge *m.*

euphemism /'ju:fəmɪzəm/ *n.* euphémisme *m.*

euphoria /ju:'fɔ:rɪə/ *n.* euphorie *f.*

eurocheque /'jʊərəʊtʃek/ *n.* eurochèque *m.*
Europe /'jʊərəp/ *n.* Europe *f.* **~an** /-'pɪən/ *a.* & *n.* européen(ne) (*m.* (*f.*)). **E~an Community,** Communauté Européenne *f.*
euthanasia /ju:θə'neɪzɪə/ *n.* euthanasie *f.*
evacuat|e /ɪ'vækjʊeɪt/ *v.t.* évacuer. **~ion** /-'eɪʃn/ *n.* évacuation *f.*
evade /ɪ'veɪd/ *v.t.* esquiver. **~ tax,** frauder le fisc.
evaluate /ɪ'væljʊeɪt/ *v.t.* évaluer.
evangelical /i:væn'dʒelɪkl/ *a.* évangélique.
evangelist /ɪ'vændʒəlɪst/ *n.* évangéliste *m.*
evaporat|e /ɪ'væpəreɪt/ *v.i.* s'évaporer. **~ed milk,** lait concentré *m.* **~ion** /-'reɪʃn/ *n.* évaporation *f.*
evasion /ɪ'veɪʒn/ *n.* fuite *f.* (**of,** devant); (*excuse*) subterfuge *m.* **tax ~,** fraude fiscale.
evasive /ɪ'veɪsɪv/ *a.* évasif.
eve /i:v/ *n.* veille *f.* (**of,** de).
even /'i:vn/ *a.* régulier; (*surface*) uni; (*equal, unvarying*) égal; (*number*) pair. ● *v.t./i.* **~ (out** *or* **up),** (s')égaliser. ● *adv.* même. **~ better**/*etc.*, (*still*) encore mieux/*etc.* **get ~ with,** se venger de. **~ly** *adv.* régulièrement; (*equally*) de manière égale.
evening /'i:vnɪŋ/ *n.* soir *m.*; (*whole evening, event*) soirée *f.*
event /ɪ'vent/ *n.* événement *m.*; (*sport*) épreuve *f.* **in the ~ of,** en cas de. **~ful** *a.* mouvementé.
eventual /ɪ'ventʃʊəl/ *a.* final, définitif. **~ity** /-'ælətɪ/ *n.* éventualité *f.* **~ly** *adv.* en fin de compte; (*in future*) un jour ou l'autre.
ever /'evə(r)/ *adv.* jamais; (*at all times*) toujours. **~ since** *prep.* & *adv.* depuis (ce moment-là); *conj.* depuis que. **~ so,** (*fam.*) vraiment.
evergreen /'evəgri:n/ *n.* arbre à feuilles persistantes *m.*
everlasting /evə'lɑ:stɪŋ/ *a.* éternel.
every /'evrɪ/ *a.* chaque. **~ one,** chacun(e). **~ other day,** un jour sur deux, tous les deux jours.
everybody /'evrɪbɒdɪ/ *pron.* tout le monde.
everyday /'evrɪdeɪ/ *a.* quotidien.
everyone /'evrɪwʌn/ *pron.* tout le monde.
everything /'evrɪθɪŋ/ *pron.* tout.
everywhere /'evrɪweə(r)/ *adv.* partout. **~ he goes,** partout où il va.
evict /ɪ'vɪkt/ *v.t.* expulser. **~ion** /-kʃn/ *n.* expulsion *f.*
evidence /'evɪdəns/ *n.* (*proof*) preuve(s) *f.* (*pl.*); (*certainty*) évidence *f.*; (*signs*) signes *m. pl.*; (*testimony*) témoignage *m.* **give ~,** témoigner. **in ~,** en vue.
evident /'evɪdənt/ *a.* évident. **~ly** *adv.* de toute évidence.
evil /'i:vl/ *a.* mauvais. ● *n.* mal *m.*
evo|ke /ɪ'vəʊk/ *v.t.* évoquer. **~cative** /ɪ'vɒkətɪv/ *a.* évocateur.
evolution /i:və'lu:ʃn/ *n.* évolution *f.*
evolve /ɪ'vɒlv/ *v.i.* se développer, évoluer. ● *v.t.* développer.
ewe /ju:/ *n.* brebis *f.*
ex- /eks/ *pref.* ex-, ancien.
exacerbate /ɪg'zæsəbeɪt/ *v.t.* exacerber.
exact[1] /ɪg'zækt/ *a.* exact. **~ly** *adv.* exactement. **~ness** *n.* exactitude *f.*
exact[2] /ɪg'zækt/ *v.t.* exiger (**from,** de). **~ing** *a.* exigeant.
exaggerat|e /ɪg'zædʒəreɪt/ *v.t./i.* exagérer. **~ion** /-'reɪʃn/ *n.* exagération *f.*
exalted /ɪg'zɔ:ltɪd/ *a.* (*in rank*) de haut rang; (*ideal*) élevé.
exam /ɪg'zæm/ *n.* (*fam.*) examen *m.*
examination /ɪgzæmɪ'neɪʃn/ *n.* examen *m.*
examine /ɪg'zæmɪn/ *v.t.* examiner; (*witness etc.*) interroger. **~r** /-ə(r)/ *n.* examina|teur, -trice *m., f.*
example /ɪg'zɑ:mpl/ *n.* exemple *m.* **for ~,** par exemple. **make an ~ of,** punir pour l'exemple.
exasperat|e /ɪg'zæspəreɪt/ *v.t.* exaspérer. **~ion** /-'reɪʃn/ *n.* exaspération *f.*
excavat|e /'ekskəveɪt/ *v.t.* creuser; (*uncover*) déterrer. **~ions** /-'veɪʃnz/ *n. pl.* (*archaeol.*) fouilles *f. pl.*
exceed /ɪk'si:d/ *v.t.* dépasser. **~ingly** *adv.* extrêmement.
excel /ɪk'sel/ *v.i.* (*p.t.* **excelled**) exceller. ● *v.t.* surpasser.
excellen|t /'eksələnt/ *a.* excellent. **~ce** *n.* excellence *f.* **~tly** *adv.* admirablement, parfaitement.
except /ɪk'sept/ *prep.* sauf, excepté. ● *v.t.* excepter. **~ for,** à part. **~ing** *prep.* sauf, excepté.
exception /ɪk'sepʃn/ *n.* exception *f.* **take ~ to,** s'offenser de.

exceptional /ɪk'sepʃənl/ *a.* exceptionnel. **~ly** *adv.* exceptionnellement.
excerpt /'eksɜ:pt/ *n.* extrait *m.*
excess[1] /ɪk'ses/ *n.* excès *m.*
excess[2] /'ekses/ *a.* excédentaire. **~ fare,** supplément *m.* **~ luggage,** excédent de bagages *m.*
excessive /ɪk'sesɪv/ *a.* excessif. **~ly** *adv.* excessivement.
exchange /ɪks'tʃeɪndʒ/ *v.t.* échanger. ● *n.* échange *m.*; (*between currencies*) change *m.* **~ rate,** taux d'échange *m.* **(telephone) ~,** central (téléphonique) *m.*
exchequer /ɪks'tʃekə(r)/ *n.* (*British pol.*) Échiquier *m.*
excise /'eksaɪz/ *n.* impôt (indirect) *m.*
excit|e /ɪk'saɪt/ *v.t.* exciter; (*enthuse*) enthousiasmer. **~able** *a.* excitable. **~ed** *a.* excité. **get ~ed,** s'exciter. **~ement** *n.* excitation *f.* **~ing** *a.* passionnant.
exclaim /ɪk'skleɪm/ *v.t./i.* exclamer, s'écrier.
exclamation /eksklə'meɪʃn/ *n.* exclamation *f.* **~ mark** *or* **point** (*Amer.*), point d'exclamation *m.*
exclu|de /ɪk'sklu:d/ *v.t.* exclure. **~sion** *n.* exclusion *f.*
exclusive /ɪk'sklu:sɪv/ *a.* (*rights etc.*) exclusif; (*club etc.*) sélect; (*news item*) en exclusivité. **~ of service/***etc.*, service/*etc.* non compris. **~ly** *adv.* exclusivement.
excrement /'ekskrəmənt/ *n.* excrément(s) *m.* (*pl.*).
excruciating /ɪk'skru:ʃɪeɪtɪŋ/ *a.* atroce, insupportable.
excursion /ɪk'skɜ:ʃn/ *n.* excursion *f.*
excus|e[1] /ɪk'skju:z/ *v.t.* excuser. **~e from,** (*exempt*) dispenser de. **~e me!,** excusez-moi!, pardon! **~able** *a.* excusable.
excuse[2] /ɪk'skju:s/ *n.* excuse *f.*
ex-directory /eksdɪ'rektərɪ/ *a.* qui n'est pas dans l'annuaire.
execute /'eksɪkju:t/ *v.t.* exécuter.
execution /eksɪ'kju:ʃn/ *n.* exécution *f.* **~er** *n.* bourreau *m.*
executive /ɪg'zekjʊtɪv/ *n.* (pouvoir) exécutif *m.*; (*person*) cadre *m.* ● *a.* exécutif.
exemplary /ɪg'zemplərɪ/ *a.* exemplaire.
exemplify /ɪg'zemplɪfaɪ/ *v.t.* illustrer.
exempt /ɪg'zempt/ *a.* exempt (**from,** de). ● *v.t.* exempter. **~ion** /-pʃn/ *n.* exemption *f.*
exercise /'eksəsaɪz/ *n.* exercice *m.* ● *v.t.* exercer; (*restraint, patience*) faire preuve de. ● *v.i.* prendre de l'exercice. **~ book,** cahier *m.*
exert /ɪg'zɜ:t/ *v.t.* exercer. **~ o.s.,** se dépenser, faire des efforts. **~ion** /-ʃn/ *n.* effort *m.*
exhaust /ɪg'zɔ:st/ *v.t.* épuiser. ● *n.* (*auto.*) (pot d')échappement *m.* **~ed** *a.* épuisé. **~ion** /-stʃən/ *n.* épuisement *m.*
exhaustive /ɪg'zɔ:stɪv/ *a.* complet.
exhibit /ɪg'zɪbɪt/ *v.t.* exposer; (*fig.*) faire preuve de. ● *n.* objet exposé *m.* **~or** *n.* exposant(e) *m.* (*f.*).
exhibition /eksɪ'bɪʃn/ *n.* exposition *f.*; (*act of showing*) démonstration *f.* **~ist** *n.* exhibitionniste *m./f.*
exhilarat|e /ɪg'zɪləreɪt/ *v.t.* transporter de joie; (*invigorate*) stimuler. **~ing** *a.* euphorisant. **~ion** /-'reɪʃn/ *n.* joie *f.*
exhort /ɪg'zɔ:t/ *v.t.* exhorter (**to,** à).
exhume /eks'hju:m/ *v.t.* exhumer.
exile /'eksaɪl/ *n.* exil *m.*; (*person*) exilé(e) *m.* (*f.*). ● *v.t.* exiler.
exist /ɪg'zɪst/ *v.i.* exister. **~ence** *n.* existence *f.* **be in ~ence,** exister. **~ing** *a.* actuel.
exit /'eksɪt/ *n.* sortie *f.* ● *v.t./i.* (*comput.*) sortir (de).
exodus /'eksədəs/ *n.* exode *m.*
exonerate /ɪg'zɒnəreɪt/ *v.t.* disculper, innocenter.
exorbitant /ɪg'zɔ:bɪtənt/ *a.* exorbitant.
exorcize /'eksɔ:saɪz/ *v.t.* exorciser.
exotic /ɪg'zɒtɪk/ *a.* exotique.
expan|d /ɪk'spænd/ *v.t./i.* (*develop*) (se) développer; (*extend*) (s')étendre; (*metal, liquid*) (se) dilater. **~sion** *n.* développement *m.*; dilatation *f.*; (*pol., comm.*) expansion *f.*
expanse /ɪk'spæns/ *n.* étendue *f.*
expatriate /eks'pætrɪət, *Amer.* eks'peɪtrɪət/ *a.* & *n.* expatrié(e) (*m.* (*f.*)).
expect /ɪk'spekt/ *v.t.* attendre, s'attendre à; (*suppose*) supposer; (*demand*) exiger; (*baby*) attendre. **~ to do,** compter faire. **~ation** /ekspek'teɪʃn/ *n.* attente *f.*
expectan|t /ɪk'spektənt/ *a.* **~t look,** air d'attente *m.* **~t mother,** future maman *f.* **~cy** *n.* attente *f.*
expedient /ɪk'spi:dɪənt/ *a.* opportun. ● *n.* expédient *m.*
expedite /'ekspɪdaɪt/ *v.t.* hâter.

expedition /ekspɪ'dɪʃn/ *n.* expédition *f.*
expel /ɪk'spel/ *v.t.* (*p.t.* **expelled**) expulser; (*from school*) renvoyer.
expend /ɪk'spend/ *v.t.* dépenser. **~able** *a.* remplaçable.
expenditure /ɪk'spendɪtʃə(r)/ *n.* dépense(s) *f.* (*pl.*).
expense /ɪk'spens/ *n.* dépense *f.*; frais *m. pl.* **at s.o.'s ~,** aux dépens de qn. **~ account,** note de frais *f.*
expensive /ɪk'spensɪv/ *a.* cher, coûteux; (*tastes, habits*) de luxe. **~ly** *adv.* coûteusement.
experience /ɪk'spɪərɪəns/ *n.* expérience *f.*; (*adventure*) aventure *f.* ● *v.t.* (*undergo*) connaître; (*feel*) éprouver. **~d** *a.* expérimenté.
experiment /ɪk'sperɪmənt/ *n.* expérience *f.* ● *v.i.* faire une expérience. **~al** /-'mentl/ *a.* expérimental.
expert /'ekspɜ:t/ *n.* expert(e) *m.* (*f.*). ● *a.* expert. **~ly** *adv.* habilement.
expertise /ekspɜ:'ti:z/ *n.* compétence *f.* (**in,** en).
expir|e /ɪk'spaɪə(r)/ *v.i.* expirer. **~ed** *a.* périmé. **~y** *n.* expiration *f.*
expl|ain /ɪk'spleɪn/ *v.t.* expliquer. **~anation** /eksplə'neɪʃn/ *n.* explication *f.* **~anatory** /-ænətərɪ/ *a.* explicatif.
expletive /ɪk'spli:tɪv, *Amer.* 'eksplətɪv/ *n.* juron *m.*
explicit /ɪk'splɪsɪt/ *a.* explicite.
explo|de /ɪk'spləʊd/ *v.t./i.* (faire) exploser. **~sion** *n.* explosion *f.* **~sive** *a.* & *n.* explosif (*m.*).
exploit[1] /'eksplɔɪt/ *n.* exploit *m.*
exploit[2] /ɪk'splɔɪt/ *v.t.* exploiter. **~ation** /eksplɔɪ'teɪʃn/ *n.* exploitation *f.*
exploratory /ɪk'splɒrətrɪ/ *a.* (*talks: pol.*) exploratoire.
explor|e /ɪk'splɔ:(r)/ *v.t.* explorer; (*fig.*) examiner. **~ation** /eksplə'reɪʃn/ *n.* exploration *f.* **~er** *n.* explora|teur, -trice *m., f.*
exponent /ɪk'spəʊnənt/ *n.* interprète *m.* (**of,** de).
export[1] /ɪk'spɔ:t/ *v.t.* exporter. **~er** *n.* exportateur *m.*
export[2] /'ekspɔ:t/ *n.* exportation *f.*
expos|e /ɪk'spəʊz/ *v.t.* exposer; (*disclose*) dévoiler. **~ure** /-ʒə(r)/ *n.* exposition *f.*; (*photo.*) pose *f.* **die of ~ure,** mourir de froid.
expound /ɪk'spaʊnd/ *v.t.* exposer.
express[1] /ɪk'spres/ *a.* formel, exprès; (*letter*) exprès *invar.* ● *adv.* (*by express post*) (par) exprès. ● *n.* (*train*) rapide *m.*; (*less fast*) express *m.* **~ly** *adv.* expressément.
express[2] /ɪk'spres/ *v.t.* exprimer. **~ion** /-ʃn/ *n.* expression *f.* **~ive** *a.* expressif.
expressway /ɪk'spresweɪ/ *n.* voie express *f.*
expulsion /ɪk'spʌlʃn/ *n.* expulsion *f.*; (*from school*) renvoi *m.*
expurgate /'ekspəgeɪt/ *v.t.* expurger.
exquisite /'ekskwɪzɪt/ *a.* exquis. **~ly** *adv.* d'une façon exquise.
ex-serviceman /eks'sɜ:vɪsmən/ *n.* (*pl.* **-men**) ancien combattant *m.*
extant /ek'stænt/ *a.* existant.
extempore /ek'stempərɪ/ *a.* & *adv.* impromptu.
exten|d /ɪk'stend/ *v.t.* (*increase*) étendre, agrandir; (*arm, leg*) étendre; (*prolong*) prolonger; (*house*) agrandir; (*grant*) offrir. ● *v.i.* (*stretch*) s'étendre; (*in time*) se prolonger. **~sion** *n.* (*of line, road*) prolongement *m.*; (*in time*) prolongation *f.*; (*building*) annexe *f.*; (*of phone*) appareil supplémentaire *m.*; (*phone number*) poste *m.*; (*cable, hose, etc.*) rallonge *f.*
extensive /ɪk'stensɪv/ *a.* vaste; (*study*) profond; (*damage etc.*) important. **~ly** *adv.* (*much*) beaucoup; (*very*) très.
extent /ɪk'stent/ *n.* (*size, scope*) étendue *f.*; (*degree*) mesure *f.* **to some ~,** dans une certaine mesure. **to such an ~ that,** à tel point que.
extenuating /ɪk'stenjʊeɪtɪŋ/ *a.* **~ circumstances,** circonstances atténuantes.
exterior /ɪk'stɪərɪə(r)/ *a.* & *n.* extérieur (*m.*).
exterminat|e /ɪk'stɜ:mɪneɪt/ *v.t.* exterminer. **~ion** /-'neɪʃn/ *n.* extermination *f.*
external /ɪk'stɜ:nl/ *a.* extérieur; (*cause, medical use*) externe. **~ly** *adv.* extérieurement.
extinct /ɪk'stɪŋkt/ *a.* (*species*) disparu; (*volcano, passion*) éteint. **~ion** /-kʃn/ *n.* extinction *f.*
extinguish /ɪk'stɪŋgwɪʃ/ *v.t.* éteindre. **~er** *n.* extincteur *m.*
extol /ɪk'stəʊl/ *v.t.* (*p.t.* **extolled**) exalter, chanter les louanges de.
extort /ɪk'stɔ:t/ *v.t.* extorquer (**from,** à). **~ion** /-ʃn/ *n.* (*jurid.*) extorsion (de fonds) *f.*

extortionate /ɪk'stɔ:ʃənət/ *a.* exorbitant.

extra /'ekstrə/ *a.* de plus, supplémentaire. ● *adv.* plus (que d'habitude). **~ strong,** extra-fort. ● *n.* (*additional thing*) supplément *m.*; (*cinema*) figurant(e) *m.* (*f.*). **~ charge,** supplément *m.* **~ time,** (*football*) prolongation *f.*

extra- /'ekstrə/ *pref.* extra-.

extract[1] /ɪk'strækt/ *v.t.* extraire; (*promise, tooth*) arracher; (*fig.*) obtenir. **~ion** /-kʃn/ *n.* extraction *f.*

extract[2] /'ekstrækt/ *n.* extrait *m.*

extra-curricular /ekstrəkə'rɪkjʊlə(r)/ *a.* parascolaire.

extradit|e /'ekstrədaɪt/ *v.t.* extrader. **~ion** /-'dɪʃn/ *n.* extradition *f.*

extramarital /ekstrə'mærɪtl/ *a.* extra-conjugal.

extramural /ekstrə'mjʊərəl/ *a.* (*univ.*) hors faculté.

extraordinary /ɪk'strɔ:dnrɪ/ *a.* extraordinaire.

extravagan|t /ɪk'strævəgənt/ *a.* extravagant; (*wasteful*) prodigue. **~ce** *n.* extravagance *f.*; prodigalité *f.*

extrem|e /ɪk'stri:m/ *a.* & *n.* extrême (*m.*). **~ely** *adv.* extrêmement. **~ist** *n.* extrémiste *m./f.*

extremity /ɪk'stremətɪ/ *n.* extrémité *f.*

extricate /'ekstrɪkeɪt/ *v.t.* dégager.

extrovert /'ekstrəvɜ:t/ *n.* extraverti(e) *m.* (*f.*).

exuberan|t /ɪg'zju:bərənt/ *a.* exubérant. **~ce** *n.* exubérance *f.*

exude /ɪg'zju:d/ *v.t.* (*charm etc.*) dégager.

exult /ɪg'zʌlt/ *v.i.* exulter.

eye /aɪ/ *n.* œil *m.* (*pl.* yeux). ● *v.t.* (*p.t.* **eyed,** *pres. p.* **eyeing**) regarder. **keep an ~ on,** surveiller. **~-catching** *a.* qui attire l'attention. **~-opener** *n.* révélation *f.* **~-shadow** *n.* ombre à paupières *f.*

eyeball /'aɪbɔ:l/ *n.* globe oculaire *m.*

eyebrow /'aɪbraʊ/ *n.* sourcil *m.*

eyeful /'aɪfʊl/ *n.* **get an ~,** (*fam.*) se rincer l'œil.

eyelash /'aɪlæʃ/ *n.* cil *m.*

eyelet /'aɪlɪt/ *n.* œillet *m.*

eyelid /'aɪlɪd/ *n.* paupière *f.*

eyesight /'aɪsaɪt/ *n.* vue *f.*

eyesore /'aɪsɔ:(r)/ *n.* horreur *f.*

eyewitness /'aɪwɪtnɪs/ *n.* témoin oculaire *m.*

F

fable /'feɪbl/ *n.* fable *f.*

fabric /'fæbrɪk/ *n.* (*cloth*) tissu *m.*

fabrication /fæbrɪ'keɪʃn/ *n.* (*invention*) invention *f.*

fabulous /'fæbjʊləs/ *a.* fabuleux; (*marvellous*: *fam.*) formidable.

façade /fə'sɑ:d/ *n.* façade *f.*

face /feɪs/ *n.* visage *m.*, figure *f.*; (*aspect*) face *f.*; (*of clock*) cadran *m.* ● *v.t.* être en face de; (*risk*) devoir affronter; (*confront*) faire face à, affronter. ● *v.i.* se tourner; (*of house*) être exposé. **~-flannel** *n.* gant de toilette *m.* **~-lift** *n.* lifting *m.* **give a ~-lift to,** donner un coup de neuf à. **~ value,** (*comm.*) valeur nominale. **take sth. at ~ value,** prendre qch. au premier degré. **~ to face,** face à face. **~ up/down,** tourné vers le haut/bas. **~ up to,** faire face à. **in the ~ of, ~d with,** face à. **make a (funny) ~,** faire une grimace.

faceless /'feɪslɪs/ *a.* anonyme.

facet /'fæsɪt/ *n.* facette *f.*

facetious /fə'si:ʃəs/ *a.* facétieux.

facial /'feɪʃl/ *a.* de la face, facial. ● *n.* soin du visage *m.*

facile /'fæsaɪl, *Amer.* 'fæsl/ *a.* facile, superficiel.

facilitate /fə'sɪlɪteɪt/ *v.t.* faciliter.

facilit|y /fə'sɪlətɪ/ *n.* facilité *f.* **~ies,** (*equipment*) équipements *m. pl.*

facing /'feɪsɪŋ/ *n.* parement *m.* ● *prep.* en face de. ● *a.* en face.

facsimile /fæk'sɪməlɪ/ *n.* facsimilé *m.* **~ transmission,** télécopie *f.*

fact /fækt/ *n.* fait *m.* **as a matter of ~, in ~,** en fait.

faction /'fækʃn/ *n.* faction *f.*

factor /'fæktə(r)/ *n.* facteur *m.*

factory /'fæktərɪ/ *n.* usine *f.*

factual /'fæktʃʊəl/ *a.* basé sur les faits.

faculty /'fækltɪ/ *n.* faculté *f.*

fad /fæd/ *n.* manie *f.*, folie *f.*

fade /feɪd/ *v.i.* (*sound*) s'affaiblir; (*memory*) s'évanouir; (*flower*) se faner; (*material*) déteindre; (*colour*) passer.

fag /fæg/ *n.* (*chore*: *fam.*) corvée *f.*; (*cigarette*: *sl.*) sèche *f.*; (*homosexual*: *Amer., sl.*) pédé *m.*

fagged /fægd/ *a.* (*tired*) éreinté.

fail /feɪl/ *v.i.* échouer; (*grow weak*) (s'af)faiblir; (*run short*) manquer; (*engine etc.*) tomber en panne. ● *v.t.* (*exam*) échouer à; (*candidate*) refuser, recaler; (*disappoint*) décevoir. **~ s.o.,** (*of words etc.*) manquer à qn. **~ to do,** (*not do*) ne pas faire; (*not be able*) ne pas réussir à faire. **without ~,** à coup sûr.

failing /ˈfeɪlɪŋ/ *n.* défaut *m.* ● *prep.* à défaut de.

failure /ˈfeɪljə(r)/ *n.* échec *m.*; (*person*) raté(e) *m.* (*f.*); (*breakdown*) panne *f.* **~ to do,** (*inability*) incapacité de faire *f.*

faint /feɪnt/ *a.* (**-er, -est**) léger, faible. ● *v.i.* s'évanouir. ● *n.* évanouissement *m.* **feel ~,** (*ill*) se trouver mal. **I haven't the ~est idea,** je n'en ai pas la moindre idée. **~-hearted** *a.* timide. **~ly** *adv.* (*weakly*) faiblement; (*slightly*) légèrement. **~ness** *n.* faiblesse *f.*

fair[1] /feə(r)/ *n.* foire *f.* **~-ground** *n.* champ de foire *m.*

fair[2] /feə(r)/ *a.* (**-er, -est**) (*hair, person*) blond; (*skin etc.*) clair; (*just*) juste, équitable; (*weather*) beau; (*amount, quality*) raisonnable. ● *adv.* (*play*) loyalement. **~ play,** le fair-play. **~ly** *adv.* (*justly*) équitablement; (*rather*) assez. **~ness** *n.* justice *f.*

fairy /ˈfeərɪ/ *n.* fée *f.* **~ story, ~-tale** *n.* conte de fées *m.*

faith /feɪθ/ *n.* foi. *f.* **~-healer** *n.* guérisseu|r, -se *m., f.*

faithful /ˈfeɪθfl/ *a.* fidèle. **~ly** *adv.* fidèlement. **~ness** *n.* fidélité *f.*

fake /feɪk/ *n.* (*forgery*) faux *m.*; (*person*) imposteur *m.* **it is a ~,** c'est faux. ● *a.* faux. ● *v.t.* (*copy*) faire un faux de; (*alter*) falsifier, truquer; (*illness*) simuler.

falcon /ˈfɔːlkən/ *n.* faucon *m.*

fall /fɔːl/ *v.i.* (*p.t.* **fell**, *p.p.* **fallen**) tomber. ● *n.* chute *f.*; (*autumn: Amer.*) automne *m.* **Niagara F~s,** chutes de Niagara. **~ back on,** se rabattre sur. **~ behind,** prendre du retard. **~ down** *or* **off,** tomber. **~ for,** (*person: fam.*) tomber amoureux de; (*a trick: fam.*) se laisser prendre à. **~ in,** (*mil.*) se mettre en rangs. **~ off,** (*decrease*) diminuer. **~ out,** se brouiller (**with,** avec). **~-out** *n.* retombées *f. pl.* **~ over,** tomber (par terre). **~ short,** être insuffisant. **~ through,** (*plans*) tomber à l'eau.

fallacy /ˈfæləsɪ/ *n.* erreur *f.*

fallible /ˈfæləbl/ *a.* faillible.

fallow /ˈfæləʊ/ *a.* en jachère.

false /fɔːls/ *a.* faux. **~hood** *n.* mensonge *m.* **~ly** *adv.* faussement. **~ness** *n.* fausseté *f.*

falsetto /fɔːlˈsetəʊ/ *n.* (*pl.* **-os**) fausset *m.*

falsify /ˈfɔːlsɪfaɪ/ *v.t.* falsifier.

falter /ˈfɔːltə(r)/ *v.i.* vaciller; (*nerve*) faire défaut.

fame /feɪm/ *n.* renommée *f.*

famed /feɪmd/ *a.* renommé.

familiar /fəˈmɪlɪə(r)/ *a.* familier. **be ~ with,** connaître. **~ity** /-ˈærətɪ/ *n.* familiarité *f.* **~ize** *v.t.* familiariser.

family /ˈfæməlɪ/ *n.* famille *f.* ● *a.* de famille, familial.

famine /ˈfæmɪn/ *n.* famine *f.*

famished /ˈfæmɪʃt/ *a.* affamé.

famous /ˈfeɪməs/ *a.* célèbre. **~ly** *adv.* (*very well: fam.*) à merveille.

fan[1] /fæn/ *n.* ventilateur *m.*; (*hand-held*) éventail *m.* ● *v.t.* (*p.t.* **fanned**) éventer; (*fig.*) attiser. ● *v.i.* **~ out,** se déployer en éventail. **~ belt,** courroie de ventilateur *f.*

fan[2] /fæn/ *n.* (*of person*) fan *m./f.*, admira|teur, -trice *m., f.*; (*enthusiast*) fervent(e) *m.* (*f.*), passionné(e) *m.* (*f.*).

fanatic /fəˈnætɪk/ *n.* fanatique *m./f.* **~al** *a.* fanatique. **~ism** /-sɪzəm/ *n.* fanatisme *m.*

fancier /ˈfænsɪə(r)/ *n.* (**dog**/*etc.*) **~,** amateur (de chiens/*etc.*) *m.*

fanciful /ˈfænsɪfl/ *a.* fantaisiste.

fancy /ˈfænsɪ/ *n.* (*whim, fantasy*) fantaisie *f.*; (*liking*) goût *m.* ● *a.* (*buttons etc.*) fantaisie *invar.*; (*prices*) extravagant; (*impressive*) impressionnant. ● *v.t.* s'imaginer; (*want: fam.*) avoir envie de; (*like: fam.*) aimer. **take a ~ to s.o.,** se prendre d'affection pour qn. **it took my ~,** ça m'a plu. **~ dress,** déguisement *m.*

fanfare /ˈfænfeə(r)/ *n.* fanfare *f.*

fang /fæŋ/ *n.* (*of dog etc.*) croc *m.*; (*of snake*) crochet *m.*

fanlight /ˈfænlaɪt/ *n.* imposte *f.*

fantastic /fænˈtæstɪk/ *a.* fantastique.

fantas|y /ˈfæntəsɪ/ *n.* fantaisie *f.*; (*day-dream*) fantasme *m.* **~ize** *v.i.* fantasmer.

far /fɑ:(r)/ *adv.* loin; (*much*) beaucoup; (*very*) très. ● *a.* lointain; (*end, side*) autre. **~ away, ~ off,** au loin. **as ~ as,** (*up to*) jusqu'à. **as ~ as I know,** autant que je sache. **~-away** *a.* lointain. **by ~,** de loin. **~ from,** loin de. **the Far East,** l'Extrême-Orient *m.* **~-fetched** *a.* bizarre, exagéré. **~-reaching** *a.* de grande portée.

farc|e /fɑ:s/ *n.* farce *f.* **~ical** *a.* ridicule, grotesque.

fare /feə(r)/ *n.* (prix du) billet *m.*; (*food*) nourriture *f.* ● *v.i.* (*progress*) aller; (*manage*) se débrouiller.

farewell /feə'wel/ *int.* & *n.* adieu (*m.*).

farm /fɑ:m/ *n.* ferme *f.* ● *v.t.* cultiver. ● *v.i.* être fermier. **~ out,** céder en sous-traitance. **~ worker,** ouvri|er, -ère agricole *m., f.* **~er** *n.* fermier *m.* **~ing** *n.* agriculture *f.*

farmhouse /'fɑ:mhaʊs/ *n.* ferme *f.*

farmyard /'fɑ:mjɑ:d/ *n.* basse-cour *f.*

fart /fɑ:t/ *v.i.* péter. ● *n.* pet *m.*

farth|er /'fɑ:ðə(r)/ *adv.* plus loin. ● *a.* plus éloigné. **~est** *adv.* le plus loin; *a.* le plus éloigné.

fascinat|e /'fæsmeɪt/ *v.t.* fasciner. **~ion** /-'neɪʃn/ *n.* fascination *f.*

Fascis|t /'fæʃɪst/ *n.* fasciste *m./f.* **~m** /-zəm/ *n.* fascisme *m.*

fashion /'fæʃn/ *n.* (*current style*) mode *f.*; (*manner*) façon *f.* ● *v.t.* façonner. **~ designer,** styliste *m./f.* **in ~,** à la mode. **out of ~,** démodé. **~able** *a.*, **~ably** *adv.* à la mode.

fast[1] /fɑ:st/ *a.* (**-er, -est**) rapide; (*colour*) grand teint *invar.*, fixe; (*firm*) fixe, solide. ● *adv.* vite; (*firmly*) ferme. **be ~,** (*clock etc.*) avancer. **~ asleep,** profondément endormi. **~ food,** fast food *m.* restauration rapide *f.*

fast[2] /fɑ:st/ *v.i.* (*go without food*) jeûner. ● *n.* jeûne *m.*

fasten /'fɑ:sn/ *v.t./i.* (s')attacher. **~er, ~ing** *ns.* attache *f.*, fermeture *f.*

fastidious /fə'stɪdɪəs/ *a.* difficile.

fat /fæt/ *n.* graisse *f.*; (*on meat*) gras *m.* ● *a.* (**fatter, fattest**) gros, gras; (*meat*) gras; (*sum, volume*: *fig.*) gros. **a ~ lot,** (*sl.*) bien peu (**of,** de). **~-head** *n.* (*fam.*) imbécile *m.,/f.* **~ness** *n.* corpulence *f.*

fatal /'feɪtl/ *a.* mortel; (*fateful, disastrous*) fatal. **~ity** /fə'tælətɪ/ *n.* mort *m.* **~ly** *adv.* mortellement.

fatalist /'feɪtəlɪst/ *n.* fataliste *m./f.*

fate /feɪt/ *n.* (*controlling power*) destin *m.*, sort *m.*; (*one's lot*) sort *m.* **~ful** *a.* fatidique.

fated /'feɪtɪd/ *a.* destiné (**to,** à).

father /'fɑ:ðə(r)/ *n.* père *m.* **~-in-law** *n.* (*pl.* **~s-in-law**) beau-père *m.* **~hood** *n.* paternité *f.* **~ly** *a.* paternel.

fathom /'fæðəm/ *n.* brasse *f.* (*=1.8 m.*). ● *v.t.* **~ (out),** comprendre.

fatigue /fə'ti:g/ *n.* fatigue *f.* ● *v.t.* fatiguer.

fatten /'fætn/ *v.t./i.* engraisser. **~ing** *a.* qui fait grossir.

fatty /'fætɪ/ *a.* gras; (*tissue*) adipeux. ● *n.* (*person*: *fam.*) gros(se) *m.* (*f.*).

fatuous /'fætʃʊəs/ *a.* stupide.

faucet /'fɔ:sɪt/ *n.* (*Amer.*) robinet *m.*

fault /fɔ:lt/ *n.* (*defect, failing*) défaut *m.*; (*blame*) faute *f.*; (*geol.*) faille *f.* ● *v.t.* **~ sth./s.o.,** trouver des défauts à qch./chez qn. **at ~,** fautif. **find ~ with,** critiquer. **~less** *a.* irréprochable. **~y** *a.* défectueux.

fauna /'fɔ:nə/ *n.* faune *f.*

favour, (*Amer.*) **favor** /'feɪvə(r)/ *n.* faveur *f.* ● *v.t.* favoriser; (*support*) être en faveur de; (*prefer*) préférer. **do s.o. a ~,** rendre service à qn. **in ~ of,** pour. **~able** *a.* favorable. **~ably** *adv.* favorablement.

favourit|e /'feɪvərɪt/ *a.* & *n.* favori(te) (*m.* (*f.*)). **~ism** *n.* favoritisme *m.*

fawn[1] /fɔ:n/ *n.* faon *m.* ● *a.* fauve.

fawn[2] /fɔ:n/ *v.i.* **~ on,** flatter bassement, flagorner.

fax /fæks/ *n.* fax *m.*, télécopie *f.* ● *v.t.* faxer, envoyer par télécopie. **~ machine,** télécopieur *m.*

FBI *abbr.* (*Federal Bureau of Investigation*) (*Amer.*) service d'enquêtes du Ministère de la Justice *m.*

fear /fɪə(r)/ *n.* crainte *f.*, peur *f.*; (*fig.*) risque *m.* ● *v.t.* craindre. **for ~ of/that,** de peur de/que. **~ful** *a.* (*terrible*) affreux; (*timid*) craintif. **~less** *a.* intrépide. **~lessness** *n.* intrépidité *f.*

fearsome /'fɪəsəm/ *a.* redoutable.

feasib|le /'fi:zəbl/ *a.* faisable; (*likely*) plausible. **~ility** /-'bɪlətɪ/ *n.* possibilité *f.*; plausibilité *f.*

feast /fi:st/ *n.* festin *m.*; (*relig.*) fête *f.* ● *v.i.* festoyer. ● *v.t.* régaler. **~ on,** se régaler de.

feat /fi:t/ *n.* exploit *m.*

feather /'feðə(r)/ *n.* plume *f.* ● *v.t.* **~ one's nest,** s'enrichir. **~ duster,** plumeau *m.*

featherweight /ˈfeðəweɪt/ *n.* poids plume *m. invar.*
feature /ˈfiːtʃə(r)/ *n.* caractéristique *f.*; (*of person, face*) trait *m.*; (*film*) long métrage *m.*; (*article*) article vedette *m.* ● *v.t.* représenter; (*give prominence to*) mettre en vedette. ● *v.i.* figurer (**in,** dans).
February /ˈfebrʊərɪ/ *n.* février *m.*
feckless /ˈfeklɪs/ *a.* inepte.
fed /fed/ *see* feed. ● *a.* **be ~ up,** (*fam.*) en avoir marre (**with,** de).
federa|l /ˈfedərəl/ *a.* fédéral. **~tion** /-ˈreɪʃn/ *n.* fédération *f.*
fee /fiː/ *n.* (*for entrance*) prix *m.* **~(s),** (*of doctor etc.*) honoraires *m. pl.*; (*of actor, artist*) cachet *m.*; (*for tuition*) frais *m. pl.*; (*for enrolment*) droits *m. pl.*
feeble /fiːbl/ *a.* (**-er, -est**) faible. **~-minded** *a.* faible d'esprit.
feed /fiːd/ *v.t.* (*p.t.* **fed**) nourrir, donner à manger à; (*suckle*) allaiter; (*supply*) alimenter. ● *v.i.* se nourrir (**on,** de). ● *n.* nourriture *f.*; (*of baby*) tétée *f.* **~ in information,** rentrer des données. **~er** *n.* alimentation. *f.*
feedback /ˈfiːdbæk/ *n.* réaction(s) *f.* (*pl.*); (*med., techn.*) feed-back *m.*
feel /fiːl/ *v.t.* (*p.t.* **felt**) (*touch*) tâter; (*be conscious of*) sentir; (*emotion*) ressentir; (*experience*) éprouver; (*think*) estimer. ● *v.i.* (*tired, lonely, etc.*) se sentir. **~ hot/thirsty/***etc.*, avoir chaud/soif/*etc.* **~ as if,** avoir l'impression que. **~ awful,** (*ill*) se sentir malade. **~ like,** (*want: fam.*) avoir envie de.
feeler /ˈfiːlə(r)/ *n.* antenne *f.* **put out a ~,** lancer un ballon d'essai.
feeling /ˈfiːlɪŋ/ *n.* sentiment *m.*; (*physical*) sensation *f.*
feet /fiːt/ *see* foot.
feign /feɪn/ *v.t.* feindre.
feint /feɪnt/ *n.* feinte *f.*
felicitous /fəˈlɪsɪtəs/ *a.* heureux.
feline /ˈfiːlaɪn/ *a.* félin.
fell[1] /fel/ *v.t.* (*cut down*) abattre.
fell[2] /fel/ *see* fall.
fellow /ˈfeləʊ/ *n.* compagnon *m.*, camarade *m.*; (*of society*) membre *m.*; (*man: fam.*) type *m.* **~-countryman** *n.* compatriote *m.* **~-passenger, ~-traveller** *n.* compagnon de voyage *m.* **~ship** *n.* camaraderie *f.*; (*group*) association *f.*
felony /ˈfelənɪ/ *n.* crime *m.*
felt[1] /felt/ *n.* feutre *m.* **~-tip** *n.* feutre *m.*
felt[2] /felt/ *see* feel.
female /ˈfiːmeɪl/ *a.* (*animal etc.*) femelle; (*voice, sex, etc.*) féminin. ● *n.* femme *f.*; (*animal*) femelle *f.*
feminin|e /ˈfemənɪn/ *a.* & *n.* féminin (*m.*). **~ity** /-ˈnɪnətɪ/ *n.* féminité *f.*
feminist /ˈfemɪnɪst/ *n.* féministe *m./f.*
fenc|e /fens/ *n.* barrière *f.*; (*person: jurid.*) receleu|r, -se *m., f.* ● *v.t.* **~e (in),** clôturer. ● *v.i.* (*sport*) faire de l'escrime. **~er** *n.* escrimeu|r, -se *m., f.* **~ing** *n.* escrime *f.*
fend /fend/ *v.i.* **~ for o.s.,** se débrouiller tout seul. ● *v.t.* **~ off,** (*blow, attack*) parer.
fender /ˈfendə(r)/ *n.* (*for fireplace*) garde-feu *m. invar.*; (*mudguard: Amer.*) garde-boue *m. invar.*
fennel /ˈfenl/ *n.* (*culin.*) fenouil *m.*
ferment[1] /fəˈment/ *v.t./i.* (faire) fermenter. **~ation** /fɜːmenˈteɪʃn/ *n.* fermentation *f.*
ferment[2] /ˈfɜːment/ *n.* ferment *m.*; (*excitement: fig.*) agitation *f.*
fern /fɜːn/ *n.* fougère *f.*
feroc|ious /fəˈrəʊʃəs/ *a.* féroce. **~ity** /-ˈrɒsətɪ/ *n.* férocité *f.*
ferret /ˈferɪt/ *n.* (*animal*) furet *m.* ● *v.i.* (*p.t.* **ferreted**) fureter. ● *v.t.* **~ out,** dénicher.
ferry /ˈferɪ/ *n.* ferry *m.*, bac *m.* ● *v.t.* transporter.
fertil|e /ˈfɜːtaɪl, *Amer* ˈfɜːtl/ *a.* fertile; (*person, animal*) fécond. **~ity** /fəˈtɪlətɪ/ *n.* fertilité *f.*; fécondité *f.* **~ize** /-əlaɪz/ *v.t.* fertiliser; féconder.
fertilizer /ˈfɜːtəlaɪzə(r)/ *n.* engrais *m.*
fervent /ˈfɜːvənt/ *a.* fervent.
fervour /ˈfɜːvə(r)/ *n.* ferveur *f.*
fester /ˈfestə(r)/ *v.i.* (*wound*) suppurer; (*fig.*) rester sur le cœur.
festival /ˈfestɪvl/ *n.* festival *m.*; (*relig.*) fête *f.*
festiv|e /ˈfestɪv/ *a.* de fête, gai. **~e season,** période des fêtes *f.* **~ity** /feˈstɪvətɪ/ *n.* réjouissances *f. pl.*
festoon /feˈstuːn/ *v.i.* **~ with,** orner de.
fetch /fetʃ/ *v.t.* (*go for*) aller chercher; (*bring person*) amener; (*bring thing*) apporter; (*be sold for*) rapporter.
fête /feɪt/ *n.* fête *f.* ● *v.t.* fêter.
fetid /ˈfetɪd/ *a.* fétide.
fetish /ˈfetɪʃ/ *n.* (*object*) fétiche *m.*; (*psych.*) obsession *f.*

fetter /'fetə(r)/ *v.t.* enchaîner. **~s** *n. pl.* chaînes *f. pl.*
feud /fju:d/ *n.* querelle *f.*
feudal /'fju:dl/ *a.* féodal.
fever /'fi:və(r)/ *n.* fièvre *f.* **~ish** *a.* fiévreux.
few /fju:/ *a. & n.* peu (de). **~ books,** peu de livres. **they are ~,** ils sont peu nombreux. **a ~** *a.* quelques; *n.* quelques-un(e)s. **a good ~, quite a ~,** (*fam.*) bon nombre (de). **~er** *a. & n.* moins (de). **be ~er,** être moins nombreux (**than,** que). **~est** *a. & n.* le moins (de).
fiancé /fɪ'ɒnseɪ/ *n.* fiancé *m.*
fiancée /fɪ'ɒnseɪ/ *n.* fiancée *f.*
fiasco /fɪ'æskəʊ/ *n.* (*pl.* **-os**) fiasco *m.*
fib /fɪb/ *n.* mensonge *m.* **~ber** *n.* menteu|r, -se *m., f.*
fibre, *Amer.* **fiber** /'faɪbə(r)/ *n.* fibre *f.* **~ optics,** fibres optiques.
fibreglass, *Amer.* **fiberglass** /'faɪbəglɑ:s/ *n.* fibre de verre *f.*
fickle /'fɪkl/ *a.* inconstant.
fiction /'fɪkʃn/ *n.* fiction *f.* **(works of) ~,** romans *m. pl.* **~al** *a.* fictif.
fictitious /fɪk'tɪʃəs/ *a.* fictif.
fiddle /'fɪdl/ *n.* (*fam.*) violon *m.*; (*swindle*: *sl.*) combine *f.* ● *v.i.* (*sl.*) frauder. ● *v.t.* (*sl.*) falsifier. **~ with,** (*fam.*) tripoter. **~r** /-ə(r)/ *n.* (*fam.*) violoniste *m./f.*
fidelity /fɪ'delətɪ/ *n.* fidélité *f.*
fidget /'fɪdʒɪt/ *v.i.* (*p.t.* **fidgeted**) remuer sans cesse. ● *n.* **be a ~,** être remuant. **~ with,** tripoter. **~y** *a.* remuant.
field /fi:ld/ *n.* champ *m.*; (*sport*) terrain *m.*; (*fig.*) domaine *m.* ● *v.t.* (*ball*: *cricket*) bloquer. **~-day** *n.* grande occasion *f.* **~-glasses** *n. pl.* jumelles *f. pl.* **F~ Marshal,** maréchal *m.*
fieldwork /'fi:ldwɜ:k/ *n.* travaux pratiques *m. pl.*
fiend /fi:nd/ *n.* démon *m.* **~ish** *a.* diabolique.
fierce /fɪəs/ *a.* (**-er, -est**) féroce; (*storm, attack*) violent. **~ness** *n.* férocité *f.*; violence *f.*
fiery /'faɪərɪ/ *a.* (**-ier, -iest**) (*hot*) ardent; (*spirited*) fougueux.
fiesta /fɪ'estə/ *n.* fiesta *f.*
fifteen /fɪf'ti:n/ *a. & n.* quinze (*m.*). **~th** *a. & n.* quinzième (*m./f.*).
fifth /fɪfθ/ *a. & n.* cinquième (*m./f.*). **~ column,** cinquième colonne *f.*
fift|y /'fɪftɪ/ *a. & n.* cinquante (*m.*). **~ieth** *a. & n.* cinquantième (*m./f.*). **a ~y-fifty chance,** (*equal*) une chance sur deux.
fig /fɪg/ *n.* figue *f.*
fight /faɪt/ *v.i.* (*p.t.* **fought**) se battre; (*struggle*: *fig.*) lutter; (*quarrel*) se disputer. ● *v.t.* se battre avec; (*evil etc.*: *fig.*) lutter contre. ● *n.* (*struggle*) lutte *f.*; (*quarrel*) dispute *f.*; (*brawl*) bagarre *f.*; (*mil.*) combat *m.* **~ back,** se défendre. **~ off,** surmonter. **~ over sth.,** se disputer qch. **~ shy of,** fuir devant. **~er** *n.* (*brawler, soldier*) combattant *m.*; (*fig.*) battant *m.*; (*aircraft*) chasseur *m.* **~ing** *n.* combats *m. pl.*
figment /'fɪgmənt/ *n.* invention *f.*
figurative /'fɪgjərətɪv/ *a.* figuré.
figure /'fɪgə(r)/ *n.* (*number*) chiffre *m.*; (*diagram*) figure *f.*; (*shape*) forme *f.*; (*body*) ligne *f.* **~s,** arithmétique *f.* ● *v.t.* s'imaginer. ● *v.i.* (*appear*) figurer. **~ out,** comprendre. **~-head** *n.* (*person with no real power*) prête-nom *m.* **~ of speech,** façon de parler *f.* **that ~s,** (*Amer., fam.*) c'est logique.
filament /'fɪləmənt/ *n.* filament *m.*
filch /fɪltʃ/ *v.t.* voler, piquer.
fil|e[1] /faɪl/ *n.* (*tool*) lime *f.* ● *v.t.* limer. **~ings** *n. pl.* limaille *f.*
fil|e[2] /faɪl/ *n.* dossier *m.*, classeur *m.*; (*comput.*) fichier *m.*; (*row*) file *f.* ● *v.t.* (*papers*) classer; (*jurid.*) déposer. ● *v.i.* **~e in,** entrer en file. **~e past,** défiler devant. **~ing cabinet,** classeur *m.*
fill /fɪl/ *v.t./i.* (se) remplir. ● *n.* **eat one's ~,** manger à sa faim. **have had one's ~,** en avoir assez. **~ in** *or* **up,** (*form*) remplir. **~ out,** (*get fat*) grossir. **~ up,** (*auto.*) faire le plein (d'essence).
fillet /'fɪlɪt, *Amer.* fɪ'leɪ/ *n.* filet *m.* ● *v.t.* (*p.t.* **filleted**) découper en filets.
filling /'fɪlɪŋ/ *n.* (*of tooth*) plombage *m.*; (*of sandwich*) garniture *f.* **~ station,** station-service *f.*
filly /'fɪlɪ/ *n.* pouliche *f.*
film /fɪlm/ *n.* film *m.*; (*photo.*) pellicule *f.* ● *v.t.* filmer. **~-goer** *n.* cinéphile *m./f.* **~ star,** vedette de cinéma *f.*
filter /'fɪltə(r)/ *n.* filtre *m.*; (*traffic signal*) flèche *f.* ● *v.t./i.* filtrer; (*of traffic*) suivre la flèche. **~ coffee,** café-filtre *m.* **~-tip** *n.* bout filtre *m.*
filth, ~iness, /fɪlθ, fɪlθɪnəs/ *n.* saleté *f.* **~y** *a.* sale.

fin /fɪn/ *n.* (*of fish, seal*) nageoire *f.*; (*of shark*) aileron *m.*

final /'faɪnl/ *a.* dernier; (*conclusive*) définitif. ● *n.* (*sport*) finale *f.* **~ist** *n.* finaliste *m./f.* **~ly** *adv.* (*lastly, at last*) enfin, finalement; (*once and for all*) définitivement.

finale /fɪ'nɑ:lɪ/ *n.* (*mus.*) final(e) *m.*

finalize /'faɪnəlaɪz/ *v.t.* mettre au point, fixer.

financ|e /'faɪnæns/ *n.* finance *f.* ● *a.* financier. ● *v.t.* financer. **~ier** /-'nænsɪə(r)/ *n.* financier *m.*

financial /faɪ'nænʃl/ *a.* financier. **~ly** *adv.* financièrement.

find /faɪnd/ *v.t.* (*p.t.* **found**) trouver; (*sth. lost*) retrouver. ● *n.* trouvaille *f.* **~ out** *v.t.* découvrir; *v.i.* se renseigner (**about,** sur). **~ings** *n. pl.* conclusions *f. pl.*

fine [1] /faɪn/ *n.* amende *f.* ● *v.t.* condamner à une amende.

fine [2] /faɪn/ *a.* (**-er, -est**) fin; (*excellent*) beau. ● *adv.* (très) bien; (*small*) fin. **~ arts,** beaux-arts *m. pl.* **~ly** *adv.* (*admirably*) magnifiquement; (*cut*) fin.

finery /'faɪnərɪ/ *n.* atours *m. pl.*

finesse /fɪ'nes/ *n.* finesse *f.*

finger /'fɪŋgə(r)/ *n.* doigt *m.* ● *v.t.* palper. **~-nail** *n.* ongle *m.* **~-stall** *n.* doigtier *m.*

fingerprint /'fɪŋgəprɪnt/ *n.* empreinte digitale *f.*

fingertip /'fɪŋgətɪp/ *n.* bout du doigt *m.*

finicking, finicky /'fɪnɪkɪŋ, 'fɪnɪkɪ/ *adjs.* méticuleux.

finish /'fɪnɪʃ/ *v.t./i.* finir. ● *n.* fin *f.*; (*of race*) arrivée *f.*; (*appearance*) finition *f.* **~ doing,** finir de faire. **~ up doing,** finir par faire. **~ up in,** (*land up in*) se retrouver à.

finite /'faɪnaɪt/ *a.* fini.

Fin|land /'fɪnlənd/ *n.* Finlande *f.* **~n** *n.* Finlandais(e) *m.* (*f.*). **~nish** *a.* finlandais; *n.* (*lang.*) finnois *m.*

fir /fɜ:(r)/ *n.* sapin *m.*

fire /'faɪə(r)/ *n.* feu *m.*; (*conflagration*) incendie *m.*; (*heater*) radiateur *m.* ● *v.t.* (*bullet etc.*) tirer; (*dismiss*) renvoyer; (*fig.*) enflammer. ● *v.i.* tirer (**at,** sur). **~ a gun,** tirer un coup de revolver *or* de fusil. **set ~ to,** mettre le feu à. **~ alarm,** avertisseur d'incendie *m.* **~ brigade,** pompiers *m. pl.* **~-engine** *n.* voiture de pompiers *f.* **~-escape** *n.* escalier de secours *m.* **~ extinguisher,** extincteur d'incendie *m.* **~ station,** caserne de pompiers *f.*

firearm /'faɪərɑ:m/ *n.* arme à feu *f.*

firecracker /'faɪəkrækə(r)/ *n.* (*Amer.*) pétard *m.*

firelight /'faɪəlaɪt/ *n.* lueur du feu *f.*

fireman /'faɪəmən/ *n.* (*pl.* **-men**) pompier *m.*

fireplace /'faɪəpleɪs/ *n.* cheminée *f.*

fireside /'faɪəsaɪd/ *n.* coin du feu *m.*

firewood /'faɪəwʊd/ *n.* bois de chauffage *m.*

firework /'faɪəwɜ:k/ *n.* feu d'artifice *m.*

firing-squad /'faɪərɪŋskwɒd/ *n.* peloton d'exécution *m.*

firm [1] /fɜ:m/ *n.* firme *f.*, société *f.*

firm [2] /fɜ:m/ *a.* (**-er, -est**) ferme; (*belief*) solide. **~ly** *adv.* fermement. **~ness** *n.* fermeté *f.*

first /fɜ:st/ *a.* premier. ● *n.* prem|ier, -ière *m., f.* ● *adv.* d'abord, premièrement; (*arrive etc.*) le premier, la première. **at ~,** d'abord. **at ~ hand,** de première main. **at ~ sight,** à première vue. **~ aid,** premiers soins *m. pl.* **~-class** *a.* de première classe. **~ floor,** (*Amer.*) rez-de-chaussée *m. invar.* **~ (gear),** première (vitesse) *f.* **F~ Lady,** (*Amer.*) épouse du Président *f.* **~ name,** prénom *m.* **~ of all,** tout d'abord. **~-rate** *a.* de premier ordre. **~ly** *adv.* premièrement.

fiscal /'fɪskl/ *a.* fiscal.

fish /fɪʃ/ *n.* (*usually invar.*) poisson *m.* ● *v.i.* pêcher. **~ for,** (*cod etc.*) pêcher. **~ out,** (*from water*) repêcher; (*take out: fam.*) sortir. **~ shop,** poissonnerie *f.* **~ing** *n.* pêche *f.* **go ~ing,** aller à la pêche. **~ing rod,** canne à pêche *f.* **~y** *a.* de poisson; (*fig.*) louche.

fisherman /'fɪʃəmən/ *n.* (*pl.* **-men**) *n.* pêcheur *m.*

fishmonger /'fɪʃmʌŋgə(r)/ *n.* poissonn|ier, -ière *m., f.*

fission /'fɪʃn/ *n.* fission *f.*

fist /fɪst/ *n.* poing *m.*

fit [1] /fɪt/ *n.* (*bout*) accès *m.*, crise *f.*

fit [2] /fɪt/ *a.* (**fitter, fittest**) en bonne santé; (*proper*) convenable; (*good enough*) bon; (*able*) capable. ● *v.t./i.* (*p.t.* **fitted**) (*clothes*) aller (à); (*match*) s'accorder (avec); (*put or go in or on*) (s')adapter (**to,** à); (*into space*) aller; (*install*) poser. ● *n.* **be a good ~,** (*dress*) être à la bonne taille. **in no ~ state to do,**

pas en état de faire. **~ in,** *v.t.* caser; *v.i.* (*newcomer*) s'intégrer. **~ out, ~ up,** équiper. **~ness** *n.* santé *f.*; (*of remark*) justesse *f.*

fitful /'fɪtfl/ *a.* irrégulier.

fitment /'fɪtmənt/ *n.* meuble fixe *m.*

fitted /'fɪtɪd/ *a.* (*wardrobe*) encastré. **~ carpet,** moquette *f.*

fitting /'fɪtɪŋ/ *a.* approprié. ● *n.* essayage *m.* **~ room,** cabine d'essayage *f.*

fittings /'fɪtɪŋz/ *n. pl.* (*in house*) installations *f. pl.*

five /faɪv/ *a.* & *n.* cinq (*m.*).

fiver /'faɪvə(r)/ *n.* (*fam.*) billet de cinq livres *m.*

fix /fɪks/ *v.t.* (*make firm, attach, decide*) fixer; (*mend*) réparer; (*deal with*) arranger. ● *n.* **in a ~,** dans le pétrin. **~ s.o. up with sth.,** trouver qch. à qn. **~ed** *a.* fixe.

fixation /fɪk'seɪʃn/ *n.* fixation *f.*

fixture /'fɪkstʃə(r)/ *n.* (*sport*) match *m.* **~s,** (*in house*) installations *f. pl.*

fizz /fɪz/ *v.i.* pétiller. ● *n.* pétillement *m.* **~y** *a.* gazeux.

fizzle /'fɪzl/ *v.i.* pétiller. **~ out,** (*plan etc.*) finir en queue de poisson.

flab /flæb/ *n.* (*fam.*) corpulence *f.* **~by** /'flæbɪ/ *a.* flasque.

flabbergast /'flæbəgɑ:st/ *v.t.* sidérer, ahurir.

flag[1] /flæg/ *n.* drapeau *m.*; (*naut.*) pavillon *m.* ● *v.t.* (*p.t.* **flagged**). **~ (down),** faire signe de s'arrêter à. **~-pole** *n.* mât *m.*

flag[2] /flæg/ *v.i.* (*p.t.* **flagged**) (*weaken*) faiblir; (*sick person*) s'affaiblir; (*droop*) dépérir.

flagon /'flægən/ *n.* bouteille *f.*

flagrant /'fleɪgrənt/ *a.* flagrant.

flagstone /'flægstəʊn/ *n.* dalle *f.*

flair /fleə(r)/ *n.* flair *m.*

flak /flæk/ *n.* (*fam.*) critiques *f. pl.*

flak|e /fleɪk/ *n.* flocon *m.*; (*of paint, metal*) écaille *f.* ● *v.i.* s'écailler. **~y** *a.* (*paint*) écailleux.

flamboyant /flæm'bɔɪənt/ *a.* (*colour*) éclatant; (*manner*) extravagant.

flame /fleɪm/ *n.* flamme *f.* ● *v.i.* flamber. **burst into ~s,** exploser. **go up in ~s,** brûler.

flamingo /flə'mɪŋgəʊ/ *n.* (*pl.* **-os**) flamant (rose) *m.*

flammable /'flæməbl/ *a.* inflammable.

flan /flæn/ *n.* tarte *f.*; (*custard tart*) flan *m.*

flank /flæŋk/ *n.* flanc *m.* ● *v.t.* flanquer.

flannel /'flænl/ *n.* flannelle *f.*; (*for face*) gant de toilette *m.*

flannelette /flænə'let/ *n.* pilou *m.*

flap /flæp/ *v.i.* (*p.t.* **flapped**) battre. ● *v.t.* **~ its wings,** battre des ailes. ● *n.* (*of pocket*) rabat *m.*; (*of table*) abattant *m.* **get into a ~,** (*fam.*) s'affoler.

flare /fleə(r)/ *v.i.* **~ up,** s'enflammer, flamber; (*fighting*) éclater; (*person*) s'emporter. ● *n.* flamboiement *m.*; (*mil.*) fusée éclairante *f.*; (*in skirt*) évasement *m.* **~d** *a.* (*skirt*) évasé.

flash /flæʃ/ *v.i.* briller; (*on and off*) clignoter. ● *v.t.* faire briller; (*aim torch*) diriger (**at,** sur); (*flaunt*) étaler. ● *n.* éclair *m.*, éclat *m.*; (*of news, camera*) flash *m.* **in a ~,** en un éclair. **~ one's headlights,** faire un appel de phares. **~ past,** passer à toute vitesse.

flashback /'flæʃbæk/ *n.* retour en arrière *m.*

flashlight /'flæʃlaɪt/ *n.* (*torch*) lampe électrique *f.*

flashy /'flæʃɪ/ *a.* voyant.

flask /flɑ:sk/ *n.* flacon *m.*; (*vacuum flask*) thermos *m./f. invar.* (P.).

flat /flæt/ *a.* (**flatter, flattest**) plat; (*tyre*) à plat; (*refusal*) catégorique; (*fare, rate*) fixe. ● *adv.* (*say*) carrément. ● *n.* (*rooms*) appartement *m.*; (*tyre: fam.*) crevaison *f.*; (*mus.*) bémol *m.* **~ out,** (*drive*) à toute vitesse; (*work*) d'arrache-pied. **~-pack** *a.* en kit. **~ly** *adv.* catégoriquement. **~ness** *n.* égalité *f.*

flatten /'flætn/ *v.t./i.* (s')aplatir.

flatter /'flaetə(r)/ *v.t.* flatter. **~er** *n.* flatteu|r, -se *m., f.* **~ing** *a.* flatteur. **~y** *n.* flatterie *f.*

flatulence /'flætjʊləns/ *n.* flatulence *f.*

flaunt /flɔ:nt/ *v.t.* étaler, afficher.

flautist /'flɔ:tɪst/ *n.* flûtiste *m./f.*

flavour, (*Amer.*) **flavor** /'fleɪvə(r)/ *n.* goût *m.*; (*of ice-cream etc.*) parfum *m.* ● *v.t.* parfumer, assaisonner. **~ing** *n.* arôme artificiel *m.*

flaw /flɔ:/ *n.* défaut *m.* **~ed** *a.* imparfait. **~less** *a.* parfait.

flax /flæks/ *n.* lin *m.* **~en** *a.* de lin.

flea /fli:/ *n.* puce *f.* **~ market,** marché aux puces *m.*

fleck /flek/ *n.* petite tache *f.*

fled /fled/ *see* flee.

fledged /fledʒd/ *a.* **fully-~,** (*doctor etc.*) diplômé; (*member, citizen*) à part entière.

flee /fli:/ *v.i.* (*p.t.* **fled**) s'enfuir. ● *v.t.* s'enfuir de; (*danger*) fuir.

fleece /fli:s/ *n.* toison *f.* ● *v.t.* voler.

fleet /fli:t/ *n.* (*naut., aviat.*) flotte *f.* **a ~ of vehicles,** un parc automobile.

fleeting /'fli:tɪŋ/ *a.* très bref.

Flemish /'flemɪʃ/ *a.* flamand. ● *n.* (*lang.*) flamand *m.*

flesh /fleʃ/ *n.* chair *f.* **one's (own) ~ and blood,** les siens *m. pl.* **~y** *a.* charnu.

flew /flu:/ *see* fly².

flex¹ /fleks/ *v.t.* (*knee etc.*) fléchir; (*muscle*) faire jouer.

flex² /fleks/ *n.* (*electr.*) fil souple *m.*

flexib|le /'fleksəbl/ *a.* flexible. **~ility** /-'bɪlətɪ/ *n.* flexibilité *f.*

flexitime /'fleksɪtaɪm/ *n.* horaire variable *m.*

flick /flɪk/ *n.* petit coup *m.* ● *v.t.* donner un petit coup à. **~-knife** *n.* couteau à cran d'arrêt *m.* **~ through,** feuilleter.

flicker /'flɪkə(r)/ *v.i.* vaciller. ● *n.* vacillement *m.*; (*light*) lueur *f.*

flier /'flaɪə(r)/ *n.* = **flyer**.

flies /flaɪz/ *n. pl.* (*on trousers*: *fam.*) braguette *f.*

flight¹ /flaɪt/ *n.* (*of bird, plane, etc.*) vol *m.* **~-deck** *n.* poste de pilotage *m.* **~ of stairs,** escalier *m.*

flight² /flaɪt/ *n.* (*fleeing*) fuite *f.* **put to ~,** mettre en fuite. **take ~,** prendre la fuite.

flimsy /'flɪmzɪ/ *a.* (**-ier, -iest**) (*pej.*) mince, peu solide.

flinch /flɪntʃ/ *v.i.* (*wince*) broncher; (*draw back*) reculer.

fling /flɪŋ/ *v.t.* (*p.t.* **flung**) jeter. ● *n.* **have a ~,** faire la fête.

flint /flɪnt/ *n.* silex *m.*; (*for lighter*) pierre *f.*

flip /flɪp/ *v.t.* (*p.t.* **flipped**) donner un petit coup à. ● *n.* chiquenaude *f.* **~ through,** feuilleter. **~-flops** *n. pl.* tongs *f. pl.*

flippant /'flɪpənt/ *a.* désinvolte.

flipper /'flɪpə(r)/ *n.* (*of seal etc.*) nageoire *f.*; (*of swimmer*) palme *f.*

flirt /flɜ:t/ *v.i.* flirter. ● *n.* flirteu|r, -se *m., f.* **~ation** /-'teɪʃn/ *n.* flirt *m.*

flit /flɪt/ *v.i.* (*p.t.* **flitted**) voltiger.

float /fləʊt/ *v.t./i.* (faire) flotter. ● *n.* flotteur *m.*; (*cart*) char *m.*

flock /flɒk/ *n.* (*of sheep etc.*) troupeau *m.*; (*of people*) foule *f.* ● *v.i.* venir en foule.

flog /flɒg/ *v.t.* (*p.t.* **flogged**) (*beat*) fouetter; (*sell*: *sl.*) vendre.

flood /flʌd/ *n.* inondation *f.*; (*fig.*) flot *m.* ● *v.t.* inonder. ● *v.i.* (*building etc.*) être inondé; (*river*) déborder; (*people*: *fig.*) affluer.

floodlight /'flʌdlaɪt/ *n.* projecteur *m.* ● *v.t.* (*p.t.* **floodlit**) illuminer.

floor /flɔ:(r)/ *n.* sol *m.*, plancher *m.*; (*for dancing*) piste *f.*; (*storey*) étage *m.* ● *v.t.* (*knock down*) terrasser; (*baffle*) stupéfier. **~-board** *n.* planche *f.*

flop /flɒp/ *v.i.* (*p.t.* **flopped**) s'agiter faiblement; (*drop*) s'affaler; (*fail*: *sl.*) échouer. ● *n.* (*sl.*) échec *m.*, fiasco *m.* **~py** *a.* lâche, flasque. **~py (disk),** disquette *f.*

flora /'flɔ:rə/ *n.* flore *f.*

floral /'flɔ:rəl/ *a.* floral.

florid /'flɒrɪd/ *a.* fleuri.

florist /'flɒrɪst/ *n.* fleuriste *m./f.*

flounce /flaʊns/ *n.* volant *m.*

flounder¹ /'flaʊndə(r)/ *v.i.* patauger (avec difficulté).

flounder² /'flaʊndə(r)/ *n.* (*fish*: *Amer.*) flet *m.*, plie *f.*

flour /'flaʊə(r)/ *n.* farine *f.* **~y** *a.* farineux.

flourish /'flʌrɪʃ/ *v.i.* prospérer. ● *v.t.* brandir. ● *n.* geste élégant *m.*; (*curve*) fioriture *f.*

flout /flaʊt/ *v.t.* faire fi de.

flow /fləʊ/ *v.i.* couler; (*circulate*) circuler; (*traffic*) s'écouler; (*hang loosely*) flotter. ● *n.* (*of liquid, traffic*) écoulement *m.*; (*of tide*) flux *m.*; (*of orders, words*: *fig.*) flot *m.* **~ chart,** organigramme *m.* **~ in,** affluer. **~ into,** (*of river*) se jeter dans.

flower /'flaʊə(r)/ *n.* fleur *f.* ● *v.i.* fleurir. **~-bed** *n.* plate-bande *f.* **~ed** *a.* à fleurs. **~y** *a.* fleuri.

flown /fləʊn/ *see* fly².

flu /flu:/ *n.* (*fam.*) grippe *f.*

fluctuat|e /'flʌktʃʊeɪt/ *v.i.* varier. **~ion** /-'eɪʃn/ *n.* variation *f.*

flue /flu:/ *n.* (*duct*) tuyau *m.*

fluen|t /'flu:ənt/ *a.* (*style*) aisé. **be ~t (in a language),** parler (une langue) couramment. **~cy** *n.* facilité *f.* **~tly** *adv.* avec facilité; (*lang.*) couramment.

fluff /flʌf/ *n.* peluche(s) *f.* (*pl.*); (*down*) duvet *m.* **~y** *a.* pelucheux.

fluid /ˈflu:ɪd/ *a. & n.* fluide (*m.*).
fluke /flu:k/ *n.* coup de chance *m.*
flung /flʌŋ/ *see* fling.
flunk /flʌŋk/ *v.t./i.* (*Amer., fam.*) être collé (à).
fluorescent /flʊəˈresnt/ *a.* fluorescent.
fluoride /ˈflʊəraɪd/ *n.* (*in toothpaste, water*) fluor *m.*
flurry /ˈflʌrɪ/ *n.* (*squall*) rafale *f.*; (*fig.*) agitation *f.*
flush[1] /flʌʃ/ *v.i.* rougir. ● *v.t.* nettoyer à grande eau. ● *n.* (*blush*) rougeur *f.*; (*fig.*) excitation *f.* ● *a.* ~ **with,** (*level with*) au ras de. ~ **the toilet,** tirer la chasse d'eau.
flush[2] /flʌʃ/ *v.t.* ~ **out,** chasser.
fluster /ˈflʌstə(r)/ *v.t.* énerver.
flute /flu:t/ *n.* flûte *f.*
flutter /ˈflʌtə(r)/ *v.i.* voleter; (*of wings*) battre. ● *n.* (*of wings*) battement *m.*; (*fig.*) agitation *f.*; (*bet: fam.*) pari *m.*
flux /flʌks/ *n.* changement continuel *m.*
fly[1] /flaɪ/ *n.* mouche *f.*
fly[2] /flaɪ/ *v.i.* (*p.t.* **flew,** *p.p.* **flown**) voler; (*of passengers*) voyager en avion; (*of flag*) flotter; (*rush*) filer. ● *v.t.* (*aircraft*) piloter; (*passengers, goods*) transporter par avion; (*flag*), arborer. ● *n.* (*of trousers*) braguette *f.* ~ **off,** s'envoler.
flyer /ˈflaɪə(r)/ *n.* aviateur *m.*; (*circular: Amer.*) prospectus *m.*
flying /ˈflaɪɪŋ/ *a.* (*saucer etc.*) volant. ● *n.* (*activity*) aviation *f.* ~ **buttress,** arc-boutant *m.* **with** ~ **colours,** haut la main. ~ **start,** excellent départ *m.* ~ **visit,** visite éclair *f.* (*a. invar.*).
flyover /ˈflaɪəʊvə(r)/ *n.* (*road*) toboggan *m.*, saut-de-mouton *m.*
flyweight /ˈflaɪweɪt/ *n.* poids mouche *m.*
foal /fəʊl/ *n.* poulain *m.*
foam /fəʊm/ *n.* écume *f.*, mousse *f.* ● *v.i.* écumer, mousser. ~ **(rubber)** *n.* caoutchouc mousse *m.*
fob /fɒb/ *v.t.* (*p.t.* **fobbed**) ~ **off on (to) s.o.,** (*palm off*) refiler à qn. ~ **s.o. off with,** forcer qn. à se contenter de.
focal /ˈfəʊkl/ *a.* focal.
focus /ˈfəʊkəs/ *n.* (*pl.* **-cuses** *or* **-ci** /-saɪ/) foyer *m.*; (*fig.*) centre *m.* ● *v.t./i.* (*p.t.* **focused**) (faire) converger; (*instrument*) mettre au point; (*with camera*) faire la mise au point (**on,** sur); (*fig.*) (se) concentrer. **be in/out of** ~, être/ne pas être au point.
fodder /ˈfɒdə(r)/ *n.* fourrage *m.*
foe /fəʊ/ *n.* ennemi(e) *m.(f.)*.
foetus /ˈfi:təs/ *n.* (*pl.* **-tuses**) fœtus *m.*
fog /fɒg/ *n.* brouillard *m.* ● *v.t./i.* (*p.t.* **fogged**) (*window etc.*) (s')embuer. ~**-horn** *n.* (*naut.*) corne de brume *f.* ~**gy** *a.* brumeux. **it is** ~**gy,** il fait du brouillard.
fog(e)y /ˈfəʊgɪ/ *n.* **(old)** ~, vieille baderne *f.*
foible /ˈfɔɪbl/ *n.* faiblesse *f.*
foil[1] /fɔɪl/ *n.* (*tin foil*) papier d'aluminium *m.*; (*fig.*) repoussoir *m.*
foil[2] /fɔɪl/ *v.t.* (*thwart*) déjouer.
foist /fɔɪst/ *v.t.* imposer (**on,** à).
fold[1] /fəʊld/ *v.t./i.* (se) plier; (*arms*) croiser; (*fail*) s'effondrer. ● *n.* pli *m.* ~**er** *n.* (*file*) chemise *f.*; (*leaflet*) dépliant *m.* ~**ing** *a.* pliant.
fold[2] /fəʊld/ *n.* (*for sheep*) parc à moutons *m.*; (*relig.*) bercail *m.*
foliage /ˈfəʊlɪɪdʒ/ *n.* feuillage *m.*
folk /fəʊk/ *n.* gens *m. pl.* ~**s,** parents *m. pl.* ● *a.* folklorique.
folklore /ˈfəʊklɔ:(r)/ *n.* folklore *m.*
follow /ˈfɒləʊ/ *v.t./i.* suivre. **it** ~**s that,** il s'ensuit que. ~ **suit,** en faire autant. ~ **up,** (*letter etc.*) donner suite à. ~**er** *n.* partisan *m.* ~**ing** *n.* partisans *m. pl.*; *a.* suivant; *prep.* à la suite de.
folly /ˈfɒlɪ/ *n.* sottise *f.*
foment /fəʊˈment/ *v.t.* fomenter.
fond /fɒnd/ *a.* **(-er, -est)** (*loving*) affectueux; (*hope*) cher. **be** ~ **of,** aimer. ~**ness** *n.* affection *f.*; (*for things*) attachement *m.*
fondle /ˈfɒndl/ *v.t.* caresser.
food /fu:d/ *n.* nourriture *f.* ● *a.* alimentaire. **French** ~, la cuisine française. ~ **processor,** robot (ménager) *m.*
fool /fu:l/ *n.* idiot(e) *m.* (*f.*). ● *v.t.* duper. ● *v.i.* ~ **around,** faire l'idiot.
foolhardy /ˈfu:lhɑ:dɪ/ *a.* téméraire.
foolish /ˈfu:lɪʃ/ *a.* idiot. ~**ly** *adv.* sottement. ~**ness** *n.* sottise *f.*
foolproof /ˈfu:lpru:f/ *a.* infaillible.
foot /fʊt/ *n.* (*pl.* **feet**) pied *m.*; (*measure*) pied *m.* (= *30.48 cm.*); (*of stairs, page*) bas *m.* ● *v.t.* (*bill*) payer. ~**-bridge** *n.* passerelle *f.* **on** ~, à pied. **on** *or* **to one's feet,** debout. **under s.o.'s feet,** dans les jambes de qn.

footage /'fʊtɪdʒ/ *n.* (*of film*) métrage *m.*
football /'fʊtbɔ:l/ *n.* (*ball*) ballon *m.*; (*game*) football *m.* **~ pools,** paris sur les matchs de football *m. pl.* **~er** *n.* footballeur *m.*
foothills /'fʊthɪlz/ *n. pl.* contreforts *m. pl.*
foothold /'fʊthəʊld/ *n.* prise *f.*
footing /'fʊtɪŋ/ *n.* prise (de pied) *f.*, équilibre *m.*; (*fig.*) situation *f.* **on an equal ~,** sur un pied d'égalité.
footlights /'fʊtlaɪts/ *n. pl.* rampe *f.*
footman /'fʊtmən/ *n.* (*pl.* **-men**) valet de pied *m.*
footnote /'fʊtnəʊt/ *n.* note (en bas de la page) *f.*
footpath /'fʊtpɑ:θ/ *n.* sentier *m.*; (*at the side of the road*) chemin *m.*
footprint /'fʊtprɪnt/ *n.* empreinte (de pied) *f.*
footsore /'fʊtsɔ:(r)/ *a.* **be ~,** avoir les pieds douloureux.
footstep /'fʊtstep/ *n.* pas *m.*
footwear /'fʊtweə(r)/ *n.* chaussures *f. pl.*
for /fɔ:(r), *unstressed* fə(r)/ *prep.* pour; (*during*) pendant; (*before*) avant. ● *conj.* car. **a liking ~,** le goût de. **look ~,** chercher. **pay ~,** payer. **he has been away ~,** il est absent depuis. **he stopped ~ ten minutes,** il s'est arrêté (pendant) dix minutes. **it continues ~ ten kilometres,** ça continue pendant dix kilomètres. **~ ever,** pour toujours. **~ good,** pour de bon. **~ all my work,** malgré mon travail.
forage /'fɒrɪdʒ/ *v.i.* fourrager. ● *n.* fourrage *m.*
foray /'fɒreɪ/ *n.* incursion *f.*
forbade /fə'bæd/ *see* forbid.
forbear /fɔ:'beə(r)/ *v.t./i.* (*p.t.* **forbore,** *p.p.* **forborne**) s'abstenir. **~ance** *n.* patience *f.*
forbid /fə'bɪd/ *v.t.* (*p.t.* **forbade,** *p.p.* **forbidden**) interdire, défendre (**s.o. to do,** à qn. de faire). **~ s.o. sth.,** interdire *or* défendre qch. à qn. **you are ~den to leave,** il vous est interdit de partir.
forbidding /fə'bɪdɪŋ/ *a.* menaçant.
force /fɔ:s/ *n.* force *f.* ● *v.t.* forcer. **~ into,** faire entrer de force. **~ on,** imposer à. **come into ~,** entrer en vigueur. **the ~s,** les forces armées *f. pl.* **~d** *a.* forcé. **~ful** *a.* énergique.
force-feed /'fɔ:sfi:d/ *v.t.* (*p.t.* **-fed**) nourrir de force.
forceps /'fɔ:seps/ *n. invar.* forceps *m.*
forcibl|e /'fɔ:səbl/ *a.*, **~y** *adv.* de force.
ford /fɔ:d/ *n.* gué *m.* ● *v.t.* passer à gué.
fore /fɔ:(r)/ *a.* antérieur. ● *n.* **to the ~,** en évidence.
forearm /'fɔ:rɑ:m/ *n.* avant-bras *m. invar.*
foreboding /fɔ:'bəʊdɪŋ/ *n.* pressentiment *m.*
forecast /'fɔ:kɑ:st/ *v.t.* (*p.t.* **forecast**) prévoir. ● *n.* prévision *f.*
forecourt /'fɔ:kɔ:t/ *n.* (*of garage*) devant *m.*; (*of station*) cour *f.*
forefathers /'fɔ:fɑ:ðəz/ *n. pl.* aïeux *m. pl.*
forefinger /'fɔ:fɪŋgə(r)/ *n.* index *m.*
forefront /'fɔ:frʌnt/ *n.* premier rang *m.*
foregone /'fɔ:gɒn/ *a.* **~ conclusion,** résultat à prévoir *m.*
foreground /'fɔ:graʊnd/ *n.* premier plan *m.*
forehead /'fɒrɪd/ *n.* front *m.*
foreign /'fɒrən/ *a.* étranger; (*trade*) extérieur; (*travel*) à l'étranger. **~er** *n.* étrang|er, -ère *m., f.*
foreman /'fɔ:mən/ *n.* (*pl.* **-men**) contremaître *m.*
foremost /'fɔ:məʊst/ *a.* le plus éminent. ● *adv.* **first and ~,** tout d'abord.
forename /'fɔ:neɪm/ *n.* prénom *m.*
forensic /fə'rensɪk/ *a.* médico-légal **~ medicine,** médecine légale *f.*
foreplay /'fɔ:pleɪ/ *n.* préliminaires *m. pl.*
forerunner /'fɔ:rʌnə(r)/ *n.* précurseur *m.*
foresee /fɔ:'si:/ *v.t.* (*p.t.* **-saw,** *p.p.* **-seen**) prévoir. **~able** *a.* prévisible.
foreshadow /fɔ:'ʃædəʊ/ *v.t.* présager, laisser prévoir.
foresight /'fɔ:saɪt/ *n.* prévoyance *f.*
forest /'fɒrɪst/ *n.* forêt *f.*
forestall /fɔ:'stɔ:l/ *v.t.* devancer.
forestry /'fɒrɪstrɪ/ *n.* sylviculture *f.*
foretaste /'fɔ:teɪst/ *n.* avant-goût *m.*
foretell /fɔ:'tel/ *v.t.* (*p.t.* **foretold**) prédire.
forever /fə'revə(r)/ *adv.* toujours.
forewarn /fɔ:'wɔ:n/ *v.t.* avertir.
foreword /'fɔ:wɜ:d/ *n.* avant-propos *m. invar.*
forfeit /'fɔ:fɪt/ *n.* (*penalty*) peine *f.*; (*in game*) gage *m.* ● *v.t.* perdre.
forgave /fə'geɪv/ *see* forgive.

forge[1] /fɔ:dʒ/ *v.i.* **~ ahead,** aller de l'avant, avancer.

forge[2] /fɔ:dʒ/ *n.* forge *f.* ● *v.t.* (*metal, friendship*) forger; (*copy*) contrefaire, falsifier. **~r** /-ə(r)/ *n.* faussaire *m.* **~ry** /-ərɪ/ *n.* faux *m.*, contrefaçon *f.*

forget /fə'get/ *v.t./i.* (*p.t.* **forgot,** *p.p.* **forgotten**) oublier. **~-me-not** *n.* myosotis *m.* **~ o.s.,** s'oublier. **~ful** *a.* distrait. **~ful of,** oublieux de.

forgive /fə'gɪv/ *v.t.* (*p.t.* **forgave,** *p.p.* **forgiven**) pardonner (**s.o. for sth.,** qch. à qn.). **~ness** *n.* pardon *m.*

forgo /fɔ:'gəʊ/ *v.t.* (*p.t.* **forwent,** *p.p.* **forgone**) renoncer à.

fork /fɔ:k/ *n.* fourchette *f.*; (*for digging etc.*) fourche *f.*; (*in road*) bifurcation *f.* ● *v.i.* (*road*) bifurquer. **~-lift truck,** chariot élévateur *m.* **~ out,** (*sl.*) payer. **~ed** *a.* fourchu.

forlorn /fə'lɔ:n/ *a.* triste, abandonné. **~ hope,** mince espoir *m.*

form /fɔ:m/ *n.* forme *f.*; (*document*) formulaire *m.*; (*schol.*) classe *f.* ● *v.t./i.* (se) former. **on ~,** en forme.

formal /'fɔ:ml/ *a.* officiel, en bonne et due forme; (*person*) compassé, cérémonieux; (*dress*) de cérémonie; (*denial, grammar*) formel; (*language*) soutenu. **~ity** /-'mælətɪ/ *n.* cérémonial *m.*; (*requirement*) formalité *f.* **~ly** *adv.* officiellement.

format /'fɔ:mæt/ *n.* format *m.* ● *v.t.* (*p.t.* **formatted**) (*disk*) initialiser, formater.

formation /fɔ:'meɪʃn/ *n.* formation *f.*

formative /'fɔ:mətɪv/ *a.* formateur.

former /'fɔ:mə(r)/ *a.* ancien; (*first of two*) premier. ● *n.* **the ~,** celui-là, celle-là. **~ly** *adv.* autrefois.

formidable /'fɔ:mɪdəbl/ *a.* redoutable, terrible.

formula /'fɔ:mjʊlə/ *n.* (*pl.* **-ae** /-i:/ *or* **-as**) formule *f.*

formulate /'fɔ:mjʊleɪt/ *v.t.* formuler.

forsake /fə'seɪk/ *v.t.* (*p.t.* **forsook,** *p.p.* **forsaken**) abandonner.

fort /fɔ:t/ *n.* (*mil.*) fort *m.*

forte /'fɔ:teɪ/ *n.* (*talent*) fort *m.*

forth /fɔ:θ/ *adv.* en avant. **and so ~,** et ainsi de suite. **go back and ~,** aller et venir.

forthcoming /fɔ:θ'kʌmɪŋ/ *a.* à venir, prochain; (*sociable: fam.*) communicatif.

forthright /'fɔ:θraɪt/ *a.* direct.

forthwith /fɔ:θ'wɪθ/ *adv.* sur-le-champ.

fortif|y /'fɔ:tɪfaɪ/ *v.t.* fortifier. **~ication** /-ɪ'keɪʃn/ *n.* fortification *f.*

fortitude /'fɔ:tɪtju:d/ *n.* courage *m.*

fortnight /'fɔ:tnaɪt/ *n.* quinze jours *m. pl.*, quinzaine *f.* **~ly** *a.* bimensuel; *adv.* tous les quinze jours.

fortress /'fɔ:trɪs/ *n.* forteresse *f.*

fortuitous /fɔ:'tju:ɪtəs/ *a.* fortuit.

fortunate /'fɔ:tʃənət/ *a.* heureux. **be ~,** avoir de la chance. **~ly** *adv.* heureusement.

fortune /'fɔ:tʃu:n/ *n.* fortune *f.* **~-teller** *n.* diseuse de bonne aventure *f.* **have the good ~ to,** avoir la chance de.

fort|y /'fɔ:tɪ/ *a.* & *n.* quarante (*m.*). **~y winks,** un petit somme. **~ieth** *a.* & *n.* quarantième (*m./f.*).

forum /'fɔ:rəm/ *n.* forum *m.*

forward /'fɔ:wəd/ *a.* en avant; (*advanced*) précoce; (*pert*) effronté. ● *n.* (*sport*) avant *m.* ● *adv.* en avant. ● *v.t.* (*letter*) faire suivre; (*goods*) expédier; (*fig.*) favoriser. **come ~,** se présenter. **go ~,** avancer. **~ness** *n.* précocité *f.*

forwards /'fɔ:wədz/ *adv.* en avant.

fossil /'fɒsl/ *n.* & *a.* fossile (*m.*).

foster /'fɒstə(r)/ *v.t.* (*promote*) encourager; (*child*) élever. **~-child** *n.* enfant adoptif *m.* **~-mother** *n.* mère adoptive *f.*

fought /fɔ:t/ *see* fight.

foul /faʊl/ *a.* (**-er, -est**) (*smell, weather, etc.*) infect; (*place, action*) immonde; (*language*) ordurier. ● *n.* (*football*) faute *f.* ● *v.t.* souiller, encrasser. **~-mouthed** *a.* au langage ordurier. **~ play,** jeu irrégulier *m.*; (*crime*) acte criminel *m.* **~ up,** (*sl.*) gâcher.

found[1] /faʊnd/ *see* find.

found[2] /faʊnd/ *v.t.* fonder. **~ation** /-'deɪʃn/ *n.* fondation *f.*; (*basis*) fondement *m.*; (*make-up*) fond de teint *m.* **~er**[1] *n.* fonda|teur, -trice *m., f.*

founder[2] /'faʊndə(r)/ *v.i.* sombrer.

foundry /'faʊndrɪ/ *n.* fonderie *f.*

fountain /'faʊntɪn/ *n.* fontaine *f.* **~-pen** *n.* stylo à encre *m.*

four /fɔ:(r)/ *a.* & *n.* quatre (*m.*). **~fold** *a.* quadruple; *adv.* au quadruple. **~th** *a.* & *n.* quatrième (*m./f.*). **~-wheel drive,** quatre roues motrices; (*car*) quatre-quatre *m.*

foursome /'fɔ:səm/ *n.* partie à quatre *f.*

fourteen /fɔ:'ti:n/ *a.* & *n.* quatorze (*m.*). **~th** *a.* & *n.* quatorzième (*m./f.*).
fowl /faʊl/ *n.* volaille *f.*
fox /fɒks/ *n.* renard *m.* ● *v.t.* (*baffle*) mystifier; (*deceive*) tromper.
foyer /'fɔɪeɪ/ *n.* (*hall*) foyer *m.*
fraction /'frækʃn/ *n.* fraction *f.*
fracture /'fræktʃə(r)/ *n.* fracture *f.* ● *v.t./i.* (se) fracturer.
fragile /'frædʒaɪl, *Amer.* 'frædʒəl/ *a.* fragile.
fragment /'frægmənt/ *n.* fragment *m.* **~ary** *a.* fragmentaire.
fragran|t /'freɪgrənt/ *a.* parfumé. **~ce** *n.* parfum *m.*
frail /freɪl/ *a.* (**-er, -est**) frêle.
frame /freɪm/ *n.* charpente *f.*; (*of picture*) cadre *m.*; (*of window*) châssis *m.*; (*of spectacles*) monture *f.* ● *v.t.* encadrer; (*fig.*) formuler; (*jurid., sl.*) monter un coup contre. **~ of mind,** humeur *f.*
framework /'freɪmwɜ:k/ *n.* structure *f.*; (*context*) cadre *m.*
franc /fræŋk/ *n.* franc *m.*
France /frɑ:ns/ *n.* France *f.*
franchise /'fræntʃaɪz/ *n.* (*pol.*) droit de vote *m.*; (*comm.*) franchise *f.*
Franco- /'fræŋkəʊ/ *pref.* franco-.
frank[1] /fræŋk/ *a.* franc. **~ly** *adv.* franchement. **~ness** *n.* franchise *f.*
frank[2] /fræŋk/ *v.t.* affranchir.
frantic /'fræntɪk/ *a.* frénétique. **~ with,** fou de.
fratern|al /frə'tɜ:nl/ *a.* fraternel. **~ity** *n.* (*bond*) fraternité *f.*; (*group, club*) confrérie *f.*
fraternize /'frætənaɪz/ *v.i.* fraterniser (**with,** avec).
fraud /frɔ:d/ *n.* (*deception*) fraude *f.*; (*person*) imposteur *m.* **~ulent** *a.* frauduleux.
fraught /frɔ:t/ *a.* (*tense*) tendu. **~ with,** chargé de.
fray[1] /freɪ/ *n.* rixe *f.*
fray[2] /freɪ/ *v.t./i.* (s')effilocher.
freak /fri:k/ *n.* phénomène *m.* ● *a.* anormal. **~ish** *a.* anormal.
freckle /'frekl/ *n.* tache de rousseur *f.* **~d** *a.* couvert de taches de rousseur.
free /fri:/ *a.* (**freer** /'fri:ə(r)/, **freest** /'fri:ɪst/) libre; (*gratis*) gratuit; (*lavish*) généreux. ● *v.t.* (*p.t.* **freed**) libérer; (*clear*) dégager. **~ enterprise,** la libre entreprise. **a ~ hand,** carte blanche *f.* **~ kick,** coup franc *m.* **~lance** *a.* & *n.* free-lance (*m./f.*), indépendant(e) *m., f.* **~ (of charge),** gratuit(ement). **~-range** *a.* (*eggs*) de ferme. **~-wheel** *v.i.* descendre en roue libre. **~-wheeling** *a.* sans contraintes. **~ly** *adv.* librement.
freedom /'fri:dəm/ *n.* liberté *f.*
Freemason /'fri:meɪsn/ *n.* franc-maçon *m.* **~ry** *n.* francmaçonnerie *f.*
freeway /'fri:weɪ/ *n.* (*Amer.*) autoroute *f.*
freez|e /fri:z/ *v.t./i.* (*p.t.* **froze,** *p.p.* **frozen**) geler; (*culin.*) (se) congeler; (*wages etc.*) bloquer. ● *n.* gel *m.*; blocage *m.* **~e-dried** *a.* lyophilisé. **~er** *n.* congélateur *m.* **~ing** *a.* glacial. **below ~ing,** au-dessous de zéro.
freight /freɪt/ *n.* fret *m.* **~er** *n.* (*ship*) cargo *m.*
French /frentʃ/ *a.* français. ● *n.* (*lang.*) français *m.* **~ bean,** haricot vert *m.* **~ fries,** frites *f. pl.* **~-speaking** *a.* francophone. **~ window** *n.* porte-fenêtre *f.* **the ~,** les Français *m. pl.* **~man** *n.* Français *m.* **~woman** *n.* Française *f.*
frenz|y /'frenzɪ/ *n.* frénésie *f.* **~ied** *a.* frénétique.
frequen|t[1] /'fri:kwənt/ *a.* fréquent. **~cy** *n.* fréquence *f.* **~tly** *adv.* fréquemment.
frequent[2] /frɪ'kwent/ *v.t.* fréquenter.
fresco /'freskəʊ/ *n.* (*pl.* **-os**) fresque *f.*
fresh /freʃ/ *a.* (**-er, -est**) frais; (*different, additional*) nouveau; (*cheeky: fam.*) culotté. **~ly** *adv.* nouvellement. **~ness** *n.* fraîcheur *f.*
freshen /'freʃn/ *v.i.* (*weather*) fraîchir. **~ up,** (*person*) se rafraîchir.
fresher /'freʃə(r)/ *n.*, **freshman** /'freʃmən/ *n.* (*pl.* **-men**) bizuth *m./f.*
freshwater /'freʃwɔ:tə(r)/ *a.* d'eau douce.
fret /fret/ *v.i.* (*p.t.* **fretted**) se tracasser. **~ful** *a.* ronchon, insatisfait.
friar /'fraɪə(r)/ *n.* moine *m.*, frère *m.*
friction /'frɪkʃn/ *n.* friction *f.*
Friday /'fraɪdɪ/ *n.* vendredi *m.*
fridge /frɪdʒ/ *n.* frigo *m.*
fried /fraɪd/ *see* fry. ● *a.* frit. **~ eggs,** œufs sur le plat *m. pl.*
friend /frend/ *n.* ami(e) *m.* (*f.*). **~ship** *n.* amitié *f.*
friendl|y /'frendlɪ/ *a.* (**-ier, -iest**) amical, gentil. **F~y Society,** mutuelle *f.*, société de prévoyance *f.* **~iness** *n.* gentillesse *f.*
frieze /fri:z/ *n.* frise *f.*

frigate /'frɪgət/ *n.* frégate *f.*
fright /fraɪt/ *n.* peur *f.*; (*person, thing*) horreur *f.* **~ful** *a.* affreux. **~fully** *adv.* affreusement.
frighten /'fraɪtn/ *v.t.* effrayer. **~ off,** faire fuir. **~ed** *a.* effrayé. **be ~ed,** avoir peur (**of,** de). **~ing** *a.* effrayant.
frigid /'frɪdʒɪd/ *a.* froid, glacial; (*psych.*) frigide. **~ity** /-'dʒɪdətɪ/ *n.* frigidité *f.*
frill /frɪl/ *n.* (*trimming*) fanfreluche *f.* **with no ~s,** très simple.
fringe /frɪndʒ/ *n.* (*edging, hair*) frange *f.*; (*of area*) bordure *f.*; (*of society*) marge *f.* **~ benefits,** avantages sociaux *m. pl.*
frisk /frɪsk/ *v.t.* (*search*) fouiller.
frisky /'frɪskɪ/ *a.* (**-ier, -iest**) fringant, frétillant.
fritter[1] /'frɪtə(r)/ *n.* beignet *m.*
fritter[2] /'frɪtə(r)/ *v.t.* **~ away,** gaspiller.
frivol|ous /'frɪvələs/ *a.* frivole. **~ity** /-'vɒlətɪ/ *n.* frivolité *f.*
frizzy /'frɪzɪ/ *a.* crépu, crêpelé.
fro /frəʊ/ *see* to and fro.
frock /frɒk/ *n.* robe *f.*
frog /frɒg/ *n.* grenouille *f.* **a ~ in one's throat,** un chat dans la gorge.
frogman /'frɒgmən/ *n.* (*pl.* **-men**) homme-grenouille *m.*
frolic /'frɒlɪk/ *v.i.* (*p.t.* **frolicked**) s'ébattre. ● *n.* ébats *m. pl.*
from /frɒm, *unstressed* frəm/ *prep.* de; (*with time, prices, etc.*) à partir de, de; (*habit, conviction, etc.*) par; (*according to*) d'après. **take ~ s.o.,** prendre à qn. **take ~ one's pocket,** prendre dans sa poche.
front /frʌnt/ *n.* (*of car, train, etc.*) avant *m.*; (*of garment, building*) devant *m.*; (*mil., pol.*) front *m.*; (*of book, pamphlet, etc.*) début *m.*; (*appearance: fig.*) façade *f.* ● *a.* de devant, avant *invar.*; (*first*) premier. **~ door,** porte d'entrée *f.* **~-wheel drive,** traction avant *f.* **in ~ (of),** devant. **~age** *n.* façade *f.* **~al** *a.* frontal; (*attack*) de front.
frontier /'frʌntɪə(r)/ *n.* frontière *f.*
frost /frɒst/ *n.* gel *m.*, gelée *f.*; (*on glass etc.*) givre *m.* ● *v.t./i.* (se) givrer. **~-bite** *n.* gelure *f.* **~-bitten** *a.* gelé. **~ed** *a.* (*glass*) dépoli. **~ing** *n.* (*icing: Amer.*) glace *f.* **~y** *a.* (*weather, welcome*) glacial; (*window*) givré.
froth /frɒθ/ *n.* mousse *f.*, écume *f.* ● *v.i.* mousser, écumer. **~y** *a.* mousseux.
frown /fraʊn/ *v.i.* froncer les sourcils. ● *n.* froncement de sourcils *m.* **~ on,** désapprouver.
froze /frəʊz/ *see* freeze.
frozen /'frəʊzn/ *see* **freeze.** ● *a.* congelé.
frugal /'fru:gl/ *a.* (*person*) économe; (*meal, life*) frugal. **~ly** *adv.* (*live*) simplement.
fruit /fru:t/ *n.* fruit *m.*; (*collectively*) fruits *m. pl.* **~ machine,** machine à sous *f.* **~ salad,** salade de fruits *f.* **~erer** *n.* fruit|ier, -ière *m., f.* **~y** *a.* (*taste*) fruité.
fruit|ful /'fru:tfl/ *a.* (*discussions*) fructueux. **~less** *a.* stérile.
fruition /fru:'ɪʃn/ *n.* **come to ~,** se réaliser.
frustrat|e /frʌ'streɪt/ *v.t.* (*plan*) faire échouer; (*person: psych.*) frustrer; (*upset: fam.*) exaspérer. **~ion** /-ʃn/ *n.* (*psych.*) frustration *f.*; (*disappointment*) déception *f.*
fry[1] /fraɪ/ *v.t./i.* (*p.t.* **fried**) (faire) frire. **~ing-pan** *n.* poêle (à frire) *f.*
fry[2] /fraɪ/ *n.* **the small ~,** le menu fretin.
fuddy-duddy /'fʌdɪdʌdɪ/ *n.* **be a ~,** (*sl.*) être vieux jeu *invar.*
fudge /fʌdʒ/ *n.* (sorte de) caramel mou *m.* ● *v.t.* se dérober à.
fuel /'fju:əl/ *n.* combustible *m.*; (*for car engine*) carburant *m.* ● *v.t.* (*p.t.* **fuelled**) alimenter en combustible.
fugitive /'fju:dʒətɪv/ *n.* & *a.* fugiti|f, -ve (*m., f.*).
fugue /fju:g/ *n.* (*mus.*) fugue *f.*
fulfil /fʊl'fɪl/ *v.t.* (*p.t.* **fulfilled**) accomplir, réaliser; (*condition*) remplir. **~ o.s.,** s'épanouir. **~ling** *a.* satisfaisant. **~ment** *n.* réalisation *f.*; épanouissement *m.*
full /fʊl/ *a.* (**-er, -est**) plein (**of,** de); (*bus, hotel*) complet; (*programme*) chargé; (*name*) complet; (*skirt*) ample. ● *n.* **in ~,** intégral(ement). **to the ~,** complètement. **be ~ (up),** n'avoir plus faim. **~ back,** (*sport*) arrière *m.* **~ moon,** pleine lune *f.* **~-scale** *a.* (*drawing etc.*) grandeur nature *invar.*; (*fig.*) de grande envergure. **at ~ speed,** à toute vitesse. **~ stop,** point *m.* **~-time** *a.* & *adv.* à plein temps. **~y** *adv.* complètement.
fulsome /'fʊlsəm/ *a.* excessif.

fumble /ˈfʌmbl/ *v.i.* tâtonner, fouiller. ~ **with,** tripoter.
fume /fjuːm/ *v.i.* rager. ~**s** *n. pl.* exhalaisons *f. pl.*, vapeurs *f. pl.*
fumigate /ˈfjuːmɪgeɪt/ *v.t.* désinfecter.
fun /fʌn/ *n.* amusement *m.* **be ~,** être chouette. **for ~,** pour rire. **~-fair** *n.* fête foraine *f.* **make ~ of,** se moquer de.
function /ˈfʌŋkʃn/ *n.* (*purpose, duty*) fonction *f.*; (*event*) réception *f.* ● *v.i.* fonctionner. ~**al** *a.* fonctionnel.
fund /fʌnd/ *n.* fonds *m.* ● *v.t.* fournir les fonds pour.
fundamental /fʌndəˈmentl/ *a.* fondamental. ~**ist** *n.* intégriste *m./f.* ~**ism** *n.* intégrisme *m.*
funeral /ˈfjuːnərəl/ *n.* enterrement *m.*, funérailles *f. pl.* ● *a.* funèbre.
fungus /ˈfʌŋgəs/ *n.* (*pl.* **-gi** /-gaɪ/) (*plant*) champignon *m.*; (*mould*) moisissure *f.*
funicular /fjuːˈnɪkjʊlə(r)/ *n.* funiculaire *m.*
funk /fʌŋk/ *m.* **be in a ~,** (*afraid*: *sl.*) avoir la frousse; (*depressed*: *Amer., sl.*) être déprimé.
funnel /ˈfʌnl/ *n.* (*for pouring*) entonnoir *m.*; (*of ship*) cheminée *f.*
funn|y /ˈfʌnɪ/ *a.* (**-ier, -iest**) drôle; (*odd*) bizarre. ~**y business,** quelque chose de louche. ~**ily** *adv.* drôlement; bizarrement.
fur /fɜː(r)/ *n.* fourrure *f.*; (*in kettle*) tartre *m.*
furious /ˈfjʊərɪəs/ *a.* furieux. ~**ly** *adv.* furieusement.
furnace /ˈfɜːnɪs/ *n.* fourneau *m.*
furnish /ˈfɜːnɪʃ/ *v.t.* (*with furniture*) meubler; (*supply*) fournir. ~**ings** *n. pl.* ameublement *m.*
furniture /ˈfɜːnɪtʃə(r)/ *n.* meubles *m. pl.*, mobilier *m.*
furrow /ˈfʌrəʊ/ *n.* sillon *m.*
furry /ˈfɜːrɪ/ *a.* (*animal*) à fourrure; (*toy*) en peluche.
furth|er /ˈfɜːðə(r)/ *a.* plus éloigné; (*additional*) supplémentaire. ● *adv.* plus loin; (*more*) davantage. ● *v.t.* avancer. ~**er education,** formation continue *f.* ~**est** *a.* le plus éloigné; *adv.* le plus loin.
furthermore /ˈfɜːðəmɔː(r)/ *adv.* en outre, de plus.
furtive /ˈfɜːtɪv/ *a.* furtif.
fury /ˈfjʊərɪ/ *n.* fureur *f.*
fuse[1] /fjuːz/ *v.t./i.* (*melt*) fondre; (*unite*: *fig.*) fusionner. ● *n.* fusible *m.*, plomb *m.* ~ **the lights** *etc.*, faire sauter les plombs.
fuse[2] /fjuːz/ *n.* (*of bomb*) amorce *f.*
fuselage /ˈfjuːzəlɑːʒ/ *n.* fuselage *m.*
fusion /ˈfjuːʒn/ *n.* fusion *f.*
fuss /fʌs/ *n.* (*when upset*) histoire(s) *f.* (*pl.*); (*when excited*) agitation *f.* ● *v.i.* s'agiter. **make a ~,** faire des histoires; s'agiter; (*about food*) faire des chichis. **make a ~ of,** faire grand cas de. ~**y** *a.* (*finicky*) tatillon; (*hard to please*) difficile.
futile /ˈfjuːtaɪl/ *a.* futile, vain.
future /ˈfjuːtʃə(r)/ *a.* futur. ● *n.* avenir *m.*; (*gram.*) futur *m.* **in ~,** à l'avenir.
fuzz /fʌz/ *n.* (*fluff, growth*) duvet *m.*; (*police*: *sl.*) flics *m. pl.*
fuzzy /ˈfʌzɪ/ *a.* (*hair*) crépu; (*photograph*) flou; (*person*: *fam.*) à l'esprit confus.

G

gabardine /gæbəˈdiːn/ *n.* gabardine *f.*
gabble /ˈgæbl/ *v.t./i.* bredouiller. ● *n.* baragouin *m.*
gable /ˈgeɪbl/ *n.* pignon *m.*
gad /gæd/ *v.i.* (*p.t.* **gadded**). ~ **about,** se promener, aller çà et là.
gadget /ˈgædʒɪt/ *n.* gadget *m.*
Gaelic /ˈgeɪlɪk/ *n.* gaélique *m.*
gaffe /gæf/ *n.* (*blunder*) gaffe *f.*
gag /gæg/ *n.* bâillon *m.*; (*joke*) gag *m.* ● *v.t.* (*p.t.* **gagged**) bâillonner.
gaiety /ˈgeɪətɪ/ *n.* gaieté *f.*
gaily /ˈgeɪlɪ/ *adv.* gaiement.
gain /geɪn/ *v.t.* gagner; (*speed, weight*) prendre. ● *v.i.* (*of clock*) avancer. ● *n.* acquisition *f.*; (*profit*) gain *m.* ~**ful** *a.* profitable.
gait /geɪt/ *n.* démarche *f.*
gala /ˈgɑːlə/ *n.* (*festive occasion*) gala *m.*; (*sport*) concours *m.*
galaxy /ˈgæləksɪ/ *n.* galaxie *f.*
gale /geɪl/ *n.* tempête *f.*
gall /gɔːl/ *n.* bile *f.*; (*fig.*) fiel *m.*; (*impudence*: *sl.*) culot *m.* **~-bladder** *n.* vésicule biliaire *f.*
gallant /ˈgælənt/ *a.* (*brave*) courageux; (*chivalrous*) galant. ~**ry** *n.* courage *m.*
galleon /ˈgælɪən/ *n.* galion *m.*
gallery /ˈgælərɪ/ *n.* galerie *f.* **(art) ~,** (*public*) musée *m.*

galley /'gælɪ/ *n.* (*ship*) galère *f.*; (*kitchen*) cambuse *f.*
Gallic /'gælɪk/ *a.* français. **~ism** /-sɪzəm/ *n.* gallicisme *m.*
gallivant /gælɪ'vænt/ *v.i.* (*fam.*) se promener, aller çà et là.
gallon /'gælən/ *n.* gallon *m.* (*imperial = 4.546 litres; Amer. = 3.785 litres*).
gallop /'gæləp/ *n.* galop *m.* ● *v.i.* (*p.t.* **galloped**) galoper.
gallows /'gæləʊz/ *n.* potence *f.*
galore /gə'lɔ:(r)/ *adv.* en abondance, à gogo.
galosh /gə'lɒʃ/ *n.* (*overshoe*) caoutchouc *m.*
galvanize /'gælvənaɪz/ *v.t.* galvaniser.
gambit /'gæmbɪt/ *n.* **(opening) ~,** (*move*) première démarche *f.*; (*ploy*) stratagème *m.*
gambl|e /'gæmbl/ *v.t./i.* jouer. ● *n.* (*venture*) entreprise risquée *f.*; (*bet*) pari *m.*; (*risk*) risque *m.* **~e on,** miser sur. **~er** *n.* joueu|r, -se *m., f.* **~ing** *n.* le jeu.
game[1] /geɪm/ *n.* jeu *m.*; (*football*) match *m.*; (*tennis*) partie *f.*; (*animals, birds*) gibier *m.* ● *a.* (*brave*) brave. **~ for,** prêt à.
game[2] /geɪm/ *a.* (*lame*) estropié.
gamekeeper /'geɪmki:pə(r)/ *n.* garde-chasse *m.*
gammon /'gæmən/ *n.* jambon fumé *m.*
gamut /'gæmət/ *n.* gamme *f.*
gamy /'geɪmɪ/ *a.* faisandé.
gang /gæŋ/ *n.* bande *f.*; (*of workmen*) équipe *f.* ● *v.i.* **~ up,** se liguer (**on, against,** contre).
gangling /'gæŋglɪŋ/ *a.* dégingandé, grand et maigre.
gangrene /'gæŋgri:n/ *n.* gangrène *f.*
gangster /'gæŋstə(r)/ *n.* gangster *m.*
gangway /'gæŋweɪ/ *n.* passage *m.*; (*aisle*) allée *f.*; (*of ship*) passerelle *f.*
gaol /dʒeɪl/ *n.* & *v.t.* = **jail.**
gap /gæp/ *n.* trou *m.*, vide *m.*; (*in time*) intervalle *m.*; (*in education*) lacune *f.*; (*difference*) écart *m.*
gap|e /geɪp/ *v.i.* rester bouche bée. **~ing** *a.* béant.
garage /'gærɑ:ʒ, *Amer.* gə'rɑ:ʒ/ *n.* garage *m.* ● *v.t.* mettre au garage.
garb /gɑ:b/ *n.* costume *m.*
garbage /'gɑ:bɪdʒ/ *n.* ordures *f. pl.*
garble /'gɑ:bl/ *v.t.* déformer.
garden /'gɑ:dn/ *n.* jardin *m.* ● *v.i.* jardiner. **~er** *n.* jardin|ier, -ière *m., f.* **~ing** *n.* jardinage *m.*
gargle /'gɑ:gl/ *v.i.* se gargariser. ● *n.* gargarisme *m.*
gargoyle /'gɑ:gɔɪl/ *n.* gargouille *f.*
garish /'geərɪʃ/ *a.* voyant, criard.
garland /'gɑ:lənd/ *n.* guirlande *f.*
garlic /'gɑ:lɪk/ *n.* ail *m.*
garment /'gɑ:mənt/ *n.* vêtement *m.*
garnish /'gɑ:nɪʃ/ *v.t.* garnir (**with,** de). ● *n.* garniture *f.*
garret /'gærət/ *n.* mansarde *f.*
garrison /'gærɪsn/ *n.* garnison *f.*
garrulous /'gærələs/ *a.* loquace.
garter /'gɑ:tə(r)/ *n.* jarretière *f.* **~-belt** *n.* porte-jarretelles *n.m. invar.*
gas /gæs/ *n.* (*pl.* **gases**) gaz *m.*; (*med.*) anesthésique *m.*; (*petrol: Amer., fam.*) essence *f.* ● *a.* (*mask, pipe*) à gaz. ● *v.t.* asphyxier; (*mil.*) gazer. ● *v.i.* (*fam.*) bavarder.
gash /gæʃ/ *n.* entaille *f.* ● *v.t.* entailler.
gasket /'gæskɪt/ *n.* (*auto.*) joint de culasse *m.*; (*for pressure cooker*) rondelle *f.*
gasoline /'gæsəli:n/ *n.* (*petrol: Amer.*) essence *f.*
gasp /gɑ:sp/ *v.i.* haleter; (*in surprise: fig.*) avoir le souffle coupé. ● *n.* halètement *m.*
gassy /'gæsɪ/ *a.* gazeux.
gastric /'gæstrɪk/ *a.* gastrique.
gastronomy /gæ'strɒnəmɪ/ *n.* gastronomie *f.*
gate /geɪt/ *n.* porte *f.*; (*of metal*) grille *f.*; (*barrier*) barrière *f.*
gatecrash /'geɪtkræʃ/ *v.t./i.* venir sans invitation (à). **~er** *n.* intrus(e) *m.(f).*
gateway /'geɪtweɪ/ *n.* porte *f.*
gather /'gæðə(r)/ *v.t.* (*people, objects*) rassembler; (*pick up*) ramasser; (*flowers*) cueillir; (*fig.*) comprendre; (*sewing*) froncer. ● *v.i.* (*people*) se rassembler; (*crowd*) se former; (*pile up*) s'accumuler. **~ speed,** prendre de la vitesse. **~ing** *n.* rassemblement *m.*
gaudy /'gɔ:dɪ/ *a.* (**-ier, -iest**) voyant, criard.
gauge /geɪdʒ/ *n.* jauge *f.*, indicateur *m.* ● *v.t.* jauger, évaluer.
gaunt /gɔ:nt/ *a.* (*lean*) émacié; (*grim*) lugubre.
gauntlet /'gɔ:ntlɪt/ *n.* **run the ~ of,** subir (l'assaut de).
gauze /gɔ:z/ *n.* gaze *f.*
gave /geɪv/ *see* give.
gawky /'gɔ:kɪ/ *a.* (**-ier, -iest**) gauche, maladroit.

gawp (*or* **gawk**) /gɔ:p, gɔ:k/ *v.i.* ~ **(at)**, regarder bouche bée.

gay /geɪ/ *a.* **(-er, -est)** (*joyful*) gai; (*fam.*) gay *invar.* ● *n.* gay *m./f.*

gaze /geɪz/ *v.i.* ~ **(at)**, regarder (fixement). ● *n.* regard (fixe) *m.*

gazelle /gə'zel/ *n.* gazelle *f.*

gazette /gə'zet/ *n.* journal (officiel) *m.*

GB *abbr. see* Great Britain.

gear /gɪə(r)/ *n.* équipement *m.*; (*techn.*) engrenage *m.*; (*auto.*) vitesse *f.* ● *v.t.* adapter. **~-lever**, (*Amer.*) **~-shift** *ns.* levier de vitesse *m.* **in ~**, en prise. **out of ~**, au point mort.

gearbox /'gɪəbɒks/ *n.* (*auto.*) boîte de vitesses *f.*

geese /gi:s/ *see* goose.

gel /dʒel/ *n.* gelée *f.*; (*for hair*) gel *m.*

gelatine /'dʒeləti:n/ *n.* gélatine *f.*

gelignite /'dʒelɪgnaɪt/ *n.* nitroglycérine *f.*

gem /dʒem/ *n.* pierre précieuse *f.*

Gemini /'dʒemɪnaɪ/ *n.* les Gémeaux *m. pl.*

gender /'dʒendə(r)/ *n.* genre *m.*

gene /dʒi:n/ *n.* gène *m.*

genealogy /dʒi:nɪ'ælədʒɪ/ *n.* généalogie *f.*

general /'dʒenrəl/ *a.* général. ● *n.* général *m.* ~ **election**, élections législatives *f. pl.* ~ **practitioner**, (*med.*) généraliste *m.* **in ~**, en général. **~ly** *adv.* généralement.

generaliz|e /'dʒenrəlaɪz/ *v.t./i.* généraliser. **~ation** /-'zeɪʃn/ *n.* généralisation *f.*

generate /'dʒenəreɪt/ *v.t.* produire.

generation /dʒenə'reɪʃn/ *n.* génération *f.*

generator /'dʒenəreɪtə(r)/ *n.* (*electr.*) groupe électrogène *m.*

gener|ous /'dʒenərəs/ *a.* généreux; (*plentiful*) copieux. **~osity** /-'rɒsətɪ/ *n.* générosité *f.*

genetic /dʒɪ'netɪk/ *a.* génétique. **~s** *n.* génétique *f.*

Geneva /dʒɪ'ni:və/ *n.* Genève *m./f.*

genial /'dʒi:nɪəl/ *a.* affable, sympathique; (*climate*) doux.

genital /'dʒenɪtl/ *a.* génital. **~s** *n. pl.* organes génitaux *m. pl.*

genius /'dʒi:nɪəs/ *n.* (*pl.* **-uses**) génie *m.*

genocide /'dʒenəsaɪd/ *n.* génocide *m.*

gent /dʒent/ *n.* (*sl.*) monsieur *m.*

genteel /dʒen'ti:l/ *a.* distingué.

gentl|e /'dʒentl/ *a.* **(-er, -est)** (*mild, kind*) doux; (*slight*) léger; (*hint*) discret. **~eness** *n.* douceur *f.* **~y** *adv.* doucement.

gentleman /'dʒentlmən/ *n.* (*pl.* **-men**) (*man*) monsieur *m.*; (*wellbred*) gentleman *m.*

genuine /'dʒenjʊɪn/ *a.* (*true*) véritable; (*person, belief*) sincère.

geograph|y /dʒɪ'ɒgrəfɪ/ *n.* géographie *f.* **~er** *n.* géographe *m./f.* **~ical** /dʒɪə'græfɪkl/ *a.* géographique.

geolog|y /dʒɪ'ɒlədʒɪ/ *n.* géologie *f.* **~ical** /dʒɪə'lɒdʒɪkl/ *a.* géologique. **~ist** *n.* géologue *m./f.*

geometr|y /dʒɪ'ɒmətrɪ/ *n.* géométrie *f.* **~ic(al)** /dʒɪə'metrɪk(l)/ *a.* géométrique.

geranium /dʒə'reɪnɪəm/ *n.* géranium *m.*

geriatric /dʒerɪ'ætrɪk/ *a.* gériatrique.

germ /dʒɜ:m/ *n.* (*rudiment, seed*) germe *m.*; (*med.*) microbe *m.*

German /'dʒɜ:mən/ *a.* & *n.* allemand(e) (*m.* (*f.*)); (*lang.*) allemand *m.* ~ **measles**, rubéole *f.* ~ **shepherd**, (*dog: Amer.*) berger allemand *m.* **~ic** /dʒə'mænɪk/ *a.* germanique. **~y** *n.* Allemagne *f.*

germinate /'dʒɜ:mɪneɪt/ *v.t./i.* (faire) germer.

gestation /dʒe'steɪʃn/ *n.* gestation *f.*

gesticulate /dʒe'stɪkjʊleɪt/ *v.i.* gesticuler.

gesture /'dʒestʃə(r)/ *n.* geste *m.*

get /get/ *v.t.* (*p.t.* & *p.p.* **got**, *p.p. Amer.* **gotten**, *pres. p.* **getting**) avoir, obtenir, recevoir; (*catch*) prendre; (*buy*) acheter, prendre; (*find*) trouver; (*fetch*) aller chercher; (*understand: sl.*) comprendre. ~ **s.o. to do sth.**, faire faire qch. à qn. ~ **sth. done**, faire faire qch. **did you ~ that number?**, tu as relevé le numéro? ● *v.i.* aller, arriver (**to**, à); (*become*) devenir; (*start*) se mettre (**to**, à); (*manage*) parvenir (**to**, à). ~ **married/ready**/*etc.*, se marier/se préparer/*etc.* ~ **promoted/hurt**/*etc.*, être promu/blessé/*etc.* ~ **arrested/robbed**/*etc.*, se faire arrêter/voler/*etc.* **you ~ to use the computer**, vous utilisez l'ordinateur. **it's ~ting to be annoying**, ça commence a être agaçant. ~ **about**, (*person*) se déplacer. ~ **across**, (*cross*) traverser. ~ **along** *or* **by**, (*manage*) se débrouiller. **~ along** *or* **on,** (*progress*) avancer. **~ along** *or* **on with,** s'entendre avec. **~ at,** (*reach*) parvenir à. **what are you ~ting at?,** où veux-tu en venir? **~ away,** partir; (*escape*) s'échapper. **~ back** *v.i.* revenir; *v.t.* (*recover*) récupérer. **~ by** *or* **through,** (*pass*) passer. **~ down** *v.t./i.* descendre; (*depress*) déprimer. **~ in,** entrer, arriver. **~ into,** (*car*) monter dans; (*dress*) mettre. **~ into trouble,** avoir des ennuis. **~ off** *v.i.* (*from bus etc.*) descendre; (*leave*) partir; (*jurid.*) être acquitté; *v.t.* (*remove*) enlever. **~ on,** (*on train etc.*) monter; (*succeed*) réussir. **~ on with,** (*job*) attaquer; (*person*) s'entendre avec. **~ out,** sortir. **~ out of,** (*fig.*) se soustraire à. **~ over,** (*illness*) se remettre de. **~ round,** (*rule*) contourner; (*person*) entortiller. **~ through,** (*finish*) finir. **~ up** *v.i.* se lever; *v.t.* (*climb, bring*) monter. **~-up** *n.* (*clothes: fam.*) mise *f.*

getaway /'getəweɪ/ *n.* fuite *f.*

geyser /'gi:zə(r)/ *n.* chauffe-eau *m. invar.*; (*geol.*) geyser *m.*

Ghana /'gɑ:nə/ *n.* Ghana *m.*

ghastly /'gɑ:stlɪ/ *a.* (**-ier, -iest**) affreux; (*pale*) blême.

gherkin /'gɜ:kɪn/ *n.* cornichon *m.*

ghetto /'getəʊ/ *n.* (*pl.* **-os**) ghetto *m.*

ghost /gəʊst/ *n.* fantôme *m.* **~ly** *a.* spectral.

giant /'dʒaɪənt/ *n.* & *a.* géant (*m.*).

gibberish /'dʒɪbərɪʃ/ *n.* baragouin *m.*, charabia *m.*

gibe /dʒaɪb/ *n.* raillerie *f.* ● *v.i.* **~ (at),** railler.

giblets /'dʒɪblɪts/ *n. pl.* abattis *m. pl.*, abats *m. pl.*

gidd|y /'gɪdɪ/ *a.* (**-ier, -iest**) vertigineux. **be** *or* **feel ~y,** avoir le vertige. **~iness** *n.* vertige *m.*

gift /gɪft/ *n.* cadeau *m.*; (*ability*) don *m.* **~-wrap** *v.t.* (*p.t.* **-wrapped**) faire un paquet-cadeau de.

gifted /'gɪftɪd/ *a.* doué.

gig /gɪg/ *n.* (*fam.*) concert *m.*

gigantic /dʒaɪ'gæntɪk/ *a.* gigantesque.

giggle /'gɪgl/ *v.i.* ricaner (sottement), glousser. ● *n.* ricanement *m.* **the ~s,** le fou rire.

gild /gɪld/ *v.t.* dorer.

gill /dʒɪl/ *n.* (*approx.*) décilitre (*imperial = 0.15 litre; Amer. = 0.12 litre*).

gills /gɪlz/ *n. pl.* ouïes *f. pl.*

gilt /gɪlt/ *a.* doré. ● *n.* dorure *f.* **~-edged** *a.* (*comm.*) de tout repos.

gimmick /'gɪmɪk/ *n.* truc *m.*

gin /dʒɪn/ *n.* gin *m.*

ginger /'dʒɪndʒə(r)/ *n.* gingembre *m.* ● *a.* roux. **~ ale, ~ beer,** boisson gazeuse au gingembre *f.*

gingerbread /'dʒɪndʒəbred/ *n.* pain d'épice *m.*

gingerly /'dʒɪndʒəlɪ/ *adv.* avec précaution.

gipsy /'dʒɪpsɪ/ *n.* = **gypsy**.

giraffe /dʒɪ'rɑ:f/ *n.* girafe *f.*

girder /'gɜ:də(r)/ *n.* poutre *f.*

girdle /'gɜ:dl/ *n.* (*belt*) ceinture *f.*; (*corset*) gaine *f.*

girl /gɜ:l/ *n.* (petite) fille *f.*; (*young woman*) (jeune) fille *f.* **~-friend** *n.* amie *f.*; (*of boy*) petite amie *f.* **~hood** *n.* enfance *f.*, jeunesse *f.* **~ish** *a.* de (jeune) fille.

giro /'dʒaɪərəʊ/ *n.* (*pl.* **-os**) virement bancaire *m.*; (*cheque: fam.*) mandat *m.*

girth /gɜ:θ/ *n.* circonférence *f.*

gist /dʒɪst/ *n.* essentiel *m.*

give /gɪv/ *v.t.* (*p.t.* **gave**, *p.p.* **given**) donner; (*gesture*) faire; (*laugh, sigh, etc.*) pousser. **~ s.o. sth.,** donner qch. à qn. ● *v.i.* donner; (*yield*) céder; (*stretch*) se détendre. ● *n.* élasticité *f.* **~ away,** donner; (*secret*) trahir. **~ back,** rendre. **~ in,** (*yield*) se rendre. **~ off,** dégager. **~ out** *v.t.* distribuer; *v.i.* (*become used up*) s'épuiser. **~ over,** (*devote*) consacrer; (*stop: fam.*) cesser. **~ up** *v.t./i.* (*renounce*) renoncer (à); (*yield*) céder. **~ o.s. up,** se rendre. **~ way,** céder; (*collapse*) s'effondrer.

given /'gɪvn/ *see* give. ● *a.* donné. **~ name,** prénom *m.*

glacier /'glæsɪə(r), *Amer.* 'gleɪʃər/ *n.* glacier *m.*

glad /glæd/ *a.* content. **~ly** *adv.* avec plaisir.

gladden /'glædn/ *v.t.* réjouir.

gladiolus /glædɪ'əʊləs/ *n.* (*pl.* **-li** /-laɪ/) glaïeul *m.*

glam|our /'glæmə(r)/ *n.* enchantement *m.*, séduction *f.* **~orize** *v.t.* rendre séduisant. **~orous** *a.* séduisant, ensorcelant.

glance /glɑ:ns/ *n.* coup d'œil *m.* ● *v.i.* **~ at,** jeter un coup d'œil à.

gland /glænd/ *n.* glande *f.*

glar|e /gleə(r)/ *v.i.* briller très fort. ● *n.* éclat (aveuglant) *m.*; (*stare: fig.*) regard furieux *m.* **~e at,** regarder d'un air furieux. **~ing** *a.* éblouissant; (*obvious*) flagrant.

glass /glɑ:s/ *n.* verre *m.*; (*mirror*) miroir *m.* **~es,** (*spectacles*) lunettes *f. pl.* **~y** *a.* vitreux.

glaze /gleɪz/ *v.t.* (*door etc.*) vitrer; (*pottery*) vernisser. ● *n.* vernis *m.*

gleam /gli:m/ *n.* lueur *f.* ● *v.i.* luire.

glean /gli:n/ *v.t.* glaner.

glee /gli:/ *n.* joie *f.* **~ club,** chorale *f.* **~ful** *a.* joyeux.

glen /glen/ *n.* vallon *m.*

glib /glɪb/ *a.* (*person*: *pej.*) qui a la parole facile *or* du bagou; (*reply, excuse*) désinvolte, spécieux. **~ly** *adv.* avec désinvolture.

glide /glaɪd/ *v.i.* glisser; (*of plane*) planer. **~r** /-ə(r)/ *n.* planeur *m.*

glimmer /'glɪmə(r)/ *n.* lueur *f.* ● *v.i.* luire.

glimpse /glɪmps/ *n.* aperçu *m.* **catch a ~ of,** entrevoir.

glint /glɪnt/ *n.* éclair *m.* ● *v.i.* étinceler.

glisten /'glɪsn/ *v.i.* briller, luire.

glitter /'glɪtə(r)/ *v.i.* scintiller. ● *n.* scintillement *m.*

gloat /gləʊt/ *v.i.* jubiler (**over,** à l'idée de).

global /'gləʊbl/ *a.* (*world-wide*) mondial; (*all-embracing*) global.

globe /gləʊb/ *n.* globe *m.*

gloom /glu:m/ *n.* obscurité *f.*; (*sadness: fig.*) tristesse *f.* **~y** *a.* triste; (*pessimistic*) pessimiste.

glorif|y /'glɔ:rɪfaɪ/ *v.t.* glorifier. **a ~ied waitress**/*etc.*, à peine plus qu'une serveuse/*etc.*

glorious /'glɔ:rɪəs/ *a.* splendide; (*deed, hero, etc.*) glorieux.

glory /'glɔ:rɪ/ *n.* gloire *f.*; (*beauty*) splendeur *f.* ● *v.i.* **~ in,** s'enorgueillir de.

gloss /glɒs/ *n.* lustre *m.*, brillant *m.* ● *a.* brillant. ● *v.i.* **~ over,** (*make light of*) glisser sur; (*cover up*) dissimuler. **~y** *a.* brillant.

glossary /'glɒsərɪ/ *n.* glossaire *m.*

glove /glʌv/ *n.* gant *m.* **~ compartment,** (*auto.*) vide-poches *m. invar.* **~d** *a.* ganté.

glow /gləʊ/ *v.i.* rougeoyer; (*person, eyes*) rayonner. ● *n.* rougeoiement *m.*, éclat *m.* **~ing** *a.* (*account etc.*) enthousiaste.

glucose /'glu:kəʊs/ *n.* glucose *m.*

glue /glu:/ *n.* colle *f.* ● *v.t.* (*pres. p.* **gluing**) coller.

glum /glʌm/ *a.* (**glummer, glummest**) triste, morne.

glut /glʌt/ *n.* surabondance *f.*

glutton /'glʌtn/ *n.* glouton(ne) *m.* (*f.*). **~ous** *a.* glouton. **~y** *n.* gloutonnerie *f.*

glycerine /'glɪsəri:n/ *n.* glycérine *f.*

gnarled /nɑ:ld/ *a.* noueux.

gnash /næʃ/ *v.t.* **~ one's teeth,** grincer des dents.

gnat /næt/ *n.* (*fly*) cousin *m.*

gnaw /nɔ:/ *v.t./i.* ronger.

gnome /nəʊm/ *n.* gnome *m.*

go /gəʊ/ *v.i.* (*p.t.* **went,** *p.p.* **gone**) aller; (*leave*) partir; (*work*) marcher; (*become*) devenir; (*be sold*) se vendre; (*vanish*) disparaître. **my coat's gone,** mon manteau n'est plus là. **~ via Paris,** passer par Paris. **~ by car/on foot,** aller en voiture/à pied. **~ for a walk/ride,** aller se promener/faire un tour en voiture. **go red/dry**/*etc.*, rougir/tarir/*etc.* **don't ~ telling him,** ne va pas lui dire. **~ riding/shopping**/*etc.*, faire du cheval/les courses/*etc.* ● *n.* (*pl.* **goes**) (*try*) coup *m.*; (*success*) réussite *f.*; (*turn*) tour *m.*; (*energy*) dynamisme *m.* **have a ~,** essayer. **be ~ing to do,** aller faire. **~ across,** traverser. **~ ahead!,** allez-y! **~-ahead** *n.* feu vert *m.*; *a.* dynamique. **~ away,** s'en aller. **~ back,** retourner; (*go home*) rentrer. **~ back on,** (*promise etc.*) revenir sur. **~ bad** *or* **off,** se gâter. **~-between** *n.* intermédiaire *m./f.* **~ by,** (*pass*) passer. **~ down,** descendre; (*sun*) se coucher. **~ for,** aller chercher; (*like*) aimer; (*attack*: *sl.*) attaquer. **~ in,** (r)entrer. **~ in for,** (*exam*) se présenter à. **~ into,** entrer dans; (*subject*) examiner. **~-kart** *n.* kart *m.* **~ off,** partir; (*explode*) sauter; (*ring*) sonner; (*take place*) se dérouler; (*dislike*) revenir de. **~ on,** continuer; (*happen*) se passer. **~ out,** sortir; (*light, fire*) s'éteindre. **~ over,** (*cross*) traverser; (*pass*) passer. **~ over** *or* **through,** (*check*) vérifier; (*search*) fouiller. **~ round,** (*be enough*) suffire. **~-slow** *n.* grève perlée *f.* **~ through,** (*suffer*) subir. **~ under,** (*sink*) couler; (*fail*) échouer. **~ up,** monter. **~ without,** se passer de. **on the ~,** actif.

goad /gəʊd/ *v.t.* aiguillonner.

goal /gəʊl/ *n.* but *m.* **~-post** *n.* poteau de but *m.*
goalkeeper /'gəʊlki:pə(r)/ *n.* gardien de but *m.*
goat /gəʊt/ *n.* chèvre *f.*
goatee /gəʊ'ti:/ *n.* barbiche *f.*
gobble /'gɒbl/ *v.t.* engouffrer.
goblet /'gɒblɪt/ *n.* verre à pied *m.*
goblin /'gɒblɪn/ *n.* lutin *m.*
God /gɒd/ *n.* Dieu *m.* **~-forsaken** *a.* perdu.
god /gɒd/ *n.* dieu *m.* **~dess** *n.* déesse *f.* **~ly** *a.* dévot.
god|child /'gɒdtʃaɪld/ *n.* (*pl.* **-children**) filleul(e) *m.* (*f.*). **~daughter** *n.* filleule *f.* **~father** *n.* parrain *m.* **~mother** *n.* marraine *f.* **~son** *n.* filleul *m.*
godsend /'gɒdsend/ *n.* aubaine *f.*
goggle /'gɒgl/ *v.i.* **~ (at),** regarder avec de gros yeux.
goggles /'gɒglz/ *n. pl.* lunettes (protectrices) *f. pl.*
going /'gəʊɪŋ/ *n.* **it is slow/hard ~,** c'est lent/difficile. ● *a.* (*price, rate*) actuel. **~s-on** *n. pl.* activités (bizarres) *f. pl.*
gold /gəʊld/ *n.* or *m.* ● *a.* en or, d'or. **~-mine** *n.* mine d'or *f.*
golden /'gəʊldən/ *a.* d'or; (*in colour*) doré; (*opportunity*) unique. **~ wedding,** noces d'or *f. pl.*
goldfish /'gəʊldfɪʃ/ *n. invar.* poisson rouge *m.*
gold-plated /gəʊld'pleɪtɪd/ *a.* plaqué or.
goldsmith /'gəʊldsmɪθ/ *n.* orfèvre *m.*
golf /gɒlf/ *n.* golf *m.* **~ ball,** balle de golf *f.*; (*on typewriter*) boule *f.* **~-course** *n.* terrain de golf *m.* **~er** *n.* joueu|r, -se de golf *m.*, *f.*
gondol|a /'gɒndələ/ *n.* gondole *f.* **~ier** /-'lɪə(r)/ *n.* gondolier *m.*
gone /gɒn/ *see* go. ● *a.* parti. **~ six o'clock,** six heures passées. **the butter's all ~,** il n'y a plus de beurre.
gong /gɒŋ/ *n.* gong *m.*
good /gʊd/ *a.* (**better, best**) bon; (*weather*) beau; (*well-behaved*) sage. ● *n.* bien *m.* **as ~ as,** (*almost*) pratiquement. **that's ~ of you,** c'est gentil (de ta part). **be ~ with,** savoir s'y prendre avec. **do ~,** faire du bien. **feel ~,** se sentir bien. **~-for-nothing** *a.* & *n.* propre à rien (*m./f.*). **G~ Friday,** Vendredi saint *m.* **~-afternoon, ~-morning** *ints.* bonjour. **~-evening** *int.* bonsoir. **~-looking** *a.* beau. **~-natured** *a.* gentil. **~ name,** réputation *f.* **~-night** *int.* bonsoir, bonne nuit. **it is ~ for you,** ça vous fait du bien. **is it any ~?,** est-ce que c'est bien? **it's no ~,** ça ne vaut rien. **it is no ~ shouting**/*etc.*, ça ne sert à rien de crier/*etc.* **for ~,** pour toujours. **~ness** *n.* bonté *f.* **my ~ness!,** mon Dieu!
goodbye /gʊd'baɪ/ *int.* & *n.* au revoir (*m. invar.*).
goods /gʊdz/ *n. pl.* marchandises *f. pl.*
goodwill /gʊd'wɪl/ *n.* bonne volonté *f.*
goody /'gʊdɪ/ *n.* (*fam.*) bonne chose *f.* **~-goody** *n.* petit(e) saint(e) *m.* (*f.*).
gooey /'gu:ɪ/ *a.* (*sl.*) poisseux.
goof /gu:f/ *v.i.* (*Amer.*) gaffer.
goose /gu:s/ *n.* (*pl.* **geese**) oie *f.* **~-flesh, ~-pimples** *ns.* chair de poule *f.*
gooseberry /'gʊzbərɪ/ *n.* groseille à maquereau *f.*
gore[1] /gɔ:(r)/ *n.* (*blood*) sang *m.*
gore[2] /gɔ:(r)/ *v.t.* encorner.
gorge /gɔ:dʒ/ *n.* (*geog.*) gorge *f.* ● *v.t.* **~ o.s.,** se gorger.
gorgeous /'gɔ:dʒəs/ *a.* magnifique, splendide, formidable.
gorilla /gə'rɪlə/ *n.* gorille *m.*
gormless /'gɔ:mlɪs/ *a.* (*sl.*) stupide.
gorse /gɔ:s/ *n. invar.* ajonc(s) *m.* (*pl.*).
gory /'gɔ:rɪ/ *a.* (**-ier, -iest**) sanglant; (*horrific: fig.*) horrible.
gosh /gɒʃ/ *int.* mince (alors).
gospel /'gɒspl/ *n.* évangile *m.* **the G~,** l'Évangile *m.*
gossip /'gɒsɪp/ *n.* bavardage(s) *m.* (*pl.*), commérage(s) *m.* (*pl.*); (*person*) bavard(e) *m.* (*f.*). ● *v.i.* (*p.t.* **gossiped**) bavarder. **~y** *a.* bavard.
got /gɒt/ *see* get. ● **have ~,** avoir. **have ~ to do,** devoir faire.
Gothic /'gɒθɪk/ *a.* gothique.
gouge /gaʊdʒ/ *v.t.* **~ out,** arracher.
gourmet /'gʊəmeɪ/ *n.* gourmet *m.*
gout /gaʊt/ *n.* (*med.*) goutte *f.*
govern /'gʌvn/ *v.t./i.* gouverner. **~ess** /-ənɪs/ *n.* gouvernante *f.* **~or** /-ənə(r)/ *n.* gouverneur *m.*
government /'gʌvənmənt/ *n.* gouvernement *m.* **~al** /-'mentl/ *a.* gouvernemental.
gown /gaʊn/ *n.* robe *f.*; (*of judge, teacher*) toge *f.*
GP *abbr. see* general practitioner.
grab /græb/ *v.t.* (*p.t.* **grabbed**) saisir.

grace /greɪs/ *n.* grâce *f.* ● *v.t.* (*honour*) honorer; (*adorn*) orner. **~ful** *a.* gracieux.

gracious /'greɪʃəs/ *a.* (*kind*) bienveillant; (*elegant*) élégant.

gradation /grə'deɪʃn/ *n.* gradation *f.*

grade /greɪd/ *n.* catégorie *f.*; (*of goods*) qualité *f.*; (*on scale*) grade *m.*; (*school mark*) note *f.*; (*class: Amer.*) classe *f.* ● *v.t.* classer; (*school work*) noter. **~ crossing,** (*Amer.*) passage à niveau *m.* **~ school,** (*Amer.*) école primaire *f.*

gradient /'greɪdɪənt/ *n.* (*slope*) inclinaison *f.*

gradual /'grædʒʊəl/ *a.* progressif, graduel. **~ly** *adv.* progressivement, peu à peu.

graduate[1] /'grædʒʊət/ *n.* (*univ.*) diplômé(e) *m.* (*f.*).

graduat|e[2] /'grædʒʊeɪt/ *v.i.* obtenir son diplôme. ● *v.t.* graduer. **~ion** /-'eɪʃn/ *n.* remise de diplômes *f.*

graffiti /grə'fi:ti:/ *n. pl.* graffiti *m. pl.*

graft[1] /grɑ:ft/ *n.* (*med., bot.*) greffe *f.* (*work*) boulot *m.* ● *v.t.* greffer; (*work*) trimer.

graft[2] /grɑ:ft/ *n.* (*bribery: fam.*) corruption *f.*

grain /greɪn/ *n.* (*seed, quantity, texture*) grain *m.*; (*in wood*) fibre *f.*

gram /græm/ *n.* gramme *m.*

gramm|ar /'græmə(r)/ *n.* grammaire *f.* **~atical** /grə'mætɪkl/ *a.* grammatical.

grand /grænd/ *a.* (**-er, -est**) magnifique; (*duke, chorus*) grand. **~ piano,** piano à queue *m.*

grandad /'grændæd/ *n.* (*fam.*) papy *m.*

grand|child /'græn(d)tʃaɪld/ *n.* (*pl.* **-children**) petit(e)-enfant *m.* (*f.*). **~daughter** *n.* petite-fille *f.* **~father** *n.* grand-père *m.* **~mother** *n.* grand-mère *f.* **~parents** *n. pl.* grands-parents *m. pl.* **~son** *n.* petit-fils *m.*

grandeur /'grændʒə(r)/ *n.* grandeur *f.*

grandiose /'grændɪəʊs/ *a.* grandiose.

grandma /'grændmɑ:/ *n.* = **granny.**

grandstand /'græn(d)stænd/ *n.* tribune *f.*

granite /'grænɪt/ *n.* granit *m.*

granny /'grænɪ/ *n.* (*fam.*) grandmaman *f.*, mémé *f.*, mamie *f.*

grant /grɑ:nt/ *v.t.* (*give*) accorder; (*request*) accéder à; (*admit*) admettre (**that,** que). ● *n.* subvention *f.*; (*univ.*) bourse *f.* **take sth. for ~ed,** considérer qch. comme une chose acquise.

granulated /'grænjʊleɪtɪd/ *a.* **~ sugar,** sucre semoule *m.*

granule /'grænju:l/ *n.* granule *m.*

grape /greɪp/ *n.* grain de raisin *m.* **~s,** raisin(s) *m.* (*pl.*).

grapefruit /'greɪpfru:t/ *n. invar.* pamplemousse *m.*

graph /grɑ:f/ *n.* graphique *m.*

graphic /'græfɪk/ *a.* (*arts etc.*) graphique; (*fig.*) vivant, explicite. **~s** *n. pl.* (*comput.*) graphiques *m. pl.*

grapple /græpl/ *v.i.* **~ with,** affronter, être aux prises avec.

grasp /grɑ:sp/ *v.t.* saisir. ● *n.* (*hold*) prise *f.*; (*strength of hand*) poigne *f.*; (*reach*) portée *f.*; (*fig.*) compréhension *f.*

grasping /'grɑ:spɪŋ/ *a.* rapace.

grass /grɑ:s/ *n.* herbe *f.* **~ roots,** peuple *m.*; (*pol.*) base *f.* **~-roots** *a.* populaire. **~y** *a.* herbeux.

grasshopper /'grɑ:shɒpə(r)/ *n.* sauterelle *f.*

grassland /'grɑ:slænd/ *n.* prairie *f.*

grate[1] /greɪt/ *n.* (*fireplace*) foyer *m.*; (*frame*) grille *f.*

grate[2] /greɪt/ *v.t.* râper. ● *v.i.* grincer. **~r** /-ə(r)/ *n.* râpe *f.*

grateful /'greɪtfl/ *a.* reconnaissant. **~ly** *adv.* avec reconnaissance.

gratif|y /'grætɪfaɪ/ *v.t.* satisfaire; (*please*) faire plaisir à **~ied** *a.* très heureux. **~ying** *a.* agréable.

grating /'greɪtɪŋ/ *n.* grille *f.*

gratis /'greɪtɪs, 'grætɪs/ *a.* & *adv.* gratis (*a. invar.*).

gratitude /'grætɪtju:d/ *n.* gratitude *f.*

gratuitous /grə'tju:ɪtəs/ *a.* gratuit.

gratuity /grə'tju:ətɪ/ *n.* (*tip*) pourboire *m.*; (*bounty: mil.*) prime *f.*

grave[1] /greɪv/ *n.* tombe *f.* **~-digger** *n.* fossoyeur *m.*

grave[2] /greɪv/ *a.* (**-er, -est**) (*serious*) grave. **~ly** *adv.* gravement.

grave[3] /grɑ:v/ *a.* **~ accent,** accent grave *m.*

gravel /'grævl/ *n.* gravier *m.*

gravestone /'greɪvstəʊn/ *n.* pierre tombale *f.*

graveyard /'greɪvjɑ:d/ *n.* cimetière *m.*

gravitat|e /'grævɪteɪt/ *v.i.* graviter. **~ion** /-'teɪʃn/ *n.* gravitation *f.*

gravity /'grævətɪ/ *n.* (*seriousness*) gravité *f.*; (*force*) pesanteur *f.*

gravy /'greɪvɪ/ *n.* jus (de viande) *m.*

gray /greɪ/ *a.* & *n.* = **grey.**

graze[1] /greɪz/ *v.t./i.* (*eat*) paître.

graze[2] /greɪz/ *v.t.* (*touch*) frôler; (*scrape*) écorcher. ● *n.* écorchure *f.*

greas|e /gri:s/ *n.* graisse *f.* ● *v.t.* graisser. **~e-proof paper,** papier sulfurisé *m.* **~y** *a.* graisseux.

great /greɪt/ *a.* (**-er, -est**) grand; (*very good*: *fam.*) magnifique. **~ Britain,** Grande-Bretagne *f.* **~-grandfather** *n.* arrière-grand-père *m.* **~-grandmother** *n.* arrière-grand-mère *f.* **~ly** *adv.* (*very*) très; (*much*) beaucoup. **~ness** *n.* grandeur *f.*

Greece /gri:s/ *n.* Grèce *f.*

greed /gri:d/ *n.* avidité *f.*; (*for food*) gourmandise *f.* **~y** *a.* avide; gourmand.

Greek /gri:k/ *a.* & *n.* grec(que) (*m.* (*f.*)); (*lang.*) grec *m.*

green /gri:n/ *a.* (**-er, -est**) vert; (*fig.*) naïf. ● *n.* vert *m.*; (*grass*) pelouse *f.*; (*golf*) green *m.* **~s,** légumes verts *m. pl.* **~ belt,** ceinture verte *f.* **~ light,** feu vert *m.* **~ery** *n.* verdure *f.*

greengage /'gri:ngeɪdʒ/ *n.* (*plum*) reine-claude *f.*

greengrocer /'gri:ngrəʊsə(r)/ *n.* marchand(e) de fruits et légumes *m.* (*f.*).

greenhouse /'gri:nhaʊs/ *n.* serre *f.*

greet /gri:t/ *v.t.* (*receive*) accueillir; (*address politely*) saluer. **~ing** *n.* accueil *m.* **~ings** *n. pl.* compliments *m. pl.*; (*wishes*) vœux *m. pl.* **~ings card,** carte de vœux *f.*

gregarious /grɪ'geərɪəs/ *a.* (*instinct*) grégaire; (*person*) sociable.

grenade /grɪ'neɪd/ *n.* grenade *f.*

grew /gru:/ *see* grow.

grey /greɪ/ *a.* (**-er, -est**) gris; (*fig.*) triste. ● *n.* gris *m.* **go ~,** (*hair, person*) grisonner.

greyhound /'greɪhaʊnd/ *n.* lévrier *m.*

grid /grɪd/ *n.* grille *f.*; (*network*: *electr.*) réseau *m.*; (*culin.*) gril *m.*

grief /gri:f/ *n.* chagrin *m.* **come to ~,** (*person*) avoir un malheur; (*fail*) tourner mal.

grievance /'gri:vns/ *n.* grief *m.*

grieve /gri:v/ *v.t./i.* (s')affliger. **~ for,** pleurer.

grill /grɪl/ *n.* (*cooking device*) gril *m.*; (*food*) grillade *f.*; (*auto.*) calandre *f.* ● *v.t./i.* griller; (*interrogate*) cuisiner.

grille /grɪl/ *n.* grille *f.*

grim /grɪm/ *a.* (**grimmer, grimmest**) sinistre.

grimace /grɪ'meɪs/ *n.* grimace *f.* ● *v.i.* grimacer.

grim|e /graɪm/ *n.* crasse *f.* **~y** *a.* crasseux.

grin /grɪn/ *v.i.* (*p.t.* **grinned**) sourire. ● *n.* (large) sourire *m.*

grind /graɪnd/ *v.t.* (*p.t.* **ground**) écraser; (*coffee*) moudre; (*sharpen*) aiguiser. ● *n.* corvée *f.* **~ one's teeth,** grincer des dents. **~ to a halt,** devenir paralysé.

grip /grɪp/ *v.t.* (*p.t.* **gripped**) saisir; (*interest*) passionner. ● *n.* prise *f.*; (*strength of hand*) poigne *f.*; (*bag*) sac de voyage *m.* **come to ~s,** en venir aux prises.

gripe /graɪp/ *n.* **~s,** (*med.*) coliques *f. pl.* ● *v.i.* (*grumble*: *sl.*) râler.

grisly /'grɪzlɪ/ *a.* (**-ier, -iest**) macabre, horrible.

gristle /'grɪsl/ *n.* cartilage *m.*

grit /grɪt/ *n.* gravillon *m.*, sable *m.*; (*fig.*) courage *m.* ● *v.t.* (*p.t.* **gritted**) (*road*) sabler; (*teeth*) serrer.

grizzle /'grɪzl/ *v.i.* (*cry*) pleurnicher.

groan /grəʊn/ *v.i.* gémir. ● *n.* gémissement *m.*

grocer /'grəʊsə(r)/ *n.* épic|ier, -ière *m., f.* **~ies** *n. pl.* (*goods*) épicerie *f.* **~y** *n.* (*shop*) épicerie *f.*

grog /grɒg/ *n.* grog *m.*

groggy /'grɒgɪ/ *a.* (*weak*) faible; (*unsteady*) chancelant; (*ill*) mal fichu.

groin /grɔɪn/ *n.* aine *f.*

groom /gru:m/ *n.* marié *m.*; (*for horses*) valet d'écurie *m.* ● *v.t.* (*horse*) panser; (*fig.*) préparer.

groove /gru:v/ *n.* (*for door etc.*) rainure *f.*; (*in record*) sillon *m.*

grope /grəʊp/ *v.i.* tâtonner. **~ for,** chercher à tâtons.

gross /grəʊs/ *a.* (**-er, -est**) (*coarse*) grossier; (*comm.*) brut. ● *n. invar.* grosse *f.* **~ly** *adv.* grossièrement; (*very*) extrêmement.

grotesque /grəʊ'tesk/ *a.* grotesque, horrible.

grotto /'grɒtəʊ/ *n.* (*pl.* **-oes**) grotte *f.*

grotty /'grɒtɪ/ *a.* (*sl.*) moche.

grouch /graʊtʃ/ *v.i.* (*grumble*: *fam.*) rouspéter, râler.

ground[1] /graʊnd/ *n.* terre *f.*, sol *m.*; (*area*) terrain *m.*; (*reason*) raison *f.*; (*electr., Amer.*) masse *f.* **~s,** terres *f. pl.*, parc *m.*; (*of coffee*) marc *m.* ● *v.t./i.* (*naut.*) échouer; (*aircraft*) retenir au sol. **on the ~,** par terre. **lose ~,** perdre du terrain. **~ floor,**

rez-de-chaussée *m. invar.* **~ rule,** règle de base *f.* **~less** *a.* sans fondement. **~ swell,** lame de fond *f.*

ground² /graʊnd/ *see* grind. ● *a.* **~ beef,** (*Amer.*) bifteck haché *m.*

grounding /ˈgraʊndɪŋ/ *n.* connaissances (de base) *f. pl.*

groundsheet /ˈgraʊndʃi:t/ *n.* tapis de sol *m.*

groundwork /ˈgraʊndwɜ:k/ *n.* travail préparatoire *m.*

group /gru:p/ *n.* groupe *m.* ● *v.t./i.* (se) grouper.

grouse¹ /graʊs/ *n. invar.* (*bird*) coq de bruyère *m.*, grouse *f.*

grouse² /graʊs/ *v.i.* (*grumble: fam.*) rouspéter, râler.

grove /grəʊv/ *n.* bocage *m.*

grovel /ˈgrɒvl/ *v.i.* (*p.t.* **grovelled**) ramper. **~ling** *a.* rampant.

grow /grəʊ/ *v.i.* (*p.t.* **grew,** *p.p.* **grown**) grandir; (*of plant*) pousser; (*become*) devenir. ● *v.t.* cultiver. **~ up,** devenir adulte, grandir. **~er** *n.* cultiva|teur, -trice *m., f.* **~ing** *a.* grandissant.

growl /graʊl/ *v.i.* grogner. ● *n.* grognement *m.*

grown /grəʊn/ *see* grow. ● *a.* adulte. **~-up** *a.* & *n.* adulte (*m./f.*).

growth /grəʊθ/ *n.* croissance *f.*; (*in numbers*) accroissement *m.*; (*of hair, tooth*) pousse *f.*; (*med.*) tumeur *f.*

grub /grʌb/ *n.* (*larva*) larve *f.*; (*food: sl.*) bouffe *f.*

grubby /ˈgrʌbɪ/ *a.* (**-ier, -iest**) sale.

grudge /grʌdʒ/ *v.t.* **~ doing,** faire à contrecœur. **~ s.o. sth.,** (*success, wealth*) en vouloir à qn. de qch. ● *n.* rancune *f.* **have a ~ against,** en vouloir à. **grudgingly** *adv.* à contrecœur.

gruelling /ˈgru:əlɪŋ/ *a.* exténuant.

gruesome /ˈgru:səm/ *a.* macabre.

gruff /grʌf/ *a.* (**-er, -est**) bourru.

grumble /ˈgrʌmbl/ *v.i.* ronchonner, grogner (**at,** après).

grumpy /ˈgrʌmpɪ/ *a.* (**-ier, -iest**) grincheux, grognon.

grunt /grʌnt/ *v.i.* grogner. ● *n.* grognement *m.*

guarant|ee /gærənˈti:/ *n.* garantie *f.* ● *v.t.* garantir. **~or** *n.* garant(e) *m.* (*f.*).

guard /gɑ:d/ *v.t.* protéger; (*watch*) surveiller. ● *v.i.* **~ against,** se protéger contre. ● *n.* (*vigilance, mil., group*) garde *f.*; (*person*) garde *m.*; (*on train*) chef de train *m.* **~ian** *n.* gardien(ne) *m.* (*f.*); (*of orphan*) tu|teur, -trice *m., f.*

guarded /ˈgɑ:dɪd/ *a.* prudent.

guerrilla /gəˈrɪlə/ *n.* guérillero *m.* **~ warfare,** guérilla *f.*

guess /ges/ *v.t./i.* deviner; (*suppose*) penser. ● *n.* conjecture *f.*

guesswork /ˈgeswɜ:k/ *n.* conjectures *f. pl.*

guest /gest/ *n.* invité(e) *m.* (*f.*); (*in hotel*) client(e) *m.* (*f.*). **~-house** *n.* pension *f.* **~-room** *n.* chambre d'ami *f.*

guffaw /gəˈfɔ:/ *n.* gros rire *m.* ● *v.i.* s'esclaffer, rire bruyamment.

guidance /ˈgaɪdns/ *n.* (*advice*) conseils *m. pl.*; (*information*) information *f.*

guide /gaɪd/ *n.* (*person, book*) guide *m.* ● *v.t.* guider. **~d** /ɪd/ *a.* **~d missile,** missile téléguidé *m.* **~-dog** *n.* chien d'aveugle *m.* **~-lines** *n. pl.* grandes lignes *f. pl.*

Guide /gaɪd/ *n.* (*girl*) guide *f.*

guidebook /ˈgaɪdbʊk/ *n.* guide *m.*

guild /gɪld/ *n.* corporation *f.*

guile /gaɪl/ *n.* ruse *f.*

guillotine /ˈgɪləti:n/ *n.* guillotine *f.*; (*for paper*) massicot *m.*

guilt /gɪlt/ *n.* culpabilité *f.* **~y** *a.* coupable.

guinea-pig /ˈgɪnɪpɪg/ *n.* cobaye *m.*

guinea-fowl /ˈgɪnɪfaʊl/ *n.* pintade *f.*

guise /gaɪz/ *n.* apparence *f.*

guitar /gɪˈtɑ:(r)/ *n.* guitare *f.* **~ist** *n.* guitariste *m./f.*

gulf /gʌlf/ *n.* (*part of sea*) golfe *m.*; (*hollow*) gouffre *m.*

gull /gʌl/ *n.* mouette *f.*, goéland *m.*

gullet /ˈgʌlɪt/ *n.* gosier *m.*

gullible /ˈgʌləbl/ *a.* crédule.

gully /ˈgʌlɪ/ *n.* (*ravine*) ravine *f.*; (*drain*) rigole *f.*

gulp /gʌlp/ *v.t.* **~ (down),** avaler en vitesse. ● *v.i.* (*from fear etc.*) avoir un serrement de gorge. ● *n.* gorgée *f.*

gum¹ /gʌm/ *n.* (*anat.*) gencive *f.*

gum² /gʌm/ *n.* (*from tree*) gomme *f.*; (*glue*) colle *f.*; (*for chewing*) chewing-gum *m.* ● *v.t.* (*p.t.* **gummed**) gommer.

gumboil /ˈgʌmbɔɪl/ *n.* abcès dentaire *m.*

gumboot /ˈgʌmbu:t/ *n.* botte de caoutchouc *f.*

gumption /ˈgʌmpʃn/ *n.* (*fam.*) initiative *f.*, courage *m.*, audace *f.*

gun /gʌn/ *n.* (*pistol*) revolver *m.*; (*rifle*) fusil *m.*; (*large*) canon *m.* ● *v.t.* (*p.t.* **gunned**). **~ down,** abattre. **~ner** *n.* artilleur *m.*
gunfire /'gʌnfaɪə(r)/ *n.* fusillade *f.*
gunge /gʌndʒ/ *n.* (*sl.*) crasse *f.*
gunman /'gʌnmən/ *n.* (*pl.* **-men**) bandit armé *m.*
gunpowder /'gʌnpaʊdə(r)/ *n.* poudre à canon *f.*
gunshot /'gʌnʃɒt/ *n.* coup de feu *m.*
gurgle /'gɜːgl/ *n.* glouglou *m.* ● *v.i.* glouglouter.
guru /'gʊruː/ *n.* (*pl.* **-us**) gourou *m.*
gush /gʌʃ/ *v.i.* **~ (out),** jaillir. ● *n.* jaillissement *m.*
gust /gʌst/ *n.* rafale *f.*; (*of smoke*) bouffée *f.* **~y** *a.* venteux.
gusto /'gʌstəʊ/ *n.* enthousiasme *m.*
gut /gʌt/ *n.* boyau *m.* **~s,** boyaux *m. pl.*, ventre *m.*; (*courage*: *fam.*) cran *m.* ● *v.t.* (*p.t.* **gutted**) (*fish*) vider; (*of fire*) dévaster.
gutter /'gʌtə(r)/ *n.* (*on roof*) gouttière *f.*; (*in street*) caniveau *m.*
guttural /'gʌtərəl/ *a.* guttural.
guy /gaɪ/ *n.* (*man*: *fam.*) type *m.*
guzzle /'gʌzl/ *v.t./i.* (*eat*) bâfrer; (*drink*: *Amer.*) boire d'un trait.
gym /dʒɪm/ *n.* (*fam.*) gymnase *m.*; (*fam.*) gym(nastique) *f.* **~-slip** *n.* tunique *f.* **~nasium** *n.* gymnase *m.*
gymnast /'dʒɪmnæst/ *n.* gymnaste *m./f.* **~ics** /-'næstɪks/ *n. pl.* gymnastique *f.*
gynaecolog|y /gaɪnɪ'kɒlədʒɪ/ *n.* gynécologie *f.* **~ist** *n.* gynécologue *m./f.*
gypsy /'dʒɪpsɪ/ *n.* bohémien(ne) *m.* (*f.*).
gyrate /dʒaɪ'reɪt/ *v.i.* tournoyer.

H

haberdashery /hæbə'dæʃərɪ/ *n.* mercerie *f.*
habit /'hæbɪt/ *n.* habitude *f.*; (*costume*: *relig.*) habit *m.* **be in/get into the ~ of,** avoir/prendre l'habitude de.
habit|able /'hæbɪtəbl/ *a.* habitable. **~ation** /-'teɪʃn/ *n.* habitation *f.*
habitat /'hæbɪtæt/ *n.* habitat *m.*
habitual /hə'bɪtʃʊəl/ *a.* (*usual*) habituel; (*smoker, liar*) invétéré. **~ly** *adv.* habituellement.
hack[1] /hæk/ *n.* (*old horse*) haridelle *f.*; (*writer*) nègre *m.*, écrivailleu|r, -se *m., f.*
hack[2] /hæk/ *v.t.* hacher, tailler.
hackneyed /'hæknɪd/ *a.* rebattu.
had /hæd/ *see* have.
haddock /'hædək/ *n. invar.* églefin *m.* **smoked ~,** haddock *m.*
haemorrhage /'hemərɪdʒ/ *n.* hémorragie *f.*
haemorrhoids /'hemərɔɪdz/ *n. pl.* hémorroïdes *f. pl.*
hag /hæg/ *n.* (vieille) sorcière *f.*
haggard /'hægəd/ *a.* (*person*) qui a le visage défait; (*face, look*) défait, hagard.
haggle /'hægl/ *v.i.* marchander. **~ over,** (*object*) marchander; (*price*) discuter.
Hague (The) /(ðə)'heɪg/ *n.* La Haye.
hail[1] /heɪl/ *v.t.* (*greet*) saluer; (*taxi*) héler. ● *v.i.* **~ from,** venir de.
hail[2] /heɪl/ *n.* grêle *f.* ● *v.i.* grêler.
hailstone /'heɪlstəʊn/ *n.* grêlon *m.*
hair /heə(r)/ *n.* (*on head*) cheveux *m. pl.*; (*on body, of animal*) poils *m. pl.*; (*single strand on head*) cheveu *m.*; (*on body*) poil *m.* **~-do** *n.* (*fam.*) coiffure *f.* **~-drier** *n.* séchoir (à cheveux) *m.* **~-grip** *n.* pince à cheveux *f.* **~-raising** *a.* horrifiant. **~ remover,** dépilatoire *m.* **~-style** *n.* coiffure *f.*
hairbrush /'heəbrʌʃ/ *n.* brosse à cheveux *f.*
haircut /'heəkʌt/ *n.* coupe de cheveux *f.* **have a ~,** se faire couper les cheveux.
hairdresser /'heədresə(r)/ *n.* coiffeu|r, -se *m., f.*
hairpin /'heəpɪn/ *n.* épingle à cheveux *f.*
hairy /'heərɪ/ *a.* (**-ier, -iest**) poilu; (*terrifying*: *sl.*) horrifiant.
hake /heɪk/ *n. invar.* colin *m.*
hale /heɪl/ *a.* vigoureux.
half /hɑːf/ *n.* (*pl.* **halves**) moitié *f.*, demi(e) *m.* (*f.*). ● *a.* demi. ● *adv.* à moitié. **~ a dozen,** une demi-douzaine. **~ an hour,** une demi-heure. **four and a ~,** quatre et demi(e). **~ and half,** moitié moitié. **in ~,** en deux. **~-back** *n.* (*sport*) demi *m.* **~-caste** *n.* métis(se) *m.* (*f.*). **~-hearted** *a.* tiède. **at ~-mast** *adv.* en berne. **~ measure,** demi-mesure *f.* **~ price,** moitié prix. **~-term** *n.* congé de (de)mi-trimestre *m.* **~-time**

n. mi-temps *f.* **~-way** *adv.* à mi-chemin. **~-wit** *n.* imbécile *m./f.*

halibut /'hælɪbət/ *n. invar.* (*fish*) flétan *m.*

hall /hɔ:l/ *n.* (*room*) salle *f.*; (*entrance*) vestibule *m.*; (*mansion*) manoir *m.*; (*corridor*) couloir *m.* **~ of residence,** foyer d'étudiants *m.*

hallelujah /hælɪ'lu:jə/ *int. & n.* = **alleluia.**

hallmark /'hɔ:lmɑ:k/ *n.* (*on gold etc.*) poinçon *m.*; (*fig.*) sceau *m.*

hallo /hə'ləʊ/ *int. & n.* bonjour (*m.*). **~!,** (*on telephone*) allô!; (*in surprise*) tiens!

hallow /'hæləʊ/ *v.t.* sanctifier.

Hallowe'en /hæləʊ'i:n/ *n.* la veille de la Toussaint.

hallucination /həlu:sɪ'neɪʃn/ *n.* hallucination *f.*

halo /'heɪləʊ/ *n.* (*pl.* **-oes**) auréole *f.*

halt /hɔ:lt/ *n.* halte *f.* ● *v.t./i.* (s')arrêter.

halve /hɑ:v/ *v.t.* diviser en deux; (*time etc.*) réduire de moitié.

ham /hæm/ *n.* jambon *m.*; (*theatre: sl.*) cabotin(e) *m.* (*f.*). **~-fisted** *a.* maladroit.

hamburger /'hæmbɜ:gə(r)/ *n.* hamburger *m.*

hamlet /'hæmlɪt/ *n.* hameau *m.*

hammer /'hæmə(r)/ *n.* marteau *m.* ● *v.t./i.* marteler, frapper; (*defeat*) battre à plate couture. **~ out,** (*differences*) arranger; (*agreement*) arriver à.

hammock /'hæmək/ *n.* hamac *m.*

hamper [1] /'hæmpə(r)/ *n.* panier *m.*

hamper [2] /'hæmpə(r)/ *v.t.* gêner.

hamster /'hæmstə(r)/ *n.* hamster *m.*

hand /hænd/ *n.* main *f.*; (*of clock*) aiguille *f.*; (*writing*) écriture *f.*; (*worker*) ouvr|ier, -ière *m., f.*; (*cards*) jeu *m.* ● *v.t.* donner. **at ~,** proche. **~-baggage** *n.* bagages à main *m. pl.* **give s.o. a ~,** donner un coup de main à qn. **~ in** *or* **over,** remettre. **~ out,** distribuer. **~-out** *n.* prospectus *m.*; (*money*) aumône *f.* **on ~,** disponible. **on one's ~s,** (*fig.*) sur les bras. **on the one ~ . . . on the other ~,** d'une part . . . d'autre part. **to ~,** à portée de la main.

handbag /'hændbæg/ *n.* sac à main *m.*

handbook /'hændbʊk/ *n.* manuel *m.*

handbrake /'hændbreɪk/ *n.* frein à main *m.*

handcuffs /'hændkʌfs/ *n. pl.* menottes *f. pl.*

handful /'hændfʊl/ *n.* poignée *f.*; **he's a ~!,** c'est du boulot!

handicap /'hændɪkæp/ *n.* handicap *m.* ● *v.t.* (*p.t.* **handicapped**) handicaper.

handicraft /'hændɪkrɑ:ft/ *n.* travaux manuels *m. pl.*, artisanat *m.*

handiwork /'hændɪwɜ:k/ *n.* ouvrage *m.*

handkerchief /'hæŋkətʃɪf/ *n.* (*pl.* **-fs**) mouchoir *m.*

handle /'hændl/ *n.* (*of door etc.*) poignée *f.*; (*of implement*) manche *m.*; (*of cup etc.*) anse *f.*; (*of pan etc.*) queue *f.*; (*for turning*) manivelle *f.* ● *v.t.* manier; (*deal with*) s'occuper de; (*touch*) toucher à.

handlebar /'hændlbɑ:(r)/ *n.* guidon *m.*

handshake /'hændʃeɪk/ *n.* poignée de main *f.*

handsome /'hænsəm/ *a.* (*goodlooking*) beau; (*generous*) généreux; (*large*) considérable.

handwriting /'hændraɪtɪŋ/ *n.* écriture *f.*

handy /'hændɪ/ *a.* (**-ier, -iest**) (*useful*) commode, utile; (*person*) adroit; (*near*) accessible.

handyman /'hændɪmæn/ *n.* (*pl.* **-men**) bricoleur *m.*; (*servant*) homme à tout faire *m.*

hang /hæŋ/ *v.t.* (*p.t.* **hung**) suspendre, accrocher; (*p.t.* **hanged**) (*criminal*) pendre. ● *v.i.* pendre. ● *n.* **get the ~ of doing,** trouver le truc pour faire. **~ about,** traîner. **~-gliding** *n.* vol libre *m.* **~ on,** (*hold out*) tenir bon; (*wait: sl.*) attendre. **~ out** *v.i.* pendre; (*live: sl.*) crécher; (*spend time: sl.*) passer son temps; *v.t.* (*washing*) étendre. **~ up,** (*telephone*) raccrocher. **~-up** *n.* (*sl.*) complexe *m.*

hangar /'hæŋə(r)/ *n.* hangar *m.*

hanger /'hæŋə(r)/ *n.* (*for clothes*) cintre *m.* **~-on** *n.* parasite *m.*

hangover /'hæŋəʊvə(r)/ *n.* (*after drinking*) gueule de bois *f.*

hanker /'hæŋkə(r)/ *v.i.* **~ after,** avoir envie de. **~ing** *n.* envie *f.*

hanky-panky /'hæŋkɪpæŋkɪ/ *n.* (*trickery: sl.*) manigances *f. pl.*

haphazard /hæp'hæzəd/ *a.*, **~ly** *adv.* au petit bonheur, au hasard.

hapless /'hæplɪs/ *a.* infortuné.

happen /'hæpən/ *v.i.* arriver, se passer. **it so ~s that,** il se trouve que. **he ~s to know that,** il se trouve qu'il sait que. **~ing** *n.* événement *m.*

happ|y /'hæpɪ/ *a.* (**-ier, -iest**) heureux. **I'm not ~y about the idea,** je n'aime pas trop l'idée. **~y with sth.,** satisfait de qch. **~y medium** *or* **mean,** juste milieu *m.* **~ily** *adv.* joyeusement; (*fortunately*) heureusement. **~iness** *n.* bonheur *m.* **~y-go-lucky** *a.* insouciant.

harass /'hærəs/ *v.t.* harceler. **~ment** *n.* harcèlement *m.*

harbour, (*Amer.*) **harbor** /'hɑ:bə(r)/ *n.* port *m.* ● *v.t.* (*shelter*) héberger.

hard /hɑ:d/ *a.* (**-er, -est**) dur; (*difficult*) difficile, dur. ● *adv.* dur; (*think*) sérieusement; (*pull*) fort. **~ and fast,** concret. **~-boiled egg,** œuf dur *m.* **~ by,** tout près. **~ disk,** disque dur *m.* **~ done by,** mal traité. **~-headed** *a.* réaliste. **~ of hearing,** dur d'oreille. **the ~ of hearing,** les malentendants *m. pl.* **~-line** *a.* pur et dur. **~ shoulder,** accotement stabilisé *m.* **~ up,** (*fam.*) fauché. **~-wearing** *a.* solide. **~-working** *a.* travailleur. **~ness** *n.* dureté *f.*

hardboard /'hɑ:dbɔ:d/ *n.* Isorel *m.* (P.).

harden /'hɑ:dn/ *v.t./i.* durcir.

hardly /'hɑ:dlɪ/ *adv.* à peine. **~ ever,** presque jamais.

hardship /'hɑ:dʃɪp/ *n.* **~(s),** épreuves *f. pl.*, souffrance *f.*

hardware /'hɑ:dweə(r)/ *n.* (*metal goods*) quincaillerie *f.*; (*machinery, of computer*) matériel *m.*

hardy /'hɑ:dɪ/ *a.* (**-ier, iest**) résistant.

hare /heə(r)/ *n.* lièvre *m.* **~ around,** courir partout. **~-brained** *a.* écervelé.

hark /hɑ:k/ *v.i.* écouter. **~ back to,** revenir sur.

harm /hɑ:m/ *n.* (*hurt*) mal *m.*; (*wrong*) tort *m.* ● *v.t.* (*hurt*) faire du mal à; (*wrong*) faire du tort à; (*object*) endommager. **there is no ~ in,** il n'y a pas de mal à. **~ful** *a.* nuisible. **~less** *a.* inoffensif.

harmonica /hɑ:'mɒnɪkə/ *n.* harmonica *m.*

harmon|y /'hɑ:mənɪ/ *n.* harmonie *f.* **~ious** /-'məʊnɪəs/ *a.* harmonieux. **~ize** *v.t./i.* (s')harmoniser.

harness /'hɑ:nɪs/ *n.* harnais *m.* ● *v.t.* (*horse*) harnacher; (*control*) maîtriser; (*use*) exploiter.

harp /hɑ:p/ *n.* harpe *f.* ● *v.i.* **~ on (about),** rabâcher. **~ist** *n.* harpiste *m./f.*

harpoon /hɑ:'pu:n/ *n.* harpon *m.*

harpsichord /'hɑ:psɪkɔ:d/ *n.* clavecin *m.*

harrowing /'hærəʊɪŋ/ *a.* déchirant, qui déchire le cœur.

harsh /hɑ:ʃ/ *a.* (**-er, -est**) dur, rude; (*taste*) âpre; (*sound*) rude, âpre. **~ly** *adv.* durement. **~ness** *n.* dureté *f.*

harvest /'hɑ:vɪst/ *n.* moisson *f.*, récolte *f.* **the wine ~,** les vendanges *f. pl.* ● *v.t.* moissonner, récolter. **~er** *n.* moissonneuse *f.*

has /hæz/ *see* have.

hash /hæʃ/ *n.* (*culin.*) hachis *m.*; (*fig.*) gâchis *m.* **make a ~ of,** (*bungle*: *sl.*) saboter.

hashish /'hæʃi:ʃ/ *n.* ha(s)chisch *m.*

hassle /'hæsl/ *n.* (*fam.*) difficulté(s) *f.* (*pl.*); (*bother, effort*: *fam.*) mal *m.*, peine *f.*; (*quarrel*: *fam.*) chamaillerie *f.* ● *v.t.* (*harass*: *fam.*) harceler.

haste /heɪst/ *n.* hâte *f.* **in ~,** à la hâte. **make ~,** se hâter.

hasten /'heɪsn/ *v.t./i.* (se) hâter.

hast|y /'heɪstɪ/ *a.* (**-ier, -iest**) précipité. **~ily** *adv.* à la hâte.

hat /hæt/ *n.* chapeau *m.* **a ~ trick,** trois succès consécutifs.

hatch[1] /hætʃ/ *n.* (*for food*) passeplat *m.*; (*naut.*) écoutille *f.*

hatch[2] /hætʃ/ *v.t./i.* (faire) éclore.

hatchback /'hætʃbæk/ *n.* voiture avec hayon arrière *f.*

hatchet /'hætʃɪt/ *n.* hachette *f.*

hate /heɪt/ *n.* haine *f.* ● *v.t.* haïr. **~ful** *a.* haïssable.

hatred /'heɪtrɪd/ *n.* haine *f.*

haughty /'hɔ:tɪ/ *a.* (**-ier, -iest**) hautain.

haul /hɔ:l/ *v.t.* traîner, tirer. ● *n.* (*of thieves*) butin *m.*; (*catch*) prise *f.*; (*journey*) voyage *m.* **~age** *n.* camionnage *m.* **~ier** *n.* camionneur *m.*

haunch /hɔ:ntʃ/ *n.* **on one's ~es,** accroupi.

haunt /hɔ:nt/ *v.t.* hanter. ● *n.* endroit favori *m.*

have /hæv/ *v.t.* (*3 sing. present tense* **has;** *p.t.* **had**) avoir; (*meal, bath, etc.*) prendre; (*walk, dream, etc.*) faire. ● *v. aux.* avoir; (*with aller, partir, etc. & pronominal verbs*) être. **~ it out with,** s'expliquer avec. **~ just**

done, venir de faire. **~ sth. done,** faire faire qch. **~ to do,** devoir faire. **the ~s and have-nots,** les riches et les pauvres *m. pl.*

haven /'heɪvn/ *n.* havre *m.*, abri *m.*

haversack /'hævəsæk/ *n.* musette *f.*

havoc /'hævək/ *n.* ravages *m. pl.*

haw /hɔ:/ *see* hum.

hawk[1] /hɔ:k/ *n.* faucon *m.*

hawk[2] /hɔ:k/ *v.t.* colporter. **~er** *n.* colporteu|r, -se *m., f.*

hawthorn /'hɔ:θɔ:n/ *n.* aubépine *f.*

hay /heɪ/ *n.* foin *m.* **~ fever,** rhume des foins *m.*

haystack /'heɪstæk/ *n.* meule de foin *f.*

haywire /'heɪwaɪə(r)/ *a.* **go ~,** (*plans*) se désorganiser; (*machine*) se détraquer.

hazard /'hæzəd/ *n.* risque *m.* ● *v.t.* risquer, hasarder. **~ warning lights,** feux de détresse *m. pl.* **~ous** *a.* hasardeux, risqué.

haze /heɪz/ *n.* brume *f.*

hazel /'heɪzl/ *n.* (*bush*) noisetier *m.* **~-nut** *n.* noisette *f.*

hazy /'heɪzɪ/ *a.* (**-ier, -iest**) (*misty*) brumeux; (*fig.*) flou, vague.

he /hi:/ *pron.* il; (*emphatic*) lui. ● *n.* mâle *m.*

head /hed/ *n.* tête *f.*; (*leader*) chef *m.*; (*of beer*) mousse *f.* ● *a.* principal. ● *v.t.* être à la tête de. ● *v.i.* **~ for,** se diriger vers. **~-dress** *n.* coiffure *f.*; (*lady's*) coiffe *f.* **~-on** *a.* & *adv.* de plein fouet. **~ first,** la tête la première. **~s or tails?,** pile ou face? **~ office,** siège *m.* **~ rest,** appui-tête *m.* **~ the ball,** faire une tête. **~ waiter,** maître d'hôtel *m.* **~er** *n.* (*football*) tête *f.*

headache /'hedeɪk/ *n.* mal de tête *m.*

heading /'hedɪŋ/ *n.* titre *m.*; (*subject category*) rubrique *f.*

headlamp /'hedlæmp/ *n.* phare *m.*

headland /'hedlənd/ *n.* cap *m.*

headlight /'hedlaɪt/ *n.* phare *m.*

headline /'hedlaɪn/ *n.* titre *m.*

headlong /'hedlɒŋ/ *adv.* (*in a rush*) à toute allure.

head|master /hed'mɑ:stə(r)/ *n.* (*of school*) directeur *m.* **~mistress** *n.* directrice *f.*

headphone /'hedfəʊn/ *n.* écouteur *m.* **~s,** casque (à écouteurs) *m.*

headquarters /'hedkwɔ:təz/ *n. pl.* siège *m.*, bureau central *m.*; (*mil.*) quartier général *m.*

headstrong /'hedstrɒŋ/ *a.* têtu.

headway /'hedweɪ/ *n.* progrès *m.* (*pl.*) **make ~,** faire des progrès.

heady /'hedɪ/ *a.* (**-ier, -iest**) (*wine*) capiteux; (*exciting*) grisant.

heal /hi:l/ *v.t./i.* guérir.

health /helθ/ *n.* santé *f.* **~ centre,** dispensaire *m.* **~ foods,** aliments diététiques *m. pl.* **~ insurance,** assurance médicale *f.* **~y** *a.* sain; (*person*) en bonne santé.

heap /hi:p/ *n.* tas *m.* ● *v.t.* entasser. **~s of,** (*fam.*) des tas de.

hear /hɪə(r)/ *v.t./i.* (*p.t.* **heard** /hɜ:d/) entendre. **hear, hear!,** bravo! **~ from,** recevoir des nouvelles de. **~ of or about,** entendre parler de. **not ~ of,** (*refuse to allow*) ne pas entendre parler de. **~ing** *n.* ouïe *f.*; (*of witness*) audition *f.*; (*of case*) audience *f.* **~ing-aid** *n.* appareil acoustique *m.*

hearsay /'hɪəseɪ/ *n.* ouï-dire *m. invar.* **from ~,** par ouï-dire.

hearse /hɜ:s/ *n.* corbillard *m.*

heart /hɑ:t/ *n.* cœur *m.* **~s,** (*cards*) cœur *m.* **at ~,** au fond. **by ~,** par cœur. **~ attack,** crise cardiaque *f.* **~-break** *n.* chagrin *m.* **~-breaking** *a.* navrant. **be ~-broken,** avoir le cœur brisé. **~-to-heart** *a.* à cœur ouvert. **lose ~,** perdre courage.

heartache /'hɑ:teɪk/ *n.* chagrin *m.*

heartburn /'hɑ:tbɜ:n/ *n.* brûlures d'estomac *f. pl.*

hearten /'hɑ:tn/ *v.t.* encourager.

heartfelt /'hɑ:tfelt/ *a.* sincère.

hearth /hɑ:θ/ *n.* foyer *m.*

heartless /'hɑ:tlɪs/ *a.* cruel.

heart|y /'hɑ:tɪ/ *a.* (**-ier, -iest**) (*sincere*) chaleureux; (*meal*) gros. **~ily** *adv.* (*eat*) avec appétit.

heat /hi:t/ *n.* chaleur *f.*; (*excitement: fig.*) feu *m.*; (*contest*) éliminatoire *f.* ● *v.t./i.* chauffer. **~ stroke,** insolation *f.* **~ up,** (*food*) réchauffer. **~ wave,** vague de chaleur *f.* **~er** *n.* radiateur *m.* **~ing** *n.* chauffage *m.*

heated /'hi:tɪd/ *a.* (*fig.*) passionné.

heath /hi:θ/ *n.* (*area*) lande *f.*

heathen /'hi:ðn/ *n.* païen(ne) *m.* (*f.*).

heather /'heðə(r)/ *n.* bruyère *f.*

heave /hi:v/ *v.t./i.* (*lift*) (se) soulever; (*a sigh*) pousser; (*throw: fam.*) lancer; (*retch*) avoir des nausées.

heaven /'hevn/ *n.* ciel *m.* **~ly** *a.* céleste; (*pleasing: fam.*) divin.

heav|y /'hevɪ/ *a.* (**-ier, -iest**) lourd; (*cold, work, etc.*) gros; (*traffic*) dense. **~y goods vehicle,** poids lourd *m.* **~y-handed** *a.* maladroit. **~ily** *adv.* lourdement; (*smoke, drink*) beaucoup.

heavyweight /'hevɪweɪt/ *n.* poids lourd *m.*

Hebrew /'hi:bru:/ *a.* hébreu (*m. only*), hébraïque. ● *n.* (*lang.*) hébreu *m.*

heckle /'hekl/ *v.t.* (*speaker*) interrompre, interpeller.

hectic /'hektɪk/ *a.* très bousculé, trépidant, agité.

hedge /hedʒ/ *n.* haie *f.* ● *v.t.* entourer. ● *v.i.* (*in answering*) répondre évasivement. **~ one's bets,** protéger ses arrières.

hedgehog /'hedʒhɒg/ *n.* hérisson *m.*

heed /hi:d/ *v.t.* faire attention à. ● *n.* **pay ~ to,** faire attention à. **~less** *a.* **~less of,** inattentif à.

heel /hi:l/ *n.* talon *m.*; (*man: sl.*) salaud *m.* **down at ~,** (*Amer.*) **down at the ~s,** miteux.

hefty /'heftɪ/ *a.* (**-ier, -iest**) gros, lourd.

heifer /'hefə(r)/ *n.* génisse *f.*

height /haɪt/ *n.* hauteur *f.*; (*of person*) taille *f.*; (*of plane, mountain*) altitude *f.*; (*of fame, glory*) apogée *m.*; (*of joy, folly, pain*) comble *m.*

heighten /'haɪtn/ *v.t.* (*raise*) rehausser; (*fig.*) augmenter.

heinous /'heɪnəs/ *a.* atroce.

heir /eə(r)/ *n.* héritier *m.* **~ess** *n.* héritière *f.*

heirloom /'eəlu:m/ *n.* bijou (meuble, tableau, *etc.*) de famille *m.*

held /held/ *see* hold[1].

helicopter /'helɪkɒptə(r)/ *n.* hélicoptère *m.*

heliport /'helɪpɔ:t/ *n.* héliport *m.*

hell /hel/ *n.* enfer *m.* **~-bent** *a.* acharné (**on,** à). **~ish** *a.* infernal.

hello /hə'ləʊ/ *int. & n.* = **hallo.**

helm /helm/ *n.* (*of ship*) barre *f.*

helmet /'helmɪt/ *n.* casque *m.*

help /help/ *v.t./i.* aider. ● *n.* aide *f.*; (*employees*) personnel *m.*; (*charwoman*) femme de ménage *f.* **~ o.s. to,** se servir de. **he cannot ~ laughing,** il ne peut pas s'empêcher de rire. **~er** *n.* aide *m./f.* **~ful** *a.* utile; (*person*) serviable. **~less** *a.* impuissant.

helping /'helpɪŋ/ *n.* portion *f.*

helter-skelter /heltə'skeltə(r)/ *n.* toboggan *m.* ● *adv.* pêle-mêle.

hem /hem/ *n.* ourlet *m.* ● *v.t.* (*p.t.* **hemmed**) ourler. **~ in,** enfermer.

hemisphere /'hemɪsfɪə(r)/ *n.* hémisphère *m.*

hemorrhage /'hemərɪdʒ/ *n.* (*Amer.*) = **haemorrhage.**

hemorrhoids /'hemərɔɪdz/ *n. pl.* (*Amer.*) = **haemorrhoids.**

hen /hen/ *n.* poule *f.*

hence /hens/ *adv.* (*for this reason*) d'où; (*from now*) d'ici. **~forth** *adv.* désormais.

henchman /'hentʃmən/ *n.* (*pl.* **-men**) acolyte *m.*, homme de main *m.*

henpecked /'henpekt/ *a.* dominé *or* harcelé par sa femme.

hepatitis /hepə'taɪtɪs/ *n.* hépatite *f.*

her /hɜ:(r)/ *pron.* la, l'*; (*after prep.*) elle. **(to) ~,** lui. **I know ~,** je la connais. ● *a.* son, sa, *pl.* ses.

herald /'herəld/ *v.t.* annoncer.

herb /hɜ:b, *Amer.* ɜ:b/ *n.* herbe *f.* **~s,** (*culin.*) fines herbes *f. pl.*

herd /hɜ:d/ *n.* troupeau *m.* ● *v.t./i.* **~ together,** (s')entasser.

here /hɪə(r)/ *adv.* ici. **~!,** (*take this*) tenez! **~ is, ~ are,** voici. **I'm ~,** je suis là. **~abouts** *adv.* par ici.

hereafter /hɪər'ɑ:ftə(r)/ *adv.* après; (*in book*) ci-après.

hereby /hɪə'baɪ/ *adv.* par le présent acte; (*in letter*) par la présente.

hereditary /hə'redɪtərɪ/ *a.* héréditaire.

heredity /hə'redətɪ/ *n.* hérédité *f.*

here|sy /'herəsɪ/ *n.* hérésie *f.* **~tic** *n.* hérétique *m./f.*

herewith /hɪə'wɪð/ *adv.* (*comm.*) avec ceci, ci-joint.

heritage /'herɪtɪdʒ/ *n.* patrimoine *m.*, héritage *m.*

hermit /'hɜ:mɪt/ *n.* ermite *m.*

hernia /'hɜ:nɪə/ *n.* hernie *f.*

hero /'hɪərəʊ/ *n.* (*pl.* **-oes**) héros *m.* **~ine** /'herəʊɪn/ *n.* héroïne *f.* **~ism** /'herəʊɪzəm/ *n.* héroïsme *m.*

heroic /hɪ'rəʊɪk/ *a.* héroïque.

heroin /'herəʊɪn/ *n.* héroïne *f.*

heron /'herən/ *n.* héron *m.*

herpes /'hɜ:pi:z/ *n.* herpès *m.*

herring /'herɪŋ/ *n.* hareng *m.*

hers /hɜ:z/ *poss. pron.* le sien, la sienne, les sien(ne)s. **it is ~,** c'est à elle *or* le sien.

herself /hɜ:'self/ *pron.* elle-même; (*reflexive*) se; (*after prep.*) elle.

hesitant /'hezɪtənt/ *a.* hésitant.

hesitat|e /'hezɪteɪt/ *v.i.* hésiter. **~ion** /-'teɪʃn/ *n.* hésitation *f.*

het /het/ *a.* **~ up,** (*sl.*) énervé.

heterosexual /hetərəʊ'seksjʊəl/ *a. & n.* hétérosexuel(le) (*m.* (*f.*)).

hexagon /'heksəgən/ *n.* hexagone *m.* **~al** /-'ægənl/ *a.* hexagonal.

hey /heɪ/ *int.* dites donc.

heyday /'heɪdeɪ/ *n.* apogée *m.*

HGV *abbr. see* heavy goods vehicle.

hi /haɪ/ *int.* (*greeting*: *Amer.*) salut.

hibernat|e /'haɪbəneɪt/ *v.i.* hiberner. **~ion** /-'neɪʃn/ *n.* hibernation *f.*

hiccup /'hɪkʌp/ *n.* hoquet *m.* ● *v.i.* hoqueter. **(the) ~s,** le hoquet.

hide[1] /haɪd/ *v.t.* (*p.t.* **hid,** *p.p.* **hidden**) cacher (**from,** à). ● *v.i.* se cacher (**from,** de). **go into hiding,** se cacher. **~-out** *n.* (*fam.*) cachette *f.*

hide[2] /haɪd/ *n.* (*skin*) peau *f.*

hideous /'hɪdɪəs/ *a.* (*dreadful*) atroce; (*ugly*) hideux.

hiding /'haɪdɪŋ/ *n.* (*thrashing*: *fam.*) correction *f.*

hierarchy /'haɪərɑːkɪ/ *n.* hiérarchie *f.*

hi-† /haɪ'faɪ/ *a. & n.* hi-fi *a. & f. invar.*; (*machine*) chaîne hi-fi *f.*

high /haɪ/ *a.* (**-er, -est**) haut; (*price, number*) élevé; (*priest, speed*) grand; (*voice*) aigu. ● *n.* **a (new) ~,** (*recorded level*) un record. ● *adv.* haut. **~ chair,** chaise haute *f.* **~-handed** *a.* autoritaire. **~-jump,** saut en hauteur *m.* **~-level** *a.* de haut niveau. **~-rise building,** tour *f.* **~ road,** grand-route *f.* **~ school,** lycée *m.* **in the ~ season,** en pleine saison. **~- speed** *a.* ultra-rapide. **~ spot,** (*fam.*) point culminant *m.* **~ street,** grand-rue *f.* **~-strung** *a.* (*Amer.*) nerveux. **~ tea,** goûter-dîner *m.* **~er education,** enseignement supérieur *m.*

highbrow /'haɪbraʊ/ *a. & n.* intellectuel(le) (*m.* (*f.*)).

highlight /'haɪlaɪt/ *n.* (*vivid moment*) moment fort *m.* **~s,** (*in hair*) balayage *m.* **recorded ~s,** extraits enregistrés *m. pl.* ● *v.t.* (*emphasize*) souligner.

highly /'haɪlɪ/ *adv.* extrêmement; (*paid*) très bien. **~-strung** *a.* nerveux. **speak/think ~ of,** dire/penser du bien de.

Highness /'haɪnɪs/ *n.* Altesse *f.*

highway /'haɪweɪ/ *n.* route nationale *f.* **~ code,** code de la route *m.*

hijack /'haɪdʒæk/ *v.t.* détourner. ● *n.* détournement *m.* **~er** *n.* pirate (de l'air) *m.*

hike /haɪk/ *n.* randonnée *f.* ● *v.i.* faire de la randonnée. **price ~,** hausse de prix *f.* **~r** /-ə(r)/ *n.* randonneu|r, -se *m., f.*

hilarious /hɪ'leərɪəs/ *a.* (*funny*) désopilant.

hill /hɪl/ *n.* colline *f.*; (*slope*) côte *f.* **~y** *a.* accidenté.

hillside /'hɪlsaɪd/ *n.* coteau *m.*

hilt /hɪlt/ *n.* (*of sword*) garde *f.* **to the ~,** tout à fait, au maximum.

him /hɪm/ *pron.* le, l'*; (*after prep.*) lui. **(to) ~,** lui. **I know ~,** je le connais.

himself /hɪm'self/ *pron.* lui-même; (*reflexive*) se; (*after prep.*) lui.

hind /haɪnd/ *a.* de derrière.

hind|er /'hɪndə(r)/ *v.t.* (*hamper*) gêner; (*prevent*) empêcher. **~rance** *n.* obstacle *m.*, gêne *f.*

hindsight /'haɪndsaɪt/ *n.* **with ~,** rétrospectivement.

Hindu /hɪn'duː/ *a. & n.* hindou(e) (*m.* (*f.*)). **~ism** /'hɪnduːɪzəm/ *n.* hindouisme *m.*

hinge /hɪndʒ/ *n.* charnière *f.* ● *v.i.* **~ on,** (*depend on*) dépendre de.

hint /hɪnt/ *n.* allusion *f.*; (*advice*) conseil *m.* ● *v.t.* laisser entendre. ● *v.i.* **~ at,** faire allusion à.

hip /hɪp/ *n.* hanche *f.*

hippie /'hɪpɪ/ *n.* hippie *m./f.*

hippopotamus /hɪpə'pɒtəməs/ *n.* (*pl.* **-muses**) hippopotame *m.*

hire /'haɪə(r)/ *v.t.* (*thing*) louer; (*person*) engager. ● *n.* location *f.* **~-car** *n.* voiture de location *f.* **~-purchase** *n.* achat à crédit *m.*, vente à crédit *f.*

his /hɪz/ *a.* son, sa, *pl.* ses. ● *poss. pron.* le sien, la sienne, les sien(ne)s. **it is ~,** c'est à lui *or* le sien.

hiss /hɪs/ *n.* sifflement *m.* ● *v.t./i.* siffler.

historian /hɪ'stɔːrɪən/ *n.* historien(ne) *m.* (*f.*).

histor|y /'hɪstərɪ/ *n.* histoire *f.* **make ~y,** entrer dans l'histoire. **~ic(al)** /hɪ'stɒrɪk(l)/ *a.* historique.

hit /hɪt/ *v.t.* (*p.t.* **hit,** *pres. p.* **hitting**) frapper; (*knock against, collide with*) heurter; (*find*) trouver; (*affect, reach*) toucher. ● *v.i.* **~ on,** (*find*) tomber sur. ● *n.* (*blow*) coup *m.*; (*fig.*) succès *m.*; (*song*) tube *m.* **~ it off,** s'entendre bien (**with,** avec). **~-or-miss** *a.* fait au petit bonheur.

hitch /hɪtʃ/ *v.t.* (*fasten*) accrocher. ● *n.* (*snag*) anicroche *f.* **~ a lift, ~-hike** *v.i.* faire de l'auto-stop. **~-hiker** *n.* auto-stoppeu|r, -se *m., f.* **~ up,** (*pull up*) remonter.

hi-tech /haɪ'tek/ *a.* & *n.* high-tech (*m.*) *invar.*

hitherto /hɪðə'tu:/ *adv.* jusqu'ici.

HIV *abbr.* HIV. **~-positive** *a.* séropositif.

hive /haɪv/ *n.* ruche *f.* ● *v.t.* **~ off,** séparer; (*industry*) vendre.

hoard /hɔ:d/ *v.t.* amasser. ● *n.* réserve(s) *f.* (*pl.*); (*of money*) magot *m.*, trésor *m.*

hoarding /'hɔ:dɪŋ/ *n.* panneau d'affichage *m.*

hoar-frost /'hɔ:frɒst/ *n.* givre *m.*

hoarse /hɔ:s/ *a.* (**-er, -est**) enroué. **~ness** *n.* enrouement *m.*

hoax /həʊks/ *n.* canular *m.* ● *v.t.* faire un canular à.

hob /hɒb/ *n.* plaque chauffante *f.*

hobble /'hɒbl/ *v.i.* clopiner.

hobby /'hɒbɪ/ *n.* passe-temps *m.* *invar.* **~-horse** *n.* (*fig.*) dada *m.*

hob-nob /'hɒbnɒb/ *v.i.* (*p.t.* **hob-nobbed**) **~ with,** frayer avec.

hock[1] /hɒk/ *n.* vin du Rhin *m.*

hock[2] /hɒk/ *v.t.* (*pawn*: *sl.*) mettre au clou.

hockey /'hɒkɪ/ *n.* hockey *m.*

hoe /həʊ/ *n.* binette *f.* ● *v.t.* (*pres. p.* **hoeing**) biner.

hog /hɒg/ *n.* cochon *m.* ● *v.t.* (*p.t.* **hogged**) (*fam.*) accaparer.

hoist /hɔɪst/ *v.t.* hisser. ● *n.* palan *m.*

hold[1] /həʊld/ *v.t.* (*p.t.* **held**) tenir; (*contain*) contenir; (*interest, breath, etc.*) retenir; (*possess*) avoir; (*believe*) maintenir. ● *v.i.* (*of rope, weather, etc.*) tenir. ● *n.* prise *f.* **get ~ of,** saisir; (*fig.*) trouver. **on ~,** en suspens. **~ back,** (*contain*) retenir; (*hide*) cacher. **~ down,** (*job*) garder; (*in struggle*) retenir. **~ on,** (*stand firm*) tenir bon; (*wait*) attendre. **~ on to,** (*keep*) garder; (*cling to*) se cramponner à. **~ one's tongue,** se taire. **~ out** *v.t.* (*offer*) offrir; *v.i.* (*resist*) tenir le coup. **~ (the line), please,** ne quittez pas. **~ up,** (*support*) soutenir; (*delay*) retarder; (*rob*) attaquer. **~-up** *n.* retard *m.*; (*of traffic*) bouchon *m.*; (*robbery*) hold-up *m. invar.* **not ~ with,** désapprouver. **~er** *n.* déten|teur, -trice *m., f.*; (*of post*) titulaire *m./f.*; (*for object*) support *m.*

hold[2] /həʊld/ *n.* (*of ship*) cale *f.*

holdall /'həʊldɔ:l/ *n.* (*bag*) fourre-tout *m. invar.*

holding /'həʊldɪŋ/ *n.* (*possession, land*) possession *f.* **~ company,** holding *m.*

hole /həʊl/ *n.* trou *m.* ● *v.t.* trouer.

holiday /'hɒlədeɪ/ *n.* vacances *f. pl.*; (*public*) jour férié *m.*; (*day off*) congé *m.* ● *v.i.* passer ses vacances. ● *a.* de vacances. **~-maker** *n.* vacanc|ier, -ière *m., f.*

holiness /'həʊlɪnɪs/ *n.* sainteté *f.*

holistic /həʊ'lɪstɪk/ *a.* holistique.

Holland /'hɒlənd/ *n.* Hollande *f.*

hollow /'hɒləʊ/ *a.* creux; (*fig.*) faux. ● *n.* creux *m.* ● *v.t.* creuser.

holly /'hɒlɪ/ *n.* houx *m.*

holster /'həʊlstə(r)/ *n.* étui de revolver *m.*

holy /'həʊlɪ/ *a.* (**-ier, -iest**) saint, sacré; (*water*) bénit. **H~ Ghost, H~ Spirit,** Saint-Esprit *m.*

homage /'hɒmɪdʒ/ *n.* hommage *m.*

home /həʊm/ *n.* maison *f.*, foyer *m.*; (*institution*) maison *f.*; (*for soldiers, workers*) foyer *m.*; (*country*) pays natal *m.* ● *a.* de la maison, du foyer; (*of family*) de famille; (*pol.*) national, intérieur; (*match, visit*) à domicile. ● *adv.* **(at) ~,** à la maison, chez soi. **come** *or* **go ~,** rentrer; (*from abroad*) rentrer dans son pays. **feel at ~ with,** être à l'aise avec. **H~ Counties,** région autour de Londres *f.* **~-made** *a.* (*food*) fait maison; (*clothes*) fait à la maison. **H~ Office,** ministère de l'Intérieur *m.* **H~ Secretary,** ministre de l'Intérieur *m.* **~ town,** ville natale *f.* **~ truth,** vérité bien sentie *f.* **~less** *a.* sans abri.

homeland /'həʊmlænd/ *n.* patrie *f.*

homely /'həʊmlɪ/ *a.* (**-ier, -iest**) simple; (*person*: *Amer.*) assez laid.

homesick /'həʊmsɪk/ *a.* **be ~,** avoir le mal du pays.

homeward /'həʊmwəd/ *a.* (*journey*) de retour.

homework /'həʊmwɜ:k/ *n.* devoirs *m. pl.*

homicide /'hɒmɪsaɪd/ *n.* homicide *m.*

homœopath|y /həʊmɪ'ɒpəθɪ/ *n.* homéopathie *f.* **~ic** *a.* homéopathique.

homogeneous /hɒmə'dʒi:nɪəs/ *a.* homogène.

homosexual /hɒmə'sekʃʊəl/ *a.* & *n.* homosexuel(le) (*m.* (*f.*)).

honest /'ɒnɪst/ *a.* honnête; (*frank*) franc. **~ly** *adv.* honnêtement; franchement. **~y** *n.* honnêteté *f.*

honey /'hʌnɪ/ *n.* miel *m.*; (*person*: *fam.*) chéri(e) *m.* (*f.*).

honeycomb /'hʌnɪkəʊm/ *n.* rayon de miel *m.*

honeymoon /'hʌnɪmu:n/ *n.* lune de miel *f.*

honk /hɒŋk/ *v.i.* klaxonner.

honorary /'ɒnərərɪ/ *a.* (*person*) honoraire; (*duties*) honorifique.

honour, (*Amer.*) **honor** /'ɒnə(r)/ *n.* honneur *m.* ● *v.t.* honorer. **~able** *a.* honorable.

hood /hʊd/ *n.* capuchon *m.*; (*car roof*) capote *f.*; (*car engine cover*: *Amer.*) capot *m.*

hoodlum /'hu:dləm/ *n.* voyou *m.*

hoodwink /'hʊdwɪŋk/ *v.t.* tromper.

hoof /hu:f/ *n.* (*pl.* **-fs**) sabot *m.*

hook /hʊk/ *n.* crochet *m.*; (*on garment*) agrafe *f.*; (*for fishing*) hameçon *m.* ● *v.t./i.* (s')accrocher; (*garment*) (s')agrafer. **off the ~**, tiré d'affaire; (*phone*) décroché.

hooked /hʊkt/ *a.* crochu. **~ on**, (*sl.*) adonné à.

hooker /'hʊkə(r)/ *n.* (*rugby*) talonneur *m.*; (*Amer.*, *sl.*) prostituée *f.*

hookey /'hʊkɪ/ *n.* **play ~**, (*Amer.*, *sl.*) faire l'école buissonnière.

hooligan /'hu:lɪgən/ *n.* houligan *m.*

hoop /hu:p/ *n.* (*toy etc.*) cerceau *m.*

hooray /hu:'reɪ/ *int.* & *n.* = **hurrah**.

hoot /hu:t/ *n.* (h)ululement *m.*; coup de klaxon *m.*; huée *f.* ● *v.i.* (*owl*) (h)ululer; (*of car*) klaxonner; (*jeer*) huer. **~er** *n.* klaxon *m.* (P.); (*of factory*) sirène *f.*

Hoover /'hu:və(r)/ *n.* (P.) aspirateur *m.* ● *v.t.* passer à l'aspirateur.

hop[1] /hɒp/ *v.i.* (*p.t.* **hopped**) sauter (à cloche-pied). ● *n.* saut *m.*; (*flight*) étape *f.* **~ in**, (*fam.*) monter. **~ it**, (*sl.*) décamper. **~ out**, (*fam.*) descendre.

hop[2] /hɒp/ *n.* **~(s)**, houblon *m.*

hope /həʊp/ *n.* espoir *m.* ● *v.t./i.* espérer. **~ for**, espérer (avoir). **I ~ so**, je l'espère. **~ful** *a.* encourageant. **be ~ful (that)**, avoir bon espoir (que). **~fully** *adv.* avec espoir; (*it is hoped*) on l'espère. **~less** *a.* sans espoir; (*useless*: *fig.*) nul. **~lessly** *adv.* sans espoir *m.*

hopscotch /'hɒpskɒtʃ/ *n.* marelle *f.*

horde /hɔ:d/ *n.* horde *f.*, foule *f.*

horizon /hə'raɪzn/ *n.* horizon *m.*

horizontal /hɒrɪ'zɒntl/ *a.* horizontal.

hormone /'hɔ:məʊn/ *n.* hormone *f.*

horn /hɔ:n/ *n.* corne *f.*; (*of car*) klaxon *m.* (P.); (*mus.*) cor *m.* ● *v.i.* **~ in**, (*sl.*) interrompre. **~y** *a.* (*hands*) calleux.

hornet /'hɔ:nɪt/ *n.* frelon *m.*

horoscope /'hɒrəskəʊp/ *n.* horoscope *m.*

horrible /'hɒrəbl/ *a.* horrible.

horrid /'hɒrɪd/ *a.* horrible.

horrific /hə'rɪfɪk/ *a.* horrifiant.

horr|or /'hɒrə(r)/ *n.* horreur *f.* ● *a.* (*film etc.*) d'épouvante. **~ify** *v.t.* horrifier.

hors-d'œuvre /ɔ:'dɜ:vrə/ *n.* hors-d'œuvre *m. invar.*

horse /hɔ:s/ *n.* cheval *m.* **~-chestnut** *n.* marron (d'Inde) *m.* **~-race** *n.* course de chevaux *f.* **~-radish** *n.* raifort *m.* **~ sense**, (*fam.*) bon sens *m.*

horseback /'hɔ:sbæk/ *n.* **on ~**, à cheval.

horseman /'hɔ:smən/ *n.* (*pl.* **-men**) cavalier *m.*

horsepower /'hɔ:spaʊə(r)/ *n.* (*unit*) cheval (vapeur) *m.*

horseshoe /'hɔ:sʃu:/ *n.* fer à cheval *m.*

horsy /'hɔ:sɪ/ *a.* (*face etc.*) chevalin.

horticultur|e /'hɔ:tɪkʌltʃə(r)/ *n.* horticulture *f.* **~al** /-'kʌltʃərəl/ *a.* horticole.

hose /həʊz/ *n.* (*tube*) tuyau *m.* ● *v.t.* arroser. **~-pipe** *n.* tuyau *m.*

hosiery /'həʊzɪərɪ/ *n.* bonneterie *f.*

hospice /'hɒspɪs/ *n.* hospice *m.*

hospit|able /hɒ'spɪtəbl/ *a.* hospitalier. **~ably** *adv.* avec hospitalité. **~ality** /-'tælətɪ/ *n.* hospitalité *f.*

hospital /'hɒspɪtl/ *n.* hôpital *m.*

host[1] /həʊst/ *n.* (*to guests*) hôte *m.*; (*on TV*) animateur *m.* **~ess** *n.* hôtesse *f.*

host[2] /həʊst/ *n.* **a ~ of**, une foule de.

host[3] /həʊst/ *n.* (*relig.*) hostie *f.*

hostage /'hɒstɪdʒ/ *n.* otage *m.*

hostel /'hɒstl/ *n.* foyer *m.* **(youth) ~**, auberge (de jeunesse) *f.*

hostil|e /'hɒstaɪl, *Amer.* /'hɒstl/ *a.* hostile. **~ity** /hɒ'stɪlətɪ/ *n.* hostilité *f.*

hot /hɒt/ *a.* (**hotter, hottest**) chaud; (*culin.*) épicé; (*news*) récent. **be** *or* **feel ~**, avoir chaud. **it is ~**, il fait chaud. ● *v.t./i.* (*p.t.* **hotted**) **~ up**, (*fam.*) chauffer. **~ dog**, hot-dog *m.* **~ line**, téléphone rouge *m.* **~ shot**, (*Amer.*, *sl.*) crack *m.* **~-water bot-**

tle, bouillotte *f.* **in ~ water,** (*fam.*) dans le pétrin. **~ly** *adv.* vivement.

hotbed /ˈhɒtbed/ *n.* foyer *m.*

hotchpotch /ˈhɒtʃpɒtʃ/ *n.* fatras *m.*

hotel /həʊˈtel/ *n.* hôtel *m.* **~ier** /-ɪeɪ/ *n.* hôtel|ier, -ière *m., f.*

hothead /ˈhɒthed/ *n.* tête brûlée *f.* **~ed** *a.* impétueux.

hotplate /ˈhɒtpleɪt/ *n.* plaque chauffante *f.*

hound /haʊnd/ *n.* chien courant *m.* ● *v.t.* poursuivre.

hour /ˈaʊə(r)/ *n.* heure *f.* **~ly** *a.* & *adv.* toutes les heures. **~ly rate,** tarif horaire *m.* **paid ~ly,** payé à l'heure.

house[1] /haʊs/ *n.* (*pl.* **-s** /ˈhaʊzɪz/) *n.* maison *f.*; (*theatre*) salle *f.*; (*pol.*) chambre *f.* **~-proud** *a.* méticuleux. **~-warming** *n.* pendaison de la crémaillère *f.*

house[2] /haʊz/ *v.t.* loger; (*of building*) abriter; (*keep*) garder.

housebreaking /ˈhaʊsbreɪkɪŋ/ *n.* cambriolage *m.*

housecoat /ˈhaʊskəʊt/ *n.* blouse *f.*, tablier *m.*

household /ˈhaʊshəʊld/ *n.* (*house, family*) ménage *m.* ● *a.* ménager. **~er** *n.* occupant(e) *m.* (*f.*); (*owner*) propriétaire *m./f.*

housekeep|er /ˈhaʊski:pə(r)/ *n.* gouvernante *f.* **~ing** *n.* ménage *m.*

housewife /ˈhaʊswaɪf/ *n.* (*pl.* **-wives**) ménagère *f.*

housework /ˈhaʊswɜ:k/ *n.* ménage *m.* travaux de ménage *m. pl.*

housing /ˈhaʊzɪŋ/ *n.* logement *m.* **~ association,** service de logement *m.* **~ development,** cité *f.*

hovel /ˈhɒvl/ *n.* taudis *m.*

hover /ˈhɒvə(r)/ *v.i.* (*bird, threat, etc.*) planer; (*loiter*) rôder.

hovercraft /ˈhɒvəkrɑ:ft/ *n.* aéroglisseur *m.*

how /haʊ/ *adv.* comment. **~ long/tall is . . .?,** quelle est la longueur/hauteur de . . .? **~ pretty!,** comme *or* que c'est joli! **~ about a walk?,** si on faisait une promenade? **~ are you?,** comment allez-vous? **~ do you do?,** (*introduction*) enchanté. **~ many?, ~ much?,** combien?

however /haʊˈevə(r)/ *adv.* de quelque manière que; (*nevertheless*) cependant. **~ small/delicate/***etc.* **it may be,** quelque petit/délicat/*etc.* que ce soit.

howl /haʊl/ *n.* hurlement *m.* ● *v.i.* hurler.

howler /ˈhaʊlə(r)/ *n.* (*fam.*) bévue *f.*

HP *abbr. see* hire-purchase.

hp *abbr. see* horsepower.

HQ *abbr. see* headquarters.

hub /hʌb/ *n.* moyeu *m.*; (*fig.*) centre *m.* **~-cap** *n.* enjoliveur *m.*

hubbub /ˈhʌbʌb/ *n.* vacarme *m.*

huddle /ˈhʌdl/ *v.i.* se blottir.

hue[1] /hju:/ *n.* (*colour*) teinte *f.*

hue[2] /hju:/ *n.* **~ and cry,** clameur *f.*

huff /hʌf/ *n.* **in a ~,** fâché, vexé.

hug /hʌg/ *v.t.* (*p.t.* **hugged**) serrer dans ses bras; (*keep close to*) serrer. ● *n.* étreinte *f.*

huge /hju:dʒ/ *a.* énorme. **~ly** *adv.* énormément.

hulk /hʌlk/ *n.* (*of ship*) épave *f.*; (*person*) mastodonte *m.*

hull /hʌl/ *n.* (*of ship*) coque *f.*

hullo /həˈləʊ/ *int.* & *n.* = **hallo.**

hum /hʌm/ *v.t./i.* (*p.t.* **hummed**) (*person*) fredonner; (*insect*) bourdonner; (*engine*) vrombir. ● *n.* bourdonnement *m.*; vrombissement *m.* **~ and haw,** hésiter.

human /ˈhju:mən/ *a.* humain. ● *n.* être humain *m.* **~itarian** /-mænɪˈteərɪən/ *a.* humanitaire.

humane /hju:ˈmeɪn/ *a.* humain, plein d'humanité.

humanity /hju:ˈmænətɪ/ *n.* humanité *f.*

humbl|e /ˈhʌmbl/ *a.* (**-er, -est**) humble. ● *v.t.* humilier. **~y** *adv.* humblement.

humbug /ˈhʌmbʌg/ *n.* (*false talk*) hypocrisie *f.*

humdrum /ˈhʌmdrʌm/ *a.* monotone.

humid /ˈhju:mɪd/ *a.* humide. **~ity** /-ˈmɪdətɪ/ *n.* humidité *f.*

humiliat|e /hju:ˈmɪlɪeɪt/ *v.t.* humilier. **~ion** /-ˈeɪʃn/ *n.* humiliation *f.*

humility /hju:ˈmɪlətɪ/ *n.* humilité *f.*

humorist /ˈhju:mərɪst/ *n.* humoriste *m./f.*

hum|our, (*Amer.*) **hum|or** /ˈhju:mə(r)/ *n.* humour *m.*; (*mood*) humeur *f.* ● *v.t.* ménager. **~orous** *a.* humoristique; (*person*) plein d'humour. **~orously** *adv.* avec humour.

hump /hʌmp/ *n.* bosse *f.* ● *v.t.* voûter. **the ~,** (*sl.*) le cafard.

hunch[1] /hʌntʃ/ *v.t.* voûter.

hunch[2] /hʌntʃ/ *n.* petite idée *f.*

hunchback /ˈhʌntʃbæk/ *n.* bossu(e) *m.* (*f.*).

hundred /ˈhʌndrəd/ *a.* & *n.* cent (*m.*). **~s of,** des centaines de. **~fold** *a.* centuple; *adv.* au centuple. **~th** *a.* & *n.* centième (*m./f.*).

hundredweight /ˈhʌndrədweɪt/ *n.* 50.8 kg.; (*Amer.*) 45.36 kg.

hung /hʌŋ/ *see* hang.

Hungar|y /ˈhʌŋgərɪ/ *n.* Hongrie *f.* **~ian** /-ˈgeərɪən/ *a.* & *n.* hongrois(e) (*m.* (*f.*)).

hunger /ˈhʌŋgə(r)/ *n.* faim *f.* ● *v.i.* **~ for,** avoir faim de. **~-strike** *n.* grève de la faim *f.*

hungr|y /ˈhʌŋgrɪ/ *a.* (**-ier, -iest**) affamé. **be ~y,** avoir faim. **~ily** *adv.* avidement.

hunk /hʌŋk/ *n.* gros morceau *m.*

hunt /hʌnt/ *v.t./i.* chasser. ● *n.* chasse *f.* **~ for,** chercher. **~er** *n.* chasseur *m.* **~ing** *n.* chasse *f.*

hurdle /ˈhɜ:dl/ *n.* (*sport*) haie *f.*; (*fig.*) obstacle *m.*

hurl /hɜ:l/ *v.t.* lancer.

hurrah, hurray /hʊˈrɑ:, hʊˈreɪ/ *int.* & *n.* hourra (*m.*).

hurricane /ˈhʌrɪkən, *Amer.* ˈhʌrɪkeɪn/ *n.* ouragan *m.*

hurried /ˈhʌrɪd/ *a.* précipité. **~ly** *adv.* précipitamment.

hurry /ˈhʌrɪ/ *v.i.* se dépêcher, se presser. ● *v.t.* presser, activer. ● *n.* hâte *f.* **in a ~,** pressé.

hurt /hɜ:t/ *v.t./i.* (*p.t.* **hurt**) faire mal (à); (*injure, offend*) blesser. ● *a.* blessé. ● *n.* mal *m.* **~ful** *a.* blessant.

hurtle /ˈhɜ:tl/ *v.t.* lancer. ● *v.i.* **~ along,** avancer à toute vitesse.

husband /ˈhʌzbənd/ *n.* mari *m.*

hush /hʌʃ/ *v.t.* faire taire. ● *n.* silence *m.* **~-hush** *a.* (*fam.*) ultra-secret. **~ up,** (*news etc.*) étouffer.

husk /hʌsk/ *n.* (*of grain*) enveloppe *f.*

husky /ˈhʌskɪ/ *a.* (**-ier, -iest**) (*hoarse*) rauque; (*burly*) costaud. ● *n.* chien de traîneau *m.*

hustle /ˈhʌsl/ *v.t.* (*push, rush*) bousculer. ● *v.i.* (*work busily*: *Amer.*) se démener. ● *n.* bousculade *f.* **~ and bustle,** agitation *f.*

hut /hʌt/ *n.* cabane *f.*

hutch /hʌtʃ/ *n.* clapier *m.*

hyacinth /ˈhaɪəsɪnθ/ *n.* jacinthe *f.*

hybrid /ˈhaɪbrɪd/ *a.* & *n.* hybride (*m.*).

hydrangea /haɪˈdreɪndʒə/ *n.* hortensia *m.*

hydrant /ˈhaɪdrənt/ *n.* (**fire**) **~,** bouche d'incendie *f.*

hydraulic /haɪˈdrɔ:lɪk/ *a.* hydraulique.

hydroelectric /haɪdrəʊɪˈlektrɪk/ *a.* hydro-électrique.

hydrofoil /ˈhaɪdrəʊfɔɪl/ *n.* hydroptère *m.*

hydrogen /ˈhaɪdrədʒən/ *n.* hydrogène *m.* **~ bomb,** bombe à hydrogène *f.*

hyena /haɪˈi:nə/ *n.* hyène *f.*

hygiene /ˈhaɪdʒi:n/ *n.* hygiène *f.*

hygienic /haɪˈdʒi:nɪk/ *a.* hygiénique.

hymn /hɪm/ *n.* cantique *m.*, hymne *m.*

hype /haɪp/ *n.* tapage publicitaire *m.* ● *v.t.* faire du tapage autour de.

hyper- /ˈhaɪpə(r)/ *pref.* hyper-.

hypermarket /ˈhaɪpəmɑ:kɪt/ *n.* hypermarché *m.*

hyphen /ˈhaɪfn/ *n.* trait d'union *m.* **~ate** *v.t.* mettre un trait d'union à.

hypno|sis /hɪpˈnəʊsɪs/ *n.* hypnose *f.* **~tic** /-ˈnɒtɪk/ *a.* hypnotique.

hypnot|ize /ˈhɪpnətaɪz/ *v.t.* hypnotiser. **~ism** *n.* hypnotisme *m.*

hypochondriac /haɪpəˈkɒndrɪæk/ *n.* malade imaginaire *m./f.*

hypocrisy /hɪˈpɒkrəsɪ/ *n.* hypocrisie *f.*

hypocrit|e /ˈhɪpəkrɪt/ *n.* hypocrite *m./f.* **~ical** /-ˈkrɪtɪkl/ *a.* hypocrite.

hypodermic /haɪpəˈdɜ:mɪk/ *a.* hypodermique. ● *n.* seringue hypodermique *f.*

hypothermia /haɪpəˈθɜ:mɪə/ *n.* hypothermie *f.*

hypothe|sis /haɪˈpɒθəsɪs/ *n.* (*pl.* **-theses** /-si:z/) hypothèse *f.* **~tical** /-əˈθetɪkl/ *a.* hypothétique.

hyster|ia /hɪˈstɪərɪə/ *n.* hystérie *f.* **~ical** /-erɪkl/ *a.* hystérique; (*person*) surexcité.

hysterics /hɪˈsterɪks/ *n. pl.* crise de nerfs *or* de rire *f.*

I

I /aɪ/ *pron.* je, j'*; (*stressed*) moi.

ice /aɪs/ *n.* glace *f.*; (*on road*) verglas *m.* ● *v.t.* (*cake*) glacer. ● *v.i.* **~ (up),** (*window*) se givrer; (*river*) geler. **~-cream** *n.* glace *f.* **~-cube** *n.* glaçon *m.* **~ hockey,** hockey sur glace *m.* **~ lolly,** glace (*sur bâtonnet*) *f.* **~ rink,** patinoire *f.* **~ skate,** patin à glace *m.*

iceberg /ˈaɪsbɜ:g/ *n.* iceberg *m.*

icebox /'aɪsbɒks/ *n.* (*Amer.*) réfrigérateur *m.*
Iceland /'aɪslənd/ *n.* Islande *f.* **~er** *n.* Islandais(e) *m.* (*f.*). **~ic** /-'lændɪk/ *a.* islandais; *n.* (*lang.*) islandais *m.*
icicle /'aɪsɪkl/ *n.* glaçon *m.*
icing /'aɪsɪŋ/ *n.* (*sugar*) glace *f.*
icon /'aɪkɒn/ *n.* icône *f.*
icy /'aɪsɪ/ *a.* (**-ier, -iest**) (*hands, wind*) glacé; (*road*) verglacé; (*manner, welcome*) glacial.
idea /aɪ'dɪə/ *n.* idée *f.*
ideal /aɪ'dɪəl/ *a.* idéal. ● *n.* idéal *m.* **~ize** *v.t.* idéaliser. **~ly** *adv.* idéalement.
idealis|t /aɪ'dɪəlɪst/ *n.* idéaliste *m./f.* **~m** /-zəm/ *n.* idéalisme *m.* **~tic** /-'lɪstɪk/ *a.* idéaliste.
identical /aɪ'dentɪkl/ *a.* identique.
identif|y /aɪ'dentɪfaɪ/ *v.t.* identifier. ● *v.i.* **~y with,** s'identifier à. **~ication** /-ɪ'keɪʃn/ *n.* identification *f.*; (*papers*) une pièce d'identité.
identikit /aɪ'dentɪkɪt/ *n.* **~ picture,** portrait-robot *m.*
identity /aɪ'dentətɪ/ *n.* identité *f.*
ideolog|y /aɪdɪ'ɒlədʒɪ/ *n.* idéologie *f.* **~ical** /-ə'lɒdʒɪkl/ *a.* idéologique.
idiocy /'ɪdɪəsɪ/ *n.* idiotie *f.*
idiom /'ɪdɪəm/ *n.* expression idiomatique *f.*; (*language*) idiome *m.* **~atic** /-'mætɪk/ *a.* idiomatique.
idiosyncrasy /ɪdɪə'sɪŋkrəsɪ/ *n.* particularité *f.*
idiot /'ɪdɪət/ *n.* idiot(e) *m.* (*f.*). **~ic** /-'ɒtɪk/ *a.* idiot.
idle /'aɪdl/ *a.* (**-er, -est**) désœuvré, oisif; (*lazy*) paresseux; (*unemployed*) sans travail; (*machine*) au repos; (*fig.*) vain. ● *v.i.* (*engine*) tourner au ralenti. ● *v.t.* **~ away,** gaspiller. **~ness** *n.* oisiveté *f.* **~r** /-ə(r)/ *n.* oisi|f, -ve *m.*, *f.*
idol /'aɪdl/ *n.* idole *f.* **~ize** *v.t.* idolâtrer.
idyllic /ɪ'dɪlɪk, *Amer.* aɪ'dɪlɪk/ *a.* idyllique.
i.e. *abbr.* c'est-à-dire.
if /ɪf/ *conj.* si.
igloo /'ɪglu:/ *n.* igloo *m.*
ignite /ɪg'naɪt/ *v.t./i.* (s')enflammer.
ignition /ɪg'nɪʃn/ *n.* (*auto.*) allumage *m.* **~ key,** clé de contact *f.* **~ (switch),** contact *m.*
ignoran|t /'ɪgnərənt/ *a.* ignorant (**of,** de). **~ce** *n.* ignorance *f.* **~tly** *adv.* par ignorance.
ignore /ɪg'nɔ:(r)/ *v.t.* ne faire *or* prêter aucune attention à; (*person in street etc.*) faire semblant de ne pas voir; (*facts*) ne pas tenir compte de.
ilk /ɪlk/ *n.* (*kind: fam.*) acabit *m.*
ill /ɪl/ *a.* malade; (*bad*) mauvais. ● *adv.* mal. ● *n.* mal *m.* **~-advised** *a.* peu judicieux. **~ at ease,** mal à l'aise. **~-bred** *a.* mal élevé. **~-fated** *a.* malheureux. **~ feeling,** ressentiment *m.* **~-gotten** *a.* mal acquis. **~-natured** *a.* désagréable. **~-treat** *v.t.* maltraiter. **~ will,** malveillance *f.*
illegal /ɪ'li:gl/ *a.* illégal.
illegible /ɪ'ledʒəbl/ *a.* illisible.
illegitima|te /ɪlɪ'dʒɪtɪmət/ *a.* illégitime. **~cy** *n.* illégitimité *f.*
illitera|te /ɪ'lɪtərət/ *a.* & *n.* illettré(e) (*m.* (*f.*)), analphabète *m./f.* **~cy** *n.* analphabétisme *m.*
illness /'ɪlnɪs/ *n.* maladie *f.*
illogical /ɪ'lɒdʒɪkl/ *a.* illogique.
illuminat|e /ɪ'lu:mɪneɪt/ *v.t.* éclairer; (*decorate with lights*) illuminer. **~ion** /-'neɪʃn/ *n.* éclairage *m.*; illumination *f.*
illusion /ɪ'lu:ʒn/ *n.* illusion *f.*
illusory /ɪ'lu:sərɪ/ *a.* illusoire.
illustrat|e /'ɪləstreɪt/ *v.t.* illustrer. **~ion** /-'streɪʃn/ *n.* illustration *f.* **~ive** /-ətɪv/ *a.* qui illustre.
illustrious /ɪ'lʌstrɪəs/ *a.* illustre.
image /'ɪmɪdʒ/ *n.* image *f.* **(public) ~,** (*of firm, person*) image de marque *f.* **~ry** /-ərɪ/ *n.* images *f. pl.*
imaginary /ɪ'mædʒɪnərɪ/ *a.* imaginaire.
imaginat|ion /ɪmædʒɪ'neɪʃn/ *n.* imagination *f.* **~ive** /ɪ'mædʒɪnətɪv/ *a.* plein d'imagination.
imagin|e /ɪ'mædʒɪn/ *v.t.* (*picture to o.s.*) (s')imaginer; (*suppose*) imaginer. **~able** *a.* imaginable.
imbalance /ɪm'bæləns/ *n.* déséquilibre *m.*
imbecile /'ɪmbəsi:l/ *n.* & *a.* imbécile (*m./f.*).
imbue /ɪm'bju:/ *v.t.* imprégner.
imitat|e /'ɪmɪteɪt/ *v.t.* imiter. **~ion** /-'teɪʃn/ *n.* imitation *f.* **~or** *n.* imita|teur, -trice *m.*, *f.*
immaculate /ɪ'mækjʊlət/ *a.* (*room, dress, etc.*) impeccable.
immaterial /ɪmə'tɪərɪəl/ *a.* sans importance (**to,** pour; **that,** que).
immature /ɪmə'tjʊə(r)/ *a.* pas mûr; (*person*) immature.
immediate /ɪ'mi:dɪət/ *a.* immédiat. **~ly** *adv.* immédiatement; *conj.* dès que.

immens|e /ɪ'mens/ *a.* immense. **~ely** *adv.* extrêmement, immensément. **~ity** *n.* immensité *f.*

immers|e /ɪ'mɜ:s/ *v.t.* plonger, immerger. **~ion** /-ɜ:ʃn/ *n.* immersion *f.* **~ion heater,** chauffe-eau (électrique) *m. invar.*

immigr|ate /'ɪmɪgreɪt/ *v.i.* immigrer. **~ant** *n.* & *a.* immigré(e) (*m.* (*f.*)); (*newly-arrived*) immigrant(e) (*m.* (*f.*)). **~ation** /-'greɪʃn/ *n.* immigration *f.* **go through ~ation,** passer le contrôle des passeports.

imminen|t /'ɪmɪnənt/ *a.* imminent. **~ce** *n.* imminence *f.*

immobil|e /ɪ'məʊbaɪl, *Amer.* ɪ'məʊbl/ *a.* immobile. **~ize** /-əlaɪz/ *v.t.* immobiliser.

immoderate /ɪ'mɒdərət/ *a.* immodéré.

immoral /ɪ'mɒrəl/ *a.* immoral. **~ity** /ɪmə'ræləti/ *n.* immoralité *f.*

immortal /ɪ'mɔ:tl/ *a.* immortel. **~ity** /-'tæləti/ *n.* immortalité *f.* **~ize** *v.t.* immortaliser.

immun|e /ɪ'mju:n/ *a.* immunisé (**from, to,** contre). **~ity** *n.* immunité *f.*

immuniz|e /'ɪmjʊnaɪz/ *v.t.* immuniser. **~ation** /-'zeɪʃn/ *n.* immunisation *f.*

imp /ɪmp/ *n.* lutin *m.*

impact /'ɪmpækt/ *n.* impact *m.*

impair /ɪm'peə(r)/ *v.t.* détériorer.

impart /ɪm'pɑ:t/ *v.t.* communiquer, transmettre.

impartial /ɪm'pɑ:ʃl/ *a.* impartial. **~ity** /-ɪ'æləti/ *n.* impartialité *f.*

impassable /ɪm'pɑ:səbl/ *a.* (*barrier etc.*) infranchissable; (*road*) impraticable.

impasse /'æmpɑ:s, *Amer.* 'ɪmpæs/ *n.* impasse *f.*

impassioned /ɪm'pæʃnd/ *n.* passionné.

impassive /ɪm'pæsɪv/ *a.* impassible.

impatien|t /ɪm'peɪʃnt/ *a.* impatient. **get ~t,** s'impatienter. **~ce** *n.* impatience *f.* **~tly** *adv.* impatiemment.

impeccable /ɪm'pekəbl/ *a.* impeccable.

impede /ɪm'pi:d/ *v.t.* gêner.

impediment /ɪm'pedɪmənt/ *n.* obstacle *m.* **(speech) ~,** défaut d'élocution *m.*

impel /ɪm'pel/ *v.t.* (*p.t.* **impelled**) pousser, forcer (**to do,** à faire).

impending /ɪm'pendɪŋ/ *a.* imminent.

impenetrable /ɪm'penɪtrəbl/ *a.* impénétrable.

imperative /ɪm'perətɪv/ *a.* nécessaire; (*need etc.*) impérieux. ● *n.* (*gram.*) impératif *m.*

imperceptible /ɪmpə'septəbl/ *a.* imperceptible.

imperfect /ɪm'pɜ:fɪkt/ *a.* imparfait; (*faulty*) défectueux. **~ion** /-ə'fekʃn/ *n.* imperfection *f.*

imperial /ɪm'pɪərɪəl/ *a.* impérial; (*measure*) légal (au Royaume-Uni). **~ism** *n.* impérialisme *m.*

imperil /ɪm'perəl/ *v.t.* (*p.t.* **imperilled**) mettre en péril.

imperious /ɪm'pɪərɪəs/ *a.* impérieux.

impersonal /ɪm'pɜ:sənl/ *a.* impersonnel.

impersonat|e /ɪm'pɜ:səneɪt/ *v.t.* se faire passer pour; (*mimic*) imiter. **~ion** /-'neɪʃn/ *n.* imitation *f.* **~or** *n.* imita|teur, -trice *m., f.*

impertinen|t /ɪm'pɜ:tɪnənt/ *a.* impertinent. **~ce** *n.* impertinence *f.* **~tly** *adv.* avec impertinence.

impervious /ɪm'pɜ:vɪəs/ *a.* **~ to,** imperméable à.

impetuous /ɪm'petʃʊəs/ *a.* impétueux.

impetus /'ɪmpɪtəs/ *n.* impulsion *f.*

impinge /ɪm'pɪndʒ/ *v.i.* **~ on,** affecter; (*encroach*) empiéter sur.

impish /'ɪmpɪʃ/ *a.* espiègle.

implacable /ɪm'plækəbl/ *a.* implacable.

implant /ɪm'plɑ:nt/ *v.t.* implanter. ● *n.* implant *m.*

implement[1] /'ɪmplɪmənt/ *n.* (*tool*) outil *m.*; (*utensil*) ustensile *m.*

implement[2] /'ɪmplɪment/ *v.t.* exécuter, mettre en pratique.

implicat|e /'ɪmplɪkeɪt/ *v.t.* impliquer. **~ion** /-'keɪʃn/ *n.* implication *f.*

implicit /ɪm'plɪsɪt/ *a.* (*implied*) implicite; (*unquestioning*) absolu.

implore /ɪm'plɔ:(r)/ *v.t.* implorer.

impl|y /ɪm'plaɪ/ *v.t.* (*assume, mean*) impliquer; (*insinuate*) laisser entendre. **~ied** *a.* implicite.

impolite /ɪmpə'laɪt/ *a.* impoli.

imponderable /ɪm'pɒndərəbl/ *a.* & *n.* impondérable (*m.*).

import[1] /ɪm'pɔ:t/ *v.t.* importer. **~ation** /-'teɪʃn/ *n.* importation *f.* **~er** *n.* importa|teur, -trice *m., f.*

import[2] /'ɪmpɔ:t/ *n.* (*article*) importation *f.*; (*meaning*) sens *m.*

importan|t /ɪm'pɔ:tnt/ *a.* important. **~ce** *n.* importance *f.*

impos|e /ɪm'pəʊz/ *v.t.* imposer. ● *v.i.* **~e on,** abuser de l'amabilité de. **~ition** /-ə'zɪʃn/ *n.* imposition *f.*; (*fig.*) dérangement *m.*

imposing /ɪm'pəʊzɪŋ/ *a.* imposant.

impossib|le /ɪm'pɒsəbl/ *a.* impossible. **~ility** /-'bɪlətɪ/ *n.* impossibilité *f.*

impostor /ɪm'pɒstə(r)/ *n.* imposteur *m.*

impoten|t /'ɪmpətənt/ *a.* impuissant. **~ce** *n.* impuissance *f.*

impound /ɪm'paʊnd/ *v.t.* confisquer, saisir.

impoverish /ɪm'pɒvərɪʃ/ *v.t.* appauvrir.

impracticable /ɪm'præktɪkəbl/ *a.* impraticable.

impractical /ɪm'præktɪkl/ *a.* peu pratique.

imprecise /ɪmprɪ'saɪs/ *a.* imprécis.

impregnable /ɪm'pregnəbl/ *a.* imprenable; (*fig.*) inattaquable.

impregnate /'ɪmpregneɪt/ *v.t.* imprégner (**with,** de).

impresario /ɪmprɪ'sɑ:rɪəʊ/ *n.* (*pl.* **-os**) impresario *m.*

impress /ɪm'pres/ *v.t.* impressionner; (*imprint*) imprimer. **~ on s.o.,** faire comprendre à qn.

impression /ɪm'preʃn/ *n.* impression *f.* **~able** *a.* impressionnable.

impressive /ɪm'presɪv/ *a.* impressionnant.

imprint[1] /'ɪmprɪnt/ *n.* empreinte *f.*

imprint[2] /ɪm'prɪnt/ *v.t.* imprimer.

imprison /ɪm'prɪzn/ *v.t.* emprisonner. **~ment** *n.* emprisonnement *m.*, prison *f.*

improbab|le /ɪm'prɒbəbl/ *a.* (*not likely*) improbable; (*incredible*) invraisemblable. **~ility** /-'bɪlətɪ/ *n.* improbabilité *f.*

impromptu /ɪm'prɒmptju:/ *a. & adv.* impromptu.

improp|er /ɪm'prɒpə(r)/ *a.* inconvenant, indécent; (*wrong*) incorrect. **~riety** /-ə'praɪətɪ/ *n.* inconvenance *f.*

improve /ɪm'pru:v/ *v.t./i.* (s')améliorer. **~ment** *n.* amélioration *f.*

improvis|e /'ɪmprəvaɪz/ *v.t./i.* improviser. **~ation** /-'zeɪʃn/ *n.* improvisation *f.*

imprudent /ɪm'pru:dnt/ *a.* imprudent.

impuden|t /'ɪmpjʊdənt/ *a.* impudent. **~ce** *n.* impudence *f.*

impulse /'ɪmpʌls/ *n.* impulsion *f.* **on ~,** sur un coup de tête.

impulsive /ɪm'pʌlsɪv/ *a.* impulsif. **~ly** *adv.* par impulsion.

impunity /ɪm'pju:nətɪ/ *n.* impunité *f.* **with ~,** impunément.

impur|e /ɪm'pjʊə(r)/ *a.* impur. **~ity** *n.* impureté *f.*

impute /ɪm'pju:t/ *v.t.* imputer.

in /ɪn/ *prep.* dans, à, en. ● *adv.* (*inside*) dedans; (*at home*) là, à la maison; (*in fashion*) à la mode. **in the box/garden,** dans la boîte/le jardin. **in Paris/school,** à Paris/l'école. **in town,** en ville. **in the country,** à la campagne. **in English,** en anglais. **in India,** en Inde. **in Japan,** au Japon. **in a firm manner/voice,** d'une manière/voix ferme. **in blue,** en bleu. **in ink,** à l'encre. **in uniform,** en uniforme. **in a skirt,** en jupe. **in a whisper,** en chuchotant. **in a loud voice,** d'une voix forte. **in winter,** en hiver. **in spring,** au printemps. **in an hour,** (*at end of*) au bout d'une heure. **in an hour('s time),** dans une heure. **in (the space of) an hour,** en une heure. **in doing,** en faisant. **in the evening,** le soir. **one in ten,** un sur dix. **in between,** entre les deux; (*time*) entretemps. **the best in,** le meilleur de. **we are in for,** on va avoir. **in-laws** *n. pl.* (*fam.*) beaux-parents *m. pl.* **~-patient** *n.* malade hospitalisé(e) *m.*(*f.*). **the ins and outs of,** les tenants et aboutissants de. **in so far as,** dans la mesure où.

inability /ɪnə'bɪlətɪ/ *n.* incapacité *f.* (**to do,** de faire).

inaccessible /ɪnæk'sesəbl/ *a.* inaccessible.

inaccurate /ɪn'ækjərət/ *a.* inexact.

inaction /ɪn'ækʃn/ *n.* inaction *f.*

inactiv|e /ɪn'æktɪv/ *a.* inactif. **~ity** /-'tɪvətɪ/ *n.* inaction *f.*

inadequa|te /ɪn'ædɪkwət/ *a.* insuffisant. **~cy** *n.* insuffisance *f.*

inadmissible /ɪnəd'mɪsəbl/ *a.* inadmissible.

inadvertently /ɪnəd'vɜ:təntlɪ/ *adv.* par mégarde.

inadvisable /ɪnəd'vaɪzəbl/ *a.* déconseillé, pas recommandé.

inane /ɪ'neɪn/ *a.* inepte.

inanimate /ɪn'ænɪmət/ *a.* inanimé.

inappropriate /ɪnə'prəʊprɪət/ *a.* inopportun; (*term*) inapproprié.

inarticulate /ɪnɑː'tɪkjʊlət/ *a.* qui a du mal à s'exprimer.
inasmuch as /ɪnəz'mʌtʃəz/ *adv.* en ce sens que; (*because*) vu que.
inattentive /ɪnə'tentɪv/ *a.* inattentif.
inaudible /ɪn'ɔːdɪbl/ *a.* inaudible.
inaugural /ɪ'nɔːgjʊrəl/ *a.* inaugural.
inaugurat|e /ɪ'nɔːgjʊreɪt/ *v.t.* (*open, begin*) inaugurer; (*person*) investir. **~ion** /-'reɪʃn/ *n.* inauguration *f.*; investiture *f.*
inauspicious /ɪnɔː'spɪʃəs/ *a.* peu propice.
inborn /ɪn'bɔːn/ *a.* inné.
inbred /ɪn'bred/ *a.* (*inborn*) inné.
inc. *abbr.* (*incorporated*) S.A.
incalculable /ɪn'kælkjʊləbl/ *a.* incalculable.
incapable /ɪn'keɪpəbl/ *a.* incapable.
incapacit|y /ɪnkə'pæsətɪ/ *n.* incapacité *f.* **~ate** *v.t.* rendre incapable (*de travailler etc.*).
incarcerate /ɪn'kɑːsəreɪt/ *v.t.* incarcérer.
incarnat|e /ɪn'kɑːneɪt/ *a.* incarné. **~ion** /-'neɪʃn/ *n.* incarnation *f.*
incendiary /ɪn'sendɪərɪ/ *a.* incendiaire. ● *n.* (*bomb*) bombe incendiaire *f.*
incense[1] /'ɪnsens/ *n.* encens *m.*
incense[2] /ɪn'sens/ *v.t.* mettre en fureur.
incentive /ɪn'sentɪv/ *n.* motivation *f.*; (*payment*) prime (d'encouragement) *f.*
inception /ɪn'sepʃn/ *n.* début *m.*
incessant /ɪn'sesnt/ *a.* incessant. **~ly** *adv.* sans cesse.
incest /'ɪnsest/ *n.* inceste *m.* **~uous** /ɪn'sestjʊəs/ *a.* incestueux.
inch /ɪntʃ/ *n.* pouce *m.* (*=2.54 cm.*). ● *v.i.* avancer doucement.
incidence /'ɪnsɪdəns/ *n.* fréquence *f.*
incident /'ɪnsɪdənt/ *n.* incident *m.*; (*in play, film, etc.*) épisode *m.*
incidental /ɪnsɪ'dentl/ *a.* accessoire. **~ly** *adv.* accessoirement; (*by the way*) à propos.
incinerat|e /ɪn'sɪnəreɪt/ *v.t.* incinérer. **~or** *n.* incinérateur *m.*
incipient /ɪn'sɪpɪənt/ *a.* naissant.
incision /ɪn'sɪʒn/ *n.* incision *f.*
incisive /ɪn'saɪsɪv/ *a.* incisif.
incite /ɪn'saɪt/ *v.t.* inciter, pousser. **~ment** *n.* incitation *f.*
inclement /ɪn'klemənt/ *a.* inclément, rigoureux.
inclination /ɪnklɪ'neɪʃn/ *n.* (*propensity, bowing*) inclination *f.*
incline[1] /ɪn'klaɪn/ *v.t./i.* incliner. **be ~d to,** avoir tendance à.
incline[2] /'ɪnklaɪn/ *n.* pente *f.*
inclu|de /ɪn'kluːd/ *v.t.* comprendre, inclure. **~ding** *prep.* (y) compris. **~sion** *n.* inclusion *f.*
inclusive /ɪn'kluːsɪv/ *a. & adv.* inclus, compris. **be ~ of,** comprendre, inclure.
incognito /ɪnkɒg'niːtəʊ/ *adv.* incognito.
incoherent /ɪnkəʊ'hɪərənt/ *a.* incohérent.
income /'ɪnkʌm/ *n.* revenu *m.* **~ tax,** impôt sur le revenu *m.*
incoming /'ɪnkʌmɪŋ/ *a.* (*tide*) montant; (*tenant etc.*) nouveau.
incomparable /ɪn'kɒmprəbl/ *a.* incomparable.
incompatible /ɪnkəm'pætəbl/ *a.* incompatible.
incompeten|t /ɪn'kɒmpɪtənt/ *a.* incompétent. **~ce** *n.* incompétence *f.*
incomplete /ɪnkəm'pliːt/ *a.* incomplet.
incomprehensible /ɪnkɒmprɪ'hensəbl/ *a.* incompréhensible.
inconceivable /ɪnkən'siːvəbl/ *a.* inconcevable.
inconclusive /ɪnkən'kluːsɪv/ *a.* peu concluant.
incongruous /ɪn'kɒŋgrʊəs/ *a.* déplacé, incongru.
inconsequential /ɪnkɒnsɪ'kwenʃl/ *a.* sans importance.
inconsiderate /ɪnkən'sɪdərət/ *a.* (*person*) qui ne se soucie pas des autres; (*act*) irréfléchi.
inconsisten|t /ɪnkən'sɪstənt/ *a.* (*treatment*) sans cohérence, inconséquent; (*argument*) contradictoire; (*performance*) irrégulier. **~t with,** incompatible avec. **~cy** *n.* inconséquence *f.*, contradiction *f.*; irrégularité *f.*
inconspicuous /ɪnkən'spɪkjʊəs/ *a.* peu en évidence.
incontinen|t /ɪn'kɒntɪnənt/ *a.* incontinent. **~ce** *n.* incontinence *f.*
inconvenien|t /ɪnkən'viːnɪənt/ *a.* incommode, peu pratique; (*time*) mal choisi. **be ~t for,** ne pas convenir à. **~ce** *n.* dérangement *m.*; (*drawback*) inconvénient *m.*; *v.t.* déranger.
incorporate /ɪn'kɔːpəreɪt/ *v.t.* incorporer; (*include*) contenir.
incorrect /ɪnkə'rekt/ *a.* inexact.

incorrigible /ɪn'kɒrɪdʒəbl/ *a.* incorrigible.
incorruptible /ɪnkə'rʌptəbl/ *a.* incorruptible.
increas|e[1] /ɪn'kri:s/ *v.t./i.* augmenter. **~ing** *a.* croissant. **~ingly** *adv.* de plus en plus.
increase[2] /'ɪnkri:s/ *n.* augmentation *f.* (**in, of,** de). **be on the ~,** augmenter.
incredible /ɪn'kredəbl/ *a.* incroyable.
incredulous /ɪn'kredjʊləs/ *a.* incrédule.
increment /'ɪnkrəmənt/ *n.* augmentation *f.*
incriminat|e /ɪn'krɪmɪneɪt/ *v.t.* incriminer. **~ing** *a.* compromettant.
incubat|e /'ɪnkjʊbeɪt/ *v.t.* (*eggs*) couver. **~ion** /-'beɪʃn/ *n.* incubation *f.* **~or** *n.* couveuse *f.*
inculcate /'ɪnkʌlkeɪt/ *v.t.* inculquer.
incumbent /ɪn'kʌmbənt/ *n.* (*pol., relig.*) titulaire *m./f.*
incur /ɪn'kɜ:(r)/ *v.t.* (*p.t.* **incurred**) encourir; (*debts*) contracter; (*anger*) s'exposer à.
incurable /ɪn'kjʊərəbl/ *a.* incurable.
incursion /ɪn'kɜ:ʃn/ *n.* incursion *f.*
indebted /ɪn'detɪd/ *a.* **~ to s.o.,** redevable à qn. (**for,** de).
indecen|t /ɪn'di:snt/ *a.* indécent. **~cy** *n.* indécence *f.*
indecision /ɪndɪ'sɪʒn/ *n.* indécision *f.*
indecisive /ɪndɪ'saɪsɪv/ *a.* indécis; (*ending*) peu concluant.
indeed /ɪn'di:d/ *adv.* en effet, vraiment.
indefensible /ɪndɪ'fensɪbl/ *a.* indéfendable.
indefinable /ɪndɪ'faɪnəbl/ *a.* indéfinissable.
indefinite /ɪn'defɪnɪt/ *a.* indéfini; (*time*) indéterminé. **~ly** *adv.* indéfiniment.
indelible /ɪn'deləbl/ *a.* indélébile.
indemni|fy /ɪn'demnɪfaɪ/ *v.t.* (*compensate*) indemniser (**for,** de); (*safeguard*) garantir. **~ty** /-nətɪ/ *n.* indemnité *f.*; garantie *f.*
indent /ɪn'dent/ *v.t.* (*text*) renfoncer. **~ation** /-'teɪʃn/ *n.* (*outline*) découpure *f.*
independen|t /ɪndɪ'pendənt/ *a.* indépendant. **~ce** *n.* indépendance *f.* **~tly** *adv.* de façon indépendante. **~tly of,** indépendamment de.
indescribable /ɪndɪ'skraɪbəbl/ *a.* indescriptible.
indestructible /ɪndɪ'strʌktəbl/ *a.* indestructible.
indeterminate /ɪndɪ'tɜ:mɪnət/ *a.* indéterminé.
index /'ɪndeks/ *n.* (*pl.* **indexes**) (*figure*) indice *m.*; (*in book*) index *m.*; (*in library*) catalogue *m.* ● *v.t.* classer. **~ card,** fiche *f.* **~ finger** index *m.* **~-linked** *a.* indexé.
India /'ɪndɪə/ *n.* Inde *f.* **~n** *a.* & *n.* indien(ne) (*m.* (*f.*)). **~n summer,** été de la Saint-Martin *m.*
indicat|e /'ɪndɪkeɪt/ *v.t.* indiquer. **~ion** /-'keɪʃn/ *n.* indication *f.* **~or** *n.* (*device*) indicateur *m.*; (*on vehicle*) clignotant *m.*; (*board*) tableau *m.*
indicative /ɪn'dɪkətɪv/ *a.* indicatif. ● *n.* (*gram.*) indicatif *m.*
indict /ɪn'daɪt/ *v.t.* accuser. **~ment** *n.* accusation *f.*
indifferen|t /ɪn'dɪfrənt/ *a.* indifférent; (*not good*) médiocre. **~ce** *n.* indifférence *f.*
indigenous /ɪn'dɪdʒɪnəs/ *a.* indigène.
indigest|ion /ɪndɪ'dʒestʃən/ *n.* indigestion *f.* **~ible** /-təbl/ *a.* indigeste.
indign|ant /ɪn'dɪgnənt/ *a.* indigné. **~ation** /-'neɪʃn/ *n.* indignation *f.*
indigo /'ɪndɪgəʊ/ *n.* indigo *m.*
indirect /ɪndɪ'rekt/ *a.* indirect. **~ly** *adv.* indirectement.
indiscr|eet /ɪndɪ'skri:t/ *a.* indiscret; (*not wary*) imprudent. **~etion** /-eʃn/ *n.* indiscrétion *f.*
indiscriminate /ɪndɪ'skrɪmɪnət/ *a.* qui manque de discernement; (*random*) fait au hasard. **~ly** *adv.* sans discernement; au hasard.
indispensable /ɪndɪ'spensəbl/ *a.* indispensable.
indispos|ed /ɪndɪ'spəʊzd/ *a.* indisposé, souffrant. **~ition** /-ə'zɪʃn/ *n.* indisposition *f.*
indisputable /ɪndɪ'spju:təbl/ *a.* incontestable.
indistinct /ɪndɪ'stɪŋkt/ *a.* indistinct.
indistinguishable /ɪndɪ'stɪŋgwɪʃəbl/ *a.* indifférenciable.
individual /ɪndɪ'vɪdʒʊəl/ *a.* individuel. ● *n.* individu *m.* **~ist** *n.* individualiste *m./f.* **~ity** /-'ælətɪ/ *n.* individualité *f.* **~ly** *adv.* individuellement.
indivisible /ɪndɪ'vɪzəbl/ *a.* indivisible.
indoctrinat|e /ɪn'dɒktrɪneɪt/ *v.t.* endoctriner. **~ion** /-'neɪʃn/ *n.* endoctrinement *m.*

indolen|t /ˈɪndələnt/ *a.* indolent. **~ce** *n.* indolence *f.*

indomitable /ɪnˈdɒmɪtəbl/ *a.* indomptable.

Indonesia /ɪndəʊˈniːzɪə/ *n.* Indonésie *f.* **~n** *a.* & *n.* indonésien(ne) (*m.* (*f.*)).

indoor /ˈɪndɔː(r)/ *a.* (*clothes etc.*) d'intérieur; (*under cover*) couvert. **~s** /ɪnˈdɔːz/ *adv.* à l'intérieur.

induce /ɪnˈdjuːs/ *v.t.* (*influence*) persuader; (*cause*) provoquer. **~ment** *n.* encouragement *m.*

induct /ɪnˈdʌkt/ *v.t.* investir, installer; (*mil., Amer.*) incorporer.

indulge /ɪnˈdʌldʒ/ *v.t.* (*desires*) satisfaire; (*person*) se montrer indulgent pour, gâter. ● *v.i.* **~ in,** se livrer à, s'offrir.

indulgen|t /ɪnˈdʌldʒənt/ *a.* indulgent. **~ce** *n.* indulgence *f.*; (*treat*) gâterie *f.*

industrial /ɪnˈdʌstrɪəl/ *a.* industriel; (*unrest etc.*) ouvrier; (*action*) revendicatif; (*accident*) du travail. **~ist** *n.* industriel(le) *m.*(*f.*). **~ized** *a.* industrialisé.

industrious /ɪnˈdʌstrɪəs/ *a.* travailleur, appliqué.

industry /ˈɪndəstrɪ/ *n.* industrie *f.*; (*zeal*) application *f.*

inebriated /ɪˈniːbrɪeɪtɪd/ *a.* ivre.

inedible /ɪnˈedɪbl/ *a.* (*food*) immangeable.

ineffective /ɪnɪˈfektɪv/ *a.* inefficace; (*person*) incapable.

ineffectual /ɪnɪˈfektʃʊəl/ *a.* inefficace; (*person*) incapable.

inefficien|t /ɪnɪˈfɪʃnt/ *a.* inefficace; (*person*) incompétent. **~cy** *n.* inefficacité *f.*; incompétence *f.*

ineligible /ɪnˈelɪdʒəbl/ *a.* inéligible. **be ~ for,** ne pas avoir droit à.

inept /ɪˈnept/ *a.* (*absurd*) inepte; (*out of place*) mal à propos.

inequality /ɪnɪˈkwɒlətɪ/ *n.* inégalité *f.*

inert /ɪˈnɜːt/ *a.* inerte.

inertia /ɪˈnɜːʃə/ *n.* inertie *f.*

inescapable /ɪnɪˈskeɪpəbl/ *a.* inéluctable.

inevitabl|e /ɪnˈevɪtəbl/ *a.* inévitable. **~y** *adv.* inévitablement.

inexact /ɪnɪgˈzækt/ *a.* inexact.

inexcusable /ɪnɪkˈskjuːzəbl/ *a.* inexcusable.

inexhaustible /ɪnɪgˈzɔːstəbl/ *a.* inépuisable.

inexorable /ɪnˈeksərəbl/ *a.* inexorable.

inexpensive /ɪnɪkˈspensɪv/ *a.* bon marché *invar.*, pas cher.

inexperience /ɪnɪkˈspɪərɪəns/ *n.* inexpérience *f.* **~d** *a.* inexpérimenté.

inexplicable /ɪnɪkˈsplɪkəbl/ *a.* inexplicable.

inextricable /ɪnɪkˈstrɪkəbl/ *a.* inextricable.

infallib|le /ɪnˈfæləbl/ *a.* infaillible. **~ility** /-ˈbɪlətɪ/ *n.* infaillibilité *f.*

infam|ous /ˈɪnfəməs/ *a.* infâme. **~y** *n.* infamie *f.*

infan|t /ˈɪnfənt/ *n.* (*baby*) nourrisson *m.*; (*at school*) petit(e) enfant *m.*(*f.*). **~cy** *n.* petite enfance *f.*; (*fig.*) enfance *f.*

infantile /ˈɪnfəntaɪl/ *a.* infantile.

infantry /ˈɪnfəntrɪ/ *n.* infanterie *f.*

infatuat|ed /ɪnˈfætʃʊeɪtɪd/ *a.* **~ed with,** engoué de. **~ion** /-ˈeɪʃn/ *n.* engouement *m.*, béguin *m.*

infect /ɪnˈfekt/ *v.t.* infecter. **~ s.o. with,** communiquer à qn. **~ion** /-kʃn/ *n.* infection *f.*

infectious /ɪnˈfekʃəs/ *a.* (*med.*) infectieux; (*fig.*) contagieux.

infer /ɪnˈfɜː(r)/ *v.t.* (*p.t.* **inferred**) déduire. **~ence** /ˈɪnfərəns/ *n.* déduction *f.*

inferior /ɪnˈfɪərɪə(r)/ *a.* inférieur (**to,** à); (*work, product*) de qualité inférieure. ● *n.* inférieur(e) *m.* (*f.*). **~ity** /-ˈɒrətɪ/ *n.* infériorité *f.*

infernal /ɪnˈfɜːnl/ *a.* infernal. **~ly** *adv.* (*fam.*) atrocement.

inferno /ɪnˈfɜːnəʊ/ *n.* (*pl.* **-os**) (*hell*) enfer *m.*; (*blaze*) incendie *m.*

infertil|e /ɪnˈfɜːtaɪl, *Amer.* ɪnˈfɜːtl/ *a.* infertile. **~ity** /-əˈtɪlətɪ/ *n.* infertilité *f.*

infest /ɪnˈfest/ *v.t.* infester.

infidelity /ɪnfɪˈdelətɪ/ *n.* infidélité *f.*

infighting /ˈɪnfaɪtɪŋ/ *n.* querelles internes *f. pl.*

infiltrat|e /ˈɪnfɪltreɪt/ *v.t./i.* s'infiltrer (dans). **~ion** /-ˈtreɪʃn/ *n.* infiltration *f.*

infinite /ˈɪnfɪnɪt/ *a.* infini. **~ly** *adv.* infiniment.

infinitesimal /ɪnfɪnɪˈtesɪml/ *a.* infinitésimal.

infinitive /ɪnˈfɪnətɪv/ *n.* infinitif *m.*

infinity /ɪnˈfɪnətɪ/ *n.* infinité *f.*

infirm /ɪnˈfɜːm/ *a.* infirme. **~ity** *n.* infirmité *f.*

infirmary /ɪnˈfɜːmərɪ/ *n.* hôpital *m.*; (*sick-bay*) infirmerie *f.*

inflam|e /ɪnˈfleɪm/ *v.t.* enflammer. **~mable** /-æməbl/ *a.* inflammable.

~mation /-ə'meɪʃn/ *n.* inflammation *f.*

inflammatory /ɪn'flæmətrɪ/ *a.* incendiaire.

inflat|e /ɪn'fleɪt/ *v.t.* (*balloon, prices, etc.*) gonfler. **~able** *a.* gonflable.

inflation /ɪn'fleɪʃn/ *n.* inflation *f.* **~ary** *a.* inflationniste.

inflection /ɪn'flekʃn/ *n.* inflexion *f.*; (*suffix: gram.*) désinence *f.*

inflexible /ɪn'fleksəbl/ *a.* inflexible.

inflict /ɪn'flɪkt/ *v.t.* infliger (**on,** à).

influence /'ɪnflʊəns/ *n.* influence *f.* ● *v.t.* influencer. **under the ~,** (*drunk: fam.*) en état d'ivresse.

influential /ɪnflʊ'enʃl/ *a.* influent.

influenza /ɪnflʊ'enzə/ *n.* grippe *f.*

influx /'ɪnflʌks/ *n.* afflux *m.*

inform /ɪn'fɔ:m/ *v.t.* informer (**of,** de). **keep ~ed,** tenir au courant. **~ant** *n.* informa|teur, -trice *m., f.* **~er** *n.* indica|teur, -trice *m., f.*

informal /ɪn'fɔ:ml/ *a.* (*simple*) simple, sans cérémonie; (*unofficial*) officieux; (*colloquial*) familier. **~ity** /-'mælətɪ/ *n.* simplicité *f.* **~ly** *adv.* sans cérémonie.

information /ɪnfə'meɪʃn/ *n.* renseignement(s) *m.* (*pl.*), information(s) *f.* (*pl.*). **some ~,** un renseignement. **~ technology,** informatique *f.*

informative /ɪn'fɔ:mətɪv/ *a.* instructif.

infra-red /ɪnfrə'red/ *a.* infrarouge.

infrastructure /'ɪnfrəstrʌktʃə(r)/ *n.* infrastructure *f.*

infrequent /ɪn'fri:kwənt/ *a.* peu fréquent. **~ly** *adv.* rarement.

infringe /ɪn'frɪndʒ/ *v.t.* contrevenir à. **~ on,** empiéter sur. **~ment** *n.* infraction *f.*

infuriate /ɪn'fjʊərɪeɪt/ *v.t.* exaspérer, rendre furieux.

infus|e /ɪn'fju:z/ *v.t.* infuser. **~ion** /-ʒn/ *n.* infusion *f.*

ingen|ious /ɪn'dʒi:nɪəs/ *a.* ingénieux. **~uity** /-ɪ'nju:ətɪ/ *n.* ingéniosité *f.*

ingenuous /ɪn'dʒenjʊəs/ *a.* ingénu.

ingot /'ɪŋgət/ *n.* lingot *m.*

ingrained /ɪn'greɪnd/ *a.* enraciné.

ingratiate /ɪn'greɪsɪeɪt/ *v.t.* **~ o.s. with,** gagner les bonnes grâces de.

ingratitude /ɪn'grætɪtju:d/ *n.* ingratitude *f.*

ingredient /ɪn'gri:dɪənt/ *n.* ingrédient *m.*

inhabit /ɪn'hæbɪt/ *v.t.* habiter. **~able** *a.* habitable. **~ant** *n.* habitant(e) *m.* (*f.*).

inhale /ɪn'heɪl/ *v.t.* inhaler; (*tobacco smoke*) avaler. **~r** *n.* spray *m.*

inherent /ɪn'hɪərənt/ *a.* inhérent. **~ly** *adv.* en soi, intrinsèquement.

inherit /ɪn'herɪt/ *v.t.* hériter (de). **~ance** *n.* héritage *m.*

inhibit /ɪn'hɪbɪt/ *v.t.* (*hinder*) gêner; (*prevent*) empêcher. **be ~ed,** avoir des inhibitions. **~ion** /-'bɪʃn/ *n.* inhibition *f.*

inhospitable /ɪnhɒ'spɪtəbl/ *a.* inhospitalier.

inhuman /ɪn'hju:mən/ *a.* (*brutal, not human*) inhumain. **~ity** /-'mænətɪ/ *n.* inhumanité *f.*

inhumane /ɪnhju:'meɪn/ *a.* (*unkind*) inhumain.

inimitable /ɪ'nɪmɪtəbl/ *a.* inimitable.

iniquit|ous /ɪ'nɪkwɪtəs/ *a.* inique. **~y** /-ətɪ/ *n.* iniquité *f.*

initial /ɪ'nɪʃl/ *n.* initiale *f.* ● *v.t.* (*p.t.* **initialled**) parapher. ● *a.* initial. **~ly** *adv.* initialement.

initiat|e /ɪ'nɪʃɪeɪt/ *v.t.* (*begin*) amorcer; (*scheme*) lancer; (*person*) initier (**into,** à). **~ion** /-'eɪʃn/ *n.* initiation *f.*; (*start*) amorce *f.*

initiative /ɪ'nɪʃətɪv/ *n.* initiative *f.*

inject /ɪn'dʒekt/ *v.t.* injecter; (*new element: fig.*) insuffler. **~ion** /-kʃn/ *n.* injection *f.*, piqûre *f.*

injunction /ɪn'dʒʌŋkʃn/ *n.* (*court order*) ordonnance *f.*

injure /'ɪndʒə(r)/ *v.t.* blesser; (*do wrong to*) nuire à.

injury /'ɪndʒərɪ/ *n.* (*physical*) blessure *f.*; (*wrong*) préjudice *m.*

injustice /ɪn'dʒʌstɪs/ *n.* injustice *f.*

ink /ɪŋk/ *n.* encre *f.* **~-well** *n.* encrier *m.* **~y** *a.* taché d'encre.

inkling /'ɪŋklɪŋ/ *n.* petite idée *f.*

inland /'ɪnlənd/ *a.* l'intérieur. ● *adv.* /ɪn'lænd/ à l'intérieur. **I~ Revenue,** fisc *m.*

in-laws /'ɪnlɔ:z/ *n. pl.* (*parents*) beaux-parents *m. pl.*; (*family*) belle-famille *f.*

inlay[1] /ɪn'leɪ/ *v.t.* (*p.t.* **inlaid**) incruster.

inlay[2] /'ɪnleɪ/ *n.* incrustation *f.*

inlet /'ɪnlet/ *n.* bras de mer *m.*; (*techn.*) arrivée *f.*

inmate /'ɪnmeɪt/ *n.* (*of asylum*) interné(e) *m.* (*f.*); (*of prison*) détenu(e) *m.* (*f.*).

inn /ɪn/ *n.* auberge *f.*

innards /'ɪnədz/ *n. pl.* (*fam.*) entrailles *f. pl.*
innate /ɪ'neɪt/ *a.* inné.
inner /'ɪnə(r)/ *a.* intérieur, interne; (*fig.*) profond, intime. **~ city**, quartiers défavorisés *m. pl.* **~most** *a.* le plus profond. **~ tube**, chambre à air *f.*
innings /'ɪnɪŋz/ *n. invar.* tour de batte *m.*; (*fig.*) tour *m.*
innkeeper /'ɪnki:pə(r)/ *n.* aubergiste *m./f.*
innocen|t /'ɪnəsnt/ *a.* & *n.* innocent(e) (*m.* (*f.*)). **~ce** *n.* innocence *f.*
innocuous /ɪ'nɒkjʊəs/ *a.* inoffensif.
innovat|e /'ɪnəveɪt/ *v.i.* innover. **~ion** /-'veɪʃn/ *n.* innovation *f.* **~or** *n.* innova|teur, -trice *m.*, *f.*
innuendo /ɪnju:'endəʊ/ *n.* (*pl.* **-oes**) insinuation *f.*
innumerable /ɪ'nju:mərəbl/ *a.* innombrable.
inoculat|e /ɪ'nɒkjʊleɪt/ *v.t.* inoculer. **~ion** /-'leɪʃn/ *n.* inoculation *f.*
inoffensive /ɪnə'fensɪv/ *a.* inoffensif.
inoperative /ɪn'ɒpərətɪv/ *a.* inopérant.
inopportune /ɪn'ɒpətju:n/ *a.* inopportun.
inordinate /ɪ'nɔ:dɪnət/ *a.* excessif. **~ly** *adv.* excessivement.
input /'ɪnpʊt/ *n.* (*data*) données *f. pl.*; (*computer process*) entrée *f.*; (*power: electr.*) énergie *f.*
inquest /'ɪnkwest/ *n.* enquête *f.*
inquire /ɪn'kwaɪə(r)/ *v.t./i.* = **enquire.**
inquiry /ɪn'kwaɪərɪ/ *n.* enquête *f.*
inquisition /ɪnkwɪ'zɪʃn/ *n.* inquisition *f.*
inquisitive /ɪn'kwɪzətɪv/ *a.* curieux; (*prying*) indiscret.
inroad /'ɪnrəʊd/ *n.* incursion *f.*
insan|e /ɪn'seɪn/ *a.* fou. **~ity** /ɪn'sænətɪ/ *n.* folie *f.*, démence *f.*
insanitary /ɪn'sænɪtrɪ/ *a.* insalubre, malsain.
insatiable /ɪn'seɪʃəbl/ *a.* insatiable.
inscri|be /ɪn'skraɪb/ *v.t.* inscrire; (*book*) dédicacer. **~ption** /-ɪpʃn/ *n.* inscription *f.*; dédicace *f.*
inscrutable /ɪn'skru:təbl/ *a.* impénétrable.
insect /'ɪnsekt/ *n.* insecte *m.*
insecticide /ɪn'sektɪsaɪd/ *n.* insecticide *m.*
insecur|e /ɪnsɪ'kjʊə(r)/ *a.* (*not firm*) peu solide; (*unsafe*) peu sûr; (*worried*) anxieux. **~ity** *n.* insécurité *f.*
insemination /ɪnsemɪ'neɪʃn/ *n.* insémination *f.*
insensible /ɪn'sensəbl/ *a.* insensible; (*unconscious*) inconscient.
insensitive /ɪn'sensətɪv/ *a.* insensible.
inseparable /ɪn'seprəbl/ *a.* inséparable.
insert[1] /ɪn'sɜ:t/ *v.t.* insérer. **~ion** /-ʃn/ *n.* insertion *f.*
insert[2] /'ɪnsɜ:t/ *n.* insertion *f.*; (*advertising*) encart *m.*
in-service /'ɪnsɜ:vɪs/ *a.* (*training*) continu.
inshore /ɪn'ʃɔ:(r)/ *a.* côtier.
inside /ɪn'saɪd/ *n.* intérieur *m.* **~(s)**, (*fam.*) entrailles *f. pl.* ● *a.* intérieur. ● *adv.* à l'intérieur, dedans. ● *prep.* à l'intérieur de; (*of time*) en moins de. **~ out**, à l'envers; (*thoroughly*) à fond.
insidious /ɪn'sɪdɪəs/ *a.* insidieux.
insight /'ɪnsaɪt/ *n.* (*perception*) perspicacité *f.*; (*idea*) aperçu *m.*
insignia /ɪn'sɪgnɪə/ *n. pl.* insignes *m. pl.*
insignificant /ɪnsɪg'nɪfɪkənt/ *a.* insignifiant.
insincer|e /ɪnsɪn'sɪə(r)/ *a.* peu sincère. **~ity** /-'serətɪ/ *n.* manque de sincérité *m.*
insinuat|e /ɪn'sɪnjʊeɪt/ *v.t.* insinuer. **~ion** /-'eɪʃn/ *n.* insinuation *f.*
insipid /ɪn'sɪpɪd/ *a.* insipide.
insist /ɪn'sɪst/ *v.t./i.* insister. **~ on**, affirmer; (*demand*) exiger. **~ on doing**, insister pour faire.
insisten|t /ɪn'sɪstənt/ *a.* insistant. **~ce** *n.* insistance *f.* **~tly** *adv.* avec insistance.
insole /'ɪnsəʊl/ *n.* (*separate*) semelle *f.*
insolen|t /'ɪnsələnt/ *a.* insolent. **~ce** *n.* insolence *f.*
insoluble /ɪn'sɒljʊbl/ *a.* insoluble.
insolvent /ɪn'sɒlvənt/ *a.* insolvable.
insomnia /ɪn'sɒmnɪə/ *n.* insomnie *f.* **~c** /-ɪæk/ *n.* insomniaque *m./f.*
inspect /ɪn'spekt/ *v.t.* inspecter; (*tickets*) contrôler. **~ion** /-kʃn/ *n.* inspection *f.*; contrôle *m.* **~or** *n.* inspec|teur, -trice *m.*, *f.*; (*on train, bus*) contrôleu|r, -se *m.*, *f.*
inspir|e /ɪn'spaɪə(r)/ *v.t.* inspirer. **~ation** /-ə'reɪʃn/ *n.* inspiration *f.*
instability /ɪnstə'bɪlətɪ/ *n.* instabilité *f.*
install /ɪn'stɔ:l/ *v.t.* installer. **~ation** /-ə'leɪʃn/ *n.* installation *f.*

instalment /ɪn'stɔ:lmənt/ *n.* (*payment*) acompte *m.*, versement *m.*; (*of serial*) épisode *m.*

instance /'ɪnstəns/ *n.* exemple *m.*; (*case*) cas *m.* **for ~,** par exemple. **in the first ~,** en premier lieu.

instant /'ɪnstənt/ *a.* immédiat; (*food*) instantané. ● *n.* instant *m.* **~ly** *adv.* immédiatement.

instantaneous /ɪnstən'teɪnɪəs/ *a.* instantané.

instead /ɪn'sted/ *adv.* plutôt. **~ of doing,** au lieu de faire. **~ of s.o.,** à la place de qn.

instep /'ɪnstep/ *n.* cou-de-pied *m.*

instigat|e /'ɪnstɪgeɪt/ *v.t.* provoquer. **~ion** /-'geɪʃn/ *n.* instigation *f.* **~or** *n.* instiga|teur, -trice *m., f.*

instil /ɪn'stɪl/ *v.t.* (*p.t.* **instilled**) inculquer; (*inspire*) insuffler.

instinct /'ɪnstɪŋkt/ *n.* instinct *m.* **~ive** /ɪn'stɪŋktɪv/ *a.* instinctif.

institut|e /'ɪnstɪtju:t/ *n.* institut *m.* ● *v.t.* instituer; (*inquiry etc.*) entamer. **~ion** /-'tju:ʃn/ *n.* institution *f.*; (*school, hospital*) établissement *m.*

instruct /ɪn'strʌkt/ *v.t.* instruire; (*order*) ordonner. **~ s.o. in sth.,** enseigner qch. à qn. **~ s.o. to do,** ordonner à qn. de faire. **~ion** /-kʃn/ *n.* instruction *f.* **~ions** /-kʃnz/ *n. pl.* (*for use*) mode d'emploi *m.* **~ive** *a.* instructif. **~or** *n.* professeur *m.*; (*skiing, driving*) moni|teur, -trice *m., f.*

instrument /'ɪnstrʊmənt/ *n.* instrument *m.* **~ panel,** tableau de bord *m.*

instrumental /ɪnstrʊ'mentl/ *a.* instrumental. **be ~ in,** contribuer à. **~ist** *n.* instrumentaliste *m./f.*

insubordinat|e /ɪnsə'bɔ:dɪnət/ *a.* insubordonné. **~ion** /-'neɪʃn/ *n.* insubordination *f.*

insufferable /ɪn'sʌfrəbl/ *a.* intolérable, insupportable.

insufficient /ɪnsə'fɪʃnt/ *a.* insuffisant. **~ly** *adv.* insuffisamment.

insular /'ɪnsjʊlə(r)/ *a.* insulaire; (*mind, person: fig.*) borné.

insulat|e /'ɪnsjʊleɪt/ *v.t.* (*room, wire, etc.*) isoler. **~ing tape,** chatterton *m.* **~ion** /-'leɪʃn/ *n.* isolation *f.*

insulin /'ɪnsjʊlɪn/ *n.* insuline *f.*

insult[1] /ɪn'sʌlt/ *v.t.* insulter.

insult[2] /'ɪnsʌlt/ *n.* insulte *f.*

insuperable /ɪn'sju:prəbl/ *a.* insurmontable.

insur|e /ɪn'ʃʊə(r)/ *v.t.* assurer. **~e that,** (*ensure: Amer.*) s'assurer que. **~ance** *n.* assurance *f.*

insurmountable /ɪnsə'maʊntəbl/ *a.* insurmontable.

insurrection /ɪnsə'rekʃn/ *n.* insurrection *f.*

intact /ɪn'tækt/ *a.* intact.

intake /'ɪnteɪk/ *n.* admission(s) *f.* (*pl.*); (*techn.*) prise *f.*

intangible /ɪn'tændʒəbl/ *a.* intangible.

integral /'ɪntɪgrəl/ *a.* intégral. **be an ~ part of,** faire partie intégrante de.

integrat|e /'ɪntɪgreɪt/ *v.t./i.* (s')intégrer. **~ion** /-'greɪʃn/ *n.* intégration *f.*; (*racial*) déségrégation *f.*

integrity /ɪn'tegrətɪ/ *n.* intégrité *f.*

intellect /'ɪntəlekt/ *n.* intelligence *f.* **~ual** /-'lektʃʊəl/ *a.* & *n.* intellectuel(le) (*m.* (*f.*)).

intelligen|t /ɪn'telɪdʒənt/ *a.* intelligent. **~ce** *n.* intelligence *f.*; (*mil.*) renseignements *m. pl.* **~tly** *adv.* intelligemment.

intelligentsia /ɪntelɪ'dʒentsɪə/ *n.* intelligentsia *f.*

intelligible /ɪn'telɪdʒəbl/ *a.* intelligible.

intemperance /ɪn'tempərəns/ *n.* (*drunkenness*) ivrognerie *f.*

intend /ɪn'tend/ *v.t.* destiner. **~ to do,** avoir l'intention de faire. **~ed** *a.* (*deliberate*) intentionnel; (*planned*) prévu; *n.* (*future spouse: fam.*) promis(e) *m.* (*f.*).

intens|e /ɪn'tens/ *a.* intense; (*person*) passionné. **~ely** *adv.* (*to live etc.*) intensément; (*very*) extrêmement. **~ity** *n.* intensité *f.*

intensif|y /ɪn'tensɪfaɪ/ *v.t.* intensifier. **~ication** /-ɪ'keɪʃn/ *n.* intensification *f.*

intensive /ɪn'tensɪv/ *a.* intensif. **in ~ care,** en réanimation.

intent /ɪn'tent/ *n.* intention *f.* ● *a.* attentif. **~ on,** absorbé par. **~ on doing,** résolu à faire. **~ly** *adv.* attentivement.

intention /ɪn'tenʃn/ *n.* intention *f.* **~al** *a.* intentionnel.

inter /ɪn'tɜ:(r)/ *v.t.* (*p.t.* **interred**) enterrer.

inter- /'ɪntə(r)/ *pref.* inter-.

interact /ɪntə'rækt/ *v.i.* avoir une action réciproque. **~ion** /-kʃn/ *n.* interaction *f.*

intercede /ɪntə'si:d/ *v.i.* intercéder.

intercept /ɪntə'sept/ *v.t.* intercepter. **~ion** /-pʃn/ *n.* interception *f.*
interchange /'ɪntətʃeɪndʒ/ *n.* (*road junction*) échangeur *m.*
interchangeable /ɪntə'tʃeɪndʒəbl/ *a.* interchangeable.
intercom /'ɪntəkɒm/ *n.* interphone *m.*
interconnected /ɪntəkə'nektɪd/ *a.* (*facts, events, etc.*) lié.
intercourse /'ɪntəkɔ:s/ *n.* (*sexual, social*) rapports *m. pl.*
interest /'ɪntrəst/ *n.* intérêt *m.*; (*stake*) intérêts *m. pl.* ● *v.t.* intéresser. **~ rates**, taux d'intérêt *m. pl.* **~ed** *a.* intéressé. **be ~ed in**, s'intéresser à. **~ing** *a.* intéressant.
interface /'ɪntəfeɪs/ *n.* (*comput.*) interface *f.*; (*fig.*) zone de rencontre *f.*
interfer|e /ɪntə'fɪə(r)/ *v.i.* se mêler des affaires des autres. **~e in**, s'ingérer dans. **~e with**, (*plans*) créer un contretemps avec; (*work*) s'immiscer dans; (*radio*) faire des interférences avec; (*lock*) toucher à. **~ence** *n.* ingérence *f.*; (*radio*) parasites *m. pl.*
interim /'ɪntərɪm/ *n.* intérim *m.* ● *a.* intérimaire.
interior /ɪn'tɪərɪə(r)/ *n.* intérieur *m.* ● *a.* intérieur.
interjection /ɪntə'dʒekʃn/ *n.* interjection *f.*
interlinked /ɪntə'lɪŋkt/ *a.* lié.
interlock /ɪntə'lɒk/ *v.t./i.* (*techn.*) (s')emboîter, (s')enclencher.
interloper /'ɪntələʊpə(r)/ *n.* intrus(e) *m.* (*f.*).
interlude /'ɪntəlu:d/ *n.* intervalle *m.*; (*theatre, mus.*) intermède *m.*
intermarr|iage /ɪntə'mærɪdʒ/ *n.* mariage entre membres de races différentes *m.* **~y** *v.i.* se marier (entre eux).
intermediary /ɪntə'mi:dɪərɪ/ *a.* & *n.* intermédiaire (*m./f.*).
intermediate /ɪntə'mi:dɪət/ *a.* intermédiaire; (*exam etc.*) moyen.
interminable /ɪn'tɜ:mɪnəbl/ *a.* interminable.
intermission /ɪntə'mɪʃn/ *n.* pause *f.*; (*theatre etc.*) entracte *m.*
intermittent /ɪntə'mɪtnt/ *a.* intermittent. **~ly** *adv.* par intermittence.
intern[1] /ɪn'tɜ:n/ *v.t.* interner. **~ee** /-'ni:/ *n.* interné(e) *m.* (*f.*). **~ment** *n.* internement *m.*
intern[2] /'ɪntɜ:n/ *n.* (*doctor*: *Amer.*) interne *m./f.*
internal /ɪn'tɜ:nl/ *a.* interne; (*domestic*: *pol.*) intérieur. **I~ Revenue**, (*Amer.*) fisc *m.* **~ly** *adv.* intérieurement.
international /ɪntə'næʃnəl/ *a.* & *n.* international (*m.*).
interplay /'ɪntəpleɪ/ *n.* jeu *m.*, interaction *f.*
interpolate /ɪn'tɜ:pəleɪt/ *v.t.* interpoler.
interpret /ɪn'tɜ:prɪt/ *v.t.* interpréter. ● *v.i.* faire l'interprète. **~ation** /-'teɪʃn/ *n.* interprétation *f.* **~er** *n.* interprète *m./f.*
interrelated /ɪntərɪ'leɪtɪd/ *a.* en corrélation, lié.
interrogat|e /ɪn'terəgeɪt/ *v.t.* interroger. **~ion** /-'geɪʃn/ *n.* interrogation *f.* (**of**, de); (*session of questions*) interrogatoire *m.*
interrogative /ɪntə'rɒgətɪv/ *a.* & *n.* interrogatif (*m.*).
interrupt /ɪntə'rʌpt/ *v.t.* interrompre. **~ion** /-pʃn/ *n.* interruption *f.*
intersect /ɪntə'sekt/ *v.t./i.* (*lines, roads*) (se) couper. **~ion** /-kʃn/ *n.* intersection *f.*; (*crossroads*) croisement *m.*
interspersed /ɪntə'spɜ:st/ *a.* (*scattered*) dispersé. **~ with**, parsemé de.
intertwine /ɪntə'twaɪn/ *v.t./i.* (s')entrelacer.
interval /'ɪntəvl/ *n.* intervalle *m.*; (*theatre*) entracte *m.* **at ~s**, par intervalles.
interven|e /ɪntə'vi:n/ *v.i.* intervenir; (*of time*) s'écouler (**between**, entre); (*happen*) survenir. **~tion** /-'venʃn/ *n.* intervention *f.*
interview /'ɪntəvju:/ *n.* (*with reporter*) interview *f.*; (*for job etc.*) entrevue *f.* ● *v.t.* interviewer. **~er** *n.* interviewer *m.*
intestin|e /ɪn'testɪn/ *n.* intestin *m.* **~al** *a.* intestinal.
intima|te[1] /'ɪntɪmət/ *a.* intime; (*detailed*) profond. **~cy** *n.* intimité *f.* **~tely** *adv.* intimement.
intimate[2] /'ɪntɪmeɪt/ *v.t.* (*state*) annoncer; (*imply*) suggérer.
intimidat|e /ɪn'tɪmɪdeɪt/ *v.t.* intimider. **~ion** /-'deɪʃn/ *n.* intimidation *f.*
into /'ɪntu:, *unstressed* 'ɪntə/ *prep.* (*put, go, fall, etc.*) dans; (*divide, translate, etc.*) en.

intolerable /ɪn'tɒlərəbl/ *a.* intolérable.

intoleran|t /ɪn'tɒlərənt/ *a.* intolérant. **~ce** *n.* intolérance *f.*

intonation /ɪntə'neɪʃn/ *n.* intonation *f.*

intoxicat|e /ɪn'tɒksɪkeɪt/ *v.t.* enivrer. **~ed** *a.* ivre. **~ion** /-'keɪʃn/ *n.* ivresse *f.*

intra- /'ɪntrə/ *pref.* intra-.

intractable /ɪn'træktəbl/ *a.* très difficile.

intransigent /ɪn'trænsɪdʒənt/ *a.* intransigeant.

intransitive /ɪn'trænsətɪv/ *a.* (*verb*) intransitif.

intravenous /ɪntrə'vi:nəs/ *a.* (*med.*) intraveineux.

intrepid /ɪn'trepɪd/ *a.* intrépide.

intrica|te /'ɪntrɪkət/ *a.* complexe. **~cy** *n.* complexité *f.*

intrigu|e /ɪn'tri:g/ *v.t./i.* intriguer. ● *n.* intrigue *f.* **~ing** *a.* très intéressant; (*curious*) curieux.

intrinsic /ɪn'trɪnsɪk/ *a.* intrinsèque. **~ally** /-klɪ/ *adv.* intrinsèquement.

introduce /ɪntrə'dju:s/ *v.t.* (*bring in, insert*) introduire; (*programme, question*) présenter. **~ s.o. to,** (*person*) présenter qn. à; (*subject*) faire connaître à qn.

introduct|ion /ɪntrə'dʌkʃn/ *n.* introduction *f.*; (*to person*) présentation *f.* **~ory** /-tərɪ/ *a.* (*letter, words*) d'introduction.

introspective /ɪntrə'spektɪv/ *a.* introspectif.

introvert /'ɪntrəvɜ:t/ *n.* introverti(e) *m.* (*f.*).

intru|de /ɪn'tru:d/ *v.i.* (*person*) s'imposer (**on s.o.,** à qn.), déranger. **~der** *n.* intrus(e) *m.* (*f.*). **~sion** *n.* intrusion *f.*

intuit|ion /ɪntju:'ɪʃn/ *n.* intuition *f.* **~ive** /ɪn'tju:ɪtɪv/ *a.* intuitif.

inundat|e /'ɪnʌndeɪt/ *v.t.* inonder (**with,** de). **~ion** /-'deɪʃn/ *n.* inondation *f.*

invade /ɪn'veɪd/ *v.t.* envahir. **~r** /-ə(r)/ *n.* envahisseu|r, -se *m., f.*

invalid[1] /'ɪnvəlɪd/ *n.* malade *m./f.*; (*disabled*) infirme *m./f.*

invalid[2] /ɪn'vælɪd/ *a.* non valable. **~ate** *v.t.* invalider.

invaluable /ɪn'væljʊəbl/ *a.* inestimable.

invariabl|e /ɪn'veərɪəbl/ *a.* invariable. **~y** *adv.* invariablement.

invasion /ɪn'veɪʒn/ *n.* invasion *f.*

invective /ɪn'vektɪv/ *n.* invective *f.*

inveigh /ɪn'veɪ/ *v.i.* invectiver.

inveigle /ɪn'veɪgl/ *v.t.* persuader.

invent /ɪn'vent/ *v.t.* inventer. **~ion** /-enʃn/ *n.* invention *f.* **~ive** *a.* inventif. **~or** *n.* inven|teur, -trice *m., f.*

inventory /'ɪnvəntrɪ/ *n.* inventaire *m.*

inverse /ɪn'vɜ:s/ *a.* & *n.* inverse (*m.*). **~ly** *adv.* inversement.

inver|t /ɪn'vɜ:t/ *v.t.* intervertir. **~ted commas,** guillemets *m. pl.* **~sion** *n.* inversion *f.*

invest /ɪn'vest/ *v.t.* investir; (*time, effort*: *fig.*) consacrer. ● *v.i.* faire un investissement. **~ in,** (*buy*: *fam.*) se payer. **~ment** *n.* investissement *m.* **~or** *n.* actionnaire *m./f.*; (*saver*) épargnant(e) *m.* (*f.*).

investigat|e /ɪn'vestɪgeɪt/ *v.t.* étudier; (*crime etc.*) enquêter sur. **~ion** /-'geɪʃn/ *n.* investigation *f.* **under ~ion,** à l'étude. **~or** *n.* (*police*) enquêteu|r, -se *m., f.*

inveterate /ɪn'vetərət/ *a.* invétéré.

invidious /ɪn'vɪdɪəs/ *a.* (*hateful*) odieux; (*unfair*) injuste.

invigilat|e /ɪn'vɪdʒɪleɪt/ *v.i.* (*schol.*) être de surveillance. **~or** *n.* surveillant(e) *m.* (*f.*).

invigorate /ɪn'vɪgəreɪt/ *v.t.* vivifier; (*encourage*) stimuler.

invincible /ɪn'vɪnsəbl/ *a.* invincible.

invisible /ɪn'vɪzəbl/ *a.* invisible.

invit|e /ɪn'vaɪt/ *v.t.* inviter; (*ask for*) demander. **~ation** /ɪnvɪ'teɪʃn/ *n.* invitation *f.* **~ing** *a.* (*meal, smile, etc.*) engageant.

invoice /'ɪnvɔɪs/ *n.* facture *f.* ● *v.t.* facturer.

invoke /ɪn'vəʊk/ *v.t.* invoquer.

involuntary /ɪn'vɒləntrɪ/ *a.* involontaire.

involve /ɪn'vɒlv/ *v.t.* entraîner; (*people*) faire participer. **~d** *a.* (*complex*) compliqué; (*at stake*) en jeu. **be ~d in,** (*work*) participer à; (*crime*) être mêlé à. **~ment** *n.* participation *f.* (**in,** à).

invulnerable /ɪn'vʌlnərəbl/ *a.* invulnérable.

inward /'ɪnwəd/ *a.* & *adv.* vers l'intérieur; (*feeling etc.*) intérieur. **~ly** *adv.* intérieurement. **~s** *adv.* vers l'intérieur.

iodine /'aɪədi:n/ *n.* iode *m.*; (*antiseptic*) teinture d'iode *f.*

iota /aɪ'əʊtə/ *n.* (*amount*) brin *m.*

IOU /aɪəʊ'ju:/ *abbr.* (*I owe you*) reconnaissance de dette *f.*
IQ /aɪ'kju:/ *abbr.* (*intelligence quotient*) QI *m.*
Iran /ɪ'rɑ:n/ *n.* Iran *m.* **~ian** /ɪ'reɪnɪən/ *a.* & *n.* iranien(ne) (*m.* (*f.*)).
Iraq /ɪ'rɑ:k/ *n.* Irak *m.* **~i** *a.* & *n.* irakien(ne) (*m.* (*f.*)).
irascible /ɪ'ræsəbl/ *a.* irascible.
irate /aɪ'reɪt/ *a.* en colère, furieux.
ire /'aɪə(r)/ *n.* courroux *m.*
Ireland /'aɪələnd/ *n.* Irlande *f.*
iris /'aɪərɪs/ *n.* (*anat.*, *bot.*) iris *m.*
Irish /'aɪərɪʃ/ *a.* irlandais. ● *n.* (*lang.*) irlandais *m.* **~man** *n.* Irlandais *m.* **~woman** *n.* Irlandaise *f.*
irk /ɜ:k/ *v.t.* ennuyer. **~some** *a.* ennuyeux.
iron /'aɪən/ *n.* fer *m.*; (*appliance*) fer (à repasser) *m.* ● *a.* de fer. ● *v.t.* repasser. **I~ Curtain,** rideau de fer *m.* **~ out,** faire disparaître. **~ing-board** *n.* planche à repasser *f.*
ironic(al) /aɪ'rɒnɪk(l)/ *a.* ironique.
ironmonger /'aɪənmʌŋgə(r)/ *n.* quincaillier *m.* **~y** *n.* quincaillerie *f.*
ironwork /'aɪənwɜ:k/ *n.* ferronnerie *f.*
irony /'aɪərənɪ/ *n.* ironie *f.*
irrational /ɪ'ræʃənl/ *a.* irrationnel; (*person*) pas rationnel.
irreconcilable /ɪrekən'saɪləbl/ *a.* irréconciliable; (*incompatible*) inconciliable.
irrefutable /ɪ'refjʊtəbl/ *a.* irréfutable.
irregular /ɪ'regjʊlə(r)/ *a.* irrégulier. **~ity** /-'lærətɪ/ *n.* irrégularité *f.*
irrelevan|t /ɪ'reləvənt/ *a.* sans rapport (**to,** avec). **~ce** *n.* manque de rapport *m.*
irreparable /ɪ'repərəbl/ *a.* irréparable, irrémédiable.
irreplaceable /ɪrɪ'pleɪsəbl/ *a.* irremplaçable.
irrepressible /ɪrɪ'presəbl/ *a.* irrépressible.
irresistible /ɪrɪ'zɪstəbl/ *a.* irrésistible.
irresolute /ɪ'rezəlu:t/ *a.* irrésolu.
irrespective /ɪrɪ'spektɪv/ *a.* **~ of,** sans tenir compte de.
irresponsible /ɪrɪ'spɒnsəbl/ *a.* irresponsable.
irretrievable /ɪrɪ'tri:vəbl/ *a.* irréparable.
irreverent /ɪ'revərənt/ *a.* irrévérencieux.
irreversible /ɪrɪ'vɜ:səbl/ *a.* irréversible; (*decision*) irrévocable.
irrevocable /ɪ'revəkəbl/ *a.* irrévocable.
irrigat|e /'ɪrɪgeɪt/ *v.t.* irriguer. **~ion** /-'geɪʃn/ *n.* irrigation *f.*
irritable /'ɪrɪtəbl/ *a.* irritable.
irritat|e /'ɪrɪteɪt/ *v.t.* irriter. **be ~ed by,** être énervé par. **~ing** *a.* énervant. **~ion** /-'teɪʃn/ *n.* irritation *f.*
is /ɪz/ *see* be.
Islam /'ɪzlɑ:m/ *n.* Islam *m.* **~ic** /ɪz'læmɪk/ *a.* islamique.
island /'aɪlənd/ *n.* île *f.* **traffic ~,** refuge *m.* **~er** *n.* insulaire *m./f.*
isle /aɪl/ *n.* île *f.*
isolat|e /'aɪsəleɪt/ *v.t.* isoler. **~ion** /-'leɪʃn/ *n.* isolement *m.*
isotope /'aɪsətəʊp/ *n.* isotope *m.*
Israel /'ɪzreɪl/ *n.* Israël *m.* **~i** /ɪz'reɪlɪ/ *a.* & *n.* israélien(ne) (*m.* (*f.*)).
issue /'ɪʃu:/ *n.* question *f.*; (*outcome*) résultat *m.*; (*of magazine etc.*) numéro *m.*; (*of stamps etc.*) émission *f.*; (*offspring*) descendance *f.* ● *v.t.* distribuer, donner; (*stamps etc.*) émettre; (*book*) publier; (*order*) donner. ● *v.i.* **~ from,** sortir de. **at ~,** en cause. **take ~,** engager une controverse.
isthmus /'ɪsməs/ *n.* isthme *m.*
it /ɪt/ *pron.* (*subject*) il, elle; (*object*) le, la, l'*; (*impersonal subject*) il; (*non-specific*) ce, c'*, cela, ça. **it is,** (*quiet, my book, etc.*) c'est. **it is/cold/warm/late/** *etc.*, il fait froid/chaud/tard/*etc.* **that's it,** c'est ça. **who is it?,** qui est-ce? **of it, from it,** en. **in it, at it, to it,** y.
IT *abbr. see* information technology.
italic /ɪ'tælɪk/ *a.* italique. **~s** *n. pl.* italique *m.*
Ital|y /'ɪtəlɪ/ *n.* Italie *f.* **~ian** /ɪ'tælɪən/ *a.* & *n.* italien(ne) (*m.* (*f.*)); (*lang.*) italien *m.*
itch /ɪtʃ/ *n.* démangeaison *f.* ● *v.i.* démanger. **my arm ~es,** mon bras me démange. **I am ~ing to,** ça me démange de. **~y** *a.* qui démange.
item /'aɪtəm/ *n.* article *m.*, chose *f.*; (*on agenda*) question *f.* **news ~,** nouvelle *f.* **~ize** *v.t.* détailler.
itinerant /aɪ'tɪnərənt/ *a.* itinérant; (*musician, actor*) ambulant.
itinerary /aɪ'tɪnərərɪ/ *n.* itinéraire *m.*
its /ɪts/ *a.* son, sa, *pl.* ses.
it's /ɪts/ = **it is, it has.**

itself /ɪt'self/ *pron.* lui-même, elle-même; (*reflexive*) se.
IUD *abbr.* (*intrauterine device*) stérilet *m.*
ivory /'aɪvərɪ/ *n.* ivoire *m.* **~ tower,** tour d'ivoire *f.*
ivy /'aɪvɪ/ *n.* lierre *m.*

J

jab /dʒæb/ *v.t.* (*p.t.* **jabbed**) (*thrust*) enfoncer; (*prick*) piquer. ● *n.* coup *m.*; (*injection*) piqûre *f.*
jabber /'dʒæbə(r)/ *v.i.* jacasser, bavarder; (*indistinctly*) bredouiller. ● *n.* bavardage *m.*
jack /dʒæk/ *n.* (*techn.*) cric *m.*; (*cards*) valet *m.*; (*plug*) fiche *f.* ● *v.t.* **~ up,** soulever (avec un cric).
jackal /'dʒækɔ:l/ *n.* chacal *m.*
jackass /'dʒækæs/ *n.* âne *m.*
jackdaw /'dʒækdɔ:/ *n.* choucas *m.*
jacket /'dʒækɪt/ *n.* veste *f.*, veston *m.*; (*of book*) jaquette *f.*
jack-knife /'dʒæknaɪf/ *n.* couteau pliant *m.* ● *v.i.* (*lorry*) faire un tête-à-queue.
jackpot /'dʒækpɒt/ *n.* gros lot *m.* **hit the ~,** gagner le gros lot.
Jacuzzi /dʒə'ku:zi:/ *n.* (P.) bain à remous *m.*
jade /dʒeɪd/ *n.* (*stone*) jade *m.*
jaded /'dʒeɪdɪd/ *a.* las; (*appetite*) blasé.
jagged /'dʒægɪd/ *a.* dentelé.
jail /dʒeɪl/ *n.* prison *f.* ● *v.t.* mettre en prison. **~er** *n.* geôlier *m.*
jalopy /dʒə'lɒpɪ/ *n.* vieux tacot *m.*
jam[1] /dʒæm/ *n.* confiture *f.*
jam[2] /dʒæm/ *v.t./i.* (*p.t.* **jammed**) (*wedge, become wedged*) (se) coincer; (*cram*) (s')entasser; (*street etc.*) encombrer; (*thrust*) enfoncer; (*radio*) brouiller. ● *n.* foule *f.*; (*of traffic*) embouteillage *m.*; (*situation*: *fam.*) pétrin *m.* **~-packed** *a.* (*fam.*) bourré.
Jamaica /dʒə'meɪkə/ *n.* Jamaïque *f.*
jangle /'dʒæŋgl/ *n.* cliquetis *m.* ● *v.t./i.* (faire) cliqueter.
janitor /'dʒænɪtə(r)/ *n.* concierge *m.*
January /'dʒænjʊərɪ/ *n.* janvier *m.*
Japan /dʒə'pæn/ *n.* Japon *m.* **~ese** /dʒæpə'ni:z/ *a.* & *n.* japonais(e) (*m.* (*f.*)); (*lang.*) japonais *m.*
jar[1] /dʒɑ:(r)/ *n.* pot *m.*, bocal *m.*
jar[2] /dʒɑ:(r)/ *v.i.* (*p.t.* **jarred**) grincer; (*of colours etc.*) détonner. ● *v.t.* ébranler. ● *n.* son discordant *m.* **~ring** *a.* discordant.
jargon /'dʒɑ:gən/ *n.* jargon *m.*
jasmine /'dʒæsmɪn/ *n.* jasmin *m.*
jaundice /'dʒɔ:ndɪs/ *n.* jaunisse *f.*
jaundiced /'dʒɔ:ndɪst/ *a.* (*envious*) envieux; (*bitter*) aigri.
jaunt /dʒɔ:nt/ *n.* (*trip*) balade *f.*
jaunty /'dʒɔ:ntɪ/ *a.* (**-ier, -iest**) (*cheerful, sprightly*) allègre.
javelin /'dʒævlɪn/ *n.* javelot *m.*
jaw /dʒɔ:/ *n.* mâchoire *f.* ● *v.i.* (*talk*: *sl.*) jacasser.
jay /dʒeɪ/ *n.* geai *m.* **~-walk** *v.i.* traverser la chaussée imprudemment.
jazz /dʒæz/ *n.* jazz *m.* ● *v.t.* **~ up,** animer. **~y** *a.* tape-à-l'œil *invar.*
jealous /'dʒeləs/ *a.* jaloux. **~y** *n.* jalousie *f.*
jeans /dʒi:nz/ *n. pl.* (blue-)jean *m.*
jeep /dʒi:p/ *n.* jeep *f.*
jeer /dʒɪə(r)/ *v.t./i.* **~ (at),** railler; (*boo*) huer. ● *n.* raillerie *f.*; huée *f.*
jell /dʒel/ *v.i.* (*set*: *fam.*) prendre. **~ied** *a.* en gelée.
jelly /'dʒelɪ/ *n.* gelée *f.*
jellyfish /'dʒelɪfɪʃ/ *n.* méduse *f.*
jeopard|y /'dʒepədɪ/ *n.* péril *m.* **~ize** *v.t.* mettre en péril.
jerk /dʒɜ:k/ *n.* secousse *f.*; (*fool*: *sl.*) idiot *m.*; (*creep*: *sl.*) salaud *m.* ● *v.t.* donner une secousse à. **~ily** *adv.* par saccades. **~y** *a.* saccadé.
jersey /'dʒɜ:zɪ/ *n.* (*garment*) chandail *m.*, tricot *m.*; (*fabric*) jersey *m.*
jest /dʒest/ *n.* plaisanterie *f.* ● *v.i.* plaisanter. **~er** *n.* bouffon *m.*
Jesus /'dʒi:zəs/ *n.* Jésus *m.*
jet[1] /dʒet/ *n.* (*mineral*) jais *m.* **~-black** *a.* de jais.
jet[2] /dʒet/ *n.* (*stream*) jet *m.*; (*plane*) avion à réaction *m.*, jet *m.* **~ lag,** fatigue due au décalage horaire *f.* **~-propelled** *a.* à réaction.
jettison /'dʒetɪsn/ *v.t.* jeter à la mer; (*aviat.*) larguer; (*fig.*) abandonner.
jetty /'dʒetɪ/ *n.* (*breakwater*) jetée *f.*
Jew /dʒu:/ *n.* Juif *m.* **~ess** *n.* Juive *f.*
jewel /'dʒu:əl/ *n.* bijou *m.* **~led** *a.* orné de bijoux. **~ler** *n.* bijout|ier, -ière *m., f.* **~lery** *n.* bijoux *m. pl.*
Jewish /'dʒu:ɪʃ/ *a.* juif.
Jewry /'dʒʊərɪ/ *n.* les Juifs *m. pl.*
jib /dʒɪb/ *v.i.* (*p.t.* **jibbed**) regimber (**at,** devant). ● *n.* (*sail*) foc *m.*
jibe /dʒaɪb/ *n.* = **gibe**.

jiffy /'dʒɪfɪ/ *n.* (*fam.*) instant *m.*

jig /dʒɪg/ *n.* (*dance*) gigue *f.*

jiggle /'dʒɪgl/ *v.t.* secouer légèrement.

jigsaw /'dʒɪgsɔ:/ *n.* puzzle *m.*

jilt /dʒɪlt/ *v.t.* laisser tomber.

jingle /'dʒɪŋgl/ *v.t./i.* (faire) tinter. ● *n.* tintement *m.*; (*advertising*) jingle *m.*, sonal *m.*

jinx /dʒɪŋks/ *n.* (*person*: *fam.*) porte-malheur *m. invar.*; (*spell*: *fig.*) mauvais sort *m.*

jitter|s /'dʒɪtəz/ *n. pl.* **the ~s,** (*fam.*) la frousse *f.* **~y** /-ərɪ/ *a.* **be ~y,** (*fam.*) avoir la frousse.

job /dʒɒb/ *n.* travail *m.*; (*post*) poste *m.* **have a ~ doing,** avoir du mal à faire. **it is a good ~ that,** heureusement que. **~less** *a.* sans travail, au chômage.

jobcentre /'dʒɒbsentə(r)/ *n.* agence (nationale) pour l'emploi *f.*

jockey /'dʒɒkɪ/ *n.* jockey *m.* ● *v.i.* (*manœuvre*) manœuvrer.

jocular /'dʒɒkjʊlə(r)/ *a.* jovial.

jog /dʒɒg/ *v.t.* (*p.t.* **jogged**) pousser; (*memory*) rafraîchir. ● *v.i.* faire du jogging. **~ging** *n.* jogging *m.*

join /dʒɔɪn/ *v.t.* joindre, unir; (*club*) devenir membre de; (*political group*) adhérer à; (*army*) s'engager dans. **~ s.o.,** (*in activity*) se joindre à qn.; (*meet*) rejoindre qn. ● *v.i.* (*roads etc.*) se rejoindre. ● *n.* joint *m.* **~ in,** participer (à). **~ up,** (*mil.*) s'engager.

joiner /'dʒɔɪnə(r)/ *n.* menuisier *m.*

joint /dʒɔɪnt/ *a.* (*account, venture*) commun. ● *n.* (*join*) joint *m.*; (*anat.*) articulation *f.*; (*culin.*) rôti *m.*; (*place*: *sl.*) boîte *f.* **~ author,** coauteur *m.* **out of ~,** déboîté. **~ly** *adv.* conjointement.

joist /dʒɔɪst/ *n.* solive *f.*

jok|e /dʒəʊk/ *n.* plaisanterie *f.*; (*trick*) farce *f.* ● *v.i.* plaisanter. **it's no ~e,** ce n'est pas drôle. **~er** *n.* blagueu|r, -se *m.*, *f.*; (*pej.*) petit malin *m.*; (*cards*) joker *m.* **~ingly** *adv.* pour rire.

joll|y /'dʒɒlɪ/ *a.* (**-ier, -iest**) gai. ● *adv.* (*fam.*) rudement. **~ification** /-fɪ'keɪʃn/, **~ity** *ns.* réjouissances *f. pl.*

jolt /dʒəʊlt/ *v.t./i.* (*vehicle, passenger*) cahoter; (*shake*) secouer. ● *n.* cahot *m.*; secousse *f.*

Jordan /'dʒɔ:dn/ *n.* Jordanie *f.*

jostle /'dʒɒsl/ *v.t./i.* (*push*) bousculer; (*push each other*) se bousculer.

jot /dʒɒt/ *n.* brin *m.* ● *v.t.* (*p.t.* **jotted**) **~ down,** noter. **~ter** *n.* (*pad*) bloc-notes *m.*

journal /'dʒɜ:nl/ *n.* journal *m.* **~ism** *n.* journalisme *m.* **~ist** *n.* journaliste *m./f.* **~ese** /-'li:z/ *n.* jargon des journalistes *m.*

journey /'dʒɜ:nɪ/ *n.* voyage *m.*; (*distance*) trajet *m.* ● *v.i.* voyager.

jovial /'dʒəʊvɪəl/ *a.* jovial.

joy /dʒɔɪ/ *n.* joie *f.* **~-riding** *n.* courses en voitures volées *f. pl.* **~ful, ~ous** *adjs.* joyeux.

joystick /'dʒɔɪstɪk/ *n.* (*comput.*) manette *f.*

jubil|ant /'dʒu:bɪlənt/ *a.* débordant de joie. **be ~ant,** jubiler. **~ation** /-'leɪʃn/ *n.* jubilation *f.*

jubilee /'dʒu:bɪli:/ *n.* jubilé *m.*

Judaism /'dʒu:deɪɪzəm/ *n.* judaïsme *m.*

judder /'dʒʌdə(r)/ *v.i.* vibrer. ● *n.* vibration *f.*

judge /dʒʌdʒ/ *n.* juge *m.* ● *v.t.* juger. **judging by,** à juger de. **~ment** *n.* jugement *m.*

judic|iary /dʒu:'dɪʃərɪ/ *n.* magistrature *f.* **~ial** *a.* judiciaire.

judicious /dʒu:'dɪʃəs/ *a.* judicieux.

judo /'dʒu:dəʊ/ *n.* judo *m.*

jug /dʒʌg/ *n.* cruche *f.*, pichet *m.*

juggernaut /'dʒʌgənɔ:t/ *n.* (*lorry*) poids lourd *m.*, mastodonte *m.*

juggle /'dʒʌgl/ *v.t./i.* jongler (avec). **~r** /-ə(r)/ *n.* jongleu|r, -se *m.*, *f.*

juic|e /dʒu:s/ *n.* jus *m.* **~y** *a.* juteux; (*details etc.*: *fam.*) croustillant.

juke-box /'dʒu:kbɒks/ *n.* juke-box *m.*

July /dʒu:'laɪ/ *n.* juillet *m.*

jumble /'dʒʌmbl/ *v.t.* mélanger. ● *n.* (*muddle*) fouillis *m.* **~ sale,** vente (de charité) *f.*

jumbo /'dʒʌmbəʊ/ *a.* **~ jet,** avion géant *m.*, jumbo-jet *m.*

jump /dʒʌmp/ *v.t./i.* sauter; (*start*) sursauter; (*of price etc.*) faire un bond. ● *n.* saut *m.*; sursaut *m.*; (*increase*) hausse *f.* **~ at,** sauter sur. **~-leads** *n. pl.* câbles de démarrage *m. pl.* **~ the gun,** agir prématurément. **~ the queue,** resquiller.

jumper /'dʒʌmpə(r)/ *n.* pull(-over) *m.*; (*dress*: *Amer.*) robe chasuble *f.*

jumpy /'dʒʌmpɪ/ *a.* nerveux.

junction /'dʒʌŋkʃn/ *n.* jonction *f.*; (*of roads etc.*) embranchement *m.*

juncture /'dʒʌŋktʃə(r)/ *n.* moment *m.*; (*state of affairs*) conjoncture *f.*

June /dʒu:n/ *n.* juin *m.*

jungle /'dʒʌŋgl/ *n.* jungle *f.*

junior /'dʒu:nɪə(r)/ *a.* (*in age*) plus jeune (**to,** que); (*in rank*) subalterne; (*school*) élémentaire; (*executive, doctor*) jeune. ● *n.* cadet(te) *m.* (*f.*); (*schol.*) petit(e) élève *m.*(*f.*); (*sport*) junior *m./f.*

junk /dʒʌŋk/ *n.* bric-à-brac *m. invar.*; (*poor material*) camelote *f.* ● *v.t.* (*Amer., sl.*) balancer. **~ food,** saloperies *f. pl.* **~-shop** *n.* boutique de brocanteur *f.*

junkie /'dʒʌŋkɪ/ *n.* (*sl.*) drogué(e) *m.* (*f.*).

junta /'dʒʌntə/ *n.* junte *f.*

jurisdiction /dʒʊərɪs'dɪkʃn/ *n.* juridiction *f.*

jurisprudence /dʒʊərɪs'pru:dəns/ *n.* jurisprudence *f.*

juror /'dʒʊərə(r)/ *n.* juré *m.*

jury /'dʒʊərɪ/ *n.* jury *m.*

just /dʒʌst/ *a.* (*fair*) juste. ● *adv.* juste, exactement; (*only, slightly*) juste; (*simply*) tout simplement. **he has/had ~ left**/*etc.*, il vient/venait de partir/*etc.* **have ~ missed,** avoir manqué de peu. **it's ~ a cold,** ce n'est qu'un rhume. **~ as tall**/*etc.*, tout aussi grand/*etc.* (**as,** que). **~ as well,** heureusement (que). **~ listen!,** écoutez donc! **~ly** *adv.* avec justice.

justice /'dʒʌstɪs/ *n.* justice *f.* **J~ of the Peace,** juge de paix *m.*

justifiabl|e /dʒʌstɪ'faɪəbl/ *a.* justifiable. **~y** *adv.* avec raison.

justif|y /'dʒʌstɪfaɪ/ *v.t.* justifier. **~ication** /-ɪ'keɪʃn/ *n.* justification *f.*

jut /dʒʌt/ *v.i.* (*p.t.* **jutted**). **~ out,** faire saillie, dépasser.

juvenile /'dʒu:vənaɪl/ *a.* (*youthful*) juvénile; (*childish*) puéril; (*delinquent*) jeune; (*court*) pour enfants. ● *n.* jeune *m./f.*

juxtapose /dʒʌkstə'pəʊz/ *v.t.* juxtaposer.

K

kaleidoscope /kə'laɪdəskəʊp/ *n.* kaléidoscope.

kangaroo /kæŋgə'ru:/ *n.* kangourou *m.*

karate /kə'rɑ:tɪ/ *n.* karaté *m.*

kebab /kə'bæb/ *n.* brochette *f.*

keel /ki:l/ *n.* (*of ship*) quille *f.* ● *v.i.* **~ over,** chavirer.

keen /ki:n/ *a.* (**-er, -est**) (*interest, wind, feeling, etc.*) vif; (*mind, analysis*) pénétrant; (*edge, appetite*) aiguisé; (*eager*) enthousiaste. **be ~ on,** (*person, thing: fam.*) aimer beaucoup. **be ~ to do** *or* **on doing,** tenir beaucoup à faire. **~ly** *adv.* vivement; avec enthousiasme. **~ness** *n.* vivacité *f.*; enthousiasme *m.*

keep /ki:p/ *v.t.* (*p.t.* **kept**) garder; (*promise, shop, diary, etc.*) tenir; (*family*) entretenir; (*animals*) élever; (*rule etc.*) respecter; (*celebrate*) célébrer; (*delay*) retenir; (*prevent*) empêcher; (*conceal*) cacher. ● *v.i.* (*food*) se garder; (*remain*) rester. **~ (on),** continuer (**doing,** à faire). ● *n.* subsistance *f.*; (*of castle*) donjon *m.* **for ~s,** (*fam.*) pour toujours. **~ back** *v.t.* retenir; *v.i.* ne pas s'approcher. **~ s.o. from doing,** empêcher qn. de faire. **~ in/out,** empêcher d'entrer/de sortir. **~ up,** (se) maintenir. **~ up (with),** suivre. **~er** *n.* gardien(ne) *m.* (*f.*). **~-fit** *n.* exercices physiques *m. pl.*

keeping /'ki:pɪŋ/ *n.* garde *f.* **in ~ with,** en accord avec.

keepsake /'ki:pseɪk/ *n.* (*thing*) souvenir *m.*

keg /keg/ *n.* tonnelet *m.*

kennel /'kenl/ *n.* niche *f.*

Kenya /'kenjə/ *n.* Kenya *m.*

kept /kept/ *see* keep.

kerb /kɜ:b/ *n.* bord du trottoir *m.*

kerfuffle /kə'fʌfl/ *n.* (*fuss: fam.*) histoire(s) *f.* (*pl.*).

kernel /'kɜ:nl/ *n.* amande *f.*

kerosene /'kerəsi:n/ *n.* (*aviation fuel*) kérosène *m.*; (*paraffin*) pétrole (lampant) *m.*

ketchup /'ketʃəp/ *n.* ketchup *m.*

kettle /'ketl/ *n.* bouilloire *f.*

key /ki:/ *n.* clef *f.*; (*of piano etc.*) touche *f.* ● *a.* clef (*f. invar.*). **~-ring** *n.* porte-clefs *m. invar.* ● *v.t.* **~ in,** (*comput.*) saisir. **~ up,** surexciter.

keyboard /'ki:bɔ:d/ *n.* clavier *m.*

keyhole /'ki:həʊl/ *n.* trou de la serrure *m.*

keynote /'ki:nəʊt/ *n.* (*of speech etc.*) note dominante *f.*

keystone /'ki:stəʊn/ *n.* (*archit., fig.*) clef de voûte *f.*

khaki /'kɑ:kɪ/ *a.* kaki *invar.*

kibbutz /kɪ'bʊts/ *n.* (*pl.* **-im** /-i:m/) *n.* kibboutz *m.*

kick /kɪk/ *v.t./i.* donner un coup de pied (à); (*of horse*) ruer. ● *n.* coup de pied *m.*; ruade *f.*; (*of gun*) recul *m.*; (*thrill*: *fam.*) (malin) plaisir *m.* **~-off** *n.* coup d'envoi *m.* **~ out,** (*fam.*) flanquer dehors. **~ up,** (*fuss, racket*: *fam.*) faire.

kid /kɪd/ *n.* (*goat, leather*) chevreau *m.*; (*child*: *sl.*) gosse *m./f.* ● *v.t./i.* (*p.t.* **kidded**) blaguer.

kidnap /'kɪdnæp/ *v.t.* (*p.t.* **kidnapped**) enlever, kidnapper. **~ping** *n.* enlèvement *m.*

kidney /'kɪdnɪ/ *n.* rein *m.*; (*culin.*) rognon *m.*

kill /kɪl/ *v.t.* tuer; (*fig.*) mettre fin à. ● *n.* mise à mort *f.* **~er** *n.* tueu|r, -se *m., f.* **~ing** *n.* massacre *m.*, meurtre *m.*; *a.* (*funny*: *fam.*) tordant; (*tiring*: *fam.*) tuant.

killjoy /'kɪldʒɔɪ/ *n.* rabat-joie *m. invar.*, trouble-fête *m./f. invar.*

kiln /kɪln/ *n.* four *m.*

kilo /'ki:ləʊ/ *n.* (*pl.* **-os**) kilo *m.*

kilobyte /'kɪləbaɪt/ *n.* kilo-octet *m.*

kilogram /'kɪləgræm/ *n.* kilogramme *m.*

kilohertz /'kɪləhɜ:ts/ *n.* kilohertz *m.*

kilometre /'kɪləmi:tə(r)/ *n.* kilomètre *m.*

kilowatt /'kɪləwɒt/ *n.* kilowatt *m.*

kilt /kɪlt/ *n.* kilt *m.*

kin /kɪn/ *n.* parents *m. pl.*

kind[1] /kaɪnd/ *n.* genre *m.*, sorte *f.*, espèce *f.* **in ~,** en nature *f.* **~ of,** (*somewhat*: *fam.*) un peu. **be two of a ~,** se rassembler.

kind[2] /kaɪnd/ *a.* (**-er, -est**) gentil, bon. **~-hearted** *a.* bon. **~ness** *n.* bonté *f.*

kindergarten /'kɪndəgɑ:tn/ *n.* jardin d'enfants *m.*

kindle /'kɪndl/ *v.t./i.* (s')allumer.

kindly /'kaɪndlɪ/ *a.* (**-ier, -iest**) bienveillant. ● *adv.* avec bonté. **~ wait**/*etc.*, voulez-vous avoir la bonté d'attendre/*etc.*

kindred /'kɪndrɪd/ *a.* apparenté. **~ spirit,** personne qui a les mêmes goûts *f.*, âme sœur *f.*

kinetic /kɪ'netɪk/ *a.* cinétique.

king /kɪŋ/ *n.* roi *m.* **~-size(d)** *a.* géant.

kingdom /'kɪŋdəm/ *n.* royaume *m.*; (*bot.*) règne *m.*

kingfisher /'kɪŋfɪʃə(r)/ *n.* martin-pêcheur *m.*

kink /kɪŋk/ *n.* (*in rope*) entortillement *m.*, déformation *f.*; (*fig.*) perversion *f.* **~y** *a.* (*fam.*) perverti.

kiosk /'ki:ɒsk/ *n.* kiosque *m.* **telephone ~,** cabine téléphonique *f.*

kip /kɪp/ *n.* (*sl.*) roupillon *m.* ● *v.i.* (*p.t.* **kipped**) (*sl.*) roupiller.

kipper /'kɪpə(r)/ *n.* hareng fumé *m.*

kirby-grip /'kɜ:bɪgrɪp/ *n.* pince à cheveux *f.*

kiss /kɪs/ *n.* baiser *m.* ● *v.t./i.* (s')embrasser.

kit /kɪt/ *n.* équipement *m.*; (*clothing*) affaires *f. pl.*; (*set of tools etc.*) trousse *f.*; (*for assembly*) kit *m.* ● *v.t.* (*p.t.* **kitted**). **~ out,** équiper.

kitbag /'kɪtbæg/ *n.* sac *m.* (*de marin etc.*).

kitchen /'kɪtʃɪn/ *n.* cuisine *f.* **~ garden,** jardin potager *m.*

kitchenette /kɪtʃɪ'net/ *n.* kitchenette *f.*

kite /kaɪt/ *n.* (*toy*) cerf-volant *m.*

kith /kɪθ/ *n.* **~ and kin,** parents et amis *m. pl.*

kitten /'kɪtn/ *n.* chaton *m.*

kitty /'kɪtɪ/ *n.* (*fund*) cagnotte *f.*

knack /næk/ *n.* truc *m.*, chic *m.*

knapsack /'næpsæk/ *n.* sac à dos *m.*

knave /neɪv/ *n.* (*cards*) valet *m.*

knead /ni:d/ *v.t.* pétrir.

knee /ni:/ *n.* genou *m.*

kneecap /'ni:kæp/ *n.* rotule *f.*

kneel /ni:l/ *v.i.* (*p.t.* **knelt**). **~ (down),** s'agenouiller.

knell /nel/ *n.* glas *m.*

knew /nju:/ *see* know.

knickers /'nɪkəz/ *n. pl.* (*woman's undergarment*) culotte *f.*, slip *m.*

knife /naɪf/ *n.* (*pl.* **knives**) couteau *m.* ● *v.t.* poignarder.

knight /naɪt/ *n.* chevalier *m.*; (*chess*) cavalier *m.* ● *v.t.* faire *or* armer chevalier. **~hood** *n.* titre de chevalier *m.*

knit /nɪt/ *v.t./i.* (*p.t.* **knitted** *or* **knit**) tricoter; (*bones etc.*) (se) souder. **~ one's brow,** froncer les sourcils. **~ting** *n.* tricot *m.*

knitwear /'nɪtweə(r)/ *n.* tricots *m. pl.*

knob /nɒb/ *n.* bouton *m.*

knock /nɒk/ *v.t./i.* frapper, cogner; (*criticize*: *sl.*) critiquer. ● *n.* coup *m.* **~ about** *v.t.* malmener; *v.i.* vadrouiller. **~ down,** (*chair, pedestrian*) renverser; (*demolish*) abattre; (*reduce*) baisser. **~-down** *a.* (*price*) très bas. **~-kneed** *a.* cagneux. **~ off** *v.t.* faire tomber; (*fam.*) expédier; *v.i.*

(*fam.*) s'arrêter de travailler. ~ **out,** (*by blow*) assommer; (*tire*) épuiser. **~-out** *n.* (*boxing*) knock-out *m.* ~ **over,** renverser. ~ **up,** (*meal etc.*) préparer en vitesse. **~er** *n.* heurtoir *m.*

knot /nɒt/ *n.* nœud *m.* ● *v.t.* (*p.t.* **knotted**) nouer. **~ty** /'nɒtɪ/ *a.* noueux; (*problem*) épineux.

know /nəʊ/ *v.t./i.* (*p.t.* **knew,** *p.p.* **known**) savoir (**that,** que); (*person, place*) connaître. ~ **how to do,** savoir comment faire. ● *n.* **in the ~,** (*fam.*) dans le secret, au courant. ~ **about,** (*cars etc.*) s'y connaître en. **~-all,** (*Amer.*) **~-it-all** *n.* je-sais-tout *m./f.* **~-how** *n.* technique *f.* ~ **of,** connaître, avoir entendu parler de. **~ingly** *adv.* (*consciously*) sciemment.

knowledge /'nɒlɪdʒ/ *n.* connaissance *f.*; (*learning*) connaissances *f. pl.* **~able** *a.* bien informé.

known /nəʊn/ *see* know. ● *a.* connu; (*recognized*) reconnu.

knuckle /'nʌkl/ *n.* articulation du doigt *f.* ● *v.i.* ~ **under,** se soumettre.

Koran /kə'rɑːn/ *n.* Coran *m.*

Korea /kə'rɪə/ *n.* Corée *f.*

kosher /'kəʊʃə(r)/ *a.* kascher *invar.*

kowtow /kaʊ'taʊ/ *v.i.* se prosterner (**to,** devant).

kudos /'kjuːdɒs/ *n.* (*fam.*) gloire *f.*

Kurd /kɜːd/ *a.* & *n.* kurde *m./f.*

L

lab /læb/ *n.* (*fam.*) labo *m.*

label /'leɪbl/ *n.* étiquette *f.* ● *v.t.* (*p.t.* **labelled**) étiqueter.

laboratory /lə'bɒrətrɪ, *Amer.* 'læbrətɔːrɪ/ *n.* laboratoire *m.*

laborious /lə'bɔːrɪəs/ *a.* laborieux.

labour /'leɪbə(r)/ *n.* travail *m.*; (*workers*) main-d'œuvre *f.* ● *v.i.* peiner. ● *v.t.* trop insister sur. **in ~,** en train d'accoucher, en couches. **~ed** *a.* laborieux.

Labour /'leɪbə(r)/ *n.* le parti travailliste *m.* ● *a.* travailliste.

labourer /'leɪbərə(r)/ *n.* manœuvre *m.*; (*on farm*) ouvrier agricole *m.*

labyrinth /'læbərɪnθ/ *n.* labyrinthe *m.*

lace /leɪs/ *n.* dentelle *f.*; (*of shoe*) lacet *m.* ● *v.t.* (*fasten*) lacer; (*drink*) arroser. **~-ups** *n. pl.* chaussures à lacets *f. pl.*

lacerate /'læsəreɪt/ *v.t.* lacérer.

lack /læk/ *n.* manque *m.* ● *v.t.* manquer de. **be ~ing,** manquer (**in,** de). **for ~ of,** faute de.

lackadaisical /lækə'deɪzɪkl/ *a.* indolent, apathique.

lackey /'lækɪ/ *n.* laquais *m.*

laconic /lə'kɒnɪk/ *a.* laconique.

lacquer /'lækə(r)/ *n.* laque *f.*

lad /læd/ *n.* garçon *m.*, gars *m.*

ladder /'lædə(r)/ *n.* échelle *f.*; (*in stocking*) maille filée *f.* ● *v.t./i.* (*stocking*) filer.

laden /'leɪdn/ *a.* chargé (**with,** de).

ladle /'leɪdl/ *n.* louche *f.*

lady /'leɪdɪ/ *n.* dame *f.* ~ **friend,** amie *f.* **~-in-waiting** *n.* dame d'honneur *f.* **young ~,** jeune femme *or* fille *f.* **~like** *a.* distingué.

lady|bird /'leɪdɪbɜːd/ *n.* coccinelle *f.* **~bug** *n.* (*Amer.*) coccinelle *f.*

lag[1] /læg/ *v.i.* (*p.t.* **lagged**) traîner. ● *n.* (*interval*) décalage *m.*

lag[2] /læg/ *v.t.* (*p.t.* **lagged**) (*pipes*) calorifuger.

lager /'lɑːgə(r)/ *n.* bière blonde *f.*

lagoon /lə'guːn/ *n.* lagune *f.*

laid /leɪd/ *see* lay[2]. ● **~-back** *a.* (*fam.*) cool.

lain /leɪn/ *see* lie[2].

lair /leə(r)/ *n.* tanière *f.*

laity /'leɪətɪ/ *n.* laïques *m. pl.*

lake /leɪk/ *n.* lac *m.*

lamb /læm/ *n.* agneau *m.*

lambswool /'læmzwʊl/ *n.* laine d'agneau *f.*

lame /leɪm/ *a.* (**-er, -est**) boiteux; (*excuse*) faible. **~ly** *adv.* (*argue*) sans conviction. ~ **duck,** canard boiteux *m.*

lament /lə'ment/ *n.* lamentation *f.* ● *v.t./i.* se lamenter (sur). **~able** *a.* lamentable.

laminated /'læmɪneɪtɪd/ *a.* laminé.

lamp /læmp/ *n.* lampe *f.*

lamppost /'læmppəʊst/ *n.* réverbère *m.*

lampshade /'læmpʃeɪd/ *n.* abat-jour *m. invar.*

lance /lɑːns/ *n.* lance *f.* ● *v.t.* (*med.*) inciser.

lancet /'lɑːnsɪt/ *n.* bistouri *m.*

land /lænd/ *n.* terre *f.*; (*plot*) terrain *m.*; (*country*) pays *m.* ● *a.* terrestre; (*policy, reform*) agraire. ● *v.t./i.*

débarquer; (*aircraft*) (se) poser, (faire) atterrir; (*fall*) tomber; (*obtain*) décrocher; (*put*) mettre; (*a blow*) porter. **~-locked** *a.* sans accès à la mer. **~ up,** se retrouver.

landed /'lændɪd/ *a.* foncier.

landing /'lændɪŋ/ *n.* débarquement *m.*; (*aviat.*) atterrissage *m.*; (*top of stairs*) palier *m.* **~-stage** débarcadère *m.*

land|lady /'lændleɪdɪ/ *n.* propriétaire *f.*; (*of inn*) patronne *f.* **~lord** *n.* propriétaire *m.*; patron *m.*

landmark /'lændmɑ:k/ *n.* (point de) repère *m.*

landscape /'læn(d)skeɪp/ *n.* paysage *m.* ● *v.t.* aménager.

landslide /'lændslaɪd/ *n.* glissement de terrain *m.*; (*pol.*) raz-de-marée (électoral) *m. invar.*

lane /leɪn/ *n.* (*path, road*) chemin *m.*; (*strip of road*) voie *f.*; (*of traffic*) file *f.*; (*aviat.*) couloir *m.*

language /'læŋgwɪdʒ/ *n.* langue *f.*; (*speech, style*) langage *m.* **~ laboratory,** laboratoire de langue *m.*

languid /'læŋgwɪd/ *a.* languissant.

languish /'læŋgwɪʃ/ *v.i.* languir.

lank /læŋk/ *a.* grand et maigre.

lanky /'læŋkɪ/ *a.* (**-ier, -iest**) dégingandé, grand et maigre.

lanolin /'lænəʊlɪn/ *n.* lanoline *f.*

lantern /'læntən/ *n.* lanterne *f.*

lap[1] /læp/ *n.* genoux *m. pl.*; (*sport*) tour (de piste) *m.* ● *v.t./i.* (*p.t.* **lapped**) **~ over,** (se) chevaucher.

lap[2] /læp/ *v.t.* (*p.t.* **lapped**). **~ up,** laper. ● *v.i.* (*waves*) clapoter.

lapel /lə'pel/ *n.* revers *m.*

lapse /læps/ *v.i.* (*decline*) se dégrader; (*expire*) se périmer. ● *n.* défaillance *f.*, erreur *f.*; (*of time*) intervalle *m.* **~ into,** retomber dans.

larceny /'lɑ:sənɪ/ *n.* vol simple *m.*

lard /lɑ:d/ *n.* saindoux *m.*

larder /'lɑ:də(r)/ *n.* garde-manger *m. invar.*

large /lɑ:dʒ/ *a.* (**-er, -est**) grand, gros. **at ~,** en liberté. **by and ~,** en général. **~ly** *adv.* en grande mesure. **~ness** *n.* grandeur *f.*

lark[1] /lɑ:k/ *n.* (*bird*) alouette *f.*

lark[2] /lɑ:k/ *n.* (*bit of fun: fam.*) rigolade *f.* ● *v.i.* (*fam.*) rigoler.

larva /'lɑ:və/ *n.* (*pl.* **-vae** /-vi:/) larve *f.*

laryngitis /lærɪn'dʒaɪtɪs/ *n.* laryngite *f.*

larynx /'lærɪŋks/ *n.* larynx *m.*

lasagne /lə'zænjə/ *n.* lasagne *f.*

lascivious /lə'sɪvɪəs/ *a.* lascif.

laser /'leɪzə(r)/ *n.* laser *m.* **~ printer,** imprimante laser *f.*

lash /læʃ/ *v.t.* fouetter. ● *n.* coup de fouet *m.*; (*eyelash*) cil *m.* **~ out,** (*spend*) dépenser follement. **~ out against,** attaquer.

lashings /'læʃɪŋz/ *n. pl.* **~ of,** (*cream etc.: sl.*) des masses de.

lass /læs/ *n.* jeune fille *f.*

lasso /læ'su:/ *n.* (*pl.* **-os**) lasso *m.*

last[1] /lɑ:st/ *a.* dernier. ● *adv.* en dernier; (*most recently*) la dernière fois. ● *n.* dern|ier, -ière *m., f.*; (*remainder*) reste *m.* **at (long) ~,** enfin. **~-ditch** *a.* ultime. **~-minute** *a.* de dernière minute. **~ night,** hier soir. **the ~ straw,** le comble. **the ~ word,** le mot de la fin. **on its ~ legs,** sur le point de rendre l'âme. **~ly** *adv.* en dernier lieu.

last[2] /lɑ:st/ *v.i.* durer. **~ing** *a.* durable.

latch /lætʃ/ *n.* loquet *m.*

late /leɪt/ *a.* (**-er, -est**) (*not on time*) en retard; (*recent*) récent; (*former*) ancien; (*hour, fruit, etc.*) tardif; (*deceased*) défunt. **the ~ Mrs X,** feu Mme X. **~st** /-ɪst/ (*last*) dernier. ● *adv.* (*not early*) tard; (*not on time*) en retard. **in ~ July,** fin juillet. **of ~,** dernièrement. **~ness** *n.* retard *m.*; (*of event*) heure tardive *f.*

latecomer /'leɪtkʌmə(r)/ *n.* retardataire *m./f.*

lately /'leɪtlɪ/ *adv.* dernièrement.

latent /'leɪtnt/ *a.* latent.

lateral /'lætərəl/ *a.* latéral.

lathe /leɪð/ *n.* tour *m.*

lather /'lɑ:ðə(r)/ *n.* mousse *f.* ● *v.t.* savonner. ● *v.i.* mousser.

Latin /'lætɪn/ *n.* (*lang.*) latin *m.* ● *a.* latin. **~ America,** Amérique latine *f.*

latitude /'lætɪtju:d/ *n.* latitude *f.*

latrine /lə'tri:n/ *n.* latrines *f. pl.*

latter /'lætə(r)/ *a.* dernier. ● *n.* **the ~,** celui-ci, celle-ci. **~-day** *a.* moderne. **~ly** *adv.* dernièrement.

lattice /'lætɪs/ *n.* treillage *m.*

laudable /'lɔ:dəbl/ *a.* louable.

laugh /lɑ:f/ *v.i.* rire (**at,** de). ● *n.* rire *m.* **~able** *a.* ridicule. **~ing-stock** *n.* objet de risée *m.*

laughter /'lɑ:ftə(r)/ *n.* (*act*) rire *m.*; (*sound of laughs*) rires *m. pl.*

launch[1] /lɔ:ntʃ/ *v.t.* lancer. ● *n.* lancement *m.* **~ (out) into,** se lancer dans. **~ing pad,** aire de lancement *f.*

launch[2] /lɔ:ntʃ/ *n.* (*boat*) vedette *f.*

launder /'lɔ:ndə(r)/ *v.t.* blanchir.

launderette /lɔ:n'dret/ *n.* laverie automatique *f.*
laundry /'lɔ:ndrɪ/ *n.* (*place*) blanchisserie *f.*; (*clothes*) linge *m.*
laurel /'lɒrəl/ *n.* laurier *m.*
lava /'lɑ:və/ *n.* lave *f.*
lavatory /'lævətrɪ/ *n.* cabinets *m. pl.*
lavender /'lævəndə(r)/ *n.* lavande *f.*
lavish /'lævɪʃ/ *a.* (*person*) prodigue; (*plentiful*) copieux; (*lush*) somptueux. ● *v.t.* prodiguer (**on,** à). **~ly** *adv.* copieusement.
law /lɔ:/ *n.* loi *f.*; (*profession, subject of study*) droit *m.* **~-abiding** *a.* respectueux des lois. **~ and order,** l'ordre public. **~ful** *a.* légal. **~fully** *adv.* légalement. **~less** *a.* sans loi.
lawcourt /'lɔ:kɔ:t/ *n.* tribunal *m.*
lawn /lɔ:n/ *n.* pelouse *f.*, gazon *m.* **~-mower** *n.* tondeuse à gazon *f.* **~ tennis,** tennis (sur gazon) *m.*
lawsuit /'lɔ:su:t/ *n.* procès *m.*
lawyer /'lɔ:jə(r)/ *n.* avocat *m.*
lax /læks/ *a.* négligent; (*morals etc.*) relâché. **~ity** *n.* négligence *f.*
laxative /'læksətɪv/ *n.* laxatif *m.*
lay[1] /leɪ/ *a.* (*non-clerical*) laïque; (*opinion etc.*) d'un profane.
lay[2] /leɪ/ *v.t.* (*p.t.* **laid**) poser, mettre; (*trap*) tendre; (*table*) mettre; (*plan*) former; (*eggs*) pondre. ● *v.i.* pondre. **~ aside,** mettre de côté. **~ down,** (dé)poser; (*condition*) (im)poser. **~ hold of,** saisir. **~ off** *v.t.* (*worker*) licencier; *v.i.* (*fam.*) arrêter. **~-off** *n.* licenciement *m.* **~ on,** (*provide*) fournir. **~ out,** (*design*) dessiner; (*display*) disposer; (*money*) dépenser. **~ up,** (*store*) amasser. **~ waste,** ravager.
lay[3] /leɪ/ *see* lie[2].
layabout /'leɪəbaʊt/ *n.* fainéant(e) *m.* (*f.*).
lay-by /'leɪbaɪ/ *n.* (*pl.* **-bys**) petite aire de stationnement *f.*
layer /'leɪə(r)/ *n.* couche *f.*
layman /'leɪmən/ *n.* (*pl.* **-men**) profane *m.*
layout /'leɪaʊt/ *n.* disposition *f.*
laze /leɪz/ *v.i.* paresser.
laz|y /'leɪzɪ/ *a.* (**-ier, -iest**) paresseux. **~iness** *n.* paresse *f.* **~y-bones** *n.* flemmard(e) *m.* (*f.*).
lead[1] /li:d/ *v.t./i.* (*p.t.* **led**) mener; (*team etc.*) diriger; (*life*) mener; (*induce*) amener. **~ to,** conduire à, mener à. ● *n.* avance *f.*; (*clue*) indice *m.*; (*leash*) laisse *f.*; (*theatre*) premier rôle *m.*; (*wire*) fil *m.*; (*example*) exemple *m.* **in the ~,** en tête. **~ away,** emmener. **~ up to,** (*come to*) en venir à; (*precede*) précéder.
lead[2] /led/ *n.* plomb *m.*; (*of pencil*) mine *f.* **~en** *a.* (*sky*) de plomb; (*humour*) lourd.
leader /'li:də(r)/ *n.* chef *m.*; (*of country, club, etc.*) dirigeant(e) *m.* (*f.*); (*leading article*) éditorial *m.* **~ship** *n.* direction *f.*
leading /'li:dɪŋ/ *a.* principal. **~ article,** éditorial *m.*
leaf /li:f/ *n.* (*pl.* **leaves**) feuille *f.*; (*of table*) rallonge *f.* ● *v.i.* **~ through,** feuilleter. **~y** *a.* feuillu.
leaflet /'li:flɪt/ *n.* prospectus *m.*
league /li:g/ *n.* ligue *f.*; (*sport*) championnat *m.* **in ~ with,** de mèche avec.
leak /li:k/ *n.* fuite *f.* ● *v.i.* fuir; (*news: fig.*) s'ébruiter. ● *v.t.* répandre; (*fig.*) divulguer. **~age** *n.* fuite *f.* **~y** *a.* qui a une fuite.
lean[1] /li:n/ *a.* (**-er, -est**) maigre. ● *n.* (*of meat*) maigre *m.* **~ness** *n.* maigreur *f.*
lean[2] /li:n/ *v.t./i.* (*p.t.* **leaned** *or* **leant** /lent/) (*rest*) (s')appuyer; (*slope*) pencher. **~ out,** se pencher à l'extérieur. **~ over,** (*of person*) se pencher. **~-to** *n.* appentis *m.*
leaning /'li:nɪŋ/ *a.* penché ● *n.* tendance *f.*
leap /li:p/ *v.i.* (*p.t.* **leaped** *or* **leapt** /lept/) bondir. ● *n.* bond *m.* **~-frog** *n.* saute-mouton *m. invar.*; *v.i.* (*p.t.* **-frogged**) sauter (**over,** par-dessus). **~ year,** année bissextile *f.*
learn /lɜ:n/ *v.t./i.* (*p.t.* **learned** *or* **learnt**) apprendre (**to do,** à faire). **~er** *n.* débutant(e) *m.* (*f.*).
learn|ed /'lɜ:nɪd/ *a.* érudit. **~ing** *n.* érudition *f.*, connaissances *f. pl.*
lease /li:s/ *n.* bail *m.* ● *v.t.* louer à bail.
leaseback /'li:sbæk/ *n.* cession-bail *f.*
leash /li:ʃ/ *n.* laisse *f.*
least /li:st/ *a.* **the ~,** (*smallest amount of*) le moins de; (*slightest*) le *or* la moindre. ● *n.* le moins. ● *adv.* le moins; (*with adjective*) le *or* la moins. **at ~,** au moins.
leather /'leðə(r)/ *n.* cuir *m.*
leave /li:v/ *v.t.* (*p.t.* **left**) laisser; (*depart from*) quitter. ● *v.i.* partir. ● *n.* (*holiday*) congé *m.*; (*consent*) permission *f.* **be left (over),** rester. **~ alone,** (*thing*) ne pas toucher à; (*person*) laisser

tranquille. **~ behind,** laisser. **~ out,** omettre. **on ~,** (*mil.*) en permission. **take one's ~,** prendre congé (**of,** de).

leavings /'li:vɪŋz/ *n. pl.* restes *m. pl.*

Leban|on /'lebənən/ *n.* Liban *m.* **~ese** /-'ni:z/ *a.* & *n.* libanais(e) (*m.* (*f.*)).

lecher /'letʃə(r)/ *n.* débauché *m.* **~ous** *a.* lubrique. **~y** *n.* lubricité *f.*

lectern /'lektən/ *n.* lutrin *m.*

lecture /'lektʃə(r)/ *n.* cours *m.*, conférence *f.*; (*rebuke*) réprimande *f.* ● *v.t./i.* faire un cours *or* une conférence (à); (*rebuke*) réprimander. **~r** /-ə(r)/ *n.* conférenc|ier, -ière *m.*, *f.*, (*univ.*) enseignant(e) *m.* (*f.*).

led /led/ *see* lead[1].

ledge /ledʒ/ *n.* (*window*) rebord *m.*; (*rock*) saillie *f.*

ledger /'ledʒə(r)/ *n.* grand livre *m.*

lee /li:/ *n.* côté sous le vent *m.*

leech /li:tʃ/ *n.* sangsue *f.*

leek /li:k/ *n.* poireau *m.*

leer /lɪə(r)/ *v.i.* **~ (at),** lorgner. ● *n.* regard sournois *m.*

leeway /'li:weɪ/ *n.* (*naut.*) dérive *f.*; (*fig.*) liberté d'action *f.* **make up ~,** rattraper le retard.

left[1] /left/ *see* leave. **~ luggage (office),** consigne *f.* **~-overs** *n. pl.* restes *m. pl.*

left[2] /left/ *a.* gauche. ● *adv.* à gauche. ● *n.* gauche *f.* **~-hand** *a.* à *or* de gauche. **~-handed** *a.* gaucher. **~-wing** *a.* (*pol.*) de gauche.

leftist /'leftɪst/ *n.* gauchiste *m./f.*

leg /leg/ *n.* jambe *f.*; (*of animal*) patte *f.*; (*of table*) pied *m.*; (*of chicken*) cuisse *f.*; (*of lamb*) gigot *m.*; (*of journey*) étape *f.* **~-room** *n.* place pour les jambes *f.* **~-warmers** *n. pl.* jambières *f. pl.*

legacy /'legəsɪ/ *n.* legs *m.*

legal /'li:gl/ *a.* légal; (*affairs etc.*) juridique. **~ity** /li:'gælətɪ/ *n.* légalité *f.* **~ly** *adv.* légalement.

legalize /'li:gəlaɪz/ *v.t.* légaliser.

legend /'ledʒənd/ *n.* légende *f.* **~ary** *a.* légendaire.

leggings /'legɪŋz/ *n. pl.* collant sans pieds *m.*

legib|le /'ledʒəbl/ *a.* lisible. **~ility** /-'bɪlətɪ/ *n.* lisibilité *f.* **~ly** *adv.* lisiblement.

legion /'li:dʒən/ *n.* légion *f.* **~naire** *n.* légionnaire *m.* **~naire's disease,** maladie du légionnaire *f.*

legislat|e /'ledʒɪsleɪt/ *v.i.* légiférer. **~ion** /-'leɪʃn/ *n.* (*body of laws*) législation *f.*; (*law*) loi *f.*

legislat|ive /'ledʒɪslətɪv/ *a.* législatif. **~ure** /-eɪtʃə(r)/ *n.* corps législatif *m.*

legitima|te /lɪ'dʒɪtɪmət/ *a.* légitime. **~cy** *n.* légitimité *f.*

leisure /'leʒə(r)/ *n.* loisir(s) *m.* (*pl.*). **at one's ~,** à tête reposée. **~ centre,** centre de loisirs *m.* **~ly** *a.* lent; *adv.* sans se presser.

lemon /'lemən/ *n.* citron *m.*

lemonade /lemə'neɪd/ *n.* (*fizzy*) limonade *f.*; (*still*) citronnade *f.*

lend /lend/ *v.t.* (*p.t.* **lent**) prêter; (*contribute*) donner. **~ itself to,** se prêter à. **~er** *n.* prêteu|r, -se *m.*, *f.* **~ing** *n.* prêt *m.*

length /leŋθ/ *n.* longueur *f.*; (*in time*) durée *f.*; (*section*) morceau *m.* **at ~,** (*at last*) enfin. **at (great) ~,** longuement. **~y** *a.* long.

lengthen /'leŋθən/ *v.t./i.* (s')allonger.

lengthways /'leŋθweɪz/ *adv.* dans le sens de la longueur.

lenien|t /'li:nɪənt/ *a.* indulgent. **~cy** *n.* indulgence *f.* **~tly** *adv.* avec indulgence.

lens /lenz/ *n.* lentille *f.*; (*of spectacles*) verre *m.*; (*photo.*) objectif *m.*

lent /lent/ *see* lend.

Lent /lent/ *n.* Carême *m.*

lentil /'lentl/ *n.* (*bean*) lentille *f.*

Leo /'li:əʊ/ *n.* le Lion.

leopard /'lepəd/ *n.* léopard *m.*

leotard /'li:ətɑ:d/ *n.* body *m.*

leper /'lepə(r)/ *n.* lépreu|x, -se *m.*, *f.*

leprosy /'leprəsɪ/ *n.* lèpre *f.*

lesbian /'lezbɪən/ *n.* lesbienne *f.* ● *a.* lesbien.

lesion /'li:ʒn/ *n.* lésion *f.*

less /les/ *a.* (*in quantity etc.*) moins de (**than,** que). ● *adv.*, *n.* & *prep.* moins. **~ than,** (*with numbers*) moins de. **work/etc. ~ than,** travailler/*etc.* moins que. **ten pounds/etc. ~,** dix livres/*etc.* de moins. **~ and less,** de moins en moins. **~er** *a.* moindre.

lessen /'lesn/ *v.t./i.* diminuer.

lesson /'lesn/ *n.* leçon *f.*

lest /lest/ *conj.* de peur que *or* de.

let /let/ *v.t.* (*p.t.* **let,** *pres. p.* **letting**) laisser; (*lease*) louer. ● *v. aux.* **~ us do, ~'s do,** faisons. **~ him do,** qu'il fasse. **~ me know the results,** informe-moi des résultats. ● *n.* location *f.* **~ alone,** (*thing*) ne pas toucher à; (*person*) laisser tranquille; (*never mind*) encore moins. **~ down,** baisser; (*deflate*) dégonfler; (*fig.*) décevoir. **~-down** *n.* déception *f.* **~ go** *v.t.* lâcher; *v.i.* lâcher prise. **~ sb. in/out,** laisser *or* faire entrer/sortir qn. **~ a dress out,** élargir une robe. **~ o.s. in for,** (*task*) s'engager à; (*trouble*) s'attirer. **~ off,** (*explode, fire*) faire éclater *or* partir; (*excuse*) dispenser; (*not punish*) ne pas punir. **~ up,** (*fam.*) s'arrêter. **~-up** *n.* répit *m.*

lethal /'li:θl/ *a.* mortel; (*weapon*) meurtrier.

letharg|y /'leθədʒɪ/ *n.* léthargie *f.* **~ic** /lɪ'θɑ:dʒɪk/ *a.* léthargique.

letter /'letə(r)/ *n.* lettre *f.* **~-bomb** *n.* lettre piégée *f.* **~-box** *n.* boîte à *or* aux lettres *f.* **~ing** *n.* (*letters*) caractères *m. pl.*

lettuce /'letɪs/ *n.* laitue *f.*, salade *f.*

leukaemia /lu:'ki:mɪə/ *n.* leucémie *f.*

level /'levl/ *a.* plat, uni; (*on surface*) horizontal; (*in height*) au même niveau (**with,** que); (*in score*) à égalité. ● *n.* niveau *m.* **(spirit) ~,** niveau à bulle *m.* ● *v.t.* (*p.t.* **levelled**) niveler; (*aim*) diriger. **be on the ~,** (*fam.*) être franc. **~ crossing,** passage à niveau *m.* **~-headed** *a.* équilibré.

lever /'li:və(r)/ *n.* levier *m.* ● *v.t.* soulever au moyen d'un levier.

leverage /'li:vərɪdʒ/ *n.* influence *f.*

levity /'levətɪ/ *n.* légèreté *f.*

levy /'levɪ/ *v.t.* (*tax*) (pré)lever. ● *n.* impôt *m.*

lewd /lju:d/ *a.* (**-er, -est**) obscène.

liable /'laɪəbl/ *a.* **be ~ to do,** avoir tendance à faire, pouvoir faire. **~ to,** (*illness etc.*) sujet à; (*fine*) passible de. **~ for,** responsable de.

liabilit|y /laɪə'bɪlətɪ/ *n.* responsabilité *f.*; (*fam.*) handicap *m.* **~ies,** (*debts*) dettes *f. pl.*

liais|e /lɪ'eɪz/ *v.i.* (*fam.*) faire la liaison. **~on** /-ɒn/ *n.* liaison *f.*

liar /'laɪə(r)/ *n.* menteu|r, -se *m., f.*

libel /'laɪbl/ *n.* diffamation *f.* ● *v.t.* (*p.t.* **libelled**) diffamer.

liberal /'lɪbərəl/ *a.* libéral; (*generous*) généreux, libéral. **~ly** *adv.* libéralement.

Liberal /'lɪbərəl/ *a.* & *n.* (*pol.*) libéral(e) (*m.* (*f.*)).

liberat|e /'lɪbəreɪt/ *v.t.* libérer. **~ion** /-'reɪʃn/ *n.* libération *f.*

libert|y /'lɪbətɪ/ *n.* liberté *f.* **at ~y to,** libre de. **take ~ies,** prendre des libertés.

libido /lɪ'bi:dəʊ/ *n.* libido *f.*

Libra /'li:brə/ *n.* la Balance.

librar|y /'laɪbrərɪ/ *n.* bibliothèque *f.* **~ian** /-'breərɪən/ *n.* bibliothécaire *m./f.*

libretto /lɪ'bretəʊ/ *n.* (*pl.* **-os**) (*mus.*) livret *m.*

Libya /'lɪbɪə/ *n.* Libye *f.* **~n** *a.* & *n.* libyen(ne) (*m.* (*f.*)).

lice /laɪs/ *see* louse.

licence, *Amer.* **license** [1] /'laɪsns/ *n.* permis *m.*; (*for television*) redevance *f.*; (*comm.*) licence *f.*; (*liberty: fig.*) licence *f.* **~ plate,** plaque minéralogique *f.*

license [2] /'laɪsns/ *v.t.* accorder un permis à, autoriser.

licentious /laɪ'senʃəs/ *a.* licencieux.

lichen /'laɪkən/ *n.* lichen *m.*

lick /lɪk/ *v.t.* lécher; (*defeat: sl.*) rosser. ● *n.* coup de langue *m.* **~ one's chops,** se lécher les babines.

licorice /'lɪkərɪs/ *n.* (*Amer.*) réglisse *f.*

lid /lɪd/ *n.* couvercle *m.*

lido /'laɪdəʊ/ *n.* (*pl.* **-os**) piscine en plein air *f.*

lie [1] /laɪ/ *n.* mensonge *m.* ● *v.i.* (*p.t.* **lied,** *pres. p.* **lying**) (*tell lies*) mentir. **give the ~ to,** démentir.

lie [2] /laɪ/ *v.i.* (*p.t.* **lay,** *p.p.* **lain,** *pres. p.* **lying**) s'allonger; (*remain*) rester; (*be*) se trouver, être; (*in grave*) reposer. **be lying,** être allongé. **~ down,** s'allonger. **~ in, have a ~-in,** faire la grasse matinée. **~ low,** se cacher.

lieu /lju:/ *n.* **in ~ of,** au lieu de.

lieutenant /lef'tenənt, *Amer.* lu:'tenənt/ *n.* lieutenant *m.*

life /laɪf/ *n.* (*pl.* **lives**) vie *f.* **~ cycle,** cycle de vie *m.* **~-guard** *n.* sauveteur *m.* **~ insurance,** assurance-vie *f.* **~-jacket, ~ preserver,** *n.* gilet de sauvetage *m.* **~- size(d)** *a.* grandeur nature *invar.* **~-style** *n.* style de vie *m.*

lifebelt /'laɪfbelt/ *n.* bouée de sauvetage *f.*

lifeboat /'laɪfbəʊt/ *n.* canot de sauvetage *m.*

lifebuoy /'laɪfbɔɪ/ *n.* bouée de sauvetage *f.*

lifeless /'laɪflɪs/ *a.* sans vie.

lifelike /'laɪflaɪk/ *a.* très ressemblant.

lifelong /'laɪflɒŋ/ *a.* de toute la vie.

lifetime /'laɪftaɪm/ *n.* vie *f.* **in one's ~,** de son vivant.

lift /lɪft/ *v.t.* lever; (*steal: fam.*) voler. ● *v.i.* (*of fog*) se lever. ● *n.* (*in building*) ascenseur *m.* **give a ~ to,** emmener (en voiture). **~-off** *n.* (*aviat.*) décollage *m.*

ligament /'lɪgəmənt/ *n.* ligament *m.*

light[1] /laɪt/ *n.* lumière *f.*; (*lamp*) lampe *f.*; (*for fire, on vehicle, etc.*) feu *m.*; (*headlight*) phare *m.* ● *a.* (*not dark*) clair. ● *v.t.* (*p.t.* **lit** *or* **lighted**) allumer; (*room etc.*) éclairer; (*match*) frotter. **bring to ~,** révéler. **come to ~,** être révélé. **have you got a ~?,** vous avez du feu? **~ bulb,** ampoule *f.* **~ pen,** crayon optique *m.* **~ up** *v.i.* s'allumer; *v.t.* (*room*) éclairer. **~-year** *n.* année lumière *f.*

light[2] /laɪt/ *a.* (**-er, -est**) (*not heavy*) léger. **~-fingered** *a.* chapardeur. **~-headed** *a.* (*dizzy*) qui a un vertige; (*frivolous*) étourdi. **~-hearted** *a.* gai. **~ly** *adv.* légèrement. **~ness** *n.* légèreté *f.*

lighten[1] /'laɪtn/ *v.t.* (*give light to*) éclairer; (*make brighter*) éclaircir.

lighten[2] /'laɪtn/ *v.t.* (*make less heavy*) alléger.

lighter /'laɪtə(r)/ *n.* briquet *m.*; (*for stove*) allume-gaz *m. invar.*

lighthouse /'laɪthaʊs/ *n.* phare *m.*

lighting /'laɪtɪŋ/ *n.* éclairage *m.* **~ technician,** éclairagiste *m./f.*

lightning /'laɪtnɪŋ/ *n.* éclair(s) *m.* (*pl.*), foudre *f.* ● *a.* éclair *invar.*

lightweight /'laɪtweɪt/ *a.* léger. ● *n.* (*boxing*) poids léger *m.*

like[1] /laɪk/ *a.* semblable, pareil. ● *prep.* comme. ● *conj.* (*fam.*) comme. ● *n.* pareil *m.* **be ~-minded,** avoir les mêmes sentiments. **the ~s of you,** des gens comme vous.

like[2] /laɪk/ *v.t.* aimer (bien). **~s** *n. pl.* goûts *m. pl.* **I should ~,** je voudrais, j'aimerais. **would you ~?,** voulez-vous? **~able** *a.* sympathique.

likel|y /'laɪklɪ/ *a.* (**-ier, -iest**) probable. ● *adv.* probablement. **he is ~y to do,** il fera probablement. **not ~y!,** (*fam.*) pas question! **~ihood** *n.* probabilité *f.*

liken /'laɪkən/ *v.t.* comparer.

likeness /'laɪknɪs/ *n.* ressemblance *f.*

likewise /'laɪkwaɪz/ *adv.* de même.

liking /'laɪkɪŋ/ *n.* (*for thing*) penchant *m.*; (*for person*) affection *f.*

lilac /'laɪlək/ *n.* lilas *m.* ● *a.* lilas *invar.*

lily /'lɪlɪ/ *n.* lis *m.*, lys *m.* **~ of the valley,** muguet *m.*

limb /lɪm/ *n.* membre *m.* **out on a ~,** isolé (et vulnérable).

limber /'lɪmbə(r)/ *v.i.* **~ up,** faire des exercices d'assouplissement.

limbo /'lɪmbəʊ/ *n.* **be in ~,** (*forgotten*) être tombé dans l'oubli.

lime[1] /laɪm/ *n.* chaux *f.*

lime[2] /laɪm/ *n.* (*fruit*) citron vert *m.*

lime[3] /laɪm/ *n.* **~(-tree),** tilleul *m.*

limelight /'laɪmlaɪt/ *n.* **in the ~,** en vedette.

limerick /'lɪmərɪk/ *n.* poème humoristique *m.* (*de cinq vers*).

limit /'lɪmɪt/ *n.* limite *f.* ● *v.t.* limiter. **~ed company,** société anonyme *f.* **~ation** /-'teɪʃn/ *n.* limitation *f.* **~less** *a.* sans limites.

limousine /'lɪməzi:n/ *n.* (*car*) limousine *f.*

limp[1] /lɪmp/ *v.i.* boiter. ● *n.* **have a ~,** boiter.

limp[2] /lɪmp/ *a.* (**-er, -est**) mou.

limpid /'lɪmpɪd/ *a.* limpide.

linctus /'lɪŋktəs/ *n.* sirop *m.*

line[1] /laɪn/ *n.* ligne *f.*; (*track*) voie *f.*; (*wrinkle*) ride *f.*; (*row*) rangée *f.*, file *f.*; (*of poem*) vers *m.*; (*rope*) corde *f.*; (*of goods*) gamme *f.*; (*queue: Amer.*) queue *f.* ● *v.t.* (*paper*) régler; (*streets etc.*) border. **be in ~ for,** avoir de bonnes chances d'avoir. **in ~ with,** en accord avec. **stand in ~,** faire la queue. **~ up,** (s')aligner; (*in queue*) faire la queue. **~ sth. up,** prévoir qch.

line[2] /laɪn/ *v.t.* (*garment*) doubler; (*fill*) remplir, garnir.

lineage /'lɪnɪɪdʒ/ *n.* lignée *f.*

linear /'lɪnɪə(r)/ *a.* linéaire.

linen /'lɪnɪn/ *n.* (*sheets etc.*) linge *m.*; (*material*) lin *m.*, toile de lin *f.*

liner /'laɪnə(r)/ *n.* paquebot *m.*

linesman /'laɪnzmən/ *n.* (*football*) juge de touche *m.*

linger /'lɪŋgə(r)/ *v.i.* s'attarder; (*smells etc.*) persister.

lingerie /'lænʒərɪ/ *n.* lingerie *f.*

lingo /'lɪŋgəʊ/ *n.* (*pl.* **-os**) (*hum., fam.*) jargon *m.*

linguist /'lɪŋgwɪst/ *n.* linguiste *m./f.*

linguistic /lɪŋ'gwɪstɪk/ *a.* linguistique. **~s** *n.* linguistique *f.*

lining /'laɪnɪŋ/ *n.* doublure *f.*

link /lɪŋk/ *n.* lien *m.*; (*of chain*) maillon *m.* ● *v.t.* relier; (*relate*) (re)lier. **~ up,** (*of roads*) se rejoindre. **~age** *n.* lien *m.* **~-up** *n.* liaison *f.*

links /'lɪŋks/ *n. invar.* terrain de golf *m.*

lino /'laɪnəʊ/ *n.* (*pl.* **-os**) lino *m.*

linoleum /lɪ'nəʊlɪəm/ *n.* linoléum *m.*

lint /lɪnt/ *n.* (*med.*) tissu ouaté *m.*; (*fluff*) peluche(s) *f.* (*pl.*).

lion /'laɪən/ *n.* lion *m.* **take the ~'s share,** se tailler la part du lion. **~ess** *n.* lionne *f.*

lip /lɪp/ *n.* lèvre *f.*; (*edge*) rebord *m.* **~-read** *v.t./i.* lire sur les lèvres. **pay ~-service to,** n'approuver que pour la forme.

lipsalve /'lɪpsælv/ *n.* baume pour les lèvres *m.*

lipstick /'lɪpstɪk/ *n.* rouge (à lèvres) *m.*

liquefy /'lɪkwɪfaɪ/ *v.t./i.* (se) liquéfier.

liqueur /lɪ'kjʊə(r)/ *n.* liqueur *f.*

liquid /'lɪkwɪd/ *n.* & *a.* liquide (*m.*). **~ize** *v.t.* passer au mixeur. **~izer** *n.* mixeur *m.*

liquidat|e /'lɪkwɪdeɪt/ *v.t.* liquider. **~ion** /-'deɪʃn/ *n.* liquidation *f.* **go into ~ion,** déposer son bilan.

liquor /'lɪkə(r)/ *n.* alcool *m.*

liquorice /'lɪkərɪs/ *n.* réglisse *f.*

lira /'lɪərə/ *n.* (*pl.* **lire** /'lɪəreɪ/ *or* **liras**) lire *f.*

lisp /lɪsp/ *n.* zézaiement *m.* ● *v.i.* zézayer. **with a ~,** en zézayant.

list[1] /lɪst/ *n.* liste *f.* ● *v.t.* dresser la liste de.

list[2] /lɪst/ *v.i.* (*ship*) gîter.

listen /'lɪsn/ *v.i.* écouter. **~ to, ~ in (to),** écouter. **~er** *n.* audi|teur, -trice *m./f.*

listless /'lɪstlɪs/ *a.* apathique.

lit /lɪt/ *see* light[1].

litany /'lɪtənɪ/ *n.* litanie *f.*

liter /'li:tə(r)/ *see* litre.

literal /'lɪtərəl/ *a.* littéral; (*person*) prosaïque. **~ly** *adv.* littéralement.

literary /'lɪtərərɪ/ *a.* littéraire.

litera|te /'lɪtərət/ *a.* qui sait lire et écrire. **~cy** *n.* capacité de lire et écrire *f.*

literature /'lɪtrətʃə(r)/ *n.* littérature *f.*; (*fig.*) documentation *f.*

lithe /laɪð/ *a.* souple, agile.

litigation /lɪtɪ'geɪʃn/ *n.* litige *m.*

litre, (*Amer.*) **liter** /'li:tə(r)/ *n.* litre *m.*

litter /'lɪtə(r)/ *n.* détritus *m. pl.*, papiers *m. pl.*; (*animals*) portée *f.* ● *v.t.* éparpiller; (*make untidy*) laisser des détritus dans. **~-bin** *n.* poubelle *f.* **~ed with,** jonché de.

little /'lɪtl/ *a.* petit; (*not much*) peu de. ● *n.* peu *m.* ● *adv.* peu. **a ~,** un peu (de).

liturgy /'lɪtədʒɪ/ *n.* liturgie *f.*

live[1] /laɪv/ *a.* vivant; (*wire*) sous tension; (*broadcast*) en direct. **be a ~ wire,** être très dynamique.

live[2] /lɪv/ *v.t./i.* vivre; (*reside*) habiter, vivre. **~ down,** faire oublier. **~ it up,** mener la belle vie. **~ on,** (*feed o.s. on*) vivre de; (*continue*) survivre. **~ up to,** se montrer à la hauteur de.

livelihood /'laɪvlɪhʊd/ *n.* moyens d'existence *m. pl.*

livel|y /'laɪvlɪ/ *a.* (**-ier, -iest**) vif, vivant. **~iness** *n.* vivacité *f.*

liven /'laɪvn/ *v.t./i.* **~ up,** (s')animer; (*cheer up*) (s')égayer.

liver /'lɪvə(r)/ *n.* foie *m.*

livery /'lɪvərɪ/ *n.* livrée *f.*

livestock /'laɪvstɒk/ *n.* bétail *m.*

livid /'lɪvɪd/ *a.* livide; (*angry*: *fam.*) furieux.

living /'lɪvɪŋ/ *a.* vivant. ● *n.* vie *f.* **make a ~,** gagner sa vie. **~ conditions,** conditions de vie *f. pl.* **~-room** *n.* salle de séjour *f.*

lizard /'lɪzəd/ *n.* lézard *m.*

llama /'lɑ:mə/ *n.* lama *m.*

load /ləʊd/ *n.* charge *f.*; (*loaded goods*) chargement *m.*, charge *f.*; (*weight, strain*) poids *m.* **~s of,** (*fam.*) des masses de. ● *v.t.* charger. **~ed** *a.* (*dice*) pipé; (*wealthy*: *sl.*) riche.

loaf[1] /ləʊf/ *n.* (*pl.* **loaves**) pain *m.*

loaf[2] /ləʊf/ *v.i.* **~ (about),** fainéanter. **~er** *n.* fainéant(e) *m.* (*f.*).

loam /ləʊm/ *n.* terreau *m.*

loan /ləʊn/ *n.* prêt *m.*; (*money borrowed*) emprunt *m.* ● *v.t.* (*lend*: *fam.*) prêter.

loath /ləʊθ/ *a.* peu disposé (**to,** à).

loath|e /ləʊð/ *v.t.* détester. **~ing** *n.* dégoût *m.* **~some** *a.* dégoûtant.

lobby /'lɒbɪ/ *n.* entrée *f.*, vestibule *m.*; (*pol.*) lobby *m.*, groupe de pression *m.* ● *v.t.* faire pression sur.

lobe /ləʊb/ *n.* lobe *m.*

lobster /'lɒbstə(r)/ *n.* homard *m.*

local /'ləʊkl/ *a.* local; (*shops etc.*) du quartier. ● *n.* personne du coin *f.*; (*pub*: *fam.*) pub du coin *m.* **~ government,** administration locale *f.* **~ly** *adv.* localement; (*nearby*) dans les environs.

locale /ləʊ'kɑ:l/ *n.* lieu *m.*

locality /ləʊ'kæləti/ *n.* (*district*) région *f.*; (*position*) lieu *m.*

localized /'ləʊkəlaɪzd/ *a.* localisé.

locat|e /ləʊ'keɪt/ *v.t.* (*situate*) situer; (*find*) repérer. **~ion** /-ʃn/ *n.* emplacement *m.* **on ~ion,** (*cinema*) en extérieur.

lock[1] /lɒk/ *n.* mèche (de cheveux) *f.*

lock[2] /lɒk/ *n.* (*of door etc.*) serrure *f.*; (*on canal*) écluse *f.* ● *v.t./i.* fermer à clef; (*wheels: auto.*) (se) bloquer. **~ in** *or* **up,** (*person*) enfermer. **~ out,** (*by mistake*) enfermer dehors. **~-out** *n.* lockout *m. invar.* **~-up** *n.* (*shop*) boutique *f.*; (*garage*) box *m.*

locker /'lɒkə(r)/ *n.* casier *m.*

locket /'lɒkɪt/ *n.* médaillon *m.*

locksmith /'lɒksmɪθ/ *n.* serrurier *m.*

locomotion /ləʊkə'məʊʃn/ *n.* locomotion *f.*

locomotive /'ləʊkəməʊtɪv/ *n.* locomotive *f.*

locum /'ləʊkəm/ *n.* (*doctor etc.*) remplaçant(e) *m.* (*f.*).

locust /'ləʊkəst/ *n.* criquet *m.*, sauterelle *f.*

lodge /lɒdʒ/ *n.* (*house*) pavillon (de gardien *or* de chasse) *m.*; (*of porter*) loge *f.* ● *v.t.* loger; (*money, complaint*) déposer. ● *v.i.* être logé (**with,** chez); (*become fixed*) se loger. **~r** /-ə(r)/ *n.* locataire *m./f.*, pensionnaire *m./f.*

lodgings /'lɒdʒɪŋz/ *n.* chambre (meublée) *f.*; (*flat*) logement *m.*

loft /lɒft/ *n.* grenier *m.*

lofty /'lɒftɪ/ *a.* (**-ier, -iest**) (*tall, noble*) élevé; (*haughty*) hautain.

log /lɒg/ *n.* (*of wood*) bûche *f.* **~(-book),** (*naut.*) journal de bord *m.*; (*auto.*) (*équivalent de la*) carte grise *f.* ● *v.t.* (*p.t.* **logged**) noter; (*distance*) parcourir. **~ on,** entrer. **~ off,** sortir.

logarithm /'lɒgərɪðəm/ *n.* logarithme *m.*

loggerheads /'lɒgəhedz/ *n. pl.* **at ~,** en désaccord.

logic /'lɒdʒɪk/ *a.* logique. **~al** *a.* logique. **~ally** *adv.* logiquement.

logistics /lə'dʒɪstɪks/ *n.* logistique *f.*

logo /'ləʊgəʊ/ *n.* (*pl.* **-os**) (*fam.*) emblème *m.*

loin /lɔɪn/ *n.* (*culin.*) filet *m.* **~s,** reins *m. pl.*

loiter /'lɔɪtə(r)/ *v.i.* traîner.

loll /lɒl/ *v.i.* se prélasser.

loll|ipop /'lɒlɪpɒp/ *n.* sucette *f.* **~y** *n.* (*fam.*) sucette *f.*; (*sl.*) fric *m.*

London /'lʌndən/ *n.* Londres *m./f.* **~er** *n.* Londonien(ne) *m.* (*f.*).

lone /ləʊn/ *a.* solitaire. **~r** /-ə(r)/ *n.* solitaire *m./f.* **~some** *a.* solitaire.

lonely /'ləʊnlɪ/ *a.* (**-ier, -iest**) solitaire; (*person*) seul, solitaire.

long[1] /lɒŋ/ *a.* (**-er, -est**) long. ● *adv.* longtemps. **how ~ is?,** quelle est la longueur de?; (*in time*) quelle est la durée de? **how ~?,** combien de temps? **he will not be ~,** il n'en a pas pour longtemps. **a ~ time,** longtemps. **as** *or* **so ~ as,** pourvu que. **before ~,** avant peu. **I no ~er do,** je ne fais plus. **~-distance** *a.* (*flight*) sur long parcours; (*phone call*) interurbain. **~ face,** grimace *f.* **~ johns,** (*fam.*) caleçon long *m.* **~ jump,** saut en longueur *m.* **~-playing record,** microsillon *m.* **~-range** *a.* à longue portée; (*forecast*) à long terme. **~-sighted** *a.* presbyte. **~-standing** *a.* de longue date. **~-suffering** *a.* très patient. **~-term** *a.* à long terme. **~ wave,** grandes ondes *f. pl.* **~-winded** *a.* (*speaker etc.*) verbeux.

long[2] /lɒŋ/ *v.i.* avoir bien *or* très envie (**for, to,** de). **~ for s.o.,** (*pine for*) languir après qn. **~ing** *n.* envie *f.*; (*nostalgia*) nostalgie *f.*

longevity /lɒn'dʒevətɪ/ *n.* longévité *f.*

longhand /'lɒŋhænd/ *n.* écriture courante *f.*

longitude /'lɒndʒɪtju:d/ *n.* longitude *f.*

loo /lu:/ *n.* (*fam.*) toilettes *f. pl.*

look /lʊk/ *v.t./i.* regarder; (*seem*) avoir l'air. ● *n.* regard *m.*; (*appearance*) air *m.*, aspect *m.* **(good) ~s,** beauté *f.* **~ after,** s'occuper de, soigner. **~ at,** regarder. **~ back on,** repenser à. **~ down on,** mépriser. **~ for,** chercher. **~ forward to,** attendre avec impatience. **~ in on,** passer voir. **~ into,** examiner. **~ like,** ressembler à, avoir l'air de. **~ out,** faire attention. **~ out for,** chercher; (*watch*) guetter. **~-out** *n.* (*mil.*) poste de guet *m.*; (*person*) guetteur *m.* **be on the ~-out for,** rechercher. **~ round,** se retourner. **~ up,** (*word*) chercher; (*visit*) passer voir. **~ up to,** respecter. **~-alike** *n.* sosie *m.* **~ing-glass** *n.* glace *f.*

loom[1] /lu:m/ *n.* métier à tisser *m.*

loom[2] /lu:m/ *v.i.* surgir; (*event etc.*: *fig.*) paraître imminent.

loony /'lu:nɪ/ *n.* & *a.* (*sl.*) fou, folle (*m.*, *f.*).

loop /lu:p/ *n.* boucle *f.* ● *v.t.* boucler.

loophole /'lu:phəʊl/ *n.* (*in rule*) échappatoire *f.*

loose /lu:s/ *a.* (**-er, -est**) (*knot etc.*) desserré; (*page etc.*) détaché; (*clothes*) ample, lâche; (*tooth*) qui bouge; (*lax*) relâché; (*not packed*) en vrac; (*inexact*) vague; (*pej.*) immoral. **at a ~ end,** (*Amer.*) **at ~ ends,** désœuvré. **come ~,** bouger. **~ly** *adv.* sans serrer; (*roughly*) vaguement.

loosen /'lu:sn/ *v.t.* (*slacken*) desserrer; (*untie*) défaire.

loot /lu:t/ *n.* butin *m.* ● *v.t.* piller. **~er** *n.* pillard(e) *m.* (*f.*). **~ing** *n.* pillage *m.*

lop /lɒp/ *v.t.* (*p.t.* **lopped**). **~ off,** couper.

lop-sided /lɒp'saɪdɪd/ *a.* de travers.

lord /lɔ:d/ *n.* seigneur *m.*; (*British title*) lord *m.* **the L~,** le Seigneur. **(good) L~!,** mon Dieu! **~ly** *a.* noble; (*haughty*) hautain.

lore /lɔ:(r)/ *n.* traditions *f. pl.*

lorry /'lɒrɪ/ *n.* camion *m.*

lose /lu:z/ *v.t./i.* (*p.t.* **lost**) perdre. **get lost,** se perdre. **~r** /-ə(r)/ *n.* perdant(e) *m.* (*f.*).

loss /lɒs/ *n.* perte *f.* **be at a ~,** être perplexe. **be at a ~ to,** être incapable de. **heat ~,** déperdition de chaleur *f.*

lost /lɒst/ *see* lose. ● *a.* perdu. **~ property,** (*Amer.*) **~ and found,** objets trouvés *m. pl.*

lot[1] /lɒt/ *n.* (*fate*) sort *m.*; (*at auction*) lot *m.*; (*land*) lotissement *m.*

lot[2] /lɒt/ *n.* **the ~,** (le) tout *m.*; (*people*) tous *m. pl.*, toutes *f. pl.* **a ~ (of), ~s (of),** (*fam.*) beaucoup (de). **quite a ~ (of),** (*fam.*) pas mal (de).

lotion /'ləʊʃn/ *n.* lotion *f.*

lottery /'lɒtərɪ/ *n.* loterie *f.*

loud /laʊd/ *a.* (**-er, -est**) bruyant, fort. ● *adv.* fort. **~ hailer,** portevoix *m. invar.* **out ~,** tout haut. **~ly** *adv.* fort.

loudspeaker /laʊd'spi:kə(r)/ *n.* haut-parleur *m.*

lounge /laʊndʒ/ *v.i.* paresser. ● *n.* salon *m.* **~ suit,** costume *m.*

louse /laʊs/ *n.* (*pl.* **lice**) pou *m.*

lousy /'laʊzɪ/ *a.* (**-ier, -iest**) pouilleux; (*bad*: *sl.*) infect.

lout /laʊt/ *n.* rustre *m.*

lovable /'lʌvəbl/ *a.* adorable.

love /lʌv/ *n.* amour *m.*; (*tennis*) zéro *m.* ● *v.t.* aimer; (*like greatly*) aimer (beaucoup) (**to do,** faire). **in ~,** amoureux (**with,** de). **~ affair,** liaison amoureuse *f.* **~ life,** vie amoureuse *f.* **make ~,** faire l'amour.

lovely /'lʌvlɪ/ *a.* (**-ier, -iest**) joli; (*delightful*: *fam.*) très agréable.

lover /'lʌvə(r)/ *n.* amant *m.*; (*devotee*) amateur *m.* (**of,** de).

lovesick /'lʌvsɪk/ *a.* amoureux.

loving /'lʌvɪŋ/ *a.* affectueux.

low[1] /ləʊ/ *v.i.* meugler.

low[2] /ləʊ/ *a.* & *adv.* (**-er, -est**) bas. ● *n.* (*low pressure*) dépression *f.* **reach a (new) ~,** atteindre son niveau le plus bas. **~ in sth.,** à faible teneur en qch. **~-calorie** *a.* basses-calories. **~-cut** *a.* décolleté. **~-down** *a.* méprisable; *n.* (*fam.*) renseignements *m. pl.* **~-fat** *a.* maigre. **~-key** *a.* modéré; (*discreet*) discret. **~-lying** *a.* à faible altitude.

lowbrow /'ləʊbraʊ/ *a.* peu intellectuel.

lower /'ləʊə(r)/ *a.* & *adv.* *see* low[2]. ● *v.t.* baisser. **~ o.s.,** s'abaisser.

lowlands /'ləʊləndz/ *n. pl.* plaine(s) *f.* (*pl.*).

lowly /'ləʊlɪ/ *a.* (**-ier, -iest**) humble.

loyal /'lɔɪəl/ *a.* loyal. **~ly** *adv.* loyalement. **~ty** *n.* loyauté *f.*

lozenge /'lɒzɪndʒ/ *n.* (*shape*) losange *m.*; (*tablet*) pastille *f.*

LP *abbr. see* long-playing record.

Ltd. *abbr.* (*Limited*) SA.

lubric|ate /'lu:brɪkeɪt/ *v.t.* graisser, lubrifier. **~ant** *n.* lubrifiant *m.* **~ation** /-'keɪʃn/ *n.* graissage *m.*

lucid /'lu:sɪd/ *a.* lucide. **~ity** /lu:'sɪdətɪ/ *n.* lucidité *f.*

luck /lʌk/ *n.* chance *f.* **bad ~,** malchance *f.* **good ~!,** bonne chance!

luck|y /'lʌkɪ/ *a.* (**-ier, -iest**) qui a de la chance, heureux; (*event*) heureux; (*number*) qui porte bonheur. **it's ~y that,** c'est une chance que. **~ily** *adv.* heureusement.

lucrative /'lu:krətɪv/ *a.* lucratif.

ludicrous /'lu:dɪkrəs/ *a.* ridicule.

lug /lʌg/ *v.t.* (*p.t.* **lugged**) traîner.

luggage /'lʌgɪdʒ/ *n.* bagages *m. pl.* **~-rack** *n.* porte-bagages *m. invar.*

lukewarm /'lu:kwɔ:m/ *a.* tiède.

lull /lʌl/ *v.t.* (*soothe, send to sleep*) endormir. ● *n.* accalmie *f.*
lullaby /ˈlʌləbaɪ/ *n.* berceuse *f.*
lumbago /lʌmˈbeɪgəʊ/ *n.* lumbago *m.*
lumber /ˈlʌmbə(r)/ *n.* bric-à-brac *m. invar.*; (*wood*) bois de charpente *m.* ● *v.t.* **~ s.o. with,** (*chore etc.*) coller à qn.
lumberjack /ˈlʌmbədʒæk/ *n.* (*Amer.*) bûcheron *m.*
luminous /ˈlu:mɪnəs/ *a.* lumineux.
lump /lʌmp/ *n.* morceau *m.*; (*swelling on body*) grosseur *f.*; (*in liquid*) grumeau *m.* ● *v.t.* **~ together,** réunir. **~ sum,** somme globale *f.* **~y** *a.* (*sauce*) grumeleux; (*bumpy*) bosselé.
lunacy /ˈlu:nəsɪ/ *n.* folie *f.*
lunar /ˈlu:nə(r)/ *a.* lunaire.
lunatic /ˈlu:nətɪk/ *n.* fou, folle *m.*, *f.*
lunch /lʌntʃ/ *n.* déjeuner *m.* ● *v.i.* déjeuner. **~ box,** cantine *f.*
luncheon /ˈlʌntʃən/ *n.* déjeuner *m.* **~ meat,** (*approx.*) saucisson *m.* **~ voucher,** chèque-repas *m.*
lung /lʌŋ/ *n.* poumon *m.*
lunge /lʌndʒ/ *n.* mouvement brusque en avant *m.* ● *v.i.* s'élancer (**at,** sur).
lurch[1] /lɜ:tʃ/ *n.* **leave in the ~,** planter là, laisser en plan.
lurch[2] /lɜ:tʃ/ *v.i.* (*person*) tituber.
lure /lʊə(r)/ *v.t.* appâter, attirer. ● *n.* (*attraction*) attrait *m.*, appât *m.*
lurid /ˈlʊərɪd/ *a.* choquant, affreux; (*gaudy*) voyant.
lurk /lɜ:k/ *v.i.* se cacher; (*in ambush*) s'embusquer; (*prowl*) rôder. **a ~ing suspicion,** un petit soupçon.
luscious /ˈlʌʃəs/ *a.* appétissant.
lush /lʌʃ/ *a.* luxuriant. ● *n.* (*Amer., fam.*) ivrogne(sse) *m.* (*f.*).
lust /lʌst/ *n.* luxure *f.*; (*fig.*) convoitise *f.* ● *v.i.* **~ after,** convoiter.
lustre /ˈlʌstə(r)/ *n.* lustre *m.*
lusty /ˈlʌstɪ/ *a.* (**-ier, -iest**) robuste.
lute /lu:t/ *n.* (*mus.*) luth *m.*
Luxemburg /ˈlʌksəmbɜ:g/ *n.* Luxembourg *m.*
luxuriant /lʌgˈʒʊərɪənt/ *a.* luxuriant.
luxurious /lʌgˈʒʊərɪəs/ *a.* luxueux.
luxury /ˈlʌkʃərɪ/ *n.* luxe *m.* ● *a.* de luxe.
lying /ˈlaɪɪŋ/ *see* lie[1], lie[2]. ● *n.* le mensonge.
lynch /lɪntʃ/ *v.t.* lyncher.
lynx /lɪŋks/ *n.* lynx *m.*
lyric /ˈlɪrɪk/ *a.* lyrique. **~s** *n. pl.* paroles *f. pl.* **~al** *a.* lyrique. **~ism** /-sɪzəm/ *n.* lyrisme *m.*

M

MA *abbr. see* Master of Arts
mac /mæk/ *n.* (*fam.*) imper *m.*
macaroni /mækəˈrəʊnɪ/ *n.* macaronis *m. pl.*
macaroon /mækəˈru:n/ *n.* macaron *m.*
mace /meɪs/ *n.* (*staff*) masse *f.*
Mach /mɑ:k/ *n.* **~ (number),** (nombre de) Mach *m.*
machiavellian /mækɪəˈvelɪən/ *a.* machiavélique.
machinations /mækɪˈneɪʃnz/ *n. pl.* machinations *f. pl.*
machine /məˈʃi:n/ *n.* machine *f.* ● *v.t.* (*sew*) coudre à la machine; (*techn.*) usiner. **~ code,** code machine *m.* **~-gun** *n.* mitrailleuse *f.*; *v.t.* (*p.t.* **-gunned**) mitrailler. **~-readable** *a.* en langage machine. **~ tool,** machine-outil *f.*
machinery /məˈʃi:nərɪ/ *n.* machinerie *f.*; (*working parts & fig.*) mécanisme(s) *m.* (*pl.*).
machinist /məˈʃi:nɪst/ *n.* (*operator*) opéra|teur, -trice sur machine *m.*, *f.*; (*on sewing-machine*) piqueu|r, -se *m.*, *f.*
macho /ˈmætʃəʊ/ *n.* (*pl.* **-os**) macho *m.* ● *a.* macho *invar.*
mackerel /ˈmækrəl/ *n. invar.* (*fish*) maquereau *m.*
mackintosh /ˈmækɪntɒʃ/ *n.* imperméable *m.*
macrobiotic /mækrəʊbaɪˈɒtɪk/ *a.* macrobiotique.
mad /mæd/ *a.* (**madder, maddest**) fou; (*foolish*) insensé; (*dog etc.*) enragé; (*angry: fam.*) furieux. **be ~ about,** se passionner pour; (*person*) être fou de. **drive s.o. ~,** exaspérer qn. **like ~,** comme un fou. **~ly** *adv.* (*interested, in love, etc.*) follement; (*frantically*) comme un fou. **~ness** *n.* folie *f.*
Madagascar /mædəˈgæskə(r)/ *n.* Madagascar *f.*
madam /ˈmædəm/ *n.* madame *f.*; (*unmarried*) mademoiselle *f.*
madden /ˈmædn/ *v.t.* exaspérer.
made /meɪd/ *see* make. **~ to measure,** fait sur mesure.
Madeira /məˈdɪərə/ *n.* (*wine*) madère *m.*
madhouse /ˈmædhaʊs/ *n.* (*fam.*) maison de fous *f.*

madman /'mædmən/ *n.* (*pl.* **-men**) fou *m.*
madrigal /'mædrɪgl/ *n.* madrigal *m.*
magazine /mægə'zi:n/ *n.* revue *f.*, magazine *m.*; (*of gun*) magasin *m.*
magenta /mə'dʒentə/ *a.* magenta (*invar.*).
maggot /'mægət/ *n.* ver *m.*, asticot *m.* **~y** *a.* véreux.
magic /'mædʒɪk/ *n.* magie *f.* ● *a.* magique. **~al** *a.* magique.
magician /mə'dʒɪʃn/ *n.* magicien(ne) *m.* (*f.*).
magistrate /'mædʒɪstreɪt/ *n.* magistrat *m.*
magnanim|ous /mæg'nænɪməs/ *a.* magnanime. **~ity** /-ə'nɪmətɪ/ *n.* magnanimité *f.*
magnate /'mægneɪt/ *n.* magnat *m.*
magnesia /mæg'ni:ʃə/ *n.* magnésie *f.*
magnet /'mægnɪt/ *n.* aimant *m.* **~ic** /-'netɪk/ *a.* magnétique. **~ism** *n.* magnétisme *m.* **~ize** *v.t.* magnétiser.
magneto /mæg'ni:təʊ/ *n.* (*pl.* **os**) magnéto *m.*
magnificen|t /mæg'nɪfɪsnt/ *a.* magnifique. **~ce** *n.* magnificence *f.*
magnif|y /'mægnɪfaɪ/ *v.t.* grossir; (*sound*) amplifier; (*fig.*) exagérer. **~ication** /-ɪ'keɪʃn/ *n.* grossissement *m.*; amplification *f.* **~ier** *n.*, **~ying glass,** loupe *f.*
magnitude /'mægnɪtju:d/ *n.* (*importance*) ampleur *f.*; (*size*) grandeur *f.*
magnolia /mæg'nəʊlɪə/ *n.* magnolia *m.*
magnum /'mægnəm/ *n.* magnum *m.*
magpie /'mægpaɪ/ *n.* pie *f.*
mahogany /mə'hɒgənɪ/ *n.* acajou *m.*
maid /meɪd/ *n.* (*servant*) bonne *f.*; (*girl*: *old use*) jeune fille *f.*
maiden /'meɪdn/ *n.* (*old use*) jeune fille *f.* ● *a.* (*aunt*) célibataire; (*voyage*) premier. **~ name,** nom de jeune fille *m.* **~hood** *n.* virginité *f.* **~ly** *a.* virginal.
mail[1] /meɪl/ *n.* poste *f.*; (*letters*) courrier *m.* ● *a.* (*bag*, *van*) postal. ● *v.t.* envoyer par la poste. **mail box,** boîte à lettres *f.* **~ing list,** liste d'adresses *f.* **~ order,** vente par correspondance *f.* **~ shot,** publipostage *m.*
mail[2] /meɪl/ *n.* (*armour*) cotte de mailles *f.*
mailman /'meɪlmæn/ *n.* (*pl.* **-men**) (*Amer.*) facteur *m.*
maim /meɪm/ *v.t.* mutiler.
main[1] /meɪn/ *a.* principal. ● *n.* **in the ~,** en général. **~ line,** grande ligne *f.* **a ~ road,** une grande route. **~ly** *adv.* principalement, surtout.
main[2] /meɪn/ *n.* **(water/gas) ~,** conduite d'eau/de gaz *f.* **the ~s,** (*electr.*) le secteur.
mainframe *n.* unité centrale *f.*
mainland /'meɪnlənd/ *n.* continent *m.*
mainspring /'meɪnsprɪŋ/ *n.* ressort principal *m.*; (*motive*: *fig.*) mobile principal *m.*
mainstay /'meɪnsteɪ/ *n.* soutien *m.*
mainstream /'meɪnstri:m/ *n.* tendance principale *f.*, ligne *f.*
maintain /meɪn'teɪn/ *v.t.* (*continue, keep, assert*) maintenir; (*house, machine, family*) entretenir; (*rights*) soutenir.
maintenance /'meɪntənəns/ *n.* (*care*) entretien *m.*; (*continuation*) maintien *m.*; (*allowance*) pension alimentaire *f.*
maisonette /meɪzə'net/ *n.* duplex *m.*
maize /meɪz/ *n.* maïs *m.*
majestic /mə'dʒestɪk/ *a.* majestueux.
majesty /'mædʒəstɪ/ *n.* majesté *f.*
major /'meɪdʒə(r)/ *a.* majeur. ● *n.* commandant *m.* ● *v.i.* **~ in,** (*univ.*, *Amer.*) se spécialiser en. **~ road,** route à priorité *f.*
Majorca /mə'dʒɔ:kə/ *n.* Majorque *f.*
majority /mə'dʒɒrətɪ/ *n.* majorité *f.* ● *a.* majoritaire. **the ~ of people,** la plupart des gens.
make /meɪk/ *v.t./i.* (*p.t.* **made**) faire; (*manufacture*) fabriquer; (*friends*) se faire; (*money*) gagner, se faire; (*decision*) prendre; (*destination*) arriver à; (*cause to be*) rendre. **~ s.o. do sth.,** faire faire qch. à qn.; (*force*) obliger qn. à faire qch. ● *n.* fabrication *f.*; (*brand*) marque *f.* **be made of,** être fait de. **~ o.s. at home,** se mettre à l'aise. **~ s.o. happy,** rendre qn. heureux. **~ it,** arriver; (*succeed*) réussir. **I ~ it two o'clock,** j'ai deux heures. **I ~ it 150,** d'après moi, ça fait 150. **I cannot ~ anything of it,** je n'y comprends rien. **can you ~ Friday?,** vendredi, c'est possible? **~ as if to,** faire mine de. **~ believe,** faire semblant. **~-believe,** *a.* feint, illusoire; *n.* fantaisie *f.* **~ do,** (*manage*) se débrouiller (**with,** avec). **~ do with,** (*content o.s.*) se contenter de. **~ for,** se diriger vers; (*cause*) tendre à créer. **~ good** *v.i.* réussir;

v.t. compenser; (*repair*) réparer. **~ off,** filer (**with,** avec). **~ out** *v.t.* distinguer; (*understand*) comprendre; (*draw up*) faire; (*assert*) prétendre; *v.i.* (*fam.*) se débrouiller. **~ over,** céder (**to,** à); (*convert*) transformer. **~ up** *v.t.* faire, former; (*story*) inventer; (*deficit*) combler; *v.i.* se réconcilier. **~ up (one's face),** se maquiller. **~-up** *n.* maquillage *m.*; (*of object*) constitution *f.*; (*psych.*) caractère *m.* **~ up for,** compenser; (*time*) rattraper. **~ up one's mind,** se décider. **~ up to,** se concilier les bonnes grâces de.

maker /'meɪkə(r)/ *n.* fabricant *m.*

makeshift /'meɪkʃɪft/ *n.* expédient *m.* ● *a.* provisoire.

making /'meɪkɪŋ/ *n.* **be the ~ of,** faire le succès de. **he has the ~s of,** il a l'étoffe de.

maladjusted /mælə'dʒʌstɪd/ *a.* inadapté.

maladministration /mælədmɪnɪ'streɪʃn/ *n.* mauvaise gestion *f.*

malaise /mæ'leɪz/ *n.* malaise *m.*

malaria /mə'leərɪə/ *n.* malaria *f.*

Malay /mə'leɪ/ *a.* & *n.* malais(e) (*m.* (*f.*)). **~sia** *n.* Malaisie *f.*

Malaya /mə'leɪə/ *n.* Malaisie *f.*

male /meɪl/ *a.* (*voice, sex*) masculin; (*bot., techn.*) mâle. ● *n.* mâle *m.*

malevolen|t /mə'levələnt/ *a.* malveillant. **~ce** *n.* malveillance *f.*

malform|ation /mælfɔ:'meɪʃn/ *n.* malformation *f.* **~ed** *a.* difforme.

malfunction /mæl'fʌŋkʃn/ *n.* mauvais fonctionnement *m.* ● *v.i.* mal fonctionner.

malice /'mælɪs/ *n.* méchanceté *f.*

malicious /mə'lɪʃəs/ *a.* méchant. **~ly** *adv.* méchamment.

malign /mə'laɪn/ *a.* pernicieux. ● *v.t.* calomnier.

malignan|t /mə'lɪgnənt/ *a.* malveillant; (*tumour*) malin. **~cy** *n.* malveillance *f.*; malignité *f.*

malinger /mə'lɪŋgə(r)/ *v.i.* feindre la maladie. **~er** *n.* simula|teur, -trice *m., f.*

mall /mɔ:l/ *n.* **(shopping) ~,** centre commercial *m.*

malleable /'mælɪəbl/ *a.* malléable.

mallet /'mælɪt/ *n.* maillet *m.*

malnutrition /mælnju:'trɪʃn/ *n.* sous-alimentation *f.*

malpractice /mæl'præktɪs/ *n.* faute professionnelle *f.*

malt /mɔ:lt/ *n.* malt *m.* **~ whisky,** whisky pur malt *m.*

Malt|a /'mɔ:ltə/ *n.* Malte *f.* **~ese** /-'ti:z/ *a.* & *n.* maltais(e) (*m.* (*f.*)).

maltreat /mæl'tri:t/ *v.t.* maltraiter. **~ment** *n.* mauvais traitement *m.*

mammal /'mæml/ *n.* mammifère *m.*

mammoth /'mæməθ/ *n.* mammouth *m.* ● *a.* monstre.

man /mæn/ *n.* (*pl.* **men**) homme *m.*; (*in sports team*) joueur *m.*; (*chess*) pièce *f.* ● *v.t.* (*p.t.* **manned**) pourvoir en hommes; (*ship*) armer; (*guns*) servir; (*be on duty at*) être de service à. **~-hour** *n.* heure de main-d'œuvre *f.* **~ in the street,** homme de la rue *m.* **~-made** *a.* artificiel. **~-sized** *a.* grand. **~ to man,** d'homme à homme. **~ned space flight,** vol spatial habité *m.*

manage /'mænɪdʒ/ *v.t.* diriger; (*shop, affairs*) gérer; (*handle*) manier. **I could ~ another drink,** (*fam.*) je prendrais bien encore un verre. **can you ~ Friday?,** vendredi, c'est possible? ● *v.i.* se débrouiller. **~ to do,** réussir à faire. **~able** *a.* (*tool, size, person, etc.*) maniable; (*job*) faisable. **~ment** *n.* direction *f.*; (*of shop*) gestion *f.* **managing director,** directeur général *m.*

manager /'mænɪdʒə(r)/ *n.* direc|teur, -trice *m.,f.*; (*of shop*) gérant(e) *m.*(*f.*); (*of actor*) impresario *m.* **~ess** /-'res/ *n.* directrice *f.*; gérante *f.* **~ial** /-'dʒɪərɪəl/ *a.* directorial. **~ial staff,** cadres *m. pl.*

mandarin /'mændərɪn/ *n.* mandarin *m.*; (*orange*) mandarine *f.*

mandate /'mændeɪt/ *n.* mandat *m.*

mandatory /'mændətrɪ/ *a.* obligatoire.

mane /meɪn/ *n.* crinière *f.*

manful /'mænfl/ *a.* courageux.

manganese /mæŋgə'ni:z/ *n.* manganèse *m.*

mangetout /mɑnʒ'tu:/ *n.* mange-tout *m. invar.*

mangle[1] /'mæŋgl/ *n.* (*for wringing*) essoreuse *f.*; (*for smoothing*) calandre *f.*

mangle[2] /'mæŋgl/ *v.t.* mutiler.

mango /'mæŋgəʊ/ *n.* (*pl.* **-oes**) mangue *f.*

manhandle /'mænhændl/ *v.t.* maltraiter, malmener.

manhole /'mænhəʊl/ *n.* trou d'homme *m.*, regard *m.*

manhood /'mænhʊd/ *n.* âge d'homme *m.*; (*quality*) virilité *f.*
mania /'meɪnɪə/ *n.* manie *f.* **~c** /-ɪæk/ *n.* maniaque *m./f.*, fou *m.*, folle *f.*
manic-depressive /'mænɪk-dɪ'presɪv/ *a & n.* maniaco-dépressif(-ive) (*m.* (*f.*)).
manicur|e /'mænɪkjʊə(r)/ *n.* soin des mains *m.* ● *v.t.* soigner, manucurer. **~ist** *n.* manucure *m./f.*
manifest /'mænɪfest/ *a.* manifeste. ● *v.t.* manifester. **~ation** /-'steɪʃn/ *n.* manifestation *f.*
manifesto /mænɪ'festəʊ/ *n.* (*pl.* **-os**) manifeste *m.*
manifold /'mænɪfəʊld/ *a.* multiple. ● *n.* (*auto.*) collecteur *m.*
manipulat|e /mə'nɪpjʊleɪt/ *v.t.* (*tool, person*) manipuler. **~ion** /-'leɪʃn/ *n.* manipulation *f.*
mankind /mæn'kaɪnd/ *n.* genre humain *m.*
manly /'mænlɪ/ *a.* viril.
manner /'mænə(r)/ *n.* manière *f.*; (*attitude*) attitude *f.*; (*kind*) sorte *f.* **~s,** (*social behaviour*) manières *f. pl.* **~ed** *a.* maniéré.
mannerism /'mænərɪzəm/ *n.* trait particulier *m.*
manœuvre /mə'nu:və(r)/ *n.* manœuvre *f.* ● *v.t./i.* manœuvrer.
manor /'mænə(r)/ *n.* manoir *m.*
manpower /'mænpaʊə(r)/ *n.* main-d'œuvre *f.*
manservant /'mænsɜ:vənt/ *n.* (*pl.* **menservants**) domestique *m.*
mansion /'mænʃn/ *n.* château *m.*
manslaughter /'mænslɔ:tə(r)/ *n.* homicide involontaire *m.*
mantelpiece /'mæntlpi:s/ *n.* (*shelf*) cheminée *f.*
manual /'mænjʊəl/ *a.* manuel. ● *n.* (*handbook*) manuel *m.*
manufacture /mænjʊ'fæktʃə(r)/ *v.t.* fabriquer. ● *n.* fabrication *f.* **~r** /-ə(r)/ *n.* fabricant *m.*
manure /mə'njʊə(r)/ *n.* fumier *m.*; (*artificial*) engrais *m.*
manuscript /'mænjʊskrɪpt/ *n.* manuscrit *m.*
many /'menɪ/ *a.* & *n.* beaucoup (de). **a great** *or* **good ~,** un grand nombre (de). **~ a,** bien des.
Maori /'maʊrɪ/ *a.* maori. ● *n.* Maori(e) *m.* (*f.*).
map /mæp/ *n.* carte *f.*; (*of streets etc.*) plan *m.* ● *v.t.* (*p.t.* **mapped**) faire la carte de. **~ out,** (*route*) tracer; (*arrange*) organiser.
maple /'meɪpl/ *n.* érable *m.*
mar /mɑ:(r)/ *v.t.* (*p.t.* **marred**) gâter; (*spoil beauty of*) déparer.
marathon /'mærəθən/ *n.* marathon *m.*
marble /'mɑ:bl/ *n.* marbre *m.*; (*for game*) bille *f.*
March /mɑ:tʃ/ *n.* mars *m.*
march /mɑ:tʃ/ *v.i.* (*mil.*) marcher (au pas). **~ off**/*etc.*, partir/*etc.* allégrement. ● *v.t.* **~ off,** (*lead away*) emmener. ● *n.* marche *f.* **~-past** *n.* défilé *m.*
mare /meə(r)/ *n.* jument *f.*
margarine /mɑ:dʒə'ri:n/ *n.* margarine *f.*
margin /'mɑ:dʒɪn/ *n.* marge *f.* **~al** *a.* marginal; (*increase etc.*) léger, faible. **~al seat,** (*pol.*) siège chaudement disputé *m.* **~alize** *v.t.* marginaliser. **~ally** *adv.* très légèrement.
marigold /'mærɪgəʊld/ *n.* souci *m.*
marijuana /mærɪ'wɑ:nə/ *n.* marijuana *f.*
marina /mə'ri:nə/ *n.* marina *f.*
marinate /'mærɪneɪt/ *v.t.* mariner.
marine /mə'ri:n/ *a.* marin. ● *n.* (*shipping*) marine *f.*; (*sailor*) fusilier marin *m.*
marionette /mærɪə'net/ *n.* marionnette *f.*
marital /'mærɪtl/ *a.* conjugal. **~ status,** situation de famille *f.*
maritime /'mærɪtaɪm/ *a.* maritime.
marjoram /'mɑ:dʒərəm/ *n.* marjolaine *f.*
mark[1] /mɑ:k/ *n.* (*currency*) mark *m.*
mark[2] /mɑ:k/ *n.* marque *f.*; (*trace*) trace *f.*, marque *f.*; (*schol.*) note *f.*; (*target*) but *m.* ● *v.t.* marquer; (*exam*) corriger. **~ out,** délimiter; (*person*) désigner. **~ time,** marquer le pas. **~er** *n.* marque *f.* **~ing** *n.* (*marks*) marques *f.pl.*
marked /mɑ:kt/ *a.* marqué. **~ly**/-ɪdlɪ/ *adv.* visiblement.
market /'mɑ:kɪt/ *n.* marché *m.* ● *v.t.* (*sell*) vendre; (*launch*) commercialiser. **~ garden,** jardin maraîcher *m.* **~-place** *n.* marché *m.* **~ research,** étude de marché *f.* **~ value,** valeur marchande *f.* **on the ~,** en vente. **~ing** *n.* marketing *m.*
marksman /'mɑ:ksmən/ *n.* (*pl.* **-men**) tireur d'élite *m.*
marmalade /'mɑ:məleɪd/ *n.* confiture d'oranges *f.*

maroon /mə'ru:n/ *n.* bordeaux *m. invar.* ● *a.* bordeaux *invar.*
marooned /mə'ru:nd/ *a.* abandonné; (*snow-bound etc.*) bloqué.
marquee /mɑ:'ki:/ *n.* grande tente *f.*; (*awning*: *Amer.*) marquise *f.*
marquis /'mɑ:kwɪs/ *n.* marquis *m.*
marriage /'mærɪdʒ/ *n.* mariage *m.* **~able** *a.* nubile, mariable.
marrow /'mærəʊ/ *n.* (*of bone*) moelle *f.*; (*vegetable*) courge *f.*
marr|y /'mærɪ/ *v.t.* épouser; (*give or unite in marriage*) marier. ● *v.i.* se marier. **~ied** *a.* marié; (*life*) conjugal. **get ~ied**, se marier (**to**, avec).
Mars /mɑ:z/ *n.* (*planet*) Mars *f.*
marsh /mɑ:ʃ/ *n.* marais *m.* **~y** *a.* marécageux.
marshal /'mɑ:ʃl/ *n.* maréchal *m.*; (*at event*) membre du service d'ordre *m.* ● *v.t.* (*p.t.* **marshalled**) rassembler.
marshmallow /mɑ:ʃ'mæləʊ/ *n.* guimauve *f.*
martial /'mɑ:ʃl/ *a.* martial. **~ law**, loi martiale *f.*
martyr /'mɑ:tə(r)/ *n.* martyr(e) *m.* (*f.*). ● *v.t.* martyriser. **~dom** *n.* martyre *m.*
marvel /'mɑ:vl/ *n.* merveille *f.* ● *v.i.* (*p.t.* **marvelled**) s'émerveiller (**at**, de).
marvellous /'mɑ:vələs/ *a.* merveilleux.
Marxis|t /'mɑ:ksɪst/ *a.* & *n.* marxiste (*m./f.*). **~m** /-zəm/ *n.* marxisme *m.*
marzipan /'mɑ:zɪpæn/ *n.* pâte d'amandes *f.*
mascara /mæ'skɑ:rə/ *n.* mascara *m.*
mascot /'mæskət/ *n.* mascotte *f.*
masculin|e /'mæskjʊlɪn/ *a.* & *n.* masculin (*m.*). **~ity** /-'lɪnətɪ/ *n.* masculinité *f.*
mash /mæʃ/ *n.* pâtée *f.*; (*potatoes*: *fam.*) purée *f.* ● *v.t.* écraser. **~ed potatoes**, purée (de pommes de terre) *f.*
mask /mɑ:sk/ *n.* masque *m.* ● *v.t.* masquer.
masochis|t /'mæsəkɪst/ *n.* masochiste *m./f.* **~m** /-zəm/ *n.* masochisme *m.*
mason /'meɪsn/ *n.* (*builder*) maçon *m.* **~ry** *n.* maçonnerie *f.*
Mason /'meɪsn/ *n.* maçon *m.* **~ic** /mə'sɒnɪk/ *a.* maçonnique
masquerade /mɑ:skə'reɪd/ *n.* mascarade *f.* ● *v.i.* **~ as**, se faire passer pour.
mass[1] /mæs/ *n.* (*relig.*) messe *f.*
mass[2] /mæs/ *n.* masse *f.* ● *v.t./i.* (se) masser. **~-produce** *v.t.* fabriquer en série. **the ~es**, les masses *f.pl.* **the ~ media**, les média *m.pl.*
massacre /'mæsəkə(r)/ *n.* massacre *m.* ● *v.t.* massacrer.
massage /'mæsɑ:ʒ, *Amer.* mə'sɑ:ʒ/ *n.* massage *m.* ● *v.t.* masser.
masseu|r /mæ'sɜ:(r)/ *n.* masseur *m.* **~se** /-ɜ:z/ *n.* masseuse *f.*
massive /'mæsɪv/ *a.* (*large*) énorme; (*heavy*) massif.
mast /mɑ:st/ *n.* mât *m.*; (*for radio, TV*) pylône *m.*
master /'mɑ:stə(r)/ *n.* maître *m.*; (*in secondary school*) professeur *m.* ● *v.t.* maîtriser. **~-key** *n.* passe-partout *m. invar.* **~-mind** *n.* (*of scheme etc.*) cerveau *m.*; *v.t.* diriger. **M~ of Arts**/*etc.*, titulaire d'une maîtrise ès lettres/*etc. m./f.* **~-stroke** *n.* coup de maître *m.* **~y** *n.* maîtrise *f.*
masterly /'mɑ:stəlɪ/ *a.* magistral.
masterpiece /'mɑ:stəpi:s/ *n.* chef-d'œuvre *m.*
mastiff /'mæstɪf/ *n.* dogue *m.*
masturbat|e /'mæstəbeɪt/ *v.i.* se masturber. **~ion** /-'beɪʃn/ *n.* masturbation *f.*
mat /mæt/ *n.* (petit) tapis *m.*, natte *f.*; (*at door*) paillasson *m.*
match[1] /mætʃ/ *n.* allumette *f.*
match[2] /mætʃ/ *n.* (*sport*) match *m.*; (*equal*) égal(e) *m.* (*f.*); (*marriage*) mariage *m.*; (*s.o. to marry*) parti *m.* ● *v.t.* opposer; (*go with*) aller avec; (*cups etc.*) assortir; (*equal*) égaler. **be a ~ for**, pouvoir tenir tête à. ● *v.i.* (*be alike*) être assorti. **~ing** *a.* assorti.
matchbox /'mætʃbɒks/ *n.* boîte à allumettes *f.*
mate[1] /meɪt/ *n.* camarade *m./f.*; (*of animal*) compagnon *m.*, compagne *f.*; (*assistant*) aide *m./f.* ● *v.t./i.* (s')accoupler (**with**, avec).
mate[2] /meɪt/ *n.* (*chess*) mat *m.*
material /mə'tɪərɪəl/ *n.* matière *f.*; (*fabric*) tissu *m.*; (*documents, for building*) matériau(x) *m.* (*pl.*). **~s**, (*equipment*) matériel *m.* ● *a.* matériel; (*fig.*) important. **~istic** /-'lɪstɪk/ *a.* matérialiste.

materialize /mə'tɪərɪəlaɪz/ *v.i.* se matérialiser, se réaliser.

maternal /mə'tɜ:nl/ *a.* maternel.

maternity /mə'tɜ:nətɪ/ *n.* maternité *f.* ● *a.* (*clothes*) de grossesse. **~ hospital,** maternité *f.* **~ leave,** congé maternité *m.*

mathematic|s /mæθə'mætɪks/ *n.* & *n. pl.* mathématiques *f. pl.* **~ian** /-ə'tɪʃn/ *n.* mathématicien(ne) *m.* (*f.*). **~al** *a.* mathématique.

maths /mæθs/ (*Amer.* **math** /mæθ/) *n.* & *n. pl.* (*fam.*) maths *f. pl.*

matinée /'mætɪneɪ/ *n.* matinée *f.*

mating /'meɪtɪŋ/ *n.* accouplement *m.* **~ season,** saison des amours *f.*

matriculat|e /mə'trɪkjʊleɪt/ *v.t./i.* (s')inscrire. **~ion** /-'leɪʃn/ *n.* inscription *f.*

matrimon|y /'mætrɪmənɪ/ *n.* mariage *m.* **~ial** /-'məʊnɪəl/ *a.* matrimonial.

matrix /'meɪtrɪks/ *n.* (*pl.* **matrices** /-ɪsi:z/) matrice *f.*

matron /'meɪtrən/ *n.* (*married, elderly*) dame âgée *f.*; (*in hospital: former use*) infirmière-major *f.* **~ly** *a.* d'âge mûr; (*manner*) très digne.

matt /mæt/ *a.* mat.

matted /'mætɪd/ *a.* (*hair*) emmêlé.

matter /'mætə(r)/ *n.* (*substance*) matière *f.*; (*affair*) affaire *f.*; (*pus*) pus *m.* ● *v.i.* importer. **as a ~ of fact,** en fait. **it does not ~,** ça ne fait rien. **~-of-fact** *a.* terre à terre *invar.* **no ~ what happens,** quoi qu'il arrive. **what is the ~?,** qu'est-ce qu'il y a?

mattress /'mætrɪs/ *n.* matelas *m.*

matur|e /mə'tjʊə(r)/ *a.* mûr. ● *v.t./i.* (se) mûrir. **~ity** *n.* maturité *f.*

maul /mɔ:l/ *v.t.* déchiqueter.

Mauritius /mə'rɪʃəs/ *n.* île Maurice *f.*

mausoleum /mɔ:sə'lɪəm/ *n.* mausolée *m.*

mauve /məʊv/ *a.* & *n.* mauve (*m.*).

maverick /'mævərɪk/ *n.* non-conformiste.

maxim /'mæksɪm/ *n.* maxime *f.*

maxim|um /'mæksɪməm/ *a.* & *n.* (*pl.* **-ima**) maximum (*m.*). **~ize** *v.t.* porter au maximum.

may /meɪ/ *v. aux.* (*p.t.* **might**) pouvoir. **he ~/might come,** il peut/pourrait venir. **you might have,** vous auriez pu. **you ~ leave,** vous pouvez partir. **~ I smoke?,** puis-je fumer? **~ he be happy,** qu'il soit heureux. **I ~ *or* might as well stay,** je ferais aussi bien de rester.

May /meɪ/ *n.* mai *m.* **~ Day,** le Premier Mai.

maybe /'meɪbi:/ *adv.* peut-être.

mayhem /'meɪhem/ *n.* (*havoc*) ravages *m. pl.*

mayonnaise /meɪə'neɪz/ *n.* mayonnaise *f.*

mayor /meə(r)/ *n.* maire *m.* **~ess** *n.* (*wife*) femme du maire *f.*

maze /meɪz/ *n.* labyrinthe *m.*

MBA (*abbr.*) (*Master of Business Administration*) magistère en gestion commerciale *m.*

me /mi:/ *pron.* me, m'*; (*after prep.*) moi. (**to**) **~,** me, m'*. **he knows ~,** il me connaît.

meadow /'medəʊ/ *n.* pré *m.*

meagre /'mi:gə(r)/ *a.* maigre.

meal[1] /mi:l/ *n.* repas *m.*

meal[2] /mi:l/ *n.* (*grain*) farine *f.*

mealy-mouthed /mi:lɪ'maʊðd/ *a.* mielleux.

mean[1] /mi:n/ *a.* (**-er, -est**) (*poor*) misérable; (*miserly*) avare; (*unkind*) méchant. **~ness** *n.* avarice *f.*; méchanceté *f.*

mean[2] /mi:n/ *a.* moyen. ● *n.* milieu *m.*; (*average*) moyenne *f.* **in the ~ time,** en attendant.

mean[3] /mi:n/ *v.t.* (*p.t.* **meant**) vouloir dire, signifier; (*involve*) entraîner. **I ~ that!,** je suis sérieux. **be meant for,** être destiné à. **~ to do,** avoir l'intention de faire.

meander /mɪ'ændə(r)/ *v.i.* faire des méandres.

meaning /'mi:nɪŋ/ *n.* sens *m.*, signification *f.* **~ful** *a.* significatif. **~less** *a.* denué de sens.

means /mi:nz/ *n.* moyen(s) *m.* (*pl.*). **by ~ of sth.,** au moyen de qch. ● *n. pl.* (*wealth*) moyens financiers *m. pl.* **by all ~,** certainement. **by no ~,** nullement.

meant /ment/ *see* mean[2].

mean|time /'mi:ntaɪm/, **~while** *advs.* en attendant.

measles /'mi:zlz/ *n.* rougeole *f.*

measly /'mi:zlɪ/ *a.* (*sl.*) minable.

measurable /'meʒərəbl/ *a.* mesurable.

measure /'meʒə(r)/ *n.* mesure *f.*; (*ruler*) règle *f.* ● *v.t./i.* mesurer. **~ up to,** être à la hauteur de. **~d** *a.* mesuré. **~ment** *n.* mesure *f.*

meat /mi:t/ *n.* viande *f.* **~y** *a.* de viande; (*fig.*) substantiel.

mechanic /mɪ'kænɪk/ *n.* mécanicien(ne) *m.* (*f.*).

mechanic|al /mɪ'kænɪkl/ *a.* mécanique. **~s** *n.* (*science*) mécanique *f.*; *n. pl.* mécanisme *m.*

mechan|ism /'mekənɪzəm/ *n.* mécanisme *m.* **~ize** *v.t.* mécaniser.

medal /'medl/ *n.* médaille *f.* **~list** *n.* médaillé(e) *m.* (*f.*). **be a gold ~list,** être médaillé d'or.

medallion /mɪ'dælɪən/ *n.* (*medal, portrait, etc.*) médaillon *m.*

meddle /'medl/ *v.i.* (*interfere*) se mêler (**in,** de); (*tinker*) toucher (**with,** à). **~some** *a.* importun.

media /'mi:dɪə/ *see* **medium.** ● *n. pl.* **the ~,** les média *m. pl.* **talk to the ~,** parler à la presse.

median /'mi:dɪən/ *a.* médian. ● *n.* médiane *f.*

mediat|e /'mi:dɪeɪt/ *v.i.* servir d'intermédiaire. **~ion** /-'eɪʃn/ *n.* médiation *f.* **~or** *n.* média|teur, -trice *m., f.*

medical /'medɪkl/ *a.* médical; (*student*) en médecine. ● *n.* (*fam.*) visite médicale *f.*

medicat|ed /'medɪkeɪtɪd/ *a.* médical. **~ion** /-'keɪʃn/ *n.* médicaments *m. pl.*

medicin|e /'medsn/ *n.* (*science*) médecine *f.*; (*substance*) médicament *m.* **~al** /mɪ'dɪsɪnl/ *a.* médicinal.

medieval /medɪ'i:vl/ *a.* médiéval.

mediocr|e /mi:dɪ'əʊkə(r)/ *a.* médiocre. **~ity** /-'ɒkrətɪ/ *n.* médiocrité *f.*

meditat|e /'medɪteɪt/ *v.t./i.* méditer. **~ion** /-'teɪʃn/ *n.* méditation *f.*

Mediterranean /medɪtə'reɪnɪən/ *a.* méditerranéen. ● *n.* **the ~,** la Méditerranée *f.*

medium /'mi:dɪəm/ *n.* (*pl.* **media**) milieu *m.*; (*for transmitting data etc.*) support *m.*; (*pl.* **mediums**) (*person*) médium *m.* ● *a.* moyen.

medley /'medlɪ/ *n.* mélange *m.*; (*mus.*) pot-pourri *m.*

meek /mi:k/ *a.* (**-er, -est**) doux.

meet /mi:t/ *v.t.* (*p.t.* **met**) rencontrer; (*see again*) retrouver; (*fetch*) (aller) chercher; (*be introduced to*) faire la connaissance de; (*face*) faire face à; (*requirement*) satisfaire. ● *v.i.* se rencontrer; (*see each other again*) se retrouver; (*in session*) se réunir.

meeting /'mi:tɪŋ/ *n.* réunion *f.*; (*between two people*) rencontre *f.*

megalomania /megələʊ'meɪnɪə/ *n.* mégalomanie *f.* **~c** /-æk/ *n.* mégalomane *m./f.*

megaphone /'megəfəʊn/ *n.* porte-voix *m. invar.*

melamine /'meləmi:n/ *n.* mélamine *f.*

melanchol|y /'melənkəlɪ/ *n.* mélancolie *f.* ● *a.* mélancolique. **~ic** /-'kɒlɪk/ *a.* mélancolique.

mellow /'meləʊ/ *a.* (**-er, -est**) (*fruit*) mûr; (*sound, colour*) moelleux, doux; (*person*) mûri. ● *v.t./i.* (*mature*) mûrir; (*soften*) (s')adoucir.

melodious /mɪ'ləʊdɪəs/ *a.* mélodieux.

melodrama /'melədrɑ:mə/ *n.* mélodrame *m.* **~tic** /-ə'mætɪk/ *a.* mélodramatique.

melod|y /'melədɪ/ *n.* mélodie *f.* **~ic** /mɪ'lɒdɪk/ *a.* mélodique.

melon /'melən/ *n.* melon *m.*

melt /melt/ *v.t./i.* (faire) fondre. **~ing-pot** *n.* creuset *m.*

member /'membə(r)/ *n.* membre *m.* **M~ of Parliament,** député *m.* **~ship** *n.* adhésion *f.*; (*members*) membres *m. pl.*; (*fee*) cotisation *f.*

membrane /'membreɪn/ *n.* membrane *f.*

memento /mɪ'mentəʊ/ *n.* (*pl.* **-oes**) (*object*) souvenir *m.*

memo /'meməʊ/ *n.* (*pl.* **-os**) (*fam.*) note *f.*

memoir /'memwɑ:(r)/ *n.* (*record, essay*) mémoire *m.*

memorable /'memərəbl/ *a.* mémorable.

memorandum /memə'rændəm/ *n.* (*pl.* **-ums**) note *f.*

memorial /mɪ'mɔ:rɪəl/ *n.* monument *m.* ● *a.* commémoratif.

memorize /'meməraɪz/ *v.t.* apprendre par cœur.

memory /'memərɪ/ *n.* (*mind, in computer*) mémoire *f.*; (*thing remembered*) souvenir *m.* **from ~,** de mémoire. **in ~ of,** à la mémoire de.

men /men/ *see* **man.**

menac|e /'menəs/ *n.* menace *f.*; (*nuisance*) peste *f.* ● *v.t.* menacer. **~ing** *a.* menaçant.

menagerie /mɪ'nædʒərɪ/ *n.* ménagerie *f.*

mend /mend/ *v.t.* réparer; (*darn*) raccommoder. ● *n.* raccommodage *m.* **~ one's ways,** s'amender. **on the ~,** en voie de guérison.

menial /'mi:nɪəl/ *a.* servile.

meningitis /menɪn'dʒaɪtɪs/ *n.* méningite *f.*
menopause /'menəpɔ:z/ *n.* ménopause *f.*
menstruation /menstrʊ'eɪʃn/ *n.* menstruation *f.*
mental /'mentl/ *a.* mental; (*hospital*) psychiatrique. **~ block,** blocage *m.*
mentality /men'tælətɪ/ *n.* mentalité *f.*
menthol /'menθɒl/ *n.* menthol *m.* ● *a.* mentholé.
mention /'menʃn/ *v.t.* mentionner. ● *n.* mention *f.* **don't ~ it!,** il n'y a pas de quoi!, je vous en prie!
mentor /'mentɔ:(r)/ *n.* mentor *m.*
menu /'menju:/ *n.* (*food, on computer*) menu *m.*; (*list*) carte *f.*
MEP (*abbr.*) (*member of the European Parliament*) député européen *m.*
mercenary /'mɜ:sɪnərɪ/ *a.* & *n.* mercenaire (*m.*).
merchandise /'mɜ:tʃəndaɪz/ *n.* marchandises *f. pl.*
merchant /'mɜ:tʃənt/ *n.* marchand *m.* ● *a.* (*ship, navy*) marchand. **~ bank,** banque de commerce *f.*
merciful /'mɜ:sɪfl/ *a.* miséricordieux. **~ly** *adv.* (*fortunately*: *fam.*) Dieu merci.
merciless /'mɜ:sɪlɪs/ *a.* impitoyable, implacable.
mercury /'mɜ:kjʊrɪ/ *n.* mercure *m.*
mercy /'mɜ:sɪ/ *n.* pitié *f.* **at the ~ of,** à la merci de.
mere /mɪə(r)/ *a.* simple. **~ly** *adv.* simplement.
merest /'mɪərɪst/ *a.* moindre.
merge /mɜ:dʒ/ *v.t./i.* (se) mêler (**with,** à); (*companies*: *comm.*) fusionner. **~r** /-ə(r)/ *n.* fusion *f.*
meridian /mə'rɪdɪən/ *n.* méridien *m.*
meringue /mə'ræŋ/ *n.* meringue *f.*
merit /'merɪt/ *n.* mérite *m.* ● *v.t.* (*p.t.* **merited**) mériter.
mermaid /'mɜ:meɪd/ *n.* sirène *f.*
merriment /'merɪmənt/ *n.* gaieté. *f.*
merry /'merɪ/ *a.* (**-ier, -iest**) gai. **make ~,** faire la fête. **~-go-round** *n.* manège *m.* **~-making** *n.* réjouissances *f. pl.* **merrily** *adv.* gaiement.
mesh /meʃ/ *n.* maille *f.*; (*fabric*) tissu à mailles *m.*; (*network*) réseau *m.*
mesmerize /'mezməraɪz/ *v.t.* hypnotiser.
mess /mes/ *n.* désordre *m.*, gâchis *m.*; (*dirt*) saleté *f.*; (*mil.*) mess *m.* ● *v.t.* **~ up,** gâcher. ● *v.i.* **~ about,** s'amuser; (*dawdle*) traîner. **~ with,** (*tinker with*) tripoter. **make a ~ of,** gâcher.
message /'mesɪdʒ/ *n.* message *m.*
messenger /'mesɪndʒə(r)/ *n.* messager *m.*
Messrs /'mesəz/ *n. pl.* **~ Smith,** Messieurs *or* MM. Smith.
messy /'mesɪ/ *a.* (**-ier, -iest**) en désordre; (*dirty*) sale.
met /met/ *see* meet.
metabolic /metə'bɒlɪk/ *adj.* métabolique.
metabolism /mɪ'tæbəlɪzəm/ *n.* métabolisme *m.*
metal /'metl/ *n.* métal *m.* ● *a.* de métal. **~lic** /mɪ'tælɪk/ *a.* métallique; (*paint, colour*) métallisé.
metallurgy /mɪ'tælədʒɪ, *Amer.* 'metəlɜ:dʒɪ/ *n.* métallurgie *f.*
metamorphosis /metə'mɔ:fəsɪs/ *n.* (*pl.* **-phoses** /-si:z/) métamorphose *f.*
metaphor /'metəfə(r)/ *n.* métaphore *f.* **~ical** /-'fɒrɪkl/ *a.* métaphorique.
mete /mi:t/ *v.t.* **~ out,** donner, distribuer; (*justice*) rendre.
meteor /'mi:tɪə(r)/ *n.* météore *m.*
meteorite /'mi:tɪəraɪt/ *n.* météorite *m.*
meteorolog|y /mi:tɪə'rɒlədʒɪ/ *n.* météorologie *f.* **~ical** /-ə'lɒdʒɪkl/ *a.* météorologique.
meter[1] /'mi:tə(r)/ *n.* compteur *m.*
meter[2] /'mi:tə(r)/ *n.* (*Amer.*) = **metre.**
method /'meθəd/ *n.* méthode *f.*
methodical /mɪ'θɒdɪkl/ *a.* méthodique.
Methodist /'meθədɪst/ *n.* & *a.* méthodiste (*m./f.*).
methodology /meθə'dɒlədʒɪ/ *n.* méthodologie *f.*
methylated /'meθɪleɪtɪd/ *a.* **~ spirit,** alcool à brûler *m.*
meticulous /mɪ'tɪkjʊləs/ *a.* méticuleux.
metre /'mi:tə(r)/ *n.* mètre *m.*
metric /'metrɪk/ *a.* métrique. **~ation** /-'keɪʃn/ *n.* adoption du système métrique *f.*
metropol|is /mə'trɒpəlɪs/ *n.* (*city*) métropole *f.* **~itan** /metrə'pɒlɪtən/ *a.* métropolitain.
mettle /'metl/ *n.* courage *m.*
mew /mju:/ *n.* miaulement *m.* ● *v.i.* miauler.
mews /mju:z/ *n. pl.* (*dwellings*) appartements chic aménagés dans des anciennes écuries *m. pl.*

Mexic|o /'meksɪkəʊ/ *n.* Mexique *m.* **~an** *a.* & *n.* mexicain(e) (*m.* (*f.*)).
miaow /mi:'aʊ/ *n.* & *v.i.* = **mew**.
mice /maɪs/ *see* mouse.
mickey /'mɪkɪ/ *n.* **take the ~ out of,** (*sl.*) se moquer de.
micro- /'maɪkrəʊ/ *pref.* micro-.
microbe /'maɪkrəʊb/ *n.* microbe *m.*
microchip /'maɪkrəʊtʃɪp/ *n.* microplaquette *f.*, puce *f.*
microclimate /'maɪkrəʊklaɪmət/ *n.* microclimat *n.*
microcomputer /maɪkrəʊkəm'pju:tə(r)/ *n.* micro(-ordinateur) *m.*
microcosm /'maɪkrəʊkɒzm/ *n.* microcosme *m.*
microfilm /'maɪkrəʊfɪlm/ *n.* microfilm *m.*
microlight /'maɪkrəʊlaɪt/ *n.* U.L.M. *m.*
microphone /'maɪkrəfəʊn/ *n.* microphone *m.*
microprocessor /maɪkrəʊ'prəʊsesə(r)/ *n.* microprocesseur *m.*
microscop|e /'maɪkrəskəʊp/ *n.* microscope *m.* **~ic** /-'skɒpɪk/ *a.* microscopique.
microwave /'maɪkrəʊweɪv/ *n.* micro-onde *f.* **~ oven,** four à micro-ondes *m.*
mid /mɪd/ *a.* **in ~ air**/*etc.*, en plein ciel/*etc.* **in ~ March**/*etc.*, à la mi-mars/*etc.* **in ~ ocean**/*etc.*, au milieu de l'océan/*etc.*
midday /mɪd'deɪ/ *n.* midi *m.*
middle /'mɪdl/ *a.* du milieu; (*quality*) moyen. ● *n.* milieu *m.* **in the ~ of,** au milieu de. **~-aged** *a.* d'un certain âge. **M~ Ages,** moyen âge *m.* **~ class,** classe moyenne *f.* **~-class** *a.* bourgeois. **M~ East,** Proche-Orient *m.*
middleman /'mɪdlmæn/ *n.* (*pl.* **-men**) intermédiaire *m.*
middling /'mɪdlɪŋ/ *a.* moyen.
midge /mɪdʒ/ *n.* moucheron *m.*
midget /'mɪdʒɪt/ *n.* nain(e) *m.* (*f.*). ● *a.* minuscule.
Midlands /'mɪdləndz/ *n. pl.* région du centre de l'Angleterre *f.*
midnight /'mɪdnaɪt/ *n.* minuit *f.*
midriff /'mɪdrɪf/ *n.* ventre *m.*
midst /mɪdst/ *n.* **in the ~ of,** au milieu de. **in our ~,** parmi nous.
midsummer /mɪd'sʌmə(r)/ *n.* milieu de l'été *m.*; (*solstice*) solstice d'été *m.*
midway /mɪdweɪ/ *adv.* à mi-chemin.
midwife /'mɪdwaɪf/ *n.* (*pl.* **-wives**) sage-femme *f.*
might [1] /maɪt/ *n.* puissance *f.* **~y** *a.* puissant; (*very great*: *fam.*) très grand; *adv.* (*fam.*) rudement.
might [2] /maɪt/ *see* may.
migraine /'mi:greɪn, *Amer.* 'maɪgreɪn/ *n.* migraine *f.*
migrant /'maɪgrənt/ *a.* & *n.* (*bird*) migrateur (*m.*); (*worker*) migrant(e) (*m.* (*f.*)).
migrat|e /maɪ'greɪt/ *v.i.* émigrer. **~ion** /-ʃn/ *n.* migration *f.*
mike /maɪk/ *n.* (*fam.*) micro *m.*
mild /maɪld/ *a.* (**-er, -est**) doux; (*illness*) bénin. **~ly** *adv.* doucement. **to put it ~ly,** pour ne rien exagérer. **~ness** *n.* douceur *f.*
mildew /'mɪldju:/ *n.* moisissure *f.*
mile /maɪl/ *n.* mille *m.* (= *1.6 km.*). **~s too big**/*etc.*, (*fam.*) beaucoup trop grand/*etc.* **~age** *n.* (*loosely*) kilométrage *m.*
milestone /'maɪlstəʊn/ *n.* borne *f.*; (*event, stage*: *fig.*) jalon *m.*
militant /'mɪlɪtənt/ *a.* & *n.* militant(e) (*m.* (*f.*)).
military /'mɪlɪtrɪ/ *a.* militaire.
militate /'mɪlɪteɪt/ *v.i.* militer.
militia /mɪ'lɪʃə/ *n.* milice *f.*
milk /mɪlk/ *n.* lait *m.* ● *a.* (*product*) laitier. ● *v.t.* (*cow etc.*) traire; (*fig.*) exploiter. **~ shake,** milk-shake *m.* **~y** *a.* (*diet*) lacté; (*colour*) laiteux; (*tea etc.*) au lait. **M~y Way,** Voie lactée *f.*
milkman /'mɪlkmən, *Amer.* 'mɪlkmæn/ *n.* (*pl.* **-men**) laitier *m.*
mill /mɪl/ *n.* moulin *m.*; (*factory*) usine *f.* ● *v.t.* moudre. ● *v.i.* **~ around,** tourner en rond; (*crowd*) grouiller. **~er** *n.* meunier *m.*
millennium /mɪ'lenɪəm/ *n.* (*pl.* **-ums**) millénaire *m.*
millet /'mɪlɪt/ *n.* millet *m.*
milli- /'mɪlɪ/ *pref.* milli-.
millimetre /'mɪlɪmi:tə(r)/ *n.* millimètre *m.*
milliner /'mɪlɪnə(r)/ *n.* modiste *f.*
million /'mɪljən/ *n.* million *m.* **a ~ pounds,** un million de livres. **~aire** /-'neə(r)/ *n.* millionnaire *m.*
millstone /'mɪlstəʊn/ *n.* meule *f.*; (*burden*: *fig.*) boulet *m.*
milometer /maɪ'lɒmɪtə(r)/ *n.* compteur kilométrique *m.*
mime /maɪm/ *n.* (*actor*) mime *m.*/*f.*; (*art*) (art du) mime *m.* ● *v.t.*/*i.* mimer.

mimic /'mɪmɪk/ *v.t.* (*p.t.* **mimicked**) imiter. ● *n.* imita|teur, -trice *m., f.* **~ry** *n.* imitation *f.*

mince /mɪns/ *v.t.* hacher. ● *n.* viande hachée *f.* **~ pie,** tarte aux fruits confits *f.* **not to ~ matters,** ne pas mâcher ses mots. **~r** /-ə(r)/ *n.* (*machine*) hachoir *m.*

mincemeat /'mɪnsmi:t/ *n.* hachis de fruits confits *m.* **make ~ of,** anéantir, pulvériser.

mind /maɪnd/ *n.* esprit *m.*; (*sanity*) raison *f.*; (*opinion*) avis *m.* ● *v.t.* (*have charge of*) s'occuper de; (*heed*) faire attention à. **be on s.o.'s ~,** préoccuper qn. **bear that in ~,** ne l'oubliez pas. **change one's ~,** changer d'avis. **make up one's ~,** se décider (**to,** à). **I do not ~ the noise/etc.,** le bruit/*etc.* ne me dérange pas. **I do not ~,** ça m'est égal. **would you ~ checking?,** je peux vous demander de vérifier? **~ful** *a.* attentif (**of,** à). **~less** *a.* irréfléchi.

minder /'maɪndə(r)/ *n.* (*for child*) gardien(ne) *m.* (*f.*); (*for protection*) ange gardien *m.*

mine[1] /maɪn/ *poss. pron.* le mien, la mienne, les mien(ne)s. **it is ~,** c'est à moi *or* le mien.

min|e[2] /maɪn/ *n.* mine *f.* ● *v.t.* extraire; (*mil.*) miner. **~er** *n.* mineur *m.* **~ing** *n.* exploitation minière *f.*; *a.* minier.

minefield /'maɪnfi:ld/ *n.* champ de mines *m.*

mineral /'mɪnərəl/ *n.* & *a.* minéral (*m.*). **~ (water),** (*fizzy soft drink*) boisson gazeuse *f.* **~ water,** (*natural*) eau minérale *f.*

minesweeper /'maɪnswi:pə(r)/ *n.* (*ship*) dragueur de mines *m.*

mingle /'mɪŋgl/ *v.t./i.* (se) mêler (**with,** à).

mingy /'mɪndʒɪ/ *a.* (*fam.*) radin.

mini- /'mɪnɪ/ *pref.* mini-.

miniatur|e /'mɪnɪtʃə(r)/ *a.* & *n.* miniature (*f.*). **~ize** *v.t.* miniaturiser.

minibus /'mɪnɪbʌs/ *n.* minibus *m.*

minicab /'mɪnɪkæb/ *n.* taxi *m.*

minim /'mɪnɪm/ *n.* blanche *f.*

minim|um /'mɪnɪməm/ *a.* & *n.* (*pl.* **-ima**) minimum (*m.*). **~al** *a.* minimal. **~ize** *v.t.* minimiser.

minist|er /'mɪnɪstə(r)/ *n.* ministre *m.* **~erial** /-'stɪərɪəl/ *a.* ministériel. **~ry** *n.* ministère *m.*

mink /mɪŋk/ *n.* vison *m.*

minor /'maɪnə(r)/ *a.* petit, mineur. ● *n.* (*jurid.*) mineur(e) *m.* (*f.*).

minority /maɪ'nɒrətɪ/ *n.* minorité *f.* ● *a.* minoritaire.

mint[1] /mɪnt/ *n.* **the M~,** l'Hôtel de la Monnaie *m.* **a ~,** une fortune. ● *v.t.* frapper. **in ~ condition,** à l'état neuf.

mint[2] /mɪnt/ *n.* (*plant*) menthe *f.*; (*sweet*) pastille de menthe *f.*

minus /'maɪnəs/ *prep.* moins; (*without: fam.*) sans. ● *n.* (*sign*) moins *m.* **~ sign,** moins *m.*

minute[1] /'mɪnɪt/ *n.* minute *f.* **~s,** (*of meeting*) procès-verbal *m.*

minute[2] /maɪ'nju:t/ *a.* (*tiny*) minuscule; (*detailed*) minutieux.

mirac|le /'mɪrəkl/ *n.* miracle *m.* **~ulous** /mɪ'rækjʊləs/ *a.* miraculeux.

mirage /'mɪrɑ:ʒ/ *n.* mirage *m.*

mire /maɪə(r)/ *n.* fange *f.*

mirror /'mɪrə(r)/ *n.* miroir *m.*, glace *f.* ● *v.t.* refléter.

mirth /mɜ:θ/ *n.* gaieté *f.*

misadventure /mɪsəd'ventʃə(r)/ *n.* mésaventure *f.*

misanthropist /mɪs'ænθrəpɪst/ *n.* misanthrope *m./f.*

misapprehension /mɪsæprɪ'henʃn/ *n.* malentendu *m.*

misbehav|e /mɪsbɪ'heɪv/ *v.i.* se conduire mal. **~iour** *n.* mauvaise conduite *f.*

miscalculat|e /mɪs'kælkjʊleɪt/ *v.t.* mal calculer. ● *v.i.* se tromper. **~ion** /-'leɪʃn/ *n.* erreur de calcul *f.*

miscarr|y /mɪs'kærɪ/ *v.i.* faire une fausse couche. **~iage** /-ɪdʒ/ *n.* fausse couche *f.* **~iage of justice,** erreur judiciaire *f.*

miscellaneous /mɪsə'leɪnɪəs/ *a.* divers.

mischief /'mɪstʃɪf/ *n.* (*foolish conduct*) espièglerie *f.*; (*harm*) mal *m.* **get into ~,** faire des sottises.

mischievous /'mɪstʃɪvəs/ *a.* espiègle; (*malicious*) méchant.

misconception /mɪskən'sepʃn/ *n.* idée fausse *f.*

misconduct /mɪs'kɒndʌkt/ *n.* mauvaise conduite *f.*

misconstrue /mɪskən'stru:/ *v.t.* mal interpréter.

misdeed /mɪs'di:d/ *n.* méfait *m.*

misdemeanour /mɪsdɪ'mi:nə(r)/ *n.* (*jurid.*) délit *m.*

misdirect /mɪsdɪ'rekt/ *v.t.* (*person*) mal renseigner.

miser /'maɪzə(r)/ *n.* avare *m./f.* **~ly** *a.* avare.

miserable /'mɪzrəbl/ *a.* (*sad*) malheureux; (*wretched*) misérable; (*unpleasant*) affreux.

misery /'mɪzərɪ/ *n.* (*unhappiness*) malheur *m.*; (*pain*) souffrances *f. pl.*; (*poverty*) misère *f.*; (*person: fam.*) grincheu|x, -se *m., f.*

misfire /mɪs'faɪə(r)/ *v.i.* (*plan etc.*) rater; (*engine*) avoir des ratés.

misfit /'mɪsfɪt/ *n.* inadapté(e) *m.* (*f.*).

misfortune /mɪs'fɔ:tʃu:n/ *n.* malheur *m.*

misgiving /mɪs'gɪvɪŋ/ *n.* (*doubt*) doute *m.*; (*apprehension*) crainte *f.*

misguided /mɪs'gaɪdɪd/ *a.* (*foolish*) imprudent; (*mistaken*) erroné. **be ~,** (*person*) se tromper.

mishap /'mɪshæp/ *n.* mésaventure *f.*, contretemps *m.*

misinform /mɪsɪn'fɔ:m/ *v.t.* mal renseigner.

misinterpret /mɪsɪn'tɜ:prɪt/ *v.t.* mal interpréter.

misjudge /mɪs'dʒʌdʒ/ *v.t.* mal juger.

mislay /mɪs'leɪ/ *v.t.* (*p.t.* **mislaid**) égarer.

mislead /mɪs'li:d/ *v.t.* (*p.t.* **misled**) tromper. **~ing** *a.* trompeur.

mismanage /mɪs'mænɪdʒ/ *v.t.* mal gérer. **~ment** *n.* mauvaise gestion *f.*

misnomer /mɪs'nəʊmə(r)/ *n.* terme impropre *m.*

misplace /mɪs'pleɪs/ *v.t.* mal placer; (*lose*) égarer.

misprint /'mɪsprɪnt/ *n.* faute d'impression *f.*, coquille *f.*

misread /mɪs'ri:d/ *v.t.* (*p.t.* **misread** /mɪs'red/) mal lire; (*intentions*) mal comprendre.

misrepresent /mɪsreprɪ'zent/ *v.t.* présenter sous un faux jour.

miss[1] /mɪs/ *v.t./i.* manquer; (*deceased person etc.*) regretter. **he ~es her/Paris/*etc.***, elle/Paris/*etc.* lui manque. **I ~ you,** tu me manques. **you're ~ing the point,** vous n'avez rien compris. ● *n.* coup manqué *m.* **it was a near ~,** on l'a échappé belle *or* de peu. **~ out,** omettre. **~ out on sth,** rater qch.

miss[2] /mɪs/ *n.* (*pl.* **misses**) mademoiselle *f.* (*pl.* mesdemoiselles). **M~ Smith,** Mademoiselle *or* Mlle Smith.

misshapen /mɪs'ʃeɪpən/ *a.* difforme.

missile /'mɪsaɪl/ *n.* (*mil.*) missile *m.*; (*object thrown*) projectile *m.*

missing /'mɪsɪŋ/ *a.* (*person*) disparu; (*thing*) qui manque. **something's ~,** il manque quelque chose.

mission /'mɪʃn/ *n.* mission *f.*

missionary /'mɪʃənrɪ/ *n.* missionnaire *m./f.*

missive /'mɪsɪv/ *n.* missive *f.*

misspell /mɪs'spel/ *v.t.* (*p.t.* **misspelt** *or* **misspelled**) mal écrire.

mist /mɪst/ *n.* brume *f.*; (*on window*) buée *f.* ● *v.t./i.* (s')embuer.

mistake /mɪ'steɪk/ *n.* erreur *f.* ● *v.t.* (*p.t.* **mistook,** *p.p.* **mistaken**) mal comprendre; (*choose wrongly*) se tromper de. **by ~,** par erreur. **make a ~,** faire une erreur. **~ for,** prendre pour. **~n** /-ən/ *a.* erroné. **be ~n,** se tromper. **~nly** /-ənlɪ/ *adv.* par erreur.

mistletoe /'mɪsltəʊ/ *n.* gui *m.*

mistreat /mɪs'tri:t/ *v.t.* maltraiter.

mistress /'mɪstrɪs/ *n.* maîtresse *f.*

mistrust /mɪs'trʌst/ *v.t.* se méfier de. ● *n.* méfiance *f.*

misty /'mɪstɪ/ *a.* (**-ier, -iest**) brumeux; (*window*) embué.

misunderstand /mɪsʌndə'stænd/ *v.t.* (*p.t.* **-stood**) mal comprendre. **~ing** *n.* malentendu *m.*

misuse[1] /mɪs'ju:z/ *v.t.* mal employer; (*power etc.*) abuser de.

misuse[2] /mɪs'ju:s/ *n.* mauvais emploi *m.*; (*unfair use*) abus *m.*

mitigat|e /'mɪtɪgeɪt/ *v.t.* atténuer. **~ing circumstances,** circonstances atténuantes *f. pl.*

mitten /'mɪtn/ *n.* moufle *f.*

mix /mɪks/ *v.t./i.* (se) mélanger. ● *n.* mélange *m.* **~ up,** mélanger; (*bewilder*) embrouiller; (*mistake, confuse*) confondre (**with,** avec). **~-up** *n.* confusion *f.* **~ with,** (*people*) fréquenter. **~er** *n.* (*culin.*) mélangeur *m.* **be a good ~er,** être sociable. **~er tap,** mélangeur *m.*

mixed /mɪkst/ *a.* (*school etc.*) mixte; (*assorted*) assorti. **be ~-up,** (*fam.*) avoir des problèmes.

mixture /'mɪkstʃə(r)/ *n.* mélange *m.*; (*for cough*) sirop *m.*

moan /məʊn/ *n.* gémissement *m.* ● *v.i.* gémir; (*complain*) grogner. **~er** *n.* (*grumbler*) grognon *m.*

moat /məʊt/ *n.* douve(s) *f.* (*pl.*).

mob /mɒb/ *n.* (*crowd*) cohue *f.*; (*gang: sl.*) bande *f.* ● *v.t.* (*p.t.* **mobbed**) assiéger.

mobil|e /'məʊbaɪl/ *a.* mobile. **~e home,** caravane *f.* ● *n.* mobile *m.* **~ity** /-'bɪlətɪ/ *n.* mobilité *f.*

mobiliz|e /'məʊbɪlaɪz/ *v.t./i.* mobiliser. **~ation** /-'zeɪʃn/ *n.* mobilisation *f.*

moccasin /'mɒkəsɪn/ *n.* mocassin *m.*

mock /mɒk/ *v.t./i.* se moquer (de). ● *a.* faux. **~-up** *n.* maquette *f.*

mockery /'mɒkərɪ/ *n.* moquerie *f.* **a ~ of,** une parodie de.

mode /məʊd/ *n.* (*way, method*) mode *m.*; (*fashion*) mode *f.*

model /'mɒdl/ *n.* modèle *m.*; (*of toy*) modèle réduit *m.*; (*artist's*) modèle *m.*; (*for fashion*) mannequin *m.* ● *a.* modèle; (*car etc.*) modèle réduit *invar.* ● *v.t.* (*p.t.* **modelled**) modeler; (*clothes*) présenter. ● *v.i.* être mannequin; (*pose*) poser. **~ling** *n.* métier de mannequin *m.*

modem /'məʊdem/ *n.* modem *m.*

moderate[1] /'mɒdərət/ *a.* & *n.* modéré(e) (*m.* (*f.*)). **~ly** *adv.* (*in moderation*) modérément; (*fairly*) moyennement.

moderat|e[2] /'mɒdəreɪt/ *v.t./i.* (se) modérer. **~ion** /-'reɪʃn/ *n.* modération *f.* **in ~ion,** avec modération.

modern /'mɒdn/ *a.* moderne. **~ languages,** langues vivantes *f. pl.* **~ize** *v.t.* moderniser.

modest /'mɒdɪst/ *a.* modeste. **~y** *n.* modestie *f.*

modicum /'mɒdɪkəm/ *n.* **a ~ of,** un peu de.

modif|y /'mɒdɪfaɪ/ *v.t.* modifier. **~ication** /-ɪ'keɪʃn/ *n.* modification *f.*

modular /'mɒdjʊlə(r)/ *a.* modulaire

modulat|e /'mɒdjʊleɪt/ *v.t./i.* moduler. **~ion** /-'leɪʃn/ *n.* modulation *f.*

module /'mɒdju:l/ *n.* module *m.*

mohair /'məʊheə(r)/ *n.* mohair *m.*

moist /mɔɪst/ *a.* (**-er, -est**) humide, moite. **~ure** /'mɔɪstʃə(r)/ *n.* humidité *f.* **~urizer** /'mɔɪstʃəraɪzə(r)/ *n.* produit hydratant *m.*

moisten /'mɔɪsn/ *v.t.* humecter.

molar /'məʊlə(r)/ *n.* molaire *f.*

molasses /mə'læsɪz/ *n.* mélasse *f.*

mold /məʊld/ (*Amer.*) = **mould.**

mole[1] /məʊl/ *n.* grain de beauté *m.*

mole[2] /məʊl/ *n.* (*animal*) taupe *f.*

molecule /'mɒlɪkju:l/ *n.* molécule *f.*

molest /mə'lest/ *v.t.* (*pester*) importuner; (*ill-treat*) molester.

mollusc /'mɒləsk/ *n.* mollusque *m.*

mollycoddle /'mɒlɪkɒdl/ *v.t.* dorloter, chouchouter.

molten /'məʊltən/ *a.* en fusion.

mom /mɒm/ *n.* (*Amer.*) maman *f.*

moment /'məʊmənt/ *n.* moment *m.*

momentar|y /'məʊməntrɪ, *Amer.* -terɪ/ *a.* momentané. **~ily** (*Amer.* /-'terəlɪ/) *adv.* momentanément; (*soon*: *Amer.*) très bientôt.

momentous /mə'mentəs/ *a.* important.

momentum /mə'mentəm/ *n.* élan *m.*

Monaco /'mɒnəkəʊ/ *n.* Monaco *f.*

monarch /'mɒnək/ *n.* monarque *m.* **~y** *n.* monarchie *f.*

monast|ery /'mɒnəstrɪ/ *n.* monastère *m.* **~ic** /mə'næstɪk/ *a.* monastique.

Monday /'mʌndɪ/ *n.* lundi *m.*

monetarist /'mʌnɪtərɪst/ *n.* monétariste *m./f.*

monetary /'mʌnɪtrɪ/ *a.* monétaire.

money /'mʌnɪ/ *n.* argent *m.* **~s,** sommes d'argent *f. pl.* **~-box** *n.* tirelire *f.* **~-lender** *n.* prêteu|r, -se *m., f.* **~ order,** mandat *m.* **~-spinner** *n.* mine d'or *f.*

mongrel /'mʌŋgrəl/ *n.* (chien) bâtard *m.*

monitor /'mɒnɪtə(r)/ *n.* (*pupil*) chef de classe *m.*; (*techn.*) moniteur *m.* ● *v.t.* contrôler; (*a broadcast*) écouter.

monk /mʌŋk/ *n.* moine *m.*

monkey /'mʌŋkɪ/ *n.* singe *m.* **~-nut** *n.* cacahuète *f.* **~-wrench** *n.* clef à molette *f.*

mono /'mɒnəʊ/ *n.* (*pl.* **-os**) mono *f.* ● *a.* mono *invar.*

monochrome /'mɒnəkrəʊm/ *a.* & *n.* (en) noir et blanc (*m.*).

monogram /'mɒnəgræm/ *n.* monogramme *m.*

monologue /'mɒnəlɒg/ *n.* monologue *m.*

monopol|y /mə'nɒpəlɪ/ *n.* monopole *m.* **~ize** *v.t.* monopoliser.

monotone /'mɒnətəʊn/ *n.* ton uniforme *m.*

monoton|ous /mə'nɒtənəs/ *a.* monotone. **~y** *n.* monotonie *f.*

monsoon /mɒn'su:n/ *n.* mousson *f.*

monst|er /'mɒnstə(r)/ *n.* monstre *m.* **~rous** *a.* monstrueux.

monstrosity /mɒn'strɒsətɪ/ *n.* monstruosité *f.*

month /mʌnθ/ *n.* mois *m.*

monthly /'mʌnθlɪ/ *a.* mensuel. ● *adv.* mensuellement. ● *n.* (*periodical*) mensuel *m.*

monument /'mɒnjʊmənt/ *n.* monument *m.* **~al** /-'mentl/ *a.* monumental.

moo /mu:/ *n.* meuglement *m.* ● *v.i.* meugler.

mooch /mu:tʃ/ *v.i.* (*sl.*) flâner. ● *v.t.* (*Amer., sl.*) se procurer.

mood /mu:d/ *n.* humeur *f.* **in a good/bad ~,** de bonne/mauvaise humeur. **~y** *a.* d'humeur changeante; (*sullen*) maussade.

moon /mu:n/ *n.* lune *f.*

moon|light /'mu:nlaɪt/ *n.* clair de lune *m.* **~lit** *a.* éclairé par la lune.

moonlighting /'mu:nlaɪtɪŋ/ *n.* (*fam.*) travail au noir *m.*

moor[1] /mʊə(r)/ *n.* lande *f.*

moor[2] /mʊə(r)/ *v.t.* amarrer. **~ings** *n. pl.* (*chains etc.*) amarres *f. pl.*; (*place*) mouillage *m.*

moose /mu:s/ *n. invar.* élan *m.*

moot /mu:t/ *a.* discutable. ● *v.t.* (*question*) soulever.

mop /mɒp/ *n.* balai à franges *m.* ● *v.t.* (*p.t.* **mopped**). **~ (up),** éponger. **~ of hair,** tignasse *f.*

mope /məʊp/ *v.i.* se morfondre.

moped /'məʊped/ *n.* cyclomoteur *m.*

moral /'mɒrəl/ *a.* moral. ● *n.* morale *f.* **~s,** moralité *f.* **~ize** *v.i.* moraliser. **~ly** *adv.* moralement.

morale /mə'rɑ:l/ *n.* moral *m.*

morality /mə'rælətɪ/ *n.* moralité *f.*

morass /mə'ræs/ *n.* marais *m.*

morbid /'mɔ:bɪd/ *a.* morbide.

more /mɔ:(r)/ *a.* (*a greater amount of*) plus de (**than,** que). ● *n.* & *adv.* plus (**than,** que). **(some) ~ tea/pens/***etc.*, (*additional*) encore du thé/des stylos/*etc.* **no ~ bread/***etc.*, plus de pain/*etc.* **I want no ~, I do not want any ~,** je n'en veux plus. **~ or less,** plus ou moins.

moreover /mɔ:'rəʊvə(r)/ *adv.* de plus, en outre.

morgue /mɔ:g/ *n.* morgue *f.*

moribund /'mɒrɪbʌnd/ *a.* moribond.

morning /'mɔ:nɪŋ/ *n.* matin *m.*; (*whole morning*) matinée *f.*

Morocc|o /mə'rɒkəʊ/ *n.* Maroc *m.* **~an** *a.* & *n.* marocain(e) (*m.* (*f.*)).

moron /'mɔ:rɒn/ *n.* crétin(e) *m.* (*f.*).

morose /mə'rəʊs/ *a.* morose.

morphine /'mɔ:fi:n/ *n.* morphine *f.*

Morse /mɔ:s/ *n.* **~ (code),** morse *m.*

morsel /'mɔ:sl/ *n.* petit morceau *m.*; (*of food*) bouchée *f.*

mortal /'mɔ:tl/ *a.* & *n.* mortel(le) (*m.*(*f.*)). **~ity** /mɔ:'tælətɪ/ *n.* mortalité *f.*

mortar /'mɔ:tə(r)/ *n.* mortier *m.*

mortgage /'mɔ:gɪdʒ/ *n.* crédit immobilier *m.* ● *v.t.* hypothéquer.

mortify /'mɔ:tɪfaɪ/ *v.t.* mortifier.

mortise /'mɔ:tɪs/ *n.* **~ lock** serrure encastrée *f.*

mortuary /'mɔ:tʃərɪ/ *n.* morgue *f.*

mosaic /məʊ'zeɪɪk/ *n.* mosaïque *f.*

Moscow /'mɒskəʊ/ *n.* Moscou *m./f.*

Moses /'məʊzɪz/ *a.* **~ basket,** moïse *m.*

mosque /mɒsk/ *n.* mosquée *f.*

mosquito /mə'ski:təʊ/ *n.* (*pl.* **-oes**) moustique *m.*

moss /mɒs/ *n.* mousse *f.* **~y** *a.* moussu.

most /məʊst/ *a.* (*the greatest amount of*) le plus de; (*the majority of*) la plupart de. ● *n.* le plus. ● *adv.* (le) plus; (*very*) fort. **~ of,** la plus grande partie de; (*majority*) la plupart de. **at ~,** tout au plus. **for the ~ part,** pour la plupart. **make the ~ of,** profiter de. **~ly** *adv.* surtout.

motel /məʊ'tel/ *n.* motel *m.*

moth /mɒθ/ *n.* papillon de nuit *m.*; (*in cloth*) mite *f.* **~-ball** *n.* boule de naphtaline *f.*; *v.t.* mettre en réserve. **~-eaten** *a.* mité.

mother /'mʌðə(r)/ *n.* mère *f.* ● *v.t.* entourer de soins maternels, materner. **~hood** *n.* maternité *f.* **~-in-law** *n.* (*pl.* **~s-in-law**) belle-mère *f.* **~-of-pearl** *n.* nacre *f.* **M~'s Day,** la fête des mères. **~-to-be** *n.* future maman *f.* **~ tongue,** langue maternelle *f.*

motherly /'mʌðəlɪ/ *a.* maternel.

motif /məʊ'ti:f/ *n.* motif *m.*

motion /'məʊʃn/ *n.* mouvement *m.*; (*proposal*) motion *f.* ● *v.t./i.* **~ (to) s.o. to,** faire signe à qn. de. **~less** *a.* immobile. **~ picture,** (*Amer.*) film *m.*

motivat|e /'məʊtɪveɪt/ *v.t.* motiver. **~ion** /-'veɪʃn/ *n.* motivation *f.*

motive /'məʊtɪv/ *n.* motif *m.*

motley /'mɒtlɪ/ *a.* bigarré.

motor /'məʊtə(r)/ *n.* moteur *m.*; (*car*) auto *f.* ● *a.* (*anat.*) moteur; (*boat*) à moteur. ● *v.i.* aller en auto. **~ bike,** (*fam.*) moto *f.* **~ car,** auto *f.* **~ cycle,** motocyclette *f.* **~-cyclist** *n.* motocycliste *m./f.* **~ home,** (*Amer.*) camping-car *m.* **~ing** *n.* (*sport*) l'automobile *f.* **~ized** *a.* motorisé **~ vehicle,** véhicule automobile *m.*

motorist /'məʊtərɪst/ *n.* automobiliste *m./f.*

motorway /'məʊtəweɪ/ *n.* autoroute *f.*

mottled /'mɒtld/ *a.* tacheté.

motto /'mɒtəʊ/ *n.* (*pl.* **-oes**) devise *f.*

mould [1] /məʊld/ *n.* moule *m.* ● *v.t.* mouler; (*influence*) former. **~ing** *n.* (*on wall etc.*) moulure *f.*

mould [2] /məʊld/ *n.* (*fungus, rot*) moisissure *f.* **~y** *a.* moisi.

moult /məʊlt/ *v.i.* muer.

mound /maʊnd/ *n.* monticule *m.*, tertre *m.*; (*pile: fig.*) tas *m.*

mount [1] /maʊnt/ *n.* (*hill*) mont *m.*

mount [2] /maʊnt/ *v.t./i.* monter. ● *n.* monture *f.* **~ up,** s'accumuler; (*add up*) chiffrer (**to,** à).

mountain /'maʊntɪn/ *n.* montagne *f.* **~ bike,** (vélo) tout terrain *m.*, vtt *m.* **~ous** *a.* montagneux.

mountaineer /maʊntɪ'nɪə(r)/ *n.* alpiniste *m./f.* **~ing** *n.* alpinisme *m.*

mourn /mɔ:n/ *v.t./i.* **~ (for),** pleurer. **~er** *n.* personne qui suit le cortège funèbre *f.* **~ing** *n.* deuil *m.*

mournful /'mɔ:nfl/ *a.* triste.

mouse /maʊs/ *n.* (*pl.* **mice**) souris *f.*

mousetrap /'maʊstræp/ *n.* souricière *f.*

mousse /mu:s/ *n.* mousse *f.*

moustache /mə'stɑ:ʃ, *Amer.* 'mʌstæʃ/ *n.* moustache *f.*

mousy /'maʊsɪ/ *a.* (*hair*) d'un brun terne; (*fig.*) timide.

mouth /maʊθ/ *n.* bouche *f.*; (*of dog, cat, etc.*) gueule *f.* **~-organ** *n.* harmonica *m.*

mouthful /'maʊθfʊl/ *n.* bouchée *f.*

mouthpiece /'maʊθpi:s/ *n.* (*mus.*) embouchure *f.*; (*person: fig.*) porte-parole *m. invar.*

mouthwash /'maʊθwɒʃ/ *n.* eau dentifrice *f.*

mouthwatering /'maʊθwɔ:trɪŋ/ *a.* qui fait venir l'eau à la bouche.

movable /'mu:vəbl/ *a.* mobile.

move /mu:v/ *v.t./i.* remuer, (se) déplacer, bouger; (*incite*) pousser; (*emotionally*) émouvoir; (*propose*) proposer; (*depart*) partir; (*act*) agir. **~ (out),** déménager. ● *n.* mouvement *m.*; (*in game*) coup *m.*; (*player's turn*) tour *m.*; (*procedure: fig.*) démarche *f.*; (*house change*) déménagement *m.* **~ back,** (faire) reculer. **~ forward** *or* **on,** (faire) avancer. **~ in,** emménager. **~ over,** se pousser. **on the ~,** en marche.

movement /'mu:vmənt/ *n.* mouvement *m.*

movie /'mu:vɪ/ *n.* (*Amer.*) film *m.* **the ~s,** le cinéma. **~ camera,** (*Amer.*) caméra *f.*

moving /'mu:vɪŋ/ *a.* en mouvement; (*touching*) émouvant.

mow /məʊ/ *v.t.* (*p.p.* **mowed** *or* **mown**) (*corn etc.*) faucher; (*lawn*) tondre. **~ down,** faucher. **~er** *n.* (*for lawn*) tondeuse *f.*

MP *abbr. see* Member of Parliament.

Mr /'mɪstə(r)/ *n.* (*pl.* **Messrs**). **~ Smith,** Monsieur *or* M. Smith.

Mrs /'mɪsɪz/ *n.* (*pl.* **Mrs**). **~ Smith,** Madame *or* Mme Smith. **the ~ Smith,** Mesdames *or* Mmes Smith.

Ms /mɪz/ *n.* (*title of married or unmarried woman*). **~ Smith,** Madame *or* Mme Smith.

much /mʌtʃ/ *a.* beaucoup de. ● *adv.* & *n.* beaucoup.

muck /mʌk/ *n.* fumier *m.*; (*dirt: fam.*) saleté *f.* ● *v.i.* **~ about,** (*sl.*) s'amuser. **~ about with,** (*sl.*) tripoter. **~ in,** (*sl.*) participer. ● *v.t.* **~ up,** (*sl.*) gâcher. **~y** *a.* sale.

mucus /'mju:kəs/ *n.* mucus *m.*

mud /mʌd/ *n.* boue *f.* **~dy** *a.* couvert de boue.

muddle /'mʌdl/ *v.t.* embrouiller. ● *v.i.* **~ through,** se débrouiller. ● *n.* désordre *m.*, confusion *f.*; (*mix-up*) confusion *f.*

mudguard /'mʌdgɑ:d/ *n.* garde-boue *m. invar.*

muff /mʌf/ *n.* manchon *m.*

muffin /'mʌfɪn/ *n.* muffin *m.* (*petit pain rond et plat*).

muffle /'mʌfl/ *v.t.* emmitoufler; (*sound*) assourdir. **~r** /-ə(r)/ *n.* (*scarf*) cache-nez *m. invar.*; (*Amer.: auto.*) silencieux *m.*

mug /mʌg/ *n.* tasse *f.*; (*in plastic, metal*) gobelet *m.*; (*for beer*) chope *f.*; (*face: sl.*) gueule *f.*; (*fool: sl.*) idiot(e) *m.*(*f.*) ● *v.t.* (*p.t.* **mugged**) agresser. **~ger** *n.* agresseur *m.* **~ging** *n.* agression *f.*

muggy /'mʌgɪ/ *a.* lourd.

mule /mju:l/ *n.* (*male*) mulet *m.*; (*female*) mule *f.*

mull [1] /mʌl/ *v.t.* (*wine*) chauffer.

mull [2] /mʌl/ *v.t.* **~ over,** ruminer.

multi- /'mʌltɪ/ *pref.* multi-.

multicoloured /'mʌltɪkʌləd/ *a.* multicolore.

multifarious /mʌltɪ'feərɪəs/ *a.* divers.
multinational /mʌltɪ'næʃnəl/ *a.* & *n.* multinational(e) (*f.*).
multiple /'mʌltɪpl/ *a.* & *n.* multiple (*m.*). **~ sclerosis,** sclérose en plaques *f.*
multipl|y /'mʌltɪplaɪ/ *v.t./i.* (se) multiplier. **~ication** /-ɪ'keɪʃn/ *n.* multiplication *f.*
multistorey /mʌltɪ'stɔːrɪ/ *a.* (*car park*) à étages.
multitude /'mʌltɪtjuːd/ *n.* multitude *f.*
mum [1] /mʌm/ *a.* **keep ~,** (*fam.*) garder le silence.
mum [2] /mʌm/ *n.* (*fam.*) maman *f.*
mumble /'mʌmbl/ *v.t./i.* marmotter, marmonner.
mummy [1] /'mʌmɪ/ *n.* (*embalmed body*) momie *f.*
mummy [2] /'mʌmɪ/ *n.* (*mother*: *fam.*) maman *f.*
mumps /mʌmps/ *n.* oreillons *m. pl.*
munch /mʌntʃ/ *v.t./i.* mastiquer.
mundane /mʌn'deɪn/ *a.* banal.
municipal /mjuː'nɪsɪpl/ *a.* municipal. **~ity** /-'pælətɪ/ *n.* municipalité *f.*
munitions /mjuː'nɪʃnz/ *n. pl.* munitions *f. pl.*
mural /'mjʊərəl/ *a.* mural. ● *n.* peinture murale *f.*
murder /'mɜːdə(r)/ *n.* meurtre *m.* ● *v.t.* assassiner; (*ruin*: *fam.*) massacrer. **~er** *n.* meurtrier *m.*, assassin *m.* **~ous** *a.* meurtrier.
murky /'mɜːkɪ/ *a.* (**-ier, -iest**) (*night, plans, etc.*) sombre, ténébreux; (*liquid*) épais, sale.
murmur /'mɜːmə(r)/ *n.* murmure *m.* ● *v.t./i.* murmurer.
muscle /'mʌsl/ *n.* muscle *m.* ● *v.i.* **~ in,** (*sl.*) s'introduire de force (**on,** dans).
muscular /'mʌskjʊlə(r)/ *a.* musculaire; (*brawny*) musclé.
muse /mjuːz/ *v.i.* méditer.
museum /mjuː'zɪəm/ *n.* musée *m.*
mush /mʌʃ/ *n.* (*pulp, soft food*) bouillie *f.* **~y** *a.* mou.
mushroom /'mʌʃrʊm/ *n.* champignon *m.* ● *v.i.* pousser comme des champignons.
music /'mjuːzɪk/ *n.* musique *f.* **~al** *a.* musical; (*instrument*) de musique; (*talented*) doué pour la musique; *n.* comédie musicale *f.*
musician /mjuː'zɪʃn/ *n.* musicien(ne) *m.* (*f.*).
musk /mʌsk/ *n.* musc *m.*
Muslim /'mʊzlɪm/ *a.* & *n.* musulman(e) (*m.* (*f.*)).
muslin /'mʌzlɪn/ *n.* mousseline *f.*
mussel /'mʌsl/ *n.* moule *f.*
must /mʌst/ *v. aux.* devoir. **you ~ go,** vous devez partir, il faut que vous partiez. **he ~ be old,** il doit être vieux. **I ~ have done it,** j'ai dû le faire. ● *n.* **be a ~,** (*fam.*) être un must.
mustard /'mʌstəd/ *n.* moutarde *f.*
muster /'mʌstə(r)/ *v.t./i.* (se) rassembler.
musty /'mʌstɪ/ *a.* (**-ier, -iest**) (*room, etc.*) qui sent le moisi; (*smell, taste*) de moisi.
mutant /'mjuːtənt/ *a.* & *n.* mutant. (*m.*)
mutation /mjuː'teɪʃn/ *n.* mutation *f.*
mute /mjuːt/ *a.* & *n.* muet(te) (*m.* (*f.*)). **~d** /-ɪd/ *a.* (*colour, sound*) sourd, atténué; (*criticism*) voilé.
mutilat|e /'mjuːtɪleɪt/ *v.t.* mutiler. **~ion** /-'leɪʃn/ *n.* mutilation *f.*
mutin|y /'mjuːtɪnɪ/ *n.* mutinerie *f.* ● *v.i.* se mutiner. **~ous** *a.* (*sailor etc.*) mutiné; (*fig.*) rebelle.
mutter /'mʌtə(r)/ *v.t./i.* marmonner, murmurer.
mutton /'mʌtn/ *n.* mouton *m.*
mutual /'mjuːtʃʊəl/ *a.* mutuel; (*common to two or more*: *fam.*) commun. **~ly** *adv.* mutuellement.
muzzle /'mʌzl/ *n.* (*snout*) museau *m.*; (*device*) muselière *f.*; (*of gun*) gueule *f.* ● *v.t.* museler.
my /maɪ/ *a.* mon, ma, *pl.* mes.
myopic /maɪ'ɒpɪk/ *a.* myope.
myself /maɪ'self/ *pron.* moi-même; (*reflexive*) me, m'*; (*after prep.*) moi.
mysterious /mɪ'stɪərɪəs/ *a.* mystérieux.
mystery /'mɪstərɪ/ *n.* mystère *m.*
mystic /'mɪstɪk/ *a.* & *n.* mystique (*m./f.*) **~al** *a.* mystique. **~ism** /-sɪzəm/ *n.* mysticisme *m.*
mystify /'mɪstɪfaɪ/ *v.t.* laisser perplexe.
mystique /mɪ'stiːk/ *n.* mystique *f.*
myth /mɪθ/ *n.* mythe *m.* **~ical** *a.* mythique.
mythology /mɪ'θɒlədʒɪ/ *n.* mythologie *f.*

N

nab /næb/ *v.t.* (*p.t.* **nabbed**) (*arrest: sl.*) épingler, attraper.

nag /næg/ *v.t./i.* (*p.t.* **nagged**) critiquer; (*pester*) harceler.

nagging /'nægɪŋ/ *a.* persistant.

nail /neɪl/ *n.* clou *m.*; (*of finger, toe*) ongle *m.* ● *v.t.* clouer. **~-brush** *n.* brosse à ongles *f.* **~-file** *n.* lime à ongles *f.* **~ polish,** vernis à ongles *m.* **on the ~,** (*pay*) sans tarder, tout de suite.

naïve /naɪ'i:v/ *a.* naïf.

naked /'neɪkɪd/ *a.* nu. **to the ~ eye,** à l'œil nu. **~ly** *adv.* à nu. **~ness** *n.* nudité *f.*

name /neɪm/ *n.* nom *m.*; (*fig.*) réputation *f.* ● *v.t.* nommer; (*fix*) fixer. **be ~d after,** porter le nom de. **~less** *a.* sans nom, anonyme.

namely /'neɪmlɪ/ *adv.* à savoir.

namesake /'neɪmseɪk/ *n.* (*person*) homonyme *m.*

nanny /'nænɪ/ *n.* nounou *f.* **~-goat** *n.* chèvre *f.*

nap /næp/ *n.* somme *m.* ● *v.i.* (*p.t.* **napped**) faire un somme. **catch ~ping,** prendre au dépourvu.

nape /neɪp/ *n.* nuque *f.*

napkin /'næpkɪn/ *n.* (*at meals*) serviette *f.*; (*for baby*) couche *f.*

nappy /'næpɪ/ *n.* couche *f.*

narcotic /nɑ:'kɒtɪk/ *a.* & *n.* narcotique (*m.*).

narrat|e /nə'reɪt/ *v.t.* raconter. **~ion** /-ʃn/ *n.* narration *f.* **~or** *n.* narra|teur, -trice *m., f.*

narrative /'nærətɪv/ *n.* récit *m.*

narrow /'nærəʊ/ *a.* (**-er, -est**) étroit. ● *v.t./i.* (se) rétrécir; (*limit*) (se) limiter. **~ down the choices,** limiter les choix. **~ly** *adv.* étroitement; (*just*) de justesse. **~-minded** *a.* à l'esprit étroit; (*ideas etc.*) étroit. **~ness** *n.* étroitesse *f.*

nasal /'neɪzl/ *a.* nasal.

nast|y /'nɑ:stɪ/ *a.* (**-ier, -iest**) mauvais, désagréable; (*malicious*) méchant. **~ily** *adv.* désagréablement; méchamment. **~iness** *n.* (*malice*) méchanceté *f.*

nation /'neɪʃn/ *n.* nation *f.* **~-wide** *a.* dans l'ensemble du pays.

national /'næʃnəl/ *a.* national. ● *n.* ressortissant(e) *m.* (*f.*). **~ anthem,** hymne national *m.* **~ism** *n.* nationalisme *m.* **~ize** *v.t.* nationaliser. **~ly** *adv.* à l'échelle nationale.

nationality /næʃə'nælətɪ/ *n.* nationalité *f.*

native /'neɪtɪv/ *n.* (*local inhabitant*) autochtone *m./f.*; (*non-European*) indigène *m./f.* ● *a.* indigène; (*country*) natal; (*inborn*) inné. **be a ~ of,** être originaire de. **~ language,** langue maternelle *f.* **~ speaker of French,** personne de langue maternelle française *f.*

Nativity /nə'tɪvətɪ/ *n.* **the ~,** la Nativité *f.*

natter /'nætə(r)/ *v.i.* bavarder.

natural /'nætʃrəl/ *a.* naturel. **~ history,** histoire naturelle *f.* **~ist** *n.* naturaliste *m./f.* **~ly** *adv.* (*normally, of course*) naturellement; (*by nature*) de nature.

naturaliz|e /'nætʃrəlaɪz/ *v.t.* naturaliser. **~ation** /-'zeɪʃn/ *n.* naturalisation *f.*

nature /'neɪtʃə(r)/ *n.* nature *f.*

naught /nɔ:t/ *n.* (*old use*) rien *m.*

naught|y /'nɔ:tɪ/ *a.* (**-ier, -iest**) vilain, méchant; (*indecent*) grivois. **~ily** *adv.* mal.

nause|a /'nɔ:sɪə/ *n.* nausée *f.* **~ous** *a.* nauséabond.

nauseate /'nɔ:sɪeɪt/ *v.t.* écœurer.

nautical /'nɔ:tɪkl/ *a.* nautique.

naval /'neɪvl/ *a.* (*battle etc.*) naval; (*officer*) de marine.

nave /neɪv/ *n.* (*of church*) nef *f.*

navel /'neɪvl/ *n.* nombril *m.*

navigable /'nævɪgəbl/ *a.* navigable.

navigat|e /'nævɪgeɪt/ *v.t.* (*sea etc.*) naviguer sur; (*ship*) piloter. ● *v.i.* naviguer. **~ion** /-'geɪʃn/ *n.* navigation *f.* **~or** *n.* navigateur *m.*

navvy /'nævɪ/ *n.* terrassier *m.*

navy /'neɪvɪ/ *n.* marine *f.* **~ (blue),** bleu marine *invar.*

near /nɪə(r)/ *adv.* près. ● *prep.* près de. ● *a.* proche. ● *v.t.* approcher de. **draw ~,** (s')approcher (**to,** de). **~ by** *adv.* tout près. **N~ East,** Proche-Orient *m.* **~ to,** près de. **~ness** *n.* proximité *f.* **~-sighted** *a.* myope.

nearby /nɪə'baɪ/ *a.* proche.

nearly /'nɪəlɪ/ *adv.* presque. **I ~ forgot,** j'ai failli oublier. **not ~ as pretty/*etc.* as,** loin d'être aussi joli/*etc.* que.

nearside /'nɪəsaɪd/ *a.* (*auto.*) du côté du passager.

neat /ni:t/ *a.* (**-er, -est**) soigné, net; (*room etc.*) bien rangé; (*clever*) habile; (*whisky, brandy, etc.*) sec. **~ly** *adv.* avec soin; habilement. **~ness** *n.* netteté *f.*

nebulous /'nebjʊləs/ *a.* nébuleux.

necessar|y /'nesəsərɪ/ *a.* nécessaire. **~ies** *n. pl.* nécessaire *m.* **~ily** *adv.* nécessairement.

necessitate /nɪ'sesɪteɪt/ *v.t.* nécessiter.

necessity /nɪ'sesətɪ/ *n.* nécessité *f.*; (*thing*) chose indispensable *f.*

neck /nek/ *n.* cou *m.*; (*of dress*) encolure *f.* **~ and neck,** à égalité.

necklace /'neklɪs/ *n.* collier *m.*

neckline /'neklaɪn/ *n.* encolure *f.*

necktie /'nektaɪ/ *n.* cravate *f.*

nectarine /'nektərɪn/ *n.* brugnon *m.*, nectarine *f.*

need /ni:d/ *n.* besoin *m.* ● *v.t.* avoir besoin de; (*demand*) demander. **you ~ not come,** vous n'êtes pas obligé de venir. **~less** *a.* inutile. **~lessly** *adv.* inutilement.

needle /'ni:dl/ *n.* aiguille *f.* ● *v.t.* (*annoy: fam.*) asticoter, agacer.

needlework /'ni:dlwɜ:k/ *n.* couture *f.*; (*object*) ouvrage (à l'aiguille) *m.*

needy /'ni:dɪ/ *a.* (**-ier, -iest**) nécessiteux, indigent.

negation /nɪ'geɪʃn/ *n.* négation *f.*

negative /'negətɪv/ *a.* négatif. ● *n.* (*of photograph*) négatif *m.*; (*word: gram.*) négation *f.* **in the ~,** (*answer*) par la négative; (*gram.*) à la forme négative. **~ly** *adv.* négativement.

neglect /nɪ'glekt/ *v.t.* négliger, laisser à l'abandon. ● *n.* manque de soins *m.* **(state of) ~,** abandon *m.* **~ to do,** négliger de faire. **~ful** *a.* négligent.

négligé /'neglɪʒeɪ/ *n.* négligé *m.*

negligen|t /'neglɪdʒənt/ *a.* négligent. **~ce** *a.* négligence *f.*

negligible /'neglɪdʒəbl/ *a.* négligeable.

negotiable /nɪ'gəʊʃəbl/ *a.* négociable.

negotiat|e /nɪ'gəʊʃɪeɪt/ *v.t./i.* négocier. **~ion** /-'eɪʃn/ *n.* négociation *f.* **~or** *n.* négocia|teur, -trice *m., f.*

Negr|o /'ni:grəʊ/ *n.* (*pl.* **-oes**) Noir *m.* ● *a.* noir; (*art, music*) nègre. **~ess** *n.* Noire *f.*

neigh /neɪ/ *n.* hennissement *m.* ● *v.i.* hennir.

neighbour, *Amer.* **neighbor** /'neɪbə(r)/ *n.* voisin(e) *m.* (*f.*). **~hood** *n.* voisinage *m.*, quartier *m.* **in the ~hood of,** aux alentours de. **~ing** *a.* voisin.

neighbourly /'neɪbəlɪ/ *a.* amical.

neither /'naɪðə(r)/ *a.* & *pron.* aucun(e) des deux, ni l'un(e) ni l'autre. ● *adv.* ni. ● *conj.* (ne) non plus. **~ big nor small,** ni grand ni petit. **~ am I coming,** je ne viendrai pas non plus.

neon /'ni:ɒn/ *n.* néon *m.* ● *a.* (*lamp etc.*) au néon.

nephew /'nevju:, *Amer.* 'nefju:/ *n.* neveu *m.*

nerve /nɜ:v/ *n.* nerf *m.*; (*courage*) courage *m.*; (*calm*) sang-froid *m.*; (*impudence: fam.*) culot *m.* **~s,** (*before exams etc.*) le trac **~-racking** *a.* éprouvant.

nervous /'nɜ:vəs/ *a.* nerveux. **be** *or* **feel ~,** (*afraid*) avoir peur. **~ breakdown,** dépression nerveuse *f.* **~ly** *adv.* (*tensely*) nerveusement; (*timidly*) craintivement. **~ness** *n.* nervosité *f.*; (*fear*) crainte *f.*

nervy /'nɜ:vɪ/ *a.* = **nervous**; (*Amer., fam.*) effronté.

nest /nest/ *n.* nid *m.* ● *v.i.* nicher. **~-egg** *n.* pécule *m.*

nestle /'nesl/ *v.i.* se blottir.

net[1] /net/ *n.* filet *m.* ● *v.t.* (*p.t.* **netted**) prendre au filet. **~ting** *n.* (*nets*) filets *m. pl.*; (*wire*) treillis *m.*; (*fabric*) voile *m.*

net[2] /net/ *a.* (*weight etc.*) net.

netball /'netbɔ:l/ *n.* netball *m.*

Netherlands /'neðələndz/ *n. pl.* **the ~,** les Pays-Bas *m. pl.*

nettle /'netl/ *n.* ortie *f.*

network /'netwɜ:k/ *n.* réseau *m.*

neuralgia /njʊə'rældʒə/ *n.* névralgie *f.*

neuro|sis /njʊə'rəʊsɪs/ *n.* (*pl.* **-oses** /-si:z/) névrose *f.* **~tic** /-'rɒtɪk/ *a.* & *n.* névrosé(e) (*m.* (*f.*)).

neuter /'nju:tə(r)/ *a.* & *n.* neutre (*m.*). ● *v.t.* (*castrate*) castrer.

neutral /'nju:trəl/ *a.* neutre. **~ (gear),** (*auto.*) point mort *m.* **~ity** /-'trælətɪ/ *n.* neutralité *f.*

neutron /'nju:trɒn/ *n.* neutron *m.* **~ bomb,** bombe à neutrons *f.*

never /'nevə(r)/ *adv.* (ne) jamais; (*not: fam.*) (ne) pas. **he ~ refuses,** il ne refuse jamais. **I ~ saw him,** (*fam.*) je ne l'ai pas vu. **~ again,** plus jamais. **~ mind,** (*don't worry*) ne vous en faites pas; (*it doesn't* *matter*) peu importe. **~-ending** *a.* interminable.

nevertheless /nəvəðə'les/ *adv.* néanmoins, toutefois.

new /nju:/ *a.* (**-er, -est**) nouveau; (*brand-new*) neuf. **~-born** *a.* nouveau-né. **~-laid egg,** œuf frais *m.* **~ moon,** nouvelle lune *f.* **~ year,** nouvel an *m.* **New Year's Day,** le jour de l'an. **New Year's Eve,** la Saint-Sylvestre. **New Zealand,** Nouvelle-Zélande *f.* **New Zealander,** Néo-Zélandais(e) *m.* (*f.*). **~ness** *n.* nouveauté *f.*

newcomer /'nju:kʌmə(r)/ *n.* nouveau venu *m.*, nouvelle venue *f.*

newfangled /nju:'fæŋgld/ *a.* (*pej.*) moderne, neuf.

newly /'nju:lɪ/ *adv.* nouvellement. **~-weds** *n. pl.* nouveaux mariés *m. pl.*

news /nju:z/ *n.* nouvelle(s) *f.* (*pl.*); (*radio, press*) informations *f. pl.*; (*TV*) actualités *f. pl.*, informations *f. pl.* **~ agency,** agence de presse *f.* **~caster, ~-reader** *ns.* présenta|teur, trice *m.,f.*

newsagent /'nju:zeɪdʒənt/ *n.* marchand(e) de journaux *m.*(*f.*).

newsletter /'nju:zletə(r)/ *n.* bulletin *m.*

newspaper /'nju:speɪpə(r)/ *n.* journal *m.*

newsreel /'nju:zri:l/ *n.* actualités *f. pl.*

newt /nju:t/ *n.* triton *m.*

next /nekst/ *a.* prochain; (*adjoining*) voisin; (*following*) suivant. ● *adv.* la prochaine fois; (*afterwards*) ensuite. ● *n.* suivant(e) *m.*(*f.*). **~ door,** à côté (**to,** de). **~-door** *a.* d'à côté. **~ of kin,** parent le plus proche *m.* **~ to,** à côté de.

nib /nɪb/ *n.* bec *m.*, plume *f.*

nibble /'nɪbl/ *v.t./i.* grignoter.

nice /naɪs/ *a.* (**-er, -est**) agréable, bon; (*kind*) gentil; (*pretty*) joli; (*respectable*) bien *invar.*; (*subtle*) délicat. **~ly** *adv.* agréablement; gentiment; (*well*) bien.

nicety /'naɪsətɪ/ *n.* subtilité *f.*

niche /nɪtʃ, ni:ʃ/ *n.* (*recess*) niche *f.*; (*fig.*) place *f.*, situation *f.*

nick /nɪk/ *n.* petite entaille *f.* ● *v.t.* (*steal, arrest*: *sl.*) piquer. **in the ~ of time,** juste à temps.

nickel /'nɪkl/ *n.* nickel *m.*; (*Amer.*) pièce de cinq cents *f.*

nickname /'nɪkneɪm/ *n.* surnom *m.*; (*short form*) diminutif *m.* ● *v.t.* surnommer.

nicotine /'nɪkəti:n/ *n.* nicotine *f.*

niece /ni:s/ *n.* nièce *f.*

nifty /'nɪftɪ/ *a.* (*sl.*) chic *invar.*

Nigeria /naɪ'dʒɪərɪə/ *n.* Nigéria *m./f.* **~n** *a.* & *n.* nigérian(e) (*m.* (*f.*)).

niggardly /'nɪgədlɪ/ *a.* chiche.

niggling /'nɪglɪŋ/ *a.* (*person*) tatillon; (*detail*) insignifiant.

night /naɪt/ *n.* nuit *f.*; (*evening*) soir *m.* ● *a.* de nuit. **~-cap** *n.* boisson *f.* (*avant d'aller se coucher*). **~-club** *n.* boîte de nuit *f.* **~-dress, ~-gown, ~ie** *ns.* chemise de nuit *f.* **~-life** *n.* vie nocturne *f.* **~-school** *n.* cours du soir *m. pl.* **~-time** *n.* nuit *f.* **~-watchman** *n.* veilleur de nuit *m.*

nightfall /'naɪtfɔ:l/ *n.* tombée de la nuit *f.*

nightingale /'naɪtɪŋgeɪl/ *n.* rossignol *m.*

nightly /'naɪtlɪ/ *a.* & *adv.* (de) chaque nuit *or* soir.

nightmare /'naɪtmeə(r)/ *n.* cauchemar *m.*

nil /nɪl/ *n.* rien *m.*; (*sport*) zéro *m.* ● *a.* (*chances, risk, etc.*) nul.

nimble /'nɪmbl/ *a.* (**-er, -est**) agile.

nin|e /naɪn/ *a.* & *n.* neuf (*m.*). **~th** *a.* & *n.* neuvième (*m./f.*).

nineteen /naɪn'ti:n/ *a.* & *n.* dix-neuf (*m.*). **~th** *a.* & *n.* dix-neuvième (*m./f.*).

ninet|y /'naɪntɪ/ *a.* & *n.* quatre-vingt-dix (*m.*). **~tieth** *a.* & *n.* quatre-vingt-dixième (*m./f.*).

nip /nɪp/ *v.t./i.* (*p.t.* **nipped**) (*pinch*) pincer; (*rush*: *sl.*) courir. **~ out/back/***etc.*, sortir/rentrer/*etc.* rapidement. ● *n.* pincement *m.*; (*cold*) fraîcheur *f.*

nipper /'nɪpə(r)/ *n.* (*sl.*) gosse *m./f.*

nipple /'nɪpl/ *n.* bout de sein *m.*; (*of baby's bottle*) tétine *f.*

nippy /'nɪpɪ/ *a.* (**-ier, -iest**) (*fam.*) alerte; (*chilly*: *fam.*) frais.

nitrogen /'naɪtrədʒən/ *n.* azote *m.*

nitwit /'nɪtwɪt/ *n.* (*fam.*) imbécile *m./f.*

no /nəʊ/ *a.* aucun(e); pas de. ● *adv.* non. ● *n.* (*pl.* **noes**) non *m. invar.* **~ man/***etc.*, aucun homme/*etc.* **~ money/time/***etc.*, pas d'argent/de temps/*etc.* **~ man's land,** no man's land *m.* **~ one** = **nobody**. **~ smoking/entry,** défense de fumer/

d'entrer. **~ way!,** (*fam.*) pas question!
nob|le /'nəʊbl/ *a.* (**-er, -est**) noble. **~ility** /-'bɪlətɪ/ *n.* noblesse *f.*
nobleman /'nəʊblmən/ *n.* (*pl.* **-men**) noble *m.*
nobody /'nəʊbədɪ/ *pron.* (ne) personne. ● *n.* nullité *f.* **he knows ~,** il ne connaît personne. **~ is there,** personne n'est là.
nocturnal /nɒk'tɜ:nl/ *a.* nocturne.
nod /nɒd/ *v.t./i.* (*p.t.* **nodded**). **~ (one's head),** faire un signe de tête. **~ off,** s'endormir. ● *n.* signe de tête *m.*
noise /nɔɪz/ *n.* bruit *m.* **~less** *a.* silencieux.
nois|y /'nɔɪzɪ/ *a.* (**-ier, -iest**) bruyant. **~ily** *adv.* bruyamment.
nomad /'nəʊmæd/ *n.* nomade *m./f.* **~ic** /-'mædɪk/ *a.* nomade.
nominal /'nɒmɪnl/ *a.* symbolique, nominal; (*value*) nominal. **~ly** *adv.* nominalement.
nominat|e /'nɒmɪneɪt/ *v.t.* nommer; (*put forward*) proposer. **~ion** /-'neɪʃn/ *n.* nomination *f.*
non- /nɒn/ *pref.* non-. **~-iron** *a.* qui ne se repasse pas. **~-skid** *a.* antidérapant. **~-stick** *a.* à revêtement antiadhésif.
non-commissioned /nɒnkə'mɪʃnd/ *a.* **~ officer,** sous-officier *m.*
non-committal /nɒnkə'mɪtl/ *a.* évasif.
nondescript /'nɒndɪskrɪpt/ *a.* indéfinissable.
none /nʌn/ *pron.* aucun(e). **~ of us,** aucun de nous. **I have ~,** je n'en ai pas. **~ of the money was used,** l'argent n'a pas du tout été utilisé. ● *adv.* **~ too,** (ne) pas tellement. **he is ~ the happier,** il n'en est pas plus heureux.
nonentity /nɒ'nentətɪ/ *n.* nullité *f.*
non-existent /nɒnɪg'zɪstənt/ *a.* inexistant.
nonplussed /nɒn'plʌst/ *a.* perplexe, déconcerté.
nonsens|e /'nɒnsəns/ *n.* absurdités *f. pl.* **~ical** /-'sensɪkl/ *a.* absurde.
non-smoker /nɒn'sməʊkə(r)/ *n.* non-fumeur *m.*
non-stop /nɒn'stɒp/ *a.* (*train, flight*) direct. ● *adv.* sans arrêt.
noodles /'nu:dlz/ *n. pl.* nouilles *f. pl.*
nook /nʊk/ *n.* (re)coin *m.*
noon /nu:n/ *n.* midi *m.*
noose /nu:s/ *n.* nœud coulant *m.*
nor /nɔ:(r)/ *adv.* ni. ● *conj.* (ne) non plus. **~ shall I come,** je ne viendrai pas non plus.
norm /nɔ:m/ *n.* norme *f.*
normal /'nɔ:ml/ *a.* normal. **~ity** /nɔ:'mælətɪ/ *n.* normalité *f.* **~ly** *adv.* normalement.
Norman /'nɔ:mən/ *a.* & *n.* normand(e) (*m.*(*f.*)). **~dy** *n.* Normandie *f.*
north /nɔ:θ/ *n.* nord *m.* ● *a.* nord *invar.*, du nord. ● *adv.* vers le nord. **N~ America,** Amérique du Nord *f.* **N~ American** *a.* & *n.* nord-américain(e) (*m.* (*f.*)). **~-east** *n.* nord-est *m.* **~erly** /'nɔ:ðəlɪ/ *a.* du nord. **~ward** *a.* au nord. **~wards** *adv.* vers le nord. **~-west** *n.* nord-ouest *m.*
northern /'nɔ:ðən/ *a.* du nord. **~er** *n.* habitant(e) du nord *m.* (*f.*).
Norw|ay /'nɔ:weɪ/ *n.* Norvège *f.* **~egian** /nɔ:'wi:dʒən/ *a.* & *n.* norvégien(ne) (*m.* (*f.*)).
nose /nəʊz/ *n.* nez *m.* ● *v.i.* **~ about,** fouiner.
nosebleed /'nəʊzbli:d/ *n.* saignement de nez *m.*
nosedive /'nəʊzdaɪv/ *n.* piqué *m.* ● *v.i.* descendre en piqué.
nostalg|ia /nɒ'stældʒə/ *n.* nostalgie *f.* **~ic** *a.* nostalgique.
nostril /'nɒstrəl/ *n.* narine *f.*; (*of horse*) naseau *m.*
nosy /'nəʊzɪ/ *a.* (**-ier, -iest**) (*fam.*) curieux, indiscret.
not /nɒt/ *adv.* (ne) pas. **I do ~ know,** je ne sais pas. **~ at all,** pas du tout. **~ yet,** pas encore. **I suppose ~,** je suppose que non.
notable /'nəʊtəbl/ *a.* notable. ● *n.* (*person*) notable *m.*
notably /'nəʊtəblɪ/ *adv.* notamment.
notary /'nəʊtərɪ/ *n.* notaire *m.*
notation /nəʊ'teɪʃn/ *n.* notation *f.*
notch /nɒtʃ/ *n.* entaille *f.* ● *v.t.* **~ up,** (*score etc.*) marquer.
note /nəʊt/ *n.* note *f.*; (*banknote*) billet *m.*; (*short letter*) mot *m.* ● *v.t.* noter; (*notice*) remarquer.
notebook /'nəʊtbʊk/ *n.* carnet *m.*
noted /'nəʊtɪd/ *a.* connu (**for,** pour).
notepaper /'nəʊtpeɪpə(r)/ *n.* papier à lettres *m.*
noteworthy /'nəʊtwɜ:ðɪ/ *a.* remarquable.
nothing /'nʌθɪŋ/ *pron.* (ne) rien. ● *n.* rien *m.*; (*person*) nullité *f.* ● *adv.* nullement. **he eats ~,** il ne

mange rien. ~ **big**/*etc.*, rien de grand/*etc.* ~ **else,** rien d'autre. ~ **much,** pas grand-chose. **for ~,** pour rien, gratis.

notice /'nəʊtɪs/ *n.* avis *m.*, annonce *f.*; (*poster*) affiche *f.* **(advance) ~,** préavis *m.* **at short ~,** dans des délais très brefs. **give in one's ~,** donner sa démission. ● *v.t.* remarquer, observer. **~-board** *n.* tableau d'affichage *m.* **take ~,** faire attention (**of,** à).

noticeabl|e /'nəʊtɪsəbl/ *a.* visible. **~y** *adv.* visiblement.

notif|y /'nəʊtɪfaɪ/ *v.t.* (*inform*) aviser; (*make known*) notifier. **~ication** /-ɪ'keɪʃn/ *n.* avis *m.*

notion /'nəʊʃn/ *n.* idée *f.*, notion *f.* **~s,** (*sewing goods etc.*: *Amer.*) mercerie *f.*

notor|ious /nəʊ'tɔ:rɪəs/ *a.* (tristement) célèbre. **~iety** /-ə'raɪətɪ/ *n.* notoriété *f.* **~iously** *adv.* notoirement.

notwithstanding /nɒtwɪθ'stændɪŋ/ *prep.* malgré. ● *adv.* néanmoins.

nougat /'nu:gɑ:/ *n.* nougat *m.*

nought /nɔ:t/ *n.* zéro *m.*

noun /naʊn/ *n.* nom *m.*

nourish /'nʌrɪʃ/ *v.t.* nourrir. **~ing** *a.* nourrissant. **~ment** *n.* nourriture *f.*

novel /'nɒvl/ *n.* roman *m.* ● *a.* nouveau. **~ist** *n.* romanc|ier, -ière *m.*, *f.* **~ty** *n.* nouveauté *f.*

November /nəʊ'vembə(r)/ *n.* novembre *m.*

novice /'nɒvɪs/ *n.* novice *m./f.*

now /naʊ/ *adv.* maintenant. ● *conj.* maintenant que. **just ~,** maintenant; (*a moment ago*) tout à l'heure. **~ and again, ~ and then,** de temps à autre.

nowadays /'naʊədeɪz/ *adv.* de nos jours.

nowhere /'nəʊweə(r)/ *adv.* nulle part.

nozzle /'nɒzl/ *n.* (*tip*) embout *m.*; (*of hose*) lance *f.*

nuance /'nju:ɑ:ns/ *n.* nuance *f.*

nuclear /'nju:klɪə(r)/ *a.* nucléaire.

nucleus /'nju:klɪəs/ *n.* (*pl.* **-lei** /-lɪaɪ/) noyau *m.*

nud|e /nju:d/ *a.* nu. ● *n.* nu *m.* **in the ~e,** tout nu. **~ity** *n.* nudité *f.*

nudge /nʌdʒ/ *v.t.* pousser du coude. ● *n.* coup de coude *m.*

nudis|t /'nju:dɪst/ *n.* nudiste *m./f.* **~m** /-zəm/ *n.* nudisme *m.*

nuisance /'nju:sns/ *n.* (*thing*, *event*) ennui *m.*; (*person*) peste *f.* **be a ~,** être embêtant.

null /nʌl/ *a.* nul. **~ify** *v.t.* infirmer.

numb /nʌm/ *a.* engourdi. ● *v.t.* engourdir.

number /'nʌmbə(r)/ *n.* nombre *m.*; (*of ticket*, *house*, *page*, *etc.*) numéro *m.* ● *v.t.* numéroter; (*count*, *include*) compter. **a ~ of people,** plusieurs personnes. **~-plate** *n.* plaque d'immatriculation *f.*

numeral /'nju:mərəl/ *n.* chiffre *m.*

numerate /'nju:mərət/ *a.* qui sait calculer.

numerical /nju:'merɪkl/ *a.* numérique.

numerous /'nju:mərəs/ *a.* nombreux.

nun /nʌn/ *n.* religieuse *f.*

nurs|e /nɜ:s/ *n.* infirmière *f.*, infirmier *m.*; (*nanny*) nurse *f.* ● *v.t.* soigner; (*hope etc.*) nourrir. **~ing home,** clinique *f.*

nursemaid /'nɜ:smeɪd/ *n.* bonne d'enfants *f.*

nursery /'nɜ:sərɪ/ *n.* chambre d'enfants *f.*; (*for plants*) pépinière *f.* **(day) ~,** crèche *f.* **~ rhyme,** chanson enfantine *f.*, comptine *f.* **~ school,** (école) maternelle *f.* **~ slope,** piste facile *f.*

nurture /'nɜ:tʃə(r)/ *v.t.* élever.

nut /nʌt/ *n.* (*walnut*, *Brazil nut*, *etc.*) noix *f.*; (*hazelnut*) noisette *f.*; (*peanut*) cacahuète *f.*; (*techn.*) écrou *m.*; (*sl.*) idiot(e) *m.* (*f.*).

nutcrackers /'nʌtkrækəz/ *n. pl.* casse-noix *m. invar.*

nutmeg /'nʌtmeg/ *n.* muscade *f.*

nutrient /'nju:trɪənt/ *n.* substance nutritive *f.*

nutrit|ion /nju:'trɪʃn/ *n.* nutrition *f.* **~ious** *a.* nutritif.

nuts /nʌts/ *a.* (*crazy*: *sl.*) cinglé.

nutshell /'nʌtʃel/ *n.* coquille de noix *f.* **in a ~,** en un mot.

nuzzle /'nʌzl/ *v.i.* **~ up to,** coller son museau à.

nylon /'naɪlɒn/ *n.* nylon *m.* **~s,** bas nylon *m. pl.*

O

oaf /əʊf/ *n.* (*pl.* **oafs**) lourdaud(e) *m.* (*f.*).

oak /əʊk/ *n.* chêne *m.*

OAP *abbr.* (*old-age pensioner*) retraité(e) *m.* (*f.*), personne âgée *f.*
oar /ɔ:(r)/ *n.* aviron *m.*, rame *f.*
oasis /əʊ'eɪsɪs/ *n.* (*pl.* **oases** /-si:z/) oasis *f.*
oath /əʊθ/ *n.* (*promise*) serment *m.*; (*swear-word*) juron *m.*
oatmeal /'əʊtmi:l/ *n.* farine d'avoine *f.*, flocons d'avoine *m. pl.*
oats /əʊts/ *n. pl.* avoine *f.*
obedien|t /ə'bi:dɪənt/ *a.* obéissant. **~ce** *n.* obéissance *f.* **~tly** *adv.* docilement, avec soumission.
obes|e /əʊ'bi:s/ *a.* obèse. **~ity** *n.* obésité *f.*
obey /ə'beɪ/ *v.t./i.* obéir (à).
obituary /ə'bɪtʃʊərɪ/ *n.* nécrologie *f.*
object[1] /'ɒbdʒɪkt/ *n.* (*thing*) objet *m.*; (*aim*) but *m.*, objet *m.*; (*gram.*) complément (d'objet) *m.* **money/ etc. is no ~,** l'argent/*etc.* ne pose pas de problèmes.
object[2] /əb'dʒekt/ *v.i.* protester. ● *v.t.* **~ that,** objecter que. **~ to,** (*behaviour*) désapprouver; (*plan*) protester contre. **~ion** /-kʃn/ *n.* objection *f.*; (*drawback*) inconvénient *m.*
objectionable /əb'dʒekʃnəbl/ *a.* désagréable.
objectiv|e /əb'dʒektɪv/ *a.* objectif. ● *n.* objectif *m.* **~ity** /ɒbdʒek'tɪvətɪ/ *n.* objectivité *f.*
obligat|e /'ɒblɪgeɪt/ *v.t.* obliger. **~ion** /-'geɪʃn/ *n.* obligation *f.* **under an ~ion to s.o.,** redevable à qn. (**for,** de).
obligatory /ə'blɪgətrɪ/ *a.* obligatoire.
oblig|e /ə'blaɪdʒ/ *v.t.* obliger. **~e to do,** obliger à faire. **~ed** *a.* obligé (**to,** de). **~ed to s.o.,** redevable à qn. **~ing** *a.* obligeant. **~ingly** *adv.* obligeamment.
oblique /ə'bli:k/ *a.* oblique; (*reference etc.: fig.*) indirect.
obliterat|e /ə'blɪtəreɪt/ *v.t.* effacer. **~ion** /-'reɪʃn/ *n.* effacement *m.*
oblivion /ə'blɪvɪən/ *n.* oubli *m.*
oblivious /ə'blɪvɪəs/ *a.* (*unaware*) inconscient (**to, of,** de).
oblong /'ɒblɒŋ/ *a.* oblong. ● *n.* rectangle *m.*
obnoxious /əb'nɒkʃəs/ *a.* odieux.
oboe /'əʊbəʊ/ *n.* hautbois *m.*
obscen|e /əb'si:n/ *a.* obscène. **~ity** /-enətɪ/ *n.* obscénité *f.*
obscur|e /əb'skjʊə(r)/ *a.* obscur. ● *v.t.* obscurcir; (*conceal*) cacher. **~ely** *adv.* obscurément. **~ity** *n.* obscurité *f.*
obsequious /əb'si:kwɪəs/ *a.* obséquieux.
observan|t /əb'zɜ:vənt/ *a.* observateur. **~ce** *n.* observance *f.*
observatory /əb'zɜ:vətrɪ/ *n.* observatoire *m.*
observ|e /əb'zɜ:v/ *v.t.* observer; (*remark*) remarquer. **~ation** /ɒbzə'veɪʃn/ *n.* observation *f.* **~er** *n.* observa|teur, -trice *m., f.*
obsess /əb'ses/ *v.t.* obséder. **~ion** /-ʃn/ *n.* obsession *f.* **~ive** *a.* obsédant; (*psych.*) obsessionnel.
obsolete /'ɒbsəli:t/ *a.* dépassé.
obstacle /'ɒbstəkl/ *n.* obstacle *m.*
obstetric|s /əb'stetrɪks/ *n.* obstétrique *f.* **~ian** /ɒbstɪ'trɪʃn/ *n.* médecin accoucheur *m.*
obstina|te /'ɒbstɪnət/ *a.* obstiné. **~cy** *n.* obstination *f.* **~tely** *adv.* obstinément.
obstruct /əb'strʌkt/ *v.t.* (*block*) boucher; (*congest*) encombrer; (*hinder*) entraver. **~ion** /-kʃn/ *n.* (*act*) obstruction *f.*; (*thing*) obstacle *m.*; (*traffic jam*) encombrement *m.*
obtain /əb'teɪn/ *v.t.* obtenir. ● *v.i.* avoir cours. **~able** *a.* disponible.
obtrusive /əb'tru:sɪv/ *a.* importun; (*thing*) trop en évidence.
obtuse /əb'tju:s/ *a.* obtus.
obviate /'ɒbvɪeɪt/ *v.t.* éviter.
obvious /'ɒbvɪəs/ *a.* évident, manifeste. **~ly** *adv.* manifestement.
occasion /ə'keɪʒn/ *n.* occasion *f.*; (*big event*) événement *m.* ● *v.t.* occasionner. **on ~,** à l'occasion.
occasional /ə'keɪʒənl/ *a.* fait, pris, *etc.* de temps en temps; (*visitor etc.*) qui vient de temps en temps. **~ly** *adv.* de temps en temps. **very ~ly,** rarement.
occult /ɒ'kʌlt/ *a.* occulte.
occupation /ɒkjʊ'peɪʃn/ *n.* (*activity, occupying*) occupation *f.*; (*job*) métier *m.*, profession *f.* **~al** *a.* professionnel, du métier. **~al therapy** ergothérapie *f.*
occup|y /'ɒkjʊpaɪ/ *v.t.* occuper. **~ant, ~ier** *ns.* occupant(e) *m.* (*f.*).
occur /ə'kɜ:(r)/ *v.i.* (*p.t.* **occurred**) se produire; (*arise*) se présenter. **~ to s.o.,** venir à l'esprit de qn.
occurrence /ə'kʌrəns/ *n.* événement *m.* **a frequent ~,** une chose qui arrive souvent.
ocean /'əʊʃn/ *n.* océan *m.*

o'clock /ə'klɒk/ *adv.* **it is six ~/***etc.*, il est six heures/*etc.*

octagon /'ɒktəgən/ *n.* octogone *m.*

octane /'ɒkteɪn/ *n.* octane *m.*

octave /'ɒktɪv/ *n.* octave *f.*

October /ɒk'təʊbə(r)/ *n.* octobre *m.*

octopus /'ɒktəpəs/ *n.* (*pl.* **-puses**) pieuvre *f.*

odd /ɒd/ *a.* (**-er, -est**) bizarre; (*number*) impair; (*left over*) qui reste; (*not of set*) dépareillé; (*occasional*) fait, pris, *etc.* de temps en temps. **~ jobs,** menus travaux *m. pl.* **twenty ~,** vingt et quelques. **~ity** *n.* bizarrerie *f.*; (*thing*) curiosité *f.* **~ly** *adv.* bizarrement.

oddment /'ɒdmənt/ *n.* fin de série *f.*

odds /ɒdz/ *n. pl.* chances *f. pl.*; (*in betting*) cote *f.* (**on,** de). **at ~,** en désaccord. **it makes no ~,** ça ne fait rien. **~ and ends,** des petites choses.

ode /əʊd/ *n.* ode *f.*

odious /'əʊdɪəs/ *a.* odieux.

odour, *Amer.* **odor** /'əʊdə(r)/ *n.* odeur *f.* **~less** *a.* inodore.

of /ɒv, *unstressed* əv/ *prep.* de. **of the,** du, de la, *pl.* des. **of it, of them,** en. **a friend of mine,** un de mes amis. **six of them,** six d'entre eux. **the fifth of June/***etc.*, le cinq juin/*etc.* **a litre of water,** un litre d'eau; **made of steel,** en acier.

off /ɒf/ *adv.* parti, absent; (*switched off*) éteint; (*tap*) fermé; (*taken off*) enlevé, détaché; *cancelled*) annulé. ● *prep.* de; (*distant from*) éloigné de. **go ~,** (*leave*) partir; (*milk*) tourner; (*food*) s'abîmer. **be better ~,** (*in a better position, richer*) être mieux. **a day ~,** un jour de congé. **20% ~,** une réduction de 20%. **take sth. ~,** (*a surface*) prendre qch. sur. **~-beat** *a.* original. **on the ~ chance (that),** au cas où. **~ colour,** (*ill*) patraque. **~ color,** (*improper*: *Amer.*) scabreux. **~-licence** *n.* débit de vins *m.* **~-line** *a.* autonome; (*switched off*) déconnecté. **~-load** *v.t.* décharger. **~-peak** *a.* (*hours*) creux; (*rate*) des heures creuses. **~-putting** *a.* (*fam.*) rebutant. **~-stage** *a.* & *adv.* dans les coulisses. **~-white** *a.* blanc cassé *invar.*

offal /'ɒfl/ *n.* abats *m. pl.*

offence /ə'fens/ *n.* délit *m.* **give ~ to,** offenser. **take ~,** s'offenser (**at,** de).

offend /ə'fend/ *v.t.* offenser; (*fig.*) choquer. **be ~ed,** s'offenser (**at,** de). **~er** *n.* délinquant(e) *m.* (*f.*).

offensive /ə'fensɪv/ *a.* offensant; (*disgusting*) dégoûtant; (*weapon*) offensif. ● *n.* offensive *f.*

offer /'ɒfə(r)/ *v.t.* (*p.t.* **offered**) offrir. ● *n.* offre *f.* **on ~,** en promotion. **~ing** *n.* offrande *f.*

offhand /ɒf'hænd/ *a.* désinvolte. ● *adv.* à l'improviste.

office /'ɒfɪs/ *n.* bureau *m.*; (*duty*) fonction *f.*; (*surgery*: *Amer.*) cabinet *m.* ● *a.* de bureau. **good ~s,** bons offices *m. pl.* **in ~,** au pouvoir. **~ building,** immeuble de bureaux *m.*

officer /'ɒfɪsə(r)/ *n.* (*army etc.*) officier *m.*; (*policeman*) agent *m.*

official /ə'fɪʃl/ *a.* officiel. ● *n.* officiel *m.*; (*civil servant*) fonctionnaire *m./f.* **~ly** *adv.* officiellement.

officiate /ə'fɪʃɪeɪt/ *v.i.* (*priest*) officier; (*president*) présider.

officious /ə'fɪʃəs/ *a.* trop zélé.

offing /'ɒfɪŋ/ *n.* **in the ~,** en perspective.

offset /'ɒfset/ *v.t.* (*p.t.* **-set,** *pres. p.* **-setting**) compenser.

offshoot /'ɔfʃu:t/ *n.* (*bot.*) rejeton *m.*; (*fig.*) ramification *f.*

offshore /ɒf'ʃɔ:(r)/ *a.* (*waters*) côtier; (*exploration*) en mer; (*banking*) dans les paladis fiscaux.

offside /ɒf'saɪd/ *a.* (*sport*) hors jeu *invar.*; (*auto.*) du côté du conducteur.

offspring /'ɒfsprɪŋ/ *n. invar.* progéniture *f.*

often /'ɒfn/ *adv.* souvent. **how ~?,** combien de fois? **every so ~,** de temps en temps.

ogle /'əʊgl/ *v.t.* lorgner.

ogre /'əʊgə(r)/ *n.* ogre *m.*

oh /əʊ/ *int.* oh, ah.

oil /ɔɪl/ *n.* huile *f.*; (*petroleum*) pétrole *m.*; (*for heating*) mazout *m.* ● *v.t.* graisser. **~-painting** *n.* peinture à l'huile *f.* **~-tanker** *n.* pétrolier *m.* **~y** *a.* graisseux.

oilfield /'ɔɪlfi:ld/ *n.* gisement pétrolifère *m.*

oilskins /'ɔɪlskɪnz/ *n. pl.* ciré *m.*

ointment /'ɔɪntmənt/ *n.* pommade *f.*, onguent *m.*

OK /əʊ'keɪ/ *a.* & *adv.* (*fam.*) bien.

old /əʊld/ *a.* (**-er, -est**) vieux; (*person*) vieux, âgé; (*former*) ancien. **how ~ is he?,** quel âge a-t-il? **he is eight years ~,** il a huit ans. **of ~,** jadis. **~ age,** vieillesse *f.* **~-age pensioner,** retraité(e) *m.* (*f.*) **~ boy,** ancien élève *m.*; (*fellow*: *fam.*) vieux *m.*

~er, ~est, (*son etc.*) aîné. **~-fashioned** *a.* démodé; (*person*) vieux jeu *invar.* **~ maid,** vieille fille *f.* **~ man,** vieillard *m.*, vieux *m.* **~-time** *a.* ancien. **~ woman,** vieille *f.*

olive /'ɒlɪv/ *n.* olive *f.* ● *a.* olive *invar.* **~ oil,** huile d'olive *f.*

Olympic /ə'lɪmpɪk/ *a.* olympique. **~s** *n. pl.*, **~ Games,** Jeux olympiques *m. pl.*

omelette /'ɒmlɪt/ *n.* omelette *f.*

omen /'əʊmen/ *n.* augure *m.*

ominous /'ɒmɪnəs/ *a.* de mauvais augure; (*fig.*) menaçant.

omi|t /ə'mɪt/ *v.t.* (*p.t.* **omitted**) omettre. **~ssion** *n.* omission *f.*

on /ɒn/ *prep.* sur. ● *adv.* en avant; (*switched on*) allumé; (*tap*) ouvert; (*machine*) en marche; (*put on*) mis. **on foot/time/***etc.*, à pied/l'heure/*etc.* **on arriving,** en arrivant. **on Tuesday,** mardi. **on Tuesdays,** le mardi. **walk/***etc.* **on,** continuer à marcher/*etc.* **be on,** (*of film*) passer. **the meeting/deal is still on,** la réunion/le marché est maintenu(e). **be on at,** (*fam.*) être après. **on and off,** de temps en temps.

once /wʌns/ *adv.* une fois; (*formerly*) autrefois. ● *conj.* une fois que. **all at ~,** tout à coup. **~-over** *n.* (*fam.*) coup d'œil rapide *m.*

oncoming /'ɒnkʌmɪŋ/ *a.* (*vehicle etc.*) qui approche.

one /wʌn/ *a.* & *n.* un(e) (*m.* (*f.*)). ● *pron.* un(e) *m.* (*f.*); (*impersonal*) on. **~ (and only),** seul (et unique). **a big/red/***etc.*. **~,** un(e) grand(e)/rouge/*etc.* **this/that ~,** celui-ci/-là, celle-ci/-là. **~ another,** l'un(e) l'autre. **~-eyed,** borgne. **~-off** *a.* (*fam.*), **~ of a kind,** (*Amer.*) unique, exceptionnel. **~-sided** *a.* (*biased*) partial; (*unequal*) inégal. **~-way** *a.* (*street*) à sens unique; (*ticket*) simple.

oneself /wʌn'self/ *pron.* soi-même; (*reflexive*) se.

ongoing /'ɒngəʊɪŋ/ *a.* qui continue à évoluer.

onion /'ʌnjən/ *n.* oignon *m.*

onlooker /'ɒnlʊkə(r)/ *n.* specta|teur, -trice *m.*, *f.*

only /'əʊnlɪ/ *a.* seul. **an ~ son/** *etc.*, un fils/*etc.* unique. ● *adv.* & *conj.* seulement. **he ~ has six,** il n'en a que six, il en a six seulement. **~ too,** extrêmement.

onset /'ɒnset/ *n.* début *m.*

onslaught /'ɒnslɔ:t/ *n.* attaque *f.*

onus /'əʊnəs/ *n.* **the ~ is on me/***etc.*, c'est ma/*etc.* responsabilité (**to,** de).

onward(s) /'ɒnwəd(z)/ *adv.* en avant.

onyx /'ɒnɪks/ *n.* onyx *m.*

ooze /u:z/ *v.i.* suinter.

opal /'əʊpl/ *n.* opale *f.*

opaque /əʊ'peɪk/ *a.* opaque.

open /'əʊpən/ *a.* ouvert; (*view*) dégagé; (*free to all*) public; (*undisguised*) manifeste; (*question*) en attente. ● *v.t./i.* (s')ouvrir; (*of shop, play*) ouvrir. **in the ~ air,** en plein air. **~-ended** *a.* sans limite (*de durée etc.*); (*system*) qui peut évoluer. **~-heart** *a.* (*surgery*) à cœur ouvert. **keep ~ house,** tenir table ouverte. **~ out** *or* **up,** (s')ouvrir. **~-minded** *a.* à l'esprit ouvert. **~-plan** *a.* sans cloisons. **~ secret,** secret de Polichinelle *m.*

opener /'əʊpənə(r)/ *n.* ouvre-boîte(s) *m.*, ouvre-bouteille(s) *m.*

opening /'əʊpənɪŋ/ *n.* ouverture *f.*; (*job*) débouché *m.*, poste vacant *m.*

openly /'əʊpənlɪ/ *adv.* ouvertement.

opera /'ɒpərə/ *n.* opéra *m.* **~-glasses** *n. pl.* jumelles *f. pl.* **~tic** /ɒpə'rætɪk/ *a.* d'opéra.

operat|e /'ɒpəreɪt/ *v.t./i.* opérer; (*techn.*) (faire) fonctionner. **~e on,** (*med.*) opérer. **~ing theatre,** salle d'opération *f.* **~ion** /-'reɪʃn/ *n.* opération *f.* **have an ~ion,** se faire opérer. **in ~ion,** en vigueur; (*techn.*) en service. **~or** *n.* opéra|teur, -trice *m.*, *f.*; (*telephonist*) standardiste *m./f.*

operational /ɒpə'reɪʃənl/ *a.* opérationnel.

operative /'ɒpərətɪv/ *a.* (*med.*) opératoire; (*law etc.*) en vigueur.

operetta /ɒpə'retə/ *n.* opérette *f.*

opinion /ə'pɪnjən/ *n.* opinion *f.*, avis *m.* **~ated** *a.* dogmatique.

opium /'əʊpɪəm/ *n.* opium *m.*

opponent /ə'pəʊnənt/ *n.* adversaire *m./f.*

opportune /'ɒpətju:n/ *a.* opportun.

opportunist /ɒpə'tju:nɪst/ *n.* opportuniste *m./f.*

opportunity /ɒpə'tju:nətɪ/ *n.* occasion *f.* (**to do,** de faire).

oppos|e /ə'pəʊz/ *v.t.* s'opposer à. **~ed to,** opposé à. **~ing** *a.* opposé.

opposite /'ɒpəzɪt/ *a.* opposé. ● *n.* contraire *m.*, opposé *m.* ● *adv.* en face. ● *prep.* **~ (to),** en face de.

one's ~ number, son homologue *m./f.*

opposition /ɒpə'zɪʃn/ *n.* opposition *f.*; (*mil.*) résistance *f.*

oppress /ə'pres/ *v.t.* opprimer. **~ion** /-ʃn/ *n.* oppression *f.* **~ive** *a.* (*cruel*) oppressif; (*heat*) oppressant. **~or** *n.* oppresseur *m.*

opt /ɒpt/ *v.i.* **~ for**, opter pour. **~ out**, refuser de participer (**of**, à). **~ to do**, choisir de faire.

optical /'ɒptɪkl/ *a.* optique. **~ illusion**, illusion d'optique *f.*

optician /ɒp'tɪʃn/ *n.* opticien(ne) *m.* (*f.*).

optimis|t /'ɒptɪmɪst/ *n.* optimiste *m./f.* **~m** /-zəm/ *n.* optimisme *m.* **~tic** /-'mɪstɪk/ *a.* optimiste. **~tically** /-'mɪstɪklɪ/ *adv.* avec optimisme.

optimum /'ɒptɪməm/ *a.* & *n.* (*pl.* **-ima**) optimum (*m.*).

option /'ɒpʃn/ *n.* choix *m.*, option *f.*

optional /'ɒpʃənl/ *a.* facultatif. **~ extras**, accessoires en option *m. pl.*

opulen|t /'ɒpjʊlənt/ *a.* opulent. **~ce** *n.* opulence *f.*

or /ɔ:(r)/ *conj.* ou; (*with negative*) ni.

oracle /'ɒrəkl/ *n.* oracle *m.*

oral /'ɔ:rəl/ *a.* oral. ● *n.* (*examination*: *fam.*) oral *m.*

orange /'ɒrɪndʒ/ *n.* (*fruit*) orange *f.* ● *a.* (*colour*) orange *invar.*

orangeade /ɒrɪndʒ'eɪd/ *n.* orangeade *f.*

orator /'ɒrətə(r)/ *n.* ora|teur, -trice *m., f.* **~y** /-trɪ/ *n.* rhétorique *f.*

oratorio /ɒrə'tɔ:rɪəʊ/ *n.* (*pl.* **-os**) oratorio *m.*

orbit /'ɔ:bɪt/ *n.* orbite *f.* ● *v.t.* graviter autour de, orbiter.

orchard /'ɔ:tʃəd/ *n.* verger *m.*

orchestra /'ɔ:kɪstrə/ *n.* orchestre *m.* **~ stalls** (*Amer.*), fauteuils d'orchestre *m. pl.* **~l** /-'kestrəl/ *a.* orchestral.

orchestrate /'ɔ:kɪstreɪt/ *v.t.* orchestrer.

orchid /'ɔ:kɪd/ *n.* orchidée *f.*

ordain /ɔ:'deɪn/ *v.t.* décréter (**that**, que); (*relig.*) ordonner.

ordeal /ɔ:'di:l/ *n.* épreuve *f.*

order /'ɔ:də(r)/ *n.* ordre *m.*; (*comm.*) commande *f.* ● *v.t.* ordonner; (*goods etc.*) commander. **in ~**, (*tidy*) en ordre; (*document*) en règle; (*fitting*) de règle. **in ~ that**, pour que. **in ~ to**, pour. **~ s.o. to**, ordonner à qn. de.

orderly /'ɔ:dəlɪ/ *a.* (*tidy*) ordonné; (*not unruly*) discipliné. ● *n.* (*mil.*) planton *m.*; (*med.*) garçon de salle *m.*

ordinary /'ɔ:dɪnrɪ/ *a.* (*usual*) ordinaire; (*average*) moyen.

ordination /ɔ:dɪ'neɪʃn/ *n.* (*relig.*) ordination *f.*

ore /ɔ:(r)/ *n.* mineral *m.*

organ /'ɔ:gən/ *n.* organe *m.*; (*mus.*) orgue *m.* **~ist** *n.* organiste *m./f.*

organic /ɔ:'gænɪk/ *a.* organique.

organism /'ɔ:gənɪzəm/ *n.* organisme *m.*

organiz|e /'ɔ:gənaɪz/ *v.t.* organiser. **~ation** /-'zeɪʃn/ *n.* organisation *f.* **~er** *n.* organisa|teur, -trice *m., f.*

orgasm /'ɔ:gæzəm/ *n.* orgasme *m.*

orgy /'ɔ:dʒɪ/ *n.* orgie *f.*

Orient /'ɔ:rɪənt/ *n.* **the ~**, l'Orient *m.* **~al** /-'entl/ *n.* Oriental(e) *m.* (*f.*).

oriental /ɔ:rɪ'entl/ *a.* oriental.

orient(at|e) /'ɔ:rɪənt(eɪt)/ *v.t.* orienter. **~ion** /-'teɪʃn/ *n.* orientation *f.*

orifice /'ɒrɪfɪs/ *n.* orifice *m.*

origin /'ɒrɪdʒɪn/ *n.* origine *f.*

original /ə'rɪdʒənl/ *a.* (*first*) originel; (*not copied*) original. **~ity** /-'nælətɪ/ *n.* originalité *f.* **~ly** *adv.* (*at the outset*) à l'origine; (*write etc.*) originalement.

originat|e /ə'rɪdʒɪneɪt/ *v.i.* (*plan*) prendre naissance. ● *v.t.* être l'auteur de. **~e from**, provenir de; (*person*) venir de. **~or** *n.* auteur *m.*

ornament /'ɔ:nəmənt/ *n.* (*decoration*) ornement *m.*; (*object*) objet décoratif *m.* **~al** /-'mentl/ *a.* ornemental. **~ation** /- en'teɪʃn/ *n.* ornementation *f.*

ornate /ɔ:'neɪt/ *a.* richement orné.

ornithology /ɔ:nɪ'θɒlədʒɪ/ *n.* ornithologie *f.*

orphan /'ɔ:fn/ *n.* orphelin(e) *m.* (*f.*). ● *v.t.* rendre orphelin. **~age** *n.* orphelinat *m.*

orthodox /'ɔ:θədɒks/ *a.* orthodoxe. **~y** *n.* orthodoxie *f.*

orthopaedic /ɔ:θə'pi:dɪk/ *a.* orthopédique.

oscillate /'ɒsɪleɪt/ *v.i.* osciller.

ostensibl|e /ɒs'tensəbl/ *a.* apparent, prétendu. **~y** *adv.* apparemment, prétendument.

ostentati|on /ɒsten'teɪʃn/ *n.* ostentation *f.* **~ous** *a.* prétentieux.

osteopath /'ɒstɪəpæθ/ *n.* ostéopathe *m./f.*

ostracize /ˈɒstrəsaɪz/ *v.t.* frapper d'ostracisme.
ostrich /ˈɒstrɪtʃ/ *n.* autruche *f.*
other /ˈʌðə(r)/ *a.* autre. ● *n. & pron.* autre *m./f.* ● *adv.* ~ **than,** autrement que; (*except*) à part. **(some) ~s,** d'autres. **the ~ one,** l'autre *m./f.*
otherwise /ˈʌðəwaɪz/ *adv.* autrement.
otter /ˈɒtə(r)/ *n.* loutre *f.*
ouch /aʊtʃ/ *int.* aïe!
ought /ɔːt/ *v. aux.* devoir. **you ~ to stay,** vous devriez rester. **he ~ to succeed,** il devrait réussir. **I ~ to have done it,** j'aurais dû le faire.
ounce /aʊns/ *n.* once *f.* (= *28.35 g.*).
our /ˈaʊə(r)/ *a.* notre, *pl.* nos.
ours /ˈaʊəz/ *poss.* le *or* la nôtre, les nôtres.
ourselves /aʊəˈselvz/ *pron.* nous-mêmes; (*reflexive & after prep.*) nous.
oust /aʊst/ *v.t.* évincer.
out /aʊt/ *adv.* dehors; (*sun*) levé. **be ~,** (*person, book*) être sorti; (*light*) être éteint; (*flower*) être épanoui; (*tide*) être bas; (*secret*) se savoir; (*wrong*) se tromper. **be ~ to do,** être résolu à faire. **run**/*etc.* **~,** sortir en courant/*etc.* **~-and-out** *a.* absolu. **~ of,** hors de; (*without*) sans, à court de. **~ of pity**/*etc.*, par pitié/*etc.* **made ~ of,** fait en *or* de. **take ~ of,** prendre dans. **5 ~ of 6,** 5 sur 6. **~ of date,** démodé; (*not valid*) périmé. **~ of doors,** dehors. **~ of hand,** (*situation*) dont on n'est plus maître. **~ of line,** (*impertinent: Amer.*) incorrect. **~ of one's mind,** fou. **~ of order,** (*broken*) en panne. **~ of place,** (*object, remark*) déplacé. **~ of the way,** écarté. **get ~ of the way!** écarte-toi! **~ of work,** sans travail. **~-patient** *n.* malade en consultation externe *m./f.*
outbid /aʊtˈbɪd/ *v.t.* (*p.t.* **-bid,** *pres. p.* **-bidding**) enchérir sur.
outboard /ˈaʊtbɔːd/ *a.* (*motor*) hors-bord *invar.*
outbreak /ˈaʊtbreɪk/ *n.* (*of war etc.*) début *m.*; (*of violence, boils*) éruption *f.*
outburst /ˈaʊtbɜːst/ *n.* explosion *f.*
outcast /ˈaʊtkɑːst/ *n.* paria *m.*
outclass /aʊtˈklɑːs/ *v.t.* surclasser.
outcome /ˈaʊtkʌm/ *n.* résultat *m.*
outcrop /ˈaʊtkrɒp/ *n.* affleurement.
outcry /ˈaʊtkraɪ/ *n.* tollé *m.*
outdated /aʊtˈdeɪtɪd/ *a.* démodé.
outdo /aʊtˈduː/ *v.t.* (*p.t.* **-did,** *p.p.* **-done**) surpasser.
outdoor /ˈaʊtdɔː(r)/ *a.* de *or* en plein air. **~s** /-ˈdɔːz/ *adv.* dehors.
outer /ˈaʊtə(r)/ *a.* extérieur. **~ space,** espace (cosmique) *m.*
outfit /ˈaʊtfɪt/ *n.* (*articles*) équipement *m.*; (*clothes*) tenue *f.*; (*group: fam.*) équipe *f.* **~ter** *n.* spécialiste de confection *m./f.*
outgoing /ˈaʊtgəʊɪŋ/ *a.* (*minister, tenant*) sortant; (*sociable*) ouvert. **~s** *n. pl.* dépenses *f. pl.*
outgrow /aʊtˈgrəʊ/ *v.t.* (*p.t.* **-grew,** *p.p.* **-grown**) (*clothes*) devenir trop grand pour; (*habit*) dépasser.
outhouse /ˈaʊthaʊs/ *n.* appentis *m.*; (*of mansion*) dépendance *f.*; (*Amer.*) cabinets extérieurs *m. pl.*
outing /ˈaʊtɪŋ/ *n.* sortie *f.*
outlandish /aʊtˈlændɪʃ/ *a.* bizarre, étrange.
outlaw /ˈaʊtlɔː/ *n.* hors-la-loi *m. invar.* ● *v.t.* proscrire.
outlay /ˈaʊtleɪ/ *n.* dépenses *f. pl.*
outlet /ˈaʊtlet/ *n.* (*for water, gases*) sortie *f.*; (*for goods*) débouché *m.*; (*for feelings*) exutoire *m.*
outline /ˈaʊtlaɪn/ *n.* contour *m.*; (*summary*) esquisse *f.* **(main) ~s,** grandes lignes *f. pl.* ● *v.t.* tracer le contour de; (*summarize*) exposer sommairement.
outlive /aʊtˈlɪv/ *v.t.* survivre à.
outlook /ˈaʊtlʊk/ *n.* perspective *f.*
outlying /ˈaʊtlaɪɪŋ/ *a.* écarté.
outmoded /aʊtˈməʊdɪd/ *a.* démodé.
outnumber /aʊtˈnʌmbə(r)/ *v.t.* surpasser en nombre.
outpost /ˈaʊtpəʊst/ *n.* avant-poste *m.*
output /ˈaʊtpʊt/ *n.* rendement *m.*; (*comput.*) sortie *f.* ● *v.t./i.* (*comput.*) sortir.
outrage /ˈaʊtreɪdʒ/ *n.* atrocité *f.*; (*scandal*) scandale *m.* ● *v.t.* (*morals*) outrager; (*person*) scandaliser.
outrageous /aʊtˈreɪdʒəs/ *a.* scandaleux, atroce.
outright /aʊtˈraɪt/ *adv.* complètement; (*at once*) sur le coup; (*frankly*) carrément. ● *a.* /ˈaʊtraɪt/ complet; (*refusal*) net.
outset /ˈaʊtset/ *n.* début *m.*
outside[1] /aʊtˈsaɪd/ *n.* extérieur *m.* ● *adv.* (au) dehors. ● *prep.* en dehors de; (*in front of*) devant.
outside[2] /ˈaʊtsaɪd/ *a.* extérieur.

outsider /aʊt'saɪdə(r)/ *n.* étrang|er, -ère *m., f.*; (*sport*) outsider *m.*
outsize /'aʊtsaɪz/ *a.* grande taille *invar.*
outskirts /'aʊtskɜ:ts/ *n. pl.* banlieue *f.*
outspoken /aʊt'spəʊkən/ *a.* franc.
outstanding /aʊt'stændɪŋ/ *a.* exceptionnel; (*not settled*) en suspens.
outstretched /əʊt'stretʃt/ *a.* (*arm*) tendu.
outstrip /aʊt'strɪp/ *v.t.* (*p.t.* **-stripped**) devancer, surpasser.
outward /'aʊtwəd/ *a.* & *adv.* vers l'extérieur; (*sign etc.*) extérieur; (*journey*) d'aller. **~ly** *adv.* extérieurement. **~s** *adv.* vers l'extérieur.
outweigh /aʊt'weɪ/ *v.t.* (*exceed in importance*) l'emporter sur.
outwit /aʊt'wɪt/ *v.t.* (*p.t.* **-witted**) duper, être plus malin que.
oval /'əʊvl/ *n.* & *a.* ovale (*m.*).
ovary /'əʊvərɪ/ *n.* ovaire *m.*
ovation /ə'veɪʃn/ *n.* ovation *f.*
oven /'ʌvn/ *n.* four *m.*
over /'əʊvə(r)/ *prep.* sur, au-dessus de; (*across*) de l'autre côté de; (*during*) pendant; (*more than*) plus de. ● *adv.* (par-)dessus; (*ended*) fini; (*past*) passé; (*too*) trop; (*more*) plus. **jump/***etc.* **~,** sauter/*etc.* par-dessus. **~ the radio,** à la radio. **ask ~,** inviter chez soi. **he has some ~,** il lui en reste. **all ~ (the table),** partout (sur la table). **~ and above,** en plus de. **~ and over,** à maintes reprises. **~ here,** par ici. **~ there,** là-bas.
over- /'əʊvə(r)/ *pref.* sur-, trop.
overall [1] /'əʊvərɔ:l/ *n.* blouse *f.* **~s,** bleu(s) de travail *m.* (*pl.*).
overall [2] /əʊvər'ɔ:l/ *a.* global, d'ensemble; (*length, width*) total. ● *adv.* globalement.
overawe /əʊvər'ɔ:/ *v.t.* intimider.
overbalance /əʊvə'bæləns/ *v.t./i.* (faire) basculer.
overbearing /əʊvə'beərɪŋ/ *a.* autoritaire.
overboard /'əʊvəbɔ:d/ *adv.* par-dessus bord.
overbook /əʊvə'bʊk/ *v.t.* accepter trop de réservations pour.
overcast /'əʊvəkɑ:st/ *a.* couvert.
overcharge /əʊvə'tʃɑ:dʒ/ *v.t.* **~ s.o. (for),** faire payer trop cher à qn.
overcoat /'əʊvəkəʊt/ *n.* pardessus *m.*
overcome /əʊvə'kʌm/ *v.t.* (*p.t.* **-came,** *p.p.* **-come**) triompher de; (*difficulty*) surmonter, triompher de. **~ by,** accablé de.
overcrowded /əʊvə'kraʊdɪd/ *a.* bondé; (*country*) surpeuplé.
overdo /əʊvə'du:/ *v.t.* (*p.t.* **-did,** *p.p.* **-done**) exagérer; (*culin.*) trop cuire. **~ it,** (*overwork*) se surmener.
overdose /'əʊvədəʊs/ *n.* overdose *f.*, surdose *f.*
overdraft /'əʊvədrɑ:ft/ *n.* découvert *m.*
overdraw /əʊvə'drɔ:/ *v.t.* (*p.t.* **-drew,** *p.p.* **-drawn**) (*one's account*) mettre à découvert.
overdrive /'əʊvədraɪv/ *n.* surmultipliée *f.*
overdue /əʊvə'dju:/ *a.* en retard; (*belated*) tardif; (*bill*) impayé.
overestimate /əʊvər'estɪmeɪt/ *v.t.* surestimer.
overexposed /əʊvərɪk'spəʊzd/ *a.* surexposé.
overflow [1] /əʊvə'fləʊ/ *v.i.* déborder.
overflow [2] /'əʊvəfləʊ/ *n.* (*outlet*) trop-plein *m.*
overgrown /əʊvə'grəʊn/ *a.* (*garden etc.*) envahi par la végétation.
overhang /əʊvə'hæŋ/ *v.t.* (*p.t.* **-hung**) surplomber. ● *v.i.* faire saillie.
overhaul [1] /əʊvə'hɔ:l/ *v.t.* réviser.
overhaul [2] /'əʊvəhɔ:l/ *n.* révision *f.*
overhead [1] /əʊvə'hed/ *adv.* au-dessus; (*in sky*) dans le ciel.
overhead [2] /'əʊvəhed/ *a.* aérien. **~s** *n. pl.* frais généraux *m. pl.* **~ projector,** rétroprojecteur *m.*
overhear /əʊvə'hɪə(r)/ *v.t.* (*p.t.* **-heard**) surprendre, entendre.
overjoyed /əʊvə'dʒɔɪd/ *a.* ravi.
overland *a.* /'əʊvəlænd/, *adv.* /ɔʊvə'lænd/ par voie de terre.
overlap /əʊvə'læp/ *v.t./i.* (*p.t.* **-lapped**) (se) chevaucher.
overleaf /əʊvə'li:f/ *adv.* au verso.
overload /əʊvə'ləʊd/ *v.t.* surcharger.
overlook /əʊvə'lʊk/ *v.t.* oublier, négliger; (*of window, house*) donner sur; (*of tower*) dominer.
overly /'əʊvəlɪ/ *adv.* excessivement.
overnight /əʊvə'naɪt/ *adv.* (pendant) la nuit; (*instantly: fig.*) du jour au lendemain. ● *a.* /'əʊvənaɪt/ (*train etc.*) de nuit; (*stay etc.*) d'une nuit; (*fig.*) soudain.
overpay /əʊvə'peɪ/ *v.t.* (*p.t.* **-paid**) (*person*) surpayer.
overpower /əʊvə'paʊə(r)/ *v.t.* subjuguer; (*opponent*) maîtriser; (*fig.*)

accabler. **~ing** *a.* irrésistible; (*heat, smell*) accablant.
overpriced /əʊvə'praɪst/ *a.* trop cher.
overrate /əʊvə'reɪt/ *v.t.* surestimer. **~d** /-ɪd/ *a.* surfait.
overreach /əʊvə'ri:tʃ/ *v. pr.* **~ o.s.,** trop entreprendre.
overreact /əʊvərɪ'ækt/ *v.i.* réagir excessivement.
overrid|e /əʊvə'raɪd/ *v.t.* (*p.t.* **-rode,** *p.p.* **-ridden**) passer outre à. **~ing** *a.* prépondérant; (*importance*) majeur.
overripe /'əʊvəraɪp/ *a.* trop mûr.
overrule /əʊvə'ru:l/ *v.t.* rejeter.
overrun /əʊvə'rʌn/ *v.t.* (*p.t.* **-ran,** *p.p.* **-run,** *pres. p.* **-running**) envahir; (*a limit*) aller au-delà de. ● *v.i.* (*meeting*) durer plus longtemps que prévu.
overseas /əʊvə'si:z/ *a.* d'outre-mer, étranger. ● *adv.* outre-mer, à l'étranger.
oversee /əʊvə'si:/ *v.t.* (*p.t.* **-saw,** *p.p.* **-seen**) surveiller. **~r** /'əʊvəsɪə(r)/ *n.* contremaître *m.*
overshadow /əʊvə'ʃædəʊ/ *v.t.* (*darken*) assombrir; (*fig.*) éclipser.
overshoot /əʊvə'ʃu:t/ *v.t.* (*p.t.* **-shot**) dépasser.
oversight /'əʊvəsaɪt/ *n.* omission *f.*
oversleep /əʊvə'sli:p/ *v.i.* (*p.t.* **-slept**) se réveiller trop tard.
overt /'əʊvɜ:t/ *a.* manifeste.
overtake /əʊvə'teɪk/ *v.t./i.* (*p.t.* **-took,** *p.p.* **-taken**) dépasser; (*vehicle*) doubler, dépasser; (*surprise*) surprendre.
overtax /əʊvə'tæks/ *v.t.* (*strain*) fatiguer; (*taxpayer*) surimposer.
overthrow /əʊvə'θrəʊ/ *v.t.* (*p.t.* **-threw,** *p.p.* **-thrown**) renverser.
overtime /'əʊvətaɪm/ *n.* heures supplémentaires *f. pl.*
overtone /'əʊvətəʊn/ *n.* nuance *f.*
overture /'əʊvətjʊə(r)/ *n.* ouverture *f.*
overturn /əʊvə'tɜ:n/ *v.t./i.* (se) renverser.
overweight /əʊvə'weɪt/ *a.* **be ~,** peser trop.
overwhelm /əʊvə'welm/ *v.t.* accabler; (*defeat*) écraser; (*amaze*) bouleverser. **~ing** *a.* accablant; (*victory*) écrasant; (*urge*) irrésistible.
overwork /əʊvə'wɜ:k/ *v.t./i.* (se) surmener. ● *n.* surmenage *m.*
overwrought /əʊvə'rɔ:t/ *a.* à bout.
ow|e /əʊ/ *v.t.* devoir. **~ing** *a.* dû. **~ing to,** à cause de.
owl /aʊl/ *n.* hibou *m.*
own[1] /əʊn/ *a.* propre. **a house/***etc.* **of one's ~,** sa propre maison/*etc.*, une maison/*etc.* à soi. **get one's ~ back,** (*fam.*) prendre sa revanche. **hold one's ~,** bien se défendre. **on one's ~,** tout seul.
own[2] /əʊn/ *v.t.* posséder. **~ up (to),** (*fam.*) avouer. **~er** *n.* propriétaire *m./f.* **~ership** *n.* possession *f.* (**of,** de); (*right*) propriété *f.*
ox /ɒks/ *n.* (*pl.* **oxen**) bœuf *m.*
oxygen /'ɒksɪdʒən/ *n.* oxygène *m.*
oyster /'ɔɪstə(r)/ *n.* huître *f.*
ozone /'əʊzəʊn/ *n.* ozone *m.* **~ layer,** couche d'ozone *f.*

P

pace /peɪs/ *n.* pas *m.*; (*speed*) allure *f.*; ● *v.t.* (*room etc.*) arpenter. ● *v.i.* **~ (up and down),** faire les cent pas. **keep ~ with,** suivre.
pacemaker /'peɪsmeɪkə(r)/ *n.* (*med.*) stimulateur cardiaque *m.*
Pacific /pə'sɪfɪk/ *a.* pacifique. ● *n.* **~ (Ocean),** Pacifique *m.*
pacifist /'pæsɪfɪst/ *n.* pacifiste *m./f.*
pacif|y /'pæsɪfaɪ/ *v.t.* (*country*) pacifier; (*person*) apaiser. **~ier** *n.* (*Amer.*) sucette *f.*
pack /pæk/ *n.* paquet *m.*; (*mil.*) sac *m.*; (*of hounds*) meute *f.*; (*of thieves*) bande *f.*; (*of lies*) tissu *m.* ● *v.t.* emballer; (*suitcase*) faire; (*box, room*) remplir; (*press down*) tasser. ● *v.i.* **~ (one's bags),** faire ses valises. **~ into,** (*cram*) (s')entasser dans. **~ off,** expédier. **send ~ing,** envoyer promener. **~ed** *a.* (*crowded*) bondé. **~ed lunch,** repas froid *m.* **~ing** *n.* (*action, material*) emballage *m.* **~ing case,** caisse *f.*
package /'pækɪdʒ/ *n.* paquet *m.* ● *v.t.* empaqueter. **~ deal,** forfait *m.* **~ tour,** voyage organisé *m.*
packet /'pækɪt/ *n.* paquet *m.*
pact /pækt/ *n.* pacte *m.*
pad[1] /pæd/ *n.* bloc(-notes) *m.*; (*for ink*) tampon *m.* **(launching) ~,** rampe (de lancement) *f.* ● *v.t.* (*p.t.* **padded**) rembourrer; (*text: fig.*) délayer. **~ding** *n.* rembourrage *m.*; délayage *m.*
pad[2] /pæd/ *v.i.* (*p.t.* **padded**) (*walk*) marcher à pas feutrés.

paddle[1] /'pædl/ *n.* pagaie *f.* ● *v.t.* **~ a canoe,** pagayer. **~-steamer** *n.* bateau à roues *m.*

paddl|e[2] /'pædl/ *v.i.* barboter, se mouiller les pieds. **~ing pool,** pataugeoire *f.*

paddock /'pædək/ *n.* paddock *m.*

paddy(-field) /'pædɪ(fi:ld)/ *n.* rizière *f.*

padlock /'pædlɒk/ *n.* cadenas *m.* ● *v.t.* cadenasser.

paediatrician /pi:dɪə'trɪʃn/ *n.* pédiatre *m./f.*

pagan /'peɪgən/ *a.* & *n.* païen(ne) (*m.* (*f.*)).

page[1] /peɪdʒ/ *n.* (*of book etc.*) page *f.*

page[2] /peɪdʒ/ *n.* (*in hotel*) chasseur *m.* (*at wedding*) page *m.* ● *v.t.* (faire) appeler.

pageant /'pædʒənt/ *n.* spectacle (historique) *m.* **~ry** *n.* pompe *f.*

pagoda /pə'gəʊdə/ *n.* pagode *f.*

paid /peɪd/ *see* pay. ● *a.* **put ~ to,** (*fam.*) mettre fin à.

pail /peɪl/ *n.* seau *m.*

pain /peɪn/ *n.* douleur *f.* **~s,** efforts *m. pl.* ● *v.t.* (*grieve*) peiner. **be in ~,** souffrir. **take ~s to,** se donner du mal pour. **~-killer** *n.* analgésique *m.* **~less** *a.* indolore.

painful /'peɪnfl/ *a.* douloureux; (*laborious*) pénible.

painstaking /'peɪnzteɪkɪŋ/ *a.* assidu, appliqué.

paint /peɪnt/ *n.* peinture *f.* **~s,** (*in tube, box*) couleurs *f. pl.* ● *v.t./i.* peindre. **~er** *n.* peintre *m.* **~ing** *n.* peinture *f.*

paintbrush /'peɪntbrʌʃ/ *n.* pinceau *m.*

paintwork /'peɪntwɜ:k/ *n.* peintures *f. pl.*

pair /peə(r)/ *n.* paire *f.*; (*of people*) couple *m.* **a ~ of trousers,** un pantalon. ● *v.i.* **~ off,** (*at dance etc.*) former un couple.

pajamas /pə'dʒɑ:məz/ *n.pl.* (*Amer.*) pyjama *m.*

Pakistan /pɑ:kɪ'stɑ:n/ *n.* Pakistan. *m.* **~i** *a.* & *n.* pakistanais(e) (*m.* (*f.*)).

pal /pæl/ *n.* (*fam.*) cop|ain, -ine *m., f.*

palace /'pælɪs/ *n.* palais *m.*

palat|e /'pælət/ *n.* (*of mouth*) palais *m.* **~able** *a.* agréable au goût.

palatial /pə'leɪʃl/ *a.* somptueux.

palaver /pə'lɑ:və(r)/ *n.* (*fuss: fam.*) histoire(s) *f.* (*pl.*).

pale /peɪl/ *a.* **(-er, -est)** pâle. ● *v.i.* pâlir. **~ness** *n.* pâleur *f.*

Palestin|e /'pælɪstaɪn/ *n.* Palestine *f.* **~ian** /-'stɪnɪən/ *a.* & *n.* palestinien(ne) (*m.* (*f.*)).

palette /'pælɪt/ *n.* palette *f.*

pall /pɔ:l/ *v.i.* devenir insipide.

pallet /'pælɪt/ *n.* palette *f.*

pallid /'pælɪd/ *a.* pâle.

palm /pɑ:m/ *n.* (*of hand*) paume *f.*; (*tree*) palmier *m.*; (*symbol*) palme *f.* ● *v.t.* **~ off,** (*thing*) refiler, coller **(on,** à); (*person*) coller. **P~ Sunday,** dimanche des Rameaux *m.*

palmist /'pɑ:mɪst/ *n.* chiromancien(ne) *m.* (*f.*).

palpable /'pælpəbl/ *a.* manifeste.

palpitat|e /'pælpɪteɪt/ *v.i.* palpiter. **~ion** /-'teɪʃn/ *n.* palpitation *f.*

paltry /'pɔ:ltrɪ/ *a.* **(-ier, -iest)** dérisoire, piètre.

pamper /'pæmpə(r)/ *v.t.* dorloter.

pamphlet /'pæmflɪt/ *n.* brochure *f.*

pan /pæn/ *n.* casserole *f.*; (*for frying*) poêle *f.*; (*of lavatory*) cuvette *f.* ● *v.t.* (*p.t.* **panned**) (*fam.*) critiquer.

panacea /pænə'sɪə/ *n.* panacée *f.*

panache /pə'næʃ/ *n.* panache *m.*

pancake /'pænkeɪk/ *n.* crêpe *f.*

pancreas /'pæŋkrɪəs/ *n.* pancréas *m.*

panda /'pændə/ *n.* panda *m.* **~ car,** voiture pie (de la police) *f.*

pandemonium /pændɪ'məʊnɪəm/ *n.* tumulte *m.*, chaos *m.*

pander /'pændə(r)/ *v.i.* **~ to,** (*person, taste*) flatter bassement.

pane /peɪn/ *n.* carreau *m.*, vitre *f.*

panel /'pænl/ *n.* (*of door etc.*) panneau *m.*; (*jury*) jury *m.*; (*speakers: TV*) invités *m. pl.* **(instrument) ~,** tableau de bord *m.* **~ of experts,** groupe d'experts *m.* **~led** *a.* lambrissé. **~ling** *n.* lambrissage *m.* **~list** *n.* (*TV*) invité(e) (de tribune) *m.* (*f.*).

pang /pæŋ/ *n.* pincement au cœur *m.* **~s,** (*of hunger, death*) affres *f. pl.* **~s of conscience,** remords *m. pl.*

panic /'pænɪk/ *n.* panique *f.* ● *v.t./ i.* (*p.t.* **panicked**) (s')affoler, paniquer. **~-stricken** *a.* pris de panique, affolé.

panorama /pænə'rɑ:mə/ *n.* panorama *m.*

pansy /'pænzɪ/ *n.* (*bot.*) pensée *f.*

pant /pænt/ *v.i.* haleter.

panther /'pænθə(r)/ *n.* panthère *f.*

panties /'pæntɪz/ *n. pl.* (*fam.*) slip *m.*, culotte *f.* (*de femme*).

pantihose /'pæntɪhəʊz/ *n.* (*Amer.*) collant *m.*

pantomime /'pæntəmaɪm/ *n.* (*show*) spectacle de Noël *m.*; (*mime*) pantomime *f.*

pantry /'pæntrɪ/ *n.* office *m.*

pants /pænts/ *n. pl.* (*underwear: fam.*) slip *m.*; (*trousers: fam. & Amer.*) pantalon *m.*

papacy /'peɪpəsɪ/ *n.* papauté *f.*

papal /'peɪpl/ *a.* papal.

paper /'peɪpə(r)/ *n.* papier *m.*; (*newspaper*) journal *m.*; (*exam*) épreuve *f.*; (*essay*) exposé *m.*; (*wallpaper*) papier peint *m.* (*identity*) **~s** papiers (d'identité) *m. pl.* ● *v.t.* (*room*) tapisser. **on ~,** par écrit. **~-clip** *n.* trombone *m.*

paperback /'peɪpəbæk/ *a. & n.* **~ (book),** livre broché *m.*

paperweight /'peɪpəweɪt/ *n.* presse-papiers *m. invar.*

paperwork /'peɪpəwɜ:k/ *n.* paperasserie *f.*

paprika /'pæprɪkə/ *n.* paprika *m.*

par /pɑ:(r)/ *n.* **be below ~,** ne pas être en forme. **on a ~ with,** à égalité avec.

parable /'pærəbl/ *n.* parabole *f.*

parachut|e /'pærəʃu:t/ *n.* parachute *m.* ● *v.i.* descendre en parachute. **~ist** *n.* parachutiste *m./f.*

parade /pə'reɪd/ *n.* (*procession*) défilé *m.*; (*ceremony, display*) parade *f.*; (*street*) avenue *f.* ● *v.i.* défiler. ● *v.t.* faire parade de.

paradise /'pærədaɪs/ *n.* paradis *m.*

paradox /'pærədɒks/ *n.* paradoxe *m.* **~ical** /-'dɒksɪkl/ *a.* paradoxal.

paraffin /'pærəfɪn/ *n.* pétrole (lampant) *m.*; (*wax*) paraffine *f.*

paragon /'pærəgən/ *n.* modèle *m.*

paragraph /'pærəgrɑ:f/ *n.* paragraphe *m.*

parallel /'pærəlel/ *a.* parallèle. ● *n.* (*line*) parallèle *f.*; (*comparison & geog.*) parallèle *m.* ● *v.t.* (*p.t.* **paralleled**) être semblable à; (*match*) égaler.

paralyse /'pærəlaɪz/ *v.t.* paralyser.

paraly|sis /pə'ræləsɪs/ *n.* paralysie *f.* **~tic** /pærə'lɪtɪk/ *a. & n.* paralytique (*m./f.*).

paramedic /pærə'medɪk/ *n.* auxiliaire médical(e) *m.* (*f.*).

parameter /pə'ræmɪtə(r)/ *n.* paramètre *m.*

paramount /'pærəmaʊnt/ *a.* primordial, fondamental.

paranoi|a /pærə'nɔɪə/ *n.* paranoïa *f.* **~d** *a.* paranoïaque; (*fam.*) parano *invar.*

parapet /'pærəpɪt/ *n.* parapet *m.*

paraphernalia /pærəfə'neɪlɪə/ *n.* attirail *m.*, équipement *m.*

paraphrase /'pærəfreɪz/ *n.* paraphrase *f.* ● *v.t.* paraphraser.

parasite /'pærəsaɪt/ *n.* parasite *m.*

parasol /'pærəsɒl/ *n.* ombrelle *f.*; (*on table, at beach*) parasol *m.*

paratrooper /'pærətru:pə(r)/ *n.* (*mil.*) parachutiste *m/f.*

parcel /'pɑ:sl/ *n.* colis *m.*, paquet *m.* ● *v.t.* (*p.t.* **parcelled**). **~ out,** diviser en parcelles.

parch /pɑ:tʃ/ *v.t.* dessécher. **be ~ed,** (*person*) avoir très soif.

parchment /'pɑ:tʃmənt/ *n.* parchemin *m.*

pardon /'pɑ:dn/ *n.* pardon *m.*; (*jurid.*) grâce *m.* ● *v.t.* (*p.t.* **pardoned**) pardonner (**s.o. for sth.,** qch. à qn.); gracier. **I beg your ~,** pardon.

pare /peə(r)/ *v.t.* (*clip*) rogner; (*peel*) éplucher.

parent /'peərənt/ *n.* père *m.*, mère *f.* **~s,** parents *m. pl.* **~al** /pə'rentl/ *a.* des parents. **~hood** *n.* l'état de parent *m.*

parenthesis /pə'renθəsɪs/ *n.* (*pl.* **-theses** /-si:z/) parenthèse *f.*

Paris /'pærɪs/ *n.* Paris *m./f.* **~ian** /pə'rɪzɪən, *Amer.* pə'ri:ʒn/ *a. & n.* parisien(ne) (*m.* (*f.*)).

parish /'pærɪʃ/ *n.* (*relig.*) paroisse *f.*; (*municipal*) commune *f.* **~ioner** /pə'rɪʃənə(r)/ *n.* paroissien(ne) *m.* (*f.*).

parity /'pærətɪ/ *n.* parité *f.*

park /pɑ:k/ *n.* parc *m.* ● *v.t./i.* (se) garer; (*remain parked*) stationner. **~ing-lot** *n.* (*Amer.*) parking *m.* **~ing-meter** *n.* parcmètre *m.* **~ing ticket,** procès-verbal *m.*

parka /'pɑ:kə/ *n.* parka *m./f.*

parlance /'pɑ:ləns/ *n.* langage *m.*

parliament /'pɑ:ləmənt/ *n.* parlement *m.* **~ary** /-'mentrɪ/ *a.* parlementaire.

parlour, (*Amer.*) **parlor** /'pɑ:lə(r)/ *n.* salon *m.*

parochial /pə'rəʊkɪəl/ *a.* (*relig.*) paroissial; (*fig.*) borné, provincial.

parody /'pærədɪ/ *n.* parodie *f.* ● *v.t.* parodier.

parole /pə'rəʊl/ *n.* **on ~,** en liberté conditionnelle.

parquet /'pɑ:keɪ/ *n.* parquet *m.*

parrot /'pærət/ *n.* perroquet *m.*

parry /'pærɪ/ *v.t.* (*sport*) parer; (*question etc.*) esquiver. ● *n.* parade *f.*

parsimonious /pɑ:sɪ'məʊnɪəs/ *a.* parcimonieux.

parsley /'pɑ:slɪ/ *n.* persil *m.*

parsnip /'pɑ:snɪp/ *n.* panais *m.*

parson /'pɑ:sn/ *n.* pasteur *m.*

part /pɑ:t/ *n.* partie *f.*; (*of serial*) épisode *m.*; (*of machine*) pièce *f.*; (*theatre*) rôle *m.*; (*side in dispute*) parti *m.* ● *a.* partiel. ● *adv.* en partie. ● *v.t./i.* (*separate*) (se) séparer. **in ~,** en partie. **on the ~ of,** de la part de. **~-exchange** *n.* reprise *f.* **~ of speech,** catégorie grammaticale *f.* **~-time** *a.* & *adv.* à temps partiel. **~ with,** se séparer de. **take ~ in,** participer à. **in these ~s,** dans la région, dans le coin.

partake /pɑ:'teɪk/ *v.i.* (*p.t.* **-took,** *p.p.* **-taken**) participer (**in,** à).

partial /'pɑ:ʃl/ *a.* partiel; (*biased*) partial. **be ~ to,** avoir une prédilection pour. **~ity** /-ɪ'ælətɪ/ *n.* (*bias*) partialité *f.*; (*fondness*) prédilection *f.* **~ly** *adv.* partiellement.

particip|ate /pɑ:'tɪsɪpeɪt/ *v.i.* participer (**in,** à). **~ant** *n.* participant(e) *m.* (*f.*). **~ation** /-'peɪʃn/ *n.* participation *f.*

participle /'pɑ:tɪsɪpl/ *n.* participe *m.*

particle /'pɑ:tɪkl/ *n.* particule *f.*

particular /pə'tɪkjʊlə(r)/ *a.* particulier; (*fussy*) difficile; (*careful*) méticuleux. **that ~ man,** cet homme-là en particulier. **~s** *n. pl.* détails *m. pl.* **in ~,** en particulier. **~ly** *adv.* particulièrement.

parting /'pɑ:tɪŋ/ *n.* séparation *f.*; (*in hair*) raie *f.* ● *a.* d'adieu.

partisan /pɑ:tɪ'zæn, *Amer.* 'pɑ:tɪzn/ *n.* partisan(e) *m.* (*f.*).

partition /pɑ:'tɪʃn/ *n.* (*of room*) cloison *f.*; (*pol.*) partage *m.*, partition *f.* ● *v.t.* (*room*) cloisonner; (*country*) partager.

partly /'pɑ:tlɪ/ *adv.* en partie.

partner /'pɑ:tnə(r)/ *n.* associé(e) *m.* (*f.*); (*sport*) partenaire *m./f.* **~ship** *n.* association *f.*

partridge /'pɑ:trɪdʒ/ *n.* perdrix *f.*

party /'pɑ:tɪ/ *n.* fête *f.*; (*formal*) réception *f.*; (*for young people*) boum *f.*; (*group*) groupe *m.*, équipe *f.*; (*pol.*) parti *m.*; (*jurid.*) partie *f.* **~ line,** (*telephone*) ligne commune *f.*

pass /pɑ:s/ *v.t./i.* (*p.t.* **passed**) passer; (*overtake*) dépasser; (*in exam*) être reçu (à); (*approve*) accepter, autoriser; (*remark*) faire; (*judgement*) prononcer; (*law, bill*) voter. **~ (by),** (*building*) passer devant; (*person*) croiser. ● *n.* (*permit*) laissez-passer *m. invar.*; (*ticket*) carte (d'abonnement) *f.*; (*geog.*) col *m.*; (*sport*) passe *f.* **~ (mark),** (*in exam*) moyenne *f.* **make a ~ at,** (*fam.*) faire des avances à. **~ away,** mourir. **~ out** *or* **round,** distribuer. **~ out,** (*faint*: *fam.*) s'évanouir. **~ over,** (*overlook*) passer sur. **~ up,** (*forego*: *fam.*) laisser passer.

passable /'pɑ:səbl/ *a.* (*adequate*) passable; (*road*) praticable.

passage /'pæsɪdʒ/ *n.* (*way through, text, etc.*) passage *m.*; (*voyage*) traversée *f.*; (*corridor*) couloir *m.*

passenger /'pæsɪndʒə(r)/ *n.* passag|er, -ère *m., f.*; (*in train*) voyageu|r, -se *m., f.*

passer-by /pɑ:sə'baɪ/ *n.* (*pl.* **passers-by**) passant(e) *m.* (*f.*).

passing /'pɑ:sɪŋ/ *a.* (*fleeting*) fugitif, passager.

passion /'pæʃn/ *n.* passion *f.* **~ate** *a.* passionné. **~ately** *adv.* passionnément.

passive /'pæsɪv/ *a.* passif. **~ness** *n.* passivité *f.*

Passover /'pɑ:səʊvə(r)/ *n.* Pâque *f.*

passport /'pɑ:spɔ:t/ *n.* passeport *m.*

password /'pɑ:swɜ:d/ *n.* mot de passe *m.*

past /pɑ:st/ *a.* passé; (*former*) ancien. ● *n.* passé *m.* ● *prep.* au-delà de; (*in front of*) devant. ● *adv.* devant. **the ~ months,** ces derniers mois. **~ midnight,** minuit passé. **10 ~ 6,** six heures dix.

pasta /'pæstə/ *n.* pâtes *f. pl.*

paste /peɪst/ *n.* (*glue*) colle *f.*; (*dough*) pâte *f.*; (*of fish, meat*) pâté *m.*; (*jewellery*) strass *m.* ● *v.t.* coller.

pastel /'pæstl/ *n.* pastel *m.* ● *a.* pastel *invar.*

pasteurize /'pæstʃəraɪz/ *v.t.* pasteuriser.

pastiche /pæ'sti:ʃ/ *n.* pastiche *m.*

pastille /'pæstɪl/ *n.* pastille *f.*

pastime /'pɑ:staɪm/ *n.* passetemps *m. invar.*

pastoral /'pɑ:stərəl/ *a.* pastoral.

pastry /'peɪstrɪ/ *n.* (*dough*) pâte *f.*; (*tart*) pâtisserie *f.*

pasture /'pɑ:stʃə(r)/ *n.* pâturage *m.*

pasty[1] /'pæstɪ/ *n.* petit pâté *m.*

pasty[2] /'peɪstɪ/ *a.* pâteux.

pat /pæt/ *v.t.* (*p.t.* **patted**) tapoter. ● *n.* petite tape *f.* ● *adv.* & *a.* à propos; (*ready*) tout prêt.

patch /pætʃ/ *n.* pièce *f.*; (*over eye*) bandeau *m.*; (*spot*) tache *f.*; (*of vegetables*) carré *m.* ● *v.t.* ~ **up**, rapiécer; (*fig.*) régler. **bad ~**, période difficile *f.* **not be a ~ on**, ne pas arriver à la cheville de. **~y** *a.* inégal.

patchwork /'pætʃwɜ:k/ *n.* patchwork *m.*

pâté /'pæteɪ/ *n.* pâté *m.*

patent /'peɪtnt/ *a.* patent. ● *n.* brevet (d'invention) *m.* ● *v.t.* breveter. **~ leather**, cuir verni *m.* **~ly** *adv.* manifestement.

paternal /pə'tɜ:nl/ *a.* paternel.

paternity /pə'tɜ:nətɪ/ *n.* paternité *f.*

path /pɑ:θ/ *n.* (*pl.* **-s** /pɑ:ðz/) sentier *m.*, chemin *m.*; (*in park*) allée *f.*; (*of rocket*) trajectoire *f.*

pathetic /pə'θetɪk/ *a.* pitoyable; (*bad*: *fam.*) minable.

pathology /pə'θɒlədʒɪ/ *n.* pathologie *f.*

pathos /'peɪθɒs/ *n.* pathétique *m.*

patience /'peɪʃns/ *n.* patience *f.*

patient /'peɪʃnt/ *a.* patient. ● *n.* malade *m./f.*, patient(e) *m.* (*f.*). **~ly** *adv.* patiemment.

patio /'pætɪəʊ/ *n.* (*pl.* **-os**) patio *m.*

patriot /'pætrɪət, 'peɪtrɪət/ *n.* patriote *m./f.* **~ic** /-'ɒtɪk/ *a.* patriotique; (*person*) patriote. **~ism** *n.* patriotisme *m.*

patrol /pə'trəʊl/ *n.* patrouille *f.* ● *v.t./i.* patrouiller (dans). **~ car**, voiture de police *f.*

patrolman /pə'trəʊlmən/ *n.* (*pl.* **-men** /-men/) (*Amer.*) agent de police *m.*

patron /'peɪtrən/ *n.* (*of the arts*) mécène *m.* (*customer*) client(e) *m.* (*f.*). **~ saint**, saint(e) patron(ne) *m.* (*f.*).

patron|age /'pætrənɪdʒ/ *n.* clientèle *f.*; (*support*) patronage *m.* **~ize** *v.t.* être client de; (*fig.*) traiter avec condescendance.

patter[1] /'pætə(r)/ *n.* (*of steps*) bruit *m.*; (*of rain*) crépitement *m.*

patter[2] /'pætə(r)/ *n.* (*speech*) baratin *m.*

pattern /'pætn/ *n.* motif *m.*, dessin *m.*; (*for sewing*) patron *m.*; (*procedure, type*) schéma *m.*; (*example*) exemple *m.*

paunch /pɔ:ntʃ/ *n.* panse *f.*

pauper /'pɔ:pə(r)/ *n.* indigent(e) *m.* (*f.*), pauvre *m.*, pauvresse *f.*

pause /pɔ:z/ *n.* pause *f.* ● *v.i.* faire une pause; (*hesitate*) hésiter.

pav|e /peɪv/ *v.t.* paver. **~e the way**, ouvrir la voie (**for**, à). **~ing-stone** *n.* pavé *m.*

pavement /'peɪvmənt/ *n.* trottoir *m.*; (*Amer.*) chaussée *f.*

pavilion /pə'vɪljən/ *n.* pavillon *m.*

paw /pɔ:/ *n.* patte *f.* ● *v.t.* (*of animal*) donner des coups de patte à; (*touch*: *fam.*) tripoter.

pawn[1] /pɔ:n/ *n.* (*chess* & *fig.*) pion *m.*

pawn[2] /pɔ:n/ *v.t.* mettre en gage. ● *n.* **in ~**, en gage. **~-shop** *n.* mont-de-piété *m.*

pawnbroker /'pɔ:nbrəʊkə(r)/ *n.* prêteur sur gages *m.*

pay /peɪ/ *v.t./i.* (*p.t.* **paid**) payer; (*yield*: *comm.*) rapporter; (*compliment, visit*) faire. ● *n.* salaire *m.*, paie *f.* **in the ~ of**, à la solde de. **~ attention**, faire attention (**to**, à). **~ back**, rembourser. **~ for**, payer. **~ homage**, rendre hommage (**to**, à). **~ in**, verser (**to**, à). **~ off**, (finir de) payer; (*succeed*: *fam.*) être payant. **~ out**, payer, verser.

payable /'peɪəbl/ *a.* payable.

payment /'peɪmənt/ *n.* paiement *m.*; (*regular*) versement *m.* (*reward*) récompense *f.*

payroll /'peɪrəʊl/ *n.* registre du personnel *m.* **be on the ~ of**, être membre du personnel de.

pea /pi:/ *n.* (petit) pois *m.* **~-shooter** *n.* sarbacane *f.*

peace /pi:s/ *n.* paix *f.* **~ of mind**, tranquillité d'esprit *f.* **~able** *a.* pacifique.

peaceful /'pi:sfl/ *a.* paisible; (*intention, measure*) pacifique.

peacemaker /'pi:smeɪkə(r)/ *n.* concilia|teur, -trice *m.*, *f.*

peach /pi:tʃ/ *n.* pêche *f.*

peacock /'pi:kɒk/ *n.* paon *m.*

peak /pi:k/ *n.* sommet *m.*; (*of mountain*) pic *m.*; (*maximum*) maximum *m.* **~ hours**, heures de pointe *f. pl.* **~ed cap**, casquette *f.*

peaky /'pi:kɪ/ *a.* (*pale*) pâlot; (*puny*) chétif; (*ill*) patraque.

peal /pi:l/ *n.* (*of bells*) carillon *m.*; (*of laughter*) éclat *m.*

peanut /'pi:nʌt/ *n.* cacahuète *f.* **~s**, (*money*: *sl.*) une bagatelle.

pear /peə(r)/ *n.* poire *f.*

pearl /pɜ:l/ *n.* perle *f.* **~y** *a.* nacré.

peasant /ˈpeznt/ *n.* paysan(ne) *m.* (*f.*).
peat /piːt/ *n.* tourbe *f.*
pebble /ˈpebl/ *n.* caillou *m.*; (*on beach*) galet *m.*
peck /pek/ *v.t./i.* (*food etc.*) picorer; (*attack*) donner des coups de bec (à). ● *n.* coup de bec *m.* **a ~ on the cheek,** une bise.
peckish /ˈpekɪʃ/ *a.* **be ~,** (*fam.*) avoir faim.
peculiar /pɪˈkjuːlɪə(r)/ *a.* (*odd*) bizarre; (*special*) particulier (**to,** à). **~ity** /-ˈærətɪ/ *n.* bizarrerie *f.*
pedal /ˈpedl/ *n.* pédale *f.* ● *v.i.* pédaler.
pedantic /pɪˈdæntɪk/ *a.* pédant.
peddle /ˈpedl/ *v.t.* colporter; (*drugs*) revendre.
pedestal /ˈpedɪstl/ *n.* piédestal *m.*
pedestrian /pɪˈdestrɪən/ *n.* piéton *m.* ● *a.* (*precinct, street*) piétonnier; (*fig.*) prosaïque. **~ crossing,** passage piétons *m.*
pedigree /ˈpedɪgriː/ *n.* (*of person*) ascendance *f.*; (*of animal*) pedigree *m.* ● *a.* (*cattle etc.*) de race.
pedlar /ˈpedlə(r)/ *n.* camelot *m.*; (*door-to-door*) colporteu|r, -se *m., f.*
pee /piː/ *v.i.* (*fam.*) faire pipi.
peek /piːk/ *v.i.* & *n.* = peep[1].
peel /piːl/ *n.* épluchure(s) *f.* (*pl.*); (*of orange*) écorce *f.* ● *v.t.* (*fruit, vegetables*) éplucher. ● *v.i.* (*of skin*) peler; (*of paint*) s'écailler. **~ings** *n. pl.* épluchures *f. pl.*
peep[1] /piːp/ *v.i.* jeter un coup d'œil (furtif) (**at,** à). ● *n.* coup d'œil (furtif) *m.* **~-hole** *n.* judas *m.* **P~ing Tom,** voyeur *m.*
peep[2] /piːp/ *v.i.* (*chirp*) pépier.
peer[1] /pɪə(r)/ *v.i.* **~ (at),** regarder attentivement, scruter.
peer[2] /pɪə(r)/ *n.* (*equal, noble*) pair *m.* **~age** *n.* pairie *f.*
peeved /piːvd/ *a.* (*sl.*) irrité.
peevish /ˈpiːvɪʃ/ *a.* grincheux.
peg /peg/ *n.* cheville *f.*; (*for clothes*) pince à linge *f.*; (*to hang coats etc.*) patère *f.*; (*for tent*) piquet *m.* ● *v.t.* (*p.t.* **pegged**) (*prices*) stabiliser. **buy off the ~,** acheter en prêt-à-porter.
pejorative /pɪˈdʒɒrətɪv/ *a.* péjoratif.
pelican /ˈpelɪkən/ *n.* pélican *m.* **~ crossing,** passage clouté (avec feux de signalisation) *m.*
pellet /ˈpelɪt/ *n.* (*round mass*) boulette *f.*; (*for gun*) plomb *m.*
pelt[1] /pelt/ *n.* (*skin*) peau *f.*
pelt[2] /pelt/ *v.t.* bombarder (**with,** de). ● *v.i.* pleuvoir à torrents.
pelvis /ˈpelvɪs/ *n.* (*anat.*) bassin *m.*
pen[1] /pen/ *n.* (*for sheep etc.*) enclos *m.*; (*for baby, cattle*) parc *m.*
pen[2] /pen/ *n.* stylo *m.*; (*to be dipped in ink*) plume *f.* ● *v.t.* (*p.t.* **penned**) écrire. **~-friend** *n.* correspondant(e) *m.* (*f.*). **~-name** *n.* pseudonyme *m.*
penal /ˈpiːnl/ *a.* pénal. **~ize** *v.t.* pénaliser; (*fig.*) handicaper.
penalty /ˈpenltɪ/ *n.* peine *f.*; (*fine*) amende *f.*; (*sport*) pénalité *f.*
penance /ˈpenəns/ *n.* pénitence *f.*
pence /pens/ *see* penny.
pencil /ˈpensl/ *n.* crayon *m.* ● *v.t.* (*p.t.* **pencilled**) crayonner. **~ in,** noter provisoirement. **~-sharpener** *n.* taille-crayon(s) *m.*
pendant /ˈpendənt/ *n.* pendentif *m.*
pending /ˈpendɪŋ/ *a.* en suspens. ● *prep.* (*until*) en attendant.
pendulum /ˈpendjʊləm/ *n.* pendule *m.*; (*of clock*) balancier *m.*
penetrat|e /ˈpenɪtreɪt/ *v.t.* (*enter*) pénétrer dans; (*understand, permeate*) pénétrer. ● *v.i.* pénétrer. **~ing** *a.* pénétrant. **~ion** /-ˈtreɪʃn/ *n.* pénétration *f.*
penguin /ˈpeŋgwɪn/ *n.* manchot *m.*, pingouin *m.*
penicillin /penɪˈsɪlɪn/ *n.* pénicilline *f.*
peninsula /pəˈnɪnsjʊlə/ *n.* péninsule *f.*
penis /ˈpiːnɪs/ *n.* pénis *m.*
peniten|t /ˈpenɪtənt/ *a.* & *n.* pénitent(e) (*m.* (*f.*)). **~ce** *n.* pénitence *f.*
penitentiary /penɪˈtenʃərɪ/ *n.* (*Amer.*) prison *f.*, pénitencier *m.*
penknife /ˈpennaɪf/ *n.* (*pl.* **-knives**) canif *m.*
pennant /ˈpenənt/ *n.* flamme *f.*
penniless /ˈpenɪlɪs/ *a.* sans le sou.
penny /ˈpenɪ/ *n.* (*pl.* **pennies** *or* **pence**) penny *m.*; (*fig.*) sou *m.*
pension /ˈpenʃn/ *n.* pension *f.*; (*for retirement*) retraite *f.* ● *v.t.* **~ off,** mettre à la retraite. **~ scheme,** caisse de retraite *f.* **~able** *a.* qui a droit à une retraite. **~er** *n.* (**old-age**) **~er,** retraité(e) *m.* (*f.*), personne âgée *f.*
pensive /ˈpensɪv/ *a.* pensif.
Pentecost /ˈpentɪkɒst/ *n.* Pentecôte *f.* **~al** *a.* pentecôtiste.
penthouse /ˈpenthaʊs/ *n.* appartement de luxe *m.* (*sur le toit d'un immeuble*).
pent-up /pentˈʌp/ *a.* refoulé.

penultimate /pen'ʌltɪmət/ *a.* avant-dernier.

people /'pi:pl/ *n. pl.* gens *m. pl.*, personnes *f. pl.* ● *n.* peuple *m.* ● *v.t.* peupler. **English/etc. ~,** les Anglais/ *etc. m. pl.* **~ say,** on dit.

pep /pep/ *n.* entrain *m.* ● *v.t.* **~ up,** donner de l'entrain à. **~ talk,** discours d'encouragement *m.*

pepper /'pepə(r)/ *n.* poivre *m.*; (*vegetable*) poivron *m.* ● *v.t.* (*culin.*) poivrer. **~y** *a.* poivré.

peppermint /'pepəmɪnt/ *n.* (*plant*) menthe poivrée *f.*; (*sweet*) bonbon à la menthe *m.*

per /pɜ:(r)/ *prep.* par. **~ annum,** par an. **~ cent,** pour cent. **~ kilo/***etc.*, le kilo/*etc.* **ten km. ~ hour,** dix km à l'heure.

perceive /pə'si:v/ *v.t.* percevoir; (*notice*) s'apercevoir de. **~ that,** s'apercevoir que.

percentage /pə'sentɪdʒ/ *n.* pourcentage *m.*

perceptible /pə'septəbl/ *a.* perceptible.

percept|ion /pə'sepʃn/ *n.* perception *f.* **~ive** /-tɪv/ *a.* pénétrant.

perch /pɜ:tʃ/ *n.* (*of bird*) perchoir *m.* ● *v.i.* (se) percher.

percolat|e /'pɜ:kəleɪt/ *v.t.* passer. ● *v.i.* filtrer. **~or** *n.* cafetière *f.*

percussion /pə'kʌʃn/ *n.* percussion *f.*

peremptory /pə'remptərɪ/ *a.* péremptoire.

perennial /pə'renɪəl/ *a.* perpétuel; (*plant*) vivace.

perfect[1] /'pɜ:fɪkt/ *a.* parfait. **~ly** *adv.* parfaitement.

perfect[2] /pə'fekt/ *v.t.* parfaire, mettre au point. **~ion** /-kʃn/ *n.* perfection *f.* **to ~ion,** à la perfection. **~ionist** /-kʃənɪst/ *n.* perfectionniste *m./f.*

perforat|e /'pɜ:fəreɪt/ *v.t.* perforer. **~ion** /-'reɪʃn/ *n.* perforation *f.*; (*line of holes*) pointillé *m.*

perform /pə'fɔ:m/ *v.t.* exécuter, faire; (*a function*) remplir; (*mus., theatre*) interpréter, jouer. ● *v.i.* jouer; (*behave, function*) se comporter. **~ance** *n.* exécution *f.*; interprétation *f.*; (*of car, team*) performance *f.*; (*show*) représentation *f.*; séance *f.*; (*fuss*) histoire *f.* **~er** *n.* artiste *m./f.*

perfume /'pɜ:fju:m/ *n.* parfum *m.*

perfunctory /pə'fʌŋktərɪ/ *a.* négligent, superficiel.

perhaps /pə'hæps/ *adv.* peut-être.

peril /'perəl/ *n.* péril *m.* **~ous** *a.* périlleux.

perimeter /pə'rɪmɪtə(r)/ *n.* périmètre *m.*

period /'pɪərɪəd/ *n.* période *f.*, époque *f.*; (*era*) époque *f.*; (*lesson*) cours *m.*; (*gram.*) point *m.*; (*med.*) règles *f. pl.* ● *a.* d'époque. **~ic** /-'ɒdɪk/ *a.* périodique. **~ically** /-'ɒdɪklɪ/ *adv.* périodiquement.

periodical /pɪərɪ'ɒdɪkl/ *n.* périodique *m.*

peripher|y /pə'rɪfərɪ/ *n.* périphérie *f.* **~al** *a.* périphérique; (*of lesser importance: fig.*) accessoire; *n.* (*comput.*) périphérique *m.*

periscope /'perɪskəʊp/ *n.* périscope *m.*

perish /'perɪʃ/ *v.i.* périr; (*rot*) se détériorer. **~able** *a.* périssable.

perjur|e /'pɜ:dʒə(r)/ *v. pr.* **~e o.s.,** se parjurer. **~y** *n.* parjure *m.*

perk[1] /pɜ:k/ *v.t./i.* **~ up,** (*fam.*) (se) remonter. **~y** *a.* (*fam.*) gai.

perk[2] /pɜ:k/ *n.* (*fam.*) avantage *m.*

perm /pɜ:m/ *n.* permanente *f.* ● *v.t.* **have one's hair ~ed,** se faire faire une permanente.

permanen|t /'pɜ:mənənt/ *a.* permanent. **~ce** *n.* permanence *f.* **~tly** *adv.* à titre permanent.

permeable /'pɜ:mɪəbl/ *a.* perméable.

permeate /'pɜ:mɪeɪt/ *v.t.* imprégner, se répandre dans.

permissible /pə'mɪsəbl/ *a.* permis.

permission /pə'mɪʃn/ *n.* permission *f.*

permissive /pə'mɪsɪv/ *a.* tolérant, laxiste. **~ness** *n.* laxisme *m.*

permit[1] /pə'mɪt/ *v.t.* (*p.t.* **permitted**) permettre (**s.o. to,** à qn. de), autoriser (**s.o. to,** qn. à).

permit[2] /'pɜ:mɪt/ *n.* permis *m.*; (*pass*) laissez-passer *m. invar.*

permutation /pɜ:mjʊ'teɪʃn/ *n.* permutation *f.*

pernicious /pə'nɪʃəs/ *a.* nocif, pernicieux; (*med.*) pernicieux.

peroxide /pə'rɒksaɪd/ *n.* eau oxygénée *f.*

perpendicular /pɜ:pən'dɪkjʊlə(r)/ *a.* & *n.* perpendiculaire (*f.*).

perpetrat|e /'pɜ:pɪtreɪt/ *v.t.* perpétrer. **~or** *n.* auteur *m.*

perpetual /pə'petʃʊəl/ *a.* perpétuel.

perpetuate /pə'petʃʊeɪt/ *v.t.* perpétuer.

perplex /pə'pleks/ *v.t.* rendre perplexe. **~ed** *a.* perplexe. **~ing** *a.* déroutant. **~ity** *n.* perplexité *f.*

persecut|e /'pɜ:sɪkju:t/ *v.t.* persécuter. **~ion** /-'kju:ʃn/ *n.* persécution *f.*

persever|e /pɜ:sɪ'vɪə(r)/ *v.i.* persévérer. **~ance** *n.* persévérance *f.*

Persian /'pɜ:ʃn/ *a.* & *n.* (*lang.*) persan (*m.*). **~ Gulf,** golfe persique *m.*

persist /pə'sɪst/ *v.i.* persister (**in doing,** à faire). **~ence** *n.* persistance *f.* **~ent** *a.* (*cough, snow, etc.*) persistant; (*obstinate*) obstiné; (*continual*) continuel. **~ently** *adv.* avec persistance.

person /'pɜ:sn/ *n.* personne *f.* **in ~,** en personne. **~able** *a.* beau.

personal /'pɜ:sənl/ *a.* personnel; (*hygiene, habits*) intime; (*secretary*) particulier. **~ly** *adv.* personnellement. **~ stereo,** baladeur *m.*

personality /pɜ:sə'nælətɪ/ *n.* personnalité *f.*; (*on TV*) vedette *f.*

personify /pə'sɒnɪfaɪ/ *v.t.* personnifier.

personnel /pɜ:sə'nel/ *n.* personnel *m.*

perspective /pə'spektɪv/ *n.* perspective *f.*

Perspex /'pɜ:speks/ *n.* (P.) plexiglas *m.* (P.).

perspir|e /pə'spaɪə(r)/ *v.i.* transpirer. **~ation** /-ə'reɪʃn/ *n.* transpiration *f.*

persua|de /pə'sweɪd/ *v.t.* persuader (**to,** de). **~sion** /-eɪʒn/ *n.* persuasion *f.*

persuasive /pə'sweɪsɪv/ *a.* (*person, speech, etc.*) persuasif. **~ly** *adv.* d'une manière persuasive.

pert /pɜ:t/ *a.* (*saucy*) impertinent; (*lively*) plein d'entrain. **~ly** *adv.* avec impertinence.

pertain /pə'teɪn/ *v.i.* **~ to,** se rapporter à.

pertinent /'pɜ:tɪnənt/ *a.* pertinent. **~ly** *adv.* pertinemment.

perturb /pə'tɜ:b/ *v.t.* troubler.

Peru /pə'ru:/ *n.* Pérou *m.* **~vian** *a.* & *n.* péruvien(ne) (*m.* (*f.*)).

perus|e /pə'ru:z/ *v.t.* lire (attentivement). **~al** *n.* lecture *f.*

perva|de /pə'veɪd/ *v.t.* imprégner, envahir. **~sive** *a.* (*mood, dust*) envahissant.

pervers|e /pə'vɜ:s/ *a.* (*stubborn*) entêté; (*wicked*) pervers. **~ity** *n.* perversité *f.*

perver|t[1] /pə'vɜ:t/ *v.t.* pervertir. **~sion** *n.* perversion *f.*

perver|t[2] /'pɜ:vɜ:t/ *n.* perverti(e) *m.* (*f.*), dépravé(e) *m.* (*f.*).

peseta /pə'seɪtə/ *n.* peseta *f.*

pessimis|t /'pesɪmɪst/ *n.* pessimiste *m./f.* **~m** /-zəm/ *n.* pessimisme *m.* **~tic** /-'mɪstɪk/ *a.* pessimiste. **~tically** /-'mɪstɪklɪ/ *adv.* avec pessimisme.

pest /pest/ *n.* insecte *or* animal nuisible *m.*; (*person: fam.*) enquiquineu|r, -se *m., f.*

pester /'pestə(r)/ *v.t.* harceler.

pesticide /'pestɪsaɪd/ *n.* pesticide *m.*, insecticide *m.*

pet /pet/ *n.* animal (domestique) *m.*; (*favourite*) chouchou(te) *m.* (*f.*). ● *a.* (*tame*) apprivoisé. ● *v.t.* (*p.t.* **petted**) caresser; (*sexually*) peloter. **~ hate,** bête noire *f.* **~ name,** diminutif *m.*

petal /'petl/ *n.* pétale *m.*

peter /'pi:tə(r)/ *v.i.* **~ out,** (*supplies*) s'épuiser; (*road*) finir.

petite /pə'ti:t/ *a.* (*woman*) menue.

petition /pɪ'tɪʃn/ *n.* pétition *f.* ● *v.t.* adresser une pétition à.

petrify /'petrɪfaɪ/ *v.t.* pétrifier; (*scare: fig.*) pétrifier de peur.

petrol /'petrəl/ *n.* essence *f.* **~ bomb,** cocktail molotov *m.* **~ station,** station-service *f.* **~ tank,** réservoir d'essence *m.*

petroleum /pɪ'trəʊlɪəm/ *n.* pétrole *m.*

petticoat /'petɪkəʊt/ *n.* jupon *m.*

petty /'petɪ/ *a.* (**-ier, -iest**) (*minor*) petit; (*mean*) mesquin. **~ cash,** petite caisse *f.*

petulan|t /'petjʊlənt/ *a.* irritable. **~ce** *n.* irritabilité *f.*

pew /pju:/ *n.* banc (d'église) *m.*

pewter /'pju:tə(r)/ *n.* étain *m.*

phallic /'fælɪk/ *a.* phallique.

phantom /'fæntəm/ *n.* fantôme *m.*

pharmaceutical /fɑ:mə'sju:tɪkl/ *a.* pharmaceutique.

pharmac|y /'fɑ:məsɪ/ *n.* pharmacie *f.* **~ist** *n.* pharmacien(ne) *m.* (*f.*).

pharyngitis /færɪn'dʒaɪtɪs/ *n.* pharyngite *f.*

phase /feɪz/ *n.* phase *f.* ● *v.t.* **~ in/out,** introduire/retirer progressivement.

pheasant /'feznt/ *n.* faisan *m.*

phenomen|on /fɪ'nɒmɪnən/ *n.* (*pl.* **-ena**) phénomène *m.* **~al** *a.* phénoménal.

phew /fju:/ *int.* ouf.

phial /'faɪəl/ *n.* fiole *f.*

philanderer /fɪ'lændərə(r)/ *n.* coureur (de femmes) *m.*

philanthrop|ist /fɪ'lænθrəpɪst/ *n.* philanthrope *m./f.* **~ic** /-ən'θrɒpɪk/ *a.* philanthropique.

philatel|y /fɪ'lætəlɪ/ *n.* philatélie *f.* **~ist** *n.* philatéliste *m./f.*

philharmonic /fɪlɑ:'mɒnɪk/ *a.* philharmonique.

Philippines /'fɪlɪpi:nz/ *n. pl.* **the ~,** les Philippines *f. pl.*

philistine /'fɪlɪstaɪn, *Amer.* 'fɪlɪsti:n/ *n.* philistin *m.*

philosoph|y /fɪ'lɒsəfɪ/ *n.* philosophie *f.* **~er** *n.* philosophe *m./f.* **~ical** /-ə'sɒfɪkl/ *a.* philosophique; (*resigned*) philosophe.

phlegm /flem/ *n.* (*med.*) mucosité *f.*

phlegmatic /fleg'mætɪk/ *a.* flegmatique.

phobia /'fəʊbɪə/ *n.* phobie *f.*

phone /fəʊn/ *n.* téléphone *m.* ● *v.t.* (*person*) téléphoner à; (*message*) téléphoner. ● *v.i.* téléphoner. **~ back,** rappeler. **on the ~,** au téléphone. **~ book,** annuaire *m.* **~ box, ~ booth,** cabine téléphonique *f.* **~ call,** coup de fil *m.* **~-in** *n.* émission à ligne ouverte *f.*

phonecard /'fəʊnkɑ:d/ *n.* télécarte *f.*

phonetic /fə'netɪk/ *a.* phonétique.

phoney /'fəʊnɪ/ *a.* (**-ier, -iest**) (*sl.*) faux. ● *n.* (*person*: *sl.*) charlatan *m.* **it's a ~,** (*sl.*) c'est faux.

phosphate /'fɒsfeɪt/ *n.* phosphate *m.*

phosphorus /'fɒsfərəs/ *n.* phosphore *m.*

photo /'fəʊtəʊ/ *n.* (*pl.* **-os**) (*fam.*) photo *f.*

photocop|y /'fəʊtəʊkɒpɪ/ *n.* photocopie *f.* ● *v.t.* photocopier. **~ier** *n.* photocopieuse *f.*

photogenic /fəʊtəʊ'dʒenɪk/ *a.* photogénique.

photograph /'fəʊtəgrɑ:f/ *n.* photographie *f.* ● *v.t.* photographier. **~er** /fə'tɒgrəfə(r)/ *n.* photographe *m./f.* **~ic** /-'græfɪk/ *a.* photographique. **~y** /fə'tɒgrəfɪ/ *n.* (*activity*) photographie *f.*

phrase /freɪz/ *n.* expression *f.*; (*idiom & gram.*) locution *f.* ● *v.t.* exprimer, formuler. **~-book** *n.* guide de conversation *m.*

physical /'fɪzɪkl/ *a.* physique. **~ly** *adv.* physiquement.

physician /fɪ'zɪʃn/ *n.* médecin *m.*

physicist /'fɪzɪsɪst/ *n.* physicien(ne) *m.* (*f.*).

physics /'fɪzɪks/ *n.* physique *f.*

physiology /fɪzɪ'ɒlədʒɪ/ *n.* physiologie *f.*

physiotherap|y /fɪzɪəʊ'θerəpɪ/ *n.* kinésithérapie *f.* **~ist** *n.* kinésithérapeute *m./f.*

physique /fɪ'zi:k/ *n.* constitution *f.*; (*appearance*) physique *m.*

pian|o /pɪ'ænəʊ/ *n.* (*pl.* **-os**) piano *m.* **~ist** /'pɪənɪst/ *n.* pianiste *m./f.*

piazza /pɪ'ætsə/ *n.* (*square*) place *f.*

pick[1] /pɪk/ (*tool*) *n.* pioche *f.*

pick[2] /pɪk/ *v.t.* choisir; (*flower etc.*) cueillir; (*lock*) crocheter; (*nose*) se curer; (*pockets*) faire. **~ (off),** enlever. ● *n.* choix *m.*; (*best*) meilleur(e) *m.* (*f.*). **~ a quarrel with,** chercher querelle à. **~ holes in,** relever les défauts de. **the ~ of,** ce qu'il y a de mieux dans. **~ off,** (*mil.*) abattre un à un. **~ on,** harceler. **~ out,** choisir; (*identify*) distinguer. **~ up** *v.t.* ramasser; (*sth. fallen*) relever; (*weight*) soulever; (*habit, passenger, speed, etc.*) prendre; (*learn*) apprendre; *v.i.* s'améliorer. **~-me-up** *n.* remontant *m.* **~-up** *n.* partenaire de rencontre *m./f.*; (*truck, stylus-holder*) pick-up *m.*

pickaxe /'pɪkæks/ *n.* pioche *f.*

picket /'pɪkɪt/ *n.* (*single striker*) gréviste *m./f.*; (*stake*) piquet *m.* **~ (line),** piquet de grève *m.* ● *v.t.* (*p.t.* **picketed**) mettre un piquet de grève devant.

pickings /'pɪkɪŋz/ *n. pl.* restes *m. pl.*

pickle /'pɪkl/ *n.* vinaigre *m.*; (*brine*) saumure *f.* **~s,** pickles *m. pl.*; (*Amer.*) concombres *m.pl.* ● *v.t.* conserver dans du vinaigre *or* de la saumure. **in a ~,** (*fam.*) dans le pétrin.

pickpocket /'pɪkpɒkɪt/ *n.* (*thief*) pickpocket *m.*

picnic /'pɪknɪk/ *n.* pique-nique *m.* ● *v.i.* (*p.t.* **picnicked**) piqueniquer.

pictorial /pɪk'tɔ:rɪəl/ *a.* illustré.

picture /'pɪktʃə(r)/ *n.* image *f.*; (*painting*) tableau *m.*; (*photograph*) photo *f.*; (*drawing*) dessin *m.*; (*film*) film *m.*; (*fig.*) description *f.*, tableau *m.* ● *v.t.* s'imaginer; (*describe*) dépeindre. **the ~s,** (*cinema*) le cinéma. **~ book,** livre d'images *m.*

picturesque /pɪktʃə'resk/ *a.* pittoresque.

piddling /ˈpɪdlɪŋ/ *a.* (*fam.*) dérisoire.
pidgin /ˈpɪdʒɪn/ *a.* ~ **English,** pidgin *m.*
pie /paɪ/ *n.* tarte *f.*; (*of meat*) pâté en croûte *m.* ~ **chart,** camembert *m.*
piebald /ˈpaɪbɔːld/ *a.* pie *invar.*
piece /piːs/ *n.* morceau *m.*; (*of currency, machine, etc.*) pièce *f.* ● *v.t.* ~ **(together),** (r)assembler. **a ~ of advice/furniture/*etc.*,** un conseil/meuble/*etc.* **~-work** *n.* travail à la pièce *m.* **go to ~s,** (*fam.*) s'effondrer. **take to ~s,** démonter.
piecemeal /ˈpiːsmiːl/ *a.* par bribes.
pier /pɪə(r)/ *n.* (*promenade*) jetée *f.*
pierc|e /pɪəs/ *v.t.* percer. **~ing** *a.* perçant; (*cold*) glacial.
piety /ˈpaɪətɪ/ *n.* piété *f.*
piffl|e /ˈpɪfl/ *n.* (*sl.*) fadaises *f. pl.* **~ing** *a.* (*sl.*) insignifiant.
pig /pɪg/ *n.* cochon *m.* **~-headed** *a.* entêté.
pigeon /ˈpɪdʒən/ *n.* pigeon *m.* **~-hole** *n.* casier *m.*; *v.t.* classer.
piggy /ˈpɪgɪ/ *a.* porcin; (*greedy: fam.*) goinfre. **~-back** *adv.* sur le dos. **~ bank,** tirelire *f.*
pigment /ˈpɪgmənt/ *n.* pigment *m.* **~ation** /-enˈteɪʃn/ *n.* pigmentation *f.*
pigsty /ˈpɪgstaɪ/ *n.* porcherie *f.*
pigtail /ˈpɪgteɪl/ *n.* natte *f.*
pike /paɪk/ *n. invar.* (*fish*) brochet *m.*
pilchard /ˈpɪltʃəd/ *n.* pilchard *m.*
pile /paɪl/ *n.* pile *f.*, tas *m.*; (*of carpet*) poils *m.pl.* ● *v.t.* ~ **(up),** (*stack*) empiler. ● *v.i.* ~ **into,** s'empiler dans. ~ **up,** (*accumulate*) (s')accumuler. **a ~ of,** (*fam.*) un tas de. **~-up** *n.* (*auto.*) carambolage *m.*
piles /paɪlz/ *n. pl.* (*fam.*) hémorroïdes *f. pl.*
pilfer /ˈpɪlfə(r)/ *v.t.* chaparder. **~age** *n.* chapardage *m.*
pilgrim /ˈpɪlgrɪm/ *n.* pèlerin *m.* **~age** *n.* pèlerinage *m.*
pill /pɪl/ *n.* pilule *f.*
pillage /ˈpɪlɪdʒ/ *n.* pillage *m.* ● *v.t.* piller. ● *v.i.* se livrer au pillage.
pillar /ˈpɪlə(r)/ *n.* pilier *m.* **~-box** *n.* boîte à *or* aux lettres *f.*
pillion /ˈpɪljən/ *n.* siège arrière *m.* **ride ~,** monter derrière.
pillory /ˈpɪlərɪ/ *n.* pilori *m.*
pillow /ˈpɪləʊ/ *n.* oreiller *m.*
pillowcase /ˈpɪləʊkeɪs/ *n.* taie d'oreiller *f.*
pilot /ˈpaɪlət/ *n.* pilote *m.* ● *a.* pilote. ● *v.t.* (*p.t.* **piloted**) piloter. **~-light** *n.* veilleuse *f.*
pimento /pɪˈmentəʊ/ *n.* (*pl.* **-os**) piment *m.*
pimp /pɪmp/ *n.* souteneur *m.*
pimpl|e /ˈpɪmpl/ *n.* bouton *m.* **~y** *a.* boutonneux.
pin /pɪn/ *n.* épingle *f.*; (*techn.*) goupille *f.* ● *v.t.* (*p.t.* **pinned**) épingler, attacher; (*hold down*) clouer. **have ~s and needles,** avoir des fourmis. **~ s.o. down,** (*fig.*) forcer qn. à se décider. **~-point** *v.t.* repérer, définir. ~ **up,** afficher. **~-up** *n.* (*fam.*) pin-up *f. invar.*
pinafore /ˈpɪnəfɔː(r)/ *n.* tablier *m.*
pincers /ˈpɪnsəz/ *n. pl.* tenailles *f. pl.*
pinch /pɪntʃ/ *v.t.* pincer; (*steal: sl.*) piquer. ● *v.i.* (*be too tight*) serrer. ● *n.* (*mark*) pinçon *m.*; (*of salt*) pincée *f.* **at a ~,** au besoin.
pincushion /ˈpɪnkʊʃn/ *n.* pelote à épingles *f.*
pine[1] /paɪn/ *n.* (*tree*) pin *m.* **~-cone** *n.* pomme de pin *f.*
pine[2] /paɪn/ *v.i.* ~ **away,** dépérir. ~ **for,** languir après.
pineapple /ˈpaɪnæpl/ *n.* ananas *m.*
ping /pɪŋ/ *n.* bruit métallique *m.*
ping-pong /ˈpɪŋpɒŋ/ *n.* ping-pong *m.*
pink /pɪŋk/ *a.* & *n.* rose (*m.*).
pinnacle /ˈpɪnəkl/ *n.* pinacle *m.*
pint /paɪnt/ *n.* pinte *f.* (*imperial = 0.57 litre; Amer. = 0.47 litre*).
pioneer /paɪəˈnɪə(r)/ *n.* pionnier *m.* ● *v.t.* être le premier à faire, utiliser, étudier, *etc.*
pious /ˈpaɪəs/ *a.* pieux.
pip[1] /pɪp/ *n.* (*seed*) pépin *m.*
pip[2] /pɪp/ *n.* (*sound*) top *m.*
pipe /paɪp/ *n.* tuyau *m.*; (*of smoker*) pipe *f.*; (*mus.*) pipeau *m.* ● *v.t.* transporter par tuyau. **~-cleaner** *n.* cure-pipe *m.* ~ **down,** se taire. **~-dream** *n.* chimère *f.*
pipeline /ˈpaɪplaɪn/ *n.* pipeline *m.* **in the ~,** en route.
piping /ˈpaɪpɪŋ/ *n.* tuyau(x) *m.* (*pl.*). ~ **hot,** très chaud.
piquant /ˈpiːkənt/ *a.* piquant.
pique /piːk/ *n.* dépit *m.*
pira|te /ˈpaɪərət/ *n.* pirate *m.* ● *v.t.* pirater. **~cy** *n.* piraterie *f.*
Pisces /ˈpaɪsiːz/ *n.* les Poissons *m. pl.*
pistachio /pɪˈstæʃɪəʊ/ *n.* (*pl.* **-os**) pistache *f.*
pistol /ˈpɪstl/ *n.* pistolet *m.*
piston /ˈpɪstən/ *n.* piston *m.*
pit /pɪt/ *n.* fosse *f.*, trou *m.*; (*mine*) puits *m.*; (*quarry*) carrière *f.*; (*for orchestra*) fosse *f.*; (*of stomach*)

creux *m.*; (*of cherry etc.*: *Amer.*) noyau *m.* ● *v.t.* (*p.t.* **pitted**) trouer; (*fig.*) opposer. ~ **o.s. against,** se mesurer à.

pitch[1] /pɪtʃ/ *n.* (*tar*) poix *f.* **~-black** *a.* d'un noir d'ébène.

pitch[2] /pɪtʃ/ *v.t.* lancer; (*tent*) dresser. ● *v.i.* (*of ship*) tanguer. ● *n.* degré *m.*; (*of voice*) hauteur *f.*; (*mus.*) ton *m.*; (*sport*) terrain *m.* **~ed battle,** bataille rangée *f.* **a high-~ed voice,** une voix aigüe. **~ in,** (*fam.*) contribuer. **~ into,** (*fam.*) s'attaquer à.

pitcher /ˈpɪtʃə(r)/ *n.* cruche *f.*

pitchfork /ˈpɪtʃfɔːk/ *n.* fourche à foin *f.*

pitfall /ˈpɪtfɔːl/ *n.* piège *m.*

pith /pɪθ/ *n.* (*of orange*) peau blanche *f.*; (*essence*: *fig.*) moelle *f.*

pithy /ˈpɪθɪ/ *a.* (**-ier, -iest**) (*terse*) concis; (*forceful*) vigoureux.

piti|ful /ˈpɪtɪfl/ *a.* pitoyable. **~less** *a.* impitoyable.

pittance /ˈpɪtns/ *n.* revenu *or* salaire dérisoire *m.*

pity /ˈpɪtɪ/ *n.* pitié *f.*; (*regrettable fact*) dommage *m.* ● *v.t.* plaindre. **take ~ on,** avoir pitié de. **what a ~,** quel dommage. **it's a ~,** c'est dommage.

pivot /ˈpɪvət/ *n.* pivot *m.* ● *v.i.* (*p.t.* **pivoted**) pivoter.

pixie /ˈpɪksɪ/ *n.* lutin *m.*

pizza /ˈpiːtsə/ *n.* pizza *f.*

placard /ˈplækɑːd/ *n.* affiche *f.*

placate /pləˈkeɪt, *Amer.* ˈpleɪkeɪt/ *v.t.* calmer.

place /pleɪs/ *n.* endroit *m.*, lieu *m.*; (*house*) maison *f.*; (*seat, rank, etc.*) place *f.* ● *v.t.* placer; (*an order*) passer; (*remember*) situer. **at** *or* **to my ~,** chez moi. **be ~d,** (*in race*) se placer. **change ~s,** changer de place. **in the first ~,** d'abord. **out of ~,** déplacé. **take ~,** avoir lieu. **~-mat** *n.* set *m.*

placenta /pləˈsentə/ *n.* placenta *m.*

placid /ˈplæsɪd/ *a.* placide.

plagiar|ize /ˈpleɪdʒəraɪz/ *v.t.* plagier. **~ism** *n.* plagiat *m.*

plague /pleɪɡ/ *n.* peste *f.*; (*nuisance*: *fam.*) fléau *m.* ● *v.t.* harceler.

plaice /pleɪs/ *n. invar.* carrelet *m.*

plaid /plæd/ *n.* tissu écossais *m.*

plain /pleɪn/ *a.* (**-er, -est**) clair; (*candid*) franc; (*simple*) simple; (*not pretty*) sans beauté; (*not patterned*) uni. ● *adv.* franchement. ● *n.* plaine *f.* **~ chocolate,** chocolat noir *m.* **in ~ clothes,** en civil. **~ly** *adv.* clairement; franchement; simplement. **~ness** *n.* simplicité *f.*

plaintiff /ˈpleɪntɪf/ *n.* plaignant(e) *m.* (*f.*).

plaintive /ˈpleɪntɪv/ *a.* plaintif.

plait /plæt/ *v.t.* tresser, natter. ● *n.* tresse *f.*, natte *f.*

plan /plæn/ *n.* projet *m.*, plan *m.*; (*diagram*) plan *m.* ● *v.t.* (*p.t.* **planned**) prévoir, projeter; (*arrange*) organiser; (*design*) concevoir; (*economy, work*) planifier. ● *v.i.* faire des projets. **~ to do,** avoir l'intention de faire.

plane[1] /pleɪn/ *n.* (*tree*) platane *m.*

plane[2] /pleɪn/ *n.* (*level*) plan *m.*; (*aeroplane*) avion *m.* ● *a.* plan.

plane[3] /pleɪn/ *n.* (*tool*) rabot *m.* ● *v.t.* raboter.

planet /ˈplænɪt/ *n.* planète *f.* **~ary** *a.* planétaire.

plank /plæŋk/ *n.* planche *f.*

plankton /plæŋktn/ *n.* plancton *m.*

planning /ˈplænɪŋ/ *n.* (*pol., comm.*) planification *f.* **family ~,** planning familial *m.* **~ permission,** permis de construire *m.*

plant /plɑːnt/ *n.* plante *f.*; (*techn.*) matériel *m.*; (*factory*) usine *f.* ● *v.t.* planter; (*bomb*) (dé)poser. **~ation** /-ˈteɪʃn/ *n.* plantation *f.*

plaque /plɑːk/ *n.* plaque *f.*

plasma /ˈplæzmə/ *n.* plasma *m.*

plaster /ˈplɑːstə(r)/ *n.* plâtre *m.*; (*adhesive*) sparadrap *m.* ● *v.t.* plâtrer; (*cover*) tapisser (**with,** de). **in ~,** dans le plâtre. **~ of Paris,** plâtre à mouler *m.* **~er** *n.* plâtrier *m.*

plastic /ˈplæstɪk/ *a.* en plastique; (*art, substance*) plastique. ● *n.* plastique *m.* **~ surgery,** chirurgie esthétique *f.*

Plasticine /ˈplæstɪsiːn/ *n.* (P.) pâte à modeler *f.*

plate /pleɪt/ *n.* assiette *f.*; (*of metal*) plaque *f.*; (*gold or silver dishes*) vaisselle plate *f.*; (*in book*) gravure *f.* ● *v.t.* (*metal*) plaquer. **~ful** *n.* (*pl.* **-fuls**) assiettée *f.*

plateau /ˈplætəʊ/ *n.* (*pl.* **-eaux** /-əʊz/) plateau *m.*

platform /ˈplætfɔːm/ *n.* (*in classroom, hall, etc.*) estrade *f.*; (*for speaking*) tribune *f.*; (*rail.*) quai *m.*; (*of bus & pol.*) plate-forme *f.*

platinum /ˈplætɪnəm/ *n.* platine *m.*

platitude /ˈplætɪtjuːd/ *n.* platitude *f.*

platonic /pləˈtɒnɪk/ *a.* platonique.

platoon /plə'tu:n/ *n.* (*mil.*) section *f.*
platter /'plætə(r)/ *n.* plat *m.*
plausible /'plɔ:zəbl/ *a.* plausible.
play /pleɪ/ *v.t./i.* jouer; (*instrument*) jouer de; (*record*) passer; (*game*) jouer à; (*opponent*) jouer contre; (*match*) disputer. ● *n.* jeu *m.*; (*theatre*) pièce *f.* **~-act** *v.i.* jouer la comédie. **~ down,** minimiser. **~-group, ~-school** *ns.* garderie *f.* **~-off** *n.* (*sport*) belle *f.* **~ on,** (*take advantage of*) jouer sur. **~ on words,** jeu de mots *m.* **~ed out,** épuisé. **~-pen** *n.* parc *m.* **~ safe,** ne pas prendre de risques. **~ up,** (*fam.*) créer des problèmes (à). **~ up to,** flatter. **~er** *n.* joueu|r, -se *m., f.*
playboy /'pleɪbɔɪ/ *n.* play-boy *m.*
playful /'pleɪfl/ *a.* enjoué; (*child*) joueur. **~ly** *adv.* avec espièglerie.
playground /'pleɪgraʊnd/ *n.* cour de récréation *f.*
playing /'pleɪɪŋ/ *n.* jeu *m.* **~-card** *n.* carte à jouer *f.* **~-field** *n.* terrain de sport *m.*
playmate /'pleɪmeɪt/ *n.* camarade *m./f.*, cop|ain, -ine *m., f.*
plaything /'pleɪθɪŋ/ *n.* jouet *m.*
playwright /'pleɪraɪt/ *n.* dramaturge *m./f.*
plc *abbr.* (*public limited company*) SA.
plea /pli:/ *n.* (*entreaty*) supplication *f.*; (*reason*) excuse *f.*; (*jurid.*) défense *f.*
plead /pli:d/ *v.t./i.* (*jurid.*) plaider; (*as excuse*) alléguer. **~ for,** (*beg for*) implorer. **~ with,** (*beg*) implorer.
pleasant /'pleznt/ *a.* agréable. **~ly** *adv.* agréablement.
please /pli:z/ *v.t./i.* plaire (à), faire plaisir (à). ● *adv.* s'il vous *or* te plaît. **~ o.s., do as one ~s,** faire ce qu'on veut. **~d** *a.* content (**with,** de). **pleasing** *a.* agréable.
pleasur|e /'pleʒə(r)/ *n.* plaisir *m.* **~able** *a.* très agréable.
pleat /pli:t/ *n.* pli *m.* ● *v.t.* plisser.
plebiscite /'plebɪsɪt/ *n.* plébiscite *m.*
pledge /pledʒ/ *n.* (*token*) gage *m.*; (*fig.*) promesse *f.* ● *v.t.* promettre; (*pawn*) engager.
plentiful /'plentɪfl/ *a.* abondant.
plenty /'plentɪ/ *n.* abondance *f.* **~ (of),** (*a great deal*) beaucoup (de); (*enough*) assez (de).
pleurisy /'plʊərəsɪ/ *n.* pleurésie *f.*
pliable /'plaɪəbl/ *a.* souple.
pliers /'plaɪəz/ *n. pl.* pince(s) *f.* (*pl.*).
plight /plaɪt/ *n.* triste situation *f.*
plimsoll /'plɪms(ə)l/ *n.* chaussure de gym *f.*
plinth /plɪnθ/ *n.* socle *m.*
plod /plɒd/ *v.i.* (*p.t.* **plodded**) avancer péniblement *or* d'un pas lent; (*work*) bûcher. **~der** *n.* bûcheu|r, -se *m., f.* **~ding** *a.* lent.
plonk /plɒŋk/ *n.* (*sl.*) pinard *m.* ● *v.t.* **~ down,** poser lourdement.
plot /plɒt/ *n.* complot *m.*; (*of novel etc.*) intrigue *f.* **~ (of land),** terrain *m.* ● *v.t./i.* (*p.t.* **plotted**) comploter; (*mark out*) tracer.
plough /plaʊ/ *n.* charrue *f.* ● *v.t./i.* labourer. **~ back,** réinvestir. **~ into,** rentrer dans. **~ through,** avancer péniblement dans.
plow /plaʊ/ *n.* & *v.t./i.* (*Amer.*) = **plough**.
ploy /plɔɪ/ *n.* (*fam.*) stratagème *m.*
pluck /plʌk/ *v.t.* cueillir; (*bird*) plumer; (*eyebrows*) épiler; (*strings*: *mus.*) pincer. ● *n.* courage *m.* **~ up courage,** prendre son courage à deux mains. **~y** *a.* courageux.
plug /plʌg/ *n.* (*of cloth, paper, etc.*) tampon *m.*; (*for sink etc.*) bonde *f.*; (*electr.*) fiche *f.*, prise *f.* ● *v.t.* (*p.t.* **plugged**) (*hole*) boucher; (*publicize*: *fam.*) faire du battage autour de. ● *v.i.* **~ away,** (*work*: *fam.*) bosser. **~ in,** brancher. **~-hole** *n.* vidange *f.*
plum /plʌm/ *n.* prune *f.* **~ job,** travail en or *m.* **~ pudding,** (plum-) pudding *m.*
plumb /plʌm/ *adv.* tout à fait. ● *v.t.* (*probe*) sonder. **~-line** *n.* fil à plomb *m.*
plumb|er /'plʌmə(r)/ *n.* plombier *m.* **~ing** *n.* plomberie *f.*
plum|e /plu:m/ *n.* plume(s) *f.* (*pl.*). **~age** *n.* plumage *m.*
plummet /'plʌmɪt/ *v.i.* (*p.t.* **plummeted**) tomber, plonger.
plump /plʌmp/ *a.* (**-er, -est**) potelé, dodu. ● *v.i.* **~ for,** choisir. **~ness** *n.* rondeur *f.*
plunder /'plʌndə(r)/ *v.t.* piller. ● *n.* (*act*) pillage *m.*; (*goods*) butin *m.*
plunge /plʌndʒ/ *v.t./i.* (*dive, thrust*) plonger; (*fall*) tomber. ● *n.* plongeon *m.*; (*fall*) chute *f.* **take the ~,** se jeter à l'eau.
plunger /'plʌndʒə(r)/ *n.* (*for sink etc.*) ventouse *f.*, déboucholr *m.*
plural /'plʊərəl/ *a.* pluriel; (*noun*) au pluriel. ● *n.* pluriel *m.*

plus /plʌs/ *prep.* plus. ● *a.* (*electr.* & *fig.*) positif. ● *n.* signe plus *m.*; (*fig.*) atout *m.* **ten ~,** plus de dix.

plush(y) /'plʌʃ(ɪ)/ *a.* somptueux.

ply /plaɪ/ *v.t.* (*tool*) manier; (*trade*) exercer. ● *v.i.* faire la navette. **~ s.o. with drink,** offrir continuellement à boire à qn.

plywood /'plaɪwʊd/ *n.* contreplaqué *m.*

p.m. /pi:'em/ *adv.* de l'après-midi *or* du soir.

pneumatic /nju:'mætɪk/ *a.* pneumatique. **~ drill,** marteau-piqueur *m.*

pneumonia /nju:'məʊnɪə/ *n.* pneumonie *f.*

PO *abbr. see* Post Office.

poach /pəʊtʃ/ *v.t./i.* (*game*) braconner; (*staff*) débaucher; (*culin.*) pocher. **~er** *n.* braconnier *m.*

pocket /'pɒkɪt/ *n.* poche *f.* ● *a.* de poche. ● *v.t.* empocher. **be out of ~,** avoir perdu de l'argent. **~-book** *n.* (*notebook*) carnet *m.*; (*wallet*: *Amer.*) portefeuille *m.*; (*handbag*: *Amer.*) sac à main *m.* **~-money** *n.* argent de poche *m.*

pock-marked /'pɒkmɑ:kt/ *a.* (*face etc.*) grêlé.

pod /pɒd/ *n.* (*peas etc.*) cosse *f.*; (*vanilla*) gousse *f.*

podgy /'pɒdʒɪ/ *a.* (**-ier, -iest**) dodu.

poem /'pəʊɪm/ *n.* poème *m.*

poet /'pəʊɪt/ *n.* poète *m.* **~ic** /-'etɪk/ *a.* poétique.

poetry /'pəʊɪtrɪ/ *n.* poésie *f.*

poignant /'pɔɪnjənt/ *a.* poignant.

point /pɔɪnt/ *n.* point *m.*; (*tip*) pointe *f.*; (*decimal point*) virgule *f.*; (*meaning*) sens *m.*, intérêt *m.*; (*remark*) remarque *f.* **~s,** (*rail.*) aiguillage *m.* ● *v.t.* (*aim*) braquer; (*show*) indiquer. ● *v.i.* indiquer du doigt (**at** *or* **to s.o.,** qn.). **~ out that, make the ~ that,** faire remarquer que. **good ~s,** qualités *f. pl.* **make a ~ of doing,** ne pas manquer de faire. **on the ~ of,** sur le point de. **~-blank** *a.* & *adv.* à bout portant. **~ in time,** moment *m.* **~ of view,** point de vue *m.* **~ out,** signaler. **to the ~,** pertinent. **what is the ~?,** à quoi bon?

pointed /'pɔɪntɪd/ *a.* pointu; (*remark*) lourd de sens.

pointer /'pɔɪntə(r)/ *n.* (*indicator*) index *m.*; (*dog*) chien d'arrêt *m.*; (*advice*: *fam.*) tuyau *m.*

pointless /'pɔɪntlɪs/ *a.* inutile.

poise /pɔɪz/ *n.* équilibre *m.*; (*carriage*) maintien *m.*; (*fig.*) assurance *f.* **~d** *a.* en équilibre; (*confident*) assuré. **~d for,** prêt à.

poison /'pɔɪzn/ *n.* poison *m.* ● *v.t.* empoisonner. **~ous** *a.* (*substance etc.*) toxique; (*plant*) vénéneux; (*snake*) venimeux.

poke /pəʊk/ *v.t./i.* (*push*) pousser; (*fire*) tisonner; (*thrust*) fourrer. ● *n.* (petit) coup *m.* **~ about,** fureter. **~ fun at,** se moquer de. **~ out,** (*head*) sortir.

poker[1] /'pəʊkə(r)/ *n.* tisonnier *m.*

poker[2] /'pəʊkə(r)/ *n.* (*cards*) poker *m.*

poky /'pəʊkɪ/ *a.* (**-ier, -iest**) (*small*) exigu; (*slow*: *Amer.*) lent.

Poland /'pəʊlənd/ *n.* Pologne *f.*

polar /'pəʊlə(r)/ *a.* polaire. **~ bear,** ours blanc *m.*

polarize /'pəʊləraɪz/ *v.t.* polariser.

Polaroid /'pəʊlərɔɪd/ *n.* (P.) polaroïd (P.) *m.*

pole[1] /pəʊl/ *n.* (*fixed*) poteau *m.*; (*rod*) perche *f.*; (*for flag*) mât *m.* **~-vault** *n.* saut à la perche *m.*

pole[2] /pəʊl/ *n.* (*geog.*) pôle *m.*

Pole /pəʊl/ *n.* Polonais(e) *m.* (*f.*).

polemic /pə'lemɪk/ *n.* polémique *f.*

police /pə'li:s/ *n.* police *f.* ● *v.t.* faire la police dans. **~ state,** état policier *m.* **~ station,** commissariat de police *m.*

police|man /pə'li:smən/ *n.* (*pl.* **-men**) agent de police *m.* **~woman** (*pl.* **-women**) femme-agent *f.*

policy[1] /'pɒlɪsɪ/ *n.* politique *f.*

policy[2] /'pɒlɪsɪ/ *n.* (*insurance*) police (d'assurance) *f.*

polio(myelitis) /'pəʊlɪəʊ(maɪə'laɪtɪs)/ *n.* polio(myélite) *f.*

polish /'pɒlɪʃ/ *v.t.* polir; (*shoes, floor*) cirer. ● *n.* (*for shoes*) cirage *m.*; (*for floor*) encaustique *f.*; (*for nails*) vernis *m.*; (*shine*) poli *m.*; (*fig.*) raffinement *m.* **~ off,** finir en vitesse. **~ up,** (*language*) perfectionner. **~ed** *a.* raffiné.

Polish /'pəʊlɪʃ/ *a.* polonais. ● *n.* (*lang.*) polonais *m.*

polite /pə'laɪt/ *a.* poli. **~ly** *adv.* poliment. **~ness** *n.* politesse *f.*

political /pə'lɪtɪkl/ *a.* politique.

politician /pɒlɪ'tɪʃn/ *n.* homme politique *m.*, femme politique *f.*

politics /'pɒlətɪks/ *n.* politique *f.*

polka /'pɒlkə, *Amer.* 'pəʊlkə/ *n.* polka *f.* ~ **dots,** pois *m. pl.*
poll /pəʊl/ *n.* scrutin *m.*; (*survey*) sondage *m.* ● *v.t.* (*votes*) obtenir. **go to the ~s,** aller aux urnes. **~ing-booth** *n.* isoloir *m.* **~ing station,** bureau de vote *m.*
pollen /'pɒlən/ *n.* pollen *m.*
pollut|e /pə'lu:t/ *v.t.* polluer. **~ion** /-ʃn/ *n.* pollution *f.*
polo /'pəʊləʊ/ *n.* polo *m.* ~ **neck,** col roulé *m.* ~ **shirt,** polo *m.*
polyester /pɒlɪ'estə(r)/ *n.* polyester *m.*
polygamy /pə'lɪgəmɪ/ *n.* polygamie *f.*
polytechnic /pɒlɪ'teknɪk/ *n.* institut universitaire de technologie *m.*
polythene /'pɒlɪθi:n/ *n.* polythène *m.*, polyéthylène *m.*
pomegranate /'pɒmɪgrænɪt/ *n.* (*fruit*) grenade *f.*
pomp /pɒmp/ *n.* pompe *f.*
pompon /'pɒmpɒn/ *n.* pompon *m.*
pomp|ous /'pɒmpəs/ *a.* pompeux. **~osity** /-'pɒsətɪ/ *n.* solennité *f.*
pond /pɒnd/ *n.* étang *m.*; (*artificial*) bassin *m.*; (*stagnant*) mare *f.*
ponder /'pɒndə(r)/ *v.t./i.* réfléchir (à), méditer (sur).
ponderous /'pɒndərəs/ *a.* pesant.
pong /pɒŋ/ *n.* (*stink*: *sl.*) puanteur *f.* ● *v.i.* (*sl.*) puer.
pony /'pəʊnɪ/ *n.* poney *m.* **~-tail** *n.* queue de cheval *f.*
poodle /'pu:dl/ *n.* caniche *m.*
pool[1] /pu:l/ *n.* (*puddle*) flaque *f.*; (*pond*) étang *m.*; (*of blood*) mare *f.*; (*for swimming*) piscine *f.*
pool[2] /pu:l/ *n.* (*fund*) fonds commun *m.*, (*of ideas*) réservoir *m.*; (*of typists*) pool *m.*; (*snooker*) billard américain *m.* **~s,** pari mutuel sur le football *m.* ● *v.t.* mettre en commun.
poor /pɔ:(r)/ *a.* (**-er, -est**) pauvre; (*not good*) médiocre, mauvais. **~ly** *adv.* mal; *a.* malade.
pop[1] /pɒp/ *n.* (*noise*) bruit sec *m.* ● *v.t./i.* (*p.t.* **popped**) (*burst*) crever; (*put*) mettre. ~ **in/out/off,** entrer/sortir/partir. ~ **over,** faire un saut (**to see s.o.,** chez qn.). ~ **up,** surgir.
pop[2] /pɒp/ *n.* (*mus.*) musique pop *f.* ● *a.* pop *invar.*
popcorn /'pɒpkɔ:n/ *n.* pop-corn *m.*
pope /pəʊp/ *n.* pape *m.*
poplar /'pɒplə(r)/ *n.* peuplier *m.*
poppy /'pɒpɪ/ *n.* pavot *m.*; (*wild*) coquelicot *m.*
popsicle /'pɒpsɪkl/ *n.* (P.) (*Amer.*) glace à l'eau *f.*
popular /'pɒpjʊlə(r)/ *a.* populaire; (*in fashion*) en vogue. **be ~ with,** plaire à. **~ity** /-'lærətɪ/ *n.* popularité *f.* **~ize** *v.t.* populariser. **~ly** *adv.* communément.
populat|e /'pɒpjʊleɪt/ *v.t.* peupler. **~ion** /-'leɪʃn/ *n.* population *f.*
populous /'pɒpjʊləs/ *a.* populeux.
porcelain /'pɔ:səlɪn/ *n.* porcelaine *f.*
porch /pɔ:tʃ/ *n.* porche *m.*
porcupine /'pɔ:kjʊpaɪn/ *n.* (*rodent*) porc-épic *m.*
pore[1] /pɔ:(r)/ *n.* pore *m.*
pore[2] /pɔ:(r)/ *v.i.* ~ **over,** étudier minutieusement.
pork /pɔ:k/ *n.* (*food*) porc *m.*
pornograph|y /pɔ:'nɒgrəfɪ/ *n.* pornographie *f.* **~ic** /-ə'græfɪk/ *a.* pornographique.
porous /'pɔ:rəs/ *a.* poreux.
porpoise /'pɔ:pəs/ *n.* marsouin *m.*
porridge /'pɒrɪdʒ/ *n.* porridge *m.*
port[1] /pɔ:t/ *n.* (*harbour*) port *m.* ~ **of call,** escale *f.*
port[2] /pɔ:t/ *n.* (*left*: *naut.*) bâbord *m.*
port[3] /pɔ:t/ *n.* (*wine*) porto *m.*
portable /'pɔ:təbl/ *a.* portatif.
portal /'pɔ:tl/ *n.* portail *m.*
porter[1] /'pɔ:tə(r)/ *n.* (*carrier*) porteur *m.*
porter[2] /'pɔ:tə(r)/ *n.* (*door-keeper*) portier *m.*
portfolio /pɔ:t'fəʊlɪəʊ/ *n.* (*pl.* **-os**) (*pol., comm.*) portefeuille *m.*
porthole /'pɔ:thəʊl/ *n.* hublot *m.*
portico /'pɔ:tɪkəʊ/ *n.* (*pl.* **-oes**) portique *m.*
portion /'pɔ:ʃn/ *n.* (*share, helping*) portion *f.*; (*part*) partie *f.*
portly /'pɔ:tlɪ/ *a.* (**-ier, -iest**) corpulent (et digne).
portrait /'pɔ:trɪt/ *n.* portrait *m.*
portray /pɔ:'treɪ/ *v.t.* représenter. **~al** *n.* portrait *m.*, peinture *f.*
Portug|al /'pɔ:tjʊgl/ *n.* Portugal *m.* **~uese** /-'gi:z/ *a.* & *n. invar.* portugais(e) (*m.* (*f.*)).
pose /pəʊz/ *v.t./i.* poser. ● *n.* pose *f.* ~ **as,** (*expert etc.*) se poser en.
poser /'pəʊzə(r)/ *n.* colle *f.*
posh /pɒʃ/ *a.* (*sl.*) chic *invar.*
position /pə'zɪʃn/ *n.* position *f.*; (*job, state*) situation *f.* ● *v.t.* placer.
positive /'pɒzətɪv/ *a.* (*test, help, etc.*) positif; (*sure*) sûr, certain; (*real*)

réel, vrai. **~ly** *adv.* positivement; (*absolutely*) complètement.

possess /pə'zes/ *v.t.* posséder. **~ion** /-ʃn/ *n.* possession *f.* **take ~ion of,** prendre possession de. **~or** *n.* possesseur *m.*

possessive /pə'zesɪv/ *a.* possessif.

possib|le /'pɒsəbl/ *a.* possible. **~ility** /-'bɪlətɪ/ *n.* possibilité *f.*

possibly /'pɒsəblɪ/ *adv.* peut-être. **if I ~ can,** si cela m'est possible. **I cannot ~ leave,** il m'est impossible de partir.

post[1] /pəʊst/ *n.* (*pole*) poteau *m.* ● *v.t.* **~ (up),** (*a notice*) afficher.

post[2] /pəʊst/ *n.* (*station, job*) poste *m.* ● *v.t.* poster; (*appoint*) affecter.

post[3] /pəʊst/ *n.* (*mail service*) poste *f.*; (*letters*) courrier *m.* ● *a.* postal. ● *v.t.* (*put in box*) poster; (*send*) envoyer (par la poste). **catch the last ~,** attraper la dernière levée. **keep ~ed,** tenir au courant. **~box** *n.* boîte à *or* aux lettres *f.* **~ code** *n.* code postal *m.* **P~ Office,** postes *f. pl.*; (*in France*) Postes et Télécommunications *f. pl.* **~ office,** bureau de poste *m.*, poste *f.*

post- /pəʊst/ *pref.* post-.

postage /'pəʊstɪdʒ/ *n.* tarif postal *m.*, frais de port *m.pl.*

postal /'pəʊstl/ *a.* postal. **~ order,** mandat *m.* **~ worker,** employé(e) des postes *m.* (*f.*).

postcard /'pəʊstkɑ:d/ *n.* carte postale *f.*

poster /'pəʊstə(r)/ *n.* affiche *f.*; (*for decoration*) poster *m.*

posterior /pɒ'stɪərɪə(r)/ *n.* postérieur *m.*

posterity /pɒ'sterətɪ/ *n.* postérité *f.*

postgraduate /pəʊst'grædʒʊət/ *n.* étudiant(e) de troisième cycle *m.* (*f.*).

posthumous /'pɒstjʊməs/ *a.* posthume. **~ly** *adv.* à titre posthume.

postman /'pəʊstmən/ *n.* (*pl.* **-men**) facteur *m.*

postmark /'pəʊstmɑ:k/ *n.* cachet de la poste *m.*

postmaster /'pəʊstmɑ:stə(r)/ *n.* receveur des postes *m.*

post-mortem /pəʊst'mɔ:təm/ *n.* autopsie *f.*

postpone /pə'spəʊn/ *v.t.* remettre. **~ment** *n.* ajournement *m.*

postscript /'pəʊskrɪpt/ *n.* (*to letter*) post-scriptum *m. invar.*

postulate /'pɒstjʊleɪt/ *v.t.* postuler.

posture /'pɒstʃə(r)/ *n.* posture *f.* ● *v.i.* (*affectedly*) prendre des poses.

post-war /'pəʊstwɔ:(r)/ *a.* d'après-guerre.

pot /pɒt/ *n.* pot *m.*; (*for cooking*) marmite *f.*; (*drug: sl.*) marie-jeanne *f.* ● *v.t.* (*plants*) mettre en pot. **go to ~,** (*sl.*) aller à la ruine. **~-belly** *n.* gros ventre *m.* **take ~ luck,** tenter sa chance. **take a ~-shot at,** faire un carton sur.

potato /pə'teɪtəʊ/ *n.* (*pl.* **-oes**) pomme de terre *f.*

poten|t /'pəʊtnt/ *a.* puissant; (*drink*) fort. **~cy** *n.* puissance *f.*

potential /pə'tenʃl/ *a.* & *n.* potentiel (*m.*). **~ly** *adv.* potentiellement.

pot-hol|e /'pɒthəʊl/ *n.* (*in rock*) caverne *f.*; (*in road*) nid de poule *m.* **~ing** *n.* spéléologie *f.*

potion /'pəʊʃn/ *n.* potion *f.*

potted /'pɒtɪd/ *a.* (*plant etc.*) en pot; (*preserved*) en conserve; (*abridged*) condensé.

potter[1] /'pɒtə(r)/ *n.* potier *m.* **~y** *n.* (*art*) poterie *f.*; (*objects*) poteries *f.pl.*

potter[2] /'pɒtə(r)/ *v.i.* bricoler.

potty /'pɒtɪ/ *a.* (**-ier, -iest**) (*crazy: sl.*) toqué. ● *n.* pot *m.*

pouch /paʊtʃ/ *n.* poche *f.*; (*for tobacco*) blague *f.*

pouffe /pu:f/ *n.* pouf *m.*

poultice /'pəʊltɪs/ *n.* cataplasme *m.*

poult|ry /'pəʊltrɪ/ *n.* volaille *f.* **~erer** *n.* marchand de volailles *m.*

pounce /paʊns/ *v.i.* bondir (**on,** sur). ● *n.* bond *m.*

pound[1] /paʊnd/ *n.* (*weight*) livre *f.* (= *454 g.*); (*money*) livre *f.*

pound[2] /paʊnd/ *n.* (*for dogs, cars*) fourrière *f.*

pound[3] /paʊnd/ *v.t.* (*crush*) piler; (*bombard*) pilonner. ● *v.i.* frapper fort; (*of heart*) battre fort; (*walk*) marcher à pas lourds.

pour /pɔ:(r)/ *v.t.* verser. ● *v.i.* couler, ruisseler (**from,** de); (*rain*) pleuvoir à torrents. **~ in/out,** (*people*) arriver/sortir en masse. **~ off** *or* **out,** vider. **~ing rain,** pluie torrentielle *f.*

pout /paʊt/ *v.t./i.* **~ (one's lips),** faire la moue. ● *n.* moue *f.*

poverty /'pɒvətɪ/ *n.* misère *f.*, pauvreté *f.*

powder /'paʊdə(r)/ *n.* poudre *f.* ● *v.t.* poudrer. **~ed** *a.* en poudre. **~y** *a.* poudreux. **~-room** *n.* toilettes pour dames *f. pl.*

power /'paʊə(r)/ *n.* puissance *f.*; (*ability, authority*) pouvoir *m.*; (*energy*) énergie *f.*; (*electr.*) courant *m.* **~ cut**, coupure de courant *f.* **~ed by**, fonctionnant à; (*jet etc.*) propulsé par. **~less** *a.* impuissant. **~ point**, prise de courant *f.* **~-station** *n.* centrale électrique *f.*

powerful /'paʊəfl/ *a.* puissant. **~ly** *adv.* puissamment.

practicable /'præktɪkəbl/ *a.* praticable.

practical /'præktɪkl/ *a.* pratique. **~ity** /-'kælətɪ/ *n.* sens *or* aspect pratique *m.* **~ joke**, farce *f.*

practically /'præktɪklɪ/ *adv.* pratiquement.

practice /'præktɪs/ *n.* pratique *f.*; (*of profession*) exercice *m.*; (*sport*) entraînement *m.*; (*clients*) clientèle *f.* **be in ~**, (*doctor, lawyer*) exercer. **in ~**, (*in fact*) en pratique; (*well-trained*) en forme. **out of ~**, rouillé. **put into ~**, mettre en pratique.

practis|e /'præktɪs/ *v.t./i.* (*musician, typist, etc.*) s'exercer (à); (*sport*) s'entraîner (à); (*put into practice*) pratiquer; (*profession*) exercer. **~ed** *a.* expérimenté. **~ing** *a.* (*Catholic etc.*) pratiquant.

practitioner /præk'tɪʃənə(r)/ *n.* praticien(ne) *m.* (*f.*).

pragmatic /præg'mætɪk/ *a.* pragmatique.

prairie /'preərɪ/ *n.* (*in North America*) prairie *f.*

praise /preɪz/ *v.t.* louer. ● *n.* éloge(s) *m.* (*pl.*), louange(s) *f.* (*pl.*).

praiseworthy /'preɪzwɜ:ðɪ/ *a.* digne d'éloges.

pram /præm/ *n.* voiture d'enfant *f.*, landau *m.*

prance /prɑ:ns/ *v.i.* caracoler.

prank /præŋk/ *n.* farce *f.*

prattle /'prætl/ *v.i.* jaser.

prawn /prɔ:n/ *n.* crevette rose *f.*

pray /preɪ/ *v.i.* prier.

prayer /preə(r)/ *n.* prière *f.*

pre- /pri:/ *pref.* pré-.

preach /pri:tʃ/ *v.t./i.* prêcher. **~ at** *or* **to**, prêcher. **~er** *n.* prédicateur *m.*

preamble /pri:'æmbl/ *n.* préambule *m.*

pre-arrange /pri:ə'reɪndʒ/ *v.t.* fixer à l'avance.

precarious /prɪ'keərɪəs/ *a.* précaire.

precaution /prɪ'kɔ:ʃn/ *n.* précaution *f.* **~ary** *a.* de précaution.

preced|e /prɪ'si:d/ *v.t.* précéder. **~ing** *a.* précédent.

precedence /'presɪdəns/ *n.* priorité *f.*; (*in rank*) préséance *f.*

precedent /'presɪdənt/ *n.* précédent *m.*

precept /'pri:sept/ *n.* précepte *m.*

precinct /'pri:sɪŋkt/ *n.* enceinte *f.*; (*pedestrian area*) zone *f.*; (*district: Amer.*) circonscription *f.*

precious /'preʃəs/ *a.* précieux. ● *adv.* (*very: fam.*) très.

precipice /'presɪpɪs/ *n.* (*geog.*) à-pic *m. invar.*; (*fig.*) précipice *m.*

precipitat|e /prɪ'sɪpɪteɪt/ *v.t.* (*person, event, chemical*) précipiter. ● *a.* /-ɪtət/ précipité. **~ion** /-'teɪʃn/ *n.* précipitation *f.*

précis /'preɪsi:/ *n. invar.* précis *m.*

precis|e /prɪ'saɪs/ *a.* précis; (*careful*) méticuleux. **~ely** *adv.* précisément. **~ion** /-'sɪʒn/ *n.* précision *f.*

preclude /prɪ'klu:d/ *v.t.* (*prevent*) empêcher; (*rule out*) exclure.

precocious /prɪ'kəʊʃəs/ *a.* précoce.

preconc|eived /pri:kən'si:vd/ *a.* préconçu. **~eption** *n.* préconception *f.*

pre-condition /pri:kən'dɪʃn/ *n.* condition requise *f.*

predator /'predətə(r)/ *n.* prédateur *m.* **~y** *a.* rapace.

predecessor /'pri:dɪsesə(r)/ *n.* prédécesseur *m.*

predicament /prɪ'dɪkəmənt/ *n.* mauvaise situation *or* passe *f.*

predict /prɪ'dɪkt/ *v.t.* prédire. **~able** *a.* prévisible. **~ion** /-kʃn/ *n.* prédiction *f.*

predispose /pri:dɪ'spəʊz/ *v.t.* prédisposer (**to do**, à faire).

predominant /prɪ'dɒmɪnənt/ *a.* prédominant. **~ly** *adv.* pour la plupart.

predominate /prɪ'dɒmɪneɪt/ *v.i.* prédominer.

pre-eminent /pri:'emɪnənt/ *a.* prééminent.

pre-empt /pri:'empt/ *v.t.* (*buy*) acquérir d'avance; (*stop*) prévenir. **~ive** *a.* preventif.

preen /pri:n/ *v.t.* (*bird*) lisser. **~ o.s.**, (*person*) se bichonner.

prefab /'pri:fæb/ *n.* (*fam.*) bâtiment préfabriqué *m.* **~ricated** /-'fæbrɪkeɪtɪd/ *a.* préfabriqué.

preface /'prefɪs/ *n.* préface *f.*

prefect /'pri:fekt/ *n.* (*pupil*) élève chargé(e) de la discipline *m.(f.)*; (*official*) préfet *m.*

prefer /prɪ'fɜ:(r)/ *v.t.* (*p.t.* **preferred**) préférer (**to do,** faire). **~able** /'prefrəbl/ *a.* préférable. **~ably** *adv.* de préférence.

preferen|ce /'prefrəns/ *n.* préférence *f.* **~tial** /-ə'renʃl/ *a.* préférentiel.

prefix /'pri:fɪks/ *n.* préfixe *m.*

pregnan|t /'pregnənt/ *a.* (*woman*) enceinte; (*animal*) pleine. **~cy** *n.* (*of woman*) grossesse *f.*

prehistoric /pri:hɪ'stɒrɪk/ *a.* préhistorique.

prejudge /pri:'dʒʌdʒ/ *v.t.* préjuger de; (*person*) juger d'avance.

prejudice /'predʒʊdɪs/ *n.* préjugé(s) *m.* (*pl.*); (*harm*) préjudice *m.* ● *v.t.* (*claim*) porter préjudice à; (*person*) prévenir. **~d** *a.* partial; (*person*) qui a des préjugés.

preliminar|y /prɪ'lɪmɪnərɪ/ *a.* préliminaire. **~ies** *n. pl.* préliminaires *m. pl.*

prelude /'prelju:d/ *n.* prélude *m.*

pre-marital /pri:'mærɪtl/ *a.* avant le mariage.

premature /'premətjʊə(r)/ *a.* prématuré.

premeditated /pri:'medɪteɪtɪd/ *a.* prémédité.

premier /'premɪə(r)/ *a.* premier. ● *n.* premier ministre *m.*

première /'premɪeə(r)/ *n.* première *f.*

premises /'premɪsɪz/ *n. pl.* locaux *m. pl.* **on the ~,** sur les lieux.

premiss /'premɪs/ *n.* prémisse *f.*

premium /'pri:mɪəm/ *n.* prime *f.* **be at a ~,** faire prime.

premonition /pri:mə'nɪʃn/ *n.* prémonition *f.*, pressentiment *m.*

preoccup|ation /pri:ɒkjʊ'peɪʃn/ *n.* préoccupation *f.* **~ied** /-'ɒkjʊpaɪd/ *a.* préoccupé.

prep /prep/ *n.* (*work*) devoirs *m.pl.* **~ school = preparatory school**.

preparation /prepə'reɪʃn/ *n.* préparation *f.* **~s,** préparatifs *m. pl.*

preparatory /prɪ'pærətrɪ/ *a.* préparatoire. **~ school,** école primaire privée *f.*; (*Amer.*) école secondaire privée *f.*

prepare /prɪ'peə(r)/ *v.t./i.* (se) préparer (**for,** à). **be ~d for,** (*expect*) s'attendre à **~d to,** prêt à.

prepay /pri:'peɪ/ *v.t.* (*p.t.* **-paid**) payer d'avance.

preponderance /prɪ'pɒndərəns/ *n.* prédominance *f.*

preposition /prepə'zɪʃn/ *n.* préposition *f.*

preposterous /prɪ'pɒstərəs/ *a.* absurde, ridicule.

prerequisite /pri:'rekwɪzɪt/ *n.* condition préalable *f.*

prerogative /prɪ'rɒgətɪv/ *n.* prérogative *f.*

Presbyterian /prezbɪ'tɪərɪən/ *a.* & *n.* presbytérien(ne) (*m.* (*f.*)).

prescri|be /prɪ'skraɪb/ *v.t.* prescrire. **~ption** /-ɪpʃn/ *n.* prescription *f.*; (*med.*) ordonnance *f.*

presence /'prezns/ *n.* présence *f.* **~ of mind,** présence d'esprit *f.*

present[1] /'preznt/ *a.* présent. ● *n.* présent *m.* **at ~,** à présent. **for the ~,** pour le moment. **~-day** *a.* actuel.

present[2] /'preznt/ *n.* (*gift*) cadeau *m.*

present[3] /prɪ'zent/ *v.t.* présenter; (*film, concert, etc.*) donner. **~ s.o. with,** offrir à qn. **~able** *a.* présentable. **~ation** /prezn'teɪʃn/ *n.* présentation *f.* **~er** *n.* présenta|teur, -trice *m., f.*

presently /'prezntlɪ/ *adv.* bientôt; (*now*: *Amer.*) en ce moment.

preservative /prɪ'zɜ:vətɪv/ *n.* (*culin.*) agent de conservation *m.*

preserv|e /prɪ'zɜ:v/ *v.t.* préserver; (*maintain & culin.*) conserver. ● *n.* réserve *f.*; (*fig.*) domaine *m.*; (*jam*) confiture *f.* **~ation** /prezə'veɪʃn/ *n.* conservation *f.*

preside /prɪ'zaɪd/ *v.i.* présider. **~ over,** présider.

presiden|t /'prezɪdənt/ *n.* président(e) *m.* (*f.*). **~cy** *n.* présidence *f.* **~tial** /-'denʃl/ *a.* présidentiel.

press /pres/ *v.t./i.* (*button etc.*) appuyer (sur); (*squeeze*) presser; (*iron*) repasser; (*pursue*) poursuivre. ● *n.* (*newspapers, machine*) presse *f.*; (*for wine*) pressoir *m.* **be ~ed for,** (*time etc.*) manquer de. **~ for sth.,** faire pression pour avoir qch. **~ s.o. to do sth.,** pousser qn. à faire qch. **~ conference/cutting,** conférence/coupure de presse *f.* **~ on,** continuer (**with sth.,** qch.). **~ release,** communiqué de presse *m.* **~-stud** *n.* bouton-pression *m.* **~-up** *n.* traction *f.*

pressing /'presɪŋ/ *a.* pressant.

pressure /'preʃə(r)/ *n.* pression *f.* ● *v.t.* faire pression sur. **~-cooker**

n. cocotte-minute *f.* **~ group,** groupe de pression *m.*

pressurize /ˈpreʃəraɪz/ *v.t.* (*cabin etc.*) pressuriser; (*person*) faire pression sur.

prestige /preˈsti:ʒ/ *n.* prestige *m.*

prestigious /preˈstɪdʒəs/ *a.* prestigieux.

presumably /prɪˈzju:məblɪ/ *adv.* vraisemblablement.

presum|e /prɪˈzju:m/ *v.t.* (*suppose*) présumer. **~e to,** (*venture*) se permettre de. **~ption** /-ˈzʌmpʃn/ *n.* présomption *f.*

presumptuous /prɪˈzʌmptʃʊəs/ *a.* présomptueux.

pretence, (*Amer.*) **pretense** /prɪˈtens/ *n.* feinte *f.*, simulation *f.*; (*claim*) prétention *f.*; (*pretext*) prétexte *m.*

pretend /prɪˈtend/ *v.t./i.* faire semblant (**to do,** de faire). **~ to,** (*lay claim to*) prétendre à.

pretentious /prɪˈtenʃəs/ *a.* prétentieux.

pretext /ˈpri:tekst/ *n.* prétexte *m.*

pretty /ˈprɪtɪ/ *a.* (**-ier, -iest**) joli. ● *adv.* assez. **~ much,** presque.

prevail /prɪˈveɪl/ *v.i.* prédominer; (*win*) prévaloir. **~ on,** persuader (**to do,** de faire). **~ing** *a.* actuel; (*wind*) dominant.

prevalen|t /ˈprevələnt/ *a.* répandu. **~ce** *n.* fréquence *f.*

prevent /prɪˈvent/ *v.t.* empêcher (**from doing,** de faire). **~able** *a.* évitable. **~ion** /-enʃn/ *n.* prévention *f.* **~ive** *a.* préventif.

preview /ˈpri:vju:/ *n.* avant-première *f.*; (*fig.*) aperçu *m.*

previous /ˈpri:vɪəs/ *a.* précédent, antérieur. **~ to,** avant. **~ly** *adv.* précédemment, auparavant.

pre-war /ˈpri:wɔ:(r)/ *a.* d'avant-guerre.

prey /preɪ/ *n.* proie *f.* ● *v.i.* **~ on,** faire sa proie de; (*worry*) préoccuper. **bird of ~,** rapace *m.*

price /praɪs/ *n.* prix *m.* ● *v.t.* fixer le prix de. **~less** *a.* inestimable; (*amusing*: *sl.*) impayable.

pricey /ˈpraɪsɪ/ *a.* (*fam.*) coûteux.

prick /prɪk/ *v.t.* (*with pin etc.*) piquer. ● *n.* piqûre *f.* **~ up one's ears,** dresser l'oreille.

prickl|e /ˈprɪkl/ *n.* piquant *m.*; (*sensation*) picotement *m.* **~y** *a.* piquant; (*person*) irritable.

pride /praɪd/ *n.* orgueil *m.*; (*satisfaction*) fierté *f.* ● *v. pr.* **~ o.s. on,** s'enorgueillir de. **~ of place,** place d'honneur *f.*

priest /pri:st/ *n.* prêtre *m.* **~hood** *n.* sacerdoce *m.* **~ly** *a.* sacerdotal.

prig /prɪg/ *n.* petit saint *m.*, pharisien(ne) *m.* (*f.*). **~gish** *a.* hypocrite.

prim /prɪm/ *a.* (**primmer, primmest**) guindé, méticuleux.

primar|y /ˈpraɪmərɪ/ *a.* (*school, elections, etc.*) primaire; (*chief, basic*) premier, fondamental. ● *n.* (*pol.*: *Amer.*) primaire *m.* **~ily** *Amer.* /-ˈmerılɪ/ *adv.* essentiellement.

prime[1] /praɪm/ *a.* principal, premier; (*first-rate*) excellent. **P~ Minister,** Premier Ministre *m.* **the ~ of life,** la force de l'âge.

prime[2] /praɪm/ *v.t.* (*pump, gun*) amorcer; (*surface*) apprêter. **~r**[1] /-ə(r)/ *n.* (*paint etc.*) apprêt *m.*

primer[2] /ˈpraɪmə(r)/ *n.* (*school-book*) premier livre *m.*

primeval /praɪˈmi:vl/ *a.* primitif.

primitive /ˈprɪmɪtɪv/ *a.* primitif.

primrose /ˈprɪmrəʊz/ *n.* primevère (jaune) *f.*

prince /prɪns/ *n.* prince *m.* **~ly** *a.* princier.

princess /prɪnˈses/ *n.* princesse *f.*

principal /ˈprɪnsəpl/ *a.* principal. ● *n.* (*of school etc.*) direc|teur, -trice *m.*, *f.* **~ly** *adv.* principalement.

principle /ˈprɪnsəpl/ *n.* principe *m.* **in/on ~,** en/par principe.

print /prɪnt/ *v.t.* imprimer; (*write in capitals*) écrire en majuscules. ● *n.* (*of foot etc.*) empreinte *f.*; (*letters*) caractères *m. pl.*; (*photograph*) épreuve *f.*; (*engraving*) gravure *f.* **in ~,** disponible. **out of ~,** épuisé. **~-out** *n.* listage *m.* **~ed matter,** imprimés *m. pl.*

print|er /ˈprɪntə(r)/ *n.* (*person*) imprimeur *m.*; (*comput.*) imprimante *f.* **~ing** *n.* impression *f.*

prior[1] /ˈpraɪə(r)/ *a.* précédent. **~ to,** *prep.* avant (de).

prior[2] /ˈpraɪə(r)/ *n.* (*relig.*) prieur *m.* **~y** *n.* prieuré *m.*

priority /praɪˈɒrətɪ/ *n.* priorité *f.* **take ~,** avoir la priorité (**over,** sur).

prise /praɪz/ *v.t.* forcer. **~ open,** ouvrir en forçant.

prism /ˈprɪzəm/ *n.* prisme *m.*

prison /ˈprɪzn/ *n.* prison *f.* **~er** *n.* prisonn|ier, -ière *m.*, *f.* **~ officer,** gardien(ne) de prison *m.* (*f.*).

pristine /'prɪsti:n/ *a.* primitif; (*condition*) parfait.

privacy /'prɪvəsɪ/ *n.* intimité *f.*, solitude *f.*

private /'praɪvɪt/ *a.* privé; (*confidential*) personnel; (*lessons, house, etc.*) particulier; (*ceremony*) intime. ● *n.* (*soldier*) simple soldat *m.* **in ~,** en privé; (*of ceremony*) dans l'intimité. **~ly** *adv.* en privé; dans l'intimité; (*inwardly*) intérieurement.

privation /praɪ'veɪʃn/ *n.* privation *f.*

privet /'prɪvɪt/ *n.* (*bot.*) troène *m.*

privilege /'prɪvəlɪdʒ/ *n.* privilège *m.* **~d** *a.* privilégié. **be ~d to,** avoir le privilège de.

privy /'prɪvɪ/ *a.* **~ to,** au fait de.

prize /praɪz/ *n.* prix *m.* ● *a.* (*entry etc.*) primé; (*fool etc.*) parfait. ● *v.t.* (*value*) priser. **~-fighter** *n.* boxeur professionnel *m.* **~-winner** *n.* lauréat(e) *m.* (*f.*); (*in lottery etc.*) gagnant(e) *m.* (*f.*).

pro /prəʊ/ *n.* **the ~s and cons,** le pour et le contre.

pro- /prəʊ/ *pref.* pro-.

probab|le /'prɒbəbl/ *a.* probable. **~ility** /-'bɪlətɪ/ *n.* probabilité *f.* **~ly** *adv.* probablement.

probation /prə'beɪʃn/ *n.* (*testing*) essai *m.*; (*jurid.*) liberté surveillée *f.* **~ary** *a.* d'essai.

probe /prəʊb/ *n.* (*device*) sonde *f.*; (*fig.*) enquête *f.* ● *v.t.* sonder. ● *v.i.* **~ into,** sonder.

problem /'prɒbləm/ *n.* problème *m.* ● *a.* difficile. **~atic** /-'mætɪk/ *a.* problématique.

procedure /prə'si:dʒə(r)/ *n.* procédure *f.*; (*way of doing sth.*) démarche à suivre *f.*

proceed /prə'si:d/ *v.i.* (*go*) aller, avancer; (*pass*) passer (**to,** à); (*act*) procéder. **~ (with),** (*continue*) continuer. **~ to do,** se mettre à faire. **~ing** *n.* procédé *m.*

proceedings /prə'si:dɪŋz/ *n. pl.* (*discussions*) débats *m. pl.*; (*meeting*) réunion *f.*; (*report*) actes *m. pl.*; (*jurid.*) poursuites *f. pl.*

proceeds /'prəʊsi:dz/ *n. pl.* (*profits*) produit *m.*, bénéfices *m. pl.*

process /'prəʊses/ *n.* processus *m.*; (*method*) procédé *m.* ● *v.t.* (*material, data*) traiter. **in ~,** en cours. **in the ~ of doing,** en train de faire.

procession /prə'seʃn/ *n.* défilé *m.*

procl|aim /prə'kleɪm/ *v.t.* proclamer. **~amation** /prɒklə'meɪʃn/ *n.* proclamation *f.*

procrastinate /prə'kræstɪneɪt/ *v.i.* différer, tergiverser.

procreation /prəʊkrɪ'eɪʃn/ *n.* procréation *f.*

procure /prə'kjʊə(r)/ *v.t.* obtenir.

prod /prɒd/ *v.t./i.* (*p.t.* **prodded**) pousser. ● *n.* poussée *f.*, coup *m.*

prodigal /'prɒdɪgl/ *a.* prodigue.

prodigious /prə'dɪdʒəs/ *a.* prodigieux.

prodigy /'prɒdɪdʒɪ/ *n.* prodige *m.*

produc|e[1] /prə'dju:s/ *v.t./i.* produire; (*bring out*) sortir; (*show*) présenter; (*cause*) provoquer; (*theatre, TV*) mettre en scène; (*radio*) réaliser; (*cinema*) produire. **~er** *n.* metteur en scène *m.*; réalisateur *m.*; producteur *m.* **~tion** /-'dʌkʃn/ *n.* production *f.*; mise en scène *f.*; réalisation *f.*

produce[2] /'prɒdju:s/ *n.* (*food etc.*) produits *m. pl.*

product /'prɒdʌkt/ *n.* produit *m.*

productiv|e /prə'dʌktɪv/ *a.* productif. **~ity** /prɒdʌk'tɪvətɪ/ *n.* productivité *f.*

profan|e /prə'feɪn/ *a.* sacrilège; (*secular*) profane. **~ity** /-'fænətɪ/ *n.* (*oath*) juron *m.*

profess /prə'fes/ *v.t.* professer. **~ to do,** prétendre faire.

profession /prə'feʃn/ *n.* profession *f.* **~al** *a.* professionnel; (*of high quality*) de professionnel; (*person*) qui exerce une profession libérale; *n.* professionnel(le) *m.* (*f.*).

professor /prə'fesə(r)/ *n.* professeur (titulaire d'une chaire) *m.*

proficien|t /prə'fɪʃnt/ *a.* compétent. **~cy** *n.* compétence *f.*

profile /'prəʊfaɪl/ *n.* profil *m.*

profit /'prɒfɪt/ *n.* profit *m.*, bénéfice *m.* ● *v.i.* (*p.t.* **profited**). **~ by,** tirer profit de. **~able** *a.* rentable.

profound /prə'faʊnd/ *a.* profond. **~ly** *adv.* profondément.

profus|e /prə'fju:s/ *a.* abondant. **~e in,** (*lavish in*) prodigue de. **~ely** *adv.* en abondance; (*apologize*) avec effusion. **~ion** /-ʒn/ *n.* profusion *f.*

progeny /'prɒdʒənɪ/ *n.* progéniture *f.*

program /'prəʊgræm/ *n.* (*Amer.*) = **programme. (computer) ~,** programme *m.* ● *v.t.* (*p.t.* **programmed**) programmer. **~mer** *n.* programmeu|r, -se *m., f.* **~ming** *n.* (*on computer*) programmation *f.*

programme /'prəʊgræm/ *n.* programme *m.*; (*broadcast*) émission *f.*

progress[1] /'prəʊgres/ *n.* progrès *m.* (*pl.*). **in ~,** en cours. **make ~,** faire des progrès. **~ report,** compte-rendu *m.*

progress[2] /prə'gres/ *v.i.* (*advance, improve*) progresser. **~ion** /-ʃn/ *n.* progression *f.*

progressive /prə'gresɪv/ *a.* progressif; (*reforming*) progressiste. **~ly** *adv.* progressivement.

prohibit /prə'hɪbɪt/ *v.t.* interdire (**s.o. from doing,** à qn. de faire).

prohibitive /prə'hɪbətɪv/ *a.* (*price etc.*) prohibitif.

project[1] /prə'dʒekt/ *v.t.* projeter. ● *v.i.* (*jut out*) être en saillie. **~ion** /-kʃn/ *n.* projection *f.*; saillie *f.*

project[2] /'prɒdʒekt/ *n.* (*plan*) projet *m.*; (*undertaking*) entreprise *f.*; (*schol.*) dossier *m.*

projectile /prə'dʒektaɪl/ *n.* projectile *m.*

projector /prə'dʒektə(r)/ *n.* (*cinema etc.*) projecteur *m.*

proletari|at /prəʊlɪ'teərɪət/ *n.* prolétariat *m.* **~an** *a.* prolétarien; *n.* prolétaire *m./f.*

proliferat|e /prə'lɪfəreɪt/ *v.i.* proliférer. **~ion** /-'reɪʃn/ *n.* prolifération *f.*

prolific /prə'lɪfɪk/ *a.* prolifique.

prologue /'prəʊlɒg/ *n.* prologue *m.*

prolong /prə'lɒŋ/ *v.t.* prolonger.

promenade /prɒmə'nɑ:d/ *n.* promenade *f.* ● *v.t./i.* (se) promener.

prominen|t /'prɒmɪnənt/ *a.* (*projecting*) proéminent; (*conspicuous*) bien en vue; (*fig.*) important. **~ce** *n.* proéminence *f.*; importance *f.* **~tly** *adv.* bien en vue.

promiscu|ous /prə'mɪskjʊəs/ *a.* qui a plusieurs partenaires; (*pej.*) de mœurs faciles. **~ity** /prɒmɪ'skju:ətɪ/ *n.* les partenaires multiples; (*pej.*) liberté de mœurs *f.*

promis|e /'prɒmɪs/ *n.* promesse *f.* ● *v.t./i.* promettre. **~ing** *a.* prometteur; (*person*) qui promet.

promot|e /prə'məʊt/ *v.t.* promouvoir; (*advertise*) faire la promotion de. **~ion** /-'məʊʃn/ *n.* (*of person, sales, etc.*) promotion *f.*

prompt /prɒmpt/ *a.* rapide; (*punctual*) à l'heure, ponctuel. ● *adv.* (*on the dot*) pile. ● *v.t.* inciter; (*cause*) provoquer; (*theatre*) souffler (son rôle) à. **~er** *n.* souffleu|r, -se *m., f.* **~ly** *adv.* rapidement; ponctuellement. **~ness** *n.* rapidité *f.*

prone /prəʊn/ *a.* couché sur le ventre. **~ to,** prédisposé à.

prong /prɒŋ/ *n.* (*of fork*) dent *f.*

pronoun /'prəʊnaʊn/ *n.* pronom *m.*

pron|ounce /prə'naʊns/ *v.t.* prononcer. **~ouncement** *n.* déclaration *f.* **~unciation** /-ʌnsɪ'eɪʃn/ *n.* prononciation *f.*

pronounced /prə'naʊnst/ *a.* (*noticeable*) prononcé.

proof /pru:f/ *n.* (*evidence*) preuve *f.*; (*test, trial copy*) épreuve *f.*; (*of liquor*) teneur en alcool *f.* ● *a.* **~ against,** à l'épreuve de.

prop[1] /prɒp/ *n.* support *m.* ● *v.t.* (*p.t.* **propped**). **~ (up),** (*support*) étayer; (*lean*) appuyer.

prop[2] /prɒp/ *n.* (*theatre, fam.*) accessoire *m.*

propaganda /prɒpə'gændə/ *n.* propagande *f.*

propagat|e /'prɒpəgeɪt/ *v.t./i.* (se) propager. **~ion** /-'geɪʃn/ *n.* propagation *f.*

propane /'prəʊpeɪn/ *n.* propane *m.*

propel /prə'pel/ *v.t.* (*p.t.* **propelled**) propulser. **~ling pencil,** porte-mine *m. invar.*

propeller /prə'pelə(r)/ *n.* hélice *f.*

proper /'prɒpə(r)/ *a.* correct, bon; (*seemly*) convenable; (*real*) vrai; (*thorough*: *fam.*) parfait. **~ noun,** nom propre *m.* **~ly** *adv.* correctement, comme il faut; (*rightly*) avec raison.

property /'prɒpətɪ/ *n.* propriété *f.*; (*things owned*) biens *m. pl.*, propriété *f.* ● *a.* immobilier, foncier.

prophecy /'prɒfəsɪ/ *n.* prophétie *f.*

prophesy /'prɒfɪsaɪ/ *v.t./i.* prophétiser. **~ that,** prédire que.

prophet /'prɒfɪt/ *n.* prophète *m.* **~ic** /prə'fetɪk/ *a.* prophétique.

proportion /prə'pɔ:ʃn/ *n.* (*ratio, dimension*) proportion *f.*; (*amount*) partie *f.* **~al, ~ate** *adjs.* proportionnel.

proposal /prə'pəʊzl/ *n.* proposition *f.*; (*of marriage*) demande en mariage *f.*

propos|e /prə'pəʊz/ *v.t.* proposer. ● *v.i.* **~e to,** faire une demande en mariage à. **~e to do,** se proposer de faire. **~ition** /prɒpə'zɪʃn/ *n.* proposition *f.*; (*matter*: *fam.*) affaire *f.*; *v.t.* (*fam.*) faire des propositions malhonnêtes à.

propound /prə'paʊnd/ *v.t.* (*theory etc.*) proposer.

proprietor /prə'praɪətə(r)/ *n.* propriétaire *m./f.*

propriety /prə'praɪətɪ/ *n.* (*correct behaviour*) bienséance *f.*

propulsion /prə'pʌlʃn/ *n.* propulsion *f.*

prosaic /prə'zeɪɪk/ *a.* prosaïque.

proscribe /prə'skraɪb/ *v.t.* proscrire.

prose /prəʊz/ *n.* prose *f.*; (*translation*) thème *m.*

prosecut|e /'prɒsɪkju:t/ *v.t.* poursuivre. **~ion** /-'kju:ʃn/ *n.* poursuites *f. pl.* **~or** *n.* procureur *m.*

prospect[1] /'prɒspekt/ *n.* perspective *f.*; (*chance*) espoir *m.* **a job with ~s,** un travail avec des perspectives d'avenir.

prospect[2] /prə'spekt/ *v.t./i.* prospecter. **~or** *n.* prospecteur *m.*

prospective /prə'spektɪv/ *a.* (*future*) futur; (*possible*) éventuel.

prospectus /prə'spektəs/ *n.* prospectus *m.*; (*univ.*) guide *m.*

prosper /'prɒspə(r)/ *v.i.* prospérer.

prosper|ous /'prɒspərəs/ *a.* prospère. **~ity** /-'sperətɪ/ *n.* prospérité *f.*

prostate /'prɒsteɪt/ *n.* prostate *f.*

prostitut|e /'prɒstɪtju:t/ *n.* prostituée *f.* **~ion** /-'tju:ʃn/ *n.* prostitution *f.*

prostrate /'prɒstreɪt/ *a.* (*prone*) à plat ventre; (*submissive*) prosterné; (*exhausted*) prostré.

protagonist /prə'tægənɪst/ *n.* protagoniste *m.*

protect /prə'tekt/ *v.t.* protéger. **~ion** /-kʃn/ *n.* protection *f.* **~or** *n.* protec|teur, -trice *m., f.*

protective /prə'tektɪv/ *a.* protecteur; (*clothes*) de protection.

protégé /'prɒtɪʒeɪ/ *n.* protégé *m.* **~e** *n.* protégée *f.*

protein /'prəʊti:n/ *n.* protéine *f.*

protest[1] /'prəʊtest/ *n.* protestation *f.* **under ~,** en protestant.

protest[2] /prə'test/ *v.t./i.* protester. **~er** *n.* (*pol.*) manifestant(e) *m.* (*f.*).

Protestant /'prɒtɪstənt/ *a.* & *n.* protestant(e) (*m.* (*f.*)).

protocol /'prəʊtəkɒl/ *n.* protocole *m.*

prototype /'prəʊtətaɪp/ *n.* prototype *m.*

protract /prə'trækt/ *v.t.* prolonger, faire traîner. **~ed** *a.* prolongé.

protractor /prə'træktə(r)/ *n.* (*for measuring*) rapporteur *m.*

protrude /prə'tru:d/ *v.i.* dépasser.

proud /praʊd/ *a.* (**-er, -est**) fier, orgueilleux. **~ly** *adv.* fièrement.

prove /pru:v/ *v.t.* prouver. ● *v.i.* **~ (to be) easy/*etc.*,** se révéler facile/*etc.* **~ o.s.,** faire ses preuves. **~n** *a.* prouvé.

proverb /'prɒvɜ:b/ *n.* proverbe *m.* **~ial** /prə'vɜ:bɪəl/ *a.* proverbial.

provide /prə'vaɪd/ *v.t.* fournir (**s.o. with sth.,** qch. à qn.). ● *v.i.* **~ for,** (*allow for*) prévoir; (*guard against*) parer à; (*person*) pourvoir aux besoins de.

provided /prə'vaɪdɪd/ *conj.* **~ that,** à condition que.

providence /'prɒvɪdəns/ *n.* providence *f.*

providing /prə'vaɪdɪŋ/ *conj.* = **provided.**

provinc|e /'prɒvɪns/ *n.* province *f.*; (*fig.*) compétence *f.* **~ial** /prə'vɪnʃl/ *a.* & *n.* provincial(e) (*m.* (*f.*)).

provision /prə'vɪʒn/ *n.* (*stock*) provision *f.*; (*supplying*) fourniture *f.*; (*stipulation*) disposition *f.* **~s,** (*food*) provisions *f. pl.*

provisional /prə'vɪʒənl/ *a.* provisoire. **~ly** *adv.* provisoirement.

proviso /prə'vaɪzəʊ/ *n.* (*pl.* **-os**) condition *f.*, stipulation *f.*

provo|ke /prə'vəʊk/ *v.t.* provoquer. **~cation** /prɒvə'keɪʃn/ *n.* provocation *f.* **~cative** /-'vɒkətɪv/ *a.* provocant.

prow /praʊ/ *n.* proue *f.*

prowess /'praʊɪs/ *n.* prouesse *f.*

prowl /praʊl/ *v.i.* rôder. ● *n.* **be on the ~,** rôder. **~er** *n.* rôdeu|r, -se *m., f.*

proximity /prɒk'sɪmətɪ/ *n.* proximité *f.*

proxy /'prɒksɪ/ *n.* **by ~,** par procuration.

prud|e /pru:d/ *n.* prude *f.* **~ish** *a.* prude.

pruden|t /'pru:dnt/ *a.* prudent. **~ce** *n.* prudence *f.* **~tly** *adv.* prudemment.

prune[1] /pru:n/ *n.* pruneau *m.*

prune[2] /pru:n/ *v.t.* (*cut*) tailler.

pry[1] /praɪ/ *v.i.* être indiscret. **~ into,** fourrer son nez dans.

pry[2] /praɪ/ *v.t.* (*Amer.*) = **prise.**

psalm /sɑ:m/ *n.* psaume *m.*

pseudo- /'sju:dəʊ/ *pref.* pseudo-.

pseudonym /'sju:dənɪm/ *n.* pseudonyme *m.*

psoriasis /sə'raɪəsɪs/ *n.* psoriasis *m.*

psyche /'saɪkɪ/ *n.* psyché *f.*
psychiatr|y /saɪ'kaɪətrɪ/ *n.* psychiatrie *f.* **~ic** /-ɪ'ætrɪk/ *a.* psychiatrique. **~ist** *n.* psychiatre *m./f.*
psychic /'saɪkɪk/ *a.* (*phenomenon etc.*) métapsychique; (*person*) doué de télépathie.
psychoanalys|e /saɪkəʊ'ænəlaɪz/ *v.t.* psychanalyser. **~t** /-ɪst/ *n.* psychanalyste *m./f.*
psychoanalysis /saɪkəʊə'næləsɪs/ *n.* psychanalyse *f.*
psycholog|y /saɪ'kɒlədʒɪ/ *n.* psychologie *f.* **~ical** /-ə'lɒdʒɪkl/ *a.* psychologique. **~ist** *n.* psychologue *m./f.*
psychopath /'saɪkəʊpæθ/ *n.* psychopathe *m./f.*
psychosomatic /saɪkəʊsə'mætɪk/ *a.* psychosomatique.
psychotherap|y /saɪkəʊ'θerəpɪ/ *n.* psychothérapie *f.* **~ist** *n.* psychothérapeute *m./f.*
pub /pʌb/ *n.* pub *m.*
puberty /'pju:bətɪ/ *n.* puberté *f.*
public /'pʌblɪk/ *a.* public; (*library etc.*) municipal. **in ~,** en public. **~ address system,** sonorisation *f.* (*dans un lieu public*). **~ house,** pub *m.* **~ relations,** relations publiques *f. pl.* **~ school,** école privée *f.*; (*Amer.*) école publique *f.* **~ servant,** fonctionnaire *m./f.* **~-spirited** *a.* dévoué au bien public. **~ transport,** transports en commun *m. pl.* **~ly** *adv.* publiquement.
publican /'pʌblɪkən/ *n.* patron(ne) de pub *m.* (*f.*).
publication /pʌblɪ'keɪʃn/ *n.* publication *f.*
publicity /pʌb'lɪsətɪ/ *n.* publicité *f.*
publicize /'pʌblɪsaɪz/ *v.t.* faire connaître au public.
publish /'pʌblɪʃ/ *v.t.* publier. **~er** *n.* éditeur *m.* **~ing** *n.* édition *f.*
puck /pʌk/ *n.* (*ice hockey*) palet *m.*
pucker /'pʌkə(r)/ *v.t./i.* (se) plisser.
pudding /'pʊdɪŋ/ *n.* dessert *m.*; (*steamed*) pudding *m.* **black ~,** boudin *m.* **rice ~,** riz au lait *m.*
puddle /'pʌdl/ *n.* flaque d'eau *f.*
pudgy /'pʌdʒɪ/ *a.* (**-ier, -iest**) dodu.
puerile /'pjʊəraɪl/ *a.* puéril.
puff /pʌf/ *n.* bouffée *f.* ● *v.t./i.* souffler. **~ at,** (*cigar*) tirer sur. **~ out,** (*swell*) (se) gonfler.
puffy /'pʌfɪ/ *a.* gonflé.
pugnacious /pʌg'neɪʃəs/ *a.* batailleur, combatif.
pug-nosed /'pʌgnəʊzd/ *a.* camus.
pull /pʊl/ *v.t./i.* tirer; (*muscle*) se froisser. ● *n.* traction *f.*; (*fig.*) attraction *f.*; (*influence*) influence *f.* **give a ~,** tirer. **~ a face,** faire une grimace. **~ one's weight,** faire sa part du travail. **~ s.o.'s leg,** faire marcher qn. **~ apart,** mettre en morceaux. **~ away,** (*auto.*) démarrer. **~ back** *or* **out,** (*withdraw*) (se) retirer. **~ down,** baisser; (*building*) démolir. **~ in,** (*enter*) entrer; (*stop*) s'arrêter. **~ off,** enlever; (*fig.*) réussir. **~ out,** (*from bag etc.*) sortir; (*extract*) arracher; (*auto.*) déboîter. **~ over,** (*auto.*) se ranger. **~ round** *or* **through,** s'en tirer. **~ o.s. together,** se ressaisir. **~ up,** remonter; (*uproot*) déraciner; (*auto.*) (s')arrêter.
pulley /'pʊlɪ/ *n.* poulie *f.*
pullover /'pʊləʊvə(r)/ *n.* pull(-over) *m.*
pulp /pʌlp/ *n.* (*of fruit*) pulpe *f.*; (*for paper*) pâte à papier *f.*
pulpit /'pʊlpɪt/ *n.* chaire *f.*
pulsate /pʌl'seɪt/ *v.i.* battre.
pulse /pʌls/ *n.* (*med.*) pouls *m.*
pulverize /'pʌlvəraɪz/ *v.t.* (*grind, defeat*) pulvériser.
pummel /'pʌml/ *v.t.* (*p.t.* **pummelled**) bourrer de coups.
pump[1] /pʌmp/ *n.* pompe *f.* ● *v.t./i.* pomper; (*person*) soutirer des renseignements à. **~ up,** gonfler.
pump[2] /pʌmp/ *n.* (*plimsoll*) tennis *m.*; (*for dancing*) escarpin *m.*
pumpkin /'pʌmpkɪn/ *n.* potiron *m.*
pun /pʌn/ *n.* jeu de mots *m.*
punch[1] /pʌntʃ/ *v.t.* donner un coup de poing à; (*perforate*) poinçonner; (*a hole*) faire. ● *n.* coup de poing *m.*; (*vigour: sl.*) punch *m.*; (*device*) poinçonneuse *f.* **~-drunk** *a.* sonné. **~-line,** chute *f.* **~-up** *n.* (*fam.*) bagarre *f.*
punch[2] /pʌntʃ/ *n.* (*drink*) punch *m.*
punctual /'pʌŋktʃʊəl/ *a.* à l'heure; (*habitually*) ponctuel. **~ity** /-'ælətɪ/ *n.* ponctualité *f.* **~ly** *adv.* à l'heure; ponctuellement.
punctuat|e /'pʌŋktʃʊeɪt/ *v.t.* ponctuer. **~ion** /-'eɪʃn/ *n.* ponctuation *f.*
puncture /'pʌŋktʃə(r)/ *n.* (*in tyre*) crevaison *f.* ● *v.t./i.* crever.
pundit /'pʌndɪt/ *n.* expert *m.*
pungent /'pʌndʒənt/ *a.* âcre.

punish /'pʌnɪʃ/ *v.t.* punir (**for sth.,** de qch.). **~able** *a.* punissable (**by,** de). **~ment** *n.* punition *f.*
punitive /'pju:nɪtɪv/ *a.* punitif.
punk /pʌŋk/ *n.* (*music, fan*) punk *m.*; (*person: Amer., fam.*) salaud *m.*
punt[1] /pʌnt/ *n.* (*boat*) bachot *m.*
punt[2] /pʌnt/ *v.i.* (*bet*) parier.
puny /'pju:nɪ/ *a.* (**-ier, -iest**) chétif.
pup(py) /'pʌp(ɪ)/ *n.* chiot *m.*
pupil /'pju:pl/ *n.* (*person*) élève *m./f.*; (*of eye*) pupille *f.*
puppet /'pʌpɪt/ *n.* marionnette *f.*
purchase /'pɜ:tʃəs/ *v.t.* acheter (**from s.o.,** à qn.). ● *n.* achat *m.* **~r** /-ə(r)/ *n.* acheteu|**r, -se** *m., f.*
pur|e /pjʊə(r)/ *a.* (**-er, -est**) pur. **~ely** *adv.* purement. **~ity** *n.* pureté *f.*
purgatory /'pɜ:gətrɪ/ *n.* purgatoire *m.*
purge /pɜ:dʒ/ *v.t.* purger (**of,** de). ● *n.* purge *f.*
purif|y /'pjʊərɪfaɪ/ *v.t.* purifier. **~ication** /-ɪ'keɪʃn/ *n.* purification *f.*
purist /'pjʊərɪst/ *n.* puriste *m./f.*
puritan /'pjʊərɪtən/ *n.* puritain(e) *m.* (*f.*). **~ical** /-'tænɪkl/ *a.* puritain.
purple /'pɜ:pl/ *a.* & *n.* violet (*m.*).
purport /pə'pɔ:t/ *v.t.* **~ to be,** (*claim*) prétendre être.
purpose /'pɜ:pəs/ *n.* but *m.*; (*fig.*) résolution *f.* **on ~,** exprès. **~-built** *a.* construit spécialement. **to no ~,** sans résultat.
purr /pɜ:(r)/ *n.* ronronnement *m.* ● *v.i.* ronronner.
purse /pɜ:ʃ/ *n.* porte-monnaie *m. invar.*; (*handbag: Amer.*) sac à main *m.* ● *v.t.* (*lips*) pincer.
pursue /pə'sju:/ *v.t.* poursuivre. **~r** /-ə(r)/ *n.* poursuivant(e) *m.* (*f.*).
pursuit /pə'sju:t/ *n.* poursuite *f.*; (*fig.*) activité *f.*, occupation *f.*
purveyor /pə'veɪə(r)/ *n.* fournisseur *m.*
pus /pʌs/ *n.* pus *m.*
push /pʊʃ/ *v.t./i.* pousser; (*button*) appuyer sur; (*thrust*) enfoncer; (*recommend: fam.*) proposer avec insistance. ● *n.* poussée *f.*; (*effort*) gros effort *m.*; (*drive*) dynamisme *m.* **be ~ed for,** (*time etc.*) manquer de. **be ~ing thirty**/ *etc.*, (*fam.*) friser la trentaine/*etc.* **give the ~ to,** (*sl.*) flanquer à la porte. **~ s.o. around,** bousculer qn. **~ back,** repousser. **~-chair** *n.* poussette *f.* **~er** *n.* revendeu|r, -se (de drogue) *m., f.* **~ off,** (*sl.*) filer. **~ on,** continuer. **~-over** *n.* jeu d'enfant *m.* **~ up,** (*lift*) relever; (*prices*) faire monter. **~-up** *n.* (*Amer.*) traction *f.* **~y** *a.* (*fam.*) autoritaire.
pushing /'pʊʃɪŋ/ *a.* arriviste.
puss /pʊs/ *n.* (*cat*) minet(te) *m.* (*f.*).
put /pʊt/ *v.t./i.* (*p.t.* **put,** *pres. p.* **putting**) mettre, placer, poser; (*question*) poser. **~ the damage at a million,** estimer les dégâts à un million; **I'd ~ it at a thousand,** je dirais un millier. **~ sth. tactfully,** dire qch. avec tact. **~ across,** communiquer. **~ away,** ranger; (*fig.*) enfermer. **~ back,** remettre; (*delay*) retarder. **~ by,** mettre de côté. **~ down,** (dé)poser; (*write*) inscrire; (*pay*) verser; (*suppress*) réprimer. **~ forward,** (*plan*) soumettre. **~ in,** (*insert*) introduire; (*fix*) installer; (*submit*) soumettre. **~ in for,** faire une demande de. **~ off,** (*postpone*) renvoyer à plus tard; (*disconcert*) déconcerter; (*displease*) rebuter. **~ s.o. off sth.,** dégoûter qn. de qch. **~ on,** (*clothes, radio*) mettre; (*light*) allumer; (*speed, accent, weight*) prendre. **~ out,** sortir; (*stretch*) (é)tendre; (*extinguish*) éteindre; (*disconcert*) déconcerter; (*inconvenience*) déranger. **~ up,** lever, remonter; (*building*) construire; (*notice*) mettre; (*price*) augmenter; (*guest*) héberger; (*offer*) offrir. **~-up job,** coup monté *m.* **~ up with,** supporter.
putt /pʌt/ *n.* (*golf*) putt *m.*
putter /'pʌtə(r)/ *v.i.* (*Amer.*) bricoler.
putty /'pʌtɪ/ *n.* mastic *m.*
puzzle /'pʌzl/ *n.* énigme *f.*; (*game*) casse-tête *m. invar.*; (*jigsaw*) puzzle *m.* ● *v.t.* rendre perplexe. ● *v.i.* se creuser la tête.
pygmy /'pɪgmɪ/ *n.* pygmée *m.*
pyjamas /pə'dʒɑ:məz/ *n. pl.* pyjama *m.*
pylon /'paɪlɒn/ *n.* pylône *m.*
pyramid /'pɪrəmɪd/ *n.* pyramide *f.*
Pyrenees /pɪrə'ni:z/ *n. pl.* **the ~,** les Pyrénées *f. pl.*
python /'paɪθn/ *n.* python *m.*

Q

quack[1] /kwæk/ *n.* (*of duck*) coin-coin *m. invar.*

quack[2] /kwæk/ *n.* charlatan *m.*
quad /kwɒd/ (*fam.*) = **quadrangle, quadruplet.**
quadrangle /'kwɒdræŋgl/ (*of college*) *n.* cour *f.*
quadruped /'kwɒdrʊped/ *n.* quadrupède *m.*
quadruple /kwɒ'dru:pl/ *a. & n.* quadruple (*m.*). ● *v.t./i.* quadrupler. **~ts** /-plɪts/ *n. pl.* quadruplé(e)s *m.* (*f.*) *pl.*
quagmire /'kwægmaɪə(r)/ *n.* (*bog*) bourbier *m.*
quail /kweɪl/ *n.* (*bird*) caille *f.*
quaint /kweɪnt/ *a.* (**-er, -est**) pittoresque; (*old*) vieillot; (*odd*) bizarre. **~ness** *n.* pittoresque *m.*
quake /kweɪk/ *v.i.* trembler. ● *n.* (*fam.*) tremblement de terre *m.*
Quaker /'kweɪkə(r)/ *n.* quaker(esse) *m.* (*f.*).
qualification /kwɒlɪfɪ'keɪʃn/ *n.* diplôme *m.*; (*ability*) compétence *f.*; (*fig.*) réserve *f.*, restriction *f.*
qualif|y /'kwɒlɪfaɪ/ *v.t.* qualifier; (*modify*: *fig.*) mettre des réserves à; (*statement*) nuancer. ● *v.i.* obtenir son diplôme (**as,** de); (*sport*) se qualifier; (*fig.*) remplir les conditions requises. **~ied** *a.* diplômé; (*able*) qualifié (**to do,** pour faire); (*fig.*) conditionnel; (*success*) modéré. **~ying** *a.* (*round*) éliminatoire; (*candidates*) qualifiés.
qualit|y /'kwɒlətɪ/ *n.* qualité *f.* **~ative** /-ɪtətɪv/ *a.* qualitatif.
qualm /kwɑ:m/ *n.* scrupule *m.*
quandary /'kwɒndərɪ/ *n.* embarras *m.*, dilemme *m.*
quantit|y /'kwɒntətɪ/ *n.* quantité *f.* **~ative** /-ɪtətɪv/ *a.* quantitatif.
quarantine /'kwɒrənti:n/ *n.* (*isolation*) quarantaine *f.*
quarrel /'kwɒrəl/ *n.* dispute *f.*, querelle *f.* ● *v.i.* (*p.t.* **quarrelled**) se disputer. **~some** *a.* querelleur.
quarry[1] /'kwɒrɪ/ *n.* (*prey*) proie *f.*
quarry[2] /'kwɒrɪ/ *n.* (*excavation*) carrière *f.* ● *v.t.* extraire.
quart /kwɔ:t/ *n.* (*approx.*) litre *m.*
quarter /'kwɔ:tə(r)/ *n.* quart *m.*; (*of year*) trimestre *m.*; (*25 cents*: *Amer.*) quart de dollar *m.*; (*district*) quartier *m.* **~s,** logement(s) *m.* (*pl.*) ● *v.t.* diviser en quatre; (*mil.*) cantonner. **from all ~s,** de toutes parts. **~-final** *n.* quart de finale *m.* **~ly** *a.* trimestriel; *adv.* trimestriellement.
quartermaster /'kwɔ:təmɑ:stə(r)/ *n.* (*mil.*) intendant *m.*
quartet /kwɔ:'tet/ *n.* quatuor *m.*
quartz /kwɔ:ts/ *n.* quartz *m.* ● *a.* (*watch etc.*) à quartz.
quash /kwɒʃ/ *v.t.* (*suppress*) étouffer; (*jurid.*) annuler.
quasi- /'kweɪsaɪ/ *pref.* quasi-.
quaver /'kweɪvə(r)/ *v.i.* trembler, chevroter. ● *n.* (*mus.*) croche *f.*
quay /ki:/ *n.* (*naut.*) quai *m.* **~side** *n.* (*edge of quay*) quai *m.*
queasy /'kwi:zɪ/ *a.* (*stomach*) délicat. **feel ~,** avoir mal au cœur.
queen /kwi:n/ *n.* reine *f.*; (*cards*) dame *f.* **~ mother,** reine mère *f.*
queer /kwɪə(r)/ *a.* (**-er, -est**) étrange; (*dubious*) louche; (*ill*) patraque. ● *n.* (*sl.*) homosexuel *m.*
quell /kwel/ *v.t.* réprimer.
quench /kwentʃ/ *v.t.* éteindre; (*thirst*) étancher; (*desire*) étouffer.
query /'kwɪərɪ/ *n.* question *f.* ● *v.t.* mettre en question.
quest /kwest/ *n.* recherche *f.*
question /'kwestʃən/ *n.* question *f.* ● *v.t.* interroger; (*doubt*) mettre en question, douter de. **a ~ of money,** une question d'argent. **in ~,** en question. **no ~ of,** pas question de. **out of the ~,** hors de question. **~ mark,** point d'interrogation *m.*
questionable /'kwestʃənəbl/ *a.* discutable.
questionnaire /kwestʃə'neə(r)/ *n.* questionnaire *m.*
queue /kju:/ *n.* queue *f.* ● *v.i.* (*pres. p.* **queuing**) faire la queue.
quibble /'kwɪbl/ *v.i.* ergoter.
quick /kwɪk/ *a.* (**-er, -est**) rapide. ● *adv.* vite. ● *n.* **a ~ one,** (*fam.*) un petit verre. **cut to the ~,** piquer au vif. **be ~,** (*hurry*) se dépêcher. **have a ~ temper,** s'emporter facilement. **~ly** *adv.* rapidement, vite. **~-witted** *a.* vif.
quicken /'kwɪkən/ *v.t./i.* (s')accélérer.
quicksand /'kwɪksænd/ *n.* **~(s),** sables mouvants *m. pl.*
quid /kwɪd/ *n. invar.* (*sl.*) livre *f.*
quiet /'kwaɪət/ *a.* (**-er, -est**) (*calm, still*) tranquille; (*silent*) silencieux; (*gentle*) doux; (*discreet*) discret. ● *n.* tranquillité *f.* **keep ~,** se taire. **on the ~,** en cachette. **~ly** *adv.* tranquillement; silencieusement; doucement; discrètement. **~ness** *n.* tranquillité *f.*
quieten /'kwaɪətn/ *v.t./i.* (se) calmer.

quill /kwɪl/ *n.* plume (d'oie) *f.*

quilt /kwɪlt/ *n.* édredon *m.* **(continental) ~,** couette *f.* ● *v.t.* matelasser.

quinine /'kwɪni:n, *Amer.* 'kwaɪnaɪn/ *n.* quinine *f.*

quintet /kwɪn'tet/ *n.* quintette *m.*

quintuplets /kwɪn'tju:plɪts/ *n. pl.* quintuplé(e)s *m.* (*f.*) *pl.*

quip /kwɪp/ *n.* mot piquant *m.*

quirk /kwɜ:k/ *n.* bizarrerie *f.*

quit /kwɪt/ *v.t.* (*p.t.* **quitted**) quitter. ● *v.i.* abandonner; (*resign*) démissionner. **~ doing,** (*cease: Amer.*) cesser de faire.

quite /kwaɪt/ *adv.* tout à fait, vraiment; (*rather*) assez. **~ (so)!,** parfaitement! **~ a few,** un assez grand nombre (de).

quits /kwɪts/ *a.* quitte (**with,** envers). **call it ~,** en rester là.

quiver /'kwɪvə(r)/ *v.i.* trembler.

quiz /kwɪz/ *n.* (*pl.* **quizzes**) test *m.*; (*game*) jeu-concours *m.* ● *v.t.* (*p.t.* **quizzed**) questionner.

quizzical /'kwɪzɪkl/ *a.* moqueur.

quorum /'kwɔ:rəm/ *n.* quorum *m.*

quota /'kwəʊtə/ *n.* quota *m.*

quotation /kwəʊ'teɪʃn/ *n.* citation *f.*; (*price*) devis *m.*; (*stock exchange*) cotation *f.* **~ marks,** guillemets *m. pl.*

quote /kwəʊt/ *v.t.* citer; (*reference: comm.*) rappeler; (*price*) indiquer; (*share price*) coter. ● *v.i.* **~ for,** faire un devis pour. **~ from,** citer. ● *n.* (*estimate*) devis; (*fam.*) = **quotation. in ~s,** (*fam.*) entre guillemets.

quotient /'kwəʊʃnt/ *n.* quotient *m.*

R

rabbi /'ræbaɪ/ *n.* rabbin *m.*

rabbit /'ræbɪt/ *n.* lapin *m.*

rabble /'ræbl/ *n.* (*crowd*) cohue *f.* **the ~,** (*pej.*) la populace.

rabid /'ræbɪd/ *a.* enragé.

rabies /'reɪbi:z/ *n.* (*disease*) rage *f.*

race[1] /reɪs/ *n.* course *f.* ● *v.t.* (*horse*) faire courir; (*engine*) emballer. **~ (against),** faire la course à. ● *v.i.* courir; (*rush*) foncer. **~-track** *n.* piste *f.*; (*for horses*) champ de courses *m.*

race[2] /reɪs/ *n.* (*group*) race *f.* ● *a.* racial; (*relations*) entre les races.

racecourse /'reɪskɔ:s/ *n.* champ de courses *m.*

racehorse /'reɪshɔ:s/ *n.* cheval de course *m.*

racial /'reɪʃl/ *a.* racial.

racing /'reɪsɪŋ/ *n.* courses *f. pl.* **~ car,** voiture de course *f.*

racis|t /'reɪsɪst/ *a.* & *n.* raciste (*m./f.*). **~m** /-zəm/ *n.* racisme *m.*

rack[1] /ræk/ *n.* (*shelf*) étagère *f.*; (*pigeon-holes*) casier *m.*; (*for luggage*) porte-bagages *m. invar.*; (*for dishes*) égouttoir *m.*; (*on car roof*) galerie *f.* ● *v.t.* **~ one's brains,** se creuser la cervelle.

rack[2] /ræk/ *n.* **go to ~ and ruin,** aller à la ruine; (*building*) tomber en ruine.

racket[1] /'rækɪt/ *n.* raquette *f.*

racket[2] /'rækɪt/ *n.* (*din*) tapage *m.*; (*dealings*) combine *f.*; (*crime*) racket *m.* **~eer** /-ə'tɪə(r)/ *n.* racketteur *m.*

racy /'reɪsɪ/ *a.* (**-ier, -iest**) fougueux, piquant; (*Amer.*) risqué.

radar /'reɪdɑ:(r)/ *n.* radar *m.* ● *a.* (*system etc.*) radar *invar.*

radial /'reɪdɪəl/ *a.* (*tyre*) à carcasse radiale.

radian|t /'reɪdɪənt/ *a.* rayonnant. **~ce** *n.* éclat *m.* **~tly** *adv.* avec éclat.

radiat|e /'reɪdɪeɪt/ *v.t.* dégager. ● *v.i.* rayonner (**from,** de). **~ion** /-'eɪʃn/ *n.* rayonnement *m.*; (*radioactivity*) radiation *f.*

radiator /'reɪdɪeɪtə(r)/ *n.* radiateur *m.*

radical /'rædɪkl/ *a.* radical. ● *n.* (*person: pol.*) radical(e) *m.* (*f.*).

radio /'reɪdɪəʊ/ *n.* (*pl.* **-os**) radio *f.* ● *v.t.* (*message*) envoyer par radio; (*person*) appeler par radio.

radioactiv|e /reɪdɪəʊ'æktɪv/ *a.* radioactif. **~ity** /-'tɪvətɪ/ *n.* radioactivité *f.*

radiographer /reɪdɪ'ɒgrəfə(r)/ *n.* radiologue *m./f.*

radish /'rædɪʃ/ *n.* radis *m.*

radius /'reɪdɪəs/ *n.* (*pl.* **-dii** /-dɪaɪ/) rayon *m.*

raffle /'ræfl/ *n.* tombola *f.*

raft /rɑ:ft/ *n.* radeau *m.*

rafter /'rɑ:ftə(r)/ *n.* chevron *m.*

rag[1] /ræg/ *n.* lambeau *m.*, loque *f.*; (*for wiping*) chiffon *m.*; (*newspaper*) torchon *m.* **in ~s,** (*person*) en haillons; (*clothes*) en lambeaux. **~ doll,** poupée de chiffon *f.*

rag[2] /ræg/ *v.t.* (*p.t.* **ragged**) (*tease*: *sl.*) taquiner. ● *n.* (*univ.*, *sl.*) carnaval *m.* (*pour une œuvre de charité*).

ragamuffin /ˈrægəmʌfɪn/ *n.* va-nu-pieds *m. invar.*

rage /reɪdʒ/ *n.* rage *f.*, fureur *f.* ● *v.i.* rager; (*storm, battle*) faire rage. **be all the ~,** faire fureur.

ragged /ˈrægɪd/ *a.* (*clothes, person*) loqueteux; (*edge*) déchiqueté.

raging /ˈreɪdʒɪŋ/ *a.* (*storm, fever, etc.*) violent.

raid /reɪd/ *n.* (*mil.*) raid *m.*; (*by police*) rafle *f.*; (*by criminals*) hold-up *m. invar.* ● *v.t.* faire un raid *or* une rafle *or* un hold-up dans. **~er** *n.* (*person*) bandit *m.*, pillard *m.* **~ers** *n. pl.* (*mil.*) commando *m.*

rail /reɪl/ *n.* (*on balcony*) balustrade *f.*; (*stairs*) main courante *f.*, rampe *f.*; (*for train*) rail *m.*; (*for curtain*) tringle *f.* **by ~,** par chemin de fer.

railing /ˈreɪlɪŋ/ *n.* **~s,** grille *f.*

railroad /ˈreɪlrəʊd/ *n.* (*Amer.*) = **railway.**

railway /ˈreɪlweɪ/ *n.* chemin de fer *m.* **~ line,** voie ferrée *f.* **~man** *n.* (*pl.* **-men**) cheminot *m.* **~ station,** gare *f.*

rain /reɪn/ *n.* pluie *f.* ● *v.i.* pleuvoir. **~ forest,** forêt (humide) tropicale *f.* **~-storm** *n.* trombe d'eau *f.* **~-water** *n.* eau de pluie *f.*

rainbow /ˈreɪnbəʊ/ *n.* arc-en-ciel *m.*

raincoat /ˈreɪnkəʊt/ *n.* imperméable *m.*

rainfall /ˈreɪnfɔːl/ *n.* précipitation *f.*

rainy /ˈreɪnɪ/ *a.* (**-ier, -iest**) pluvieux; (*season*) des pluies.

raise /reɪz/ *v.t.* lever; (*breed, build*) élever; (*question etc.*) soulever; (*price etc.*) relever; (*money etc.*) obtenir; (*voice*) élever. ● *n.* (*Amer.*) augmentation *f.*

raisin /ˈreɪzn/ *n.* raisin sec *m.*

rake[1] /reɪk/ *n.* râteau *m.* ● *v.t.* (*garden*) ratisser; (*search*) fouiller dans. **~ in,** (*money*) amasser. **~-off** *n.* (*fam.*) profit *m.* **~ up,** (*memories, past*) remuer.

rake[2] /reɪk/ *n.* (*man*) débauché *m.*

rally /ˈrælɪ/ *v.t./i.* (se) rallier; (*strength*) reprendre; (*after illness*) aller mieux. ● *n.* rassemblement *m.*; (*auto.*) rallye *m.*; (*tennis*) échange *m.* **~ round,** venir en aide.

ram /ræm/ *n.* bélier *m.* ● *v.t.* (*p.t.* **rammed**) (*thrust*) enfoncer; (*crash into*) emboutir, percuter.

RAM /ræm/ *abbr.* (*random access memory*) mémoire vive *f.*

rambl|e /ˈræmbl/ *n.* randonnée *f.* ● *v.i.* faire une randonnée. **~e on,** parler (sans cesse), divaguer. **~er** *n.* randonneu|r, -se, *m.*, *f.* **~ing** *a.* (*speech*) décousu.

ramification /ræmɪfɪˈkeɪʃn/ *n.* ramification *f.*

ramp /ræmp/ *n.* (*slope*) rampe *f.*; (*in garage*) pont de graissage *m.*

rampage[1] /ræmˈpeɪdʒ/ *v.i.* se livrer à des actes de violence, se déchaîner.

rampage[2] /ˈræmpeɪdʒ/ *n.* **go on the ~ = rampage**[1].

rampant /ˈræmpənt/ *a.* **be ~,** (*disease etc.*) sévir, être répandu.

rampart /ˈræmpɑːt/ *n.* rempart *m.*

ramshackle /ˈræmʃækl/ *a.* délabré.

ran /ræn/ *see* run.

ranch /rɑːntʃ/ *n.* ranch *m.*

rancid /ˈrænsɪd/ *a.* rance.

rancour /ˈræŋkə(r)/ *n.* rancœur *f.*

random /ˈrændəm/ *a.* fait, pris, *etc.* au hasard, aléatoire (*techn.*). ● *n.* **at ~,** au hasard.

randy /ˈrændɪ/ *a.* (**-ier, -iest**) (*fam.*) excité, en chaleur.

rang /ræŋ/ *see* ring[2].

range /reɪndʒ/ *n.* (*distance*) portée *f.*; (*of aircraft etc.*) rayon d'action *m.*; (*series*) gamme *f.*; (*scale*) échelle *f.*; (*choice*) choix *m.*; (*domain*) champ *m.*; (*of mountains*) chaîne *f.*; (*stove*) cuisinière *f.* ● *v.i.* s'étendre; (*vary*) varier.

ranger /ˈreɪndʒə(r)/ *n.* garde forestier *m.*

rank[1] /ræŋk/ *n.* rang *m.*; (*grade*: *mil.*) grade *m.*, rang *m.* ● *v.t./i.* **~ among,** compter parmi. **the ~ and file,** les gens ordinaires.

rank[2] /ræŋk/ *a.* (**-er, -est**) (*plants*: *pej.*) luxuriant; (*smell*) fétide; (*complete*) absolu.

rankle /ˈræŋkl/ *v.i.* **~ with s.o.,** rester sur le cœur à qn.

ransack /ˈrænsæk/ *v.t.* (*search*) fouiller; (*pillage*) saccager.

ransom /ˈrænsəm/ *n.* rançon *f.* ● *v.t.* rançonner; (*redeem*) racheter. **hold to ~,** rançonner.

rant /rænt/ *v.i.* tempêter.

rap /ræp/ *n.* petit coup sec *m.* ● *v.t./i.* (*p.t.* **rapped**) frapper.

rape /reɪp/ *v.t.* violer. ● *n.* viol *m.*

rapid /ˈræpɪd/ *a.* rapide. **~ity** /rəˈpɪdətɪ/ *n.* rapidité *f.* **~s** *n. pl.* (*of river*) rapides *m. pl.*

rapist /'reɪpɪst/ *n.* violeur *m.*
rapport /ræ'pɔ:(r)/ *n.* rapport *m.*
rapt /ræpt/ *a.* (*attention*) profond. **~ in,** plongé dans.
raptur|e /'ræptʃə(r)/ *n.* extase *f.* **~ous** *a.* (*person*) en extase; (*welcome etc.*) frénétique.
rar|e[1] /reə(r)/ *a.* (**-er, -est**) rare. **~ely** *adv.* rarement. **~ity** *n.* rareté *f.*
rare[2] /reə(r)/ *a.* (**-er, -est**) (*culin.*) saignant.
rarefied /'reərɪfaɪd/ *a.* raréfié.
raring /'reərɪŋ/ *a.* **~ to,** (*fam.*) impatient de.
rascal /'rɑ:skl/ *n.* coquin(e) *m.* (*f.*).
rash[1] /ræʃ/ *n.* (*med.*) éruption *f.*, rougeurs *f. pl.*
rash[2] /ræʃ/ *a.* (**-er, -est**) imprudent. **~ly** *adv.* imprudemment. **~ness** *n.* imprudence *f.*
rasher /'ræʃə(r)/ *n.* tranche (de lard) *f.*
raspberry /'rɑ:zbrɪ/ *n.* framboise *f.*
rasping /'rɑ:spɪŋ/ *a.* grinçant.
rat /ræt/ *n.* rat *m.* • *v.i.* (*p.t.* **ratted**). **~ on,** (*desert*) lâcher; (*inform on*) dénoncer. **~ race,** foire d'empoigne *f.*
rate /reɪt/ *n.* (*ratio, level*) taux *m.*; (*speed*) allure *f.*; (*price*) tarif *m.* **~s,** (*taxes*) impôts locaux *m. pl.* • *v.t.* évaluer; (*consider*) considérer; (*deserve*: *Amer.*) mériter. • *v.i.* **~ as,** être considéré comme. **at any ~,** en tout cas. **at the ~ of,** (*on the basis of*) à raison de.
ratepayer /'reɪtpeɪə(r)/ *n.* contribuable *m./f.*
rather /'rɑ:ðə(r)/ *adv.* (*by preference*) plutôt; (*fairly*) assez, plutôt; (*a little*) un peu. **I would ~ go,** j'aimerais mieux partir. **~ than go,** plutôt que de partir.
ratif|y /'rætɪfaɪ/ *v.t.* ratifier. **~ication** /-ɪ'keɪʃn/ *n.* ratification *f.*
rating /'reɪtɪŋ/ *n.* classement *m.*; (*sailor*) matelot *m.*; (*number*) indice *m.* **the ~s,** (*TV*) l'audimat (P.).
ratio /'reɪʃɪəʊ/ *n.* (*pl.* **-os**) proportion *f.*
ration /'ræʃn/ *n.* ration *f.* • *v.t.* rationner.
rational /'ræʃənl/ *a.* rationnel; (*person*) raisonnable.
rationalize /'ræʃənəlaɪz/ *v.t.* tenter de justifier; (*organize*) rationaliser.
rattle /'rætl/ *v.i.* faire du bruit; (*of bottles*) cliqueter. • *v.t.* secouer; (*sl.*) agacer. • *n.* bruit (de ferraille) *m.*; cliquetis *m.*; (*toy*) hochet *m.* **~ off,** débiter en vitesse.
rattlesnake /'rætlsneɪk/ *n.* serpent à sonnette *m.*, crotale *m.*
raucous /'rɔ:kəs/ *a.* rauque.
raunchy /'rɔ:ntʃɪ/ *a.* (**-ier, -iest**) (*Amer., sl.*) cochon.
ravage /'rævɪdʒ/ *v.t.* ravager. **~s** /-ɪz/ *n. pl.* ravages *m. pl.*
rav|e /reɪv/ *v.i.* divaguer; (*in anger*) tempêter. **~e about,** s'extasier sur. **~ings** *n. pl.* divagations *f. pl.*
raven /'reɪvn/ *n.* corbeau *m.*
ravenous /'rævənəs/ *a.* vorace. **I am ~,** je meurs de faim.
ravine /rə'vi:n/ *n.* ravin *m.*
raving /'reɪvɪŋ/ *a.* **~ lunatic,** fou furieux *m.*, folle furieuse *f.*
ravioli /rævɪ'əʊlɪ/ *n.* ravioli *m. pl.*
ravish /'rævɪʃ/ *v.t.* (*rape*) ravir. **~ing** *a.* (*enchanting*) ravissant.
raw /rɔ:/ *a.* (**-er, -est**) cru; (*not processed*) brut; (*wound*) à vif; (*immature*) inexpérimenté. **get a ~ deal,** être mal traité. **~ materials,** matières premières *f. pl.*
ray /reɪ/ *n.* (*of light etc.*) rayon *m.* **~ of hope,** lueur d'espoir *f.*
raze /reɪz/ *v.t.* (*destroy*) raser.
razor /'reɪzə(r)/ *n.* rasoir *m.* **~-blade** *n.* lame de rasoir *f.*
re /ri:/ *prep.* concernant.
re- /ri:/ *pref.* re-, ré-, r-.
reach /ri:tʃ/ *v.t.* atteindre, arriver à; (*contact*) joindre; (*hand over*) passer. • *v.i.* s'étendre. • *n.* portée *f.* **~ for,** tendre la main pour prendre. **within ~ of,** à portée de, (*close to*) à proximité de.
react /rɪ'ækt/ *v.i.* réagir.
reaction /rɪ'ækʃn/ *n.* réaction *f.* **~ary** *a.* & *n.* réactionnaire (*m./f.*).
reactor /rɪ'æktə(r)/ *n.* réacteur *m.*
read /ri:d/ *v.t./i.* (*p.t.* **read** /red/) lire; (*fig.*) comprendre; (*study*) étudier; (*of instrument*) indiquer. • *n.* (*fam.*) lecture *f.* **~ about s.o.,** lire un article sur qn. **~ out,** lire à haute voix. **~able** *a.* agréable *or* facile à lire. **~ing** *n.* lecture *f.*; indication *f.* **~ing-glasses** *pl. n.* lunettes pour lire *f. pl.* **~ing-lamp** *n.* lampe de bureau *f.* **~-out** *n.* affichage *m.*
reader /'ri:də(r)/ *n.* lec|teur, -trice *m., f.* **~ship** *n.* lecteurs *m. pl.*
readily /'redɪlɪ/ *adv.* (*willingly*) volontiers; (*easily*) facilement.
readiness /'redɪnɪs/ *n.* empressement *m.* **in ~,** prêt (**for,** à).

readjust /ri:ə'dʒʌst/ *v.t.* rajuster. • *v.i.* se réadapter (**to,** à).

ready /'redɪ/ *a.* (**-ier, -iest**) prêt; (*quick*) prompt. • *n.* **at the ~,** tout prêt. **~-made** *a.* tout fait. **~ money,** (argent) liquide *m.* **~ reckoner,** barème *m.* **~-to-wear** *a.* prêt-à-porter.

real /rɪəl/ *a.* vrai, véritable, réel. • *adv.* (*Amer., fam.*) vraiment. **~ estate,** biens fonciers *m. pl.*

realis|t /'rɪəlɪst/ *n.* réaliste *m./f.* **~m** /-zəm/ *n.* réalisme *m.* **~tic** /-'lɪstɪk/ *a.* réaliste. **~tically** /-'lɪstɪklɪ/ *adv.* avec réalisme.

reality /rɪ'ælətɪ/ *n.* réalité *f.*

realiz|e /'rɪəlaɪz/ *v.t.* se rendre compte de, comprendre; (*fulfil, turn into cash*) réaliser; (*price*) atteindre. **~ation** /-'zeɪʃn/ *n.* prise de conscience *f.*; réalisation *f.*

really /'rɪəlɪ/ *adv.* vraiment.

realtor /'rɪəltə(r)/ *n.* (*Amer.*) agent immobilier *m.*

realm /relm/ *n.* royaume *m.*

reap /ri:p/ *v.t.* (*crop, field*) moissonner; (*fig.*) récolter.

reappear /ri:ə'pɪə(r)/ *v.i.* réapparaître, reparaître.

reappraisal /ri:ə'preɪzl/ *n.* réévaluation *f.*

rear[1] /rɪə(r)/ *n.* arrière *m.*, derrière *m.* • *a.* arrière *invar.*, de derrière. **~-view mirror,** rétroviseur *m.*

rear[2] /rɪə(r)/ *v.t.* (*bring up, breed*) élever. • *v.i.* (*horse*) se cabrer. **~ one's head,** dresser la tête.

rearguard /'rɪəgɑ:d/ *n.* (*mil.*) arrière-garde *f.*

rearm /ri:'ɑ:m/ *v.t./i.* réarmer.

rearrange /ri:ə'reɪndʒ/ *v.t.* réarranger.

reason /'ri:zn/ *n.* raison *f.* • *v.i.* raisonner. **it stands to ~ that,** de toute évidence. **we have ~ to believe that,** on a tout lieu de croire que. **there is no ~ to panic,** il n'y a pas de raison de paniquer. **~ with,** raisonner. **everything within ~,** tout dans les limites normales. **~ing** *n.* raisonnement *m.*

reasonable /'ri:znəbl/ *a.* raisonnable.

reassur|e /ri:ə'ʃʊə(r)/ *v.t.* rassurer. **~ance** *n.* réconfort *m.*

rebate /'ri:beɪt/ *n.* remboursement (partiel) *m.*; (*discount*) rabais *m.*

rebel[1] /'rebl/ *n.* & *a.* rebelle (*m./f.*).

rebel[2] /rɪ'bel/ *v.i.* (*p.t.* **rebelled**) se rebeller. **~lion** *n.* rébellion *f.* **~lious** *a.* rebelle.

rebound /rɪ'baʊnd/ *v.i.* rebondir. **~ on,** (*backfire*) se retourner contre. • *n.* /'ri:baʊnd/ *n.* rebond *m.*

rebuff /rɪ'bʌf/ *v.t.* repousser. • *n.* rebuffade *f.*

rebuild /ri:'bɪld/ *v.t.* reconstruire.

rebuke /rɪ'bju:k/ *v.t.* réprimander. • *n.* réprimande *f.*, reproche *m.*

rebuttal /rɪ'bʌtl/ *n.* réfutation *f.*

recall /rɪ'kɔ:l/ *v.t.* (*to s.o., call back*) rappeler; (*remember*) se rappeler. • *n.* rappel *m.*

recant /rɪ'kænt/ *v.i.* se rétracter.

recap /'ri:kæp/ *v.t./i.* (*p.t.* **recapped**) (*fam.*) récapituler. • *n.* (*fam.*) récapitulation *f.*

recapitulat|e /ri:kə'pɪtʃʊleɪt/ *v.t./i.* récapituler. **~ion** /-'leɪʃn/ *n.* récapitulation *f.*

recapture /ri:'kæptʃə(r)/ *v.t.* reprendre; (*recall*) recréer.

reced|e /rɪ'si:d/ *v.i.* s'éloigner. **his hair is ~ing,** son front se dégarnit. **~ing** *a.* (*forehead*) fuyant.

receipt /rɪ'si:t/ *n.* (*written*) reçu *m.*; (*of letter*) réception *f.* **~s,** (*money: comm.*) recettes *f. pl.*

receive /rɪ'si:v/ *v.t.* recevoir. **~r** /-ə(r)/ *n.* (*of stolen goods*) receleu|r, -se *m., f.*; (*telephone*) combiné *m.*

recent /'ri:snt/ *a.* récent. **~ly** *adv.* récemment.

receptacle /rɪ'septəkl/ *n.* récipient *m.*

reception /rɪ'sepʃn/ *n.* réception *f.* **give s.o. a warm ~,** donner un accueil chaleureux à qn. **~ist** *n.* réceptionniste *m./f.*

receptive /rɪ'septɪv/ *a.* réceptif.

recess /rɪ'ses/ *n.* (*alcove*) renfoncement *m.*; (*nook*) recoin *m.*; (*holiday*) vacances *f. pl.*; (*schol., Amer.*) récréation *f.*

recession /rɪ'seʃn/ *n.* récession *f.*

recharge /ri:'tʃɑ:dʒ/ *v.t.* recharger.

recipe /'resəpɪ/ *n.* recette *f.*

recipient /rɪ'sɪpɪənt/ *n.* (*of honour*) récipiendaire *m.*; (*of letter*) destinataire *m./f.*

reciprocal /rɪ'sɪprəkl/ *a.* réciproque.

reciprocate /rɪ'sɪprəkeɪt/ *v.t.* offrir en retour. • *v.i.* en faire autant.

recital /rɪ'saɪtl/ *n.* récital *m.*

recite /rɪ'saɪt/ *v.t.* (*poem, lesson, etc.*) réciter; (*list*) énumérer.

reckless /'reklɪs/ *a.* imprudent. **~ly** *adv.* imprudemment.

reckon /'rekən/ *v.t./i.* calculer; (*judge*) considérer; (*think*) penser. **~ on/with,** compter sur/avec. **~ing** *n.* calcul(s) *m.* (*pl.*).

reclaim /rɪ'kleɪm/ *v.t.* (*seek return of*) réclamer; (*land*) défricher; (*flooded land*) assécher.

reclin|e /rɪ'klaɪn/ *v.i.* être étendu. **~ing** *a.* (*person*) étendu; (*seat*) à dossier réglable.

recluse /rɪ'klu:s/ *n.* reclus(e) *m.* (*f.*), ermite *m.*

recognition /rekəg'nɪʃn/ *n.* reconnaissance *f.* **beyond ~,** méconnaissable. **gain ~,** être reconnu.

recognize /'rekəgnaɪz/ *v.t.* reconnaître.

recoil /rɪ'kɔɪl/ *v.i.* reculer (**from,** devant).

recollect /rekə'lekt/ *v.t.* se souvenir de, se rappeler. **~ion** /-kʃn/ *n.* souvenir *m.*

recommend /rekə'mend/ *v.t.* recommander. **~ation** /-'deɪʃn/ *n.* recommandation *f.*

recompense /'rekəmpens/ *v.t.* (ré)compenser. ● *n.* récompense *f.*

reconcil|e /'rekənsaɪl/ *v.t.* (*people*) réconcilier; (*facts*) concilier. **~e o.s. to,** se résigner à. **~iation** /-sɪlɪ'eɪʃn/ *n.* réconciliation *f.*

recondition /ri:kən'dɪʃn/ *v.t.* remettre à neuf, réviser.

reconn|oitre /rekə'nɔɪtə(r)/ *v.t.* (*pres. p.* **-tring**) (*mil.*) reconnaître. **~aissance** /rɪ'kɒnɪsns/ *n.* reconnaissance *f.*

reconsider /ri:kən'sɪdə(r)/ *v.t.* reconsidérer. ● *v.i.* se déjuger.

reconstruct /ri:kən'strʌkt/ *v.t.* reconstruire; (*crime*) reconstituer.

record[1] /rɪ'kɔ:d/ *v.t./i.* (*in register, on tape, etc.*) enregistrer; (*in diary*) noter. **~ that,** rapporter que. **~ing** *n.* enregistrement *m.*

record[2] /'rekɔ:d/ *n.* (*report*) rapport *m.*; (*register*) registre *m.*; (*mention*) mention *f.*; (*file*) dossier *m.*; (*fig.*) résultats *m. pl.*; (*mus.*) disque *m.*; (*sport*) record *m.* **(criminal) ~,** casier judiciaire *m.* ● *a.* record *invar.* **off the ~,** officieusement. **~-holder** *n.* déten|teur, -trice du record *m.*, *f.* **~-player** *n.* électrophone *m.*

recorder /rɪ'kɔ:də(r)/ *n.* (*mus.*) flûte à bec *f.*

recount /rɪ'kaʊnt/ *v.t.* raconter.

re-count /ri:'kaʊnt/ *v.t.* recompter.

recoup /rɪ'ku:p/ *v.t.* récupérer.

recourse /rɪ'kɔ:s/ *n.* recours *m.* **have ~ to,** avoir recours à.

recover /rɪ'kʌvə(r)/ *v.t.* récupérer. ● *v.i.* se remettre; (*med.*) se rétablir; (*economy*) se redresser. **~y** *n.* récupération *f.*; (*med.*) rétablissement *m.*

recreation /rekrɪ'eɪʃn/ *n.* récréation *f.* **~al** *a.* de récréation.

recrimination /rɪkrɪmɪ'neɪʃn/ *n.* contre-accusation *f.*

recruit /rɪ'kru:t/ *n.* recrue *f.* ● *v.t.* recruter. **~ment** *n.* recrutement *m.*

rectang|le /'rektæŋgl/ *n.* rectangle *m.* **~ular** /-'tæŋgjʊlə(r)/ *a.* rectangulaire.

rectif|y /'rektɪfaɪ/ *v.t.* rectifier. **~ication** /-ɪ'keɪʃn/ *n.* rectification *f.*

recuperate /rɪ'kju:pəreɪt/ *v.t.* récupérer. ● *v.i.* (*med.*) se rétablir.

recur /rɪ'kɜ:(r)/ *v.i.* (*p.t.* **recurred**) revenir, se répéter.

recurren|t /rɪ'kʌrənt/ *a.* fréquent. **~ce** *n.* répétition *f.*, retour *m.*

recycle /ri:'saɪkl/ *v.t.* recycler.

red /red/ *a.* (**redder, reddest**) rouge; (*hair*) roux. ● *n.* rouge *m.* **in the ~,** en déficit. **roll out the ~ carpet for,** recevoir en grande pompe. **Red Cross,** Croix-Rouge *f.* **~-handed** *a.* en flagrant délit. **~ herring,** fausse piste *f.* **~-hot** *a.* brûlant. **the ~ light,** le feu rouge *m.* **~ tape,** paperasserie *f.*, bureaucratie *f.*

redcurrant /red'kʌrənt/ *n.* groseille *f.*

redden /'redn/ *v.t./i.* rougir.

reddish /'redɪʃ/ *a.* rougeâtre.

redecorate /ri:'dekəreɪt/ *v.t.* (*repaint etc.*) repeindre, refaire.

redeem /rɪ'di:m/ *v.t.* racheter. **~ing quality,** qualité qui rachète les défauts *f.*

redemption *n.* /rɪ'dempʃn/ rachat *m.*

redeploy /ri:dɪ'plɔɪ/ *v.t.* réorganiser; (*troops*) répartir.

redirect /ri:daɪə'rekt/ *v.t.* (*letter*) faire suivre.

redness /'rednɪs/ *n.* rougeur *f.*

redo /ri:'du:/ *v.t.* (*p.t.* **-did,** *p.p.* **-done**) refaire.

redolent /'redələnt/ *a.* **~ of,** qui évoque.

redouble /rɪ'dʌbl/ *v.t.* redoubler.

redress /rɪ'dres/ *v.t.* (*wrong etc.*) redresser. ● *n.* réparation *f.*

reduc|e /rɪ'dju:s/ *v.t.* réduire; (*temperature etc.*) faire baisser. **~tion** /rɪ'dʌkʃn/ *n.* réduction *f.*

redundan|t /rɪ'dʌndənt/ *a.* superflu; (*worker*) licencié. **make ~,** licencier. **~cy** *n.* licenciement *m.*; (*word, phrase*) pléonasme *m.*

reed /ri:d/ *n.* (*plant*) roseau *m.*; (*mus.*) anche *f.*

reef /ri:f/ *n.* récif *m.*, écueil *m.*

reek /ri:k/ *n.* puanteur *f.* ● *v.i.* **~ (of),** puer.

reel /ri:l/ *n.* (*of thread*) bobine *f.*; (*of film*) bande *f.*; (*winding device*) dévidoir *m.* ● *v.i.* chanceler. ● *v.t.* **~ off,** réciter.

refectory /rɪ'fektərɪ/ *n.* réfectoire *m.*

refer /rɪ'fɜ:(r)/ *v.t./i.* (*p.t.* **referred**). **~ to,** (*allude to*) faire allusion à; (*concern*) s'appliquer à; (*consult*) consulter; (*submit*) soumettre à; (*direct*) renvoyer à.

referee /refə'ri:/ *n.* arbitre *m.*; (*for job*) répondant(e) *m.* (*f.*). ● *v.t.* (*p.t.* **refereed**) arbitrer.

reference /'refrəns/ *n.* référence *f.*; (*mention*) allusion *f.*; (*person*) répondant(e) *m.* (*f.*). **in** *or* **with ~ to,** en ce qui concerne; (*comm.*) suite à. **~ book,** ouvrage de référence *m.*

referendum /refə'rendəm/ *n.* (*pl.* **-ums**) référendum *m.*

refill[1] /ri:fɪl/ *v.t.* remplir (à nouveau); (*pen etc.*) recharger.

refill[2] /'ri:fɪl/ *n.* (*of pen, lighter, lipstick*) recharge *f.*

refine /rɪ'faɪn/ *v.t.* raffiner. **~d** *a.* raffiné. **~ment** *n.* raffinement *m.*; (*techn.*) raffinage *m.* **~ry** /-ərɪ/ *n.* raffinerie *f.*

reflate /ri:'fleɪt/ *v.t.* relancer.

reflect /rɪ'flekt/ *v.t.* refléter; (*of mirror*) réfléchir, refléter. ● *v.i.* réfléchir (**on,** à). **~ on s.o.,** (*glory etc.*) (faire) rejaillir sur qn.; (*pej.*) donner une mauvaise impression de qn. **~ion** /-kʃn/ *n.* réflexion *f.*; (*image*) reflet *m.* **on ~ion,** réflexion faite. **~or** *n.* réflecteur *m.*

reflective /rɪ'flektɪv/ *a.* réfléchissant.

reflex /'ri:fleks/ *a.* & *n.* réflexe (*m.*).

reflexive /rɪ'fleksɪv/ *a.* (*gram.*) réfléchi.

reform /rɪ'fɔ:m/ *v.t.* réformer. ● *v.i.* (*person*) s'amender. ● *n.* réforme *f.* **~er** *n.* réforma|teur, -trice *m.*, *f.*

refract /rɪ'frækt/ *v.t.* réfracter.

refrain[1] /rɪ'freɪn/ *n.* refrain *m.*

refrain[2] /rɪ'freɪn/ *v.i.* s'abstenir (**from,** de).

refresh /rɪ'freʃ/ *v.t.* rafraîchir; (*of rest etc.*) ragaillardir, délasser. **~ing** *a.* (*drink*) rafraîchissant; (*sleep*) réparateur. **~ments** *n. pl.* rafraîchissements *m. pl.*

refresher /rɪ'freʃə(r)/ *a.* (*course*) de perfectionnement.

refrigerat|e /rɪ'frɪdʒəreɪt/ *v.t.* réfrigérer. **~or** *n.* réfrigérateur *m.*

refuel /ri:'fju:əl/ *v.t./i.* (*p.t.* **refuelled**) (se) ravitailler.

refuge /'refju:dʒ/ *n.* refuge *m.* **take ~,** se réfugier.

refugee /refjʊ'dʒi:/ *n.* réfugié(e) *m.* (*f.*).

refund /rɪ'fʌnd/ *v.t.* rembourser. ● *n.* /'ri:fʌnd/ remboursement *m.*

refurbish /ri:'fɜ:bɪʃ/ *v.t.* remettre à neuf.

refus|e[1] /rɪ'fju:z/ *v.t./i.* refuser. **~al** *n.* refus *m.*

refuse[2] /'refju:s/ *n.* ordures *f. pl.*

refute /rɪ'fju:t/ *v.t.* réfuter.

regain /rɪ'geɪn/ *v.t.* retrouver; (*lost ground*) regagner.

regal /'ri:gl/ *a.* royal, majestueux.

regalia /rɪ'geɪlɪə/ *n. pl.* (*insignia*) insignes (royaux) *m. pl.*

regard /rɪ'gɑ:d/ *v.t.* considérer. ● *n.* considération *f.*, estime *f.* **~s,** amitiés *f. pl.* **in this ~,** à cet égard. **as ~s, ~ing** *prep.* en ce qui concerne.

regardless /rɪ'gɑ:dlɪs/ *adv.* quand même. **~ of,** sans tenir compte de.

regatta /rɪ'gætə/ *n.* régates *f. pl.*

regenerat|e /rɪ'dʒenəreɪt/ *v.t.* régénérer. **~ion** /-'reɪʃn/ *n.* régénération *f.*

regen|t /'ri:dʒənt/ *n.* régent(e) *m.* (*f.*). **~cy** *n.* régence *f.*

regime /reɪ'ʒi:m/ *n.* régime *m.*

regiment /'redʒɪmənt/ *n.* régiment *m.* **~al** /-'mentl/ *a.* d'un régiment. **~ation** /-en'teɪʃn/ *n.* discipline excessive *f.*

region /'ri:dʒən/ *n.* région *f.* **in the ~ of,** environ. **~al** *a.* régional.

regist|er /'redʒɪstə(r)/ *n.* registre *m.* ● *v.t.* enregistrer; (*vehicle*) immatriculer; (*birth*) déclarer; (*letter*) recommander; (*indicate*) indiquer; (*express*) exprimer. ● *v.i.* (*enrol*) s'inscrire; (*fig.*) être compris. **~er office,** bureau d'état civil *m.* **~ration** /-'streɪʃn/ *n.* enregistrement *m.*; inscription *f.*; (*vehicle document*) carte grise *f.* **~ration**

(number), (*auto.*) numéro d'immatriculation *m.*
registrar /redʒɪ'strɑ:(r)/ *n.* officier de l'état civil *m.*; (*univ.*) secrétaire général *m.*
regret /rɪ'gret/ *n.* regret *m.* ● *v.t.* (*p.t.* **regretted**) regretter (**to do,** de faire). **~fully** *adv.* à regret. **~table** *a.* regrettable, fâcheux. **~tably** *adv.* malheureusement; (*small, poor, etc.*) fâcheusement.
regroup /ri:'gru:p/ *v.t./i.* (se) regrouper.
regular /'regjʊlə(r)/ *a.* régulier; (*usual*) habituel; (*thorough: fam.*) vrai. ● *n.* (*fam.*) habitué(e) *m.* (*f.*). **~ity** /-'lærətɪ/ *n.* régularité *f.* **~ly** *adv.* régulièrement.
regulat|e /'regjʊleɪt/ *v.t.* régler. **~ion** /-'leɪʃn/ *n.* réglage *m.*; (*rule*) règlement *m.*
rehabilitat|e /ri:ə'bɪlɪteɪt/ *v.t.* réadapter; (*in public esteem*) réhabiliter. **~ion** /-'teɪʃn/ *n.* réadaptation *f.*; réhabilitation *f.*
rehash[1] /ri:'hæʃ/ *v.t.* remanier.
rehash[2] /'ri:hæʃ/ *n.* réchauffé *m.*
rehears|e /rɪ'hɜ:s/ *v.t./i.* (*theatre*) répéter. **~al** *n.* répétition *f.*
re-heat /ri:'hi:t/ *v.t.* réchauffer.
reign /reɪn/ *n.* règne *m.* ● *v.i.* régner (**over,** sur).
reimburse /ri:ɪm'bɜ:s/ *v.t.* rembourser.
rein /reɪn/ *n.* rêne *f.*
reindeer /'reɪndɪə(r)/ *n. invar.* renne *m.*
reinforce /ri:ɪn'fɔ:s/ *v.t.* renforcer. **~ment** *n.* renforcement *m.* **~ments** *n. pl.* renforts *m. pl.* **~d concrete,** béton armé *m.*
reinstate /ri:ɪn'steɪt/ *v.t.* réintégrer, rétablir.
reiterate /ri:'ɪtəreɪt/ *v.t.* réitérer.
reject[1] /rɪ'dʒekt/ *v.t.* (*offer, plea, etc.*) rejeter; (*book, goods, etc.*) refuser. **~ion** /-kʃn/ *n.* rejet *m.*; refus *m.*
reject[2] /'ri:dʒekt/ *n.* (article de) rebut *m.*
rejoic|e /rɪ'dʒɔɪs/ *v.i.* se réjouir. **~ing** *n.* réjouissance *f.*
rejuvenate /rɪ'dʒu:vəneɪt/ *v.t.* rajeunir.
relapse /rɪ'læps/ *n.* rechute *f.* ● *v.i.* rechuter. **~ into,** retomber dans.
relate /rɪ'leɪt/ *v.t.* raconter; (*associate*) rapprocher. ● *v.i.* **~ to,** se rapporter à; (*get on with*) s'entendre avec. **~d** /-ɪd/ *a.* (*ideas etc.*) lié. **~d to s.o.,** parent(e) de qn.
relation /rɪ'leɪʃn/ *n.* rapport *m.*; (*person*) parent(e) *m.* (*f.*). **~ship** *n.* lien de parenté *m.*; (*link*) rapport *m.*; (*affair*) liaison *f.*
relative /'relətɪv/ *n.* parent(e) *m.* (*f.*). ● *a.* relatif; (*respective*) respectif. **~ly** *adv.* relativement.
relax /rɪ'læks/ *v.t./i.* (*less tense*) (se) relâcher; (*for pleasure*) (se) détendre. **~ation** /ri:læk'seɪʃn/ *n.* relâchement *m.*; détente *f.* **~ing** *a.* délassant.
relay[1] /'ri:leɪ/ *n.* relais *m.* **~ race,** course de relais *f.*
relay[2] /rɪ'leɪ/ *v.t.* relayer.
release /rɪ'li:s/ *v.t.* libérer; (*bomb*) lâcher; (*film*) sortir; (*news*) publier; (*smoke*) dégager; (*spring*) déclencher. ● *n.* libération *f.*; sortie *f.*; (*record*) nouveau disque *m.* (*of pollution*) émission *f.*
relegate /'relɪgeɪt/ *v.t.* reléguer.
relent /rɪ'lent/ *v.i.* se laisser fléchir. **~less** *a.* impitoyable.
relevan|t /'reləvənt/ *a.* pertinent. **be ~t to,** avoir rapport à. **~ce** *n.* pertinence *f.*, rapport *m.*
reliab|le /rɪ'laɪəbl/ *a.* sérieux, sûr; (*machine*) fiable. **~ility** /-'bɪlətɪ/ *n.* sérieux *m.*; fiabilité *f.*
reliance /rɪ'laɪəns/ *n.* dépendance *f.*; (*trust*) confiance *f.*
relic /'relɪk/ *n.* relique *f.* **~s,** (*of past*) vestiges *m. pl.*
relief /rɪ'li:f/ *n.* soulagement *m.* (**from,** à); (*assistance*) secours *m.*; (*outline, design*) relief *m.* **~ road,** route de délestage *f.*
relieve /rɪ'li:v/ *v.t.* soulager; (*help*) secourir; (*take over from*) relayer.
religion /rɪ'lɪdʒən/ *n.* religion *f.*
religious /rɪ'lɪdʒəs/ *a.* religieux.
relinquish /rɪ'lɪŋkwɪʃ/ *v.t.* abandonner; (*relax hold of*) lâcher.
relish /'relɪʃ/ *n.* plaisir *m.*, goût *m.*; (*culin.*) assaisonnement *m.* ● *v.t.* savourer; (*idea etc.*) aimer.
relocate /ri:ləʊ'keɪt/ *v.t.* (*company*) déplacer; (*employee*) muter. ● *v.i.* se déplacer, déménager.
reluctan|t /rɪ'lʌktənt/ *a.* fait, donné, *etc.* à contrecœur. **~t to,** peu disposé à. **~ce** *n.* répugnance *f.* **~tly** *adv.* à contrecœur.
rely /rɪ'laɪ/ *v.i.* **~ on,** compter sur; (*financially*) dépendre de.

remain /rɪ'meɪn/ *v.i.* rester. **~s** *n. pl.* restes *m. pl.*

remainder /rɪ'meɪndə(r)/ *n.* reste *m.*; (*book*) invendu soldé *m.*

remand /rɪ'mɑ:nd/ *v.t.* mettre en détention préventive. ● *n.* **on ~,** en détention préventive.

remark /rɪ'mɑ:k/ *n.* remarque *f.* ● *v.t.* remarquer. ● *v.i.* **~ on,** faire des commentaires sur. **~able** *a.* remarquable.

remarry /ri:'mærɪ/ *v.i.* se remarier.

remed|y /'remədɪ/ *n.* remède *m.* ● *v.t.* remédier à. **~ial** /rɪ'mi:dɪəl/ *a.* (*class etc.*) de rattrapage; (*treatment: med.*) curatif.

rememb|er /rɪ'membə(r)/ *v.t.* se souvenir de, se rappeler. **~er to do,** ne pas oublier de faire. **~rance** *n.* souvenir *m.*

remind /rɪ'maɪnd/ *v.t.* rappeler (**s.o. of sth.,** qch. à qn.). **~ s.o. to do,** rappeler à qn. qu'il doit faire. **~er** *n.* (*letter, signal*) rappel *m.*

reminisce /remɪ'nɪs/ *v.i.* évoquer ses souvenirs. **~nces** *n. pl.* réminiscences *f. pl.*

reminiscent /remɪ'nɪsnt/ *a.* **~ of,** qui rappelle, qui évoque.

remiss /rɪ'mɪs/ *a.* négligent.

remission /rɪ'mɪʃn/ *n.* rémission *f.*; (*jurid.*) remise (de peine) *f.*

remit /rɪ'mɪt/ *v.t.* (*p.t.* **remitted**) (*money*) envoyer; (*debt*) remettre. **~tance** *n.* paiement *m.*

remnant /'remnənt/ *n.* reste *m.*, débris *m.*; (*trace*) vestige *m.*; (*of cloth*) coupon *m.*

remodel /ri:'mɒdel/ *v.t.* (*p.t.* **remodelled**) remodeler.

remorse /rɪ'mɔ:s/ *n.* remords *m.* (*pl.*). **~ful** *a.* plein de remords. **~less** *a.* implacable.

remote /rɪ'məʊt/ *a.* (*place, time*) lointain; (*person*) distant; (*slight*) vague. **~ control,** télécommande *f.* **~ly** *adv.* au loin; vaguement. **~ness** *n.* éloignement *m.*

removable /rɪ'mu:vəbl/ *a.* (*detachable*) amovible.

remov|e /rɪ'mu:v/ *v.t.* enlever; (*lead away*) emmener; (*dismiss*) renvoyer; (*do away with*) supprimer. **~al** *n.* enlèvement *m.*; renvoi *m.*; suppression *f.*; (*from house*) déménagement *m.* **~al men,** déménageurs *m. pl.* **~er** *n.* (*for paint*) décapant *m.*

remunerat|e /rɪ'mju:nəreɪt/ *v.t.* rémunérer. **~ion** /-'reɪʃn/ *n.* rémunération *f.*

rename /ri:'neɪm/ *v.t.* rebaptiser.

render /'rendə(r)/ *v.t.* (*give, make*) rendre; (*mus.*) interpréter. **~ing** *n.* interprétation *f.*

rendezvous /'rɒndeɪvu:/ *n.* (*pl.* **-vous** /-vu:z/) rendez-vous *m. invar.*

renegade /'renɪgeɪd/ *n.* renégat(e) *m.* (*f.*).

renew /rɪ'nju:/ *v.t.* renouveler; (*resume*) reprendre. **~able** *a.* renouvelable. **~al** *n.* renouvellement *m.*; reprise *f.*

renounce /rɪ'naʊns/ *v.t.* renoncer à; (*disown*) renier.

renovat|e /renəveɪt/ *v.t.* rénover. **~ion** /-'veɪʃn/ *n.* rénovation *f.*

renown /rɪ'naʊn/ *n.* renommée *f.* **~ed** *a.* renommé.

rent /rent/ *n.* loyer *m.* ● *v.t.* louer. **for ~,** à louer. **~al** *n.* prix de location *m.*

renunciation /rɪnʌnsɪ'eɪʃn/ *n.* renonciation *f.*

reopen /ri:'əʊpən/ *v.t./i.* rouvrir. **~ing** *n.* réouverture *f.*

reorganize /ri:'ɔ:gənaɪz/ *v.t.* réorganiser.

rep /rep/ *n.* (*comm., fam.*) représentant(e) *m.* (*f.*).

repair /rɪ'peə(r)/ *v.t.* réparer. ● *n.* réparation *f.* **in good/bad ~,** en bon/mauvais état. **~er** *n.* réparateur *m.*

repartee /repɑ:'ti:/ *n.* repartie *f.*

repatriat|e /ri:'pætrɪeɪt/ *v.t.* rapatrier. **~ion** /-'eɪʃn/ *n.* rapatriement *m.*

repay /ri:'peɪ/ *v.t.* (*p.t.* **repaid**) rembourser; (*reward*) récompenser. **~ment** *n.* remboursement *m.*; récompense *f.* **monthly ~ments,** mensualités *f. pl.*

repeal /rɪ'pi:l/ *v.t.* abroger, annuler. ● *n.* abrogation *f.*

repeat /rɪ'pi:t/ *v.t./i.* répéter; (*renew*) renouveler. ● *n.* répétition *f.*; (*broadcast*) reprise *f.* **~ itself, ~ o.s.,** se répéter.

repeatedly /rɪ'pi:tɪdlɪ/ *adv.* à maintes reprises.

repel /rɪ'pel/ *v.t.* (*p.t.* **repelled**) repousser. **~lent** *a.* repoussant.

repent /rɪ'pent/ *v.i.* se repentir (**of,** de). **~ance** *n.* repentir *m.* **~ant** *a.* repentant.

repercussion /ri:pə'kʌʃn/ *n.* répercussion *f.*

repertoire /'repətwɑ:(r)/ *n.* répertoire *m.*

repertory /'repətrɪ/ *n.* répertoire *m.* **~ (theatre),** théâtre de répertoire *m.*

repetit|ion /repɪ'tɪʃn/ *n.* répétition *f.* **~ious** /-'tɪʃəs/, **~ive** /rɪ'petətɪv/ *adjs.* plein de répétitions.

replace /rɪ'pleɪs/ *v.t.* remettre; (*take the place of*) remplacer. **~ment** *n.* remplacement *m.* (**of,** de); (*person*) remplaçant(e) *m.* (*f.*); (*new part*) pièce de rechange *f.*

replay /'ri:pleɪ/ *n.* (*sport*) match rejoué *m.*; (*recording*) répétition immédiate *f.*

replenish /rɪ'plenɪʃ/ *v.t.* (*refill*) remplir; (*renew*) renouveler.

replica /'replɪkə/ *n.* copie exacte *f.*

reply /rɪ'plaɪ/ *v.t./i.* répondre. ● *n.* réponse *f.*

report /rɪ'pɔ:t/ *v.t.* rapporter, annoncer (**that,** que); (*notify*) signaler; (*denounce*) dénoncer. ● *v.i.* faire un rapport. **~ (on),** (*news item*) faire un reportage sur. **~ to,** (*go*) se présenter chez. ● *n.* rapport *m.*; (*in press*) reportage *m.*; (*schol.*) bulletin *m.*; (*sound*) détonation *f.* **~edly** *adv.* selon ce qu'on dit.

reporter /rɪ'pɔ:tə(r)/ *n.* reporter *m.*

repose /rɪ'pəʊz/ *n.* repos *m.*

repossess /ri:pə'zes/ *v.t.* reprendre.

represent /reprɪ'zent/ *v.t.* représenter. **~ation** /-'teɪʃn/ *n.* représentation *f.* **make ~ations to,** protester auprès de.

representative /reprɪ'zentətɪv/ *a.* représentatif, typique (**of,** de). ● *n.* représentant(e) *m.* (*f.*).

repress /rɪ'pres/ *v.t.* réprimer. **~ion** /-ʃn/ *n.* répression *f.* **~ive** *a.* répressif.

reprieve /rɪ'pri:v/ *n.* (*delay*) sursis *m.*; (*pardon*) grâce *f.* ● *v.t.* accorder un sursis à; gracier.

reprimand /'reprɪmɑ:nd/ *v.t.* réprimander. ● *n.* réprimande *f.*

reprint /'ri:prɪnt/ *n.* réimpression *f.*; (*offprint*) tiré à part *m.*

reprisals /rɪ'praɪzlz/ *n. pl.* représailles *f. pl.*

reproach /rɪ'prəʊtʃ/ *v.t.* reprocher (**s.o. for sth.,** qch. à qn.). ● *n.* reproche *m.* **~ful** *a.* de reproche, réprobateur. **~fully** *adv.* avec reproche.

reproduc|e /ri:prə'dju:s/ *v.t./i.* (se) reproduire. **~tion** /-'dʌkʃn/ *n.* reproduction *f.* **~tive** /-'dʌktɪv/ *a.* reproducteur.

reptile /'reptaɪl/ *n.* reptile *m.*

republic /rɪ'pʌblɪk/ *n.* république *f.* **~an** *a.* & *n.* républicain(e) (*m.* (*f.*)).

repudiate /rɪ'pju:dɪeɪt/ *v.t.* répudier; (*treaty*) refuser d'honorer.

repugnan|t /rɪ'pʌgnənt/ *a.* répugnant. **~ce** *n.* répugnance *f.*

repuls|e /rɪ'pʌls/ *v.t.* repousser. **~ion** /-ʃn/ *n.* répulsion *f.* **~ive** *a.* repoussant.

reputable /'repjʊtəbl/ *a.* honorable, de bonne réputation.

reputation /repjʊ'teɪʃn/ *n.* réputation *f.*

repute /rɪ'pju:t/ *n.* réputation *f.* **~d** /ɪd/ *a.* réputé. **~dly** /-ɪdlɪ/ *adv.* d'après ce qu'on dit.

request /rɪ'kwest/ *n.* demande *f.* ● *v.t.* demander (**of, from,** à). **~ stop,** arrêt facultatif *m.*

requiem /'rekwɪem/ *n.* requiem *m.*

require rɪ'kwaɪə(r) *v.t.* (*of thing*) demander; (*of person*) avoir besoin de; (*demand, order*) exiger. **~d** *a.* requis. **~ment** *n.* exigence *f.*; (*condition*) condition (requise) *f.*

requisite /'rekwɪzɪt/ *a.* nécessaire. ● *n.* chose nécessaire *f.* **~s,** (*for travel etc.*) articles *m. pl.*

requisition /rekwɪ'zɪʃn/ *n.* réquisition *f.* ● *v.t.* réquisitionner.

re-route /ri:'ru:t/ *v.t.* dérouter.

resale /'ri:seɪl/ *n.* revente *f.*

rescind /rɪ'sɪnd/ *v.t.* annuler.

rescue /'reskju:/ *v.t.* sauver. ● *n.* sauvetage *m.* (**of,** de); (*help*) secours *m.* **~r** /-ə(r)/ *n.* sauveteur *m.*

research /rɪ'sɜ:tʃ/ *n.* recherche(s) *f.*(*pl.*). ● *v.t./i.* faire des recherches (sur). **~er** *n.* chercheu|r, -se *m.*, *f.*

resembl|e /rɪ'zembl/ *v.t.* ressembler à **~ance** *n.* ressemblance *f.*

resent /rɪ'zent/ *v.t.* être indigné de, s'offenser de. **~ful** *a.* plein de ressentiment, indigné. **~ment** *n.* ressentiment *m.*

reservation /rezə'veɪʃn/ *n.* réserve *f.*; (*booking*) réservation *f.*; (*Amer.*) réserve (indienne) *f.* **make a ~,** réserver.

reserve /rɪ'zɜ:v/ *v.t.* réserver. ● *n.* (*reticence, stock, land*) réserve *f.*; (*sport*) remplaçant(e) *m.* (*f.*). **in ~,** en réserve. **the ~s,** (*mil.*) les réserves *f. pl.* **~d** *a.* (*person, room*) réservé.

reservist /rɪ'zɜ:vɪst/ *n.* (*mil.*) réserviste *m.*

reservoir /'rezəvwɑ:(r)/ *n.* (*lake, supply, etc.*) réservoir *m.*

reshape /ri:'ʃeɪp/ *v.t.* remodeler.

reshuffle /ri:'ʃʌfl/ *v.t.* (*pol.*) remanier. ● *n.* (*pol.*) remaniement (ministériel) *m.*

reside /rɪ'zaɪd/ *v.i.* résider.

residen|t /'rezɪdənt/ *a.* résidant. **be ~t,** résider. ● *n.* habitant(e) *m.* (*f.*); (*foreigner*) résident(e) *m.* (*f.*); (*in hotel*) pensionnaire *m./f.* **~ce** *n.* résidence *f.*; (*of students*) foyer *m.* **in ~ce,** (*doctor*) résidant; (*students*) au foyer.

residential /rezɪ'denʃl/ *a.* résidentiel.

residue /'rezɪdju:/ *n.* résidu *m.*

resign /rɪ'zaɪn/ *v.t.* abandonner; (*job*) démissionner de. ● *v.i.* démissionner. **~ o.s. to,** se résigner à. **~ation** /rezɪg'neɪʃn/ *n.* résignation *f.*; (*from job*) démission *f.* **~ed** *a.* résigné.

resilien|t /rɪ'zɪlɪənt/ *a.* élastique; (*person*) qui a du ressort. **~ce** *n.* élasticité *f.*; ressort *m.*

resin /'rezɪn/ *n.* résine *f.*

resist /rɪ'zɪst/ *v.t./i.* résister (à). **~ance** *n.* résistance *f.* **~ant** *a.* (*med.*) rebelle; (*metal*) résistant.

resolut|e /'rezəlu:t/ *a.* résolu. **~ion** /-'lu:ʃn/ *n.* résolution *f.*

resolve /rɪ'zɒlv/ *v.t.* résoudre (**to do,** de faire). ● *n.* résolution *f.* **~d** *a.* résolu (**to do,** à faire).

resonan|t /'rezənənt/ *a.* résonnant. **~ce** *n.* résonance *f.*

resort /rɪ'zɔ:t/ *v.i.* **~ to,** avoir recours à. ● *n.* (*recourse*) recours *m.*; (*place*) station *f.* **in the last ~,** en dernier ressort.

resound /rɪ'zaʊnd/ *v.i.* retentir (**with,** de). **~ing** *a.* retentissant.

resource /rɪ'sɔ:s/ *n.* (*expedient*) ressource *f.* **~s,** (*wealth etc.*) ressources *f. pl.* **~ful** *a.* ingénieux. **~fulness** *n.* ingéniosité *f.*

respect /rɪ'spekt/ *n.* respect *m.*; (*aspect*) égard *m.* ● *v.t.* respecter. **with ~ to,** à l'égard de, relativement à. **~ful** *a.* respectueux.

respectab|le /rɪ'spektəbl/ *a.* respectable. **~ility** /-'bɪlətɪ/ *n.* respectabilité *f.* **~ly** *adv.* convenablement.

respective /rɪ'spektɪv/ *a.* respectif. **~ly** *adv.* respectivement.

respiration /respə'reɪʃn/ *n.* respiration *f.*

respite /'resp(a)ɪt/ *n.* répit *m.*

resplendent /rɪ'splendənt/ *a.* resplendissant.

respond /rɪ'spɒnd/ *v.i.* répondre (**to,** à) **~ to,** (*react to*) réagir à.

response /rɪ'spɒns/ *n.* réponse *f.*

responsib|le /rɪ'spɒnsəbl/ *a.* responsable: (*job*) qui comporte des responsabilités. **~ility** /-'bɪlətɪ/ *n.* responsabilité *f.* **~ly** *adv.* de façon responsable.

responsive /rɪ'spɒnsɪv/ *a.* qui réagit bien. **~ to,** sensible à.

rest[1] /rest/ *v.t./i.* (se) reposer; (*lean*) (s')appuyer (**on,** sur); (*be buried, lie*) reposer. ● *n.* (*repose*) repos *m.*; (*support*) support *m.* **have a ~,** se reposer; (*at work*) prendre une pause. **~-room** *n.* (*Amer.*) toilettes *f. pl.*

rest[2] /rest/ *v.i.* (*remain*) demeurer. ● *n.* (*remainder*) reste *m.* (**of,** de). **the ~ (of the),** (*others, other*) les autres. **it ~s with him to,** il lui appartient de.

restaurant /'restərɒnt/ *n.* restaurant *m.*

restful /'restfl/ *a.* reposant.

restitution /restɪ'tju:ʃn/ *n.* (*for injury*) compensation *f.*

restive /'restɪv/ *a.* rétif.

restless /'restlɪs/ *a.* agité. **~ly** *adv.* avec agitation, fébrilement.

restor|e /rɪ'stɔ:(r)/ *v.t.* rétablir; (*building*) restaurer. **~e sth. to s.o.,** restituer qch. à qn. **~ation** /restə'reɪʃn/ *n.* rétablissement *m.*; restauration *f.* **~er** *n.* (*art*) restaura|teur, -trice *m., f.*

restrain /rɪ'streɪn/ *v.t.* contenir. **~ s.o. from,** retenir qn. de. **~ed** *a.* (*moderate*) mesuré; (*in control of self*) maître de soi. **~t** *n.* contrainte *f.*; (*moderation*) retenue *f.*

restrict /rɪ'strɪkt/ *v.t.* restreindre. **~ion** /-kʃn/ *n.* restriction *f.* **~ive** *a.* restrictif.

restructure /ri:'strʌktʃə(r)/ *v.t.* restructurer.

result /rɪ'zʌlt/ *n.* résultat *m.* ● *v.i.* résulter. **~ in,** aboutir à.

resum|e /rɪ'zju:m/ *v.t./i.* reprendre. **~ption** /rɪ'zʌmpʃn/ *n.* reprise *f.*

résumé /'rezju:meɪ/ *n.* résumé *m.*; (*of career: Amer.*) CV *m.*, curriculum vitae *m.*
resurgence /rɪ'sɜ:dʒəns/ *n.* réapparition *f.*
resurrect /rezə'rekt/ *v.t.* ressusciter. **~ion** /-kʃn/ *n.* résurrection *f.*
resuscitate /rɪ'sʌsɪteɪt/ *v.t.* réanimer.
retail /'ri:teɪl/ *n.* détail *m.* ● *a. & adv.* au détail. ● *v.t./i.* (se) vendre (au détail). **~er** *n.* détaillant(e) *m.* (*f.*).
retain /rɪ'teɪn/ *v.t.* (*hold back, remember*) retenir; (*keep*) conserver.
retaliat|e /rɪ'tælɪeɪt/ *v.i.* riposter. **~ion** /-'eɪʃn/ *n.* représailles *f. pl.*
retarded /rɪ'tɑ:dɪd/ *a.* arriéré.
retch /retʃ/ *v.i.* avoir un haut-le-cœur.
retentive /rɪ'tentɪv/ *a.* (*memory*) fidèle. **~ of,** qui retient.
rethink /ri:'θɪŋk/ *v.t.* (*p.t.* **rethought**) repenser.
reticen|t /'retɪsnt/ *a.* réticent. **~ce** *n.* réticence *f.*
retina /'retɪnə/ *n.* rétine *f.*
retinue /'retɪnju:/ *n.* suite *f.*
retire /rɪ'taɪə(r)/ *v.i.* (*from work*) prendre sa retraite; (*withdraw*) se retirer; (*go to bed*) se coucher. ● *v.t.* mettre à la retraite. **~d** *a.* retraité. **~ment** *n.* retraite *f.*
retiring /rɪ'taɪərɪŋ/ *a.* réservé.
retort /rɪ'tɔ:t/ *v.t./i.* répliquer. ● *n.* réplique *f.*
retrace /ri:'treɪs/ *v.t.* **~ one's steps,** revenir sur ses pas.
retract /rɪ'trækt/ *v.t./i.* (se) rétracter.
retrain /ri:'treɪn/ *v.t./i.* (se) recycler.
retread /ri:'tred/ *n.* pneu rechapé *m.*
retreat /rɪ'tri:t/ *v.i.* (*mil.*) battre en retraite. ● *n.* retraite *f.*
retrial /ri:'traɪəl/ *n.* nouveau procès *m.*
retribution /retrɪ'bju:ʃn/ *n.* châtiment *m.*; (*vengeance*) vengeance *f.*
retriev|e /rɪ'tri:v/ *v.t.* (*recover*) récupérer; (*restore*) rétablir; (*put right*) réparer. **~al** *n.* récupération *f.*; (*of information*) recherche documentaire *f.* **~er** *n.* (*dog*) chien d'arrêt *m.*
retrograde /'retrəgreɪd/ *a.* rétrograde ● *v.i.* rétrograder.
retrospect /'retrəspekt/ *n.* **in ~,** rétrospectivement.
return /rɪ'tɜ:n/ *v.i.* (*come back*) revenir; (*go back*) retourner; (*go home*) rentrer. ● *v.t.* (*give back*) rendre; (*bring back*) rapporter; (*send back*) renvoyer; (*put back*) remettre. ● *n.* retour *m.*; (*yield*) rapport *m.* **~s,** (*comm.*) bénéfices *m. pl.* **in ~ for,** en échange de. **~ journey,** voyage de retour *m.* **~ match,** match retour *m.* **~ ticket,** aller-retour *m.*
reunion /ri:'ju:nɪən/ *n.* réunion *f.*
reunite /ri:ju:'naɪt/ *v.t.* réunir.
rev /rev/ *n.* (*auto., fam.*) tour *m.* ● *v.t./i.* (*p.t.* **revved**). **~ (up),** (*engine: fam.*) (s')emballer.
revamp /ri:'væmp/ *v.t.* rénover.
reveal /rɪ'vi:l/ *v.t.* révéler; (*allow to appear*) laisser voir. **~ing** *a.* révélateur.
revel /'revl/ *v.i.* (*p.t.* **revelled**) faire bombance. **~ in,** se délecter de. **~ry** *n.* festivités *f. pl.*
revelation /revə'leɪʃn/ *n.* révélation *f.*
revenge /rɪ'vendʒ/ *n.* vengeance *f.*; (*sport*) revanche *f.* ● *v.t.* venger.
revenue /'revənju:/ *n.* revenu *m.*
reverberate /rɪ'vɜ:bəreɪt/ *v.i.* (*sound, light*) se répercuter.
revere /rɪ'vɪə(r)/ *v.t.* révérer. **~nce** /'revərəns/ *n.* vénération *f.*
reverend /'revərənd/ *a.* révérend.
reverent /'revərənt/ *a.* respectueux.
reverie /'revərɪ/ *n.* rêverie *f.*
revers|e /rɪ'vɜ:s/ *a.* contraire, inverse. ● *n.* contraire *m.*; (*back*) revers *m.*, envers *m.*; (*gear*) marche arrière *f.* ● *v.t.* (*situation, bracket, etc.*) renverser; (*order*) inverser; (*decision*) annuler. ● *v.i.* (*auto.*) faire marche arrière. **~al** *n.* renversement *m.*; (*of view*) revirement *m.*
revert /rɪ'vɜ:t/ *v.i.* **~ to,** revenir à.
review /rɪ'vju:/ *n.* (*inspection, magazine*) revue *f.*; (*of book etc.*) critique *f.* ● *v.t.* passer en revue; (*situation*) réexaminer; faire la critique de. **~er** *n.* critique *m.*
revis|e /rɪ'vaɪz/ *v.t.* réviser; (*text*) revoir. **~ion** /-ɪʒn/ *n.* révision *f.*
revitalize /ri:'vaɪtəlaɪz/ *v.t.* revitaliser, revivifier.
reviv|e /rɪ'vaɪv/ *v.t.* (*person, hopes*) ranimer; (*play*) reprendre; (*custom*) rétablir. ● *v.i.* se ranimer. **~al** *n.* (*resumption*) reprise *f.*; (*of faith*) renouveau *m.*
revoke /rɪ'vəʊk/ *v.t.* révoquer.
revolt /rɪ'vəʊlt/ *v.t./i.* (se) révolter. ● *n.* révolte *f.*
revolting /rɪ'vəʊltɪŋ/ *a.* dégoûtant.
revolution /revə'lu:ʃn/ *n.* révolution *f.* **~ary** *a. & n.* révolutionnaire (*m./f.*). **~ize** *v.t.* révolutionner.

revolv|e /rɪ'vɒlv/ *v.i.* tourner. **~ing door,** tambour *m.*
revolver /rɪ'vɒlvə(r)/ *n.* revolver *m.*
revulsion /rɪ'vʌlʃn/ *n.* dégoût *m.*
reward /rɪ'wɔ:d/ *n.* récompense *f.* ● *v.t.* récompenser (**for,** de). **~ing** *a.* rémunérateur; (*worthwhile*) qui (en) vaut la peine.
rewind /ri:'waɪnd/ *v.t.* (*p.t.* **rewound**) (*tape, film*) rembobiner.
rewire /ri:'waɪə(r)/ *v.t.* refaire l'installation électrique de.
reword /ri:'wɜ:d/ *v.t.* reformuler.
rewrite /ri:'raɪt/ *v.t.* récrire.
rhapsody /'ræpsədɪ/ *n.* rhapsodie *f.*
rhetoric /'retərɪk/ *n.* rhétorique *f.* **~al** /rɪ'tɒrɪkl/ *a.* (de) rhétorique; (*question*) de pure forme.
rheumati|c /ru:'mætɪk/ *a.* (*pain*) rhumatismal; (*person*) rhumatisant. **~sm** /'ru:mətɪzəm/ *n.* rhumatisme *m.*
rhinoceros /raɪ'nɒsərəs/ *n.* (*pl.* **-oses**) rhinocéros *m.*
rhubarb /'ru:bɑ:b/ *n.* rhubarbe *f.*
rhyme /raɪm/ *n.* rime *f.*; (*poem*) vers *m. pl.* ● *v.t./i.* (faire) rimer.
rhythm /'rɪðəm/ *n.* rythme *m.* **~ic(al)** /'rɪðmɪk(l)/ *a.* rythmique.
rib /rɪb/ *n.* côte *f.*
ribald /'rɪbld/ *a.* grivois.
ribbon /'rɪbən/ *n.* ruban *m.* **in ~s,** (*torn pieces*) en lambeaux.
rice /raɪs/ *n.* riz *m.*
rich /rɪtʃ/ *a.* (**-er, -est**) riche. **~es** *n. pl.* richesses *f. pl.* **~ly** *adv.* richement. **~ness** *n.* richesse *f.*
rickety /'rɪkətɪ/ *a.* branlant.
ricochet /'rɪkəʃeɪ/ *n.* ricochet *m.* ● *v.i.* (*p.t.* **ricocheted** /-ʃeɪd/) ricocher.
rid /rɪd/ *v.t.* (*p.t.* **rid,** *pres. p.* **ridding**) débarrasser (**of,** de). **get ~ of,** se débarrasser de.
riddance /'rɪdns/ *n.* **good ~!,** bon débarras!
ridden /'rɪdn/ *see* ride.
riddle[1] /'rɪdl/ *n.* énigme *f.*
riddle[2] /'rɪdl/ *v.t.* **~ with,** (*bullets*) cribler de; (*mistakes*) bourrer de.
ride /raɪd/ *v.i.* (*p.t.* **rode,** *p.p.* **ridden**) aller (à bicyclette, à cheval, *etc.*); (*in car*) rouler. **~ (a horse),** (*go riding as sport*) monter (à cheval). ● *v.t.* (*a particular horse*) monter; (*distance*) parcourir. ● *n.* promenade *f.*, tour *m.*; (*distance*) trajet *m.* **give s.o. a ~,** (*Amer.*) prendre qn. en voiture. **go for a ~,** aller faire un tour (à bicyclette, à cheval, *etc.*). **~r** /-ə(r)/ *n.* caval|ier, -ière *m., f.*; (*in horse race*) jockey *m.*; (*cyclist*) cycliste *m./f.*; (*motorcyclist*) motocycliste *m./f.*; (*in document*) annexe *f.*
ridge /rɪdʒ/ *n.* arête *f.*, crête *f.*
ridicule /'rɪdɪkju:l/ *n.* ridicule *m.* ● *v.t.* ridiculiser.
ridiculous /rɪ'dɪkjʊləs/ *a.* ridicule.
riding /'raɪdɪŋ/ *n.* équitation *f.*
rife /raɪf/ *a.* **be ~,** être répandu, sévir. **~ with,** abondant en.
riff-raff /'rɪfræf/ *n.* canaille *f.*
rifle /'raɪfl/ *n.* fusil *m.* ● *v.t.* (*rob*) dévaliser.
rift /rɪft/ *n.* (*crack*) fissure *f.*; (*between people*) désaccord *m.*
rig[1] /rɪg/ *v.t.* (*p.t.* **rigged**) (*equip*) équiper. ● *n.* (*for oil*) derrick *m.* **~ out,** habiller. **~-out** *n.* (*fam.*) tenue *f.* **~ up,** (*arrange*) arranger.
rig[2] /rɪg/ *v.t.* (*p.t.* **rigged**) (*election, match, etc.*) truquer.
right /raɪt/ *a.* (*morally*) bon; (*fair*) juste; (*best*) bon, qu'il faut; (*not left*) droit. **be ~,** (*person*) avoir raison (**to,** de); (*calculation, watch*) être exact. ● *n.* (*entitlement*) droit *m.*; (*not left*) droite *f.*; (*not evil*) le bien. ● *v.t.* (*a wrong, sth. fallen, etc.*) redresser. ● *adv.* (*not left*) à droite; (*directly*) tout droit; (*exactly*) bien, juste; (*completely*) tout (à fait). **be in the ~,** avoir raison. **by ~s,** normalement. **on the ~,** à droite. **put ~,** arranger, rectifier. **~ angle,** angle droit *m.* **~ away,** tout de suite. **~-hand** *a.* à *or* de droite. **~-hand man,** bras droit *m.* **~-handed** *a.* droitier. **~ now,** (*at once*) tout de suite; (*at present*) en ce moment. **~ of way,** (*auto.*) priorité *f.* **~-wing** *a.* (*pol.*) de droite.
righteous /'raɪtʃəs/ *a.* (*person*) vertueux; (*cause, anger*) juste.
rightful /'raɪtfl/ *a.* légitime. **~ly** *adv.* à juste titre.
rightly /'raɪtlɪ/ *adv.* correctement; (*with reason*) à juste titre.
rigid /'rɪdʒɪd/ *a.* rigide. **~ity** /rɪ'dʒɪdətɪ/ *n.* rigidité *f.*
rigmarole /'rɪgmərəʊl/ *n.* charabia *m.*; (*procedure*) comédie *f.*
rig|our /'rɪgə(r)/ *n.* rigueur *f.* **~orous** *a.* rigoureux.
rile /raɪl/ *v.t.* (*fam.*) agacer.
rim /rɪm/ *n.* bord *m.*; (*of wheel*) jante *f.* **~med** *a.* bordé.

rind /raɪnd/ *n.* (*on cheese*) croûte *f.*; (*on bacon*) couenne *f.*; (*on fruit*) écorce *f.*

ring [1] /rɪŋ/ *n.* anneau *m.*; (*with stone*) bague *f.*; (*circle*) cercle *m.*; (*boxing*) ring *m.*; (*arena*) piste *f.* ● *v.t.* entourer; (*word in text etc.*) entourer d'un cercle. **(wedding) ~,** alliance *f.* **~ road,** périphérique *m.*

ring [2] /rɪŋ/ *v.t./i.* (*p.t.* **rang,** *p.p.* **rung**) sonner; (*of words etc.*) retentir. ● *n.* sonnerie *f.* **give s.o. a ~,** donner un coup de fil à qn. **~ the bell,** sonner. **~ back,** rappeler. **~ off,** raccrocher. **~ up,** téléphoner (à). **~ing** *n.* (*of bell*) sonnerie *f.* **~ing tone,** tonalité *f.*

ringleader /ˈrɪŋliːdə(r)/ *n.* chef *m.*

rink /rɪŋk/ *n.* patinoire *f.*

rinse /rɪns/ *v.t.* rincer. **~ out,** rincer. ● *n.* rinçage *m.*

riot /ˈraɪət/ *n.* émeute *f.*; (*of colours*) orgie *f.* ● *v.i.* faire une émeute. **run ~,** se déchaîner. **~er** *n.* émeut|ier, -ière *m., f.*

riotous /ˈraɪətəs/ *a.* turbulent.

rip /rɪp/ *v.t./i.* (*p.t.* **ripped**) (se) déchirer. ● *n.* déchirure *f.* **let ~,** (*not check*) laisser courir. **~ off,** (*sl.*) rouler. **~-off** *n.* (*sl.*) vol *m.*

ripe /raɪp/ *a.* (**-er, -est**) mûr. **~ness** *n.* maturité *f.*

ripen /ˈraɪpən/ *v.t./i.* mûrir.

ripple /ˈrɪpl/ *n.* ride *f.*, ondulation *f.*; (*sound*) murmure *m.* ● *v.t./i.* (*water*) (se) rider.

rise /raɪz/ *v.i.* (*p.t.* **rose,** *p.p.* **risen**) (*go upwards, increase*) monter, s'élever; (*stand up, get up from bed*) se lever; (*rebel*) se soulever; (*sun, curtain*) se lever; (*water*) monter. ● *n.* (*slope*) pente *f.*; (*of curtain*) lever *m.*; (*increase*) hausse *f.*; (*in pay*) augmentation *f.*; (*progress, boom*) essor *m.* **give ~ to,** donner lieu à. **~ up,** se soulever. **~r** /-ə(r)/ *n.* **be an early ~r,** se lever tôt.

rising /ˈraɪzɪŋ/ *n.* (*revolt*) soulèvement *m.* ● *a.* (*increasing*) croissant; (*price*) qui monte; (*tide*) montant; (*sun*) levant. **~ generation,** nouvelle génération *f.*

risk /rɪsk/ *n.* risque *m.* ● *v.t.* risquer. **at ~,** menacé. **~ doing,** (*venture*) se risquer à faire. **~y** *a.* risqué.

rissole /ˈrɪsəʊl/ *n.* croquette *f.*

rite /raɪt/ *n.* rite *m.* **last ~s,** derniers sacrements *m. pl.*

ritual /ˈrɪtʃʊəl/ *a.* & *n.* rituel (*m.*).

rival /ˈraɪvl/ *n.* rival(e) *m.* (*f.*). ● *a.* rival; (*claim*) opposé. ● *v.t.* (*p.t.* **rivalled**) rivaliser avec. **~ry** *n.* rivalité *f.*

river /ˈrɪvə(r)/ *n.* rivière *f.*; (*flowing into sea & fig.*) fleuve *m.* ● *a.* (*fishing, traffic, etc.*) fluvial.

rivet /ˈrɪvɪt/ *n.* (*bolt*) rivet *m.* ● *v.t.* (*p.t.* **riveted**) river, riveter. **~ing** *a.* fascinant.

Riviera /rɪvɪˈeərə/ *n.* **the (French) ~,** la Côte d'Azur.

road /rəʊd/ *n.* route *f.*; (*in town*) rue *f.*; (*small*) chemin *m.* ● *a.* (*sign, safety*) routier. **the ~ to,** (*glory etc.: fig.*) le chemin de. **~-block** *n.* barrage routier *m.* **~- hog** *n.* chauffard *m.* **~-map** *n.* carte routière *f.* **~-works** *n. pl.* travaux *m. pl.*

roadside /ˈrəʊdsaɪd/ *n.* bord de la route *m.*

roadway /ˈrəʊdweɪ/ *n.* chaussée *f.*

roadworthy /ˈrəʊdwɜːðɪ/ *a.* en état de marche.

roam /rəʊm/ *v.i.* errer. ● *v.t.* (*streets, seas, etc.*) parcourir.

roar /rɔː(r)/ *n.* hurlement *m.*; rugissement *m.*; grondement *m.* ● *v.t./i.* hurler; (*of lion, wind*) rugir; (*of lorry, thunder*) gronder. **~ with laughter,** rire aux éclats.

roaring /ˈrɔːrɪŋ/ *a.* (*trade, success*) très gros. **~ fire,** belle flambée *f.*

roast /rəʊst/ *v.t./i.* rôtir. ● *n.* (*roast or roasting meat*) rôti *m.* ● *a.* rôti. **~ beef,** rôti de bœuf *m.*

rob /rɒb/ *v.t.* (*p.t.* **robbed**) voler (**s.o. of sth.,** qch. à qn.); (*bank, house*) dévaliser; (*deprive*) priver (**of,** de). **~ber** *n.* voleu|r, -se *m., f.* **~bery** *n.* vol *m.*

robe /rəʊb/ *n.* (*of judge etc.*) robe *f.*; (*dressing-gown*) peignoir *m.*

robin /ˈrɒbɪn/ *n.* rouge-gorge *m.*

robot /ˈrəʊbɒt/ *n.* robot *m.*

robust /rəʊˈbʌst/ *a.* robuste.

rock [1] /rɒk/ *n.* roche *f.*; (*rock face, boulder*) rocher *m.*; (*hurled stone*) pierre *f.*; (*sweet*) sucre d'orge *m.* **on the ~s,** (*drink*) avec des glaçons; (*marriage*) en crise. **~-bottom** *a.* (*fam.*) très bas. **~-climbing** *n.* varappe *f.*

rock [2] /rɒk/ *v.t./i.* (se) balancer; (*shake*) (faire) trembler; (*child*) bercer. ● *n.* (*mus.*) rock *m.* **~ing-chair** *n.* fauteuil à bascule *m.*

rockery /ˈrɒkərɪ/ *n.* rocaille *f.*

rocket /ˈrɒkɪt/ *n.* fusée *f.*

rocky /'rɒkɪ/ *a.* (**-ier, -iest**) (*ground*) rocailleux; (*hill*) rocheux; (*shaky*: *fig.*) branlant.

rod /rɒd/ *n.* (*metal*) tige *f.*; (*for curtain*) tringle *f.*; (*wooden*) baguette *f.*; (*for fishing*) canne à pêche *f.*

rode /rəʊd/ *see* ride.

rodent /'rəʊdnt/ *n.* rongeur *m.*

rodeo /rəʊ'deɪəʊ, *Amer.* 'rəʊdɪəʊ/ *n.* (*pl.* **-os**) rodéo *m.*

roe[1] /rəʊ/ *n.* œufs de poisson *m. pl.*

roe[2] /rəʊ/ *n.* (*pl.* **roe** *or* **roes**) (*deer*) chevreuil *m.*

rogu|e /rəʊg/ *n.* (*dishonest*) bandit *m.*, voleu|r, -se *m.*, *f.*; (*mischievous*) coquin(e) *m.* (*f.*). **~ish** *a.* coquin.

role /rəʊl/ *n.* rôle *m.* **~-playing** *n.* jeu de rôle *m.*

roll /rəʊl/ *v.t./i.* rouler. **~ (about),** (*child, dog*) se rouler. ● *n.* rouleau *m.*; (*list*) liste *f.*; (*bread*) petit pain *m.*; (*of drum, thunder*) roulement *m.*; (*of ship*) roulis *m.* **be ~ing (in money),** (*fam.*) rouler sur l'or. **~-bar** *n.* arceau de sécurité *m.* **~-call** *n.* appel *m.* **~ing-pin** *n.* rouleau à pâtisserie *m.* **~ out,** étendre. **~ over,** (*turn over*) se retourner. **~ up** *v.t.* (*sleeves*) retrousser; *v.i.* (*fam.*) s'amener.

roller /'rəʊlə(r)/ *n.* rouleau *m.* **~-blind** *n.* store *m.* **~-coaster** *n.* montagnes russes *f. pl.* **~-skate** *n.* patin à roulettes *m.*

rollicking /'rɒlɪkɪŋ/ *a.* exubérant.

rolling /'rəʊlɪŋ/ *a.* onduleux.

ROM (*abbr.*) (*read-only memory*) mémoire morte *f.*

Roman /'rəʊmən/ *a.* & *n.* romain(e) (*m.* (*f.*)). **~ Catholic** *a.* & *n.* catholique (*m./f.*). **~ numerals,** chiffres romains *m. pl.*

romance /rə'mæns/ *n.* roman d'amour *m.*; (*love*) amour *m.*; (*affair*) idylle *f.*; (*fig.*) poésie *f.*

Romania /rəʊ'meɪnɪə/ *n.* Roumanie *f.* **~n** *a.* & *n.* roumain(e) (*m.* (*f.*)).

romantic /rə'mæntɪk/ *a.* (*of love etc.*) romantique; (*of the imagination*) romanesque. **~ally** *adv.* (*behave*) en romantique.

romp /rɒmp/ *v.i.* s'ébattre; (*fig.*) réussir. ● *n.* **have a ~**, s'ébattre.

roof /ru:f/ *n.* (*pl.* **roofs**) toit *m.*; (*of tunnel*) plafond *m.*; (*of mouth*) palais *m.* ● *v.t.* recouvrir. **~ing** *n.* toiture *f.* **~-rack** *n.* galerie *f.* **~-top** *n.* toit *m.*

rook[1] /rʊk/ *n.* (*bird*) corneille *f.*

rook[2] /rʊk/ *n.* (*chess*) tour *f.*

room /ru:m/ *n.* pièce *f.*; (*bedroom*) chambre *f.*; (*large hall*) salle *f.*; (*space*) place *f.* **~-mate** *n.* camarade de chambre *m./f.* **~y** *a.* spacieux; (*clothes*) ample.

roost /ru:st/ *n.* perchoir *m.* ● *v.i.* percher. **~er** /'ru:stə(r)/ *n.* coq *m.*

root[1] /ru:t/ *n.* racine *f.*; (*source*) origine *f.* ● *v.t./i.* (s')enraciner. **~out,** extirper. **take ~,** prendre racine. **~less** *a.* sans racines.

root[2] /ru:t/ *v.i.* **~ about,** fouiller. **~ for,** (*Amer., fam.*) encourager.

rope /rəʊp/ *n.* corde *f.* ● *v.t.* attacher. **know the ~s,** être au courant. **~ in,** (*person*) enrôler.

rosary /'rəʊzərɪ/ *n.* chapelet *m.*

rose[1] /rəʊz/ *n.* (*flower*) rose *f.*; (*colour*) rose *m.*; (*nozzle*) pomme *f.*

rose[2] /rəʊz/ *see* rise.

rosé /'rəʊzeɪ/ *n.* rosé *m.*

rosette /rəʊ'zet/ *n.* (*sport*) cocarde *f.*; (*officer's*) rosette *f.*

roster /'rɒstə(r)/ *n.* liste (de service) *f.*, tableau (de service) *m.*

rostrum /'rɒstrəm/ *n.* (*pl.* **-tra**) tribune *f.*; (*sport*) podium *m.*

rosy /'rəʊzɪ/ *a.* (**-ier, -iest**) rose; (*hopeful*) plein d'espoir.

rot /rɒt/ *v.t./i.* (*p.t.* **rotted**) pourrir. ● *n.* pourriture *f.*; (*nonsense*: *sl.*) bêtises *f. pl.*, âneries *f. pl.*

rota /'rəʊtə/ *n.* liste (de service) *f.*

rotary /'rəʊtərɪ/ *a.* rotatif.

rotat|e /rəʊ'teɪt/ *v.t./i.* (faire) tourner; (*change round*) alterner. **~ing** *a.* tournant. **~ion** /-ʃn/ *n.* rotation *f.*

rote /rəʊt/ *n.* **by ~,** machinalement.

rotten /'rɒtn/ *a.* pourri; (*tooth*) gâté; (*bad*: *fam.*) mauvais, sale.

rotund /rəʊ'tʌnd/ *a.* rond.

rouge /ru:ʒ/ *n.* rouge (à joues) *m.*

rough /rʌf/ *a.* (**-er, -est**) (*manners*) rude; (*to touch*) rugueux; (*ground*) accidenté; (*violent*) brutal; (*bad*) mauvais; (*estimate etc.*) approximatif; (*diamond*) brut. ● *adv.* (*live*) à la dure; (*play*) brutalement. ● *n.* (*ruffian*) voyou *m.* ● *v.t.* **~ it,** vivre à la dure. **~-and-ready** *a.* (*solution etc.*) grossier (mais efficace). **~-and-tumble** *n.* mêlée *f.* **~ out,** ébaucher. **~ paper,** papier brouillon *m.* **~ly** *adv.* rudement; (*approximately*) à peu près. **~ness** *n.* rudesse *f.*; brutalité *f.*

roughage /'rʌfɪdʒ/ *n.* fibres (alimentaires) *f. pl.*

roulette /ru:ˈlet/ *n.* roulette *f.*

round /raʊnd/ *a.* (**-er, -est**) rond. ● *n.* (*circle*) rond *m.*; (*slice*) tranche *f.*; (*of visits, drinks*) tournée *f.*; (*mil.*) ronde *f.*; (*competition*) partie *f.*, manche *f.*; (*boxing*) round *m.*; (*of talks*) série *f.* ● *prep.* autour de. ● *adv.* autour. ● *v.t.* (*object*) arrondir; (*corner*) tourner. **go** *or* **come ~ to,** (*a friend etc.*) passer chez. **I'm going ~ the corner,** je vais juste à côté. **enough to go ~,** assez pour tout le monde. **go the ~ s,** circuler. **she lives ~ here** elle habite par ici. **~ about,** (*near by*) par ici; (*fig.*) à peu près. **~ of applause,** applaudissements *m. pl.* **~ off,** terminer. **~ the clock,** vingt-quatre heures sur vingt-quatre. **~ trip,** voyage aller-retour *m.* **~ up,** rassembler. **~-up** *n.* rassemblement *m.*; (*of suspects*) rafle *f.*

roundabout /ˈraʊndəbaʊt/ *n.* manège *m.*; (*for traffic*) rond-point (à sens giratoire) *m.* ● *a.* indirect.

rounders /ˈraʊndəz/ *n.* sorte de baseball *f.*

roundly /ˈraʊndlɪ/ *adv.* (*bluntly*) franchement.

rous|e /raʊz/ *v.t.* éveiller; (*wake up*) réveiller. **be ~ed,** (*angry*) être en colère. **~ing** *a.* (*speech, music*) excitant; (*cheers*) frénétique.

rout /raʊt/ *n.* (*defeat*) déroute *f.* ● *v.t.* mettre en déroute.

route /ru:t/ *n.* itinéraire *m.*, parcours *m.*; (*naut., aviat.*) route *f.*

routine /ru:ˈti:n/ *n.* routine *f.* ● *a.* de routine. **daily ~,** travail quotidien *m.*

rov|e /rəʊv/ *v.t./i.* errer (dans). **~ing** *a.* (*life*) vagabond.

row[1] /rəʊ/ *n.* rangée *f.*, rang *m.* **in a ~,** (*consecutive*) consécutif.

row[2] /rəʊ/ *v.i.* ramer; (*sport*) faire de l'aviron. ● *v.t.* faire aller à la rame. **~ing** *n.* aviron *m.* **~(ing)-boat** *n.* bateau à rames *m.*

row[3] /raʊ/ *n.* (*noise: fam.*) tapage *m.*; (*quarrel; fam.*) engueulade *f.* ● *v.i.* (*fam.*) s'engueuler.

rowdy /ˈraʊdɪ/ *a.* (**-ier, -iest**) tapageur. ● *n.* voyou *m.*

royal /ˈrɔɪəl/ *a.* royal. **~ly** *adv.* (*treat, live, etc.*) royalement.

royalt|y /ˈrɔɪəltɪ/ *n.* famille royale *f.* **~ies,** droits d'auteur *m. pl.*

rub /rʌb/ *v.t./i.* (*p.t.* **rubbed**) frotter. ● *n.* friction *f.* **~ it in,** insister là-dessus. **~ off on,** déteindre sur. **~ out,** (s')effacer.

rubber /ˈrʌbə(r)/ *n.* caoutchouc *m.*; (*eraser*) gomme *f.* **~ band,** élastique *m.* **~ stamp,** tampon *m.* **~-stamp** *v.t.* approuver. **~y** *a.* caoutchouteux.

rubbish /ˈrʌbɪʃ/ *n.* (*refuse*) ordures *f. pl.*; (*junk*) saletés *f. pl.*; (*fig.*) bêtises *f. pl.* **~y** *a.* sans valeur.

rubble /ˈrʌbl/ *n.* décombres *m. pl.*

ruby /ˈru:bɪ/ *n.* rubis *m.*

rucksack /ˈrʌksæk/ *n.* sac à dos *m.*

rudder /ˈrʌdə(r)/ *n.* gouvernail *m.*

ruddy /ˈrʌdɪ/ *a.* (**-ier, -iest**) coloré, rougeâtre; (*damned: sl.*) fichu.

rude /ru:d/ *a.* (**-er, -est**) impoli, grossier; (*improper*) indécent; (*shock, blow*) brutal. **~ly** *adv.* impoliment. **~ness** *n.* impolitesse *f.*; indécence *f.*; brutalité *f.*

rudiment /ˈru:dɪmənt/ *n.* rudiment *m.* **~ary** /-ˈmentrɪ/ *a.* rudimentaire.

rueful /ˈru:fl/ *a.* triste.

ruffian /ˈrʌfɪən/ *n.* voyou *m.*

ruffle /ˈrʌfl/ *v.t.* (*hair*) ébouriffer; (*clothes*) froisser; (*person*) contrarier. ● *n.* (*frill*) ruche *f.*

rug /rʌg/ *n.* petit tapis *m.*

Rugby /ˈrʌgbɪ/ *n.* **~ (football),** rugby *m.*

rugged /ˈrʌgɪd/ *a.* (*surface*) rude, rugueux; (*ground*) accidenté; (*character, features*) rude.

ruin /ˈru:ɪn/ *n.* ruine *f.* ● *v.t.* (*destroy*) ruiner; (*damage*) abîmer; (*spoil*) gâter. **~ous** *a.* ruineux.

rule /ru:l/ *n.* règle *f.*; (*regulation*) règlement *m.*; (*pol.*) gouvernement *m.* ● *v.t.* gouverner; (*master*) dominer; (*decide*) décider. ● *v.i.* régner. **as a ~,** en règle générale. **~ out,** exclure. **~d paper,** papier réglé *m.* **~r** /-ə(r)/ *n.* dirigeant(e) *m.* (*f.*), gouvernant *m.*; (*measure*) règle *f.*

ruling /ˈru:lɪŋ/ *a.* (*class*) dirigeant; (*party*) au pouvoir. ● *n.* décision *f.*

rum /rʌm/ *n.* rhum *m.*

rumble /rʌmbl/ *v.i.* gronder; (*stomach*) gargouiller. ● *n.* grondement *m.*; gargouillement *m.*

rummage /ˈrʌmɪdʒ/ *v.i.* fouiller.

rumour, (*Amer.*) **rumor** /ˈru:mə(r)/ *n.* bruit *m.*, rumeur *f.* **there's a ~ that,** le bruit court que.

rump /rʌmp/ *n.* (*of horse etc.*) croupe *f.*; (*of fowl*) croupion *m.*; (*steak*) romsteck *m.*

rumpus /ˈrʌmpəs/ *n.* (*uproar: fam.*) chahut *m.*

run /rʌn/ *v.i.* (*p.t.* **ran,** *p.p.* **run,** *pres. p.* **running**) courir; (*flow*) couler; (*pass*) passer; (*function*) marcher; (*melt*) fondre; (*extend*) s'étendre; (*of bus etc.*) circuler; (*of play*) se jouer; (*last*) durer; (*of colour in washing*) déteindre; (*in election*) être candidat. ● *v.t.* (*manage*) diriger; (*event*) organiser; (*risk, race*) courir; (*house*) tenir; (*blockade*) forcer; (*temperature, errand*) faire; (*comput.*) exécuter. ● *n.* course *f.*; (*journey*) parcours *m.*; (*outing*) promenade *f.*; (*rush*) ruée *f.*; (*series*) série *f.*; (*in cricket*) point *m.* **have the ~ of,** avoir à sa disposition. **in the long ~,** avec le temps. **on the ~,** en fuite. **~ across,** rencontrer par hasard. **~ away,** s'enfuir. **~ down,** descendre en courant; (*of vehicle*) renverser; (*production*) réduire progressivement; (*belittle*) dénigrer. **be ~ down,** (*weak etc.*) être sans forces *or* mal fichu. **~ in,** (*vehicle*) roder. **~ into,** (*hit*) heurter. **~ off,** (*copies*) tirer. **~-of-the-mill** *a.* ordinaire. **~ out,** (*be used up*) s'épuiser; (*of lease*) expirer. **~ out of,** manquer de. **~ over,** (*of vehicle*) écraser; (*details*) revoir. **~ through sth.,** regarder qch. rapidement. **~ sth. through sth.,** passer qch. à travers qch. **~ up,** (*bill*) accumuler. **the ~-up to,** la période qui précède.

runaway /'rʌnəweɪ/ *n.* fugiti|f, -ve *m.*, *f.* ● *a.* fugitif; (*horse, vehicle*) fou; (*inflation*) galopant.

rung [1] /rʌŋ/ *n.* (*of ladder*) barreau *m.*

rung [2] /rʌŋ/ *see* ring[2].

runner /'rʌnə(r)/ *n.* coureu|r, -se *m.*, *f.* **~ bean,** haricot (grimpant) *m.* **~-up** *n.* second(e) *m.* (*f.*).

running /'rʌnɪŋ/ *n.* course *f.*; (*of business*) gestion *f.*; (*of machine*) marche *f.* ● *a.* (*commentary*) suivi; (*water*) courant. **be in the ~ for,** être sur les rangs pour. **four days/etc. ~,** quatre jours/*etc.* de suite.

runny /'rʌnɪ/ *a.* (*nose*) qui coule.

runt /rʌnt/ *n.* avorton *m.*

runway /'rʌnweɪ/ *n.* piste *f.*

rupture /'rʌptʃə(r)/ *n.* (*breaking, breach*) rupture *f.*; (*med.*) hernie *f.* ● *v.t./i.* (se) rompre. **~ o.s.,** se donner une hernie.

rural /'rʊərəl/ *a.* rural.

ruse /ru:z/ *n.* (*trick*) ruse *f.*

rush [1] /rʌʃ/ *n.* (*plant*) jonc *m.*

rush [2] /rʌʃ/ *v.i.* (*move*) se précipiter; (*be in a hurry*) se dépêcher. ● *v.t.* faire, envoyer, *etc.* en vitesse; (*person*) bousculer; (*mil.*) prendre d'assaut. ● *n.* ruée *f.*; (*haste*) bousculade *f.* **in a ~,** pressé. **~-hour** *n.* heure de pointe *f.*

rusk /rʌsk/ *n.* biscotte *f.*

russet /'rʌsɪt/ *a.* roussâtre, roux.

Russia /'rʌʃə/ *n.* Russie *f.* **~n** *a.* & *n.* russe (*m./f.*); (*lang.*) russe *m.*

rust /rʌst/ *n.* rouille *f.* ● *v.t./i.* rouiller. **~-proof** *a.* inoxydable. **~y** *a.* (*tool, person, etc.*) rouillé.

rustic /'rʌstɪk/ *a.* rustique.

rustle /'rʌsl/ *v.t./i.* (*leaves*) (faire) bruire; (*steal*: *Amer.*) voler. **~ up,** (*food etc.*: *fam.*) préparer.

rut /rʌt/ *n.* ornière *f.* **be in a ~,** rester dans l'ornière.

ruthless /'ru:θlɪs/ *a.* impitoyable. **~ness** *n.* cruauté *f.*

rye /raɪ/ *n.* seigle *m.*; (*whisky*) whisky *m.* (*à base de seigle*).

S

sabbath /'sæbəθ/ *n.* (*Jewish*) sabbat *m.*; (*Christian*) dimanche *m.*

sabbatical /sə'bætɪkl/ *a.* (*univ.*) sabbatique.

sabot|age /'sæbətɑ:ʒ/ *n.* sabotage *m.* ● *v.t.* saboter. **~eur** /-'tɜ:(r)/ *n.* saboteu|r, -se *m.*, *f.*

saccharin /'sækərɪn/ *n.* saccharine *f.*

sachet /'sæʃeɪ/ *n.* sachet *m.*

sack [1] /sæk/ *n.* (*bag*) sac *m.* ● *v.t.* (*fam.*) renvoyer. **get the ~,** (*fam.*) être renvoyé. **~ing** *n.* toile à sac *f.*; (*dismissal*: *fam.*) renvoi *m.*

sack [2] /sæk/ *v.t.* (*plunder*) saccager.

sacrament /'sækrəmənt/ *n.* sacrement *m.*

sacred /'seɪkrɪd/ *a.* sacré.

sacrifice /'sækrɪfaɪs/ *n.* sacrifice *m.* ● *v.t.* sacrifier.

sacrileg|e /'sækrɪlɪdʒ/ *n.* sacrilège *m.* **~ious** /-'lɪdʒəs/ *a.* sacrilège.

sad /sæd/ *a.* (**sadder, saddest**) triste. **~ly** *adv.* tristement; (*unfortunately*) malheureusement. **~ness** *n.* tristesse *f.*

sadden /'sædn/ *v.t.* attrister.

saddle /'sædl/ *n.* selle *f.* ● *v.t.* (*horse*) seller. **~ s.o. with,** (*task,* *person*) coller à qn. **in the ~,** bien en selle. **~-bag** *n.* sacoche *f.*

sadis|t /'seɪdɪst/ *n.* sadique *m./f.* **~m** /-zəm/ *n.* sadisme *m.* **~tic** /sə'dɪstɪk/ *a.* sadique.

safari /sə'fɑːrɪ/ *n.* safari *m.*

safe /seɪf/ *a.* (**-er, -est**) (*not dangerous*) sans danger; (*reliable*) sûr; (*out of danger*) en sécurité; (*after accident*) sain et sauf; (*wise*: *fig.*) prudent. ● *n.* coffre-fort *m.* **to be on the ~ side,** pour être sûr. **in ~ keeping,** en sécurité. **~ conduct,** sauf-conduit *m.* **~ from,** à l'abri de. **~ly** *adv.* sans danger; (*in safe place*) en sûreté.

safeguard /'seɪfgɑːd/ *n.* sauvegarde *f.* ● *v.t.* sauvegarder.

safety /'seɪftɪ/ *n.* sécurité *f.* **~-belt** *n.* ceinture de sécurité *f.* **~-pin** *n.* épingle de sûreté *f.* **~-valve** *n.* soupape de sûreté *f.*

saffron /'sæfrən/ *n.* safran *m.*

sag /sæg/ *v.i.* (*p.t.* **sagged**) s'affaisser, fléchir. **~ging** *a.* affaissé.

saga /'sɑːgə/ *n.* saga *f.*

sage[1] /seɪdʒ/ *n.* (*herb*) sauge *f.*

sage[2] /seɪdʒ/ *a.* & *n.* sage (*m.*).

Sagittarius /sædʒɪ'teərɪəs/ *n.* le Sagittaire.

said /sed/ *see* say.

sail /seɪl/ *n.* voile *f.*; (*journey*) tour en bateau *m.* ● *v.i.* naviguer; (*leave*) partir; (*sport*) faire de la voile; (*glide*) glisser. ● *v.t.* (*boat*) piloter. **~ing-boat, ~ing ship** *ns* bateau à voiles *m.*

sailor /'seɪlə(r)/ *n.* marin *m.*

saint /seɪnt/ *n.* saint(e) *m.* (*f.*). **~ly** *a.* (*person, act, etc.*) saint.

sake /seɪk/ *n.* **for the ~ of,** pour, pour l'amour de.

salad /'sæləd/ *n.* salade *f.* **~-dressing** *n.* vinaigrette *f.*

salami /sə'lɑːmɪ/ *n.* salami *m.*

salar|y /'sælərɪ/ *n.* traitement *m.*, salaire *m.* **~ied** *a.* salarié.

sale /seɪl/ *n.* vente *f.* **~s,** (*at reduced prices*) soldes *m. pl.* **~s assistant,** (*Amer.*) **~s clerk,** vendeu|r, -se *m., f.* **for ~,** à vendre. **on ~,** en vente; (*at a reduced price*: *Amer.*) en solde. **~-room** *n.* salle des ventes *f.*

saleable /'seɪləbl/ *a.* vendable.

sales|man /'seɪlzmən/ *n.* (*pl.* **-men**) (*in shop*) vendeur *m.*; (*traveller*) représentant *m.* **~woman** *n.* (*pl.* **-women**) vendeuse *f.*; représentante *f.*

salient /'seɪlɪənt/ *a.* saillant.

saline /'seɪlaɪn/ *a.* salin. ● *n.* sérum physiologique *m.*

saliva /sə'laɪvə/ *n.* salive *f.*

sallow /'sæləʊ/ *a.* (**-er, -est**) (*complexion*) jaunâtre.

salmon /'sæmən/ *n. invar.* saumon *m.*

salon /'sælɒn/ *n.* salon *m.*

saloon /sə'luːn/ *n.* (*on ship*) salon *m.*; (*bar*: *Amer.*) bar *m.*, saloon *m.* **~ (car),** berline *f.*

salt /sɔːlt/ *n.* sel *m.* ● *a.* (*culin.*) salé; (*water*) de mer. ● *v.t.* saler. **~-cellar** *n.* salière *f.* **~y** *a.* salé.

salutary /'sæljʊtrɪ/ *a.* salutaire.

salute /sə'luːt/ *n.* (*mil.*) salut *m.* ● *v.t.* saluer. ● *v.i.* faire un salut.

salvage /'sælvɪdʒ/ *n.* sauvetage *m.*; (*of waste*) récupération *f.*; (*goods*) objets sauvés *m. pl.* ● *v.t.* sauver; (*for re-use*) récupérer.

salvation /sæl'veɪʃn/ *n.* salut *m.*

salvo /'sælvəʊ/ *n.* (*pl.* **-oes**) salve *f.*

same /seɪm/ *a.* même (**as,** que). ● *pron.* **the ~,** le *or* la même, les mêmes. **at the ~ time,** en même temps. **the ~ (thing),** la même chose.

sample /'sɑːmpl/ *n.* échantillon *m.*; (*of blood*) prélèvement *m.* ● *v.t.* essayer; (*food*) goûter.

sanatorium /sænə'tɔːrɪəm/ *n.* (*pl.* **-iums**) sanatorium *m.*

sanctify /'sæŋktɪfaɪ/ *v.t.* sanctifier.

sanctimonious /sæŋktɪ'məʊnɪəs/ *a.* (*person*) bigot; (*air, tone*) de petit saint.

sanction /'sæŋkʃn/ *n.* sanction *f.* ● *v.t.* sanctionner.

sanctity /'sæŋktətɪ/ *n.* sainteté *f.*

sanctuary /'sæŋktʃʊərɪ/ *n.* (*relig.*) sanctuaire *m.*; (*for animals*) réserve *f.*; (*refuge*) asile *m.*

sand /sænd/ *n.* sable *m.* **~s,** (*beach*) plage *f.* ● *v.t.* sabler. **~-castle** *n.* château de sable *m.* **~-pit,** (*Amer.*) **~-box** *n.* bac à sable *m.*

sandal /'sændl/ *n.* sandale *f.*

sandpaper /'sændpeɪpə(r)/ *n.* papier de verre *m.* ● *v.t.* poncer.

sandstone /'sændstəʊn/ *n.* grès *m.*

sandwich /'sænwɪdʒ/ *n.* sandwich *m.* ● *v.t.* **~ed between,** pris en sandwich entre. **~ course,** stage de formation continue à mi-temps *m.*

sandy /'sændɪ/ *a.* sablonneux, de sable; (*hair*) blond roux *invar.*

sane /seɪn/ *a.* (**-er, -est**) (*view etc.*) sain; (*person*) sain d'esprit. **~ly** *adv.* sainement.
sang /sæŋ/ *see* sing.
sanitary /'sænɪtrɪ/ *a.* (*clean*) hygiénique; (*system etc.*) sanitaire. **~ towel,** (*Amer.*) **~ napkin,** serviette hygiénique *f.*
sanitation /sænɪ'teɪʃn/ *n.* hygiène (publique) *f.*; (*drainage etc.*) système sanitaire *m.*
sanity /'sænətɪ/ *n.* santé mentale *f.*; (*good sense*: *fig.*) bon sens *m.*
sank /sæŋk/ *see* sink.
Santa Claus /'sæntəklɔ:z/ *n.* le père Noël.
sap /sæp/ *n.* (*of plants*) sève *f.* ● *v.t.* (*p.t.* **sapped**) (*undermine*) saper.
sapphire /'sæfaɪə(r)/ *n.* saphir *m.*
sarcas|m /'sɑ:kæzəm/ *n.* sarcasme *m.* **~tic** /sɑ:'kæstɪk/ *a.* sarcastique.
sardine /sɑ:'di:n/ *n.* sardine *f.*
Sardinia /sɑ:'dɪnɪə/ *n.* Sardaigne *f.*
sardonic /sɑ:'dɒnɪk/ *a.* sardonique.
sash /sæʃ/ *n.* (*on uniform*) écharpe *f.*; (*on dress*) ceinture *f.* **~-window** *n.* fenêtre à guillotine *f.*
sat /sæt/ *see* sit.
satanic /sə'tænɪk/ *a.* satanique.
satchel /'sætʃl/ *n.* cartable *m.*
satellite /'sætəlaɪt/ *n.* & *a.* satellite (*m.*). **~ dish,** antenne parabolique *f.*
satin /'sætɪn/ *n.* satin *m.*
satir|e /'sætaɪə(r)/ *n.* satire *f.* **~ical** /sə'tɪrɪkl/ *a.* satirique.
satisfactor|y /sætɪs'fæktərɪ/ *a.* satisfaisant. **~ily** *adv.* d'une manière satisfaisante.
satisf|y /'sætɪsfaɪ/ *v.t.* satisfaire; (*convince*) convaincre. **~action** /-'fækʃn/ *n.* satisfaction *f.* **~ying** *a.* satisfaisant.
satsuma /sæt'su:mə/ *n.* mandarine *f.*
saturat|e /'sætʃəreɪt/ *v.t.* saturer. **~ed** *a.* (*wet*) trempé. **~ion** /-'reɪʃn/ *n.* saturation *f.*
Saturday /'sætədɪ/ *n.* samedi *m.*
sauce /sɔ:s/ *n.* sauce *f.*; (*impudence*: *sl.*) toupet *m.*
saucepan /'sɔ:spən/ *n.* casserole *f.*
saucer /'sɔ:sə(r)/ *n.* soucoupe *f.*
saucy /'sɔ:sɪ/ *a.* (**-ier, -iest**) impertinent; (*boldly smart*) coquin.
Saudi Arabia /saʊdɪə'reɪbɪə/ *n.* Arabie Séoudite *f.*
sauna /'sɔ:nə/ *n.* sauna *m.*
saunter /'sɔ:ntə(r)/ *v.i.* flâner.
sausage /'sɒsɪdʒ/ *n.* saucisse *f.*; (*precooked*) saucisson *m.*
savage /'sævɪdʒ/ *a.* (*fierce*) féroce; (*wild*) sauvage. ● *n.* sauvage *m./f.* ● *v.t.* attaquer férocement. **~ry** *n.* sauvagerie *f.*
sav|e /seɪv/ *v.t.* sauver; (*money*) économiser; (*time*) (faire) gagner; (*keep*) garder; (*prevent*) éviter (**from,** de). ● *n.* (*football*) arrêt *m.* ● *prep.* sauf. **~er** *n.* épargnant(e) *m.* (*f.*). **~ing** *n.* (*of time, money*) économie *f.* **~ings** *n. pl.* économies *f. pl.*
saviour, (*Amer.*) **savior** /'seɪvɪə(r)/ *n.* sauveur *m.*
savour, (*Amer.*) **savor** /'seɪvə(r)/ *n.* saveur *f.* ● *v.t.* savourer. **~y** *a.* (*tasty*) savoureux; (*culin.*) salé.
saw[1] /sɔ:/ *see* see[1].
saw[2] /sɔ:/ *n.* scie *f.* ● *v.t.* (*p.t.* **sawed,** *p.p.* **sawn** /sɔ:n/ *or* **sawed**) scier.
sawdust /'sɔ:dʌst/ *n.* sciure *f.*
saxophone /'sæksəfəʊn/ *n.* saxophone *m.*
say /seɪ/ *v.t./i.* (*p.t.* **said** /sed/) dire; (*prayer*) faire. ● *n.* **have a ~,** dire son mot; (*in decision*) avoir voix au chapitre. **I ~!,** dites donc!
saying /'seɪɪŋ/ *n.* proverbe *m.*
scab /skæb *n.* (*on sore*) croûte *f.*; (*blackleg*: *fam.*) jaune *m.*
scaffold /'skæfəʊld/ *n.* (*gallows*) échafaud *m.* **~ing** /-əldɪŋ/ *n.* (*for workmen*) échafaudage *m.*
scald /skɔ:ld/ *v.t.* (*injure, cleanse*) ébouillanter. ● *n.* brûlure *f.*
scale[1] /skeɪl/ *n.* (*of fish*) écaille *f.*
scale[2] /skeɪl/ *n.* (*for measuring, size, etc.*) échelle *f.*; (*mus.*) gamme *f.*; (*of salaries, charges*) barême *m.* **on a small/***etc.* **~,** sur une petite *etc.* échelle. **~ model,** maquette *f.* ● *v.t.* (*climb*) escalader. **~ down,** réduire (proportionnellement).
scales /skeɪlz/ *n. pl.* (*for weighing*) balance *f.*
scallop /'skɒləp/ *n.* coquille Saint-Jacques *f.*
scalp /skælp/ *n.* cuir chevelu *m.* ● *v.t.* (*mutilate*) scalper.
scalpel /'skælp(ə)l/ *n.* scalpel *m.*
scamper /'skæmpə(r)/ *v.i.* courir, trotter. **~ away,** détaler.
scampi /'skæmpɪ/ *n. pl.* grosses crevettes *f. pl.*, gambas *f. pl.*
scan /skæn/ *v.t.* (*p.t.* **scanned**) scruter; (*quickly*) parcourir; (*poetry*) scander; (*of radar*) balayer. ● *n.* (*ultrasound*) échographie *f.*

scandal /ˈskændl/ *n.* (*disgrace, outrage*) scandale *m.*; (*gossip*) cancans *m. pl.* **~ous** *a.* scandaleux.

scandalize /ˈskændəlaɪz/ *v.t.* scandaliser.

Scandinavia /skændɪˈneɪvɪə/ *n.* Scandinavie *f.* **~n** *a.* & *n.* scandinave (*m./f.*).

scant /skænt/ *a.* insuffisant.

scant|y /ˈskæntɪ/ *a.* (**-ier, -iest**) insuffisant; (*clothing*) sommaire. **~ily** *adv.* insuffisamment. **~ily dressed,** à peine vêtu.

scapegoat /ˈskeɪpgəʊt/ *n* bouc émissaire *m.*

scar /skɑː(r)/ *n.* cicatrice *f.* ● *v.t.* (*p.t.* **scarred**) marquer d'une cicatrice; (*fig.*) marquer.

scarc|e /skeəs/ *a.* (**-er, -est**) rare. **make o.s. ~e,** (*fam.*) se sauver. **~ity** *n.* rareté *f.*, pénurie *f.*

scarcely /ˈskeəslɪ/ *adv.* à peine.

scare /ˈskeə(r)/ *v.t.* faire peur à. ● *n.* peur *f.* **be ~d,** avoir peur. **bomb ~,** alerte à la bombe *f.*

scarecrow /ˈskeəkrəʊ/ *n.* épouvantail *m.*

scarf /skɑːf/ *n.* (*pl.* **scarves**) écharpe *f.*; (*over head*) foulard *m.*

scarlet /ˈskɑːlət/ *a.* écarlate. **~ fever,** scarlatine *f.*

scary /ˈskeərɪ/ *a.* (**-ier, -iest**) (*fam.*) qui fait peur, effrayant.

scathing /ˈskeɪðɪŋ/ *a.* cinglant.

scatter /ˈskætə(r)/ *v.t.* (*throw*) éparpiller, répandre; (*disperse*) disperser. ● *v.i.* se disperser. **~brain** *n.* écervelé(e) *m.* (*f.*).

scavenge /ˈskævɪndʒ/ *v.i.* fouiller (dans les ordures). **~r** /-ə(r)/ *n.* (*vagrant*) personne qui fouille dans les ordures *f.*

scenario /sɪˈnɑːrɪəʊ/ *n.* (*pl.* **-os**) scénario *m.*

scene /siːn/ *n.* scène *f.*; (*of accident, crime*) lieu(x) *m.* (*pl.*); (*sight*) spectacle *m.*; (*incident*) incident *m.* **behind the ~s,** en coulisse. **to make a ~,** faire un esclandre.

scenery /ˈsiːnərɪ/ *n.* paysage *m.*; (*theatre*) décor(s) *m.* (*pl.*).

scenic /ˈsiːnɪk/ *a.* pittoresque.

scent /sent/ *n.* (*perfume*) parfum *m.*; (*trail*) piste *f.* ● *v.t.* flairer; (*make fragrant*) parfumer.

sceptic /ˈskeptɪk/ *n.* sceptique *m./f.* **~al** *a.* sceptique. **~ism** /-sɪzəm/ *n.* scepticisme *m.*

schedule /ˈʃedjuːl, *Amer.* ˈskedʒʊl/ *n.* horaire *m.*; (*for job*) planning *m.* ● *v.t.* prévoir. **behind ~,** en retard. **on ~,** (*train*) à l'heure; (*work*) dans les temps. **~d flight,** vol régulier *m.*

scheme /skiːm/ *n.* plan *m.*; (*dishonest*) combine *f.*; (*fig.*) arrangement *m.* ● *v.i.* intriguer. **pension ~,** caisse de retraite *f.* **~r** /-ə(r)/ *n.* intrigant(e) *m.* (*f.*).

schism /ˈsɪzəm/ *n.* schisme *m.*

schizophrenic /skɪtsəʊˈfrenɪk/ *a.* & *n.* schizophrène (*m./f.*).

scholar /ˈskɒlə(r)/ *n.* érudit(e) *m.* (*f.*) **~ly** *a.* érudit. **~ship** *n.* érudition *f.*; (*grant*) bourse *f.*

school /skuːl/ *n.* école *f.*; (*secondary*) lycée *m.*; (*of university*) faculté *f.* ● *a.* (*age, year, holidays*) scolaire. ● *v.t.* (*person*) éduquer; (*animal*) dresser. **~ing** *n.* (*education*) instruction *f.*; (*attendance*) scolarité *f.*

school|boy /ˈskuːlbɔɪ/ *n.* écolier *m.* **~girl** *n.* écolière *f.*

school|master /ˈskuːlmɑːstə(r)/, **~mistress, ~teacher** *ns.* (*primary*) institu|teur, -trice *m., f.*; (*secondary*) professeur *m.*

schooner /ˈskuːnə(r)/ *n.* goélette *f.*

sciatica /saɪˈætɪkə/ *n.* sciatique *f.*

scien|ce /ˈsaɪəns/ *n.* science *f.* **~ce fiction,** science-fiction *f.* **~tific** /-ˈtɪfɪk/ *a.* scientifique.

scientist /ˈsaɪəntɪst/ *n.* scientifique *m./f.*

scintillate /ˈsɪntɪleɪt/ *v.i.* scintiller; (*person: fig.*) briller.

scissors /ˈsɪzəz/ *n. pl.* ciseaux *m. pl.*

scoff[1] /skɒf/ *v.i.* **~ at,** se moquer de.

scoff[2] /skɒf/ *v.t.* (*eat: sl.*) bouffer.

scold /skəʊld/ *v.t.* réprimander. **~ing** *n.* réprimande *f.*

scone /skɒn/ *n.* petit pain au lait *m.*, galette *f.*

scoop /skuːp/ *n.* (*for grain, sugar*) pelle (à main) *f.*; (*for food*) cuiller *f.*; (*ice cream*) boule *f.*; (*news*) exclusivité *f.* ● *v.t.* (*pick up*) ramasser. **~ out,** creuser. **~ up,** ramasser.

scoot /skuːt/ *v.i.* (*fam.*) filer.

scooter /ˈskuːtə(r)/ *n.* (*child's*) trottinette *f.*; (*motor cycle*) scooter *m.*

scope /skəʊp/ *n.* étendue *f.*; (*competence*) compétence *f.*; (*opportunity*) possibilité(s) *f.* (*pl.*).

scorch /skɔːtʃ/ *v.t.* brûler, roussir. **~ing** *a.* brûlant, très chaud.

score /skɔː(r)/ *n.* score *m.*; (*mus.*) partition *f.* ● *v.t.* marquer; (*suc-*

cess) remporter. ● *v.i.* marquer un point; (*football*) marquer un but; (*keep score*) compter les points. **a ~ (of)**, (*twenty*) vingt. **on that ~**, à cet égard. **~ out**, rayer. **~-board** *n.* tableau *m.* **~r** /-ə(r)/ *n.* (*sport*) marqueur *m.*

scorn /skɔ:n/ *n.* mépris *m.* ● *v.t.* mépriser. **~ful** *a.* méprisant. **~fully** *adv.* avec mépris.

Scorpio /'skɔ:pɪəʊ/ *n.* le Scorpion.

scorpion /'skɔ:pɪən/ *n.* scorpion *m.*

Scot /skɒt/ *n.* Écossais(e) *m.* (*f.*). **~tish** *a.* écossais.

Scotch /skɒtʃ/ *a.* écossais. ● *n.* whisky *m.*, scotch *m.*

scotch /skɒtʃ/ *v.t.* mettre fin à.

scot-free /skɒt'fri:/ *a.* & *adv.* sans être puni; (*gratis*) sans payer.

Scotland /'skɒtlənd/ *n.* Écosse *f.*

Scots /skɒts/ *a.* écossais. **~man** *n.* Écossais *m.* **~woman** *n.* Écossaise *f.*

scoundrel /'skaʊndrəl/ *n.* vaurien *m.*, bandit *m.*, gredin(e) *m.* (*f.*).

scour[1] /'skaʊə(r)/ *v.t.* (*pan*) récurer. **~er** *n.* tampon à récurer *m.*

scour[2] /'skaʊə(r)/ *v.t.* (*search*) parcourir.

scourge /skɜ:dʒ/ *n.* fléau *m.*

scout /skaʊt/ *n.* (*mil.*) éclaireur *m.* ● *v.i.* **~ around (for)**, chercher.

Scout /skaʊt/ *n.* (*boy*) scout *m.*, éclaireur *m.* **~ing** *n.* scoutisme *m.*

scowl /skaʊl/ *n.* air renfrogné *m.* ● *v.i.* faire la tête (**at**, à).

scraggy /'skrægɪ/ *a.* (**-ier, -iest**) décharné, efflanqué.

scram /skræm/ *v.i.* (*sl.*) se tirer.

scramble /'skræmbl/ *v.i.* (*clamber*) grimper. ● *v.t.* (*eggs*) brouiller. ● *n.* bousculade *f.*, ruée *f.* **~ for**, se bousculer pour avoir.

scrap[1] /skræp/ *n.* petit morceau *m.* **~s**, (*of metal, fabric, etc.*) déchets *m. pl.*; (*of food*) restes *m. pl.* ● *v.t.* (*p.t.* **scrapped**) mettre au rebut; (*plan etc.*) abandonner. **~-book** *n.* album *m.* **on the ~-heap**, mis au rebut. **~-iron** *n.* ferraille *f.* **~-paper** *n.* brouillon *m.* **~py** *a.* fragmentaire.

scrap[2] /skræp/ *n.* (*fight*: *fam.*) bagarre *f.*, dispute *f.*

scrape /skreɪp/ *v.t.* racler, gratter; (*graze*) érafler. ● *v.i.* (*rub*) frotter. ● *n.* raclement *m.*; éraflure *f.* **in a ~**, dans une mauvaise passe. **~ through**, réussir de justesse. **~ together**, réunir. **~r** /-ə(r)/ *n.* racloir *m.*

scratch /skrætʃ/ *v.t./i.* (se) gratter; (*with claw, nail*) griffer; (*graze*) érafler; (*mark*) rayer. ● *n.* éraflure *f.* **start from ~**, partir de zéro. **up to ~**, au niveau voulu.

scrawl /skrɔ:l/ *n.* gribouillage *m.* ● *v.t./i.* gribouiller.

scrawny /'skrɔ:nɪ/ *a.* (**-ier, -iest**) décharné, émacié.

scream /skri:m/ *v.t./i.* crier, hurler. ● *n.* cri (perçant) *m.*

scree /skri:/ *n.* éboulis *m.*

screech /skri:tʃ/ *v.i.* (*scream*) hurler; (*of brakes*) grincer. ● *n.* hurlement *m.*; grincement *m.*

screen /skri:n/ *n.* écran *m.*; (*folding*) paravent *m.* ● *v.t.* masquer; (*protect*) protéger; (*film*) projeter; (*candidates*) filtrer; (*med.*) faire subir un test de dépistage. **~ing** *n.* projection *f.*

screenplay /'skri:npleɪ/ *n.* scénario *m.*

screw /skru:/ *n.* vis *f.* ● *v.t.* visser. **~ up**, (*eyes*) plisser; (*ruin*: *sl.*) bousiller.

screwdriver /'skru:draɪvə(r)/ *n.* tournevis *m.*

screwy /'skru:ɪ/ *a.* (**-ier, -iest**) (*crazy*: *sl.*) cinglé.

scribble /'skrɪbl/ *v.t./i.* griffonner. ● *n.* griffonnage *m.*

scribe /skraɪb/ *n.* scribe *m.*

script /skrɪpt/ *n.* écriture *f.*; (*of film*) scénario *m.*; (*of play*) texte *m.* **~-writer** *n.* scénariste *m./f.*

Scriptures /'skrɪptʃəz/ *n. pl.* **the ~**, l'Écriture (sainte) *f.*

scroll /skrəʊl/ *n.* rouleau *m.* ● *v.t./i.* (*comput.*) (faire) défiler.

scrounge /skraʊndʒ/ *v.t.* (*meal*) se faire payer; (*steal*) chiper. ● *v.i.* (*beg*) quémander. **~ money from**, taper. **~r** /-ə(r)/ *n.* parasite *m.*; (*of money*) tapeu|r, -se *m.*, *f.*

scrub[1] /skrʌb/ *n.* (*land*) broussailles *f. pl.*

scrub[2] /skrʌb/ *v.t./i.* (*p.t.* **scrubbed**) nettoyer (à la brosse), frotter. ● *n.* nettoyage *m.*

scruff /skrʌf/ *n.* **by the ~ of the neck**, par la peau du cou.

scruffy /'skrʌfɪ/ *a.* (**-ier, -iest**) (*fam.*) miteux, sale.

scrum /skrʌm/ *n.* (*Rugby*) mêlée *f.*

scruple /'skru:pl/ *n.* scrupule *m.*

scrupulous /'skru:pjʊləs/ *a.* scrupuleux. **~ly** *adv.* scrupu-

leusement. **~ly clean,** impeccable.
scrutin|y /'skru:tɪnɪ/ *n.* examen minutieux *m.* **~ize** *v.t.* scruter.
scuba-diving /'sku:bədaɪvɪŋ/ *n.* plongée sous-marine *f.*
scuff /skʌf/ *v.t.* (*scratch*) érafler.
scuffle /'skʌfl/ *n.* bagarre *f.*
sculpt /skʌlpt/ *v.t./i.* sculpter. **~or** *n.* sculpteur *m.* **~ure** /-tʃə(r)/ *n.* sculpture *f.*; *v.t./i.* sculpter.
scum /skʌm/ *n.* (*on liquid*) écume *f.*; (*people: pej.*) racaille *f.*
scurf /skɜ:f/ *n.* pellicules *f. pl.*
scurrilous /'skʌrɪləs/ *a.* grossier, injurieux, venimeux.
scurry /'skʌrɪ/ *v.i.* courir (**for,** pour chercher). **~ off,** filer.
scuttle[1] /'skʌtl/ *v.t.* (*ship*) saborder.
scuttle[2] /'skʌtl/ *v.i.* **~ away,** se sauver, filer.
scythe /saɪð/ *n.* faux *f.*
sea /si:/ *n.* mer *f.* ● *a.* de (la) mer, marin. **at ~,** en mer. **by ~,** par mer. **~-green** *a.* vert glauque *invar.* **~-level** *n.* niveau de la mer *m.* **~ shell,** coquillage *m.* **~shore** *n.* rivage *m.*
seaboard /'si:bɔ:d/ *n.* littoral *m.*
seafarer /'si:feərə(r)/ *n.* marin *m.*
seafood /'si:fu:d/ *n.* fruits de mer *m. pl.*
seagull /'si:gʌl/ *n.* mouette *f.*
seal[1] /si:l/ *n.* (*animal*) phoque *m.*
seal[2] /si:l/ *n.* sceau *m.*; (*with wax*) cachet *m.* ● *v.t.* sceller; cacheter; (*stick down*) coller. **~ing-wax** *n.* cire à cacheter *f.* **~ off,** (*area*) boucler.
seam /si:m/ *n.* (*in cloth etc.*) couture *f.*; (*of coal*) veine *f.*
seaman /'si:mən/ *n.* (*pl.* **-men**) marin *m.*
seamy /'si:mɪ/ *a.* **~ side,** côté sordide *m.*
seance /'seɪɑ:ns/ *n.* séance de spiritisme *f.*
seaplane /'si:pleɪn/ *n.* hydravion *m.*
seaport /'si:pɔ:t/ *n.* port de mer *m.*
search /sɜ:tʃ/ *v.t./i.* fouiller; (*study*) examiner. ● *n.* fouille *f.*; (*quest*) recherche(s) *f.* (*pl.*). **in ~ of,** à la recherche de. **~ for,** chercher. **~-party** *n.* équipe de secours *f.* **~-warrant** *n.* mandat de perquisition *m.* **~ing** *a.* (*piercing*) pénétrant.
searchlight /'sɜ:tʃlaɪt/ *n.* projecteur *m.*
seasick /'si:sɪk/ *a.* **be ~,** avoir le mal de mer.
seaside /'si:saɪd/ *n.* bord de la mer *m.*
season /'si:zn/ *n.* saison *f.* ● *v.t.* assaisonner. **in ~,** de saison. **~able** *a.* qui convient à la saison. **~al** *a.* saisonnier. **~ing** *n.* assaisonnement *m.* **~-ticket** *n.* carte d'abonnement *f.*
seasoned /'si:znd/ *a.* expérimenté.
seat /si:t/ *n.* siège *m.*; (*place*) place *f.*; (*of trousers*) fond *m.* ● *v.t.* (*put*) placer; (*have seats for*) avoir des places assises pour. **be ~ed, take a ~,** s'asseoir. **~-belt** *n.* ceinture de sécurité *f.*
seaweed /'si:wi:d/ *n.* algues *f. pl.*
seaworthy /'si:wɜ:ðɪ/ *a.* en état de naviguer.
secateurs /sekə'tɜ:z/ *n. pl.* sécateur *m.*
sece|de /sɪ'si:d/ *v.i.* faire sécession. **~ssion** /-eʃn/ *n.* sécession *f.*
seclu|de /sɪ'klu:d/ *v.t.* isoler. **~ded** *a.* isolé. **~sion** /-ʒn/ *n.* solitude *f.*
second[1] /'sekənd/ *a.* deuxième, second. ● *n.* deuxième *m./f.*, second(e) *m.* (*f.*); (*unit of time*) seconde *f.* **~s,** (*goods*) articles de second choix *m. pl.* ● *adv.* (*in race etc.*) en seconde place. ● *v.t.* (*proposal*) appuyer. **~-best** *a.* de second choix, numéro deux *invar.* **~-class** *a.* de deuxième classe. **at ~ hand,** de seconde main. **~-hand** *a. & adv.* d'occasion; *n.* (*on clock*) trotteuse *f.* **~-rate** *a.* médiocre. **have ~ thoughts,** avoir des doutes, changer d'avis. **on ~ thoughts,** (*Amer.*) **on ~ thought,** à la réflexion. **~ly** *adv.* deuxièmement.
second[2] /sɪ'kɒnd/ *v.t.* (*transfer*) détacher (**to,** à). **~ment** *n.* détachement *m.*
secondary /'sekəndrɪ/ *a.* secondaire. **~ school,** lycée *m.*, collège *m.*
secrecy /'si:krəsɪ/ *n.* secret *m.*
secret /'si:krɪt/ *a.* secret. ● *n.* secret *m.* **in ~,** en secret. **~ly** *adv.* en secret, secrètement.
secretariat /sekrə'teərɪət/ *n.* secrétariat *m.*
secretar|y /'sekrətrɪ/ *n.* secrétaire *m./f.* **S~y of State,** ministre *m.*; (*Amer.*) ministre des Affaires étrangères *m.* **~ial** /-'teərɪəl/ *a.* (*work etc.*) de secrétaire.
secret|e /sɪ'kri:t/ *v.t.* (*med.*) sécréter. **~ion** /-ʃn/ *n.* sécrétion *f.*
secretive /'si:krətɪv/ *a.* cachottier.

sect /sekt/ *n.* secte *f.* **~arian** /-'teərɪən/ *a.* sectaire.

section /'sekʃn/ *n.* section *f.*; (*of country, town*) partie *f.*; (*in store*) rayon *m.*; (*newspaper column*) rubrique *f.*

sector /'sektə(r)/ *n.* secteur *m.*

secular /'sekjʊlə(r)/ *a.* (*school etc.*) laïque; (*art, music, etc.*) profane.

secure /sɪ'kjʊə(r)/ *a.* (*safe*) en sûreté; (*in mind*) tranquille; (*psychologically*) sécurisé; (*firm*) solide; (*against attack*) sûr; (*window etc.*) bien fermé. ● *v.t.* attacher; (*obtain*) s'assurer; (*ensure*) assurer. **~ly** *adv.* solidement; (*safely*) en sûreté.

security /sɪ'kjʊərətɪ/ *n.* (*safety*) sécurité *f.*; (*for loan*) caution *f.* **~ guard,** vigile *m.*

sedan /sɪ'dæn/ *n.* (*Amer.*) berline *f.*

sedate[1] /sɪ'deɪt/ *a.* calme.

sedat|e[2] /sɪ'deɪt/ *v.t.* donner un sédatif à. **~ion** /-ʃn/ *n.* sédation *f.*

sedative /'sedətɪv/ *n.* sédatif *m.*

sedentary /'sedntrɪ/ *a.* sédentaire.

sediment /'sedɪmənt/ *n.* sédiment *m.*

sedition /sɪ'dɪʃn/ *n.* sédition *f.*

seduce /sɪ'dju:s/ *v.t.* séduire. **~r** /-ə(r)/ *n.* séduc|teur, -trice *m., f.*

seduct|ion /sɪ'dʌkʃn/ *n.* séduction *f.* **~ive** /-tɪv/ *a.* séduisant.

see[1] /si:/ *v.t./i.* (*p.t.* **saw,** *p.p.* **seen**) voir; (*escort*) (r)accompagner. **~ about** *or* **to,** s'occuper de. **~ through,** (*task*) mener à bonne fin; (*person*) deviner (le jeu de). **~ (to it) that,** veiller à ce que. **see you (soon)!,** à bientôt! **~ing that,** vu que.

see[2] /si:/ *n.* (*of bishop*) évêché *m.*

seed /si:d/ *n.* graine *f.*; (*collectively*) graines *f. pl.*; (*origin: fig.*) germe *m.*; (*tennis*) tête de série *f.* **go to ~,** (*plant*) monter en graine; (*person*) se laisser aller. **~ling** *n.* plant *m.*

seedy /'si:dɪ/ *a.* (**-ier, -iest**) miteux.

seek /si:k/ *v.t.* (*p.t.* **sought**) chercher. **~ out,** aller chercher.

seem /si:m/ *v.i.* sembler. **~ingly** *adv.* apparemment.

seemly /'si:mlɪ/ *adv.* convenable.

seen /si:n/ *see* see[1].

seep /si:p/ *v.i.* (*ooze*) suinter. **~ into,** s'infiltrer dans. **~age** *n.* suintement *m.*; infiltration *f.*

see-saw /'si:sɔ:/ *n.* balançoire *f.*, tapecul *m.* ● *v.t.* osciller.

seethe /si:ð/ *v.i.* **~ with,** (*anger*) bouillir de; (*people*) grouiller de.

segment /'segmənt/ *n.* segment *m.*; (*of orange*) quartier *m.*

segregat|e /'segrɪgeɪt/ *v.t.* séparer. **~ion** /-'geɪʃn/ *n.* ségrégation *f.*

seize /si:z/ *v.t.* saisir; (*take possession of*) s'emparer de. ● *v.i.* **~ on,** (*chance etc.*) saisir. **~ up,** (*engine etc.*) se gripper.

seizure /'si:ʒə(r)/ *n.* (*med.*) crise *f.*

seldom /'seldəm/ *adv.* rarement.

select /sɪ'lekt/ *v.t.* choisir, sélectionner. ● *a.* choisi; (*exclusive*) sélect. **~ion** /-kʃn/ *n.* sélection *f.*

selective /sɪ'lektɪv/ *a.* sélectif.

self /self/ *n.* (*pl.* **selves**) (*on cheque*) moi-même. **the ~,** le moi *m. invar.* **your good ~,** vous-même.

self- /self/ *pref.* **~-assurance** *n.* assurance *f.* **~-assured** *a.* sûr de soi. **~-catering** *a.* où l'on fait la cuisine soi-même. **~-centred,** (*Amer.*) **~-entered** *a.* égocentrique. **~-coloured,** (*Amer.*) **~-colored** *a.* uni. **~-confidence** *n.* confiance en soi *f.* **~-confident** *a.* sûr de soi. **~-conscious** *a.* gêné, timide. **~-contained** *a.* (*flat*) indépendant. **~-control** *n.* maîtrise de soi *f.* **~-defence** *n.* autodéfense *f.*; (*jurid.*) légitime défense *f.* **~-denial** *n.* abnégation *f.* **~-employed** *a.* qui travaille à son compte. **~-esteem** *n.* amour-propre *m.* **~-evident** *a.* évident. **~-government** *n.* autonomie *f.* **~-indulgent** *a.* qui se permet tout. **~-interest** *n.* intérêt personnel *m.* **~-portrait** *n.* autoportrait *m.* **~-possessed** *a.* assuré. **~-reliant** *a.* indépendant. **~-respect** *n.* respect de soi *m.*, dignité *f.* **~-righteous** *a.* satisfait de soi. **~-sacrifice** *n.* abnégation *f.* **~-satisfied** *a.* content de soi. **~-seeking** *a.* égoïste. **~-service** *n.* & *a.* libre-service (*m.*). **~-styled** *a.* soi-disant. **~-sufficient** *a.* indépendant. **~-willed** *a.* entêté.

selfish /'selfɪʃ/ *a.* égoïste; (*motive*) intéressé. **~ness** *n.* égoïsme *m.*

selfless /'selflɪs/ *a.* désintéressé.

sell /sel/ *v.t./i.* (*p.t.* **sold**) (se) vendre. **~-by date,** date limite de vente *f.* **be sold out of,** n'avoir plus de. **~ off,** liquider. **~-out,** *n.* trahison *f.* **it was a ~-out,** on a vendu tous les billets. **~ up,** vendre son fonds, sa maison, *etc.* **~er** *n.* vendeu|r, -se *m., f.*

Sellotape /'seləʊteɪp/ *n.* (P.) scotch *m.* (P.).

semantic /sɪ'mæntɪk/ *a.* sémantique. **~s** *n.* sémantique *f.*
semaphore /'seməfɔ:(r)/ *n.* signaux à bras *m. pl.*; (*device: rail.*) sémaphore *m.*
semblance /'sembləns/ *n.* semblant *m.*
semen /'si:mən/ *n.* sperme *m.*
semester /sɪ'mestə(r)/ *n.* (*univ., Amer.*) semestre *m.*
semi- /'semɪ/ *pref.* semi-, demi-.
semibreve /'semɪbri:v/ *n.* (*mus.*) ronde *f.*
semicirc|le /'semɪsɜ:kl/ *n.* demi-cercle *m.* **~ular** /-'sɜ:kjʊlə(r)/ *a.* en demi-cercle.
semicolon /semɪ'kəʊlən/ *n.* point-virgule *m.*
semiconductor /semɪkən'dʌktə(r)/ *n.* semi-conducteur *n.*
semi-detached /semɪ'dɪtætʃt/ *a.* **~ house,** maison jumelée *f.*
semifinal /semɪ'faɪnl/ *n.* demi-finale *f.*
seminar /'semɪnɑ:(r)/ *n.* séminaire *m.*
seminary /'semɪnərɪ/ *n.* séminaire *m.*
semiquaver /'semɪkweɪvə(r)/ *n.* (*mus.*) double croche *f.*
Semit|e /'si:maɪt, *Amer.* 'semaɪt/ *n.* Sémite *m./f.* **~ic** /sɪ'mɪtɪk/ *a.* sémite; (*lang.*) sémitique.
semolina /semə'li:nə/ *n.* semoule *f.*
senat|e /'senɪt/ *n.* sénat *m.* **~or** /-ətə(r)/ *n.* sénateur *m.*
send /send/ *v.t./i.* (*p.t.* **sent**) envoyer. **~ away,** (*dismiss*) renvoyer. **~ (away** *or* **off) for,** commander (par la poste). **~ back,** renvoyer. **~ for,** (*person, help*) envoyer chercher. **~ a player off,** renvoyer un joueur. **~-off** *n.* adieux chaleureux *m. pl.* **~ up,** (*fam.*) parodier. **~er** *n.* expédi|teur, -trice *m., f.*
senil|e /'si:naɪl/ *a.* sénile. **~ity** /sɪ'nɪlətɪ/ *n.* sénilité *f.*
senior /'si:nɪə(r)/ *a.* plus âgé (**to,** que); (*in rank*) supérieur; (*teacher, partner*) principal. ● *n.* aîné(e) *m.* (*f.*); (*schol.*) grand(e) *m.* (*f.*). **~ citizen,** personne âgée *f.* **~ity** /-'ɒrətɪ/ *n.* priorité d'âge *f.*; supériorité *f.*; (*in service*) ancienneté *f.*
sensation /sen'seɪʃn/ *n.* sensation *f.* **~al** *a.* (*event*) qui fait sensation; (*wonderful*) sensationnel.
sense /sens/ *n.* sens *m.*; (*sensation*) sensation *f.*; (*mental impression*) sentiment *m.*; (*common sense*) bon sens *m.* **~s,** (*mind*) raison *f.* ● *v.t.* (pres)sentir. **make ~,** avoir du sens. **make ~ of,** comprendre. **~less** *a.* stupide; (*med.*) sans connaissance.
sensibilit|y /sensə'bɪlətɪ/ *n.* sensibilité *f.* **~ies,** susceptibilité *f.*
sensible /'sensəbl/ *a.* raisonnable, sensé; (*clothing*) fonctionnel.
sensitiv|e /'sensətɪv/ *a.* sensible (**to,** à); (*touchy*) susceptible. **~ity** /-'tɪvətɪ/ *n.* sensibilité *f.*
sensory /'sensərɪ/ *a.* sensoriel.
sensual /'senʃʊəl/ *a.* sensuel. **~ity** /-'ælətɪ/ *n.* sensualité *f.*
sensuous /'senʃʊəs/ *a.* sensuel.
sent /sent/ *see* send.
sentence /'sentəns/ *n.* phrase *f.*; (*decision: jurid.*) jugement *m.*, condamnation *f.*; (*punishment*) peine *f.* ● *v.t.* **~ to,** condamner à.
sentiment /'sentɪmənt/ *n.* sentiment *m.*
sentimental /sentɪ'mentl/ *a.* sentimental. **~ity** /-'tælətɪ/ *n.* sentimentalité *f.*
sentry /'sentrɪ/ *n.* sentinelle *f.*
separable /'sepərəbl/ *a.* séparable.
separate[1] /'seprət/ *a.* séparé, différent; (*independent*) indépendant. **~s** *n. pl.* coordonnés *m. pl.* **~ly** *adv.* séparément.
separat|e[2] /'sepəreɪt/ *v.t./i.* (se) séparer. **~ion** /-'reɪʃn/ *n.* séparation *f.*
September /sep'tembə(r)/ *n.* septembre *m.*
septic /'septɪk/ *a.* (*wound*) infecté. **~ tank,** fosse septique *f.*
sequel /'si:kwəl/ *n.* suite *f.*
sequence /'si:kwəns/ *n.* (*order*) ordre *m.*; (*series*) suite *f.*; (*of film*) séquence *f.*
sequin /'si:kwɪn/ *n.* paillette *f.*
serenade /serə'neɪd/ *n.* sérénade *f.* ● *v.t.* donner une sérénade à.
seren|e /sɪ'ri:n/ *a.* serein. **~ity** /-enətɪ/ *n.* sérénité *f.*
sergeant /'sɑ:dʒənt/ *n.* (*mil.*) sergent *m.*; (*policeman*) brigadier *m.*
serial /'sɪərɪəl/ *n.* (*story*) feuilleton *m.* ● *a.* (*number*) de série.
series /'sɪərɪz/ *n. invar.* série *f.*
serious /'sɪərɪəs/ *a.* sérieux; (*very bad, critical*) grave, sérieux. **~ly** *adv.* sérieusement, gravement. **take ~ly,** prendre au sérieux. **~ness** *n.* sérieux *m.*
sermon /'sɜ:mən/ *n.* sermon *m.*
serpent /'sɜ:pənt/ *n.* serpent *m.*

serrated /sɪ'reɪtɪd/ *a.* (*edge*) en dents de scie.
serum /'sɪərəm/ *n.* (*pl.* **-a**) sérum *m.*
servant /'sɜ:vənt/ *n.* domestique *m./f.*; (*of God etc.*) serviteur *m.*
serve /sɜ:v/ *v.t./i.* servir; (*undergo, carry out*) faire; (*of transport*) desservir. ● *n.* (*tennis*) service *m.* **~ as/to,** servir de/à. **~ its purpose,** remplir sa fonction.
service /'sɜ:vɪs/ *n.* service *m.*; (*maintenance*) révision *f.*; (*relig.*) office *m.* **~s,** (*mil.*) forces armées *f. pl.* ● *v.t.* (*car etc.*) réviser. **of ~ to,** utile à. **~ area,** (*auto.*) aire de services *f.* **~ charge,** service *m.* **~ station,** station-service *f.*
serviceable /'sɜ:vɪsəbl/ *a.* (*usable*) utilisable; (*useful*) commode; (*durable*) solide.
serviceman /'sɜ:vɪsmən/ *n.* (*pl.* **-men**) militaire *m.*
serviette /sɜ:vɪ'et/ *n.* serviette *f.*
servile /'sɜ:vaɪl/ *a.* servile.
session /'seʃn/ *n.* séance *f.*; (*univ.*) année (universitaire) *f.*; (*univ., Amer.*) semestre *m.*
set /set/ *v.t.* (*p.t.* **set,** *pres. p.* **setting**) mettre; (*put down*) poser, mettre; (*limit etc.*) fixer; (*watch, clock*) régler; (*example, task*) donner; (*for printing*) composer; (*in plaster*) plâtrer. ● *v.i.* (*of sun*) se coucher; (*of jelly*) prendre. ● *n.* (*of chairs, stamps, etc.*) série *f.*; (*of knives, keys, etc.*) jeu *m.*; (*of people*) groupe *m.*; (*TV, radio*) poste *m.*; (*style of hair*) mise en plis *f.*; (*theatre*) décor *m.*; (*tennis*) set *m.*; (*mathematics*) ensemble *m.* ● *a.* fixe; (*in habits*) régulier; (*meal*) à prix fixe; (*book*) au programme. **~ against sth.,** opposé à. **be ~ on doing,** être résolu à faire. **~ about** *or* **to,** se mettre à. **~ back,** (*delay*) retarder; (*cost: sl.*) coûter. **~-back** *n.* revers *m.* **~ fire to,** mettre le feu à. **~ free,** libérer. **~ in,** (*take hold*) s'installer, commencer. **~ off** *or* **out,** partir. **~ off,** (*mechanism, activity*) déclencher; (*bomb*) faire éclater. **~ out,** (*state*) exposer; (*arrange*) disposer. **~ out to do sth.,** entreprendre de faire qch. **~ sail,** partir. **~ square,** équerre *f.* **~ to,** (*about to*) sur le point de. **~-to** *n.* querelle *f.* **~ to music,** mettre en musique. **~ up,** (*establish*) fonder, établir; (*launch*) lancer. **~-up** *n.* (*fam.*) affaire *f.*
settee /se'ti:/ *n.* canapé *m.*
setting /'setɪŋ/ *n.* cadre *m.*
settle /'setl/ *v.t.* (*arrange, pay*) régler; (*date*) fixer; (*nerves*) calmer. ● *v.i.* (*come to rest*) se poser; (*live*) s'installer. **~ down,** se calmer; (*become orderly*) se ranger. **~ for,** accepter. **~ in,** s'installer. **~ up (with),** régler. **~r** /-ə(r)/ *n.* colon *m.*
settlement /'setlmənt/ *n.* règlement *m.* (**of,** de); (*agreement*) accord *m.*; (*place*) colonie *f.*
seven /'sevn/ *a. & n.* sept (*m.*). **~th** *a. & n.* septième (*m./f.*).
seventeen /sevn'ti:n/ *a. & n.* dix-sept (*m.*). **~th** *a. & n.* dix-septième (*m./f.*).
sevent|y /'sevntɪ/ *a. & n.* soixante-dix (*m.*). **~ieth** *a. & n.* soixante-dixième (*m./f.*).
sever /'sevə(r)/ *v.t.* (*cut*) couper; (*relations*) rompre. **~ance** *n.* (*breaking off*) rupture *f.* **~ance pay,** indemnité de licenciement *f.*
several /'sevrəl/ *a. & pron.* plusieurs.
sever|e /sɪ'vɪə(r)/ *a.* (**-er, -est**) sévère; (*violent*) violent; (*serious*) grave. **~ely** *adv.* sévèrement; gravement. **~ity** /sɪ'verətɪ/ *n.* sévérité *f.*; violence *f.*; gravité *f.*
sew /səʊ/ *v.t./i.* (*p.t.* **sewed,** *p.p.* **sewn** *or* **sewed**) coudre. **~ing** *n.* couture *f.* **~ing-machine** *n.* machine à coudre *f.*
sewage /'sju:ɪdʒ/ *n.* eaux d'égout *f. pl.*, vidanges *f. pl.*
sewer /'su:ə(r)/ *n.* égout *m.*
sewn /səʊn/ *see* sew.
sex /seks/ *n.* sexe *m.* ● *a.* sexuel. **have ~,** avoir des rapports (sexuels). **~ maniac,** obsédé(e) sexuel(le) *m.* (*f.*). **~y** *a.* sexy *invar.*
sexist /'seksɪst/ *a. & n.* sexiste (*m./f.*).
sextet /seks'tet/ *n.* sextuor *m.*
sexual /'sekʃʊəl/ *a.* sexuel. **~ intercourse,** rapports sexuels *m. pl.* **~ity** /-'ælətɪ/ *n.* sexualité *f.*
shabb|y /'ʃæbɪ/ *a.* (**-ier, -iest**) (*place, object*) minable, miteux; (*person*) pauvrement vêtu; (*mean*) mesquin. **~ily** *adv.* (*dress*) pauvrement; (*act*) mesquinement.
shack /ʃæk/ *n.* cabane *f.*
shackles /'ʃæklz/ *n. pl.* chaînes *f. pl.*
shade /ʃeɪd/ *n.* ombre *f.*; (*of colour, opinion*) nuance *f.*; (*for lamp*) abat-jour *m.*; (*blind: Amer.*) store *m.* **a ~**

bigger/*etc.*, légèrement plus grand/*etc.* ● *v.t.* (*of person etc.*) abriter; (*of tree*) ombrager.

shadow /ˈʃædəʊ/ *n.* ombre *f.* ● *v.t.* (*follow*) filer. **S~ Cabinet,** cabinet fantôme *m.* **~y** *a.* ombragé; (*fig.*) vague.

shady /ˈʃeɪdɪ/ *a.* (**-ier, -iest**) ombragé; (*dubious: fig.*) louche.

shaft /ʃɑːft/ *n.* (*of arrow*) hampe *f.*; (*axle*) arbre *m.*; (*of mine*) puits *m.*; (*of light*) rayon *m.*

shaggy /ˈʃægɪ/ *a.* (**-ier, -iest**) (*beard*) hirsute; (*hair*) broussailleux; (*animal*) à longs poils.

shake /ʃeɪk/ *v.t.* (*p.t.* **shook,** *p.p.* **shaken**) secouer; (*bottle*) agiter; (*house, belief, etc.*) ébranler. ● *v.i.* trembler. ● *n.* secousse *f.* **~ hands with,** serrer la main à. **~ off,** (*get rid of*) se débarrasser de. **~ one's head,** (*in refusal*) dire non de la tête. **~ up,** (*disturb, rouse, mix contents of*) secouer. **~-up** *n.* (*upheaval*) remaniement *m.*

shaky /ˈʃeɪkɪ/ *a.* (**-ier, -iest**) (*hand, voice*) tremblant; (*table etc.*) branlant; (*weak: fig.*) faible.

shall /ʃæl, *unstressed* ʃ(ə)l/ *v. aux.* **I ~ do,** je ferai. **we ~ do,** nous ferons.

shallot /ʃəˈlɒt/ *n.* échalote *f.*

shallow /ˈʃæləʊ/ *a.* (**-er, -est**) peu profond; (*fig.*) superficiel.

sham /ʃæm/ *n.* comédie *f.*; (*person*) imposteur *m.*; (*jewel*) imitation *f.* ● *a.* faux; (*affected*) feint. ● *v.t.* (*p.t.* **shammed**) feindre.

shambles /ˈʃæmblz/ *n. pl.* (*mess: fam.*) désordre *m.*, pagaille *f.*

shame /ʃeɪm/ *n.* honte *f.* ● *v.t.* faire honte à. **it's a ~,** c'est dommage. **~ful** *a.* honteux. **~fully** *adv.* honteusement. **~less** *a.* éhonté.

shamefaced /ˈʃeɪmfeɪst/ *a.* honteux.

shampoo /ʃæmˈpuː/ *n.* shampooing *m.* ● *v.t.* faire un shampooing à, shampooiner.

shandy /ˈʃændɪ/ *n.* panaché *m.*

shan't /ʃɑːnt/ = shall not.

shanty /ˈʃæntɪ/ *n.* (*shack*) baraque *f.* **~ town,** bidonville *m.*

shape /ʃeɪp/ *n.* forme *f.* ● *v.t.* (*fashion, mould*) façonner; (*future etc.: fig.*) déterminer. ● *v.i.* **~ up,** (*plan etc.*) prendre tournure *or* forme; (*person etc.*) faire des progrès. **~less** *a.* informe.

shapely /ˈʃeɪplɪ/ *a.* (**-ier, -iest**) (*leg, person*) bien tourné.

share /ʃeə(r)/ *n.* part *f.*; (*comm.*) action *f.* ● *v.t./i.* partager; (*feature*) avoir en commun. **~-out** *n.* partage *m.*

shareholder /ˈʃeəhəʊldə(r)/ *n.* actionnaire *m./f.*

shark /ʃɑːk/ *n.* requin *m.*

sharp /ʃɑːp/ *a.* (**-er, -est**) (*knife etc.*) tranchant; (*pin etc.*) pointu; (*point*) aigu; (*acute*) vif; (*sudden*) brusque; (*dishonest*) peu scrupuleux. ● *adv.* (*stop*) net. **six o'clock**/*etc.* **~,** six heures/*etc.* pile. ● *n.* (*mus.*) dièse *m.* **~ly** *adv.* (*harshly*) vivement; (*suddenly*) brusquement.

sharpen /ˈʃɑːpən/ *v.t.* aiguiser; (*pencil*) tailler. **~er** *n.* (*for pencil*) taille-crayon(s) *m.*

shatter /ˈʃætə(r)/ *v.t./i.* (*glass etc.*) (faire) voler en éclats, (se) briser; (*upset, ruin*) anéantir.

shav|e /ʃeɪv/ *v.t./i.* (se) raser. ● *n.* **have a ~e,** se raser. **~en** *a.* rasé. **~er** *n.* rasoir électrique *m.* **~ing-brush** *n.* blaireau *m.* **~ing-cream** *n.* crème à raser *f.*

shaving /ˈʃeɪvɪŋ/ *n.* copeau *m.*

shawl /ʃɔːl/ *n.* châle *m.*

she /ʃiː/ *pron.* elle. ● *n.* femelle *f.*

sheaf /ʃiːf/ *n.* (*pl.* **sheaves**) gerbe *f.*

shear /ʃɪə(r)/ *v.t.* (*p.p.* **shorn** *or* **sheared**) (*sheep etc.*) tondre. **~ off,** se détacher.

shears /ʃɪəz/ *n. pl.* cisaille(s) *f.* (*pl.*).

sheath /ʃiːθ/ *n.* (*pl.* **-s** /ʃiːðz/) gaine *f.*, fourreau *m.*; (*contraceptive*) préservatif *m.*

sheathe /ʃiːð/ *v.t.* rengainer.

shed[1] /ʃed/ *n.* remise *f.*

shed[2] /ʃed/ *v.t.* (*p.t.* **shed,** *pres. p.* **shedding**) perdre; (*light, tears*) répandre.

sheen /ʃiːn/ *n.* lustre *m.*

sheep /ʃiːp/ *n. invar.* mouton *m.* **~-dog** *n.* chien de berger *m.*

sheepish /ˈʃiːpɪʃ/ *a.* penaud. **~ly** *adv.* d'un air penaud.

sheepskin /ˈʃiːpskɪn/ *n.* peau de mouton *f.*

sheer /ʃɪə(r)/ *a.* pur (et simple); (*steep*) à pic; (*fabric*) très fin. ● *adv.* à pic, verticalement.

sheet /ʃiːt/ *n.* drap *m.*; (*of paper*) feuille *f.*; (*of glass, ice*) plaque *f.*

sheikh /ʃeɪk/ *n.* cheik *m.*

shelf /ʃelf/ *n.* (*pl.* **shelves**) rayon *m.* étagère *f.* **on the ~,** (*person*) laissé pour compte.

shell /ʃel/ *n.* coquille *f.*; (*on beach*) coquillage *m.*; (*of building*) carcasse *f.*; (*explosive*) obus *m.* ● *v.t.* (*nut etc.*) décortiquer; (*peas*) écosser; (*mil.*) bombarder.

shellfish /ˈʃelfɪʃ/ *n. invar.* (*lobster etc.*) crustacé(s) *m.* (*pl.*); (*mollusc*) coquillage(s) *m.* (*pl.*).

shelter /ˈʃeltə(r)/ *n.* abri *m.* ● *v.t./i.* (s')abriter; (*give lodging to*) donner asile à. **~ed** *a.* (*life etc.*) protégé.

shelve /ʃelv/ *v.t.* (*plan etc.*) laisser en suspens, remettre à plus tard.

shelving /ˈʃelvɪŋ/ *n.* (*shelves*) rayonnage(s) *m.* (*pl.*).

shepherd /ˈʃepəd/ *n.* berger *m.* ● *v.t.* (*people*) guider. **~'s pie,** hachis Parmentier *m.*

sherbet /ˈʃɜːbət/ *n.* jus de fruits *m.*; (*powder*) poudre acidulée *f.*; (*water-ice: Amer.*) sorbet *m.*

sheriff /ˈʃerɪf/ *n.* shérif *m.*

sherry /ˈʃerɪ/ *n.* xérès *m.*

shield /ʃiːld/ *n.* bouclier *m.*; (*screen*) écran *m.* ● *v.t.* protéger.

shift /ʃɪft/ *v.t./i.* (se) déplacer, bouger; (*exchange, alter*) changer de. ● *n.* changement *m.*; (*workers*) équipe *f.*; (*work*) poste *m.*; (*auto.: Amer.*) levier de vitesse *m.* **make ~,** se débrouiller. **~ work,** travail par roulement *m.*

shiftless /ˈʃɪftlɪs/ *a.* paresseux.

shifty /ˈʃɪftɪ/ *a.* (**-ier, -iest**) louche.

shilling /ˈʃɪlɪŋ/ *n.* shilling *m.*

shilly-shally /ˈʃɪlɪʃælɪ/ *v.i.* hésiter, balancer.

shimmer /ˈʃɪmə(r)/ *v.i.* chatoyer. ● *n.* chatoiement *m.*

shin /ʃɪn/ *n.* tibia *m.*

shine /ʃaɪn/ *v.t./i.* (*p.t.* **shone** /ʃɒn/) (faire) briller. ● *n.* éclat *m.*, brillant *m.* **~ one's torch** *or* **the light (on),** éclairer.

shingle /ˈʃɪŋgl/ *n.* (*pebbles*) galets *m. pl.*; (*on roof*) bardeau *m.*

shingles /ˈʃɪŋglz/ *n. pl.* (*med.*) zona *m.*

shiny /ˈʃaɪnɪ/ *a.* (**-ier, -iest**) brillant.

ship /ʃɪp/ *n.* bateau *m.*, navire *m.* ● *v.t.* (*p.t.* **shipped**) transporter; (*send*) expédier; (*load*) embarquer. **~ment** *n.* cargaison *f.*, envoi *m.* **~per** *n.* expéditeur *m.* **~ping** *n.* (*ships*) navigation *f.*, navires *m. pl.*

shipbuilding /ˈʃɪpbɪldɪŋ/ *n.* construction navale *f.*

shipshape /ˈʃɪpʃeɪp/ *adv.* & *a.* parfaitement en ordre.

shipwreck /ˈʃɪprek/ *n.* naufrage *m.* **~ed** *a.* naufragé. **be ~ed,** faire naufrage.

shipyard /ˈʃɪpjɑːd/ *n.* chantier naval *m.*

shirk /ʃɜːk/ *v.t.* esquiver. **~er** *n.* tire-au-flanc *m. invar.*

shirt /ʃɜːt/ *n.* chemise *f.*; (*of woman*) chemisier *m.* **in ~-sleeves,** en bras de chemise.

shiver /ˈʃɪvə(r)/ *v.i.* frissonner. ● *n.* frisson *m.*

shoal /ʃəʊl/ *n.* (*of fish*) banc *m.*

shock /ʃɒk/ *n.* choc *m.*, secousse *f.*; (*electr.*) décharge *f.*; (*med.*) choc *m.* ● *a.* (*result*) choc *invar.*; (*tactics*) de choc. ● *v.t.* choquer. **~ absorber,** amortisseur *m.* **be a ~er,** (*fam.*) être affreux. **~ing** *a.* choquant; (*bad: fam.*) affreux. **~ingly** *adv.* (*fam.*) affreusement.

shodd|y /ˈʃɒdɪ/ *a.* (**-ier, -iest**) mal fait, mauvais. **~ily** *adv.* mal.

shoe /ʃuː/ *n.* chaussure *f.*, soulier *m.*; (*of horse*) fer (à cheval) *m.*; (*in vehicle*) sabot (de frein) *m.* ● *v.t.* (*p.t.* **shod** /ʃɒd/, *pres. p.* **shoeing**) (*horse*) ferrer. **~ repairer,** cordonnier *m.* **on a ~string,** avec très peu d'argent.

shoehorn /ˈʃuːhɔːn/ *n.* chausse-pied *m.*

shoelace /ˈʃuːleɪs/ *n.* lacet *m.*

shoemaker /ˈʃuːmeɪkə(r)/ *n.* cordonnier *m.*

shone /ʃɒn/ *see* shine.

shoo /ʃuː/ *v.t.* chasser.

shook /ʃʊk/ *see* shake.

shoot /ʃuːt/ *v.t.* (*p.t.* **shot**) (*gun*) tirer un coup de; (*missile, glance*) lancer; (*kill, wound*) tuer, blesser (d'un coup de fusil, de pistolet, *etc.*); (*execute*) fusiller; (*hunt*) chasser; (*film*) tourner. ● *v.i.* tirer (**at,** sur). ● *n.* (*bot.*) pousse *f.* **~ down,** abattre. **~ out,** (*rush*) sortir en vitesse. **~ up,** (*spurt*) jaillir; (*grow*) pousser vite. **hear ~ing,** entendre des coups de feu. **~ing-range** *n.* stand de tir *m.* **~ing star,** étoile filante *f.*

shop /ʃɒp/ *n.* magasin *m.*, boutique *f.*; (*workshop*) atelier *m.* ● *v.i.* (*p.t.* **shopped**) faire ses courses. **~ around,** comparer les prix. **~ assistant,** vendeu|r, -se *m., f.* **~- floor** *n.* (*workers*) ouvriers *m. pl.* **~per** *n.* acheteu|r, -se *m., f.* **~-soiled,** (*Amer.*) **~-worn** *adjs.* abîmé. **~**

steward, délégué(e) syndical(e) *m.* (*f.*). **~ window,** vitrine *f.*

shopkeeper /'ʃɒpki:pə(r)/ *n.* commerçant(e) *m.* (*f.*).

shoplift|er /'ʃɒplɪftə(r)/ *n.* voleu|r, -se à l'étalage *m., f.* **~ing** *n.* vol à l'étalage *m.*

shopping /'ʃɒpɪŋ/ *n.* (*goods*) achats *m. pl.* **go ~,** faire ses courses. **~ bag,** sac à provisions *m.* **~ centre,** centre commercial *m.*

shore /ʃɔ:(r)/ *n.* rivage *m.*

shorn /ʃɔ:n/ *see* shear. ● *a.* **~ of,** dépouillé de.

short /ʃɔ:t/ *a.* (**-er, -est**) court; (*person*) petit; (*brief*) court, bref; (*curt*) brusque. **be ~ (of),** (*lack*) manquer (de). ● *adv.* (*stop*) net. ● *n.* (*electr.*) court-circuit *m.*; (*film*) court-métrage *m.* **~s,** (*trousers*) short *m.* **~ of money,** à court d'argent. **I'm two ~,** il m'en manque deux. **~ of doing sth,** à moins de faire qch. **everything ~ of,** tout sauf. **nothing ~ of,** rien de moins que. **cut ~,** écourter. **cut s.o. ~,** couper court à qn. **fall ~ of,** ne pas arriver à. **he is called Tom for ~,** son diminutif est Tom. **in ~,** en bref. **~-change** *v.t.* (*cheat*) rouler. **~ circuit,** court-circuit *m.* **~-circuit** *v.t.* court-circuiter. **~ cut,** raccourci *m.* **~-handed** *a.* à court de personnel. **~ list,** liste des candidats choisis *f.* **~-lived** *a.* éphémère. **~-sighted** *a.* myope. **~-staffed** *a.* à court de personnel. **~ story,** nouvelle *f.* **~-term** *a.* à court terme. **~ wave,** ondes courtes *f. pl.*

shortage /'ʃɔ:tɪdʒ/ *n.* manque *m.*

shortbread /'ʃɔ:tbred/ *n.* sablé *m.*

shortcoming /'ʃɔ:tkʌmɪŋ/ *n.* défaut *m.*

shorten /'ʃɔ:tn/ *v.t.* raccourcir.

shortfall /'ʃɔ:tfɔ:l/ *n.* déficit *m.*

shorthand /'ʃɔ:thænd/ *n.* sténo(-graphie) *f.* **~ typist,** sténodactylo *f.*

shortly /'ʃɔ:tlɪ/ *adv.* bientôt.

shot /ʃɒt/ *see* shoot. ● *n.* (*firing, attempt, etc.*) coup de feu *m.*; (*person*) tireur *m.*; (*bullet*) balle *f.*; (*photograph*) photo *f.*; (*injection*) piqûre *f.* **like a ~,** comme une flèche. **~-gun** *n.* fusil de chasse *m.*

should /ʃʊd, *unstressed* ʃəd/ *v.aux.* devoir. **you ~ help me,** vous devriez m'aider. **I ~ have stayed,** j'aurais dû rester. **I ~ like to,** j'aimerais bien. **if he ~ come,** s'il vient.

shoulder /'ʃəʊldə(r)/ *n.* épaule *f.* ● *v.t.* (*responsibility*) endosser; (*burden*) se charger de. **~-bag** *n.* sac à bandoulière *m.* **~-blade** *n.* omoplate *f.* **~-pad** *n.* épaulette *f.*

shout /ʃaʊt/ *n.* cri *m.* ● *v.t./i.* crier. **~ at,** engueuler. **~ down,** huer.

shove /ʃʌv/ *n.* poussée *f.* ● *v.t./i.* pousser; (*put*: *fam.*) ficher. **~ off,** (*depart*: *fam.*) se tirer.

shovel /'ʃʌvl/ *n.* pelle *f.* ● *v.t.* (*p.t.* **shovelled**) pelleter.

show /ʃəʊ/ *v.t.* (*p.t.* **showed,** *p.p.* **shown**) montrer; (*of dial, needle*) indiquer; (*put on display*) exposer; (*film*) donner; (*conduct*) conduire. ● *v.i.* (*be visible*) se voir. ● *n.* démonstration *f.*; (*ostentation*) parade *f.*; (*exhibition*) exposition *f.*, salon *m.*; (*theatre*) spectacle *m.*; (*cinema*) séance *f.* **for ~,** pour l'effet. **on ~,** exposé. **~-down** *n.* épreuve de force *f.* **~-jumping** *n.* concours hippique *m.* **~ off** *v.t.* étaler; *v.i.* poser, crâner. **~-off** *n.* poseu|r, -se *m., f.* **~-piece** *n.* modèle du genre *m.* **~ s.o. in/out,** faire entrer/sortir qn. **~ up,** (faire) ressortir; (*appear*: *fam.*) se montrer. **~ing** *n.* performance *f.*; (*cinema*) séance *f.*

shower /'ʃaʊə(r)/ *n.* (*of rain*) averse *f.*; (*of blows etc.*) grêle *f.*; (*for washing*) douche *f.* ● *v.t.* **~ with,** couvrir de. ● *v.i.* se doucher. **~y** *a.* pluvieux.

showerproof /'ʃaʊəpru:f/ *a.* imperméable.

showmanship /'ʃəʊmənʃɪp/ *n.* art de la mise en scène *m.*

shown /ʃəʊn/ *see* show.

showroom /'ʃəʊrʊm/ *n.* salle d'exposition *f.*

showy /'ʃəʊɪ/ *a.* (**-ier, -iest**) voyant; (*manner*) prétentieux.

shrank /ʃræŋk/ *see* shrink.

shrapnel /'ʃræpn(ə)l/ *n.* éclats d'obus *m. pl.*

shred /ʃred/ *n.* lambeau *m.*; (*least amount*: *fig.*) parcelle *f.* ● *v.t.* (*p.t.* **shredded**) déchiqueter; (*culin.*) râper. **~der** *n.* destructeur de documents *m.*

shrew /ʃru:/ *n.* (*woman*) mégère *f.*

shrewd /ʃru:d/ *a.* (**-er, -est**) astucieux. **~ness** *n.* astuce *f.*

shriek /ʃri:k/ *n.* hurlement *m.* ● *v.t./i.* hurler.
shrift /ʃrɪft/ *n.* **give s.o. short ~,** traiter qn. sans ménagement.
shrill /ʃrɪl/ *a.* strident, aigu.
shrimp /ʃrɪmp/ *n.* crevette *f.*
shrine /ʃraɪn/ *n.* (*place*) lieu saint *m.*; (*tomb*) châsse *f.*
shrink /ʃrɪŋk/ *v.t./i.* (*p.t.* **shrank,** *p.p.* **shrunk**) rétrécir; (*lessen*) diminuer. **~ from,** reculer devant. **~age** *n.* rétrécissement *m.*
shrivel /ˈʃrɪvl/ *v.t./i.* (*p.t.* **shrivelled**) (se) ratatiner.
shroud /ʃraʊd/ *n.* linceul *m.* ● *v.t.* (*veil*) envelopper.
Shrove /ʃrəʊv/ *n.* **~ Tuesday,** Mardi gras *m.*
shrub /ʃrʌb/ *n.* arbuste *m.* **~bery** *n.* arbustes *m. pl.*
shrug /ʃrʌg/ *v.t.* (*p.t.* **shrugged**). **~ one's shoulders,** hausser les épaules. ● *n.* haussement d'épaules *m.* **~ sth. off,** réagir avec indifférence à qch.
shrunk /ʃrʌŋk/ *see* shrink. **~en** *a.* rétréci; (*person*) ratatiné.
shudder /ˈʃʌdə(r)/ *v.i.* frémir. ● *n.* frémissement *m.*
shuffle /ˈʃʌfl/ *v.t.* (*feet*) traîner; (*cards*) battre. ● *v.i.* traîner les pieds. ● *n.* démarche traînante *f.*
shun /ʃʌn/ *v.t.* (*p.t.* **shunned**) éviter, fuir.
shunt /ʃʌnt/ *v.t.* (*train*) aiguiller.
shush /ʃʊʃ/ *int.* (*fam.*) chut.
shut /ʃʌt/ *v.t.* (*p.t.* **shut,** *pres. p.* **shutting**) fermer. ● *v.i.* se fermer; (*of shop, bank, etc.*) fermer. **~ down** *or* **up,** fermer. **~-down** *n.* fermeture *f.* **~ in** *or* **up,** enfermer. **~ up** *v.i.* (*fam.*) se taire; *v.t.* (*fam.*) faire taire.
shutter /ˈʃʌtə(r)/ *n.* volet *m.*; (*photo.*) obturateur *m.*
shuttle /ˈʃʌtl/ *n.* (*bus etc.*) navette *f.* ● *v.i.* faire la navette. ● *v.t.* transporter. **~ service,** navette *f.*
shuttlecock /ˈʃʌtlkɒk/ *n.* (*badminton*) volant *m.*
shy /ʃaɪ/ *a.* (**-er, -est**) timide. ● *v.i.* reculer. **~ness** *n.* timidité *f.*
Siamese /saɪəˈmi:z/ *a.* siamois.
sibling /ˈsɪblɪŋ/ *n.* frère *m.*, sœur *f.*
Sicily /ˈsɪsɪlɪ/ *n.* Sicile *f.*
sick /sɪk/ *a.* malade; (*humour*) macabre. **be ~,** (*vomit*) vomir. **be ~ of,** en avoir assez *or* marre de. **feel ~,** avoir mal au cœur. **~-bay** *n.* infirmerie *f.* **~-leave** *n.* congé maladie *m.* **~-pay** *n.* assurance-maladie *f.* **~room** *n.* chambre de malade *f.*
sicken /ˈsɪkən/ *v.t.* écœurer. ● *v.i.* **be ~ing for,** (*illness*) couver.
sickle /ˈsɪkl/ *n.* faucille *f.*
sickly /ˈsɪklɪ/ *a.* (**-ier, -iest**) (*person*) maladif; (*taste, smell, etc.*) écœurant.
sickness /ˈsɪknɪs/ *n.* maladie *f.*
side /saɪd/ *n.* côté *m.*; (*of road, river*) bord *m.*; (*of hill*) flanc *m.*; (*sport*) équipe *f.* ● *a.* latéral. ● *v.i.* **~ with,** se ranger du côté de. **on the ~,** (*extra*) en plus; (*secretly*) en catimini. **~ by side,** côte à côte. **~-car** *n.* side-car *m.* **~-effect** *n.* effet secondaire *m.* **~-saddle** *adv.* en amazone. **~-show** *n.* petite attraction *f.* **~-step** *v.t.* (*p.t.* **-stepped**) éviter. **~-street** *n.* rue latérale *f.* **~-track** *v.t.* faire dévier de son sujet.
sideboard /ˈsaɪdbɔ:d/ *n.* buffet *m.* **~s,** (*whiskers*: *sl.*) pattes *f. pl.*
sideburns /ˈsaɪdbɜ:nz/ *n. pl.* pattes *f. pl.*, rouflaquettes *f. pl.*
sidelight /ˈsaɪdlaɪt/ *n.* (*auto.*) veilleuse *f.*, lanterne *f.*
sideline /ˈsaɪdlaɪn/ *n.* activité secondaire *f.*
sidewalk /ˈsaɪdwɔ:k/ *n.* (*Amer.*) trottoir *m.*
side|ways /ˈsaɪdweɪz/, **~long** *adv.* & *a.* de côté.
siding /ˈsaɪdɪŋ/ *n.* voie de garage *f.*
sidle /ˈsaɪdl/ *v.i.* avancer furtivement (**up to,** vers).
siege /si:dʒ/ *n.* siège *m.*
siesta /sɪˈestə/ *n.* sieste *f.*
sieve /sɪv/ *n.* tamis *m.*; (*for liquids*) passoire *f.* ● *v.t.* tamiser.
sift /sɪft/ *v.t.* tamiser. ● *v.i.* **~ through,** examiner.
sigh /saɪ/ *n.* soupir *m.* ● *v.t./i.* soupirer.
sight /saɪt/ *n.* vue *f.*; (*scene*) spectacle *m.*; (*on gun*) mire *f.* ● *v.t.* apercevoir. **at** *or* **on ~,** à vue. **catch ~ of,** apercevoir. **in ~,** visible. **lose ~ of,** perdre de vue.
sightsee|ing /ˈsaɪtsi:ɪŋ/ *n.* tourisme *m.* **~r** /-ə(r)/ *n.* touriste *m./f.*
sign /saɪn/ *n.* signe *m.*; (*notice*) panneau *m.* ● *v.t./i.* signer. **~ language,** (*for deaf*) langage des sourds-muets *m.* **~ on,** (*when unemployed*) s'inscrire au chômage. **~ up,** (s')enrôler.
signal /ˈsɪgnəl/ *n.* signal *m.* ● *v.t.* (*p.t.* **signalled**) communiquer (par

signaux); (*person*) faire signe à. **~-box** *n.* poste d'aiguillage *m.*

signalman /'sɪgnəlmən/ *n.* (*pl.* **-men**) (*rail.*) aiguilleur *m.*

signatory /'sɪgnətrɪ/ *n.* signataire *m./f.*

signature /'sɪgnətʃə(r)/ *n.* signature *f.* **~ tune,** indicatif musical *m.*

signet-ring /'sɪgnɪtrɪŋ/ *n.* chevalière *f.*

significan|t /sɪg'nɪfɪkənt/ *a.* important; (*meaningful*) significatif. **~ce** *n.* importance *f.*; (*meaning*) signification *f.* **~tly** *adv.* (*much*) sensiblement.

signify /'sɪgnɪfaɪ/ *v.t.* signifier.

signpost /'saɪnpəʊst/ *n.* poteau indicateur *m.*

silence /'saɪləns/ *n.* silence *m.* ● *v.t.* faire taire. **~r** /-ə(r)/ *n.* (*on gun, car*) silencieux *m.*

silent /'saɪlənt/ *a.* silencieux; (*film*) muet. **~ly** *adv.* silencieusement.

silhouette /sɪlu:'et/ *n.* silhouette *f.* ● *v.t.* **be ~d against,** se profiler contre.

silicon /'sɪlɪkən/ *n.* silicium *m.* **~ chip,** microplaquette *f.*

silk /sɪlk/ *n.* soie *f.* **~en, ~y** *adjs.* soyeux.

sill /sɪl/ *n.* rebord *m.*

silly /'sɪlɪ/ *a.* (**-ier, -iest**) bête, idiot.

silo /'saɪləʊ/ *n.* (*pl.* **-os**) silo *m.*

silt /sɪlt/ *n.* vase *f.*

silver /'sɪlvə(r)/ *n.* argent *m.*; (*silverware*) argenterie *f.* ● *a.* en argent, d'argent. **~ wedding,** noces d'argent *f. pl.* **~y** *a.* argenté; (*sound*) argentin.

silversmith /'sɪlvəsmɪθ/ *n.* orfèvre *m.*

silverware /'sɪlvəweə(r)/ *n.* argenterie *f.*

similar /'sɪmɪlə(r)/ *a.* semblable (**to,** à). **~ity** /-ə'lærətɪ/ *n.* ressemblance *f.* **~ly** *adv.* de même.

simile /'sɪmɪlɪ/ *n.* comparaison *f.*

simmer /'sɪmə(r)/ *v.t./i.* (*soup etc.*) mijoter; (*water*) (laisser) frémir; (*smoulder: fig.*) couver. **~ down,** se calmer.

simper /'sɪmpə(r)/ *v.i.* minauder. **~ing** *a.* minaudier.

simpl|e /'sɪmpl/ *a.* (**-er, -est**) simple. **~e-minded** *a.* simple d'esprit. **~icity** /-'plɪsətɪ/ *n.* simplicité *f.* **~y** *adv.* simplement; (*absolutely*) absolument.

simplif|y /'sɪmplɪfaɪ/ *v.t.* simplifier. **~ication** /-ɪ'keɪʃn/ *n.* simplification *f.*

simplistic /sɪm'plɪstɪk/ *a.* simpliste.

simulat|e /'sɪmjʊleɪt/ *v.t.* simuler. **~ion** /-'leɪʃn/ *n.* simulation *f.*

simultaneous /sɪml'teɪnɪəs, *Amer.* saɪml'teɪnɪəs/ *a.* simultané. **~ly** *adv.* simultanément.

sin /sɪn/ *n.* péché *m.* ● *v.i.* (*p.t.* **sinned**) pécher.

since /sɪns/ *prep.* & *adv.* depuis. ● *conj.* depuis que; (*because*) puisque. **~ then,** depuis.

sincer|e /sɪn'sɪə(r)/ *a.* sincère. **~ely** *adv.* sincèrement. **~ity** /-'serətɪ/ *n.* sincérité *f.*

sinew /'sɪnju:/ *n.* tendon *m.* **~s,** muscles *m. pl.*

sinful /'sɪnfl/ *a.* (*act*) coupable, qui constitue un péché; (*shocking*) scandaleux.

sing /sɪŋ/ *v.t./i.* (*p.t.* **sang,** *p.p.* **sung**) chanter. **~er** *n.* chanteu|r, -se *m., f.*

singe /sɪndʒ/ *v.t.* (*pres. p.* **singeing**) brûler légèrement, roussir.

single /'sɪŋgl/ *a.* seul; (*not double*) simple; (*unmarried*) célibataire; (*room, bed*) pour une personne; (*ticket*) simple. ● *n.* (*ticket*) aller simple *m.*; (*record*) 45 tours *m. invar.* **~s,** (*tennis*) simple *m.* **~s bar,** bar pour les célibataires *m.* ● *v.t.* **~ out,** choisir. **in ~ file,** en file indienne. **~-handed** *a.* sans aide. **~-minded** *a.* tenace. **~ parent,** parent seul *m.* **singly** *adv.* un à un.

singlet /'sɪŋglɪt/ *n.* maillot de corps *m.*

singsong /'sɪŋsɒŋ/ *n.* **have a ~,** chanter en chœur. ● *a.* (*voice*) monotone.

singular /'sɪŋgjʊlə(r)/ *n.* singulier *m.* ● *a.* (*uncommon & gram.*) singulier; (*noun*) au singulier. **~ly** *adv.* singulièrement.

sinister /'sɪnɪstə(r)/ *a.* sinistre.

sink /sɪŋk/ *v.t./i.* (*p.t.* **sank,** *p.p.* **sunk**) (faire) couler; (*of ground, person*) s'affaisser; (*well*) creuser; (*money*) investir. ● *n.* (*in kitchen*) évier *m.*; (*wash-basin*) lavabo *m.* **~ in,** (*fig.*) être compris. **~ into** *v.t.* (*thrust*) enfoncer dans; *v.i.* (*go deep*) s'enfoncer dans. **~ unit,** bloc-évier *m.*

sinner /'sɪnə(r)/ *n.* péch|eur, -eresse *m., f.*

sinuous /'sɪnjʊəs/ *a.* sinueux.

sinus /'saɪnəs/ *n.* (*pl.* **-uses**) (*anat.*) sinus *m.*

sip /sɪp/ *n.* petite gorgée *f.* ● *v.t.* (*p.t.* **sipped**) boire à petites gorgées.

siphon /'saɪfn/ *n.* siphon *m.* ● *v.t.* ~ **off**, siphonner.

sir /sɜ:(r)/ *n.* monsieur *m.* **Sir**, (*title*) Sir *m.*

siren /'saɪərən/ *n.* sirène *f.*

sirloin /'sɜ:lɔɪn/ *n.* faux-filet *m.*, aloyau *m.*; (*Amer.*) romsteck *m.*

sissy /'sɪsɪ/ *n.* personne efféminée *f.*; (*coward*) dégonflé(e) *m.* (*f.*).

sister /'sɪstə(r)/ *n.* sœur *f.*; (*nurse*) infirmière en chef *f.* **~-in-law** (*pl.* **~s-in-law**) belle-sœur *f.* **~ly** *a.* fraternel.

sit /sɪt/ *v.t./i.* (*p.t.* **sat**, *pres. p.* **sitting**) (s')asseoir; (*of committee etc.*) siéger. **~ (for)**, (*exam*) se présenter à. **be ~ting**, être assis. **~ around**, ne rien faire. **~ down**, s'asseoir. **~ in on a meeting**, assister à une réunion pour écouter. **~-in** *n.* sit-in *m. invar.* **~ting** *n.* séance *f.*; (*in restaurant*) service *m.* **~ting-room** *n.* salon *m.*

site /saɪt/ *n.* emplacement *m.* **(building) ~**, chantier *m.* ● *v.t.* placer, construire, situer.

situat|e /'sɪtʃʊeɪt/ *v.t.* situer. **be ~ed**, être situé. **~ion** /-'eɪʃn/ *n.* situation *f.*

six /sɪks/ *a.* & *n.* six (*m.*). **~th** *a.* & *n.* sixième (*m./f.*).

sixteen /sɪk'sti:n/ *a.* & *n.* seize (*m.*). **~th** *a.* & *n.* seizième (*m./f.*).

sixt|y /'sɪkstɪ/ *a.* & *n.* soixante (*m.*). **~ieth** *a.* & *n.* soixantième (*m./f.*).

size /saɪz/ *n.* dimension *f.*; (*of person, garment, etc.*) taille *f.*; (*of shoes*) pointure *f.*; (*of sum, salary*) montant *m.*; (*extent*) ampleur *f.* ● *v.t.* **~ up**, (*fam.*) jauger, juger. **~able** *a.* assez grand.

sizzle /'sɪzl/ *v.i.* grésiller.

skate[1] /skeɪt/ *n. invar.* (*fish*) raie *f.*

skat|e[2] /skeɪt/ *n.* patin *m.* ● *v.i.* patiner. **~er** *n.* patineu|r, -se *m.*, *f.* **~ing** *n.* patinage *m.* **~ing-rink** *n.* patinoire *f.*

skateboard /'skeɪtbɔ:d/ *n.* skateboard *m.*, planche à roulettes *f.*

skelet|on /'skelɪtən/ *n.* squelette *m.* **~on crew** *or* **staff**, effectifs minimums *m. pl.* **~al** *a.* squelettique.

sketch /sketʃ/ *n.* esquisse *f.*, croquis *m.*; (*theatre*) sketch *m.* ● *v.t.* faire un croquis de, esquisser. ● *v.i.* faire des esquisses. **~ out**, esquisser. **~ pad**, bloc à dessins *m.*

sketchy /'sketʃɪ/ *a.* (**-ier**, **-iest**) sommaire, incomplet.

skew /skju:/ *n.* **on the ~**, de travers. **~-whiff** *a.* (*fam.*) de travers.

skewer /'skjʊə(r)/ *n.* brochette *f.*

ski /ski:/ *n.* (*pl.* **-is**) ski *m.* ● *a.* de ski. ● *v.i.* (*p.t.* **ski'd** *or* **skied**, *pres. p.* **skiing**) skier; (*go skiing*) faire du ski. **~ jump**, saut à skis *m.* **~ lift**, remonte-pente *m.* **~er** *n.* skieu|r, -se *m.*, *f.* **~ing** *n.* ski *m.*

skid /skɪd/ *v.i.* (*p.t.* **skidded**) déraper. ● *n.* dérapage *m.*

skilful /'skɪlfl/ *a.* habile.

skill /skɪl/ *n.* habileté *f.*; (*craft*) métier *m.* **~s**, aptitudes *f. pl.* **~ed** *a.* habile; (*worker*) qualifié.

skim /skɪm/ *v.t.* (*p.t.* **skimmed**) écumer; (*milk*) écrémer; (*pass or glide over*) effleurer. ● *v.i.* **~ through**, parcourir.

skimp /skɪmp/ *v.t./i.* **~ (on)**, lésiner (sur).

skimpy /'skɪmpɪ/ *a.* (**-ier**, **-iest**) (*clothes*) étriqué; (*meal*) chiche.

skin /skɪn/ *n.* peau *f.* ● *v.t.* (*p.t.* **skinned**) (*animal*) écorcher; (*fruit*) éplucher. **~-diving** *n.* plongée sous-marine *f.* **~-tight** *a.* collant.

skinflint /'skɪnflɪnt/ *n.* avare *m./f.*

skinny /'skɪnɪ/ *a.* (**-ier**, **-iest**) maigre, maigrichon.

skint /skɪnt/ *a.* (*sl.*) fauché.

skip[1] /skɪp/ *v.i.* (*p.t.* **skipped**) sautiller; (*with rope*) sauter à la corde. ● *v.t.* (*page, class, etc.*) sauter. ● *n.* petit saut *m.* **~ping-rope** *n.* corde à sauter *f.*

skip[2] /skɪp/ *n.* (*container*) benne *f.*

skipper /'skɪpə(r)/ *n.* capitaine *m.*

skirmish /'skɜ:mɪʃ/ *n.* escarmouche *f.*, accrochage *m.*

skirt /skɜ:t/ *n.* jupe *f.* ● *v.t.* contourner. **~ing-board** *n.* plinthe *f.*

skit /skɪt/ *n.* sketch satirique *m.*

skittle /'skɪtl/ *n.* quille *f.*

skive /skaɪv/ *v.i.* (*sl.*) tirer au flanc.

skivvy /'skɪvɪ/ *n.* (*fam.*) boniche *f.*

skulk /skʌlk/ *v.i.* (*move*) rôder furtivement; (*hide*) se cacher.

skull /skʌl/ *n.* crâne *m.* **~-cap** *n.* calotte *f.*

skunk /skʌŋk/ *n.* (*animal*) mouffette *f.*; (*person*: *sl.*) salaud *m.*

sky /skaɪ/ *n.* ciel *m.* **~-blue** *a.* & *n.* bleu ciel *m. invar.*

skylight /'skaɪlaɪt/ *n.* lucarne *f.*
skyscraper /'skaɪskreɪpə(r)/ *n.* gratte-ciel *m. invar.*
slab /slæb/ *n.* plaque *f.*, bloc *m.*; (*of paving-stone*) dalle *f.*
slack /slæk/ *a.* (**-er, -est**) (*rope*) lâche; (*person*) négligent; (*business*) stagnant; (*period*) creux. ● *n.* **the ~,** (*in rope*) du mou ● *v.t./i.* (se) relâcher.
slacken /'slækən/ *v.t./i.* (se) relâcher; (*slow*) (se) ralentir.
slacks /slæks/ *n. pl.* pantalon *m.*
slag /slæg/ *n.* scories *f. pl.* **~-heap** *n.* crassier *m.*
slain /sleɪn/ *see* slay.
slake /sleɪk/ *v.t.* étancher.
slalom /'slɑ:ləm/ *n.* slalom *m.*
slam /slæm/ *v.t./i.* (*p.t.* **slammed**) (*door etc.*) claquer; (*throw*) flanquer; (*criticize*: *sl.*) critiquer. ● *n.* (*noise*) claquement *m.*
slander /'slɑ:ndə(r)/ *n.* diffamation *f.*, calomnie *f.* ● *v.t.* diffamer, calomnier. **~ous** *a.* diffamatoire.
slang /slæŋ/ *n.* argot *m.* **~y** *a.* argotique.
slant /slɑ:nt/ *v.t./i.* (faire) pencher; (*news*) présenter sous un certain jour. ● *n.* inclinaison *f.*; (*bias*) angle *m.* **~ed** *a.* partial. **be ~ing,** être penché.
slap /slæp/ *v.t.* (*p.t.* **slapped**) (*strike*) donner une claque à; (*face*) gifler; (*put*) flanquer. ● *n.* claque *f.*; gifle *f.* ● *adv.* tout droit. **~-happy** *a.* (*carefree*: *fam.*) insouciant; (*dazed*: *fam.*) abruti. **~-up meal,** (*sl.*) gueuleton *m.*
slapdash /'slæpdæʃ/ *a.* fait, qui travaille *etc.* n'importe comment.
slapstick /'slæpstɪk/ *n.* grosse farce *f.*
slash /slæʃ/ *v.t.* (*cut*) taillader; (*sever*) trancher; (*fig.*) réduire (radicalement). ● *n.* taillade *f.*
slat /slæt/ *n.* (*in blind*) lamelle *f.*; (*on bed*) latte *f.*
slate /sleɪt/ *n.* ardoise *f.* ● *v.t.* (*fam.*) critiquer, éreinter.
slaughter /'slɔ:tə(r)/ *v.t.* massacrer; (*animals*) abattre. ● *n.* massacre *m.*; abattage *m.*
slaughterhouse /'slɔ:təhaʊs/ *n.* abattoir *m.*
Slav /slɑ:v/ *a.* & *n.* slave (*m./f.*). **~onic** /slə'vɒnɪk/ *a.* (*lang.*) slave.
slave /sleɪv/ *n.* esclave *m./f.* ● *v.i.* trimer. **~-driver** *n.* négr|ier, -ière *m., f.* **~ry** /-ərɪ/ *n.* esclavage *m.*
slavish /'sleɪvɪʃ/ *a.* servile.
slay /sleɪ/ *v.t.* (*p.t.* **slew,** *p.p.* **slain**) tuer.
sleazy /'sli:zɪ/ *a.* (**-ier, -iest**) (*fam.*) sordide, miteux.
sledge /sledʒ/ *n.* luge *f.*; (*horse-drawn*) traîneau *m.* **~-hammer** *n.* marteau de forgeron *m.*
sleek /sli:k/ *a.* (**-er, -est**) lisse, brillant; (*manner*) onctueux.
sleep /sli:p/ *n.* sommeil *m.* ● *v.i.* (*p.t.* **slept**) dormir; (*spend the night*) coucher. ● *v.t.* loger. **go to ~,** s'endormir. **~ in,** faire la grasse matinée. **~er** *n.* dormeu|r, -se *m., f.*; (*beam*: *rail*) traverse *f.*; (*berth*) couchette *f.* **~ing-bag** *n.* sac de couchage *m.* **~ing pill,** somnifère *m.* **~less** *a.* sans sommeil. **~-walker** *n.* somnambule *m./f.*
sleep|y /'sli:pɪ/ *a.* (**-ier, -iest**) somnolent. **be ~y,** avoir sommeil. **~ily** *adv.* à moitié endormi.
sleet /sli:t/ *n.* neige fondue *f.*; (*coat of ice*: *Amer.*) verglas *m.* ● *v.i.* tomber de la neige fondue.
sleeve /sli:v/ *n.* manche *f.*; (*of record*) pochette *f.* **up one's ~,** en réserve. **~less** *a.* sans manches.
sleigh /sleɪ/ *n.* traîneau *m.*
sleight /slaɪt/ *n.* **~ of hand,** prestidigitation *f.*
slender /'slendə(r)/ *a.* mince, svelte; (*scanty*: *fig.*) faible.
slept /slept/ *see* sleep.
sleuth /slu:θ/ *n.* limier *m.*
slew[1] /slu:/ *v.i.* (*turn*) virer.
slew[2] /slu:/ *see* slay.
slice /slaɪs/ *n.* tranche *f.* ● *v.t.* couper (en tranches).
slick /slɪk/ *a.* (*unctuous*) mielleux; (*cunning*) astucieux. ● *n.* **(oil) ~,** nappe de pétrole *f.*, marée noire *f.*
slide /slaɪd/ *v.t./i.* (*p.t.* **slid**) glisser. ● *n.* glissade *f.*; (*fall*: *fig.*) baisse *f.*; (*in playground*) toboggan *m.*; (*for hair*) barrette *f.*; (*photo.*) diapositive *f.* **~ into,** (*go silently*) se glisser dans. **~-rule** *n.* règle à calcul *f.* **sliding** *a.* (*door*, *panel*) à glissière, à coulisse. **sliding scale,** échelle mobile *f.*
slight /slaɪt/ *a.* (**-er, -est**) petit, léger; (*slender*) mince; (*frail*) frêle. ● *v.t.* (*insult*) offenser. ● *n.* affront *m.* **~est** *a.* moindre. **~ly** *adv.* légèrement, un peu.

slim /slɪm/ *a.* (**slimmer, slimmest**) mince. ● *v.i.* (*p.t.* **slimmed**) maigrir. **~ness** *n.* minceur *f.*

slim|e /slaɪm/ *n.* boue (visqueuse) *f.*; (*on river-bed*) vase *f.* **~y** *a.* boueux; vaseux; (*sticky, servile*) visqueux.

sling /slɪŋ/ *n.* (*weapon, toy*) fronde *f.*; (*bandage*) écharpe *f.* ● *v.t.* (*p.t.* **slung**) jeter, lancer.

slip /slɪp/ *v.t./i.* (*p.t.* **slipped**) glisser. ● *n.* faux pas *m.*; (*mistake*) erreur *f.*; (*petticoat*) combinaison *f.*; (*paper*) fiche *f.* **give the ~ to,** fausser compagnie à. **~ away,** s'esquiver. **~-cover** *n.* (*Amer.*) housse *f.* **~ into,** (*go*) se glisser dans; (*clothes*) mettre. **~ of the tongue,** lapsus *m.* **~ped disc,** hernie discale *f.* **~-road** *n.* bretelle *f.* **~ s.o.'s mind,** échapper à qn. **~-stream** *n.* sillage *m.* **~ up,** (*fam.*) gaffer. **~-up** *n.* (*fam.*) gaffe *f.*

slipper /ˈslɪpə(r)/ *n.* pantoufle *f.*

slippery /ˈslɪpərɪ/ *a.* glissant.

slipshod /ˈslɪpʃɒd/ *a.* (*person*) négligent; (*work*) négligé.

slit /slɪt/ *n.* fente *f.* ● *v.t.* (*p.t.* **slit,** *pres. p.* **slitting**) couper, fendre.

slither /ˈslɪðə(r)/ *v.i.* glisser.

sliver /ˈslɪvə(r)/ *n.* (*of cheese etc.*) lamelle *f.*; (*splinter*) éclat *m.*

slob /slɒb/ *n.* (*fam.*) rustre *m.*

slobber /ˈslɒbə(r)/ *v.i.* baver.

slog /slɒg/ *v.t.* (*p.t.* **slogged**) (*hit*) frapper dur. ● *v.i.* (*work*) trimer. ● *n.* (*work*) travail dur *m.*; (*effort*) gros effort *m.*

slogan /ˈsləʊgən/ *n.* slogan *m.*

slop /slɒp/ *v.t./i.* (*p.t.* **slopped**) (se) répandre. **~s** *n. pl.* eaux sales *f. pl.*

slop|e /sləʊp/ *v.i.* être en pente; (*of handwriting*) pencher. ● *n.* pente *f.*; (*of mountain*) flanc *m.* **~ing** *a.* en pente.

sloppy /ˈslɒpɪ/ *a.* (**-ier, -iest**) (*ground*) détrempé; (*food*) liquide; (*work*) négligé; (*person*) négligent; (*fig.*) sentimental.

slosh /slɒʃ/ *v.t.* (*fam.*) répandre; (*hit: sl.*) frapper. ● *v.i.* patauger.

slot /slɒt/ *n.* fente *f.* ● *v.t./i.* (*p.t.* **slotted**) (s')insérer. **~-machine** *n.* distributeur automatique *m.*; (*for gambling*) machine à sous *f.*

sloth /sləʊθ/ *n.* paresse *f.*

slouch /slaʊtʃ/ *v.i.* avoir le dos voûté; (*move*) marcher le dos voûté.

slovenl|y /ˈslʌvnlɪ/ *a.* débraillé. **~iness** *n.* débraillé *m.*

slow /sləʊ/ *a.* (**-er, -est**) lent. ● *adv.* lentement. ● *v.t./i.* ralentir. **be ~,** (*clock etc.*) retarder. **in ~ motion,** au ralenti. **~ly** *adv.* lentement. **~ness** *n.* lenteur *f.*

slow|coach /ˈsləʊkəʊtʃ/, (*Amer.*) **~poke** *ns.* lambin(e) *m.* (*f.*).

sludge /slʌdʒ/ *n.* gadoue *f.*, boue *f.*

slug /slʌg/ *n.* (*mollusc*) limace *f.*; (*bullet*) balle *f.*; (*blow*) coup *m.*

sluggish /ˈslʌgɪʃ/ *a.* lent, mou.

sluice /slu:s/ *n.* (*gate*) vanne *f.*

slum /slʌm/ *n.* taudis *m.*

slumber /ˈslʌmbə(r)/ *n.* sommeil. *m.* ● *v.i.* dormir.

slump /slʌmp/ *n.* effondrement *m.*; baisse *f.*; (*in business*) marasme *m.* ● *v.i.* (*collapse, fall limply*) s'effondrer; (*decrease*) baisser.

slung /slʌŋ/ *see* sling.

slur /slɜ:(r)/ *v.t./i.* (*p.t.* **slurred**) (*spoken words*) mal articuler. ● *n.* bredouillement *m.*; (*discredit*) atteinte *f.* (**on,** à).

slush /slʌʃ/ *n.* (*snow*) neige fondue *f.* **~ fund,** fonds servant à des pots-de-vin *m.* **~y** *a.* (*road*) couvert de neige fondue.

slut /slʌt/ *n.* (*dirty*) souillon *f.*; (*immoral*) dévergondée *f.*

sly /slaɪ/ *a.* (**slyer, slyest**) (*crafty*) rusé; (*secretive*) sournois. ● *n.* **on the ~,** en cachette. **~ly** *adv.* sournoisement.

smack[1] /smæk/ *n.* tape *f.*; (*on face*) gifle *f.* ● *v.t.* donner une tape à; gifler. ● *adv.* (*fam.*) tout droit.

smack[2] /smæk/ *v.i.* **~ of sth.,** (*have flavour*) sentir qch.

small /smɔ:l/ *a.* (**-er, -est**) petit. ● *n.* **~ of the back,** creux des reins *m.* ● *adv.* (*cut etc.*) menu. **~ness** *n.* petitesse *f.* **~ ads,** petites annonces *f. pl.* **~ businesses,** les petites entreprises. **~ change,** petite monnaie *f.* **~ talk,** menus propos *m. pl.* **~-time** *a.* petit, peu important.

smallholding /ˈsmɔ:lhəʊldɪŋ/ *n.* petite ferme *f.*

smallpox /ˈsmɔ:lpɒks/ *n.* variole *f.*

smarmy /ˈsmɑ:mɪ/ *a.* (**-ier, -iest**) (*fam.*) obséquieux, patelin.

smart /smɑ:t/ *a.* (**-er, -est**) élégant; (*clever*) astucieux, intelligent; (*brisk*) rapide. ● *v.i.* (*of wound etc.*) brûler. **~ly** *adv.* élégamment. **~ness** *n.* élégance *f.*

smarten /'smɑ:tn/ *v.t./i.* **~ (up),** embellir. **~ (o.s.) up,** se faire beau; (*tidy*) s'arranger.

smash /smæʃ/ *v.t./i.* (se) briser, (se) fracasser; (*opponent, record*) pulvériser. ● *n.* (*noise*) fracas *m.*; (*blow*) coup *m.*; (*fig.*) collision *f.*

smashing /'smæʃɪŋ/ *a.* (*fam.*) formidable, épatant.

smattering /'smætərɪŋ/ *n.* **a ~ of,** des notions de.

smear /smɪə(r)/ *v.t.* (*stain*) tacher; (*coat*) enduire; (*discredit: fig.*) entacher. ● *n.* tache *f.* **~ test,** frottis *m.*

smell /smel/ *n.* odeur *f.*; (*sense*) odorat *m.* ● *v.t./i.* (*p.t.* **smelt** *or* **smelled**) sentir. **~ of,** sentir. **~y** *a.* malodorant, qui pue.

smelt[1] /smelt/ *see* smell.

smelt[2] /smelt/ *v.t.* (*ore*) fondre.

smil|e /smaɪl/ *n.* sourire. ● *v.i.* sourire. **~ing** *a.* souriant.

smirk /smɜ:k/ *n.* sourire affecté *m.*

smith /smɪθ/ *n.* forgeron *m.*

smithereens /smɪðə'ri:nz/ *n. pl.* **to** *or* **in ~,** en mille morceaux.

smitten /'smɪtn/ *a.* (*in love*) épris (**with,** de).

smock /smɒk/ *n.* blouse *f.*

smog /smɒg/ *n.* brouillard mélangé de fumée *m.*, smog *m.*

smoke /sməʊk/ *n.* fumée *f.* ● *v.t./i.* fumer. **have a ~,** fumer. **~d** *a.* fumé. **~less** *a.* (*fuel*) non polluant. **~r** /-ə(r)/ *n.* fumeu|r, -se *m., f.* **~-screen** *n.* écran de fumée *m.*; (*fig.*) manœuvre de diversion *f.* **smoky** *a.* (*air*) enfumé.

smooth /smu:ð/ *a.* (**-er, -est**) lisse; (*movement*) régulier; (*manners, cream*) onctueux; (*flight*) sans turbulence; (*changes*) sans heurt. ● *v.t.* lisser. **~ out,** (*fig.*) faire disparaître. **~ly** *adv.* facilement, doucement.

smother /'smʌðə(r)/ *v.t.* (*stifle*) étouffer; (*cover*) couvrir.

smoulder /'sməʊldə(r)/ *v.i.* (*fire, discontent, etc.*) couver.

smudge /smʌdʒ/ *n.* tache *f.* ● *v.t./i.* (se) salir, (se) tacher.

smug /smʌg/ *a.* (**smugger, smuggest**) suffisant. **~ly** *adv.* avec suffisance. **~ness** *n.* suffisance *f.*

smuggl|e /'smʌgl/ *v.t.* passer (en contrebande). **~er** *n.* contreband|ier, -ière *m., f.* **~ing** *n.* contrebande *f.*

smut /smʌt/ *n.* saleté *f.* **~ty** *a.* indécent.

snack /snæk/ *n.* casse-croûte *m. invar.* **~-bar** *n.* snack(-bar) *m.*

snag /snæg/ *n.* difficulté *f.*, inconvénient *m.*; (*in cloth*) accroc *m.*

snail /sneɪl/ *n.* escargot *m.* **at a ~'s pace,** à un pas de tortue.

snake /sneɪk/ *n.* serpent *m.*

snap /snæp/ *v.t./i.* (*p.t.* **snapped**) (*whip, fingers, etc.*) (faire) claquer; (*break*) (se) casser net; (*say*) dire sèchement. ● *n.* claquement *m.*; (*photograph*) instantané *m.*; (*press-stud: Amer.*) bouton-pression *m.* ● *a.* soudain. **~ at,** (*bite*) happer; (*angrily*) être cassant avec. **~ up,** (*buy*) sauter sur.

snappy /'snæpɪ/ *a.* (**-ier, -iest**) (*brisk: fam.*) prompt, rapide. **make it ~,** (*fam.*) se dépêcher.

snapshot /'snæpʃɒt/ *n.* instantané *m.*, photo *f.*

snare /sneə(r)/ *n.* piège *m.*

snarl /snɑ:l/ *v.i.* gronder (en montrant les dents). ● *n.* grondement *m.* **~-up,** *n.* embouteillage *m.*

snarl /snɑ:l/ *v.i.* gronder (en montrant les dents). ● *n.* grondement *m.* **~-up** *n.* embouteillage *m.*

snatch /snætʃ/ *v.t.* (*grab*) saisir; (*steal*) voler. **~ from s.o.,** arracher à qn. ● *n.* (*theft*) vol *m.*; (*short part*) fragment *m.*

sneak /sni:k/ *v.i.* aller furtivement. ● *n.* (*schol., sl.*) rapporteu|r, -se *m., f.* **~y** *a.* sournois.

sneakers /'sni:kəz/ *n. pl.* (*shoes*) tennis *m. pl.*

sneaking /'sni:kɪŋ/ *a.* caché.

sneer /snɪə(r)/ *n.* ricanement *m.* ● *v.i.* ricaner.

sneeze /sni:z/ *n.* éternuement *m.* ● *v.i.* éternuer.

snide /snaɪd/ *a.* (*fam.*) narquois.

sniff /snɪf/ *v.t./i.* renifler. ● *n.* reniflement *m.*

snigger /'snɪgə(r)/ *n.* ricanement *m.* ● *v.i.* ricaner.

snip /snɪp/ *v.t.* (*p.t.* **snipped**) couper. ● *n.* morceau coupé *m.*; (*bargain: sl.*) bonne affaire *f.*

snipe /snaɪp/ *v.i.* canarder. **~r** /-ə(r)/ *n.* tireur embusqué *m.*

snippet /'snɪpɪt/ *n.* bribe *f.*

snivel /'snɪvl/ *v.i.* (*p.t.* **snivelled**) pleurnicher.

snob /snɒb/ *n.* snob *m./f.* **~bery** *n.* snobisme *m.* **~bish** *a.* snob *invar.*

snooker /'snu:kə(r)/ *n.* (*sorte de*) jeu de billard *m.*

snoop /snu:p/ *v.i.* (*fam.*) fourrer son nez partout. **~ on,** espionner.

snooty /'snu:tɪ/ *a.* (**-ier, -iest**) (*fam.*) snob *invar.*, hautain.

snooze /snu:z/ *n.* petit somme *m.* ● *v.i.* faire un petit somme.

snore /snɔ:(r)/ *n.* ronflement *m.* ● *v.i.* ronfler.

snorkel /'snɔ:kl/ *n.* tuba *m.*

snort /snɔ:t/ *n.* grognement *m.* ● *v.i.* (*person*) grogner; (*horse*) s'ébrouer.

snotty /'snɒtɪ/ *a.* morveux.

snout /snaʊt/ *n.* museau *m.*

snow /snəʊ/ *n.* neige *f.* ● *v.i.* neiger. **be ~ed under with,** être submergé de. **~-bound** *a.* bloqué par la neige. **~-drift** *n.* congère *f.* **~-plough** *n.* chasse-neige *m. invar.* **~-shoe** *n.* raquette *f.* **~y** *a.* neigeux.

snowball /'snəʊbɔ:l/ *n.* boule de neige *f.* ● *v.i.* faire boule de neige.

snowdrop /'snəʊdrɒp/ *n.* perce-neige *m./f. invar.*

snowfall /'snəʊfɔ:l/ *n.* chute de neige *f.*

snowflake /'snəʊfleɪk/ *n.* flocon de neige *m.*

snowman /'snəʊmæn/ *n.* (*pl.* **-men**) bonhomme de neige *m.*

snowstorm /'snəʊstɔ:m/ *n.* tempête de neige *f.*

snub /snʌb/ *v.t.* (*p.t.* **snubbed**) (*person*) snober; (*offer*) repousser. ● *n.* rebuffade *f.*

snub-nosed /'snʌbnəʊzd/ *a.* au nez retroussé.

snuff [1] /snʌf/ *n.* tabac à priser *m.*

snuff [2] /snʌf/ *v.t.* (*candle*) moucher.

snuffle /'snʌfl/ *v.i.* renifler.

snug /snʌg/ *a.* (**snugger, snuggest**) (*cosy*) confortable; (*tight*) bien ajusté; (*safe*) sûr.

snuggle /'snʌgl/ *v.i.* se pelotonner.

so /səʊ/ *adv.* si, tellement; (*thus*) ainsi. ● *conj.* donc, alors. **so am I,** moi aussi. **so good/***etc.* **as,** aussi bon/*etc.* que. **so does he,** lui aussi. **that is so,** c'est ça. **I think so,** je pense que oui. **five or so,** environ cinq. **so-and-so** *n.* un(e) tel(le) *m.* (*f.*). **so as to,** de manière à. **so-called** *a.* soi-disant *invar.* **~ far,** jusqu'ici. **so long!,** (*fam.*) à bientôt! **so many, so much,** tant (de). **so-so** *a.* & *adv.* comme ci comme ça. **so that,** pour que.

soak /səʊk/ *v.t./i.* (faire) tremper (**in,** dans). **~ in** *or* **up,** absorber. **~ing** *a.* trempé.

soap /səʊp/ *n.* savon *m.* ● *v.t.* savonner. **~ opera,** feuilleton *m.* **~ powder,** lessive *f.* **~y** *a.* savonneux.

soar /sɔ:(r)/ *v.i.* monter (en flèche).

sob /sɒb/ *n.* sanglot *m.* ● *v.i.* (*p.t.* **sobbed**) sangloter.

sober /'səʊbə(r)/ *a.* qui n'est pas ivre; (*serious*) sérieux; (*colour*) sobre. ● *v.t./i.* **~ up,** dessoûler.

soccer /'sɒkə(r)/ *n.* (*fam.*) football *m.*

sociable /'səʊʃəbl/ *a.* sociable.

social /'səʊʃl/ *a.* social; (*gathering, life*) mondain. ● *n.* réunion (amicale) *f.*, fête *f.* **~ly** *adv.* socialement; (*meet*) en société. **~ security,** aide sociale *f.*; (*for old age*: *Amer.*) pension (de retraite) *f.* **~ worker,** assistant(e) social(e) *m.* (*f.*).

socialis|t /'səʊʃəlɪst/ *n.* socialiste *m./f.* **~m** /-zəm/ *n.* socialisme *m.*

socialize /'səʊʃəlaɪz/ *v.i.* se mêler aux autres. **~ with,** fréquenter.

society /sə'saɪətɪ/ *n.* société *f.*

sociolog|y /səʊsɪ'ɒlədʒɪ/ *n.* sociologie *f.* **~ical** /-ə'lɒdʒɪkl/ *a.* sociologique. **~ist** *n.* sociologue *m./f.*

sock [1] /sɒk/ *n.* chaussette *f.*

sock [2] /sɒk/ *v.t.* (*hit*: *sl.*) flanquer un coup (de poing) à.

socket /'sɒkɪt/ *n.* cavité *f.*; (*for lamp*) douille *f.*; (*electr.*) prise (de courant) *f.*; (*of tooth*) alvéole *f.*

soda /'səʊdə/ *n.* soude *f.* **~(-pop),** (*Amer.*) soda *m.* **~(-water),** soda *m.*, eau de Seltz *f.*

sodden /'sɒdn/ *a.* détrempé.

sodium /'səʊdɪəm/ *n.* sodium *m.*

sofa /'səʊfə/ *n.* canapé *m.*, sofa *m.*

soft /sɒft/ *a.* (**-er, -est**) (*gentle, lenient*) doux; (*not hard*) doux, mou; (*heart, wood*) tendre; (*silly*) ramolli; (*easy*: *sl.*) facile. **~ drink,** boisson non alcoolisée *f.* **~ly** *adv.* doucement. **~ness** *n.* douceur *f.* **~ spot,** faible *m.*

soften /'sɒfn/ *v.t./i.* (se) ramollir; (*tone down, lessen*) (s')adoucir.

software /'sɒftweə(r)/ *n.* (*for computer*) logiciel *m.*

softwood /'sɒftwʊd/ *n.* bois tendre *m.*

soggy /'sɒgɪ/ *a.* (**-ier, -iest**) détrempé; (*bread etc.*) ramolli.

soil [1] /sɔɪl/ *n.* sol *m.*, terre *f.*

soil [2] /sɔɪl/ *v.t./i.* (se) salir.

solar /'səʊlə(r)/ *a.* solaire.

sold /səʊld/ *see* sell. ● *a.* **~ out,** épuisé.
solder /'sɒldə(r), *Amer.* 'sɒdər/ *n.* soudure *f.* ● *v.t.* souder. **~ing iron,** fer à souder *m.*
soldier /'səʊldʒə(r)/ *n.* soldat *m.* ● *v.i.* **~ on,** (*fam.*) persévérer.
sole[1] /səʊl/ *n.* (*of foot*) plante *f.*; (*of shoe*) semelle *f.*
sole[2] /səʊl/ *n.* (*fish*) sole *f.*
sole[3] /səʊl/ *a.* unique, seul. **~ly** *adv.* uniquement.
solemn /'sɒləm/ *a.* (*formal*) solennel; (*not cheerful*) grave. **~ity** /sə'lemnətɪ/ *n.* solennité *f.* **~ly** *adv.* solennellement; gravement.
solicit /sə'lɪsɪt/ *v.t.* (*seek*) solliciter. ● *v.i.* (*of prostitute*) racoler.
solicitor /sə'lɪsɪtə(r)/ *n.* avoué *m.*
solid /'sɒlɪd/ *a.* solide; (*not hollow*) plein; (*gold*) massif; (*mass*) compact; (*meal*) substantiel. ● *n.* solide *m.* **~s,** (*food*) aliments solides *m. pl.* **~-state** *a.* à circuits intégrés. **~ity** /sə'lɪdətɪ/ *n.* solidité *f.* **~ly** *adv.* solidement.
solidarity /sɒlɪ'dærətɪ/ *n.* solidarité *f.*
solidify /sə'lɪdɪfaɪ/ *v.t./i.* (se) solidifier.
soliloquy /sə'lɪləkwɪ/ *n.* monologue *m.*, soliloque *m.*
solitary /'sɒlɪtrɪ/ *a.* (*alone, lonely*) solitaire; (*only, single*) seul.
solitude /'sɒlɪtju:d/ *n.* solitude *f.*
solo /'səʊləʊ/ *n.* (*pl.* **-os**) solo *m.* ● *a.* (*mus.*) solo *invar.*; (*flight*) en solitaire. **~ist** *n.* soliste *m./f.*
solstice /'sɒlstɪs/ *n.* solstice *m.*
soluble /'sɒljʊbl/ *a.* soluble.
solution /sə'lu:ʃn/ *n.* solution *f.*
solv|e /sɒlv/ *v.t.* résoudre. **~able** *a.* soluble.
solvent /'sɒlvənt/ *a.* (*comm.*) solvable. ● *n.* (dis)solvant *m.*
sombre /'sɒmbə(r)/ *a.* sombre.
some /sʌm/ *a.* (*quantity, number*) du, de l'*, de la, des; (*unspecified, some or other*) un(e), quelque; (*a little*) un peu de; (*a certain*) un(e) certain(e), quelque; (*contrasted with others*) quelques, certain(e)s. ● *pron.* quelques-un(e)s; (*certain quantity of it or them*) en; (*a little*) un peu. ● *adv.* (*approximately*) quelque. **pour ~ milk,** versez du lait. **buy ~ flowers,** achetez des fleurs. **~ people like them,** il y a des gens qui les aiment. **~ of my friends,** quelques amis à moi. **he wants ~,** il en veut. **~ book (or other),** un livre (quelconque), quelque livre. **~ time ago,** il y a un certain temps.
somebody /'sʌmbədɪ/ *pron.* quelqu'un. ● *n.* **be a ~,** être quelqu'un.
somehow /'sʌmhaʊ/ *adv.* d'une manière ou d'une autre; (*for some reason*) je ne sais pas pourquoi.
someone /'sʌmwʌn/ *pron.* & *n.* = somebody.
someplace /'sʌmpleɪs/ *adv.* (*Amer.*) = somewhere.
somersault /'sʌməsɔ:lt/ *n.* culbute *f.* ● *v.i.* faire la culbute.
something /'sʌmθɪŋ/ *pron.* & *n.* quelque chose (*m.*). **~ good/***etc.* quelque chose de bon/*etc.* **~ like,** un peu comme.
sometime /'sʌmtaɪm/ *adv.* un jour. ● *a.* (*former*) ancien. **~ in June,** en juin.
sometimes /'sʌmtaɪmz/ *adv.* quelquefois, parfois.
somewhat /'sʌmwɒt/ *adv.* quelque peu, un peu.
somewhere /'sʌmweə(r)/ *adv.* quelque part.
son /sʌn/ *n.* fils *m.* **~-in-law** *n.* (*pl.* **~s-in-law**) beau-fils *m.*, gendre *m.*
sonar /'səʊnɑ:(r)/ *n.* sonar *m.*
sonata /sə'nɑ:tə/ *n.* sonate *f.*
song /sɒŋ/ *n.* chanson *f.* **going for a ~,** à vendre pour une bouchée de pain.
sonic /'sɒnɪk/ *a.* **~ boom,** bang supersonique *m.*
sonnet /'sɒnɪt/ *n.* sonnet *m.*
sonny /'sʌnɪ/ *n.* (*fam.*) fiston *m.*
soon /su:n/ *adv.* (**-er, -est**) bientôt; (*early*) tôt. **I would ~er stay,** j'aimerais mieux rester. **~ after,** peu après. **~er or later,** tôt ou tard.
soot /sʊt/ *n.* suie *f.* **~y** *a.* couvert de suie.
sooth|e /su:ð/ *v.t.* calmer. **~ing** *a.* (*remedy, words, etc.*) calmant.
sophisticated /sə'fɪstɪkeɪtɪd/ *a.* raffiné; (*machine etc.*) sophistiqué.
sophomore /'sɒfəmɔ:(r)/ *n.* (*Amer.*) étudiant(e) de seconde année *m.* (*f.*).
soporific /sɒpə'rɪfɪk/ *a.* soporifique.
sopping /'sɒpɪŋ/ *a.* trempé.
soppy /'sɒpɪ/ *a.* (**-ier, -iest**) (*fam.*) sentimental; (*silly*: *fam.*) bête.
soprano /sə'prɑ:nəʊ/ *n.* (*pl.* **-os**) (*voice*) soprano *m.*; (*singer*) soprano *m./f.*
sorcerer /'sɔ:sərə(r)/ *n.* sorcier *m.*

sordid /'sɔ:dɪd/ *a.* sordide.

sore /'sɔ:(r)/ *a.* (**-er, -est**) douloureux; (*vexed*) en rogne (**at, with,** contre). ● *n.* plaie *f.*

sorely /'sɔ:lɪ/ *adv.* fortement.

sorrow /'sɒrəʊ/ *n.* chagrin *m.* **~ful** *a.* triste.

sorry /'sɒrɪ/ *a.* (**-ier, -iest**) (*regretful*) désolé (**to,** de; **that,** que); (*wretched*) triste. **feel ~ for,** plaindre. **~!,** pardon!

sort /sɔ:t/ *n.* genre *m.*, sorte *f.*, espèce *f.*; (*person*: *fam.*) type *m.* ● *v.t.* **~ (out),** (*classify*) trier. **what ~ of?,** quel genre de? **be out of ~s,** ne pas être dans son assiette. **~ out,** (*tidy*) ranger; (*arrange*) arranger; (*problem*) régler.

SOS /esəʊ'es/ *n.* SOS *m.*

soufflé /'su:fleɪ/ *n.* soufflé *m.*

sought /sɔ:t/ *see* seek.

soul /səʊl/ *n.* âme *f.* **~-destroying** *a.* démoralisant.

soulful /'səʊlfl/ *a.* plein de sentiment, très expressif.

sound[1] /saʊnd/ *n.* son *m.*, bruit *m.* ● *v.t./i.* sonner; (*seem*) sembler (**as if,** que). **~ a horn,** klaxonner. **~ barrier,** mur du son *m.* **~ like,** sembler être. **~-proof** *a.* insonorisé; *v.t.* insonoriser. **~-track** *n.* bande sonore *f.*

sound[2] /saʊnd/ *a.* (**-er, -est**) solide; (*healthy*) sain; (*sensible*) sensé. **~ asleep,** profondément endormi. **~ly** *adv.* solidement; (*sleep*) profondément.

sound[3] /saʊnd/ *v.t.* (*test*) sonder. **~ out,** sonder.

soup /su:p/ *n.* soupe *f.*, potage *m.* **in the ~,** (*sl.*) dans le pétrin.

sour /'saʊə(r)/ *a.* (**-er, -est**) aigre. ● *v.t./i.* (s')aigrir.

source /sɔ:s/ *n.* source *f.*

south /saʊθ/ *n.* sud *m.* ● *a.* sud *invar.*, du sud. ● *adv.* vers le sud. **S~ Africa/America,** Afrique/Amérique du Sud *f.* **S~ African** *a.* & *n.* sud-africain(e) (*m.* (*f.*)). **S~ American** *a.* & *n.* sud-américain(e) (*m.* (*f.*)). **~-east** *n.* sud-est *m.* **~erly** /'sʌðəlɪ/ *a.* du sud. **~ward** *a.* au sud. **~wards** *adv.* vers le sud. **~-west** *n.* sud-ouest *m.*

southern /'sʌðən/ *a.* du sud. **~er** *n.* habitant(e) du sud *m.* (*f.*).

souvenir /su:və'nɪə(r)/ *n.* (*thing*) souvenir *m.*

sovereign /'sɒvrɪn/ *n.* & *a.* souverain(e) (*m.* (*f.*)). **~ty** *n.* souveraineté *f.*

Soviet /'səʊvɪət/ *a.* soviétique. **the ~ Union,** l'Union soviétique *f.*

sow[1] /səʊ/ *v.t.* (*p.t.* **sowed,** *p.p.* **sowed** *or* **sown**) (*seed etc.*) semer; (*land*) ensemencer.

sow[2] /saʊ/ *n.* (*pig*) truie *f.*

soya, soy /'sɔɪə, sɔɪ/ *n.* **~ bean,** graine de soja *f.* **~ sauce,** sauce soja *f.*

spa /spɑ:/ *n.* station thermale *f.*

space /speɪs/ *n.* espace *m.*; (*room*) place *f.*; (*period*) période *f.* ● *a.* (*research etc.*) spatial. ● *v.t.* **~ (out),** espacer.

space|craft /'speɪskrɑ:ft/ *n. invar.*, **~ship** *n.* engin spatial *m.*

spacesuit /'speɪssu:t/ *n.* scaphandre *m.*

spacious /'speɪʃəs/ *a.* spacieux.

spade[1] /speɪd/ *n.* (*large, for garden*) bêche *f.*; (*child's*) pelle *f.*

spade[2] /speɪd/ *n.* (*cards*) pique *m.*

spadework /'speɪdwɜ:k/ *n.* (*fig.*) travail préparatoire *m.*

spaghetti /spə'getɪ/ *n.* spaghetti *m. pl.*

Spa|in /speɪn/ *n.* Espagne *f.* **~niard** /'spænɪəd/ *n.* Espagnol(e) *m.* (*f.*). **~nish** /'spænɪʃ/ *a.* espagnol; *n.* (*lang.*) espagnol *m.*

span[1] /spæn/ *n.* (*of arch*) portée *f.*; (*of wings*) envergure *f.*; (*of time*) durée *f.* ● *v.t.* (*p.t.* **spanned**) enjamber; (*in time*) embrasser.

span[2] /spæn/ *see* spick.

spaniel /'spænɪəl/ *n.* épagneul *m.*

spank /spæŋk/ *v.t.* donner une fessée à. **~ing** *n.* fessée *f.*

spanner /'spænə(r)/ *n.* (*tool*) clé (plate) *f.*; (*adjustable*) clé à molette *f.*

spar /spɑ:(r)/ *v.i.* (*p.t.* **sparred**) s'entraîner (à la boxe).

spare /speə(r)/ *v.t.* épargner; (*do without*) se passer de; (*afford to give*) donner, accorder; (*use with restraint*) ménager. ● *a.* en réserve; (*surplus*) de trop; (*tyre, shoes, etc.*) de rechange; (*room, bed*) d'ami. ● *n.* **~ (part),** pièce de rechange *f.* **~ time,** loisirs *m. pl.* **are there any ~ tickets?** y a-t-il encore des places?

sparing /'speərɪŋ/ *a.* frugal. **~ of,** avare de. **~ly** *adv.* en petite quantité.

spark /spɑ:k/ *n.* étincelle *f.* ● *v.t.* **~ off,** (*initiate*) provoquer. **~(ing)-plug** *n.* bougie *f.*
sparkle /'spɑ:kl/ *v.i.* étinceler. ● *n.* étincellement *m.*
sparkling /'spɑ:klɪŋ/ *a.* (*wine*) mousseux, pétillant; (*eyes*) pétillant.
sparrow /'spærəʊ/ *n.* moineau *m.*
sparse /spɑ:s/ *a.* clairsemé. **~ly** *adv.* (*furnished etc.*) peu.
spartan /'spɑ:tn/ *a.* spartiate.
spasm /'spæzəm/ *n.* (*of muscle*) spasme *m.*; (*of coughing, anger, etc.*) accès *m.*
spasmodic /spæz'mɒdɪk/ *a.* intermittent.
spastic /'spæstɪk/ *n.* handicapé(e) moteur *m.* (*f.*).
spat /spæt/ *see* spit[1].
spate /speɪt/ *n.* **a ~ of,** (*letters etc.*) une avalanche de.
spatter /'spætə(r)/ *v.t.* éclabousser (**with,** de).
spatula /'spætjʊlə/ *n.* spatule *f.*
spawn /spɔ:n/ *n.* frai *m.*, œufs *m. pl.* ● *v.t.* pondre. ● *v.i.* frayer.
speak /spi:k/ *v.i.* (*p.t.* **spoke,** *p.p.* **spoken**) parler. ● *v.t.* (*say*) dire; (*language*) parler. **~ up,** parler plus fort.
speaker /'spi:kə(r)/ *n.* (*in public*) orateur *m.*; (*pol.*) président *m.*; (*loudspeaker*) baffle *m.* **be a French/a good/***etc.* **~,** parler français/bien/ *etc.*
spear /spɪə(r)/ *n.* lance *f.*
spearhead /'spɪəhed/ *n.* fer de lance *m.* ● *v.t.* (*lead*) mener.
spearmint /'spɪəmɪnt/ *n.* menthe verte *f.* ● *a.* à la menthe.
spec /spek/ *n.* **on ~,** (*as speculation: fam.*) à tout hasard.
special /'speʃl/ *a.* spécial; (*exceptional*) exceptionnel. **~ity** /-ɪ'ælətɪ/, (*Amer.*) **~ty** *n.* spécialité *f.* **~ly** *adv.* spécialement.
specialist /'speʃəlɪst/ *n.* spécialiste *m./f.*
specialize /'speʃəlaɪz/ *v.i.* se spécialiser (**in,** en). **~d** *a.* spécialisé.
species /'spi:ʃɪz/ *n. invar.* espèce *f.*
specific /spə'sɪfɪk/ *a.* précis, explicite. **~ally** *adv.* explicitement; (*exactly*) précisément.
specif|y /'spesɪfaɪ/ *v.t.* spécifier. **~ication** /-ɪ'keɪʃn/ *n.* spécification *f.*; (*details*) prescriptions *f. pl.*
specimen /'spesɪmɪn/ *n.* spécimen *m.*, échantillon *m.*
speck /spek/ *n.* (*stain*) (petite) tache *f.*; (*particle*) grain *m.*
speckled /'spekld/ *a.* tacheté.
specs /speks/ *n. pl.* (*fam.*) lunettes *f. pl.*
spectacle /'spektəkl/ *n.* spectacle *m.* **~s,** lunettes *f. pl.*
spectacular /spek'tækjʊlə(r)/ *a.* spectaculaire.
spectator /spek'teɪtə(r)/ *n.* specta|teur, -trice *m., f.*
spectre /'spektə(r)/ *n.* spectre *m.*
spectrum /'spektrəm/ *n.* (*pl.* **-tra**) spectre *m.*; (*of ideas etc.*) gamme *f.*
speculat|e /'spekjʊleɪt/ *v.i.* s'interroger (**about,** sur); (*comm.*) spéculer. **~ion** /-'leɪʃn/ *n.* conjectures *f. pl.*; (*comm.*) spéculation *f.* **~or** *n.* spécula|teur, -trice *m., f.*
speech /spi:tʃ/ *n.* (*faculty*) parole *f.*; (*diction*) élocution *f.*; (*dialect*) langage *m.*; (*address*) discours *m.* **~less** *a.* muet (**with,** de).
speed /spi:d/ *n.* (*of movement*) vitesse *f.*; (*swiftness*) rapidité *f.* ● *v.i.* (*p.t.* **sped** /sped/) aller vite; (*p.t.* **speeded**) (*drive too fast*) aller trop vite. **~ limit,** limitation de vitesse *f.* **~ up,** accélérer; (*of pace*) s'accélérer. **~ing** *n.* excès de vitesse *m.*
speedboat /'spi:dbəʊt/ *n.* vedette *f.*
speedometer /spi:'dɒmɪtə(r)/ *n.* compteur (de vitesse) *m.*
speedway /'spi:dweɪ/ *n.* piste pour motos *f.*; (*Amer.*) autodrome *m.*
speed|y /'spi:dɪ/ *a.* (**-ier, -iest**) rapide. **~ily** *adv.* rapidement.
spell[1] /spel/ *n.* (*magic*) charme *m.*, sortilège *m.*; (*curse*) sort *m.*
spell[2] /spel/ *v.t./i.* (*p.t.* **spelled** *or* **spelt**) écrire; (*mean*) signifier. **~ out,** épeler; (*explain*) expliquer. **~ing** *n.* orthographe *f.* **~ing mistake,** faute d'orthographe *f.*
spell[3] /spel/ *n.* (courte) période *f.*
spend /spend/ *v.t.* (*p.t.* **spent**) (*money*) dépenser (**on,** pour); (*time, holiday*) passer; (*energy*) consacrer (**on,** à). ● *v.i.* dépenser.
spendthrift /'spendθrɪft/ *n.* dépens|ier, -ière *m., f.*
spent /spent/ *see* spend. ● *a.* (*used*) utilisé; (*person*) épuisé.
sperm /spɜ:m/ *n.* (*pl.* **sperms** *or* **sperm**) (*semen*) sperme *m.*; (*cell*) spermatozoïde *m.* **~icide** *n.* spermicide *m.*
spew /spju:/ *v.t./i.* vomir.

sphere /sfɪə(r)/ *n.* sphère *f.*

spherical /'sferɪkl/ *a.* sphérique.

spic|e /spaɪs/ *n.* épice *f.*; (*fig.*) piquant *m.* **~y** *a.* épicé; piquant.

spick /spɪk/ *a.* **~ and span,** impeccable, d'une propreté parfaite.

spider /'spaɪdə(r)/ *n.* araignée *f.*

spiel /ʃpi:l, (*Amer.*) spi:l/ *n.* baratin *m.*

spik|e /spaɪk/ *n.* (*of metal etc.*) pointe *f.* **~y** *a.* garni de pointes.

spill /spɪl/ *v.t.* (*p.t.* **spilled** *or* **spilt**) renverser, répandre. ● *v.i.* se répandre. **~ over,** déborder.

spin /spɪn/ *v.t./i.* (*p.t.* **spun,** *pres. p.* **spinning**) (*wool, web, of spinner*) filer; (*turn*) (faire) tourner; (*story*) débiter. ● *n.* (*movement, excursion*) tour *m.* **~ out,** faire durer. **~-drier** *n.* essoreuse *f.* **~ning-wheel** *n.* rouet *m.* **~-off** *n.* avantage accessoire *m.*; (*by-product*) dérivé *m.*

spinach /'spɪnɪdʒ/ *n.* (*plant*) épinard *m.*; (*as food*) épinards *m. pl.*

spinal /'spaɪnl/ *a.* vertébral. **~ cord,** moelle épinière *f.*

spindl|e /'spɪndl/ *n.* fuseau *m.* **~y** *a.* filiforme, grêle.

spine /spaɪn/ *n.* colonne vertébrale *f.*; (*prickle*) piquant *m.*

spineless /'spaɪnlɪs/ *a.* (*fig.*) sans caractère, mou, lâche.

spinster /'spɪnstə(r)/ *n.* célibataire *f.*; (*pej.*) vieille fille *f.*

spiral /'spaɪərəl/ *a.* en spirale; (*staircase*) en colimaçon. ● *n.* spirale *f.* ● *v.i.* (*p.t.* **spiralled**) (*prices*) monter (en flèche).

spire /'spaɪə(r)/ *n.* flèche *f.*

spirit /'spɪrɪt/ *n.* esprit *m.*; (*boldness*) courage *m.* **~s,** (*morale*) moral *m.*; (*drink*) spiritueux *m. pl.* ● *v.t.* **~ away,** faire disparaître. **~-level** *n.* niveau à bulle *m.*

spirited /'spɪrɪtɪd/ *a.* fougueux.

spiritual /'spɪrɪtʃʊəl/ *a.* spirituel. ● *n.* (*song*) (negro-)spiritual *m.*

spit[1] /spɪt/ *v.t./i.* (*p.t.* **spat** *or* **spit,** *pres. p.* **spitting**) cracher; (*of rain*) crachiner. ● *n.* crachat(s) *m.* (*pl.*) **~ out,** cracher. **the ~ting image of,** le portrait craché *or* vivant de.

spit[2] /spɪt/ *n.* (*for meat*) broche *f.*

spite /spaɪt/ *n.* rancune *f.* ● *v.t.* contrarier. **in ~ of,** malgré. **~ful** *a.* méchant, rancunier. **~fully** *adv.* méchamment.

spittle /'spɪtl/ *n.* crachat(s) *m.* (*pl.*).

splash /splæʃ/ *v.t.* éclabousser. ● *v.i.* faire des éclaboussures. **~ (about),** patauger. ● *n.* (*act, mark*) éclaboussure *f.*; (*sound*) plouf *m.*; (*of colour*) tache *f.*

spleen /spli:n/ *n.* (*anat.*) rate *f.*

splendid /'splendɪd/ *a.* magnifique, splendide.

splendour /'splendə(r)/ *n.* splendeur *f.*, éclat *m.*

splint /splɪnt/ *n.* (*med.*) attelle *f.*

splinter /'splɪntə(r)/ *n.* éclat *m.*; (*in finger*) écharde *f.* **~ group,** groupe dissident *m.*

split /splɪt/ *v.t./i.* (*p.t.* **split,** *pres. p.* **splitting**) (se) fendre; (*tear*) (se) déchirer; (*divide*) (se) diviser; (*share*) partager. ● *n.* fente *f.*; déchirure *f.*; (*share: fam.*) part *f.*, partage *m.*; (*quarrel*) rupture *f.*; (*pol.*) scission *f.* **~ up,** (*couple*) rompre. **a ~ second,** un rien de temps. **~ one's sides,** se tordre (de rire).

splurge /splɜ:dʒ/ *v.i.* (*fam.*) faire de folles dépenses.

splutter /'splʌtə(r)/ *v.i.* crachoter; (*stammer*) bafouiller; (*engine*) tousser; (*fat*) crépiter.

spoil /spɔɪl/ *v.t.* (*p.t.* **spoilt** *or* **spoiled**) (*pamper*) gâter; (*ruin*) abîmer; (*mar*) gâcher, gâter. ● *n.* **~(s),** (*plunder*) butin *m.* **~- sport** *n.* trouble-fête *m./f. invar.*

spoke[1] /spəʊk/ *n.* rayon *m.*

spoke[2]**, spoken** /spəʊk, 'spəʊkən/ *see* speak.

spokesman /spəʊksmən/ *n.* (*pl.* **-men**) porte-parole *m. invar.*

sponge /spʌndʒ/ *n.* éponge *f.* ● *v.t.* éponger. ● *v.i.* **~ on,** vivre aux crochets de. **~-bag** *n.* trousse de toilette *f.* **~-cake** *n.* génoise *f.* **~r** /-ə(r)/ *n.* parasite *m.* **spongy** *a.* spongieux.

sponsor /'spɒnsə(r)/ *n.* (*of concert*) parrain *m.*, sponsor *m.*; (*surety*) garant *m.*; (*for membership*) parrain *m.*, marraine *f.* ● *v.t.* parrainer, sponsoriser; (*member*) parrainer. **~ship** *n.* patronage *m.*; parrainage *m.*

spontane|ous /spɒn'teɪnɪəs/ *a.* spontané. **~ity** /-tə'ni:ətɪ/ *n.* spontanéité *f.* **~ously** *adv.* spontanément.

spoof /spu:f/ *n.* (*fam.*) parodie *f.*

spool /spu:l/ *n.* bobine *f.*

spoon /spu:n/ *n.* cuiller *f.* **~-feed** *v.t.* (*p.t.* **-fed**) nourrir à la cuiller; (*help:*

fig.) mâcher la besogne à. **~ful** *n.* (*pl.* **-fuls**) cuillerée *f.*

sporadic /spəˈrædɪk/ *a.* sporadique.

sport /spɔːt/ *n.* sport *m.* **(good)** **~**, (*person*: *sl.*) chic type *m.* ● *v.t.* (*display*) exhiber, arborer. **~s car/coat,** voiture/veste de sport *f.* **~y** *a.* (*fam.*) sportif.

sporting /ˈspɔːtɪŋ/ *a.* sportif. **a ~ chance,** une assez bonne chance.

sports|man /ˈspɔːtsmən/ *n.* (*pl.* **-men**) sportif *m.* **~manship** *n.* sportivité *f.* **~woman** *n.* (*pl.* **-women**) sportive *f.*

spot /spɒt/ *n.* (*mark, stain*) tache *f.*; (*dot*) point *m.*; (*in pattern*) pois *m.*; (*drop*) goutte *f.*; (*place*) endroit *m.*; (*pimple*) bouton *m.* ● *v.t.* (*p.t.* **spotted**) (*fam.*) apercevoir. **a ~ of,** (*fam.*) un peu de. **be in a ~,** (*fam.*) avoir un problème. **on the ~,** sur place; (*without delay*) sur le coup. **~ check,** contrôle à l'improviste *m.* **~ted** *a.* tacheté; (*fabric*) à pois. **~ty** *a.* (*skin*) boutonneux.

spotless /ˈspɒtlɪs/ *a.* impeccable.

spotlight /ˈspɒtlaɪt/ *n.* (*lamp*) projecteur *m.*, spot *m.*

spouse /spaʊs/ *n.* époux *m.*, épouse *f.*

spout /spaʊt/ *n.* (*of vessel*) bec *m.*; (*of liquid*) jet *m.* ● *v.i.* jaillir. **up the ~,** (*ruined*: *sl.*) fichu.

sprain /spreɪn/ *n.* entorse *f.*, foulure *f.* ● *v.t.* **~ one's wrist**/*etc.*, se fouler le poignet/*etc.*

sprang /spræŋ/ *see* spring.

sprawl /sprɔːl/ *v.i.* (*town, person, etc.*) s'étaler. ● *n.* étalement *m.*

spray[1] /spreɪ/ *n.* (*of flowers*) gerbe *f.*

spray[2] /spreɪ/ *n.* (*water*) gerbe d'eau *f.*; (*from sea*) embruns *m. pl.*; (*device*) bombe *f.*, atomiseur *m.* ● *v.t.* (*surface, insecticide*) vaporiser; (*plant etc.*) arroser; (*crops*) traiter.

spread /spred/ *v.t./i.* (*p.t.* **spread**) (*stretch, extend*) (s')étendre; (*news, fear, etc.*) (se) répandre; (*illness*) (se) propager; (*butter etc.*) (s')étaler. ● *n.* propagation *f.*; (*of population*) distribution *f.*; (*paste*) pâte à tartiner *f.*; (*food*) belle table *f.* **~-eagled** *a.* bras et jambes écartés.

spreadsheet /ˈspredʃiːt/ *n.* tableur *m.*

spree /spriː/ *n.* **go on a ~,** (*have fun*: *fam.*) faire la noce.

sprig /sprɪg/ *n.* (*shoot*) brin *m.*; (*twig*) brindille *f.*

sprightly /ˈspraɪtlɪ/ *a.* (**-ier, -iest**) alerte, vif.

spring /sprɪŋ/ *v.i.* (*p.t.* **sprang,** *p.p.* **sprung**) bondir. ● *v.t.* faire, annoncer, *etc.* à l'improviste (**on,** à). ● *n.* bond *m.*; (*device*) ressort *m.*; (*season*) printemps *m.*; (*of water*) source *f.* **~-clean** *v.t.* nettoyer de fond en comble. **~ from,** provenir de. **~ onion,** oignon blanc *m.* **~ up,** surgir.

springboard /ˈsprɪŋbɔːd/ *n.* tremplin *m.*

springtime /ˈsprɪŋtaɪm/ *n.* printemps *m.*

springy /ˈsprɪŋɪ/ *a.* (**-ier, -iest**) élastique.

sprinkle /ˈsprɪŋkl/ *v.t.* (*with liquid*) arroser (**with,** de); (*with salt, flour*) saupoudrer (**with,** de). **~ sand**/*etc.*, répandre du sable/*etc.* **~r** /-ə(r)/ *n.* (*in garden*) arroseur *m.*; (*for fires*) extincteur (à déclenchement) automatique *m.*

sprinkling /ˈsprɪŋklɪŋ/ *n.* (*amount*) petite quantité *f.*

sprint /sprɪnt/ *v.i.* (*sport*) sprinter. ● *n.* sprint *m.* **~er** *n.* sprinteu|r, -se *m., f.*

sprout /spraʊt/ *v.t./i.* pousser. ● *n.* (*on plant etc.*) pousse *f.* **(Brussels) ~s,** choux de Bruxelles *m. pl.*

spruce[1] /spruːs/ *a.* pimpant. ● *v.t.* **~ o.s. up,** se faire beau.

spruce[2] /spruːs/ *n.* (*tree*) épicéa *m.*

sprung /sprʌŋ/ *see* spring. ● *a.* (*mattress etc.*) à ressorts.

spry /spraɪ/ *a.* (**spryer, spryest**) alerte, vif.

spud /spʌd/ *n.* (*sl.*) patate *f.*

spun /spʌn/ *see* spin.

spur /spɜː(r)/ *n.* (*of rider, cock, etc.*) éperon *m.*; (*stimulus*) aiguillon *m.* ● *v.t.* (*p.t.* **spurred**) éperonner. **on the ~ of the moment,** sous l'impulsion du moment.

spurious /ˈspjʊərɪəs/ *a.* faux.

spurn /spɜːn/ *v.t.* repousser.

spurt /spɜːt/ *v.i.* jaillir; (*fig.*) accélérer. ● *n.* jet *m.*; (*at work*) coup de collier *m.*

spy /spaɪ/ *n.* espion(ne) *m.* (*f.*). ● *v.i.* espionner. ● *v.t.* apercevoir. **~ on,** espionner. **~ out,** reconnaître.

squabble /ˈskwɒbl/ *v.i.* se chamailler. ● *n.* chamaillerie *f.*

squad /skwɒd/ *n.* (*of soldiers etc.*) escouade *f.*; (*sport*) équipe *f.*

squadron /'skwɒdrən/ *n.* (*mil.*) escadron *m.*; (*aviat.*) escadrille *f.*; (*naut.*) escadre *f.*

squal|id /'skwɒlɪd/ *a.* sordide. **~or** *n.* conditions sordides *f. pl.*

squall /skwɔ:l/ *n.* rafale *f.*

squander /'skwɒndə(r)/ *v.t.* (*money, time, etc.*) gaspiller.

square /skweə(r)/ *n.* carré *m.*; (*open space in town*) place *f.*; (*instrument*) équerre *f.* ● *a.* carré; (*honest*) honnête; (*meal*) solide; (*fam.*) ringard. **(all) ~,** (*quits*) quitte. ● *v.t.* (*settle*) régler. ● *v.i.* (*agree*) cadrer (**with,** avec). **~ up to,** faire face à. **~ metre,** mètre carré *m.* **~ly** *adv.* carrément.

squash /skwɒʃ/ *v.t.* écraser; (*crowd*) serrer. ● *n.* (*game*) squash *m.*; (*marrow*: *Amer.*) courge *f.* **lemon ~,** citronnade *f.* **orange ~,** orangeade *f.* **~y** *a.* mou.

squat /skwɒt/ *v.i.* (*p.t.* **squatted**) s'accroupir. ● *a.* (*dumpy*) trapu. **~ in a house,** squatteriser une maison. **~ter** *n.* squatter *m.*

squawk /skwɔ:k/ *n.* cri rauque *m.* ● *v.i.* pousser un cri rauque.

squeak /skwi:k/ *n.* petit cri *m.*; (*of door etc.*) grincement *m.* ● *v.i.* crier; grincer. **~y** *a.* grinçant.

squeal /skwi:l/ *n.* cri aigu *m.* ● *v.i.* pousser un cri aigu. **~ on,** (*inform on*: *sl.*) dénoncer.

squeamish /'skwi:mɪʃ/ *a.* (trop) délicat, facilement dégoûté.

squeeze /skwi:z/ *v.t.* presser; (*hand, arm*) serrer; (*extract*) exprimer (**from,** de); (*extort*) soutirer (**from,** à). ● *v.i.* (*force one's way*) se glisser. ● *n.* pression *f.*; (*comm.*) restrictions de crédit *f. pl.*

squelch /skweltʃ/ *v.i.* faire flic flac. ● *v.t.* (*suppress*) supprimer.

squid /skwɪd/ *n.* calmar *m.*

squiggle /'skwɪgl/ *n.* ligne onduleuse *f.*

squint /skwɪnt/ *v.i.* loucher; (*with half-shut eyes*) plisser les yeux. ● *n.* (*med.*) strabisme *m.*

squire /'skwaɪə(r)/ *n.* propriétaire terrien *m.*

squirm /skwɜ:m/ *v.i.* se tortiller.

squirrel /'skwɪrəl, *Amer.* 'skwɜ:rəl/ *n.* écureuil *m.*

squirt /skwɜ:t/ *v.t./i.* (faire) jaillir. ● *n.* jet *m.*

stab /stæb/ *v.t.* (*p.t.* **stabbed**) (*with knife etc.*) poignarder. ● *n.* coup (de couteau) *m.* **have a ~ at sth.,** essayer de faire qch.

stabilize /'steɪbəlaɪz/ *v.t.* stabiliser.

stab|le[1] /'steɪbl/ *a.* (**-er, -est**) stable. **~ility** /stə'bɪlətɪ/ *n.* stabilité *f.*

stable[2] /'steɪbl/ *n.* écurie *f.* **~-boy** *n.* lad *m.*

stack /stæk/ *n.* tas *m.* ● *v.t.* **~ (up),** entasser, empiler.

stadium /'steɪdɪəm/ *n.* stade *m.*

staff /stɑ:f/ *n.* personnel *m.*; (*in school*) professeurs *m. pl.*; (*mil.*) état-major *m.*; (*stick*) bâton *m.* ● *v.t.* pourvoir en personnel.

stag /stæg/ *n.* cerf *m.* **have a ~-party,** enterrer sa vie de garçon.

stage /steɪdʒ/ *n.* (*theatre*) scène *f.*; (*phase*) stade *m.*, étape *f.*; (*platform in hall*) estrade *f.* ● *v.t.* mettre en scène; (*fig.*) organiser. **go on the ~,** faire du théâtre. **~-coach** *n.* (*old use*) diligence *f.* **~ door,** entrée des artistes *f.* **~ fright,** trac *m.* **~-manage** *v.t.* monter, organiser. **~-manager** *n.* régisseur *m.*

stagger /'stægə(r)/ *v.i.* chanceler. ● *v.t.* (*shock*) stupéfier; (*holidays etc.*) étaler. **~ing** *a.* stupéfiant.

stagnant /'stægnənt/ *a.* stagnant.

stagnat|e /stæg'neɪt/ *v.i.* stagner. **~ion** /-ʃn/ *n.* stagnation *f.*

staid /steɪd/ *a.* sérieux.

stain /steɪn/ *v.t.* tacher; (*wood etc.*) colorer. ● *n.* tache *f.*; (*colouring*) colorant *m.* **~ed glass window,** vitrail *m.* **~less steel,** acier inoxydable *m.* **~ remover,** détachant *m.*

stair /steə(r)/ *n.* marche *f.* **the ~s,** l'escalier *m.*

stair|case /'steəkeɪs/, **~way** *ns.* escalier *m.*

stake /steɪk/ *n.* (*post*) pieu *m.*; (*wager*) enjeu *m.* ● *v.t.* (*area*) jalonner; (*wager*) jouer. **at ~,** en jeu. **~ a claim to,** revendiquer.

stale /steɪl/ *a.* (**-er, -est**) pas frais; (*bread*) rassis; (*smell*) de renfermé; (*news*) vieux. **~ness** *n.* manque de fraîcheur *m.*

stalemate /'steɪlmeɪt/ *n.* (*chess*) pat *m.*; (*fig.*) impasse *f.*

stalk[1] /stɔ:k/ *n.* (*of plant*) tige *f.*

stalk[2] /stɔ:k/ *v.i.* marcher de façon guindée. ● *v.t.* (*prey*) traquer.

stall /stɔ:l/ *n.* (*in stable*) stalle *f.*; (*in market*) éventaire *m.* **~s,** (*theatre*) orchestre *m.* ● *v.t./i.* (*auto.*) caler. **~ (for time),** temporiser.

stallion /'stæljən/ *n.* étalon *m.*

stalwart /'stɔ:lwət/ *n.* (*supporter*) partisan(e) fidèle *m.* (*f.*).

stamina /'stæmɪnə/ *n.* résistance *f.*

stammer /'stæmə(r)/ *v.t./i.* bégayer. ● *n.* bégaiement *m.*

stamp /stæmp/ *v.t./i.* **~ (one's foot),** taper du pied. ● *v.t.* (*letter etc.*) timbrer. ● *n.* (*for postage, marking*) timbre *m.*; (*mark: fig.*) sceau *m.* **~-collecting** *n.* philatélie *f.* **~ out,** supprimer.

stampede /stæm'pi:d/ *n.* fuite désordonnée *f.*; (*rush: fig.*) ruée *f.* ● *v.i.* s'enfuir en désordre; se ruer.

stance /stæns/ *n.* position *f.*

stand /stænd/ *v.i.* (*p.t.* **stood**) être *or* se tenir (debout); (*rise*) se lever; (*be situated*) se trouver; (*rest*) reposer; (*pol.*) être candidat (**for,** à). ● *v.t.* mettre (debout); (*tolerate*) supporter. ● *n.* position *f.*; (*mil.*) résistance *f.*; (*for lamp etc.*) support *m.*; (*at fair*) stand *m.*; (*in street*) kiosque *m.*; (*for spectators*) tribune *f.*; (*jurid., Amer.*) barre *f.* **make a ~,** prendre position. **~ a chance,** avoir une chance. **~ back,** reculer. **~ by** *or* **around,** ne rien faire. **~ by,** (*be ready*) se tenir prêt; (*promise, person*) rester fidèle à. **~-by** *a.* de réserve; *n.* **be a ~-by,** être de réserve. **~ down,** se désister. **~ for,** représenter; (*fam.*) supporter. **~ in for,** remplacer. **~-in** *n.* remplaçant(e) *m.* (*f.*). **~ in line,** (*Amer.*) faire la queue. **~-offish** *a.* (*fam.*) distant. **~ out,** (*be conspicuous*) ressortir. **~ to reason,** être logique. **~ up,** se lever. **~ up for,** défendre. **~ up to,** résister à.

standard /'stændəd/ *n.* norme *f.*; (*level*) niveau (voulu) *m.*; (*flag*) étendard *m.* **~s,** (*morals*) principes *m. pl.* ● *a.* ordinaire. **~ lamp,** lampadaire *m.* **~ of living,** niveau de vie *m.*

standardize /'stændədaɪz/ *v.t.* standardiser.

standing /'stændɪŋ/ *a.* debout *invar.*; (*army, offer*) permanent. ● *n.* position *f.*, réputation *f.*; (*duration*) durée *f.* **~ order,** prélèvement bancaire *m.* **~ room,** places debout *f. pl.*

standpoint /'stændpɔɪnt/ *n.* point de vue *m.*

standstill /'stændstɪl/ *n.* **at a ~,** immobile. **bring/come to a ~,** (s')immobiliser.

stank /stæŋk/ *see* stink.

stanza /'stænzə/ *n.* strophe *f.*

staple[1] /'steɪpl/ *n.* agrafe *f.* ● *v.t.* agrafer. **~r** /-ə(r)/ *n.* agrafeuse *f.*

staple[2] /'steɪpl/ *a.* principal, de base.

star /stɑ:(r)/ *n.* étoile *f.*; (*famous person*) vedette *f.* ● *v.t.* (*p.t.* **starred**) (*of film*) avoir pour vedette. ● *v.i.* **~ in,** être la vedette de. **~dom** *n.* célébrité *f.*

starboard /'stɑ:bəd/ *n.* tribord *m.*

starch /stɑ:tʃ/ *n.* amidon *m.*; (*in food*) fécule *f.* ● *v.t.* amidonner. **~y** *a.* féculent; (*stiff*) guindé.

stare /steə(r)/ *v.i.* **~ at,** regarder fixement. ● *n.* regard fixe *m.*

starfish /'stɑ:fɪʃ/ *n.* étoile de mer *f.*

stark /stɑ:k/ *a.* (**-er, -est**) (*desolate*) désolé; (*severe*) austère; (*utter*) complet; (*fact etc.*) brutal. ● *adv.* complètement.

starling /'stɑ:lɪŋ/ *n.* étourneau *m.*

starlit /'stɑ:lɪt/ *a.* étoilé.

starry /'stɑ:rɪ/ *a.* étoilé. **~-eyed** *a.* naïf, (trop) optimiste.

start /stɑ:t/ *v.t./i.* commencer; (*machine*) (se) mettre en marche; (*fashion etc.*) lancer; (*cause*) provoquer; (*jump*) sursauter; (*of vehicle*) démarrer. ● *n.* commencement *m.*, début *m.*; (*of race*) départ *m.*; (*lead*) avance *f.*; (*jump*) sursaut *m.* **~ to do,** commencer *or* se mettre à faire. **~ off doing,** commencer par faire. **~ out,** partir. **~ up a business,** lancer une affaire. **~er** *n.* (*auto.*) démarreur *m.*; (*runner*) partant *m.*; (*culin.*) entrée *f.* **~ing point,** point de départ *m.* **~ing tomorrow,** à partir de demain.

startle /'stɑ:tl/ *v.t.* (*make jump*) faire tressaillir; (*shock*) alarmer.

starv|e /stɑ:v/ *v.i.* mourir de faim. ● *v.t.* affamer; (*deprive*) priver. **~ation** /-'veɪʃn/ *n.* faim *f.*

stash /stæʃ/ *v.t.* (*hide: sl.*) cacher.

state /steɪt/ *n.* état *m.*; (*pomp*) apparat *m.* **S~,** (*pol.*) État *m.* ● *a.* d'État, de l'État; (*school*) public. ● *v.t.* affirmer (**that,** que); (*views*) exprimer; (*fix*) fixer. **the S~s,** les États-Unis. **get into a ~,** s'affoler.

stateless /'steɪtlɪs/ *a.* apatride.

stately /'steɪtlɪ/ *a.* (**-ier, -iest**) majestueux. **~ home,** château *m.*

statement /'steɪtmənt/ *n.* déclaration *f.*; (*of account*) relevé *m.*

statesman /'steɪtsmən/ *n.* (*pl.* **-men**) homme d'État *m.*

static /'stætɪk/ *a.* statique. ● *n.* (*radio, TV*) parasites *m. pl.*

station /'steɪʃn/ *n.* station *f.*; (*rail.*) gare *f.*; (*mil.*) poste *m.*; (*rank*) condition *f.* ● *v.t.* poster, placer. **~ed at** *or* **in,** (*mil.*) en garnison à. **~ wagon,** (*Amer.*) break *m.*

stationary /'steɪʃənrɪ/ *a.* immobile, stationnaire; (*vehicle*) à l'arrêt.

stationer /'steɪʃnə(r)/ *n.* papet|ier, -ière *m., f.* **~'s shop,** papeterie *f.* **~y** *n.* papeterie *f.*

statistic /stə'tɪstɪk/ *n.* statistique *f.* **~s,** statistique *f.* **~al** *a.* statistique.

statue /'stætʃu:/ *n.* statue *f.*

stature /'stætʃə(r)/ *n.* stature *f.*

status /'steɪtəs/ *n.* (*pl.* **-uses**) situation *f.*, statut *m.*; (*prestige*) standing *m.* **~ quo,** statu quo *m.*

statut|e /'stætʃu:t/ *n.* loi *f.* **~es,** (*rules*) statuts *m. pl.* **~ory** /-ʊtrɪ/ *a.* statutaire; (*holiday*) légal.

staunch /stɔ:ntʃ/ *a.* (**-er, -est**) (*friend etc.*) loyal, fidèle.

stave /steɪv/ *n.* (*mus.*) portée *f.* ● *v.t.* **~ off,** éviter, conjurer.

stay /steɪ/ *v.i.* rester; (*spend time*) séjourner; (*reside*) loger. ● *v.t.* (*hunger*) tromper. ● *n.* séjour *m.* **~ away from,** (*school etc.*) ne pas aller à. **~ behind/on/late/***etc.*, rester. **~ in/out,** rester à la maison/dehors. **~ up (late),** veiller, se coucher tard.

stead /sted/ *n.* **stand s.o. in good ~,** être bien utile à qn.

steadfast /'stedfɑ:st/ *a.* ferme.

stead|y /'stedɪ/ *a.* (**-ier, -iest**) stable; (*hand, voice*) ferme; (*regular*) régulier; (*staid*) sérieux. ● *v.t.* maintenir, assurer; (*calm*) calmer. **~ily** *adv.* fermement; régulièrement.

steak /steɪk/ *n.* steak *m.*, bifteck *m.*; (*of fish*) darne *f.*

steal /sti:l/ *v.t./i.* (*p.t.* **stole,** *p.p.* **stolen**) voler (**from s.o.,** à qn.).

stealth /stelθ/ *n.* **by ~,** furtivement. **~y** *a.* furtif.

steam /sti:m/ *n.* vapeur *f.*; (*on glass*) buée *f.* ● *v.t.* (*cook*) cuire à la vapeur; (*window*) embuer. ● *v.i.* fumer. **~-engine** *n.* locomotive à vapeur *f.* **~ iron,** fer à vapeur *m.* **~y** *a.* humide.

steam|er /'sti:mə(r)/ *n.* (*culin.*) cuit-vapeur *m.*; (*also* **~ship**) (bateau à) vapeur *m.*

steamroller /'sti:mrəʊlə(r)/ *n.* rouleau compresseur *m.*

steel /sti:l/ *n.* acier *m.* ● *v. pr.* **~ o.s.,** s'endurcir, se cuirasser. **~ industry,** sidérurgie *f.*

steep[1] /sti:p/ *v.t.* (*soak*) tremper. **~ed in,** (*fig.*) imprégné de.

steep[2] /sti:p/ *a.* (**-er, -est**) raide, rapide; (*price*: *fam.*) excessif. **~ly** *adv.* **rise ~ly,** (*slope, price*) monter rapidement.

steeple /'sti:pl/ *n.* clocher *m.*

steeplechase /'sti:pltʃeɪs/ *n.* (*race*) steeple(-chase) *m.*

steer[1] /stɪə(r)/ *n.* (*ox*) bouvillon *m.*

steer[2] /stɪə(r)/ *v.t.* diriger; (*ship*) gouverner; (*fig.*) guider. ● *v.i.* (*in ship*) gouverner. **~ clear of,** éviter. **~ing** *n.* (*auto.*) direction *f.* **~ing-wheel** *n.* volant *m.*

stem[1] /stem/ *n.* tige *f.*; (*of glass*) pied *m.* ● *v.i.* (*p.t.* **stemmed**). **~ from,** provenir de.

stem[2] /stem/ *v.t.* (*p.t.* **stemmed**) (*check, stop*) endiguer, contenir.

stench /stentʃ/ *n.* puanteur *f.*

stencil /'stensl/ *n.* pochoir *m.*; (*for typing*) stencil *m.* ● *v.t.* (*p.t.* **stencilled**) (*document*) polycopier.

stenographer /ste'nɒgrəfə(r)/ *n.* (*Amer.*) sténodactylo *f.*

step /step/ *v.i.* (*p.t.* **stepped**) marcher, aller. ● *v.t.* **~ up,** augmenter. ● *n.* pas *m.*; (*stair*) marche *f.*; (*of train*) marchepied *m.*; (*action*) mesure *f.* **~s,** (*ladder*) escabeau *m.* **in ~,** au pas; (*fig.*) conforme (**with,** à). **~ down,** (*resign*) démissionner; (*from ladder*) descendre. **~ forward,** (faire un) pas en avant. **~ up,** (*pressure*) augmenter. **~ in,** (*intervene*) intervenir. **~-ladder** *n.* escabeau *m.* **~ping-stone** *n.* (*fig.*) tremplin *m.*

step|brother /'stepbrʌðə(r)/ *n.* demi-frère *m.* **~daughter** *n.* belle-fille *f.* **~father** *n.* beau-père *m.* **~mother** *n.* belle-mère *f.* **~sister** *n.* demi-sœur *f.* **~son** *n.* beau-fils *m.*

stereo /'sterɪəʊ/ *n.* (*pl.* **-os**) stéréo *f.*; (*record-player*) chaîne stéréo *f.* ● *a.* stéréo *invar.* **~phonic** /-ə'fɒnɪk/ *a.* stéréophonique.

stereotype /'sterɪətaɪp/ *n.* stéréotype *m.* **~d** *a.* stéréotypé.

steril|e /'steraɪl, *Amer.* 'sterəl/ *a.* stérile. **~ity** /stə'rɪlətɪ/ *n.* stérilité *f.*

steriliz|e /'sterəlaɪz/ *v.t.* stériliser. **~ation** /-'zeɪʃn/ *n.* stérilisation *f.*

sterling /'stɜ:lɪŋ/ *n.* livre(s) sterling *f.* (*pl.*). ● *a.* sterling *invar.*; (*silver*) fin; (*fig.*) excellent.

stern [1] /stɜ:n/ *a.* (**-er, -est**) sévère.

stern [2] /stɜ:n/ *n.* (*of ship*) arrière *m.*

steroid /'sterɔɪd/ *n.* stéroïde *m.*

stethoscope /'steθəskəʊp/ *n.* stéthoscope *m.*

stew /stju:/ *v.t./i.* cuire à la casserole. ● *n.* ragoût *m.* **~ed fruit,** compote *f.* **~ed tea,** thé trop infusé *m.* **~-pan** *n.* cocotte *f.*

steward /stjʊəd/ *n.* (*of club etc.*) intendant *m.*; (*on ship etc.*) steward *m.* **~ess** /-'des/ *n.* hôtesse *f.*

stick [1] /stɪk/ *n.* bâton *m.*; (*for walking*) canne *f.*

stick [2] /stɪk/ *v.t.* (*p.t.* **stuck**) (*glue*) coller; (*thrust*) enfoncer; (*put: fam.*) mettre; (*endure: sl.*) supporter. ● *v.i.* (*adhere*) coller, adhérer; (*to pan*) attacher; (*remain: fam.*) rester; (*be jammed*) être coincé. **be stuck with s.o.,** (*fam.*) se farcir qn. **~-in-the-mud** *n.* encroûté(e) *m.* (*f.*). **~ at,** persévérer dans. **~ out** *v.t.* (*head etc.*) sortir; (*tongue*) tirer; *v.i.* (*protrude*) dépasser. **~ to,** (*promise etc.*) rester fidèle à. **~ up for,** (*fam.*) défendre. **~ing-plaster** *n.* sparadrap *m.*

sticker /'stɪkə(r)/ *n.* autocollant *m.*

stickler /'stɪklə(r)/ *n.* **be a ~ for,** insister sur.

sticky /'stɪkɪ/ *a.* (**-ier, -iest**) poisseux; (*label, tape*) adhésif.

stiff /stɪf/ *a.* (**-er, -est**) raide; (*limb, joint*) ankylosé; (*tough*) dur; (*drink*) fort; (*price*) élevé; (*manner*) guindé. **~ neck,** torticolis *m.* **~ness** *n.* raideur *f.*

stiffen /'stɪfn/ *v.t./i.* (se) raidir.

stifle /'staɪfl/ *v.t./i.* étouffer.

stigma /'stɪgmə/ *n.* (*pl.* **-as**) stigmate *m.* **~tize** *v.t.* stigmatiser.

stile /staɪl/ *n.* échalier *m.*

stiletto /stɪ'letəʊ/ *a.* & *n.* (*pl.* **-os**) **~s, ~ heels** talons aiguille *m. pl.*

still [1] /stɪl/ *a.* immobile; (*quiet*) calme, tranquille. ● *n.* silence *m.* ● *adv.* encore, toujours; (*even*) encore; (*nevertheless*) tout de même. **keep ~!,** arrête de bouger! **~ life,** nature morte *f.*

still [2] /stɪl/ *n.* (*apparatus*) alambic *m.*

stillborn /'stɪlbɔ:n/ *a.* mort-né.

stilted /'stɪltɪd/ *a.* guindé.

stilts /stɪlts/ *n. pl.* échasses *f. pl.*

stimul|ate /'stɪmjʊleɪt/ *v.t.* stimuler. **~ant** *n.* stimulant *m.* **~ation** /-'leɪʃn/ *n.* stimulation *f.*

stimulus /'stɪmjʊləs/ *n.* (*pl.* **-li** /-laɪ/) (*spur*) stimulant *m.*

sting /stɪŋ/ *n.* piqûre *f.*; (*organ*) dard *m.* ● *v.t./i.* (*p.t.* **stung**) piquer. **~ing** *a.* (*fig.*) cinglant.

stingy /'stɪndʒɪ/ *a.* (**-ier, -iest**) avare (**with,** de).

stink /stɪŋk/ *n.* puanteur *f.* ● *v.i.* (*p.t.* **stank** *or* **stunk,** *p.p.* **stunk**). **~ (of),** puer. ● *v.t.* **~ out,** (*room etc.*) empester.

stinker /'stɪŋkə(r)/ *n.* (*thing: sl.*) vacherie *f.*; (*person: sl.*) vache *f.*

stint /stɪnt/ *v.i.* **~ on,** lésiner sur. ● *n.* (*work*) tour *m.*

stipulat|e /'stɪpjʊleɪt/ *v.t.* stipuler. **~ion** /-'leɪʃn/ *n.* stipulation *f.*

stir /stɜ:(r)/ *v.t./i.* (*p.t.* **stirred**) (*move*) remuer; (*excite*) exciter. ● *n.* agitation *f.* **~ up,** (*trouble etc.*) provoquer.

stirrup /'stɪrəp/ *n.* étrier *m.*

stitch /stɪtʃ/ *n.* point *m.*; (*in knitting*) maille *f.*; (*med.*) point de suture *m.*; (*muscle pain*) point de côté *m.* ● *v.t.* coudre. **be in ~es,** (*fam.*) avoir le fou rire.

stoat /stəʊt/ *n.* hermine *f.*

stock /stɒk/ *n.* réserve *f.*; (*comm.*) stock *m.*; (*financial*) valeurs *f. pl.*; (*family*) souche *f.*; (*soup*) bouillon *m.* ● *a.* (*goods*) courant. ● *v.t.* (*shop etc.*) approvisionner; (*sell*) vendre. ● *v.i.* **~ up,** s'approvisionner (**with,** de). **~-car** *n.* stock-car *m.* **~ cube,** bouillon-cube *m.* **S~ Exchange, ~ market,** Bourse *f.* **~ phrase,** cliché *m.* **~-taking** *n.* (*comm.*) inventaire *m.* **in ~,** en stock. **we're out of ~,** il n'y en a plus. **take ~,** (*fig.*) faire le point.

stockbroker /'stɒkbrəʊkə(r)/ *n.* agent de change *m.*

stocking /'stɒkɪŋ/ *n.* bas *m.*

stockist /'stɒkɪst/ *n.* stockiste *m.*

stockpile /'stɒkpaɪl/ *n.* stock *m.* ● *v.t.* stocker; (*arms*) amasser.

stocky /'stɒkɪ/ *a.* (**-ier, -iest**) trapu.

stodg|e /stɒdʒ/ *n.* (*fam.*) aliment(s) lourd(s) *m.* (*pl.*). **~y** *a.* lourd.

stoic /'stəʊɪk/ *n.* stoïque *m./f.* **~al** *a.* stoïque. **~ism** /-sɪzəm/ *n.* stoïcisme *m.*

stoke /stəʊk/ *v.t.* (*boiler, fire*) garnir, alimenter.

stole [1] /stəʊl/ *n.* (*garment*) étole *f.*

stole[2], **stolen** /stəʊl, 'stəʊlən/ *see* steal.
stolid /'stɒlɪd/ *a.* flegmatique.
stomach /'stʌmək/ *n.* estomac *m.*; (*abdomen*) ventre *m.* ● *v.t.* (*put up with*) supporter. **~-ache** *n.* mal à l'estomac *or* au ventre *m.*
ston|e /stəʊn/ *n.* pierre *f.*; (*pebble*) caillou *m.*; (*in fruit*) noyau *m.*; (*weight*) 6.350 kg. ● *a.* de pierre. ● *v.t.* lapider; (*fruit*) dénoyauter. **~e-cold/-deaf,** complètement froid/sourd. **~y** *a.* pierreux. **~y-broke** *a.* (*sl.*) fauché.
stonemason /'stəʊnmeɪsn/ *n.* maçon *m.*, tailleur de pierre *m.*
stood /stʊd/ *see* stand.
stooge /stu:dʒ/ *n.* (*actor*) comparse *m./f.*; (*fig.*) fantoche *m.*, laquais *m.*
stool /stu:l/ *n.* tabouret *m.*
stoop /stu:p/ *v.i.* (*bend*) se baisser; (*condescend*) s'abaisser. ● *n.* **have a ~,** être voûté.
stop /stɒp/ *v.t./i.* (*p.t.* **stopped**) arrêter (**doing,** de faire); (*moving, talking*) s'arrêter; (*prevent*) empêcher (**from,** de); (*hole, leak, etc.*) boucher; (*of pain, noise, etc.*) cesser; (*stay*: *fam.*) rester. ● *n.* arrêt *m.*; (*full stop*) point *m.* **~ off,** s'arrêter. **~ up,** boucher. **~(-over),** halte *f.*; (*port of call*) escale *f.* **~-light** *n.* (*on vehicle*) stop *m.* **~-watch** *n.* chronomètre *m.*
stopgap /'stɒpgæp/ *n.* bouche-trou *m.* ● *a.* intérimaire.
stoppage /'stɒpɪdʒ/ *n.* arrêt *m.*; (*of work*) arrêt de travail *m.*; (*of pay*) retenue *f.*
stopper /'stɒpə(r)/ *n.* bouchon *m.*
storage /'stɔ:rɪdʒ/ *n.* (*of goods, food, etc.*) emmagasinage *m.* **~ heater,** radiateur électrique à accumulation *m.* **~ space,** espace de rangement *m.*
store /stɔ:(r)/ *n.* réserve *f.*; (*warehouse*) entrepôt *m.*; (*shop*) grand magasin *m.*; (*Amer.*) magasin *m.* ● *v.t.* (*for future*) mettre en réserve; (*in warehouse, mind*) emmagasiner. **have in ~ for,** réserver à. **set ~ by,** attacher du prix à. **~-room** *n.* réserve *f.*
storey /'stɔ:rɪ/ *n.* étage *m.*
stork /stɔ:k/ *n.* cigogne *f.*
storm /stɔ:m/ *n.* tempête *f.*, orage *m.* ● *v.t.* prendre d'assaut. ● *v.i.* (*rage*) tempêter. **~y** *a.* orageux.
story /'stɔ:rɪ/ *n.* histoire *f.*; (*in press*) article *m.*; (*storey*: *Amer.*) étage *m.* **~ book,** livre d'histoires *m.* **~-teller** *n.* conteu|r, -se *m.*, *f.*; (*liar*: *fam.*) menteu|r, -se *m.*, *f.*
stout /staʊt/ *a.* (**-er, -est**) corpulent; (*strong*) solide. ● *n.* bière brune *f.* **~ness** *n.* corpulence *f.*
stove /stəʊv/ *n.* (*for cooking*) cuisinière *f.*; (*heater*) poêle *m.*
stow /stəʊ/ *v.t.* **~ away,** (*put away*) ranger; (*hide*) cacher. ● *v.i.* voyager clandestinement.
stowaway /'stəʊəweɪ/ *n.* passag|er, -ère clandestin(e) *m.*, *f.*
straddle /'strædl/ *v.t.* être à cheval sur, enjamber.
straggle /'strægl/ *v.i.* (*lag behind*) traîner en désordre. **~r** /-ə(r)/ *n.* traînard(e) *m.* (*f.*).
straight /streɪt/ *a.* (**-er, -est**) droit; (*tidy*) en ordre; (*frank*) franc. ● *adv.* (*in straight line*) droit; (*direct*) tout droit. ● *n.* ligne droite *f.* **~ ahead** *or* **on,** tout droit. **~ away,** tout de suite. **~ face,** visage sérieux *m.* **get sth. ~,** mettre qch. au clair. **~ off,** (*fam.*) sans hésiter.
straighten /'streɪtn/ *v.t.* (*nail, situation, etc.*) redresser; (*tidy*) arranger.
straightforward /streɪt'fɔ:wəd/ *a.* honnête; (*easy*) simple.
strain[1] /streɪn/ *n.* (*breed*) race *f.*; (*streak*) tendance *f.*
strain[2] /streɪn/ *v.t.* (*rope, ears*) tendre; (*limb*) fouler; (*eyes*) fatiguer; (*muscle*) froisser; (*filter*) passer; (*vegetables*) égoutter; (*fig.*) mettre à l'épreuve. ● *v.i.* fournir des efforts. ● *n.* tension *f.*; (*fig.*) effort *m.* **~s,** (*tune*: *mus.*) accents *m. pl.* **~ed** *a.* forcé; (*relations*) tendu. **~er** *n.* passoire *f.*
strait /streɪt/ *n.* détroit *m.* **~s,** détroit *m.*; (*fig.*) embarras *m.* **~-jacket** *n.* camisole de force *f.* **~-laced** *a.* collet monté *invar.*
strand /strænd/ *n.* (*thread*) fil *m.*, brin *m.*; (*lock of hair*) mèche *f.*
stranded /'strændɪd/ *a.* (*person*) en rade; (*ship*) échoué.
strange /streɪndʒ/ *a.* (**-er, -est**) étrange; (*unknown*) inconnu. **~ly** *adv.* étrangement. **~ness** *n.* étrangeté *f.*
stranger /'streɪndʒə(r)/ *n.* inconnu(e) *m.* (*f.*).
strangle /'stræŋgl/ *v.t.* étrangler.
stranglehold /'stræŋglhəʊld/ *n.* **have a ~ on,** tenir à la gorge.

strap /stræp/ *n.* (*of leather etc.*) courroie *f.*; (*of dress*) bretelle *f.*; (*of watch*) bracelet *m.* ● *v.t.* (*p.t.* **strapped**) attacher.

strapping /'stræpɪŋ/ *a.* costaud.

stratagem /'strætədʒəm/ *n.* stratagème *m.*

strategic /strə'ti:dʒɪk/ *a.* stratégique.

strategy /'strætədʒɪ/ *n.* stratégie *f.*

stratum /'strɑ:təm/ *n.* (*pl.* **strata**) couche *f.*

straw /strɔ:/ *n.* paille *f.* **the last ~,** le comble.

strawberry /'strɔ:brɪ/ *n.* fraise *f.*

stray /streɪ/ *v.i.* s'égarer; (*deviate*) s'écarter. ● *a.* perdu; (*isolated*) isolé. ● *n.* animal perdu *m.*

streak /stri:k/ *n.* raie *f.*, bande *f.*; (*trace*) trace *f.*; (*period*) période *f.*; (*tendency*) tendance *f.* ● *v.t.* (*mark*) strier. ● *v.i.* filer à toute allure. **~y** *a.* strié.

stream /stri:m/ *n.* ruisseau *m.*; (*current*) courant *m.*; (*flow*) flot *m.*; (*in schools*) classe (de niveau) *f.* ● *v.i.* ruisseler (**with,** de); (*eyes, nose*) couler.

streamer /'stri:mə(r)/ *n.* (*of paper*) serpentin *m.*; (*flag*) banderole *f.*

streamline /'stri:mlaɪn/ *v.t.* rationaliser. **~d** *a.* (*shape*) aérodynamique.

street /stri:t/ *n.* rue *f.* **~ lamp,** réverbère *m.* **~ map,** plan des rues *m.*

streetcar /'stri:tkɑ:(r)/ *n.* (*Amer.*) tramway *m.*

strength /streŋθ/ *n.* force *f.*; (*of wall, fabric, etc.*) solidité *f.* **on the ~ of,** en vertu de.

strengthen /'streŋθn/ *v.t.* renforcer, fortifier.

strenuous /'strenjʊəs/ *a.* énergique; (*arduous*) ardu; (*tiring*) fatigant. **~ly** *adv.* énergiquement.

stress /stres/ *n.* accent *m.*; (*pressure*) pression *f.*; (*med.*) stress *m.* ● *v.t.* souligner, insister sur.

stretch /stretʃ/ *v.t.* (*pull taut*) tendre; (*arm, leg*) étendre; (*neck*) tendre; (*clothes*) étirer; (*truth etc.*) forcer. ● *v.i.* s'étendre; (*of person, clothes*) s'étirer. ● *n.* étendue *f.*; (*period*) période *f.*; (*of road*) tronçon *m.* ● *a.* (*fabric*) extensible. **~ one's legs,** se dégourdir les jambes. **at a ~,** d'affilée.

stretcher /'stretʃə(r)/ *n.* brancard *m.*

strew /stru:/ *v.t.* (*p.t.* **strewed,** *p.p.* **strewed** *or* **strewn**) (*scatter*) répandre; (*cover*) joncher.

stricken /'strɪkən/ *a.* **~ with,** frappé *or* atteint de.

strict /strɪkt/ *a.* (**-er, -est**) strict. **~ly** *adv.* strictement. **~ness** *n.* sévérité *f.*

stride /straɪd/ *v.i.* (*p.t.* **strode,** *p.p.* **stridden**) faire de grands pas. ● *n.* grand pas *m.*

strident /'straɪdnt/ *a.* strident.

strife /straɪf/ *n.* conflit(s) *m.* (*pl.*).

strike /straɪk/ *v.t.* (*p.t.* **struck**) frapper; (*blow*) donner; (*match*) frotter; (*gold etc.*) trouver. ● *v.i.* faire grève; (*attack*) attaquer; (*clock*) sonner. ● *n.* (*of workers*) grève *f.*; (*mil.*) attaque *f.*; (*find*) découverte *f.* **on ~,** en grève. **~ off** *or* **out,** rayer. **~ up a friendship,** lier amitié (**with,** avec).

striker /'straɪkə(r)/ *n.* gréviste *m./f.*; (*football*) buteur *m.*

striking /'straɪkɪŋ/ *a.* frappant.

string /strɪŋ/ *n.* ficelle *f.*; (*of violin, racket, etc.*) corde *f.*; (*of pearls*) collier *m.*; (*of lies etc.*) chapelet *m.* ● *v.t.* (*p.t.* **strung**) (*thread*) enfiler. **the ~s,** (*mus.*) les cordes. **~ bean,** haricot vert *m.* **pull ~s,** faire jouer ses relations, faire marcher le piston. **~ out,** (s')échelonner. **~ed** *a.* (*instrument*) à cordes. **~y** *a.* filandreux.

stringent /'strɪndʒənt/ *a.* rigoureux, strict.

strip[1] /strɪp/ *v.t./i.* (*p.t.* **stripped**) (*undress*) (se) déshabiller; (*machine*) démonter; (*deprive*) dépouiller. **~per** *n.* strip-teaseuse *f.*; (*solvent*) décapant *m.* **~-tease** *n.* strip-tease *m.*

strip[2] /strɪp/ *n.* bande *f.* **comic ~,** bande dessinée *f.* **~ light,** néon *m.*

stripe /straɪp/ *n.* rayure *f.*, raie *f.* **~d** *a.* rayé.

strive /straɪv/ *v.i.* (*p.t.* **strove,** *p.p.* **striven**) s'efforcer (**to,** de).

strode /strəʊd/ *see* stride.

stroke[1] /strəʊk/ *n.* coup *m.*; (*of pen*) trait *m.*; (*swimming*) nage *f.*; (*med.*) attaque *f.*, congestion *f.* **at a ~,** d'un seul coup.

stroke[2] /strəʊk/ *v.t.* (*with hand*) caresser. ● *n.* caresse *f.*

stroll /strəʊl/ *v.i.* flâner. ● *n.* petit tour *m.* **~ in**/*etc.*, entrer/*etc.*

tranquillement. **~er** *n.* (*Amer.*) poussette *f.*

strong /strɒŋ/ *a.* (**-er, -est**) fort; (*shoes, fabric, etc.*) solide. **be fifty/** *etc.* **~,** être au nombre de cinquante/ *etc.* **~-box** *n.* coffre-fort *m.* **~-minded** *a.* résolu. **~- room** *n.* chambre forte *f.* **~ly** *adv.* (*greatly*) fortement; (*with energy*) avec force; (*deeply*) profondément.

stronghold /'strɒŋhəʊld/ *n.* bastion *m.*

strove /strəʊv/ *see* strive.

struck /strʌk/ *see* strike. ● *a.* **~ on,** (*sl.*) impressionné par.

structur|e /'strʌktʃə(r)/ *n.* (*of cell, poem, etc.*) structure *f.*; (*building*) construction *f.* **~al** *a.* structural; de (la) construction.

struggle /'strʌgl/ *v.i.* lutter, se battre. ● *n.* lutte *f.*; (*effort*) effort *m.* **have a ~ to,** avoir du mal à.

strum /strʌm/ *v.t.* (*p.t.* **strummed**) (*banjo etc.*) gratter de.

strung /strʌŋ/ *see* string. ● *a.* **~ up,** (*tense*) nerveux.

strut /strʌt/ *n.* (*support*) étai *m.* ● *v.i.* (*p.t.* **strutted**) se pavaner.

stub /stʌb/ *n.* bout *m.*; (*of tree*) souche *f.*; (*counterfoil*) talon *m.* ● *v.t.* (*p.t.* **stubbed**). **~ one's toe,** se cogner le doigt de pied. **~ out,** écraser.

stubble /'stʌbl/ *n.* (*on chin*) barbe de plusieurs jours *f.*; (*remains of wheat*) chaume *m.*

stubborn /'stʌbən/ *a.* opiniâtre, obstiné. **~ly** *adv.* obstinément. **~ness** *n.* opiniâtreté *f.*

stubby /'stʌbɪ/ *a.* (**-ier, -iest**) (*finger*) épais; (*person*) trapu.

stuck /stʌk/ *see* stick[2]. ● *a.* (*jammed*) coincé. **I'm ~,** (*for answer*) je sèche. **~-up** *a.* (*sl.*) prétentieux.

stud[1] /stʌd/ *n.* clou *m.*; (*for collar*) bouton *m.* ● *v.t.* (*p.t.* **studded**) clouter. **~ded with,** parsemé de.

stud[2] /stʌd/ *n.* (*horses*) écurie *f.* **~ (-farm)** *n.* haras *m.*

student /'stju:dnt/ *n.* (*univ.*) étudiant(e) *m.* (*f.*); (*schol.*) élève *m./f.* ● *a.* (*restaurant, life, residence*) universitaire.

studied /'stʌdɪd/ *a.* étudié.

studio /'stju:dɪəʊ/ *n.* (*pl.* **-os**) studio *m.* **~ flat,** studio *m.*

studious /'stju:dɪəs/ *a.* (*person*) studieux; (*deliberate*) étudié. **~ly** *adv.* (*carefully*) avec soin.

study /'stʌdɪ/ *n.* étude *f.*; (*office*) bureau *m.* ● *v.t./i.* étudier.

stuff /stʌf/ *n.* substance *f.*; (*sl.*) chose(s) *f.* (*pl.*). ● *v.t.* rembourrer; (*animal*) empailler; (*cram*) bourrer; (*culin.*) farcir; (*block up*) boucher; (*put*) fourrer. **~ing** *n.* bourre *f.*; (*culin.*) farce *f.*

stuffy /'stʌfɪ/ *a.* (**-ier, -iest**) mal aéré; (*dull*: *fam.*) vieux jeu *invar.*

stumbl|e /'stʌmbl/ *v.i.* trébucher. **~e across** *or* **on,** tomber sur. **~ing-block** *n.* pierre d'achoppement *f.*

stump /stʌmp/ *n.* (*of tree*) souche *f.*; (*of limb*) moignon *m.*; (*of pencil*) bout *m.*

stumped /stʌmpt/ *a.* (*baffled*: *fam.*) embarrassé.

stun /stʌn/ *v.t.* (*p.t.* **stunned**) étourdir; (*bewilder*) stupéfier.

stung /stʌŋ/ *see* sting.

stunk /stʌŋk/ *see* stink.

stunning /'stʌnɪŋ/ *a.* (*delightful*: *fam.*) sensationnel.

stunt[1] /stʌnt/ *v.t.* (*growth*) retarder. **~ed** *a.* (*person*) rabougri.

stunt[2] /stʌnt/ *n.* (*feat*: *fam.*) tour de force *m.*; (*trick*: *fam.*) truc *m.*; (*dangerous*) cascade *f.* **~man** *n.* cascadeur *m.*

stupefy /'stju:pɪfaɪ/ *v.t.* abrutir; (*amaze*) stupéfier.

stupendous /stju:'pendəs/ *a.* prodigieux, formidable.

stupid /'stju:pɪd/ *a.* stupide, bête. **~ity** /-'pɪdətɪ/ *n.* stupidité *f.* **~ly** *adv.* stupidement, bêtement.

stupor /'stju:pə(r)/ *n.* stupeur *f.*

sturd|y /'stɜ:dɪ/ *a.* (**-ier, -iest**) robuste. **~iness** *n.* robustesse *f.*

stutter /'stʌtə(r)/ *v.i.* bégayer. ● *n.* bégaiement *m.*

sty[1] /staɪ/ *n.* (*pigsty*) porcherie *f.*

sty[2] /staɪ/ *n.* (*on eye*) orgelet *m.*

styl|e /staɪl/ *n.* style *m.*; (*fashion*) mode *f.*; (*sort*) genre *m.*; (*pattern*) modèle *m.* ● *v.t.* (*design*) créer. **do sth. in ~e,** faire qch. avec classe. **~e s.o.'s hair,** coiffer qn. **~ist** *n.* (*of hair*) coiffeu|r, -se *m., f.*

stylish /'staɪlɪʃ/ *a.* élégant.

stylized /'staɪlaɪzd/ *a.* stylisé.

stylus /'staɪləs/ *n.* (*pl.* **-uses**) (*of record-player*) saphir *m.*

suave /swɑ:v/ *a.* (*urbane*) courtois; (*smooth*: *pej.*) doucereux.

sub- /sʌb/ *pref.* sous-, sub-.
subconscious /sʌb'kɒnʃəs/ *a.* & *n.* inconscient (*m.*), subconscient (*m.*). **~ly** *adv.* inconsciemment.
subcontract /sʌbkən'trækt/ *v.t.* sous-traiter.
subdivide /sʌbdɪ'vaɪd/ *v.t.* subdiviser.
subdue /səb'dju:/ *v.t.* (*feeling*) maîtriser; (*country*) subjuguer. **~d** *a.* (*weak*) faible; (*light*) tamisé; (*person, criticism*) retenu.
subject[1] /'sʌbdʒɪkt/ *a.* (*state etc.*) soumis. ● *n.* sujet *m.*; (*schol., univ.*) matière *f.*; (*citizen*) ressortissant(e) *m.* (*f.*), sujet(te) *m.* (*f.*). **~-matter** *n.* contenu *m.* **~ to,** soumis à; (*liable to, dependent on*) sujet à.
subject[2] /səb'dʒekt/ *v.t.* soumettre. **~ion** /-kʃn/ *n.* soumission *f.*
subjective /səb'dʒektɪv/ *a.* subjectif.
subjunctive /səb'dʒʌŋktɪv/ *a.* & *n.* subjonctif (*m.*).
sublet /sʌb'let/ *v.t.* sous-louer.
sublime /sə'blaɪm/ *a.* sublime.
submarine /sʌbmə'ri:n/ *n.* sous-marin *m.*
submerge /səb'mɜ:dʒ/ *v.t.* submerger. ● *v.i.* plonger.
submissive /səb'mɪsɪv/ *a.* soumis.
submi|t /səb'mɪt/ *v.t./i.* (*p.t.* **submitted**) (se) soumettre (**to,** à). **~ssion** *n.* soumission *f.*
subordinate[1] /sə'bɔ:dɪnət/ *a.* subalterne; (*gram.*) subordonné. ● *n.* subordonné(e) *m.* (*f.*).
subordinate[2] /sə'bɔ:dɪneɪt/ *v.t.* subordonner (**to,** à).
subpoena /səb'pi:nə/ *n.* (*pl.* **-as**) (*jurid.*) citation *f.*, assignation *f.*
subroutine /'sʌbru:ti:n/ *n.* sous-programme *m.*
subscribe /səb'skraɪb/ *v.t./i.* verser (de l'argent) (**to,** à). **~ to,** (*loan, theory*) souscrire à; (*newspaper*) s'abonner à, être abonné à. **~r** /-ə(r)/ *n.* abonné(e) *m.* (*f.*).
subscription /səb'skrɪpʃn/ *n.* souscription *f.*; abonnement *m.*; (*membership dues*) cotisation *f.*
subsequent /'sʌbsɪkwənt/ *a.* (*later*) ultérieur; (*next*) suivant. **~ly** *adv.* par la suite.
subside /səb'saɪd/ *v.i.* (*land etc.*) s'affaisser; (*flood, wind*) baisser. **~nce** /-əns/ *n.* affaissement *m.*
subsidiary /səb'sɪdɪərɪ/ *a.* accessoire. ● *n.* (*comm.*) filiale *f.*
subsid|y /'sʌbsədɪ/ *n.* subvention *f.* **~ize** /-ɪdaɪz/ *v.t.* subventionner.
subsist /səb'sɪst/ *v.i.* subsister. **~ence** *n.* subsistance *f.*
substance /'sʌbstəns/ *n.* substance *f.*
substandard /sʌb'stændəd/ *a.* de qualité inférieure.
substantial /səb'stænʃl/ *a.* considérable; (*meal*) substantiel. **~ly** *adv.* considérablement.
substantiate /səb'stænʃɪeɪt/ *v.t.* justifier, prouver.
substitut|e /'sʌbstɪtju:t/ *n.* succédané *m.*; (*person*) remplaçant(e) *m.* (*f.*). ● *v.t.* substituer (**for,** à). **~ion** /-'tju:ʃn/ *n.* substitution *f.*
subterfuge /'sʌbtəfju:dʒ/ *n.* subterfuge *m.*
subterranean /sʌbtə'reɪnɪən/ *a.* souterrain.
subtitle /'sʌbtaɪtl/ *n.* sous-titre *m.*
subtle /'sʌtl/ *a.* (**-er, -est**) subtil. **~ty** *n.* subtilité *f.*
subtotal /sʌb'təʊtl/ *n.* total partiel *m.*
subtract /səb'trækt/ *v.t.* soustraire. **~ion** /-kʃn/ *n.* soustraction *f.*
suburb /'sʌbɜ:b/ *n.* faubourg *m.*, banlieue *f.* **~s,** banlieue *f.* **~an** /sə'bɜ:bən/ *a.* de banlieue.
suburbia /sə'bɜ:bɪə/ *n.* la banlieue.
subversive /səb'vɜ:sɪv/ *a.* subversif.
subver|t /səb'vɜ:t/ *v.t.* renverser. **~sion** /-ʃn/ *n.* subversion *f.*
subway /'sʌbweɪ/ *n.* passage souterrain *m.*; (*Amer.*) métro *m.*
succeed /sək'si:d/ *v.i.* réussir (**in doing,** à faire). ● *v.t.* (*follow*) succéder à. **~ing** *a.* suivant.
success /sək'ses/ *n.* succès *m.*, réussite *f.*
successful /sək'sesfl/ *a.* réussi, couronné de succès; (*favourable*) heureux; (*in exam*) reçu. **be ~ in doing,** réussir à faire. **~ly** *adv.* avec succès.
succession /sək'seʃn/ *n.* succession *f.* **in ~,** de suite.
successive /sək'sesɪv/ *a.* successif. **six ~ days,** six jours consécutifs.
successor /sək'sesə(r)/ *n.* successeur *m.*
succinct /sək'sɪŋkt/ *a.* succinct.
succulent /'sʌkjʊlənt/ *a.* succulent.
succumb /sə'kʌm/ *v.i.* succomber.
such /sʌtʃ/ *a.* & *pron.* tel(le), tel(le)s; (*so much*) tant (de). ● *adv.* si. **~ a book**/*etc.*, un tel livre/*etc.* **~ books**/*etc.*, de tels livres/*etc.* **~ courage**/*etc.*, tant de courage/ *etc.* **~ a big house,** une si grande maison. **~ as,**

comme, tel que. **as ~,** en tant que tel. **there's no ~ thing,** ça n'existe pas. **~-and-such** *a.* tel ou tel.

suck /sʌk/ *v.t.* sucer. **~ in** *or* **up,** aspirer. **~er** *n.* (*rubber pad*) ventouse *f.*; (*person*: *sl.*) dupe *f.*

suction /ˈsʌkʃn/ *n.* succion *f.*

sudden /ˈsʌdn/ *a.* soudain, subit. **all of a ~,** tout à coup. **~ly** *adv.* subitement, brusquement. **~ness** *n.* soudaineté *f.*

suds /sʌdz/ *n. pl.* (*froth*) mousse de savon *f.*

sue /su:/ *v.t.* (*pres. p.* **suing**) poursuivre (en justice).

suede /sweɪd/ *n.* daim *m.*

suet /ˈsu:ɪt/ *n.* graisse de rognon *f.*

suffer /ˈsʌfə(r)/ *v.t./i.* souffrir; (*loss, attack, etc.*) subir. **~er** *n.* victime *f.*, malade *m./f.* **~ing** *n.* souffrance(s) *f.* (*pl.*).

suffice /səˈfaɪs/ *v.i.* suffire.

sufficient /səˈfɪʃnt/ *a.* (*enough*) suffisamment de; (*big enough*) suffisant. **~ly** *adv.* suffisamment.

suffix /ˈsʌfɪks/ *n.* suffixe *m.*

suffocat|e /ˈsʌfəkeɪt/ *v.t./i.* suffoquer. **~ion** /-ˈkeɪʃn/ *n.* suffocation *f.*; (*med.*) asphyxie *f.*

suffused /səˈfju:zd/ *a.* **~ with,** (*light, tears*) baigné de.

sugar /ˈʃʊgə(r)/ *n.* sucre *m.* ● *v.t.* sucrer. **~y** *a.* sucré.

suggest /səˈdʒest/ *v.t.* suggérer. **~ion** /-tʃn/ *n.* suggestion *f.*

suggestive /səˈdʒestɪv/ *a.* suggestif. **be ~ of,** suggérer.

suicid|e /ˈsu:ɪsaɪd/ *n.* suicide *m.* **commit ~e,** se suicider. **~al** /-ˈsaɪdl/ *a.* suicidaire.

suit /su:t/ *n.* costume *m.*; (*woman's*) tailleur *m.*; (*cards*) couleur *f.* ● *v.t.* convenir à; (*of garment, style, etc.*) aller à; (*adapt*) adapter. **~ability** *n.* (*of action etc.*) à-propos *m.*; (*of candidate*) aptitude(s) *f.* (*pl.*). **~able** *a.* qui convient (**for,** à), convenable. **~ably** *adv.* convenablement. **~ed** *a.* **(well) ~ed,** (*matched*) bien assorti. **~ed to,** fait pour, apte à.

suitcase /ˈsu:tkeɪs/ *n.* valise *f.*

suite /swi:t/ *n.* (*rooms, retinue*) suite *f.*; (*furniture*) mobilier *m.*

suitor /ˈsu:tə(r)/ *n.* soupirant *m.*

sulfur /ˈsʌlfər/ *n.* (*Amer.*) = **sulphur**.

sulk /sʌlk/ *v.i.* bouder. **~y** *a.* boudeur, maussade.

sullen /ˈsʌlən/ *a.* maussade. **~ly** *adv.* d'un air maussade.

sulphur /ˈsʌlfə(r)/ *n.* soufre *m.* **~ic** /-ˈfjʊərɪk/ *a.* **~ic acid,** acide sulfurique *m.*

sultan /ˈsʌltən/ *n.* sultan *m.*

sultana /sʌlˈtɑ:nə/ *n.* raisin de Smyrne *m.*, raisin sec *m.*

sultry /ˈsʌltrɪ/ *a.* (**-ier, -iest**) étouffant, lourd; (*fig.*) sensuel.

sum /sʌm/ *n.* somme *f.*; (*in arithmetic*) calcul *m.* ● *v.t./i.* (*p.t.* **summed**). **~ up,** résumer, récapituler; (*assess*) évaluer.

summar|y /ˈsʌmərɪ/ *n.* résumé *m.* ● *a.* sommaire. **~ize** *v.t.* résumer.

summer /ˈsʌmə(r)/ *n.* été *m.* ● *a.* d'été. **~-time** *n.* (*season*) été *m.* **~y** *a.* estival.

summit /ˈsʌmɪt/ *n.* sommet *m.* **~ (conference),** (*pol.*) (conférence *f.* au) sommet *m.*

summon /ˈsʌmən/ *v.t.* appeler; (*meeting, s.o. to meeting*) convoquer. **~ up,** (*strength, courage, etc.*) rassembler.

summons /ˈsʌmənz/ *n.* (*jurid.*) assignation *f.* ● *v.t.* assigner.

sump /sʌmp/ *n.* (*auto.*) carter *m.*

sumptuous /ˈsʌmptʃʊəs/ *a.* somptueux, luxueux.

sun /sʌn/ *n.* soleil *m.* ● *v.t.* (*p.t.* **sunned**). **~ o.s.,** se chauffer au soleil. **~-glasses** *n. pl.* lunettes de soleil *f. pl.* **~-roof** *n.* toit ouvrant *m.* **~-tan** *n.* bronzage *m.* **~-tanned** *a.* bronzé.

sunbathe /ˈsʌnbeɪð/ *v.i.* prendre un bain de soleil.

sunburn /ˈsʌnbɜ:n/ *n.* coup de soleil *m.* **~t** *a.* brûlé par le soleil.

Sunday /ˈsʌndɪ/ *n.* dimanche *m.* **~ school,** catéchisme *m.*

sundial /ˈsʌndaɪəl/ *n.* cadran solaire *m.*

sundown /ˈsʌndaʊn/ *n.* = sunset.

sundr|y /ˈsʌndrɪ/ *a.* divers. **~ies** *n. pl.* articles divers *m. pl.* **all and ~y,** tout le monde.

sunflower /ˈsʌnflaʊə(r)/ *n.* tournesol *m.*

sung /sʌŋ/ *see* sing.

sunk /sʌŋk/ *see* sink.

sunken /ˈsʌŋkən/ *a.* (*ship etc.*) submergé; (*eyes*) creux.

sunlight /ˈsʌnlaɪt/ *n.* soleil *m.*

sunny /ˈsʌnɪ/ *a.* (**-ier, -iest**) (*room, day, etc.*) ensoleillé.

sunrise /ˈsʌnraɪz/ *n.* lever du soleil *m.*

sunset /'sʌnset/ *n.* coucher du soleil *m.*
sunshade /'sʌnʃeɪd/ *n.* (*lady's*) ombrelle *f.*; (*awning*) parasol *m.*
sunshine /'sʌnʃaɪn/ *n.* soleil *m.*
sunstroke /'sʌnstrəʊk/ *n.* insolation *f.*
super /'su:pə(r)/ *a.* (*sl.*) formidable.
superb /su:'pɜ:b/ *a.* superbe.
supercilious /su:pə'sɪlɪəs/ *a.* hautain, dédaigneux.
superficial /su:pə'fɪʃl/ *a.* superficiel. **~ity** /-ɪ'ælətɪ/ *n.* caractère superficiel *m.* **~ly** *adv.* superficiellement.
superfluous /su:'pɜ:flʊəs/ *a.* superflu.
superhuman /su:pə'hju:mən/ *a.* surhumain.
superimpose /su:pərɪm'pəʊz/ *v.t.* superposer (**on,** à).
superintendent /su:pərɪn'tendənt/ *n.* direc|teur, -trice *m., f.*; (*of police*) commissaire *m.*
superior /su:'pɪərɪə(r)/ *a. & n.* supérieur(e) (*m.* (*f.*)). **~ity** /-'ɒrətɪ/ *n.* supériorité *f.*
superlative /su:'pɜ:lətɪv/ *a.* suprême. ● *n.* (*gram.*) superlatif *m.*
superman /'su:pəmæn/ *n.* (*pl.* **-men**) surhomme *m.*
supermarket /'su:pəmɑ:kɪt/ *n.* supermarché *m.*
supernatural /su:pə'nætʃrəl/ *a.* surnaturel.
superpower /'su:pəpaʊə(r)/ *n.* superpuissance *f.*
supersede /su:pə'si:d/ *v.t.* remplacer, supplanter.
supersonic /su:pə'sɒnɪk/ *a.* supersonique.
superstiti|on /su:pə'stɪʃn/ *n.* superstition *f.* **~ous** *a.* superstitieux.
superstore /'su:pəstɔ:(r)/ *n.* hypermarché *m.*
supertanker /'su:pətæŋkə(r)/ *n.* pétrolier géant *m.*
supervis|e /'su:pəvaɪz/ *v.t.* surveiller, diriger. **~ion** /-'vɪʒn/ *n.* surveillance *f.* **~or** *n.* surveillant(e) *m.* (*f.*); (*shop*) chef de rayon *m.*; (*firm*) chef de service *m.* **~ory** /-'vaɪzərɪ/ *a.* de surveillance.
supper /'sʌpə(r)/ *n.* dîner *m.*; (*late at night*) souper *m.*
supple /'sʌpl/ *a.* souple.
supplement[1] /'sʌplɪmənt/ *n.* supplément *m.* **~ary** /-'mentrɪ/ *a.* supplémentaire.
supplement[2] /'sʌplɪment/ *v.t.* compléter.
supplier /sə'plaɪə(r)/ *n.* fournisseur *m.*
suppl|y /sə'plaɪ/ *v.t.* fournir; (*equip*) pourvoir; (*feed*) alimenter (**with,** en). ● *n.* provision *f.*; (*of gas etc.*) alimentation *f.* **~ies,** (*food*) vivres *m. pl.*; (*material*) fournitures *f. pl.* **~y teacher,** (professeur) suppléant(e) *m.* (*f.*).
support /sə'pɔ:t/ *v.t.* soutenir; (*family*) assurer la subsistance de; (*endure*) supporter. ● *n.* soutien *m.*, appui *m.*; (*techn.*) support *m.* **~er** *n.* partisan(e) *m.* (*f.*); (*sport*) supporter *m.* **~ive** *a.* qui soutient et encourage.
suppos|e /sə'pəʊz/ *v.t./i.* supposer. **be ~ed to do,** être censé faire, devoir faire. **~ing he comes,** supposons qu'il vienne. **~ition** /sʌpə'zɪʃn/ *n.* supposition *f.*
supposedly /sə'pəʊzɪdlɪ/ *adv.* soi-disant, prétendument.
suppress /sə'pres/ *v.t.* (*put an end to*) supprimer; (*restrain*) réprimer; (*stifle*) étouffer. **~ion** /-ʃn/ *n.* suppression *f.*; répression *f.*
suprem|e /su:'pri:m/ *a.* suprême. **~acy** /-eməsɪ/ *n.* suprématie *f.*
surcharge /'sɜ:tʃɑ:dʒ/ *n.* prix supplémentaire *m.*; (*tax*) surtaxe *f.*; (*on stamp*) surcharge *f.*
sure /ʃɔ:(r)/ *a.* (**-er, -est**) sûr. ● *adv.* (*Amer., fam.*) pour sûr. **make ~ of,** s'assurer de. **make ~ that,** vérifier que. **~ly** *adv.* sûrement.
surety /ʃɔ:rətɪ/ *n.* caution *f.*
surf /sɜ:f/ *n.* (*waves*) ressac *m.* **~ing** *n.* surf *m.*
surface /'sɜ:fɪs/ *n.* surface *f.* ● *a.* superficiel. ● *v.t.* revêtir. ● *v.i.* faire surface; (*fig.*) réapparaître. **~ mail,** courrier maritime *m.*
surfboard /'sɜ:fbɔ:d/ *n.* planche de surf *f.*
surfeit /'sɜ:fɪt/ *n.* excès *m.* (**of,** de).
surge /sɜ:dʒ/ *v.i.* (*of crowd*) déferler; (*of waves*) s'enfler; (*increase*) monter. ● *n.* (*wave*) vague *f.*; (*rise*) montée *f.*
surgeon /'sɜ:dʒən/ *n.* chirurgien *m.*
surg|ery /'sɜ:dʒərɪ/ *n.* chirurgie *f.*; (*office*) cabinet *m.*; (*session*) consultation *f.* **need ~ery,** devoir être opéré. **~ical** *a.* chirurgical. **~ical spirit,** alcool à 90 degrés *m.*
surly /'sɜ:lɪ/ *a.* (**-ier, -iest**) bourru.

surmise /sə'maɪz/ *v.t.* conjecturer. ● *n.* conjecture *f.*
surmount /sə'maʊnt/ *v.t.* (*overcome, cap*) surmonter.
surname /'sɜ:neɪm/ *n.* nom de famille *m.*
surpass /sə'pɑ:s/ *v.t.* surpasser.
surplus /'sɜ:pləs/ *n.* surplus *m.* ● *a.* en surplus.
surpris|e /sə'praɪz/ *n.* surprise *f.* ● *v.t.* surprendre. **~ed** *a.* surpris (**at**, de). **~ing** *a.* surprenant. **~ingly** *adv.* étonnamment.
surrender /sə'rendə(r)/ *v.i.* se rendre. ● *v.t.* (*hand over*) remettre; (*mil.*) rendre. ● *n.* (*mil.*) reddition *f.*; (*of passport etc.*) remise *f.*
surreptitious /sʌrəp'tɪʃəs/ *a.* subreptice, furtif.
surround /sə'raʊnd/ *v.t.* entourer; (*mil.*) encercler. **~ing** *a.* environnant. **~ings** *n. pl.* environs *m. pl.*; (*setting*) cadre *m.*
surveillance /sɜ:'veɪləns/ *n.* surveillance *f.*
survey[1] /sə'veɪ/ *v.t.* (*review*) passer en revue; (*inquire into*) enquêter sur; (*building*) inspecter. **~or** *n.* expert (géomètre) *m.*
survey[2] /'sɜ:veɪ/ *n.* (*inquiry*) enquête *f.*; inspection *f.*; (*general view*) vue d'ensemble *f.*
survival /sə'vaɪvl/ *n.* survie *f.*; (*relic*) vestige *m.*
surviv|e /sə'vaɪv/ *v.t./i.* survivre (à). **~or** *n.* survivant(e) *m.* (*f.*).
susceptib|le /sə'septəbl/ *a.* sensible (**to**, à). **~le to**, (*prone to*) prédisposé à. **~ility** /-'bɪlətɪ/ *n.* sensibilité *f.*; prédisposition *f.*
suspect[1] /sə'spekt/ *v.t.* soupçonner; (*doubt*) douter de.
suspect[2] /'sʌspekt/ *n. & a.* suspect(e) (*m.* (*f.*)).
suspen|d /sə'spend/ *v.t.* (*hang, stop*) suspendre; (*licence*) retirer provisoirement. **~ded sentence**, condamnation avec sursis *f.* **~sion** *n.* suspension *f.*; retrait provisoire *m.* **~sion bridge**, pont suspendu *m.*
suspender /sə'spendə(r)/ *n.* jarretelle *f.* **~s**, (*braces*: *Amer.*) bretelles *f. pl.* **~ belt**, porte-jarretelles *m.*
suspense /sə'spens/ *n.* attente *f.*; (*in book etc.*) suspense *m.*
suspicion /sə'spɪʃn/ *n.* soupçon *m.*; (*distrust*) méfiance *f.*
suspicious /səs'pɪʃəs/ *a.* soupçonneux; (*causing suspicion*) suspect. **be ~ of**, (*distrust*) se méfier de. **~ly** *adv.* de façon suspecte.
sustain /səs'teɪn/ *v.t.* supporter; (*effort etc.*) soutenir; (*suffer*) subir.
sustenance /'sʌstɪnəns/ *n.* (*food*) nourriture *f.*; (*quality*) valeur nutritive *f.*
swab /swɒb/ *n.* (*pad*) tampon *m.*
swagger /'swægə(r)/ *v.i.* (*walk*) se pavaner, parader.
swallow[1] /'swɒləʊ/ *v.t./i.* avaler. **~ up**, (*absorb, engulf*) engloutir.
swallow[2] /'swɒləʊ/ *n.* hirondelle *f.*
swam /swæm/ *see* swim.
swamp /swɒmp/ *n.* marais *m.* ● *v.t.* (*flood, overwhelm*) submerger. **~y** *a.* marécageux.
swan /swɒn/ *n.* cygne *m.* **~-song** *n.* (*fig.*) chant du cygne *m.*
swank /swæŋk/ *n.* (*behaviour*: *fam.*) épate *f.*, esbroufe *f.*; (*person*: *fam.*) crâneu|r, -se *m.*, *f.* ● *v.i.* (*show off*: *fam.*) crâner.
swap /swɒp/ *v.t./i.* (*p.t.* **swapped**) (*fam.*) échanger. ● *n.* (*fam.*) échange *m.*
swarm /swɔ:m/ *n.* (*of insects, people*) essaim *m.* ● *v.i.* fourmiller. **~ into** *or* **round**, (*crowd*) envahir.
swarthy /'swɔ:ðɪ/ *a.* (**-ier, -iest**) noiraud; (*complexion*) basané.
swastika /'swɒstɪkə/ *n.* (*Nazi*) croix gammée *f.*
swat /swɒt/ *v.t.* (*p.t.* **swatted**) (*fly etc.*) écraser.
sway /sweɪ/ *v.t./i.* (se) balancer; (*influence*) influencer. ● *n.* balancement *m.*; (*rule*) empire *m.*
swear /sweə(r)/ *v.t./i.* (*p.t.* **swore**, *p.p.* **sworn**) jurer (**to sth.**, de qch.). **~ at**, injurier. **~ by sth.**, (*fam.*) ne jurer que par qch. **~-word** *n.* juron *m.*
sweat /swet/ *n.* sueur *f.* ● *v.i.* suer. **~-shirt** *n.* sweat-shirt *m.* **~y** *a.* en sueur.
sweater /'swetə(r)/ *n.* pull-over *m.*
swede /swi:d/ *n.* rutabaga *m.*
Swed|e /swi:d/ *n.* Suédois(e) *m.* (*f.*). **~en** *n.* Suède *f.* **~ish** *a.* suédois; *n.* (*lang.*) suédois *m.*
sweep /swi:p/ *v.t./i.* (*p.t.* **swept**) balayer; (*carry away*) emporter, entraîner; (*chimney*) ramonner. ● *n.* coup de balai *m.*; (*curve*) courbe *f.*; (*mouvement*) geste *m.*, mouvement *m.*; (*for chimneys*) ramonneur *m.* **~ by**, passer rapidement *or* majestueusement. **~ out**, balayer.

~er *n.* (*for carpet*) balai mécanique *m.*; (*football*) arrière volant *m.* **~ing** *a.* (*gesture*) large; (*action*) qui va loin; (*statement*) trop général.

sweet /swi:t/ *a.* (**-er, -est**) (*not sour, pleasant*) doux; (*not savoury*) sucré; (*charming: fam.*) gentil. ● *n.* bonbon *m.*; (*dish*) dessert *m.*; (*person*) chéri(e) *m.* (*f.*). **have a ~ tooth,** aimer les sucreries. **~ corn,** maïs *m.* **~ pea,** pois de senteur *m.* **~ shop,** confiserie *f.* **~ly** *adv.* gentiment. **~ness** *n.* douceur *f.*; goût sucré *m.*

sweeten /'swi:tn/ *v.t.* sucrer; (*fig.*) adoucir. **~er** *n.* édulcorant *m.*

sweetheart /'swi:thɑ:t/ *n.* petit(e) ami(e) *m.* (*f.*); (*term of endearment*) chéri(e) *m.* (*f.*).

swell /swel/ *v.t./i.* (*p.t.* **swelled,** *p.p.* **swollen** *or* **swelled**) (*increase*) grossir; (*expand*) (se) gonfler; (*of hand, face*) enfler. ● *n.* (*of sea*) houle *f.* ● *a.* (*fam.*) formidable. **~ing** *n.* (*med.*) enflure *f.*

swelter /'sweltə(r)/ *v.i.* étouffer. **~ing** *a.* étouffant.

swept /swept/ *see* sweep.

swerve /swɜ:v/ *v.i.* faire un écart.

swift /swɪft/ *a.* (**-er, -est**) rapide. ● *n.* (*bird*) martinet *m.* **~ly** *adv.* rapidement. **~ness** *n.* rapidité *f.*

swig /swɪg/ *v.t.* (*p.t.* **swigged**) (*drink: fam.*) lamper. ● *n.* (*fam.*) lampée *f.*, coup *m.*

swill /swɪl/ *v.t.* rincer; (*drink*) lamper. ● *n.* (*pig-food*) pâtée *f.*

swim /swɪm/ *v.i.* (*p.t.* **swam,** *p.p.* **swum,** *pres. p.* **swimming**) nager; (*be dizzy*) tourner. ● *v.t.* traverser à la nage; (*distance*) nager. ● *n.* baignade *f.* **go for a ~,** aller se baigner. **~mer** *n.* nageu|r, -se *m., f.* **~ming** *n.* natation *f.* **~ming-bath, ~ming-pool** *ns.* piscine *f.* **~-suit** *n.* maillot (de bain) *m.*

swindle /'swɪndl/ *v.t.* escroquer. ● *n.* escroquerie *f.* **~r** /-ə(r)/ *n.* escroc *m.*

swine /swaɪn/ *n. pl.* (*pigs*) pourceaux *m. pl.* ● *n. invar.* (*person: fam.*) salaud *m.*

swing /swɪŋ/ *v.t./i.* (*p.t.* **swung**) (se) balancer; (*turn round*) tourner; (*of pendulum*) osciller. ● *n.* balancement *m.*; (*seat*) balançoire *f.*; (*of opinion*) revirement *m.* (**towards,** en faveur de); (*mus.*) rythme *m.* **be in full ~,** battre son plein. **~ round,** (*of person*) se retourner.

swingeing /'swɪndʒɪŋ/ *a.* écrasant.

swipe /swaɪp/ *v.t.* (*hit: fam.*) frapper; (*steal: fam.*) piquer. ● *n.* (*hit: fam.*) grand coup *m.*

swirl /swɜ:l/ *v.i.* tourbillonner. ● *n.* tourbillon *m.*

swish /swɪʃ/ *v.i.* (*hiss*) siffler, cingler l'air. ● *a.* (*fam.*) chic *invar.*

Swiss /swɪs/ *a.* suisse. ● *n. invar.* Suisse(sse) *m.* (*f.*).

switch /swɪtʃ/ *n.* bouton (électrique) *m.*, interrupteur *m.*; (*shift*) changement *m.*, revirement *m.* ● *v.t.* (*transfer*) transférer; (*exchange*) échanger (**for,** contre); (*reverse positions of*) changer de place. **~ trains/** *etc.*, (*change*) changer de train/*etc.* ● *v.i.* (*go over*) passer. **~ off,** éteindre. **~ on,** mettre, allumer.

switchback /'swɪtʃbæk/ *n.* montagnes russes *f. pl.*

switchboard /'swɪtʃbɔ:d/ *n.* (*telephone*) standard *m.*

Switzerland /'swɪtsələnd/ *n.* Suisse *f.*

swivel /'swɪvl/ *v.t./i.* (*p.t.* **swivelled**) (faire) pivoter.

swollen /'swəʊlən/ *see* swell.

swoon /swu:n/ *v.i.* se pâmer.

swoop /swu:p/ *v.i.* (*bird*) fondre; (*police*) faire une descente, foncer. ● *n.* (*police raid*) descente *f.*

sword /sɔ:d/ *n.* épée *f.*

swore /swɔ:(r)/ *see* swear.

sworn /swɔ:n/ *see* swear. ● *a.* (*enemy*) juré; (*ally*) dévoué.

swot /swɒt/ *v.t./i.* (*p.t.* **swotted**) (*study: sl.*) bûcher. ● *n.* (*sl.*) bûcheu|r, -se *m., f.*

swum /swʌm/ *see* swim.

swung /swʌŋ/ *see* swing.

sycamore /'sɪkəmɔ:(r)/ *n.* (*maple*) sycomore *m.*; (*Amer.*) platane *m.*

syllable /'sɪləbl/ *n.* syllabe *f.*

syllabus /'sɪləbəs/ *n.* (*pl.* **-uses**) (*schol., univ.*) programme *m.*

symbol /'sɪmbl/ *n.* symbole *m.* **~ic(al)** /-'bɒlɪk(l)/ *a.* symbolique. **~ism** *n.* symbolisme *m.*

symbolize /'sɪmbəlaɪz/ *v.t.* symboliser.

symmetr|y /'sɪmətrɪ/ *n.* symétrie *f.* **~ical** /sɪ'metrɪkl/ *a.* symétrique.

sympathize /'sɪmpəθaɪz/ *v.i.* **~ with,** (*pity*) plaindre; (*fig.*) comprendre les sentiments de. **~r** /ə(r)/ *n.* sympathisant(e) *m.* (*f.*).

sympath|y /'sɪmpəθɪ/ *n.* (*pity*) compassion *f.*; (*fig.*) compréhension *f.*; (*solidarity*) solidarité *f.*; (*condo-*

lences) condoléances *f. pl.* **be in ~y with,** comprendre, être en accord avec. **~etic** /-'θetɪk/ *a.* compatissant; (*fig.*) compréhensif. **~etically** /-'θetɪklɪ/ *adv.* avec compassion; (*fig.*) avec compréhension.

symphon|y /'sɪmfənɪ/ *n.* symphonie *f.* ● *a.* symphonique. **~ic** /-'fɒnɪk/ *a.* symphonique.

symposium /sɪm'pəʊzɪəm/ *n.* (*pl.* **-ia**) symposium *m.*

symptom /'sɪmptəm/ *n.* symptôme *m.* **~atic** /-'mætɪk/ *a.* symptomatique (**of,** de).

synagogue /'sɪnəgɒg/ *n.* synagogue *f.*

synchronize /'sɪŋkrənaɪz/ *v.t.* synchroniser.

syndicate /'sɪndɪkət/ *n.* syndicat *m.*

syndrome /'sɪndrəʊm/ *n.* syndrome *m.*

synonym /'sɪnənɪm/ *n.* synonyme *m.* **~ous** /sɪ'nɒnɪməs/ *a.* synonyme.

synopsis /sɪ'nɒpsɪs/ *n.* (*pl.* **-opses** /-si:z/) résumé *m.*

syntax /'sɪntæks/ *n.* syntaxe *f.*

synthesis /'sɪnθəsɪs/ *n.* (*pl.* **-theses** /-si:z/) synthèse *f.*

synthetic /sɪn'θetɪk/ *a.* synthétique.

syphilis /'sɪfɪlɪs/ *n.* syphilis *f.*

Syria /'sɪrɪə/ *n.* Syrie *f.* **~n** *a.* & *n.* syrien(ne) (*m.* (*f.*)).

syringe /sɪ'rɪndʒ/ *n.* seringue *f.*

syrup /'sɪrəp/ *n.* (*liquid*) sirop *m.*; (*treacle*) mélasse raffinée *f.* **~y** *a.* sirupeux.

system /'sɪstəm/ *n.* système *m.*; (*body*) organisme *m.*; (*order*) méthode *f.* **~s analyst,** analyste-programmeu|r, -se *m., f.* **~s disk,** disque système *m.*

systematic /sɪstə'mætɪk/ *a.* systématique.

T

tab /tæb/ *n.* (*flap*) languette *f.*, patte *f.*; (*loop*) attache *f.*; (*label*) étiquette *f.*; (*Amer., fam.*) addition *f.* **keep ~s on,** (*fam.*) surveiller.

table /'teɪbl/ *n.* table *f.* ● *v.t.* présenter; (*postpone*) ajourner. ● *a.* (*lamp, wine*) de table. **at ~,** à table. **lay** *or* **set the ~,** mettre la table. **~-cloth** *n.* nappe *f.* **~-mat** *n.* dessous-de-plat *m. invar.*; (*cloth*) set *m.* **~ of contents,** table des matières *f.* **~ tennis,** ping-pong *m.*

tablespoon /'teɪblspu:n/ *n.* cuiller à soupe *f.* **~ful** *n.* (*pl.* **~fuls**) cuillerée à soupe *f.*

tablet /'tæblɪt/ *n.* (*of stone*) plaque *f.*; (*drug*) comprimé *m.*

tabloid /'tæblɔɪd/ *n.* tabloïd *m.* **the ~ press,** la presse populaire.

taboo /tə'bu:/ *n.* & *a.* tabou (*m.*).

tabulator /'tæbjʊleɪtə(r)/ *n.* (*on typewriter*) tabulateur *m.*

tacit /'tæsɪt/ *a.* tacite.

taciturn /'tæsɪtɜ:n/ *a.* taciturne.

tack /tæk/ *n.* (*nail*) broquette *f.*; (*stitch*) point de bâti *m.*; (*course of action*) voie *f.* ● *v.t.* (*nail*) clouer; (*stitch*) bâtir; (*add*) ajouter. ● *v.i.* (*naut.*) louvoyer.

tackle /'tækl/ *n.* équipement *m.*, matériel *m.*; (*football*) plaquage *m.* ● *v.t.* (*problem etc.*) s'attaquer à; (*football player*) plaquer.

tacky /'tækɪ/ *a.* (**-ier, -iest**) poisseux, pas sec; (*shabby, mean*: *Amer.*) moche.

tact /tækt/ *n.* tact *m.* **~ful** *a.* plein de tact. **~fully** *adv.* avec tact. **~less** *a.* qui manque de tact. **~lessly** *adv.* sans tact.

tactic /'tæktɪk/ *n.* tactique *f.* **~s** *n.* & *n. pl.* tactique *f.* **~al** *a.* tactique.

tactile /'tæktaɪl/ *a.* tactile.

tadpole /'tædpəʊl/ *n.* têtard *m.*

tag /tæg/ *n.* (*label*) étiquette *f.*; (*end piece*) bout *m.*; (*phrase*) cliché *m.* ● *v.t.* (*p.t.* **tagged**) étiqueter; (*join*) ajouter. ● *v.i.* **~ along,** (*fam.*) suivre.

tail /teɪl/ *n.* queue *f.*; (*of shirt*) pan *m.* **~s,** (*coat*) habit *m.* **~s!,** (*tossing coin*) pile! ● *v.t.* (*follow*) filer. ● *v.i.* **~ away** *or* **off,** diminuer. **~-back** *n.* (*traffic*) bouchon *m.* **~-end** *n.* fin *f.*, bout *m.* **~-gate** *n.* hayon arrière *m.*

tailcoat /'teɪlkəʊt/ *n.* habit *m.*

tailor /'teɪlə(r)/ *n.* tailleur *m.* ● *v.t.* (*garment*) façonner; (*fig.*) adapter. **~-made** *a.* fait sur mesure. **~-made for,** (*fig.*) fait pour.

tainted /'teɪntɪd/ *a.* (*infected*) infecté; (*decayed*) gâté; (*fig.*) souillé.

take /teɪk/ *v.t./i.* (*p.t.* **took,** *p.p.* **taken**) prendre; (*carry*) (ap)porter (**to,** à); (*escort*) accompagner, amener; (*contain*) contenir; (*tolerate*) supporter; (*prize*) remporter; (*exam*) passer; (*choice*) faire; (*precedence*) avoir. **~ sth. from s.o.,** prendre qch. à qn. **~ sth. from a place,** prendre qch. d'un endroit. **~ s.o. home,** ramener qn. chez lui. **be ~n by** *or* **with,** être impressionné par. **be ~n ill,** tomber malade. **it ~s time/courage/***etc.* **to,** il faut du temps/du courage/*etc.* pour. **~ after,** ressembler à. **~ apart,** démonter. **~ away,** (*object*) emporter; (*person*) emmener; (*remove*) enlever (**from,** à). **~-away** *n.* (*meal*) plat à emporter *m.*; (*shop*) restaurant qui fait des plats à emporter *m.* **~ back,** reprendre; (*return*) rendre; (*accompany*) raccompagner; (*statement*) retirer. **~ down,** (*object*) descendre; (*notes*) prendre. **~ in,** (*object*) rentrer; (*include*) inclure; (*cheat*) tromper; (*grasp*) saisir. **~ it that,** supposer que. **~ off** *v.t.* enlever; (*mimic*) imiter; *v.i.* (*aviat.*) décoller. **~-off** *n.* imitation *f.*; (*aviat.*) décollage *m.* **~ on,** (*task, staff, passenger, etc.*) prendre; (*challenger*) relever le défi de. **~ out,** sortir; (*stain etc.*) enlever. **~ over** *v.t.* (*factory, country, etc.*) prendre la direction de; (*firm: comm.*) racheter; *v.i.* (*of dictator*) prendre le pouvoir. **~ over from,** (*relieve*) prendre la relève de; (*succeed*) prendre la succession de. **~-over** *n.* (*pol.*) prise de pouvoir *f.*; (*comm.*) rachat *m.* **~ part,** participer (**in,** à). **~ place,** avoir lieu. **~ sides,** prendre parti (**with,** pour). **~ to,** se prendre d'amitié pour; (*activity*) prendre goût à. **~ to doing,** se mettre à faire. **~ up,** (*object*) monter; (*hobby*) se mettre à; (*occupy*) prendre; (*resume*) reprendre. **~ up with,** se lier avec.

takings /ˈteɪkɪŋz/ *n. pl.* recette *f.*

talcum /ˈtælkəm/ *n.* talc *m.* **~ powder,** talc *m.*

tale /teɪl/ *n.* conte *m.*; (*report*) récit *m.*; (*lie*) histoire *f.*

talent /ˈtælənt/ *n.* talent *m.* **~ed** *a.* doué, qui a du talent.

talk /tɔːk/ *v.t./i.* parler; (*say*) dire; (*chat*) bavarder. ● *n.* conversation *f.*, entretien *m.*; (*words*) propos *m. pl.*; (*lecture*) exposé *m.* **~ into doing,** persuader de faire. **~ over,** discuter (de). **~-show** *n.* talk-show *m.* **~er** *n.* causeu|r, -se *m., f.* **~ing-to** *n.* (*fam.*) réprimande *f.*

talkative /ˈtɔːkətɪv/ *a.* bavard.

tall /tɔːl/ *a.* (**-er, -est**) (*high*) haut; (*person*) grand. **~ story,** (*fam.*) histoire invraisemblable *f.*

tallboy /ˈtɔːlbɔɪ/ *n.* commode *f.*

tally /ˈtælɪ/ *v.i.* correspondre (**with,** à), s'accorder (**with,** avec).

tambourine /tæmbəˈriːn/ *n.* tambourin *m.*

tame /teɪm/ *a.* (**-er, -est**) apprivoisé; (*dull*) insipide. ● *v.t.* apprivoiser; (*lion*) dompter. **~r** /-ə(r)/ *n.* dompteu|r, -se *m., f.*

tamper /ˈtæmpə(r)/ *v.i.* **~ with,** toucher à, tripoter; (*text*) altérer.

tampon /ˈtæmpɒn/ *n.* (*med.*) tampon hygiénique *m.*

tan /tæn/ *v.t./i.* (*p.t.* **tanned**) bronzer; (*hide*) tanner. ● *n.* bronzage *m.* ● *a.* marron clair *invar.*

tandem /ˈtændəm/ *n.* (*bicycle*) tandem *m.* **in ~,** en tandem.

tang /tæŋ/ *n.* (*taste*) saveur forte *f.*; (*smell*) odeur forte *f.*

tangent /ˈtændʒənt/ *n.* tangente *f.*

tangerine /tændʒəˈriːn/ *n.* mandarine *f.*

tangible /ˈtændʒəbl/ *a.* tangible.

tangle /ˈtæŋgl/ *v.t.* enchevêtrer. ● *n.* enchevêtrement *m.* **become ~d,** s'enchevêtrer.

tango /ˈtæŋgəʊ/ *n.* (*pl.* **-os**) tango *m.*

tank /tæŋk/ *n.* réservoir *m.*; (*vat*) cuve *f.*; (*for fish*) aquarium *m.*; (*mil.*) char *m.*, tank *m.*

tankard /ˈtæŋkəd/ *n.* chope *f.*

tanker /ˈtæŋkə(r)/ *n.* camion-citerne *m.*; (*ship*) pétrolier *m.*

tantaliz|e /ˈtæntəlaɪz/ *v.t.* tourmenter. **~ing** *a.* tentant.

tantamount /ˈtæntəmaʊnt/ *a.* **be ~ to,** équivaloir à.

tantrum /ˈtæntrəm/ *n.* crise de colère *or* de rage *f.*

tap[1] /tæp/ *n.* (*for water etc.*) robinet *m.* ● *v.t.* (*p.t.* **tapped**) (*resources*) exploiter; (*telephone*) mettre sur table d'écoute. **on ~,** (*fam.*) disponible.

tap[2] /tæp/ *v.t./i.* (*p.t.* **tapped**) frapper (doucement). ● *n.* petit coup *m.* **~-dance** *n.* claquettes *f. pl.*

tape /teɪp/ *n.* ruban *m.*; (*sticky*) ruban adhésif *m.* **(magnetic) ~,** bande (magnétique) *f.* ● *v.t.* (*tie*) attacher; (*stick*) coller; (*record*) enregistrer. **~-measure** *n.* mètre (à) ruban *m.* **~ recorder,** magnétophone *m.*

taper /'teɪpə(r)/ *n.* (*for lighting*) bougie *f.* ● *v.t./i.* (s')effiler. ~ **off,** (*diminish*) diminuer. **~ed, ~ing** *adjs.* (*fingers etc.*) effilé, fuselé; (*trousers*) étroit du bas.

tapestry /'tæpɪstrɪ/ *n.* tapisserie *f.*

tapioca /tæpɪ'əʊkə/ *n.* tapioca *m.*

tar /tɑ:(r)/ *n.* goudron *m.* ● *v.t.* (*p.t.* **tarred**) goudronner.

tardy /'tɑ:dɪ/ *a.* (**-ier, -iest**) (*slow*) lent; (*belated*) tardif.

target /'tɑ:gɪt/ *n.* cible *f.*; (*objective*) objectif *m.* ● *v.t.* prendre pour cible.

tariff /'tærɪf/ *n.* (*charges*) tarif *m.*; (*on imports*) tarif douanier *m.*

Tarmac /'tɑ:mæk/ *n.* (P.) macadam (goudronné) *m.*; (*runway*) piste *f.*

tarnish /'tɑ:nɪʃ/ *v.t./i.* (se) ternir.

tarpaulin /tɑ:'pɔ:lɪn/ *n.* bâche goudronnée *f.*

tarragon /'tærəgən/ *n.* estragon *m.*

tart[1] /tɑ:t/ *a.* (**-er, -est**) acide.

tart[2] /tɑ:t/ *n.* tarte *f.*; (*prostitute*; *sl.*) poule *f.* ● *v.t.* ~ **up,** (*pej.*, *sl.*) embellir (sans le moindre goût).

tartan /'tɑ:tn/ *n.* tartan *m.* ● *a.* écossais.

tartar /'tɑ:tə(r)/ *n.* tartre *m.* ~ **sauce,** sauce tartare *f.*

task /tɑ:sk/ *n.* tâche *f.*, travail *m.* **take to ~,** réprimander. ~ **force,** détachement spécial *m.*

tassel /'tæsl/ *n.* gland *m.*, pompon *m.*

taste /teɪst/ *n.* goût *m.* ● *v.t.* (*eat, enjoy*) goûter; (*try*) goûter à; (*perceive taste of*) sentir le goût de. ● *v.i.* ~ **of** *or* **like,** avoir un goût de. **have a ~ of,** (*experience*) goûter de. **~less** *a.* sans goût; (*fig.*) de mauvais goût.

tasteful /'teɪstfl/ *a.* de bon goût. **~ly** *adv.* avec goût.

tasty /'teɪstɪ/ *a.* (**-ier, -iest**) délicieux, savoureux.

tat /tæt/ *see* tit[2].

tatter|s /'tætəz/ *n. pl.* lambeaux *m. pl.* **~ed** /'tætəd/ *a.* en lambeaux.

tattoo[1] /tə'tu:/ *n.* (*mil.*) spectacle militaire *m.*

tattoo[2] /tə'tu:/ *v.t.* tatouer. ● *n.* tatouage *m.*

tatty /'tætɪ/ *a.* (**-ier, -iest**) (*shabby*: *fam.*) miteux, minable.

taught /tɔ:t/ *see* teach.

taunt /tɔ:nt/ *v.t.* railler. ● *n.* raillerie *f.* **~ing** *a.* railleur.

Taurus /'tɔ:rəs/ *n.* le Taureau.

taut /tɔ:t/ *a.* tendu.

tavern /'tævn/ *n.* taverne *f.*

tawdry /'tɔ:drɪ/ *a.* (**-ier, -iest**) (*showy*) tape-à-l'œil *invar.*

tax /tæks/ *n.* taxe *f.*, impôt *m.*; (*on income*) impôts *m. pl.* ● *v.t.* imposer; (*put to test*: *fig.*) mettre à l'épreuve. **~able** *a.* imposable. **~ation** /-'seɪʃn/ *n.* imposition *f.*; (*taxes*) impôts *m. pl.* **~-collector** *n.* percepteur *m.* **~-deductible** *a.* déductible d'impôts. ~ **disc,** vignette *f.* **~-free** *a.* exempt d'impôts. **~ing** *a.* (*fig.*) éprouvant. ~ **haven** paradis fiscal *m.* ~ **inspector,** inspecteur des impôts *m.* ~ **relief,** dégrèvement fiscal *m.* ~ **return,** déclaration d'impôts *f.*

taxi /'tæksɪ/ *n.* (*pl.* **-is**) taxi *m.* ● *v.i.* (*p.t.* **taxied,** *pres. p.* **taxiing**) (*aviat.*) rouler au sol. **~-cab** *n.* taxi *m.* ~ **rank,** (*Amer.*) ~ **stand,** station de taxi *f.*

taxpayer /'tækspeɪə(r)/ *n.* contribuable *m./f.*

tea /ti:/ *n.* thé *m.*; (*snack*) goûter *m.* **~-bag** *n.* sachet de thé *m.* **~-break** *n.* pause-thé *f.* **~-leaf** *n.* feuille de thé *f.* **~-set** *n.* service à thé *m.* **~-shop** *n.* salon de thé *m.* **~-towel** *n.* torchon *m.*

teach /ti:tʃ/ *v.t.* (*p.t.* **taught**) apprendre (**s.o. sth.,** qch. à qn.); (*in school*) enseigner (**s.o. sth.,** qch. à qn.). ● *v.i.* enseigner. **~er** *n.* professeur *m.*; (*primary*) institu|teur, -trice *m.*, *f.*; (*member of teaching profession*) enseignant(e) *m.* (*f.*). **~ing** *n.* enseignement *m.*; *a.* pédagogique; (*staff*) enseignant.

teacup /'ti:kʌp/ *n.* tasse à thé *f.*

teak /ti:k/ *n.* (*wood*) teck *m.*

team /ti:m/ *n.* équipe *f.*; (*of animals*) attelage *m.* ● *v.i.* ~ **up,** faire équipe (**with,** avec). **~- work** *n.* travail d'équipe *m.*

teapot /'ti:pɒt/ *n.* théière *f.*

tear[1] /teə(r)/ *v.t./i.* (*p.t.* **tore,** *p.p.* **torn**) (se) déchirer; (*snatch*) arracher (**from,** à); (*rush*) aller à toute vitesse. ● *n.* déchirure *f.*

tear[2] /tɪə(r)/ *n.* larme *f.* **in ~s,** en larmes. **~-gas** *n.* gaz lacrymogène *m.*

tearful /'tɪəfl/ *a.* (*voice*) larmoyant; (*person*) en larmes. **~ly** *adv.* en pleurant, les larmes aux yeux.

tease /ti:z/ *v.t.* taquiner. ● *n.* (*person*: *fam.*) taquin(e) *m.* (*f.*).

teaspoon /'ti:spu:n/ *n.* petite cuiller *f.* **~ful** *n.* (*pl.* **-fuls**) cuillerée à café *f.*

teat /ti:t/ *n.* (*of bottle, animal*) tétine *f.*
technical /'teknɪkl/ *a.* technique. **~ity** /-'kælətɪ/ *n.* détail technique *m.* **~ly** *adv.* techniquement.
technician /tek'nɪʃn/ *n.* technicien(ne) *m.* (*f.*).
technique /tek'ni:k/ *n.* technique *f.*
technolog|y /tek'nɒlədʒɪ/ *n.* technologie *f.* **~ical** /-ə'lɒdʒɪkl/ *a.* technologique.
teddy /'tedɪ/ *a.* **~ bear,** ours en peluche *m.*
tedious /'ti:dɪəs/ *a.* fastidieux.
tedium /'ti:dɪəm/ *n.* ennui *m.*
tee /ti:/ *n.* (*golf*) tee *m.*
teem[1] /ti:m/ *v.i.* (*swarm*) grouiller (**with,** de).
teem[2] /ti:m/ *v.i.* **~ (with rain),** pleuvoir à torrents.
teenage /'ti:neɪdʒ/ *a.* (d')adolescent. **~d** *a.* adolescent. **~r** /-ə(r)/ *n.* adolescent(e) *m.* (*f.*).
teens /ti:nz/ *n. pl.* **in one's ~,** adolescent.
teeny /'ti:nɪ/ *a.* (**-ier, -iest**) (*tiny: fam.*) minuscule.
teeter /'ti:tə(r)/ *v.i.* chanceler.
teeth /ti:θ/ *see* tooth.
teeth|e /ti:ð/ *v.i.* faire ses dents. **~ing troubles,** (*fig.*) difficultés initiales *f. pl.*
teetotaller /ti:'təʊtlə(r)/ *n.* personne qui ne boit pas d'alcool *f.*
telecommunications /telɪkəmju:nɪ'keɪʃnz/ *n. pl.* télécommunications *f. pl.*
telegram /'telɪgræm/ *n.* télégramme *m.*
telegraph /'telɪgrɑ:f/ *n.* télégraphe *m.* ● *a.* télégraphique. **~ic** /-'græfɪk/ *a.* télégraphique.
telepath|y /tɪ'lepəθɪ/ *n.* télépathie *f.* **~ic** /telɪ'pæθɪk/ *a.* télépathique.
telephone /'telɪfəʊn/ *n.* téléphone *m.* ● *v.t.* (*person*) téléphoner à; (*message*) téléphoner. ● *v.i.* téléphoner. **~ book,** annuaire *m.* **~-box** *n.*, **~ booth,** cabine téléphonique *f.* **~ call,** coup de téléphone *m.* **~ number,** numéro de téléphone *m.*
telephonist /tɪ'lefənɪst/ *n.* (*in exchange*) téléphoniste *m./f.*
telephoto /telɪ'fəʊtəʊ/ *a.* **~ lens,** téléobjectif *m.*
telescop|e /'telɪskəʊp/ *n.* télescope *m.* ● *v.t./i.* (se) télescoper. **~ic** /-'skɒpɪk/ *a.* télescopique.
teletext /'telɪtekst/ *n.* télétexte *m.*
televise /'telɪvaɪz/ *v.t.* téléviser.
television /'telɪvɪʒn/ *n.* télévision *f.* **~ set,** poste de télévision *m.*
telex /'teleks/ *n.* télex *m.* ● *v.t.* envoyer par télex.
tell /tel/ *v.t.* (*p.t.* **told**) dire (**s.o. sth.,** qch. à qn.); (*story*) raconter; (*distinguish*) distinguer. ● *v.i.* avoir un effet; (*know*) savoir. **~ of,** parler de. **~ off,** (*fam.*) gronder. **~-tale** *n.* rapporteu|r, -se *m., f.*; *a.* révélateur. **~ tales,** rapporter.
teller /'telə(r)/ *n.* (*in bank*) caiss|ier, -ière *m., f.*
telling /'telɪŋ/ *a.* révélateur.
telly /'telɪ/ *n.* (*fam.*) télé *f.*
temerity /tɪ'merətɪ/ *n.* témérité *f.*
temp /temp/ *n.* (*temporary employee: fam.*) intérimaire *m./f.* ● *v.i.* faire de l'intérim.
temper /'tempə(r)/ *n.* humeur *f.*; (*anger*) colère *f.* ● *v.t.* (*metal*) tremper; (*fig.*) tempérer. **lose one's ~,** se mettre en colère.
temperament /'temprəmənt/ *n.* tempérament *m.* **~al** /-'mentl/ *a.* capricieux; (*innate*) inné.
temperance /'tempərəns/ *n.* (*in drinking*) tempérance *f.*
temperate /'tempərət/ *a.* tempéré.
temperature /'temprətʃə(r)/ *n.* température *f.* **have a ~,** avoir (de) la fièvre *or* de la température.
tempest /'tempɪst/ *n.* tempête *f.*
tempestuous /tem'pestʃʊəs/ *a.* (*meeting etc.*) orageux.
template /'templ(e)ɪt/ *n.* patron *m.*
temple[1] /'templ/ *n.* temple *m.*
temple[2] /'templ/ *n.* (*of head*) tempe *f.*
tempo /'tempəʊ/ *n.* (*pl.* **-os**) tempo *m.*
temporal /'tempərəl/ *a.* temporel.
temporar|y /'temprərɪ/ *a.* temporaire, provisoire. **~ily** *adv.* temporairement, provisoirement.
tempt /tempt/ *v.t.* tenter. **~ s.o. to do,** donner envie à qn. de faire. **~ation** /-'teɪʃn/ *n.* tentation *f.* **~ing** *a.* tentant.
ten /ten/ *a.* & *n.* dix (*m.*).
tenable /'tenəbl/ *a.* défendable.
tenac|ious /tɪ'neɪʃəs/ *a.* tenace. **~ity** /-æsətɪ/ *n.* ténacité *f.*
tenancy /'tenənsɪ/ *n.* location *f.*
tenant /'tenənt/ *n.* locataire *m./f.*
tend[1] /tend/ *v.t.* s'occuper de.
tend[2] /tend/ *v.i.* **~ to,** (*be apt to*) avoir tendance à.
tendency /'tendənsɪ/ *n.* tendance *f.*

tender[1] /'tendə(r)/ *a.* tendre; (*sore, painful*) sensible. **~ly** *adv.* tendrement. **~ness** *n.* tendresse *f.*

tender[2] /'tendə(r)/ *v.t.* offrir, donner. ● *v.i.* faire une soumission. ● *n.* (*comm.*) soumission *f.* **be legal ~,** (*money*) avoir cours. **put sth. out to ~,** faire un appel d'offres pour qch.

tendon /'tendən/ *n.* tendon *m.*

tenement /'tenəmənt/ *n.* maison de rapport *f.*, H.L.M. *m./f.*; (*slum: Amer.*) taudis *m.*

tenet /'tenɪt/ *n.* principe *m.*

tenner /'tenə(r)/ *n.* (*fam.*) billet de dix livres *m.*

tennis /'tenɪs/ *n.* tennis *m.* ● *a.* de tennis **~ shoes,** tennis *m. pl.*

tenor /'tenə(r)/ *n.* (*meaning*) sens général *m.*; (*mus.*) ténor *m.*

tense[1] /tens/ *n.* (*gram.*) temps *m.*

tense[2] /tens/ *a.* (**-er, -est**) tendu. ● *v.t.* (*muscles*) tendre, raidir. ● *v.i.* (*of face*) se crisper. **~ness** *n.* tension *f.*

tension /'tenʃn/ *n.* tension *f.*

tent /tent/ *n.* tente *f.*

tentacle /'tentəkl/ *n.* tentacule *m.*

tentative /'tentətɪv/ *a.* provisoire; (*hesitant*) timide. **~ly** *adv.* provisoirement; timidement.

tenterhooks /'tentəhʊks/ *n. pl.* **on ~,** sur des charbons ardents.

tenth /tenθ/ *a. & n.* dixième (*m./f.*).

tenuous /'tenjʊəs/ *a.* ténu.

tenure /'tenjʊə(r)/ *n.* (*in job, office*) (période de) jouissance *f.* **have ~,** être titulaire.

tepid /'tepɪd/ *a.* tiède.

term /tɜ:m/ *n.* (*word, limit*) terme *m.*; (*of imprisonment*) temps *m.*; (*in school etc.*) trimestre *m.*; (*Amer.*) semestre *m.* **~s,** conditions *f. pl.* ● *v.t.* appeler, **on good/bad ~s,** en bons/mauvais termes. **in the short/long ~,** à court/long terme **come to ~s,** arriver à un accord. **come to ~s with sth.,** accepter qch. **~ of office,** (*pol.*) mandat *m.*

terminal /'tɜ:mɪnl/ *a.* terminal, final; (*med.*) en phase terminale. ● *n.* (*oil, computer*) terminal *m.*; (*rail.*) terminus *m.*; (*electr.*) borne *f.* **(air) ~,** aérogare *f.*

terminat|e /'tɜ:mɪneɪt/ *v.t.* mettre fin à. ● *v.i.* prendre fin. **~ion** /-'neɪʃn/ *n.* fin *f.*

terminology /tɜ:mɪ'nɒlədʒɪ/ *n.* terminologie *f.*

terminus /'tɜ:mɪnəs/ *n.* (*pl.* **-ni** /-naɪ/) (*station*) terminus *m.*

terrace /'terəs/ *n.* terrasse *f.*; (*houses*) rangée de maisons contiguës *f.* **the ~s,** (*sport*) les gradins *m. pl.*

terracotta /terə'kɒtə/ *n.* terre cuite *f.*

terrain /te'reɪn/ *n.* terrain *m.*

terribl|e /'terəbl/ *a.* affreux, atroce. **~y** *adv.* affreusement; (*very*) terriblement.

terrier /'terɪə(r)/ *n.* (*dog*) terrier *m.*

terrific /tə'rɪfɪk/ *a.* (*fam.*) terrible. **~ally** /-klɪ/ *adv.* (*very: fam.*) terriblement; (*very well: fam.*) terriblement bien.

terrif|y /'terɪfaɪ/ *v.t.* terrifier. **be ~ied of,** avoir très peur de.

territorial /terɪ'tɔ:rɪəl/ *a.* territorial.

territory /'terɪtərɪ/ *n.* territoire *m.*

terror /'terə(r)/ *n.* terreur *f.*

terroris|t /'terərɪst/ *n.* terroriste *m./f.* **~m** /-zəm/ *n.* terrorisme *m.*

terrorize /'terəraɪz/ *v.t.* terroriser.

terse /tɜ:s/ *a.* concis, laconique.

test /test/ *n.* examen *m.*, analyse *f.*; (*of goods*) contrôle *m.*; (*of machine etc.*) essai *m.*; (*in school*) interrogation *f.*; (*of strength etc.: fig.*) épreuve *f.* ● *v.t.* examiner, analyser; (*check*) contrôler; (*try*) essayer; (*pupil*) donner une interrogation à; (*fig.*) éprouver. **driving ~,** (épreuve *f.* du) permis de conduire *m.* **~ match,** match international *m.* **~ pilot** pilote d'essai *m.* **~-tube** *n.* éprouvette *f.*

testament /'testəmənt/ *n.* testament *m.* **Old/New T~,** Ancien/Nouveau Testament *m.*

testicle /'testɪkl/ *n.* testicule *m.*

testify /'testɪfaɪ/ *v.t./i.* témoigner (**to,** de). **~ that,** témoigner que.

testimony /'testɪmənɪ/ *n.* témoignage *m.*

testy /'testɪ/ *a.* grincheux.

tetanus /'tetənəs/ *n.* tétanos *m.*

tetchy /'tetʃɪ/ *a.* grincheux.

tether /'teðə(r)/ *v.t.* attacher. ● *n.* **at the end of one's ~,** à bout.

text /tekst/ *n.* texte *m.*

textbook /'tekstbʊk/ *n.* manuel *m.*

textile /'tekstaɪl/ *n. & a.* textile (*m.*).

texture /'tekstʃə(r)/ *n.* (*of paper etc.*) grain *m.*; (*of fabric*) texture *f.*

Thai /taɪ/ *a. & n.* thaïlandais(e) (*m.* (*f.*)). **~land** *n.* Thaïlande *f.*

Thames /temz/ *n.* Tamise *f.*

than /ðæn, *unstressed* ðən/ *conj.* que, qu'*; (*with numbers*) de. **more/less ~ ten,** plus/moins de dix.

thank /θæŋk/ *v.t.* remercier. **~s** *n. pl.* remerciements *m. pl.* **~ you!,** merci! **~s!,** (*fam.*) merci! **~s to,** grâce à. **T~sgiving (Day),** (*Amer.*) jour d'action de grâces *m.* (*fête nationale*).

thankful /'θæŋkfl/ *a.* reconnaissant (**for,** de). **~ly** *adv.* (*happily*) heureusement.

thankless /'θæŋklɪs/ *a.* ingrat.

that /ðæt, *unstressed* ðət/ *a. pl.* **those**) ce *or* cet*, cette. **those,** ces. ● *pron.* ce *or* c'*, cela, ça. **~ (one),** celui-là, celle-là. **those (ones),** ceux-là, celles-là. ● *adv.* si, aussi. ● *rel. pron.* (*subject*) qui; (*object*) que, qu'*. ● *conj.* que, qu'*. **~ boy,** ce garçon (*with emphasis*) ce garçon-là. **~ is,** c'est. **~ is (to say),** c'est-à-dire. **after ~,** après ça *or* cela. **the day ~,** le jour où. **the man ~ married her,** l'homme qui l'a épousée. **the man ~ she married,** l'homme qu'elle a épousé. **the car ~ I came in,** la voiture dans laquelle je suis venu. **~ big,** grand comme ça. **~ many, ~ much,** tant que ça.

thatch /θætʃ/ *n.* chaume *m.* **~ed** *a.* en chaume. **~ed cottage,** chaumière *f.*

thaw /θɔ:/ *v.t./i.* (faire) dégeler; (*snow*) (faire) fondre. ● *n.* dégel *m.*

the /*before vowel* ðɪ, *before consonant* ðə, *stressed* ði:/ *a.* le *or* l'*, la *or* l'*, *pl.* les. **of ~, from ~,** du, de l'*, de la, *pl.* des. **to ~, at ~,** au, à l'*, à la, *pl.* aux. **~ third of June,** le trois juin.

theatre /'θɪətə(r)/ *n.* théâtre *m.*

theatrical /θɪ'ætrɪkl/ *a.* théâtral.

theft /θeft/ *n.* vol *m.*

their /ðeə(r)/ *a.* leur, *pl.* leurs.

theirs /ðeəz/ *poss. pron.* le *or* la leur, les leurs.

them /ðem, *unstressed* ðəm/ *pron.* les; (*after prep.*) eux, elles. **(to) ~,** leur. **I know ~,** je les connais.

theme /θi:m/ *n.* thème *m.* **~ song,** (*in film etc.*) chanson principale *f.*

themselves /ðəm'selvz/ *pron.* eux-mêmes, elles-mêmes; (*reflexive*) se; (*after prep.*) eux, elles.

then /ðen/ *adv.* alors; (*next*) ensuite, puis; (*therefore*) alors, donc. ● *a.* d'alors. **from ~ on,** dès lors.

theolog|y /θɪ'ɒlədʒɪ/ *n.* théologie *f.* **~ian** /θɪə'ləʊdʒən/ *n.* théologien(ne) *m.* (*f.*).

theorem /'θɪərəm/ *n.* théorème *m.*

theor|y /'θɪərɪ/ *n.* théorie *f.* **~etical** /-'retɪkl/ *a.* théorique.

therapeutic /θerə'pju:tɪk/ *a.* thérapeutique.

therapy /'θerəpɪ/ *n.* thérapie *f.*

there /ðeə(r)/ *adv.* là; (*with verb*) y; (*over there*) là-bas. ● *int.* allez. **he goes ~,** il y va. **on ~,** là-dessus. **~ is, ~ are,** il y a; (*pointing*) voilà. **~, ~!,** allons, allons! **~abouts** *adv.* par là. **~after** *adv.* par la suite. **~by** *adv.* de cette manière.

therefore /'ðeəfɔ:(r)/ *adv.* donc.

thermal /'θɜ:ml/ *a.* thermique.

thermometer /θə'mɒmɪtə(r)/ *n.* thermomètre *m.*

thermonuclear /θɜ:məʊ'nju:klɪə(r)/ *a.* thermonucléaire.

Thermos /'θɜ:məs/ *n.* (P.) thermos *m./f. invar.* (P.).

thermostat /'θɜ:məstæt/ *n.* thermostat *m.*

thesaurus /θɪ'sɔ:rəs/ *n.* (*pl.* **-ri** /-raɪ/) dictionnaire de synonymes *m.*

these /ði:z/ *see* this.

thesis /'θi:sɪs/ *n.* (*pl.* **theses** /-si:z/) thèse *f.*

they /ðeɪ/ *pron.* ils, elles; (*emphatic*) eux, elles; (*people in general*) on.

thick /θɪk/ *a.* (**-er, -est**) épais; (*stupid*) bête; (*friends*: *fam.*) très lié. ● *adv.* = **thickly.** ● *n.* **in the ~ of,** au plus gros de. **~ly** *adv.* (*grow*) dru; (*spread*) en couche épaisse. **~ness** *n.* épaisseur *f.* **~-skinned** *a.* peu sensible.

thicken /'θɪkən/ *v.t./i.* (s')épaissir.

thickset /θɪk'set/ *a.* trapu.

thief /θi:f/ *n.* (*pl.* **thieves**) voleu|**r, -se** *m., f.*

thigh /θaɪ/ *n.* cuisse *f.*

thimble /'θɪmbl/ *n.* dé (à coudre) *m.*

thin /θɪn/ *a.* (**thinner, thinnest**) mince; (*person*) maigre, mince; (*sparse*) clairsemé; (*fine*) fin. ● *adv.* = **thinly.** ● *v.t./i.* (*p.t.* **thinned**) (*liquid*) (s')éclaircir. **~ out,** (*in quantity*) (s')éclaircir. **~ly** *adv.* (*slightly*) légèrement. **~ner** *n.* diluant *m.* **~ness** *n.* minceur *f.*; maigreur *f.*

thing /θɪŋ/ *n.* chose *f.* **~s,** (*belongings*) affaires *f. pl.* **the best ~ is to,** le mieux est de. **the (right) ~,** ce qu'il faut (**for s.o.,** à qn.).

think /θɪŋk/ *v.t./i.* (*p.t.* **thought**) penser (**about, of,** à); (*carefully*) réfléchir (**about, of,** à); (*believe*) croire. **I ~ so,** je crois que oui. **~ better of it,** se raviser. **~ nothing of,** trouver naturel de. **~ of,** (*hold opinion of*) penser de. **I'm ~ing of going,** je pense que j'irai peut-être. **~ over,** bien réfléchir à. **~-tank** *n.* comité d'experts *m.* **~ up,** inventer. **~er** *n.* penseu|r, -se *m., f.*

third /θɜ:d/ *a.* troisième. ● *n.* troisième *m./f.*; (*fraction*) tiers *m.* **~ly** *adv.* troisièmement. **~-rate** *a.* très inférieur. **T~ World,** Tiers-Monde *m.*

thirst /θɜ:st/ *n.* soif *f.* **~y** *a.* **be ~y,** avoir soif. **make ~y,** donner soif à.

thirteen /θɜ:'ti:n/ *a.* & *n.* treize (*m.*). **~th** *a.* & *n.* treizième (*m./f.*).

thirt|y /'θɜ:tɪ/ *a.* & *n.* trente (*m.*). **~ieth** *a.* & *n.* trentième (*m./f.*).

this /ðɪs/ *a.* (*pl.* **these**) ce *or* cet*, cette. **these,** ces. ● *pron.* ce *or* c'*, ceci. **~ (one),** celui-ci, celle-ci. **these (ones),** ceux-ci, celles-ci. **~ boy,** ce garçon; (*with emphasis*) ce garçon-ci. **~ is a mistake,** c'est une erreur. **~ is the book,** voici le livre. **~ is my son,** je vous présente mon fils. **~ is Anne speaking,** c'est Anne à l'appareil. **after ~,** après ceci.

thistle /'θɪsl/ *n.* chardon *m.*

thorn /θɔ:n/ *n.* épine *f.* **~y** *a.* épineux.

thorough /'θʌrə/ *a.* consciencieux; (*deep*) profond; (*cleaning, washing*) à fond. **~ly** *adv.* (*clean, study, etc.*) à fond; (*very*) tout à fait.

thoroughbred /'θʌrəbred/ *n.* (*horse etc.*) pur-sang *m. invar.*

thoroughfare /'θʌrəfeə(r)/ *n.* grande artère *f.*

those /ðəʊz/ *see* that.

though /ðəʊ/ *conj.* bien que. ● *adv.* (*fam.*) cependant.

thought /θɔ:t/ *see* think. ● *n.* pensée *f.*; (*idea*) idée *f.*

thoughtful /'θɔ:tfl/ *a.* pensif; (*considerate*) attentionné. **~ly** *adv.* pensivement; avec considération.

thoughtless /'θɔ:tlɪs/ *a.* étourdi. **~ly** *adv.* étourdiment.

thousand /'θaʊznd/ *a.* & *n.* mille (*m. invar.*). **~s of,** des milliers de.

thrash /θræʃ/ *v.t.* rosser; (*defeat*) écraser. **~ about,** se débattre. **~ out,** discuter à fond.

thread /θred/ *n.* (*yarn & fig.*) fil *m.*; (*of screw*) pas *m.* ● *v.t.* enfiler. **~ one's way,** se faufiler.

threadbare /'θredbeə(r)/ *a.* râpé.

threat /θret/ *n.* menace *f.*

threaten /'θretn/ *v.t./i.* menacer (**with,** de). **~ingly** *adv.* d'un air menaçant.

three /θri:/ *a.* & *n.* trois (*m.*). **~-dimensional** *a.* en trois dimensions.

thresh /θreʃ/ *v.t.* (*corn etc.*) battre.

threshold /'θreʃəʊld/ *n.* seuil *m.*

threw /θru:/ *see* throw.

thrift /θrɪft/ *n.* économie *f.* **~y** *a.* économe.

thrill /θrɪl/ *n.* émotion *f.*, frisson *m.* ● *v.t.* transporter (de joie). ● *v.i.* frissonner (de joie). **be ~ed,** être ravi. **~ing** *a.* excitant.

thriller /'θrɪlə(r)/ *n.* livre *or* film à suspense *m.*

thriv|e /θraɪv/ *v.i.* (*p.t.* **thrived** *or* **throve,** *p.p.* **thrived** *or* **thriven**) prospérer. **he ~es on it,** cela lui réussit. **~ing** *a.* prospère.

throat /θrəʊt/ *n.* gorge *f.* **have a sore ~,** avoir mal à la gorge.

throb /θrɒb/ *v.i.* (*p.t.* **throbbed**) (*wound*) causer des élancements; (*heart*) palpiter; (*fig.*) vibrer. ● *n.* (*pain*) élancement *m.*; palpitation *f.* **~bing** *a.* (*pain*) lancinant.

throes /θrəʊz/ *n. pl.* **in the ~ of,** au milieu de, aux prises avec.

thrombosis /θrɒm'bəʊsɪs/ *n.* thrombose *f.*

throne /θrəʊn/ *n.* trône *m.*

throng /θrɒŋ/ *n.* foule *f.* ● *v.t.* (*streets etc.*) se presser dans. ● *v.i.* (*arrive*) affluer.

throttle /'θrɒtl/ *n.* (*auto.*) accélérateur *m.* ● *v.t.* étrangler.

through /θru:/ *prep.* à travers; (*during*) pendant; (*by means or way of, out of*) par; (*by reason of*) grâce à, à cause de. ● *adv.* à travers; (*entirely*) jusqu'au bout. ● *a.* (*train etc.*) direct. **be ~,** (*finished*) avoir fini. **come** *or* **go ~,** (*cross, pierce*) traverser. **I'm putting you ~,** je vous passe votre correspondant.

throughout /θru:'aʊt/ *prep.* **~ the country/***etc.*, dans tout le pays/*etc.* **~ the day/***etc.*, pendant toute la journée/*etc.* ● *adv.* (*place*) partout; (*time*) tout le temps.

throw /θrəʊ/ *v.t.* (*p.t.* **threw,** *p.p.* **thrown**) jeter, lancer; (*baffle: fam.*) déconcerter. ● *n.* jet *m.*; (*of dice*) coup *m.* **~ a party,** (*fam.*) faire une fête. **~ away,** jeter. **~-away** *a.* à jeter. **~ off,** (*get rid of*) se débarrasser de. **~ out,** jeter; (*person*) expulser; (*reject*) rejeter. **~ over,** (*desert*) plaquer. ~ **up,** (*one's arms*) lever; (*resign from*) abandonner; (*vomit: fam.*) vomir.

thru /θru:/ *prep., adv. & a.* (*Amer.*) = **through.**

thrush /θrʌʃ/ *n.* (*bird*) grive *f.*

thrust /θrʌst/ *v.t.* (*p.t.* **thrust**) pousser. ● *n.* poussée *f.* ~ **into,** (*put*) enforcer dans, mettre dans. ~ **upon,** (*force on*) imposer à.

thud /θʌd/ *n.* bruit sourd *m.*

thug /θʌg/ *n.* voyou *m.*, bandit *m.*

thumb /θʌm/ *n.* pouce *m.* ● *v.t.* (*book*) feuilleter. ~ **a lift,** faire de l'auto-stop. **~-index,** répertoire à onglets *m.*

thumbtack /'θʌmtæk/ *n.* (*Amer.*) punaise *f.*

thump /θʌmp/ *v.t./i.* cogner (sur); (*of heart*) battre fort. ● *n.* grand coup *m.* **~ing** *a.* (*fam.*) énorme.

thunder /'θʌndə(r)/ *n.* tonnerre *m.* ● *v.i.* (*weather, person, etc.*) tonner. ~ **past,** passer dans un bruit de tonnerre. **~y** *a.* orageux.

thunderbolt /'θʌndəbəʊlt/ *n.* coup de foudre *m.*; (*event: fig.*) coup de tonnerre *m.*

thunderstorm /'θʌndəstɔ:m/ *n.* orage *m.*

Thursday /'θɜ:zdɪ/ *n.* jeudi *m.*

thus /ðʌs/ *adv.* ainsi.

thwart /θwɔ:t/ *v.t.* contrecarrer.

thyme /taɪm/ *n.* thym *m.*

thyroid /'θaɪrɔɪd/ *n.* thyroïde *f.*

tiara /tɪ'ɑ:rə/ *n.* diadème *m.*

tic /tɪk/ *n.* tic (nerveux) *m.*

tick[1] /tɪk/ *n.* (*sound*) tic-tac *m.*; (*mark*) coche *f.*; (*moment: fam.*) instant *m.* ● *v.i.* faire tic-tac. ● *v.t.* ~ **(off),** cocher. ~ **off,** (*fam.*) réprimander. ~ **over,** (*engine, factory*) tourner au ralenti.

tick[2] /tɪk/ *n.* (*insect*) tique *f.*

ticket /'tɪkɪt/ *n.* billet *m.*; (*for bus, cloakroom, etc.*) ticket *m.*; (*label*) étiquette *f.* **~-collector** *n.* contrôleu|r, -se *m., f.* **~-office** *n.* guichet *m.*

tickle /'tɪkl/ *v.t.* chatouiller; (*amuse: fig.*) amuser. ● *n.* chatouillement *m.*

ticklish /'tɪklɪʃ/ *a.* chatouilleux.

tidal /'taɪdl/ *a.* qui a des marées. ~ **wave,** raz-de-marée *m. invar.*

tiddly-winks /'tɪdlɪwɪŋks/ *n.* (*game*) jeu de puce *m.*

tide /taɪd/ *n.* marée *f.*; (*of events*) cours *m.* ● *v.t.* ~ **over,** dépanner.

tidings /'taɪdɪŋz/ *n. pl.* nouvelles *f. pl.*

tid|y /'taɪdɪ/ *a.* (**-ier, -iest**) (*room*) bien rangé; (*appearance, work*) soigné; (*methodical*) ordonné; (*amount: fam.*) joli. ● *v.t./i.* ranger. **~y o.s.,** s'arranger. **~ily** *adv.* avec soin. **~iness** *n.* ordre *m.*

tie /taɪ/ *v.t.* (*pres. p.* **tying**) attacher, nouer; (*a knot*) faire; (*link*) lier. ● *v.i.* (*darts etc.*) finir à égalité de points; (*football*) faire match nul; (*in race*) être ex aequo. ● *n.* attache *f.*; (*necktie*) cravate *f.*; (*link*) lien *m.*; égalité (de points) *f.*, match nul *m.* ~ **down,** attacher; (*job*) bloquer. ~ **s.o. down to,** (*date*) forcer qn. à respecter. ~ **in with,** être lié à. ~ **up,** attacher; (*money*) immobiliser; (*occupy*) occuper. **~-up** *n.* (*link*) lien *m.*; (*auto., Amer.*) bouchon *m.*

tier /tɪə(r)/ *n.* étage *m.*, niveau *m.*; (*in stadium etc.*) gradin *m.*

tiff /tɪf/ *n.* petite querelle *f.*

tiger /'taɪgə(r)/ *n.* tigre *m.*

tight /taɪt/ *a.* (**-er, -est**) (*clothes*) étroit, juste; (*rope*) tendu; (*lid*) solidement fixé; (*control*) strict; (*knot, collar, schedule*) serré; (*drunk: fam.*) ivre. ● *adv.* (*hold, sleep, etc.*) bien; (*squeeze*) fort. ~ **corner,** situation difficile *f.* **~-fisted** *a.* avare. **~ly** *adv.* bien; (*squeeze*) fort.

tighten /'taɪtn/ *v.t./i.* (se) tendre; (*bolt etc.*) (se) resserrer; (*control etc.*) renforcer. ~ **up on,** se montrer plus strict à l'égard de.

tightrope /'taɪtrəʊp/ *n.* corde raide *f.* ~ **walker,** funambule *m./f.*

tights /taɪts/ *n. pl.* collant *m.*

tile /taɪl/ *n.* (*on wall, floor*) carreau *m.*; (*on roof*) tuile *f.* ● *v.t.* carreler; couvrir de tuiles.

till[1] /tɪl/ *v.t.* (*land*) cultiver.

till[2] /tɪl/ *prep. & conj.* = **until.**

till[3] /tɪl/ *n.* caisse (enregistreuse) *f.*

tilt /tɪlt/ *v.i./i.* pencher. ● *n.* (*slope*) inclinaison *f.* **(at) full ~,** à toute vitesse.

timber /'tɪmbə(r)/ *n.* bois (de construction) *m.*; (*trees*) arbres *m. pl.*

time /taɪm/ *n.* temps *m.*; (*moment*) moment *m.*; (*epoch*) époque *f.*; (*by clock*) heure *f.*; (*occasion*) fois *f.*; (*rhythm*) mesure *f.* **~s,** (*multiplying*) fois *f. pl.* ● *v.t.* choisir le moment de; (*measure*) minuter; (*sport*) chronométrer. **any ~,** n'importe quand. **behind the ~s,** en retard sur son temps. **for the ~ being,** pour le moment. **from ~ to time,** de temps en temps. **have a good ~,** s'amuser. **in no ~,** en un rien de temps. **in ~,** à temps; (*eventually*) avec le temps. **a long ~,** longtemps. **on ~,** à l'heure. **what's the ~?,** quelle heure est-il? **~ bomb,** bombe à retardement *f.* **~-honoured** *a.* consacré (par l'usage). **~-lag** *n.* décalage *m.* **~-limit** *n.* délai *m.* **~-scale** *n.* délais fixés *m. pl.* **~ off,** du temps libre. **~ zone,** fuseau horaire *m.*

timeless /'taɪmlɪs/ *a.* éternel.

timely /'taɪmlɪ/ *a.* à propos.

timer /'taɪmə(r)/ *n.* (*for cooker etc.*) minuteur *m.*; (*on video*) programmateur; (*culin.*) compte-minutes *m. invar.*; (*with sand*) sablier *m.*

timetable /'taɪmteɪbl/ *n.* horaire *m.*

timid /'tɪmɪd/ *a.* timide; (*fearful*) peureux. **~ly** *adv.* timidement.

timing /'taɪmɪŋ/ *n.* (*measuring*) minutage *m.*; (*moment*) moment *m.*; (*of artist*) rythme *m.*

tin /tɪn/ *n.* étain *m.*; (*container*) boîte *f.* **~(plate),** fer-blanc *m.* ● *v.t.* (*p.t.* **tinned**) mettre en boîte. **~ foil,** papier d'aluminium *m.* **~ny** *a.* métallique. **~-opener** *n.* ouvre-boîte(s) *m.*

tinge /tɪndʒ/ *v.t.* teinter (**with,** de). ● *n.* teinte *f.*

tingle /'tɪŋgl/ *v.i.* (*prickle*) picoter. ● *n.* picotement *m.*

tinker /'tɪŋkə(r)/ *n.* rétameur *m.* ● *v.i.* **~ (with),** bricoler.

tinkle /'tɪŋkl/ *n.* tintement *m.*; (*fam.*) coup de téléphone *m.*

tinsel /'tɪnsl/ *n.* cheveux d'ange *m. pl.*, guirlandes de Noël *f. pl.*

tint /tɪnt/ *n.* teinte *f.*; (*for hair*) shampooing colorant *m.* ● *v.t.* (*glass, paper*) teinter.

tiny /'taɪnɪ/ *a.* (**-ier, -iest**) minuscule, tout petit.

tip[1] /tɪp/ *n.* bout *m.*; (*cover*) embout *m.* **~ped cigarette,** cigarette (à bout) filtre *f.*

tip[2] /tɪp/ *v.t./i.* (*p.t.* **tipped**) (*tilt*) pencher; (*overturn*) (faire) basculer; (*pour*) verser; (*empty*) déverser; (*give money*) donner un pourboire à. ● *n.* (*money*) pourboire *m.*; (*advice*) tuyau *m.*; (*for rubbish*) décharge *f.* **~ off,** prévenir. **~-off** *n.* tuyau *m.* (*pour prévenir*).

tipsy /'tɪpsɪ/ *a.* un peu ivre, gris.

tiptoe /'tɪptəʊ/ *n.* **on ~,** sur la pointe des pieds.

tiptop /'tɪptɒp/ *a.* (*fam.*) excellent.

tir|e[1] /'taɪə(r)/ *v.t./i.* (se) fatiguer. **~e of,** se lasser de. **~eless** *a.* infatigable. **~ing** *a.* fatigant.

tire[2] /'taɪə(r)/ *n.* (*Amer.*) pneu *m.*

tired /'taɪəd/ *a.* fatigué. **be ~ of,** en avoir assez de.

tiresome /'taɪəsəm/ *a.* ennuyeux.

tissue /'tɪʃu:/ *n.* tissu *m.*; (*handkerchief*) mouchoir en papier *m.* **~-paper** *n.* papier de soie *m.*

tit[1] /tɪt/ *n.* (*bird*) mésange *f.*

tit[2] /tɪt/ *n.* **give ~ for tat,** rendre coup pour coup.

titbit /'tɪtbɪt/ *n.* friandise *f.*

titillate /'tɪtɪleɪt/ *v.t.* exciter.

title /'taɪtl/ *n.* titre *m.* **~-deed** *n.* titre de propriété *m.* **~-role** *n.* rôle principal *m.*

titter /'tɪtə(r)/ *v.i.* rigoler.

titular /'tɪtjʊlə(r)/ *a.* (*ruler etc.*) nominal.

to /tu:, *unstressed* tə/ *prep.* à; (*towards*) vers; (*of attitude*) envers. ● *adv.* **push** *or* **pull to,** (*close*) fermer. **to France**/*etc.*, en France/*etc.* **to town,** en ville. **to Canada**/*etc.*, au Canada/*etc.* **to the baker's**/*etc.*, chez le boulanger/*etc.* **the road/door/** *etc.* **to,** la route/porte/*etc.* de. **to me/her**/*etc.*, me/lui/*etc.* **to do/sit**/*etc.*, faire/s'asseoir/*etc.* **I wrote to tell her,** j'ai écrit pour lui dire. **I tried to help you,** j'ai essayé de t'aider. **ten to six,** (*by clock*) six heures moins dix. **go to and fro,** aller et venir. **husband**/*etc.*-**to-be** *n.* futur mari/ *etc. m.*

toad /təʊd/ *n.* crapaud *m.*

toadstool /'təʊdstu:l/ *n.* champignon (vénéneux) *m.*

toast /təʊst/ *n.* pain grillé *m.*, toast *m.*; (*drink*) toast *m.* ● *v.t.* (*bread*) faire griller; (*drink to*) porter un toast à; (*event*) arroser. **~er** *n.* grille-pain *m. invar.*

tobacco /tə'bækəʊ/ *n.* tabac *m.*

tobacconist /tə'bækənɪst/ *n.* marchand(e) de tabac *m.* (*f.*). **~'s shop,** tabac *m.*

toboggan /tə'bɒgən/ *n.* toboggan *m.*, luge *f.*

today /tə'deɪ/ *n.* & *adv.* aujourd'hui (*m.*).

toddler /'tɒdlə(r)/ *n.* tout(e) petit(e) enfant *m.*(*f*).

toddy /'tɒdɪ/ *n.* (*drink*) grog *m.*

toe /təʊ/ *n.* orteil *m.*; (*of shoe*) bout *m.* ● *v.t.* **~ the line,** se conformer. **on one's ~s,** vigilant. **~-hold** *n.* prise (précaire) *f.*

toffee /'tɒfɪ/ *n.* caramel *m.* **~-apple** *n.* pomme caramélisée *f.*

together /tə'geðə(r)/ *adv.* ensemble; (*at same time*) en même temps. **~ with,** avec. **~ness** *n.* camaraderie *f.*

toil /tɔɪl/ *v.i.* peiner. ● *n.* labeur *m.*

toilet /'tɔɪlɪt/ *n.* toilettes *f. pl.*; (*grooming*) toilette *f.* **~-paper** *n.* papier hygiénique *m.* **~-roll** *n.* rouleau de papier hygiénique *m.* **~ water,** eau de toilette *f.*

toiletries /'tɔɪlɪtrɪz/ *n. pl.* articles de toilette *m. pl.*

token /'təʊkən/ *n.* témoignage *m.*, marque *f.*; (*voucher*) bon *m.*; (*coin*) jeton *m.* ● *a.* symbolique.

told /təʊld/ *see* tell. ● *a.* **all ~,** (*all in all*) en tout.

tolerabl|e /'tɒlərəbl/ *a.* tolérable; (*not bad*) passable. **~y** *adv.* (*work, play, etc.*) passablement.

toleran|t /'tɒlərənt/ *a.* tolérant (**of,** à l'égard de). **~ce** *n.* tolérance *f.* **~tly** *adv.* avec tolérance.

tolerate /'tɒləreɪt/ *v.t.* tolérer.

toll[1] /təʊl/ *n.* péage *m.* **death ~,** nombre de morts *m.* **take its ~,** (*of age*) faire sentir son poids.

toll[2] /təʊl/ *v.i.* (*of bell*) sonner.

tom /tɒm/, **~-cat** *ns.* matou *m.*

tomato /tə'mɑːtəʊ, *Amer.* tə'meɪtəʊ/ *n.* (*pl.* **-oes**) tomate *f.*

tomb /tuːm/ *n.* tombeau *m.*

tombola /tɒm'bəʊlə/ *n.* tombola *f.*

tomboy /'tɒmbɔɪ/ *n.* garçon manqué *m.*

tombstone /'tuːmstəʊn/ *n.* pierre tombale *f.*

tomfoolery /tɒm'fuːlərɪ/ *n.* âneries *f. pl.*, bêtises *f. pl.*

tomorrow /tə'mɒrəʊ/ *n.* & *adv.* demain (*m.*). **~ morning/night,** demain matin/soir. **the day after ~,** après-demain.

ton /tʌn/ *n.* tonne *f.* (= *1016 kg.*). **(metric) ~,** tonne *f.* (= *1000 kg.*). **~s of,** (*fam.*) des masses de.

tone /təʊn/ *n.* ton *m.*; (*of radio, telephone, etc.*) tonalité *f.* ● *v.t.* **~ down,** atténuer. ● *v.i.* **~ in,** s'harmoniser (**with,** avec). **~-deaf** *a.* qui n'a pas d'oreille. **~ up,** (*muscles*) tonifier.

tongs /tɒŋz/ *n. pl.* pinces *f. pl.*; (*for sugar*) pince *f.*; (*for hair*) fer *m.*

tongue /tʌŋ/ *n.* langue *f.* **~-tied** *a.* muet. **~-twister** *n.* phrase difficile à prononcer *f.* **with one's ~ in one's cheek,** ironiquement.

tonic /'tɒnɪk/ *n.* (*med.*) tonique *m.* ● *a.* (*effect, accent*) tonique. **~ (water),** tonic *m.*

tonight /tə'naɪt/ *n.* & *adv.* cette nuit (*f.*); (*evening*) ce soir (*m.*).

tonne /tʌn/ *n.* (*metric*) tonne *f.*

tonsil /'tɒnsl/ *n.* amygdale *f.*

tonsillitis /tɒnsɪ'laɪtɪs/ *n.* amygdalite *f.*

too /tuː/ *adv.* trop; (*also*) aussi. **~ many** *a.* trop de; *n.* trop. **~ much** *a.* trop de; *adv.* & *n.* trop.

took /tʊk/ *see* take.

tool /tuːl/ *n.* outil *m.* **~-bag** *n.* trousse à outils *f.*

toot /tuːt/ *n.* coup de klaxon *m.* ● *v.t./i.* **~ (the horn),** klaxonner.

tooth /tuːθ/ *n.* (*pl.* **teeth**) dent *f.* **~less** *a.* édenté.

toothache /'tuːθeɪk/ *n.* mal de dents *m.*

toothbrush /'tuːθbrʌʃ/ *n.* brosse à dents *f.*

toothcomb /'tuːθkəʊm/ *n.* peigne fin *m.*

toothpaste /'tuːθpeɪst/ *n.* dentifrice *m.*, pâte dentifrice *f.*

toothpick /'tuːθpɪk/ *n.* cure-dent *m.*

top[1] /tɒp/ *n.* (*highest point*) sommet *m.*; (*upper part*) haut *m.*; (*upper surface*) dessus *m.*; (*lid*) couvercle *m.*; (*of bottle, tube*) bouchon *m.*; (*of beer bottle*) capsule *f.*; (*of list*) tête *f.* ● *a.* (*shelf etc.*) du haut; (*floor*) dernier; (*in rank*) premier; (*best*) meilleur; (*distinguished*) éminent; (*maximum*) maximum. ● *v.t.* (*p.t.* **topped**) (*exceed*) dépasser; (*list*) venir en tête de. **from ~ to bottom,** de fond en comble. **on ~ of,** sur; (*fig.*) en plus de. **~ hat,** haut-de-forme *m.* **~-heavy** *a.* trop lourd du haut. **~-level** *a.* du plus haut niveau. **~-notch** *a.* excellent. **~-quality** *a.* de la plus haute qualité. **~ secret,** ultra-secret. **~ up,** remplir. **~ped with,** surmonté de; (*cream etc.*: *culin.*) nappé de.

top[2] /tɒp/ *n.* (*toy*) toupie *f.*

topic /'tɒpɪk/ *n.* sujet *m.*

topical /'tɒpɪkl/ *a.* d'actualité.

topless /'tɒplɪs/ *a.* aux seins nus.

topple /'tɒpl/ *v.t./i.* (faire) tomber, (faire) basculer.

topsy-turvy /tɒpsɪ'tɜ:vɪ/ *adv.* & *a.* sens dessus dessous.

torch /tɔ:tʃ/ *n.* (*electric*) lampe de poche *f.*; (*flaming*) torche *f.*

tore /tɔ:(r)/ *see* tear[1].

torment[1] /'tɔ:ment/ *n.* tourment *m.*

torment[2] /tɔ:'ment/ *v.t.* tourmenter; (*annoy*) agacer.

torn /tɔ:n/ *see* tear[1].

tornado /tɔ:'neɪdəʊ/ *n.* (*pl.* **-oes**) tornade *f.*

torpedo /tɔ:'pi:dəʊ/ *n.* (*pl.* **-oes**) torpille *f.* ● *v.t.* torpiller.

torrent /'tɒrənt/ *n.* torrent *m.* **~ial** /tə'renʃl/ *a.* torrentiel.

torrid /'tɒrɪd/ *a.* (*climate etc.*) torride; (*fig.*) passionné.

torso /'tɔ:səʊ/ *n.* (*pl.* **-os**) torse *m.*

tortoise /'tɔ:təs/ *n.* tortue *f.*

tortoiseshell /'tɔ:təsʃel/ *n.* (*for ornaments etc.*) écaille *f.*

tortuous /'tɔ:tʃʊəs/ *a.* tortueux.

torture /'tɔ:tʃə(r)/ *n.* torture *f.*, supplice *m.* ● *v.t.* torturer. **~r** /-ə(r)/ *n.* tortionnaire *m.*

Tory /'tɔ:rɪ/ *n.* tory *m.* ● *a.* tory (*f. invar.*).

toss /tɒs/ *v.t.* jeter, lancer; (*shake*) agiter. ● *v.i.* s'agiter. **~ a coin, ~ up,** tirer à pile ou face (**for,** pour).

tot[1] /tɒt/ *n.* petit(e) enfant *m.*(*f.*; (*glass*: *fam.*) petit verre *m.*

tot[2] /tɒt/ *v.t.* (*p.t.* **totted**). **~ up,** (*fam.*) additionner.

total /'təʊtl/ *a.* total. ● *n.* total *m.* ● *v.t.* (*p.t.* **totalled**) (*find total of*) totaliser; (*amount to*) s'élever à. **~ity** /-'tælətɪ/ *n.* totalité *f.* **~ly** *adv.* totalement.

totalitarian /təʊtælɪ'teərɪən/ *a.* totalitaire.

totter /'tɒtə(r)/ *v.i.* chanceler.

touch /tʌtʃ/ *v.t./i.* toucher; (*of ends, gardens, etc.*) se toucher; (*tamper with*) toucher à. ● *n.* (*sense*) toucher *m.*; (*contact*) contact *m.*; (*of colour*) touche *f.*; (*football*) touche *f.* **a ~ of,** (*small amount*) un peu de. **get in ~ with,** contacter. **lose ~,** perdre contact. **be out of ~,** n'être plus dans le coup. **~-and-go** *a.* douteux. **~ down,** (*aviat.*) atterrir. **~-line** *n.* (ligne de) touche *f.* **~ off,** (*explode*) faire partir; (*cause*) déclencher. **~ on,** (*mention*) aborder. **~ up,** retoucher.

touchdown /'tʌtʃdaʊn/ *n.* atterrissage *m.*; (*sport, Amer.*) but *m.*

touching /'tʌtʃɪŋ/ *a.* touchant.

touchstone /'tʌtʃstəʊn/ *n.* pierre de touche *f.*

touchy /'tʌtʃɪ/ *a.* susceptible.

tough /tʌf/ *a.* (**-er, -est**) (*hard, difficult*) dur; (*strong*) solide; (*relentless*) acharné. ● *n.* **~ (guy),** dur *m.* **~ luck!,** (*fam.*) tant pis! **~ness** *n.* dureté *f.*; solidité *f.*

toughen /'tʌfn/ *v.t.* (*strengthen*) renforcer; (*person*) endurcir.

toupee /'tu:peɪ/ *n.* postiche *m.*

tour /tʊə(r)/ *n.* voyage *m.*; (*visit*) visite *f.*; (*by team etc.*) tournée *f.* ● *v.t.* visiter. **on ~,** en tournée. **~ operator,** voyagiste *m.*

tourism /'tʊərɪzəm/ *n.* tourisme *m.*

tourist /'tʊərɪst/ *n.* touriste *m./f.* ● *a.* touristique. **~ office,** syndicat d'initiative *m.*

tournament /'tɔ:nəmənt/ *n.* (*sport & medieval*) tournoi *m.*

tousle /'taʊzl/ *v.t.* ébouriffer.

tout /taʊt/ *v.i.* **~ (for),** racoler. ● *v.t.* (*sell*) revendre. ● *n.* racoleu|r, -se *m., f.*; revendeu|r, -se *m., f.*

tow /təʊ/ *v.t.* remorquer. ● *n.* remorque *f.* **on ~,** en remorque. **~ away,** (*vehicle*) (faire) enlever. **~-path** *n.* chemin de halage *m.* **~ truck,** dépanneuse *f.*

toward(s) /tə'wɔ:d(z), *Amer.* tɔ:d(z)/ *prep.* vers; (*of attitude*) envers.

towel /'taʊəl/ *n.* serviette *f.*; (*teatowel*) torchon *m.* **~ling** *n.* tissu-éponge *m.*

tower /'taʊə(r)/ *n.* tour *f.* ● *v.i.* **~ above,** dominer. **~ block,** tour *f.*, immeuble *m.* **~ing** *a.* très haut.

town /taʊn/ *n.* ville *f.* **go to ~,** (*fam.*) mettre le paquet. **~ council,** conseil municipal *m.* **~ hall,** hôtel de ville *m.*

toxic /'tɒksɪk/ *a.* toxique.

toxin /'tɒksɪn/ *n.* toxine *f.*

toy /tɔɪ/ *n.* jouet *m.* ● *v.i.* **~ with,** (*object*) jouer avec; (*idea*) caresser.

toyshop /'tɔɪʃɒp/ *n.* magasin de jouets *m.*

trace /treɪs/ *n.* trace *f.* ● *v.t.* suivre *or* retrouver la trace de; (*draw*) tracer; (*with tracing-paper*) décalquer; (*relate*) retracer.

tracing /'treɪsɪŋ/ *n.* calque *m.* **~-paper** *n.* papier-calque *m. invar.*

track /træk/ *n.* (*of person etc.*) trace *f.*, piste *f.*; (*path, race-track & of tape*) piste *f.*; (*on disc*) plage *f.*; (*of rocket etc.*) trajectoire *f.*; (*rail.*) voie *f.* ● *v.t.* suivre la trace *or* la trajectoire de. **keep ~ of,** suivre. **~ down,** (*find*) retrouver; (*hunt*) traquer. **~ suit,** survêtement *m.*; (*with sweat-shirt*) jogging *m.*

tract[1] /trækt/ *n.* (*land*) étendue *f.*; (*anat.*) appareil *m.*

tract[2] /trækt/ *n.* (*pamphlet*) tract *m.*

tractor /'træktə(r)/ *n.* tracteur *m.*

trade /treɪd/ *n.* commerce *m.*; (*job*) métier *m.*; (*swap*) échange *m.* ● *v.i.* faire du commerce. ● *v.t.* échanger. **~ deficit,** déficit commercial *m.* **~ in,** (*used article*) faire reprendre. **~-in** *n.* reprise *f.* **~ mark,** marque de fabrique *f.*; (*name*) marque déposée *f.* **~-off** *n.* (*fam.*) compromis *m.* **~ on,** (*exploit*) abuser de. **~ union,** syndicat *m.* **~-unionist** *n.* syndicaliste *m./f.* **~r** /-ə(r)/ *n.* négociant(e) *m.* (*f.*), commerçant(e) *m.* (*f.*)

tradesman /'treɪdzmən/ *n.* (*pl.* **-men**) commerçant *m.*

trading /'treɪdɪŋ/ *n.* commerce *m.* **~ estate,** zone industrielle *f.*

tradition /trə'dɪʃn/ *n.* tradition *f.* **~al** *a.* traditionnel.

traffic /'træfɪk/ *n.* trafic *m.*; (*on road*) circulation *f.* ● *v.i.* (*p.t.* **trafficked**) trafiquer (**in,** de). **~ circle,** (*Amer.*) rond-point *m.* **~ cone,** cône de délimitation de voie *m.* **~ jam,** embouteillage *m.* **~-lights** *n. pl.* feux (de circulation) *m. pl.* **~ warden,** contractuel(le) *m.* (*f.*).

tragedy /'trædʒədɪ/ *n.* tragédie *f.*

tragic /'trædʒɪk/ *a.* tragique.

trail /treɪl/ *v.t./i.* traîner; (*of plant*) ramper; (*track*) suivre. ● *n.* (*of powder etc.*) traînée *f.*; (*track*) piste *f.*; (*beaten path*) sentier *m.* **~ behind,** traîner.

trailer /'treɪlə(r)/ *n.* remorque *f.*; (*caravan: Amer.*) caravane *f.*; (*film*) bande-annonce *f.*

train /treɪn/ *n.* (*rail.*) train *m.*; (*underground*) rame *f.*; (*procession*) file *f.*; (*of dress*) traîne *f.* ● *v.t.* (*instruct, develop*) former; (*sportsman*) entraîner; (*animal*) dresser; (*ear*) exercer; (*aim*) braquer. ● *v.i.* recevoir une formation; s'entraîner. **~ed** *a.* (*skilled*) qualifié; (*doctor etc.*) diplômé. **~er** *n.* (*sport*) entraîneu|r, -se *m., f.* **~ers,** (*shoes*) chaussures de sport *f. pl.* **~ing** *n.* formation *f.*; entraînement *m.*; dressage *m.*

trainee /treɪ'ni:/ *n.* stagiaire *m./f.*

traipse /treɪps/ *v.i.* (*fam.*) traîner.

trait /treɪ(t)/ *n.* trait *m.*

traitor /'treɪtə(r)/ *n.* traître *m.*

tram /træm/ *n.* tram(way) *m.*

tramp /træmp/ *v.i.* marcher (d'un pas lourd). ● *v.t.* parcourir. ● *n.* pas lourds *m. pl.*; (*vagrant*) clochard(e) *m.* (*f.*); (*Amer., sl.*) dévergondée *f.*; (*hike*) randonnée *f.*

trample /'træmpl/ *v.t./i.* **~ (on),** piétiner; (*fig.*) fouler aux pieds.

trampoline /'træmpəli:n/ *n.* (*canvas sheet*) trampoline *m.*

trance /trɑ:ns/ *n.* transe *f.*

tranquil /'træŋkwɪl/ *a.* tranquille. **~lity** /-'kwɪlətɪ/ *n.* tranquillité *f.*

tranquillizer /'træŋkwɪlaɪzə(r)/ *n.* (*drug*) tranquillisant *m.*

transact /træn'zækt/ *v.t.* traiter. **~ion** /-kʃn/ *n.* transaction *f.*

transatlantic /trænzət'læntɪk/ *a.* transatlantique.

transcend /træn'send/ *v.t.* transcender. **~ent** *a.* transcendant.

transcript /'trænskrɪpt/ *n.* (*written copy*) transcription *f.*

transfer[1] /træns'fɜ:(r)/ *v.t.* (*p.t.* **transferred**) transférer; (*power*) faire passer. ● *v.i.* être transféré. **~ the charges,** (*telephone*) téléphoner en PCV.

transfer[2] /'trænsfɜ:(r)/ *n.* transfert *m.*; (*of power*) passation *f.*; (*image*) décalcomanie *f.*; (*sticker*) autocollant *m.*

transform /træns'fɔ:m/ *v.t.* transformer. **~ation** /-ə'meɪʃn/ *n.* transformation *f.* **~er** *n.* (*electr.*) transformateur *m.*

transfusion /træns'fju:ʒn/ *n.* (*of blood*) transfusion *f.*

transient /'trænzɪənt/ *a.* transitoire, éphémère.

transistor /træn'zɪstə(r)/ *n.* (*device, radio set*) transistor *m.*

transit /'trænsɪt/ *n.* transit *m.*

transition /træn'zɪʃn/ *n.* transition *f.* **~al** *a.* transitoire.

transitive /'trænsətɪv/ *a.* transitif.

transitory /'trænsɪtərɪ/ *a.* transitoire.

translat|e /trænz'leɪt/ *v.t.* traduire. **~ion** /-ʃn/ *n.* traduction *f.* **~or** *n.* traduc|teur, -trice *m., f.*

translucent /trænz'lu:snt/ *a.* translucide.

transmi|t /trænz'mɪt/ *v.t.* (*p.t.* **transmitted**) (*pass on etc.*) transmettre; (*broadcast*) émettre. **~ssion** *n.* transmission *f.*; émission *f.* **~tter** *n.* émetteur *m.*

transparen|t /træns'pærənt/ *a.* transparent. **~cy** *n.* transparence *f.*; (*photo.*) diapositive *f.*
transpire /træn'spaɪə(r)/ *v.i.* s'avérer; (*happen: fam.*) arriver.
transplant[1] /træns'plɑ:nt/ *v.t.* transplanter; (*med.*) greffer.
transplant[2] /'trænsplɑ:nt/ *n.* transplantation *f.*; greffe *f.*
transport[1] /træn'spɔ:t/ *v.t.* (*carry, delight*) transporter. **~ation** /-'teɪʃn/ *n.* transport *m.*
transport[2] /'trænspɔ:t/ *n.* (*of goods, delight, etc.*) transport *m.*
transpose /træn'spəʊz/ *v.t.* transposer.
transverse /'trænzvɜ:s/ *a.* transversal.
transvestite /trænz'vestaɪt/ *n.* travesti(e) *m.* (*f.*).
trap /træp/ *n.* piège *m.* ● *v.t.* (*p.t.* **trapped**) (*jam, pin down*) coincer; (*cut off*) bloquer; (*snare*) prendre au piège. **~per** *n.* trappeur *m.*
trapdoor /træp'dɔ:(r)/ *n.* trappe *f.*
trapeze /trə'pi:z/ *n.* trapèze *m.*
trappings /'træpɪŋz/ *n. pl.* (*fig.*) signes extérieurs *m. pl.*, apparat *m.*
trash /træʃ/ *n.* (*junk*) saleté(s) *f.* (*pl.*); (*refuse*) ordures *f. pl.*; (*nonsense*) idioties *f. pl.* **~-can** *n.* (*Amer.*) poubelle *f.* **~y** *a.* qui ne vaut rien, de mauvaise qualité.
trauma /'trɔ:mə/ *n.* traumatisme *m.* **~tic** /-'mætɪk/ *a.* traumatisant.
travel /'trævl/ *v.i.* (*p.t.* **travelled,** *Amer.* **traveled**) voyager; (*of vehicle, bullet, etc.*) aller. ● *v.t.* parcourir. ● *n.* voyage(s) *m.* (*pl.*). **~ agent,** agent de voyage *m.* **~ler** *n.* voyageu|r, -se *m., f.* **~ler's cheque,** chèque de voyage *m.* **~ling** *n.* voyage(s) *m.* (*pl.*). **~ sickness,** mal des transports *m.*
travesty /'trævəstɪ/ *n.* parodie *f.*, simulacre *m.* ● *v.t.* travestir.
trawler /'trɔ:lə(r)/ *n.* chalutier *m.*
tray /treɪ/ *n.* plateau *m.*; (*on office desk*) corbeille *f.*
treacherous /'tretʃərəs/ *a.* traître. **~ly** *adv.* traîtreusement.
treachery /'tretʃərɪ/ *n.* traîtrise *f.*
treacle /'tri:kl/ *n.* mélasse *f.*
tread /tred/ *v.i.* (*p.t.* **trod,** *p.p.* **trodden**) marcher (**on,** sur). ● *v.t.* parcourir (à pied); (*soil: fig.*) fouler. ● *n.* démarche *f.*; (*sound*) (bruit *m.* de) pas *m. pl.*; (*of tyre*) chape *f.* **~ sth. into,** (*carpet*) étaler qch. sur (avec les pieds).
treason /'tri:zn/ *n.* trahison *f.*
treasure /'treʒə(r)/ *n.* trésor *m.* ● *v.t.* attacher une grande valeur à; (*store*) conserver. **~r** /-ə(r)/ *n.* trésor|ier, -ière *m., f.*
treasury /'treʒərɪ/ *n.* trésorerie *f.* **the T~,** le ministère des Finances.
treat /tri:t/ *v.t.* traiter; (*consider*) considérer. ● *n.* (*pleasure*) plaisir *m.*, régal *m.*; (*present*) gâterie *f.*; (*food*) régal *m.* **~ s.o. to sth.,** offrir qch. à qn.
treatise /'tri:tɪz/ *n.* traité *m.*
treatment /'tri:tmənt/ *n.* traitement *m.*
treaty /'tri:tɪ/ *n.* (*pact*) traité *m.*
trebl|e /'trebl/ *a.* triple. ● *v.t./i.* tripler. ● *n.* (*voice: mus.*) soprano *m.* **~e clef,** clé de sol *f.* **~y** *adv.* triplement.
tree /tri:/ *n.* arbre *m.* **~-top** *n.* cime (d'un arbre) *f.*
trek /trek/ *n.* voyage pénible *m.*; (*sport*) randonnée *f.* ● *v.i.* (*p.t.* **trekked**) voyager (péniblement); (*sport*) faire de la randonnée.
trellis /'trelɪs/ *n.* treillage *m.*
tremble /'trembl/ *v.i.* trembler.
tremendous /trɪ'mendəs/ *a.* énorme; (*excellent: fam.*) fantastique. **~ly** *adv.* fantastiquement.
tremor /'tremə(r)/ *n.* tremblement *m.* **(earth) ~,** secousse (sismique) *f.*
trench /trentʃ/ *n.* tranchée *f.*
trend /trend/ *n.* tendance *f.*; (*fashion*) mode *f.* **~-setter** *n.* lanceu|r, -se de mode *m., f.* **~y** *a.* (*fam.*) dans le vent.
trepidation /trepɪ'deɪʃn/ *n.* (*fear*) inquiétude *f.*
trespass /'trespəs/ *v.i.* s'introduire sans autorisation (**on,** dans). **~er** *n.* intrus(e) *m.* (*f.*).
tresses /'tresɪz/ *n. pl.* chevelure *f.*
trestle /'tresl/ *n.* tréteau *m.* **~-table** *n.* table à tréteaux *f.*
tri- /traɪ/ *pref.* tri-.
trial /'traɪəl/ *n.* (*jurid.*) procès *m.*; (*test*) essai *m.*; (*ordeal*) épreuve *f.* **go on ~,** passer en jugement. **~ and error,** tâtonnements *m. pl.* **~ run,** galop d'essai *m.*
triang|le /'traɪæŋgl/ *n.* triangle *m.* **~ular** /-'æŋgjʊlə(r)/ *a.* triangulaire.
trib|e /traɪb/ *n.* tribu *f.* **~al** *a.* tribal.
tribulation /trɪbjʊ'leɪʃn/ *n.* tribulation *f.*

tribunal /traɪ'bjuːnl/ *n.* tribunal *m.*; (*mil.*) commission *f.*

tributary /'trɪbjʊtərɪ/ *n.* affluent *m.*

tribute /'trɪbjuːt/ *n.* tribut *m.* **pay ~ to,** rendre hommage à.

trick /trɪk/ *n.* astuce *f.*, ruse *f.*; (*joke, feat of skill*) tour *m.*; (*habit*) manie *f.* ● *v.t.* tromper. **do the ~,** (*fam.*) faire l'affaire.

trickery /'trɪkərɪ/ *n.* ruse *f.*

trickle /'trɪkl/ *v.i.* dégouliner. **~ in/out,** arriver *or* partir en petit nombre. ● *n.* filet *m.*; (*fig.*) petit nombre *m.*

tricky /'trɪkɪ/ *a.* (*crafty*) rusé; (*problem*) délicat, difficile.

tricycle /'traɪsɪkl/ *n.* tricycle *m.*

trifle /'traɪfl/ *n.* bagatelle *f.*; (*cake*) diplomate *m.* ● *v.i.* **~ with,** jouer avec. **a ~,** (*small amount*) un peu.

trifling /'traɪflɪŋ/ *a.* insignifiant.

trigger /'trɪgə(r)/ *n.* (*of gun*) gâchette *f.*, détente *f.* ● *v.t.* **~ (off),** (*initiate*) déclencher.

trilby /'trɪlbɪ/ *n.* (*hat*) feutre *m.*

trim /trɪm/ *a.* (**trimmer, trimmest**) net, soigné; (*figure*) svelte. ● *v.t.* (*p.t.* **trimmed**) (*cut*) couper légèrement; (*hair*) rafraîchir; (*budget*) réduire. ● *n.* (*cut*) coupe légère *f.*; (*decoration*) garniture *f.* **in ~,** en bon ordre; (*fit*) en forme. **~ with,** (*decorate*) orner de. **~ming(s)** *n.* (*pl.*) garniture(s) *f.* (*pl.*).

Trinity /'trɪnətɪ/ *n.* Trinité *f.*

trinket /'trɪŋkɪt/ *n.* colifichet *m.*

trio /'triːəʊ/ *n.* (*pl.* **-os**) trio *m.*

trip /trɪp/ *v.t./i.* (*p.t.* **tripped**) (faire) trébucher; (*go lightly*) marcher d'un pas léger. ● *n.* (*journey*) voyage *m.*; (*outing*) excursion *f.*; (*stumble*) faux pas *m.*

tripe /traɪp/ *n.* (*food*) tripes *f. pl.*; (*nonsense*: *sl.*) bêtises *f. pl.*

triple /'trɪpl/ *a.* triple. ● *v.t./i.* tripler. **~ts** /-plɪts/ *n. pl.* triplé(e)s *m.* (*f.*) *pl.*

tripod /'traɪpɒd/ *n.* trépied *m.*

trite /traɪt/ *a.* banal.

triumph /'traɪəmf/ *n.* triomphe *m.* ● *v.i.* triompher (**over,** de). **~al** /-'ʌmfl/ *a.* triomphal. **~ant** /-'ʌmfənt/ *a.* triomphant, triomphal. **~antly** /-'ʌmfəntlɪ/ *adv.* en triomphe.

trivial /'trɪvɪəl/ *a.* insignifiant. **~ize** *v.t.* considérer comme insignifiant.

trod, trodden /trɒd, 'trɒdn/ *see* tread.

trolley /'trɒlɪ/ *n.* chariot *m.* **(tea-)~,** table roulante *f.* **~-bus** *n.* trolleybus *m.*

trombone /trɒm'bəʊn/ *n.* (*mus.*) trombone *m.*

troop /truːp/ *n.* bande *f.* **~s,** (*mil.*) troupes *f. pl.* ● *v.i.* **~ in/out,** entrer/sortir en bande. **~er** *n.* soldat de cavalerie *m.* **~ing the colour,** le salut au drapeau.

trophy /'trəʊfɪ/ *n.* trophée *m.*

tropic /'trɒpɪk/ *n.* tropique *m.* **~s,** tropiques *m. pl.* **~al** *a.* tropical.

trot /trɒt/ *n.* trot *m.* ● *v.i.* (*p.t.* **trotted**) trotter. **on the ~,** (*fam.*) de suite. **~ out,** (*produce*: *fam.*) sortir; (*state*: *fam.*) formuler.

trouble /'trʌbl/ *n.* ennui(s) *m.* (*pl.*), difficulté(s) *f.* (*pl.*); (*pains, effort*) mal *m.*, peine *f.* **~(s),** ennuis *m. pl.*; (*unrest*) conflits *m. pl.* ● *v.t./i.* (*bother*) (se) déranger; (*worry*) ennuyer. **be in ~,** avoir des ennuis. **go to a lot of ~,** se donner du mal. **what's the ~?,** quel est le problème? **~d** *a.* inquiet; (*period*) agité. **~-maker** *n.* provoca|teur, -trice *m., f.* **~- shooter** *n.* personne appelée pour désamorcer une crise.

troublesome /'trʌblsəm/ *a.* ennuyeux, pénible.

trough /trɒf/ *n.* (*drinking*) abreuvoir *m.*; (*feeding*) auge *f.* **~ (of low pressure),** dépression *f.*

trounce /traʊns/ *v.t.* (*defeat*) écraser; (*thrash*) rosser.

troupe /truːp/ *n.* (*theatre*) troupe *f.*

trousers /'traʊzəz/ *n. pl.* pantalon *m.* **short ~,** culotte courte *f.*

trousseau /'truːsəʊ/ *n.* (*pl.* **-s** /-əʊz/) (*of bride*) trousseau *m.*

trout /traʊt/ *n. invar.* truite *f.*

trowel /'traʊəl/ *n.* (*garden*) déplantoir *m.*; (*for mortar*) truelle *f.*

truan|t /'truːənt/ *n.* absentéiste *m./f.*; (*schol.*) élève absent(e) sans permission *m.*(*f.*). **play ~t,** sécher les cours. **~cy** *n.* absentéisme *m.*

truce /truːs/ *n.* trêve *f.*

truck /trʌk/ *n.* (*lorry*) camion *m.*; (*cart*) chariot *m.*; (*rail.*) wagon *m.*, plateforme *f.* **~-driver** *n.* camionneur *m.*

truculent /'trʌkjʊlənt/ *a.* agressif.

trudge /trʌdʒ/ *v.i.* marcher péniblement, se traîner.

true /truː/ *a.* (**-er, -est**) vrai; (*accurate*) exact; (*faithful*) fidèle.

truffle /'trʌfl/ *n.* truffe *f.*

truly /ˈtru:lɪ/ *adv.* vraiment; (*faithfully*) fidèlement; (*truthfully*) sincèrement.
trump /trʌmp/ *n.* atout *m.* ● *v.t.* **~ up,** inventer. **~ card,** atout *m.*
trumpet /ˈtrʌmpɪt/ *n.* trompette *f.*
truncate /trʌŋˈkeɪt/ *v.t.* tronquer.
trundle /ˈtrʌndl/ *v.t./i.* rouler bruyamment.
trunk /trʌŋk/ *n.* (*of tree, body*) tronc *m.*; (*of elephant*) trompe *f.*; (*box*) malle *f.*; (*auto., Amer.*) coffre *m.* **~s,** (*for swimming*) slip de bain *m.* **~-call** *n.* communication interurbaine *f.* **~-road** *n.* route nationale *f.*
truss /trʌs/ *n.* (*med.*) bandage herniaire *m.* ● *v.t.* (*fowl*) trousser.
trust /trʌst/ *n.* confiance *f.*; (*association*) trust *m.* ● *v.t.* avoir confiance en. ● *v.i.* **~ in** *or* **to,** s'en remettre à. **in ~,** en dépôt. **on ~,** de confiance. **~ s.o. with,** confier à qn. **~ed** *a.* (*friend etc.*) éprouvé, sûr. **~ful, ~ing** *adjs.* confiant. **~y** *a.* fidèle.
trustee /trʌsˈti:/ *n.* administra|teur, -trice *m., f.*
trustworthy /ˈtrʌstwɜ:ðɪ/ *a.* digne de confiance.
truth /tru:θ/ *n.* (*pl.* **-s** /tru:ðz/) vérité *f.* **~ful** *a.* (*account etc.*) véridique; (*person*) qui dit la vérité. **~fully** *adv.* sincèrement.
try /traɪ/ *v.t./i.* (*p.t.* **tried**) essayer; (*be a strain on*) éprouver; (*jurid.*) juger. ● *n.* (*attempt*) essai *m.*; (*Rugby*) essai *m.* **~ on** *or* **out,** essayer. **~ to do,** essayer de faire. **~ing** *a.* éprouvant.
tsar /zɑ:(r)/ *n.* tsar *m.*
T-shirt /ˈti:ʃɜ:t/ *n.* tee-shirt *m.*
tub /tʌb/ *n.* baquet *m.*, cuve *f.*; (*bath: fam.*) baignoire *f.*
tuba /ˈtju:bə/ *n.* tuba *m.*
tubby /ˈtʌbɪ/ *a.* (**-ier, -iest**) dodu.
tub|e /tju:b/ *n.* tube *m.*; (*railway: fam.*) métro *m.*; (*in tyre*) chambre à air *f.* **~ing** *n.* tubes *m. pl.*
tuberculosis /tju:bɜ:kjʊˈləʊsɪs/ *n.* tuberculose *f.*
tubular /ˈtju:bjʊlə(r)/ *a.* tubulaire.
tuck /tʌk/ *n.* (*fold*) rempli *m.*, (re)pli *m.* ● *v.t.* (*put away, place*) ranger; (*hide*) cacher. ● *v.i.* **~ in** *or* **into,** (*eat: sl.*) attaquer. **~ in,** (*shirt*) rentrer; (*blanket, person*) border. **~-shop** *n.* (*schol.*) boutique à provisions *f.*
Tuesday /ˈtju:zdɪ/ *n.* mardi *m.*
tuft /tʌft/ *n.* (*of hair etc.*) touffe *f.*
tug /tʌg/ *v.t.* (*p.t.* **tugged**) tirer fort (sur). ● *v.i.* tirer fort. ● *n.* (*boat*) remorqueur *m.* **~ of war,** jeu de la corde tirée *m.*
tuition /tju:ˈɪʃn/ *n.* cours *m. pl.*; (*fee*) frais de scolarité *m. pl.*
tulip /ˈtju:lɪp/ *n.* tulipe *f.*
tumble /ˈtʌmbl/ *v.i.* (*fall*) dégringoler. ● *n.* chute *f.* **~-drier** *n.* séchoir à linge (à air chaud) *m.* **~ to,** (*realize: fam.*) piger.
tumbledown /ˈtʌmbldaʊn/ *a.* délabré, en ruine.
tumbler /ˈtʌmblə(r)/ *n.* gobelet *m.*
tummy /ˈtʌmɪ/ *n.* (*fam.*) ventre *m.*
tumour /ˈtju:mə(r)/ *n.* tumeur *f.*
tumult /ˈtju:mʌlt/ *n.* tumulte *m.* **~uous** /-ˈmʌltʃʊəs/ *a.* tumultueux.
tuna /ˈtju:nə/ *n. invar.* thon *m.*
tune /tju:n/ *n.* air *m.* ● *v.t.* (*engine*) régler; (*mus.*) accorder. ● *v.i.* **~ in (to),** (*radio, TV*) écouter. **be in ~/out of ~,** (*instrument*) être accordé/désaccordé; (*singer*) chanter juste/faux. **~ful** *a.* mélodieux. **tuning-fork** *n.* diapason *m.* **~ up,** (*orchestra*) accorder leurs instruments.
tunic /ˈtju:nɪk/ *n.* tunique *f.*
Tunisia /tju:ˈnɪzɪə/ *n.* Tunisie *f.* **~n** *a.* & *n.* tunisien(ne) (*m.* (*f.*)).
tunnel /ˈtʌnl/ *n.* tunnel *m.*; (*in mine*) galerie *f.* ● *v.i.* (*p.t.* **tunnelled**) creuser un tunnel (**into,** dans).
turban /ˈtɜ:bən/ *n.* turban *m.*
turbine /ˈtɜ:baɪn/ *n.* turbine *f.*
turbo /ˈtɜ:bəʊ/ *n.* turbo *m.*
turbulen|t /ˈtɜ:bjʊlənt/ *a.* turbulent. **~ce** *n.* turbulence *f.*
tureen /tjʊˈri:n/ *n.* soupière *f.*
turf /tɜ:f/ *n.* (*pl.* **turf** *or* **turves**) gazon *m.* ● *v.t.* **~ out,** (*sl.*) jeter dehors. **the ~,** (*racing*) le turf.
turgid /ˈtɜ:dʒɪd/ *a.* (*speech, style*) boursouflé, ampoulé.
Turk /tɜ:k/ *n.* Turc *m.*, Turque *f.* **~ey** *n.* Turquie *f.* **~ish** *a.* turc; *n.* (*lang.*) turc *m.*
turkey /ˈtɜ:kɪ/ *n.* dindon *m.*, dinde *f.*; (*as food*) dinde *f.*
turmoil /ˈtɜ:mɔɪl/ *n.* trouble *m.*, chaos *m.* **in ~,** en ébullition.
turn /tɜ:n/ *v.t./i.* tourner; (*of person*) se tourner; (*to other side*) retourner; (*change*) (se) transformer (**into,** en); (*become*) devenir; (*deflect*) détourner; (*milk*) tourner. ● *n.* tour *m.*; (*in road*) tournant *m.*; (*of mind,*

events) tournure *f.*; (*illness*: *fam.*) crise *f.* **do a good ~,** rendre service. **in ~,** à tour de rôle. **speak out of ~,** commettre une indiscrétion. **take ~s,** se relayer. **~ against,** se retourner contre. **~ away** *v.i.* se détourner; *v.t.* (*avert*) détourner; (*refuse*) refuser; (*send back*) renvoyer. **~ back** *v.i.* (*return*) retourner; (*vehicle*) faire demi-tour; *v.t.* (*fold*) rabattre. **~ down,** refuser; (*fold*) rabattre; (*reduce*) baisser. **~ in,** (*go to bed*: *fam.*) se coucher. **~ off,** (*light etc.*) éteindre; (*engine*) arrêter; (*tap*) fermer; (*of driver*) tourner. **~-off** *n.* (*auto.*) embranchement *m.* **~ on,** (*light etc.*) allumer; (*engine*) allumer; (*tap*) ouvrir. **~ out** *v.t.* (*light*) éteindre; (*empty*) vider; (*produce*) produire; *v.i.* (*transpire*) s'avérer; (*come*: *fam.*) venir. **~-out** *n.* assistance *f.* **~ over,** (se) retourner. **~ round,** (*person*) se retourner. **~-round** *n.* revirement *m.* **~ up** *v.i.* arriver; (*be found*) se retrouver; *v.t.* (*find*) déterrer; (*collar*) remonter. **~-up** *n.* (*of trousers*) revers *m.*

turning /'tɜ:nɪŋ/ *n.* rue (latérale) *f.*; (*bend*) tournant *m.* **~-point** *n.* tournant *m.*

turnip /'tɜ:nɪp/ *n.* navet *m.*

turnover /'tɜ:nəʊvə(r)/ *n.* (*pie, tart*) chausson *m.*; (*money*) chiffre d'affaires *m.*

turnpike /'tɜ:npaɪk/ *n.* (*Amer.*) autoroute à péage *f.*

turnstile /'tɜ:nstaɪl/ *n.* (*gate*) tourniquet *m.*

turntable /'tɜ:nteɪbl/ *n.* (*for record*) platine *f.*, plateau *m.*

turpentine /'tɜ:pəntaɪn/ *n.* térébenthine *f.*

turquoise /'tɜ:kwɔɪz/ *a.* turquoise *invar.*

turret /'tʌrɪt/ *n.* tourelle *f.*

turtle /'tɜ:tl/ *n.* tortue (de mer) *f.* **~-neck** *a.* à col montant, roulé.

tusk /tʌsk/ *n.* (*tooth*) défense *f.*

tussle /'tʌsl/ *n.* bagarre *f.*, lutte *f.*

tutor /'tju:tə(r)/ *n.* précep|teur, -trice *m.*, *f.*; (*univ.*) direc|teur, -trice d'études *m.*, *f.*

tutorial /tju:'tɔ:rɪəl/ *n.* (*univ.*) séance d'études *or* de travaux pratiques *f.*

tuxedo /tʌk'si:dəʊ/ *n.* (*pl.* **-os**) (*Amer.*) smoking *m.*

TV /ti:'vi:/ *n.* télé *f.*

twaddle /'twɒdl/ *n.* fadaises *f. pl.*

twang /twæŋ/ *n.* (*son*: *mus.*) pincement *m.*; (*in voice*) nasillement *m.* ● *v.t./i.* (faire) vibrer.

tweed /twi:d/ *n.* tweed *m.*

tweezers /'twi:zəz/ *n. pl.* pince (à épiler) *f.*

twel|ve /twelv/ *a.* & *n.* douze (*m.*). **~fth** *a.* & *n.* douzième (*m./f.*). **~ve (o'clock),** midi *m. or* minuit *m.*

twent|y /'twentɪ/ *a.* & *n.* vingt (*m.*). **~ieth** *a.* & *n.* vingtième (*m./f.*).

twice /twaɪs/ *adv.* deux fois.

twiddle /'twɪdl/ *v.t./i.* **~ (with),** (*fiddle with*) tripoter. **~ one's thumbs,** se tourner les pouces.

twig[1] /twɪg/ *n.* brindille *f.*

twig[2] /twɪg/ *v.t./i.* (*p.t.* **twigged**) (*understand*: *fam.*) piger.

twilight /'twaɪlaɪt/ *n.* crépuscule *m.* ● *a.* crépusculaire.

twin /twɪn/ *n.* & *a.* jum|eau, -elle (*m.*, *f.*). ● *v.t.* (*p.t.* **twinned**) jumeler. **~ning** *n.* jumelage *m.*

twine /twaɪn/ *n.* ficelle *f.* ● *v.t./i.* (*wind*) (s')enlacer.

twinge /twɪndʒ/ *n.* élancement *m.*; (*remorse*) remords *m.*

twinkle /'twɪŋkl/ *v.i.* (*star etc.*) scintiller; (*eye*) pétiller. ● *n.* scintillement *m.*; pétillement *m.*

twirl /twɜ:l/ *v.t./i.* (faire) tournoyer.

twist /twɪst/ *v.t.* tordre; (*weave together*) entortiller; (*roll*) enrouler; (*distort*) déformer. ● *v.i.* (*rope etc.*) s'entortiller; (*road*) zigzaguer. ● *n.* torsion *f.*; (*in rope*) tortillon *m.*; (*in road*) tournant *m.*; (*of events*) tournure *f.*, tour *m.*

twit /twɪt/ *n.* (*fam.*) idiot(e) *m.* (*f.*).

twitch /twɪtʃ/ *v.t./i.* (se) contracter nerveusement. ● *n.* (*tic*) tic *m.*; (*jerk*) secousse *f.*

two /tu:/ *a.* & *n.* deux (*m.*). **in** *or* **of ~ minds,** indécis. **put ~ and two together,** faire le rapport. **~-faced** *a.* hypocrite. **~fold** *a.* double; *adv.* au double. **~-piece** *n.* (*garment*) deux-pièces *m. invar.*

twosome /'tu:səm/ *n.* couple *m.*

tycoon /taɪ'ku:n/ *n.* magnat *m.*

tying /'taɪɪŋ/ *see* tie.

type /taɪp/ *n.* (*example*) type *m.*; (*kind*) genre *m.*, sorte *f.*; (*person*: *fam.*) type *m.*; (*print*) caractères *m. pl.* ● *v.t./i.* (*write*) taper (à la machine). **~-cast** *a.* catégorisé (**as,** comme).

typescript /'taɪpskrɪpt/ *n.* manuscrit dactylographié *m.*

typewrit|er /'taɪpraɪtə(r)/ *n.* machine à écrire *f.* **~ten** /-ɪtn/ *a.* dactylographié.

typhoid /'taɪfɔɪd/ *n.* **~ (fever),** typhoïde *f.*

typhoon /taɪ'fu:n/ *n.* typhon *m.*

typical /'tɪpɪkl/ *a.* typique. **~ly** *adv.* typiquement.

typify /'tɪpɪfaɪ/ *v.t.* être typique de.

typing /'taɪpɪŋ/ *n.* dactylo(graphie) *f.*

typist /'taɪpɪst/ *n.* dactylo *f.*

tyrann|y /'tɪrənɪ/ *n.* tyrannie *f.* **~ical** /tɪ'rænɪkl/ *a.* tyrannique.

tyrant /'taɪərənt/ *n.* tyran *m.*

tyre /'taɪə(r)/ *n.* pneu *m.*

U

ubiquitous /ju:'bɪkwɪtəs/ *a.* omniprésent, qu'on trouve partout.

udder /'ʌdə(r)/ *n.* pis *m.*, mamelle *f.*

UFO /'ju:fəʊ/ *n.* (*pl.* **-Os**) OVNI *m.*

Uganda /ju:'gændə/ *n.* Ouganda *m.*

ugl|y /'ʌglɪ/ *a.* (**-ier, -iest**) laid. **~iness** *n.* laideur *f.*

UK *abbr. see* United Kingdom.

ulcer /'ʌlsə(r)/ *n.* ulcère *m.*

ulterior /ʌl'tɪərɪə(r)/ *a.* ultérieur. **~ motive,** arrière-pensée *f.*

ultimate /'ʌltɪmət/ *a.* dernier, ultime; (*definitive*) définitif; (*basic*) fondamental. **~ly** *adv.* à la fin; (*in the last analysis*) en fin de compte.

ultimatum /ʌltɪ'meɪtəm/ *n.* (*pl.* **-ums**) ultimatum *m.*

ultra- /'ʌltrə/ *pref.* ultra-.

ultrasound /'ʌltrəsaʊnd/ *n.* ultrason *m.*

ultraviolet /ʌltrə'vaɪələt/ *a.* ultraviolet.

umbilical /ʌm'bɪlɪkl/ *a.* **~ cord,** cordon ombilical *m.*

umbrella /ʌm'brelə/ *n.* parapluie *m.*

umpire /'ʌmpaɪə(r)/ *n.* (*sport*) arbitre *m.* ● *v.t.* arbitrer.

umpteen /'ʌmpti:n/ *a.* (*many*: *sl.*) un tas de. **~th** *a.* (*fam.*) énième.

UN *abbr.* (*United Nations*) ONU *f.*

un- /ʌn/ *pref.* in-, dé(s)-, non, peu, mal, sans.

unabated /ʌnə'beɪtɪd/ *a.* non diminué, aussi fort qu'avant.

unable /ʌn'eɪbl/ *a.* incapable; (*through circumstances*) dans l'impossibilité (**to do,** de faire).

unacceptable /ʌnək'septəbl/ *a.* inacceptable, inadmissible.

unaccountabl|e /ʌnə'kaʊntəbl/ *a.* (*strange*) inexplicable. **~y** *adv.* inexplicablement.

unaccustomed /ʌnə'kʌstəmd/ *a.* inaccoutumé. **~ to,** peu habitué à.

unadulterated /ʌnə'dʌltəreɪtɪd/ *a.* (*pure, sheer*) pur.

unaided /ʌn'eɪdɪd/ *a.* sans aide.

unanim|ous /ju:'nænɪməs/ *a.* unanime. **~ity** /-ə'nɪmətɪ/ *n.* unanimité *f.* **~ously** *adv.* à l'unanimité.

unarmed /ʌn'ɑ:md/ *a.* non armé.

unashamed /ʌnə'ʃeɪmd/ *a.* éhonté. **~ly** /-ɪdlɪ/ *adv.* sans vergogne.

unassuming /ʌnə'sju:mɪŋ/ *a.* modeste, sans prétention.

unattached /ʌnə'tætʃt/ *a.* libre.

unattainable /ʌnə'teɪnəbl/ *a.* inaccessible.

unattended /ʌnə'tendɪd/ *a.* (laissé) sans surveillance.

unattractive /ʌnə'træktɪv/ *a.* peu séduisant, laid; (*offer*) peu intéressant.

unauthorized /ʌn'ɔ:θəraɪzd/ *a.* non autorisé.

unavailable /ʌnə'veɪləbl/ *a.* pas disponible.

unavoidabl|e /ʌnə'vɔɪdəbl/ *a.* inévitable. **~y** *adv.* inévitablement.

unaware /ʌnə'weə(r)/ *a.* **be ~ of,** ignorer. **~s** /-eəz/ *adv.* au dépourvu.

unbalanced /ʌn'bælənst/ *a.* (*mind, person*) déséquilibré.

unbearable /ʌn'beərəbl/ *a.* insupportable.

unbeat|able /ʌn'bi:təbl/ *a.* imbattable. **~en** *a.* non battu.

unbeknown(st) /ʌnbɪ'nəʊn(st)/ *a.* **~(st) to,** (*fam.*) à l'insu de.

unbelievable /ʌnbɪ'li:vəbl/ *a.* incroyable.

unbend /ʌn'bend/ *v.i.* (*p.t.* **unbent**) (*relax*) se détendre.

unbiased /ʌn'baɪəst/ *a.* impartial.

unblock /ʌn'blɒk/ *v.t.* déboucher.

unborn /ʌn'bɔ:n/ *a.* futur, à venir.

unbounded /ʌn'baʊndɪd/ *a.* illimité.

unbreakable /ʌn'breɪkəbl/ *a.* incassable.

unbridled /ʌn'braɪdld/ *a.* débridé.

unbroken /ʌn'brəʊkən/ *a.* (*intact*) intact; (*continuous*) continu.

unburden /ʌn'bɜ:dn/ *v. pr.* **~ o.s.,** (*open one's heart*) s'épancher.

unbutton /ʌn'bʌtn/ *v.t.* déboutonner.

uncalled-for /ʌn'kɔ:ldfɔ:(r)/ *a.* injustifié, superflu.
uncanny /ʌn'kænɪ/ *a.* (**-ier, -iest**) étrange, mystérieux.
unceasing /ʌn'si:sɪŋ/ *a.* incessant.
unceremonious /ʌnserɪ'məʊnɪəs/ *a.* sans façon, brusque.
uncertain /ʌn'sɜ:tn/ *a.* incertain. **be ~ whether,** ne pas savoir exactement si (**to do,** on doit faire). **~ty** *n.* incertitude *f.*
unchang|ed /ʌn'tʃeɪndʒd/ *a.* inchangé. **~ing** *a.* immuable.
uncivilized /ʌn'sɪvɪlaɪzd/ *a.* barbare.
uncle /'ʌŋkl/ *n.* oncle *m.*
uncomfortable /ʌn'kʌmftəbl/ *a.* (*thing*) peu confortable; (*unpleasant*) désagréable. **feel** *or* **be ~,** (*person*) être mal à l'aise.
uncommon /ʌn'kɒmən/ *a.* rare. **~ly** *adv.* remarquablement.
uncompromising /ʌn'kɒmprəmaɪzɪŋ/ *a.* intransigeant.
unconcerned /ʌnkən'sɜ:nd/ *a.* (*indifferent*) indifférent (**by,** à).
unconditional /ʌnkən'dɪʃənl/ *a.* inconditionnel.
unconscious /ʌn'kɒnʃəs/ *a.* sans connaissance, inanimé; (*not aware*) inconscient (**of,** de) ● *n.* inconscient *m.* **~ly** *adv.* inconsciemment.
unconventional /ʌnkən'venʃənl/ *a.* peu conventionnel.
uncooperative /ʌnkəʊ'ɒpərətɪv/ *a.* peu coopératif.
uncork /ʌn'kɔ:k/ *v.t.* déboucher.
uncouth /ʌn'ku:θ/ *a.* grossier.
uncover /ʌn'kʌvə(r)/ *v.t.* découvrir.
undecided /ʌndɪ'saɪdɪd/ *a.* indécis.
undefinable /ʌndɪ'faɪnəbl/ *a.* indéfinissable.
undeniable /ʌndɪ'naɪəbl/ *a.* indéniable, incontestable.
under /'ʌndə(r)/ *prep.* sous; (*less than*) moins de; (*according to*) selon. ● *adv.* au-dessous. **~ age,** mineur. **~ it/there,** là-dessous. **~-side** *n.* dessous *m.* **~ way,** (*in progress*) en cours; (*on the way*) en route.
under- /'ʌndə(r)/ *pref.* sous-.
undercarriage /'ʌndəkærɪdʒ/ *n.* (*aviat.*) train d'atterrissage *m.*
underclothes /'ʌndəkləʊðz/ *n. pl.* sous-vêtements *m. pl.*
undercoat /'ʌndəkəʊt/ *n.* (*of paint*) couche de fond *f.*
undercover /ʌndə'kʌvə(r)/ (*agent, operation*) *a.* secret.
undercurrent /'ʌndəkʌrənt/ *n.* courant (profond) *m.*
undercut /ʌndə'kʌt/ *v.t.* (*p.t.* **undercut,** *pres. p.* **undercutting**) (*comm.*) vendre moins cher que.
underdeveloped /ʌndədɪ'veləpt/ *a.* sous-développé.
underdog /'ʌndədɒg/ *n.* (*pol.*) opprimé(e) *m.* (*f.*); (*socially*) déshérité(e) *m.* (*f.*).
underdone /'ʌndədʌn/ *a.* pas assez cuit; (*steak*) saignant.
underestimate /ʌndər'estɪmeɪt/ *v.t.* sous-estimer.
underfed /'ʌndəfed/ *a.* sous-alimenté.
underfoot /ʌndə'fʊt/ *adv.* sous les pieds.
undergo /ʌndə'gəʊ/ *v.t.* (*p.t.* **-went,** *pp.* **-gone**) subir.
undergraduate /ʌndə'grædʒʊət/ *n.* étudiant(e) (qui prépare la licence) *m.* (*f.*).
underground [1] /ʌndə'graʊnd/ *adv.* sous terre.
underground [2] /'ʌndəgraʊnd/ *a.* souterrain; (*secret*) clandestin. ● *n.* (*rail.*) métro *m.*
undergrowth /'ʌndəgrəʊθ/ *n.* sous-bois *m. invar.*
underhand /'ʌndəhænd/ *a.* (*deceitful*) sournois.
under|lie /ʌndə'laɪ/ *v.t.* (*p.t.* **-lay,** *p.p.* **-lain,** *pres. p.* **-lying**) sous-tendre. **~lying** *a.* fondamental.
underline /ʌndə'laɪn/ *v.t.* souligner.
undermine /ʌndə'maɪn/ *v.t.* (*cliff, society, etc.*) miner, saper.
underneath /ʌndə'ni:θ/ *prep.* sous. ● *adv.* (en) dessous.
underpaid /ʌndə'peɪd/ *a.* sous-payé.
underpants /'ʌndəpænts/ *n. pl.* (*man's*) slip *m.*
underpass /'ʌndəpɑ:s/ *n.* (*for cars, people*) passage souterrain *m.*
underprivileged /ʌndə'prɪvəlɪdʒd/ *a.* défavorisé.
underrate /ʌndə'reɪt/ *v.t.* sous-estimer.
undershirt /'ʌndəʃɜ:t/ *n.* (*Amer.*) maillot (de corps) *m.*
undershorts /'ʌndəʃɔ:ts/ *n. pl.* (*Amer.*) caleçon *m.*
underskirt /'ʌndəʃkɜ:t/ *n.* jupon *m.*
understand /ʌndə'stænd/ *v.t./i.* (*p.t.* **-stood**) comprendre. **~able** *a.* compréhensible. **~ing** *a.* compréhensif; *n.* compréhension *f.*; (*agreement*) entente *f.*

understatement /'ʌndəsteɪtmənt/ *n.* litote *f.* **that's an ~,** c'est en deçà de la vérité.

understudy /'ʌndəstʌdɪ/ *n.* (*theatre*) doublure *f.*

undertak|e /ʌndə'teɪk/ *v.t.* (*p.t.* **-took,** *p.p.* **-taken**) entreprendre; (*responsibility*) assumer. **~e to,** s'engager à. **~ing** *n.* (*task*) entreprise *f.*; (*promise*) promesse *f.*

undertaker /'ʌndəteɪkə(r)/ *n.* entrepreneur de pompes funèbres *m.*

undertone /'ʌndətəʊn/ *n.* **in an ~,** à mi-voix.

undervalue /ʌndə'vælju:/ *v.t.* sous-évaluer.

underwater /ʌndə'wɔ:tə(r)/ *a.* sous-marin. ● *adv.* sous l'eau.

underwear /'ʌndəweə(r)/ *n.* sous-vêtements *m. pl.*

underwent /ʌndə'went/ *see* undergo.

underworld /'ʌndəwɜ:ld/ *n.* (*of crime*) milieu *m.*, pègre *f.*

undeserved /ʌndɪ'zɜ:vd/ *a.* immérité.

undesirable /ʌndɪ'zaɪərəbl/ *a.* peu souhaitable; (*person*) indésirable.

undies /'ʌndɪz/ *n. pl.* (*female underwear: fam.*) dessous *m. pl.*

undignified /ʌn'dɪgnɪfaɪd/ *a.* qui manque de dignité, sans dignité.

undisputed /ʌndɪ'spju:tɪd/ *a.* incontesté.

undistinguished /ʌndɪ'stɪŋgwɪʃt/ *a.* médiocre.

undo /ʌn'du:/ *v.t.* (*p.t.* **-did,** *p.p.* **-done** /-dʌn/) défaire, détacher; (*a wrong*) réparer. **leave ~ne,** ne pas faire.

undoubted /ʌn'daʊtɪd/ *a.* indubitable. **~ly** *adv.* indubitablement.

undreamt /ʌn'dremt/ *a.* **~ of,** insoupçonné, inimaginable.

undress /ʌn'dres/ *v.t./i.* (se) déshabiller. **get ~ed,** se déshabiller.

undu|e /ʌn'dju:/ *a.* excessif. **~ly** *adv.* excessivement.

undulate /'ʌndjʊleɪt/ *v.i.* onduler.

undying /ʌn'daɪɪŋ/ *a.* éternel.

unearth /ʌn'ɜ:θ/ *v.t.* déterrer.

unearthly /ʌn'ɜ:θlɪ/ *a.* mystérieux. **~ hour,** (*fam.*) heure indue *f.*

uneasy /ʌn'i:zɪ/ *a.* (*ill at ease*) mal à l'aise; (*worried*) inquiet; (*situation*) difficile.

uneducated /ʌn'edʒʊkeɪtɪd/ *a.* (*person*) inculte; (*speech*) populaire.

unemploy|ed /ʌnɪm'plɔɪd/ *a.* en chômage. **~ment** *n.* chômage *m.* **~ment benefit,** allocations de chômage *f. pl.*

unending /ʌn'endɪŋ/ *a.* interminable, sans fin.

unequal /ʌn'i:kwəl/ *a.* inégal. **~led** *a.* inégalé.

unerring /ʌn'ɜ:rɪŋ/ *a.* infaillible.

uneven /ʌn'i:vn/ *a.* inégal.

uneventful /ʌnɪ'ventfl/ *a.* sans incident.

unexpected /ʌnɪk'spektɪd/ *a.* inattendu, imprévu. **~ly** *adv.* subitement; (*arrive*) à l'improviste.

unfailing /ʌn'feɪlɪŋ/ *a.* constant, continuel; (*loyal*) fidèle.

unfair /ʌn'feə(r)/ *a.* injuste. **~ness** *n.* injustice *f.*

unfaithful /ʌn'feɪθfl/ *a.* infidèle.

unfamiliar /ʌnfə'mɪlɪə(r)/ *a.* inconnu, peu familier. **be ~ with,** ne pas connaître.

unfashionable /ʌn'fæʃənəbl/ *a.* (*clothes*) démodé. **it's ~ to,** ce n'est pas à la mode de.

unfasten /ʌn'fɑ:sn/ *v.t.* défaire.

unfavourable /ʌn'feɪvərəbl/ *a.* défavorable.

unfeeling /ʌn'fi:lɪŋ/ *a.* insensible.

unfinished /ʌn'fɪnɪʃt/ *a.* inachevé.

unfit /ʌn'fɪt/ *a.* (*med.*) peu en forme: (*unsuitable*) impropre (**for,** à). **~ to,** (*unable*) pas en état de.

unflinching /ʌn'flɪntʃɪŋ/ *a.* (*fearless*) intrépide.

unfold /ʌn'fəʊld/ *v.t.* déplier; (*expose*) exposer. ● *v.i.* se dérouler.

unforeseen /ʌnfɔ:'si:n/ *a.* imprévu.

unforgettable /ʌnfə'getəbl/ *a.* inoubliable.

unforgivable /ʌnfə'gɪvəbl/ *a.* impardonnable, inexcusable.

unfortunate /ʌn'fɔ:tʃʊnət/ *a.* malheureux; (*event*) fâcheux. **~ly** *adv.* malheureusement.

unfounded /ʌn'faʊndɪd/ *a.* (*rumour etc.*) sans fondement.

unfriendly /ʌn'frendlɪ/ *a.* peu amical, froid.

ungainly /ʌn'geɪnlɪ/ *a.* gauche.

ungodly /ʌn'gɒdlɪ/ *a.* impie. **~ hour,** (*fam.*) heure indue *f.*

ungrateful /ʌn'greɪtfl/ *a.* ingrat.

unhapp|y /ʌn'hæpɪ/ *a.* (**-ier, -iest**) malheureux, triste; (*not pleased*) mécontent (**with,** de). **~ily** *adv.* malheureusement. **~iness** *n.* tristesse *f.*

unharmed /ʌn'hɑ:md/ *a.* indemne, sain et sauf.

unhealthy /ʌn'helθɪ/ *a.* **(-ier, -iest)** (*climate etc.*) malsain; (*person*) en mauvaise santé.

unheard-of /ʌn'hɜ:dɒv/ *a.* inouï.

unhinge /ʌn'hɪndʒ/ *v.t.* (*person, mind*) déséquilibrer.

unholy /ʌn'həʊlɪ/ *a.* **(-ier, -iest)** (*person, act, etc.*) impie; (*great: fam.*) invraisemblable.

unhook /ʌn'hʊk/ *v.t.* décrocher; (*dress*) dégrafer.

unhoped /ʌn'həʊpt/ *a.* **~ for,** inespéré.

unhurt /ʌn'hɜ:t/ *a.* indemne.

unicorn /'ju:nɪkɔ:n/ *n.* licorne *f.*

uniform /'ju:nɪfɔ:m/ *n.* uniforme *m.* ● *a.* uniforme. **~ity** /-'fɔ:mətɪ/ *n.* uniformité *f.* **~ly** *adv.* uniformément.

unif|y /'ju:nɪfaɪ/ *v.t.* unifier. **~ication** /-ɪ'keɪʃn/ *n.* unification *f.*

unilateral /ju:nɪ'lætrəl/ *a.* unilatéral.

unimaginable /ʌnɪ'mædʒɪnəbl/ *a.* inimaginable.

unimportant /ʌnɪm'pɔ:tnt/ *a.* peu important.

uninhabited /ʌnɪn'hæbɪtɪd/ *a.* inhabité.

unintentional /ʌnɪn'tenʃənl/ *a.* involontaire.

uninterest|ed /ʌn'ɪntrəstɪd/ *a.* indifférent **(in,** à). **~ing** *a.* peu intéressant.

union /'ju:nɪən/ *n.* union *f.*; (*trade union*) syndicat *m.* **~ist** *n.* syndiqué(e) *m.* (*f.*). **U~ Jack,** drapeau britannique *m.*

unique /ju:'ni:k/ *a.* unique. **~ly** *adv.* exceptionnellement.

unisex /'ju:nɪseks/ *a.* unisexe.

unison /'ju:nɪsn/ *n.* **in ~,** à l'unisson.

unit /'ju:nɪt/ *n.* unité *f.*; (*of furniture etc.*) élément *m.*, bloc *m.* **~ trust,** (*équivalent d'une*) SICAV *f.*

unite /ju:'naɪt/ *v.t./i.* (s')unir. **U~d Kingdom,** Royaume Uni *m.* **U~d Nations,** Nations Unies *f. pl.* **U~d States (of America),** États-Unis (d'Amérique) *m. pl.*

unity /'ju:nətɪ/ *n.* unité *f.*; (*harmony: fig.*) harmonie *f.*

universal /ju:nɪ'vɜ:sl/ *a.* universel.

universe /'ju:nɪvɜ:s/ *n.* univers *m.*

university /ju:nɪ'vɜ:sətɪ/ *n.* université *f.* ● *a.* universitaire; (*student, teacher*) d'université.

unjust /ʌn'dʒʌst/ *a.* injuste.

unkempt /ʌn'kempt/ *a.* négligé.

unkind /ʌn'kaɪnd/ *a.* pas gentil, méchant. **~ly** *adv.* méchamment.

unknowingly /ʌn'nəʊɪŋlɪ/ *adv.* sans le savoir, inconsciemment.

unknown /ʌn'nəʊn/ *a.* inconnu. ● *n.* **the ~,** l'inconnu *m.*

unleash /ʌn'li:ʃ/ *v.t.* déchaîner.

unless /ən'les/ *conj.* à moins que.

unlike /ʌn'laɪk/ *a.* (*brothers etc.*) différents. ● *prep.* à la différence de; (*different from*) très différent de.

unlikel|y /ʌn'laɪklɪ/ *a.* improbable. **~ihood** *n.* improbabilité *f.*

unlimited /ʌn'lɪmɪtɪd/ *a.* illimité.

unlisted /ʌn'lɪstɪd/ *a.* (*comm.*) non inscrit à la cote; (*Amer.*) qui n'est pas dans l'annuaire.

unload /ʌn'ləʊd/ *v.t.* décharger.

unlock /ʌn'lɒk/ *v.t.* ouvrir.

unluck|y /ʌn'lʌkɪ/ *a.* **(-ier, -iest)** malheureux; (*number*) qui porte malheur. **~ily** *adv.* malheureusement.

unmarried /ʌn'mærɪd/ *a.* célibataire, qui n'est pas marié.

unmask /ʌn'mɑ:sk/ *v.t.* démasquer.

unmistakable /ʌnmɪ'steɪkəbl/ *a.* (*voice etc.*) facilement reconnaissable; (*clear*) très net.

unmitigated /ʌn'mɪtɪgeɪtɪd/ *a.* (*absolute*) absolu.

unmoved /ʌn'mu:vd/ *a.* indifférent **(by,** à), insensible **(by,** à).

unnatural /ʌn'nætʃrəl/ *a.* pas naturel, anormal.

unnecessary /ʌn'nesəsərɪ/ *a.* inutile; (*superfluous*) superflu.

unnerve /ʌn'nɜ:v/ *v.t.* troubler.

unnoticed /ʌn'nəʊtɪst/ *a.* inaperçu.

unobtainable /ʌnəb'teɪnəbl/ *n.* impossible à obtenir.

unobtrusive /ʌnəb'tru:sɪv/ *a.* (*person, object*) discret.

unofficial /ʌnə'fɪʃl/ *a.* officieux.

unorthodox /ʌn'ɔ:θədɒks/ *a.* peu orthodoxe.

unpack /ʌn'pæk/ *v.t.* (*suitcase etc.*) défaire; (*contents*) déballer. ● *v.i.* défaire sa valise.

unpalatable /ʌn'pælətəbl/ *a.* (*food, fact, etc.*) désagréable.

unparalleled /ʌn'pærəleld/ *a.* incomparable.

unpleasant /ʌn'pleznt/ *a.* désagréable **(to,** avec).

unplug /ʌn'plʌg/ *v.t.* (*electr.*) débrancher; (*unblock*) déboucher.

unpopular /ʌn'pɒpjʊlə(r)/ *a.* impopulaire. **~ with,** mal vu de.
unprecedented /ʌn'presɪdentɪd/ *a.* sans précédent.
unpredictable /ʌnprɪ'dɪktəbl/ *a.* imprévisible.
unprepared /ʌnprɪ'peəd/ *a.* non préparé; (*person*) qui n'a rien préparé. **be ~ for,** (*not expect*) ne pas s'attendre à.
unpretentious /ʌnprɪ'tenʃəs/ *a.* sans prétention(s).
unprincipled /ʌn'prɪnsəpld/ *a.* sans scrupules.
unprofessional /ʌnprə'feʃənl/ *a.* (*work*) d'amateur; (*conduct*) contraire au code professionel.
unpublished /ʌn'pʌblɪʃt/ *a.* inédit.
unqualified /ʌn'kwɒlɪfaɪd/ *a.* non diplômé; (*success etc.*) total. **be ~ to,** ne pas être qualifié pour.
unquestionabl|e /ʌn'kwestʃənəbl/ *a.* incontestable. **~y** *adv.* incontestablement.
unravel /ʌn'rævl/ *v.t.* (*p.t.* **unravelled**) démêler, débrouiller.
unreal /ʌn'rɪəl/ *a.* irréel.
unreasonable /ʌn'ri:znəbl/ *a.* déraisonnable, peu raisonnable.
unrecognizable /ʌnrekəg'naɪzəbl/ *a.* méconnaissable.
unrelated /ʌnrɪ'leɪtɪd/ *a.* (*facts*) sans rapport (**to,** avec).
unreliable /ʌnrɪ'laɪəbl/ *a.* peu sérieux; (*machine*) peu fiable.
unremitting /ʌnrɪ'mɪtɪŋ/ *a.* (*effort*) acharné; (*emotion*) inaltérable.
unreservedly /ʌnrɪ'zɜ:vɪdlɪ/ *adv.* sans réserve.
unrest /ʌn'rest/ *n.* troubles *m. pl.*
unrivalled /ʌn'raɪvld/ *a.* sans égal, incomparable.
unroll /ʌn'rəʊl/ *v.t.* dérouler.
unruffled /ʌn'rʌfld/ *a.* (*person*) qui n'a pas perdu son calme.
unruly /ʌn'ru:lɪ/ *a.* indiscipliné.
unsafe /ʌn'seɪf/ *a.* (*dangerous*) dangereux; (*person*) en danger.
unsaid /ʌn'sed/ *a.* **leave ~,** passer sous silence.
unsatisfactory /ʌnsætɪs'fæktərɪ/ *a.* peu satisfaisant.
unsavoury /ʌn'seɪvərɪ/ *a.* désagréable, répugnant.
unscathed /ʌn'skeɪðd/ *a.* indemne.
unscheduled /ʌn'ʃedju:ld, *Amer.* ʌn'skedju:ld/ *a.* pas prévu.
unscrew /ʌn'skru:/ *v.t.* dévisser.
unscrupulous /ʌn'skru:pjʊləs/ *a.* sans scrupules, malhonnête.
unseemly /ʌn'si:mlɪ/ *a.* inconvenant, incorrect, incongru.
unseen /ʌn'si:n/ *a.* inaperçu. ● *n.* (*translation*) version *f.*
unsettle /ʌn'setl/ *v.t.* troubler. **~d** *a.* (*weather*) instable.
unshakeable /ʌn'ʃeɪkəbl/ *a.* (*person, belief, etc.*) inébranlable.
unshaven /ʌn'ʃeɪvn/ *a.* pas rasé.
unsightly /ʌn'saɪtlɪ/ *a.* laid.
unskilled /ʌn'skɪld/ *a.* inexpert; (*worker*) non qualifié.
unsociable /ʌn'səʊʃəbl/ *a.* insociable, farouche.
unsophisticated /ʌnsə'fɪstɪkeɪtɪd/ *a.* peu sophistiqué, simple.
unsound /ʌn'saʊnd/ *a.* peu solide. **of ~ mind,** fou.
unspeakable /ʌn'spi:kəbl/ *a.* indescriptible; (*bad*) innommable.
unspecified /ʌn'spesɪfaɪd/ *a.* indéterminé.
unstable /ʌn'steɪbl/ *a.* instable.
unsteady /ʌn'stedɪ/ *a.* (*step*) chancelant; (*ladder*) instable; (*hand*) mal assuré.
unstuck /ʌn'stʌk/ *a.* décollé. **come ~,** (*fail: fam.*) échouer.
unsuccessful /ʌnsək'sesfl/ *a.* (*result, candidate*) malheureux; (*attempt*) infructueux. **be ~,** ne pas réussir (**in doing,** à faire).
unsuit|able /ʌn'su:təbl/ *a.* qui ne convient pas (**for,** à), peu approprié. **~ed** *a.* inapte (**to,** à).
unsure /ʌn'ʃɔ:(r)/ *a.* incertain.
unsuspecting /ʌnsə'spektɪŋ/ *a.* qui ne se doute de rien.
unsympathetic /ʌnsɪmpə'θetɪk/ *a.* (*unhelpful*) peu compréhensif; (*unpleasant*) antipathique.
untangle /ʌn'tæŋgl/ *v.t.* démêler.
untenable /ʌn'tenəbl/ *a.* intenable.
unthinkable /ʌn'θɪŋkəbl/ *a.* impensable, inconcevable.
untid|y /ʌn'taɪdɪ/ *a.* (**-ier, -iest**) (*person*) désordonné; (*clothes, hair, room*) en désordre; (*work*) mal soigné. **~ily** *adv.* sans soin.
untie /ʌn'taɪ/ *v.t.* (*knot, parcel*) défaire; (*person*) détacher.
until /ən'tɪl/ *prep.* jusqu'à. **not ~,** pas avant. ● *conj.* jusqu'à ce que; (*before*) avant que.
untimely /ʌn'taɪmlɪ/ *a.* inopportun; (*death*) prématuré.
untold /ʌn'təʊld/ *a.* incalculable.

untoward /ʌntəˈwɔːd/ *a.* fâcheux.
untrue /ʌnˈtruː/ *a.* faux.
unused[1] /ʌnˈjuːzd/ *a.* (*new*) neuf; (*not in use*) inutilisé.
unused[2] /ʌnˈjuːst/ *a.* **~ to,** peu habitué à.
unusual /ʌnˈjuːʒʊəl/ *a.* exceptionnel; (*strange*) insolite, étrange. **~ly** *adv.* exceptionnellement.
unveil /ʌnˈveɪl/ *v.t.* dévoiler.
unwanted /ʌnˈwɒntɪd/ *a.* (*useless*) superflu; (*child*) non désiré.
unwelcome /ʌnˈwelkəm/ *a.* fâcheux; (*guest*) importun.
unwell /ʌnˈwel/ *a.* indisposé.
unwieldy /ʌnˈwiːldɪ/ *a.* difficile à manier.
unwilling /ʌnˈwɪlɪŋ/ *a.* peu disposé (**to,** à); (*victim*) récalcitrant. **~ly** *adv.* à contrecœur.
unwind /ʌnˈwaɪnd/ *v.t./i.* (*p.t.* **unwound** /ʌnˈwaʊnd/) (se) dérouler; (*relax: fam.*) se détendre.
unwise /ʌnˈwaɪz/ *a.* imprudent.
unwittingly /ʌnˈwɪtɪŋlɪ/ *adv.* involontairement.
unworkable /ʌnˈwɜːkəbl/ *a.* (*plan etc.*) irréalisable.
unworthy /ʌnˈwɜːðɪ/ *a.* indigne.
unwrap /ʌnˈræp/ *v.t.* (*p.t.* **unwrapped**) ouvrir, défaire.
unwritten /ʌnˈrɪtn/ *a.* (*agreement*) verbal, tacite.
up /ʌp/ *adv.* en haut, en l'air; (*sun, curtain*) levé; (*out of bed*) levé, debout; (*finished*) fini. **be up,** (*level, price*) avoir monté. ● *prep.* (*a hill*) en haut de; (*a tree*) dans; (*a ladder*) sur. ● *v.t.* (*p.t.* **upped**) augmenter. **come** *or* **go up,** monter. **up in the bedroom,** là-haut dans la chambre. **up there,** là-haut. **up to,** jusqu'à; (*task*) à la hauteur de. **it is up to you,** ça dépend de vous (**to,** de). **be up to sth.,** (*able*) être capable de qch.; (*do*) faire qch.; (*plot*) préparer qch. **be up to,** (*in book*) en être à. **be up against,** faire face à. **be up in,** (*fam.*) s'y connaître en. **feel up to doing,** (*able*) être de taille à faire. **have ups and downs,** connaître des hauts et des bas. **up-and-coming** *a.* prometteur. **up-market** *a.* haut-de-gamme. **up to date,** moderne; (*news*) récent.
upbringing /ˈʌpbrɪŋɪŋ/ *n.* éducation *f.*
update /ʌpˈdeɪt/ *v.t.* mettre à jour.
upgrade /ʌpˈgreɪd/ *v.t.* (*person*) promouvoir; (*job*) revaloriser.
upheaval /ʌpˈhiːvl/ *n.* bouleversement *m.*
uphill /ʌpˈhɪl/ *a.* qui monte; (*fig.*) difficile. ● *adv.* **go ~,** monter.
uphold /ʌpˈhəʊld/ *v.t.* (*p.t.* **upheld**) maintenir.
upholster /ʌpˈhəʊlstə(r)/ *v.t.* (*pad*) rembourrer; (*cover*) recouvrir. **~y** *n.* (*in vehicle*) garniture *f.*
upkeep /ˈʌpkiːp/ *n.* entretien *m.*
upon /əˈpɒn/ *prep.* sur.
upper /ˈʌpə(r)/ *a.* supérieur. ● *n.* (*of shoe*) empeigne *f.* **have the ~ hand,** avoir le dessus. **~ class,** aristocratie *f.* **~most** *a.* (*highest*) le plus haut.
upright /ˈʌpraɪt/ *a.* droit. ● *n.* (*post*) montant *m.*
uprising /ˈʌpraɪzɪŋ/ *n.* soulèvement *m.*, insurrection *f.*
uproar /ˈʌprɔː(r)/ *n.* tumulte *m.*
uproot /ʌpˈruːt/ *v.t.* déraciner.
upset[1] /ʌpˈset/ *v.t.* (*p.t.* **upset,** *pres. p.* **upsetting**) (*overturn*) renverser; (*plan, stomach*) déranger; (*person*) contrarier, affliger. ● *a.* peiné.
upset[2] /ˈʌpset/ *n.* dérangement *m.*; (*distress*) chagrin *m.*
upshot /ˈʌpʃɒt/ *n.* résultat *m.*
upside-down /ʌpsaɪdˈdaʊn/ *adv.* (*in position, in disorder*) à l'envers, sens dessus dessous.
upstairs /ʌpˈsteəz/ *adv.* en haut. ● *a.* (*flat etc.*) d'en haut.
upstart /ˈʌpstɑːt/ *n.* (*pej.*) parvenu(e) *m.* (*f.*).
upstream /ʌpˈstriːm/ *adv.* en amont.
upsurge /ˈʌpsɜːdʒ/ *n.* recrudescence *f.*; (*of anger*) accès *m.*
uptake /ˈʌpteɪk/ *n.* **be quick on the ~,** comprendre vite.
uptight /ʌpˈtaɪt/ *a.* (*tense: fam.*) crispé; (*angry: fam.*) en colère.
upturn /ˈʌptɜːn/ *n.* amélioration *f.*
upward /ˈʌpwəd/ *a.* & *adv.*, **~s** *adv.* vers le haut.
uranium /jʊˈreɪnɪəm/ *n.* uranium *m.*
urban /ˈɜːbən/ *a.* urbain.
urbane /ɜːˈbeɪn/ *a.* courtois.
urchin /ˈɜːtʃɪn/ *n.* garnement *m.*
urge /ɜːdʒ/ *v.t.* conseiller vivement (**to do,** de faire). ● *n.* forte envie *f.* **~ on,** (*impel*) encourager.
urgen|t /ˈɜːdʒənt/ *a.* urgent; (*request*) pressant. **~cy** *n.* urgence *f.*; (*of request, tone*) insistance *f.* **~tly** *adv.* d'urgence.
urinal /jʊəˈraɪnl/ *n.* urinoir *m.*

urin|e /ˈjʊərɪn/ *n.* urine *f.* **~ate** *v.i.* uriner.

urn /ɜ:n/ *n.* urne *f.*; (*for tea, coffee*) fontaine *f.*

us /ʌs, *unstressed* əs/ *pron.* nous. **(to) us,** nous.

US *abbr. see* United States.

USA *abbr. see* United States of America.

usable /ˈju:zəbl/ *a.* utilisable.

usage /ˈju:sɪdʒ/ *n.* usage *m.*

use [1] /ju:z/ *v.t.* se servir de, utiliser; (*consume*) consommer. **~ up,** épuiser. **~r** /-ə(r)/ *n.* usager *m.* **~r-friendly** *a.* facile d'emploi.

use [2] /ju:s/ *n.* usage *m.*, emploi *m.* **in ~,** en usage. **it is no ~ shouting**/*etc.*, ça ne sert à rien de crier/*etc.* **make ~ of,** se servir de. **of ~,** utile.

used [1] /ju:zd/ *a.* (*second-hand*) d'occasion.

used [2] /ju:st/ *p.t.* **he ~ to do,** il faisait (autrefois), il avait l'habitude de faire. ● *a.* **~ to,** habitué à.

use|ful /ˈju:sfl/ *a.* utile. **~fully** *adv.* utilement. **~less** *a.* inutile; (*person*) incompétent.

usher /ˈʌʃə(r)/ *n.* (*in theatre, hall*) placeur *m.* ● *v.t.* **~ in,** faire entrer. **~ette** *n.* ouvreuse *f.*

USSR *abbr.* (*Union of Soviet Socialist Republics*) URSS *f.*

usual /ˈju:ʒʊəl/ *a.* habituel, normal. **as ~,** comme d'habitude. **~ly** *adv.* d'habitude.

usurp /ju:ˈzɜ:p/ *v.t.* usurper.

utensil /ju:ˈtensl/ *n.* ustensile *m.*

uterus /ˈju:tərəs/ *n.* utérus *m.*

utilitarian /ju:tɪlɪˈteərɪən/ *a.* utilitaire.

utility /ju:ˈtɪlətɪ/ *n.* utilité *f.* **(public) ~,** service public *m.*

utilize /ˈju:tɪlaɪz/ *v.t.* utiliser.

utmost /ˈʌtməʊst/ *a.* (*furthest, most intense*) extrême. **the ~ care**/*etc.*, (*greatest*) le plus grand soin/*etc.* ● *n.* **do one's ~,** faire tout son possible.

Utopia /ju:ˈtəʊpɪə/ *n.* utopie *f.* **~n** *a.* utopique.

utter [1] /ˈʌtə(r)/ *a.* complet, absolu. **~ly** *adv.* complètement.

utter [2] /ˈʌtə(r)/ *v.t.* proférer; (*sigh, shout*) pousser. **~ance** *n.* déclaration *f.* **give ~ance to,** exprimer.

U-turn /ˈju:tɜ:n/ *n.* demi-tour *m.*

V

vacan|t /ˈveɪkənt/ *a.* (*post*) vacant; (*seat etc.*) libre; (*look*) vague. **~cy** *n.* (*post*) poste vacant *m.*; (*room*) chambre disponible *f.*

vacate /vəˈkeɪt, *Amer.* ˈveɪkeɪt/ *v.t.* quitter.

vacation /veɪˈkeɪʃn/ *n.* (*Amer.*) vacances *f. pl.*

vaccinat|e /ˈvæksɪneɪt/ *v.t.* vacciner. **~ion** /-ˈneɪʃn/ *n.* vaccination *f.*

vaccine /ˈvæksi:n/ *n.* vaccin *m.*

vacuum /ˈvækjʊəm/ *n.* (*pl.* **-cuums** *or* **-cua**) vide *m.* **~ cleaner,** aspirateur *m.* **~ flask,** bouteille thermos *f.* (P.). **~-packed** *a.* emballé sous vide.

vagabond /ˈvægəbɒnd/ *n.* vagabond(e) *m.* (*f.*).

vagina /vəˈdʒaɪnə/ *n.* vagin *m.*

vagrant /ˈveɪgrənt/ *n.* vagabond(e) *m.* (*f.*), clochard(e) *m.* (*f.*).

vague /veɪg/ *a.* (**-er, -est**) vague; (*outline*) flou. **be ~ about,** ne pas préciser. **~ly** *adv.* vaguement.

vain /veɪn/ *a.* (**-er, -est**) (*conceited*) vaniteux; (*useless*) vain. **in ~,** en vain. **~ly** *adv.* en vain.

valentine /ˈvæləntaɪn/ *n.* (*card*) carte de la Saint-Valentin *f.*

valet /ˈvælɪt, ˈvæleɪ/ *n.* (*manservant*) valet de chambre *m.*

valiant /ˈvælɪənt/ *a.* courageux.

valid /ˈvælɪd/ *a.* valable. **~ity** /vəˈlɪdətɪ/ *n.* validité *f.*

validate /ˈvælɪdeɪt/ *v.t.* valider.

valley /ˈvælɪ/ *n.* vallée *f.*

valour, (*Amer.*) **valor** /ˈvælə(r)/ *n.* courage *m.*

valuable /ˈvæljʊəbl/ *a.* (*object*) de valeur; (*help etc.*) précieux. **~s** *n. pl.* objets de valeur *m. pl.*

valuation /væljʊˈeɪʃn/ *n.* expertise *f.*; (*of house*) évaluation *f.*

value /ˈvælju:/ *n.* valeur *f.* ● *v.t.* (*appraise*) évaluer; (*cherish*) attacher de la valeur à. **~ added tax,** taxe à la valeur ajoutée *f.*, TVA *f.* **~d** *a.* estimé. **~r** /-ə(r)/ *n.* expert *m.*

valve /vælv/ *n.* (*techn.*) soupape *f.*; (*of tyre*) valve *f.*; (*radio*) lampe *f.*

vampire /ˈvæmpaɪə(r)/ *n.* vampire *m.*

van /væn/ *n.* (*vehicle*) camionnette *f.*; (*rail.*) fourgon *m.*

vandal /ˈvændl/ *n.* vandale *m./f.* **~ism** /-əlɪzəm/ *n.* vandalisme *m.*

vandalize /'vændəlaɪz/ *v.t.* abîmer, détruire, saccager.
vanguard /'vængɑ:d/ *n.* (*of army, progress, etc.*) avant-garde *f.*
vanilla /və'nɪlə/ *n.* vanille *f.*
vanish /'vænɪʃ/ *v.i.* disparaître.
vanity /'vænətɪ/ *n.* vanité *f.* **~ case,** mallette de toilette *f.*
vantage-point /'vɑ:tɪdʒpɔɪnt/ *n.* (*place*) excellent point de vue *m.*
vapour /'veɪpə(r)/ *n.* vapeur *f.*
vari|able /'veərɪəbl/ *a.* variable. **~ation** /-'eɪʃn/ *n.* variation *f.* **~ed** /-ɪd/ *a.* varié.
variance /'veərɪəns/ *n.* **at ~,** en desaccord (**with,** avec).
variant /'veərɪənt/ *a.* différent. ● *n.* variante *f.*
varicose /'værɪkəʊs/ *a.* **~ veins,** varices *f. pl.*
variety /və'raɪətɪ/ *n.* variété *f.*; (*entertainment*) variétés *f. pl.*
various /'veərɪəs/ *a.* divers. **~ly** *adv.* diversement.
varnish /'vɑ:nɪʃ/ *n.* vernis *m.* ● *v.t.* vernir.
vary /'veərɪ/ *v.t./i.* varier.
vase /vɑ:z, *Amer.* veɪs/ *n.* vase *m.*
vast /vɑ:st/ *a.* vaste, immense. **~ly** *adv.* infiniment, extrêmement. **~ness** *n.* immensité *f.*
vat /væt/ *n.* cuve *f.*
VAT /vi:eɪ'ti:, væt/ *abbr.* (*value added tax*) TVA *f.*
vault[1] /vɔ:lt/ *n.* (*roof*) voûte *f.*; (*in bank*) chambre forte *f.*; (*tomb*) caveau *m.*; (*cellar*) cave *f.*
vault[2] /vɔ:lt/ *v.t./i.* sauter. ● *n.* saut *m.*
vaunt /vɔ:nt/ *v.t.* vanter.
VCR *abbr. see* video cassette recorder.
VDU *abbr. see* visual display unit.
veal /vi:l/ *n.* (*meat*) veau *m.*
veer /vɪə(r)/ *v.i.* tourner, virer.
vegan /'vi:gən/ *a.* & *n.* végétalien(-ne) (*m.* (*f.*)).
vegetable /'vedʒtəbl/ *n.* légume *m.* ● *a.* végétal. **~ garden,** (jardin) potager *m.*
vegetarian /vedʒɪ'teərɪən/ *a.* & *n.* végétarien(ne) (*m.* (*f.*)).
vegetate /'vedʒɪteɪt/ *v.i.* végéter.
vegetation /vedʒɪ'teɪʃn/ *n.* végétation *f.*
vehement /'vi:əmənt/ *a.* véhément. **~ly** *adv.* avec véhémence.
vehicle /'vi:ɪkl/ *n.* véhicule *m.*
veil /veɪl/ *n.* voile *m.* ● *v.t.* voiler.
vein /veɪn/ *n.* (*in body, rock*) veine *f.*; (*on leaf*) nervure *f.* (*mood*) esprit *m.*
velocity /vɪ'lɒsətɪ/ *n.* vélocité *f.*
velvet /'velvɪt/ *n.* velours *m.*
vending-machine /'vendɪŋməʃi:n/ *n.* distributeur automatique *m.*
vendor /'vendə(r)/ *n.* vendeu|r, -se *m., f.*
veneer /və'nɪə(r)/ *n.* placage *m.*; (*appearance: fig.*) vernis *m.*
venerable /'venərəbl/ *a.* vénérable.
venereal /və'nɪərɪəl/ *a.* vénérien.
venetian /və'ni:ʃn/ *a.* **~ blind,** jalousie *f.*
vengeance /'vendʒəns/ *n.* vengeance *f.* **with a ~,** furieusement.
venison /'venɪzn/ *n.* venaison *f.*
venom /'venəm/ *n.* venin *m.* **~ous** /'venəməs/ *a.* venimeux.
vent[1] /vent/ *n.* (*in coat*) fente *f.*
vent[2] /vent/ *n.* (*hole*) orifice *m.*; (*for air*) bouche d'aération *f.* ● *v.t.* (*anger*) décharger (**on,** sur). **give ~ to,** donner libre cours à.
ventilat|e /'ventɪleɪt/ *v.t.* ventiler. **~ion** /-'leɪʃn/ *n.* ventilation *f.* **~or** *n.* ventilateur *m.*
ventriloquist /ven'trɪləkwɪst/ *n.* ventriloque *m./f.*
venture /'ventʃə(r)/ *n.* entreprise *f.* ● *v.t./i.* (se) risquer.
venue /'venju:/ *n.* lieu de rencontre *or* de rendez-vous *m.*
veranda /və'rændə/ *n.* véranda *f.*
verb /vɜ:b/ *n.* verbe *m.*
verbal /'vɜ:bl/ *a.* verbal.
verbatim /vɜ:'beɪtɪm/ *adv.* textuellement, mot pour mot.
verdict /'vɜ:dɪkt/ *n.* verdict *m.*
verge /vɜ:dʒ/ *n.* bord *m.* ● *v.i.* **~ on,** friser, frôler. **on the ~ of doing,** sur le point de faire.
verif|y /'verɪfaɪ/ *v.t.* vérifier. **~ication** /-ɪ'keɪʃn/ *n.* vérification *f.*
vermicelli /vɜ:mɪ'selɪ/ *n.* vermicelle(s) *m.* (*pl.*).
vermin /'vɜ:mɪn/ *n.* vermine *f.*
vermouth /'vɜ:məθ/ *n.* vermouth *m.*
vernacular /və'nækjʊlə(r)/ *n.* langue *f.*; (*regional*) dialecte *m.*
versatil|e /'vɜ:sətaɪl, *Amer.* 'vɜ:sətl/ *a.* (*person*) aux talents variés; (*mind*) souple. **~ity** /-'tɪlətɪ/ *n.* souplesse *f.* **her ~ity,** la variété de ses talents.
verse /vɜ:s/ *n.* strophe *f.*; (*of Bible*) verset *m.*; (*poetry*) vers *m. pl.*
versed /vɜ:st/ *a.* **~ in,** versé dans.
version /'vɜ:ʃn/ *n.* version *f.*
versus /'vɜ:səs/ *prep.* contre.

vertebra /'vɜ:tɪbrə/ *n.* (*pl.* **-brae** /-bri:/) vertèbre *f.*
vertical /'vɜ:tɪkl/ *a.* vertical. **~ly** *adv.* verticalement.
vertigo /'vɜ:tɪgəʊ/ *n.* vertige *m.*
verve /vɜ:v/ *n.* fougue *f.*
very /'verɪ/ *adv.* très. ● *a.* (*actual*) même. **the ~ day/***etc.*, le jour/*etc.* même. **at the ~ end,** tout à la fin. **the ~ first,** le tout premier. **~ much,** beaucoup.
vessel /'vesl/ *n.* (*duct, ship*) vaisseau *m.*
vest /vest/ *n.* maillot de corps *m.*; (*waistcoat*: *Amer.*) gilet *m.*
vested /'vestɪd/ *a.* **~ interests,** droits acquis *m. pl.*, intérêts *m. pl.*
vestige /'vestɪdʒ/ *n.* vestige *m.*
vestry /'vestrɪ/ *n.* sacristie *f.*
vet /vet/ *n.* (*fam.*) vétérinaire *m./f.* ● *v.t.* (*p.t.* **vetted**) (*candidate etc.*) examiner (de près).
veteran /'vetərən/ *n.* vétéran *m.* **(war) ~,** ancien combattant *m.*
veterinary /'vetərɪnərɪ/ *a.* vétérinaire. **~ surgeon,** vétérinaire *m./f.*
veto /'vi:təʊ/ *n.* (*pl.* **-oes**) veto *m.*; (*right*) droit de veto *m.* ● *v.t.* mettre son veto à.
vex /veks/ *v.t.* contrarier, irriter. **~ed question,** question controversée *f.*
via /'vaɪə/ *prep.* via, par.
viable /'vaɪəbl/ *a.* (*baby, plan, firm*) viable.
viaduct /'vaɪədʌkt/ *n.* viaduc *m.*
vibrant /'vaɪbrənt/ *a.* vibrant.
vibrat|e /vaɪ'breɪt/ *v.t./i.* (faire) vibrer. **~ion** /-ʃn/ *n.* vibration *f.*
vicar /'vɪkə(r)/ *n.* pasteur *m.* **~age** *n.* presbytère *m.*
vicarious /vɪ'keərɪəs/ *a.* (*emotion*) ressenti indirectement.
vice[1] /vaɪs/ *n.* (*depravity*) vice *m.*
vice[2] /vaɪs/ *n.* (*techn.*) étau *m.*
vice- /vaɪs/ *pref.* vice-.
vice versa /'vaɪsɪ'vɜ:sə/ *adv.* vice versa.
vicinity /vɪ'sɪnətɪ/ *n.* environs *m. pl.* **in the ~ of,** aux environs de.
vicious /'vɪʃəs/ *a.* (*spiteful*) méchant; (*violent*) brutal. **~ circle,** cercle vicieux *m.* **~ly** *adv.* méchamment; brutalement.
victim /'vɪktɪm/ *n.* victime *f.*
victimiz|e /'vɪktɪmaɪz/ *v.t.* persécuter, martyriser. **~ation** /-'zeɪʃn/ *n.* persécution *f.*
victor /'vɪktə(r)/ *n.* vainqueur *m.*
Victorian /vɪk'tɔ:rɪən/ *a. & n.* victorien(ne) (*m.* (*f.*)).
victor|y /'vɪktərɪ/ *n.* victoire *f.* **~ious** /-'tɔ:rɪəs/ *a.* victorieux.
video /'vɪdɪəʊ/ *a.* (*game, camera*) vidéo *invar.* ● *n.* (*recorder*) magnétoscope *m.*; (*film*) vidéo *f.* **~ cassette,** vidéocassette *f.* **~ (cassette) recorder,** magnétoscope *m.* ● *v.t.* (*programme*) enregistrer.
videotape /'vɪdɪəʊteɪp/ *n.* bande vidéo *f.* ● *v.t.* (*programme*) enregistrer; (*wedding*) filmer avec une caméra vidéo.
vie /vaɪ/ *v.i.* (*pres. p.* **vying**) rivaliser (**with,** avec).
view /vju:/ *n.* vue *f.* ● *v.t.* (*watch*) regarder; (*consider*) considérer (**as,** comme); (*house*) visiter. **in my ~,** à mon avis. **in ~ of,** compte tenu de. **on ~,** exposé. **with a ~ to,** dans le but de. **~er** *n.* (*TV*) téléspecta|teur, -trice *m., f.*; (*for slides*) visionneuse *f.*
viewfinder /'vju:faɪndə(r)/ *n.* viseur *m.*
viewpoint /'vju:pɔɪnt/ *n.* point de vue *m.*
vigil /'vɪdʒɪl/ *n.* veille *f.*; (*over sick person, corpse*) veillée *f.*
vigilan|t /'vɪdʒɪlənt/ *a.* vigilant. **~ce** *n.* vigilance *f.*
vig|our, (*Amer.*) **vigor** /'vɪgə(r)/ *n.* vigueur *f.* **~orous** *a.* vigoureux.
vile /vaɪl/ *a.* (*base*) infâme, vil; (*bad*) abominable, exécrable.
vilify /'vɪlɪfaɪ/ *v.t.* diffamer.
villa /'vɪlə/ *n.* villa *f.*, pavillon *m.*
village /'vɪlɪdʒ/ *n.* village *m.* **~r** /-ə(r)/ *n.* villageois(e) *m.* (*f.*).
villain /'vɪlən/ *n.* scélérat *m.*, bandit *m.*; (*in story etc.*) méchant *m.* **~y** *n.* infamie *f.*
vindicat|e /'vɪndɪkeɪt/ *v.t.* justifier. **~ion** /-'keɪʃn/ *n.* justification *f.*
vindictive /vɪn'dɪktɪv/ *a.* vindicatif.
vine /vaɪn/ *n.* vigne *f.*
vinegar /'vɪnɪgə(r)/ *n.* vinaigre *m.*
vineyard /'vɪnjəd/ *n.* vignoble *m.*
vintage /'vɪntɪdʒ/ *n.* (*year*) année *f.*, millésime *m.* ● *a.* (*wine*) de grand cru; (*car*) d'époque.
vinyl /'vaɪnɪl/ *n.* vinyle *m.*
viola /vɪ'əʊlə/ *n.* (*mus.*) alto *m.*
violat|e /'vaɪəleɪt/ *v.t.* violer. **~ion** /-'leɪʃn/ *n.* violation *f.*

violen|t /ˈvaɪələnt/ *a.* violent. **~ce** *n.* violence *f.* **~tly** *adv.* violemment, avec violence.

violet /ˈvaɪələt/ *n.* (*bot.*) violette *f.*; (*colour*) violet *m.* ● *a.* violet.

violin /vaɪəˈlɪn/ *n.* violon *m.* **~ist** *n.* violoniste *m./f.*

VIP /vi:aɪˈpi:/ *abbr.* (*very important person*) personnage de marque *m.*

viper /ˈvaɪpə(r)/ *n.* vipère *f.*

virgin /ˈvɜ:dʒɪn/ *n.* (*woman*) vierge *f.* ● *a.* vierge. **be a ~,** (*woman, man*) être vierge. **~ity** /vəˈdʒɪnətɪ/ *n.* virginité *f.*

Virgo /ˈvɜ:gəʊ/ *n.* la Vierge.

viril|e /ˈvɪraɪl, *Amer.* ˈvɪrəl/ *a.* viril. **~ity** /vɪˈrɪlətɪ/ *n.* virilité *f.*

virtual /ˈvɜ:tʃʊəl/ *a.* vrai. **a ~ failure**/*etc.*, pratiquement un échec/*etc.* **~ly** *adv.* pratiquement.

virtue /ˈvɜ:tʃu:/ *n.* (*goodness, chastity*) vertu *f.*; (*merit*) mérite *m.* **by** *or* **in ~ of,** en raison de.

virtuos|o /vɜ:tʃʊˈəʊsəʊ/ *n.* (*pl.* **-si** /-si:/) virtuose *m./f.* **~ity** /-ˈɒsətɪ/ *n.* virtuosité *f.*

virtuous /ˈvɜ:tʃʊəs/ *a.* vertueux.

virulent /ˈvɪrʊlənt/ *a.* virulent.

virus /ˈvaɪərəs/ *n.* (*pl.* **-uses**) virus *m.*

visa /ˈvi:zə/ *n.* visa *m.*

viscount /ˈvaɪkaʊnt/ *n.* vicomte *m.*

viscous /ˈvɪskəs/ *a.* visqueux.

vise /vaɪs/ *n.* (*Amer.*) étau *m.*

visib|le /ˈvɪzəbl/ *a.* (*discernible, obvious*) visible. **~ility** /-ˈbɪlətɪ/ *n.* visibilité *f.* **~ly** *adv.* visiblement.

vision /ˈvɪʒn/ *n.* vision *f.*

visionary /ˈvɪʒənərɪ/ *a.* & *n.* visionnaire (*m./f.*).

visit /ˈvɪzɪt/ *v.t.* (*p.t.* **visited**) (*person*) rendre visite à; (*place*) visiter. ● *v.i.* être en visite. ● *n.* (*tour, call*) visite *f.*; (*stay*) séjour *m.* **~or** *n.* visiteu|r, -se *m., f.*; (*guest*) invité(e) *m.* (*f.*); (*in hotel*) client(e) *m.* (*f.*).

visor /ˈvaɪzə(r)/ *n.* visière *f.*

vista /ˈvɪstə/ *n.* perspective *f.*

visual /ˈvɪʒʊəl/ *a.* visuel. **~ display unit,** visuel *m.*, console de visualisation *f.* **~ly** *adv.* visuellement.

visualize /ˈvɪʒʊəlaɪz/ *v.t.* se représenter; (*foresee*) envisager.

vital /ˈvaɪtl/ *a.* vital. **~ statistics,** (*fam.*) mensurations *f. pl.*

vitality /vaɪˈtælətɪ/ *n.* vitalité *f.*

vitally /ˈvaɪtəlɪ/ *adv.* extrêmement.

vitamin /ˈvɪtəmɪn/ *n.* vitamine *f.*

vivac|ious /vɪˈveɪʃəs/ *a.* plein d'entrain, animé. **~ity** /-æsətɪ/ *n.* vivacité *f.*, entrain *m.*

vivid /ˈvɪvɪd/ *a.* vif; (*graphic*) vivant. **~ly** *adv.* vivement; (*describe*) de façon vivante.

vivisection /vɪvɪˈsekʃn/ *n.* vivisection *f.*

vocabulary /vəˈkæbjʊlərɪ/ *n.* vocabulaire *m.*

vocal /ˈvəʊkl/ *a.* vocal; (*person*: *fig.*) qui s'exprime franchement. **~ cords,** cordes vocales *f. pl.* **~ist** *n.* chanteu|r, -se *m., f.*

vocation /vəˈkeɪʃn/ *n.* vocation *f.* **~al** *a.* professionnel.

vociferous /vəˈsɪfərəs/ *a.* bruyant.

vodka /ˈvɒdkə/ *n.* vodka *f.*

vogue /vəʊg/ *n.* (*fashion, popularity*) vogue *f.* **in ~,** en vogue.

voice /vɔɪs/ *n.* voix *f.* ● *v.t.* (*express*) formuler.

void /vɔɪd/ *a.* vide (**of,** de); (*not valid*) nul. ● *n.* vide *m.*

volatile /ˈvɒlətaɪl, *Amer.* ˈvɒlətl/ *a.* (*person*) versatile; (*situation*) variable.

volcan|o /vɒlˈkeɪnəʊ/ *n.* (*pl.* **-oes**) volcan *m.* **~ic** /-ænɪk/ *a.* volcanique.

volition /vəˈlɪʃn/ *n.* **of one's own ~,** de son propre gré.

volley /ˈvɒlɪ/ *n.* (*of blows etc., in tennis*) volée *f.*; (*of gunfire*) salve *f.* **~-ball** *n.* volley(-ball) *m.*

volt /vəʊlt/ *n.* (*electr.*) volt *m.* **~age** *n.* voltage *m.*

voluble /ˈvɒljʊbl/ *a.* volubile.

volume /ˈvɒlju:m/ *n.* volume *m.*

voluntar|y /ˈvɒləntərɪ/ *a.* volontaire; (*unpaid*) bénévole. **~ily** /-trəlɪ, *Amer.* -ˈterəlɪ/ *adv.* volontairement.

volunteer /vɒlənˈtɪə(r)/ *n.* volontaire *m./f.* ● *v.i.* s'offrir (**to do,** pour faire); (*mil.*) s'engager comme volontaire. ● *v.t.* offrir.

voluptuous /vəˈlʌptʃʊəs/ *a.* voluptueux.

vomit /ˈvɒmɪt/ *v.t./i.* (*p.t.* **vomited**) vomir. ● *n.* vomi(ssement) *m.*

voracious /vəˈreɪʃəs/ *a.* vorace.

vot|e /vəʊt/ *n.* vote *m.*; (*right*) droit de vote *m.* ● *v.t./i.* voter. **~ (in),** (*person*) élire. **~er** *n.* élec|teur, -trice *m., f.* **~ing** *n.* vote *m.* (**of,** de); (*poll*) scrutin *m.*

vouch /ˈvaʊtʃ/ *v.i.* **~ for,** se porter garant de, répondre de.

voucher /ˈvaʊtʃə(r)/ *n.* bon *m.*

vow /vaʊ/ *n.* vœu *m.* ● *v.t.* (*loyalty etc.*) jurer (**to,** à). ~ **to do,** jurer de faire.

vowel /ˈvaʊəl/ *n.* voyelle *f.*

voyage /ˈvɔɪɪdʒ/ *n.* voyage (par mer) *m.*

vulgar /ˈvʌlgə(r)/ *a.* vulgaire. ~**ity** /-ˈgærətɪ/ *n.* vulgarité *f.*

vulnerab|le /ˈvʌlnərəbl/ *a.* vulnérable. ~**ility** /-ˈbɪlətɪ/ *n.* vulnérabilité *f.*

vulture /ˈvʌltʃə(r)/ *n.* vautour *m.*

W

wad /wɒd/ *n.* (*pad*) tampon *m.*; (*bundle*) liasse *f.*

wadding /ˈwɒdɪŋ/ *n.* rembourrage *m.*, ouate *f.*

waddle /ˈwɒdl/ *v.i.* se dandiner.

wade /weɪd/ *v.i.* ~ **through,** (*mud etc.*) patauger dans; (*book*: *fig.*) avancer péniblement dans.

wafer /ˈweɪfə(r)/ *n.* (*biscuit*) gaufrette *f.*; (*relig.*) hostie *f.*

waffle[1] /ˈwɒfl/ *n.* (*talk*: *fam.*) verbiage *m.* ● *v.i.* (*fam.*) divaguer.

waffle[2] /ˈwɒfl/ *n.* (*cake*) gaufre *f.*

waft /wɒft/ *v.i.* flotter. ● *v.t.* porter.

wag /wæg/ *v.t./i.* (*p.t.* **wagged**) (*tail*) remuer.

wage[1] /weɪdʒ/ *v.t.* (*campaign*) mener. ~ **war,** faire la guerre.

wage[2] /weɪdʒ/ *n.* (*weekly, daily*) salaire *m.* ~**s,** salaire *m.* ~**-earner** *n.* salarié(e) *m.* (*f.*).

wager /ˈweɪdʒə(r)/ *n.* (*bet*) pari *m.* ● *v.t.* parier (**that,** que).

waggle /ˈwægl/ *v.t./i.* remuer.

wagon /ˈwægən/ *n.* (*horse-drawn*) chariot *m.*; (*rail.*) wagon (de marchandises) *m.*

waif /weɪf/ *n.* enfant abandonné(e) *m.*(*f.*).

wail /weɪl/ *v.i.* (*utter cry or complaint*) gémir. ● *n.* gémissement *m.*

waist /weɪst/ *n.* taille *f.*

waistcoat /ˈweɪskəʊt/ *n.* gilet *m.*

wait /weɪt/ *v.t./i.* attendre. ● *n.* attente *f.* **I can't** ~, je n'en peux plus d'impatience. **let's** ~ **and see,** attendons voir. **while you** ~, sur place. ~ **for,** attendre. ~ **on,** servir. ~**ing-list** *n.* liste d'attente *f.* ~**ing-room** *n.* salle d'attente *f.*

wait|er /ˈweɪtə(r)/ *n.* garçon *m.*, serveur *m.* ~**ress** *n.* serveuse *f.*

waive /weɪv/ *v.t.* renoncer à

wake[1] /weɪk/ *v.t./i.* (*p.t.* **woke,** *p.p.* **woken**). ~ **(up),** (se) réveiller.

wake[2] /weɪk/ *n.* (*track*) sillage *m.* **in the** ~ **of,** (*after*) à la suite de.

waken /ˈweɪkən/ *v.t./i.* (se) réveiller, (s')éveiller.

Wales /weɪlz/ *n.* pays de Galles *m.*

walk /wɔːk/ *v.i.* marcher; (*not ride*) aller à pied; (*stroll*) se promener. ● *v.t.* (*streets*) parcourir; (*distance*) faire à pied; (*dog*) promener. ● *n.* promenade *f.*, tour *m.*; (*gait*) démarche *f.*; (*pace*) marche *f.*, pas *m.*; (*path*) allée *f.* ~ **of life,** condition sociale *f.* ~ **out,** (*go away*) partir; (*worker*) faire grève. ~**-out** *n.* grève surprise *f.* ~ **out on,** abandonner. ~**-over** *n.* victoire facile *f.*

walker /ˈwɔːkə(r)/ *n.* (*person*) marcheu|r, -se *m.*, *f.*

walkie-talkie /wɔːkɪˈtɔːkɪ/ *n.* talkie-walkie *m.*

walking /ˈwɔːkɪŋ/ *n.* marche (à pied) *f.* ● *a.* (*corpse, dictionary*: *fig.*) vivant. ~**-stick** *n.* canne *f.*

Walkman /ˈwɔːkmən/ *n.* (P.) Walkman (P.) *m.*, baladeur *m.*

wall /wɔːl/ *n.* mur *m.*; (*of tunnel, stomach, etc.*) paroi *f.* ● *a.* mural. ● *v.t.* (*city*) fortifier. **go to the** ~, (*firm*) faire faillite.

wallet /ˈwɒlɪt/ *n.* portefeuille *m.*

wallflower /ˈwɔːlflaʊə(r)/ *n.* (*bot.*) giroflée *f.*

wallop /ˈwɒləp/ *v.t.* (*p.t.* **walloped**) (*hit*: *sl.*) taper sur. ● *n.* (*blow*: *sl.*) grand coup *m.*

wallow /ˈwɒləʊ/ *v.i.* se vautrer.

wallpaper /ˈwɔːlpeɪpə(r)/ *n.* papier peint *m.* ● *v.t.* tapisser.

walnut /ˈwɔːlnʌt/ *n.* (*nut*) noix *f.*; (*tree*) noyer *m.*

walrus /ˈwɔːlrəs/ *n.* morse *m.*

waltz /wɔːls/ *n.* valse *f.* ● *v.i.* valser.

wan /wɒn/ *a.* pâle, blême.

wand /wɒnd/ *n.* baguette (magique) *f.*

wander /ˈwɒndə(r)/ *v.i.* errer; (*stroll*) flâner; (*digress*) s'écarter du sujet; (*in mind*) divaguer. ~**er** *n.* vagabond(e) *m.* (*f.*).

wane /weɪn/ *v.i.* décroître. ● *n.* **on the** ~, (*strength, fame, etc.*) en déclin; (*person*) sur son déclin.

wangle /ˈwæŋgl/ *v.t.* (*obtain*: *sl.*) se débrouiller pour avoir.

want /wɒnt/ *v.t.* vouloir (**to do,** faire); (*need*) avoir besoin de (**doing,** d'être fait); (*ask for*) demander. ● *v.i.* **~ for,** manquer de. ● *n.* (*need, poverty*) besoin *m.*; (*desire*) désir *m.*; (*lack*) manque *m.* **I ~ you to do it,** je veux que vous le fassiez. **for ~ of,** faute de. **~ed** *a.* (*criminal*) recherché par la police.

wanting /ˈwɒntɪŋ/ *a.* **be ~,** manquer (**in,** de).

wanton /ˈwɒntən/ *a.* (*cruelty*) gratuit; (*woman*) impudique.

war /wɔː(r)/ *n.* guerre *f.* **at ~,** en guerre. **on the ~-path,** sur le sentier de la guerre.

ward /wɔːd/ *n.* (*in hospital*) salle *f.*; (*minor: jurid.*) pupille *m./f.*; (*pol.*) division électorale *f.* ● *v.t.* **~ off,** (*danger*) prévenir; (*blow, anger*) détourner.

warden /ˈwɔːdn/ *n.* direc|teur, -trice *m., f.*; (*of park*) gardien(ne) *m.* (*f.*). **(traffic) ~,** contractuel(le) *m.* (*f.*).

warder /ˈwɔːdə(r)/ *n.* gardien (de prison) *m.*

wardrobe /ˈwɔːdrəʊb/ *n.* (*place*) armoire *f.*; (*clothes*) garde-robe *f.*

warehouse /ˈweəhaʊs/ *n.* (*pl.* **-s** /-haʊzɪz/) entrepôt *m.*

wares /weəz/ *n. pl.* (*goods*) marchandises *f. pl.*

warfare /ˈwɔːfeə(r)/ *n.* guerre *f.*

warhead /ˈwɔːhed/ *n.* ogive *f.*

warily /ˈweərɪlɪ/ *adv.* avec prudence.

warm /wɔːm/ *a.* (**-er, -est**) chaud; (*hearty*) chaleureux. **be** *or* **feel ~,** avoir chaud. **it is ~,** il fait chaud. ● *v.t./i.* **~ (up),** (se) réchauffer; (*food*) chauffer; (*liven up*) (s')animer; (*exercise*) s'échauffer. **~-hearted** *a.* chaleureux. **~ly** *adv.* (*wrap up etc.*) chaudement; (*heartily*) chaleureusement. **~th** *n.* chaleur *f.*

warn /wɔːn/ *v.t.* avertir, prévenir. **~ s.o. off sth.,** (*advise against*) mettre qn. en garde contre qch.; (*forbid*) interdire qch. à qn. **~ing** *n.* avertissement *m.*; (*notice*) avis *m.* **without ~ing,** sans prévenir. **~ing light,** voyant *m.* **~ing triangle,** triangle de sécurité *m.*

warp /wɔːp/ *v.t./i.* (*wood etc.*) (se) voiler; (*pervert*) pervertir.

warrant /ˈwɒrənt/ *n.* (*for arrest*) mandat (d'arrêt) *m.*; (*comm.*) autorisation *f.* ● *v.t.* justifier.

warranty /ˈwɒrəntɪ/ *n.* garantie *f.*

warring /ˈwɔːrɪŋ/ *a.* en guerre.

warrior /ˈwɒrɪə(r)/ *n.* guerr|ier, -ière *m., f.*

warship /ˈwɔːʃɪp/ *n.* navire de guerre *m.*

wart /wɔːt/ *n.* verrue *f.*

wartime /ˈwɔːtaɪm/ *n.* **in ~,** en temps de guerre.

wary /ˈweərɪ/ *a.* (**-ier, -iest**) prudent.

was /wɒz, *unstressed* wəz/ *see* be.

wash /wɒʃ/ *v.t./i.* (se) laver; (*flow over*) baigner. ● *n.* lavage *m.*; (*clothes*) lessive *f.*; (*of ship*) sillage *m.* **have a ~,** se laver. **~-basin** *n.* lavabo *m.* **~-cloth** *n.* (*Amer.*) gant de toilette *m.* **~ down,** (*meal*) arroser. **~ one's hands of,** se laver les mains de. **~ out,** (*cup etc.*) laver; (*stain*) (faire) partir. **~-out** *n.* (*sl.*) fiasco *m.* **~-room** *n.* (*Amer.*) toilettes *f. pl.* **~ up,** faire la vaisselle; (*Amer.*) se laver. **~able** *a.* lavable. **~ing** *n.* lessive *f.* **~ing-machine** *n.* machine à laver *f.* **~ing-powder** *n.* lessive *f.* **~ing-up** *n.* vaisselle *f.*; **~ing-up liquid,** produit pour la vaisselle *m.*

washed-out /wɒʃtˈaʊt/ *a.* (*faded*) délavé; (*tired*) lessivé; (*ruined*) anéanti.

washer /ˈwɒʃə(r)/ *n.* rondelle *f.*

wasp /wɒsp/ *n.* guêpe *f.*

wastage /ˈweɪstɪdʒ/ *n.* gaspillage *m.* **some ~,** (*in goods, among candidates, etc.*) du déchet.

waste /weɪst/ *v.t.* gaspiller; (*time*) perdre. ● *v.i.* **~ away,** dépérir. ● *a.* superflu; (*product*) de rebut. ● *n.* gaspillage *m.*; (*of time*) perte *f.*; (*rubbish*) déchets *m. pl.* **lay ~,** dévaster. **~ disposal unit,** broyeur d'ordures *m.* **~ (land),** (*desolate*) terre désolée *f.*; (*unused*) terre inculte *f.*; (*in town*) terrain vague *m.* **~ paper,** vieux papiers *m. pl.* **~-paper basket,** corbeille (à papier) *f.* **~-pipe** *n.* vidange *f.*

wasteful /ˈweɪstfl/ *a.* peu économique; (*person*) gaspilleur.

watch /wɒtʃ/ *v.t./i.* (*television*) regarder; (*observe*) observer; (*guard, spy on*) surveiller; (*be careful about*) faire attention à. ● *n.* (*for telling time*) montre *f.*; (*naut.*) quart. **be on the ~,** guetter. **keep ~ on,** surveiller. **~-dog** *n.* chien de garde *m.* **~ out,** (*take care*) faire attention (**for,** à). **~ out for,** guetter. **~-tower** *n.* tour de guet *f.* **~ful** *a.* vigilant.

watchmaker /wɒtʃmeɪkə(r)/ *n.* horlog|er, -ère *m., f.*

watchman /ˈwɒtʃmən/ *n.* (*pl.* **-men**) (*of building*) gardien *m.*

water /ˈwɔːtə(r)/ *n.* eau *f.* ● *v.t.* arroser. ● *v.i.* (*of eyes*) larmoyer. **my/his/***etc.* **mouth ~s,** l'eau me/lui/*etc.* vient à la bouche. **by ~,** en bateau. **~-bottle** *n.* bouillotte *f.* **~-closet** *n.* waters *m. pl.* **~-colour** *n.* couleur pour aquarelle *f.*; (*painting*) aquarelle *f.* **~ down,** couper (d'eau); (*tone down*) édulcorer. **~ heater,** chauffe-eau *m.* **~-ice** *n.* sorbet *m.* **~-lily** *n.* nénuphar *m.* **~-main** *n.* canalisation d'eau *f.* **~-melon** *n.* pastèque *f.* **~-pistol** *n.* pistolet à eau *m.* **~ polo,** water-polo *m.* **~ power,** énergie hydraulique *f.* **~-skiing** *n.* ski nautique *m.*

watercress /ˈwɔːtəkres/ *n.* cresson (de fontaine) *m.*

waterfall /ˈwɔːtəfɔːl/ *n.* chute d'eau *f.*, cascade *f.*

watering-can /ˈwɔːtərɪŋkæn/ *n.* arrosoir *m.*

waterlogged /ˈwɔːtəlɒgd/ *a.* imprégné d'eau; (*land*) détrempé.

watermark /ˈwɔːtəmɑːk/ *n.* (*in paper*) filigrane *m.*

waterproof /ˈwɔːtəpruːf/ *a.* (*material*) imperméable.

watershed /ˈwɔːtəʃed/ *n.* (*in affairs*) tournant décisif *m.*

watertight /ˈwɔːtətaɪt/ *a.* étanche.

waterway /ˈwɔːtəweɪ/ *n.* voie navigable *f.*

waterworks /ˈwɔːtəwɜːks/ *n.* (*place*) station hydraulique *f.*

watery /ˈwɔːtərɪ/ *a.* (*colour*) délavé; (*eyes*) humide; (*soup*) trop liquide; (*tea*) faible.

watt /wɒt/ *n.* watt *m.*

wav|e /weɪv/ *n.* vague *f.*; (*in hair*) ondulation *f.*; (*radio*) onde *f.*; (*sign*) signe *m.* ● *v.t.* agiter. ● *v.i.* faire signe (de la main); (*move in wind*) flotter. **~y** *a.* (*line*) onduleux; (*hair*) ondulé.

wavelength /ˈweɪvleŋθ/ *n.* (*radio & fig.*) longueur d'ondes *f.*

waver /ˈweɪvə(r)/ *v.i.* vaciller.

wax[1] /wæks/ *n.* cire *f.*; (*for skis*) fart *m.* ● *v.t.* cirer; farter; (*car*) astiquer. **~en, ~y** *adjs.* cireux.

wax[2] /wæks/ *v.i.* (*of moon*) croître.

waxwork /ˈwækswɜːk/ *n.* (*dummy*) figure de cire *f.*

way /weɪ/ *n.* (*road, path*) chemin *m.* (**to,** de); (*distance*) distance *f.*; (*direction*) direction *f.*; (*manner*) façon *f.*; (*means*) moyen *m.*; (*particular*) égard *m.* **~s,** (*habits*) habitudes *f. pl.* ● *adv.* (*fam.*) loin. **be in the ~,** bloquer le passage; (*hindrance*: *fig.*) gêner (qn.). **be on one's** *or* **the ~,** être sur son *or* le chemin. **by the ~,** à propos. **by the ~side,** au bord de la route. **by ~ of,** comme; (*via*) par. **go out of one's ~,** se donner du mal pour. **in a ~,** dans un sens. **make one's ~ somewhere,** se rendre quelque part. **push one's ~ through,** se frayer un passage. **that ~,** par là. **this ~,** par ici. **~ in,** entrée *f.* **~ out,** sortie *f.* **~-out** *a.* (*strange*: *fam.*) original.

waylay /ˈweɪleɪ/ *v.t.* (*p.t.* **-laid**) (*assail*) assaillir; (*stop*) accrocher.

wayward /ˈweɪwəd/ *a.* capricieux.

WC /dʌb(ə)ljuːˈsiː/ *n.* w.-c. *m. pl.*

we /wiː/ *pron.* nous.

weak /wiːk/ *a.* (**-er, -est**) faible; (*delicate*) fragile. **~ly** *adv.* faiblement; *a.* faible. **~ness** *n.* faiblesse *f.*; (*fault*) point faible *m.* **a ~ness for,** (*liking*) un faible pour.

weaken /ˈwiːkən/ *v.t.* affaiblir ● *v.i.* s'affaiblir, faiblir.

weakling /ˈwiːklɪŋ/ *n.* gringalet *m.*

wealth /welθ/ *n.* richesse *f.*; (*riches, resources*) richesses *f. pl.*; (*quantity*) profusion *f.*

wealthy /ˈwelθɪ/ *a.* (**-ier, -iest**) riche. ● *n.* **the ~,** les riches *m. pl.*

wean /wiːn/ *v.t.* (*baby*) sevrer.

weapon /ˈwepən/ *n.* arme *f.*

wear /weə(r)/ *v.t.* (*p.t.* **wore,** *p.p.* **worn**) porter; (*put on*) mettre; (*expression etc.*) avoir. ● *v.i.* (*last*) durer. **~ (out),** (s')user. ● *n.* usage *m.*; (*damage*) usure *f.*; (*clothing*) vêtements *m. pl.* **~ down,** user. **~ off,** (*colour, pain*) passer. **~ on,** (*time*) passer. **~ out,** (*exhaust*) épuiser.

wear|y /ˈwɪərɪ/ *a.* (**-ier, -iest**) fatigué, las; (*tiring*) fatigant. ● *v.i.* **~y of,** se lasser de. **~ily** *adv.* avec lassitude. **~iness** *n.* lassitude *f.*, fatigue *f.*

weasel /ˈwiːzl/ *n.* belette *f.*

weather /ˈweðə(r)/ *n.* temps *m.* ● *a.* météorologique. ● *v.t.* (*survive*) réchapper de *or* à. **under the ~,** patraque. **~-beaten** *a.* tanné. **~**

forecast, météo *f.* **~-vane** *n.* girouette *f.*

weathercock /'weðəkɒk/ *n.* girouette *f.*

weave /wi:v/ *v.t./i.* (*p.t.* **wove,** *p.p.* **woven**) tisser; (*basket etc.*) tresser; (*move*) se faufiler. ● *n.* (*style*) tissage *m.* **~r** /-ə(r)/ *n.* tisserand(e) *m.* (*f.*).

web /web/ *n.* (*of spider*) toile *f.*; (*fabric*) tissu *m.*; (*on foot*) palmure *f.* **~bed** *a.* (*foot*) palmé. **~bing** *n.* (*in chair*) sangles *f. pl.*

wed /wed/ *v.t.* (*p.t.* **wedded**) épouser. ● *v.i.* se marier. **~ded to,** (*devoted to*: *fig.*) attaché à.

wedding /'wedɪŋ/ *n.* mariage *m.* **~-ring** *n.* alliance *f.*

wedge /wedʒ/ *n.* coin *m.*; (*under wheel etc.*) cale *f.* ● *v.t.* caler; (*push*) enfoncer; (*crowd*) coincer.

Wednesday /'wenzdɪ/ *n.* mercredi *m.*

wee /wi:/ *a.* (*fam.*) tout petit.

weed /wi:d/ *n.* mauvaise herbe *f.* ● *v.t./i.* désherber. **~-killer** *n.* désherbant *m.* **~ out,** extirper. **~y** *a.* (*person*: *fig.*) faible, maigre.

week /wi:k/ *n.* semaine *f.* **a ~ today/tomorrow,** aujourd'hui/demain en huit. **~ly** *adv.* toutes les semaines; *a.* & *n.* (*periodical*) hebdomadaire (*m.*).

weekday /'wi:kdeɪ/ *n.* jour de semaine *m.*

weekend /wi:k'end/ *n.* week-end *m.*, fin de semaine *f.*

weep /wi:p/ *v.t./i.* (*p.t.* **wept**) pleurer (**for s.o.,** qn.). **~ing willow,** saule pleureur *m.*

weigh /weɪ/ *v.t./i.* peser. **~ anchor,** lever l'ancre. **~ down,** lester (avec un poids); (*bend*) faire plier; (*fig.*) accabler. **~ up,** (*examine*: *fam.*) calculer.

weight /weɪt/ *n.* poids *m.* **lose/put on ~,** perdre/prendre du poids. **~lessness** *n.* apesanteur *f.* **~-lifting** *n.* haltérophilie *f.* **~y** *a.* lourd; (*subject etc.*) de poids.

weighting /'weɪtɪŋ/ *n.* indemnité *f.*

weir /wɪə(r)/ *n.* barrage *m.*

weird /wɪəd/ *a.* (**-er, -est**) mystérieux; (*strange*) bizarre.

welcome /'welkəm/ *a.* agréable; (*timely*) opportun. **be ~,** être le *or* la bienvenu(e), être les bienvenu(e)s. **you're ~!,** (*after thank you*) il n'y a pas de quoi! **~ to do,** libre de faire. ● *int.* soyez le *or* la bienvenu(e), soyez les bienvenu(e)s. ● *n.* accueil *m.* ● *v.t.* accueillir; (*as greeting*) souhaiter la bienvenue à; (*fig.*) se réjouir de.

weld /weld/ *v.t.* souder. ● *n.* soudure *f.* **~er** *n.* soudeur *m.* **~ing** *n.* soudure *f.*

welfare /'welfeə(r)/ *n.* bien-être *m.*; (*aid*) aide sociale *f.* **W~ State,** État-providence *m.*

well[1] /wel/ *n.* (*for water, oil*) puits *m.*; (*of stairs*) cage *f.*

well[2] /wel/ *adv.* (**better, best**) bien. ● *a.* bien *invar.* **as ~,** aussi. **be ~,** (*healthy*) aller bien. ● *int.* eh bien; (*surprise*) tiens. **do ~,** (*succeed*) réussir. **~-behaved** *a.* sage. **~-being** *n.* bien-être *m.* **~-built** *a.* bien bâti. **~-disposed** *a.* bien disposé. **~ done!,** bravo! **~-dressed** *a.* bien habillé. **~-heeled** *a.* (*fam.*) nanti. **~-informed** *a.* bien informé. **~-known** *a.* (bien) connu. **~-meaning** *a.* bien intentionné. **~ off,** aisé, riche. **~-read** *a.* instruit. **~-spoken** *a.* qui parle bien. **~-to-do** *a.* riche. **~-wisher** *n.* admira|teur, -trice *m.*, *f.*

wellington /'welɪŋtən/ *n.* (*boot*) botte de caoutchouc *f.*

Welsh /welʃ/ *a.* gallois. ● *n.* (*lang.*) gallois *m.* **~man** *n.* Gallois *m.* **~ rabbit,** croûte au fromage *f.* **~woman** *n.* Galloise *f.*

welsh /welʃ/ *v.i.* **~ on,** (*debt, promise*) ne pas honorer.

welterweight /'weltəweɪt/ *n.* poids mi-moyen *m.*

wench /wentʃ/ *n.* (*old use*) jeune fille *f.*

wend /wend/ *v.t.* **~ one's way,** se diriger, aller son chemin.

went /went/ *see* go.

wept /wept/ *see* weep.

were /wɜ:(r), *unstressed* wə(r)/ *see* be.

west /west/ *n.* ouest *m.* **the W~,** (*pol.*) l'Occident *m.* ● *a.* d'ouest. ● *adv.* vers l'ouest. **the W~ Country,** le sud-ouest (de l'Angleterre). **W~ Germany,** Allemagne de l'Ouest *f.* **W~ Indian** *a.* & *n.* antillais(e) (*m.* (*f.*)). **the W~ Indies,** les Antilles *f. pl.* **~erly** *a.* d'ouest. **~ern** *a.* de l'ouest; (*pol.*) occidental; *n.* (*film*) western *m.* **~erner** *n.* occidental(e) *m.* (*f.*). **~ward** *a.* à l'ouest. **~wards** *adv.* vers l'ouest.

westernize /'westənaɪz/ *v.t.* occidentaliser.

wet /wet/ *a.* (**wetter, wettest**) mouillé; (*damp, rainy*) humide; (*paint*) frais. ● *v.t.* (*p.t.* **wetted**) mouiller. ● *n.* **the ~,** l'humidité *f.*; (*rain*) la pluie *f.* **get ~,** se mouiller. **~ blanket,** rabat-joie *m. invar.* **~ness** *n.* humidité *f.* **~ suit,** combinaison de plongée *f.*

whack /wæk/ *n.* (*fam.*) grand coup *m.* ● *v.t.* (*fam.*) taper sur.

whacked /wækt/ *a.* (*fam.*) claqué.

whacking /'wækɪŋ/ *a.* énorme.

whale /weɪl/ *n.* baleine *f.*

wham /wæm/ *int.* vlan.

wharf /wɔ:f/ *n.* (*pl.* **wharfs**) (*for ships*) quai *m.*

what /wɒt/ *a.* (*in questions*) quel(le), quel(le)s. ● *pron.* (*in questions*) qu'est-ce qui; (*object*) (qu'est-ce) que *or* qu'*; (*after prep.*) quoi; (*that which*) ce qui; (*object*) ce que, ce qu'*. ● *int.* quoi, comment. **~ date?,** quelle date? **~ time?,** à quelle heure? **~ happened?,** qu'est-ce qui s'est passé? **~ did he say?,** qu'est-ce qu'il a dit? **~ he said,** ce qu'il a dit. **~ is important,** ce qui est important. **~ is it?,** qu'est-ce que c'est? **~ you need,** ce dont vous avez besoin. **~ a fool**/*etc.*, quel idiot/*etc.* **~ about me/him**/*etc.*?, et moi/lui/*etc.*? **~ about doing?,** si on faisait? **~ for?,** pourquoi?

whatever /wɒt'evə(r)/ *a.* **~ book**/*etc.*, quel que soit le livre/*etc.* ● *pron.* (*no matter what*) quoi que, quoi qu'*; (*anything that*) tout ce qui; (*object*) tout ce que *or* qu'*. **~ happens,** quoi qu'il arrive. **~ happened?,** qu'est-ce qui est arrivé? **~ the problems,** quels que soient les problèmes. **~ you want,** tout ce que vous voulez. **nothing ~,** rien du tout.

whatsoever /wɒtsəʊ'evər/ *a.* & *pron.* = **whatever.**

wheat /wi:t/ *n.* blé *m.*, froment *m.*

wheedle /'wi:dl/ *v.t.* cajoler.

wheel /wi:l/ *n.* roue *f.* ● *v.t.* pousser. ● *v.i.* tourner. **at the ~,** (*of vehicle*) au volant; (*helm*) au gouvernail. **~ and deal,** faire des combines.

wheelbarrow /'wi:lbærəʊ/ *n.* brouette *f.*

wheelchair /'wi:ltʃeə(r)/ *n.* fauteuil roulant *m.*

wheeze /wi:z/ *v.i.* siffler (en respirant). ● *n.* sifflement *m.*

when /wen/ *adv.* & *pron.* quand. ● *conj.* quand, lorsque. **the day/moment ~,** le jour/moment où.

whenever /wen'evə(r)/ *conj.* & *adv.* (*at whatever time*) quand; (*every time that*) chaque fois que.

where /weə(r)/ *adv., conj., & pron.* où; (*whereas*) alors que; (*the place that*) là où. **~abouts** *adv.* (à peu prés) où; *n.* **s.o.'s ~abouts,** l'endroit où se trouve qn. **~by** *adv.* par quoi. **~upon** *adv.* sur quoi.

whereas /weər'æz/ *conj.* alors que.

wherever /weər'evə(r)/ *conj.* & *adv.* où que; (*everywhere*) partout où; (*anywhere*) (là) où; (*emphatic where*) où donc.

whet /wet/ *v.t.* (*p.t.* **whetted**) (*appetite, desire*) aiguiser.

whether /'weðə(r)/ *conj.* si. **not know ~,** ne pas savoir si. **~ I go or not,** que j'aille ou non.

which /wɪtʃ/ *a.* (*in questions*) quel(le), quel(le)s. ● *pron.* (*in questions*) lequel, laquelle, lesquel(le)s; (*the one or ones that*) celui (celle, ceux, celles) qui; (*object*) celui (celle, ceux, celles) que *or* qu'*; (*referring to whole sentence, = and that*) ce qui; (*object*) ce que, ce qu'*; (*after prep.*) lequel/*etc.* ● *rel. pron.* qui; (*object*) que, qu'*. **~ house?,** quelle maison? **~ (one) do you want?,** lequel voulez-vous? **~ are ready?,** lesquels sont prêts? **the bird ~ flies,** l'oiseau qui vole. **the hat ~ he wears,** le chapeau qu'il porte. **of ~, from ~,** duquel/*etc.* **to ~, at ~,** auquel/*etc.* **the book of ~,** le livre dont *or* duquel. **after ~,** après quoi. **she was there, ~ surprised me,** elle était là, ce qui m'a surpris.

whichever /wɪtʃ'evə(r)/ *a.* **~ book**/*etc.*, quel que soit le livre/*etc.* que *or* qui. **take ~ book you wish,** prenez le livre que vous voulez. ● *pron.* celui (celle, ceux, celles) qui *or* que.

whiff /wɪf/ *n.* (*puff*) bouffée *f.*

while /waɪl/ *n.* moment *m.* ● *conj.* (*when*) pendant que; (*although*) bien que; (*as long as*) tant que. ● *v.t.* **~ away,** (*time*) passer.

whilst /waɪlst/ *conj.* = **while.**

whim /wɪm/ *n.* caprice *m.*

whimper /'wɪmpə(r)/ *v.i.* geindre, pleurnicher. ● *n.* pleurnichement *m.*

whimsical /'wɪmzɪkl/ *a.* (*person*) capricieux; (*odd*) bizarre.

whine /waɪn/ *v.i.* gémir, se plaindre. ● *n.* gémissement *m.*

whip /wɪp/ *n.* fouet *m.* ● *v.t.* (*p.t.* **whipped**) fouetter; (*culin.*) fouetter, battre; (*seize*) enlever brusquement. ● *v.i.* (*move*) aller en vitesse. **~-round** *n.* (*fam.*) collecte *f.* **~ out,** (*gun etc.*) sortir. **~ up,** exciter; (*cause*) provoquer; (*meal*: *fam.*) préparer.

whirl /wɜːl/ *v.t./i.* (faire) tourbillonner. ● *n.* tourbillon *m.*

whirlpool /ˈwɜːlpuːl/ *n.* (*in sea etc.*) tourbillon *m.*

whirlwind /ˈwɜːlwɪnd/ *n.* tourbillon (de vent) *m.*

whirr /wɜː(r)/ *v.i.* vrombir.

whisk /wɪsk/ *v.t.* (*snatch*) enlever *or* emmener brusquement; (*culin.*) fouetter. ● *n.* (*culin.*) fouet *m.*; (*broom, brush*) petit balai *m.* **~ away,** (*brush away*) chasser.

whisker /ˈwɪskə(r)/ *n.* poil *m.* **~s,** (*man's*) barbe *f.*, moustache *f.*; (*sideboards*) favoris *m. pl.*

whisky /ˈwɪskɪ/ *n.* whisky *m.*

whisper /ˈwɪspə(r)/ *v.t./i.* chuchoter. ● *n.* chuchotement *m.*; (*rumour*: *fig.*) rumeur *f.*, bruit *m.*

whistle /ˈwɪsl/ *n.* sifflement *m.*; (*instrument*) sifflet *m.* ● *v.t./i.* siffler. **~ at** *or* **for,** siffler.

Whit /wɪt/ *a.* **~ Sunday,** dimanche de Pentecôte *m.*

white /waɪt/ *a.* (**-er, -est**) blanc. ● *n.* blanc *m.*; (*person*) blanc(he) *m.* (*f.*). **~ coffee,** café au lait *m.* **~-collar worker,** employé(e) de bureau *m.* (*f.*). **~ elephant,** objet, projet, *etc.* inutile *m.* **~ lie,** pieux mensonge *m.* **W~ Paper,** livre blanc *m.* **~ness** *n.* blancheur *f.*

whiten /ˈwaɪtn/ *v.t./i.* blanchir.

whitewash /ˈwaɪtwɒʃ/ *n.* blanc de chaux *m.* ● *v.t.* blanchir à la chaux; (*person*: *fig.*) blanchir.

whiting /ˈwaɪtɪŋ/ *n. invar.* (*fish*) merlan *m.*

Whitsun /ˈwɪtsn/ *n.* la Pentecôte.

whittle /wɪtl/ *v.t.* **~ down,** tailler (au couteau); (*fig.*) réduire.

whiz /wɪz/ *v.i.* (*p.t.* **whizzed**) (*through air*) fendre l'air; (*hiss*) siffler; (*rush*) aller à toute vitesse. **~-kid** *n.* jeune prodige *m.*

who /huː/ *pron.* qui.

whodunit /huːˈdʌnɪt/ *n.* (*story*: *fam.*) roman policier *m.*

whoever /huːˈevə(r)/ *pron.* (*no matter who*) qui que ce soit qui *or* que; (*the one who*) quiconque. **tell ~ you want,** dites-le à qui vous voulez.

whole /həʊl/ *a.* entier; (*intact*) intact. **the ~ house**/*etc.*, toute la maison/*etc.* ● *n.* totalité *f.*; (*unit*) tout *m.* **on the ~,** dans l'ensemble. **~-hearted** *a.*, **~-heartedly** *adv.* sans réserve.

wholefoods /ˈhəʊlfuːdz/ *n. pl.* aliments naturels et diététiques *m. pl.*

wholemeal /ˈhəʊlmiːl/ *a.* **~ bread,** pain complet *m.*

wholesale /ˈhəʊlseɪl/ *n.* gros *m.* ● *a.* (*firm*) de gros; (*fig.*) systématique. ● *adv.* (*in large quantities*) en gros; (*buy or sell one item*) au prix de gros; (*fig.*) en masse. **~r** /-ə(r)/ *n.* grossiste *m./f.*

wholesome /ˈhəʊlsəm/ *a.* sain.

wholewheat /ˈhəʊlhwiːt/ *a.* = **wholemeal**.

wholly /ˈhəʊlɪ/ *adv.* entièrement.

whom /huːm/ *pron.* (*that*) que, qu'*; (*after prep. & in questions*) qui. **of ~,** dont. **with ~,** avec qui.

whooping cough /ˈhuːpɪŋkɒf/ *n.* coqueluche *f.*

whopping /ˈwɒpɪŋ/ *a.* (*sl.*) énorme.

whore /hɔː(r)/ *n.* putain *f.*

whose /huːz/ *pron. & a.* à qui, de qui. **~ hat is this?, ~ is this hat?,** à qui est ce chapeau? **~ son are you?,** de qui êtes-vous le fils? **the man ~ hat I see,** l'homme dont je vois le chapeau.

why /waɪ/ *adv.* pourquoi. ● *int.* eh bien, ma parole, tiens. **the reason ~,** la raison pour laquelle.

wick /wɪk/ *n.* (*of lamp etc.*) mèche *f.*

wicked /ˈwɪkɪd/ *a.* méchant, mauvais, vilain. **~ly** *adv.* méchamment. **~ness** *n.* méchanceté *f.*

wicker /ˈwɪkə(r)/ *n.* osier *m.* **~work** *n.* vannerie *f.*

wicket /ˈwɪkɪt/ *n.* guichet *m.*

wide /waɪd/ *a.* (**-er, -est**) large; (*ocean etc.*) vaste. ● *adv.* (*fall etc.*) loin du but. **open ~,** ouvrir tout grand. **~ open,** grand ouvert. **~-angle lens** grand-angle *m.* **~ awake,** éveillé. **~ly** *adv.* (*spread, space*) largement; (*travel*) beaucoup; (*generally*) généralement; (*extremely*) extrêmement.

widen /ˈwaɪdn/ *v.t./i.* (s')élargir.

widespread /ˈwaɪdspred/ *a.* très répandu.

widow /ˈwɪdəʊ/ *n.* veuve. *f.* **~ed** *a.* (*man*) veuf; (*woman*) veuve. **be ~ed,** (*become widower or widow*) devenir veuf *or* veuve. **~er** *n.* veuf *m.*

width /wɪdθ/ *n.* largeur *f.*

wield /wi:ld/ *v.t.* (*axe etc.*) manier; (*power: fig.*) exercer.

wife /waɪf/ *n.* (*pl.* **wives**) femme *f.*, épouse *f.* **~ly** *a.* d'épouse.

wig /wɪg/ *n.* perruque *f.*

wiggle /ˈwɪgl/ *v.t./i.* remuer; (*hips*) tortiller; (*of worm*) se tortiller.

wild /waɪld/ *a.* (**-er, -est**) sauvage; (*sea, enthusiasm*) déchaîné; (*mad*) fou; (*angry*) furieux. ● *adv.* (*grow*) à l'état sauvage. **~s** *n. pl.* régions sauvages *f. pl.* **run ~,** (*free*) courir en liberté. **~-goose chase,** fausse piste *f.* **~ly** *adv.* violemment; (*madly*) follement.

wildcat /ˈwaɪldkæt/ *a.* **~ strike,** grève sauvage *f.*

wilderness /ˈwɪldənɪs/ *n.* désert *m.*

wildlife /ˈwaɪldlaɪf/ *n.* faune *f.*

wile /waɪl/ *n.* ruse *f.*, artifice *m.*

wilful /ˈwɪlfl/ *a.* (*intentional, obstinate*) volontaire.

will[1] /wɪl/ *v. aux.* **he ~ do/you ~ sing/*etc.*,** (*future tense*) il fera/tu chanteras/*etc.* **~ you have a coffee?,** voulez-vous prendre un café?

will[2] /wɪl/ *n.* volonté *f.*; (*document*) testament *m.* ● *v.t.* (*wish*) vouloir. **at ~,** quand *or* comme on veut. **~-power** *n.* volonté *f.* **~ o.s. to do,** faire un effort de volonté pour faire.

willing /ˈwɪlɪŋ/ *a.* (*help, offer*) spontané; (*helper*) bien disposé. **~ to,** disposé à. **~ly** *adv.* (*with pleasure*) volontiers; (*not forced*) volontairement. **~ness** *n.* empressement *m.* **(to do,** à faire); (*goodwill*) bonne volonté *f.*

willow /ˈwɪləʊ/ *n.* saule *m.*

willy-nilly /wɪlɪˈnɪlɪ/ *adv.* bon gré mal gré.

wilt /wɪlt/ *v.i.* (*plant etc.*) dépérir.

wily /ˈwaɪlɪ/ *a.* (**-ier, -iest**) rusé.

win /wɪn/ *v.t./i.* (*p.t.* **won,** *pres. p.* **winning**) gagner; (*victory, prize*) remporter; (*fame, fortune*) acquérir, trouver. ● *n.* victoire *f.* **~ round,** convaincre.

winc|e /wɪns/ *v.i.* se crisper, tressaillir. **without ~ing,** sans broncher.

winch /wɪntʃ/ *n.* treuil *m.* ● *v.t.* hisser au treuil.

wind[1] /wɪnd/ *n.* vent *m.*; (*breath*) souffle *m.* ● *v.t.* essouffler. **get ~ of,** avoir vent de. **in the ~,** dans l'air. **~cheater,** (*Amer.*) **~breaker** *ns.* blouson *m.* **~ instrument,** instrument à vent *m.* **~-swept** *a.* balayé par les vents.

wind[2] /waɪnd/ *v.t./i.* (*p.t.* **wound**) (s')enrouler; (*of path, river*) serpenter. **~ (up),** (*clock etc.*) remonter. **~ up,** (*end*) (se) terminer. **~ up in hospital,** finir à l'hôpital. **~ing** *a.* (*path*) sinueux.

windfall /ˈwɪndfɔ:l/ *n.* fruit tombé *m.*; (*money: fig.*) aubaine *f.*

windmill /ˈwɪndmɪl/ *n.* moulin à vent *m.*

window /ˈwɪndəʊ/ *n.* fenêtre *f.*; (*glass pane*) vitre *f.*; (*in vehicle, train*) vitre *f.*; (*in shop*) vitrine *f.*; (*counter*) guichet *m.* **~-box** *n.* jardinière *f.* **~-cleaner** *n.* laveur de carreaux *m.* **~-dresser** *n.* étalagiste *m./f.* **~-ledge** *n.* rebord de (la) fenêtre *m.*; **~-shopping** *n.* lèche-vitrines *m.* **~-sill** *n.* (*inside*) appui de (la) fenêtre *m.*; (*outside*) rebord de (la) fenêtre *m.*

windpipe /ˈwɪndpaɪp/ *n.* trachée *f.*

windscreen /ˈwɪndskri:n/, (*Amer.*) **windshield** /ˈwɪndʃi:ld/ *n.* pare-brise *m. invar.* **~ washer,** lave-glace *m.* **~ wiper,** essuie-glace *m.*

windsurf|ing /ˈwɪndsɜ:fɪŋ/ *n.* planche à voile *f.* **~er** *n.* véliplanchiste *m./f.*

windy /ˈwɪndɪ/ *a.* (**-ier, -iest**) venteux. **it is ~,** il y a du vent.

wine /waɪn/ *n.* vin *m.* **~-cellar** *n.* cave (à vin) *f.* **~-grower** *n.* viticulteur *m.* **~-growing** *n.* viticulture *f.*; *a.* viticole. **~ list,** carte des vins *f.* **~-tasting** *n.* dégustation de vins *f.* **~ waiter,** sommelier *m.*

wineglass /ˈwaɪnglɑ:s/ *n.* verre à vin *m.*

wing /wɪŋ/ *n.* aile *f.* **~s,** (*theatre*) coulisses *f. pl.* **under one's ~,** sous son aile. **~ mirror,** rétroviseur extérieur *m.* **~ed** *a.* ailé. **~er** *n.* (*sport*) ailier *m.*

wink /wɪŋk/ *v.i.* faire un clin d'œil; (*light, star*) clignoter. ● *n.* clin d'œil *m.*; clignotement *m.*

winner /ˈwɪnə(r)/ *n.* (*of game*) gagnant(e) *m.* (*f.*); (*of fight*) vainqueur *m.*

winning /ˈwɪnɪŋ/ *see* win. ● *a.* (*number, horse*) gagnant; (*team*) victorieux; (*smile*) engageant. **~s** *n. pl.* gains *m. pl.*

wint|er /ˈwɪntə(r)/ *n.* hiver *m.* ● *v.i.* hiverner. **~ry** *a.* hivernal.

wipe /waɪp/ *v.t.* essuyer. ● *v.i.* **~ up,** essuyer la vaisselle. ● *n.* coup de torchon *or* d'éponge *m.* **~ off** *or* **out,** essuyer. **~ out,** (*destroy*) anéantir; (*remove*) effacer.

wir|e /ˈwaɪə(r)/ *n.* fil *m.*; (*Amer.*) télégramme *m.* **~e netting,** grillage *m.* **~ing** *n.* (*electr.*) installation électrique *f.*

wireless /ˈwaɪəlɪs/ *n.* radio *f.*

wiry /ˈwaɪərɪ/ *a.* (**-ier, -iest**) (*person*) nerveux et maigre.

wisdom /ˈwɪzdəm/ *n.* sagesse *f.*

wise /waɪz/ *a.* (**-er, -est**) prudent, sage; (*look*) averti. **~ guy,** (*fam.*) petit malin *m.* **~ man,** sage *m.* **~ly** *adv.* prudemment.

wisecrack /ˈwaɪzkræk/ *n.* (*fam.*) mot d'esprit *m.*, astuce *f.*

wish /wɪʃ/ *n.* (*specific*) souhait *m.*, vœu *m.*; (*general*) désir *m.* ● *v.t.* souhaiter, vouloir, désirer (**to do,** faire); (*bid*) souhaiter. ● *v.i.* **~ for,** souhaiter. **I ~ he'd leave,** je voudrais bien qu'il parte. **best ~es,** (*in letter*) amitiés *f. pl.*; (*on greeting card*) meilleurs vœux *m. pl.*

wishful /ˈwɪʃfl/ *a.* **it's ~ thinking,** on se fait des illusions.

wishy-washy /ˈwɪʃɪwɒʃɪ/ *a.* fade.

wisp /wɪsp/ *n.* (*of smoke*) volute *f.*

wistful /ˈwɪstfl/ *a.* mélancolique.

wit /wɪt/ *n.* intelligence *f.*; (*humour*) esprit *m.*; (*person*) homme d'esprit *m.*, femme d'esprit *f.* **be at one's ~'s** *or* **~s' end,** ne plus savoir que faire.

witch /wɪtʃ/ *n.* sorcière *f.* **~craft** *n.* sorcellerie *f.*

with /wɪð/ *prep.* avec; (*having*) à; (*because of*) de; (*at house of*) chez. **the man ~ the beard,** l'homme à la barbe. **fill**/*etc.* **~,** remplir/*etc.* de. **pleased/shaking**/*etc.* **~,** content/frémissant/ *etc.* de. **~ it,** (*fam.*) dans le vent.

withdraw /wɪðˈdrɔː/ *v.t./i.* (*p.t.* **withdrew,** *p.p.* **withdrawn**) (se) retirer. **~al** *n.* retrait *m.* **~n** *a.* (*person*) renfermé.

wither /ˈwɪðə(r)/ *v.t./i.* (se) flétrir. **~ed** *a.* (*person*) desséché.

withhold /wɪðˈhəʊld/ *v.t.* (*p.t.* **withheld**) refuser (de donner); (*retain*) retenir; (*conceal, not tell*) cacher (**from,** à).

within /wɪˈðɪn/ *prep. & adv.* à l'intérieur (de); (*in distances*) à moins de. **~ a month,** (*before*) avant un mois. **~ sight,** en vue.

without /wɪˈðaʊt/ *prep.* sans. **~ my knowing,** sans que je sache.

withstand /wɪðˈstænd/ *v.t.* (*p.t.* **withstood**) résister à.

witness /ˈwɪtnɪs/ *n.* témoin *m.*; (*evidence*) témoignage *m.* ● *v.t.* être le témoin de, voir; (*document*) signer. **bear ~ to,** témoigner de. **~ box** *or* **stand,** barre des témoins *f.*

witticism /ˈwɪtɪsɪzəm/ *n.* bon mot *m.*

witt|y /ˈwɪtɪ/ *a.* (**-ier, -iest**) spirituel. **~iness** *n.* esprit *m.*

wives /waɪvz/ *see* wife.

wizard /ˈwɪzəd/ *n.* magicien *m.*; (*genius*: *fig.*) génie *m.*

wobbl|e /ˈwɒbl/ *v.i.* (*of jelly, voice, hand*) trembler; (*stagger*) chanceler; (*of table, chair*) branler. **~y** *a.* tremblant; branlant.

woe /wəʊ/ *n.* malheur *m.*

woke, woken /wəʊk, ˈwəʊkən/ *see* wake[1].

wolf /wʊlf/ *n.* (*pl.* **wolves**) loup *m.* ● *v.t.* (*food*) engloutir. **cry ~,** crier au loup. **~-whistle** *n.* sifflement admiratif *m.*

woman /ˈwʊmən/ *n.* (*pl.* **women**) femme *f.* **~ doctor,** femme médecin *f.* **~ driver,** femme au volant *f.* **~ friend,** amie *f.* **~hood** *n.* féminité *f.* **~ly** *a.* féminin.

womb /wuːm/ *n.* utérus *m.*

women /ˈwɪmɪn/ *see* woman.

won /wʌn/ *see* win.

wonder /ˈwʌndə(r)/ *n.* émerveillement *m.*; (*thing*) merveille *f.* ● *v.t.* se demander (**if,** si). ● *v.i.* s'étonner (**at,** de); (*reflect*) songer (**about,** à). **it is no ~,** ce *or* il n'est pas étonnant (**that,** que).

wonderful /ˈwʌndəfl/ *a.* merveilleux. **~ly** *adv.* merveilleusement; (*work, do, etc.*) à merveille.

won't /wəʊnt/ = **will not**.

woo /wuː/ *v.t.* (*woman*) faire la cour à; (*please*) chercher à plaire à.

wood /wʊd/ *n.* bois *m.* **~ed** *a.* boisé. **~en** *a.* en *or* de bois; (*stiff*: *fig.*) raide, comme du bois.

woodcut /ˈwʊdkʌt/ *n.* gravure sur bois *f.*

woodland /ˈwʊdlənd/ *n.* région boisée *f.*, bois *m. pl.*

woodpecker /ˈwʊdpekə(r)/ *n.* (*bird*) pic *m.*, pivert *m.*

woodwind /'wʊdwɪnd/ *n.* (*mus.*) bois *m. pl.*
woodwork /'wʊdwɜ:k/ *n.* (*craft, objects*) menuiserie *f.*
woodworm /'wʊdwɜ:m/ *n.* (*larvae*) vers (de bois) *m. pl.*
woody /'wʊdɪ/ *a.* (*wooded*) boisé; (*like wood*) ligneux.
wool /wʊl/ *n.* laine *f.* **~len** *a.* de laine. **~lens** *n. pl.* lainages *m. pl.* **~ly** *a.* laineux; (*vague*) nébuleux; *n.* (*garment: fam.*) lainage *m.*
word /wɜ:d/ *n.* mot *m.*; (*spoken*) parole *f.*, mot *m.*; (*promise*) parole *f.*; (*news*) nouvelles *f. pl.* ● *v.t.* rédiger. **by ~ of mouth,** de vive voix. **give/keep one's ~,** donner/tenir sa parole. **have a ~ with,** parler à. **in other ~s,** autrement dit. **~ processor,** machine de traitement de texte *f.* **~ing** *n.* termes *m. pl.*
wordy /'wɜ:dɪ/ *a.* verbeux.
wore /wɔ:(r)/ *see* wear.
work /wɜ:k/ *n.* travail *m.*; (*product, book, etc.*) œuvre *f.*, ouvrage *m.*; (*building etc. work*) travaux *m. pl.* **~s,** (*techn.*) mécanisme *m.*; (*factory*) usine *f.* ● *v.t./i.* (*of person*) travailler; (*shape, hammer, etc.*) travailler; (*techn.*) (faire) fonctionner, (faire) marcher; (*land, mine*) exploiter; (*of drug etc.*) agir. **~ s.o.,** (*make work*) faire travailler qn. **~-force** *n.* main-d'œuvre *f.* **~ in,** (s')introduire. **~-load** *n.* travail (à faire) *m.* **~ off,** (*get rid of*) se débarrasser de. **~ out** *v.t.* (*solve*) résoudre; (*calculate*) calculer; (*elaborate*) élaborer; *v.i.* (*succeed*) marcher; (*sport*) s'entraîner. **~-station** *n.* poste de travail *m.* **~-to-rule** *n.* grève du zèle *f.* **~ up** *v.t.* développer; *v.i.* (*to climax*) monter vers. **~ed up,** (*person*) énervé.
workable /'wɜ:kəbl/ *a.* réalisable.
workaholic /wɜ:kə'hɒlɪk/ *n.* (*fam.*) bourreau de travail *m.*
worker /'wɜ:kə(r)/ *n.* travailleu|r, -se *m., f.*; (*manual*) ouvr|ier, -ière *m., f.*
working /'wɜ:kɪŋ/ *a.* (*day, lunch, etc.*) de travail. **~s** *n. pl.* mécanisme *m.* **~ class,** classe ouvrière *f.* **~-class** *a.* ouvrier. **in ~ order,** en état de marche.
workman /'wɜ:kmən/ *n.* (*pl.* **-men**) ouvrier *m.* **~ship** *n.* maîtrise *f.*
workshop /'wɜ:kʃɒp/ *n.* atelier *m.*
world /wɜ:ld/ *n.* monde *m.* ● *a.* (*power etc.*) mondial; (*record etc.*) du monde. **best in the ~,** meilleur au monde. **~-wide** *a.* universel.
worldly /'wɜ:ldlɪ/ *a.* de ce monde, terrestre. **~-wise** *a.* qui a l'expérience du monde.
worm /wɜ:m/ *n.* ver *m.* ● *v.t.* **~ one's way into,** s'insinuer dans. **~-eaten** *a.* (*wood*) vermoulu; (*fruit*) véreux.
worn /wɔ:n/ *see* wear. ● *a.* usé. **~-out** *a.* (*thing*) complètement usé; (*person*) épuisé.
worr|y /'wʌrɪ/ *v.t./i.* (s')inquiéter. ● *n.* souci *m.* **~ied** *a.* inquiet. **~ier** *n.* inqu|et, -iète *m., f.*
worse /wɜ:s/ *a.* pire, plus mauvais. ● *adv.* plus mal. ● *n.* pire *m.* **be ~ off,** perdre.
worsen /'wɜ:sn/ *v.t./i.* empirer.
worship /'wɜ:ʃɪp/ *n.* (*adoration*) culte *m.* ● *v.t.* (*p.t.* **worshipped**) adorer. ● *v.i.* faire ses dévotions. **~per** *n.* (*in church*) fidèle *m./f.*
worst /wɜ:st/ *a.* pire, plus mauvais. ● *adv.* **(the) ~,** (*sing etc.*) le plus mal. ● *n.* **the ~ (one),** (*person, object*) le *or* la pire. **the ~ (thing),** le pire (**that,** que). **get the ~ of it,** (*be defeated*) avoir le dessous.
worsted /'wʊstɪd/ *n.* worsted *m.*
worth /wɜ:θ/ *a.* **be ~,** valoir. **it is ~ waiting/***etc.*, ça vaut la peine d'attendre/*etc.* ● *n.* valeur *f.* **ten pence ~ of,** (pour) dix pence de. **it is ~ (one's) while,** ça (en) vaut la peine. **~less** *a.* qui ne vaut rien.
worthwhile /wɜ:θ'waɪl/ *a.* qui (en) vaut la peine.
worthy /'wɜ:ðɪ/ *a.* (**-ier, -iest**) digne (**of,** de); (*laudable*) louable. ● *n.* (*person*) notable *m.*
would /wʊd, *unstressed* wəd/ *v. aux.* **he ~ do/you ~ sing/***etc.*, (*conditional tense*) il ferait/tu chanterais/*etc.* **he ~ have done,** il aurait fait. **I ~ come every day,** (*used to*) je venais chaque jour. **I ~ like some tea,** je voudrais du thé. **~ you come here?,** voulez-vous venir ici? **he ~n't come,** il a refusé de venir. **~-be** *a.* soi-disant.
wound[1] /wu:nd/ *n.* blessure *f.* ● *v.t.* blesser. **the ~ed,** les blessés *m. pl.*
wound[2] /waʊnd/ *see* wind[2].
wove, woven /wəʊv, 'wəʊvn/ *see* weave.
wow /waʊ/ *int.* mince (alors).
wrangle /'ræŋgl/ *v.i.* se disputer. ● *n.* dispute *f.*

wrap /ræp/ *v.t.* (*p.t.* **wrapped**). ~ **(up)**, envelopper. ● *v.i.* ~ **up**, (*dress warmly*) se couvrir. ● *n.* châle *m.* **~ped up in**, (*engrossed*) absorbé dans. **~per** *n.* (*of book*) jaquette *f.*; (*of sweet*) papier *m.* **~ping** *n.* emballage *m.*; **~ping paper**, papier d'emballage *m.*

wrath /rɒθ/ *n.* courroux *m.*

wreak /ri:k/ *v.t.* ~ **havoc**, (*of storm etc.*) faire des ravages.

wreath /ri:θ/ *n.* (*pl.* **-s** /-ðz/) (*of flowers, leaves*) couronne *f.*

wreck /rek/ *n.* (*sinking*) naufrage *m.*; (*ship, remains, person*) épave *f.*; (*vehicle*) voiture accidentée *or* délabrée *f.* ● *v.t.* détruire; (*ship*) provoquer le naufrage de. **~age** *n.* (*pieces*) débris *m. pl.*; (*wrecked building*) décombres *m. pl.*

wren /ren/ *n.* roitelet *m.*

wrench /rentʃ/ *v.t.* (*pull*) tirer sur; (*twist*) tordre; (*snatch*) arracher (**from**, à). ● *n.* (*tool*) clé *f.*

wrest /rest/ *v.t.* arracher (**from**, à).

wrestl|e /'resl/ *v.i.* lutter, se débattre (**with**, contre). **~er** *n.* lutteu|r, -se *m., f.*; catcheu|r, -se *m., f.* **~ing** *n.* lutte *f.* **(all-in) ~ing**, catch *m.*

wretch /retʃ/ *n.* malheureu|x, -se *m., f.*; (*rascal*) misérable *m./f.*

wretched /'retʃɪd/ *a.* (*pitiful, poor*) misérable; (*bad*) affreux.

wriggle /'rɪgl/ *v.t./i.* (se) tortiller.

wring /rɪŋ/ *v.t.* (*p.t.* **wrung**) (*twist*) tordre; (*clothes*) essorer. ~ **out of**, (*obtain from*) arracher à. **~ing wet**, trempé (jusqu'aux os).

wrinkle /'rɪŋkl/ *n.* (*crease*) pli *m.*; (*on skin*) ride *f.* ● *v.t./i.* (se) rider.

wrist /rɪst/ *n.* poignet *m.* **~-watch** *n.* montre-bracelet *f.*

writ /rɪt/ *n.* acte judiciaire *m.*

write /raɪt/ *v.t./i.* (*p.t.* **wrote**, *p.p.* **written**) écrire. ~ **back**, répondre. ~ **down**, noter. ~ **off**, (*debt*) passer aux profits et pertes; (*vehicle*) considérer bon pour la casse. **~-off** *n.* perte totale *f.* ~ **up**, (*from notes*) rédiger. **~-up** *n.* compte rendu *m.*

writer /'raɪtə(r)/ *n.* auteur *m.*, écrivain *m.* ~ **of**, auteur de.

writhe /raɪð/ *v.i.* se tordre.

writing /'raɪtɪŋ/ *n.* écriture *f.* **~(s)**, (*works*) écrits *m. pl.* **in ~**, par écrit. **~-paper** *n.* papier à lettres *m.*

written /'rɪtn/ *see* write.

wrong /rɒŋ/ *a.* (*incorrect, mistaken*) faux, mauvais; (*unfair*) injuste; (*amiss*) qui ne va pas; (*clock*) pas à l'heure. **be ~**, (*person*) avoir tort (**to**, de); (*be mistaken*) se tromper. ● *adv.* mal. ● *n.* injustice *f.*; (*evil*) mal *m.* ● *v.t.* faire (du) tort à. **be in the ~**, avoir tort. **go ~**, (*err*) se tromper; (*turn out badly*) mal tourner; (*vehicle*) tomber en panne. **it is ~ to**, (*morally*) c'est mal de. **what's ~?**, qu'est-ce qui ne va pas? **what is ~ with you?**, qu'est-ce que vous avez? **~ly** *adv.* mal; (*blame etc.*) à tort.

wrongful /'rɒŋfl/ *a.* injustifié, injuste. **~ly** *adv.* à tort.

wrote /rəʊt/ *see* write.

wrought /rɔ:t/ *a.* ~ **iron**, fer forgé *m.*

wrung /rʌŋ/ *see* wring.

wry /raɪ/ *a.* (**wryer**, **wryest**) (*smile*) désabusé, forcé. ~ **face**, grimace *f.*

X

xerox /'zɪərɒks/ *v.t.* photocopier.

Xmas /'krɪsməs/ *n.* Noël *m.*

X-ray /'eksreɪ/ *n.* rayon X *m.*; (*photograph*) radio(graphie) *f.* ● *v.t.* radiographier.

xylophone /'zaɪləfəʊn/ *n.* xylophone *m.*

Y

yacht /jɒt/ *n.* yacht *m.* **~ing** *n.* yachting *m.*

yank /jæŋk/ *v.t.* tirer brusquement. ● *n.* coup brusque *m.*

Yank /jæŋk/ *n.* (*fam.*) Américain(e) *m.* (*f.*), Amerloque *m./f.*

yap /jæp/ *v.i.* (*p.t.* **yapped**) japper.

yard[1] /jɑ:d/ *n.* (*measure*) yard *m.* (= *0.9144 metre*).

yard[2] /jɑ:d/ *n.* (*of house etc.*) cour *f.*; (*garden: Amer.*) jardin *m.*; (*for storage*) chantier *m.*, dépôt *m.*

yardstick /'jɑ:dstɪk/ *n.* mesure *f.*

yarn /jɑ:n/ *n.* (*thread*) fil *m.*; (*tale: fam.*) (longue) histoire *f.*

yawn /jɔ:n/ *v.i.* bâiller. ● *n.* bâillement *m.* **~ing** *a.* (*gaping*) béant.

year /jɪə(r)/ *n.* an *m.*, année *f.*; **school/tax/***etc.* **~**, année scolaire/fiscale/*etc.* **be ten/***etc.* **~s old**, avoir dix/*etc.*

ans. **~-book** *n.* annuaire *m.* **~ly** *a.* annuel; *adv.* annuellement.
yearn /jɜ:n/ *v.i.* avoir bien *or* très envie (**for, to,** de). **~ing** *n.* envie *f.*
yeast /ji:st/ *n.* levure *f.*
yell /jel/ *v.t./i.* hurler. ● *n.* hurlement *m.*
yellow /'jeləʊ/ *a.* jaune; (*cowardly*: *fam.*) froussard. ● *n.* jaune *m.*
yelp /jelp/ *n.* (*of dog etc.*) jappement *m.* ● *v.i.* japper.
yen /jen/ *n.* (*desire*) grande envie *f.*
yes /jes/ *adv.* oui; (*as answer to negative question*) si. ● *n.* oui *m. invar.*
yesterday /'jestədɪ/ *n.* & *adv.* hier (*m.*).
yet /jet/ *adv.* encore; (*already*) déjà. ● *conj.* pourtant, néanmoins.
yew /ju:/ *n.* (*tree, wood*) if *m.*
Yiddish /'jɪdɪʃ/ *n.* yiddish *m.*
yield /ji:ld/ *v.t.* (*produce*) produire, rendre; (*profit*) rapporter; (*surrender*) céder. ● *v.i.* (*give way*) céder. ● *n.* rendement *m.*
yoga /'jəʊgə/ *n.* yoga *m.*
yoghurt /'jɒgət, *Amer.* 'jəʊgərt/ *n.* yaourt *m.*
yoke /jəʊk/ *n.* joug *m.*
yokel /'jəʊkl/ *n.* rustre *m.*
yolk /jəʊk/ *n.* jaune (d'œuf) *m.*
yonder /'jɒndə(r)/ *adv.* là-bas.
you /ju:/ *pron.* (*familiar form*) tu, *pl.* vous; (*polite form*) vous; (*object*) te, t'*, *pl.* vous; (*polite*) vous; (*after prep.*) toi, *pl.* vous; (*polite*) vous; (*indefinite*) on; (*object*) vous. (**to**) **~,** te, t'*, *pl.* vous; (*polite*) vous. **I gave ~ a pen,** je vous ai donné un stylo. **I know ~,** je te connais; je vous connais.
young /jʌŋ/ *a.* (**-er, -est**) jeune. ● *n.* (*people*) jeunes *m. pl.*; (*of animals*) petits *m. pl.* **~er** *a.* (*brother etc.*) cadet. **~est** *a.* **my ~est brother,** le cadet de mes frères.
youngster /'jʌŋstə(r)/ *n.* jeune *m./f.*
your /jɔ:(r)/ *a.* (*familiar form*) ton, ta, *pl.* tes; (*polite form, & familiar form pl.*) votre, *pl.* vos.
yours /jɔ:z/ *poss. pron.* (*familiar form*) le tien, la tienne, les tien(ne)s; (*polite form, & familiar form pl.*) le *or* la vôtre, les vôtres. **~ faithfully/ sincerely,** je vous prie d'agréer/de croire en l'expression de mes sentiments les meilleurs.
yoursel|f /jɔ:'self/ *pron.* (*familiar form*) toi-même; (*polite form*) vous-même; (*reflexive & after prep.*) te, t'*; vous. **~ves** *pron. pl.* vous-mêmes; (*reflexive*) vous.
youth /ju:θ/ *n.* (*pl.* **-s** /-ðz/) jeunesse *f.*; (*young man*) jeune *m.* **~ club,** centre de jeunes *m.* **~hostel,** auberge de jeunesse *f.* **~ful** *a.* juvénile, jeune.
yo-yo /'jəʊjəʊ/ *n.* (*pl.* **-os**) (P.) yo-yo *m. invar.* (P.).
Yugoslav /'ju:gəslɑ:v/ *a.* & *n.* Yougoslave (*m./f.*) **~ia** /-'slɑ:vɪə/ *n.* Yougoslavie *f.*
yuppie /'jʌpɪ/ *n.* yuppie *m.*

Z

zany /'zeɪnɪ/ *a.* (**-ier, -iest**) farfelu.
zap /zæp/ *v.t.* (*fam.*) (*kill*) descendre; (*comput.*) enlever; (*TV*) zapper.
zeal /zi:l/ *n.* zèle *m.*
zealous /'zeləs/ *a.* zélé. **~ly** *a.* zèle.
zebra /'zebrə, 'zi:brə/ *n.* zèbre *m.* **~ crossing,** passage pour piétons *m.*
zenith /'zenɪθ/ *n.* zénith *m.*
zero /'zɪərəʊ/ *n.* (*pl.* **-os**) zéro *m.* **~ hour,** l'heure H *f.*
zest /zest/ *n.* (*gusto*) entrain *m.*; (*spice*: *fig.*) piment *m.*; (*of orange or lemon peel*) zeste *m.*
zigzag /'zɪgzæg/ *n.* zigzag *m.* ● *a.* & *adv.* en zigzag. ● *v.i.* (*p.t.* **zigzagged**) zigzaguer.
zinc /zɪŋk/ *n.* zinc *m.*
Zionism /'zaɪənɪzəm/ *n.* sionisme *m.*
zip /zɪp/ *n.* (*vigour*) allant *m.* **~(-fastener),** fermeture éclair *f.* (P.). ● *v.t.* (*p.t.* **zipped**) fermer avec une fermeture éclair (P.). ● *v.i.* aller à toute vitesse. **Zip code,** (*Amer.*) code postal *m.*
zipper /'zɪpə(r)/ *n.* (*Amer.*) = **zip (-fastener).**
zither /'zɪðə(r)/ *n.* cithare *f.*
zodiac /'zəʊdɪæk/ *n.* zodiaque *m.*
zombie /'zɒmbɪ/ *n.* mort(e) vivant(e) *m.* (*f.*); (*fam.*) automate *m.*
zone /zəʊn/ *n.* zone *f.*
zoo /zu:/ *n.* zoo *m.*
zoolog|y /zəʊ'ɒlədʒɪ/ *n.* zoologie *f.* **~ical** /-ə'lɒdʒɪkl/ *a.* zoologique. **~ist** *n.* zoologiste *m./f.*
zoom /zu:m/ *v.i.* (*rush*) se précipiter. **~ lens,** zoom *m.* **~ off** *or* **past,** filer (comme une flèche).
zucchini /zu:'ki:nɪ/ *n. invar.* (*Amer.*) courgette *f.*

French Verb Tables

Notes: The conditional may be formed by substituting the following endings for those of the future: *ais* for *ai* and *as*, *ait* for *a*, *ions* for *ons*, *iez* for *ez*, *aient* for *ont*. The present participle is formed (unless otherwise indicated) by substituting *ant* for *ons* in the first person plural of the present tense (e.g. *finissant* and *donnant* may be derived from *finissons* and *donnons*). The imperative forms are (unless otherwise indicated) the same as the second persons singular and plural and the first person plural of the present tense. The second person singular does not take *s* after *e* or *a* (e.g. *donne*, *va*), except when followed by *y* or *en* (e.g. *vas-y*).

Regular verbs:

1. in *-er* (e.g. **donn|er**)

Present. ~e, ~es, ~e, ~ons, ~ez, ~ent.
Imperfect. ~ais, ~ais, ~ait, ~ions, ~iez, ~aient.
Past historic. ~ai, ~as, ~a, ~âmes, ~âtes, ~èrent.
Future. ~erai, ~eras, ~era, ~erons, ~erez, ~eront.
Present subjunctive. ~e, ~es, ~e, ~ions, ~iez, ~ent.
Past participle. ~é.

2. in *-ir* (e.g. **fin|ir**)

Pres. ~is, ~is, ~it, ~issons, ~issez, ~issent.
Impf. ~issais, ~issais, ~issait, ~issions, ~issiez, ~issaient.
Past hist. ~is, ~is, ~it, ~îmes, ~îtes, ~irent.
Fut. ~irai, ~iras, ~ira, ~irons, ~irez, ~iront.
Pres. sub. ~isse, ~isses, ~isse, ~issions, ~issiez, ~issent.
Past part. ~i.

3. in *-re* (e.g. **vend|re**)

Pres. ~s, ~s, ~, ~ons, ~ez, ~ent.
Impf. ~ais, ~ais, ~ait, ~ions, ~iez, ~aient.
Past hist. ~is, ~is, ~it, ~îmes, ~îtes, ~irent.
Fut. ~rai, ~ras, ~ra, ~rons, ~rez, ~ront.
Pres. sub. ~e, ~es, ~e, ~ions, ~iez, ~ent.
Past part. ~u.

Peculiarities of *-er* verbs:

In verbs in *-cer* (e.g. **commencer**) and *-ger* (e.g. **manger**), *c* becomes *ç* and *g* becomes *ge* before *a* and *o* (e.g. commença, commençons; mangea, mangeons).
In verbs in *-yer* (e.g. **nettoyer**), *y* becomes *i* before mute *e* (e.g. nettoie, nettoierai). Verbs in *-ayer* (e.g. **payer**) may retain *y* before mute *e* (e.g. paye or paie, payerai or paierai).

In verbs in *-eler* (e.g. **appeler**) and in *-eter* (e.g. **jeter**), *l* becomes *ll* and *t* becomes *tt* before a syllable containing mute *e* (e.g. appelle, appellerai; jette, jetterai). In the verbs **celer, ciseler, congeler, déceler, démanteler, écarteler, geler, marteler, modeler** and **peler**, and in the verbs **acheter, crocheter, fureter, haleter** and **racheter**, *e* becomes *è* before a syllable containing mute *e* (e.g. cèle, cèlerai; achète, achèterai).

In verbs in which the penultimate syllable contains mute *e* (e.g. **semer**) or *é* (e.g. **révéler**), both *e* and *é* become *è* before a syllable containing mute *e* (e.g. sème, sèmerai; révèle). However, in the verbs in which the penultimate syllable containx *é*, *é* remains unchanged in the future and conditional (e.g. révéleral).

Irregular verbs

At least the first persons singular and plural of the present tense are shown. Forms not listed may be derived from these. Thought the base form of the imperfect, future, and present subjunctive may be irregular, the endings of these tenses are as shown in the regular verb section. Only the first person singular of these tenses is given in most cases. The base form of the past historic may also be irregular but the endings of this tense shown in the verbs below fall (with few exceptions) into the 'u' category, listed under **être** and **avoir**, and the 'i' category shown under **finir** and **vendre** in the regular verb section.

Only the first person singular of the past historic is listed in most cases. Additional forms appear throughout when these cannot be derived from the forms given or when it is considered helpful to list them. Only those irregular verbs judged to be the most useful are shown in the tables.

abbattre *as* BATTRE.
accueillir *as* CUEILLIR.
acquérir ● *Pres.* acquiers, acquérons, acquièrent. ● *Impf.* acquérais. ● *Past hist.* acquis. ● *Fut.* acquerrai. ● *Pres. sub.* acquière. ● *Past part.* acquis.
admettre *as* METTRE.
aller ● *Pres.* vais, vas, va, allons, allez, vont. ● *Fut.* irai. ● *Pres. sub.* aille, allions.
apercevoir *as* RECEVOIR.
apparaître *as* CONNAÎTRE.
appartenir *as* TENIR.
apprendre *as* PRENDRE.
asseoir ● *Pres.* assieds, asseyons, asseyent. ● *Impf.* asseyais. ● *Past hist.* assis. ● *Fut.* assiérai. ● *Pres. sub.* asseye. ● *Past part.* assis.
atteindre ● *Pres.* atteins, atteignons, atteignent. ● *Impf.* atteignais. ● *Past hist.* atteignis. ● *Fut.* atteindrai. ● *Pres. sub.* atteigne. ● *Past part.* atteint.
avoir ● *Pres.* ai, as, a, avons, avez, ont. ● *Impf.* avais. ● *Past hist.* eus, eut, eûmes, eûtes, eurent. ● *Fut.* aurai. ● *Pres. sub.* aie, aies, ait, ayons, ayez, aient. ● *Pres. part.* ayant. ● *Past part.* eu. ● *Imp.* aie, ayons, ayez.
battre ● *Pres.* bats, bat, battons, battez, battent.
boire ● *Pres.* bois, buvons, boivent. ● *Impf.* buvais. ● *Past hist.* bus. ● *Pres. sub.* boive, buvions. ● *Past part.* bu.
bouillir ● *Pres.* bous, bouillons, bouillent. ● *Impf.* bouillais. ● *Pres. sub.* bouille.
combattre *as* BATTRE.
commettre *as* METTRE.
comprendre *as* PRENDRE.
concevoir *as* RECEVOIR.
conclure ● *Pres.* conclus, concluons, concluent. ● *Past hist.* conclus. ● *Past part.* conclu.
conduire ● *Pres.* conduis, conduisons, conduisent. ● *Impf.* conduisais. ● *Past hist.* conduisis. ● *Pres. sub.* conduise. ● *Past part.* conduit.
connaître ● *Pres.* connais, connaît, connaissons. ● *Impf.* connaissais. ● *Past hist.* connus. ● *Pres. sub.* connaisse. ● *Past part.* connu.
construire *as* CONDUIRE.
contenir *as* TENIR.
contraindre *as* ATTEINDRE (except *ai* replaces *ei*).
contredire *as* DIRE, except ● *Pres.* vous contredisez.
convaincre *as* VAINCRE.
convenir *as* TENIR.
corrompre *as* ROMPRE.
coudre ● *Pres.* couds, cousons, cousent. ● *Impf.* cousais. ● *Past hist.* cousis. ● *Pres. sub.* couse. ● *Past part.* cousu.
courir ● *Pres.* cours, courons, courent. ● *Impf.* courais. ● *Past hist.* courus. ● *Fut.* courrai. ● *Pres. sub.* coure. ● *Past part.* couru.
couvrir ● *Pres.* couvre, couvrons. ● *Impf.* couvrais. ● *Pres. sub.* couvre. ● *Past part.* couvert.
craindre *as* ATTEINDRE (except *ai* replaces *ei*).
croire ● *Pres.* crois, croit, croyons, croyez, croient. ● *Impf.* croyais. ● *Past hist.* crus. ● *Pres. sub.* croie, croyions. ● *Past part.* cru.
croître ● *Pres.* crois, croît, croissons. ● *Impf.* croissais. ● *Past hist.* crûs. ● *Pres. sub.* croisse. ● *Past part.* crû, crue.

cueillir • *Pres.* cueille, cueillons. • *Impf.* cueillais. • *Fut.* cueillerai. • *Pres. sub.* cueille.
débattre *as* BATTRE.
décevoir *as* RECEVOIR.
découvrir *as* COUVRIR.
décrire *as* ÉCRIRE.
déduire *as* CONDUIRE.
défaire *as* FAIRE.
détenir *as* TENIR.
détruire *as* CONDUIRE.
devenir *as* TENIR.
devoir • *Pres.* dois, devons, doivent. • *Impf.* devais. • *Past hist.* dus. • *Fut.* devrai. • *Pres. sub.* doive. • *Past part.* dû, due.
dire • *Pres.* dis, dit, disons, dites, disent. • *Impf.* disais. • *Past hist.* dis. • *Past part.* dit.
disparaître *as* CONNAîTRE.
dissoudre • *Pres.* dissous. dissolvons. • *Impf.* dissolvais. • *Pres. sub.* dissolve. • *Past part.* dissous, dissoute.
distraire *as* EXTRAIRE.
dormir • *Pres.* dors, dormons. • *Impf.* dormais. • *Pres. sub* dorme.
écrire • *Pres.* écris, écrivons. • *Impf.* écrivais. • *Past hist.* écrivis. • *Pres. sub.* écrive. • *Past part.* écrit.
élire *as* LIRE.
émettre *as* METTRE.
s'enfuir *as* FUIR.
entreprendre *as* PRENDRE.
entretenir *as* TENIR.
envoyer • *Fut.* enverrai.
éteindre *as* ATTEINDRE.
être • *Pres.* suis, es, est, sommes, êtes, sont. • *Impf.* étais. • *Past hist.* fus, futm fûmes, fûtes, furent. • *Fut.* serai. • *Pres. sub.* sois, soit, soyons, soyez, soient. • *Pres. part.* étant. • *Past part.* été. • *Imp.* sois, soyons, soyez.
exclure *as* CONCLURE.
extraire • *Pres.* extrais, extrayons. • *Impf.* extrayais. • Pres. sub. extraie. • *Past part.* extrait.
faire • *Pres.* fais, fait, faisons, faites, font. • *Impf.* faisais. • *Past hist.* fis. • *Fut.* ferai. • *Pres. sub.* fasse. • *Past part.* fait.
falloir (Impersonal) • *Pres.* faut. • *Impf.* fallait. • *Past hist.* fallut. • *Fut.* faudra. • *Pres. sub.* faille. • *Past part.* fallu.
feindre *as* ATTEINDRE.
fuir • *Pres.* fuis, fuyons, fuient. • *Impf.* fuyais. • *Past hist.* fuis. • *Pres sub.* fuie. • *Past part.* fui.
inscrire *as* ÉCRIRE.
instruire *as* CONDUIRE.
interdire *as* DIRE, except • *Pres.* vous interdisez.
interrompre *as* ROMPRE.
intervenir *as* TENIR.
introduire *as* CONDUIRE.
joindre *as* ATTEINDRE (except *oi* replaces *ei*).
lire • *Pres.* lis, lit, lisons, lisez, lisent. • *Impf.* lisais. • *Past hist.* lus. • *Pres. sub.* lise. • *Past part.* lu.
luire • *Pres.* luis, luisons. • *Impf.* luisais. • *Past hist.* luisis. • *Pres. sub.* luise. • *Past part.* lui.
maintenir *as* TENIR.
maudire • *Pres.* maudis, maudissons. • *Impf.* maudissais. • *Past hist.* maudis. • *Pres. sub.* maudisse. • *Past part.* maudit.
mentir *as* SORTIR *(except en replaces or).*
mettre • *Pres.* mets, met. mettons, mettez. mettent. • *Past hist.* mis. • *Past part.* mis.
mourir • *Pres.* meurs, mourons, meurent. • *Impf.* mourais. • *Past hist.* mourus. • *Fut.* mourrai. • *Pres sub.* meure, mourions. • *Past part.* mort.
mouvoir • *Pres.* meus, mouvons, meuvent. • *Impf.* mouvais. • *Fut.* mouvrai. • *Pres. sub.* meuve, mouvions.

• *Past part.* mû, mue.

naître • *Pres.* nais, nait, naissons. • *Impf.* naissais. • *Past hist.* naquis. • *Pres. sub.* naisse. • *Past part.* né.

nuire *as* LUIRE.

obtenir *as* TENIR.

offrir, ouvrir *as* COUVRIR.

omettre *as* METTRE.

paraître *as* CONNAÎTRE.

parcourir *as* COURIR.

partir *as* SORTIR (except *ar* replaces *or*).

parvenir *as* TENIR.

peindre *as* ATTEINDRE.

percevoir *as* RECEVOIR.

permettre *as* METTRE.

plaindre *as* ATTEINDRE (except *ai* replaces *ei*).

plaire • *Pres.* plais, plait, plaisons. • *Impf.* plaisais. • *Past hist.* plus. • *Pres. sub.* plaise. • *Past part.* plu.

pleuvoir (impersonal) • *Pres.* pleut. • *Impf.* pleuvait. • *Past hist.* plut. • *Fut.* pleuvra. • *Pres. sub.* pleuve. • *Past part.* plu.

poursuivre *as* SUIVRE.

pourvoir *as* VOIR, except • *Fut.* pourvoirai.

pouvoir • *Pres.* peux. peut, pouvons, pouvez, peuvent. • *Impf.* pouvais. • *Past hist.* pus. • *Fut.* pourrai. • *Pres. sub.* puisse. • *Past part.* pu.

prédirc *as* DIRE, except • *Pres* vous prédisez.

prendre • *Pres.* prends, prenons, prennent. • *Impf.* prenais. • *Past hist.* pris. • *Pres. sub.* prenne, prenions. • *Past part.* pris.

prescrire *as* éCRIRE.

prévenir *as* TENIR.

prévoir *as* VOIR, except • *Fut.* prévoirai.

produire *as* CONDUIRE.

prommettre *as* METTRE.

provenir *as* TENIR.

recevoir • *Pres.* reçois, recevons, reçoivent. • *Impf.* recevais. • *Past hist.* reçus. • *Fut.* recevrai. • *Pres. sub.* reçoive, recevions. • *Past part.* reçu.

reconduire *as* CONDUIRE.

reconnaître *as* CONNAîTRE.

reconstruire *as* CONDUIRE.

recouvrir *as* COUVRIR.

recueillir *as* CUEILLIR..

redire *as* DIRE.

réduire *as* CONDUIRE.

refaire *as* FAIRE.

rejoindre *as* ATTEINDRE (except *oi* replaces *ei*).

remettre *as* METTRE.

renvoyer *as* *ENVOYER*.

repartir *as* SORTIR (except *ar* replaces *or*.

reprendre *as* PRENDRE.

reproduire *as* vconduire.

résoudre • *Pres.* résous, résolvons. • *Impf.* résolvais. • *Past hist.* résolus. • *Pres. sub.* résolve. • *Past part.* résolu.

ressortir *as* SORTIR.

restreindre *as* ATTEINDRE.

retenir, revenir *as* TENIR.

revivre *as* vvivre.

revoir *as* VOIR.

rire • *Pres.* ris, rit, rions, riez, rient. • *Impf.* riais. • *Past hist.* ris. • *Pres. sub.* rie, riions. • *Past part.* ri.

rompre *as* VENDRE (regular), except • *Pres.* il rompt.

satisfaire *as* FAIRE.

savoir • *Pres.* sais, sait, savons, savez, savent. • *Impf.* savais. • *Past hist.* sus. • *Fut.* saurai. • *Pres. sub.* sache, sachions. • *Pres. part.* sachant. • *Past part.* su. • *Impt.* sache, sachons, sachez.

séduire *as* CONDUIRE.

sentir *as* SORTIR (except *en* replaces *or*).

servir • *Pres.* sers, servons. • *Impf.* servais. • *Pres. sub.* serve.

sortir • *Pres.* sors, sortons. • *Impf.* sortais. • *Pres. sub.* sorte.

souffrir *as* COUVRIR.

soumettre *as* METTRE.

soustraire *as* EXTRAIRE.

soutenir *as* TENIR.

suffire ● *Pres.* suffis, suffisons. ● *Impf.* suffisais. ● *Past hist.* suffis. ● *Pres. sub.* suffise. ● *Past part.* suffi.

suivre ● *Pres.* suis, suivons. ● *Impf.* suivais. ● *Past hist.* suivis. ● *Pres. sub.* suive. ● *Past part.* suivi.

surprendre *as* PRENDRE.

survivre *as* VIVRE.

taire ● *Pres.* tais, taisond. ● *Impf.* taisais. ● *Past hist.* tus. ● *Pres. sub.* taise. ● *Past part.* tu.

teindre *as* ATTEINDRE.

tenir ● *Pres.* tiens, tenons, tiennent. ● *Impf.* tenais. ● *Past hist.* tins, tint, tinmes, tintes, tinrent. ● *Fut.* tiendrai. ● *Pres. sub.* tienne. ● *Past part.* tenu.

traduire *as* CONDUIRE.

traire *as* EXTRAIRE.

transmettre *as* METTRE.

vaincre ● *Pres.* vaincs, vaine, vainquons. ● *Impf.* vain-quais. ● *Past hist.* vainquis. ● *Pres. sub.* vainque. ● *Past part.* vaincu.

valoir ● *Pres.* vaux, vaut, valons, valez, valent. ● *Impf.* valais. ● *Past hist.* valus. ● *Fut.* vaudrai. ● *Pres. sub.* vaille. ● *Past part.* valu.

venir *as* TENIR.

vivre ● *Pres.* vis, vit, vivons, vivez, vivent. ● *Impf.* vivais. ● *Past hist.* vécus. ● *Pres. sub* vive. ● *Past part.* vécu.

voir ● *Pres.* vois, voyons, voient. ● *Impf.* voyais. ● *Past hist.* vis. ● *Fut.* verrai. ● *Pres. sub.* voie, voyions. ● *Past part.* vu.

vouloir ● *Pres.* veux, veut, voulons, voulez, veulent. ● *Impf.* voulais. ● *Past hist.* voulus. ● *Fut.* voudrai. ● *Pres. sub.* veuille, voulions. ● *Past part.* voulu. ● *Imp.* veuille, veuillons, veuillez.